Gotham at War

The Final Volume of the *Gotham* Series

Gotham at War

A History of New York City from 1933 to 1945

Mike Wallace

Oxford University Press is a department of the University of Oxford.
It furthers the University's objective of excellence in research, scholarship,
and education by publishing worldwide. Oxford is a registered trade mark of
Oxford University Press in the UK and in certain other countries.

Published in the United States of America by Oxford University Press
198 Madison Avenue, New York, NY 10016, United States of America.

© Mike Wallace 2025

All rights reserved. No part of this publication may be reproduced, stored in a retrieval system, transmitted, used for text and data mining, or used for training artificial intelligence, in any form or by any means, without the prior permission in writing of Oxford University Press, or as expressly permitted by law, by license or under terms agreed with the appropriate reprographics rights organization. Inquiries concerning reproduction outside the scope of the above should be sent to the Rights Department, Oxford University Press, at the address above.

You must not circulate this work in any other form
and you must impose this same condition on any acquirer.

Library of Congress Control Number: 2025908945

ISBN 9780199384518

Printed by Sheridan Books, Inc., United States of America

The manufacturer's authorized representative in the EU for product safety is
Oxford University Press España S.A., Parque Empresarial San Fernando de Henares,
Avenida de Castilla, 2 – 28830 Madrid (www.oup.es/en).

The manufacturer's authorised representative in the EU for product safety is
Oxford University Press España S.A. of El Parque Empresarial San Fernando de
Henares, Avenida de Castilla, 2 – 28830 Madrid (www.oup.es/en or
product.safety@oup.com). OUP España S.A. also acts as importer into
Spain of products made by the manufacturer.

Contents

NAZIS AND NEW YORK

1. Boycott — 3
2. Brain Drain — 9
3. Nazis in New York — 13
4. A Fifth Column? — 20
5. Kristallnacht — 22
6. Émigrés Arrive: Manhattan — 25
7. Émigrés Arrive: Williamsburg — 28
8. Aliens and Enemies — 33

ITALIANS

9. Duce! Duce! — 39
10. Italian Anti-Fascists — 41
11. Hands off Ethiopia! — 44
12. Ambling Alp v. Brown Bomber — 47
13. "The Eagles of Rome Have Devoured the Lion of Judah" — 50
14. Italians and Jews: 1938–1941 — 55
15. Louis v. Schmeling — 57

THE IRISH

16.	The Waning of the Green	63
17.	Catholic New York	67
18.	A Church Besieged	69
19.	War in Spain	71
20.	¡Viva La Quince Brigada!	73
21.	Greens and Reds: The Transport Workers Union	77
22.	Catholics v. "Communists"	80
23.	The Christian Front	84
24.	Enter Spellman	88
25.	Spellman Takes Command	92
26.	The Cross and the Flag	95
27.	Polonia	98

ASIAN NEW YORK

28.	Japanese New York	103
29.	Chinese Gotham	105

IN UNO PLURES

30.	Pluralists	113
31.	Culture Warrior	117
32.	Building Brotherhood	121
33.	Fêteing the Folks	124
34.	Teaching Tolerance	126
35.	Americans All	132
36.	Immigrants All	135
37.	Balladeers for Brotherhood	138
38.	Common Ground	141

STUDY WAR NO MORE

39.	The Renunciator	147
40.	Antiwarriors	149
41.	Against War and Fascism	152
42.	Peace Crusade	156
43.	Unpopular Fronts	158
44.	Spanish New Yorkers	162

45.	Partisan Views	166
46.	Anti-totalitarianism	176
47.	Unpopular Front	183
48.	Red Scare Lite	186
49.	Spies	191
50.	The Yanks Are Not Coming?	196

FIGHTING LIBERALS

51.	FDR: Common Defense and General Welfare	201
52.	Moral Rearmament	206
53.	Muscular Democracy	209
54.	Playwrights and Poets	212
55.	Reality Radio	215
56.	Mars Invades New York	218
57.	Winchell Calling to All Ships at Sea	223
58.	Stern's Post, Dolly's Daily	226
59.	PM	229
60.	Brands from the Burning	235

WALL STREET WARRIORS

61.	Let's Make a Deal	243
62.	Change Agent	247
63.	The Veriest Roman	250
64.	Bankers Balked	252
65.	Council Counsel	254
66.	Anglophiliacs	257
67.	Intrepid	260
68.	Aid the Allies!	263
69.	Fifth Columnist	268
70.	Fighting Liberals v. Wall Street Warriors	270
71.	We Want Willkie!	272
72.	War Hawks at Work	278
73.	Martin, Barton, and Fish	281
74.	Arsenal of Democracy	286
75.	America First	290
76.	Second Platoon	294

77.	007 and the Stork Club Detective	299
78.	Down South America Way	304
79.	You Go to War with the Capitalists You've Got	308

GOTHAM GIRDS FOR WAR

80.	Cash and Carry	313
81.	Black Power	319
82.	Illiberal Liberals	327
83.	Battle of the Atlantic	334
84.	Civilian Defender	339
85.	La Guardia Third Term?	343
86.	Pearl Harbor	352

UNDER THE GUN

87.	Turkey Shoot	357
88.	Sabotage?	360
89.	The Mob and the Military	363
90.	Sabotage!	366
91.	Aliens	368
92.	Dissenters	377
93.	"As Dark as Hitler's Heart"	380
94.	Convoys	386
95.	"New York at War"	389

WAR PORT

96.	Anchors Aweigh	397
97.	Smaller War Plants	409

SCIENCE IN THE CITY

98.	R&D: Radar	421
99.	R&D: Manhattan Project	428
100.	The Anthropology of New York City	438

SELLING THE WAR

101.	"Any Bonds Today?"	445
102.	"What This War Is All About"	453
103.	Clashing Visions of Victory	458
104.	Writers on Demand	465

105.	War Songs	467
106.	"Smashing Thru, Captain America Came Face to Face with Hitler…"	471

HOME FRONT

107.	Women at Work	481
108.	Rosie and Charlie	490
109.	"Wenches with Wrenches"	498
110.	Bad Moms	504
111.	Controlling Consumption	507
112.	Controlling Rents	517

BLACKS

113.	A White Folks' War?	523
114.	"Checkerboarding" Worksites	525
115.	Penned In and Pissed Off	528
116.	GI Jim Crow	533
117.	Satyagraha in Madison Square Garden	537
118.	Zoots	540
119.	Clampdown	543
120.	"Get the White Man! Get the White Man!"	546
121.	Passing the Torch	552

HOLOCAUST

122.	Sounds of Distant Slaughter	557
123.	Homeland?	568
124.	Trouble at Home	584

JEWS AND BLACKS

125.	Jews and Blacks Allied	589
126.	Fighting Prejudice	593
127.	Politics	600
128.	Housing	605
129.	Jobs	609
130.	Game Changer	613

ON THE TOWN

131.	Sex and the City	621
132.	Nightclubs	627

133.	The Voice	633
134.	Bop	637
135.	Rumbamania	645
136.	Art of This Century	651
137.	Book Boom	664
138.	Broadway	673
139.	Toward a Fashion-Industrial Complex	680
140.	On the Town	689
141.	The Theater at the Center of the World	697

PLANNING THE POSTWAR CITY

142.	Presenting the Future: A Public Plan	703
143.	"Two Million Plans!"	706
144.	Housing: The Specter of Suburbanization, the Battle against Blight	710
145.	Rubber and Rails	720
146.	Sea	729
147.	Sky	732
148.	Infrastructure	736
149.	Washington or Wall Street?	741
150.	Manufacturing: Tide Going Out or Tide Coming In?	745
151.	Headquarters	751

PLANNING THE POSTWAR NATION

152.	Dueling Planners	759
153.	Paging Dr. New Deal	762
154.	Dr. New Deal: Call Only When Needed	764
155.	Dr. New Deal: Wanted, Dead or Alive, Preferably Dead	768
156.	Rightist Thrust...	776
157.	...Liberal Riposte	779
158.	The Last Subway Series	783
159.	Enter: "Red Menace"	787
160.	Cue: Cold War	791
161.	Dr. New Deal: Back in the Saddle?	795

PLANNING THE POSTWAR WORLD

| 162. | New World A-Comin' | 801 |
| 163. | An Empire of Free Trade | 806 |

164.	Racism and Imperialism	812
165.	India	816
166.	China	820
167.	Puerto Rico	825
168.	Uniting the Nations	834
	Epilogs	847
	Acknowledgments	863
	References	865
	Bibliography	881
	Index of Names	927
	Index of Subjects	938

NAZIS AND NEW YORK

The Hindenburg flies over lower Manhattan on its way to New Jersey, May 5, 1937. (Sueddeutsche Zeitung Photo / Alamy Stock Photo)

1

Boycott

On January 30, 1933, Adolf Hitler was sworn in as chancellor of Germany. Seeking to win a Nazi majority in the Reichstag, he arranged for new parliamentary elections to be held. On February 27, a week before the balloting, the Reichstag itself was set ablaze. Hitler blamed the Communists, got President Paul von Hindenburg, the aging hero of the First World War, to suspend most constitutional rights, then silenced the opposition press and arrested thousands of his political enemies (with many communist leaders imprisoned in a former gunpowder factory just outside the Bavarian town of Dachau). On election day the Nazis won only 44 percent. But with the backing of nationalist and Catholic parties, Hitler banned or cowed remaining opponents and, on March 23, won passage of a law granting him full dictatorial powers.

By then the Nazis had opened up a second front—as much economic as political—against Jewish intellectuals, professionals, and merchants. On March 8, in the Ruhr city of Essen, storm troopers had massed in front of Jewish stores and forced crowds of shoppers to turn away, lobbing stench bombs when necessary. Similar attacks spread swiftly across Germany. Jewish professors were forced to cancel classes, performers to abandon the stage. Demands were made that the entire legal profession be purged of Jewish lawyers over the next four years, that judicial benches "be cleansed immediately" of "alien races," that hospitals cancel the contracts of Jewish doctors. Brown-shirted thugs broke into Jewish lodgings, beat up (and in some instances shot) Jews in the street. Refugees began leaving Germany for nearby countries.

Consternation over what the Nazis were doing was worldwide, but it was in New York City—Brooklyn, to be precise—that a movement was launched to rein in the Nazi regime. At a March 18 meeting of militant Jewish War Veterans (JWV), Benjamin Sperling, commander of Brooklyn's JWV East Post, formally called for a national boycott of German goods, services, and shipping lines. The logic was straightforward: the Nazis had promised to combat unemployment; recovery required expanding Germany's exports; thwarting that strategy could increase joblessness, foster discontent, and perhaps foment a movement to overthrow Hitler, or at least force him to mitigate his anti-Semitic campaign.

On March 23, the very day Hitler attained führer-hood, 2,000 Jewish veterans of the First World War, accompanied by 2,000 non-Jewish veterans, hoisted American flags and marched from Cooper Square down Lafayette Street to City Hall with 10,000 onlookers cheering their progress. Mayor John Patrick O'Brien greeted them and accepted their resolutions calling for an economic protest. In short order, with each JWV post overseeing the picketing of stores in their area, $2 million worth of orders for German goods had been countermanded, and German steamship lines—valuable foreign currency earners—reported a rash of canceled bookings.

Still, this was barely a pinprick. The tiny, marginal outfit would need powerful allies. It turned, accordingly, to the major Jewish organizations, only to find them deeply divided over how to respond to the mushrooming Nazi menace.

On March 19, one of the largest of these organizations, the American Jewish Congress (AJC), at the urging of honorary president Rabbi Stephen Wise, had convened a mass meeting to plan a course of action. Over a thousand representatives of local and national Jewish groups crammed into the Hotel Astor (another 1,500 milled in the lobby and streets nearby). The meeting quickly endorsed a proposal to hold a giant Madison Square Garden rally on March 27 as the centerpiece of an international expression of outrage. But when the Jewish War Veterans proposed that those assembled also adopt their boycott proposal, Judge Joseph M. Proskauer (former governor Al Smith's friend and adviser) took the floor to urge rejection and indeed to oppose all demonstrations and marches as unproductive, even dangerous. Proskauer read aloud a letter from Judge Irving Lehman, brother of the current governor, which warned that protests would lead to Nazi reprisals and thus "kill Jews in Germany." These calls for "patience, fortitude and exemplary conduct" touched off an uproar, with the crowd booing, hissing, and storming its disapproval in English, Yiddish, and Russian.

Proskauer and Lehman were stalwarts of the American Jewish Committee, and their intervention was but the latest in a long-running series of disagreements between the Committee and the American Jewish Congress over how best to respond to anti-Semitism (and an equally long-running battle for leadership of the city's and the nation's Jews). The Committee—an unabashedly elitist, self-perpetuating oligarchy rooted in New York's commercial, banking, and Reform Judaism circles—boasted of its connections with national and metropolitan counterparts. The Committee's assimilationist leaders argued that behind-the-scenes politicking influentials would be more effective than "irresponsible" and "hysterical" public actions that, by underscoring the protesters' Jewishness, might generate an upsurge of anti-Semitism. The Congress—more socialist in politics, middle/professional in class, orthodox in religion, and Zionist in aspiration—denounced the Committee's quiescence.

Their differences also had an ethnic dimension. While the Congress chiefly represented Eastern European Jews, the Committee's members (and those of B'nai B'rith, which joined in condemning public protests) were mainly second- and third-generation German Americans. Many had relatives and associates in the Third Reich, some of whom—under Nazi duress—were frantically cabling New York, urging rejection of militancy. The fascist regime and its business backers, keenly aware an effective boycott could be lethal, had taken steps to head one off. Hermann Goering had summoned the heads of major German Jewish organizations and demanded they "make sure that the protest meeting called in New York by Dr. Stephen S. Wise is canceled." Wise, he declared, "is one of our most dangerous and unscrupulous enemies."

Some of this was a matter of the Nazis believing their own paranoid fantasies about organized Jewry. They were sure Jews had cooked up the anti-Hun propaganda campaigns that mobilized opposition to Germany back in the First World War. There was the boycott of Model T cars that in 1927 had forced the Nazis' hero Henry Ford to call off his anti-Semitic campaign and issue a humiliating plea to the Jews for forgiveness. And now a new hullaballoo over "supposed atrocities"—"pure inventions" the Nazis claimed—was emanating not only from New York but also from Europe. A mass meeting of Vilna's Jews on March 20, 1933, had sparked boycotts in Warsaw, then throughout all of Poland. On March 24 placards had gone up in store windows of London's West End calling for a ban on German goods (the English–German fur trade ground to an almost immediate halt). Boycotts were breaking out in Czechoslovakia, Holland, Belgium, Switzerland, Turkey, and Egypt.

In New York, Wise pressed ahead with the March 27 rally. By 8:00 p.m., 20,000 had jammed into the Garden, lofting banners denouncing the Third Reich, as tens of thousands more thronged outside seeking entry. Loudspeakers were hastily set up at Columbus Circle, then other nearby intersections, to draw off some of the overflow. At the same moment, 70,000 gathered at rallies in Chicago, DC, San Francisco, and Houston to hear the Garden proceedings broadcast live; in all, an estimated 1,000,000 listeners gathered around their radios for the coast-to-coast hookup, and yet another million—in Poland, Austria, and Czechoslovakia—picked up the transmission relayed from Gotham to their local stations.

Among the voices they heard denouncing Nazi persecution of Jews were those of prominent New York Christians, including Bishop William Manning, head of the city's Episcopal Diocese. Catholic bishop John J. Dunn had reneged, saying he'd been assured by the State Department that mistreatment had ended, but his coreligionist Al Smith insisted forcefully that German bigotry be given "the same treatment that we gave the Ku Klux Klan. And it don't make any difference to me whether it is a brown shirt or a night shirt." Senator Robert Wagner, himself of German descent, vehemently denounced the new order in Germany, as did William Green, president of the American Federation of Labor (AFL) whose longshoremen could, if they chose, put a serious crimp in German–American commerce.

The main speaker, however, refrained from backing a boycott. Rabbi Wise's otherwise militant remarks were greeted with roars of approval from inside and outside the Garden. Yet the Congress leader (as he wrote two days later) "spoke with absolute self-restraint"—partly in deference to the American Jewish Committee's concerns, partly from a desire to give the new Roosevelt administration a chance to act, partly from worries about a promised retaliatory boycott the Nazis had announced, and partly from fears about mass mobilization itself. As Wise wrote a friend two days later, it would have been "the easiest thing in the world" to have roused "that mighty meeting, the most wonderful meeting you have ever seen in your life, to murderous rage."

While Wise hesitated, Samuel Untermyer stepped to the helm. The man who had fought the Money Trust during the Pujo hearings in the 1910s and campaigned against Henry Ford's anti-Semitic efforts in the 1920s, was still one of the country's foremost attorneys. Untermyer had a foot in both leading Jewish camps—as a German American and as a former official of the American Jewish Congress—and he announced his support for a boycott on station WEVD (after Socialist leader Eugene Victor Debs). Untermyer then addressed the founding conference, which had been organized by Zionist leader Abe Coralnik, who called on local Jews to adopt the methods of civil disobedience Gandhi was using in India. Six hundred delegates—representing 288 fraternal, professional, religious, and mercantile groups, Jews and Gentiles alike—pledged at the Hotel Astor gathering to build an inclusive nationwide boycott movement. In mid-1933, seeking to widen its outreach he changed its name from the American League for the Defense of Jewish Rights to the Non-Sectarian Anti-Nazi League to Champion Human Rights.

Activists were galvanized anew when word came that on May 10 Nazi university students would burn thousands of "un-German" books in Berlin's Opernplatz, to "purify" their culture. In a direct riposte, 600 New York area Jewish organizations, led by the American Jewish Congress, organized a parade that same day. Over 100,000 New Yorkers, carrying thousands of antifascist placards (that of the undertakers' union read: "We Want Hitler"), marched from Madison Square to Battery Park, taking four hours to pass the City Hall reviewing stand, while countless thousands of onlookers cheered their progress and showered them with ticker tape. Unionists and black-robed rabbis, artists and professionals, city officials and Christian sympathizers—all ended up at a colossal demonstration on the island's southern edge. Speakers voiced their abhorrence of Nazi infamies, though Wise, once again, refrained from endorsing the swelling popular boycott.

By August, with an estimated 95 percent of the Congress membership now demanding action, the AJC leadership finally joined the boycott, which had scored some notable successes. By that summer of 1933, the Hamburg-American shipping line's business had been so adversely affected that the chairman and all the board directors had resigned; US imports from Germany had been cut by nearly a fourth below the 1932 level; and Germany's declining export surplus had shrunk the pool of foreign currency available for buying vital raw materials. In August, Goebbels railed against the "iron boycott with which the world has encircled us."

A matchbook distributed by the Non-Sectarian Anti-Nazi League to Champion Human Rights, 1933. (PD-US-ineligible)

That fall and winter boycotters stepped up pressure against large New York retailers (many of them Jewish-owned firms) that—citing responsibility to shareholders—continued to sell German goods. Sales plummeted: in September, twenty leading department stores, while deploring the boycott, admitted it was "extensive and effective." Slowly the big stores caved—Saks and Hearns signed on in February 1934—though Macy's president, Percy S. Straus, held out stubbornly. Untermyer blasted Straus for refusing to "cease selling German goods" and for maintaining a purchasing office in Berlin, but it wasn't until March, after Norman Thomas had set up a picket line surrounding the giant store— "Macy's Buys German Goods," read the signs, "We Want No Fascism Here"—that Straus ceased dealing in German merchandise, citing "consumer resistance."

Gimbels (as was its wont) swiftly followed suit. Three days later Woolworth's 1,941 stores severed their German connection as well.

These turnarounds had likely been spurred by the arrival of fresh boycott troops under the command of Baruch Charney Vladeck, general manager of the *Jewish Daily Forward*, housing activist, and a hero of the city's Yiddish-speaking masses. On February 25, 1934, Vladeck had presided over the founding meeting of the Jewish Labor Committee (JLC), at which over a thousand delegates representing the International Ladies' Garment Workers Union (ILGWU), Amalgamated Clothing Workers, United Hebrew Trades, Workmen's Circle, Jewish Daily Forward Association, and a number of smaller groups had chosen Vladeck as president; he quickly backed the boycott.

Though the boycott failed to derail the Nazis, it did deter them for a time: when Goebbels was asked in February 1935 why the anti-Semitic campaign hadn't proceeded more vigorously, he blamed "foreign political reasons, since further boycotts, foreign exchange difficulties and other troubles are thereby threatened." But boycotts are notoriously difficult to pull off unless the boycotters are highly organized and their target is vulnerable to pressure. Conditions had been ripe in the Anglo-German fur trade and would be so again when Holland's mostly Jewish diamond traders refused to send gems to Germany for polishing or cutting; by diverting their orders to Antwerp and Amsterdam, they managed to dismantle the Third Reich's diamond industry virtually overnight. Conditions in the US were not as favorable.

Gotham's market clout, while substantial, wasn't sufficient, and outside the metropolitan region the US boycott movement never gained traction. Retail trade, moreover, constituted only a small percentage of German–American commerce. US industrial firms were not susceptible to public pressure, and indeed many big companies (and commercial associations) were struggling to find new markets and profit centers. They were working hard to expand German–American trade. Organized labor, desperately seeking jobs, wasn't much more helpful: AFL leaders endorsed the boycott but did virtually nothing to enforce it. The country's political leadership was equally eager to combat the depression—after 1935 the US and German governments negotiated new agreements to stimulate trade—and, geostrategically, the State Department (not overly troubled by anti-Semitism in the first place) considered Hitler a useful bulwark against communism.

If Gentile allies were in short supply, the Jews themselves were divided as to the boycott's advisability (the American Jewish Committee and B'nai B'rith continued to oppose it) and diffident as to its prosecution (the American Jewish Congress rejected mass picketing, hampering their effectiveness). Even ardent advocates were unwilling to coalesce: in 1935, when the American Jewish Congress and JLC formed a Joint Boycott Council, Untermyer's Anti-Nazi League refused to join the coalition, and the American League Against War and Fascism splintered when Socialist and Communist factions came to blows.

Worse, a fledgling effort by Jews all over the world to mount a concerted global campaign was blindsided when German Zionists cut a deal with the Nazis (the "Transfer Agreement"), which allowed Jewish emigrants to put their savings (which they were barred from taking out of the country) into underwriting the export of German goods to Palestine. Untermyer, Wise, and Vladeck were incensed at this undermining of the boycott—"The Transfer Agreement is a blot on the Jews," Vladeck declared—but were powerless to halt it.

By 1935, any impact the boycotters might have had on Third Reich policies evaporated as Hitler's rearmament and public works programs drastically diminished his vulnerability to outside opinion. The movement carried on nevertheless. A push was made to torpedo US participation in the 1936 Olympic Games, to be held in Berlin. Protesters won some support from the Amateur Athletic Union, whose certification of amateur status was required of all would-be participants. AAU president Jeremiah T. Mahoney, a Catholic New York City judge appalled by Nazi anti-Semitism, pushed for an alternate location, and when that failed, suggested the US withdraw from the games. But Avery Brundage, who ran the American Olympic Committee, denounced the boycott proposal as a "Jewish-Communist conspiracy" and overcame AAU resistance. In response, the JLC held a Counter-Olympics on Randall's Island during August 1936, with Governor Lehman presenting the prizes.

These and other initiatives would keep the antifascist flame alive, if feebly, until events later in the decade would set it blazing once again. In the meantime, the city's Jews and their allies worked to provide refuge for those fleeing a growing level of persecution.

2

Brain Drain

Within weeks of the first storm trooper harassments, New Yorkers were hard at work trying to ease access for German émigrés. Their target, at first, was not the rigid structure of the exclusionary US immigration law welded in place back in 1924, because at this point, ironically, its pro-Nordic quota system inadvertently privileged Jews. Flaxen-haired Germany had been assigned one of the highest allotments—in 1933, 25,957 were eligible for access. This was deemed an adequate level at a time when, according to reports flowing into the Hebrew Sheltering and Immigrant Aid Society of America (HIAS) office on Lafayette Street, the overwhelming bulk of the first ten thousand largely Jewish refugees were opting to camp out in nearby European countries, chiefly France, while waiting to see if the Nazi storm might blow over.

The more immediate problem was that in 1930, President Hoover, as an anti-depression measure, had issued an Executive Order directing American consuls abroad to stringently enforce the 1924 law's requirement that applicants for immigration prove they would not become a "public charge." But Nazi regulations effectively pauperized departing Jews, restricting the amount of money they could take out to roughly four US dollars, and consuls routinely demanded applicants furnish certificates of good character from the local police, who were among their chief persecutors. Rabbi Wise, accordingly, went to Capitol Hill to urge revocation of Hoover's order. He received a warm welcome from Brooklyn congressman Emanuel Celler—who had led the opposition to immigration restriction back in the twenties and now claimed Hoover's order in effect slashed the nominal quota allotment by 90 percent—and from Manhattan congressman Samuel Dickstein, chairman of the House Committee on Immigration and Naturalization.

Dickstein, himself a Russian-born Jewish immigrant, had been brought to New York at the age of two, his parents in flight from pogroms. A graduate of the city's public schools, CCNY, and New York City Law School, Dickstein had been representing his overwhelmingly Jewish Lower East Side district since 1923. He and Wise were old friends. After hearing the rabbi's testimony on March 22, 1933, Dickstein submitted a resolution calling for unrestricted entry for German Jews fleeing persecution if they were dependents of naturalized

US citizens. Even this modest move was opposed by the State Department, patriotic societies, and Cyrus Adler, elderly president of the American Jewish Committee, who feared that seeking special treatment for Jews when the country was mired in depression would generate a backlash. Dickstein's plan died in committee.

The protests did win a slight alteration in the immigration rules by late 1933: the requirement that persons seeking entry have on hand sufficient funds to support themselves was waived for those with sponsors—American friends or relations who agreed to accept financial responsibility for the applicant. This precipitated a flood of letters from German Jews to people, culled from New York City phone books, who had the same (or at least a Jewish-sounding) surname, in the hopes that a possibly distant family member (or at least a coreligionist) might help obtain a visa. *New York Times* publisher Arthur Sulzberger and his wife, Iphigene, sponsored more than a score of relatives, or relatives of relatives, but drew the line at non-kin ("I wish I had signed for them all," Iphigene Sulzberger would later write, "I wish to God I had"). Even so, the total number of German Jews who entered the country in 1933 was a mere 585, and the number in 1934 had risen only slightly to 2,310.

Some New Yorkers themselves took the initiative in reaching out across the Atlantic to sponsor persecuted Jews. On April 7, 1933, the Nazis promulgated their first official anti-Semitic ordinance—as opposed to unofficial street thuggery—mandating retirement for professionals and civil servants who were "non-Aryan" (had at least one Jewish grandparent) or were "politically unreliable." Over 1,000 Jewish and socialist scholars were dismissed immediately from German universities and scientific institutions, including roughly a quarter of all the country's physicists, eleven of whom were already or would later become Nobel Prize winners. This act of intellectual decapitation was justified as a cultural cleansing and as a job-creation program for graduates of German universities, over half of whom had been unable since 1929 to find jobs in their field.

That Germany's loss might be America's gain was immediately apparent to many in the US scholarly world, especially given a provision in the 1924 immigration law that authorized issuing non-quota visas to university faculty who had been teaching for at least two years and could prove a job awaited them in the US. On the other hand, academic jobs were scarce here too—depression-era universities, hard hit by declining student enrollments, had laid off thousands of instructors, who now jostled with thousands of newly minted PhDs pursuing scarce openings. Hiring refugees was hardly a priority for most colleges, especially as anti-Semitism was widespread in American academia. In New York City, however, there was an obligation to succor persecuted colleagues as well as an opportunity to augment the ranks of their own institutions and, more generally, to enhance the standing of American scholarship.

In April 1933, Alvin Johnson, founding president of the New School for Social Research, decided the Nazi purge offered a chance to establish at one blow an entire graduate faculty of political and social scientists. Johnson announced the creation of a self-governing University in Exile and selected a dozen refugee scholars to staff it—eleven Germans, one Italian; eleven men, one woman. Almost all were Jews; nearly all were liberals or Social Democrats (no communists were considered); all were fervent antifascists; and all were thrilled by the New School's freedom from anti-Semitism, its modernist agenda, its commitment to democratic values. Collectively the newcomers were akin to New School luminaries such as John Dewey, Charles Beard, Thorstein Veblen, and James Harvey Robinson, mixing a penchant for empirical research with a bent for intellectual activism.

Johnson had assumed he could raise the funds for his ambitious program from Jewish philanthropists but quickly discovered that apart from a substantial gift from one wealthy

Pound Ridge businessman (Hiram Halle), most of those he approached worried that a University in Exile would (like the boycott) only convince anti-Semites that an international Jewish conspiracy really did exist. Johnson got a much warmer reception at the Rockefeller Foundation, in no small part because the organization had been supporting academic programs in Germany since the 1920s, as part of an effort to wean scholars there off German "metaphysics" and to US-style empirical social science.

Johnson actually believed the opposite—that American academicians, increasingly positivistic and conservative, could do with a good jolt of European-style theoretical and methodological sophistication. The Foundation, moreover, preferred to scatter refugees throughout the country, ensuring their ultimate Americanization, while Johnson wanted to concentrate them in a few institutions (especially his), where they could sustain the collective identity that would allow them to leaven American approaches. In the end, both had their way. Johnson got Rockefeller backing for the University in Exile and quickly assembled his refugees in Joseph Urban's striking building on West 12th Street, where they set about studying the nature of German and Italian fascism. And Johnson, in turn, helped the Rockefeller Foundation launch a still wider New York–based rescue operation for academics.

In May 1933, Dr. Stephen Duggan, a former City College professor and now director of the International Institute of Education (IIE), an outfit run out of a West 45th Street loft that encouraged student exchange programs, called a meeting that included Johnson, Rockefeller representatives, and other educators and scientists. The conclave agreed to establish an Emergency Committee in Aid of Displaced German Scholars, which would raise funds—the Foundation pledged to match all contributions on a dollar-for-dollar basis—to bring world-renowned scholars, in all fields, to US universities, at no cost to them; only senior scholars would be eligible, to minimize competition with entry-level American PhDs.

Understanding the moment in grand world-historical terms—the progenitors noted the epic impact on recipient cultures of prior expulsions (Greeks from Byzantium in 1453, Jews from Spain in 1492, Huguenots from France in 1685)—they set about constructing a lifeline across the Atlantic from Europe to New York. Much of the actual work of contacting refugees, potential funders, and host institutions was done by Assistant Secretary Edward R. Murrow, himself a recent (1930) migrant to New York City from Polecat Creek, North Carolina, by way of college in Washington State.

Murrow's efforts ("The most satisfying thing I ever did in my life") helped place 355 refugee academics—including Paul Tillich, Kurt Lewin, Martin Buber, Hans J. Morgenthau, Jacques Maritain, and Herbert Marcuse. Many passed through Gotham to the continent, but some major figures settled in—temporarily or permanently—at local institutions that had launched their own complementary outreach efforts.

Up in Morningside Heights, in 1933, a group of Columbia professors, including philosopher John Dewey, anthropologist Franz Boas, developmental geneticist Leslie Dunn, and economist Wesley Mitchell, met at the Faculty Club and set up a fund to aid displaced colleagues. (Dewey and Dunn became active in the Emergency Committee as well.) By year's end, 125 colleagues had contributed enough (with assistance from the EC) to bring in four visiting scholars. More remarkably, in 1934, Nicholas Murray Butler, Columbia's relatively conservative president, offered affiliation and space (at 429 West 117th Street) to a group of leftist scholars who had fled Frankfurt: the world-famous (and independently funded) Institute for Social Research. Soon such luminaries as Max Horkheimer, Theodor Adorno, Herbert Marcuse, Erich Fromm, Leo Lowenthal, and Karl Wittfogel had regrouped in

Morningside Heights, where they would spend the decade exploring the rising authoritarian threat, the collapse of liberalism, and the crisis of capitalism.

Not all drained brains belonged to academicians: the New York rescue movements—in collaboration with the trade unions—snatched political as well as intellectual brands from the burning. On July 24, 1933, at the request of the International Relief Association (IRA) headed by Albert Einstein, leading Gotham intellectuals and labor activists established a New York branch of the IRA to promote the emigration—by illegal as well as legal means—of Nazi victims. Chaired by historian Charles Beard, its members included Dewey, theologian Reinhold Niebuhr, philosopher Morris Cohen, Roger Baldwin of the American Civil Liberties Union, writer John Dos Passos, Oswald Garrison Villard and Freda Kirchwey (both from *The Nation*), and David Dubinsky from the ILGWU. The IRA channeled aid from US social democrats to the underground resistance in Germany. And in 1934, Vladeck of the Jewish Labor Committee addressed the AFL convention, casting Nazi persecution of Jews as part of a general assault on labor rights and political liberty and winning Federation creation of a Labor Chest to aid unionists and socialists in escaping the fascists.

In 1935, the Nuremberg Laws tightened the noose around "non-Aryan" necks. The new statutes—which deprived all Jews of citizenship, stripped them of almost all legal rights, and barred them from broad categories of employment—were accompanied by a rolling pogrom that intensified and extended physical persecution. Growing numbers of those who had thought they'd found a safe niche now decided they had no future in Germany. Some would be helped by the specialized assistance programs set up in New York, but most asylum seekers quickly bumped up against an exclusionary immigration apparatus designed to filter them out. The number of admitted émigrés grew modestly (to 6,346 in 1936, the first year of the program) but stayed negligible, well below the annual quota allotment.

Their dilemma was not lost on Hitler, who delighting in pointing out his critics' glasshouse hypocrisy. What right had Americans to complain about Nazi anti-Semitic policies? The US, after all, had been "the first to draw practical political consequences from the differentiation of races," the Führer taunted. "Through its immigration law, America has inhibited the unwelcome influence of such races as it has been unable to tolerate within its midst." Nor, for all its pious humanitarianism, was America ready now to harbor exiles: "I would be only too glad," Hitler told *New York Times* columnist Anne O'Hare McCormick, "if the nations which take such an enormous interest in Jews would open their gates to them."

Had he been more taunting still, Hitler might have suggested that those few Jews who did succeed in reaching Gotham—that so-called bastion of antifascism—had best prepare themselves for a rude shock, as they were about to discover that New York had its own nests of Nazis.

3

Nazis in New York

Nazism had arrived in New York in 1922 when émigré members of Hitler's National Socialist German Workers' Party established a local unit in the Bronx. In 1931 the party's Foreign Department anointed this Gotham group as nucleus of a new "Gauleitung [region] USA." When Hitler took formal power in 1933, Deputy Führer Rudolf Hess authorized Heinz Spanknoebel, a resident German national, to create (with help from the Third Reich's consul in New York) a new organization, the "Friends of the New Germany." It had two goals: in the short term, contest the boycott because of treatment of Jews and refute the "vicious lies of atrocities"; in the long run, convince German Americans to back the new regime.

From the Nazi perspective, America's Germans had—after traumatic repression during World War I—wimped out, gone native, assimilated to the point of invisibility. Though Yorkville, centered around First Avenue and 86th Street, still had an active club life revolving around musical presentations, political discussions, and sporting events, the community had indeed been doing its best to fade into the American woodwork. Many had Americanized their names, started using English at home. Theaters that once produced German plays now ran American movies. The Amerikanischer Turnerbund 33 had become the American Gymnastic Union. The community's leading organization, the Steuben Society of America, had been founded in 1919 as part of the new order of things; English was its official language. The United German Societies—a confederation of seventy metropolitan area groups that ran the German Day celebration each October—had an aggregate membership of only 10,000. And German Americans were dropping dramatically as a percentage of Gotham's population—from 22 percent in 1900, they would be a mere 4 percent by 1940.

The ethnic press, in New York as nationally, had also declined drastically since the war. In 1914 there had been over 500 German-language papers and magazines in the United States, with a combined circulation of 3.5 million; in 1933, there were fewer than 150, whose collective outreach had shrunk to a million and a half. Locally, the old *Staats-Zeitung* had retained its preeminence but gone through changes since its prewar heyday. The elderly Herman Ridder had died in 1915, leaving his sons, Bernard, Victor, and Joseph, to steer the paper through war and witch hunt. It survived in part thanks to their connections with the Catholic Church and Democratic Party. The Ridders bought up and consolidated other dailies that weathered the storms less well, including the *Herold*, and the merged *Staats-Zeitung und Herold* (1934) was still selling a respectable 80,000 copies a day in 1938.

Having won a new level of acceptance as loyal Americans, few residents of Yorkville and other German neighborhoods wished to upset the assimilationist applecart. Their response to the Third Reich was accordingly ambivalent.

Some, particularly educated workingmen on the left, came out swinging against the new regime. The old *New York Volks-Zeitung*—organ of German American labor since 1878—had also survived the hard years, though forced to switch from daily to weekly status in 1932. Renamed the *Neue Volks-Zeitung*, it was stridently anti-Nazi—sponsoring a large antifascist rally in 1933—and became more so after the editorship was assumed in 1936 by Gerhart Heinrich Seger, a former Reichstag member and one of the first to be imprisoned by the Nazis (he escaped to New York from the Oranienburg Concentration Camp). Still, the paper's message did not play well with most Germans east of Central Park, and its circulation, more than 20,000 in 1934, sagged steadily over the decade.

Many in Yorkville were in fact quite taken with the Fatherland's vigorous new leadership and resented assaults on it by other New Yorkers. In May 1933, the Steuben Society defended Hitler, asserting Americans were wrong to criticize the campaign against the Jews, which was aimed not at their religion but their (Communist) politics. The *Staats-Zeitung* was more circumspect—reliant as it was on ad revenue from local German Jewish businesses—but responded to readers' cautious curiosity about the New Germany. Editorials praised some Nazi accomplishments, remained silent about anti-Semitic abuses, and opposed the boycott. News reports passed along information obtained from the National Socialist Transocean Agency (a wire service adjunct of Goebbels's Propaganda Ministry), and the paper provided schedules of German programming available on shortwave radio.

This was nowhere near good enough for Herr Spanknoebel, who set out to bully Yorkville into more full-throated support. In July 1933 he stormed into the Ridders' office and demanded the *Staats-Zeitung* begin publishing encomiums to the Third Reich; they refused and threw him out. Spanknoebel now moved in on the United German Societies, demanding their upcoming German Day celebration fly the swastika flag over the 69th Regiment's armory and include addresses by the German ambassador and Spanknoebel himself; he also harangued the group with vicious tirades against Jews. The Society leadership, notably the Ridders, resisted, but this time it was they who were shouted down and thrown out.

Counterattacking immediately, the German Jewish societies split from the United German Societies, saying it had come "completely under the ruthless, ruinous and destructive control of the Nazis." Mayor O'Brien barred access to the armory, lest the swastika fly over a US government building, and German Day was moved to Madison Square Garden under the auspices of the Steuben Society, which disinvited Spanknoebel. Meanwhile, the Ridders had tipped off federal authorities that the Friends' leader had failed to register as a foreign agent, and just as the troublesome Bundesführer, as Spanknoebel was known, was about to be arrested he was whisked back to Germany (grabbed at Gestapo gunpoint, according to some accounts). He was replaced by a more soothing spokesman, Dr. Ignatz Theodor Griebl, who had immigrated to New York in the '20s, become a citizen, obtained a degree from Long Island Medical College, and set up a practice in Yorkville (and Harlem Hospital) specializing in obstetrics and surgery for varicose veins. Under new management, the Friends of New Germany succeeded

Nazis in New York 15

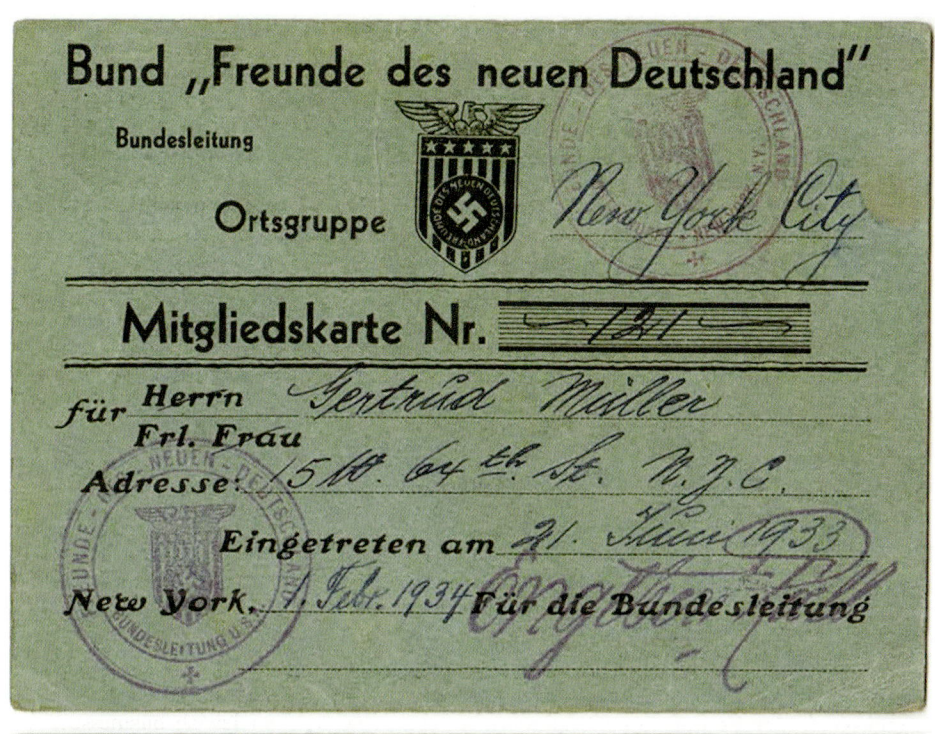

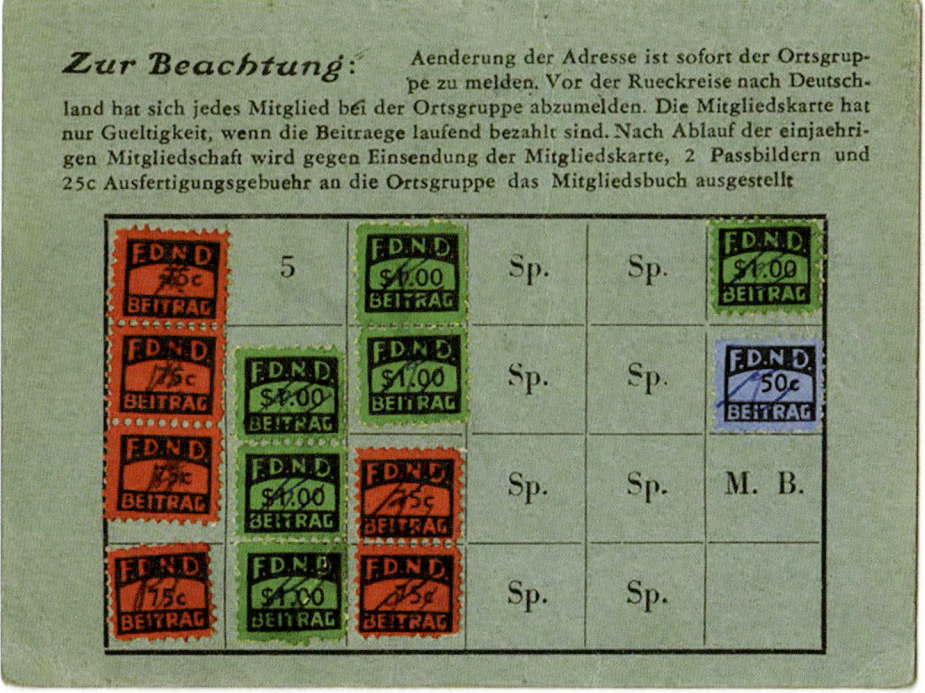

Friends of the New Germany, Membership Card, February 1, 1934. Paper. Gift of Channa and Shragai Cohen, Museum of Jewish Heritage, NY, 2000.A.335. (Gift of Channa and Shragai Cohen)

in wresting control of German Day in 1934, at which twenty thousand heiled speakers who denounced the "Jewish boycott" and called for hanging Untermyer.

The local elite was not about to cede community leadership to Nazi upstarts, and the Steuben Society commenced a tug of war over control of German Day. Yet their hearts, too, were warmed by many of Hitler's actions, and when they recaptured the fete in 1935, it was hard to tell the difference: the Garden was garlanded with swastikas, the Führer was praised vociferously, and the proceedings were broadcast to Germany (by NBC) to demonstrate the regime had substantial support in Gotham.

To counter these inroads, Congressman Dickstein prevailed on his colleagues to launch a probe of "Nazi propaganda." A special House Committee to Investigate Un-American Activities was established—with Dickstein as cochair—which held hearings and issued a 1935 report branding the Friends of New Germany as agent of a foreign power. The Nazi high command, dismayed by the brouhaha, ordered all German citizens to quit the Friends by year's end, and the group promptly collapsed.

Only to be immediately reincarnated, in 1936, now as a putatively all-American operation, the German American Bund. Its Bundesführer, Fritz Kuhn, was a Munich native who had fought in the German Army during World War I (winning the Iron Cross), gotten a degree in chemical engineering from Munich University, gone to work for Henry Ford in Detroit in the late 1920s, and become a US citizen in '34. Though humorless, vain, and unprepossessing—with the air of a Katzenjammer Kids comic strip—Kuhn initially proved an effective leader. From national headquarters in Yorkville (at 178 East 85th Street), he presided over a growing membership. Primarily New York–based (with branches in the Bronx, Brooklyn, Staten Island, Astoria, and Jamaica), it had offshoots across the country: the FBI estimated its 1937 size at 75,000 members.

Most Bundists were lower middle class or working class, first-generation German Americans, battered by the Depression and ongoing postwar prejudice—mechanics and clerks, barbers and shoemakers, waiters and owners of delicatessens. Perhaps a quarter were German nationals recently arrived from south German states, many of them Catholics, many thwarted in finding jobs of similar status in New York. The Bund offered vicarious association with a rising Reich and a network of associations, including a *Jungvolk* for children aged six to thirteen; a local version of Hitler Youth—the *Jungenschaft* for boys, the *Madchenschaft* for girls—that instructed their children in the German language, German history, and Nazi philosophy; for late teens, the Women's Command and, for young men, the *Ordnungsdienst*, whose troopers attended ever-larger rallies in smart uniforms of gray shirt, black trousers, legionnaire-style cap, black Sam Browne belt, and swastika armband (members had to buy their own regalia, at a pricey $27).

The Bund also offered entertainment venues. In the city, Ebling's Casino in the Bronx, on St. Ann's Avenue near the Third Avenue El, was one of several outlets that offered evenings of beer and music. In the surrounding suburbs, the Bund established recreational camps for the entire family, such as Camp Siegfried in New York and Camp Nordland in New Jersey. In the sweltering summer months, the Long Island Railroad put on "Camp Siegfried Specials," which pulled out of Penn Station every Sunday at 8:00 a.m. (making stops at Flatbush and Jamaica), carrying thousands of Bundists to the Yaphank station (in 1937, a day's tally of 40,000 was not unheard of). Awaiting them was a restaurant and inn (whose floral garden was arrayed as a giant swastika), farm fields crisscrossed with walking trails (named after Goering, Goebbels, et al.), and free dances (with Linden beer at 10 cents a glass) on Friday nights. There was also martial arts training for young campers, mass sing-alongs (the Horst Wessel Song, Nazism's unofficial anthem, was particularly popular), and a chance to hear Fritz Kuhn lash the "Choos."

Kuhn had become the spokesman for alienated recent immigrants but was making slower headway winning over older German Americans, despite his argument that they were being denied their proper position in the city's economy and polity by religious enemies. "The Jewish sharks own already [sic] New York City," Bundist leaders claimed, implying, in the words of the Horst Wessel Song, that "When Jewish blood drips from the knife / Then will the German people prosper." Struggling to whip up anti-Semitic sentiment, SA and SS wannabes handed out Aryan pamphlets outside Jewish-owned establishments, heckled public lectures by Jewish exiles, and initiated violent incidents against Jewish Americans.

There were two flaws to this strategy. First, *pace* the Bundists, local Germans were not locked in economic or political combat with local Jews. Second, and more to the point, they were badly outnumbered. There were two million Jews in New York, making them the largest single ethnic-religious element in town, and with each passing day they grew more organized and more politically potent. Nowhere was this more apparent than in the support they received at the highest levels of city government, most spectacularly from the mayor himself.

Even before being elected to City Hall in 1933, La Guardia had spoken out against Nazi depredations, and shortly after his inauguration in 1934 the scrappy "Little Flower" (from "Fiorello") had officially joined Untermyer's boycott organization. Then and later, La Guardia was attacked by Germans and others as an opportunist, but while he was certainly attentive to political arithmetic, his visceral antifascism had multiple sources. Though he liked to say playfully that "I have Jewish blood, but not enough to boast about," his mother, Irene Cohen, was a Jewish immigrant from Austria-Hungary. And as a staunch progressive, he viewed the Nazis as yet another pernicious vested interest—akin to the criminal mobsters and corporate malefactors he'd long been battling at home—whose organized evil must be exposed to public scrutiny. Reform at home and human rights abroad were for La Guardia a matched set.

No surprise, therefore, that on March 7, 1934, he took enthusiastic part in a mock trial in Madison Square Garden—"The Case of Civilization Against Hitler"—sponsored by the American Federation of Labor, the American Jewish Congress, and fifty or so other liberal and Jewish organizations. Before the "jury" of 20,000, twenty "witnesses" testified against the regime. La Guardia and Al Smith represented "American public opinion"; other equally notable New Yorkers detailed Nazi crimes against democracy, free speech, religion, civil liberties, academic freedom, science, world peace, women, liberals, workers, Catholics, and the arts. After former Court of Appeals Judge Samuel Seabury summed up the case, John Haynes Holmes, minister of the Community Church, presented the judgment, in which he proposed convicting the Nazis for "crimes against civilization" (though absolving the German people); and the massive jury roared its approbation.

La Guardia kept at it, to the growing dismay of local Germans. In July 1935 he blocked the granting of commercial licenses to German citizens, in retaliation for Third Reich discrimination against US Jews. Six thousand Germans and German Americans attended protest meetings at the Turnhalle and Yorkville Casino (210 East 86th Street), where the mayor was booed as "a Red and a Jew."

Two years later he escalated again, this time triggering an international incident. In March 1937, speaking to the Women's Division of the American Jewish Congress assembled at the Hotel Astor, La Guardia suggested that officials drafting plans for the 1939 World's Fair add a Chamber of Horrors that would include a figure of Hitler, that "brown-shirted fanatic." Germany lodged an official protest. Secretary of State Cordell Hull apologized for the uncontrollable mayor's behavior. La Guardia promptly repeated his characterization. The Steuben Society and United German Societies complained. So did Bundists of Brooklyn and Queens in a meeting at Schwaben Hall (on Knickerbocker and Myrtle, between Bushwick and Ridgewood). In Germany itself, the Nazi-controlled press went berserk, hurling vituperative appellations across the Atlantic—"dirty Talmud Jew," "whoremonger," "Jewish Bolshevik," "New York's chief gangster." The SS paper *Das Schwarze Korps* published a cartoon of La Guardia as King Kong. The mayor responded that he would not call Hitler to account for these insults as the Führer was "not personally or diplomatically satisfaktionsfaehig" (i.e., of such low social status that a gentleman wouldn't deign to duel him). Further German complaints, he added, would be turned over to Gotham's sewer commissioner.

The contretemps made headlines around the country. FDR, unwilling to be equally forthcoming in public, told a discomfited Hull at a cabinet meeting he completely agreed with the feisty New Yorker. And when the mayor next visited the president, he reported that Roosevelt "smiled as I entered his office. Then he extended his right arm and said, 'Heil, Fiorello!' I snapped to attention, extended my right arm and replied 'Heil, Franklin!' And that's all that was ever said about it."

Time magazine suggested La Guardia's attacks on Hitler were but the opening gun of the city's 1937 mayoral race. "In New York City," the Luce publication commented, "as any political nose-counter knows, the hooked far outnumber the Aryan noses." And indeed, the Democrats acknowledged the centrality of the Jewish vote by nominating Judge Mahoney, the Catholic who had won Jewish kudos by opposing the Berlin Olympics. But La Guardia's reelection was pretty much a shoo-in anyway, and the mayor didn't hesitate to infuriate local Jews by protecting the Bund's constitutional rights—he okayed their parade permits and even banned a counterdemonstration.

Yet for all the Bund's street presence, Kuhn was failing to enlarge the group's base. He got a standing ovation from the 20,000 gathered in Madison Square Garden for the October 4, 1937, German Day but was refused a speaking role on the platform by the Steuben Society, which had now completely repudiated the Bund. Once again, the Nazi leadership was beginning to lose patience with their protégés, even to question the very possibility that German Americans could ever be rallied to their cause, though that notion retained its currency among some of Hitler's "America experts"—like Nazi ideologue Colin Ross.

In 1936 Ross had argued (in *Our America: The German Role in the United States*) that German Americans were no different from the oppressed volk of Austria, Poland, and Czechoslovakia—restive minorities whose assimilation was reversible. Indeed, Ross suggested, the pressures of the Great Depression might fissure the US along ethnic lines, allowing German Americans—who after all constituted a good quarter of the American population—to overthrow Anglo-Saxon (and Jewish) dominance and assemble a multi-ethnic majority coalition that would ally itself with the Third Reich. In 1937 Ross went one better, in *America's House of Destiny: The United States Between Democracy and Dictatorship*, arguing that the country, again in deep economic crisis, was facing dissolution and might turn to fascism to solve its problems. Ross in fact knew better, but pandering to Nazi fantasies was a highly profitable pursuit—Hitler summoned Ross to a private audience at which Ross counseled the Führer to strengthen ties to German Americans. Other experts at the Stuttgart-based Deutsches Ausland-Institut (DAI, German Foreign Institute) seconded this perception, men such as Karl Goetz (author of *Brothers Beyond the Sea*) and DAI director Karl Strölin, who had attended the 1936 German Day at the Garden and been impressed enough to ferry forty Bundists to Stuttgart for consultations.

Privately, however, some experts were beginning to doubt the coming triumph of American fascism; the Jews were too powerful, the German Americans too cowardly. Karl Goerdeler, former Mayor of Leipzig, after visiting New York in 1937, boldly informed the Nazi elite that its consensus on the US was all wrong, that it wasn't a fragmentable pastiche of ethnic groups, that the Germans there were hopelessly assimilated. Goerdeler's assessment was forcefully echoed by the new German ambassador to the United States, Hans Heinrich Dieckhoff, who arrived in the summer of 1937. He wrote Berlin officials that the Bund would never succeed in America because no German "minority" existed in the European sense, and the organization was only stirring up anti-German feelings. Kuhn, in particular, he thought "stupid, noisy and absurd"; Dieckhoff urged the Foreign Ministry to cut him loose.

So, in March 1938, the Nazi government found itself again forced to distance itself from an embarrassing operation. The Bund was firmly declared off-limits to German citizens and barred from using Nazi emblems. Kuhn traveled to Berlin to appeal the decision, was told it was final, but returned to America bragging of his continuing connections. He seems to have been encouraged by the Auslands-Organisation der NSDAP (Foreign Organization of the Nazi Party), whose general position, *pace* the Foreign Office, was that Germans abroad were "obliged to cooperate in the work that Adolf Hitler began." The perception thus nurtured of an ongoing link between Gotham's and Germany's fascists was about to prove fatal to the former.

4

A Fifth Column?

Anschluss—Hitler's annexation of Austria in March 1938—played well in German Gotham. The Ridders' *Staats-Zeitung* applauded it, convinced that the peoples of both countries favored the merger. A Ridgewood newspaper reported that the community "glowed with pride at the annexation of Austria." The Bund was of course ecstatic, and in April, 3,500 supporters packed the Yorkville Casino to hail the seizure as a "birthday gift by Chancellor Hitler [it was his 49th] to Greater Germany."

Suddenly, New York Nazism took on a whole new complexion. Fascism in Europe had now stormed across an established frontier, and its triumph had been facilitated by complaisant compatriots inside the conquered country. Could that happen here? Kuhn's proclamation that summer, before 50,000 cheering Bundists, that Camp Siegfried was "part of Germany in America," seemed freshly menacing.

The term "Fifth Column" came into new currency, having languished since its coinage in 1936, during the Spanish Civil War, when a Franco general had boasted that not only were four of his columns advancing on Madrid, the besieged capital of Republican Loyalists, but a Fifth Column of fascists, inside the city itself, stood ready to assail the defenders from behind their own lines.

Now, in 1938, the Nazis were once again relying on behind-the-lines ethnic allies, using Sudeten Germans to make impossible demands on Czechoslovakia's government, giving Hitler an excuse to intervene on behalf of an "oppressed minority." On September 29, 1938, at Munich, England and France acquiesced in another annexation. On October 1, German troops marched across the frontier. And on October 2, in New York, Fritz Kuhn sponsored a series of extravagant Bund rallies around the metropolitan area—at Prospect Hall in Brooklyn, at Turn-Halls in Astoria and Yorkville, at Camp Nordland in Andover, New Jersey—at which thousands cheered Hitler for "liberating the Sudetens from a Bolshevist-controlled Czechoslovakia."

Seizing on these and other pro-Fascist manifestations, Congressman Dickstein, hyperbolically claiming Hitler's regime was sending millions of dollars to local Bundists for subversive purposes, pushed for another investigation. In a move he was soon to regret, Dickstein joined forces with Martin Dies, a notoriously anti–New Deal, anti-immigrant, anti-labor, anti-civil rights, and anti-Communist congressman from East Texas, who had been trying unsuccessfully to win support for an investigation of the CIO. Rallying groups like Untermyer's Anti-Nazi League and the Federal Council of Churches, he provided the margin needed for Dies to win creation of a House Committee to Investigate Un-American Activities, which the Texan promised would focus on fascists. Once empowered, Chairman Dies—Dickstein having been frozen out of the Committee—did hold hearings in August 1938 on Bund activities, airing wild charges that Kuhn had amassed 480,000 followers, before lighting into labor and the left, ignoring Dickstein's public denunciations.

Congressional alarmism about Nazi subversion gained credence when the FBI uncovered a German espionage network operating out of Gotham, with none other than Dr. Ignatz Theodor Griebl, former leader of the Friends of New Germany, at the center. The ring had begun to unravel with the arrest, in February 1938, of one Guenther Gustave Rumrich, a Chicago-born but German-educated man who had been working in New York as a dishwasher and Berlitz instructor (and attending Bund meetings) when he offered his services to the Nazis for a $50-a-month retainer. Having been assigned by his handlers the task of obtaining some blank US passports, he dimwittedly called the New York Passport Division, claimed he was the under-secretary of state, and asked to have the blanks delivered to him at a midtown hotel. The NYPD Alien Squad showed up instead. When FBI agent Leon Turrou got wind of this, he had Rumrich brought to the Bureau's Foley Square office for interrogation. After three days of grilling, Rumrich confessed to an even sillier plot. He had envisioned luring the commander of Fort Totten's 62nd Coast Artillery to a meeting at the Hotel McAlpin in Herald Square, plans in hand for the Army's entire East Coast defense strategy, at which point Rumrich would have overpowered him using gas hidden in a fountain pen.

Far more disquietingly, Rumrich disclosed to Agent Turrou that he was but a small part of a much larger (and far more competent) operation being run by Griebl, which, since 1934, had been smuggling valuable military information to Germany via couriers posing as stewards on liners of the North German Lloyd and Hamburg-America shipping companies. Griebl's operation, moreover, had linked up with an even older spy ring, run by one Wilhelm Lonkowski, which the Abwehr (German Military Intelligence) had set up back in 1927 to steal American aviation technology for the Luftwaffe then being secretly assembled. Their combined string of operatives had been stealing plans and blueprints (using Leicas to make microphotographic copies) from the Federal Shipbuilding Company in Kearny, NJ, and the Seversky Aircraft plant at Farmingdale, NY, among other sensitive venues, and reports on tactical air exercises at Mitchel Airfield. By 1938, after a virtually trouble-free decade, agents had procured nearly all that was needed to have the Luftwaffe combat ready the following year.

In June, eighteen people were indicted for conspiring to steal military secrets, but by then Griebl, Lonkowski, and twelve others had slipped away to Germany, leaving only four to stand trial in October. In December, after months of sensational coverage, the four were found guilty and negotiated a lucrative deal with the *New York Post* for a series of lurid articles—infuriating J. Edgar Hoover—which Random House then brought out as a 300-page book, *Nazi Spies in America* (1938). It became a huge bestseller.

The discovery that fascism was now for export, and that Bund-connected spies had stolen American defense plans, triggered fresh efforts by established German Americans to put daylight between themselves and Kuhn's minions. Bundists were personae non gratae at the October 2, 1938, German Day festivities—though the meeting expressed its own satisfaction with the acquisition of Sudetenland—and a dozen leading old-line groups lashed out at American Nazism in a *Staats-Zeitung* statement. But what really doomed the Bund were the horrific events that transpired a month later in the Fatherland itself.

5

Kristallnacht

On the night of November 9–10, 1938, the Nazi state launched an anti-Jewish pogrom throughout Germany and Austria—an orgy of pillage, arson, and murder. The Gestapo, SS, and police interned and brutalized nearly 30,000 people placed in concentration camps. Roughly a hundred Jews were killed. More than two hundred synagogues were torched, and almost all were desecrated in some way. Torahs were taken out, spread on the ground, danced upon. Brownshirts trashed schools, looted and burned homes. Over 7,500 Jewish-owned businesses were destroyed. Glass was the target of choice—store panes, display cases, office windows—if it was glass, the Nazis smashed it, leaving sidewalks littered with broken shards, hence crystal night, Kristallnacht. Two days later the regime announced that property damage would be repaired—by levying a huge "atonement fine" on the Jews who'd been victimized. All Jewish retail establishments were shut down. A few weeks later all Jewish assets were confiscated. The future for German Jewry evaporated virtually overnight.

The barbarities outraged Americans. Roosevelt, declaring, "I myself could scarcely believe that such things could occur in a twentieth-century civilization," recalled the US ambassador. Even bitter anti-Semites disassociated themselves from such methods—a nationwide Gallup poll on December 9 found 94 percent disapproved—and in New York there was a storm of protests from labor, religious, political, and social organizations. Prominent Christians staged a rally in Carnegie Hall. The faculty and students of Union Theological Seminary invited those of the Jewish Theological Seminary to a memorial for the victims. Demonstrations were held at North German Lloyd piers, and antifascists threatened to bomb the German consulate. La Guardia, in a coup de théâtre, responded by creating on November 16 an all-Jewish police detail, under Captain Max Finkelstein, president of the Shomrin Society (the NYPD's Jewish fraternal organization), and assigning it to protect assorted German dignitaries and institutions, infuriating the Nazis. (Here he took a leaf from Teddy Roosevelt's playbook, T.R. having assigned, when New York's police commissioner, forty Jewish cops to guard a German clergyman then in town crusading against the Jews.)

Supporters of the anti-Nazi movement protest in the Garment District, November 15, 1938. (Bettmann/Contributor/Getty Images)

Kristallnacht gave sudden life to the languishing boycott movement—on November 15, several hundred of Gotham's educational, scientific, labor, and religious leaders, paced by Dr. William Jay Schieffelin, formed a Volunteer Christian Committee to Boycott Nazi Germany. A poll that month estimated 61 percent of Americans were now prepared to sign up.

Nice gestures, but way too late in the day, especially as despite all its sympathetic outrage the country adamantly refused to open its doors to the surging number of Jews newly desperate to flee Europe. Roosevelt helped somewhat. After Anschluss he had authorized a merger of the German and Austrian quotas and ordered Jewish visa applications be expedited. A week after Kristallnacht, again pushing the limits of presidential authority, he extended the visitor visas of the approximately 15,000 refugees (including Albert Einstein) who had used these non-quota (thus temporary) documents to enter. But the paper barricades erected by State Department bureaucrats remained firmly in place—3,000 applied each day at the US Consulate in Stuttgart, which issued 850 each month.

Resistance went far beyond the striped pants set. Throughout 1938, polls showed consistently that 71–85 percent of Americans opposed increasing the immigration quotas. A Roper survey taken in December, with the pogrom still much in the news, found only 8.7 percent of those sampled favored raising the ceilings to accommodate more refugees.

Ongoing unemployment accounted for some of the rejectionism: nine million people were still jobless that winter. Ongoing anti-Semitism was also part of the mix. Polls found 60 percent of Americans thought Jews had "objectionable qualities," 45 percent thought Jews less honest than Gentiles in business, nearly 50 percent thought they had "too much power" in the US, 24 percent believed they had too many government jobs, and 35 percent thought European Jews were largely responsible for the oppression visited upon them. Ongoing isolationism exacerbated the anti-Semitism, as opponents of intervention feared that anti-Jewish atrocities—like the fictive anti-Belgian atrocities that had spurred US involvement in World War I—might provide a casus belli for warmongers.

With FDR unwilling to buck these attitudes, New Yorkers took on the task. Congressman Dickstein sponsored a law allowing the "mortgaging" of future quotas—borrowing from 1940 and 1941 to expand the allotments of 1938 and 1939. This went nowhere. Congressman Celler tried to get a quota exemption for racial or religious refugees. In vain. Senator Wagner, in February 1939, co-introduced a bill that would allow 20,000 German children under fourteen to enter outside the quota if their support was guaranteed from private, not public sources. Even the AFL supported this effort. But two-thirds of Americans told pollsters they disapproved (though perhaps few as obnoxiously as Laura Delano Houghteling, wife of the US commissioner of immigration [and FDR's cousin], who warned that "20,000 charming children would all too soon grow into 20,000 ugly adults"). FDR backed away from the bill and it died in committee, though a "Mercy Ships" law to welcome British children evacuated from England passed handily the following year.

Most Jewish organizations rejected even this degree of public agitation, fearful that continued protest would only stoke the increasingly ugly anti-Semitism. Just after Kristallnacht, representatives of the General Jewish Council decided "there should be no parades, public demonstrations or protests by Jews." Rabbi Wise of the American Jewish Congress was now at one with the American Jewish Committee, which declared that it was "neither desirable nor practicable to recommend any change in the quota provisions." When FDR asked Samuel Rosenman, his closest Jewish adviser, if more refugees should be allowed in, Rosenman opposed such a move because "it would create a Jewish problem in the U.S." These leaders weren't alone: when a *Fortune* poll asked respondents in mid-1939 how they would vote on opening the doors if they were members of Congress, 85 percent of Protestants, 84 percent of Catholics, and an astonishing 25.8 percent of Jews said they'd vote no.

6

Émigrés Arrive: Manhattan

The quotas stayed in place and succeeded in damping down Jewish immigration. The 1939 German-Austrian allotment of 27,000 was quickly oversubscribed—309,000 Jews had applied—forcing those rejected to seek other havens. America's entryway remained impeded until October 1941, when Germany's exit door swung ominously shut.

At that point, since 1933 roughly 97,000 German and Austrian Jews had been admitted on permanent visas (and perhaps another 30,000 on temporary visas)—the vast bulk of them having arrived between 1938 and 1940. Of these 127,000 refugees perhaps 70,000 settled in New York City—the first significant influx to Gotham since the immigration barriers had gone up. A relatively tiny group compared to pre-1924 cohorts—its members could have fit comfortably into Yankee Stadium—it would have an outsized impact on the city.

Because the first contingent to arrive, in 1933–35, had featured Hitler's initial victims—university professors and leftists—most subsequent German refugees were popularly thought to be radical intellectuals. The late-thirties arrivals did include some spectacularly accomplished figures in the arts and sciences, all of them antifascist, and these men and women would have an immense influence on metropolitan (and national) culture and politics. But professional intellectuals accounted for fewer than 10 percent of the total.

Still, the overall group's demographic profile differed sharply from that of late nineteenth- and early twentieth-century immigrant streams, which had consisted overwhelmingly of farmers and workers, most with rudimentary educations, who had left their small towns or rural districts for primarily economic reasons. In contrast, those escaping Nazism in the thirties were mainly upper- or middle-class businessmen, professionals (especially doctors and lawyers), and white-collar workers. They tended to be well-educated city-dwellers (especially from Berlin, which had been home to one-third of Germany's Jews in 1933), and older than their average predecessors, many having reached middle or even old age when forced to flee for their lives.

Many of the new refugees had lived comfortably in the best neighborhoods of some of Europe's most sophisticated urban centers, though few were able to sustain such a lifestyle in New York. Some affluent refugees did smuggle out portable forms of wealth, especially diamonds;

among this group were the diamond dealers themselves, those who fled Antwerp and Amsterdam when the Nazis overran Belgium and the Netherlands in 1940. However, most émigrés were forced to leave their possessions behind. And while many had moneyed sponsors, pride (or acrimony) usually brought an early end to such support. Employers were reluctant to hire them, and when they were taken on, jobless natives resented it. The academics who had been jackbooted out in 1933 had received extensive assistance, but many professors who came later never resumed their careers. Nor did many other professionals: lawyers, journalists, and chemists became butlers, factory hands, newsstand operators. Wives found it somewhat easier to adjust—often much younger than their husbands, they tended to learn the lingo more quickly—but their jobs, too, were mainly menial (domestics, salesgirls, babysitters, seamstresses), and their new breadwinner status introduced unaccustomed strains into patriarchal bourgeois households.

In search of housing, the newcomers fanned out across the city—though avoiding Bund Country. Yorkville didn't attract or accept refugees—Kuhnians were predictably hostile to "Refu-Jews"—and home-hunting Germans gave Ridgewood a similarly wide berth.

One favorite roosting place, just across Central Park from Yorkville, was the Upper West Side, a capacious chunk of Manhattan bounded by Central Park West and Riverside Drive, 70th and 100th Streets, whose economic and cultural spine was Broadway. The Upper West Side attracted perhaps 15,000 to 20,000 of the refugees, roughly a quarter of the influx. They took up lodging in the many brownstones that had been converted to residential hotels with community kitchens, moved in with relatives who had cavernous apartments to share, or were placed in local hostelries like the Milburn (West 76th) or Marseilles (West 103rd) by resettlement agencies such as HIAS, the Hebrew Immigrant Aid society mentioned earlier.

The new Upper West Siders, who came disproportionately from the ranks of big city intellectuals and professionals, were drawn by the district's familiar urban environment. There were libraries and universities; restaurants, cabarets, and cafes like Eclair on West 72nd; specialty shops that dealt in imported halvah and sauerkraut. Drawn by its European feel, they in turn reinforced Broadway's "mittel Europeanisch" flavor, imparting a slower rhythm, as people (observed a WPA writer in 1941) tended to "stroll in a comfortable pace as if walking on the boulevards of Berlin or Vienna."

They were drawn, too, by the area's Jewishness. A destination point for European Jews since the nineteenth century, by the early twenties the Upper West Side had over 50,000 Jewish residents. Successful Russian and Polish (and in lesser numbers German) manufacturers and jobbers had continued to flock there in the late 1920s and early 1930s, attracted by its speedy subway link to the Garment Center and its art deco apartment houses and grand residential hotels. By 1934, it was the only large area in Manhattan where Jews constituted over 50 percent of the population. It boasted twenty synagogues, mostly modern Orthodox, within a thirty-block radius; several Jewish Centers; a YWHA on 110th Street; and an abundance of women's groups (the 1,400-member sisterhood of Mt. Neboh Temple on West 79th was the nation's largest). The streets were well stocked with kosher butchers, kosher bakeries like Clark-Brody on 90th and Amsterdam, and Steinberg's kosher dairy restaurant on Broadway and 81st. And new ones quickly came on board that catered to émigré tastes, like Schreiber's, "Good and Strictly Kosher, Famous 25 Years in Vienna."

Religion helped newcomers fit in. Though seldom as observant as earlier immigrants, they happily made use of local cultural resources (Belgian refugees sent their children to Jewish parochial schools). But religion could also be a barrier, as émigrés stumbled over ancient animosities between Gotham's German and East European Jews. Some among the predominant Eastern Europeans considered the refugees more German than Jewish, found them arrogant and condescending (everything was better in *die Heimat*), and were infuriated by their unfamiliarity with Yiddish culture. One refugee housewife entered a delicatessen, was addressed by the owner in Yiddish, replied she didn't understand, at which he screamed at her: "Get out! You German Jews always thought you were too good for us! Go join the goyim; that's where you belong! Or learn Yiddish! It's a beautiful language!"

In fact, many West Side Germans were determined to Americanize themselves as fast as possible, the Nazi nightmare having left them deeply ambivalent about all things German, including the language. The leading émigré journal, *Aufbau/Reconstruction*, which had started as the obscure organ of a west side German-Jewish club in 1934, had by the late thirties become the most influential German language publication for exiles in the US, with a readership in the thousands. Yet *Aufbau*'s subtitle read: "Dedicated to the Americanization of the Immigrants," and its pages were full of information about New York City's history, politics, businesses, and places of recreation. (The paper also criticized the German Americans across the park for being insufficiently assimilated, as evidenced by their fondness for fascism; *Aufbau* editors scanned the *Staats-Zeitung* for hints of anti-Semitism and closely monitored Bund activities.)

A second, even larger group—more than 20,000 of the refugees—headed for the hills of northern Manhattan. The Washington Heights exiles were less cosmopolitan, less wealthy, less urban (Berliners constituted a much smaller percentage), and included more rural and small-town Jews from South Germany. Businessmen and white- or blue-collar workers loomed larger in the occupational profile, which accounted, perhaps, for the entrepreneurial alacrity with which a variety of upholstery, watch, hat, chocolate, and machine-repair shops sprouted in the area, which ran from 135th Street up to 193rd.

Emigrants were drawn by the neighborhood's parks—especially Fort Tryon—and its proximity to the river: so many settled into the brick apartment houses bordering the Hudson between 158th and 186th Streets that the territory (like the Catskills) became known as the "Jewish Alps." On Cabrini Boulevard between 181st and 186th Streets lay the massive, newly constructed cliffside complex of Castle Village—five thirteen-story towers built on seven acres by developer Charles Paterno. Having had great success in the area with his Tudor-style Hudson View Gardens (1924), Paterno in 1938 tore down his extravagant 1909 mansion (Paterno Castle) to make way for the 583 apartments that came on line in 1939, just as the inrush was cresting.

The newcomers also liked the Heights's small-town atmosphere—despite its having an overall population of 200,000, larger than many European or American cities—and they soon established a highly visible presence. A dozen synagogues sprang up, as did yeshivas, kosher butchers, German bakeries, countless small shops, mutual aid societies, and the Prospect Unity Club at 158th Street, the country's largest German Jewish club. Though constituting less than 10 percent of the area's denizens (reaching 25 percent in particular nodes), the émigrés made Washington Heights the largest and most concentrated German Jewish community in the United States. By 1940, the area around 158th Street near Broadway and Fort Washington Avenue was called the "Fourth Reich."

Religion played a stronger role up here than farther down the west side, with the Orthodox having a disproportionate influence and visibility (despite constituting only a quarter of Washington Heights Jewry). Their prominence, in turn, helped attract, in 1938, an entire Orthodox community from Frankfurt am Main—the K'hal Adath Jeshurun congregation, aka the "Breuers," after their leader, Rabbi Dr. Joseph Breuer, who moved the community to New York after Kristallnacht. Here Breuer and his impoverished followers set about reconstructing the old-country *kehilla* (caring community), rebuilding piece by piece its cradle-to-grave network of educational and religious institutions.

7

Émigrés Arrive: Williamsburg

The real center of New York Orthodoxy lay across the East River in Jewish Williamsburg, where a third contingent of refugees—primarily from Central and Eastern Europe—were attracted by the neighborhood's religious intensity and institutions. There certainly wasn't much secular appeal to the densely packed tenement district—just above the Brooklyn Navy Yard and Wallabout Market and just behind the docks, factories, and refineries lining the oil-slicked East River. Indeed, the area bounded by Broadway, Wythe Avenue, and Heyward Street had been having a very hard Depression—as chronicled in Daniel Fuchs's *Summer in Williamsburg* (1934)—and its spinal avenues (Bedford, Lee, Marcy, and Division) had seen far better days.

Elegant mansions and row houses had set the tone here through the early twentieth century, when affluent Anglo-Protestant industrialists and professionals (as well as some of the city's wealthiest German Jews) had peopled the district, constructing clubs, churches, and a few synagogues, including the borough's largest, Reform-leaning Beth Elohim's red brick Victorian temple on Keap Street (1876). But then came the Williamsburg Bridge (1903) and the massive influx over the "Jews' Highway" from the Lower East Side. As Russians and Poles poured in during the years preceding and following the First World War, most WASPs departed. So did the better-off German Jews, who headed for Flatbush, Borough Park, and Crown Heights (Beth Elohim sold off its temple to an Orthodox congregation in 1921 and moved to new quarters on Eastern Parkway). This section of Williamsburg—the wider community retained a substantial Irish and Italian presence—had become a solidly working-class Jewish district.

The availability of jobs in the garment industry, retail trade, and booming real estate and construction business kept the area relatively prosperous during the 1920s. But after the Crash, when all these sectors collapsed, Williamsburg spiraled rapidly downward. A 1936 Jewish Welfare Board study found the percentage of families on relief was 50 percent higher in Williamsburg than in Brooklyn as a whole. Housing stock deteriorated, too, and soon the area led the borough in substandard apartment buildings. Not surprisingly, when the New Deal's Williamsburg Houses 1,600 apartments went up in 1938, more than 20,000 applied to live there. With many cultural and social institutions facing financial ruin, it seemed the ghetto might implode as a residential area.

Yet while the gray and dreary slum tenements were indeed swept by dreams of escape, they also spawned more collective responses to community crisis. Most were similar to organized initiatives elsewhere in the city—radicalism, New Dealism, gangsterism—but what predominated here was religious revivalism, specifically an effort to reinvigorate, indeed to refashion, Orthodox Judaism.

Orthodoxy had proven notoriously difficult to sustain in the American environment. The great bulk of the city's Jews had long since reached varying degrees of accommodation—Reform, Conservative, or secular—with the dominant culture. In the 1920s, Orthodoxy itself had morphed into a home-grown "modern" version, making its peace with beardless English-speaking rabbis, working and shopping on the Sabbath, men going bareheaded on the job and out in public, and relaxed adherence to dietary laws and separation of the sexes. The Ashkenazic synagogues and schools occupying Williamsburg's former clubs and churches remained Orthodox in form but were increasingly assimilationist in practice.

There were, to be sure, lots of pious immigrant Jews who tried, in their *shtiebels* (small makeshift synagogues and prayer rooms in storefronts, basements, or apartments), to maintain European standards of observance. Yet even they found it all but impossible to bequeath such standards to their children, who were under enormous social and economic pressure to Americanize. Even youths who wanted to hew to tradition—like the single young men who formed a branch of Young Israel on Bedford Avenue—found it necessary to make concessions to prevailing mores, like holding mixed dances to gain members.

Part of the problem was the paucity of educational institutions dedicated to transmitting customary values. The handful of available yeshivas (religious schools) were a far cry from the imposing seminaries of Europe, offering only rudimentary religious instruction to preteens after regular school hours, in a kind of pedagogical postscript. Most Orthodox parents in the 1920s and 1930s sent their children to the city's public schools partly to comply with compulsory education statutes (though these did permit the establishment of religious schools) and partly because they feared that without a secular education the next generation would be condemned to a life of poverty. Yet if their children's Orthodoxy remained intact after years of mixing with non- (or more liberal) Jewish children, it would not likely survive attendance at one of the city's public colleges, which in the 1930s were hotbeds of radicalism and secularism.

Into this breach stepped a handful of rabbis and laymen determined to not only arrest but reverse the erosion of Orthodoxy. In 1923, a group of young men formed a Williamsburg branch of Agudath Israel ("Union of Israel"), a worldwide political movement established in 1912 to promote Orthodoxy (and oppose Zionism). The Brooklynites had the more modest goal of creating an environment in which they could practice what they considered a less compromised form of Judaism without fear of being ridiculed as outdated fanatics. Most were American born, as comfortable in English as in Yiddish, and intent on future careers in business or the professions, but they devoted their after-work hours to studying the Talmud in their basement headquarters on Rodney Street.

The Agudath chapter's informal adviser and role model was Rabbi Gedaliah Schorr, a brilliant Torah scholar and charismatic teacher-activist. Schorr promoted reverence for the great scholar-leaders of European Jewry and urged stricter standards of religious practice on Agudath members, and on the wider Williamsburg community. On Friday afternoons, wielding a loudspeaker, Schorr would mount milk boxes on Lee Avenue, the hub of the business district, and exhort shoppers not to patronize stores that opened on the Sabbath.

Agudath made minimal progress until after the Crash, when local membership expanded and additional branches emerged in other Jewish sections of the city. Among the new recruits in 1931 was the American-born, English-speaking, well-to-do, impeccably dressed Elimelech Gavriel (universally known as "Mike") Tress. Born on the Lower East Side in 1909 to immigrant parents from the Russian Pale, Tress was raised in an intensely pious home by his mother (his father having died at twenty-five). He attended public schools, parlaying good grades at Seward Park into acceptance at the free-tuition-and-books Queens College, and went on to a successful career managing a textile firm. Yet Tress continued to daven with a minyan every morning, and when he learned of Agudath's ambition to forge an Orthodox youth movement, he signed up, becoming the group's president within six months. Escalating Rabbi Schorr's Lee Avenue initiative, Tress established a grass-roots campaign that gathered signatures on a mass pledge to refrain from Saturday purchases, organized a rally of several thousand potential boycotters, and succeeded in pressuring half the street's stores into shutting up shop on Shabbos. He achieved similarly impressive results when he went after local synagogues that fielded non-religious singing stars from the Yiddish theater, rather than cantors, to enhance turnout. By decade's end, Agudath had established its own newspaper and begun building a national movement.

A third member of the revivalist brigade was Hungarian-born Rabbi Shraga Feivel Mendlowitz, who worked to shore up Orthodoxy's educational bastions. In 1923, fresh from a campaign to tighten inspection procedures for certifying meat as kosher, Rabbi Mendlowitz joined the faculty (and quickly became principal) of Yeshivah Torah Vodaath, an elementary-level religious school established in Williamsburg in 1918. In 1926 Mendlowitz added a Mesivta (high school) for boys above bar mitzvah age. Some objected that RIETS— Manhattan's Rabbi Isaac Elchanan Theological Seminary, directed by Dr. Bernard Revel— was the only institution Orthodoxy needed to produce rabbis, just as Conservatives relied solely on the Jewish Theological Seminary. Mendlowitz, however, had a different vision for Torah Vodaath. It would offer Talmudic studies to all comers, even those without a rabbinical career in mind. It would reject Revel's synthesis of torah instruction and secular learning, which led Revel in 1928 to fold RIETS into a new Yeshiva College, the first liberal arts school under Orthodox auspices; Mendlowitz considered this yet another compromise with the forces of irreligion. Torah Vodaath would, like Yeshiva, seek out intellectually rigorous teachers, especially graduates of famous Lithuanian yeshivas. Mendlowitz also intended to add to his pedagogical mix the spiritual intensity of Polish-Galician Hasidism.

Mendlowitz was himself a Hasid—"pious one" in Hebrew—and thus part of a religious revitalization movement founded in the eighteenth century by Jewish mystics, followers of the Ba'al Shem Tov. Hasidic congregational communities, organized as "courts" around "rebbes"—dynastic leaders combining religious and political authority—had spread rapidly throughout the shtetls and cities of Eastern and Central Europe, thanks to its populist appeal: it promised a direct and joyous relationship with God for the poor and uneducated, not just the ascetic scholarly elite. At its height in the first half of the nineteenth century, Hasidism had won the allegiance of millions, perhaps a majority of Eastern European Jews. Since then it had been in slow decline, but many Hasidic communities kept change at bay by holding fast to traditional practices. They adopted distinctive attire: men in black suits, coats, and hats; women in full-length dresses. Facial hair was determinedly anti-modern: men let their beards grow and sported payos (long side curls); married women kept their hair covered or shaved it off completely and wore a wig. Gender arrangements were deeply patriarchal, sexual spheres strictly partitioned: men ran religious and political affairs, women looked after the households and raised large families. Religious practices were earthy and ecstatic, not ascetic and rational. They cultivated emotional intensity and communal enthusiasm through singing, dancing, storytelling, drinking, and engaging in festive meals.

There was not a big Hasidic presence in Williamsburg in the 1930s, because European rebbes had long enjoined their followers not to go to America, which they called the *Treyfe Medina* (the Unclean Country). There were, however, numerous individual Hasids like Rabbi Mendlowitz in residence, and at least one Hasidic community, the Malochim of Williamsburg. Many of its members were Torah Vodaath Mesivta students who followed the Maloch—Rabbi Chaim Avraham Dov Levin, who had arrived after the First World War to a pulpit in the Bronx. A respected Torah scholar, Levin had studied Hasidic thought in the town of Lubavich, Belorussia, center of the Chabad movement, where he had taught the young Rabbi Yosef Yitzchak Schneersohn, then being groomed as Chabad's future leader.

By the late thirties, Torah Vodaath and Agudath Israel had helped make Williamsburg a self-confident beachhead for traditional Orthodoxy. Which is why, from 1938 on, Jews of similar theological bent began flowing into its treeless streets and decrepit tenements, heedless of the lack of refinements or creature comforts available on the Upper West Side and in Washington Heights. What drew them was partly the cheap rent but mainly the warm reception. On the first night German refugee Gershon Kranzler arrived in the city, he went straight to Agudath's Rodney Street headquarters, found dancing in full swing, and was immediately drawn into the circle, introduced to all the members, made one of the boys...

Kranzler's choice of destination was not mere happenstance. Immediately after Kristallnacht, Williamsburg's Orthodox community, paced by Tress, Schorr, and Mendlowitz, had thrown yet another New York City lifeline across the Atlantic. In 1939, Tress organized a Refugee and Immigration Division of Agudath Israel, which enlisted Torah Vodaath students and other volunteers in rounding up the financial affidavits needed for obtaining visas. Given the relative poverty of the Orthodox community, Tress arranged for a few wealthy supporters (including himself) to transfer money to others, who would then present themselves as sponsors. (Tress rapidly went through his own savings, then mortgaged his property to raise additional funds.) The trio also established contacts in Washington to speed the processing of applications. After the invasion of Poland, when 3,000 rabbis and students from leading yeshivot fled to Vilna, in neutral Lithuania, Agudath helped some escape to the US and Palestine via Russia and Japan. (So, too, did Yeshiva College, recognized as a legitimate institution of higher learning by the State Department, and the Union of Orthodox Rabbis, which in November 1939 established the Emergency Committee for War-Torn Yeshivoth, soon to be known as the Vaad ha-Hatzala, to raise funds for the rescue effort.) The New York Orthodox also sent food packages to starving Jews trapped in Poland's Nazi-organized ghettos, defying a British-imposed blockade on German-occupied Europe.

To house arriving refugees, the Williamsburg Agudath raised money from Jewish groups across the city for a down payment on a three-story mansion at 616 Bedford Avenue, into which they moved in January 1939. Within three months a mushrooming staff of volunteers had established a refugee home on the top floor for indigent unmarried male refugees, who were fed in the Torah Vodaath's dining room and nourished spiritually by Rabbi Schorr, who opened a night Yeshiva for their benefit. For the vast majority of immigrants—who arrived as families—apartments were rounded up and stocked with furniture, linens, and housewares collected by Orthodox girls going door to door.

The Williamsburg rescuers also worked at finding jobs for the newcomers and managed to place hundreds in Sabbath-observing positions. In this sphere the immigrants proved to be a source of their own salvation. Most refugee diamond merchants settled on the Upper West Side. Yet many in the industry's arriving work force of polishers, cleavers, sawyers, and setters—4,000 to 5,000 of whom made it to America, the bulk of them Belgian Orthodox Jews—opted for Williamsburg, an easy commute by subway to the Canal Street complex and the exploding 47th Street diamond district. They also set up workshops in Williamsburg itself and taught the trade to locals pulled from the wreckage of the garment industry, as well as to newcomers sent along by Agudath, generating hundreds of high-paying positions that would soon rejuvenate the neighborhood's economy.

The newcomers provided a spiritual boost as well as an economic one by moving rapidly into (and helping finance an expansion of) the refurbished Orthodox infrastructure. Yeshiva Torah Vodaath expanded so dramatically that in March 1941 thousands attended the dedication of a new Mesivta Building on South 3rd Street, an event that drew congratulations from Governor Lehman, Senator Wagner, and President Roosevelt. And soon Williamsburg would become home to some of the giants of European Jewry, those same revered Torah scholars for whom their Brooklyn devotees had been, unwittingly, preparing a place.

The very first of these immigrant Orthodox princes, however, chose to touch down in an adjacent domain. On March 19, 1940, Yosef Yitzchak Schneersohn, the sixth Chabad Lubavitch Rebbe, arrived on the Swedish-American liner *Drottningholm* at its West 57th Street pier. There, as befit the leader of a major Hasidic dynasty—"Chabad" was an acronym for the Hebrew words for wisdom, intelligence, and faith—the Rebbe was met by civic dignitaries, twenty-five orthodox rabbis, and 500 followers. Schneerson had refused to leave Warsaw when the Nazis invaded, remaining to aid the escape of as many Jews as possible. After lobbying by many Jewish leaders and the intercession of the United States Department of State, the Rebbe was finally granted diplomatic immunity and given safe conduct to go via Berlin and Riga to New York City. After a few months' stay at the Greystone Hotel on the Upper West Side, the Rebbe established his headquarters in Crown Heights, in a building at 770 Eastern Parkway, purchased for him by an investment banker supporter.

Schneerson threw himself into ongoing rescue efforts, pressuring government officials to validate visas for trapped Jews, including his daughter, Chaya Mushka, and her husband, Rabbi Menachem Mendel Schneerson (who would make good their escape to Gotham in June 1941). Already thinking, as well, of the long-term future, the Lubavitcher Rebbe quickly established his own Talmudic seminary (Tomchei Tmimim Lubavitch) and set out to promote Hasidic Orthodoxy in Gotham and throughout the United States, a missionary vision that would far transcend anything the young Williamsburgers had dared to dream.

8

Aliens and Enemies

German American Bundists found the accelerating influx of "refu-Jews" deeply disturbing. But after Kristallnacht, which Fritz Kuhn and colleagues had heartily applauded, local fascists had bigger things to worry about.

On the wintry evening of February 20, 1939, Madison Square Garden was packed with Nazis ostensibly there to celebrate George Washington's birthday—Kuhn's attempt to counter charges that the Bund was un-American. Inside the arena, a capacity crowd roared approval and screamed "Heil Hitler" as, from the rear, a drum and bugle corps stepped off, beating a tattoo, followed by 400 of the 1,200 *Ordnungsdienst* (storm troopers) in attendance, their gray-shirted arms outthrust in fascist salute as they marched toward the speakers' platform. There Bundesführer Kuhn waited beneath a towering portrait of Washington flanked by giant black swastikas and US flags. To ear-splitting applause, the corpulent Kuhn, in his thick German accent, hurled fervent denunciations at President "Franklin D. Rosenfeld" and his "Jew Deal," agents of a Bolshevik-Jewish conspiracy. "Stop Jewish Domination of Christian America!" bellowed one of the banners. "1,000,000 Bund Members by 1940!" promised another.

In fact, this crowd was numerically (and acoustically) dwarfed by the one hundred thousand protesters who flooded the blocks along Eighth Avenue from 47th to 52nd Streets—hurling imprecations and toting banners like "Smash Anti-Semitism" and "Drive the Nazis Out of New York."

The event proved to be the Bund's swan song. Within one week of the rally—notable for its massive display of storm trooper muscle—La Guardia symbolically emasculated the *Ordnungsdienst* by barring them from donning uniforms in all places of public assembly. La Guardia had long contrasted his support for freedom of speech in Gotham with Nazi practices in Germany—a stand he reiterated to a packed March 3, 1939, Carnegie Hall meeting, billed as "New York's Answer to the Bund" and sponsored by the Council Against Intolerance in America. Even as he spoke, the mayor had already directed Investigations Commissioner William Herlands to investigate the Bund's financial records to see if he could scare up tax

Mounted police hold back a protest of a German American Bund rally outside Madison Square Garden, February 20, 1939. (AP Photo/Murray Becker, File)

irregularities and provide legal cover for a crackdown. Herlands's report, issued on May 17, 1939, indeed found multiple (if petty) violations, and La Guardia sent it along to District Attorney Thomas Dewey requesting criminal prosecution.

The DA had already leapt into the fray. Dewey, who had nearly unseated Governor Lehman in 1938, and was now thinking of running for president in 1940, could hardly have failed to notice that attacking the Bund was good politics. And if he had, all doubts would have been erased by the plaudits that greeted Warner Brothers' April release of *Confessions of a Nazi Spy*, a melodramatic, quasi-documentary dramatization of the 1938 New York City spy trial, based on G-Man Leon Turrou's book. A breakthrough for Hollywood—whose largely Jewish producers had shied away from frontally confronting the Hitler regime—*Confessions*, as a Warner PR man boasted, was the first movie "to call a swastika a swastika." Forging far ahead of the facts, the film—which premiered at the Strand Theatre in Times Square on April 29—depicted the Yorkville Bundists as a Fifth Column ready and eager to take up arms against the American government at the behest of its leader, who looked and sounded remarkably like Fritz Kuhn. (The Bundesführer promptly sued the studio for libel.)

On May 2, 1939, Dewey's agents seized financial records from the Bund's West 85th Street headquarters. On perusing the ledgers, they discovered that Kuhn had misappropriated part of the $14,548 netted from the February rally. Further digging discovered the motivation. Kuhn, a notorious womanizer who was often spotted with girlfriends at Broadway nightclubs or Yorkville beer halls, had recently met a blond divorcee from LA, Mrs. Florence Camp (promptly dubbed "Meine Camp" by the tabloids), and he had run up substantial bills calling her long distance and moving her to New York. Kuhn was arrested for embezzlement, and, after trial in November—two months after the Reich invaded Poland—he was found guilty and sentenced to 2½ to 5 years in Sing Sing. "Kuhn a Prisoner of War," blared the Bund, which soon splintered and collapsed.

But if *Deutschsland, Deutschsland über alles* would no longer resound throughout Madison Square Garden, similar sentiments could still be found on display in Yorkville, as immigrant English poet W. H. Auden discovered in 1940. Visiting a crowded presentation of the Nazi propaganda film *Campaign in Poland*, at the 500-seat Ninety-sixth Street Theater, Auden was startled to hear shouts of "Kill Them" ring out when Poles put in an onscreen appearance. And while the *Staats-Zeitung* and Steuben Society had finally condemned the Nazi dictatorship, they now drew a sharp line between fascist fanatics and the mass of the German people, forcefully opposing US intervention on behalf of Britain. At a Hotel Astor Steuben Society dinner on September 17, 1939, shortly after war commenced in Europe, its leader, Theodore H. Hoffman, had called for strict enforcement of the Neutrality Act and arms embargo, in clear dissent from calls for a change of course, issued just days before by a group of German American leftist, liberal, and refugee organizations.

Hitler's May 1940 Blitzkrieg into the Low Countries raised the stakes, as many believed only perfidy could explain its astonishingly swift success. Certainly FDR thought so, and in a May 16 address to Congress he condemned "the treacherous use of the fifth column.…" Such convictions made the post-invasion assembly by 12,000 German Americans on Randall's Island, to hear an address by the Reich's vice consul and offer a stiff-armed salute as the swastika flag went by, extremely ill advised. On May 26, FDR warned in a fireside chat that the US, too, must beware "the Trojan Horse" menace—the "fifth column that betrays a nation unprepared for treachery"—and he assured listeners that "we must and will deal vigorously" with all such "spies, saboteurs and traitors."

The president's speech, and subsequent behind-the-scenes encouragement, generated a torrent of anxious prose, unswayed (perhaps even spurred) by the formation in New York that June of a German American Congress for Democracy, pledged to fight Fifth Column activities (among the dozen constituent groups was the Roland German-American Democratic Society chaired by State Assemblyman Robert F. Wagner Jr., the senator's son). That same month, the *New York World-Telegram* ran a series of articles by journalist George Britt—brought out that summer as a bestselling book entitled *The Fifth Column Is Here*—in which Britt claimed that a "cold official estimate based on investigation" suggested that more than a million Fifth Columnists were already in place, "their hearts black with hostile intentions." This conspiracy, "more sinister than any criminal underworld of the movies," lurked wherever secret information could be gleaned, such as aircraft factories (Bundists were thickly concentrated near Farmingdale) or hotels, where, Britt darkly warned potential guests, nine-tenths of the waiters, maids, and porters were Germans, especially in room service.

In August, journalist Edgar Mowrer produced a pamphlet, *Fifth Column Lessons for America*, to which Wall Street lawyer and Roosevelt confidante William Donovan—later founder of the OSS, the precursor to the CIA—lent his name as coauthor, at the president's urging; it suggested that several million Germans would happily work with the Gestapo if and when war came. August also brought the Radio City Music Hall release of the March of Time's film *The Ramparts We Watch*, which while rejecting scattershot bigotry against German Americans, implied a Fifth Column was busily undermining the country. FBI director Hoover had assured FDR that such initiatives were unlikely, given Germany's concern not to provoke the US, but when Roosevelt banged on about Fifth Columnists, Hoover changed course, and the FBI began claiming that subversives had penetrated every area of American life.

It was in this atmosphere that in June 1940 Congress passed, and FDR signed, the Alien Registration Act (or Smith Act, after one of its authors). The law required that all aliens over fourteen report to their local post office for fingerprinting and submit a sworn statement of their political affiliations. It permitted deportation of non-citizens who "advocate, abet, advise, or teach the duty, necessity, desirability or propriety of overthrowing or destroying any government in the United States by force or violence," or were members of any group that did.

According to the 1930 census an estimated 3,600,000 million people in the United States were subject to the Smith Act, of whom 1,128,217 lived in New York City. Authorities set up a host of registration sites around Gotham—City Hall, the Times Square information center, the (outer) borough halls, post offices, and designated schools—and staffed them with several thousand typists and fingerprint experts. Over a four-month period, from August 27 to December 26, close to a million aliens trooped to these sites, spurred by penalties of six months' imprisonment and a thousand-dollar fine for failure to register, and received a card that they were required to carry at all times.

Tensions in the German community would heighten steadily during the following year, fed by anxious recollections of First World War–era anti-Hun hysteria. But if the Germans kept their heads down and patriotic protestations up—"You won't find Americans of German extraction, like our members, in any fifth column," the Steuben Society's leader declared in May 1941—they stubbornly continued to oppose US participation in the growing European conflagration. Here, at least, they knew they marched in tandem with substantial numbers of Americans, and Gothamites, too, especially among the ranks of Italian Americans, who had joined them on the lengthy alien registration lines.

ITALIANS

May Day parade near Union Square, early 1930s. (Photo by Historica Graphica Collection/Heritage Images/Getty Images)

9

Duce! Duce!

Throughout the 1930s, the city's Little Italys were festooned with portraits of Benito Mussolini—his jaw-jutting visage beaming (or glowering) down from the walls of classrooms and churches, bars and groceries, homes and clubs. At parades and communal celebrations one heard cries of Duce! Duce!, saw a forest of arms upthrust in salute. New York's Italian districts supported Fascism far more enthusiastically than Gotham's Germans did Nazism.

In part this was because Mussolini worked harder than Hitler at winning friends and influencing people in America and did so more efficiently, not least because he'd been at it a decade longer. Mussolini had learned, after the Fascist League of North America had been slapped down back in 1929, to avoid noisy and off-putting tactics like having supporters strut about in black shirts and riding breeches, brandishing steel-tipped whips. Ideologically, he demanded little of Italian Americans. His minions in the Bureau of Fascists Abroad peddled an export-only Fascism-Lite, which vaguely promoted abstract virtues like order, duty, and valor. Advertising copy promulgated by the Italian Library of Information, situated appropriately on Madison Avenue, dwelt mainly on Mussolini's restoration of the Greatness That Was—and Now Was Once Again—Rome. The government's tourist office offered Italian Americans cheap group rates to see for themselves the splendors of the New Italy. And the Italian consul general worked through local cultural, educational, and civic groups to promote favorable images of Il Duce and his regime—even managing to slip books praising "the great Mussolini" into New York's public-school classrooms.

This prideful nationalism lifted the spirits of Gotham's Depression-battered Italians, hungry for affirmation after decades of derision capped by an immigration law that all but barred *paesani*. The New Italy allowed them to shine in reflected glory yet didn't conflict with their American patriotism, didn't require them to criticize democratic institutions or suggest the US adopt dictatorial rule. Italian Americans were asked only to admire Fascism from afar, not emulate it at home.

There were, to be sure, some hardliners in town, notably Domenico Trombetta, a former Fascist League capo. In 1930 Trombetta had set up a successor organization—the Lictor

Federation, housed in lower Manhattan's Little Italy—whose members did some stormtrooping about at local events: in 1932, after a Garibaldi memorial ceremony on Staten Island ended in a clash between Lictor men and the rival Duce Fascist Alliance of New York, Trombetta was indicted for murder (though later acquitted). Still, the Federation never developed equivalents of Fritz Kuhn's summer camps or Hitler Youth—though the Lictorites did pack local lads off to Italy for summer drilling with the Opera Nazionale Ballila, the Fascist organization for eight-to-fourteen-year-olds, and there were about sixty *doposcuola* (afterschool clubs) in the New York area. Trombetta concentrated on propaganda of the word, not deed. He continued to edit *Il Grido della Stirpe* (*The Cry of the Race*, established back in 1923), which was subsidized by Mussolini's Fascist Ministry of Popular Culture and hailed by Ugo Veniero d'Annunzio, the Italian Library's director (and son of the poet Gabriele d'Annunzio), as a "one-hundred-percent Fascist newspaper." Trombetta also took to the airwaves with regular broadcasts on WHOM, supplementing shortwave agitprop from Radio Rome.

But Il Duce had no need to rely on fringe elements like Trombetta when *prominenti* potentates stepped forward so willingly to support the regime—including respectable ethnic community businessmen like Wall Street financier Luigi Criscuolo, judges like Ferdinand Pecora of investigatory fame, professionals like the Columbia academics who ran Casa Italiana and proclaimed Italy's civilizing mission, and the heads of such fraternal organizations as the Sons of Italy and the Dante Alighieri Society (whose president told Mussolini the group was "proud of serving the Fascist revolution" and stood ready "to believe, to obey, to fight at your command").

Above all there was Generoso Pope. Since his emergence as Mussolini's chief cheerleader in the 1920s, his influence had swelled mightily. Pope's fleet of newspapers, flagshipped by *Il Progresso Italo-Americano* (whose average circulation of 95,000 copies made it the country's second-largest ethnic daily, after the *Forward*), were completely at Rome's service—and that of the Democratic Party. In the early 1930s, Pope welded a scattering of political clubs into a potent ethnic machine and shepherded 188 civic and cultural groups into an umbrella organization, the National United Italian Associations (NUIA). The press baron had become a power broker capable of channeling the Italian American vote to accommodating candidates and wasn't shy about proclaiming it. Italians would henceforth demand the same political respect paid other ethnic groups, he boldly announced, now that "we have today a respectable electoral force which in New York alone is more than half a million voters."

Pope made countless appearances at social functions throughout the city. Playing the Fascist card, he invariably showed up with an Italian official, underscoring his quasi-official association with Mussolini. It was no coincidence that the NUIA was headquartered, as was Trombetta's *Il Grido*, at 225 Lafayette Street, along with a large number of organizations connected to the Italian government; the building was known as a "beehive of Fascist activities." The apex of Pope's ceremonial activities came on Columbus Day—the Italian community's equivalent of German Day. In the early 1930s, thousands paraded each year into Columbus Circle, with Pope and Consul General Gaetano Vecchiotti heading the line of march, where they heard flattering addresses by the city and state's highest elected officials—like Governor Lehman—who had been put in office with their help.

10

Italian Anti-Fascists

Pope did not, however, have the Italian field to himself. Anti-Fascism had been a factor in New York City as long as Fascism had been—since the early 1920s—and in the 1930s opponents of Mussolini and Pope maintained a strong presence in New York's laboring and radical circles. At the 1934 Columbus Day affair, for instance, even as patriotic, civic, and political organizations gathered in Columbus Circle to listen to Lehman under the aegis of *Il Progresso*, an equally large gathering assembled just across the street at the base of the *Maine* monument, under the leadership of the United Anti-Fascist Committee—a constellation of unionists, socialists, Trotskyists, communists, and anarchists who lustily booed the official group.

They were led that day by Girolamo Valenti, the forty-four-year-old Italian-born editor of *La Stampa Libera (The Free Press)*. Housed downtown at 81 East 10th Street, Valenti's paper was a reincarnation (as of 1931) of *Il Nuovo Mondo*, the New York anti-Fascist daily that had been founded back in the early twenties, along with the Anti-Fascist Alliance of North America (1926).

Another old-timer on hand was radical publisher Carlo Tresca, a major thorn in the side of local blackshirts for over a decade, still going strong at fifty-five. (A 1934 headline in his paper, *Il Martello*, blared: "We Accuse Generoso Pope...of Being a Gangster and a Racketeer," a reference to Pope's reputed ties to underworld characters.) Italian communists were in the fray as well, including members of the Party's Italian American Section (which sponsored *L'Unita Operaia* [1932–38] and its successor *L'Unita del Popolo*), the Garibaldi-American Fraternal Society, and the Italian Workers Club.

Yet another powerful institution of Italian American anti-Fascism was Local 89 of the International Ladies Garment Workers Union—the Italian Dress and Waist Makers—whose roughly 40,000 members made it one of the largest locals in the US. It was steered by Luigi Antonini—who in 1934 became an ILGWU vice president—a longtime outspoken anti-Fascist and ardent anti-Stalinist. In 1934 when his ILGWU colleague David Dubinsky committed the union to combating German Nazism, Antonini convinced him to broaden it into an "anti-Nazi and anti-Fascist" campaign, which Antonini kicked off at the celebration that

A protest organized by the United Front Anti-Fascist Action Committee outside the Italian Consulate on 70th Street and Lexington Avenue demanding the release of political prisoners held by Mussolini and Hitler. June 10, 1933. (Bettmann/Contributor/Getty Images)

year of Local 89's fifteenth anniversary. Twenty thousand unionists, most of them Italian, rocked Madison Square Garden with chants of "Down with Mussolini!" and "Down with fascism!" This laboring contingent—like Pope's legions—received the support of powerful political figures like Governor Lehman and Mayor La Guardia, whose address that day (in Italian) won a tumultuous ovation.

Pope promptly attacked Antonini as "anti-Italian" in *Il Progresso*, but the labor leader slugged back on Local 89's weekly radio show on WEVD, and in its newspaper, *Giustizia*. Still, Antonini was well aware that the bulk of the city's Italian Americans were not sympathetic to the anti-Fascist position—even some of his members glowed at Mussolini's successes—and after a few months of bitter polemics, the two *prominenti* called a truce in 1935, agreeing to refrain from personal attacks. Pope and La Guardia arrived at a similar detente. The publisher had successfully backed Tammany's Jimmy Walker against La Guardia in 1929 and helped beat La Guardia again when he ran for reelection to Congress in 1932. After 1933, however, when La Guardia won City Hall with overwhelming Italian backing, Pope soft-pedaled his opposition, while the mayor muted his public reservations about Mussolini (whom privately he thought a "sawdust Caesar"). By the mid-1930s, there was something of a standoff between Gotham's pro- and anti-Fascists.

Then the pendulum swung strongly in Pope's direction.

On December 5, 1934, Mussolini used a skirmish involving an Italian garrison 80 miles inside the border of Ethiopia (aka Abyssinia) as a pretext for demanding compensation and preparing for war. He announced, moreover, that he expected Italian Americans to back his grand design of forging an East African empire. Italian America was an "outlying colony," Il Duce declared, and even naturalized Americans were his subjects: "My order," he bellowed in 1934, "is that an Italian citizen must remain an Italian citizen, no matter in what land he lives, even to the seventh generation." This was a risky gambit; even Hitler's Americanists hadn't sought this level of commitment to a foreign regime. But it worked. New York's Italians, swept up by the prospect of Mussolini's recapturing the splendors not only of Rome but of the Roman Empire, rallied behind Pope to the imperial adventure. Internal opposition to the impending assault on Ethiopia would continue, though be overwhelmed, and the burden of resistance would shift to the city's African American community.

11

Hands off Ethiopia!

Mussolini's intention to conquer the last uncolonized nation in Africa aroused enormous indignation in Harlem, and Black Gothamites took up the defense of Ethiopia with an intensity of fraternal feeling unmatched elsewhere in the US, the Caribbean, or for that matter Africa itself. Marcus Garvey remained in English exile, but his Universal Negro Improvement Association, and successor organizations like the African Patriotic League, remained a forceful presence on the New York scene. The Garvey movement—whose official anthem was "Ethiopia, Thou Land of Our Fathers"—held that the New World's African diaspora was part of a dispersed Ethiopian nation that would one day reclaim its ancient glory as a world civilization and redeem the Black race from white rule. Harlem nationalists thus saw Mussolini's threats as an affront to Blacks everywhere; street-corner soapboxers harangued passersby on the need for global Black unity against Fascist militarism; and young men took to calling themselves "Afro-Americans."

Ethiopia had iconic significance for other, overlapping circles of African American New Yorkers. Abyssinia was the focus of an emergent race scholarship—a Black Studies movement centered on the Harlem History Club. Founded in 1932 at the YMCA by Garveyite historian Dr. Willis Nathaniel Huggins (BA/MA Columbia, Fordham PhD), it was soon renamed the Blyden Society (after the influential Liberian educator and politician). Its members, dedicated to examining Africa's past, would include John Henrik Clarke, Bayard Rustin, John Glover Jackson (who had worked with Hubert Henry Harrison and Arthur Schomburg), and a visiting West African student, Kwame Nkrumah. In 1934, Huggins and Jackson produced *A Guide to the Study of African History*.

Ethiopia had signal significance for many of Gotham's Black churchgoers, too, as one of the first countries in the world to adopt Christianity; Adam Clayton Powell Sr.'s Abyssinian Baptist Church was named for the East African kingdom. Ethiopia resonated with secular Pan-Africanists as well, who argued (with WEB. Du Bois) that the safety and wellbeing of African Americans was tied to the fate of Africa itself; and with anti-imperialists, who insisted it was imperative to defend a country that had maintained its independence as the continent got carved up.

Black Harlem Communists like James Ford and Abner Berry were more critical of Ethiopia. They considered it "a feudal state," whose ruler, Emperor Haile Selassie, opposed land reform. They noted it was one of the few regions on earth where slavery retained a foothold. They nevertheless believed strongly that it should be defended against Italian aggression and were prepared to do so together with race-first nationalists they had long condemned as reactionaries.

In February 1935, with unusual unity of purpose, twenty Harlem organizations, including Communists, Garveyites, and church groups, formed a Provisional Committee for the Defense of Ethiopia (PCDE). Its first public meeting, on March 7 at the Abyssinian Baptist Church, drew 3,000 and launched a campaign to raise funds for the beleaguered country, organize mass demonstrations against Mussolini's plans, and request intervention by the League of Nations and the Vatican. The National Association for the Advancement of Colored People (NAACP)—a more cautious counterpart of the PCDE mass action organizations—hung back from vigorous public protest, though Walter White and Roy Wilkins (who had replaced Du Bois as editor of *The Crisis* after the latter resigned in 1934) did lobby the State Department.

Then, on March 19, a riot erupted, momentarily diverting attention from foreign affairs. Heightened antiwhite animosities soon spurred Black nationalists like Arthur Reid and Ira Kemp of the African Patriotic League to call for a boycott of local Italian merchants, indeed for driving them out of Harlem altogether, not only because they discriminated against Blacks in employment and should be supplanted by Black businesses, but because profits garnered by Italian shopkeepers might flow to Mussolini's war machine.

Members of the American League Against War and Fascism picket the Italian Consulate to protest actions during the invasion of Ethiopia (then known as Abyssinia). May 1936. (Photo by FPG/Hulton Archive/Getty Images)

A Pan-Africanist Reconstruction Association campaign car. (Photo by Visual Studies Workshop/Getty Images)

A surrogate battle over Ethiopia between Gotham's Blacks and Italians would indeed erupt in that summer of 1935; however, the sparring would take place not on the streets of East Harlem but in a boxing ring, just across the river in the Bronx.

12

Ambling Alp v. Brown Bomber

On the sultry evening of June 25, 60,000 spectators—including massive contingents of Blacks and Italians—crowded into Yankee Stadium. A throng of luminaries was in attendance, led by Mayor La Guardia. So were 400 members of the press (the largest fight contingent since Jack Dempsey fought Georges Carpentier fourteen years earlier) and a virtual army of 1,500 police, equipped with riot gear, commanded by Commissioner Lewis Joseph Valentine himself.

At the center of all this attention were two highly unusual combatants.

In one corner: Primo Carnera. At six foot seven and 260 pounds (he'd weighed twenty-two pounds at his birth, near Venice, in 1906), Carnera was the biggest boxer ever to step foot in an American ring. "Da Preem," as dubbed by his Italian American fans, had been working in Paris as a circus strongman in 1928—grabbing ropes attached to two cars, he'd prevent them from racing off in opposite directions—when a French promoter plucked him from obscurity and launched him on a pugilistic career, one for which he had natural ability but little skill. Nevertheless, after demolishing a series of mediocre European fighters, he was brought to the US in 1930, where his tremendous size made him an immediate box office and media sensation (bemused sportswriters tagged him the "Ambling Alp").

Carnera was quickly taken in hand by gangsters Owney Madden and the Gowanus-born Big Bill Duffy (though Big Frenchy DeMange, Dutch Schultz, Lucky Luciano, and Thomas Lucchese were also rumored to own pieces of the Italian heavyweight). The racketeers matched him up against a parade of opponents paid to take a dive—in one fight he knocked his adversary to the mat six times in the first 47 seconds without landing a single blow. The mobsters garnered hundreds of thousands in side bets, while handing Carnera little more than pocket change. Still, thus assisted, the fighter worked his way up to the threshold of the heavyweight crown, won it in 1933 (Pope threw him a party at the Hotel Delmonico), and defended his title twice, before being flattened by Max Baer in June 1934. Since then, the ex-champ had defeated four unknown challengers and remained in contention for a comeback.

In the other corner was Joe Louis, the Alabama-born sharecropper's son who had turned pro in July 1934, after brilliantly boxing his way up through the amateur ranks, and out of his job at a Detroit Ford auto plant. Over the next year Louis had fought twenty-two honest bouts against serious opponents, an average of one every two weeks, and won them all, eighteen by knockouts, gaining the sobriquet "Brown Bomber." At this point his Black managers, John Roxborough and Julian Black, asked his Black trainer, Jack "Chappie" Blackburn, if Louis was ready for the big time. "Yeah, he's ready for New York," Chappie replied, "but New York ain't ready for him."

For more than two decades, ever since the heyday of Jack Johnson, the color bar against Black heavyweight contenders had remained firmly in place. Only too aware of this, Louis's managers had spent as much time fashioning an image for him as an anti-Johnson as they had teaching him to box. They instructed the young fighter in the rudiments of personal hygiene and dinner table etiquette, hired a tutor to upgrade his grammar and manners, and ordered him never to have his picture taken with a white woman or go alone to a nightclub. He was presented as an anti–Jack Dempsey: not a natural-born killer but a scientific craftsman, a man who hated to hurt his opponents and never gloated over a conquered foe. Louis had accepted this role as a humble, modest, God-fearing, bible-reading, churchgoing, clean-living, unthreatening Negro, though so far it hadn't done him much good. Blackburn did get in touch with Madison Square Garden, the national mecca of the fight game, but (as expected) had been turned down.

Then came a call from Mike Jacobs, promoter extraordinaire. Jacobs, who had no objections to mixed matches, now circumvented the Garden by arranging to hold the fight in Yankee Stadium—a revolutionary breakthrough for interracial boxing.

Sportswriters began hyping the fight by hailing Louis's attachment to his mother and his faith. With war looming in Ethiopia, however, both Blacks and Italians imposed a different story line on the impending bout, making it a stand-in for international affairs.

Neither boxer was particularly political. Carnera was no Fascist, though it was widely known that Mussolini, who believed boxing "an exquisitely fascist means of self-expression," had closely followed Carnera's career. And in hailing the Alp's 1933 title-win, Il Duce had declared that "fascist Italy and its sport-loving people are proud that a blackshirt has become boxing champion of the world."

Though Louis was no racial spokesperson, various Afro-American nationalists began visiting his training camp and putting, as he recalled, "a heavy weight on my twenty-year-old shoulders. Now, not only did I have to beat the man, but I had to beat him for a cause."

Jacobs and the sportswriters now played up the international dimension, hoping to generate a bigger gate. A New York *Daily Mirror* cartoon depicted Carnera towering over Louis, next to Italy towering over Ethiopia. The Hearst reporters provided mountains of publicity. And on June 25, amid super-tight security, the boxers weighed in, with the "mastodonic" Carnera overmatching Louis by sixty-four pounds.

It availed him naught. Almost immediately, a lightning right from Louis to Carnera's head drove his lower teeth thru his upper lip, causing him to spurt blood, and it was all downhill from there. Carnera hung on courageously through a merciless thrashing—late in the fifth, when Louis lifted him off his feet as they struggled in a clinch, the astonished Italian said, "I should be doing this to you." The final bombardment came in the sixth, when (said John Kieran, the *New York Times*'s erudite sportswriter) Carnera "went down slowly, like a great chimney that had been dynamited"; wobbled up, was smashed back; and had staggered up a third time, reeling and utterly senseless, when the referee declared a TKO.

The city's (and country's) African American communities erupted in delirium, laced with a determination to extend the triumph to the global arena. Even as a long line of slow-moving cars of wealthy white patrons was leaving the fight, throngs of Black boys, ten or twelve years of age, raced in and out, shouting "Let's get Mussolini next."

13

"The Eagles of Rome Have Devoured the Lion of Judah"

In Harlem, the rhetoric grew more muscular. Nationalist street-corner orators moved from the merely metaphorical—"we want to knock out Mussolini like Joe Louis did Carnera"—to concrete calls for Blacks to enlist in Ethiopia's army, calls which, by July 1935, had reportedly netted nearly a thousand responses. Though Haile Selassie was glad to accept African American volunteers, the US government announced such service would violate an 1818 law forbidding Americans from fighting under foreign flags, under penalty of fine, jail time, even loss of citizenship. Despite this, a Garveyite Black Legion established a training camp in upstate New York, which allegedly drew some 3,000 volunteers, before Selassie, fearing to alienate US authorities, effectively ended recruitment.

Balked abroad, nationalists like Reid and Kemp revived plans to boycott Italian American merchants at home. They were stymied on this front, too, when the PCDE moved to divert anti-Italian and antiwhite outrage into "anti-Fascist" channels. Radical, liberal, and moderate Blacks reached out to Italian American opponents of Mussolini and organized an interracial march through Harlem. On August 3, participants stepped off in two columns. One, Black, included Pullman porters in uniforms, Garveyites in military regalia, and followers of Harlem-based religious leader Father Divine. The other, white, included hundreds of radical Italian Americans shouting, "Death to Fascism" and "Hands Off Ethiopia." The contingents merged into a unified line of march at 129th Street and 7th Avenue and proceeded, 25,000 strong, to a joint mass meeting at 141st and Edgecombe Avenue.

New York was ablaze with pro-Ethiopia activities that fall. A host of other interracial initiatives were launched, like the American Aid for Ethiopia, the Committee for Ethiopia (Adam Clayton Powell Jr. was vice chair), and the American Committee on the Ethiopian Crisis. A Medical Committee for the Defense of Ethiopia assembled two tons of medical equipment for the Ethiopian army. In August, the Provisional Committee sent Willis Huggins to Geneva to deliver an appeal from US Blacks directly to the League of Nations. In

September, the American League Against War and Fascism sponsored a "Hands Off Ethiopia" rally at Madison Square Garden, with W.E.B. Du Bois and the NAACP's Walter White among the featured speakers. And poet Langston Hughes penned "The Ballad of Ethiopia": "All you colored peoples / Be a man at last / Say to Mussolini / No! You shall not pass."

But he did: on October 3, 1935, Italian troops crossed from Eritrea into Ethiopia, preceded by bombers blasting mud hut villages and strafing defenseless horsemen. Mussolini's son Vittorio exulted at the "magnificent sport" of watching victims blown up like "a budding rose unfolding."

Anti-Italian fervor swept Black Gotham immediately, with hundreds joining protests and demonstrations that day. At 118th and Lenox, a Reid- and Kemp-led picket line of an Italian market drew counterdemonstrators, and a riot was prevented only by the dispatch of 1,200 extra police. In Brownsville fighting broke out at P.S. 178 on Dean Street (Saratoga and Hopkinson Avenues)—30 percent of the 2,200 pupils were Black, another 30 percent Italian—the combatants battling with ice picks, lead pipes, and sawed-off billiard cues. The next day, October 4, 1935, Huggins announced the formation of the Friends of Ethiopia to raise funds for the wounded; by December there were 106 branches across the country. Other relief groups merged into an umbrella organization, United Aid for Ethiopia.

The city's Italians mobilized with equal speed. Pope told a post-invasion assemblage at Manhattan's Central Opera House (67th Street and 3rd Avenue), "We can be sure that Italy will triumph under the guidance of the Duce and will be greater and more feared in the future." Anti-Fascists dissented—on Columbus Day 1935, 2,500 demonstrators carrying a huge caricature of Mussolini labeled "Public Enemy No. 1" waded into an equal number of Duce supporters in Columbus Circle—they wrestled, punched, and kicked one another until separated by club-wielding mounted police. In the months to come such police opposition was overwhelmed.

Pope organized a fundraising drive for the Italian Red Cross that in eight weeks raised half a million dollars from 350,000 local contributors. On December 14, he presented a check to the Italian consul general at a 20,000-strong Madison Square Garden rally (preceded by a concert featuring Rosa Ponselle, soprano, and Ezio Pinza, basso). Four days later, at a mass meeting in the Brooklyn Labor Lyceum (at Myrtle and Willoughby Avenues), Italian American women, following in the footsteps of Italy's Queen Elena, offered up their gold wedding bands to be melted down for the cause. The consul general promised them Mussolini would send new iron rings, blessed by a local Catholic priest, which couples could use to renew their vows. An estimated 100,000 rings (along with a shower of watches, crucifixes, and cigarette cases) were dispatched to Italy from New York, New Jersey, and New England alone, nearly a ton of gold in all.

Mussolini also urged compatriots to return home to fight though few Italian American citizens defied the ban on such enlistments. Nor did many resident Italians ship out either, in sharp contrast to the First World War, when 90,000 decamped to the killing fields.

Nonetheless the Italian community had something far more useful to contribute—electoral muscle—which it deployed to help keep the US "neutral." Four days after the October invasion, the League of Nations condemned Mussolini's aggression and recommended sanctions, possibly including an embargo on oil. This would have brought Il Duce's East African war machine to a clanking halt. Such a sanction would be meaningless without American participation, however, as the US (not a League member) produced over half the world's oil. The US Neutrality Act of 1935, whose provisions Roosevelt now put into effect, embargoed arms and ammunition to both belligerents, although not oil.

A crowd celebrates the conquest of Ethiopia on 116th street. May 17, 1936. (Photo by Walter Kelleher/NY Daily News Archive via Getty Images)

FDR disapproved of Mussolini's adventure and so announced a "moral embargo" on essential war materials, though American exporters, sniffing profit, responded by tripling the flow of oil, copper, trucks, tractors, and scrap iron to Italy (Ethiopia couldn't pay). So Roosevelt asked Congress (in January 1936) for authority to mandate a cutoff. At Rome's urging, Pope orchestrated a nationwide campaign to thwart this. The White House, along with senators and congressmen with large Italian American constituencies, were flooded with over a million letters, and Pope lobbied the president personally. With the 1936 election coming up, FDR abandoned the effort, and the League backed away from oil sanctions. (The

A crowd toasts Mussolini and Italy's victory in Ethiopia on Mott Street, May 6, 1936. (Photo by Klein/NY Daily News Archive via Getty Images)

Europeans proved equally disinclined to close the Suez Canal, which would also have doomed the invasion.)

Thus unhampered, the Italians destroyed Ethiopian resistance and on May 5, 1936, marched into the capital, Addis Ababa. That same day thousands of Gotham's Italians surged through Mulberry Street, carrying a pine coffin containing a stuffed effigy of Haile Selassie, and waved banners proclaiming, "The Eagles of Rome Have Devoured the Lion of Judah." Uptown, thousands more thronged East 116th Street to pay tribute to the victorious troops, as police warily patrolled the border between Black and Italian Harlem. On May 9, Mussolini officially annexed Ethiopia. The next day Italians filled Madison Square Garden for a Victory Ball at which Pope—to whom Mussolini cabled personal thanks—declared the conquest "a victory of civilization over barbarism."

The NAACP's *Crisis* noted that the arsenal of "civilization" included poison gas, which accounted for many of the 400,000 Ethiopian dead. And on May 18, in reaction to Fascist atrocities in occupied Addis Ababa, hundreds of Blacks marched down Lenox Avenue smashing windows of Italian stores and battling police. Thousands more swelled subsequent protest marches. When massive police reinforcements blanketed the neighborhood, the locals likened them to the army occupying Ethiopia.

In the fall 1936 elections, Pope reached the pinnacle of power. The Democratic Party, convinced the ethnic vote was crucial to FDR's reelection, established a Foreign Language Citizens Committee and made "Gene" Pope chair of its Italian Division. In return, Pope swung his papers behind Roosevelt, and the president's victory made Pope a pivotal figure in US politics. (Locally, *Il Progresso* went after Vito Marcantonio, who lost his congressional seat.) In 1937, Pope dined at the White House, then made a triumphal visit to Italy, where Mussolini granted him a private audience and made him a Commendatore dell'Ordine dei Santi Maurizio e Lazzaro. Back in New York, La Guardia, Lehman, and Dewey hastened to share the Columbus Day 1937 platform with Pope and Consul Vecchiotti. The anti-Fascist opposition wasn't completely crushed: that same day the mayor bustled to a separate and substantial gathering organized by the ousted Marcantonio and showed up with the governor at an even larger one Antonini put together at the huge Hippodrome (located on Sixth Avenue between West 43rd and West 44th Streets).

Still, anti-Fascist fortunes had flagged amid the martial fervor. Then, in 1938, the balance of power in New York's Little Italys once again swung in their direction.

14

Italians and Jews: 1938–1941

On July 14, 1938, the Fascist mouthpiece *Il Giornale d'Italia* published a *Manifesto della Razza* (*Manifesto of the Race*). It decreed the Italian population to be of Aryan origin and that, accordingly, "Jews do not belong to the Italian race." Nazi-style measures followed, mandating a progressive exclusion of Jews from economic, political, and social life and banning "interracial" marriages.

In New York, some local blackshirts, like Trombetta, hailed the anti-Semitic initiative, claiming racism was the "essence of Fascism" and purging Jews would strengthen Italian identity. Arguing that Gotham's Italians had suffered at Jewish hands, Trombetta set out to mobilize local anti-Jewish sentiment via vituperative commentaries in *Il Grido* and on WHOM (until taken off the air in September by management, fearful the FCC might revoke its license). Echoing Il Duce's bonding with Hitler, some resident Fascists linked up with New York Nazis and began speaking out at Bund rallies. One, Ralph Ninfo, was convicted of disorderly conduct for saying "if I had my way, I would hang all Jews in the country."

New York's Italian Americans were not immune to late thirties' rising anti-Semitism. Competition for jobs, patronage, housing, and relief benefits—to say nothing of religious differences—provided some bases for inter-communal strains. Yet the two groups had a great deal in common, too, not least their alliances in the labor movement and Democratic Party, which had delivered tangible benefits, and Italians weren't angry with the Jews. Traditionally, moreover, Italians were more German-averse than anti-Semitic. Few were thrilled by Mussolini's embrace of Hitler, who in *Mein Kampf* had sneered at that "bastardized, Negro cauldron of impurity, the Latin race." Most worrisome, Gotham's Jews were far more capable of inflicting retaliatory damage than were the city's African Americans. Indeed, Rabbi Wise had begun talking about an Italian boycott which, together with a decline in Italian bonds on the New York market, had deeply alarmed even Mussolini's Ministry of Foreign Affairs.

Pope tried to navigate these newly choppy waters by putting some daylight between himself and Mussolini's measures. *Il Progresso*, like most US Italian-language pro-Fascist papers, at first downplayed or explained away the anti-Semitic legislation. Pope made clear that it "would be highly deplorable should divisions and rancors develop between Jews and Italians in the United States." Nevertheless, when Germany invaded Poland in September 1939, triggering war, *Il Progresso* stoutly asserted US neutrality, a position Pope reaffirmed even more forcefully after Italy invaded France in June 1940. Roosevelt's denunciation of Il Duce's action—"the hand that held the dagger has struck it into the back of its neighbor"—infuriated many Italian Americans by its transparent referencing of stereotypes about stiletto-wielding dagos. The growing likelihood that Italy and the US might wind up on opposite sides of the barricades deeply worried Pope's constituency. Some individuals and organizations now loudly protested their American loyalty. *Il Progresso* followed suit—in its English-language editorials—though continued to praise Mussolini's regime and its initial military victories in Italian-language articles.

Anti-Fascist organizations, old and new, strove to widen the wedge between New York's Italians and Mussolini's regime. The ILGWU's Antonini denounced the anti-Semitic laws—"once racial discrimination is rampant, no one will escape"—and Marcantonio, whose reelection in 1938 signaled a turning tide, joined with Girolamo Valenti in proclaiming "the Italian people do not hate the Jews." In December 1939, historian and veteran anti-Fascist Gaetano Salvemini, along with Max Ascoli of the New School, established a Mazzini Society, which quickly attracted anti-Fascist exiles fleeing the fall of France—intellectuals, professionals, and powerful politicians like Count Carlo Sforza, Italy's former foreign minister, who arrived in July of 1940.

These anti-Fascists zeroed in on the local influence of Italian consular officials, fanning fears of a Fifth Column. Soon after Italy's invasion of France, a twenty-five-page confidential mimeographed memo entitled "The Fascist Fifth Column in New York" began circulating among the New York Police Department's borough commanders, and inspectors of the Criminal Alien, Sabotage, and Bomb Squads. The memo claimed there was hard evidence—"rumor, hearsay and unverified statements rigidly excluded"—that the Italian Consulate General in New York, under orders from Mussolini, was promoting Fascism here. This charge, which echoed assertions by Valenti and Salvemini, surfaced increasingly in the popular English-language press (*Look* magazine's December 17, 1940, issue ran an exposé entitled "Italian Fascist Propaganda in the United States").

In the first half of 1941 the campaign to discredit Pope reached a crescendo, with articles denouncing his loyalty (one by Valenti was called "Generoso Pope's Fascist Record") and rallies sponsored by the Mazzini Society. In June, FDR shuttered the Italian consulate at Rockefeller Center and ordered an FBI investigation of Pope's political activities. Finally, in September, Pope openly condemned Mussolini, though he would continue (as did his German American counterparts) to doggedly oppose intervention on behalf of the Allies.

The city's African American community moved steadily in the opposite direction, toward embracing intervention. Blacks had been among the first Americans to recognize Fascism as a global threat, and while the conquest of Ethiopia was a setback, they didn't abandon their international assessment.

15

Louis v. Schmeling

In 1938 African Americans participated in another symbolic slugfest with international Fascism, when, once again, global attention was riveted on a mano-a-mano faceoff in New York City—the "Fight of the Century" between Joe Louis and Max Schmeling.

Schmeling, designated stand-in for the Third Reich, was in many ways a most unlikely Nazi representative. Son of a Hamburg sailor, Schmeling's initial bouts in Weimar Berlin had made him the darling of a circle of avant-garde fight fans that included artists, communists, and Jews. And when he arrived in New York in 1928, he hooked up with a Jewish manager named Joe Jacobs. Jacobs promoted him as a new Dempsey, of whom Schmeling's good looks and pile-driver right reminded many. In 1930 he fought Jack Sharkey for Gene Tunney's vacated title, winning the bout while flat on his back, as officials ruled Sharkey guilty of a low blow, one which filmed replays failed to disclose. The title passed back to Sharkey, in an equally odiferous way, at the Madison Square Garden Bowl in 1932, when Sharkey was awarded the victory despite having been patently outboxed by Schmeling for fifteen rounds. The decision—and Schmeling's manager—attained a certain immortality when Joe Jacobs screamed into an open mike, "We wuz robbed!"

After a few more defeats a depressed and seemingly washed-up Schmeling returned to Germany in 1934. The boxer rehabilitated his image in Europe, partly in the ring, and partly thanks to being taken up by Hitler (an embrace he accepted publicly though he had no love for the regime). In return for giving pro-Nazi interviews—"Max Schmeling Says Germany Is Not Cruel to Jewish Folks"—the Third Reich backed his campaign to regain the heavyweight crown, which at the end of 1935 was held by Hell's Kitchen–born James Braddock. The Nazis were a bit leery about the requisite first step in such a comeback—taking on Joe Louis—fearing Schmeling might disgrace them by losing to a Black man. However, Louis—newly wed and newly enamored of golf, a sport to which he'd been recently introduced by columnist Ed Sullivan—goofed off in training and was consequently felled by the German in the twelfth round of their June 1936 encounter. Goebbels telegraphed congrats. Schmeling, though he'd refrained from racist and unsportsmanlike remarks about Louis, now credited

"Hitler's inspiration" for his win. The fighter was zeppelined back on the *Hindenburg* for a private reception with the Führer, and together they screened footage of the fight (soon to be a major motion picture: *Max Schmeling's Victory, A German Victory*).

Now an official Nazi hero, Schmeling returned to New York in December 1936 on the SS *Brehjmen* to arrange his title fight with Braddock and signed a deal with Madison Square Garden management. Mike Jacobs derailed the Braddock–Schmeling matchup, enticing the champ into fighting Louis instead. (He did so by guaranteeing Braddock that should he lose, he would get 10 percent of Jacobs's net profits from heavyweight fights over the next decade.) In June 1937, Louis trained rigorously, beat Braddock (who, busy with endorsements and other profitable ventures, hadn't entered a ring in two years), and became heavyweight champion of the world at age twenty-three.

Now the two managerial Jacobses arranged a Louis–Schmeling rematch for June 1938, almost a year later. By that time Hitler had absorbed Austria, menaced Czechoslovakia, and bombed Guernica in Spain, and the fight had become a symbolic stand-in for contending civilizations. The Germans presented it as Aryanism versus decadent Americanism. Goebbels's propaganda machine cranked out fictitious Schmeling quotes—no Black could stand up to "a super race man" like him—which the boxer, his family in Germany vulnerable to retaliation, was in no position to repudiate. White Americans—faced with the prospect of the title going to Germany, perhaps never to return—rallied behind Louis as their Great Black Hope. Joe accepted that he was "backing up America against Germany." A few weeks before the fight, Franklin Roosevelt invited the champion to the White House, gripped his arm, and told Louis, "These are the muscles we need to defeat the Germans."

On the sticky night of June 22, as 70,000 (including 1,000 police) crowded into a muggy Yankee Stadium, they were greeted by leafleting protesters from Samuel Untermyer's Anti-Nazi League and Rabbi Wise's American Jewish Congress, groups that had been trying for months to have Jacobs call off the fight, despite the promoter's having offered 10 percent of the gate to refugee groups. They argued that buying tickets to see Schmeling was like buying German-made goods. Meanwhile, as people were filing into the stadium, Jacobs was urging Louis to "murder that bum," reminding him that if Schmeling won, they both stood to lose a fortune. Louis assured him, "I ain't going back to Ford, and you ain't gonna go back to selling lemon drops on the Staten Island Ferry." The latter prediction was safe enough: Jacobs had covered his bets by quietly signing a contract with Schmeling to promote him should he win.

The radio audience was immense and far-flung. NBC combined its Blue and Red Networks to mount a broadcast that reached 146 stations. An industry report would estimate that 97 percent of radio owners in New York City listened, along with two-thirds of those in the rest of the country, audience levels rivaled only by FDR's fireside chats. Across the Atlantic, Germany's curfew was lifted so that cafés and beer gardens could carry the middle-of-the-night shortwave broadcast live. Goebbels invited Schmeling's wife to his home to listen; Hitler hunkered down next to his set at Berchtesgaden.

The fighters had circled each other for only a few seconds after the opening bell when two Louis jabs and a left hook to Schmeling's face startled the German into retreating. Piston-like lefts and rights followed, then an overhand right to the head. Then, as Louis launched another long right, Schmeling twisted his trunk, and the blow landed in his lower left back, fracturing the third lumbar vertebra and driving it into his kidney, eliciting a short piercing scream (it "sounded like a stuck pig") and leaving him partially paralyzed in mind

The weigh-in before the fight between Joe Louis and Max Schmeling, 1938.   (Photo by Popperfoto via Getty Images/Getty Images)

and legs, at which point another hard right to the chin floored him, two minutes and four seconds into the first round. (Duke Ellington had dropped his straw hat, bent down to look for it, and by the time he got up the fight was over.) It was, observers agreed, the most concentratedly destructive 124 seconds in two centuries of ring history, a prizefight version of Hitler's Blitzkrieg.

Harlem went wild. The *Daily News* said it looked like "a dozen Christmases, a score of New Year's Eves." A hundred thousand Blacks poured into the upper Manhattan streets, some goose-stepping crazily, others shouting anti-Fascist slogans. With this kind of booster shot, the city's African American community was well and truly inoculated against Nazi Aryanism. A tiny handful of Black Fascists would pop up on Lenox Avenue soapboxes and stepladders from time to time—one Ras de Killer greeted news of the invasion of Poland by declaring himself "happy to see Hitler declare war on the white man"—but everyone else was only too aware of the fate that awaited colored people should the Third Reich win.

Yet wanting Germany and Italy to lose did not mean Black Gotham had any desire to fight for imperial England and imperial France. Indeed, the Black press denied the war was a conflict between democracy and dictatorship, noting both sets of Europeans were proponents of white supremacy and equal opportunity exploiters of Africa.

England, moreover, ruled the Indies—West and East—and Gandhi's struggle was widely supported in Harlem, as was that of Caribbean nationalists. Hopefully the conflict would weaken all combatants, enhancing prospects for colonial freedom. In the spring of 1940, A. Philip Randolph summed up the prevailing mood, declaring: "Negroes should oppose America's entrance into war."

By that fall, however, with England's position deteriorating, Randolph conceded that Britain, in accepting that Blacks were human, was a lesser evil than Hitler, who thought them "half apes," and by early 1941, most Black leaders had come around to advocating armed neutrality and aid to England.

THE IRISH

Father Charles Coughlin delivers a speech for the radio at Cleveland Stadium, 1936. (Photo by Fotosearch/Getty Images)

16

The Waning of the Green

In the 1930s, Gotham's Germans, Jews, Italians, Africans, and Chinese—riveted on the fates of their respective compatriots abroad—wrestled over the appropriate American (and metropolitan) response to global developments. New York's Irish Americans had been focused on their homeland since local Fenians had come up from underground in 1865, hoisted their harp-and-sunburst flag over the old Moffat mansion in Union Square, and proclaimed New York City the headquarters of their revolutionary government-in-exile, the command post of an international campaign to free Ireland from English oppression. From the 1870s on, a Gotham-based organization—the Clan na Gael—had been the principal overseas supporter of the Irish Republican Army (IRA), hailing its Easter Rising of 1916 and in large measure funding the ensuing War of Independence (1919–1921). In 1919, Éamon de Valera, a commandant during the Rising, came to the United States to raise money for the independence struggle and to campaign for US citizenship, having been born in New York in 1882, which was one reason why, when captured by the British, he hadn't been shot for his role in the Rising. De Valera drew enormous crowds in venues around the country, raising over five million dollars for the struggle.

In 1921 an Anglo-Irish treaty granted establishment of, not a *republic*, but an Irish Free State, a twenty-six-county self-governing *dominion* in the British Commonwealth—the status held by Canada and Australia. Six northern counties, largely Protestant, opted to remain in the United Kingdom of Great Britain. Though there was widespread support for this solution, in the US as well as Ireland, a militant IRA minority demanded exclusion of the British and retention of the northern counties, and the country descended into civil war (1922–1923), which was won by the pro-treaty forces.

Quasi independence did not solve Ireland's economic problems, and widespread impoverishment generated another wave of emigration. Most of those people who left Ireland for the United States in the 1920s came from straitened rural backgrounds. But in booming New York City most of the unskilled were able to get jobs. For men: construction workers, longshoremen, auto mechanics, and truck drivers. For women: domestic servants, teachers, nurses, telephone operators.

The newcomers settled into neighborhoods with a substantial Irish presence. In Manhattan: Washington Heights and Inwood, Hell's Kitchen and Chelsea. In the Bronx: Fordham and Kingsbridge. In Brooklyn: Park Slope and Flatbush.

Though they kept up with developments in Ireland—the *Irish Echo*, *Irish Advocate*, *Irish World*, and *Gaelic American* catered to an emigrant audience—many of the newcomers, including defeated IRA veterans, were disinclined to radical politics. By 1929, the Clan na Gael had only 620 dues-paying members. Instead, they were drawn to fraternal and social groups, institutions, and bars. For many young immigrants the first introduction to their new communities (and their fellow arrivals) were the dozens of dance halls in Manhattan, Brooklyn, and the Bronx that featured Irish and American dancing.

Then came the Crash. Immigration skidded to a halt. In 1930 the *Irish World* warned potential emigrants not to leave Ireland, as "for every position vacant in New York…there are several hundred applicants," making life in the city for emigrants a "hopeless struggle." During 1931 only 801 emigrants from the Free State arrived in the US, compared to 23,445 the year before.

The economic sectors in which they had made gains in the 1920s were hard hit by hard times. Unskilled and semiskilled jobs, plentiful in the previous decade, grew scarcer. Higher up the economic ladder, those second- and third-generation Irishmen who had gotten college degrees and moved into professional careers in law, accounting, insurance, and medicine found their upward momentum rudely checked. Real estate developers and land speculators who had grown rich in the 1920s constructing middle-class outer-borough housing—much of it for their increasingly affluent compatriots—were caught out by the housing market's collapse. And those who had carved out places in Wall Street's banks, brokerages, and law firms now found themselves victims of the financial market's toboggan slide.

Still from *A Tree Grows in Brooklyn* (1945). (Allstar Picture Library Ltd/Alamy Stock Photo)

What made matters worse was the Irish sense of relative decline vis-à-vis ethnic competitors—particularly Jews and to a lesser degree Italians—who were also scrambling for a piece of the shrinking economic pie.

Nowhere was the slippage more painfully apparent than in the political arena, where a succession of blows toppled Manhattan's Tammany, ending an era of Irish domination that stretched back more than a half century to the days of John Kelly, William Russell Grace, and Richard Croker. In 1932–33, the forced resignation of Jimmy Walker; the capture of the White House by Franklin Roosevelt, not Al Smith; and Herbert Lehman's ascension to the governorship were followed by the triumph of Fiorello La Guardia on a pointedly balanced ticket (an Italian, a Jew, and an Irishman). Worse, the Little Flower immediately slashed the Irish share of mayoral cabinet appointments from the bountiful 41 percent they'd enjoyed in the administration of his immediate predecessor, John L. O'Brien, to a scanty 5 percent in his.

This reversal of fortune extended far down the governmental job chain, as La Guardia dismantled long-standing discriminations against the non-Irish. Municipal job openings were publicly advertised. The percentage of positions subject to competitive examination rose from roughly half the city's work force (in 1933) to nearly three quarters (by 1939). Multiple choice questions replaced essay exams, reducing the discretion of Irish civil service examiners. Such reforms loosened the Gaelic grip on public employment. By 1940 in the school system, long an Irish female bastion, 56 percent of all newly hired teachers were Jewish women.

Tammany itself commenced an ethnic succession, as Irish chieftains turned to Italian mobsters for alternative sources of funding, and they in turn installed their own district leaders.

The enhanced share of jobs going to Jews and Italians (even Blacks) did not go unnoticed, or unlamented, by partisans of the old order. Daniel Danaher of the Federation of Irish Societies complained that his people "as a race" were "being pushed aside to make room for other more aggressive and better organized races." And Al Smith, tongue only partly in cheek, told a Jewish audience that "I'm beginning to wonder if someone shouldn't do something for the poor Irish, here in New York."

The Irish overstated their decline. Tammany's crisis was partly locational, the consequence of a Gaelic exodus from Manhattan. Democratic machines remained alive and well in the outer boroughs, with Irish bosses firmly in command. In Brooklyn, though John H. McCooey gave ground gracefully to Jewish politicians like Irwin Steingut, in districts such as Crown Heights, where Jews had all but completely replaced Irish voters, he and his compatriots retained borough-wide power: it was Frank Kelley who took over when McCooey died in 1934. In the Bronx, Ed Flynn remained on excellent terms with Governor Lehman and President Roosevelt, receiving patronage from both. Indeed, FDR brought more Irishmen into the cabinet and federal judiciary than any of his predecessors—not a complete surprise, as it was James Aloysius Farley, chairman of both the state and national Democratic Party, who oversaw appointments. And when Roosevelt and Farley fell out in 1940, it was Flynn who assumed command of the national apparatus. In Queens, where the Irish were regrouping, Galway-born George U. Harvey opened up a new base for his compatriots inside the Republican Party. In 1928, Harvey, a crusading anti-Tammany alderman from Flushing, brought down Democratic borough president Maurice Connolly—who did a year's stretch in the Welfare Island penitentiary for his role in a sewer contract scandal. Harvey was immediately elected to replace him.

Still, Tammany's travails throughout the 1930s—the sequential woes of bosses John Curry, Peter J. Dooling, and Tim Sullivan—had great symbolic resonance in the Irish community, especially as they seemed of a piece with what appeared to be Gaelic Gotham's diminishing capacity to shape the city's (and nation's) culture in other arenas as well. Irish boxers (like Tunney, Sullivan, and Dempsey) had given way to Black and Jewish champions (like Louis and Baer); Joe DiMaggio ruled baseball's roost; Irish crooners faced mellifluous Italian competition; and the funniest comedians, more often than not, were Jewish.

Feeding their malaise was an ongoing demographic decline that was both absolute—the number of Irish stock New Yorkers (both foreign-born and second-generation) dropped from 613,006, of which 220,631 were born in Ireland, to 518,466 over the 1930s—and relative, with their percentage of the city's population sloping down from one in five (1910) to one in ten (1945). This slippage—the function of a declining birth rate, a shift to the suburbs, and diminished immigration—was most starkly registered in neighborhoods where long-established Irish settlers gave ground before an influx of German-Jewish refugees, as in Washington Heights, where Celts, retreating east from Broadway, regrouped in more dilapidated quarters along Amsterdam Avenue.

17

Catholic New York

Yet the Irish still held sway over one seemingly impregnable stronghold—the Catholic Church—organized in two vast encampments, the Archdiocese of New York (including Manhattan, the Bronx, and Staten Island, along with some upriver counties) and the Diocese of Brooklyn (encompassing Queens and the rest of Long Island). In 1938, when Cardinal Patrick Joseph Hayes jested that it seemed like half the archdiocese had moved to Queens, his dominion still embraced a million Catholics. And across the East River that year, where the flock of Thomas Edmund Molloy—Bishop of Brooklyn since 1922—was approaching 1.2 million, there was even talk (though as yet no action) of spinning off Nassau and Suffolk into a new diocese.

In the aggregate, Catholics constituted perhaps 25 percent of the city's population, and while the faithful included Poles and Puerto Ricans, Blacks and Germans and Italians, the Irish retained pride of place, not least by virtue of their overwhelming dominance of the enormous hierarchy. Together (in 1939) the two dioceses included 2,732 priests, whose ranks were replenished by seminarians trained at St. Joseph's Seminary up north in the Dunwoodie section of Yonkers (for New York) or the Seminary of the Immaculate Conception out east at Lloyd Harbor (for Brooklyn). In addition, there were thousands of male and female religious, who in New York were arrayed in forty-five separate orders, including Jesuits, Dominicans, Franciscans, Capuchins, Redemptorists, Carmelites, Augustinians, Trappists, Josephites, Salesians, Marists, and Passionist Fathers.

Aggregate numbers don't convey the true dimension of the Catholic presence in the Depression-era city. The two million weren't isolated individuals but members of vibrant parishes—371 in New York (as of 1937), 129 in Brooklyn (as of 1939)—each one a strongly held domain. Parishioners considered their neighborhoods as Catholic milieus even though others shared the space. Bronx Catholics, asked where they lived, would likely as not reply "Visitation," "Friday Good Shepherd," "St. Brendan's," or "St. Philip Neri's"—territories delineated on their mental map of an alternate New York.

Parishes, moreover, were far more than merely imagined communities. Catholic ownership claims were staked out by shrines in yards, by processions that carted statues of Mary through the neighborhood, by local businesses shutting up shop on Good Friday. More tangibly still, the Catholic presence was anchored by brick-and-mortar establishments. Each parish had at least one church: the combined dioceses boasted nearly 800 of them in New York City. Many had a school as well. Four hundred seventy-five parish, diocesan, and privately organized educational institutions offered low- (or no-) cost elementary education to pupils who were then funneled up to 123 Catholic high schools, twelve Catholic colleges, and two Catholic universities.

In addition to parochial institutions, the Church maintained a citywide social service apparatus—a Catholic welfare state—that included thirty-three orphanages (and other childcare institutions), thirty-two day nurseries, twenty-three summer homes and camps, forty-five hospitals, fourteen homes for the aged, and twelve cemeteries.

There was also a panoply of associations for the faithful to join as individuals—Catholic counterparts for virtually every imaginable secular organization. Professionals could gather in the Guild of Catholic Lawyers, the Catholic Physicians' Guild, and the Catholic Press Association. Scholars could meet at the Catholic Historical Association, Catholic Sociological Society, Catholic Philosophical Association, and Catholic Economics Association. For belletrists there were the Catholic Writers' Guild of America and the Catholic Poetry Society of America; for educators the National Catholic Education Association and the Catholic Teachers Association. For students, membership in a campus branch of the Newman Club Federation or National Federation of Catholic College Students could give way after commencement to affiliation with a Catholic alumni organization.

Businessmen rendezvoused at their local Knights of Columbus chapter. Policemen, firemen, and postal workers had their own Holy Name societies, whose monthly or annual communion breakfasts—often preceded by a packed mass at St. Patrick's Cathedral—attracted four, five, or six thousand members to ballroom venues at the Astor, St. George, or Waldorf Astoria hotels. The National Catholic Youth Organization sponsored sports leagues, boxing tournaments, and competitions with YM and YWCAs, while adults could enlist in wide-spectrum organizations like the National Council of Catholic Men and the National Council of Catholic Women. New Yorkers could subscribe to the *Catholic Digest*, *America*, *Commonweal*, *The Brooklyn Tablet*, or *Catholic World* (among many other periodicals); join the Catholic Book Club or Spiritual Book Associates; and tune in (after 1930) to the weekly *Catholic Hour*.

In New York City, one could travel life's highway, from cradle to grave, almost exclusively in Catholic company.

Yet for all the strength of its institutional structure, the vigor of its ideological resurgence, and the force of its cultural militancy, the Catholic Church, and particularly its Irish hierarchy, felt increasingly beleaguered during the Depression decade. This was partly a matter of declining revenues. Collections from hard-pressed parishioners dropped off, debts soared (by 1938 the Archdiocese of New York owed over $28 million), and the bricks-and-mortar boom of the previous decade petered out: of the sixty-five new parishes started by Cardinal Hayes, only five were established in the 1930s; and where Brooklyn had started fourteen churches in the 1920s, it created only three in the 1930s.

Far more threatening was the fact that all over the world—and increasingly in the United States, even in New York itself—Catholicism seemed to be under assault by powerful states controlled by an unholy trinity of atheists, pagans, and communists.

18

A Church Besieged

Gotham's conservative Irish clergy had worried about Red Republican anticlericalism as far back as the upheavals of 1848, in Archbishop Hughes's day. And in 1917, Russian revolutionaries having begun to persecute believers, Soviet Communism had been New York Catholicism's bête noire. But it was the disturbing events in Mexico during the 1920s and early 1930s that really put the fear of godlessness into New York prelates.

In 1926, Mexico's president, Plutarco Elías Calles, had launched a crackdown on the country's Catholic Church, considered by many revolutionaries the handmaiden of reaction. Calles decreed that those anticlerical articles of the 1917 Constitution, dormant since their adoption, were now to be ruthlessly enforced. Priests had to register with the government; clerics and nuns were denied the right to vote or to criticize government officials or to wear ecclesiastical garb; foreign priests and nuns were to be deported; religious organizations were forbidden to own property; monasteries and convents were to be closed; and Catholic schools were to be shut down and replaced by thousands of newly established secular public schools. In response, the Mexican Episcopate declared an interdict, suspending public administration of the sacraments. This triggered an uprising in west-central Mexico where, to the cry of "Viva Cristo Rey" ("Long Live Christ the King"), bands of militant Catholics attacked government officials and torched public schools. The government responded with massive force, using the army (and supplies obtained from the United States), along with its own partisan bands of "Red Shirts," to fight the "Cristeros."

Three years of vicious warfare ensued, with both sides engaging in grisly acts of terrorism. By 1929, with thousands of Cristero *campesinos* still in the field, the US decided to impose peace. Ambassador Dwight Morrow brokered an arrangement between Calles and the dominant faction of the Mexican hierarchy. The Church accepted the government's secularist ground rules de jure, while negotiating a de facto right to evade them. Once a modus vivendi was worked out, the prelates abandoned the *campesinos* (as did the Vatican), who were soon crushed, though in some states, notably Tabasco, suppression and resistance battled on through the mid-'30s.

The Cristero War, a multihued event, engendered Black and white responses in New York. Prominent liberals deprecated reports of persecution, or actively backed the Calles regime, citing the Mexican Church's presumed ties with aristocratic and counterrevolutionary classes. In fact, Mexico's deeply divided Church of the 1920s differed from its hidebound nineteenth-century predecessor, with powerful factions now supporting some social reform. New York's Catholics—deeply shocked by the murder of priests and nuns and the closure of schools and churches—universally sympathized with their Mexican brethren and denounced the failure of local liberals to demonstrate concern as manifesting KKK-style bigotry.

The rise of Euro-fascist dictatorships troubled New York's Catholic prelates far less than had the events in Mexico, in large part because Mussolini and Hitler signed formal treaties (concordats) with the Vatican that, supposedly, preserved the Church's institutional prerogatives. Pope Pius XI came to terms with Il Duce in the 1929 Lateran Accord, and Mussolini's many concessions to Catholic interests played well in New York. Cardinal Hayes applauded the dictator as a man "unusually favorably disposed to the progress of the Catholic Church."

The 1933 treaty with Germany similarly "guaranteed" freedom of religious association and the right to proselytize, in return for German Catholics dismantling their Center Party, a potential source of political resistance to Nazism. The Reich Concordat received a similar approbation in New York, where the Catholic press welcomed the emergence of another strongly anticommunist regime.

19

War in Spain

The outbreak of civil war in Spain in 1936 commanded the Catholic clergy's total attention—and total horror. Though the struggle was labyrinthian enough to make the Cristero War seem transparent by comparison, it was perceived by the New York hierarchy in the same dichotomized way they had viewed Mexican events, in part because they read the story exclusively through the eyes of their episcopal Spanish confreres.

Back in 1931, the Iberian bishops had opposed the supersession of Spain's monarchy by the Second Spanish Republic. They'd been right to worry. As in Mexico, many of the newly empowered republicans proved vehemently anticlerical, convinced (with good reason) that the Church would oppose the pluralist, democratic, secular society they sought to establish. The government moved immediately (in 1931–32) to pry apart church and state, by establishing secular public schools (thus breaking the Catholic monopoly on education); allowing civil marriages and burials; and permitting divorce. More rashly, it curtailed the hierarchy's power and privileges (priests were no longer to be paid by the state, the Jesuits were expelled altogether) and infringed on the rights and identity of the Catholic laity (silencing church bells, removing religious statuary from public squares) in ways thought petty and vindictive.

Republican initiatives trod on other powerful toes—huge estates were nationalized, many army officers were forced to retire early on half pay—generating powerful political opposition from a conservative Catholic party (CEDA), a fascist party (the Falange, or Phalanx), revanchist monarchical groups, the officer corps, wealthy industrialists, and large landowners. For a time, the country's seething cultural and political conflicts—all greatly aggravated by depression and agrarian crisis—were contained within the electoral system. Right-wing forces formed a National Front, won power in 1933, and promptly reversed the anti-Church measures and other reforms. In the 1936 election, a Spanish Popular Front of Communists, Socialists, Republicans, Anarchists, Syndicalists, and Separatists (Basques and Catalonians)—drawing on urban workers, peasants, and much of the educated middle class—regained power and reintroduced the reforms.

The Falange turned to paramilitary violence on the model of Italy's fascisti and Germany's storm troopers. On July 17, 1936, in conjunction with conservatives, monarchists, and fascists (domestic and foreign), the military high command set out to overthrow the Republic. On July 28, courtesy of Hitler and Mussolini, German and Italian transport planes began airlifting Nationalist troops commanded by General Francisco Franco from Morocco to Spain. With the government unprepared to contest a full-scale invasion, a potpourri of popular militias, of wildly varying political persuasions, sprang up almost overnight to defend the Republic and advance a social revolution. Some militias seized factories; others collectivized land; and some went after their age-old enemy, the Church, attacking not only its property (sacking and burning buildings) but murdering priests and nuns—hundreds in the first days, perhaps 5,000 in the first months.

These atrocities were but the subset of an orgy of mass executions committed by both sides: as many as 50,000 were assassinated or summarily executed in the early aftermath of the Nationalist insurrection. Religious persecutions diminished dramatically as Republican authorities reasserted control, but the general carnage continued, indeed expanded, as Franco's forces adopted a calculated program of terror. Republicans and liberals were rounded up *en masse*, tortured, raped, shot, disappeared.

In October, having won control of much of the country, Nationalists launched an all-out assault on Madrid to finish off the Republic. The odds were with them, as Britain and France had declared an embargo on arms shipments to Spain that affected only the legitimate government; the fascist powers continued to blatantly deliver planes, tanks, and troops (50,000 from Mussolini) to their Nationalist comrades. But now the Soviet Union, declaring that it, too, would ignore the embargo, rushed armaments and ammunition to the Republican forces, in return for the great bulk of Spain's gold reserves, roughly 500 million-worth in US dollars. Russian tanks and planes arrived in Madrid, slowing though not halting the Nationalist advance. Then, on November 8, with Republican lines close to breaking, 3,000 disciplined troops arrived to help defend the city. Mostly German, Polish, and Italian World War I veterans, they were the first of the International Brigades—volunteers from many countries organized and directed by the Comintern. One from the US would shortly join the fray.

20

¡Viva La Quince Brigada!

On the summer evening of August 21, 1936, just over a month after civil war had erupted in Spain, the Hapag Lloyd liner *Bremen* had been preparing to depart from Hudson River Pier 86, at the foot of West 46th Street. Unbeknownst to the 3,000 visitors on hand to see off the 800 passengers, among their number were 150 men and women who had sauntered up the gangplank, dressed in evening clothes, but who were not bent on partying. Around 11:00 p.m., occupants of a car driving slowly past the pier on the West Side Elevated Highway tossed some firecrackers to the street below, a signal for the "visitors" to whip off their outer wraps, revealing white cotton sweaters emblazoned (in red paint) with "Hands off Spain." They proceeded to march through the ship, passing out handbills, yelling "Hitler must be kept out of Spain." Crew members and pier police leapt to the attack, touching off a wild confrontation, with deck chairs swinging and spectators shrieking "Communists!"—correctly, as it turned out. Several of the CP women produced chains and padlocks and affixed themselves to the railing of the first-class decks, and crew members began chopping the chains with axes. Finally, a large contingent of New York policemen showed up, restored order, and arrested twelve protesters (eight women and four men, including two stenographers, two housewives, two office workers, two unemployed, and a pianist, teacher, pharmacist, and writer).

In the coming months, New York Communists kept ratcheting up the noise level—two days after Thanksgiving, 15,000 paraded from Union Square to the German Consulate at 17 Battery Place, singing the Internationale and carrying banners like "Make Madrid the Tomb of Fascism." November had brought a still sharper escalation, when, pursuant to a Comintern communiqué newly arrived from Moscow, the Party began seeking volunteers to fight Franco on the battlefields of Spain. Word was passed along the waterfront and to furrier shops, union halls, ethnic associations, and unemployed organizations, and by early 1937 nearly 1,000 men (of an eventual 2,800) had joined the Abraham Lincoln Brigade. (Officially it was the Abraham Lincoln Battalion, part of the Fifteenth International Brigade, but "Brigade" was the name that stuck.)

Most volunteers were in their twenties. About one in four were from Gotham. The great bulk of the Brigade—over 70 percent—were committed Communists. Over a third were Jews. The brigade included over eighty African Americans, making it the first racially integrated military unit in US history. Students were the biggest white-collar contingent—eighty-eight members of the American Student Union served—second in numbers only to volunteers from the maritime trades, with their long tradition of radicalism. Sailor Bill Bailey had taken part in an earlier CP protest on the *Bremen* (in July 1935), during which he had slashed down its black swastika flag; now Bailey signed up for service in a machine gun company.

Lincoln Brigade recruits convened several nights a week at hired halls like the Manhattan Lyceum (68 East 4th Street) and the Spartacus Club (269 West 25th Street), where they drilled with broomstick-rifles. The first group sailed the day after Christmas 1936 on the *Normandie*, traveling as "tourists," their real mission forbidden by US law. By February 1937 the first 450 had been hurried into the Battle of Jarama, where they helped win Madrid's defenders a temporary respite at a cost of 120 dead and 175 wounded. By late November Franco's advance had been stymied. Both sides settled in for a long and ferocious war.

In 1937, with German assistance, the Nationalists began a campaign against the Basques. On April 26, at Franco's request, the Luftwaffe's Condor Legion conducted a massive saturation bombing raid on Guernica, a small Basque town lacking either defenses or military significance. After pounding the village for hours with high explosives and dropping incendiary devices that set off a firestorm, Heinkel fighter planes machine-gunned the terrified civilians running through the streets and fields seeking shelter. Initially proud of the attack, the Nationalists soon realized they had shocked the world and spread the tale that Bolsheviks or Basques themselves had destroyed the city. In any case, concern for world opinion did not halt the ongoing Nationalist slaughter of civilians, captured prisoners, and Basque Catholics (including priests) who supported the Republic.

Nor were remonstrances about Franco's brutality forthcoming from Catholic quarters. Quite the opposite. The pope had already condemned the Republican Government for its "satanic hate against God" and blessed "all those who have taken the difficult and dangerous task to defend and reinstate the honor of God and of Religion." Now, on July 1, 1937, scant weeks after Guernica, the Primate of Spain, Cardinal Gomá, penned a "Collective Letter" from the Spanish hierarchy to the "Bishops of the World." Written at Franco's behest, it was aimed at convincing international Catholic opinion that the Nationalist cause was a sacred one, that the uprising was a holy war to save Catholic Spain and Western civilization from Marxism. Caught up in a crusade mentality, fearful of conspiracies by Freemasons and Jews ("the Semitic International") as well as Bolsheviks, Gomá, long an admirer of Mussolini and Hitler, offered theological cover for Franco's regime, to which the Vatican extended formal recognition on August 28.

After eighteen more months of horrific fighting, the Nationalists finally captured Madrid, on March 29, 1939, and the Republic was crushed. Pope Pius XII, "with great joy," extended "our paternal congratulations" to his "dearest sons of Catholic Spain" on their "noble" and "heroic" victory, even as Franco was well embarked on a postwar campaign to cleanse the country of all traces of the Second Republic by killing over 100,000 Loyalists. This new mountain of corpses drove the total body count, including combatants and executed civilians (55,000 murdered by Republicans, 75,000 by Nationalists), to well over 500,000, possibly as high as a million.

From the war's opening days in 1936, Catholic clerics and publications in New York, already hyper-sensitized by events in Mexico, responded to the violent anticlericalism, and growing Soviet involvement, by unequivocally supporting the Nationalist insurrection.

Local Jesuits were quickest off the mark. Francis X. Talbot, editor of the Jesuit magazine *America*, was a man of monarchical inclinations with close connections to the Spanish Right. He declared that Franco was not a fascist; that he sought only to bring a Catholic order to power in Spain; and that those who criticized him were simply "lovers of communism and Sovietism."

Equally adamant in defense of the Nationalists was Patrick Scanlan, managing editor since 1917 of *The Brooklyn Tablet* (as *The Tablet* was called between 1931 and 1939), the official weekly voice of the Brooklyn Diocese. In the 1920s, Scanlan—when not inveighing against the evils of jazz, immodest dress, and contraception—had battled the Ku Klux Klan in the US and denounced persecutions committed by the "barbaric and Caesarian" regime in Mexico. In the 1930s, from his paper's perch in the Williamsburg Savings Bank skyscraper, Scanlan told his 50,000 readers—overwhelmingly working-class, Irish Catholic Brooklynites—that not only was the Spanish conflict an Armageddon between atheistic communism and Christian civilization, but that the Nationalists were liberal democrats—the equivalents of "our Patriots of 1776"—and that Franco was the George Washington of Spain.

Another Brooklynite, the Rev. Edward Lodge Curran, pastor of St. Stephen's Church (on Summit and Hicks in Red Hook), was even more proactive. Curran, who held a PhD from Fordham and a law degree from St. Lawrence, was Dean of Brooklyn's Cathedral College until he left in 1932 to head the International Catholic Truth Society. Headquartered at 407 Bergen Street in Brooklyn since its founding in 1899, the ICTS had labored to refute calumnies against the Catholic faith. In 1936, the Society established an American Committee against Communism (ACC), also directed by Curran, which dispatched hundreds of Catholic girls across the city to collect funds for medical supplies to send to Franco's forces. In May 1937 the ACC cosponsored a mass rally at Madison Square Garden (approved by Cardinal Hayes and Bishop Molloy), at which speakers glorified the insurgents and minimized the butchery at Guernica and a choir sang a processional hymn, composed for the occasion, which asserted: "Now again over Spain, Hangs the Hammer of Hell, And the Sickle of the Bolshevik, And the Anarch's evil spell."

There were dissenters from this orthodoxy in New York, and Dorothy Day was among the first. As early as September 1936, Day argued in the *Catholic Worker* that the Spanish situation was nowhere as clear cut as Talbot, Scanlan, and Curran were arguing. The *Worker* reprinted assessments from knowledgeable European sources—notably the French Catholic philosopher Jacques Maritain—that disputed those coming from the Spanish clergy. Day also argued that the defenders of the Nationalist–Nazi alliance should look closely at Hitler's persecution of German Catholics, despite the 1933 Concordat, "to see just how much love the Catholic Church can expect" from a fascist victory in Spain. Nor should New York Catholics uncritically back the Nationalists, Day counseled, as they, too, were committing horrendous crimes.

George Shuster's was another voice cautioning against swallowing whole the Spanish bishops' interpretation of events. Managing editor since 1928 of the liberal Catholic journal *The Commonweal*, Shuster published a lengthy article entitled "Some Reflections on Spain" in the April 12, 1937, issue. Echoing Day, and drawing on German Catholic sources, he warned that Franco's admiration for Hitler and Mussolini foreshadowed a Fascist Spain, which, given the Nazi depredations that Pius XI had just denounced in a March 14 encyclical, *Mit Brennender Sorge (With Burning Anxiety)*, bode ill for Spanish Catholics. Even more sharply, Shuster raised the question of why so many Spaniards hated the Church. Had its failure to promote social justice, and its backing of the country's most reactionary classes, perhaps fueled the success of communism and anarchism? Would not its alliance with fascists, its turning a blind eye to Franco's use of immoral means, and its false assertion that all Republicans were Communists (overlooking, among others, its Basque Catholic supporters), all serve to further widen the gulf between Catholicism and the Spanish masses?

Shuster's "Reflections" set off a firestorm. A mountain of hate mail poured in, including threats to his life. Father Talbot—hitherto a friend of Shuster's—denounced him in *America* for providing "ammunition for all the communistically controlled organizations in this country." Scanlan's *Brooklyn Tablet* issued vitriolic assaults. The New York Chancery phoned Shuster's parish priest in Connecticut inquiring whether he had attended Sunday Mass regularly. With subscriptions to *The Commonweal* falling dramatically, Shuster was forced to step down as editor (in 1940 he would become president of Hunter College). Reflecting on the controversy from his relatively marginal vantage point—being of German rather than Irish background—Shuster decided that "for Catholic New York the world outside the United States was either Communist or Fascist and that therefore they had opted for Fascism."

Shuster overstated the case. It is true that the *hierarchy* all but unanimously backed the Nationalists. However, a poll in December 1938 found that—nationally—the Catholic *laity* was seriously divided. While 39 percent of American Catholics favored Franco, 30 percent were pro Loyalist, and 31 percent were uncommitted. Similarly, in response to a nationwide poll in 1939 that asked respondents to choose between fascism and communism, 34 percent of Catholics opted for the latter—admittedly only half the percentage of Jews who did so (67 percent)—but still fully one-third the total.

So nearly two-thirds of American Catholics failed to follow their leaders. *Politically organized* Catholicism was what counted on the most crucial front, the debate over whether to lift the US embargo on arms to Spain. Roosevelt, who in October 1937 had denounced the "Nazi-Fascist aggressors" in Spain, was amenable, and Eleanor Roosevelt was ardent. Widespread opposition quickly erupted, and though it came from many quarters, including anti-interventionist Protestants, it was the massive lobbying campaign undertaken by Catholic groups that most forcefully registered with FDR. By May 1938, Secretary of the Interior Harold Ickes reported, the president had become convinced that lifting it would "mean the loss of every Catholic vote next fall." The embargo stayed in place. The Republic fell.

While many New York prelates hailed the victory over communism in Spain, many feared it was on the rise in Gotham. In a troubling number of local contests—over labor unions, civil service jobs, birth control, and public education—things were not going their way.

21

Greens and Reds: The Transport Workers Union

Beneath the sidewalks of New York lay the subways of New York, notorious for their miserable working conditions. A twelve-hour day and a 7-day week fetched 33 cents an hour, with no sick leave, holidays, or pension rights provided. It was also dangerous down there; accidents were not uncommon. Repeated efforts to create a union were snuffed out by a managerial spy network that fired would-be unionists on the spot.

In 1933, two initiatives to organize a union emerged, one from within, one from outside. The inside movement emerged in the near majority of transit workers who were Irish republicans. Some were IRA veterans of the prolonged fight against the British. They were not cowed by management—they'd dealt with much worse—and were inspired by the revolutionary unionist James Connolly, organizer for the Irish Transport and General Workers Union until he was captured and executed for his participation in the Rising,

One of those who shared Connolly's vision of trade unions as citizen armies for social betterment was Mike Quill, who had arrived in 1926, having briefly served in the IRA, and been on the losing side of the battle over the Anglo-Irish treaty. Quill slotted himself into the vigorous Irish American social world of the 1920s. Given his considerable oratorical skills, he became a well-known figure, much in demand as master of ceremonies for dance hall fundraisers. He also joined the Clan na Gael and linked up with other transit worker IRA veterans to create a network of activists that held its organizing meetings in subway tunnels, in near-perfect secrecy.

These deep insiders knew, however, that they needed outside help to defeat the autocratic management. They first took their plight to the Ancient Order of Hibernians and the Friendly Sons of St. Patrick; the effort proved fruitless. Reach-outs to the Democratic Party and the Irish American press were similarly ignored or rebuffed.

The New York Communist Party, however, opened up a line of communication to the struggling organizers by establishing what they called an Irish Worker Club. As its first members were all "Jewish fellas," they had trouble communicating with the Irishmen. That passed—the mutuality of interest was manifest—and at an April 1934 sit-down between the Clan na Gael men and top Irish American CP figures like Elizabeth Gurley Flynn and William Z. Foster, a Fenian's son, a modus operandi was forged. Quill and company would hew to the party platform, and the party would supply dozens of full-time professional organizers and also provide lawyers, publicists, and operating funds, their salaries paid by the Party. In 1935 Quill was elected president of the officially named Transit Workers Union (TWU). A series of brief strikes ensued, though the union avoided large-scale confrontations until January 23, 1937, when the Brooklyn-Manhattan Transit Corporation (BMT) fired two members for union activity and the TWU responded with a massive sit-down strike.

Mike Quill, president of the Transport Workers Union, joins the picket, March 11, 1941. (Bettmann/Contributor/Getty Images)

This was followed by an overwhelming victory in a National Labor Relations Board election, which in turn drew thirty thousand men into the union. Later that year, the TWU joined the Congress of Industrial Organizations (the CIO) and plunged into municipal politics. Quill himself joined the American Labor Party and ran successfully for a seat on the City Council.

The city's Catholic clerics had at first paid little attention to the TWU's emergence, in part because the union's leaders had been very careful not to provoke its ire. As Quill noted, "Many a fellow who thought me a dangerous agitator found me more to his taste after meeting with me at the Paulist Fathers."

TWU success galvanized active resistance by more conservative Catholic groups. In 1937 Father Curran organized an American Association Against Communism intended to

Greens and Reds: The Transport Workers Union 79

Mike Quill is carried up to the speakers' platform by the Transport Workers Union, 1937. (Photo by Underwood Archives/Getty Images)

"unmask those labor leaders who are boring from within." Holy Name societies and Knights of Columbus joined the cause, and the *Brooklyn Tablet* called on members to quit the union.

To no avail. The campaign ran up against a widespread conviction that priestly authority, appropriate in Church concerns, was a writ that should not run in political or social matters. There was also a particular history of bad blood between prelates and parishioners, dating to the Irish bishops' ban on IRA membership during the troubles with England. There was resentment, too, that the hierarchy's attention to transit workers had not been paid until the TWU came along. As one Irish motorman put it, "What the hell did the Church do for us? Not a god damn thing."

22

Catholics v. "Communists"

In 1938 Mayor La Guardia appointed Paul J. Kern to head the Civil Service Commission. An outspoken liberal who had been a member of the mayor's brain trust since 1934, Kern was a member of the American Labor Party and a supporter of the Spanish Republic (evidence enough for Robert Moses, who kept voluminous files on his enemies, to claim he was a communist). What particularly riled Irish Catholics, however, was that Kern extended La Guardia's dismantlement of Tammany-era favoritism to their once impregnable bastion, the Police Department. In 1939, Kern's new competitive examinations (he boasted) produced police candidates more representative of the city's population than in former days, when "only occasionally" did a Jew or a Negro get on the force. Such results engendered complaints that Kern was now discriminating against the Irish. And similar charges were levied, by Scanlan and others, against the Department of Welfare, which the editor declared was honeycombed with Communist case workers who not only curtailed Catholic access to the relief rolls but fostered revolution among the unemployed.

Then there was the city's increasing receptivity to birth control. The decade had begun badly, from the Catholic vantage point, with a 1930 decision by the Episcopal Church to break with it on the issue. This was followed by an acceptance of contraception, in varying degrees, by various mainline religious organizations, including Universalists and Unitarians, the Central Conference of American Rabbis, and the Federal Council of Churches of Christ (embracing twenty-seven denominations with a collective membership of twenty-two million). Worse, in 1933, the Federation of Jewish Women, in convention assembled at the Hotel Astor, called (at the urging of Margaret Sanger) for repeal of the Comstock Laws. Worse still, birth control clinics sprouted throughout the city and state. In 1939, Manhattan and the Bronx alone had seventeen community health centers, which that year offered contraceptive care to more than 27,000 women, helping make New York State the country's leading purveyor of birth control information.

In response, the Catholic Church had dug in its heels. In 1930, Pius XI had issued an encyclical, *Casti Connubii*, which reaffirmed that contraception was "an offense against the law of God and of nature" and adjudged those who indulged in it as guilty of a "grave sin."

Gotham's clergy promptly followed suit. At St. Patrick's, radio priest Monsignor Fulton Sheen declared that "the public conscience is attempting to call something that is a sin not a sin." He asserted that such "private interpretation of morals"—a deplorable tendency begun centuries earlier by Protestant schismatics—was "making fools and cads of men." Michael F. Walsh, a Knights of Columbus official, affirmed that "there is no freedom from the moral law," and on this issue, the city's left-leaning Catholics, like Dorothy Day and the *Commonweal* editors, were in complete agreement (the latter opining that contraception in marriage was akin to "self-mutilation or the practice of the solitary vice"). Still, the tide in town was clearly running against them, and increasing numbers of Catholic women were ignoring Church teachings. As a defensive measure, Catholic maternity clinics were established, but in 1940 a dispirited Very Reverend Robert I. Gannon, president of Fordham, predicted that the "violent campaign for birth control" being undertaken by "our brainy society women" would depopulate the nation by 1961.

An early indicator of demographic collapse, Gannon gloomily predicted, would be declining college enrollments, which would first shutter church-related colleges (like his), leaving the field (at least for the moment) to tax-supported institutions. Catholic concern over competition from public colleges was not limited to academic chieftains—Scanlan, for one, opposed the expansion of free municipal higher education—but it was the state of K–12 public education in the city that summoned up levels of outrage that could hardly have been more choleric had the Board of Education, newly installed in the former Elks Club at 110 Livingston Street in Brooklyn, been composed of Mexican or Spanish anticlerics.

From the Catholic perspective, New York's public school system was a disaster. God had been banned from its precincts, and "child-centered" progressive educators—minions of John Dewey and his "atheistical" and "un-American" associates at Columbia's Teachers College—were in the saddle. Deweyan pedagogy, like Deweyan philosophy, promoted a "complete relativization of truth," which left students bereft of firm spiritual moorings and opened the door, warned Edward James Walsh, president of St. John's University, to the implantation by "materialistic governments" of the "poison of Godlessness and impurity into young minds and hearts that are unable to protect themselves."

Some, like Fordham's Father Gannon, thought the wolf was already at the door. In a speech to the Friendly Sons of St. Patrick, Gannon warned that New Yorkers, in warring on plundering politicians, were paving the way for far more dangerous "liberals." "They are not as crude or as simple as the ward-heeler with the big cigars," Gannon said. "What they want is not so much our money as our children. They want our schools and colleges." And later, he added, "when they have the youth of the nation in their power," they hope "to eliminate all religion and all morality that does not conform to their peculiar ideology."

Others believed the wolf had made it inside the door. In 1940, former Brooklyn district attorney William F. X. Geoghan warned the annual communion breakfast of the borough Fire Department's Holy Name Society that "there are forces at work in our secular schools and colleges which are poisoning the minds of the rising generation against American ideals and traditions and against religion," forces that, if allowed to continue, "will deal just as deadly a blow to our Republic as has already been landed by Hitler on Germany and Stalin on Russia."

Catholic schools, to be sure, offered secure bastions against creeping secular humanism or communism, their pedagogy being antithetical to that of the public schools. Catholic teachers explicated the universal moral principles that Neo-Scholastic philosophers had discerned in natural law. They put God, not the child, at the center of the curriculum. New York's parochial system, explained one cleric in 1931, existed "chiefly in order to safeguard the spiritual faith of our children; to inculcate thoroughly their duties to their God." And to country, as well: it was the task of Catholic educators, a teacher from St. Catherine of Alexandria School in Brooklyn reminded her diocesan colleagues in 1936, to impress upon their pupils a deep respect for authority, the better to ward off "skeptical attitudes toward our public officials," and to instill in students an "abhorrence for communistic radical principles and agitators."

The problem was that most school-age Catholics did not attend parochial schools. In Brooklyn, only about 40 percent of Catholic K-8 pupils were in parish institutions, leaving the majority—and the rest of the city's children—to the untender mercies of secularists.

What to do? One approach was to seek public funding for parochial education, though all such requests by the hierarchy were denied. Even their effort to get New York State to underwrite free school bus transportation to faith-based schools was vetoed by Governor Lehman (an action, said the *Brooklyn Tablet*, that "smacks of dictatorship"). As a fallback, the Church sought and won permission to liberate students from secularist clutches for at least part of the school day. In 1940, overriding objections from teachers and parents' groups, Lehman signed the McLaughlin bill, which required the Commissioner of Education to allow released time for religious instruction and observance.

Catholics also set out to police the public system. At a 1940 convention of 3,150 Catholic teachers of the Diocese of Brooklyn, Msgr. Sheen proposed creating a "central clearing house" to which New York's public-school teachers could transmit the names of any colleagues "who send out their children to a Communist parade, or who turn over their classrooms to some member of a Communist organization, or a Nazi or Fascist organization"; all such miscreant pedagogues would then be fired. The Knights of Columbus also launched a battle against schools that allowed their auditoriums to be used for the "spreading of subversive propaganda."

Purging seemed even better than policing, however, and Catholics were inadvertently handed an opportunity to accomplish this by Manhattan's borough president Stanley Isaacs. In December 1937, Isaacs, a Republican, appointed to his staff a bright and articulate young man, Simon W. Gerson, who was City Hall reporter for the *Daily Worker* and a member of the Executive Committee of the New York State Communist Party. When the Knights of Columbus protested, Isaacs stood firm, saying that the Communist Party was a perfectly legal party, that membership in it was no bar to government service, that he had chosen Gerson for his qualifications not his associations, and that civil service law precluded inquiring into political affiliations. "There will be no politics during office hours," Isaacs said stoutly, and "after office hours, I don't care what they are." Unappeased, Edward Lodge Curran, in February 1938, committed himself "and the Catholics of the Brooklyn Diocese" to a petition drive that would collect 100,000 signatures from "real Americans" demanding Gerson's immediate dismissal. Declaring that Communism now "stands up bold and brazen in the very governmental chambers of my own City of New York," Curran had his organization hand out pamphlets urging Catholics to seek Gerson's ouster, in more than a score of churches in Manhattan, the Bronx, Queens, and Brooklyn, endorsed by the parish priests.

Isaacs stuck to his guns, noting that no one had questioned Gerson's ability. Paul Kern, too, backed Gerson when the issue came before his Municipal Civil Service Commission, though Kern didn't endear himself to opponents with his tart remark: "Gerson eats with a fork and shaves every day and it would be hard to tell him in the dining room of the City Club from any stuffed shirts." The left in general backed the appointment, Vito Marcantonio attributing opposition to "the reactionaries of this city," and CIO unions warning that the rise of Nazism had started with the suppression of political opponents.

Equally undeterred, conservative Catholics now petitioned Governor Lehman to remove Isaacs himself from office. When the governor demurred, Curran and the Catholic War Veterans shifted their focus of attention to the State Legislature. With the aid of State Senator John J. McNaboe, they won passage of a law barring Communists from teaching or holding civil service positions. Opponents pointed out that the McNaboe Bill seemed markedly unconcerned with fascist subversion, and Lehman vetoed it in March 1938 as a threat to civil liberties, his message recalling the discredited Lusk laws and the Legislature's expulsion of Socialists during the postwar Red Scare. But a growing coalition—that now included the Knights of Columbus, the Catholic War Veterans, Curran's International Catholic Truth Society, the Ancient Order of Hibernians, and the Paulist Fathers—backed a new bill introduced by State Assemblyman John A. Devany Jr. This version avoided specific references to Communists, banning anyone who advocated forceable overthrow of the government, though Devany made his real target perfectly clear: "We do not want Communists in our State government and in our schools and we are ready to fight them."

The Devany Bill passed and was signed by Lehman in May 1939. Now Gerson's enemies closed in for the kill. They circulated a petition demanding his ouster under the new legislation and, in 1940, the American Legion brought a taxpayer suit seeking his dismissal. Gerson denied that Communist Party membership equaled support for a violent governmental overthrow and asked the city's Corporation Counsel to defend him. When that was refused him, Gerson, lacking funds to wage a legal battle, finally resigned in September 1940.

23

The Christian Front

During 1937 Father Curran revved up his rhetoric, opting for deeds, not words. In January, at a meeting in Corona, Queens, sponsored by his American Committee against Communism, Curran bellicosely declared that Americans should, if necessary, contest Communism "with bullets for bullets." In April, he sponsored a Hippodrome anticommunist rally—endorsed by Archbishop Hayes and Bishop Molloy—at which he told the assembled thousands that "Fascism is not our problem today, but communism is." While he hoped "we haven't waited too long, as they did in Spain where tonight they are fighting it out," he added briskly that "if the communists want it that way, we will give it to them." George U. Harvey, Queens borough president and aspirant for the Republican mayoral nomination, hailed Father Curran for "raising an army" to drive out the communists and announced that he himself was "enlisting for the duration of the war." Should he become mayor, Harvey pledged the cheering crowd, he would give each and every New York policeman "three feet of rubber hose" with which to flail every last communist out of town. Al Smith more temperately advocated the ballot box rather than brute force, though agreed with Harvey that all local communists "should be sent back to the country from which they came."

In May 1937, New York National Guard Brigadier General William J. Costigan called for "public displays of Catholic forces" to face down the Reds. Sixty thousand turned out at Holy Name rallies around Brooklyn and Queens—the Pope cabled his support—and joined a mass march from Atlantic Avenue near Bedford Avenue to Ebbets Field. And in June, Curran's organization dispatched youths throughout the city to pass out a circular—*Save the United States of America from Communism*—that warned of Russia's intention to shut down all churches and make every American boy and girl an atheist. In some cases, fearfulness approached full-fledged paranoia. In October, Father John F. Brady, the spiritual director of the Archdioceses' Holy Name, recalled that twenty years earlier he had heard an eminent preacher declare the day would come when "priests would be hanging from the lamp-posts of New York City." "Today," he insisted, citing events in Spain, "that is not fantastic"; indeed, "things that are happening in the world are just as likely to happen here."

WHILE SOME NEW YORK CATHOLICS fought "communism" in courts and government, others, urged on by yet another radio priest, battled it in the streets.

Charles E. Coughlin, pastor of a Detroit suburban church, first took to the airwaves in 1926. An Irishman with a strong and theatrical voice, Coughlin won his following by pushing hard for economic reforms that conformed with papal pronouncements. In 1930 he was picked up by CBS for nationwide distribution but dropped shortly thereafter, when he began laying into President Hoover as "the bankers' friend, the Holy Ghost of the rich, the protective angel of Wall Street." When NBC declined to take him on board, Coughlin rolled out his own network—leasing phone lines to twenty-six stations, mostly in the Midwest—and by 1932 his *Golden Hour* radio audience was estimated at ten million, the largest assemblage of ears in the United States.

Coughlin backed Roosevelt's first campaign and the early New Deal. As the Depression dragged on, however, and FDR ignored his proposals for inflating the currency, Coughlin upped the volume of his invective against Wall Street, the Federal Reserve, international bankers, and the Money Power in general. He depicted financiers as moral parasites—slothful, sybaritic, malevolent, cunning, and Eastern.

Coughlin now began linking his twin bêtes noires—international capital and international communism—claiming they had a common denominator in international Jewry. Relying on rusty conspiracy theories recently refurbished by Nazi ideologues, Coughlin argued that Jewish bankers had financed the Russian Revolution. In July 1938 he began reprinting *The Protocols of the Elders of Zion*, the anti-Semitic staple Henry Ford had peddled back in the 1920s. *Social Justice* also played to Americans' growing anxieties about a looming European conflict, with articles claiming Jews were crying up German persecutions to drag the US into war.

By 1939, *Social Justice* was running laudatory profiles of Hitler and Mussolini, and Coughlin's broadcasts were arguing that the Rome-Berlin axis was Christendom's "great political rampart against the spread of Communism." His assaults on American Jews grew more pugnacious: "Let's be militant and fight these people to the bitter end, cost what it may," he ranted in a letter to subscribers that April. "Our Christ Who was crucified was no weakling when He drove the money changers from the temple by physical force."

The whereabouts of that temple, moreover, was pinpointed with increasingly specificity. The American people, Coughlin wrote in November of 1939, were being herded toward the battlefields by "British gold and Jewish propaganda." And of these warmongers, "70 percent are from the Eastern states and 45 percent come from New York City." Gotham was host to Wall Street, of course, and it was also, increasingly, the bastion of Communists.

New York, like the United States, had better wake up and recognize that its institutions were increasingly controlled by communists, pagans, and non-Christians. It can't happen here? Coughlin queried. "IT IS HAPPENING HERE RIGHT NOW! Communism is all about us—in our factories—our theatres—our schools—our government—EVEN OUR CHURCHES! It is eating slowly—slowly—into our national vitals." "America MUST MOVE or the poison will be shot into her arteries and then—DEATH!"

Coughlin's solutions were as straightforward as his analysis. In May, June, and July of 1938, Coughlin called on Christians to come together in a popular front: "A UNITED CHRISTIAN FRONT IS OUR LAST-DITCH DEFENSE AGAINST COMMUNISM!"

This appeal galvanized a response in some Irish Catholic circles. On July 14, the founding members of New York's Christian Front met in a basement room of St. Paul's Church. (Soon ousted, once the Paulist fathers learned the group wasn't simply into peaceful proselytizing, they reassembled nearby at Donovan's Hall, 310 West 59th Street.) The midtown Christian Front group, like others that emerged around town, was manned by blue- and white-collar workers—longshoremen, truck drivers, cops, schoolteachers—along with parochial school students and the Depression-battered unemployed. Many found in anti-Semitism an appealing explanation of their precarious or fallen fortunes—the Jews hogged everything in New York—and of troubles yet to come: "The Jews want to destroy Hitler to the last Irishman."

The Christian Front's leadership—men like John Cassidy, head of the Brooklyn unit—tended to be drawn from the ranks of priests, politicians, professionals, and graduates from local Catholic colleges. Cassidy, who had attended parochial schools and studied law at Fordham, became convinced that a Red revolution was imminent. "We are determined," Cassidy declared, "to put it down as Franco put it down in Spain."

The Front boycotted Jewish businesses, first urging followers to "Buy Christian Only," then adopting more muscular tactics, like picketing Jewish department stores (notably Orbach's in Union Square), pasting anti-Semitic posters on Jewish retail establishments, and breaking store windows of Jewish merchants. Gangs of Christian Fronters began roaming the city's streets and subways, cursing "Jew bastards" and shouting "Kill the Kikes" in the faces of elderly Jewish men and women. In the summer of 1939 gangs marched into the Times Square station, heiling Hitler and screaming fascist slogans. Random anti-Semitic violence spread, with Fronters slugging and in some cases stabbing Jewish children and adults.

Particular neighborhoods—usually mixed Irish–Jewish areas—became war zones. In Washington Heights, during 1939, agitators harangued large street crowds at 162nd Street and St. Nicholas Avenue, or Sherman Avenue and Dyckman, eliciting chants of "Kill the Jews!" The same words were hurled by roving gangs of Christian Fronters when they barged into synagogue services; almost every temple in Washington Heights was desecrated in some way. In the Bronx, tensions were particularly acute in Highbridge, Fordham, and Mosholu Parkway—with Christian Front rallies also prevalent at the intersection of the Grand Concourse and Fordham Road, 138th Street and Willis Avenue, and 153rd Street and Third Avenue. In Queens, 116th Street and Rockaway Boulevard (in Rockaway Park) was a Christian Front stronghold. Brooklyn flashpoints included Flatbush Avenue and Albemarle Road, and Kings Highway and East 17th Street.

For some Christian Fronters, such wannabe-Gestapo tactics seemed insufficiently militant, and, breaking away, they founded their own ultra-reactionary outfit, the Christian Mobilizers. The new group's führer—a former grade-B movie actor named Joseph Ellsworth McWilliams—was a good-looking if somewhat vain man (it was said he bobbed and waved his hair); Walter Winchell dubbed him "Handsome Joe McNazi." McWilliams had two big ideas that won him a following: New York rightists needed to form their own multi-ethnic alliance—a municipal Axis—and escalate the level of violence.

On July 6, 1939, at the Christian Mobilizers' founding meeting in the Bronx's Triboro Palace (137th Street and Third Avenue), McWilliams announced he was going to assemble "the meanest, the toughest, the most ornery bunch of German soldiers, Italian veterans and Irish I.R.A. men in the country." Soon the group's meetings—in Innisfail (now Gaelic) Park at 240th Street and Broadway, Ebling's Casino, Schwaben Hall, and Triboro Palace—were attracting masses of German Bundists (including Fritz Kuhn before his incarceration), Italian fascisti, Spanish Nationalists, even Robert Jordan's pro-Japanese Blacks. While none of these outfits were prepared to abandon their independence, joint conclaves became common, festooned with American, Nazi, and green "Eire" flags.

Violent rhetoric was de rigueur at such gatherings. One George E. Deatherage called for a "holy war," saying "I am not content to walk in the footsteps of Christ. I will walk ahead of Him with a club." Mobilizers were urged to join the National Rifle Association and lock in 100 rounds of ammo for the coming showdown with Communism. Donovan's Hall on 59th Street became the scene of clandestine military maneuvering. Plans were laid for an assault on CPUSA headquarters in Union Square. "Terror! Terror! Terror! [cried McWilliams] That is our password from now on."

Gotham's police force did little to stop the violence. Higher-ups dismissed complaints ("Ah the boys are just playing") and beat cops turned a blind eye, or actively aided the Coughlinites—not surprisingly, given that the force's 12,000 Irish Catholic members had for years been hearing communion breakfast speeches remarkably similar to Coughlin's. Indeed, 400 cops actually admitted to being Christian Front members. There were some dissenters from this laissez-faire policy, notably Brooklyn's William O'Dwyer, who on being elected district attorney in 1939, announced that hooliganism would not be tolerated on the streets of his borough and won the enmity of the Christian Front by launching street sweeps.

O'Dwyer did not, however, petition Bishop Molloy for help, as the Brooklyn hierarchy, while maintaining an official silence about their flock's support for Coughlin, effectively greenlighted it. Patrick Scanlan praised and defended the Christian Front and appeared with Cassidy at Front rallies. Nor was Scanlan shy about grasping the anti-Semitic nettle. "Fr. Coughlin," he wrote in 1939 in the *Brooklyn Tablet*, "has fearlessly and courageously described the Jewish problem that others would pass by in cowardly silence."

In a similar vein, James Francis A. McIntyre, chancellor of the New York Archdiocese, dismissed Christian Front desecrations, saying "'the chalk doodlings of children have been used by paid publicity agents to conjure up the 'phantom of anti-Semitic hate' to injure the Catholics of New York."

Scanlan and McIntyre didn't speak for all of Gaelic Gotham. The Reverend Father James R. Cox of Old St. Pat's denounced Coughlin and declared that "attacks upon the Jews are abhorrent." The redoubtable Dorothy Day sent letters to metropolitan papers and magazines critiquing Coughlin's anti-Semitism and Scanlan's "pugnacious" defense of Coughlin (in the process drawing the ire of Christian Fronters, who now began attacking *Catholic Worker* salespeople). In May 1939, Day and others (including Al Smith; Harry Sylvester, a reporter and writer on Catholic themes; Harry McNeil, a Fordham philosophy professor; and Philip Burnham of *Commonweal*) formed a "Committee of Catholics to Fight Anti-Semitism." The group drew many priests, nuns, lawyers, educators, and labor leaders.

By mid-1939 Gotham's Catholics had arrived at a crossroads. Many, especially in Brooklyn and the Bronx, seemed willing to follow Coughlin's lead, and that of the Spanish bishops, into outright reaction. That the Church as a whole did not was thanks in no small part to the arrival on the scene of a prelate who had a very different perspective on local and global developments and had the power to enforce them.

24

Enter Spellman

On May 22, 1939, undeterred by a drizzling rain, crowds estimated at a quarter million lined Archdiocesan streets all the way from Port Chester to Manhattan, to welcome the 25-car motorcade ferrying Francis Joseph Spellman from Boston to New York. The party threaded its way southward on Fifth Avenue, looping around St. Patrick's Cathedral, to the old Renwick-designed residence on the southwest corner of Madison Avenue and 50th Street. The crowd of dignitaries awaiting Spellman there was splendid indeed, though as nothing compared to the assemblage that gathered the following morning to witness his investiture as Sixth Archbishop of New York City.

Nearly 2,000 clerics, many attired in medieval costume (black-gowned Jesuits, Dominicans in white tunics and hooded black capes, bearded Franciscans and Capuchins in coarse brown habits) walked in procession, headed by a contingent of the "Fighting Irish," from the archbishop's residence into an overflowing cathedral. The front pews were filled with over sixty members of papal orders—the Privy Chamberlains of the Cape and Sword particularly resplendent in their red military jackets, dress-black trousers, and swords—along with representatives of the city and state, including Senator Wagner, Governor Lehman, and Mayor La Guardia. Outside, loudspeakers carried the ensuing three-hour proceedings to the 50,000 thronging the surrounding streets, while microphones transmitted them to a nationwide radio audience.

The man at the center of this spectacular ceremony was singularly unimpressive in bearing and appearance. At fifty, Spellman was short, plump, and bald, with a round cherubic face and a tendency to emit from time to time a "curious gurgle that sounded something like a giggle." But the new archbishop would immediately prove a commanding figure in city affairs, in large part because he was an outsider—catapulted into New York after a cosmopolitan career at the very pinnacle of the international Church.

Spellman's early background was as undistinguished as his person. A grocer's son, he'd been born in 1889 in Whitman, Massachusetts, a predominantly Protestant town twenty miles south of Boston. Spellman had a solid green pedigree—his grandfather was a cobbler come over from Limerick—but he attended Whitman's public elementary and high schools and considered himself as much Yankee as Celt. In 1907 Spellman was sent down to New York to get a Jesuit education at Fordham, where he compiled an unremarkable academic record. On graduating, as he liked to recall, disarmingly, his father had counseled him to "always go with people who are smarter than you are—and in your case it won't be difficult." In 1911, Spellman was selected by Boston's Cardinal William O'Connell to study for the priesthood at the North American College in Rome. There the ambitious young man mastered Latin and Italian, the languages of the hierarchy, and made connections with aristocratic and influential priests. Receiving his Doctorate of Sacred Theology from the Pontifical Urban College for the Propagation of the Faith, he was ordained in 1916, at the age of twenty-seven.

Returning to Boston, Spellman found that Cardinal O'Connell—who detested "that little popinjay"—relegated him to marginal assignments, seemingly determined to squelch his career. Planning his escape, Spellman cultivated his distant Roman contacts, making himself useful to Monsignor Francesco Borgongini Duca, a former teacher and powerful prelate, by translating two of his books into English. When in 1925, after Spellman's nine years in the clerical doghouse, O'Connell incautiously granted him permission for a pilgrimage to Rome, he seized the opportunity. With Borgongini Duca's help, he got himself attached (O'Connell wasn't even consulted) to the Vatican Secretariat of State, becoming the first American ever so appointed. Spellman would stay seven years, working as a translator (he quickly won favor with Pius XI by rendering his articles and radio messages into English) and becoming an international diplomat.

More ambitious than ever—and desperate to make up for the years lost in Boston—he blatantly cultivated leading members of the Roman Curia, notably by arranging mutual introductions to rich American Catholics who were enchanted with the aristocratic world of the Vatican and generous to priests they liked. When eminent visitors hit town—Spellman paid concierges at luxury hotels to apprise him of new arrivals—the amateur photographer would snap their pictures at papal audiences, then brashly show up at their hotel rooms with the prints.

Spellman's busy brokering finally gained him entree to the Vatican's most rarefied circles after he succeeded in ingratiating himself with a wealthy couple from New York City, Mr. and Mrs. Nicholas F. Brady. Son of the public utilities emperor Anthony N. Brady, Nicholas had been president of the Brooklyn Rapid Transit Company and the New York Edison Company. A lapsed Catholic until his wife, the former Genevieve Garvan, brought him back to the Church, he became a major contributor to Catholic charities. The Bradys were not mere occasional visitors. They wintered in Rome and gave dazzling dinner parties for Vatican officials at *Casa del Sole*, their estate on Janiculum Hill overlooking St. Peter's, and it was at an event in the cathedral that the ever-watchful Spellman, noting the Bradys seated near the rear, had them moved up front. Soon he, too, was dining at *Casa del Sole*, playing tennis with Mr. Brady, fussing over Mrs. Brady, and serving as their private chaplain. When Spellman suggested to Nicholas that Cardinal Pietro Gasparri, papal secretary of state, might enjoy receiving a new Chrysler limousine, Brady replied, "Sure." When Spellman suggested to the cardinal that the Bradys might enjoy receiving papal titles, Nicholas (in 1927) was made a Knight of the Supreme Order of Christ, an honor usually reserved for Catholic heads of state. Mrs. Brady was named a Dame of Malta, to be addressed ever after as the Duchess Brady, and she became Spellman's wholehearted patroness. The Bradys also assisted Spellman financially, as did other grateful Americans for whom he arranged access to cardinals and bishops, routinely gifting him substantial sums, enabling him to play the booming stock market: by 1929 he was affluent enough to buy a thousand shares of Warner Brothers for $54,190.

Spellman, now elevated to Monsignor and well established as "the American back-door to the Vatican," moved even higher up the Vatican ladder by arranging financial favors for Pius XI himself—not only cars, but the underwriting of more substantial projects. When the Pope sought backing for the Vatican Library, Spellman went directly to New York millionaire John Raskob, bypassing the Vatican's chief fundraiser, and obtained a hefty donation (Raskob was shortly thereafter awarded the Order of Malta's Grand Cross of Magistral Grace). The Pope took to calling Spellman "Monsignor Precious."

Of even greater importance for Spellman's future was his introduction in 1927 (by the Duchess Brady) to Eugenio Maria Giuseppe Giovanni Pacelli, scion of a noble family and a leading Vatican diplomat (he'd been Apostolic Nuncio to Bavaria and Germany since 1917). The two men developed a genuine friendship, even traveling together on hiking holidays in the northern Italian countryside. They were a decidedly odd couple—the tall, aloofly aristocratic and immaculately tailored Pacelli, and the short shlumpy Spellman, but the Italian (himself a man on the way up) liked the shrewd American Mr. Fixit's ability to get things done in the sluggish Vatican bureaucracy. When Pius XI made him a cardinal in 1929, then secretary of state in 1930, Pacelli put Spellman to work on a grander stage.

In June 1931 Mussolini decided—concordat notwithstanding—to crush Italy's Catholic Action organization. Fascist squads invaded its clubhouses shouting, "Down with the Pope!" Pius XI and Pacelli decided to issue an encyclical message to the world denouncing Il Duce's actions and warning against "pagan worship of the State," though without condemning Fascism. Pacelli had Spellman translate this shot-across-the-bow, smuggle it to Paris, and distribute it to the AP, UP, and Reuters press services. It made front-page news worldwide, and Mussolini backed off his anticlerical campaign. His operatives castigated Spellman as an American agent, and, indeed, Spellman now emerged as a key liaison between the US Embassy and Vatican officials.

The following year, a grateful Pius XI appointed Spellman auxiliary bishop of Boston, and Pacelli presided over his consecration in St. Peter's, the first American ever so honored. But when he returned home in 1932, he received a frigid reception from Cardinal O'Connell, who continued to insult and sideline his heir apparent. While settling in to await that hoped-for-but-hardly-imminent succession, Spellman cultivated rich Boston Catholics—visiting their homes, marrying their sons and daughters, sailing on their yachts, providing them entree to Rome, soliciting their substantial donations to Catholic charities—and chief among his contacts was Joseph Kennedy, who introduced him, in turn, to President Roosevelt. Spellman visited Hyde Park and got an earful from Roosevelt about Father Coughlin, whose invective he wanted the Vatican to silence. In September a placatory editorial in the semi-official *Osservatore Romano* gestured in this direction—disapproving of, and distancing the Vatican from, Coughlin's attacks on the president, though not forbidding them. As a possible quid for a further quo, Roosevelt dangled before Spellman the possibility of appointing a US ambassador to the Holy See, a goal high on Pacelli's diplomatic agenda.

These dickerings culminated in a month-long visit in 1936 by Pacelli, making him the highest-ranking Vatican figure ever to step foot in the United States (indeed the first Papal Secretary of State to leave Italy since the Congress of Vienna in 1815). Ostensibly, the cardinal was coming only to spend time with his good friend the Duchess Brady, and the trip began with a huge reception on October 24 at Inisfada, the Brady estate on Long Island's

North Shore (near Manhasset, along a road nicknamed "The Irish Channel" for its string of Gaelic grandee residences). Attendees approached the mansion along winding driveways lined with thousands of tallow lights like those used at the Vatican and were received by the duchess and cardinal before a blazing fire in the Great Hall. Mrs. Brady soon found to her dismay that the social visit was mere cover for a diplomatic mission. It was, moreover, under the complete control (at Pacelli's insistence) of her good friend Bishop Spellman, who had never told her the truth. Infuriated, the Duchess broke with Spellman, even cut him out of her will (though Pacelli would receive a six-figure bequest).

Spellman now whisked the cardinal off on a coast-to-coast airplane tour, keeping himself in the center of the ensuing pageantry and press attention while sidelining (and enraging) other American bishops, notably New York's Cardinal Hayes. (When Pacelli spoke at Fordham, Hayes barred Spellman from entering his own alma mater.) The Papal Secretary of State made no comment on the raging presidential campaign, but on November 5, two days after Roosevelt's smashing victory, Spellman personally escorted the cardinal to Hyde Park for a tête-à-tête. The meeting would prove an important way station on the road to FDR's appointing a personal representative to the Holy See. It also cemented Spellman's position as the critical link between Washington and Rome, a status the president underscored in 1937 by inviting him for a stay in the White House, during which, for the first time in US history, he said a Catholic mass.

On September 4, 1938, Cardinal Hayes died after a long illness. Spellman immediately conveyed to Rome his interest in New York. The bishop's bid was generally accounted a long shot, and indeed Pius XI gave the post to John T. McNicholas, archbishop of Cincinnati. But in February 1939, the Pope died, without having signed the letter making the McNicholas offer official. In March, Pacelli was elevated to the papal throne, becoming Pius XII. And on April 12, Francis Spellman received a special airmail letter announcing his old friend's intention of appointing him archbishop of New York.

The first person outside his family to whom he relayed the news was Franklin Roosevelt. Spellman was profoundly impressed by FDR, even sympathized with his New Deal. The president, for his part, was wary of Spellman's self-promotional focus. When in October 1939, Cardinal George Mundelein died, theretofore his closest friend in the hierarchy, Roosevelt nonetheless immediately phoned Spellman with the news and began calling him "my favorite Bishop." At a blow, Spellman had become the most important churchman in the United States, his power rooted in his command of the New York see and his role as conduit between pope and president. Once again, New York was performing its ancient and quintessential function of linking Europe and the US.

For New York's Catholic communities, however, Spellman was an unknown quantity. He had not come up through the clerical ranks, was not hardwired into Irish American cultural circuits, and might well have different, more cosmopolitan, even more "liberal" perspectives on global affairs than did a Patrick Scanlan or a Generoso Pope.

25

Spellman Takes Command

Fully aware of his outsider status and cool reception, Spellman was determined to swiftly impose his authority. He set out to shake up a complacent clerical establishment—some priests having taken to leaving nuns to run their schools, orphanages, hospitals, and old-age homes and spending their resultant leisure time on the golf course. Spellman also asked Hayes's chancellor, the flinty James Francis McIntyre, to identify troublemakers, and the deeply conservative (and often vindictive) McIntyre fingered liberals like George Barry Ford, Columbia University's chaplain. McIntyre found Ford suspiciously ecumenical (he had Jewish and Protestant friends), economically radical (he allowed Con Ed employees to use his parish hall to discuss labor grievances), sartorially out of step (he fancied tailored suits and wore his hair longish like an Anglican minister), and theologically unsound (he favored liturgical reform). Still, while McIntyre harassed Ford for years, berating him as a crypto-Communist, his "boss" never moved against him. Nor did he discipline the far more radical Dorothy Day. Asked once why he hadn't silenced her, a startled Spellman paused, then replied that "she might be a saint."

Spellman served notice on the city's secular powers that an aggressive new player had arrived in town. On learning that local banks had colluded to gouge a 6 percent interest rate on the over twenty million dollars in mortgage loans that were held by hundreds of Catholic churches, schools, and hospitals, Spellman centralized archdiocesan borrowing, thus strengthening his bargaining position, then refinanced the loans by playing Boston lenders off New Yorkers: with low-interest loans in hand from John Hancock Life and First National Bank, he bludgeoned Bankers Trust down to 2.5 percent.

As Spellman had relied on Wall Street broker T. Murray McDonnell for advice on banking, so he turned to John J. Reynolds, a shrewd Bronx-Irish real estate broker, for help in revamping archdiocesan property holdings, selling some parcels, buying others.

Spellman also restarted a Depression-stalled bricks-and-mortar construction engine. Soon after his installation, he inaugurated a ten-million-dollar building program. The flagship project, touched off with a May 1940 groundbreaking ceremony, was the Cardinal Hayes Memorial High School for Boys; located in the Bronx, on the Grand Concourse at 153rd

Street, it included an auditorium honoring his former patrons, the Bradys. The same month brought announcement of a Bronx church complex that included a parochial school and a convent for housing twenty-three nuns, to meet the needs of the thousands of tenants moving into Metropolitan Life's new Parkchester development, on the site of the old Catholic Protectory. Not long after, Spellman (joined by Al Smith) laid the cornerstone for a nine-story pavilion to adjoin St. Vincent's Hospital.

To raise money for such projects, Spellman recapitulated his Boston gambit of reaching out to affluent locals, winning their support for Church initiatives and rewarding them with highly prized papal titles. This being New York, the archbishop was able to rally to his side some of the country's wealthiest and most powerful Catholics. At the top, Privy Chamberlains of the Cape and Sword—one of the greatest honors that could be accorded Catholic laymen—included Al Smith, John S. Burke (president of B. Altman's), and John Thomas Smith (general counsel of General Motors).

Nearly as exalted were members of the Sovereign Military Order of Malta, more familiarly known as the Knights of Malta. A sixteenth-century military organization evolved into a twentieth-century charitable (and, in Europe, political) institution, it was opened to US candidates only in 1926. Spellman had become acquainted with the Knights in Rome and through his Vatican connections became the American Order's official church patron while he was still auxiliary bishop of Boston. By 1941 Spellman had become its "Grand Protector" with veto power over the selection of new candidates and the right to deploy their contributions (beginning with the requisite minimum entry donation of $5,000). Among the New York heavyweights who had already joined the Order or who owed their elevation to Spellman were J. Peter Grace of W. R. Grace & Co.; Joseph Kennedy; John J. Raskob, chairman of General Motors; Nicholas Brady; Joseph J. Larkin, vice-president of Chase Manhattan Bank; John Farrell, president of U.S. Steel; Wall Street lawyer and World War I hero "Wild Bill" Donovan; John Coleman, stockbroker and head of the NYSE; Thomas E. Murray, inventor and electrical entrepreneur; and Clarence Mackay, former chairman of the board of Postal Telegraph and Cable. Equally notable and well-heeled men peopled the ranks of the Knights of St. Gregory, the Grand Knights of the Holy Sepulchre, and the Knights of the Grand Cross.

Contributions from such patrons, and the accumulated coins from the collection baskets of metropolitan churches, flowed not only to local projects but to Vatican coffers; soon the New York Archdiocese was contributing more money to the Holy See than the whole of Europe. The Vatican, in turn, stored much of its accumulated holdings in New York, starting in 1936, after Pacelli, on returning to Rome, sent Spellman $113,000 of his personal funds to look after; in 1941 the Holy See would ship its own gold across the Atlantic to be safe-housed in the Federal Reserve Bank of New York.

Spellman provided the Irish Catholic elite with more than papal honors; he cultivated their fierce allegiance by validating the cultural strivings of a class still uncertain about its welcome in the Protestant precincts of New York's high society. His personal presence at Irishtocracy gatherings—baptisms, weddings, summer weekends at Southampton (the Irish Newport)—helped a still precariously perched stratum find its social footing. Exclusive and pedigreed Catholic institutions offered similar stability. The 1881 Convent of the Sacred Heart School, housed, since 1934, in the Fifth Avenue renaissance mansion built by Otto H. Kahn (hence jocularly known as the "Kahn-vent"), was where Murray, McDonnell, and Cuddihy girls went to learn the Catholic variant of upper-class manners and morals before moving on to college at Manhattanville or, less fashionably, to Marymount.

Though the new archbishop was consolidating a position at the summit of the city's Irish American world, he was not unmindful of the very different working-class terrain that Coughlinites had been cultivating. Indeed, he actively shared some of the cultural concerns that motivated the Currans, Scanlans and Molloys and realized that such concerns, properly mobilized, could provide yet another pathway to power in the larger metropolitan community.

Thus Spellman heartily endorsed initiatives, such as those of the Legion of Decency, to strengthen a Catholic arbitership over popular culture. In December 1939 he joined Brooklyn's Bishop Molloy in arranging a citywide pledge, by Gotham's two million Catholics, to renew their vows to abstain from viewing proscribed films. Two years later he revealed a personal obsession with movies he deemed salacious, by issuing a pastoral letter that unprecedentedly singled out a specific picture—the not-yet-released Greta Garbo vehicle *Two-Faced Woman*—for condemnation as a danger to public morality.

But if the archbishop closed ranks with conservatives on metropolitan cultural issues, he parted company with them on international affairs—they staunchly backing Coughlin's anti-interventionist line, he cautiously supporting Roosevelt's interventionist one.

26

The Cross and the Flag

Spellman held no truck with anti-Semitism. *The Catholic News*, his archdiocesan official organ, made this perfectly clear, indeed spoke favorably of Jews. The archbishop was silent, however, on Christian Front depredations. In October 1939, Spellman was challenged directly by *Equality* magazine, a self-described nonsectarian journal dedicated to combating "racial and religious intolerance." That month's issue ran an open letter from the editorial board, whose members included Franz Boas, Bennett Cerf, Dashiell Hammett, Moss Hart, Dorothy Parker, and the Rev. Dr. Guy Emery Shipler, editor of *The Churchman*. Warning that the Christian Front's "hate-rousing and anti-Semitic activities" might "eventually culminate in a violent, bloody rioting such as the city has never known," the *Equality* editors urged Spellman to make a public statement clarifying the Church's position on Coughlin & company.

Spellman never replied. Three months later he was equally silent when, on January 14, 1940, the FBI arrested eighteen New York Christian Fronters and confiscated eighteen cans of cordite (an explosive), twelve Springfield rifles, and 3,500 rounds of ammo (stolen by Fronters with access to a National Guard armory). J. Edgar Hoover announced he had nipped in the bud a plot to bomb the *Jewish Daily Forward*, the *Daily Worker*, the Cameo Theater on 42nd Street (which screened Russian-made films), and the Brooklyn headquarters of the American League for Peace and Democracy. The conspirators, Hoover claimed, had also planned to assassinate many Jews, including a dozen congressmen who had voted to repeal the embargo on arms to Spain. These actions, in turn, were meant to preface an armed uprising in New York that would include the seizure of power plants, telegraph and phone networks, the US Customs House, the General Post Office, and the Federal Reserve Bank. Their ultimate aim, the FBI chief declared—and the crimes with which the men were formally accused—was to overthrow and destroy the government of the United States, replacing it with a Hitler-type dictatorship that would then eradicate the Jews.

Some thought Hoover overstated the case. It seemed fantastic that eighteen men with eighteen bombs and some antiquated rifles actually envisioned such an all-encompassing scheme, especially as their putschist qualifications seemed markedly deficient. The two arrested leaders—John F. Cassidy, Christian Front commander in Brooklyn, and William Gerald Bishop, head of a clandestine paramilitary Front group known as "the Sports Club"—had mustered a motley crew that included, among others, three salesmen, three clerks, and one baker, tailor, phone company lineman, chauffeur, elevator mechanic, swimming instructor, and WPA worker (of these, eleven were Irish, five German, and one Austrian). Hoover stuck to his guns—urging doubters to remember how far a few Bolsheviks had gotten back in 1917—but in the end, the jury members were among the skeptics and declined (in their June 24, 1940, decision) to convict any of the accused.

Coughlin was exultant at their acquittal (though initially he'd panicked, "roundly disavowed" the accused conspirators, and only later insisted he was not "running out on the fine body of New York Christians who make up the membership of the Christian Front"). The priest was sure the group would emerge more potent than ever. It's true that anti-Semitic activity continued—the stoning of synagogues, painting of swastikas, and physical attacks on Jews. The archbishop shed no tears when the sensational trial hastened Coughlin's own political demise. Station after station refused to renew Coughlin's contract and, in September 1940, he announced his retirement from the airwaves. There was not a peep of protest from Spellman, no doubt as glad as Roosevelt to be rid of the meddlesome priest.

The war in europe had triggered a different kind of Gaelic protest, however, one Spellman couldn't ignore, as it was based not in fringe elements but in the city's Irish middle class. In September 1939, Éamon de Valera announced that his government was determined to keep Ireland out of the war, partly because his country was virtually defenseless, partly because refusing to follow Britain into combat reaffirmed Ireland's independence. Neutrality quickly inflamed Anglo-Irish relations when de Valera refused to allow Britain to reassume control of the harbor defenses at three Irish ports that England had finally handed back to Eire in 1938. After the fall of France, Churchill, fearing the Germans would invade Ireland and use it as a base to assault England, demanded control of the ports, also useful for fighting U-boats in the burgeoning Battle of the Atlantic. The new US minister, David Gray, went even farther, urging FDR to seize the bases, and he led a stateside campaign to discredit de Valera and the Irish as pro Nazi. De Valera held fast to neutrality, though privately making clear his sympathy with Britain and working closely with British security services. By the start of 1941, a slew of distorted articles had begun affecting American opinion: a Gallup poll in January found that 61 percent wanted Ireland to abandon neutrality.

Insisting that Eire had as much right to remain neutral as did the US, de Valera set out to counteract Gray's pressure, and forestall a British (or American) invasion, by mobilizing Irish Americans. In November 1940, the *Irish Echo* arranged a meeting of 2,500 supporters that founded the American Friends of Irish Neutrality (AFIN). Perhaps because the recent uproar over the Christian Front had tainted conservative Irish Americans, the new organization turned for a leader to Paul O'Dwyer, brother of William O'Dwyer and a man on the Irish American left.

Born in County Mayo in 1907, O'Dwyer had arrived in New York in 1925 and worked on the docks while he went to night classes, first at Fordham, then at St. John's Law. Though a founder of the Park Slope division of the Ancient Order of Hibernians (AOH), O'Dwyer, first-generation son of a union organizer, was decidedly out of step with his comrades' politics. He realized this definitively on the day he asked his AOH fellows to oppose Father Coughlin, only to find himself a minority of one. At that point he had moved to Manhattan and gotten a job in 1940 with Louis Boudin (a distinguished constitutional scholar, Marxist theoretician, and labor lawyer) defending the left-wing Fur and Leather Workers Union; he also joined the left-leaning National Lawyers Guild and chaired its Civil Rights Committee.

O'Dwyer hired a former Hearst reporter to churn out press releases contesting the anti-neutrality propaganda flooding the media. The AFIN also initiated letter-writing campaigns and organized rallies to oppose forcing Ireland into war. One of those, held in April 1941 on the 25th anniversary of the Easter Rising, drew 1,500 to the Carmelite Church at 339 East 28th Street, including the leaders and members of a score of Irish societies. One of the speakers was General Frank Aiken, whom de Valera had sent as an emissary to buy ships, arms, and foodstuffs for the defense of Eire—against England as well as Germany—and a few days later Aiken addressed a 4,500-strong mass meeting (also under the auspices of AFIN) in the Windsor Palace Ballroom, at 69 West 66th Street.

Not all Gotham's Gaels signed on to this campaign. In March 1941, 129 Americans of Irish descent—many eminent in educational, theatrical, and judicial circles—called on de Valera to grant Britain bases. O'Dwyer acknowledged the group was unrepresentative: "The Irish societies from coast to coast are on record as unalterably opposed to any interference with Ireland's neutral position."

Spellman could not afford to dismiss this constituency, even though it vexed his ally President Roosevelt, and on June 15, 1941, in conjunction with AFIN, he offered a pontifical mass in St. Patrick's for the suffering people of Ireland. Massed Irish neutralists (including General Aiken) paraded down Fifth Avenue from 59th Street and into the cathedral, where the archbishop told the 6,000 in attendance that Eire, never an aggressor nation, was "a bright spot in the present dark, disordered world." Spellman also insisted he was "proud that in my veins flows the blood of four Irish-born ancestors" but stressed that he was "wholly American" (indeed, in his official biography the archbishop changed all references to himself as "Irishman" to "American"). He also noted that the mass was but one of a series he was offering for other nations affected by the European war, as if to underscore that the New York Catholic Church—a house of many mansions—could not simply align itself with any one of its nationalities.

27

Polonia

A case in point were the city's Polish Catholics who, even before the German invasion, had begun raising funds for their country's defense. By the end of August 1939, they had helped gather over a million dollars for the consul to send on to Warsaw and launched another drive to aid the Polish Red Cross. With war looming, delegates met at the Polish National Home at 19–25 St. Mark's Place to establish a central clearing house for information, and WHOM began daily broadcasts in Polish.

On October 11, 1939, a week after Poland's heroic resistance to the combined Wehrmacht and Soviet assaults finally crumpled, 100,000 tearful Pulaski Day marchers clogged Fifth Avenue. Both the *Nowy Świat* (*New World*)—New York's Polish daily—and the Brooklyn-based weekly *Czas* (*Time*) deplored the dismemberment of Poland and requested additional relief contributions. On December 17, 1939, 2,000 jammed into Cooper Union for a protest meeting under the auspices of the Polish National Council of New York, at which speakers gave eyewitness accounts of the invasion.

The city's Poles viewed a successful defense of England as the only hope for an eventual restoration of Polish independence, and the large Polish American community surged toward Roosevelt's side in the upcoming 1940 election. It was part of Spellman's constituency, too: deeply Catholic, the resistance forces used the idioms and imagery of Polish Marianism to mobilize supporters.

On October 14, 1939, Spellman told an assemblage of 5,000 Polish Americans on their way (accompanied by Poland's ambassador and consul general) to celebrate Polish Day at the World's Fair, that "as Catholicism will never die, Poland will never die." The following January, the archbishop arranged church collections for the war-ravaged country; in May, he offered a mass for the "suffering people" of Poland; and that October he reviewed the Pulaski parade from the steps of St. Patrick's.

Still, the Irish American priests who manned the city hierarchy remained overwhelmingly opposed to aiding the British. Patrick Scanlan shared Coughlin's conviction that the US had to avoid "foreign entanglements," and Father Curran was adamant that "decent nations who still enjoy the blessings of peace should lend no aid or comfort to the brawl."

Catholics could be counted on to rally if the US was attacked, Curran made clear, but "we shall not fight for any foreign nation on foreign soil." Leftist Catholics mostly agreed, if for different reasons. Dorothy Day's *Catholic Worker* advanced an absolutist, gospel-based pacifism, arguing that Catholic "just war" doctrine had been rendered inapplicable by modern combat's massive involvement of civilian populations. The *Commonweal* editors, divided after the fall of France, opened their pages to debate on the war, though officially hewed to neutrality through 1941. In September of that year, a poll of the city's Catholic clergy found over 90 percent opposed to US involvement in any war outside the western hemisphere.

Among that small minority backing Roosevelt's push for preparedness was the one voice that really counted. Spellman was convinced that war was inevitable, even necessary, and in December 1939, he accepted with alacrity his appointment by FDR as Bishop Ordinary for the Army and Navy, giving him spiritual charge of all Roman Catholic chaplains. (There had been some talk of moving the military vicariate to Washington, but the Holy See opted for leaving it in New York.) The archbishop's interventionism was limited by the pope's ongoing neutrality, but he nevertheless adopted an increasingly strong stance. "We Catholics and we Americans are not defeatists," he told graduating Manhattanville students in January 1940: "We shall fight to the end for our beliefs, for our rights, as well as to help others to defend their beliefs and their rights." By May 1941, he was telling the *New York Times* that "it would be worse than folly if we did not build about ourselves a strong defense that will discourage any possible effort against us." "We can no longer," he added, "be moles who cannot, or ostriches who will not, see."

There would be no schism in the metropolitan Church between interventionists and isolationists, however, partly because Spellman had the will and authority to direct events and partly because on one crucial issue—the Americanization of Irish Catholicism—both parties were moving on parallel tracks. Their religion had long been the greatest impediment to Irish American assimilation; in a culture dominated by Anglo-Protestantism they had opted for a defensive insularity. By the late thirties, however, spurred by global events and local developments, the Irish had begun pairing a newly assertive Catholicism with a vigorous American patriotism. Some even insisted that Catholics were the *real* Americans, having held fast to traditional (pre–World War I) beliefs while others succumbed to secularism or radicalism. For conservatives, attacking "Godless Communism" was a way to manifest patriotism *and* faith, to construct a truly American Catholicism.

Other Irish Catholics feared that anticommunism—which in Coughlinite hands had segued all too smoothly into anti-Semitism and philo-Fascism—might simply marginalize them in a newer and more dangerous way. For them, there was another, more time-honored way to demonstrate loyalty to both church and nation: by underscoring their past and future manly willingness to fight the nation's wars. Among the sixty prominent Catholics (clergy and laity) who signed a statement in October 1940, attacking Hitlerism and urging all-out aid to Britain, the First World War hero (and Knight of Malta) William "Wild Bill" Donovan had been particularly active. Shortly after the invasion of Poland, the Wall Street lawyer had told fellow veterans that "in an age of bullies we cannot afford to be a sissy."

Donovan helped underscore Irish-Catholic-American readiness in this regard by signing on as technical adviser to the Warner Brothers production of *The Fighting 69th*. While Donovan's own story figured in the film (he was portrayed by George Brent), and Jimmy Cagney appeared as a made-up character, the real heroes were Pat O'Brien's Father Francis Patrick Duffy and the all-Irish cast. Jack Warner heavily promoted this inspirational hymn to Irish Catholic patriotism, which became a hit even before it opened on January 26, 1940.

Days earlier, thousands of movie fans and veterans of the 69th, replete with their Regimental Band, had packed Grand Central to meet the Twentieth Century Limited bearing O'Brien and Cagney. At a special preview showing, arranged for a regimental reunion at the Waldorf Astoria, Governor Lehman hailed the "brave and kindly priest," while General Douglas MacArthur, speaking by radio from the Philippines, brought down the house with his declaration that "no finer fighting regiment ever existed than the Fighting Sixty-ninth" and his hope that should war come again he might have it under his command. The film premiered at the Strand Theater in Times Square, almost cheek-by-jowl with the eight-foot statue of Father Duffy (unveiled in 1937) in military garb, helmet at his feet and bible in his hand, atop a 17-foot-tall pedestal backed by a green granite Celtic cross.

It would be Archbishop Spellman, now chaplain-in-chief (and, in a sense, Father Duffy's heir), who, together with elite laypersons like William Donovan, would lead the Catholic community into an uneasy alliance with the New York liberals and the New York business community, the driving forces behind America's entry into war.

ASIAN NEW YORK

Chinese supporters of the People's Liberation Army protest the Japanese invasion at the 1933 May Day parade. (Bettmann / Contributor / Getty Images)

28

Japanese New York

The first significant Japan–New York encounter dates to 1860, when eighty Nipponese diplomats—dressed in traditional kimono and carrying samurai swords—were welcomed with a parade down Broadway, hailed by cheering New Yorkers. As participant observer Walt Whitman put it in his "Errand Bearers" poem—"Million-footed Manhattan" was delighted that "to us, then, at last, the orient comes. To us, my city."

The marchers were celebrating the ratification of a Treaty of Amity and Commerce between the US and Japan, which promised to enhance Gotham's standing on the international scene. And indeed it did. Linked by telegraph and ocean liners, trade flourished. Export-import firms trading in raw silk and cotton set up shop. Finance followed: in 1880 the Yokohama Specie Bank arrived. By the 1890s, conglomerates like Mitsui and Mitsubishi had established New York branches.

These private companies, and the Japanese Consulate, were managed not by local *Issei* (Japanese-born immigrants), or by *Nisei* (second-generation Japanese Americans), but by hundreds of *Kaisha* (Japanese nationals only temporarily in residence). Despite their impermanence, the wealthiest members of this rotating elite forged connections with New York's Euro-American upper class. In 1905 they founded the Nippon Club (a men's social institution), and in 1907 the Japan Society was launched (it commingled prominent New York businessmen and leading Japanese residents). Their stances on foreign affairs often overlapped, most spectacularly in 1904–5 when Jacob Schiff, head of Kuhn, Loeb, floated a bond issue of $200 million to assist Japan in its successful war with Czarist Russia.

Beneath this affluent elite lay a thin stratum of professionals—doctors, lawyers, students, artists—and small businessmen, who ran restaurants, groceries, boarding houses, and tailoring shops.

Below them lay the majority of the *Issei* population. By 1898 it amounted to roughly 1,000 people, 90 percent of whom were single males. Unwelcome at factories and offices, roughly half had found work at or near their point of arrival, the Brooklyn Navy Yard, laboring as stewards, mess boys, and cooks, on shore or aboard ships. Others worked as cooks and waiters at restaurants serving Japanese cuisine. The rest of the *Issei* bachelors served as houseboys in Manhattan residences.

By 1921, the overwhelming majority of the Japanese population were domestic workers. One estimate suggested that of the approximately 4,500 Japanese then living in New York, roughly 3,500 were bachelor servants. They lived in their employers' homes or in boarding houses scattered throughout the city, but most settled in Manhattan, clustering near Cherry, Madison, East 19th, and East 33rd Streets and in a northern enclave along West 65th Street, in African American San Juan Hill. Given the dispersed nature of their jobs and homes, they lacked collective working-class institutions such as unions.

Apart from philanthropic efforts made by the Japanese Association of New York (1914) there were few social or economic ligaments linking the upper and lower Japanese classes, hence no integrated multiclass Japanese community. Given the scattershot nature of their individual residences, there was no central place, no Japan-town, no *there* there.

Then their numbers began to decline as racist immigration restrictions took hold. In 1908, pressed by West Coast exclusionists, the American government had leaned on Japan to (informally) curtail working-class emigration to the US. It did so by refusing to issue passports to other than students, businessmen, and professionals (the so-called Gentlemen's Agreement). The National Origins Act of 1924 eliminated immigration from Japan altogether. By 1930 the US Bureau of the Census estimated that there were only 2,356 ethnic Japanese still residing in New York City. In the later thirties, given deteriorating relations, many US branches of Japanese corporations drastically reduced their staffing or shut down altogether.

Those who remained were so inconsequential a political presence that they even failed to draw direct ire from New York's Chinese when their long-standing anti-Japanese animosities boiled over.

29

Chinese Gotham

Chinese Gotham, with a population of roughly 13,000 at the end of the '30s, was not only bigger than Japanese New York, it was far more cohesive, both geographically and socially. Community did not preclude complexity, however, and Chinatown was divided along class, clan, and political lines.

At the top were the tongs—institutions run by the wealthy merchant elite. Tongs were, more or less simultaneously, business and trade associations, fraternal and benevolent societies, welfare and social service agencies, criminal and political confederations, self-defense organizations and secret societies. Their members included Chinatown's most prestigious and powerful businessmen—directors of import-export firms, owners of restaurants and stores, and administrators of illegal enterprises such as gambling halls, opium dens, and brothels. Collectively, they served as Chinatown's quasi-governing, quasi-feudal body, known as the Chinese Consolidated Benevolent Association (CCBA), housed at 16 Mott Street. Payoffs to police and politicians allowed them to run their fiefdom's affairs. The various Tong headquarters were steps away from each other—the On Leong on 41 Mott, the Hip Sing at 13 Pell—as were offices, temples, and the entertainment entities (both the illegal and legal ones, such as the Chinese Opera House on Doyers Street).

The masses were there, too. Blocked from housing elsewhere in the city, they flocked to Chinatown's accessible tenements as a safe haven, sheltered from racist assaults. Residents crammed into two-room apartments which, when divvied up, could house up to fifteen men.

"Men" was the appropriate descriptor. Like Japanese New York, Chinatown was a bachelor community. The initial wave of Chinese migrants to the US in the 1840s and '50s had worked in mines and railroads—men's jobs—and when those petered out, in the 1860s and '70s, many moved east, where the gender composition was locked in place by racist legislation. The forthrightly named Chinese Exclusion Act of 1882 barred migration for all applicants (except merchants, students, or diplomats, who were mostly male) and specifically forbade husbands from bringing in their wives. (A later law closed a loophole by decreeing that an American-born woman who married a Chinese alien would be automatically stripped of her citizenship.) As a result, of the roughly 7,000 Chinese living in New York in 1900 fewer than 150 were women.

Unlike the Japanese, the Chinese had a vigorous *there* in Chinatown, with the CCBA and Tong headquarters side by side with the principal places of pleasure and socializing.

Their principal places of employment, however, were scattered about the city. Systematically excluded from most industries and offices, they dominated the hand laundry business. These were independently owned shops, usually run by only one man, perhaps with two or three partners. Clothing was indeed painstakingly washed by hand, with no equipment beyond an ironing board. To attract patrons, prices charged were low. Clearing a profit required a six- or seven-day work week. In the '30s there were 3,350 Chinese hand laundries in Gotham, and 60 percent of the Chinese population was engaged in the trade.

The Depression was disastrous. Clients faded away. Charges were cut further and working hours extended, to no avail. By the early thirties, 30 percent of the trade was unemployed.

Worse, they were under attack. Non-Chinese rivals had recently deployed cost-cutting washing machines and steam presses, run by low-waged Black and white immigrant labor. Lacking the capital to follow suit, the laundrymen regained customers by pricing services lower still and providing free extras like pickup and delivery.

In response, the industrialized companies decided to drive the hand laundries out of business. They urged the New York City Board of Aldermen to require all one-person laundries to post a thousand-dollar security bond, which, if adopted, would be a virtual death sentence. The laundrymen asked the CCBA to intervene on their behalf. The mandarins refused.

Desperate, they did what they'd never done before: they organized. In April 1933 men representing two thousand laundries from around the city poured into the basement of a Catholic church on Mott Street and established the Chinese Hand Laundry Alliance (CHLA), the first democratic mass organization in the history of New York's Chinese community.

As its first order of business, it retained Caucasian lawyers who challenged the proposed ordinance as discriminatory. The aldermen agreed and reduced the required bond to $100. This great victory attracted a massive membership—3,200 by 1934—and reconfigured the power relations of Chinatown.

There was a third power center in New York's Chinatown—China itself. The Qing (Manchu) dynasty (in place since 1636) had a limited presence in their overseas empire, until in 1912 a revolutionary movement drove it from power. The final emperor's abdication and the establishment of a Republic of China were hailed by both sides in Chinatown, as was its new president, Dr. Sun Yat-sen, who had been in New York repeatedly to raise funds for the revolution. Sun then established a National People's Party—the Kuomintang (KMT)—to govern the new Republic. The arrangement was overturned in 1916 by ambitious militarists, and China was plunged into a decade of warlordism and Japanese incursions.

Sun Yat-sen called for a Second Revolution to reunite the country under Kuomintang rule. He set up a special Overseas Chinese Affairs Bureau within the KMT, whose New York branch became a strong presence. Promoting publications that advocated republicanism, democracy, and socialism, it raised substantial funds for KMT's Northern Campaign. Sun also accepted a Soviet Union offer to form a military "United Front" alliance with the Chinese Communist Party.

Sun died in 1925, and his chief lieutenant, General Chiang Kai-shek, assumed power. In 1927 Chiang rejected the alliance and ordered a bloody purge of Communists. In 1928, when his forces established a national government in Nanjing, he jettisoned many of Sun's social programs and suspended implementation of democratic practices. China, he claimed, needed "order" and "party tutelage."

In New York City, Chiang's KMT branch became a vigorous and authoritarian presence, aligning itself with Chinatown's elite, whose financial support was deemed critical to his regime. The party appointed CCBA leaders to prominent positions, and subsidized conservative local newspapers.

In 1931 Japan's Kwantung Army annexed southern Manchuria (90 percent Chinese) and created the puppet state of Manchukuo. In 1932 Japanese forces attacked Shanghai. In 1933 a truce agreement gave Japan all Manchuria above the Great Wall. Most Chinese were convinced it was but a matter of time before the Japanese tried to conquer their entire country.

Through all of this, Chiang steadfastly refused to resist Japan's attacks, focusing his attention on "bandit annihilation campaigns" against warlords and Communists.

In New York, the CHLA—now a significant political presence—denounced Chiang as a corrupt traitor and began to build an anti-Japanese movement. They adopted a slogan—"To Save China, To Save Ourselves"—that appealed to Chinatown residents concerned about the fate of relatives abroad and convinced their humiliating status in the US was due in part to China's weakness.

In 1934, the CHLA founded the New York Chinese Anti-Japanese Society, which held rallies and parades, stoking a nationalist enthusiasm. In 1935, elements of the CCBA began to peel off and join the swelling movement. Even the conservative On Leong tong, furious at Chiang's "betrayal of the revolution," withdrew from the KMT. Finally, the CCBA, concerned that the CHLA was supplanting it, agreed (in January 1936) to jointly establish the All-Chinatown Anti-Japanese Salvation Association, leaving Chiang Kai-shek and his Kuomintang isolated.

On December 12, 1936, Chiang was himself isolated—indeed kidnapped—by dissident generals, who forced him to call off his civil war and unite with the Communists in resisting Japan. In New York the now-united Chinese community immediately pledged their political and financial support.

In July 1937, Japan's Kwantung Army launched a full-scale invasion of China below the Great Wall. By August, the Japanese had occupied Peking (now Beijing), laid siege to Shanghai, and begun a drive up the Yangtze Valley toward the Nationalist Chinese capital at Nanking. It fell in December and was subjected to the savage murder of at least 200,000 noncombatants, the gang rape of between 20,000 and 80,000 women, and a wide variety of grotesque atrocities—spearing babies, decapitating civilians with samurai swords, mutilating corpses, machine-gunning war prisoners, plus widespread torturing, looting, and arson.

Horrified, Chinese Gotham now launched a variety of initiatives. The CCBA established a General Relief Fund Committee at its 16 Mott Street headquarters, to raise money for troop supplies and refugee relief. On November 7, 1937, the first of many parades snaked through Chinatown, its 2,000 marchers representing almost every Chinese society, club, and tong in the city. Thirty women carried a huge Chinese flag into which bills and coins were hurled as the line inched forward through streets packed with cheering bystanders. The procession also featured a giant dragon that boosted financial offerings, and a huge banner on which dollar bills blazoned the slogan: "Fight against Japan to the Very Bitter End to Save China."

More venturesomely, the CHLA reached out to the wider city, seeking support for their struggle. At first, the only responders were organizations set up by the New York Communist

Parade marchers sponsored by the New York Overseas Chinese Public School carrying the Chinese national flag in an effort to raise funds for the Sino-Japanese War. (Courtesy of the Museum of Chinese in America, Warren Chan collection)

Party: the American League against War and Fascism, and the American Friends of the Chinese People. Given Japan's reliance on global markets and consequent vulnerability to economic pressure, they proposed a boycott. On October 1, 1937, some 10,000 people, including 2,000 Chinese and the leaders of forty-seven civic, labor, and religious groups, attended a Madison Square Garden rally that endorsed a boycott. What gave the boycott legs was its single-minded focus on one particular Japanese export item—the raw silk used in making stockings. Silk stocking sales were booming, a fashion phenomenon. ("In olden days a glimpse of stocking / Was looked on as something shocking," Cole Porter had observed in 1934, "But now, God knows / Anything goes.") Silk profits, boycotters argued, were crucial to Japan's war economy—"the lifeline of the Japanese militarists"—and they hammered this lethal linkage home to American women through pamphlets with titles like, "Did Your Stockings Kill Babies?"

The response they proposed, however, was not virtuous abstinence—the moralistic approach of American boycotts as far back as the Revolution—but rather a call on female consumers to revise fashion from the bottom up. Women were urged to define substitute materials like rayon, wool, and "lisle" cotton (a long-staple variant) as the equal of silk in sexiness. ("Make Lisle the Style" went one slogan.) In December 1937, mobilized by the American Friends of the Chinese People, two thousand women (including 450 Chinese) marched down Fifth Avenue carrying banners reading "We'd Rather Wear Cotton Stockings than Silk Ones." Hundreds of similar events were held during 1938–39, many accentuating the glamorous, like a "Cotton Ball" in the Hotel Pennsylvania that featured dresses by Elizabeth Hawes and other well-known designers. Famous actresses—like Frances Farmer, starring at the Belasco Theater in Clifford Odets's *Golden Boy*, and the entire cast of Clare Boothe Luce's *The Women*—let be it known they were performing in lisle stockings.

Popular and effective in curtailing a key Japanese export to the US, the "people's boycott" turned its attention to halting American exports to Japan of crucial war materials.

Widespread indignation at the bombing of Chinese civilians had led the State Department in 1938 to propose a "moral embargo" on selling airplanes and aeronautical equipment to Japan, but the government took no action against equally critical exports of scrap metal. In 1939, Chinese picketers patrolled New York piers—notably Brooklyn's Bush Terminal—from which cargo ships departed with scrap iron and steel, pickets respected by Joe Curran's National Maritime Union (Curran himself walked the picket line). The American Friends of the Chinese People also demonstrated in front of the 42nd Street offices of the Institute of Scrap Iron and Steel, hoisting placards urging an end to Japan-bound shipments. And Manhattan Borough President Stanley M. Isaacs, who presided over dismantling of the Sixth Avenue El, inserted a clause in the demolition contract forbidding the export of its 18,742 tons of scrap iron, a provision aimed squarely at Germany and Japan.

By 1940, as Japan took advantage of Germany's defeat of France to make inroads against French Indochina, popular support for a crackdown on scrap sales swelled. In July, the Roosevelt Administration pushed the Export Control Act through Congress, which allowed the president to prohibit shipment of militarily strategic goods, an authority he invoked against Japan by totally embargoing scrap sales after October 16, 1940. Ninety-six percent of the American public approved, according to a Gallup poll, in part a response to Japan's September signing of a military alliance with Germany and Italy. Ninety percent wanted to extend the cutoff to oil and gasoline, even though it might well precipitate an armed conflict.

But while Americans were opposed to Japan's aggression in China, they were deeply disinclined to take up arms to resist it. In December 1937, when the Japanese had sunk the *Panay*, a US gunboat escorting Standard Oil barges on the Yangtze River, and strafed escaping survivors, Americans had called for withdrawal not war.

And despite the overwhelming support for China against Japan, the 1940 Smith Act made no distinction between them, and members of both New York communities—equally ineligible for naturalization—joined the lengthy lines at post offices and public schools trooping forward to register as aliens.

IN UNO PLURES

An immigrant family looks at the Statue of Liberty from Ellis Island, ca. 1930s. (Photo by Bettmann/Getty Images)

30

Pluralists

The furious disagreements among Gotham's peoples over how to respond to the rise of fascism—the incandescent rhetoric at public gatherings, the growing clashes in the streets—made some wonder if war might not break out over here before it did over there. Certainly, some fascists hoped so: "Nothing will be easier than to produce a bloody revolution in the U.S.," boasted Goebbels, dismissing the United States as a threat to Nazi interests. "No other country has so many social and racial tensions. We shall be able to play on many strings there."

Worries about the city's (and country's) fissionability spurred new efforts by old nativists to restore the population to "a desirable homogeneity." John B. Trevor, the deeply xenophobic Wall Street attorney and pedigreed New Yorker who (in the 1920s) had helped craft the immigration restriction laws, took the helm (in the 1930s) of the American Coalition of Patriotic Societies, an umbrella organization of 115 groups that sought to "keep America American." Trevor used this position, and his status as spokesman on immigration issues for the New York State Chamber of Commerce, to call on Congress (unsuccessfully at first) to require the registration and fingerprinting of all resident aliens and to mandate deportation for any violation of law, however trivial.

With anti-immigrant sentiment being stoked by global conflict and national depression, it is all the more remarkable that the 1930s witnessed the triumph of a very different reading of the city and the country, one that *celebrated* their multiethnicity as being the antithesis of—indeed the antidote to—master-race fascism.

This alternative assessment had first been advanced in the First World War by those who opposed the campaign to immerse immigrants in the Melting Pot—forcibly if need be—and boil away their alien and hyphenated identities. A handful of people—notably Randolph Bourne and Horace Kallen—had argued that 100 percent Americanization, for all its hyper-patriotic rhetoric, was little more than an effort by the "Anglo-Saxon element" to (in Bourne's words) impose "its own culture upon the minority peoples." Both men believed the campaign to suppress ethnicity violated such American ideals as freedom of choice and could be implemented only by a repressive state. And both thought the Anglo-conformist vision deeply wrong-headed in scorning precisely what was most remarkable about the society that had emerged, unplanned, on the American strand. Bourne labeled this new order "cosmopolitan" or "trans-national"; Kallen called it "cultural pluralist": similar assessments, differing emphases.

"Foreign cultures have not been melted down or run together, made into some homogeneous Americanism," Bourne had written in 1916, "but have remained distinct but cooperating to the greater glory and benefit, not only of themselves but of all the native 'Americanism' around them." The synergy between newer immigrants and older residents had created "a novel international nation, the first the world has seen." The US was a "trans-national tapestry," produced by a "weaving back and forth, with the other lands, of many threads of all sizes and colors." Hence "any movement that attempts to thwart this weaving, or to dye the fabric any one color, or disentangle the strands, is false to this cosmopolitan vision."

Kallen stressed the ongoing diversity of immigrant streams rather than their cosmopolitan confluence. The US was a confederation of cultures. Each sustained an independent existence, but all worked together, like instruments in an orchestra, to create a "symphony of civilization." It was the task of the liberal state—itself not the possession of any one group—to protect difference, not impose homogeneity, and thus sustain a "democracy of nationalities" within which citizens could freely engage in their respective cultural practices.

Both Bourne's cosmopolitan and Kallen's cultural pluralist visions had been trampled underfoot in the fervent rush to war. The Melting Pot metaphor won the day but in winning became anathema to many immigrant spokespersons, a synonym for repressive assimilation, irretrievably tarred with the brush of bigotry.

Multicultural advocates had fared no better in the 1920s. Bourne had died in the Spanish flu epidemic shortly after the Armistice, but philosopher Kallen carried on from his professorial chair at the New School, only to get steamrollered once again. *Culture and Democracy in the United States* (1924), an elaboration of his cultural pluralist argument, came out the same year that homegrown master-race advocates—nativists like Trevor and eugenicists like Trevor's friend and fellow Manhattanite Madison Grant—succeeded in throttling immigration, and Kallen's book had virtually no impact.

Nevertheless, in the 1930s these spurned multiculturalist visions were placed back on the national table by a new generation of philo-pluralists, based in Gotham's liberal and left-wing circles. By decade's end these perspectives would all but completely supplant coercive assimilationism, as a wide spectrum of Americans came to hail the country's coat-of-many-colors multiplicity, indeed proclaim it the essence of (and essential to) democracy.

While the fascist challenge was fundamental to this revaluation, so too was the presence of the new immigrants themselves. Looming largest were the eastern and southern Europeans, who had poured into the US from the 1880s until war and postwar restrictions slowed the influx to a trickle, and the second generation they had birthed, coming now to adolescence or adulthood in the depression decade. Together these parents and children constituted a colossal demographic *fact*. And nowhere was this facticity thicker on the ground than in New York, where the 1930 census revealed that of Gotham's nearly seven million souls, 74.3 percent— three-quarters!—were of "foreign stock." (Of these, 33.1 percent were "white foreign born," 1 percent were foreign-born "Negro and other races"—the latter mostly Chinese and Japanese—and 40.2 percent "native white of foreign-born parents.") In the United States as a whole, by contrast, the foreign stock percentage was just under one in three. A discomfited John Trevor complained to Congress that "New York is a foreign city."

Equally important, this enormous transplantation had taken place without seismic upheaval. Yes, there had been strenuous competition over housing, jobs, and access to public resources, and yes, the jostling had been exacerbated by economic crisis, repercussions from overseas conflicts, and ethno-racial-religious antagonisms. But the process had remained relatively peaceful; the city hadn't cracked apart; its residents, if hardly lovey-dovey, had, more or less, all just gotten along.

In part, this comparative stability was due to the restrictionist victory wrought by Trevor and his ilk. The 1920s' cutoff lowered the temperature, gave old-timers and newcomers a chance to adjust to one another, without either having to deal with yet another cohort of greenhorns, fresh off the boat. In greater part it was because New York had had such extensive experience with immigration since the days of the Dutch. Indeed, over the course of its repeated remakings, Gotham had evolved into an urban organism superbly adapted for accommodating newcomers. Even before it acquired an *ideology* of multinationalism, the city had been a consummate *practitioner* of it.

Its ethnic neighborhoods—immigrant-friendly enclaves with native-language newspapers and theaters, ethnic lodges and mutual benefit associations, public schools and settlement houses, labor and business organizations—afforded multiple points of entry. Churches, too, were invitingly ethnic oriented; even the universalistic Catholics offered national parishes. The borders of these ethnic quarters, moreover, were elastic, allowing districts to expand, checked only by counterpressure from adjoining areas. Boundaries were constantly renegotiated, occasionally through clashes at the frontiers. If further expansion became impossible, nationality-neighborhoods could easily send out runners, given the superb and cheap mass-transit system, and open up new "colonies." None of this was planned, though zoning laws set some parameters, and public housing (along with Federal Housing Authority lending practices) were becoming (still modest) factors. Nor were living spaces distributed

Children on tricycles in Brooklyn, c. 1940s. (Photo by © Joseph Schwartz/CORBIS/Corbis via Getty Images)

equitably: nationality and race and wealth and class constrained one's ability to command territory. Still, the city's cellularity allowed it to house, cheek by jowl, millions of people from wildly differing backgrounds—Czechs and Greeks, Germans and Chinese, Irish and Caribbean Blacks, Poles and Puerto Ricans—while preserving a considerable degree of domestic tranquility.

The economy was similarly cellular—a pastiche of ethnic niches—with particular occupations being overwhelmingly the possessions of specific nationalities. Official records might list job categories in nation-neutral terms—bankers, cops, construction workers, seamstresses—but New Yorkers knew these categories required additional adjectives: Anglo bankers, Irish cops, Italian construction workers, Jewish seamstresses. Even organized crime was sorted out along tribal lines. This structural segmentation provided multiple access points for immigrants and their offspring. Newcomers slotted themselves into long-established and closely held niches, passed down through generations, open only to compatriots (one had an uncle in the garment biz, a paisan in the building trades). And niches were as renegotiable as neighborhoods. A new group could muscle its way in (or up) by prying open an existing category, perhaps through political means (La Guardia's opening up teaching to Jews), perhaps through race-based campaigns (like Adam Powell's in Harlem), perhaps through violence (Italians v. Irish on the Brooklyn waterfront), perhaps through collaboration in class-based multiethnic unions, perhaps through more or less peaceable succession (Puerto Ricans replacing departing Jews in the needle trades). Again, the economic (like the spatial) order was neither equitable in its allocation of rewards nor the product of intelligent design. But it worked—in the sense that an incredibly complicated and interactive society functioned well despite being heavily freighted with cultural baggage.

Multinationality, then, was a given in New York. The city's people carried in their heads mental maps of the city's ethnic geography and economic ecology. Newcomers quickly located its portals and maneuvered their way inside. Master-race nativists might reject the patchwork status quo, but for most, pluralism was simply the way things were.

What changed in the 1930s was that cultural cosmopolitanism got consciously promoted as a worthy and workable model for the country, indeed the world.

This rethinking came courtesy of a disparate crew of women and men—social scientists and philanthropists, politicians and revolutionaries, educators and clerics, union activists and popular fronters, folklorists and ethnic advocates—who picked up the banner Bourne and Kallen had raised. Galvanized by fascism abroad and its fellow travelers at home, they articulated and applauded existing pluralism. However, they also noted its fragility and urged it be nourished and strengthened. Comity could be cultivated, they argued. Tolerance—of other nationalities, religions, races, and creeds—could be taught.

Vigorous debates would emerge over where to strike the ideal balance between unity and diversity, between cosmopolitanism and pluralism, between Bourne and Kallen. Disagreements would rage about how widely to throw open the flaps of the nation's newly expanded tent. A gulf would continue to yawn between preachment and practice concerning race relations and immigration restriction. Nonetheless, after a decade's hard work, the overall sea change in sensibility about America's identity would be startling and consequential, nowhere more so than in the undermining of the old order's theoretical underpinning—the "science" of racism itself.

31

Culture Warrior

In the fall of 1932, Franz Boas, seventy-four, was suffering from a weak heart (and a lonely one, since Marie, his wife for over forty years, had died in 1929). Boas was too frail to attend meetings at the Columbia anthropology department, from which, by rights, he should have been able to retire, heaped with honors. He had, after all, not only made Schermerhorn Hall the citadel of a new academic discipline, but an army of his students had sallied forth from New York and successfully planted his perspectives in most of the country's universities and many of its professional organizations as well. In 1931, he himself had been elected president of the American Association for the Advancement of Science.

The Boasian revolution had at its core a set of propositions concerning "race" and "culture." "Race"—a term Boas reserved for biologically based subdivisions of the human species (Caucasian, Negroid, and Mongoloid)—didn't, in his judgment, pack much explanatory punch. True, it accounted for certain physiological features, notably skin color. But it was pretty much worthless at accounting for either the customs of the world's vast variety of peoples or the attributes (such as intelligence) of any particular person. "Race" was such a capacious category, the variations inside each of the three so extensive, that biology was simply too blunt an instrument to be of use in predicting the mental or social capabilities of any given group, much less of individuals.

The behavior of any human collectivity—and in the '20s and '30s terms like "ethnic group," "minority," and "nationality" came to challenge "race" as preferred descriptors—was attributable, rather, to its "culture." Boasians understood culture not as Matthew Arnold's "the best which has been thought and said" (something to be possessed privately by "cultured" individuals), but rather as an integrated complex of traits, institutions, and practices that shaped the way a group dealt with its environment. Culture was the distillate of a collectivity's historical experience, and it was transmitted socially, not bequeathed biologically, from generation to generation.

Anthropological investigations around the world, moreover, had amply demonstrated that cultures came in innumerable forms, each in its own way complex and sophisticated. These findings had undergirded Boas's assault on the Social Darwinists' evolutionary paradigm, which assigned all the planet's peoples a position on a scale that ran from primitivism and savagery up through barbarism to civilization, wherein lay still higher peaks of refinement, culminating in the rarefied altitudes occupied by white Europeans and Americans, with Anglos or Aryans (those doing the assigning) perched smugly at the very peak.

Boasians leveled this alpine ideological landscape and portrayed instead a more even terrain upon which dwelt an immense array of cultures, each of which had survived successfully in its particular environment. By dismantling the supposedly scientific basis for racialist rankings, the Columbia anthropologists undercut the legitimacy of any would-be elite's pretension to biological superiority. And the Boasian insistence that the world be seen as a plurality of cultures, not a hierarchy of races, strengthened the hand of those who proposed the US be similarly reconceived. Boas, an activist public intellectual as well as exacting scholar, had been hammering these points home in the popular arena for decades (both Bourne and Kallen had been early adherents of "Papa Franz"), and by 1932 his campaign against "scientific" racism, anti-Semitism, and nativism had had considerable popular and academic impact.

To be sure, his old opponents hadn't simply folded their tents. Charles Davenport and Harry Laughlin continued to do business at the same old stand, the Eugenics Record Office out at Cold Spring Harbor. And Henry Fairfield Osborn and the mustachioed Madison Grant were still hawking racial betterment from their posts (president and trustee, respectively) at the American Museum of Natural History (where John Trevor, too, was on the Board). Indeed, in the summer of 1932 they had brought the Third International Congress of Eugenics to Central Park West, where attendees happily rehearsed the heritability of undesirable behaviors and the need to forestall the propagation (or immigration) of inferior breeds. ("The number of socially inadequate people in the United States is appalling," a City College professor opined.) But these redoubts no longer seemed impregnable. The Carnegie Institution was casting an ever-colder eye on the Cold Spring operation it had long funded; and with Margaret Mead's installation in the west tower as an assistant curator, Boasians had infiltrated the Natural History Museum itself. Beyond these bastions, racial eugenics in 1932 was looking ever more like a disagreeable pseudo-science, destined to fade away.

Then, in 1933, Hitler came to power and immediately set out to assault the Boasian position. Nazis swooped though the library of Boas's beloved University of Kiel, where he had gotten his doctorate in 1881, scooped up all his works, and consigned them to a roaring bonfire. Conversely, Madison Grant's *Passing of the Great Race*, which Hitler had hailed as "my Bible," became the first non-German book the regime reprinted on taking over. Beyond such symbolic gestures, the Nazis enacted the Law for Prevention of Hereditarily Diseased Offspring that June and would use it to forcibly sterilize over a quarter million people in the next four years. The fascists graciously acknowledged their debt to their New York spiritual fathers, giving Harry Laughlin, who had drafted the American model sterilization law on which they based their own, an honorary degree from Heidelberg University in 1936 (he picked it up at the German Consulate in Manhattan).

The Americans, in turn, were proud of their disciples' accomplishments—in 1934 Laughlin's *Eugenical News* devoted an entire issue to adulatory accounts of Nazi "racial hygiene." More, the German advances reinvigorated their US forebears. Madison Grant mustered up a new book, *The Conquest of a Continent, or, The Expansion of Races in America*, acclaimed as the nation's first "racial history" by Professor Osborn in his introduction. In *Conquest*, Grant again inveighed against unassimilable alien masses and urged stricter anti-miscegenation and anti-immigration laws—"racial purity" proposals which the publisher,

Charles Scribner's Sons, advertised as similar to those of "Herr Hitler." Laughlin redoubled his efforts to block interracial marriages and urged Congress (in 1934) to resist lowering immigration barriers on behalf of Jewish refugees from Germany. In truth, Laughlin—who obsessed endlessly about Jews, covering page after page with handwritten lists of "Jew traits" ("chiselers," "parasites")—would have preferred to rid the country of those already here. Still, deporting the Jews, as he resignedly wrote Madison Grant, would be even harder than shipping the more numerous Negroes back to Africa; "the Jew is doubtless here to stay," he sighed; "the Nordics' task" was "to prevent more of them from coming."

John Trevor certainly did his share in this regard, lobbying hard against granting asylum to Jewish victims of Nazi persecution—which Trevor blamed on the Jews' "beliefs in the Marxian philosophy" (he, himself, was an ardent opponent of the New Deal). And the nativist campaign acquired fresh resources when multimillionaire Wickliffe Preston Draper signed on. Draper—who owned the top three floors of one of Gotham's most fashionable apartment houses, 322 East 57th Street (he had stuffed them with military weapons and trophies acquired on numerous hunting trips)—was yet another friend and disciple of Madison Grant. Draper had dabbled in the cause of racial purity since the mid-1920s, but it was in 1937, the year Grant died and other sponsors were found flagging, that he established the Pioneer Fund. Its mission was to give scholarships to children descended from "white persons who settled in the original thirteen states" and (mainly) to promote eugenics. To run it, Draper picked Harry Laughlin.

This Nazi-inflected counterrevolution enraged and reenergized Franz Boas, and in 1933 the old lion rose from his bed and (Margaret Mead said) "flung himself back into the world." Denouncing the expulsion of Jews from German universities, he joined in raising money to bring refugees to the United States and find them jobs. He began what would prove a five-year campaign to get American scientists to speak out as a community against the Nazis' use of pseudo-science—"Nordic nonsense," he called it—though at first he found almost none of them willing to take a public stand. And he proposed a "truly educational effort based on scientific data," aimed at the American public, to "refute Hitlerist theories on the subject of Aryanism and race superiority"; in this initiative he had allies.

Foremost among them was Ruth Benedict, a former student of Boas and now his alter ego. Benedict was in effect running the Columbia anthropology department for him, despite the Butler administration's sexism—women professors were not allowed to enter the Faculty Club dining room—which all but precluded the possibility of her succeeding him officially. Another strike against her was her lesbianism, not something she trumpeted publicly, but she'd been living openly with her lover, Natalie Raymond, since separating from her husband in 1930, and she wrote sympathetically about same-sex practices in her anthropological work. Benedict's outsider status heightened her eagerness to aid Boas's campaign, and in 1934 she brought out *Patterns of Culture*. Beginning with a rousing attack on racism, the book went on to describe a variety of cultures, demonstrating (as had Mead) that an appreciation of other societies could help liberate people from the imperatives of their own. Aimed at a general audience, *Patterns* was immediately and astoundingly successful; it would go on to sell over a million copies and become the most widely read work of anthropology ever; and it won space for Boasian anti-ethnocentricity within American popular culture.

Boas remained the indispensable and indefatigable culture warrior, however, publishing pamphlets, delivering lectures, issuing critiques (like his 1934 savaging, in *The New Republic*, of Madison Grant's *Conquest*), and organizing the American Committee for Anti-Nazi Literature, which tried to coordinate the work of New York's seventy-eight antifascist organizations. In 1936, Boas's fierce, duel-scarred visage graced the cover of *Time* magazine, which hailed the septuagenarian as a leader of those "knocking the flimsy props from under Nazi ideas of race purity and race superiority." But it was not until 1938, the year of Anschluss, Munich, and Kristallnacht, that Boas's campaign to rally scientists against Hitlerism finally gained traction.

In April, the prestigious British journal *Nature* published an article by the rabidly anti-Semitic German physicist and Nobel laureate Johannes Stark. Denouncing Jewish physicists for corrupting the discipline (alongside "White Jews" like Werner Heisenberg and Max Planck, Gentile theoreticians who believed in relativity and quantum theory), Stark sought "to exterminate the Jewish spirit" in science. Upon reading the piece, Boas, together with Columbia colleagues, including geneticist Leslie Dunn and physicist Harold Urey, established an ad hoc group to craft a counterstatement—the "Scientists' Manifesto"—which condemned the "official racialism of the Nazis." Boas enlisted a history department graduate student working on ancient Greece—M. I. Finkelstein, later to be renowned as the classicist Sir Moses Finley—to distribute 12,000 copies of the Manifesto to universities and research institutes across the country. By December, it had garnered 1,284 signatures from scientists at 167 universities, including three Nobel laureates and sixty-four members of the National Academy of Science—the first major condemnation by American scientists of pseudo-scientific racism.

Emboldened by this success, Boas and Finkelstein created the American Committee for Democracy and Intellectual Freedom (ACDIF) in March 1939, to "combat propaganda for racial and religious discrimination or intolerance," and promptly embarked on another whirlwind of activity. That year the ACDIF established chapters of university professors and schoolteachers across the country, arranged for antifascist lecture series and radio shows, and created a committee of scholars to investigate misuse of the term "race" in school and college textbooks. Its report, which received wide editorial coverage around the country, discovered that of the 166 texts reviewed, nearly two-thirds confounded biological and cultural categories, with 20 percent proffering what amounted to Nazi doctrines about superior and inferior races. Boas also helped launch *Equality*, a self-described nonsectarian monthly magazine dedicated to combating "racial and religious intolerance," and which attacked the Christian Front's "hate-rousing and anti-Semitic activities."

In July, Boas paused briefly for a massive epistolary tribute, on the occasion of his eighty-first birthday, headed by President Roosevelt and including a letter from 136 leading public officials, scientists, writers, and educators that applauded him for his contributions to science and for having "in these crucial times" undertaken to "spend the last years of your life in massing your fellow scientists and educators against the lowering forces of reaction."

32

Building Brotherhood

Among Boas's staunchest allies in this campaign—and his key financial supporter—was the New York–based American Jewish Committee. Like Boas, in 1932 the Committee had been limping a bit, in part because none of its core coterie of German-Jewish influentials—Cyrus Adler, Irving Lehman, Joseph Proskauer, Samuel Rosenman, Roger W. Straus, and Morris Waldman—possessed the leadership capabilities of long-time helmsman Louis Marshall. Marshall had died in 1929, making that a doubly calamitous year for the Committee, as donations had dried up dramatically after the Crash.

At first the Nazis' accession in 1933 marginalized the group still further, as Rabbi Wise and his American Jewish Congress (along with Samuel Untermyer's Anti-Nazi League) assumed leadership of the opposition to Hitler. Committee leaders held aloof from, even opposed, public battles, partly because their mandarin style eschewed mass mobilizing in favor of behind-the-scenes diplomacy (they had excellent links to Roosevelt); partly because they feared exacerbating anti-Semitism; and partly because as firm believers in (and beneficiaries of) assimilationism, they resisted underscoring Jewish separateness.

Yet with backstairs diplomacy winning them nothing but a reputation for timidity, and with anti-Semitism burgeoning despite their circumspection, the Committee entered the lists against fascism and its domestic sympathizers. It established a semiautonomous unit called the Information and Service Associates, renamed the Survey Committee in 1936, which raised a hefty war chest for its activities—$1.25 million by decade's end. Under the able direction of Sidney Wallach, the Survey Committee kept tabs on the enemy—infiltrating and tracking outfits like the German American Bund, collecting anti-Semitic propaganda, and monitoring the press and publications for racist sentiments. It arranged with Columbia professor Allan Nevins to scrutinize history textbooks for anti-immigrant perspectives. It also underwrote production and distribution of antifascist articles, books, and pamphlets; offered subventions to anti-Nazi newspapers; backed production of radio shows (nearly 600 programs in its first five months); worked with Hollywood writers and directors to incorporate antifascist themes in their movies; and employed pollsters and public relations experts to track and assess their campaign's effectiveness.

To refute Nazi "racial science"—an essential component of their public relations war—the Committee turned to Franz Boas and contributed substantial sums to his efforts, including the ACDIF. Not only was Boas the obvious choice, but he was appealingly in sync with their insistence that apart from religion Jews were indistinguishable from other Americans. Boas, of course, had devoted much of his career to demonstrating that no inherited (hence immutable) characteristics hindered Jewish immigrants from assimilating, and even during the 1930s he continued to devise research projects to reaffirm this. One, undertaken by his student David Efron, sought to prove that even gestures, the ways people used their physical bodies, were rooted in culture, not biology, hence pliable. Comparing two generations of immigrants to New York, Efron showed that while the gestures of greenhorn Jews and Italians differed dramatically, their children's body language resembled each other's more than it did that of their parents.

Even after entering the popular arena, the Committee kept a low profile. The ideal thing, said President Cyrus Adler, would be to create "a public opinion in this country against Hitler and his party absolutely without reference to the Jews at all," lest their efforts be dismissed as special pleading, or worse, a plot to embroil America in war on behalf of German coreligionists. "I am of the opinion that we cannot be constantly thrusting ourselves before the public without danger to ourselves," Adler argued. "They will get tired of us. What I want them to do is to get tired of Hitler."

Whenever possible, therefore, the Committee worked together with Christian or nonsectarian organizations, pursuing generic goals like "tolerance" or "brotherhood." Their most successful such alliance was the National Conference of Christians and Jews, an organization devoted to fostering inter-religious harmony. The NCCJ, founded formally in 1927, had earlier roots in an ecumenical Goodwill Committee established by the Federal Council of Churches of Christ—the nationwide confederation of mainly liberal Protestant denominations, headquartered in the United Charities Building at Fourth Avenue and 22nd Street. The FCCC's mid-1920s outreach to Jews was intended to overcome Jewish anger at being targeted by evangelical missionaries. But when most members proved apathetic to the initiative, with conservatives outright opposed (they *favored* continued proselytizing), FCCC leaders, together with the wealthy industrialist and American Jewish Committee stalwart Roger W. Straus (son of the late Oscar S. Straus, Teddy Roosevelt's secretary of commerce), reformatted the committee as an independent, interfaith, nonecclesiastical group. In 1928, Everett Clinchy, a Presbyterian minister, was brought in to run it.

The group's Executive Committee quickly attracted leading liberal Protestant and Jewish religious and civic figures, like Henry Sloane Coffin, Harry Emerson Fosdick, Reinhold Niebuhr, Mordecai Kaplan, and Henry Morgenthau. Clinchy also set up an advisory committee of social scientists and intellectuals and brought Horace Kallen, Boas, and John Dewey on board. The idea, however, had been to establish a *tripartite* organization that included Catholics—another reason the enterprise had departed the Protestant FCCC—but the designated third branch proved disinclined to sign on. Straus occupied one cochair, and Newton Baker took the Protestant seat, but the third position remained vacant—though the Jesuit priest Wilfred Parsons did come to the first thousand-strong conclave at Columbia University, in January 1929, to exhibit anti-Catholic tracts circulated by anti–Al Smith Protestants the previous year. Hard-line Catholic theologians resisted the very notion of fostering mutual tolerance, as the Church, possessing truth, could tolerate erring individuals but never error itself. "We are suffering as much from tolerance as from intolerance," Msgr. Fulton Sheen roundly declared in 1930, and he waxed caustic about "sophomoric latitudinarians" who "not only say one Christian sect is as good as another but that one world religion is as good as another." Still, a liberal Catholic academic—Columbia historian Carlton J. H. Hayes—was prevailed upon to serve as third cochair. The leaders hammered out an agreement to disagree on doctrine and disavow any inclination to reconcile (much less merge) their faiths, while agreeing to work together to foster "respect for unlikeness."

The organization remained wobbly until Hitler arrived in power. Then, in May 1933, the National Conference of Jews and Christians (as it was called until 1938) published a statement denouncing Nazi persecution of Jews, written by Riverside Church's Harry Emerson Fosdick and signed by 1,200 Protestant clergymen. And in October, the leadership announced that to help ward off any duplication in the US "of the outbreak of intolerance abroad," it was dispatching from New York a traveling trio—a priest, a rabbi, and a minister—to undertake a nationwide Pilgrimage of Understanding. Together they would conduct seminars, lead discussions, and reaffirm the American tradition of religious freedom. The trip was a great success—people in forty cities flocked to see this novel three-headed clerical beast in action—and it led to yet another innovation the following year—the invention of Brotherhood Day.

The brainstorm of the American Jewish Committee's Sidney Wallach, who was proving to have a flair for public relations, Brotherhood Day was floated publicly by the very distinguished Dr. S. Parkes Cadman of Brooklyn's Central Congregational Church (and former head of the FCCC). The first (1934) Brotherhood Day was devoted to holding interfaith conclaves, in New York (with the proceedings broadcast nationally by both NBC and CBS) and in an array of towns and cities across the land. Backed by President Roosevelt as an effort to "rise above ancient and harmful suspicions and prejudices and to work together as citizens of American democracy," and endorsed by a multifaith trio of Gotham civic leaders (Al Smith, Felix Warburg, and Charles E. Hughes Jr.), Brotherhood Day caught on almost immediately, and in a big way. Nineteen thirty-five's Day was observed in 600 communities; the following year's in 1,000; and by 1938—when in response to growing intolerance abroad it was extended, becoming Brotherhood Week—2,000 localities took part. These venues held community dinners, worship services, and trialogues (interfaith mass meetings), which involved chambers of commerce, service clubs, labor unions, farm organizations, youth agencies, schools, colleges, veterans' groups, and churches of every description (by now including a fully committed Catholic hierarchy). America's faith-based society, frightened by religious warfare overseas, had followed the lead of its most theologically dissevered city and established communication links to keep the peace at home.

33

Fêteing the Folks

Another bridge-building effort—aimed at spanning ethnic rather than religious chasms—also had its roots in the 1920s when settlement house and YM/YWCA workers, repelled by anti-immigrant bigotry, set out to counter nativism. Their approach was to celebrate the "cultural gifts"—notably traditional music and dance—that newcomers brought to their adopted land. In November 1921, the "America's Making Exposition," an impressive early effort in this direction, had sponsored over one thousand folk art performances in parks and playgrounds around New York, culminating in a two-week-long program of presentations by over thirty ethnic groups at the 71st Regiment Armory at Park Avenue and 33rd Street.

But it was in the 1930s that the folk-arts movement really gained momentum, thanks to efforts by the Foreign Language Information Service (FLIS), created during the First World War to translate and distribute news to the foreign language press. The FLIS carried on as a cultural broker—adopting the motto "To interpret the Immigrant to America, and America to the Immigrant"—and in 1931 joined with seventeen different nationality groups to found the Folk Festival Council (FFC). Its goal was "to give the people of New York an opportunity to enjoy the contributions of foreign-born groups to the folk arts," while providing "foreign-born people themselves with fine and dignified opportunities for artistic expression." Even more ambitiously, the FFC wanted to put paid to the "self-styled Americanism which would destroy everything alien regardless of its worth." It was convinced, rather, in the words of a 1932 FLIS pamphlet, that "the way of growth and creative achievement for America" lay "not in uniformity but in unity tolerant of difference."

Over the next decade, the Council organized multiethnic festivals around the city—in parks (Washington Square, Prospect Park, Central Park Mall); in theaters (Hudson Guild Theater, Neighborhood Playhouse, Chanin Theater); at the Seventh Regiment Armory on Park Avenue at 66th Street; and at International House on Riverside Drive (itself dedicated since 1924 to promoting interculturalism by bringing foreign students to New York). The FFC grew rapidly—by 1934, forty nationality groups were on board—as did the size and variety of its performances. Often the participants would parade side by side, arrayed in ethnic costume, in grand multinational marches—Armenians and American Indians, Bulgarians and Danes, Cossacks and Mexicans. These events drew thousands of onlookers and seemed to prove, as John Martin, chief dance critic of the *New York Times* argued in 1932, that the "old tendency, prompted no doubt by patriotic motives, to make Americans out of immigrants by urging them to forget and to discontinue their Old World customs, has happily given place to a broader outlook."

As the storms in Europe and Asia began blowing up choppy waters in local harbors—with New York's interethnic climate turning particularly blustery—something more substantial than folk festivals seemed required if the FFC's "unity tolerant of difference" was to be attained. Gotham multiculturalists responded by enlisting the city's massive public-school system in an educational blitz intended to foster the growth of "tolerance," igniting a movement that would quickly sweep the nation.

34

Teaching Tolerance

Rachel Davis DuBois fit squarely in the Census Bureau's "native white" column, having been raised (on a farm in south New Jersey) by a Quaker family descended from seventeenth-century English-Welsh ancestors. Yet, in close and sympathetic association with Gotham's immigrant and Black communities, she pioneered a pedagogy called "intercultural education." After graduating from Bucknell College in 1914, DuBois worked in the pacifist movement during and after the First World War, along with fellow Quakers and the Women's International League for Peace and Freedom. In 1924, when she began teaching at Woodbury High School, in Woodbury, New Jersey, she set out to combat nationalist chauvinism and foster "world-mindedness" in her students by showing them what other countries had contributed to human progress. In addition, convinced by the contention of W.E.B. Du Bois (no relation) that ending foreign wars had to be linked with overcoming domestic prejudice, she introduced her charges to the "cultural gifts" various peoples had brought to the American table.

Taking a leaf from the folk festival movement, DuBois organized a sequence of school assemblies at which representatives of different groups were invited to perform, present, or discuss some collective accomplishment. Determined as she was to counter negative stereotypes about assorted "others," her assemblies tended toward the uplifting—students listened to Italian operas, watched German folk dances, observed a Japanese flower arranger or a peanut bread maker at work (the latter a nod to African American agro-scientist George Washington Carver). Even such mild measures were considered subversive by local American Legionnaires, already distressed by her pacifism. When in 1926 she proposed inviting an NAACP field secretary to address the children, they denounced her as a Bolshevik and demanded she be fired. Protected by tenure, DuBois carried on until 1929 when, feeling the need to deepen her approach, she moved to New York to study at Columbia's Teachers College (TC).

The Morningside Heights campus was once again in ferment, though in the early 1930s many of the faculty were veering away from the child-centered pedagogy they had championed in the teens and twenties. Instead, with the economy in free fall, they were urging schools to take a vanguard role in reconstructing a broken society. *Dare the School Build a New Social Order?* was the question Professor George Counts posed in 1932 to the Progressive Education Association. Counts was part of the "social reconstructionist" group of TC faculty, which advocated reorganizing education around studying and solving real-life community problems. Educators at TC's experimental Lincoln School designed projects that for example set pupils to learn chemistry by analyzing the local water supply and then tackling pollution. These "activity programs" (as opposed to conventional "passive absorption" methods) got an ambitious tryout in New York elementary schools—in 1935, the program involved 75,000 students and nearly 2,500 teachers—and swiftly spread to forty states.

John Dewey, still the institution's presiding deity, had long advocated that schools prepare students to understand and change their world, and he was a sometime associate of Counts and the reconstructionists. But Dewey was as cautious about the new enthusiasm as he had been about the previous child-centered one, warning his colleagues against overestimating the capacity (or the appropriateness) of schoolteachers leading the crusade for social reform. Dewey *was* keen, however, on having schools promote multicultural amity. Long committed to ethnic and racial diversity—he'd encouraged Horace Kallen's interventions during the First World War (though not uncritically), and Randolph Bourne had been his student—Dewey in 1923 had urged schools to adopt curricula that "will make the different racial elements in this country aware of what each has contributed." He even posited that art was the best avenue for alleviating conflict and instilling sympathy for others: "Barriers are dissolved, limiting prejudices melt away, when we enter into the spirit of Negro or Polynesian art."

TC Professor Harold Rugg was of similar mind. Another reconstructionist—he helped establish the group's journal, *The Social Frontier*—Rugg in the 1920s had authored, from his Lincoln School base, a series of experimental social-science pamphlets for elementary and junior high school students. In the 1930s these evolved into a set of volumes, under the general title *Man and His Changing Society*, aimed at making schoolbook descriptions of American society more realistic by taking on issues like unemployment, class conflict, consumerism, and social inequality. Rugg's writings were immensely popular—by decade's end over 600,000 copies had been read by over five million school children in forty states— Rachel DuBois's pupils among them. She particularly liked his highlighting, in studies like *America and Her Immigrants* and *How Nations Live Together*, of the value of cultural diversity and the importance of equal rights for minorities.

In addition to working with such like-minded TC mentors, DuBois soaked up the new social scientific thinking on race and culture coming out of Columbia's anthropology department, just across 120th Street. She visited Boas, sought his help, regularly cited his work and that of Ruth Benedict and Margaret Mead. It was not just the Boasian appreciation of diversity that attracted her—its insistence on seeing the world as a plurality of cultures, not a hierarchy of races—but also its rejection of the old idea that prejudice *itself* was a biological trait, an "instinctive reaction" impervious to reason. Mead had argued in the 1920s that children were born free of prejudice but absorbed their parents' antipathies at an early age; that they were in effect *taught* to hate all the people their relatives hate, and before they were six, or seven, or eight.

This assessment was increasingly seconded by social psychologists, who developed techniques to track the genesis of prejudice. The most extensive such analysis available to DuBois—*Race Attitudes in Children*—was brought out by Bruno Lasker the same year she arrived at Columbia, and she repeatedly sought his advice. Born in Germany in 1880, Lasker had arrived in New York in 1914, worked at the Henry Street Settlement, and served as associate editor of *Survey* magazine, before embarking on his pioneering study with funding from Rockefeller philanthropies. Lasker found that children recognized racial differences as early as age five. They picked up prejudices not only at home but from school, church, books, peers—and from segregation itself, which "carries its own lesson," impressing on children that a shunned group was deemed undesirable, inferior. Nevertheless, Lasker was positive that stereotypes, having been learned, could be unlearned. And he believed that teaching "mutual tolerance" was essential to "producing a state of social harmony in a population composed of so many elements."

Theoretically fortified, DuBois began polishing her praxis, gathering multicultural curricular materials and hunting up possible speakers for school assembly programs. In doing so, she turned for advice and counsel to leaders of Gotham's racial and ethnic groups, quickly and delightedly discovering that "to be a part of a cosmopolitan society in New York City is easy." She had already met W.E.B. Du Bois and joked with him about deciding to get a doctorate so she could be called the "other Dr. DuBois"; now she befriended Aaron Douglas and his wife, Alta, James Weldon Johnson, and A. Philip Randolph and was often the only white woman (or man) in attendance at African American events. DuBois connected with Everett Clinchy of the National Conference of Christians and Jews. She also met Mordecai Kaplan, professor at the Jewish Theological Seminary and founder of Reconstructionist Judaism, and absorbed his belief that—*pace* the American Jewish Committee—Jews were an ethnic group with a distinctive culture, not just a religious denomination.

Perhaps the most important relationship DuBois struck up in the early 1930s was with Leonard Covello, then head of Casa Italiana's Educational Bureau. Covello was able to give her information about Italian "cultural gifts" but also, more importantly, to provide insight into the strained relations between Italian immigrants and the city's schools. Here he drew upon his own extensive experience. Brought over from southern Italy to an East Harlem tenement in 1896, at the age of nine, Covello was enrolled in a Soup School on 116th Street, so called for the bowl provided each pupil at noon. Run by the American Female Guardian Society—the same group that had received a charter back in 1849 to establish schools for poor children—this private institution aimed to Americanize its immigrants ASAP, drilling them to learn English, parrot patriotic songs, and jettison old world habits, notably foodways. Pupils were given a sack of oat flakes to show their parents as an example of healthy and nutritious sustenance. When little Leonard got home with his oats, his father, remembering what he'd fed pigs back in Avigliano, flew into a fury, shouting: "They give us the food of animals to eat and send it home to us with our children!"

Things didn't improve at public school (P.S. 83 on East 100th Street), where Italy and things Italian were never mentioned, and "pretty soon," Covello recalled, "we got the idea that Italian meant something inferior." It was the same at Morris High School, which he entered in 1902, walking each day up to Boston Road and 166th Street in the Bronx to save the nickel carfare. Italian youths—made hyper-aware of their accent, appearance, and retrograde foodways—hid their bulky sandwiches of crusty bread, salami, cheese, and sausage from their white-bread-and-ham American friends, lest they be laughed at, and they discouraged parents from visiting the school, embarrassed by their greenhorn clothes and poor command of English.

Covello remembered all this when he himself began teaching (in 1911) at DeWitt Clinton High School (on Tenth Avenue between 58th and 59th Streets). Although the all-male student body—over three thousand boys—included the largest number of Italians of any high school in the city, the staff made little effort to understand the youths' social background, or, worse, criticized and ridiculed Italian customs and traditions, insisting on adherence to American ways. Italian parents, already dubious about the value of education, feared the schools were weaning away their children. And the children—caught in-between two worlds, neither greenhorns nor Americans—became (so Covello believed) disaffected, deracinated, alienated, maladjusted, truant, and eventually delinquent, drifting into the orbit of well-heeled and well-dressed gangsters.

Covello set out to bridge this school-exacerbated generation gap. He began, in 1914, by establishing a club at DeWitt Clinton—Il Circolo Italiano—that sponsored all-Italian evening entertainments of classical drama, song, and prose. By teaching students about the glorious high culture of which their parents, and they, were the inheritors—by apprising them of their *own* "cultural gifts"—Covello hoped to boost their respect for their elders (shoring up parental and community authority) and for themselves (alleviating feelings of inferiority).

Next, he pushed the Board of Education to approve the teaching of Italian as a foreign language, a privilege theretofore reserved for French, German, and Latin. He succeeded, in 1922, with help from the powerful (and philo-fascist) Order Sons of Italy in America [*sic*]. By 1925, Covello headed an Italian department that offered instruction to nearly 600 boys. The program continued to expand after Clinton High moved to Mosholu Parkway in the Bronx in 1929, eventually peaking at 900 pupils, making it by far the largest Italian studies department in the United States, at either the secondary or college level.

Success was not without its contradictions, however. The language taught to children—the classical Italian of Petrarch and Mazzini—was all but incomprehensible to most parents, who spoke Sicilian, Neapolitan, or assorted micro-dialects at home. Covello was well aware of this and deliberately had his charges learn "high" Italian in the belief that a low "broken down dialect" was a "poor medium to express one's thoughts." While this exacerbated the very intra-familial divisions he'd proposed to overcome, it did enhance the likelihood of success in the larger society. Making students conversant with high culture gave them an important *class* credential—even the snootiest nativists couldn't gainsay the cultural clout of Classical Rome—and indeed a large number of his club members went on to professional careers in education, government, medicine, and law.

In truth, for all Covello's emphasis on teaching second-generation students to be proud of Italian culture, language, and sandwiches, he was equally insistent that they master English, acquire American tastes, and "undergo a cultural change," albeit gradually, without trauma. Fiercely critical of the Melting Pot, he nevertheless believed bolstering ethnic identities would facilitate Americanization in a way that enabled the immigrants to deal from strength. Once awakened to the richness of their heritage, he reckoned, they could offer an "expanding American culture the best that is inherent in their own culture," making it a *reciprocal* relationship. "We are giving them a bridge," Covello wrote, "over which they may pass proudly into their American heritage."

By the early 1930s, Covello was himself moving out into the wider city. He helped organize Casa Italiana and (in 1931) started up its Education Bureau, which offered the kind of programming he'd pioneered at Clinton to Gotham's wider Italian community, and to Rachel DuBois, when she came calling. In 1932 he teamed up with the Folk Festival Council and launched a group, Coro D'Italia, that performed all over the city. He began teaching a course at NYU's School of Education on "The Social Background of the Italian Family in America" and became a PhD candidate there in 1934. That same year he joined DuBois in an ambitious new venture.

Drawing together the contacts she'd assembled in New York, DuBois established the Service Bureau for Intercultural Education, whose advisory board included Covello, James Weldon Johnson of the NAACP, George Counts from Teachers College, Everett Clinchy from the National Conference of Christians and Jews, and Louis Posner of the New York City Board of Education, among others. To her established goal of helping teachers promote pluralism and peace by introducing students to other people's cultures, DuBois now added Covello's emphasis on teaching second-generation immigrants about their own heritage—a consideration that gained extra force with Hitler's accession. Alienated foreign-stock youths, she argued, were subject not only to the blandishments of racketeers but "to manipulation by foreign governments intent on undermining the unity and resolve of the American people."

DuBois's plan to strengthen public commitment to tolerance while immunizing young immigrants against Hitlerism proved attractive to the American Jewish Committee, and the organization helped get the Service Bureau started. With additional resources provided by the Works Progress Administration (WPA), DuBois assembled a multicultural team of researchers (*too* multi for some: when DuBois rented an apartment for her staff near Teachers College, the landlady, on discovering they were integrated, evicted them, stoutly asserting: "I've never had any damn niggers walking in my front door before, and it's not going to start now"). Quickly relocated, her crew was dispatched to libraries around town and set to gathering and writing up information about the contributions of various peoples. Soon teachers' manuals, lesson plans, bibliographies, and resource lists were spinning off the mimeograph machines. Then, with funding supplied by the American Jewish Committee, DuBois test-ran her program at fifteen schools around the metropolitan area during the 1934–35 school year.

The flagship institution for this initial tryout was the newly created Benjamin Franklin High School. Located in East Harlem, on 108th Street, it had been birthed and was now principaled by Leonard Covello. He had campaigned for it since 1931, with backing from neighborhood institutions and, more formidably, the odd trio of Generoso Pope, Vito Marcantonio, and Fiorello La Guardia; it was the latter's mayoral win in 1933 that put the project over the top. Yet Benjamin Franklin was far from being all-Italian, though they did constitute the largest single group. When it opened in September 1934, thirty-four ethnic groups were in attendance—including substantial percentages of Blacks, Puerto Ricans, Germans, Jews, and Irish. Covello reached out to all of them. A firm believer in the community-oriented activism promoted by Teachers College reconstructionists, he set up trilingual committees (Italian, Spanish, English) of parents and residents to tackle various neighborhood issues, like winning low-income public housing. And he plunged with gusto into DuBois's intercultural assembly program, tailor-made for his variegated student body. The Service Bureau arranged presentations by (and student interaction with) Japanese actors, Jewish rabbis, African American poets, and Puerto Rican dancers, among many others, while also introducing students to the full range of ethnic–American Revolutionary heroes: Crispus Attucks, Haym Salomon, Friedrich Wilhelm Von Steuben, Casimir Pulaski, the Marquis de Lafayette, and Filippo Mazzei. Before and after each term, DuBois distributed "attitude inventory" questionnaires to students, and at year's end she was delighted to announce that Benjamin Franklin had experienced a "14 per cent improvement" in the "attitudes of the children toward their classmates."

Covello was thrilled with the program. The American Jewish Committee, however, was not. Its leaders admired the feisty DuBois but worried that her focus on boosting group pride might encourage nationalist feelings. Was it really a good idea to be inflating Italian (or German) chauvinism at the very moment Mussolini (and Fritz Kuhn) were strutting their stuff? Might not separate-assemblies programming lead to cultural fragmentation rather than intercultural rapprochement? And most importantly, was it good for the Jews to be presented as just another ethnic group, rather than the religious denomination the Committee insisted they were? "You don't have a separate program on the Baptists," one AJC official pointed out to DuBois, "why on the Jews?"

In 1935, accordingly, the Committee cut off Service Bureau funding. DuBois quickly found backers in the Progressive Education Association and elsewhere and carried on with her enterprise. Covello had urged the New York City Board of Education to adopt her approach universally, and as the global situation worsened, educational authorities increasingly warmed to DuBois's argument that the city's schools—the only "common meeting ground of all our varieties of cultures"—had a responsibility to help their 1,250,000 pupils deal with growing world and local tensions. Finally, on December 14, 1938, prompted by Kristallnacht horrors, the Board passed a "Tolerance Resolution," which required all schools to hold assemblies that stressed the importance of "tolerance and freedom for all men" and made children aware of the "contributions of all races and nationalities." DuBois's Service Bureau office was besieged by teachers seeking guidance; a manual called *Adventures in Intercultural Education* was developed, and during 1939 she offered teacher training courses at NYU.

Tolerance initiatives now broke out all over. James Waterman Wise (son of Rabbi Wise) organized the Council Against Intolerance in America (CAIA). The group crafted an "American Declaration of Tolerance and Equality"—the text denounced all who "set race against race, creed against creed" and condemned "intolerance in every form"—then launched it, with a nationwide public relations blitz, on Independence Day, 1939: La Guardia promulgated the Declaration at the New York World's Fair's Court of Peace, his words broadcast coast to coast over NBC; it was also read aloud at 5,000 gatherings across the country. (A matching visual, depicting Katharine Hepburn as the Spirit of Tolerance, was plastered on a Times Square billboard and distributed nationwide in poster format.)

Eleanor Roosevelt, having been briefed by DuBois at her Greenwich Village apartment, hailed her efforts on behalf of intercultural amity in a *My Day* column that year. By then the idea had caught fire across the country, with school districts nationwide implementing programs in "intercultural education" and local teachers colleges offering courses on using the methodology. In no small part this vast escalation was also due to DuBois, who had opened up a mass media front in the multicultural crusade.

35

Americans All

In 1938, dismayed by Father Coughlin's anti-Semitic outbursts, Rachel DuBois decided to contest him on his own medium by creating an on-air version of her assemblies. She took her idea to John Studebaker, head of the federal Office of Education, home since 1935 of the New Deal's Federal Radio Project (FRP). As the FRP had been charged with using educational programming to reveal the "rich heritages that have come to us through the many races and nationalities which make up our population," Studebaker responded enthusiastically. He agreed to have the government sponsor and produce twenty-six half-hour episodes, with dramatizations and live orchestral music, in collaboration with DuBois's Service Bureau and with CBS. Such projects helped the network fulfill its requirement, mandated by the Communication Act of 1934, to sponsor some public interest shows on a "sustaining" (noncommercial) basis. The network provided its studios in New York City; assigned the series its prime public affairs slot of Sunday afternoons at 2:00 p.m.; and turned scripting over to Gilbert Seldes, who had been hired in 1937 to become CBS's first director of television, though with no TV as yet to direct, Seldes had been posted to the educational radio beat. Additional backing was soon forthcoming from the WPA, the Carnegie Foundation, and the American Jewish Committee, which agreed to underwrite DuBois's salary, out of its desperate desire to win popular support for accepting refugees, despite its reservations about her approach.

Those reservations had not been forgotten, however, and they resurfaced almost immediately. Battles broke out over the scope and content of the series, starting with its name. DuBois had proposed "Immigrants All"; this was changed to "Immigrants All, Americans All" to signal a greater ecumenism and was then flipped ("Americans All, Immigrants All") to suggest the primacy of unity over diversity. There were struggles over whether to produce one show per group (DuBois's favored device) or (Seldes's preferred strategy) to have each show present the contributions of many groups to a particular field, like the development of American science. Studebaker split the difference, authorizing both approaches. Then came hand-to-hand fighting over each episode. Iphigene Sulzberger, wife of the publisher of the *New York Times*, said it would be a great mistake to have a separate show on Jews, implying they were a nationality "when they are merely a religious group." Studebaker overrode the objection. African American advisers—there had been none until DuBois fought for and gained the appointment of W.E.B. Du Bois and Alain Locke as consultants—were extremely sensitive to media characterizations in the era of Amos 'n' Andy. They pushed Seldes into dealing with some issues he'd tried to avoid and into excising some offensive material he'd included.

In general, the series short-shrifted the nativist resistance most immigrants had encountered, though the Irish and Italian programs did refer briefly to "unfriendly" receptions. Essentialist stereotypes remained in evidence, though only in their "positive" variants (the Irish, it was said, contributed "a light laughter, and a gay spirit"). And each episode ended on a note of triumph and achievement, underscoring the nation's commitment to equality and

A booklet supplementing the Department of the Interior's radio series, *Americans All-Immigrants All*. April, 1939. (PD-US-ineligible. United States Department of the Interior and United States Department of Education)

opportunity. Overall, the series suggested, successive arrivals fused with their new homeland "like so many wholesome grafts on a healthy virile tree and became, within less than a generation, true, loyal Americans!"

Thanks in part to such an affirmative perspective, "Americans All, Immigrants All" was a tremendous success. By the time its six-month run ended in May 1939, over a hundred thousand letters had poured in, many from deeply moved individual auditors. Others had listened collectively, in study groups, social clubs, and ethnic associations. Hundreds of fraternal organizations, foreign-language papers, religious bodies, and elementary- and secondary-school teachers wrote in asking for copies of scripts (often just the one treating "their" group). Also in demand was the glossy 120-page study guide DuBois helped draft, replete with quotations from Franz Boas debunking notions of racial inferiority.

The series resonated with immigrants because its sponsorship by the federal government signaled that they were being brought officially under the American umbrella, that their contributions were being acknowledged, that a new (albeit bowdlerized) narrative was being promulgated, one that included them as significant actors—as the subjects, not merely the objects, of American history. Still, "Americans All, Immigrants All" would probably not have struck such a chord had the newcomers not been hearing a similar message from even more authoritative quarters.

36

Immigrants All

Liberal New York politicians were mainstays of the new tolerance crusade, in no small part because their profession now revolved around the brokering and mobilization of ethnic coalitions. Gotham's politics had always been decentralized, and Tammany clubhouses had long been attuned to ethnic concerns. But Irish bosses, determined to retain their hammerlock on power, had relegated other nationalities to subaltern status. Then, in 1933, anti-Tammany reformers created the first "balanced ticket" in Gotham's history, running—and more to the point electing—an Italian for mayor, an Irish Catholic for comptroller, and a Jew for president of the Board of Aldermen. Tammany swiftly followed suit, and multiethnic slates became obligatory in metropolitan politics.

The New Yorkers running national politics in the 1930s also reached out to immigrant voters—not surprisingly, given that ethnics were a crucial component of Roosevelt's electoral coalition. In 1932, during his first presidential campaign, FDR had bid for immigrant support by denouncing the Hoover administration's callous treatment of resident aliens. On taking office, Roosevelt appointed New Yorker Daniel W. MacCormack—Labor Secretary Frances Perkins's choice—to be commissioner of immigration and naturalization. Declaring that "the New Deal means a more sympathetic and humane consideration of [the alien's] problems," MacCormack promptly curtailed warrantless arrests, dragnet raids on homes and wedding parties, and other forms of federal harassment, triggering howls of protest from xenophobes like John Trevor. In 1936, during the president's reelection campaign, the national Democratic Party institutionalized its ties to ethnic constituencies by establishing a Foreign Language Citizens Committee; its Italian representative, Generoso Pope, set about mobilizing compatriots across the country as he had those in New York City.

More momentously, Franklin Roosevelt symbolically gathered immigrants into the American fold, notably on the occasion of the fiftieth anniversary of the dedication of the Statue of Liberty. Journeying up to Gotham in October 1936, Roosevelt boated out to Bedloe's Island and gave a speech that for the first time officially acknowledged that the monument had accrued a whole new status—as secular patron saint of immigrants—in addition to the role as torchbearer of international republicanism which the sculptor Bartholdi's generation had assigned it.

The statue's connection with immigration was partly fortuitous, a function of its placement in New York's harbor athwart the sea lanes and adjacent to Ellis Island. Had Bartholdi moved it to Philadelphia, as he'd threatened to do at one point, the link might never have been made. Even so, Emma Lazarus's "The New Colossus"—her poetic 1883 response to the flight here of Czarist-persecuted Jews—remained virtually unknown for decades, along with its such signature phrases as "Mother of Exiles" and "I lift my lamp beside the golden door!" Even after admirers of Lazarus inscribed it on a bronze tablet inside the statue's entrance in 1903, visible to the accumulating thousands, the poem's message took hold only slowly. Ms. Liberty's bond saleswoman role in World War I was hardly immigrant-friendly, and her apotheosis as a National Monument was no paean to immigration, coming as it did in 1924, the year the golden door slammed shut. It was only in the 1930s that the sonnet became widely admired and quoted—in caustic counterpoint to refugee restriction.

Roosevelt did not confront this contradiction that fine fall day in 1936, but he did eloquently embrace the immigrants. For centuries, he declared, they had "followed the beacon of liberty which this light symbolizes" and "brought to us strength and moral fiber developed in a civilization centuries old but fired anew by the dream of a better life in America." Gesturing toward the pluralist persuasion, the president noted that they "brought to one new country the cultures of a hundred old ones" and declared "I am proud—America is proud—of what they have given us." He even expressed a Kallenesque "satisfaction" that those who "have left their native land to join us may still retain here their affection for some things left behind—old customs, old language, old friends." But he nodded just as vigorously in the opposite direction (as was his wont) by deploying assimilationist imagery. Praising the immigrants for "wisely choosing that their children shall live in the new language and in the new customs of this new people," he wheeled out a Grand Coulee Dam–sized version of the Americanizers' favorite metaphor: "Into this continental reservoir there has been poured untold and untapped wealth of human resources. Out of that reservoir—out of the melting pot—the rich promise which the New World held out to those who came to it from many lands is finding fulfillment." Indeed, he said, Americans old *and* new, "bound together by hope of a common future rather than by reverence for a common past," had built upon their continent "a unity in language and speech, in law and economics, in education and in general purpose which nowhere finds its match."

Ferrying back to the Battery, Roosevelt's entourage made its way through dense and cheering crowds up South Street, past the Fulton Fish Market, and into the heart of the Lower East Side. At Sara Delano Roosevelt Park he addressed an immense and fervent throng of immigrants—the assemblage dotted with black-hatted and long-coated Orthodox rabbis, beshawled old Jewish ladies, Italians from Mulberry Street, Greeks from Henry, Chinese from Mott—with thousands more hanging from windows and packed onto fire escapes and rooftops of nearby tenements. From the balcony of a Hester Street building, the patrician president in his cutaway grey coat paid his respects to "My friends of the East Side"—the opening phrase alone triggered wild applause—commending immigrant contributions to American civilization ("they wove into the pattern of American life some of the color and the richness of the cultures from which they came") and hailing them for having on occasion proven better citizens than many who had been here for generations. Later, the *New Republic*, not without justice, would twit him for having finessed the crucial issue of immigration barriers, but Roosevelt's rhetoric would have lasting consequence: ever after, the great statue—like New York City—would be indelibly identified with America's multiethnic heritage.

Multiculturalists hailed Roosevelt even more enthusiastically for the brief talk he gave two years later to the Daughters of the American Revolution. "It so happens," he told his audience on April 21, 1938, that "every one of my ancestors on both sides—and when you go back four generations or five generations it means thirty-two or sixty-four of them—every single one of them, without exception, was in this land in 1776." Having underscored his impeccable pedigree before the assembled filiopietists, he underscored his patriotic bona fides as well, adding: "And there was only one Tory among them." Then he delivered his zinger: "Remember, remember always, that all of us, and you and I especially, are descended from immigrants and revolutionists." This celebrated line—often reformatted as "We are all immigrants"—would reverberate widely in the next few years, legitimating pro-ethnicity in much the way John L. Lewis's "The President wants you to join a union" had boosted the cause of labor.

37

Balladeers for Brotherhood

"Revolutionists," too, promoted a multiethnic line in the 1930s, especially those at national Communist Party headquarters on the ninth floor of 35 East Twelfth Street, a former garment industry loft building, just below Union Square. The Party had been multinational at its inception, having originated in an alliance of foreign-language federations that split from the Socialists in 1919. But in the 1920s the Leninist leadership, disapproving of nationality as a basis for organizing, tried to disband the language-based sections, a blunder that cost them many adherents. The turn to the Popular Front in 1935 brought a reversal of this stance, and the Party embraced a vision of the American working class as itself a federation of nationalities and races. This led to a resurgence of ethnic-based organizing, most spectacularly fruitful in the growth of the International Workers Organization (IWO).

Initially overwhelmingly Jewish—product of a breakaway of Communist members from the Workmen's Circle, the fraternal organization created by Jewish socialists in 1892—the IWO recruited members into thirteen other nationality-based benefit societies—including Italians, Ukrainians, Poles, Rumanians, Croats, Serbs, Hungarians, Slovaks, Russians, Finns, African Americans, and the largely Puerto Rican membership of the Cervantes Fraternal Society—leagued in a pan-ethnic federation. Each offered low-cost insurance against sickness, disability, and death; medical and dental clinics; lodges, sports teams, choruses, dance and theater groups, schools and vacation camps; and an edition of the common IWO newspaper in their language. The federation provided some protection against Depression privation, afforded an opportunity to promote labor and leftwing initiatives (without having to join the Communist Party itself), and enabled second-wave workers to preserve their respective cultures. IWO president Rockwell Kent deliberately rejected Melting-Pot-ism and embraced a Bourneian vision: the "culture of America," Kent said, was "like a tapestry, woven of brilliant colored threads, every one of which can be distinguished, and keep its own characteristics." "Americans All, Immigrants All" was very popular with International Workers Order members, who heard it on "lodge broadcasts." Attracted by this secular left alternative to church or party-based sponsorship, overall membership grew from 3,000 in 1930 to 165,000 by 1940—making it the fastest-growing mutual-benefit operation in the country.

Communists also manifested their multinationality through solidarity campaigns protesting aggression against China, Ethiopia, and the Spanish Republic and by promoting efforts by second-wave writers, playwrights, and artists to capture the experience of life in the city's eclectic ghettos. These tales told by plebeian Jewish, Irish, Italian, and African American insiders offered a corrective to outsider perspectives published by dialect writers and literary slummers in Gotham's exotic foreign quarters. Popular Front journalism—like that of the magazine *Friday*—offered articles on national and racial histories along with coverage of contemporary cultural doings (Amateur Night at the Apollo, Chinese Opera at the Canton Theatre, Jewish celebrations of Passover) and issues of ethnic concern (a story on anti-alien campaigns was headlined, in a nod to FDR, "We are all immigrants"). And Paul Robeson's concerts offered Popular Front audiences a smorgasbord of folk songs from around the world.

Robeson—artist, actor, activist as well as singer—was also the vehicle for taking Popular Front multiculturalism to the national airwaves, six months after the triumph of "Americans All," with a thunderous performance, on the same CBS network, of the ten-minute cantata *Ballad for Americans*. *Ballad* was a collaborative venture by composer Earl Robinson and lyricist John Latouche. Robinson, a Seattle-born activist and songwriter, had moved to New York in 1934 and joined the Shock Troupe of the Workers Laboratory Theatre, a mobile corps of young worker-actors (including Nicholas Ray, Clifford Odets, and Elia Kazan) who lived collectively in a one-room apartment on the Lower East Side and performed agitprop skits at rallies and strikes at wharves and factories around town. He also entered the Composers Collective of the Pierre Degeyter Club (named for the composer of the "International") along with Aaron Copland, with whom he studied at the Downtown Music School. Robinson wrote many topical songs, most famously "Joe Hill" in 1936, and in the late 1930s he led the People's Chorus at the International Workers Order. LaTouche had written for left wing cabarets sponsored by the Theatre Arts Committee, a Popular Front entertainers alliance, and had had two songs in the 1937 ILGWU hit play, *Pins and Needles*. Together they wrote a cantata, *The Ballad of Uncle Sam*, billed as a short musical history of the United States, for the WPA Federal Theater Project musical revue *Sing for Your Supper*. The show opened in the spring of 1939, but its successful run was aborted when the FTP was itself shut down.

After it closed, Robinson suggested to his friend Norman Corwin, a CBS radio writer/producer, that he might use the piece in another "sustaining" program the network was sponsoring: "The Pursuit of Happiness," a series of half-hour salutes to democracy. Corwin renamed the cantata *Ballad for Americans* and invited Robeson to sing it, which he did, on November 5, 1939, before a live audience of 600.

Robeson's narrator relates the country's history from the Revolution ("In seventy-six the sky was red / Thunder rumbling overhead / Bad King George couldn't sleep in his bed / And on that stormy morn, Ol' Uncle Sam was born. / Some birthday!") through the Civil War ("Man in white skin can never be free / While his black brother is in slavery"), and on into the twentieth century. When the chorus now asks the singer, "Who are you?...Are you an American?" Robeson replies with a paradigmatic version of the "unity in diversity" theme: "Am I an American? I'm just an Irish, Negro, Jewish, Italian, French, and English, Spanish, Russian, Chinese, Polish, Scotch, Hungarian, Litvak, Swedish, Finnish, Canadian, Greek and Turk, and Czech and double Czech American!" Then he adds: "And that ain't all. I was baptized Baptist, Methodist, Congregationalist, Lutheran, Roman Catholic, Orthodox Jewish, Presbyterian, Seventh-Day Adventist, Mormon, Quaker, Christian Scientist—and lots more," a catalog to warm the collective heart of the National Conference of Christians and Jews. After one more historical flourish, including a reference to the country's darker legacy of "murders and lynchings," Robeson rolls on to a rapturously hyperpatriotic end, a cadenza that trumpets the word "America!"

The six hundred in the studio stamped, bravoed, and shouted for the two minutes the show remained on the air, and for another fifteen minutes thereafter, while appreciative callers jammed the switchboard, a prelude to the ensuing flood of ecstatic letters. *Ballad* was repeated by popular demand on New Year's Day 1940. Robeson, backed by Robinson's working-class chorus, soon recorded it for Victor, and it soared to the top of the charts. Its rhetorical combination of ethnicity and Americanism, of radicalism and patriotism, won it a broad-based following—"it has coursed through the country like a powerful west wind," wrote critic Howard Taubman in the *Times*—becoming simultaneously an unofficial anthem of the CIO and Popular Front and a mainstream phenomenon sung everywhere from Gimbels' basement (by a chorus of Boy Scouts) to the 1940 Republican National Convention (where it served as theme song).

38

Common Ground

The new "unity in diversity" mantra wasn't home free, however. The outbreak of war afforded an opening for the balked right wing, which had been champing at the bit to restore the 100 percent Americanism of yore. John Trevor advocated a ten-year suspension of all immigration, backed a bill to create detention camps for aliens, and his New York State Chamber of Commerce Immigration Committee brought out a report, commissioned by Harry Laughlin, that urged Congress to ban entry to anyone whose ancestors were not "all members of the white or Caucasian race." Then the Fifth Column scare, which Roosevelt helped fan, eased final passage in June 1940 of the Smith Act. Its provisions mandating registration of all aliens, and authorizing deportation of those deemed too radical, gave Trevor & Co. much of what they desired. A gloomy ACLU radio address predicted "dark days ahead" for every person with a "foreign sounding name, the faintest of foreign accents, or the slightest foreign look about them."

Yet the racialized 100 percent-ism of the First World War had not, in fact, been revived. The Chamber of Commerce report proved to be Harry's last hurrah. Boas and Benedict quickly clobbered him with a pamphlet, "Science Condemns Racism," which Senator Wagner read into the Congressional Record, and the Carnegie Institution bluntly asked him to retire. Laughlin departed the last day of 1939, when the Eugenics Record Office, too, was shut down. And shortly after the Smith Act passed, Solicitor General Francis Biddle made it a point to meet with representatives of immigrant welfare groups to allay their concerns, a gathering from which the American Legion and Daughters of the American Revolution were pointedly excluded.

The right's problem was that fascism's goose-step uniformity had discredited Trevor's coercive Americanism, along with anything that smacked of Nazism, in matters small as well as large. That fall of 1940 brought an announcement from New York's superintendent of schools, Harold Campbell, that the stiffly out-thrust right arm with which Gotham's schoolchildren greeted the flag every morning "might be confused with the Nazi salute" and would henceforth be verboten. (For a time, the schools employed a hand-to-forehead salute instead, but when military men and veterans grumbled, they shifted to the right-hand-over-heart format that a Congressional Flag Code formally sanctioned two years later.)

While the "unity in diversity" flag thus remained aloft, the onset of war in Europe did lead to a heightened emphasis on "unity" and a diminished enthusiasm for "diversity." One casualty of this recalibration was Rachel DuBois. In June 1940 she wrote Leonard Covello that their approach to interculturalism was being challenged "because of the war crisis." She was right. Many liberals, even former allies, now saw her approach to cultural pluralism as part of the problem, not the solution. Some had long been concerned that separate assemblies (and radio shows) made Americans overly conscious of what divided them. But at decade's end DuBois's fundamental premise—that prejudice was based in ignorance and could be countered by information—came to seem naive. The roots of bigotry now appeared to run deeper, into the subsoil of pathology, beyond the reach of reason. And if DuBois underplayed the obduracy of intergroup antagonisms, it appeared she also underestimated intragroup complexities. Bruno Lasker, brought in to reevaluate her material in the spring of 1940, found Service Bureau representations of immigrant culture simplistic. They focused too much on high culture "contributions" deemed compatible with Anglo values, or on "folk" images that seemed little more than positive inversions of existing stereotypes. Foreign cultures, moreover, were depicted as homogeneous, lacking internal contradictions—and static, lacking capacity for change. Individuals seemed similarly frozen in time—tethered to an inherited identity, mere carriers of tradition. Kallen himself had been prone to see immigrants as over-determined by their ancestral culture—a person "cannot change his grandfather," he'd said—though in the 1930s he had come to appreciate the confining as well as the nurturant qualities of heritage.

DuBois might have proven similarly flexible, but in the hothouse atmosphere of looming war her supporters quickly melted away. Sidelined in her own Service Bureau by funderpipers calling for a new tune—DuBois attributed their animosity to her being a strong woman—she was forced to resign from the institution she'd created. Her intercultural approach was not snuffed out, however; it had far too much momentum. In 1940 the World's Fair organized a sequence of twenty-four folk festivals, one for every week of the second season, with each immigrant group in turn displaying its "contributions" at the "American Common" pavilion.

Nevertheless, leadership of the multicultural forces passed to a man who had emerged over the 1930s as one of the new immigrants' most visible spokespersons and who would now articulate the revised standard version of American identity. Louis Adamic had come through Ellis from Slovenia in 1913 at the age of fifteen and had worked his way up from the mailroom at the New York *Glas Naroda* ("The People's Voice") to becoming the paper's traveling correspondent, reporting on Slovenian settlements around the country. After army service in the First World War, Adamic settled in California, became a bohemian literary figure, sent contributions back east to the *American Mercury*, then (in 1929) returned to New York to pursue a professional writing career. In 1931 he published *Dynamite: The Story of Class Violence in America*, a timely topic given contemporary fears of bloody upheavals, and a freshly en-Nobeled Sinclair Lewis gave the book an enthusiastic boost, while Theodore Dreiser invited its author to the famous Harlan County strategy session at his Ansonia apartment. But Adamic decided to shift his focus from labor to immigrants, beginning with himself.

After bringing out *Laughing in the Jungle: The Autobiography of an Immigrant in America* in 1932, Adamic returned to Slovenia (on a Guggenheim, which Lewis helped him get), where he rediscovered his roots and wrote up the experience in *The Native's Return*. Deluged with letters from first- and second-generation readers urging him to champion their concerns, he did so in a *Harper's* article, in November 1934, called "Thirty Million New Americans." Adamic argued it was high time the United States accepted that it was not just an offshoot of the British Isles but rather of all Europe, and Africa and Asia as well. The country's roster of talismanic sites, accordingly, should be expanded to include Ellis Island as well as Plymouth Rock. Nor, he insisted, should America consider itself "something that is finished and satisfactory" but rather as "something in the process of becoming." Ethnic cultures, moreover, were the "material out of which the future has to be wrought"—a future whose "potentialities" were "immense, exciting, and inspiring." Not surprisingly, Adamic denounced (as had Bourne) anyone who would damage this immigrant material, impede this progress. In a 1936 article, he lit into the anti-alien lobby—singling out John Trevor for special excoriation—as "fascistic or near-fascistic" xenophobes who were trying "stupidly and, in the long run, futilely—to reverse history and return the country to the past."

Given such convictions, it's not surprising that Rachel DuBois found Adamic's message inspiring, or that he joined the Foreign Language Information Service during its folk festival period or served as an adviser on CBS's "Americans All, Immigrants All."

Yet Adamic also lamented the fragmentation of American life, the way it was "chopped up into numerous racial, class, and cultural islands surrounded by vague seas," and called for creation of a unified American culture. "I am for integration and homogeneity, for the disappearance of the now sharply defined, island-like groups, and the gradual organic merging of all the groups into a nation that culturally and spiritually will be a fusion of all the races and nations here." Though rhetorically this harkened back to the Melting Pot, Adamic opposed any forced or hurried Americanization. That would lead only to further alienation and heightened tensions. Ethnic enclaves, paradoxically, could foster assimilation by providing nurturant havens for newcomers to the American jungle, but only if they simultaneously facilitated self-realization. Immigrants should honor their heritage but not be bound by it, he concluded, and the country should adopt a cosmopolitan Americanism that was open to difference and change.

This was the perspective Adamic and the FLIS—which now renamed itself the Common Council for American Unity (CCAU)—took to the Carnegie Foundation in 1939. Dedicating itself to combating intolerance, the CCAU sought support for a program of "inter-cultural interpretation." Like DuBois, Adamic and his colleagues proposed to increase public appreciation for the nation's multicultural character by fostering awareness of each group's contribution. Like DuBois, they suggested this would undermine the Nazis' ability to exploit the existing "hatred against the Jew, antagonism against Germans and Italians, and other interracial prejudices which, if permitted to continue, are of special danger." But the CCAU promised to keep its emphasis on what the varied cultures shared, rather than what set them apart.

Carnegie signed on, as did the American Jewish Committee, providing the funds which, among other things, allowed the CCAU to launch a magazine, *Common Ground*, in 1940. The new quarterly, piloted by Adamic and based in New York, pledged to tell the story of the "coming and meeting on this continent" of peoples belonging to "60 different national, racial, and religious backgrounds" and to demonstrate that "Americans despite their differences shared a common ground." Indeed, only by accepting its multiplicity, by sinking "tap roots deep into its rich and varied cultural past," could the country forge "a bond of unity no totalitarian attack can break."

Thus adjusted, "unity in diversity" became a key component of liberal Americanism. In effect, it replaced the Great Seal of the United States's old motto, *E Pluribus Unum* ("From Many, One") with a new formulation, *In Uno, Plures* ("In One, Many"). Nowhere was this concept taken up with more alacrity than in its birthplace, New York City, and by no one more enthusiastically than its mayor. "New York's heterogeneous population is made up of people of almost every race, nationality and creed," La Guardia declared, yet "with all this complexity, we are united as citizens in devotion to our country and to democratic ideals." Gotham, in Fiorello's telling, was not simply the progenitor of multiculturalism, but its emblem: "New York City," boasted the Little Flower, "is more than ample proof that in this country men of many races and religion can live together in friendship and harmony."

This was, perhaps, a bit o'er hasty. Gotham had indeed managed its ethno-racial-religious antagonisms with remarkable skill. However, it was one thing to say a multicultural nirvana was desirable, another to claim it had arrived. To believe the latter one had to gloss over contemporary hostilities in much the way "Americans All" had expurgated US history.

Such was especially the case on issues of "race," a category even Boasian anthropology had left standing. It remained to be seen if "ethnics" (Italians, Slovenians, and other former "races," now "cultures") had been ushered inside an all-embracing national identity, alongside the still extant "races," or if they'd been shepherded into an expanded racial corral—the one labeled "white," formerly reserved for Anglos, Irish, and Germans—while yellow or Black Americans got shunted off to separate enclosures. Paul Robeson could have told La Guardia, from recent personal experience, that there were ample grounds for questioning his smiley-faced perspective. On New Year's Day, 1940, fresh from his triumphant performance in the second CBS broadcast of *Ballad for Americans*, the singer went to dine with a friend staying at the nearby Hotel Elysée. They had to eat in the guest's quarters, as the hostelry refused to serve Blacks in its public dining room.

Even as an ideal, the unity in diversity formula had its problems. The notion that "Americans All" could readily rise above differences of race, color, creed, and nationality muzzily ignored some hard truths: that those differences were rooted in interests, not just attitudes; that privileged groups benefitted in very material ways from prejudice and discrimination; that racism and chauvinism were deeply embedded in social, political, and economic structures and sustained by the exercise of power; and that divisions were, accordingly, not so easily transcendable as liberals imagined. Then, too, the hope that a more united society would be attained by drawing an encompassing line around those who subscribed to "American" convictions was similarly problematic. It overlooked the fact that ideological divisions could be as ferocious as cultural ones—as battles between "true" Americans and those who held "un-American" values were about to attest (indeed, the Smith Act devoted far more attention to heterodox opinions than to ethnic cultures).

For all its limitations, the new creed's repudiation of racialism and celebration of diversity was an epochal development, virtually unprecedented in US history. Because many more people saw this more inclusive American Way as worth fighting to preserve, especially if threatened by master-race fascism, it provided the basis for a pluralist patriotism. But before the unity in diversity creed could be emblazoned on banners and carried into war, liberals and leftists would have to agree that *any* war was worth fighting, an idea considered anathema through much of the 1930s, nowhere more so than in Gotham.

STUDY WAR NO MORE

Helen Allison, Marshall of the Communist Parade, leads thousands of party members at the 1933 May Day parade. In this image, they have reached 35th Street and 7th Avenue. (Bettmann / Contributor / Getty Images)

39

The Renunciator

For his Armistice Day sermon of November 1933, Harry Emerson Fosdick, pastor of Riverside Church, chose as title "The Unknown Soldier," referring to the unidentifiable remains of a First World War veteran being honored at Arlington Cemetery. In fact, Fosdick said, "I knew him well," having been with him in the trenches back in 1918, and spoken to him often. Indeed, it had been Fosdick's mission to motivate the Unknown Soldier, "to awaken his idealism," to nerve him for his "suicidal and murderous endeavor." "They sent men like me to explain to the army the high meanings of war," Fosdick recalled, "and, by every argument we could command, to strengthen their morale." And he had succeeded, all too well. Groups of valiant men, "my admonitions in their ears," charged out into No Man's Land and returned, all too soon, "the long, long hospital trains filled with their mutilated bodies."

"I lied to the Unknown Soldier," Fosdick went on. "I deceived him. I deceived myself first, unwittingly, and then I deceived him" by offering assurances that "modern war could somehow make the world safe for democracy." He had been "a gullible fool," he now realized, and his complicity and culpability—the worse for being a Christian minister—constituted "a deep self-condemnation in my heart."

The best way he could "settle my account with the Unknown Soldier," Fosdick told his Riverside parishioners, was to reject war itself, to make clear that "we can have this monstrous thing or we can have Christ but we cannot have both." Therefore, he declared, "I renounce war." "I renounce war for its consequences, for the lies it lives on and propagates, for the undying hatreds it arouses, for the dictatorships it puts in the place of democracy, for the starvation that stalks after it." "I renounce war," he swore, "and never again, directly or indirectly, will I sanction or support another!"

In rallying to a pacifist standard Fosdick was accompanied by a host of liberal Protestant clergymen in New York. Fosdick's Riverside (ecumenical, but Baptist-based) was one of Gotham's newest churches, but leaders of the city's oldest were at his side in the burgeoning no-war ranks. They included Norman Vincent Peale of the seventeenth-century (Dutch Reformed) Marble Collegiate ("The abolition of war," said Peale, "is a crusade in which the ancient genius of the Christian Church may again flourish"); William P. Merrill of the eighteenth-century Brick Presbyterian; and Allan Knight Chalmers, whose nineteenth-century (Congregational) Broadway Tabernacle, once a haven for Gotham's antislavery and women's suffrage movements, now harbored civil rights and pacifist activists. In 1934, Chalmers and Fosdick organized a Covenant of Peace Group, consisting of local clergymen who agreed that "the way of true religion cannot be reconciled with the way of war"; in 1935, 274 of them formally took Fosdick's oath of renunciation.

The Midwest is conventionally cast as a bastion of 1930s opposition to America's entering any future war. But so, too, was Gotham. Beyond the activities of specific metropolitan ministers, and the attitude of particular ethnic groups, New York hosted three nationwide peace initiatives during the decade: a Protestant-Socialist-pacifist alliance; a Communist-led antiwar front; and an assemblage of elite business groups. None were "isolationist," in the sense of suggesting the US raise its drawbridges and hunker down behind its oceanic moats. Nevertheless, the New York–based drives were at least as influential as those centered in Chicago in keeping the country on an antiwar path, even as martial temperatures rose around the planet.

40

Antiwarriors

At 115th Street, a few blocks south of Fosdick's Riverside Church, the Fellowship of Reconciliation (FOR) had its home at 2929 Broadway. Established during the First World War, FOR was now the largest pacifist organization in the United States (and perhaps in the world). Over half its estimated 10,000 members were Protestant ministers; the remainder were chiefly students, teachers, missionaries, social workers, YMCA staffers, and religiously motivated professionals. Most hewed to the Social Gospel conviction that, through concerted action by people of good will, the Kingdom of God—a Peaceable Kingdom—could be made manifest on earth.

Fosdick was an eloquent advocate for this persuasion, but FOR's highest-profile leader was John Haynes Holmes. Pastor of the Community Church of New York—another venerable Gotham institution—the Rev. Holmes had been one of FOR's founders. He was also identified with Mohandas K. Gandhi, for whom he had taken on the role of evangelist back in 1918 when he began presenting the Hindu leader to Americans as a Christianized Mahatma. "When I think of Gandhi, I think of Jesus," Holmes had averred in 1921, and since then Gandhi had assumed the status of living saint for many liberal Protestants.

Gandhi's reputation grew rapidly after his 1930 "March to the Sea" (a massive nonviolent protest against a British salt tax) and his 1931 mission to London seeking an end to colonial rule (Holmes crossed the Atlantic to visit him there). FOR leaders—spurred by Richard Gregg—began to see Gandhi not only a religious icon but as a political figure and to see his pacifism as a tool for achieving social change. Gregg, a Quaker and a Harvard-trained labor lawyer, had spent 1925–29 in India studying Gandhi's movement and on returning to the United States became its advocate. In 1933, with Roger Baldwin and others, Gregg started the American League for India's Freedom. Chaired by Holmes, it set up shop in the old Bible House on Astor Place. The following year Gregg published *The Power of Non-Violence*, a direct-action manual that FOR promoted heavily and whose tactics it would use on the sidewalks of New York.

The FOR worked closely with the Socialist Party (the SP, also housed off Union Square, at 7 East 15th Street), particularly the militant wing supporting Norman Thomas—not surprisingly, given his history. Back in 1917, the then-Presbyterian minister, seeing an "irreconcilable gulf between Christian ethics and participation in war," had left his East Harlem pulpit, become cosecretary of FOR, and signed on with the Socialists.

Socialists and Social Gospel pacifists both believed (as SP leader Charles Solomon put it) that "competitive capitalism inexorably breeds that modern imperialism which is the parent of those international frictions that cause war." This conviction was strengthened by the appearance in spring 1934 of two books—H. C. Englebrecht's *Merchants of Death* and George Seldes's *Iron, Blood and Profits*—which argued a narrower thesis: that wars were engineered by arms manufacturers seeking to drum up business. The conspiratorial notion that global conflagrations could simply be laid at the door of (in Seldes's words) "fifty men who run the munitions racket" seemed the more plausible amid District Attorney Tom Dewey's ongoing revelations about racketeering. It gained further currency during Senator Gerald Nye's probe of the munitions industry in 1934–36.

Nye, a Progressive Republican from North Dakota, set up an office in New York to investigate the role of Gotham-based arms makers (and bankers) in fostering American entry into the First World War. His committee uncovered a history of profiteering, collusive bidding, bribery of government officials, and high-voltage lobbying but rejected the notion of a plot by gun barons and bankers. Instead, Nye highlighted a more disturbing phenomenon: hundreds of prominent US corporations (and tens of thousands of workers) had been, and continued to be, deeply invested, directly or indirectly, in war-related production.

Galvanized by such analyses, and inspired by Gandhi's activism, Gotham's pacifists took to the streets to do battle—nonviolently—with the "war system."

For all their emphasis on individual renunciation of war, pacifists were equally intent on getting the government to outlaw US involvement. To mobilize the requisite political muscle, they turned to the Federal Council of Churches of Christ (FCC), housed off Union Square. As the denominations leagued in the Federal Council embraced twenty million American Protestants, the confederation proved as potent in shaping foreign affairs as it had been in influencing domestic agendas.

More immediately, the FCC pressed to rein in munitions-makers and bankers by embargoing arms sales and loans to belligerent powers. Walter W. Van Kirk, secretary of the FCC's Commission on International Justice and Good Will, took charge of this campaign. In 1934, Van Kirk published *Religion Renounces War*, which reminded politicians that large and influential denominations backed "peace policies." In May 1935, Van Kirk chaired a mass "Keep America Out of War" meeting at Carnegie Hall, cosponsored by twenty-eight peace organizations and featuring Senator Nye. Twenty-five hundred people—including Mayor La Guardia, who in welcoming Nye declared himself "pacific, if not a pacifist"—applauded the senator's call to legislate neutrality and his droll suggestion that "If Morgans and the other bankers must get into another war, let them do it by enlisting in the Foreign Legion. That's always open."

FCC leaders were thus delighted by passage of the Neutrality Act of 1935, though many were dismayed that, in practice, its provisions facilitated Mussolini's invasion of Ethiopia. They were similarly distressed when, two years later, FDR refused to block vast (and profitable) US shipments of war matériel to Japan, on the grounds that its war with China was "undeclared." Still, Gotham's Protestant-Socialist-pacifist alliance was pleased it had helped put in place a strategy for preventing war.

Pacifists were less clear about how to respond should war come, willy-nilly. Devere Allen, editor of FOR's *The World Tomorrow*, believed that workers could stop a conflict in its tracks by nonviolently refusing to manufacture or take up arms—staging a general strike for peace. Norman Thomas speculated that civil disobedience might prove more effective at defeating an actual invasion than taking up arms against it.

Reverend Holmes suggested a more fanciful approach in *If This Be Treason*, a play he cowrote that opened on Broadway at the Music Box Theatre in September 1935. Holmes's script imagined that the Japanese bombed a US naval base in the Pacific (Manila), just as the new American president, elected on a peace platform, was arriving at his Inaugural Ball. A cabal of munitions-makers, military men, and congressional jingos demanded immediate retaliation. But the president went to Japan (as Gandhi had gone to England) and roused the Japanese people against war; then he did likewise with the American people, thus curbing militarists in both countries and forcing a negotiated settlement. "From the artistic point of view it is trash," critic Brooks Atkinson acknowledged in the *Times*, but the "sheer volatility of the idea," he reported, "enkindled the imagination of the audience." The heat proved insufficient to sustain the play beyond a six-week run. Yet Holmes rejoiced at the neutrality policy authorized that year. "I count it a sign of intelligence and moral health," he told his parishioners, "that the slogan of this hour is 'Never Again.'"

41

Against War and Fascism

Communists were not pacifists. Revolutionary violence against oppressive governments was ideologically permissible; so was armed resistance to imperialist and fascist aggression. But in the early 1930s the international Communist movement came out against "war"—defined, narrowly, as what the Japanese were doing to China and what the Nazis (with tacit approval from Western democracies) might yet do to the Soviet Union.

To denounce the first and forestall the second, the Comintern initiated a World Congress Against War, held in Amsterdam in August 1932. It drew a broad spectrum of antifascists, including Christian pacifists and Socialists. Theodore Dreiser and other American participants returned home determined to forge a similar coalition in the US. In September 1933, New York hosted the founding conference of the American League against War and Fascism (ALWF). Here, too, Communists were the prime movers, but the fledgling Popular Front organization attracted Socialists, liberals, and pacifists, convinced by the fall of Manchuria and the rise of Hitler that unity was imperative. Norman Thomas showed interest, as did Adam Clayton Powell, Roger Baldwin of the ACLU, representatives from the NAACP, and individual members of peace groups such as FOR.

The smooth launch encountered choppy waters in February 1934, when Communists and Socialists (the Dubinsky-led labor wing) came to blows in Madison Square Garden. The Socialists had organized a open rally to denounce recent Austrian Fascist assaults on unionists and socialists. The Garden was all but filled when a large contingent of Communists, who had earlier demonstrated jointly with the Socialists at the Austrian Consulate on Fifth Avenue, showed up seeking entry. Allowed in but forced by YPSL ushers to check their flags and literature at the door, they jeered and booed speakers. The Dubinskyites—whose anti-Communist antipathies dated to the East Side wars of the 1920s—responded in kind. Brawls broke around the hall, chairs flew from balconies, and in the ensuing donnybrook, the Communists were ejected from the building.

In the aftermath, many socialists, pacifists, liberals, and civil rights groups, appalled by CP "hooliganism," pulled out of the ALWF. Communist chieftain Earl Browder asked Roger

Baldwin to help salvage the situation by urging Methodist minister Harry Ward to take the organization's helm. Ward, chairperson of Baldwin's ACLU, was a professor at Union Theological Seminary (UTS). A longtime activist in the labor and Social Gospel movements, he had been the main author of the 1908 Social Creed of the Churches, which had defined the FCC's domestic agenda for a generation. He continued to lead the Methodist Federation for Social Service, housed in the Methodist Building at 150 Fifth Avenue, just north of Union Square.

Ward remained a respected figure in liberal and clerical circles—though, increasingly, more for his passion than his perspicacity. In 1919 he had embraced the revolution in Russia and continued to support the Soviet regime through the 1920s—criticizing its brutal abuses and hostility to religion but believing dictatorial measures probably inevitable in a country lacking civil libertarian traditions. The Crash, Depression, and ensuing despair on the streets of New York redoubled Ward's desire to bring the Kingdom of God to Gotham and the US. A lengthy visit to Russia during 1931–32 convinced him that the seemingly depression-proof "workers state" was a viable alternative to America's crumpling capitalism. And a worthy one, too, given Ward's credulous assumption that the democratic professions in the Soviet Constitution accurately reflected Soviet reality. In 1934, Ward went so far as to declare that Stalin was no dictator. Clearly this was someone Browder could live with. Accepting the ALWF chairmanship, Ward helped make the League a vigorous antifascist and antiwar presence, one that brought together communists with progressives who, if wary of the Party, were warier still of Hitler.

Divisions on the left were better bridged by campus-based radicals, too young to harbor bitter memories of prior sectarian wars. Communist and Socialist students at New York City colleges had struck up an alliance earlier in the Depression decade, on issues of academic freedom, aid to education, and relief for youth. Now the Communist-oriented National Student League (NSL) and the Socialist-oriented Student League for Industrial Democracy (SLID) joined forces on foreign affairs. In December of 1932—galvanized by the same Amsterdam conclave that would engender the ALWF—the NSL convened a Student Congress Against War, junking the CP "social fascist" line to ensure SLID participation. Ignoring—Romeo-and-Juliet fashion—the objections of their respective party elders, they together triggered an immense antiwar uprising among students in Gotham and across the country.

The time was ripe for such an initiative. City collegians had come of age expecting another global conflagration, and in 1933 deteriorating international relations seemed to confirm their fears. As student leaders Joseph Lash and James Wechsler would put it in a popular antiwar tract: "We live next door to the executioner's block, hearing all the preparatory noises." This generation of students believed their predecessors had been lured to the killing fields by flowery speeches (as contrite clerics now admitted from their pulpits) and that the Great War had been fought for profits, not democracy (as historians now argued in their classrooms). *They* would not be similarly hornswoggled.

Peers in England steeled their resolve. On February 9, 1933, the Oxford Union—student debating society of the country's most conservative university—voted 275 to 173 that "this House will in no circumstance fight for its King and country." The renunciatory oath quickly jumped the Atlantic to New York, where an Americanized version—"We will not support the U.S. government in any war it may conduct"—was taken up by SLID members. Communist-connected NSLers opposed such indiscriminate pacifism but went along in the interests of unity, arguing that, after all, the US government would not likely make war on Hitler, a conflict they *would* support.

In 1933, therefore, opposition to war and loathing of fascism—not fighting the Depression or supporting the New Deal—were the hot issues on campus, especially at CCNY, where the overwhelming majority of the student body was Jewish. And it was into this volatile atmosphere that City College president Robinson tossed a lighted match. The fiercely antiradical Robinson's suppression of free speech had already inspired an earlier wave of student protests. Now he laid into the emerging peace movement, banning antiwar meetings, censoring antiwar literature, and on May 29, 1933, canceling classes so students could attend a military review in Lewisohn Stadium. When antiwar activists picketed what they termed the "Jingo Day" proceedings, Robinson called in police to disperse the demonstrators and personally lashed students about their heads and shoulders with his umbrella. ("ROBINSON RUNS AMOK ON CAMPUS: MADDENED PRESIDENT ATTACKS STUDENTS," ran the campus paper's headline.) He then moved to terminate the revolt, or so he thought, by suspending a score of student leaders and various student clubs.

A year later the protesters were back in force. On April 13, 1934—anniversary of American entry into the First World War—the SLID and NSL organized and jointly led a National Student Strike Against War, the largest political demonstration by college students in the history of the United States. Twenty-five thousand undergraduates (15,000 of them in Gotham alone) staged an hour-long walkout from classes during which the Oxford Pledge was administered en masse at rallies dotted with banners reading "No, We Won't Go," "Schools, not Battleships," and "Abolish the ROTC." CCNY, Columbia, Hunter, and Brooklyn again took the lead but now were joined by students at Harvard, Vassar, Johns Hopkins, and Chicago.

Robinson—an incorrigible provocateur—riposted in October by summoning students to CCNY's Great Hall to honor an official delegation of students from fascist Italy. Radicals heckled Robinson. He denounced them as "guttersnipes." The student body president made moderate antifascist remarks. Members of the City College Italian Club rushed the stage to assault him. Radicals jumped to defend him. A full-scale riot ensued, after which Robinson expelled another twenty-one student leaders and dissolved the Student Council. NSL and SLID countered with a massive demonstration in November, at which thousands of students sported buttons reading: "I am a Guttersnipe—I Fight Fascism."

The button that students wore at City College to protest President Robinson's comments and the ensuing response. (Robert F. Wagner Labor Archives Button and Pin Collection at Tamiment Library, New York University)

The next year's "Strike for Peace," in April 1935, spread to 150 campuses across the country and drew 175,000 students out of classes to rallies demanding passage of neutrality legislation. In New York, 20,000 participated. At Columbia, nearly 3,000 students gathered on South Field to cheer history professor Harry J. Carman's call to spread "the anti-war gospel." At CCNY, 3,500 jammed into the Great Hall and booed Robinson when he objected, unsuccessfully, to a reading of the Oxford Pledge. Forty-five hundred demonstrated at NYU's two campuses, and 6,000 turned out at Brooklyn College. A nationwide *Literary Digest* poll of 65,000 college students found that 81 percent would not bear arms for the US if its forces invaded another country.

In December 1935 the NSL and SLID followed up their triumph by merging into an American Student Union (ASU), achieving a degree of unity far transcending that on the adult left. Joe Lash (ignoring Norman Thomas's displeasure) became the ASU's executive secretary. Former NSLer James Wechsler ran its national magazine, whose first issue, in February 1936, featured an interview with Senator Nye and a story on war profiteering entitled "Morgan: Wanted for Murder."

42

Peace Crusade

Ironically, Morgan chieftain Thomas Lamont, increasingly disillusioned with his bellicose Japanese and Italian clients, had become a participant in the third Gotham-based peace movement—the conservative wing headed up by the Carnegie Endowment for International Peace. Like its predecessors dating back to the New York Peace Society of 1815, the Carnegie Endowment was run by internationally minded merchants, lawyers, financiers, philanthropists, and academics who were convinced that war—all things considered—was bad for business. These peacemakers were content with the domestic status quo—unlike radical antiwarriors who insisted that peace abroad demanded change at home—but were keen to rearrange the global order.

Led by Columbia University president Nicholas Murray Butler, who had succeeded Elihu Root at the helm in 1925, the Carnegie Endowment in the early 1930s opposed narrow economic nationalism, stressed the interdependence of all countries, urged a lowering of trade barriers, and sought legal and judicial mechanisms to resolve disputes. In urging that international organizations be strengthened—a sharp divergence from isolationist strategy—the Endowment paralleled the approach (and overlapped the membership) of several other New York–based organizations. Lamont, for example was a member of both the Carnegie Endowment and the League of Nations Association (LNA), piloted by Clark Eichelberger and Columbia historian James T. Shotwell. The LNA, in turn, had made common cause with the World Peace Foundation and the Foreign Policy Association, establishing a common office at 8 West 40th Street, across from the New York Public Library. All shared a reliance on genteel tactics—holding conferences, establishing international relations clubs, and high-minded speechifying—aimed at fostering an informed public opinion that would in turn promote sensible governmental policies.

A major priority for this phalanx of elite pacifists was winning ratification of American membership in the World Court, and they were accordingly jolted when in January 1935, the Senate refused to do this, bowing instead to the mass opposition stirred up by Father Coughlin and William Randolph Hearst. The thwarted conservative paladins gathered that

April at a black-tie dinner in President Butler's Morningside residence, to consider ways of directing public opinion into the "true channel of international cooperation." Shotwell proposed mobilizing a national coalition of chambers of commerce and professional associations—their natural constituency—but Eichelberger proposed a more daring strategy of allying with the liberal pacifist groups already in the field. Negotiations at a Columbia University sit-down of forty-four representatives from the conservative Carnegie wing (like Butler, Shotwell, and Eichelberger) and the liberal-Protestant wing (such as John Nevin Sayre and Walter Van Kirk) hammered out a framework for working together.

In December 1935, a National Peace Conference (NPC) was established in New York City, formally bringing together thirty groups active in war prevention. The NPC was installed in an office (underwritten by a Carnegie grant) located in the emerging Midtown peace complex at 8 West 40th. The umbrella organization's members included the Federal Council of Churches—the FCC's Van Kirk was named director—along with WILPF, the Carnegie Endowment, the League of Nations Association, American Friends Service Committee, Committee on Militarism in Education, Institute of International Education, and various faith-based groups, ranging from the Central Conference of American Rabbis and National Council of Jewish Women to the YMCA and WCTU.

Also in December, a three-day conference of over 100 conservative and liberal pacifist leaders authorized launching an Emergency Peace Campaign, a two-year nationwide educational initiative that would combine the resources of peace organizations, religious bodies, civic groups, and trade unions in a massive pacifist push.

On April 22, 1936, the same day Fosdick kicked off the Emergency Peace Campaign (EPC) with a mass meeting at Carnegie Hall, the ASU oversaw the largest student strike ever. Some 500,000 youths, including almost half the country's undergraduates, left class to rally against war. New Yorkers again took the lead. The largest single gathering was the throng of over 5,000, from six campuses, at Brooklyn's Borough Hall, but the most eye- (and press-) catching event was staged on Morningside Heights. Three thousand students from Columbia, Barnard, Teachers College, Union Theological, and Jewish Theological marched along Broadway, led by a crutch-twirling drum major, followed by a contingent of Barnard women dressed as widows carrying doll "war orphans," and 200 members of the William Randolph Hearst Post Number One of the Veterans of Future Wars. All then repaired to Columbia's South Field, where they together took the Oxford Pledge.

During that summer and fall the Emergency Peace Campaign arranged over a thousand antiwar events in cities throughout the country, many of them politically ecumenical, like the symposium that drew 2,000 to St. Nicholas Arena (66th Street near Columbus Avenue) to hear an array of speakers that ranged from Earl Browder and Norman Thomas to John Haynes Holmes and Clark Eichelberger. In 1937, the EPC mounted a "Neutrality Campaign" from January through March and followed this with a "No-Foreign-War Crusade" launched on April 6 with network radio addresses by Fosdick in New York and Eleanor Roosevelt in the White House—mobilizations that helped win passage of the Neutrality Act of 1937.

Yet even as the massed pacifist legions achieved their most spectacular triumph, their constituent forces were peeling off in different directions, responding in very different ways to the mega disturbances breaking out around the world, notably the Spanish Civil War.

43

Unpopular Fronts

The CPUSA's pacifism evaporated completely during the Spanish conflict, though Socialists remained ambivalent about armed response. There was no disagreement over resolutely backing the Republic: within days of Franco's uprising, the SP joined the CP in mounting pro-Loyalist demonstrations in Union Square. But the New York local's call for creation of a Eugene V. Debs Column—Socialist counterpart of the Lincoln Brigade—brought vigorous dissents. John Haynes Holmes, appalled to see socialism made "identical with militarism," said that using Debs's name "for this bloody business fills me with a horror which is indescribable." The Fellowship of Reconciliation, too, deplored the Debs Column, as did Jessie Hughan of the War Resisters League. The staunchly pacifist Devere Allen, however, countered that the fighting in Spain was not a war, to be resisted, but an effort by the country's legitimate government to suppress an illegal rebellion, which should be supported. Norman Thomas agreed that the "powerful Socialist arguments against participation in international war" do not apply to armed defense of a workers republic against Fascist counterrevolutionaries. Socialists "will not yield to fascism anywhere without a struggle," Thomas declared, as "nonviolence is not its first and last commandment."

The student movement also fissured over fighting in Spain. Communists in the American Student Union (ASU) called for abandoning the Oxford Pledge and backing collective security, even American rearmament. Socialist and pacifist collegians were more reluctant to change course, though the heroism of student brigadistas captured the imagination of key leaders such as Joe Lash. Turnout for the April 1937 "peace strike" was enormous, but its meaning was ambiguous. As least 500,000, perhaps a million, participated in nationwide "assemblies for peace," including a substantial number of high school students (90,000 turned out in New York City alone, from public institutions like Stuyvesant and Washington Irving, and private ones such as Lincoln, Birch Wathen, Walden, and Dalton). But if some gatherings focused on peace, others called for backing the Loyalists; many did both at once. In May, even a Randall's Island rally of 6,000 youthful pacifists was rocked by chants of "¡No Pasaran!"—the antifascist cry of "they shall not pass." And in December, delegates to the ASU convention voted nearly 3–1 to drop the Oxford Oath, boycott Japanese goods, and reverse their call (issued the previous year) for students to refuse military service outside US borders. Still, it's likely that the ongoing Socialist attachment to pacifism accounts for the failure of the Debs Column to attract more than a handful of recruits.

Whatever their disagreements about the legitimacy (or advisability) of armed resistance, New York Communists, Socialists, progressives, and liberals threw themselves fervently—and with rare unanimity—into providing material and political support to the beleaguered Spanish Republic.

The League of American Writers (LAW) doubled in size by early 1937, attracting many prestigious progressives, who replaced Communists in positions of public leadership. Spain dominated LAW gatherings like the June 1937 Second American Writers Congress, held in Carnegie Hall, at which Ernest Hemingway delivered his first-ever public address ("Fascism Is a Lie"). He also screened snippets of *The Spanish Earth*, a documentary on the Iberian situation directed by Joris Ivens, a Dutch Communist filmmaker, narrated by Hemingway, scored by Marc Blitzstein and Virgil Thomson, and financed by a group of writers (including Lillian Hellman, John Dos Passos, and Archibald MacLeish) who called themselves the "Contemporary Historians." The film received a rapturous response from the standing-room-only crowd. (Though not everyone was swept away: Dawn Powell reported that "Ernest gave a good speech if that's what you like and his sum total was that war was pretty nice and a lot better than sitting around a hot hall and writers ought to all go to war and get killed and if they didn't they were a big sissy. Then he went to the Stork Club, followed by a pack of foxes.")

An advertisement from the American Medical Bureau and North American Committee to Aid Spanish Democracy on the back cover of *Direction* 1, no. 2 (March 1939). (PD-US-not renewed, McMaster University)

The conflict also engendered new front groups, tailored to the moment's needs. Quickest off the mark was the North American Committee to Aid Spanish Democracy (NAC), based at 149 Fifth Avenue, a few blocks north of Union Square. Launched in October 1936, the Committee was chaired by Bishop Francis J. McConnell—like Harry Ward, a pillar of Social Gospel Methodism. (McConnell, whose Silver Anniversary as Bishop was celebrated at Carnegie Hall in October 1937 by 3,000 clergy and laity, was also superintendent of the New York area, president of the Methodist Board of Foreign Missions, and former head of the Federal Council of Churches.) The Committee's rank-and-file backbone, however, was drawn from the CPUSA and the SP, and from other front groups like the ALPD and ASU. The NAC opened a warehouse at 832 Broadway, just south of Union Square, and set about filling it with canned goods, clothing, and medical supplies. Young leftists drove trucks around the city picking up donated materials or took to the streets to raise money. In Times Square, the young soprano Ethel Rosenberg sang "Tango de las Rosas" and "Ay-ay-ay," while her husband, Julius, and friends held up four corners of the Spanish Republican flag, into which passersby tossed coins and bills.

More remunerative were the benefits arranged by the NAC at venues such as Carnegie Hall by the Musicians' Committee to Aid Spanish Democracy. An NAC affiliate, chaired by Pablo Casals, Musicians' Committee sponsors included Aaron Copland, Virgil Thomson, Morton Gould, Sol Hurok, and Marc Blitzstein. Gotham's jazz community also turned out for the cause: Duke Ellington and John Hammond joined the Musicians' Committee, and Benny Goodman, Cab Calloway, Fats Waller, Count Basie, W. C. Handy, Noble Sissle, and

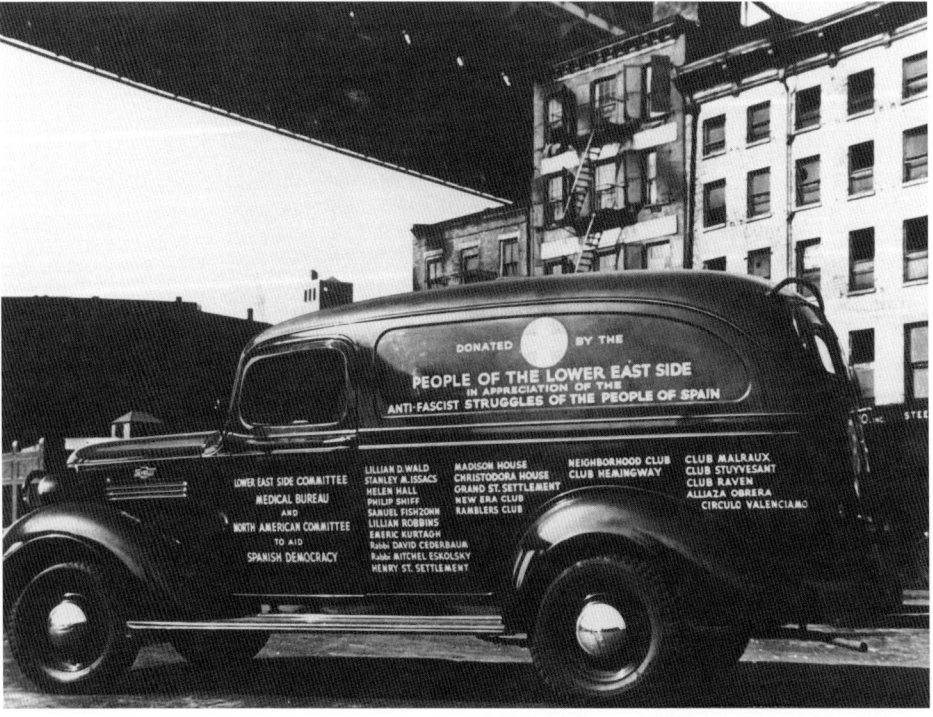

An ambulance used by the American Medical Bureau and North American Committee to Aid Spanish Democracy, c. 1930s. (Album/Science Source/Photo Researchers)

Eubie Blake all played benefit concerts. So did the city's modern dancers: in January 1938 five companies, including those of Martha Graham and Anna Sokolow, joined in a huge fundraising performance at the Hippodrome. Such revenue streams allowed the NAC, within six months of its inception, to ship 500,000 pounds of food to Spain.

Those progressives, liberals, and unionists who remained wary of the CPUSA established independent groups. Roger Baldwin, John Dewey, and Franz Boas were among the founders or supporters of the American Friends of Spanish Democracy which, in November 1936, set up a Medical Bureau to assemble supplies and personnel. In January 1937, Dewey chaired a mass meeting in Madison Square Garden at which four ambulances, intended to succor Madrid's defenders, were presented to the Spanish ambassador. David Dubinsky helped establish Trade Union Relief for Spain—with a goal of raising $100,000 for labor and socialist forces in Spain—and CIO unions sent more than 110 tons of materiel across the Atlantic. A more clandestine gesture came from Gerald O'Reilly, a Clan na Gael man who had helped found the Transit Workers Union and who now arranged a transfer to the Loyalists of arms originally obtained for the IRA.

Overlapping these efforts were those of Gotham's Spanish-speaking community.

44

Spanish New Yorkers

Roughly 200,000 strong, New York's "Hispanos" (the era's descriptive term of choice) were predominantly Puerto Rican but included a substantial representation of Cubans, and perhaps 25,000 Spaniards from such regions as Andalucía, Asturias, Catalonia, Galicia, and the Basque Country. Hispanos congregated in upper Manhattan (East Harlem, Washington Heights); along the East River waterfronts (from Red Hook to the Navy Yard in Brooklyn, and, in Manhattan, at the foot of the Brooklyn Bridge, around Cherry and Roosevelt Streets); in parts of the Bronx; and around such Little Spain survivors as the Church of Our Lady of Guadalupe (1902) and La Nacional (1868), the leading Spanish benevolent society, both situated on 14th Street between 7th and 8th Avenues.

In the mid-1930s, these barrios were aboil with pro-Loyalist activities. Soccer matches, dances, picnics, excursions to the countryside, and fiestas in Bath Beach's Ulmer Park—all doubled as Republican fundraisers; and East Harlem's Spanish-language theater/cinemas (the *Hispano*, the *Granada*, and the *Latino*) screened documentaries about the fighting. Dozens of organizations took part. Many were emigrant mutual aid societies rooted in particular regions of Spain. Others were larger umbrella associations that had coalesced during the Depression, like the Sociedad Española de Socorros Mutuos (1929), popularly known by the name of "La Nacional," its oldest constituent institution. Leftist Hispano groups were in the field, too: in Washington Heights, the Club Cubano Julio Antonio Mella (named for a founder of the Cuban Communist Party); in the Bronx, the Grupo Antifascista del Bronx and the CPUSA's José Díaz Branch (after a Spanish Communist leader); in Queens, the Frente Popular Español; and throughout the city, ten Spanish-speaking lodges of the International Workers Order, confederated in the Sociedad Fraternal Cervantes, led by Jesus Colon. During the conflict, moreover, many of these associations banded together to form the Sociedades Hispanas Confederadas, which in 1937 established a newspaper, *Frente Popular*, that, together with another new periodical, *La Voz*, reported on pro-Loyalist initiatives. The Sociedades Hispanas Confederadas also organized citywide rallies in Madison Square Garden, and the money raised under its auspices ran second only to the sums raised by the North American Committee.

Franco was not without supporters in New York, however, particularly among resident Spaniards and the upper echelons of Spanish–American shipping and commerce. Marcelino Garcia and Manuel Diaz, heads of a mercantile firm at 17 Battery Place, were dominant figures at the January 1937 gathering (at the Alhambra Coffee House on Stone Street) that organized the Casa de España (House of Spain). The first US affiliate of the Falange Exterior, the Casa was headquartered in the Park Central Hotel at Seventh Avenue and 56th Street, its office dominated by a large painting of Franco. (The venue came courtesy of Tomas Collado, a Park Central manager and brother of Casa influential Benito Collado, owner of El Chico, a Greenwich Village nightclub, and a leading promoter of the rhumba in Gotham). Here the Casa's 700-plus members gathered for fundraising dinners, forums, dances, and music recitals, and to hear lecturers expound on Franco's virtues; speakers were also dispatched, in an ecumenical gesture, to address Christian Front meetings.

The Casa de Espana stayed in close touch with Franco's official representative, Juan F. Cárdenas, housed nearby in the Ritz Carlton, who in turn received instructions from Spain via the Italian Consulate; the Park Central also accommodated Falange agents in transit to Latin America. Nevertheless, Spain wanted an even more pliable instrument in Gotham, and an organizer was dispatched to establish a New York Falange (under the less jarring name of Club Isabel y Fernando). Most Casa members quickly signed up but, with equal promptness, headed for the exits after a visiting Falangist informed them that members were expected to return to Spain and bear arms. In 1938 Falange headquarters sent their man in Havana up north to whip New Yorkers into shape; he quickly realized that a full blue-shirted Fascist operation in Gotham (on the Latin American model) was a nonstarter and, after an extensive tour of New York's brothels, headed back to Cuba.

Another Casa de Espana leader, Dr. Ramon Castroviejo, an eminent New York ophthalmologist, urged Spain to stick to establishing propaganda outlets. These were badly needed, he explained, because apart from supportive Catholic organs like the *Brooklyn Tablet* and the Jesuits' *America*, pro-Franco news was blocked by "the diabolic work" of the city's "Jewish press." (He might have added that the Hispano press was an equally unreliable read: when the managing editor of *La Prensa* came out for Franco in 1936, he was quickly forced to step down by the paper's Loyalist publisher.) Spain heeded Castroviejo's advice and, copying German and Italian initiatives, set up or subsidized a Peninsular News Service; *Spain*, a monthly magazine; and *Cara al Sol*, a weekly named for the Falangist anthem. Despite a *Cara al Sol* boast that local missionary activities had produced a growing number of "bent knees for the triumph of Franco," the more clearheaded Castroviejo reported that in Gotham's Spanish colony "supporters of our movement could be counted on the fingers of one hand."

And indeed, as the war dragged on, the Republican cause garnered ever more adherents in and beyond the Hispano communities. After Guernica, the North American Congress pulled together seventy-six high-profile figures in religion, education, politics, and business—including Senator Wagner, Bishop Manning, Rabbi Wise, Reverend Fosdick, Lillian Wald, Congresswoman Caroline O'Day, and former secretary of state Henry Stimson—to sign a letter of "overwhelming protest" ("We denounce the monstrous crime..."). After the Spanish Catholic prelates issued their pastoral letter backing Franco, the NAC published a rebuttal—*American Democracy vs the Spanish Hierarchy*—signed by 149 clergymen, educators, and laymen, including Ruth Benedict, Franz Boas, George Counts, John Dewey, Stephen Duggan, John Haynes Holmes, Harry Ward, and Harry Emerson Fosdick (who, privately, found the pastoral letter to be "one of the most vicious bits of propaganda for fascism ever issued in this country"). For sheer quantity, however, nothing topped the League of American Writers' 1938 pamphlet, *Writers Take Sides*, in whose pages 410 literary lights declared their solidarity with the Loyalists.

Yet for all their massed numbers, New York *prominenti* were unable to attain their overriding goal: getting Franklin Roosevelt to reverse the embargo he had imposed on Spain. When the insurgency first broke out, nothing in international law or historical American practice dictated denying a legitimate government, recognized by the United States, the right to import whatever it needed to defend itself against an illegal rebellion. Nor did the 1935 Neutrality Act apply to civil wars. At first, therefore, FDR only declared another "moral" embargo on arms and war matériel.

Then, in December 1936, one Robert Cuse, a Jersey City–based used aircraft dealer, applied for a license to export nearly $3,000,000 worth of planes and used parts to the Republic. Given existing law, the government found itself obliged to issue the permit, and Cuse began loading crated airplanes onto the Spanish steamer *Mar Cantabrico*, berthed at Pier 35 in the Atlantic Basin. Roosevelt, determined to frustrate its departure, acted quickly. On January 6, 1937, he sent a message to Congress requesting the Neutrality Act be extended to cover "the unfortunate civil strife in Spain." Two days later Congress passed a resolution to this effect, which FDR signed immediately, though not before the *Mar Cantabrico* had slipped its moorings and—trailed by Coast Guard ships and planes awaiting legal authorization to detain it—raced to the open sea. It would be the last shipment of arms to leave the harbor, and the *Mar Cantabrico* itself would never deliver its goods. After departing New York, the ship proceeded to Veracruz, picked up more war supplies, and sailed for Spain, only to be captured by a Franquista cruiser. Diplomatic circles in London, seconded by Senator Nye, claimed that agents of Garcia and Diaz, the Casa de España leaders, had passed along information detailing the ship's route to Franco's agents in the Ritz Carlton.

Franco hailed FDR's embargo. The Germans were equally loud in their praise. So were US Catholic spokesmen and some Protestant pacifists. The New York Left, infuriated, set out to reverse the ban. Speakers bitterly assailed it at packed Madison Square Garden rallies. Norman Thomas visited Roosevelt at the White House and told him that as the rebels were being supplied by the Germans and Italians, the US should embargo the Fascist regimes as well. Roosevelt refused, telling Thomas that would lead to American involvement in a conflict "from which our people desire so deeply to remain aloof."

As the Republic's military fortunes waned, its increasingly desperate New York supporters redoubled their pressure. The NAC held "Lift the Embargo on Spain" mass meetings and arranged parades on Broadway. The American Friends of Spanish Democracy circulated petitions among civic leaders calling for a change of course. Thousands of Protestant and Jewish clergymen telegraphed that message to FDR. In January 1939, with the Republic on the ropes, the demonstrations, motorcades, and petition drives escalated. When a Father Coughlin radio appeal to Keep the Embargo generated 100,000 telegrams to the White House, an NAC-organized counteroffensive generated 250,000 missives to Washington. A Gallup poll now found a majority of Americans backing the Republic, where a year before 67 percent had favored neutrality.

Eleanor added to the pressure on Franklin. The First Lady's commitment to the Loyalist cause was fervent and upfront. "I am not neutral in feeling," she declared, "I believe in Democracy and the right of a people to choose their own government without having it imposed on them by Hitler and Mussolini." Her close friend, war correspondent Martha Gellhorn, kept her apprised of developments. Haunted by Guernica, ER wrote anguished columns against the bombings and atrocities and arranged for Loyalist supporters to lobby her husband. In July 1937, she invited Gellhorn, Gellhorn's lover, Hemingway, and Joris Ivens to the White House for a private screening of *The Spanish Earth*, previewed a month earlier in New York. Roosevelt was riveted but remained unwilling to alienate either the Catholic, Protestant-pacifist, or isolationist vote. He was determined to avoid the kind of war that had overwhelmed Woodrow Wilson and his domestic agenda. Madrid fell on March 28, 1939. Roosevelt recognized the Franco regime five days later.

New Yorkers now took up the task of rescuing Spanish Republicans from Franco's victorious forces. The fascists began executing tens of thousands of civilians, determined to secure their rule by wholesale terror. A quarter million Loyalists fled to exile in France, where they languished in hastily set-up and disease-infested internment camps. The North American Committee organized a Spanish Refugee Relief Campaign (SRRC) to raise money for relocating them, chiefly (given US immigration restrictions) to Mexico and Latin America. By October, clothing and blankets were pouring into the SRRC warehouse at 175 Greene Street, and plans were under way for chartering rescue ships.

Some refugees didn't wait and stowed away on New York–bound ships. In May 1939, ten such were caught when it was discovered that crew members on the *Oriente* and *Yucatan*, liners of the New York and Cuba Mail Steamship Company, had secreted them away below decks. Others got through and melted into the local Hispano communities. Others still became highly visible and vocal members of the local Loyalist community and helped establish New York as an ongoing base of resistance to the Franco regime. Jesus Gonzalez Malo, a Spanish longshoreman and union organizer from Santander, arrived in 1940 and became editor of *España Libre*, which succeeded *Frente Popular* as the monthly paper of New York's Confederated Spanish Societies.

Gotham's most famous refugee was a painting. In June 1937, little more than a month after the bombing of Guernica, Picasso had displayed his huge allegorical canvas of the same name in the Spanish Pavilion at the Paris International Exposition, to great and growing acclaim. The Spanish Refugee Relief Campaign invited the artist to send *Guernica* on a US tour to raise funds for those suffering in the camps of southern France. Picasso agreed, and, three weeks after the fall of Madrid, the unstretched painting was crated up and dispatched to New York on the *Normandie*. Hoving into the harbor on May Day 1939, its art cargo was picked up at the 48th Street pier by a guard of student volunteers.

Responsibility for its exhibition was assigned to the American Artists' Congress against War and Fascism, another CP-sponsored Popular Front group, which in turn handed over control to art dealer Sidney Janis, who arranged a showing at Valentine Dudensing's spacious new Valentine Gallery at 16 East 57th. Dudensing, like MOMA's Alfred Barr, had been a New York promoter of Picasso's work since the early 1930s.

Preview night on May 4 was a glittering event, not surprisingly, given a sponsoring committee that included Eleanor Roosevelt, Mayor La Guardia, Ernest Hemingway, Georgia O'Keeffe, Mrs. Simon Guggenheim, Mrs. Averell Harriman, Mrs. Thomas Lamont, and Mr. and Mrs. William Paley. Over the next three weeks 2,000 people came to see *Guernica*, among them American artists like the relatively unknown Arshile Gorky (who was mesmerized by the work). Then it was taken out for a tour around the continent, returning in November to join *Demoiselles d'Avignon* and *Girl Before a Mirror* as a costar of Barr's Picasso retrospective. New York went Picasso mad. Over 60,000 attended the MOMA blockbuster. Bonwit Teller and Bergdorf Goodman dressed their windows with Picasso-inspired clothes. By then, war had broken out, and it was agreed that MOMA would take charge of *Guernica* until the time was right for its return to Spain (which would not come until 1981, with the end of Franco's fascist regime).

45

Partisan Views

The collapse of Spain precipitated the collapse of the Popular Front. The fight for the Republic had held together an increasingly fractious coalition of liberals, progressives, socialists, and communists, divided not only by ideology but by social and generational rivalries. Now the army of New York intellectuals and political activists that had mobilized against Franco split into contending legions, which proceeded to battle one another in the city's meeting halls, coffee shops, and editorial offices. A central issue in the swirling debates was the legitimacy of the Communist Party, which, for all the kudos it had garnered fighting the Depression at home and fascism abroad, had undermined its appeal by supporting Soviet actions many found incomprehensible or reprehensible.

In December 1934, Sergei Kirov, chief of the Leningrad Communist Party, had been assassinated, then given a hero's burial by Stalin, who falsely blamed the murder on old Bolshevik rivals and used it to justify a wave of summary arrests and secret "trials," followed swiftly by executions. The Kirov affair proved a mere curtain raiser to a sequence of four show trials, staged in Moscow between 1936 and 1938, in which virtually all living leaders of the Russian Revolution, together with many of the Red Army's general staff, were dragged to the dock and charged with conspiracy to murder Stalin, overthrow the Soviet regime, dismember the country, and re-establish capitalism—all at the behest of archfiend Leon Trotsky, in conjunction, no less, with German and Japanese fascism. Astonishingly, the Old Bolsheviks abjectly confessed themselves guilty of sabotage and treason and were executed, with countless others, during the ensuing bloody purges.

In New York, the CPUSA—officially—backed Stalin one hundred percent. Chairman Earl Browder, in full "Communism as 20th Century Americanism" mode, denounced Trotsky as an Aaron Burr, Benedict Arnold, and Jeff Davis all rolled into one. In February 1937, before 15,000 party faithful in Madison Square Garden, Browder urged Stalin to use "iron hands" to wipe out "Trotskyism and all other enemies of the Soviet Union." "Exterminating the agents of fascism," he declared, was a signal service to "progressive humanity."

Unofficially, however, many party intellectuals were severely shaken by the Moscow Trials, especially recent converts like Granville Hicks, literary editor of the *New Masses*, but

Marines practice the "Abandon Ship!" at the Sheepshead Bay Marine Service Training Station. (Library of Congress, Prints and Photographs Division, Farm Security Administration - Office of War Information photograph collection.)

also old stalwarts like Mike Gold and Joseph Freeman. The purges were a patently lose–lose proposition: either all Lenin's closest colleagues were traitors or Stalin was a monster, using terror to consolidate a personal dictatorship. Most quashed their doubts and soldiered on, convinced the Revolution's achievements were still worth defending. But with zero evidence to prove the defendants' guilt (apart from the incredible confessions), they were reduced to justifying the trials with lame formulations like Gold's 1937 syllogism: the "Soviet system is indivisible"; "Soviet nurseries, libraries, and schools are a sound development"; therefore, "Soviet justice must be as sound."

Some progressives in New York bought this line, notably Corliss Lamont, son of super-banker Thomas Lamont, head of J. P. Morgan. In an instance of generational revolt not altogether uncommon in the annals of New York radicalism, young Lamont, after graduate studies at Columbia and a revelatory trip to the Soviet Union, had switched allegiance from capitalism to communism. Though he never actually joined the Party, Lamont became an ardent and supremely uncritical advocate. Chairing the New York–based Friends of the Soviet Union (which put out a glossy called *Soviet Russia Today*), he zealously defended the trials on Gold's grounds—that Soviet justice just couldn't be out of step with Soviet accomplishments in other fields.

Few progressives supported the verdicts so wholeheartedly. Most were privately wracked by confusion and doubt. Yet they were unwilling to admit their reservations publicly and instead temporized or rationalized or apologized. *Some* flames must be flickering under all that smoke, they argued—the self-confessed defendants must be guilty of *something*—an assessment encouraged by seemingly authoritative reportage from the likes of Walter Duranty, Pulitzer Prize–winning Moscow correspondent of the *New York Times*. Or perhaps the trials *were* a bad business, but that was only to be expected, and more-or-less excused, as the Soviet Union had inherited the Czarist anti-libertarian tradition. Some progressives did dissent—among them Waldo Frank, chairman of the League of American Writers and a close ally of the party—only to retreat when fiercely attacked by Comrade Browder.

Nonetheless the main reason so many progressives went along with the verdicts was that Stalin was aiding the Spanish Republic, and no one else was. The purge trials were distant, blurry, and nothing Americans could do much about; the horrors in Spain were vivid and contestable. If Stalin was evil, he was the lesser one. If staying silent about the trials was necessary to hold the antifascist front together, they would keep mum. What they would *not* do was continue to hail Soviet domestic accomplishments—happy talk about Russia rapidly evaporated from venues like *The Nation* and *New Republic*—apart from approval for Stalin's antifascism.

For New York's liberals, however, the trials raised profound questions about the Soviet Union's antifascist credentials. They were struck, as early as 1934, by the similarities between Stalin's Kirov purge and that of Hitler against the "radical Nazis" (what the Führer himself called the "Night of the Long Knives"). The Kirov affair, said Oswald Garrison Villard of *The Nation*, "lowers the Soviet leaders to the level of Adolf Hitler." Horace Kallen, old opponent of anyone—be they Fascists or 100 percent Americanizers—who imposed unity on a plural populace, now accused Communists of that sin. Resigning from the National Committee for the Defense of Political Prisoners, Kallen attacked that front group's failure to denounce Stalin's secret trials and executions. "No true friend of the Soviet experiment," he said, "can without protest pass over conduct by the Russian government which he condemns when it is German, Italian, Polish or Spanish." The Reverend Holmes had argued—up till 1935—that for all their missteps the Bolsheviks were essentially marching forward, while Hitler was dragging Germany backward to barbarism. Now he declared: "I am unwilling to condemn ghastly horrors in Nazi Germany, and denounce dreadful crimes in my own country, and then remain silent when I see these horrors and crimes or even worse, being perpetrated in Russia." In February 1935 Holmes joined Roger Baldwin, John Dewey, George Counts, and others—Corliss Lamont excoriated them all as "wavering New York liberals"—in signing an open letter, saying they had kept silent previously so as not "to give aid and comfort to the reactionary opponents of the Soviet Union" but that now the civil liberty issue superseded that concern.

New York City socialists—longtime critics of the CPUSA, of course—agreed completely. Social Democrats like David Dubinsky said the trials reflected the undemocratic nature of communism, and their *New Leader* became a locus of anti-Soviet criticism. Dubinsky's old rival, Socialist Party leader Norman Thomas, was in full accord, arguing in 1938 that Stalin seemed the "successor not of Lenin but of Ivan the Terrible"; there was no hope for socialism, Thomas warned, unless it divorced itself from everything the trials stood for.

Organized Trotskyists, of course, rejected the trials' in absentia death sentence against their hero and presented the purges as prima facie evidence of Stalin's betrayal of the Revolution. The trials also helped midwife a new circle of radical young New York intellectuals who, influenced by Trotsky and appalled by his fate, broke what affiliations they had with the CPUSA (which they labeled a "Stalinist" entity), without signing on as official Trotskyists. Instead they set up a third camp of dissident Marxists, critical alike of American capitalism and Russian-style communism.

This "anti-Stalinist" circle was hardly a formal affair, more a network of friends and associates. Many were products of Gotham's outer-borough plebeian Jewish neighborhoods, graduates of the city's public schools, and habitués of its public libraries, though a significant segment hailed from other regions, and other religions, making this a cosmopolitan coterie. Most aspired to join the ranks of elite Manhattan writers, critics, and educators but were not yet well known—people such as Philip Rahv, William Phillips, Lionel Trilling, Meyer Schapiro, Elliot Cohen, Mary McCarthy, Herbert Solow, Fred Dupee, and Dwight Macdonald, among others. It would be Rahv and Phillips who would provide the network an institutional nucleus.

Rahv, né Ivan Greenberg, was born in Ukraine in 1908 to shopkeeper Zionist parents who fled poverty and pogroms and moved repeatedly until finally settling in Palestine in 1924. Rahv moved again, to Portland, Oregon, where he wrote ad copy (and taught Hebrew classes on the side) until, with the onset of the Depression, he lost that job and was unable to find another. In 1932 he relocated to New York, where he lived in bottom-scraping poverty—standing on breadlines, sleeping on Central Park benches—but also embarked on a passionate self-education program (and kept warm) by spending his days at the New York Public Library, steeping himself in Dostoyevsky, Henry James, and Marx. He joined the CPUSA, adopted a new surname—the Hebrew word (Rav) for "rabbi" or "teacher"—and plunged into the worker-literature movement. "We, the young writers...trudging the streets in search of employment," he wrote in Jack Conroy's *The Rebel Poet* in September 1932, had to identify "with the class-conscious proletariat." Rahv sent Joseph Freeman an unsolicited article for the *New Masses*, and Freeman encouraged the "obscure boy in the Bronx" to submit more. He began writing pieces (on Maxim Gorky, T. S. Eliot, F. Scott Fitzgerald) for the *Little Magazine*, the *Daily Worker*, and *The Nation*. He also joined the New York John Reed Club, where he taught literary criticism and met William Phillips.

Protest against fascism held by the John Reed Club and Artists' Union, 1934. (Archives of American Art, Smithsonian Institution.)

Phillips was in more comfortable circumstances than Rahv at that point, but he'd started out poor in the East Bronx. Born in 1907 to Jewish immigrants, Phillips had had the advantage of New York's free institutions (Rahv never finished high school); he attended public school and City College (in the late 1920s), while also logging many hours in the New York Public Library. An encounter with Eliot's work spurred him to become a writer and literary critic; his encounter with the Depression led him to embrace Marxism. He was teaching part time at NYU, where he had gotten his master's in 1930, but believed the economic crisis was sinking any chance for a conventional literary career. The available positions "as editors, lecturers, and readers in publishing houses," he wrote, "have been whittled down to a few sinecures." He and his plebeian contemporaries worked "in factories, in stores, and at odd jobs. Some [like himself] have had better paying jobs as teachers. But we are all in the same leaky boat now." "The bourgeoisie does not want us," he concluded; our fortunes must be "linked to the proletariat." Like other young writers who saw greater opportunities in Gotham's radical movement than its mainstream institutions, Phillips joined (and taught at) the John Reed Club, where he met Philip Rahv.

In 1933, Rahv and Phillips approached Freeman, arguing that the *New Masses* was paying insufficient attention to literary issues and suggesting the CP start a new journal to redress the deficiency. Freeman agreed, and in spring 1934, the two launched *Partisan Review* under Reed Club sponsorship—though without much by way of funding (they raised the cash themselves from lectures and dances)—to promote proletarian literature and the "defense of the Soviet Union." Soon, however, they came to resent what they considered the Party's subordination of art to politics and, in particular, of intellectuals (like themselves) to apparatchiks. They felt they'd been assigned a "servile role"—"the writing of what amounts to little more than publicity for new proletarian novels and plays"—rather than being allowed to set critical standards for a literary movement badly in need of them. While *New Masses* editor Granville Hicks argued there was no need for critics—and sniped at Phillips and Rahv as unwelcome competitors—from their perspective the work of "conventional, mediocre, and culturally backward authors" and "third-rate poets" was all too readily being passed off as "genuine literary art." Their discomfort deepened in 1935 when the Party shut down the John Reed Clubs, including the one in New York, and replaced them with the League of American Writers, aimed more at incorporating established writers than promoting new talent.

Increasingly, Rahv and Phillips came to regard the communists, and their progressive allies in the Popular Front, as themselves obstacles to the upcoming generation of New York intellectuals. They seemed to have a lock on power positions in the city's left-leaning journals, publishing houses, newspapers, radio stations, Broadway theaters, and WPA arts projects. From these perches they showered editorial jobs, fellowships, book reviews, scripts, and parts on those who kowtowed to the left liberal establishment, many of whom Phillips and Rahv thought were political and literary hacks. Worse, from 1936 on, that establishment largely supported the Moscow Trials—which Rahv considered a "massacre of the firstborn of the October Revolution"—and thus lacked political as well as artistic integrity. Righteous moral outrage now intertwined with personal and professional grievances to precipitate a schism in the New York intellectual world.

In the spring of 1936, the two editors suspended publication of *Partisan Review* and broke with the Communist Party and the League of American Writers. Their plan was to restart the journal as an avowedly anti-Stalinist magazine, somewhat akin to V. F. Calverton's independent leftist *Modern Monthly* (founded in 1923) but rooted in a younger cohort than the old Russian Mensheviks, elderly German Marxists, and prewar Village radicals who figured prominently in Calverton's Morton Street operation. Seeking out other disenchanted

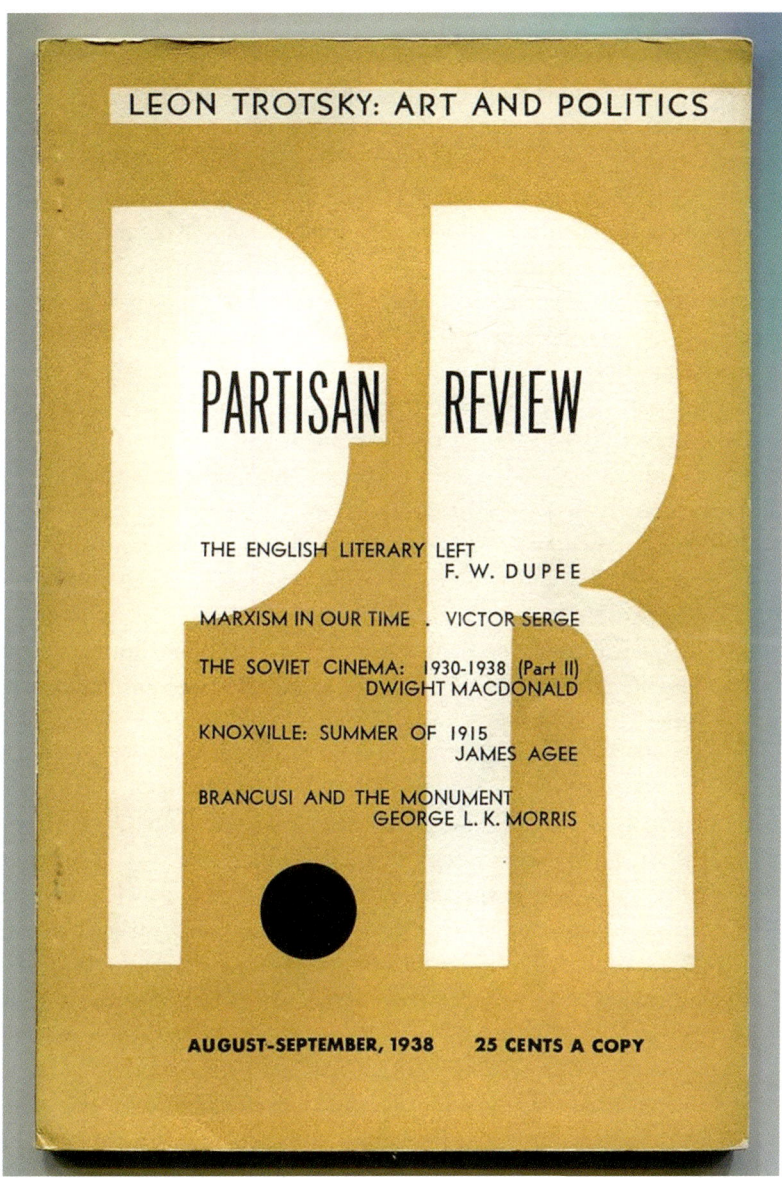

Cover of *Partisan Review* 5, no. 3 (August–September 1938). (PD-US-expired)

peers, they found an early ally in Fred Dupee, a Midwestern Yale graduate who had joined the Party, done organizing duty on the New York docks, and been appointed literary editor of the *New Masses*, only to find himself increasingly vexed at constraints imposed by Party officials.

Dupee, in turn, suggested contacting his classmate Dwight Macdonald. Born in 1906 to a prosperous Upper West Side family of Scottish descent that sent him to prestigious private academies—the Barnard School for Boys (in Riverdale), the Collegiate School (the city's oldest), and Phillips Exeter (in New Hampshire)—Macdonald graduated from Yale in 1928. Aiming to enter New York's booming corporate world, he spent three months in Macy's executive training program before deciding retailing was not for him. Another classmate landed him a lucrative job in Henry Luce's Yalie-studded empire, writing puff portraits of business leaders for *Fortune* magazine. But Macdonald was slowly radicalized by the Depression; by his research into the labor and communist movements for various *Fortune* articles; by a growing contempt for the business leaders he covered; and by meeting (and in 1934 marrying) Nancy Rodman, who introduced him to leftist politics and literature (she was the sister of Selman Rodman, an editor of the quasi-socialist magazine *Common Sense*). Intrigued by communists—though snooty about the "99 44/100% pure Yiddish" comrades, given his inherited fashionable anti-Semitism—Macdonald was viscerally outraged by the steel industry's brutal mid-'30s labor policies and turned in an article excoriating the steel barons, citing Lenin, to boot. When it was gutted by higher authorities at *Fortune*, with Luce's approval, Macdonald quit, in 1936, giving up his by-then princely income of $10,000 a year, to live (comfortably enough) off his investments and Nancy's trust fund. He now upped his level of political activism, helping organize a Newspaper Guild unit at "Il Luce's" Time-Life operations, and was considering joining the CP when Dupee introduced him to Phillips and Rahv. At a marathon session in Phillips's East 12th Street apartment, they brought him around to their anti-Stalinist point of view, and he signed on to the *Partisan Review* revival project; Nancy became its business manager.

Better still, Macdonald introduced them to yet another Yalie, the wealthy George Lovett Kingsland Morris, born and deeply rooted in Gotham, being a descendent of General Lewis Morris, a New York signer of the Declaration of Independence. Morris was less into politics than art. He had studied with realist John Sloan at the Art Students League but moved on to Modernism. In 1936, he had just helped found the American Abstract Artists group. Morris agreed to Macdonald's proposal that he sign on as the journal's art critic. He became its angel as well—providing $1,500 to underwrite the first issue.

Rahv drew one more non-Jewish writer into the inner circle, his girlfriend, Mary McCarthy, then making a name for herself as a fearless and authoritative book reviewer. Born in Seattle in 1912 and orphaned by the influenza epidemic of 1918, McCarthy had survived a grim Catholic girlhood and graduated from Vassar in 1933. At that point she married Harold Johnsrud, a radical actor, moved with him to New York, and broke into journalism. Her 1935 *Nation* series ("Our Critics, Right or Wrong"), which acerbically surveyed the leading book reviewers at august city venues like the *Times* and *Herald Tribune*, was a *sucés de scandale*. McCarthy traveled in progressive circles: attending for sharecroppers, New York waiters on strike, and the Scottsboro Boys; going to CP dances at Webster Hall; and marching down Broadway in the May Day Parade, where marshals placed the pretty Irish girl (along with assorted blue-eyed blonds) in the parade file closest to sidewalk onlookers, where they could embody the Party's new Communism-is-Americanism line (McCarthy approved of this as shrewd salesmanship). She did, however, have doubts about the proletarian literature featured in the *New Masses*. Still, in the fall of 1936, just back from a divorce in Reno and living poor on Gay Street, she was still "swollen with popular-front solidarity"—applauding the anti-Franco mobilization and buying cotton lisle stockings at Wanamaker's to boycott Japanese silk.

Yet all around her McCarthy saw the CP monopoly on leftist thought in New York breaking up "like ice floes on the Volga." At the Sunday open-house parties of her friend James T. Farrell—a left-wing novelist with whom she shared an Irish, Midwestern, and Catholic background and best known for the Studs Lonigan trilogy—guests ranted and shouted at each other around the drinks table. She found herself drawn, temperamentally, less to the successful and established, who in these circles tended to be Communists or progressives, than to dissident outsiders like Philip Rahv, to whom Farrell introduced her late in 1936. Soon McCarthy, who had landed a job reading manuscripts for Covici-Friede publishers, asked Rahv to look over a German text, and by spring 1937 they were living together at her Gay Street apartment. In June they moved to a swanky Beekman Place walk-up she borrowed from rich friends—shocking her radical ones—then settled into a place on East End Avenue.

Rahv now brought her on board as theater critic for the new *Partisan Review*—another of what he and Phillips called "our distinguished goyim." In fall 1937 McCarthy would join Saturday morning editorial meetings at the new office space just off Union Square (at 22 East 17th Street), then walk with "the boys" (as she called them) over to lunch at Pete's Tavern, nearby at 18th Street and Irving Place. The whole neighborhood, she recalled, was Communist country: "'They' were everywhere—in the streets, in the cafeterias; nearly every derelict building contained at least one of their front-groups or schools or publications." The *Partisans* enjoyed carving out an enclave inside enemy territory. Later, in an even more in-your-face gambit, they relocated to the same floor of the old Bible House on Astor Place on which the *New Masses* had its office, riding the elevator, in silence, up and down daily, with "them."

The *Partisan Review* editors intended to carve out a cultural and political space, too, wherein they would marry Marxism with Modernism. Which is why they eagerly sought out the involvement and imprimatur of Edmund Wilson, who was the very model of a modern intellectual. A preeminent literary avant-gardist—his *Axel's Castle* (1931) was their indispensable guide to Joyce, Proust, and Yeats, et al.—Wilson had also embraced socialism early in the Depression, urging Americans to take inspiration from the Soviet experiment but not to copy it. A contribution from the forty-something Wilson would validate the thirty-somethings' project, and, as it turned out, the timing of their request was perfect. Profoundly alienated by the Moscow Trials (all "fakes," he snorted), Wilson accepted their invitation to lunch in Union Square in October 1937. The boys brought McCarthy along as an extra added attraction (she donned her best outfit, a black silk dress plus silver fox fur, for the occasion). The short, stout Wilson, in his gray two-piece suit, talked mainly to the males, but his eye was on the fox-furred McCarthy, whom he soon invited to dinner, then to an affair, and then into marriage, which was celebrated the following February.

By that time the first issue of the new *Partisan Review* had appeared, in December 1937, featuring a piece by Edmund Wilson on Flaubert's politics. It also included Dwight Macdonald's essay slamming the *New Yorker* for excessive whimsy about (and neutrality in) "the class war"; Mary McCarthy's debut as scourge of Broadway progressives (starting with a dissection of Ben Hecht and Maxwell Anderson); a highly praised short story, "In Dreams Begin Responsibilities," by the twenty-four-year-old Brooklyn-born comer Delmore Schwartz; and contributions from Dupee, Morris, Wallace Stevens, Lionel Abel, Lionel Trilling, and James Agee, among others. An editorial manifesto proclaimed the journal to be the work of a new generation, opposed to the "old regime" of "yesterday's celebrities and today's philistines," who nevertheless retained the power of a "cultural bureaucracy" and would doubtless try to excommunicate the "new and dissident generation" that *Partisan Review* aspired to represent.

Liberation from dogmatic oversight was exactly what they wanted. It was also what art needed—according to the prescription they received, and published, from Leon Trotsky in 1938. In "Art and Politics," the exile in Mexico argued that "art can become a strong ally of revolution only in so far as it remains faithful to itself." Ways of seeing the world anew came from unfettered creative splinter groups, not calcified bureaucracies. It was the duty of writers and painters to retain their independence, for only if free could they germinate truly subversive and critical work. As Trotsky's manifesto "Towards a Free Revolutionary Art" (produced in collaboration with André Breton and Diego Rivera, translated by Macdonald, and also published in *Partisan Review* that year) proclaimed: "The independence of art—for the revolution; The revolution—for the complete liberation of art!"

But art was menaced by commercial as well as political pressures, *PR* people believed. It needed liberating as much from corporate bureaucrats like Henry Luce as from cultural commissars like Mike Gold. The magazine's perspective on this issue was crystallized by an over-the-transom submission from an unknown customs house clerk named Clement Greenberg. Born to a Yiddish-speaking immigrant Bronx family in 1910, Greenberg had had a relatively comfortable childhood, his father being a small manufacturer. An aspiring artist and art critic, he had studied at the Art Students League in the mid 1920s but in 1930 graduated from Syracuse into the Depression and unemployment. After years spent living with his parents, he finally landed a job in 1936 with the Civil Service Commission, then moved in 1937 to the Appraiser's Division of the Customs Service, where, like Melville, he used his spare time to write. He penned a letter to Dwight Macdonald, who encouraged him to expand it into an article, and in the fall of 1939 *Partisan Review* published Greenberg's contribution, "Avant-Garde and Kitsch."

Greenberg argued that the nineteenth century had bequeathed to the twentieth two kinds of cultural production. There was work by the avant-garde, which was bold, experimental, critical, rich, and authentic. Complex and difficult even to the point of inaccessibility, it was nevertheless forward-driving; it had transformative momentum. Then there was "kitsch"—mass-produced cultural commodities (dime novels, comic strips, pulp fiction, tabloid journalism, picture magazines, Tin Pan Alley songs, vaudeville shows, radio programs, and movies), designed for consumption by a literate working and middle class, hungry for diversion from its assembly-line and white-collar drudgery and severed from the more "authentic" folk art of the countryside.

This formulation was reminiscent of the older and equally over stark dichotomy between high(brow) art and low, but its antagonism toward the latter was fiercer. Kitsch was mechanical, something cranked out by culture industry factories according to formulaic specification, not individual inspiration. It drew on the fine arts, except in an "ersatz," "debased," and "watered down" way. (The word may have originated in the Munich art markets of the 1860s and '70s when the verb "kitschen," meaning "to scrape up mud from the street," was used to describe the inferior knockoffs of traditional art works being snapped up by nouveau riche seeking to ape elite culture; one bought kitsch to signal status, not evoke aesthetic response.) For the masses, kitsch purveyed "spurious" dreams, "vicarious" experiences, "faked" sensations; it exploited rather than satisfied the needs of audiences. However, mass culture was popular; it displaced fine art and ate the artists, drawing them into the maw of capitalist commercial culture, a diversion of talent whose "social cost," thought James T. Farrell, was "fabulous." High and low couldn't peacefully coexist, as they did before the First World War (even if each sneered at the other on occasion), because the latter was now as voraciously imperial as kudzu.

Worse, "kitsch," unlike avant-gardism, was fascist-friendly—a conviction that underlay much of the animus against it. Had not fascism conquered the masses through images and sound? (Frankfurt School exiles in New York, analyzing the catastrophe in their homeland, dwelt on the Nazis' use of film and radio.) Whereas avant-garde work had proved useless as political propaganda; indeed, the Fascists detested high modernist culture, considered it degenerate and obscure, burned its books, banned its paintings, persecuted its artists, writers, and intellectuals.

Kitsch was also being deployed by Stalin, in the form of socialist realism; it had become, in Macdonald's formulation, the dominant culture of the Soviet Union, in part because it was so readily put to propaganda purposes. And the *Partisan Review* editors (who in 1940 added Greenberg to their ranks) viewed the CPUSA's popular culture initiatives (including proletarian literature) in much the same way, which is why they found so pernicious what they saw as the growing influence of "Stalinists" in organs of mass production and communication.

Someone had to promote the avant-garde, resist kitsch, and stand up for the separation of art from politics, and the *PR* circle assigned itself that role. In doing so, the little band of critics staked out a central place for themselves in the metropolitan cultural firmament. They were no longer mere lackeys of Union Square apparatchiks, nor hirelings of the Midtown culture industry. Rather, these New York Intellectuals a-borning were the harbor pilots who would safely steer the national culture between the shallows of commerce and the shoals of communism.

46

Anti-totalitarianism

There was one contributor to *Partisan Review*'s first issue who whaled away even more vigorously at the Communists and their progressive allies than did "the boys," and who landed the most powerful blows—the short, garrulous, bespectacled, mustachioed Sidney Hook. A half generation older than they, and a good deal better known, Hook was an established professor of philosophy at NYU (Phillips had taken courses with him) and far more of a street brawler than *PR*'s would-be mandarins. Growing up in a cold-water, gas-lit, vermin-infested railroad flat in Brooklyn, where he was born in 1902 to Moravian and Galician immigrant parents, the young Hook used to fight his way through hostile Irish, Italian, and German territory, wielding a shield fashioned from a copper clothes-boiler lid, to get from his home in the Jewish section of Williamsburg, to P.S. 145 in Bushwick. At Boys High, which he entered in 1916, Hook battled his teachers, upholding the Socialist Party's antiwar stance (he soapboxed for Morris Hillquit in the 1917 mayoral race). At City College in 1919–23 he pugnaciously backed the Soviet revolution while becoming absorbed in studying philosophy (with Morris Raphael Cohen), which he pursued in graduate work at Columbia (1923–27), becoming John Dewey's favorite student. His dissertation, published immediately, helped get him hired as an instructor at NYU, and after advanced study in Berlin, Munich, and Moscow, he returned to NYU as an assistant professor in 1931.

Hook set out to use Dewey's pragmatism to liberate Marxist theory from the prevailing grip of a dogmatic and mechanical economic determinism. An engaged activist, he supported the CPUSA in the 1932 presidential campaign, working alongside John Dos Passos, Theodore Dreiser, Lewis Mumford, and Waldo Frank in the League of Professional Groups for Foster and Ford. But while Chairman Earl Browder liked and respected Hook, the philosopher's assault on reductionist Marxism alarmed Party theoreticians, and after he published *Towards the Understanding of Karl Marx: A Revolutionary Interpretation* in 1933, he was summoned to 13th Street for a grilling by CP inquisitors. Hook soon broke with the Party, and after the 1934 Madison Square Garden riot, publicly protested its "hooliganism." Arguing that the CPUSA had "brought disgrace to the term Communism," he worked that year to develop a radical alternative by joining ex-pacifist A. J. Muste in establishing the American Workers Party (AWP). Hook penned its program in an American idiom, replacing calls for a "dictatorship of the proletariat" with appeals for a "workers' democracy." The AWP didn't click with workers, but it did catch the attention of William Randolph Hearst, whose *New York American* launched an antiradical campaign that spotlit Hook's role and demanded NYU fire him. Hook turned for help to the Trotskyist-led Non-Partisan Labor Defense, which organized a 2,500-strong protest rally that denounced Hearst's red-baiting and helped save Hook's job. Through the mid-1930s he worked on the ACLU's Academic Freedom Committee to secure the right of leftists to teach.

After the Moscow Trials commenced—Hook found them "as ugly and petrifying as anything the Fascists had revealed up to that time"—he and others campaigned to help Trotsky win asylum in Mexico (granted by its President Cárdenas in January 1937), then to appeal the Moscow Trial judgment before an international body. On February 9, 1937, nearly twenty years to the day after Trotsky had sailed from New York to help launch the Russian Revolution, the American Committee for the Defense of Leon Trotsky (ACDLT) – sponsored a mass meeting at the Hippodrome, at which 6,500 assembled to hear a live phone speech from Trotsky in Mexico. When the transmission failed (someone apparently cut the wire), Trotskyite Max Schachtman read out the address, in which the old Bolshevik promised to surrender to the Soviet government if an impartial committee sustained the death-sentence verdict.

In March 1937, a Commission of Inquiry was assembled, and Hook was dispatched to persuade John Dewey to chair it. Dewey, now seventy-eight, told his former student he was too tired to shoulder the burden and in any case disliked Trotsky's "ideological fanaticism," believing that given power he'd have been as ruthless as Stalin. On the other hand, as Hook knew, Dewey was deeply disaffected from the Communists, both at the level of theory ("dictatorship of the proletariat" was an abomination for someone who believed democracy an indispensable means, not just a desirable end), and of practice (alienated by Stalin's purges, he'd announced in 1934 that, "as an unalterable opponent of Fascism in every form, I can not be a communist"). Closer to home, Dewey had battled CP delegates for control of the New York Teachers Union in the early 1930s; suffered what he called Communist "lies and character assassination"; and in 1935 had abandoned the TU and helped form a rival, the Teachers Guild.

In the end, what pushed Dewey to take on the task were the CP's hackle-raising efforts to dissuade him from doing so. In March 1937, eighty-eight progressive and Party activists—among them Heywood Broun, Malcolm Cowley, Theodore Dreiser, Lillian Hellman, Corliss Lamont, Max Lerner, Dorothy Parker, Henry Roth, Paul Sweezy, Lillian Wald, and Mary Van Kleek—signed an "Open Letter to American Liberals" denouncing the ACDLT project. Commission members were hounded with midnight phone calls urging them to resign and warning of the consequences if they did not. One thus badgered was Mary McCarthy, whose name had been added to the ACDLT letterhead without her approval, but pressure from "Stalinist" acquaintances transformed her initial inclination to withdraw into a hardened resolve to stay.

The Commission sought to bring Trotsky to Gotham, but when he was denied entry, Dewey and his colleagues headed down (in April 1937) from New York to the Coyoacan home of Diego Rivera and Frida Kahlo, just outside Mexico City, where the proceedings took place. The Dewey Commission's finding that Trotsky was innocent of all charges, made public that December, further exacerbated tensions in New York. The CP press, invoking the ventriloquist's dummy star of a popular radio show, denounced Dewey as "a Charlie McCarthy for the Trotskyites," and fifty progressive writers, artists, editors criticized him for dividing the Front. Dewey retorted in a CBS address that "If we do not insist on putting truth and justice first, the liberal movement is doomed." May 1938 brought yet another broadside, this time from over 150 writers, performers, and literary critics, in support of the third Moscow Trial.

Escalating angers were kept in check by the war with Franco—the CP fended off all critics by asking "Is Spain in flames or is it not?"—though, increasingly, Spanish developments themselves fueled the debates in New York. Russian aid to the Republic had come at the price of enhanced Soviet influence. Communist commissars were installed in the Republican army; the KGB established its own police and prisons. This new muscle gave Communists leverage in their clashes with the anarchists and syndicalists and dissident Marxists of the POUM (a small revolutionary party), who argued that winning the military struggle required a declaration of class war. Workers and peasants should undermine Franco's landed, industrial, and clerical allies by collectivizing farms and establishing workers councils. Stalin feared such measures would further alienate the capitalist powers. Revolution should await the defeat of fascism. In May 1937, accordingly, anarchists and leftists in Barcelona were attacked; POUM leaders were arrested and charged (in Moscow Trial–fashion) with being Trotskyists in the pay of Franco; and POUM leader Andres Nin was kidnapped and killed by the KGB.

In Gotham, the responses spanned the political spectrum. The CPUSA faithfully echoed the Kremlin's charges. The progressives rejected the "Charlie McCarthy for Franco" line but agreed that "war first, revolution later" was the more sensible approach—"What good are farm collectives if Franco wins?" *The Nation* asked. In general, desperate for a morally unambiguous issue, they tended to romanticize the Loyalist cause or refuse to scrutinize too closely the downside of Russian aid. Socialist Norman Thomas visited the front, protested the "lynching" of Nin, and professed himself "sorely troubled by the strength of the Communist influence in Loyalist Spain." New York anarchists—the Yiddish, Russian, Spanish, Italian, and American groups who published periodicals like *Il Martello* and *Freie Arbeiter Stimme*—formed the United Libertarian Organizations and together brought out a biweekly bulletin, *Spanish Revolution*, in support of their comrades in Spain.

The city's anti-Stalinists, who saw suppression in Spain as akin to purges in Russia, accused progressives of buying into a false version of war. At a party in Manhattan, Mary McCarthy traded angry words with Lillian Hellman over the murder of Nin, and in McCarthy's circles, *Spanish Earth* (which Hellman coproduced) was deemed sentimental agitprop, notably silent about Soviet machinations. Dos Passos was the most thoroughly alienated. Arriving in Spain in the winter of 1937 to work on *Spanish Earth* with his friend Hemingway, Dos Passos had tried to look up José Robles, a professor of Spanish literature at Johns Hopkins who had translated one of his books and who had offered his services to the Republic. Robles had disappeared, apparently shot by the Communists, and Dos Passos broke bitterly with Hemingway and many of his associates on the left.

Once Spain fell to Franco, bitter breaks came fast and furious, as Gotham's antifascist coalition shattered, its demise hastened by hammer blows from its opponents. In fact, even before Madrid surrendered, Sidney Hook set out to split New York's Popular Front the way a jeweler cleaves a diamond, along its internal fracture lines, using the newly formed League against Totalitarianism as his instrument.

The word "totalitarian" had been used by Italian Fascists in the mid-1920s to hail their own creation: a "total" state that would renew and stabilize society. This positive formulation was picked up by Germany's Nazis, who longed for their own total state to rein in Weimar "decadence" by intervening in spheres of life hitherto considered private. In the early thirties, German Protestants used the term in a negative way, to decry Hitler's efforts to subordinate their church. German theologian Paul Tillich (among others) carried this usage to New York, where he'd been offered refuge at Union Theological Seminary, and in 1934 he published "The Totalitarian State and the Claims of the Church" in the first issue of the New School's journal, *Social Research*. John Haynes Holmes employed this formulation in his contribution to a 1934 book, *Nazism: An Assault on Civilization*, denouncing the Hitlerites' subjection of opponents to "the iron régime of a totalitarian state." The term caught on because Nazism seemed such a novel phenomenon that it warranted a new word to describe its characteristics: a radically intrusive state with a single party monopoly and an infallible leader; government control of all education, media, and culture; a fanatical hostility to individualism and an unprecedented suppression of liberties; a cult of force; a fear of Others.

In the mid-1930s, sparked by the similarity of the Kirov and Soviet Army purges, some began applying the term to the Soviet Union. At first the parallels were suggested analogically, with references to "Red Fascism" and "Brown Bolshevism." Then both systems were adjudged subspecies of a common genus, totalitarianism, suggesting that their substantial differences—in historical origins, professed goals, diplomatic objectives, and ideological enemies (racial for Nazis, class for Communists)—paled before what they shared. Such language rearranged the political landscape, transforming a linear spectrum, with communism and fascism at opposite ends and capitalism in the middle, into a circle where fascism and communism met at a point called "totalitarianism," with "democracy" its diametrical opposite.

By the late 1930s, the term had come into use across the city's political spectrum, from liberals like John Dewey (whose 1939 book *Freedom and Culture* posited totalitarianism and democracy as the era's crucial combatants); to centrist Republicans like the *New York Herald Tribune* editors who in 1938 declared that the "totalitarianism of Stalin differed only in nomenclature from that of Hitler or Mussolini"; to observers on the right, like Eugene Lyons.

Lyons, born in Russia in 1899, had grown up in New York, become a left-wing journalist and Soviet sympathizer, worked for the Soviet news agency Tass in New York, then served as Russian correspondent for the United Press from 1928 to 1934. There he covered the terrible Ukrainian famine of 1932–33, in which millions died as a result of the regime's forced agricultural collectivization policies and its stripping of grain from the countryside for export abroad or distribution to the industrial cities. The Soviets played down the magnitude (and nature) of the catastrophe, and Lyons went along with the official version, as did the *Times*'s Duranty, though both knew better. His waning faith in the Soviet experiment vanished altogether with the purges, and in 1937 Lyons published *Assignment in Utopia*, which became a classic of disillusionment, and commenced a career as an anti-communist journalist. By 1939 he was editing the conservative *American Mercury*, which saw only minor differences (as "between arsenic and strychnine") betwixt "the political Tweedledum-Tweedledee which is Fascism and Communism."

Drawn into the League Against Totalitarianism, Lyons became primary author of the group's Declaration of Principles, published in *The Nation* in May 1939. The text adopted the vantage point of beleaguered intellectuals. "Never before in modern times has the integrity of the writer, the artist, the scientist, and the scholar been threatened so seriously," it argued. "The tide of totalitarianism is rising throughout the world" and "is washing away cultural and creative freedom." The list of countries where "the totalitarian idea is already enthroned" pointedly included the Soviet Union. In "Germany, Italy, Russia, Japan, and Spain," the Declaration found, "art, science, and education have been forcibly turned into lackeys for a supreme state, a deified leader, and an official pseudo-philosophy." Worse, thousands of victims of "cultural dictatorship" had been "silenced, imprisoned, tortured, or hounded into exile." Worse still, it could happen here, indeed *was* happening here. Totalitarians [read: Communists] were "infecting other countries with their false doctrines," threatening "to overwhelm nations where the democratic way of life, with its cultural liberty, is still dominant."

This argument appealed to many in New York, a city that thrived on the free creation and circulation of ideas and cultural products. So did the organization's title, changed (before the group went public) from the esoteric-sounding League Against Totalitarianism to the more accessible Committee for Cultural Freedom (CCF). Dewey assumed the chair, and ninety-six anti-Stalinists, of varying political persuasions, stepped forward to sign the Declaration.

Notably absent were the young *Partisan Review* intellectuals. Though they agreed the Soviet Union was totalitarian, and opposed the CPUSA, they faulted Hook's group for failing to pummel right-wingers as vigorously as it flayed the left. They distrusted its tone, too: the CCF (as Dwight Macdonald put it) seemed just "one more emotional, witchburning" organization "with totalitarianism substituted for fascism as the bogey-man." Macdonald, Dupee, Farrell, Phillips, Rahv, Schapiro, and others set up their own group and fired off their own manifesto to *The Nation*. Published in July 1939, it condemned the Soviet Union but also decried "deepening social reaction in the United States."

The CCF manifesto also provoked a blazing counterattack from a veritable battalion of progressives and Communists. *Four hundred* intellectuals and activists—including Roger Baldwin, Dashiell Hammett, Ernest Hemingway, Granville Hicks, Matthew Josephson, Corliss Lamont, Max Lerner, Clifford Odets, I. F. Stone, Mary Van Kleek, and Harry Ward—signed an open letter (crafted chiefly by Lamont) that appeared in *The Nation* in August. It rejected the description of the Soviets as totalitarians, insisting the term obfuscated crucial distinctions. Unlike German Nazis, Russian Communists had, the 400 argued zealously (naively equating Soviet professions with Soviet practices), criminalized anti-Semitism, eliminated racial and national prejudice, abolished unemployment, emancipated women, built trade unions, and (despite a "transitional" dictatorship of the proletariat) expanded democracy in every sphere. Finally, the 400 denounced the ninety-six as "fascists and their allies," whose real goal was to split the antifascist front.

Despite the high number of signatories, prominent progressives were missing, among them Malcolm Cowley, Dreiser, and *Nation* editor Freda Kirchwey herself, who published the 400's manifesto but refused to endorse its uncritical effusions. The "effort to promote unity on the left will fail," Kirchwey believed, "if it is predicated on a categorical declaration of faith in the virtues of the Soviet Union." She, too, believed the real motive of Hook's group was "to drop a bomb into the ranks of the liberal and left groups in the United States," creating a schism on the issue of "Russian totalitarianism," to isolate the CP. Kirchwey admitted the Party was double-dealing and intellectually dishonest, and she found its tactics "invariably provocative and often destructive." Still, she was prepared to work with it, without sacrificing essential principles, when their goals overlapped, as they appeared to on fighting fascism. The 400, in underscoring the gulf between Germany and Russia, argued similarly that, unlike the Nazis, the Soviets did not menace US interests and institutions and indeed had been "a consistent bulwark against war and aggression."

Into the Valley of Unpleasant Surprises now rode the four hundred, whose timing couldn't have been worse. On August 23, 1939, eight days after their *pronunciamento*, Hitler and Stalin agreed to a nonagression pact. The next day pictures of Stalin toasting Hitler's health flashed round the world. A week later, the Russian "bulwark against war and aggression" having been removed, German tanks rolled into Poland from the north, south, and west. Two weeks after that the Russians followed suit, invading from the east.

No one was more unpleasantly surprised then the CPUSA. Throughout the summer its leaders had repeatedly dismissed reports of a Russo–German pact as anti-Soviet slanders. "There is as much chance of [a Stalin–Hitler] agreement," said Earl Browder, "as of Earl Browder being elected President of the Chamber of Commerce." Learning of the deal through the media came as a rude, degrading shock, though it shouldn't have.

Given the Anglo–Nazi pact at Munich, which Stalin not unreasonably interpreted as an effort to direct Hitler's aggression eastward and, given also Western leaders' spurning of subsequent and repeated Russian proposals to forge an anti-Hitler alliance, a rapprochement with the Reich that would redirect Hitler westward was an obvious Russian riposte. Certainly, FDR had believed Western rebuffs were making a Nazi–Soviet pact probable; in early July he had written Stalin a prescient note warning that if he teamed up with Hitler, the Nazis would surely turn on Russia after conquering France.

In New York, much was made of the suddenness with which the CPUSA now wheeled on its heels, yet the turnaround was not that abrupt. Browder, no fool, knew that the Popular Front strategy of supporting FDR had transformed the CP (and its chieftain) into figures of consequence, a status that would be quickly punctured by a rupture with Roosevelt. So Thirteenth Street dragged its heels and continued to support the president, the Polish people, and England—authorizing *Daily Worker* headlines like "British People Determined to Crush Fascism."

Then the phone rang—metaphorically—with an impatient Moscow on the line. Actually, it was a radio, not a phone. During a trip to Russia the previous year, Comintern chief Georgi Dimitrov had told Browder to set up a powerful short-wave receiver and stay tuned. Ever since, every evening, during prearranged hours, Browder's trusted chauffeur had monitored the machine. Silence reigned until the end of September 1939, when it crackled to life and relayed a 600-word coded message, direct from Dimitrov. The line had changed. Poland was not to be defended: it was a reactionary state. England, France, and Germany were equally reactionary, their conflict a mere slugfest between rival imperialists. Americans should not die for imperialist exploiters. The CPUSA should strive to keep America out of the war. Above all, Browder and Co. should "cease to trail in the wake of FDR." A second message, in October, hammered home the point: the anti-Fascist Popular Front was history.

Even then, with his chain so rudely jerked, Browder tugged back. He hid the messages from other Party leaders and for crucial weeks ignored the injunction to break with Roosevelt. His hand was finally forced, not by the Russians but by the US, when, on October 23, federal agents arrested him on passport violation charges. It was largely his own fault. Browder had been called to testify before the Dies Committee in September. He'd done well, answering questions with suave evasions, until asked if he had ever traveled on a counterfeit passport. Browder had visited Moscow every year since 1926, back when the government refused travel documents to known Party members, and he (and others) had perforce traveled with passports obtained under assumed names. The Justice Department under both Hoover and FDR had known all this and declined to act. Now, certain that a three-year statute of limitations made it moot, he carelessly admitted the transgression. Roosevelt's enemies on the right pounced on this disclosure and used it to attack the president, who promptly threw Browder to the wolves. *Now* the CP line changed overnight. FDR, again an Enemy of the People, was attacked in the wildest terms. The Communists also jumped back to the antiwar camp. *Daily Worker* editor Louis Budenz declared that workers didn't "want their sons to die, mangled scraps of flesh...in order to enrich Wall Street." The new slogan, Budenz bellowed, was: "America, keep out of this war!"

Remarkably, the Party survived the volte face, holding on to the vast bulk of its leaders, cadre, and rank and file. Most saw the decision to divvy up Poland as a defensive move, intended to keep German soldiers as far as possible from Russia's borders and buy time to improve defenses against a certain German assault. They applied the same realpolitik to the invasion in November of Finland, whose border was 32 kilometers from Leningrad, in easy shelling range should the Germans seize Finland first. A few intellectuals quit, attacking the pact as they went out the door—mostly post-1935 recruits like Granville Hicks, for whom anti-Fascism had been the Party's chief attraction. Jewish Communists came under particular pressure—their coworkers greeted them with jeers and Nazi salutes—and when the Party abandoned even the anti-Nazi boycott, a substantial number bailed out. Still, most Yiddish-speaking Communists accepted the Pact as a painful necessity.

47

Unpopular Front

Progressives, on the other hand, were thrown from (or jumped off) the Popular Front train as it lurched around the curve of history. True, there were those who hung on tight and tracked along with the new line. Corliss Lamont was not alone in exculpating the Polish invasion and Finnish campaign as measures of self-defense. Lillian Hellman refused a request by Tallulah Bankhead, star of her play *The Little Foxes*, then running at the National Theater, to stage a benefit performance for that "lovable little Republic of Finland that everyone gets so weepy about." Still, most progressives now accepted (or ceased to oppose) the anti-totalitarian argument. *The New Republic* discerned an essential similarity between Moscow's and Berlin's foreign policy. In *The Nation*, Freda Kirchwey saw the Soviet Union as following Hitler's lead, provoking war to expand its domain, and I.F. Stone compared the incursion into Finland with Franco's invasion of Spain. (Linking Earl Browder and Adolf Hitler was perhaps facilitated by the former's astonishingly ill-advised choice of mustache, a virtual carbon copy of the latter's mid-lipped style.)

What particularly rankled progressives was the way the pact played out in New York, where the CP insisted that its allies, in front groups forged around antifascism, now pirouette with the Party and adopt a rigorous neutrality. Yes, there was a case to be made that, certainly from the perspective of colonized countries, there was little difference between the British Empire and the Third Reich, but where had that argument been up till now? It was painfully obvious that their partner's new line had been dictated by Moscow, and while local communists might hew to the faith-based assumption that whatever benefitted the Soviet Union also aided socialism, that was a conviction most local progressives no longer shared.

Some fronts deflated like a pricked balloon. In October 1939, the American League for Peace and Democracy (ALPD) held a special congress, at which the CP rammed through resolutions supporting Soviet policy. This proved a pyrrhic victory. The membership melted away, funds ceased flowing to the national office, and in February 1940, the ALPD gave Harry Ward a farewell dinner. James Lascher publicly criticized the German–Soviet pact and in December 1939 tried to get the ASU convention to condemn the attack on Finland. Voted down and viciously excoriated by the CP, Lash and Wechsler bailed out, as did two-thirds of the membership (whole chapters winked out entirely). The League of American Writers switched from antifascism to antiwar, only to have progressives bolt, taking a third of the officers with them (including Vice President MacLeish). Sufficient numbers remained, however, to keep the LAW operating for a time; it would muster one last Congress before expiring.

Other organizations became battlefields on which more evenly matched contingents struggled for control.

New York's American Labor Party (ALP) had been in turmoil since 1938, when the Communists had won control of the Manhattan unit, while the State Executive Committee remained in the hands of anti-Communist union officials, notably Alex Rose and David Dubinsky. As neither wing could displace the other, the ALP became a two-headed operation. The pact only deepened this division, as did the outbreak of war. Adolf Berle advised Dubinsky to lead his garment workers out of the ALP and into the Democratic Party. Dubinsky, however, valued his political independence too highly and decided instead to escalate the combat. Denouncing the left-wing faction as a "band of Stalinists" who wanted to make the Labor Party "another Communist front, another tail to the bloody Moscow kite," his forces won passage of a statewide resolution calling for expulsion of Communists from ALP ranks. This purge initiative won backing from the Brooklyn and Bronx units. Sidney Hillman signed on as well, the CP's value having plummeted in his eyes when it abandoned Roosevelt on orders from Moscow. Endorsement of the anti-Communist resolution, moreover, was declared a prerequisite for running on the ALP ticket. This enabled the right wing to block TWU head Mike Quill's renomination as city councilman, which cost him his seat. The left wing, ensconced in its Manhattan stronghold, held firm and hunkered down. The struggle would continue.

Another casualty was Franz Boas's anti-racist operation, the ACDIF, brought low by blows from Sidney Hook. On the occasion of launching his Committee for Cultural Freedom in May 1939, Hook gave an anonymous interview to the *New York Times*, in which he contrasted Boas's well-established group with his new (and competing) one. Hook implied that because the ACDIF deplored German racism yet did not also condemn Soviet totalitarianism, it was following the Communist line, though the "sincerity" of Professor Boas's devotion to democracy and freedom "was not doubted." Boas replied in the *Times* that the ACDIF's focus was on the United States, where racial intolerance was "unfortunately represented in our schools, colleges and universities, and has, in many instances, led to active repression." Hook now backpedaled, this time in his own name, replying that "We would be the last to assert that a person or organization who attacks Nazism and fascism but does not happen to attack communism in the same breath is therefore a Communist."

But this was indeed the subtext of his remarks, and what in fact he thought. Hook could not impugn Boas personally. Boas had denounced the Moscow Trials. He had lambasted Soviet constraints on intellectual inquiry, not least the ban on his own work ("in anthropology, there is no freedom"). And he had refused to sign the 400 letter, declaring that while he concurred with their refusal to equate fascism and communism, in Russia "free expression of opinion is ruthlessly suppressed." Nonetheless, if Boas was personally off the hook, the ACDIF did include communists—organizer Moses Finkelstein was certainly close to the Party—and for Hook their presence, together with the silence on Stalinism, meant the group was "concealing its true character."

Boas was perfectly open about his willingness to work with anyone who shared his primary concern—fighting anti-Semitic and racist propaganda. "I have always taken the point of view," he said, "that if anyone wishes to work with me in regard to a certain definite objective it is none of my business to ask what his opinion in regard to other matters may be." He also had a different threat assessment than Hook. Boas considered Hitler a far more clear-and-present danger than Stalin and was not at all convinced that domestic communists, for all their overheated rhetoric, were any threat to the Republic. Hook focused all but exclusively on the menace of communism, abroad and at home.

Hook also knew that if the ACDIF could be forced to denounce the Soviet Union, the Party-affiliated would leave the organization, depriving it of talent and energy, one reason Boas refused to do so. Balked, Hook called in supporting fire. From its inception, the ACDIF's main source of operating funds was an annual grant of $12,250 from the American Jewish Committee. Now—apparently at the instigation of Frank Trager, an AJC official who had worked with Hook to establish the rival CCF—the Committee ceased its support. In December 1939, labor reporter Benjamin Stolberg, an associate of Hook, launched a fierce attack against "M. I. Finkelstein, a notorious Stalinist." Soon J. Edgar Hoover was calling Franz Boas "one of the leading 'stooges' for Communist groups in the U.S."

Hook also brought in John Dewey, though on this issue Dewey—an old friend and colleague of Boas—was an ambivalent ally. Dewey had initially been chagrined at the zealousness of Hook's attack on Boas and tried to mediate between the two. But Hook won the battle for Dewey's allegiance, in large measure because Boas was on the opposite side in the ongoing fight over the Teachers Union (TU) and the College Teachers Union (CTU). Dewey hated the unions—partly on political grounds (both were led by communists, and both counted a substantial number of communists in their ranks), partly because he opposed their strategy of mobilizing educators on a class rather than a "professional" basis, and partly on personal grounds (he was still smarting from slashing attacks by youthful CP members). Dewey wanted the parent American Federation of Teachers (AFT) to revoke their charters, and he applauded efforts to encourage non-Communist professors to resign from the CTU.

Boas rose to the unions' defense. While others relinquished CTU membership, he took the contrarian step of signing up. Boas admired both locals—not surprisingly, as they celebrated his work on race (and that of Ruth Benedict and his other students). They also backed Rachel DuBois's intercultural education project, which relied on Boasian arguments. Boas had little patience with the burgeoning red scare. He denounced the "present hysterical search for Communist activities and the increasing tendency to denounce liberal groups as dominated by communists," noting that such attacks almost always focused on radicals, hardly ever on reactionaries. His insistence that Communist Party members had every right to hold union office acted as a red flag to Dewey and Hook.

Once again, the Nazi–Soviet pact helped CP opponents carry the day. Signed in the middle of the 1939 AFT convention, it appalled the large number of Jewish delegates. Teachers College professor George Counts (his former Soviet enthusiasm cooled by the Trials) was elected president on a pledge to eliminate CP influence in the union. Over the next year, during the fight over the ACDIF, Dewey's Teachers Guild lobbied to replace the Teachers Union, while Hook helped start up a New York Federation of College Teachers to vie with the CTU. Both campaigns were successful, and the two locals' charters were revoked and reassigned. In no small degree they won because the battle over whether communists were entitled to run labor unions got caught up in a larger struggle, over whether they were entitled to teach at all. That contest, in turn, drew more than merely private players to the fray, when the post-pact isolation of the Communist Party provided an opening for those demanding government intervention against it.

48

Red Scare Lite

On October 24, 1939, at a Waldorf-Astoria forum sponsored by the *New York Herald-Tribune*, Sidney Hook gave a speech on "Academic Freedom and 'The Trojan Horse,'" in which he argued that professors who were communists or communist sympathizers posed "a grave threat" to American education. These "Stalinist totalitarians" aimed "to impose a party line on the cultural and intellectual life of America." Ultimately, they were interested "not in education but in espionage" and in peddling "political propaganda for foreign powers." Still, the "menace to the free life of mind" they represented "*must be met* [Hook's emphasis] *not by governmental repression but by public exposure and criticism in the educational and cultural professions themselves*." Five years after beating back Hearst's calls for his dismissal from NYU, Hook demanded that "searchlights of pitiless publicity" be trained on "the Trojan horse [that] has already been drawn into our temples of learning."

To argue that "pitiless publicity" could be segregated from "governmental repression" was, in 1939, at the least disingenuous. Catholics and secular rightists, not content to let educators clean their own house, had already won a government commitment to clean it for them. In 1938 Governor Lehman had vetoed their first attempt, a State Legislature bill barring Communist Party members from teaching in the public schools. In April 1939 a more temperate-sounding version passed, shorn of references to specific parties, barring anyone who sought to overthrow the government by force. As it was axiomatic that all communists advocated violent revolution, the new version was understood as achieving the same goal. This time, Lehman signed, spurning a petition from over a thousand professors and teachers asking him to block it, and from May 1939 on membership in the CP—not in itself illegal—rendered a teacher ineligible to teach in New York.

Hook and his liberal allies might have gone along with the right on this, given their overlapping agendas. However, when the coalition behind the law first swung into action, the target was one of the liberals' own—Bertrand Russell—and he was charged with infecting youthful minds not with communism but with the "poison of Godlessness and impurity." Hook and company sprang to his defense. Dewey charged Russell's accusers with "intolerance and bigotry." Horace Kallen declared the "ecclesiastical-political assault" on Russell to be "the current phase of a warfare waged by priestcraft against men of faith and science since science first began to penetrate the dogmatic walls of churchly doctrine." Philosophy professor Morris Raphael Cohen warned New Yorkers that the "fair name of our City will suffer as did Athens for condemning Socrates as a corrupter of its youth or Tennessee for finding Scopes guilty of teaching evolution." Hook himself denounced the Catholic Church for violating "the best liberal traditions of American culture and education" and, wheeling out his heaviest epithet, declared it "the oldest and greatest totalitarian movement in history."

With Russell's cause lost, Hook warned that now "no American scholar and educator, whose views do not conform to those of fundamentalist censors of whatever creed, is safe from public calumny, from persecution, from loss of his livelihood." He was still keen on bringing "public calumny" to bear on communists; the real problem was that state-level forces had launched an insufficiently guided missile.

On the national level, too, the right threatened to discredit the anti-communist movement by promiscuous application of the term to liberals and social democrats. Congressman Dies's Committee on Un-American Activities, authorized in May 1938, had hauled in some Nazis and communists for grilling, but the ruthlessly ambitious Texas Republican had wasted no time in targeting his real enemy—New Deal Democrats—whom he accused of coddling communists. In 1939, Dies claimed he had a list of 2,850 known communists holding government positions. And Dies associate J. Parnell Thomas, rightwing Republican congressman from New Jersey, believed the CPUSA had "swallowed the New Deal"—that the New Deal was *itself* a communist front.

The pact strengthened the right's hand, which now fanned up a full-blown Red Scare, whose central tenet was the CP's putative devotion to violence. The quotes to "prove" this were conveniently cullable from William Z. Foster's 1932 compendium of bloodthirsty ravings—*Toward Soviet America*—in which he proposed that a "red guard" seize power on behalf of the "toiling masses" and establish a dictatorship that would "liquidate" all capitalist parties (Democrats, Republicans, Socialists, etc.), along with all "props" of "bourgeois rule," from Chambers of Commerce to Odd Fellows and Elks. (Hook himself cited Foster's effusions as the "true face of Communism," though they hadn't prevented his supporting Foster's presidential bid in 1932.) True, Foster's replacement, Earl Browder, was an ardent advocate of the electoral process and himself a perennial presidential candidate. Nonetheless, after the pact, Dies charged in September 1939 that the CPUSA's troops could "be turned overnight into armies of sabotage, espionage and civil war," a theme Dies elaborated in *The Trojan Horse in America*, the book to which he put his name in 1940.

Hook worried about native reactionaries (like Dies) who "would like to wipe out all liberal dissent in times of crisis." Dewey was even more worried, as he saw the specter of domestic totalitarianism in the Smith Act, which not only required aliens to register and authorized their deportation for holding radical ideas but imposed a sedition act on citizens. Scarier still, the Dies Committee, Hearst columnists, the American Legion, the Daughters of the American Revolution, and the National Association of Manufacturers launched an assault on "subversive" textbooks, with Dewey's Teachers College colleague Harold Ordway Rugg their principal target. Rugg's books were banned by schools around the country; the more zealous towns burned the offending texts in bonfires. Boas—whose own works had been consigned to flames by Nazis—spoke out strongly against this, and his ACDIF warned against a replay of the 1917 war hysteria. Boas also organized a group of educators, writers, and publishers to protest the Dies operation.

On February 25, 1940, Hook sent a telegram to Dies (with a copy to the *Times*), which took a somewhat different tack. Cosigned by Norman Thomas, John Haynes Holmes, Harry Emerson Fosdick, and other liberal and leftist anti-Communists, it applauded the Dies Committee's goals, approved its revelation of "certain dangerous activities," and agreed that there was "more work along these lines still to be done." Nonetheless, Dies's methods, they argued, constituted a "threat both to civil liberties and social progress." The hearings had all too often been used "to discredit progressive movements and moderate reforms, which are the greatest safeguards for American democracy against attacks either by foreign agents or native agitators."

How, then, to expose communists to "pitiless publicity" without lumping liberals and social democrats in with communists? It was in New York City that a strategy for doing so in a rational, coolheaded, and legalistic way would be worked out and test-driven.

In March 1940, State Senator John J. Dunnigan, Democrat of New York City and ally of the Catholic Chancellory and the Knights of Columbus, followed up the Bertrand Russell incident by demanding an investigation of the "godless, materialistic" mind set of those governing New York's schools. The legislature agreed and assigned the task of seeking out "subversive activities" in public schools and colleges to a committee chaired by Herbert Rapp, previously set up to examine (and slash) New York's school budget. Rapp turned the job over to a subcommittee chaired by Frederic R. (Fritz) Coudert Jr., the sole Republican state senator from Manhattan. Fritz Coudert was the son of lawyer Fred Coudert, and the grandson of Frederic René Coudert, founder of the powerful Coudert Brothers firm and a pillar of New York's Catholic laity. Fritz graduated from Columbia Law but turned to politics, and after losing a 1929 bid for Manhattan DA, spent the 1930s building a base in the Republican party. Since capturing his Senate seat in 1938, he'd been noted primarily for winning released time for religious instruction.

Coudert was close to the anti-communist right and capable of appealing to them with ferocious talk. Communist educators "cannot be talked to or reasoned with," he warned one Republican women's group, being "heart and soul committed to Moscow," and it would not do to be over-scrupulous about "American traditions of free assembly and free speech," which had, Coudert thought, been carried "too far." Rather, "it is going to require brutal treatment to handle these teachers." After all, he explained, "if your dog had rabies you wouldn't clap him into jail after he had bitten a number of persons—you'd put a bullet into his head."

Coudert the politician, however, was equally attuned to the desire of anti-communist liberals—powers in the city's political establishment and educational bureaucracy—to avoid witch-hunts a la Lusk or Dies. To impart the requisite aura of respectability and legitimacy, Coudert selected as chief counsel Paul Windels, La Guardia's former corporation counsel. The two then assembled a staff of respectable attorney-inquisitors who understood their task was to ferret out genuine communists, not Popular Front liberals, then turn them over to the secular arm, which in the first round meant the Board of Higher Education. The duo also set up an investigative apparatus (in a busy downtown office building where, as in Dewey's mob investigation, witnesses could come and go unobserved). It collected testimony about the political affiliations of teachers and professors, seeking not hearsay or gossip but the opinion of expert witnesses, notably liberal and leftist anti-communists, among them Sidney Hook and John Dewey (who turned over his files on communists in the Teachers Union). Then, starting in September 1940, what came to be known as the Rapp–Coudert Committee subpoenaed more than five hundred public college faculty and staff to closed-door hearings, where they were interrogated about their political activities, including Communist Party membership, and encouraged to reveal the names of colleagues who also participated in such activities. Students were subpoenaed, too, mainly members of the American Student Union, and grilled (without parents or lawyers present) about their political activities, other students, their professors. Finally, individuals fingered as communists were called before public hearings.

Anyone so summoned was in a difficult spot. They could not plead the Fifth Amendment: the New York City charter mandated city employees' cooperation with legislative inquiries; refusal constituted de facto resignation (they in effect dismissed themselves, leaving the institution's "academic freedom" credentials unblemished). But if they admitted to being communists they'd be fired. With honesty a suicidal option, most of those accused opted to lie, a strategy endorsed by the union, generaled by Bella Dodd.

The first public hearings came in December 1940, with charges brought against seven Brooklyn College professors, including some of those most popular on campus, among leftists and non-leftists alike. Bernard Grebanier, an assistant professor of English, testified that he had been politicized in the early 1930s, after the American Legion had attacked him for showing his classes pictures of First World War casualties. He'd joined the union and was pressed to join the CP, which he did in 1935, then was expelled in 1939 after he expressed doubts about the show trials and leaflets distributed to students had denounced him as a "counterrevolutionary Trotskyite." As Grebanier was the only witness, and Windels and Coudert required two (a proviso modeled on the Constitution's requirement for proving treason), none of those he named were dismissed on the spot.

At City College, William Martin Canning named fifty-four of his colleagues as being Party members, a charge denied by all (as per the union's prearrangement)—except English professor Morris Schappes, who said he had left the Party in 1939 and knew of no current City College employees who were members. The Committee refused to believe this and asked Manhattan District Attorney Thomas Dewey to prosecute him for perjury. Found guilty, he was sentenced to eighteen months to 3½ years in prison and fired. Other firings followed. Those not tenured were simply dismissed out of hand or not reappointed (among them Finkelstein, an evening adjunct in the History Department). Tenured professors were formally accused of "conduct unbecoming a teacher," meaning their perjured testimony before Rapp–Coudert.

Though the Board of Higher Education announced they would fire not only Communists but anyone who "advocates, advises, teaches or practices subversive doctrines or activities," none of the teachers were accused of any of these ill-defined breaches of law or ethics. The closest anyone came to arguing "indoctrination" was Canning's complaint that some of his fellow historians, notably the Foner twins, Philip and Jack, had "slanted" history by stressing "class struggle." They did so by "digging up various incidents which illustrate and enrich this thesis." This was not, Canning had to admit, "a very difficult task to do so"; indeed, he confessed that he himself had "indoctrinated" students by teaching that the Middle Ages (that epoch of barons and serfs and peasant uprisings) could be considered "a period of tense class struggle." Another instance of interpretive differences being classified as Machiavellian manipulations involved Dr. Max Yergan, the first Black faculty member ever hired at a New

York City public college. (He'd been brought to campus in 1937 after a vigorous campaign by the Black students' Frederick Douglass Society, the College Teachers Union, and the American Student Union.) Informers reported that Yergan's class on "Negro History and Culture" was "liberal and progressive"—and at a time when history departments (notably the one down at Columbia) routinely promulgated deeply racist interpretations of (for instance) Reconstruction, that was enough to get him ousted. In the end roughly fifty faculty and staff at CCNY were dismissed, not reappointed, or resigned—the largest political purge of a college faculty in the history of the United States. A methodology for bringing both "pitiless publicity" *and* "governmental repression" to bear on "communists" had passed its initial test.

49

Spies

Though both Congressman Dies and Sidney Hook warned that local communists were potential spies for the Soviet Union, actual Russian espionage received relatively little attention, in part because there was relatively little of it. During the 1920s Soviet intelligence agencies had focused overwhelmingly on Europe and Asia. What they did want from the US—technical industrial information—they didn't need spies to acquire. US exports to the Soviet Union had surged steadily until, by 1931, Russia was the leading purchaser of US industrial and agricultural machinery. As part of the technology transfer process, thousands of Soviet engineers and technicians spent months in US industrial plants, placing contracts and inspecting factory production. It was easy to gather up other blueprints (especially those with military applications) by visiting the patent office and reading technical journals.

What they couldn't get this way they got from spies, and what spying there was, was run out of Gotham, alongside German, Italian, and Japanese operations. Initially, cover for such espionage was provided by the Amtorg Trading Agency, the Soviet procurement organization, which had been established in 1924 in New York and through whose port flowed the bulk of Russian-bound goods. After 1933, when Roosevelt recognized the Soviet Union, urged on by businessmen eager to expand trade at a time of collapsing markets, New York's Soviet Consulate offered additional cover by affording diplomatic status to the "legal" Rezident (Station Chief). Gotham also hosted the two "illegal" branches, whose agents were more deeply clandestine, given their lack of diplomatic protection. One was military, the other civilian; they referred to one another as "the neighbors."

Russian military intelligence was the purview of the Red Army's Fourth Department—the GRU. It was run in the early 1930s by Aleksandr Ulanovsky, whose posting to New York with his wife, Nadya, they considered a demotion (though they did come to appreciate the local standard of living). Ulanovsky's base of operations for communicating with Europe was a floor-through apartment on 17 Gay Street in Greenwich Village. When a North German Lloyd or Hamburg-American ship docked in New York, a member of Ulanovsky's group met the arriving courier, usually a communist seaman or steward, and took their invisible ink message to Gay Street, where it was plunged in a chemical solution, then decoded. After this network was broken up by the Gestapo in 1933, Ulanovsky shifted operations to Brownsville. But for all the organizational sophistication, GRU spying was pitifully unfruitful under Ulanovsky, who was recalled to the USSR in 1934, and not much more productive under his successor, the Odessa-born Colonel Boris Bykov, who would supervise the network until 1939.

The GRU overlapped with, and occasionally stumbled over, its civilian neighbor, the KGB. In Russia, the KGB stamped out counterrevolutionaries; abroad, it spied on enemy governments. In the early 1930s, the New York operation was run by Valentin Markin, who liked to personally meet new agents as they checked in at the Hotel Taft. (The anonymity of the Taft's Times Square location, on 7th Avenue between 50th and 51st Streets [near the Roxy], also endeared it to the German Abwehr—one wonders about chance meetings in the lobby—though the Hotel Manhattan, nearby at Broadway and 47th, was also popular with spies.) Markin would say to the newcomer "Greetings from Fanny," and if he received the proper response—"Thank you. How is she?"—they would get down to business. Markin died in a car accident in August 1934, and a skittish Moscow, fearing exposure, temporarily shut down his network, but a new station chief, Boris Bazarov, arrived in December to start it up again.

New York was attractive for more than its hostelries. Itzhak Akhmerov, a spy who passed through the Taft in the mid-1930s, enrolled in English language studies at Columbia and soon found that "switching from the status of a foreign student to the status of an American in such a large city as New York was not difficult." Another agent, Gaik Badalovich Ovakimian, while serving as deputy head of the KGB's Scientific-Technical Intelligence Section, studied for a doctorate in chemistry at New York University.

And Gotham was home to the CPUSA, a handy source of auxiliary labor power. The communists proved considerably more useful than the ethnic volunteers upon whom German and Italian spies relied, because the Party already had a semi-pro team in place—a security apparatus set up to spy on rivals (Socialists, Trotskyites) and detect police infiltrators from Captain Michael McDermott's Radical-Alien Squad, formed in 1931 when the New York Police Department separated its long-coupled Bomb and Radical Squads and merged the latter unit with the recently created Criminal Alien Squad. The CP underground was run by Josef Peters, a dapper and mustachioed Hungarian who had fought in the First World War, joined the CP in 1918, was sent to the US in 1924, became organizational secretary of the New York party in 1930, and in 1933 was made chief of the secret apparatus, which he ran out of headquarters at Union Square.

The covert arm made itself useful by obtaining the passports that Party officials like Browder needed to travel to the USSR. Then it began furnishing them—for a fee—to Comintern officials and GRU agents as well. US passports were much in demand by globe-trotting spies; given the variety of American ethnicities, less suspicion attached to a traveling American with a Russian name. As passport applicants had only to submit a birth certificate to prove citizenship, J. (as he was known) Peters had a team of researchers at the New York Public Library's genealogical division comb through back issues of US newspapers and exhume obits of infants whose birth dates, gender, and ethnicity approximated those required for particular GRU agents. A CP member then requested a copy of "his" or "her" birth certificate and applied for the passport. In this way, during the mid 1930s, the GRU obtained hundreds of passports, and the CP made a tidy profit.

Jacob Golos, another CPUSA leader, provided similar services to the other neighbor, the KGB, in which he also held official rank. A short nondescript man with a penchant for bad suits, Golos was born in Ukraine as Jacob Rasin. An underground anti-Czarist, he was arrested in 1907 for operating a revolutionary print shop, spent two years in Siberia, escaped to Japan, and from there was spirited to the US in 1910. Becoming a citizen and a founding member of the US Party, he changed his name to Golos, after the pro-Bolshevik New York daily, *Russky Golos* (*Russian Voice*), with which he was affiliated. Golos went on to establish a company called World Tourists, with capital supplied by Browder, that facilitated international travel to and from Russia and undertook special assignments, like getting the Lincoln Brigadiers to Spain.

These back-office chores segued into actual, if amateur, espionage when Golos began collecting intelligence from Party members—most in private business—who came across information they thought the Party should know. Golos evaluated the material and passed things along to Browder. Some he also shared with Soviet intelligence, though he refused to allow them direct contact with his sources, withheld even their names. The Russians were miffed but mollified by the operation's value in vetting potential agents, recruiting couriers, furnishing safe houses, and arranging business fronts, all of which relieved them of tedious chores, provided local expertise, and enhanced productivity.

In the mid-1930s, with the world situation deteriorating, Soviet information needs broadened from the economic to the geopolitical. Increasingly Moscow wanted the scoop on Japanese and German military plans that US diplomats might have picked up at their neutral listening posts, and forecasts of American strategy as well. This necessitated cultivating governmental sources, which were based in Washington rather than New York. Again, the CP provided assistance, accessing Party members or sympathizers in federal agencies who were willing to pass along first their own assessments, and later purloined documents, to CP headquarters in New York, in the interests (so they were given to understand) of fighting fascism.

The data was couriered north by Whittaker Chambers, the communist literary wunderkind, who in 1932 left his just-attained editorship at the *New Masses* for what seemed a more glamorous assignment. Chambers had been summoned to meet Max Bedacht, a top Party official, who informed him he was being transferred to a "special institution" of whose existence he, like most party members, had been scarcely aware. Led to the nearby 14th Street subway station he was reintroduced to John Sherman, an old friend from *Daily Worker* days, now a covert comrade. That evening Sherman accompanied Chambers on an uptown IRT to 110th Street, whence they walked through Riverside Park to Grant's Tomb, where they were picked up by a car that contained KGB station chief Markin. In a thick Russian accent, Markin questioned Chambers on his politics, instructed him to quit the *New Masses*, informed him his expenses would henceforth be paid (in cash) by the underground, and told him to get a new suit. In the following days he commenced an apprenticeship, ferrying messages between Bedacht and the underground apparatus, taking circuitous routes by subway and bus to outer-borough rendezvous in deserted parks and empty movie houses, precautions scarcely necessary given that US counterintelligence barely existed.

In 1934, at a Manhattan automat, Peters introduced Chambers to Harold Ware, the Party's man in DC, and transferred him to Washington, from where he ferried material gleaned by Ware's people up to Peters and Akhmerov in New York. The KGB found his trade craft impossibly sloppy, as Chambers leaked his secret status to a host of friends (like his Columbia classmate Meyer Schapiro). In 1936 he was reassigned to GRU chief Colonel Bykov, who insisted Chambers put the amateurish operation on a professional basis and start by paying the DC contacts. When Chambers explained that most informers saw themselves as antifascist patriots and would indignantly refuse money, Bykov settled for Chambers' handing out some Bokhara rugs, picked out by art expert Schapiro, as special gifts.

When the Russians did find someone willing—indeed eager—to accept their money, they got considerably less than they bargained for. In 1937, Congressman Samuel Dickstein, then urging formation of a House Un-American Activities Committee, informed the Russians he'd be happy to keep them abreast of contacts he turned up between local Nazis and resident Russian Fascists (an elastic term the Soviets stretched to cover Trotskyites). Alas, Congress hadn't allocated funds to investigate said Russian Fascists, but Dickstein would be pleased to hire his own investigators if the KGB would come up with the requisite scratch. Dickstein seemed a great catch, their potential fox in the HUAC henhouse. The parties proceeded to haggle, Dickstein demanding $2,500 per month, the Russians countering with $500, until May 1938, when HUAC was formally established and Dickstein wasn't on it. His value and bargaining position diminishing, he settled for $1,250. A disgruntled KGB assigned the congressman the code name "Crook," and he soon lived down to his name, never supplying value for money. Legal Rezident Peter Gutzeit fired off a memo to Moscow denouncing Dickstein as "a very cunnning swindler"; and in June 1939, an outraged Ovakimian concluded their payrolled congressman was "a complete racketeer and a blackmailer."

By then, however, New York's Russian intelligence operatives, and their supporting cast of local communists, notably including Whittaker Chambers, had far bigger things to worry about. Chambers had told Meyer Schapiro in 1937 that he had developed strong doubts about the Moscow Trials, and stronger ones about his personal safety, having heard stories of Soviet agents recalled to Moscow, only to vanish into the maw of the Terror. Worse was the disappearance that year, in Gotham itself, of Juliet Stuart Poyntz. A loyal and highly visible Party member, Poyntz had studied at Barnard, Oxford, and the London School of Economics, lectured at Columbia, directed the New York Workers School, and run for Congress, state attorney general, and state assemblyman on the CP ticket. In 1934 Poyntz had left the open Party for the underground branch and begun to recruit female operatives. Shaken by a visit to Moscow in 1936, when her own loyalty had been questioned, she had been living at the American Women's Association Clubhouse at 57th Street (today's Henry Hudson Hotel), when she simply vanished, leaving all her papers and possessions in place. Carlo Tresca, an old lover, was among those convinced she'd been lured or kidnapped to Russia and killed.

Frightened, Chambers decided to quit. He held back from Bykov some stolen documents and microfilms as "life preservers," evidence of espionage he could expose if threatened, and stashed them with his wife's nephew in Brooklyn. In January 1938, with Schapiro's help, he got some translation work from Oxford University Press in New York but still laid low, sleeping with a rifle, terrified of Stalin's long arm. In fall 1938 he decided he'd be less vulnerable to assassination if he became a highly visible public figure, so on Halloween night he crashed a reception Sidney Hook and other anti-Stalinists were holding in John Dewey's honor at a pumpkin-festooned Park Slope brownstone, hoping the philosopher would take the repentant communist under his wing. But Hook, fearing a CP plot to compromise Dewey, gave Chambers a frosty reception, and he went back into hiding. In 1939, however, he surfaced again and got a plum job as a staff writer for Henry Luce's *Time*, to the KGB's apparent disinterest.

Their attention was focused elsewhere. Rezident Gutzeit was recalled to Moscow and arrested as a "people's enemy"; Colonel Bykov was summoned home, where he lived in terror of imprisonment and execution; and another seven or so agents followed, most never to be seen again, though some, like Akhmerov, would later return to New York. Some survived by simply refusing to go. Ovakimian was one who wisely refused to budge. Golos was another: the KGB, which had long disliked his independence, now suspected him of working for the Trotskyites and the FBI, and he was ordered to return to Moscow; he refused and was supported in this by Browder. In the end he was saved by the US Justice Department, which, in the post-pact crackdown, raided his office at World Tourists and arrested him for failing to register as a foreign agent. Still, by 1940, the local fallout of the purges had virtually stripped the network of American sources of professional GRU or KGB oversight, and the shattered remains of their New York apparatus devolved into the hands of the cover-blown Golos and a thirty-two-year-old Vassar graduate named Elizabeth Terrill Bentley.

A New Milford, Connecticut, Yankee, born to Republican, Episcopalian parents, Bentley, diploma in hand, had headed to New York in 1932 to do graduate work in sociology at Columbia. A 1933 fellowship took her to the University of Florence where, impressed by Mussolini, she became active in a local Fascist group. In 1934 she returned to New York, and, unemployed, she lowered her sights and took business and shorthand courses at Columbia, hoping to land a secretarial job. Befriended by a communist woman, Bentley now refashioned herself as an enemy of Mussolini and an expert on Italian fascism and began attending American League Against War and Fascism meetings at Columbia. Recruiter Juliet Poyntz spotted her and steered her to a deeper engagement with the CP. Bentley went down to Union Square headquarters, volunteered to spy on local fascists, and in 1938 was assigned to Golos, who taught her rudimentary spycraft and became her lover. After the Party plea-bargained Golos out of jail, and he registered officially as a Soviet agent, it became harder to continue running the remaining informants. So he established a new cover operation—the U.S. Shipping and Service Corporation—and made Bentley its manager, increasingly transferring the tattered network to her. When he died of a heart attack, probably hastened by stress, the entire American operation fell into Bentley's unprofessional hands, to the great dismay of Moscow intelligence authorities up to and including Lavrenty Beria. They would soon have to start all over again.

50

The Yanks Are Not Coming?

By 1939–40 the Popular Front lay in ruins, the smashed-up shards and splinters of its institutional framework strewn about the city's political landscape, with its core of communists, now severed from former allies, under attack from all directions, even its secret substratum in disarray. And yet, on the single-most-important question on the metropolitan and national agenda—whether or not the US should get involved in the worldwide warfare under way—the various remnants had reunited to form a fragile, fragmented, but nevertheless functioning de facto front, which stoutly argued the negative.

The CP, though isolated and beleaguered, remained a formidable force, and, at Moscow's orders to be sure, called vigorously for strict US neutrality in the "Second Imperialist War." One CP-promulgated ditty played off George M. Cohan's World War I–era song, "Over There," which had hailed the imminent arrival of Americans at the front. This time would be different: "Let the bugler keep on blowin, Let the drummer beat his drum; They are in for disappointment, For the Yanks will never come." The CP-run American Peace Mobilization held rallies, festooned with banners reading "We Won't Fight for Wall Street" and "Keep the Yanks in Yankee Stadium," where speakers like CP ally Vito Marcantonio thundered the anti-battle cry: "The Yanks Are Not Coming!"

The *Partisan Review* agreed completely. Evoking the memory of Randolph Bourne's opposition to the First World War, the editors denounced contemporary calls from "bourgeois" intellectuals to embrace a "new war to save democracy." It seemed, said Philip Rahv, that the "peculiar function of the intellectuals is to idealize imperialist wars when they come and debunk them after they are over." A fall 1939 statement by all editors and many contributors said that while they "loathe and abominate fascism"—the chief enemy of all culture, democracy, and social progress—1919 had shown that imperialist crusades didn't advance freedom. The last conflagration had unleashed rampant repression at home; the next would too: "Our entry into the war under the slogan of 'Stop Hitler!'" *PR* people argued, "would actually result in the immediate introduction of totalitarianism over here."

Sidney Hook agreed. To cast the war as a battle between Democracy (England and France) and Fascism (Germans and Italians) was to obscure their common colonialism (the

French in Indochina, the English in India, the Italians in North Africa, and the Germans, currently bereft, eager to get back in the Great Game). The too-neat dichotomy also elided likely effects of military mobilization on democracy itself. "The day war is declared," Hook asserted, "the Fascist emblem will flutter over the nation's capital—be it France, England, or our own United States."

John Dewey, damned by Randolph Bourne for embracing the First War, now rejected the Second one. "Resort to military force," Dewey wrote in *Freedom and Culture* (1939), "is a first sure sign that we are giving up the struggle for the democratic way of life, and that the Old World has conquered morally as well as geographically." If the US got in, it would soon be saddled with "in effect if not in name a fascist government." Hence his counsel to the country: "No Matter What Happens—Stay Out."

Many New York liberals and progressives concurred. Oswald Garrison Villard thought war would "inevitably end all social and political progress" and "turn us into a totalitarian state." Franz Boas, for all his dislike of the CP, backed the American Peace Mobilization's opposition to a war that would likely eclipse civil liberties. In 1939 Boas issued a report cataloging over seventy bills in the Congressional hopper that threatened civil rights, notably the Hobbs Bill (which passed the House 286–61 but failed in the Senate). It proposed establishing concentration camps in which "criminal aliens" along with "anarchists and similar classes" could be interned in the event of war. (Boas's old antagonist, eugenicist John Trevor, thought Hobbs's bill didn't go far enough.) Such initiatives, Boas warned, constituted "precedents of evil omen." He would have been more alarmed had he known that in 1939 J. Edgar Hoover's FBI had begun compiling a Custodial Detention List of people to be rounded up as potential dangers in wartime (it would soon include Congressman Marcantonio).

The city's pacifists also pressed the argument that total war would require total regimentation of *all* combatants and shackle even the victors with war-spawned vested interests. In June 1940 the Reverend Fosdick foresaw "totalitarian tendencies at home arising from the effort to combat totalitarianism abroad," and John Haynes Holmes thought democracy would end the minute war began. Emboldened rather than disheartened by the arrival of war, pacifist organizations redoubled their efforts to keep the US out of the fighting. The faith-based Fellowship of Reconciliation (FOR) and the secular War Resisters League (WRL) saw record gains in membership, partly thanks to the return to active duty of A. J. Muste, one of pacifism's most dynamic leaders. Having quit his pulpit and FOR in the early 1930s for secular political organizing, in 1936 Muste abandoned radical parties, regained his faith, and rejoined FOR. In 1937, he also accepted the offer of Presbyterian officials to run the New York Labor Temple on Second Avenue and East 14th Street, where he whipped up such a whirlwind of public protest against any Rooseveltian retreat from neutrality that *Time* christened him "America's Number One Pacifist." In 1940 Muste accepted full-time coleadership of FOR (with John Nevin Sayre), hoping to win a new generation to direct-action pacifism, using nonviolent Gandhian tactics.

The WRL's Jessie Hughan also argued that Gandhianism offered hard-headed solutions, even to concerns about security. Her 1939 pamphlet, *If We Should Be Invaded*, proposed shifting responsibility for national defense from the military to the entire civilian population, with women taking an equal role in a campaign of active, not passive, resistance. Invaders would be met with massive noncooperation—a refusal to obey enemy commands that would paralyze communication and transport facilities, withholding food and supplies from the occupying army. Whether tactics that had scored against the British would work with Hitler would be hotly debated and would never win serious support, even on the New York left.

There was, however, widespread agreement on the need to fight to maintain neutrality, and Norman Thomas took the lead in doing so. Thomas also saw the struggle in Europe as a battle of rival imperialisms and feared American belligerency might destroy American democracy. In January 1938 he set out to reenergize the pacifist/socialist alliance. He gathered representatives from a score of organizations in his Gramercy Park home—including FOR, WRL, the Quakers' AFSC, labor's Anti-War Council, the Methodist Episcopal Commission on World Peace, the National Council for the Prevention of War, and the Women's International League for Peace and Freedom; they together constituted the Keep America Out of War Congress (KAOWC). Within a month three hundred civic, labor, educational, and religious leaders had signed on, including A. J. Muste, John Dewey, Roger Baldwin, Algernon Black, Jay Lovestone, John Haynes Holmes, the Rev. Allan Chalmers (of Broadway Tabernacle), Rabbi Goldstein (of the Free Synagogue), Devere Allen, and Fred Libby. Stalinists were unwelcome, their antiwar stance considered contingent, not principled, all too liable to shift should Soviet policy change.

The KAOWC had a strong two years. In March 1938, 6,000 attended the KAOWC's first major rally, in the Hippodrome. In May a thousand pastors and rabbis, in forty-three states, preached on the "Keep America Out of the War" text. In January 1939 a full-blown legislative agenda was advanced, including strengthening the neutrality laws, embargoing munitions to all nations, rejecting plans for industrial mobilization and conscription, and passing a Constitutional amendment that would require a national referendum to confirm any declaration of war passed by Congress—except in the event of an invasion of US territory. In spring 1940, still the only national organization formed specifically to advocate US nonintervention in Europe, the KAOWC's program had its strongest popular support in New York, where it dovetailed with powerful antiwar sentiment in Italian, German, and Irish communities. Gotham retained its position as a center of anti-interventionism.

But the Mandate of Heaven was shifting. The outbreak of war and its ominous course in Europe eroded the popular enthusiasm for neutrality, made the pacifists' optimistic conviction that disputes could be settled by peaceful means seem increasingly naive, and in 1940 the initiative passed to two coalitions who had begun to beat the drums for intervention to halt Axis advances, one led by Franklin Roosevelt, the other by Wall Street.

FIGHTING LIBERALS

The sound effects crew for a federal radio show focused on labor, ca. 1938. (Library of Congress, Prints and Photographs Division, Harris & Ewing photograph collection)

FIGHTING LIBERALS

The sound effects crew for a federal radio show focused on labor, ca. 1938. (Library of Congress, Prints and Photographs Division, Harris & Ewing photograph collection)

51

FDR: Common Defense and General Welfare

On May 16, 1940—six days after German troops slashed into France, Belgium, Luxembourg, and Holland—Franklin Roosevelt assessed the "swift and shocking developments" before an emergency joint session of Congress. The Nazi Blitzkrieg, FDR argued, had demonstrably rewritten the rules and reach of war. Airplanes could now soften up targets by cutting communications, sowing terror, and parachuting troops behind enemy lines—establishing positions that motorized armies then raced in to secure, gobbling up enemy territory at the rate of 200 miles a day. This new ability to project power at a distance, the president warned, required that Americans immediately "recast their thinking about national protection."

The Atlantic and Pacific oceans, he suggested, had constituted "reasonably adequate defensive barriers when fleets under sail could move at an average speed of five miles an hour." (Though even in those days, Roosevelt reminded the assembled congressmen, it had proved possible for "an opponent"—a tactfully unnamed England—"actually to burn our National Capitol.") Now, should an enemy seize bases in Greenland, its aircraft could be over New England in six hours. And if "Bermuda fell into hostile hands," it would take less than three hours for "modern bombers to reach our shores." "So-called impregnable fortifications no longer exist," the president said. The US must look to its defenses.

FDR reassuringly noted that America's ability to repel would-be invaders had "very greatly improved" in recent years. In 1938, Roosevelt had gotten Congress to authorize over a billion dollars to beef up the fleet (since December of that year the Brooklyn Navy Yard had once again been running full tilt), and in 1939, fourteen of the newest cruisers and destroyers had been deployed in an Atlantic Naval Squadron. After war commenced in Poland, Congress approved the president's request for another 3.4 billion dollars for rearmament. Now, in May 1940, with the Blitzkrieg on display "in all its horror," the president asked for nearly a billion more, to underwrite a boggling increase in plane production capacity to 50,000 a year—one hundred times the aviation industry's output in the late 1930s.

Much of this firepower was to be sold to Britain and France, as the constraints of the 1935 Neutrality Act had finally been loosened. Roosevelt had first protested the law's even-handed treatment of perpetrators and victims back in 1937, three months after Japan attacked China, when he urged that we "quarantine the aggressors." But confronted with a huge uproar from anti-interventionists, the president had backed off, even expanded neutrality, by applying it to *civil* war in Spain.

In 1939 FDR had again begun to push for revising the law, insisting that Hitler's expansionary thrust constituted a clear and present danger to America. Should the Führer conquer Europe, the US would be cut off from its major trading partners. Worse: the Germans might seize the oil of the Caucasus, the grain of Ukraine, and resource-rich Africa, then jump the South Atlantic to establish Naziphile bastions throughout Latin America. If Japan succeeded in commandeering Asia's markets and resources, the US would be isolated economically and surrounded militarily, condemned to spend its diminishing treasure on garrisoning the country to ward off invasion. "The future world," Roosevelt summed up, "will be a shabby and dangerous place to live in—yes, even for Americans to live in—if it is ruled by force in the hands of a few."

Rejecting FDR's doomsday scenario, the peace bloc sent a tsunami of mail surging toward Congress, most originating in the Midwest, demanding that America retain its arms embargo. As of September 1939, when war broke out, countries resisting fascist invaders could not buy a single bullet in the US. On the other hand, an October Gallup poll made clear the country was not *feeling* neutral—it overwhelmingly (84 percent) hoped for an Allied victory rather than a German one (2 percent)—yet surveys also showed that Americans remained adamantly opposed to joining the fight. In November 1939, a compromise was struck. The arms embargo was lifted. The Allies could order war materiel in the US, though only on a cash-and-carry basis: Wall Street bankers and the Treasury alike were barred from extending credit, and foreigners had to pick up orders in their own boats. In this way, the US, it was hoped, would avoid military involvement while gaining proxy protection from a better-armed Britain, whose purchases would in turn rev up the arms industry.

Even as the administration had moved toward deeper engagement abroad, it refused to bugle retreat at home. In his Annual Message to Congress on January 3, 1940, FDR denied that the new emphasis on foreign affairs meant that "our Government is abandoning, or even overlooking, the great significance of its domestic policies." Quite the opposite, for the two were inextricably linked. European dictatorships, FDR explained, had been spawned by "the necessity for drastic action to improve internal conditions in places where democratic action for one reason or another ha[d] failed to respond to modern needs and modern demands." In the US, by contrast, Americans had fought the Depression with "a program of peaceful and democratic adjustment"—aka the New Deal. "Continued progress in the social and economic field" was imperative because "domestic betterment" would strengthen the "most valuable asset of a nation in dangerous times—its national unity."

Roosevelt expanded on this theme when he took to the airwaves again, for his fourteenth fireside chat, on May 26, 1940, at 10:30 p.m. (EST), just as the evacuation of the battered British Expeditionary Force from Dunkerque was getting under way. That very evening, the president told listeners, millions in France and Belgium were "running from their homes to escape bombs and shells and fire and machine gunning." With reassurance high on his agenda, FDR attacked domestic "calamity-howlers" who were spreading "fear bordering on panic." He rebutted claims the US was "defenseless," ticking off a lengthy list of ships commissioned, airplanes built.

But there were other things, he went on, "just as important to the sound defense of a nation as physical armament itself." Yes, ships and planes were the first line of defense, but "underlying them all, giving them their strength, sustenance and power, are the spirit and morale of a free people." To sustain this spirit and morale, Roosevelt continued, there must be "no breakdown or cancellation of any of the great social gains which we have made in these past years," because "inequalities and abuses" had "made our society weak."

The "framers of our Constitution," the president observed, wheeling out the highest supporting authority, had known perfectly well that domestic and foreign policies were inextricably intertwined. That was why in their document's preamble they "brought together in one magnificent phrase three great concepts—'common defense,' 'general welfare' and 'domestic tranquility.'" A century and a half later, Roosevelt argued, it was still the case "that our best defense is the promotion of our general welfare and domestic tranquility." Specifically: "there is nothing in our present emergency to justify making the workers of our nation toil for longer hours than now limited by statute"; nothing to justify lowering the minimum wage, or cutting back on old-age pensions, or unemployment insurance. On the contrary: such programs must be "extended to other groups who do not now enjoy them."

Alongside these pledges to rearm the country and to maintain New Deal liberalism, Roosevelt added a third—the defense of pluralism. This commitment was shadowed by his overwrought warnings about Trojan horses in America's midst. Having heard that Nazi parachute landings in Holland had been abetted by resident aliens, FDR declared in May 1940 that "today's threat to our national security is not a matter of military weapons alone" but of "new methods of attack" like "the fifth column that betrays a nation unprepared for treachery." It was in this spirit that he signed the Smith Act into law the very next month, requiring registration of all resident aliens, over a million in Gotham alone.

Yet Roosevelt used the same rhetoric to *resist* reviving the 100 percent Americanization campaigns of the First World War. He warned that foreign agents—knowing the United States was a society that commingled "the blood and genius of all the peoples of the world"—sought to "divide and weaken us in the face of danger" by playing on religious or racial or ethnic prejudices, using "false slogans and emotional appeals" to "set group against group, faith against faith, race against race." "These dividing forces," Roosevelt declared, must "not be allowed to spread in the New World as they have in the Old" what he called "undiluted poison," for America "cannot afford to face the future as a disunited people."

Foreign and domestic affairs were linked in yet another way, the president noted: the military build-up was melting the Depression. FDR did of course reject "the European solution of using the unemployed to build up excessive armaments," as that would increase the likelihood of war. He did, however, begin alluding in public to the collateral benefits of preparedness. "As more orders come in," he said in May 1940, "and as more work has to be done, tens of thousands of people, who are now unemployed, will, I believe, receive employment." And "the new speed-up of production," he added hopefully, "will cause many businesses which now pay below the minimum standards to bring their wages up."

Privately, the president noted candidly that defense expenditures could have a politically beneficial impact. "Let's be perfectly frank," FDR had told a March 1940 meeting of his cabinet: British and French "orders mean prosperity in this country and we can't elect a Democratic Party unless we get prosperity and these foreign orders are of the greatest importance."

More precisely, it was the fate of the Democratic Party's New Deal wing—and perhaps of himself—about whose fortunes in the upcoming November 1940 elections Roosevelt was concerned. Since George Washington's principled refusal of a third term, no chief executive had exceeded eight years in office. FDR was reluctant to buck this two-term tradition. Yet he feared his domestic agenda would be scrapped should a Republican or conservative Democrat take power. In 1938 and 1939 he had given some attention to grooming a liberal successor, imagining for a time that fellow New Yorker Harry Hopkins might be a credible replacement. But Hopkins was divorced, overly fond of nightclubs and racetracks, and chronically ill. By January 1940, no plausible liberal alternative had surfaced, yet Roosevelt still seemed resigned to leaving office. He signed a contract that month with *Collier's* to write a series of articles for the same $75,000 annual salary he got as president. And he busied himself that winter, and on into spring, planning a presidential library (the country's first); packing up White House papers and documents and cleaning out Hyde Park storerooms; and in general preparing to head back to New York.

The Blitzkrieg changed everything. It was probably by the end of May at the latest that FDR decided to run for reelection, convinced (not without reason) that he was uniquely prepared to deal with the deepening crisis. Yet not wanting to be seen actively pursuing a third term, he refused to announce this publicly, and with the mid-July Chicago convention looming, leading pols began to panic. Finally, on July 9, Democratic National Committee chair James Farley drove up to Hyde Park.

Though Farley had masterminded FDR's 1932 and 1936 campaigns, his political center of gravity was considerably to the right of Roosevelt's, and he had presidential aspirations of his own. The party chief told the president he should not exceed the two-term limit. Roosevelt responded that he agreed completely and didn't want to run. But when Farley advised issuing a Shermanesque refusal to serve if elected, Roosevelt replied that "in these times" he could not decline a call to office "even if I knew I would be dead within thirty days," and the canny old boss knew for a certainty the presidential hat was in the ring. Farley soon announced he would resign as DNC chair, would not run Roosevelt's third campaign, and, indeed, would enter his own name in the lists.

The New Deal high command, composed overwhelmingly of New Yorkers, rejoiced at FDR's decision, knowing perfectly well he was the only liberal who could win, and they leapt to support his third term bid and domestic/foreign agenda.

Hopkins—Roosevelt's right-hand man and himself a forceful advocate of war mobilization-cum-welfare state—went to Chicago to manage the "draft" nomination, duly achieved by acclamation. Eleanor—FDR's left-hand woman and herself on record that preparedness should include better housing and expanded health care—flew to the convention to talk balky conservatives into backing Roosevelt's vice-presidential choice, Secretary of Agriculture Henry Wallace, himself a fervent supporter of domestic liberalism and aiding the allies.

Sidney Hillman—FDR's plenipotentiary to the CIO—won wide labor backing for the Administration's defense effort despite the objections of chieftain John L. Lewis. In New York, Hillman joined David Dubinsky in putting the liberal ("right") wing of the American Labor Party squarely behind FDR's candidacy and policies. Vito Marcantonio, chief of the ALP "left," had supported the president until the Hitler–Stalin pact, when, after some initial foot dragging, he had teamed up with the Communists in attacking Roosevelt for betraying "his own New Deal" and for making the US a "military reservoir" for British imperialism; Marcantonio cast the sole vote in Congress against the major preparedness bills.

Senator Robert Wagner, the New Deal's champion domestic legislator, signed on to FDR's rearmament drive. So did brain truster Adolf Berle, who in 1938 had relinquished to Rexford Tugwell the chairmanship of the New York City Planning Commission and assumed the post of assistant secretary of state; Berle believed war preparation would revitalize domestic reform. Treasury Secretary Morgenthau was an early and earnest advocate of preparedness, as was New York's Governor Lehman, emphatically behind a third term. Mayor La Guardia, as ever a ferocious FDR advocate, was enraged that many "fusion" colleagues, notably Samuel Seabury, refused to join him in backing renomination. Seabury's objections were partly rooted in the fact that Edward J. Flynn, longtime boss of the Bronx Democratic Party, had inherited James Farley's chairmanship and was preparing to lead Roosevelt's campaign.

By mid-1940, Roosevelt and his New Deal comrades had thus planted a standard—a left-liberal ensign, blazoned with the colors of social democracy and antifascism—to which a critical cohort of like-minded New Yorkers would now repair: a constellation of churchmen and journalists, poets and playwrights, former pacifists and new-minted anti-Stalinists, around whom, in turn, would gather a broad coalition of fighting liberals, one of the two great metropolitan armies that would lead the city and country on to war.

52

Moral Rearmament

The deepening world crisis did little to change the position on foreign affairs of Gotham's Jews and Catholics. During the Blitzkrieg, prominent rabbis spoke out enthusiastically on behalf of Roosevelt's defense program at synagogues around town. Rabbi Herbert S. Goldstein was typical in telling his West Side Institutional congregation on May 18, 1940, that "we must back the President to a man, in his advocacy of full preparedness"; indeed, the United States must be ready "to meet and, if need be, to attack any potential enemy, regardless of the cost." The Catholic hierarchy, for its part, remained overwhelmingly opposed to initiatives that might lead the country into combat.

But a fissure now opened in the ranks of New York liberal Protestantism—long a pillar of the peace party—as an influential group of pastors rejected the pacifist persuasion and the optimistic social gospel theology that underlay it. More: they launched a campaign against the anti-interventionist ministers who commanded the major pulpits and presses in Gotham and Chicago, bidding boldly to replace them at the moral helm of American Protestantism.

At the forefront of this movement was Reinhold Niebuhr, Union Theological Seminary's professor of applied Christianity. As the thoroughly Americanized son of a German immigrant, Niebuhr had enthusiastically backed US involvement in the First World War, only to grow disillusioned, along with many other Protestant pastors, at the gulf between patriotic preachments and postwar practice. By 1923, Niebuhr had cast his lot with pacifism: "I am done with the war business," he said.

In the early 1930s, however, Niebuhr had broken with the pacifists over domestic issues. Finding liberal Protestantism hopelessly irrelevant to the power realities of class struggle under capitalism, he had refused to rule out using force in the fight for social justice. After 1935, Niebuhr applied his "Christian realist" precepts to the worsening international situation and decided that pacifism was as useless for confronting militaristic dictators as for contesting ruthless industrialists. Its proponents failed to recognize that strife *between* nations, like that *within* them, was rooted in inherent human sinfulness (e.g., pride and greed).

In the international arena, therefore, it was time to set aside social gospel fantasies of progress-through-reasonableness. "The historic situation in western nations does not offer the possibility of breaking through to a new society," Niebuhr wrote in *Radical Religion* in the winter of 1935–36, "it offers only the immediate possibility of defending democratic institutions, however corrupted, against the peril of fascism." Such a defense, moreover, would require more than parliamentary niceties. German Social Democrats, Niebuhr believed, had dug their own grave by relying on legal methods to resist Hitlerian brutality.

Matching word to deed with customary speed, Niebuhr in 1936 joined with the radical German exile Karl Frank in establishing the American Friends of German Freedom (AFGF). With support from the Jewish Labor Committee, the AFGF began funneling aid to the anti-Nazi underground, notably to members of Frank's *Neu Beginnen* group, situated politically between Germany's social democrats and communists.

Yet for all his hard-nosed realism, Niebuhr harbored his own optimistic hope—that in the long run, a worldwide Protestant movement, which overleapt barriers of nationality and race, might provide an antidote to war and attain justice as well as peace. This was what Samuel McCrea Cavert of the New York–based Federal Council of Churches (FCC) had been proposing, and what Niebuhr and some associates advocated forcefully in July 1937 at a momentous gathering in Oxford, England, of the *Life and Work* movement, which promoted ecumenical cooperation among Christian (read: Protestant) activists. The tall and rangy Niebuhr, with rigorous and commanding eloquence, made an electrifying speech, proffering the new Christian realist assessment, which was picked up by US newspapers and broadcast over NBC.

Sharing the international spotlight were Henry P. Van Dusen and Henry Sloane Coffin, Niebuhr's colleagues up on Morningside Heights. Van Dusen was a liberal Presbyterian—his ordination by the New York Presbytery in 1924 had been held up by fundamentalist clergy appalled by his refusal to accept a literal understanding of the virgin birth. After working with the YMCA, he joined the Union Theological Seminary faculty, where he came to adopt the new realist theology. Siding with Niebuhr, Van Dusen argued that Man's sinfulness (in particular, business-Man's gluttonous pursuit of money and power) was the fundamental cause of social conflict, an analysis he extended to the international scene. Coffin—a mentor of Van Dusen and Union Theological's president—had traveled a similar path. A New York native and Yale man, Coffin had graduated from Union in 1900, then launched a mission church atop a Bronx meat market near Bedford Park, using a chopping block for a pulpit. He'd gone on to pastor the elite Madison Avenue Presbyterian Church, building it into a premier liberal institution during the fight against fundamentalists during the early 1920s, becoming well and widely known in elite Gotham social circles.

At Oxford, the three New Yorkers helped win agreement on establishing a World Council of Churches. It would be more than a decade before the body was finally fully born, but from 1937 on, Gotham, together with Geneva and London, would be a major hub of the ecumenical Protestant movement seeking to replace competitive nationalism with international cooperation.

In the short term, however, rapacious nationalism was a fact on the ground, and the question was how to respond to it. Believing that pacifism and neutralism were part of the problem, not the solution, Niebuhr took up theological arms against Christian leaders who, in his judgment, had not taken the fascists' full moral measure. In 1937, after Japan attacked China, he blasted legislatively mandated neutrality, denying that "peace is always preferable to the exploitation of the weak by the strong." In 1938, he derided the Munich Agreement as an example of misplaced trust in reason—negotiating with an enemy intent on destroying its bargaining partner. "Is it really 'Christian,'" he asked pacifists, "is it God's will, never to call the bluff of a bully for fear that you might be involved in violence? Then we had better prepare for the complete victory of the barbarism that is spreading over Europe." After the invasion of Poland in 1939, Niebuhr castigated pacifist insensitivity to the victims of tyranny—Jews as well as Poles—and declared that those who made "non-participation in conflict" the highest good preached "a very sentimentalized version of the Christian faith."

In January 1940, Niebuhr—along with other New York lapsed pacifists like Van Dusen and Coffin—was among thirty-two lay and ministerial signers of a statement that insisted America's Christian leaders were obligated to stand against tyranny and "lead their nation to assume a responsible relationship to the present conflicts." Supporting Roosevelt's geopolitical assessments, the signatories asserted that while victory for England, France, or China "would not of itself assure the establishment of justice and peace," victory for Germany, Russia, or Japan "would inevitably preclude the justice, freedom of thought and worship, and international cooperation which are fundamental to a Christian world order."

Niebuhr remained opposed to outright intervention—so, officially, did Roosevelt—but by spring 1940 he was backing FDR's "all aid to the Allies short of war" policy, convinced— perhaps a bit unrealistically for a realist—that deeper involvement would not draw the country into combat. When the Socialists ran Norman Thomas for president on a neutralist platform, Niebuhr promptly resigned, blasting the party's position in a June 1940 *Nation* article titled "An End to Illusions." The Battle of Britain ensconced him firmly in Roosevelt's corner; he deeply admired England, and, with his English wife, had spent many months there in the late 1930s.

Also in 1940, Niebuhr and a cohort of New Yorkers girded for battle with Chicago's *Christian Century*, interdenominational Protestantism's preeminent newspaper and the journalistic stronghold of Social Gospel pacifism. With Van Dusen, Coffin, Sherwood Eddy, and Charles Culp Burlingham (La Guardia's intimate counselor and senior warden at St. George's Episcopal Church), Niebuhr proposed to publish an eight-page paper, *Christianity and Crisis*, which would be sent to several thousand members of the Federal Council of Churches. Its goal, Burlingham wrote privately, was to counteract the pacifists, "who make an awful noise and have done a lot of harm with young people." Publicly, Burlingham's more circumspect appeal for subscribers stated that the paper's "view-point will dissent from Christian pacifism." The editors would argue, he explained, "that in history men must choose between relative goods"; that pacifists who seek "an absolute perfection in historic decisions" are "betrayed into submission to tyranny"; and that Christians must "enlist their resources in defense of democratic civilization...against the totalitarian menace." Even before the first issue of *Christianity and Crisis* appeared the following February, the vigorous initiatives of Niebuhr and his colleagues had forced the Federal Council of Churches to admit its ranks were now riven: it could no longer "affirm either the pacifist or non-pacifist view to be the Christian position." This shift in sentiment, radiating out from New York City, would soon reshape the nation's religio-political landscape.

53

Muscular Democracy

A similar schism emerged among Gotham's secular intellectuals. By the late 1930s, Nazism's alarming rise had galvanized many metropolitan writers into promoting a democratic revival. Scores of books tumbled from New York presses, aimed at convincing Americans that democracy and freedom, even if imperfectly attained, were creeds worth fighting for—among them Edward L. Bernays's *Speak Up for Democracy: What You Can Do—a Practical Plan of Action for Every American Citizen*; George Counts's *The Prospects of American Democracy*; and Waldo Frank's *Chart for Rough Water*. Many of these "war intellectuals" also raised lances against other liberals they deemed insufficiently militant. Among the most truculent pro-interventionists was Lewis Mumford—an admirer of Niebuhr—and the major target of Mumford's scornful wrath was anti-interventionist John Dewey.

Mumford had never been a pacifist; he'd volunteered in the Great War (though only after efforts to avoid the draft had come to naught) and in the end never saw combat, having been sent to radio school at Harvard, where he'd had ample free time to launch his writing career. Yet, disillusioned, like so many of his generation, at the outcome of the carnage, Mumford's earliest postwar essays applauded antiwarrior Randolph Bourne's polemics against John Dewey's interventionism, especially Dewey's hope that war would galvanize reform. Through the 1920s, Mumford kept alive (after Bourne's premature death) his counterargument—that governments-at-war *stifled* reform, suppressed dissent, and aggrandized power unto themselves ("war is the health of the state," Bourne had famously aphorized).

In the 1930s, however, Dewey and Mumford completely reversed their position—Dewey turning resolutely against war, Mumford becoming its vigorous advocate—and continued to contest one another, albeit from transposed premises.

The rise of fascism had not, at first, budged Mumford from his antiwar stance. After a visit to Germany in 1932, he dismissed the Nazis as a passing phenomenon and declared himself optimistic about the country's future. In 1935, however, with Hitler now well entrenched, Mumford began suggesting that halting German expansion might become necessary, preferably by commercial blockade, by force if need be. In 1938, provoked by the Anschluss, he completed his transformation into passionate advocate of full-scale mobilization against fascism.

In May of that year Mumford published "Call to Arms" in *The New Republic*, attacking that magazine's recent publication of a "Defense Supplement" dismissing the fascist menace—on grounds that America's shining seas afforded ample protection—and calling for continued neutrality. Mumford attributed the editors' quietism to a "liberal pragmatist" (Deweyan) assumption that fascists were reasonable men who could be bargained with, but in fact the Nazi leaders were pathologically irrational (as were the German masses) and hell-bent on conquest.

In subsequent interventions—*Men Must Act* (a book brought out in January 1939); "The Corruption of Liberalism" (an April 1940 article); and *Faith for Living*, written in June 1940 as Hitler blitzkrieged into France—Mumford pressed his case with ever-escalating fervor. Dewey was accused of naively believing (as did Social Gospelers) that human conflicts were rooted in ignorance and unjust institutions, hence resolvable by education and reform. But fascists glorified war, delighted in physical cruelty, and thrived on militarism—war had become the health of the Nazi state—and could only be opposed by force of arms. Mumford called for mobilizing a million Americans to aid the British. He himself bought a .30-30 rifle with which to fight the Nazis should they invade New York.

Mumford proposed surveillance of all "active fascists" and potential fifth columnists. He called for using "any necessary amount of coercion" on "recalcitrant minorities." Shouting Sieg Heil in a crowded Madison Square Garden should be outlawed. Fascists should be denied use of the mails or access to the airwaves. Espousing fascism should be declared treason against democracy and its advocates jailed or deported. He denounced wimpy civil libertarians for being "more concerned over minor curtailments of private liberties, necessary for an effective defense against fascism," than they were "over the far more ghastly prospect of permanent servitude if fascism finally covers the earth." By "holding to the abstract principle of free speech, without regard for political reality," they were in effect asking the country "to commit suicide."

Many liberals thought Mumford's language steered dangerously close to that of the Nazis he was excoriating. One letter to *The New Republic* denounced him as the "fuhrer of anti-fascism," and Malcolm Cowley wrote that "behind Mumford's patriotic vista one can see the barbed wire of concentration camps."

Liberals tended to close ranks with Mumford against one of his domestic targets, the Catholic Church. Mumford asserted that in Europe, the Church had "chosen to ally itself with democracy's chief enemy, fascism," and at home had spawned the likes of Father Coughlin and the Christian Front. Investigative reporter George Seldes's *The Catholic Crisis* (1939) catalogued liberals' charges: the Church censored movies, suppressed books, intimidated newspapers and radio stations, blocked changes in marriage and divorce laws, opposed birth control, and consorted with wannabe totalitarians at home and fascist regimes abroad. As Adolf Berle bluntly summed up the liberal thesis: Catholicism was a "religion still in the stage of absolute dictatorship."

On this issue, Dewey and Mumford approached convergence. Dewey had long believed that democratic polities required democratic institutions to sustain them—particularly schools that taught children to resist "external authority, discipline, uniformity and dependence upon The Leader." In Dewey's opinion, Catholic educators seemed to be marching briskly in the opposite direction.

Niebuhr, too, agreed that the Church had "cast its lot with fascistic politics," one reason he praised Mumford's *Faith for Living* so effusively. He also applauded Mumford for drawing on his theological argument that modern liberals, to their peril, had ceased to believe in evil. Niebuhr disagreed, however, with Mumford's notion that Americans could willfully reknit themselves into an organic whole, finding it wrongheaded—not least because, in his judgment, no such Golden Age had ever existed. Still, by 1940, the two men's paths (one largely theological, one primarily secular) had essentially converged. In June, both resigned from institutions deemed insufficiently antifascist—Niebuhr from the Socialist Party, Mumford from *The New Republic*. And in October, both signed the manifesto of an organization of intellectuals called *The City of Man*, which aimed to "endow democracy with a fighting spirit"; the document, *A Declaration on World Democracy*, urged intervention abroad, intolerance of antidemocrats at home, and formation of a world government to safeguard democracy around the planet.

54

Playwrights and Poets

Robert Emmet Sherwood—great-great-grandson of the Thomas Addis Emmet entombed in St. Paul's churchyard—had cycled, like others in Roosevelt's growing network, from hawk to dove to hawk. In 1916, as a Harvard undergraduate, Sherwood had written a tub-thumping prowar ditty, a perishable line of which went: "For we can't stand back when the foes attack." In 1917, living up to his lyric, Sherwood, all six-foot-seven of him, had trooped to Montreal, where he joined the Canadian Black Watch Battalion, donned a kilt, and headed off to the Great War, where he was gassed, wounded, hospitalized, and (in 1919) discharged, by which time the warmonger had turned pacifist.

Sherwood entered New York's theatrical world, as drama editor of *Vanity Fair* (1919–20), and joined the Algonquin coterie with his *VF* colleagues Dorothy Parker and Robert Benchley. His first outing as a professional playwright—*The Road to Rome* (1927)—criticized the pointlessness of war. His *Idiot's Delight*, which Alfred Lunt and Lynn Fontanne staged at the Shubert in March 1936, stressed war's profitability (the villain of the piece was a munitions maker) and horror (serving up images like that of a tank rolling over a soldier, leaving him a "mass of mashed flesh and bones—a smear of purple blood—like a stepped-on snail"). The final curtain lowered on the crashing of bombs, delivering its antiwar message with a wallop that helped win Sherwood his first Pulitzer that May.

He remained antiwar through 1938, backing Chamberlain at Munich, though his *Abe Lincoln in Illinois*, which began a resounding New York run that October, featured a peace-loving democratic leader who tried to sidestep divisive issues but in the end recognized he had to take a stand, even if it meant waging war. *Lincoln* garnered Sherwood another Pulitzer, and entree to Roosevelt's circle. Sherwood had met Harry Hopkins in September, at Herbert Swope's Long Island country house, and when *Lincoln* opened in DC, Hopkins gave him a tour of the White House (especially the Lincoln bedroom).

Sherwood now was drawn directly into the president's orbit. In October, Hopkins asked him over to the Essex House on Central Park South, where he was staying. FDR had to give a speech about the need to beat Hitler; did Sherwood have any thoughts as to what the president should say? Sherwood did. Hopkins now walked him over to see Judge Sam Rosenman, who lived a few blocks away on Central Park West. Unaware that the judge had been FDR's speech writer since Albany days, the playwright told Rosenman he was convinced, having read many of FDR's speeches that, given the uniformity of style, Roosevelt had written them all himself. The judge, amused by Sherwood's naivete, told Sherwood to sit down and write some paragraphs, which he did, and was amazed a few days later to hear Roosevelt delivering the speech using many of Sherwood's formulations. Thus was Sherwood inducted into Roosevelt's writing team for the 1940 campaign.

He would be joined there by Archibald MacLeish, who had traveled a similar route. The Illinois-born MacLeish, son of a prosperous dry-goods merchant, attended Hotchkiss, Yale, and entered Harvard Law in 1915. Uncomplainingly interrupting his education, he left for France in '17 and served as an artilleryman but became embittered about the war after his brother died in combat. A successful attorney in the early 1920s, in 1923 MacLeish packed in the law, packed up his family, and spent the next five years in Paris, becoming a celebrated poet. He returned to the United States in 1928 and bought a farm in Conway, Massachusetts. When the Crash slashed his income from inherited stocks and he needed a job, MacLeish turned not to the bar and Boston, but to Henry Luce and New York.

Luce, just launching *Fortune*, was looking for major-league writers, and he made MacLeish a fabulous offer—great pay for reportage, lots of free time to write poetry. MacLeish proved spectacularly prolific on both scores. Between 1929 and 1938, from his office perch on the Chrysler Building's 52nd floor, he churned out nearly 100 stories for the magazine. From his Greenwich Village apartment at 182 Sullivan Street, he produced a torrent of poems, essays, and plays, while immersing himself in the city's literary community of writers, editors, and publishers. In an early salute to his new work base, he offered "& Forty-Second Street," a poem in his 1930 collection *New Found Land*, which celebrated Manhattan.

Politicized by the Depression, MacLeish became a zealous FDR backer and turned in many a sympathetic story about New Deal initiatives for *Fortune*. As a poet, though deeply influenced by T. S. Eliot and Ezra Pound, MacLeish rejected the modernists' emphasis on private experience, arguing that poetry, especially in the tumultuous thirties, should become "public speech."

On foreign affairs, MacLeish in 1935 was still an uncompromising pacifist, who declared he would "do everything in my power to prevent the United States from going to war under *any* circumstances." Yet he was a vigorous antifascist, too. A member of the Popular Front's League of American Writers, he played a prominent role at its Second Congress in Carnegie Hall. A strong supporter of the Spanish Republic, MacLeish was instrumental in organizing the group that produced *The Spanish Earth*. In 1937, accompanied by Robert Sherwood, he visited FDR in a fruitless effort to win him to the Loyalist cause. He had equal lack of success in getting Henry Luce to alter *Time*'s coverage of the Spanish conflict, which rested in the hands of the Francophile foreign news editor Laird "Goldie" Goldsborough. While Luce never openly declared himself on Spain, he let Goldie spin the story his way (Franco's backers were hailed as "men of property, men of God and men of the sword," Republicans were described as frog-faced and cowardly), and an outraged MacLeish quit *Fortune* in June 1938.

By then he had opened a new venue for public poetry with his pioneering verse play, *The Fall of the City*, broadcast by CBS radio's Columbia Workshop on April 11, 1937. A thirty-minute antifascist allegory, it again featured Orson Welles, this time as a radio announcer sonorously reporting the happenings in a great urban square wherein are gathered the citizenry. (It was produced in the Seventh Regiment's armory, using a cast of two hundred drama students to provide crowd noise at no cost.) A messenger brings news: a conqueror has landed. The crowd panics, what to do? A pacifist says no need to resist, reason and truth will prevail. Priests say renounce the things of this world. An old soldier says fight, but the people won't, believing the conqueror invincible. "The city is doomed! There's no holding it! Let the conqueror have it! It's his! The age is his! It's his century! Our institutions are obsolete." They bow before the conqueror, who walks into the square, armor clanking, and lifts his visor. The armor is empty, the announcer tells us, but people refuse to see. The empty armor raises its arm in salute, the people shout: "The city of masterless men has found a master! The city has fallen! The city has fallen!"

Despite being up against the *Jack Benny Program*, the parable garnered a tremendous audience and much critical praise. Anti-interventionists accused MacLeish of "fear-mongering," but he saw himself as embarked on a campaign to nerve democrats to fight fascism. By 1939, the poet had become one of the nation's strongest advocates of supporting Britain and France and preparing for full-scale war. And, like Mumford, he kept up a drumfire against the insufficiently antifascist. In April 1940 he delivered a talk called "The Irresponsibles." Printed in *The Nation* that May, it excoriated scholars and writers who remained neutral and pushed them to help prepare the nation for war. A more barbed speech followed, published in *The New Republic* in June, naming names of writers he blamed for having made Americans distrustful of moral judgments and insisting there must be "final things for which democracy will fight."

Such resolute views closely paralleled FDR's; indeed MacLeish saw himself as Roosevelt's man. So did Roosevelt, who made him Librarian of Congress. And in 1940, MacLeish was inducted into FDR's inner circle of wordsmiths, where he joined Hopkins, Rosenman, and Sherwood in drafting presidential speeches.

55

Reality Radio

Broadway plays and radio dramas could help shape the popular mood and mind, but to mobilize political support for preparedness—and a third term—Roosevelt needed something less elliptical, more direct, something that dramatized the European crisis in a way that packed a serious wallop, something equal in magnitude to the unfolding events themselves. And beginning in 1938 he got it, with the emergence in New York of a new mode of communicating news from overseas, courtesy of Bill Paley's CBS and the smoky-voiced Edward R. Murrow, the country's first on-air foreign correspondent.

In 1935, Murrow was still working at the Institute of International Education (218 Madison Avenue), helping refugee scholars find new employment, when he heard that CBS, farther up Madison (at 52nd), was looking for someone to work on educational programming. Murrow was taken on board in September, given the title Director of Talks, and put in charge of finding speakers to fill the significant amount of unsponsored airtime that the network had set aside to comply with federal regulations. The tall and lean Murrow, now twenty-eight, proved resourceful in finding talking heads, often on opposite sides of an issue, as when he arranged shortwave presentations by the crown prince of Ethiopia, who described Mussolini's aggression, and with Mussolini himself.

In 1937, CBS sent Murrow to London to serve as director of European operations. To cover the Continent, Murrow hired William L. Shirer, a Hearst wire-service reporter who'd been writing on Germany since 1934 but had just lost his job. Together they booked Europeans to broadcast on Paley's CBS—partly to show the network was au courant with the developing crisis, partly to muscle in on David Sarnoff's NBC, their great rival (abroad as at home), having gained a monopoly-like grip in that part of the world. NBC being far better wired into the circuitry of European notables, Murrow and Shirer had to settle for a more motley collection, which included speakers of stature but also novelty acts, assorted choruses, and bagpipers. And, as Shirer disappointedly told his diary, "Murrow and I are not supposed to do any talking on the radio ourselves."

The network's nervousness about live reportage stemmed from fear of on-air missteps, particularly the emitting of an opinion that might distress either a powerful sponsor or, worse, the Roosevelt Administration's Federal Communications Commission, which could giveth and taketh away broadcasting licenses. The safest approach to news was to summarize material that had previously appeared in print, a task handled smoothly by newsreader Bob Trout. It was also acceptable to offer some "analysis" of news—the purview of "commentators" like Boake Carter and H. V. Kaltenborn—but only if they refrained from offering any "opinions," especially any that might embarrass the station. What was wanted, said Ed Klauber, who had come to CBS in 1930 as Paley's #2, was "objective" and "nonpartisan" analysis in the vein of *New York Times* reporting (the brilliant if abrasive Klauber had been that paper's night city editor). Klauber told Kaltenborn so many times not to express a "point of view" that the commentator named his country home in New Jersey "Point of View," because, he said, it was the only place he could have one.

In practice, however, Paley and Klauber afforded their on-air columnists considerable leeway, depending on what their opinions were. Boake Carter—the Russian-born son of British parents, whose high-toned accent helped propel him to the front of the commentator pack—made huge sums for CBS, savaging labor unions and the New Deal without objection. Then Carter became a heated anti-interventionist and claimed Roosevelt was plotting to drag the country into war. The administration relayed its concerns to General Foods, Carter's sponsor; and to Benton & Bowles, his producers; and the CIO began talking boycott. General Foods canceled its sponsorship, and, on August 26, 1938, CBS canceled his newscast.

Kaltenborn fared better. Despite (or because of) his pontifical and much-parodied delivery style, the ex-*Brooklyn Eagle* reporter, vastly knowledgeable about foreign affairs and fluent in French and German, was widely hailed for his 1930s coverage of crises in Europe and the Far East. When his reportage on the Spanish Civil War evidenced clear Loyalist sympathy (his transcripts were gathered into book form during the summer of 1937 by Mary McCarthy), the station looked (and listened) away. Kaltenborn was even allowed to express emphatic support for each step FDR took toward intervention.

Why? Perhaps because Klauber was a New Deal Democrat, who worshiped FDR. Paley was also a Roosevelt supporter—thanks in some degree to the influence of his wife, Dorothy, a passionate partisan, but also to Paley's hyper-awareness of the president's command of the regulatory apparatus and his readiness to use it. Back in 1936, when the overwhelming majority of the print media had been vitriolically anti-Roosevelt, CBS had handed him a megaphone with which to reach the voters. Nevertheless, as of 1938, the CBS high command's de facto tolerance of editorializing did not extend to its tiny European contingent, and Edward R. Murrow, though a successful organizer (and an FDR enthusiast), remained an off-air (and fairly obscure) presence.

On March 11 of that year, Murrow was in Poland, arranging a broadcast of children's choruses, when the Nazis marched into Austria. Shirer was in Vienna, but when he tried to broadcast the story, German troops prodded him out of the Austrian state radio studio at bayonet point. Shirer flew to London to send off a belated report, and Murrow chartered a plane to fly from Warsaw to Vienna, to take over for Shirer. In the meantime, Max Jordan of NBC had arrived in Vienna, arranged air access, and—soundly scooping CBS—had beamed the first eyewitness account of Hitler's takeover to RCA's enormous receiving facilities at Riverhead, Long Island, which had relayed it by telephone line to the master control room in Radio City, whence it had gone out by wire to NBC affiliates.

Back in Gotham, Paley was in a frenzy. Faced with this competitive debacle, he not only abandoned the broadcast ban on the spot but insisted on arranging, that very evening (March 13), a thirty-minute report from various European capitals on the response to Hitler's gambit.

Shirer immediately agreed to this, though nothing exactly like it had ever been done and he had less than eight hours to pull it off. Which he did, arranging for newspaper reporters (and shortwave transmitters) to cover Berlin, Paris, and Rome, while he readied himself to report from London, as did Murrow from Vienna. At 1:00 p.m. Greenwich Mean Time—8:00 p.m. Eastern Standard Time—"through my earphones [Shirer wrote] I could hear on our transatlantic 'feedback' Bob Trout announcing the broadcast from our New York studio." As the feed switched smoothly from capital to capital, the commentators offered their assessments. When it came Murrow's turn, he dove into the medium as if born to it, adlibbing from notes, offering analysis that was immediate, engaging, perceptive, and sensitive to the significance of the historic moment. "New York" declared it a success, Shirer jotted in his diary, adding: "They want another one tonight." Soon he added this prescient entry: "I think radio talks by Ed and me are now established. Birth of the 'radio foreign correspondent' so to speak."

Indeed it was. Quickly the station upped its level of coverage from European capitals and, in September 1938, from Munich, where after eighteen days of Hitler-provoked crisis, Neville Chamberlain and Édouard Daladier agreed to the partitioning of Czechoslovakia. Throughout the tumultuous events, CBS transmitted live bulletins and news flashes from Murrow and his colleagues at listening posts around Europe to headquarters in New York, their voices crackling and stuttering their way across the Atlantic, intermittent victims of static caused by bad weather and sunspots. Their material was funneled to Kaltenborn, who camped out for the duration in Studio Nine, sleeping on a cot, subsisting on onion soup and coffee, rushing repeatedly to the microphone to elaborate on the arriving nuggets of news from Berchtesgaden or Paris; each of his more than 100 broadcasts was prefaced, at his insistence, with the announcement—"H. V. Kaltenborn, here with a keen analysis"—which they often were.

The Anschluss whetted Americans' interest in broadcast journalism; Munich made it an obsession. For the first time in the medium's history, newscasts outdrew soap operas and other entertainment. Reality radio had proven far more gripping than anything hack writers could come up with—or Archibald MacLeish, for that matter. Radio now edged out newspapers as the preferred source of updates—putting paid virtually overnight to the old tradition of newsboys hawking special editions through the streets, shouting "Extra! Extra!"; people now got their breaking news off the air.

Once again New York had reaffirmed its position as the indispensable channeler of news and information from world to country. No one realized just how potent those broadcast words had become until their power was spectacularly (if inadvertently) demonstrated, scant weeks after the Munich crisis, by live CBS coverage of a very different species of invasion.

56

Mars Invades New York

MacLeish's *Fall of the City* attracted other poets and writers to the medium—Stephen Vincent Benét, Edna St. Vincent Millay, and the young Arthur Miller—ushering in a golden era of radio drama. MacLeish himself returned to the form in 1938 with *Air Raid*, also for the Columbia Workshop. Again a conqueror arrives, this time raining destruction from the skies, Guernica style, on innocent women and children. Again the story is vividly recounted by an on-the-spot radio announcer, who reports, over the roar of planes and machine guns: "We hear them: we can't see them. / We hear the shearing metal: / We hear the tearing air." And *Air Raid*, too, was a critical and popular success.

CBS had equally high hopes for another dramatic series it launched in 1938 when it offered Orson Welles, the now twenty-three-year-old wunderkind, a chance to direct his own weekly, hour-long program, which would be called the *Mercury Theatre on the Air*. Welles's radio career had shot upward the year before, his star turn in *Fall* that April being but a blip in a blur of performances, as he dashed from stage to studio, and from studio to studio, making on average $1,000 a week, a sensational sum in Depression-era America. In July 1937 Welles had produced, written, and directed a seven-part adaptation of Hugo's *Les Misérables* for the Mutual Broadcasting System, establishing a reputation for quality programming. The show had featured many of the performers from his and John Houseman's then-in-formation Mercury Theatre, established (officially, in August) in the aftermath of their impromptu staging of Marc Blitzstein's *The Cradle Will Rock* in June. In September he had helped Mutual relaunch its sensationally successful *The Shadow*, with Welles playing Lamont Cranston, wealthy young man-about-New-York by day, and by night the Shadow, ceaseless warrior against crime. In November he'd gone back to the boards with the Mercury's staging of *Julius Caesar*, set in contemporary Fascist Italy, featuring a production "look" that Welles had patterned after Nazi rallies at Nuremberg; Brooks Atkinson thought it "superb."

The 1938 CBS offer was irresistible to Welles because the network wasn't asking him just to reproduce stage plays, as did the long-running show *First Nighter*. That effort, billed as being broadcast from "The Little Theatre off Times Square," typically had Mr. First Nighter (Don Ameche) arriving to the sound of milling crowds, honking horns, and police whistles, being shown to a seat by an "usher," hearing "Curtain going up!," then listening to a reconstructed performance. Welles didn't want to mechanically transpose plays from stage to studio; he wanted to create a new and radio-specific form of storytelling.

The *Mercury* programs, which began July 11, 1938, got off to a slow start, receiving good reviews but low ratings throughout the summer. Then came the Halloween Eve broadcast, on Sunday, October 30, almost exactly a month after Munich and three days after MacLeish's *Air Raid*. On tap was an adaptation of H. G. Wells's *War of the Worlds*, which Houseman had handed Howard Koch, a writer on the *Mercury* team, suggesting he dramatize it in the form of news bulletins. Welles accepted the script Koch produced but added a whole new level of verisimilitude. Drawing on the European broadcasts so recently branded on public consciousness, he inserted break-in bulletins ("We interrupt this program to...") and on-the-scene reports ("We take you now to...")—and backgrounded everything with the hum and static of CBS's problematic shortwave broadcasts, including apparent breakdowns in transmission.

Welles's broadcast started at 8:00 p.m. with an introduction identifying it as a dramatization of the novel, then segued into a realistic-sounding broadcast-within-the-broadcast, fading in on a weather report in progress. Next an announcer said: "We take you now to the Meridian Room in the [nonexistent] Hotel Park Plaza in downtown New York, where you'll be entertained by the music [a tango] of Ramón Raquello and his orchestra." In short order the music is interrupted by a "special bulletin" about just-sighted explosions on Mars, followed by word that balls of hydrogen were "moving towards the earth with enormous velocity." It was as if they'd been "shot from a gun," said a Professor Pierson, a (putative) Princeton astronomer, to whom the station turned for a "live" interview. Then came reports of flaming objects striking the earth, one at Grovers Mill, a New Jersey town southwest of Gotham and eleven miles from Princeton. The announcer and professor traveled to the impact site just in time to see Martian monsters slither out of their space cylinders and proceed to incinerate nearly all in sight, using heat rays. The Martians then unleashed tripodal fighting machines, which smashed all the US troops sent against them and cut the Philadelphia–New York rail tracks, precipitating a mad flight of locals that quickly clogged the roads. (The "reporter" who described this "invasion" had listened to the *Hindenburg* coverage over and over, until he'd been able to pitch-perfectly imitate its tone of rising hysteria.)

At this point—about fifteen minutes into the program—a crucial event transpired on the Edgar Bergen and Charlie McCarthy ventriloquist show, over at NBC. Bergen ended his first routine, and he (and the dummy) turned the mike over to vocalist Dorothy Lamour, at which point, a sizable percentage of listeners dialed around, planning to return later. On this night, however, 12 percent of the vast audience twiddled their way into the Welles broadcast— its audience doubled from 3.6 to 6 million—pitching them, it seemed, into the middle of a horrific (and authentic-sounding) news report about an invasion under way from Mars. A considerable portion of these newcomers were totally freaked to hear that Martian war machines had crossed the Passaic River and entered the Jersey marshes, while others were marching across the Pulaski Skyway, their "evident objective," according to the "reporter," being New York.

The "coverage" now switched to an announcer on the roof of the "Broadcasting Building, New York City," who, against a cacophonous SFX backdrop, reported breathlessly that "the bells you hear are ringing to warn the people to evacuate the city as the Martians approach. Estimated in the last two hours three million people have moved out along the

Orson Welles delivers his radio program, "First Person Singular," photo c. 1938. (Photo by Hulton Archive/Getty Images)

roads to the north.... Hutchinson River Parkway still kept open for motor traffic. Avoid bridges to Long Island...hopelessly jammed.... No more defenses. Our army is...wiped out...artillery, air force, everything wiped out."

Looking down at the harbor (cue boat whistles), the announcer saw "all manner of boats, overloaded with fleeing population, pulling out from docks." Streets were jammed and noise had reached New Year's Eve levels when the enemy hove into site above the Palisades. The first great machine crossed the Hudson "like a man wading through a brook." Others followed. They stood watching, looking over the city—their steel, cowlish heads "even with the skyscrapers"—like "a line of new towers on the city's west side." Now they emitted black smoke, which drifted over the city. "People in the streets see it now. They're running towards the East River...thousands of them, dropping in like rats. Now the smoke's spreading faster. It's reached Times Square. People are trying to run away from it, but it's no use. They're falling like flies. Now the smoke's crossing Sixth Avenue...Fifth Avenue...a...a hundred yards away...it's fifty feet...(BODY FALLS) (SOUNDS OF CITY IN TURMOIL, FOGHORNS, WHISTLES...)."

At this point the show broke frame. "You are listening to a CBS presentation of Orson Welles and the Mercury Theatre on the Air in an original dramatization of 'The War of the Worlds' by H. G. Wells. The performance will continue after a brief intermission. This is the Columbia Broadcasting System."

By this time, however, out in the real city and the surrounding region, mass hysteria reigned. People in New Jersey towns and cities leapt into their cars and roared down the highway, fleeing the imaginary invaders. One stopped to call his cousin, who lived on a farm "in the destructive path," to ask if there were Martians there. "No," his cousin replied, "but the Tuttles are, and we're about to sit down to dinner."

In Gotham, thousands milled in the streets, gathered in parks, jammed switchboards at police, newspaper, and radio stations. Callers sought advice on protective measures against the raids, asking if "the wave of poison gas will reach as far as Queens," if they would be safer in the cellar or on the roof, how could they safeguard their children—just the questions that had worried residents of London and Paris during the tense days before the Munich agreement.

Those who had stayed tuned might have found fictional relief in following Professor Pierson as he made his way toward Gotham. On the journey he met a half-mad artilleryman who planned to rally remaining humans to fight from underground bases he'd establish in New York's sewers, cellars, vaults, underground storerooms, railway tunnels, and subways. Pierson straggled on to the Holland Tunnel, walked through the "silent tube," and headed north, walking up body-littered Broadway, past Canal Street, past Fourteenth Street, past Times Square. At Columbus Circle he spotted flocks of black birds circling the sky over Central Park, where he discovered "standing in a silent row along the mall, nineteen of those great metal Titans, their cowls empty, their steel arms hanging listlessly by their sides." Below lay the Martians, "killed by the putrefactive and disease bacteria against which their systems were unprepared," the hungry birds tearing brown shreds of flesh from their corpses.

Many listeners, however, were not soothed but enraged, and they inundated CBS switchboards threatening every kind of mayhem (including bomb threats) against those who had perpetrated this malicious hoax. Welles was shaken by the furor—he held a press conference the next day to apologize—but he profited mightily from the notoriety and soon bounded off to Hollywood to raise Kane on that coast.

The print media had a field day clucking at their rival's irresponsibility. The true implications for press-radio relations, however, were spelled out in more scholarly postmortems. Paul Lazarsfeld, the Austrian émigré who had pioneered techniques to probe listener responses for purposes of facilitating market research and investigating the media's social and political implications, had established, with Rockefeller Foundation support, the Newark-based Radio Project, which he codirected with Frank Stanton and Hadley Cantril. In 1939, the project moved from Newark to Manhattan (49th and Amsterdam), changed its name to Office of Radio Research (ORR), and shifted its institutional affiliation from Princeton to Columbia (where Lazarsfeld would receive an academic post in sociology). At the same time, researchers were working on an in-depth study—*Radio and the Printed Page*—that the ORR published in 1940. It confirmed that radio news was rapidly supplanting that provided by newspapers and indeed had already done so among the working- and lower-middle-classes, women, and young people (the first "radio generation.") Also in 1940, Hadley Cantril published *The Invasion from Mars: A Study in the Psychology of Panic*, which confirmed that of the six million who'd heard the broadcast, 1.7 million had thought it an authentic newscast and 1.2 million had been genuinely frightened ("I felt the catastrophe was an attack by the Germans" was a common response among those surveyed for the study).

The networks themselves, newly aware that foreign news coverage generated prestige and profits (companies were clamoring to sponsor newscasts), professionalized their staffs and augmented their coverage, readying themselves for a possible war. At CBS, Eric Sevareid (he'd been with the *Herald Tribune*'s Paris edition and would cover the fall of France) and Elmer Davis (a former *Times* reporter and freelance writer who would pinch-hit for Kaltenborn) were taken on in 1939 as correspondent and commentator, respectively. Librarians, researchers, and editors were put in place and the newsroom refurbished, enlarged, put on promotional display. CBS made "European News Roundup" a regular feature which, together with Kaltenborn's commentary, gave CBS a solid half-hour of nightly news and left it well prepared to cover the war when it arrived.

Most of what went out on the airwaves in 1940 strongly backed Franklin Roosevelt's interventionist policies. Murrow was deeply imbricated in the English scene, and explicitly and implicitly his coverage supported aid to the Allies. (He now adopted a new opening for his broadcast—the grave "This...is London"—whose emphasis and intonation his mother had suggested.) Elmer Davis (recipient of a Rhodes scholarship to Oxford, as were "Murrow Boys" Charles Collingswood and Howard K. Smith) was a persistent advocate of intervention, who stopped just short of calling for a declaration of war. And Kaltenborn's pro-British bias became steadily more unabashed. Some advertisers protested to Paley that Kaltenborn was trying to push the nation into war, but even after General Mills dropped its sponsorship in 1939 the network kept him on the air.

In 1940, not only did the overwhelming majority of commentators—on all networks—back the Administration, so, too, did almost everything else on radio, from public service programs promoting mobilization, to privately sponsored "patriotic" broadcasts that were thinly disguised propaganda, to commercially sponsored radio dramas that not so subtly presented an interventionist perspective. Not surprisingly, when Roosevelt's adviser on media relations surveyed the radio scene a year later, he reported with satisfaction that the balance between material supporting FDR's policies, and that opposing them, was "completely in our favor" from "straight news presentation to the most elaborate dramatic presentations, of which there are many."

57

Winchell Calling to All Ships at Sea

Despite this good news, Roosevelt was well aware that he also needed some powerful mainstream newspapers on his side. The mainstream, however, had been flowing away from him with ever-increasing velocity. In 1936 nearly two-thirds of the nation's dailies had opposed his reelection. The way the 1940 contest was shaping up, three-quarters would be against him. Press barons previously in his corner—like Roy Howard, commodore of the Scripps Howard fleet flagshipped by the *New York World-Telegram*, and Henry Luce, commander of the *Time-Life-Fortune* triumvirate—were shifting their editorial support to the Republican camp. The Patterson-McCormick combine was still divided: Colonel McCormick's *Chicago Tribune* remained in vitriolic opposition to FDR, but his cousin Captain Patterson's *New York Daily News* was backing the president, though only because Patterson still believed Roosevelt was keeping us out of "Europe's war."

Hearst's papers, on the other hand, were unanimous in their animus. Which made it even odder that the president's single-biggest supporter among nationally syndicated columnists—apart from Eleanor, whose *My Day* articles in seventy-five newspapers reached over four million readers—was Hearst's superstar, Walter Winchell. "On Broadway," Winchell's column in the *New York Daily Mirror*, had a syndicated circulation of nearly nine million; and his rat-a-tat-tat radio show, aired weekly on NBC, drew an audience of twenty-five million, tying Bob Hope's program for highest rated in 1940.

FDR had begun cultivating Winchell back in 1932, and Walter had responded big time. He came to idolize Roosevelt—"If I Had an Aladdin's Lamp," he wrote, "I'd fix matters so that F.D.R. never even caught a cold"—and he became an effusive New Deal supporter. Washington officials fed him scoops for his column, and he in turn translated complex Rooseveltian initiatives into staccato bulletins for "Mr. and Mrs. America and all the ships at sea."

In 1938, by which time Winchell was virtually part of the Administration, the role of conduit to the Cub Room (the Stork Club inner sanctum where Walter held court at Table 50) was assumed by Ernest Cuneo. A New Jersey–born son of Italian immigrants, Cuneo had paid his way through Columbia College by writing for the *Daily News*. After graduating from St. John's Law, he'd worked for La Guardia, first as law clerk, then as mayoral fixer; he then joined the national Administration in a similar role. Cuneo began training up from Union to Penn Station to meet Winchell at 21, rather than the Stork, to maintain a lower profile, though at nearly 300 pounds he was hardly inconspicuous. Possessed of Falstaffian spirit as well as girth, Cuneo got on famously with Walter, who affectionately called him Fatso, but the connection rested on interlocking interests. Winchell got juicy tidbits for "the column" and a pipeline to the Administration's high command; Roosevelt got a bullhorn to promote his policies to the public; and Cuneo got entree to New York's showbiz and society worlds. In 1940 the link grew even stronger, when the profligate Cuneo, notoriously short of cash, was put on retainer (at $10,000 a year) for "legal services" which at times included ghostwriting "the column."

Liberal Democrats relied heavily on Winchell to publicize the "Draft Roosevelt" campaign—"Look, Walter, you *are* the Third Term campaign," Cuneo wanted to tell him—and increasingly to promote FDR's foreign policy as well. Winchell had recognized the threat posed by the Nazis far earlier than many others ("[Hitler's] hatred of the Israelites is contemptible—and when an assassin shoots him down some day a lot of locals won't be sorry...," he had written in 1933). Paying ever-closer attention to European events over the decade, he grew correspondingly less interested in celebrity chitchat. "I don't care who phffts on Broadway," he said in 1938, "but if Hitler and Mussolini phfft, that's news." He added an editorial segment to his broadcast that year—less gossip, more commentary—and denounced the Munich agreement. Though he opposed direct military involvement in "morally bankrupt" Europe, he aggressively backed Roosevelt's arms buildup: "We must stop kidding ourselves, ladies and gentlemen, that Americans can lick anybody. Maybe we can't." After the fall of France, he became an ardent interventionist. When Adolf Berle asked Cuneo if Walter might "help prepare the country for war," Cuneo replied, "The guy thinks Arnold's been doing it since 1930."

Winchell had little compunction about equating resistance to intervention with subservience to foreign powers. With Administration blessing he even attacked congressional opponents, calling Montana Representative Jacob Thorkelson the "mouthpiece of the Nazi movement in Congress." Thorkelson responded with relative delicacy, rebuking Winchell as a "Jewish vilifier" who slanders anyone who does not agree "with his own organized minority." Representative John E. Rankin of Mississippi, less inhibited, blasted Winchell as "a little slime-mongering kike."

Nothing daunted, in 1940 the columnist started a new feature, "The Winchell Column vs. The Fifth Column," which linked domestic right-wingers to fascists abroad. (He was unsparing of local Communists, as well.) Winchell drew on inside information from FBI chief Hoover, who become a close friend and fellow Stork Club habitué after the death of Hoover's mother in 1938. That was when Hoover and Clyde Tolson (cattily referred to as "Mrs. Hoover" by club owner Sherman Billingsley) had begun spending most weekends in New York, putatively to visit the FBI's largest field office, actually to shuttle between their complimentary Waldorf suite, the track, and various night spots (besides the Cub Room, where they hung out with Winchell at Table 50, their regular ports of call included Soulé, Maxim's, Gallaghers, 21, and Toots Shor's).

Winchell also relied on a young New York attorney named Arnold Forster, general counsel for the Anti-Defamation League of B'nai B'rith. Forster, born Arnold Fastenberg, had grown up in Hunts Point, the son of a struggling clothing manufacturer, and studied law at

St. John's. After a confrontation with a group of anti-Semitic thugs in 1937, Forster formed a group that monitored rightist outfits and filed complaints with police officials. After 1940, when he was recruited by the ADL, Forster had one of most thorough dossiers on the American right, which he put at Winchell's service. At times, like Cuneo, he drafted entire columns.

Winchell's combination of New Deal liberalism and flag-waving bellicosity was a big hit with many. It also won him enemies, such as the *World Telegram*'s Westbrook Pegler. A sportswriter turned political columnist, Pegler, with publisher Roy Howard's full blessing, had turned virulently against FDR, the New Deal, the CIO, and the Newspaper Guild. Himself possessed of a pen so venomous that Harold Ickes once said he would no more read Pegler than handle raw sewage, Pegler scathingly savaged Winchell's "gent's room journalism," suggesting he was a keyhole voyeur, a sloppy reporter, and a deadbeat who gave mentions to clubs in return for favors rendered.

Walter was also attacked by those more in tune with his politics—by intellectual elites who had once been amused by him as a gossip and were now appalled to see him taken seriously as an opinion molder; that was *their* bailiwick. In 1939, Harold Ross authorized a *New Yorker* carve-up and handed the knife to veteran newsman St. Clair McKelway, great-nephew of the longtime *Brooklyn Eagle* editor whose name he shared. When it ran in 1940—at six installments, the longest profile in the magazine's history—it skewered Winchell's credibility (41.2 percent of a representative sample of columns were pronounced "completely inaccurate," another 18.3 percent "partially inaccurate") and accused him of degrading the profession ("like a spirochete in the body of journalism"). Winchell counterattacked in his *Mirror* column, reporting that Ross wore no underwear. The editor retorted by mailing him the shorts he'd been wearing while reading the column. Winchell got the last word, as usual, by having Billingsley bar Ross from the Stork.

Far and away Winchell's most dangerous opponent, however, was his own employer. Hearst had never liked Walter but, valuing his drawing power, had given him more or less free rein so long as he'd stuck to gossip. Political columns were something else, especially those with which he disagreed. Hearst began editing out the disagreeable paragraphs, then axing whole columns. Winchell flirted with the *Daily News*, and Hearst backed off. In 1940, with the election looming, the publisher began wing-clipping again, and Walter would begin to search more seriously for an alternative outlet.

He might have considered the *New York Evening Post*, though Broadway columnist Leonard Lyons (still a friend of Winchell's) had been ensconced there since 1934. But that paper was once again in turmoil.

58

Stern's Post, Dolly's Daily

The *Post* had been owned by liberals since 1881, when it had been acquired, along with *The Nation*, by railroad magnate Henry Villard. In 1900, on Villard's death, it passed to his son Oswald Garrison Villard. In 1918, however, his opposition to the First World War having riled many readers and advertisers, Villard had agreed to sell the paper (while keeping the magazine) to Morgan banker Thomas W. Lamont. Lamont put its management in the hands of Edwin F. Gay, a former Harvard professor, and in 1922, Gay organized a syndicate that included Franklin D. Roosevelt, which purchased the *Post* from Morgan. The paper's ongoing financial troubles forced a sale in 1924 to Cyrus H. K. Curtis of Philadelphia, publisher of hugely successful magazines like the *Saturday Evening Post* (no relation) and the *Ladies' Home Journal*. Curtis expanded the *New York Evening Post*; built a modern plant for it at 75 West Street, in 1926; and—conservative that he was—switched its editorial support to the Republican Party.

When Curtis died in June 1933, his trustees were desperate to unload the *Post*, then losing well over a million dollars a year. They finally found a potential buyer in another Philadelphia publisher, David Stern, whose *Philadelphia Record* was the city's only liberal paper, a lone Democratic sheet surrounded by nine Republican ones. Profits were not the *Post*'s chief attraction for Stern; politics was. Before the 1932 convention—having been flattered, charmed, stroked, and finally captivated by FDR—he had switched his support from Al Smith to the man his competitors called "that Bolshevik governor from New York." In 1933, the victorious Roosevelt urged Stern to buy the paper of which he'd once been part owner, assuring him of full support, and Stern did the deal that December. Dropping "Evening" from the masthead, where it had been affixed by Alexander Hamilton back in 1801, he splashed a presidential letter of congratulation across four columns of his first front page (and posted a plaudit from Mayor-elect La Guardia, whom the paper had denounced, in its former incarnation, as "semi-socialistic").

Stern now set out to give the *Post* a liberal makeover. In doing so, he relied heavily on Isidor Feinstein, his chief editorial writer at the *Philadelphia Record*, who accompanied him to New York. The son and presumptive successor of a dry goods entrepreneur, Feinstein had instead been bitten by the journalism bug and drawn into radical politics by the Sacco-Vanzetti case. By 1931, age twenty-three, he'd become the *Record*'s preeminent public voice. At first, Feinstein had been far more skeptical than his boss about Roosevelt's commitment to reform. He went so far as to publish a piece in V. F. Calverton's *Modern Monthly* entitled "Roosevelt Moves Toward Fascism," referring to deflationary policies that he believed had aligned FDR with the "god-damndest bunch of Wall Streeters." But not long after he and his wife resettled into an apartment at 1 West 68th Street, Feinstein was churning out the pro-FDR editorials that would make him, and the *Post*, the toast of Gotham's liberal circles.

Thanks in part to its provision of a political perspective not seen, said Stern, "since the *World* was absorbed by the *Telegram*," the paper began to grow. Its circulation, 60,000 when Stern took over, passed 100,000 in 1934, and in 1937 hit 250,000. Many readers were liberal working-class Jews from the outer boroughs. Riders on the Brooklyn-Manhattan Transit Corporation's Sea Beach and 4th Avenue Line who perused the conservative *Wall Street Journal* or *World-Telegram*—young Brooklynite Joseph Heller noticed—would exit the car at 59th Street and transfer to the train bound for Bay Ridge; *Post* aficionados invariably carried on to Brighton Beach or Coney Island.

The paper, not surprisingly, took an antifascist stance. Stern supported the anti-German boycott early on, even though it cost him Macy's advertising business. In 1938, at Stern's urging, Isidor Feinstein changed his name, lest people dismiss his editorials as ethnic pleading. Initializing his first name, he added an "F."—a nod to "Feinstein"—then translated the German "stein" to the English "stone." I. F. Stone always denied this was an attempt to hide his identity, impossible in any case, he liked to say, as "I look like a Jewish bullfrog."

Stern and Stone soon had a falling out over, among other issues, the paper's position on the Popular Front. Stern opposed the alliance of communism and liberalism. Stone, though he denounced the Moscow Trials as a "typical governmental frame-up," soft-pedaled his reservations in the interest of antifascist unity; in '39 he signed the "400 letter" though promptly denounced the Nazi–Soviet pact. Demoted by Stern from editorials to obits, Stone began writing for Freda Kirchwey's *Nation*. In one piece he compared the Soviet incursions into Finland to Franco's into Spain. In 1940, Kirchwey made him the magazine's Washington correspondent, and "Izzy" moved down to DC.

Stern was left in command of a sinking ship, as the return of hard times in 1938 had cut into circulation, and dwindling retail sales brought ad cutbacks. Nor could he convince Percy Straus to restore Macy's now-crucial advertising. At one point they had a peace conference and worked out a deal, only to have Straus say, as they were wrapping up, "David, how about those editorials?"—at which Stern grabbed Straus by the throat, ending the short-lived truce. Stern had also signed a generous contract with the Newspaper Guild but was forced to exact worker givebacks (obtained with FDR's help), lest the *Post* (Gotham's only New Deal paper) go belly up. Even so, by spring 1939 monthly losses were mounting. Stern began looking for a buyer. No one would touch it.

Finally, George Backer Jr., a wealthy New York City real estate operator, stepped up. Backer was an ardent New Dealer, civil libertarian, anticommunist, antifascist (he ran the American Jewish Committee's program subsidizing anti-Nazi literature), and, since 1938, a New York City councilman representing the American Labor Party. Despite having all these credentials, Backer's biggest asset by far was his wife.

Dorothy (Dolly) Schiff was the daughter of investment banker Mortimer Schiff and Adele Schiff, and granddaughter of Jacob Henry Schiff, the Kuhn, Loeb magnate-philanthropist. Though Mortimer had lost half his fortune in the Crash, the family was still immensely rich.

After graduating Brearley in 1920 (age seventeen) she married Richard B. W. Hall, a socialite bond salesman (also a drunk, philanderer, and anti-Semite). Dolly spent much of the decade partying and having her own affairs (with Serge Obolensky, Averell Harriman, Jim Forrestal, and British press magnate Lord Beaverbrook). In 1931, when her father died, she divorced Hall. In 1932, when her mother died, she inherited fifteen million dollars and married Backer.

Schiff now shed her lifelong Republicanism. She studied the history of the US Progressive Movement with Max Ascoli at the New School and plunged into social welfare activism herself. She joined the boards of the Henry Street Settlement, the Women's Trade Union League of New York, and the New York Joint Committee for the Ratification of the Child Labor Amendment. La Guardia appointed her to the New York City Board of Child Welfare. As a liberal Democratic convert, she took an active role in FDR's 1936 campaign, overcoming her shyness to make speeches on his behalf. She was then invited to meet the president at Hyde Park. FDR cottoned to her—something of a snob, he liked well-bred and well-dressed women—and Dolly was regularly summoned up for weekends (and summoned to bed as well, she would claim, then deny). FDR took her for high-speed rides over back roads in his V-8 Ford touring car equipped with manual controls. At his urging, they bought adjacent parcels of nearby property together.

But it was her purchase of the *New York Post* from David Stern in July 1939 that really warmed Roosevelt's heart: "How's the paper?" became his routine greeting when he saw her. Dolly stayed out of the business, apart from paying its bills, and installed Backer as editor, publisher, and president. Backer brought in Norman Bel Geddes to redesign it, and by 1940 it was just getting back on its feet.

Then, suddenly, a competitor emerged, one that also had Franklin Roosevelt's blessing, as the newcomer perfectly represented his left-liberal, domestic-foreign perspective. And it was run, not by a novice, but by one of the most brilliant journalists on the New York City scene.

59

PM

Ralph McAllister ("Mac") Ingersoll, a New Haven–born engineer's son, had graduated Yale in 1921 as a mining engineer, but after working in the hard-rock trade for two years, left it for a reporter's job with Hearst's *New York American*. Catapulting up the world of Manhattan journalism, Ingersoll spent five years (1925–29) reinvigorating the *New Yorker* as its managing editor, then joined the Luceian empire in 1930, becoming *Fortune*'s first managing editor (1931–35), Luce's chief aide (1935–36, during which time he helped create *Life*), then, in 1937, head of *Time*.

Tall, shambling, flamboyant. and neurotic, Ingersoll loved the high life. When divorced from his first wife (in 1938) he settled into an easy bachelorhood, taking up elegant residence at the Union Club—the city's oldest, recently relocated to a Delano & Aldrich building on Park Avenue and 69th Street—whose kitchen offered a choice of thirty dishes for breakfast, any of which could be served in bed.

Yet Ingersoll—descended from Robert Ingersoll, the feisty freethinker—adopted staunchly progressive positions during the Depression decade, becoming friendly with liberals like Archibald MacLeish and leftists such as Lillian Hellman and Dashiell Hammett (though he himself never joined the CPUSA). Attuned to criticism emanating from these New York circles, Ingersoll tried to push Luce leftward. He passed along their accusations that *Time* was written by "new rich Yale boys in whose world labor movements were things to be laughed at, baited, ignored." Like *Fortune* staffers MacLeish and Dwight Macdonald, he was particularly upset about *Time*'s foreign editor Goldsborough's fawning over Franco. After Ingersoll assumed control of the magazine, he eventually convinced Luce to retire Goldie, and *Time* began attacking union-busters and refusing to condemn sit-down strikers. As former editor John Shaw Billings saw it, "Ingersoll has revolutionized and sovietized things."

Luce was slow to see Hitler as more than a Berlin bully-boy, while Ingersoll became obsessed with him. Clashes ensued. *Time*'s January 1939 issue was scheduled to feature the Führer as "Man of the Year"—not in tribute, supposedly, but only in recognition of his newsworthiness. Yet Ingersoll found the proposed cover portrait to be decidedly flattering. Fuming that it must have been sent along by Goebbels, he scrapped it and substituted a lithograph, drawn by an Austrian refugee, that depicted a diabolical Hitler accompanying, on an organ, the torture of naked bodies. The associated (distinctly un-Goldie-esque) copy portrayed the new Man of the Year "the greatest threatening force that the democratic, freedom-loving world faces today."

Luce was livid. Ingersoll decided it was time to leave, and, indeed, to become a publisher himself. He would launch a "daily news magazine" whose motto would be: "We are against people who push other people around, whether they flourish in this country or abroad." The motto perfectly captured Roosevelt's domestic-and-foreign stance, and Ingersoll discussed the project directly with the president in 1939. Not only did FDR declare his enthusiastic support for a liberal tabloid in Gotham, which could serve as foil to Hearst and Howard, he helped Ingersoll find financial backers like Jock Whitney, Elinor Gimbel, and—another heir to a department store fortune—Marshall Field III, among others.

Given Ingersoll's rep as publishing genius, most of the investors were hoping for a pecuniary as well as a political payoff. This was a risky bet. No daily paper had succeeded in entering the New York market since 1924. Quite the opposite, several had folded their tents, including the *World*, *Graphic*, and *American*. And still the field was crowded with mass circulation dailies. In 1940, there were two morning two-cent tabloids (the *News* and *Mirror*) and two three-penny, 8-column broadsheets (the *Times* and *Herald Tribune*). There was the afternoon pack of three-centers (the *Journal-American*, *World-Telegram*, *Post*, and *Evening Sun*), which the newcomer was intending to join; hence its name, *PM*. And there were yet other competitors, like the *Brooklyn Daily Eagle*, the *Daily Worker*, and a host of foreign-language dailies.

The venture was dicier still given Ingersoll's announcement that *PM* would not accept paid advertising, in order to retain its independence from "men of property," at least those who were not among its backers. Instead, it would charge a hefty five cents and live on subscriptions and newsstand sales; Ingersoll calculated the daily break-even point at 200,000 copies (the *Times* moved 500,000; the *Daily News* nearly two million).

To generate requisite sales, Ingersoll intended to revolutionize journalism, breaking with generations of encrusted convention. For starters he would incorporate into his newspaper the strategies he'd deployed at his magazines—blending texts with images as in *Life*, organizing news into departments, as in *Time*, and encouraging good writing backed by strong research, as in *Fortune*. Stories would be lively narratives, with beginnings, middles, and ends, rather than top heavy recitals starting with a "tell all lead" that crammed the main facts in the first paragraph. Nor would reporters have to adopt a solemn and "objective" tone: they could use their own voice, declare their own sympathies, and control the presentation of their stories, down to headlines and captions. In addition, they would be afforded the pay scale and protections of a model Newspaper Guild contract.

Not surprisingly, over 10,000 writers applied for fewer than 200 positions. Many were prepared to abandon the better money available working in mainstream papers, pulp fiction, advertising, or glossy magazines, to gain the promised freedom of action and self-expression. Contributors would include Ernest Hemingway, Erskine Caldwell, James Thurber, Dalton Trumbo, Dorothy Parker, Ben Hecht, Leon Edel, James Wechsler, Max Lerner, Dashiell Hammett, Lillian Hellman—and Walter Winchell: when Hearst cracked down on his *Mirror* pieces, Winchell started a regular column in *PM* under the pen name Paul Revere II.

PM would be as attentive to looks as to content. It would be a tabloid, a bit smaller than either the *News* or *Mirror*, with its thirty-two pages stapled together along the spine, facilitating its being read with one hand in a swaying subway car. The front page would use color. All the pages would attain magazine-comparable quality by using the latest technology of applying hot ink to water-cooled paper. Graphics would include award-winning typefaces, sketches, diagrams, isometric maps, and cartoons by Dr. Seuss—but above all photography (*PM* might well have stood for "picture magazine").

The paper blended photos into narratives, constructed photo-essays, and created montages that grouped images of the same subject shot by different photographers. The pictures ranged from Margaret Bourke-White's grand Soho Reflex images to the gentle street scenes of Helen Levitt, to the gritty portraits of working-class life by Weegee (born Usher Fellig in Ukraine), the closest match of photographer and journalistic mission. Though never on staff, Weegee published hundreds of images in *PM*—which were credited, unlike the anonymity with which his work in other papers was cloaked; in fact, he even got to write a column telling the (often violent) tale behind his Speed Graphic shots.

Ingersoll drew on talented promoters as well, like master advertiser William Benton, of Madison Avenue's Benton & Bowles (his partner, Chester Bowles, was a *PM* investor). Benton orchestrated the paper's launch with massive fanfare—arranging events, such as a competition-exhibition at MOMA to choose artists who could report the news by drawing it—and he managed to generate stories in all the papers in town, and by all their columnists. "We greeted it," A. J. Liebling recalled, "with the delight that bird-watchers manifest when the Department of the Interior reports the birth of a new whooping crane." Over 100,000 subscriptions were sold in advance.

Captain Patterson, however, was not pleased. Despite the *Daily News*'s 1.9 million reader advantage over the upstart, he instructed circulation manager Ivan Annenberg to inform New York's 4,200 city and suburban newsstand dealers that if they carried *PM*, they'd lose the *News*. Ingersoll stormed down to La Guardia's apartment demanding to know who was mayor—he or Joe Patterson. La Guardia, though furious, was reluctant to tackle the city's biggest publisher head on, so he suggested Ingersoll buy coin-operated racks and put them next to each newsstand, to which the mayor would extend police protection. The mayor's writ did not run in the suburbs, however, so Ingersoll had to hire a fleet of vehicles to make home deliveries.

On June 18, 1940, hundreds of the small burnt-orange delivery trucks left industrial Brooklyn (to save capital, Ingersoll had rented press time from the *Brooklyn Eagle*; to save rent, he'd set up offices at Sixth Avenue and Pacific Street, next to A. G. Spalding & Bros., manufacturer of baseballs, footballs, golf balls, and basketballs, though not yet Spaldeens). Mobbed by customers, the trucks quickly sold out their cargos; in a few hours, the whole 450,000 first run was gone, and scalpers had begun reselling them for half a dollar.

The new paper made good on its promise to deliver domestic and foreign news in punchy and innovative ways. On the national scene—covered by I. F. Stone, who signed on as *PM*'s Washington correspondent—the paper whooped it up for a third FDR term and reported on administration initiatives. But where *PM* really shone was in its hometown coverage.

Many Gotham papers covered local news spottily at best. The *Daily News* leaned heavily on crime stories lifted from police blotters. The *Journal American*, bereft of a functioning city desk, focused on gossip (Dorothy Kilgallen on show biz, "Cholly Knickerbocker" on café society). The *Brooklyn Eagle* synopsized the doings of civic and religious organizations. The *Times* offered little on neighborhood life. *PM* would cover New York from a Popular Front perspective, scrapping society news and stock market tables in favor of issues important to working people.

"We are against fraud and deceit and greed and cruelty," Ingersoll had declared in his prospectus, "and we seek to expose their practitioners." Among *PM*'s first crusades, due partly to the proximity of its Pacific Street offices to Atlantic Avenue's meat markets, was an exposé of butchers who injected water into their meat to raise its weight—an ancient ruse that at times poisoned the product with water-carried bacteria. *PM* also exposed installment loan companies who charged usurious interest; price gouging by the Sheffield and Borden milk companies; and wretched conditions at the city's mental hospitals.

PM was pro union. Its labor editor, Leo Huberman, had authored *The Labor Spy Racket* and covered labor for *The Nation*. His first article ("1700 Strike for a Decent Life") was about a CIO-led battle at a Greenpoint electrical plant, with three pages of pictures attesting to poor working conditions. *PM* covered and championed city transit strikers (riling Mayor La Guardia) and reported on unionization drives by Chinese restaurant workers, Whalen soda jerks, Staten Island clam diggers, and migrant workers on Long Island.

The paper crusaded against racial discrimination. It drew attention to the Bronx "slave market," where Black women showed up at 7 a.m. with brown paper parcels containing their work clothes, then waited for white housewives to hire them at roughly a dollar a day. It also attacked southern segregation and lynching with a fervor seldom seen in papers catering to whites. *PM* took on religious discrimination as well—exposing the housing codes that barred Jews, revealing the dental-school quotas filtering out Jewish students, and shining a spotlight on anti-Semitic street violence.

PM continued the tradition of Popular Front consumer activism, suggesting how readers could get more fun out of city life and more bang for their bucks as well. In lieu of ads, the paper's consumer column offered a digest of what was being merchandised in other papers and provided information on sales around town of everything from coats and underwear to string beans and steak. Elizabeth Hawes, long a leading dress designer, provided labor-feminist criticism of Parisian fashion and mass-produced clothing alike and called for popular price dresses specially suited to the needs of New York's thousands of women office workers. Baby and childcare issues were covered by Dr. Benjamin Spock, a pediatrician at New York Hospital, consultant to the New York City Health Department, and part-time school doctor at the Brearley School on East 83rd Street. The paper offered the first radio listings in New York (as well as a listener's digest) and was the first to provide complete movie listings with show times. It also featured top-notch criticism on everything from theater (many considered Louis Kronenberger the best drama critic in the city), to sports (from stellar writers like Tom Meany, Tom O'Reilly, and Heywood Hale Broun, son of Guild organizer Heywood Broun).

On the foreign front, *PM* was synonymous with interventionism. Its first issue, which appeared four days after the Germans entered Paris, featured an editorial cartoon of Hitler, Mussolini, and Stalin carving up Europe with Franco looking on; an analysis of how "Appeasement of Dictator Nations Put Democracies in Present Fix"; and a reprint of Churchill's ringing speech of defiance. *PM* immediately began beating the drums for preparedness. It ran stories that imagined Nazis bombing New York, then invading it (maps showed routes of attack with huge arrows directed at Gotham), then promptly banning works of local authors like Sherwood and Hellman, Odets and O'Neill. "The Fascists Are Winning," declared one of *PM*'s front-page editorials: "What Are You Going to Do About It?"

Like other fighting liberals, Ingersoll and his paper went after German American Bundists and rightwing Catholics with sledgehammer subtlety; one cartoon showed Father Curran and others marching in review before Hitler, giving him the stiff-armed salute. When Curran and Coughlin began organizing priests to force *PM* out of business, Ingersoll complained to Archbishop Spellman. "You have my sympathy," Spellman replied. "These kinds

A cotton banner from the Rebel Arts Group, 1939. (The Mitchell Wolfson, Jr. Collection, Florida International University)

of priests are a great embarrassment to the Church and I know how you feel." Alas, he could not order them to stop but suggested the problem would disappear in time.

It seemed, however, that the paper might disappear first. Barely three months after the initial issue, it had used up the entire $1.5 million in capital received from investors, newsstand purchasers, and subscribers. Readership had dropped off, as some found they missed their accustomed daily dose of scandal, racing tables, even department store ads. To make matters worse, the more than 100,000 subscription cards that had been mailed in got lost, through disorderliness or sabotage. Management had to defer payment to worried and impatient creditors. Staff layoffs followed, precipitating a war with the Guild. Red-baiting from outside against the "Uptown Daily Worker" exacerbated divisions inside between liberals and leftists. And Ingersoll made some seriously quixotic decisions: when Dubinsky offered to buy 50,000 subscriptions for his members, Ingersoll refused, saying that people threw away whatever they didn't pay for.

In September 1940, however, Marshall Field bought out the other stockholders and became the paper's guardian angel, giving Ingersoll pretty much free rein. He went to England and produced some sensational reportage, including an interview with Churchill. He argued that the Brits were ready to fight, and it was crucial to support them—and FDR. Circulation climbed again, though readership would seldom rise above 150,000 and would remain concentrated in the New York metropolitan area. Yet given its roster of readers prominent in government and media, and Field's willingness to cover deficits, *PM* would remain an influential new voice on the city and national scenes, one that helped bind together the left-liberal Rooseveltian ranks.

It could only do so in a virtual way, of course, by providing the like-minded with material that strengthened their convictions and commitments—rather as did going to a new Robert Sherwood play on Broadway; or listening to Winchell, a MacLeish radio drama, or an FDR fireside chat on the radio; or reading Niebuhr or Mumford or Kirchwey in the little magazines; or hearing militant ministers and rabbis in churches and synagogues. But the German Blitzkrieg also spurred New York's fighting liberals to undertake a dramatic action project, one that would crystallize—through praxis—a fighting liberal network, in a way that passive consumption never could have done. They would undertake a direct intervention in the European crisis, one that would mobilize the diverse talents and resources of Gotham's writers and intellectuals, politicians and media people, unionists and businessmen, socialists and theologians, reporters and politicos, nationalists and exiles, Christians and Jews, popular and highbrow artists, advertisers and PR men, and involve leading members of the Roosevelt administration up to and including the president himself.

60

Brands from the Burning

On June 22, 1940, a week after German tanks clanked down the Champs-Élysées, France signed an armistice that divided the country in two. The Nazis would occupy the north; a Gallic government would rule the rest from Vichy. Article XIX required the puppet regime to "surrender on demand" any Germans the authorities requested. This meant that refugees from fascism who had found asylum in Paris, and were now fleeing south, might still be snatched up and delivered to the Gestapo, probably no matter what their citizenship.

This provision caused great consternation in New York, especially among the two hundred people gathered for a fundraising luncheon at the Commodore Hotel on June 25, three days after the capitulation. It had been arranged by the American Friends of German Freedom (AFGF), the group founded back in '36 by Reinhold Niebuhr and the exiled Karl Frank, to underwrite the antifascist Social Democratic underground. Since the invasion of Poland the previous fall, the AFGF had shifted its work into rescuing such operatives from all but certain death. This required more money; hence the Commodore event.

After Frank and Raymond Gram Swing (Mutual radio's star commentator on European affairs) discussed the refugees' plight, Niebuhr made a pitch for contributions, and pledges of aid were made. Attendees now rose to urge a broadening of the AFGF's focus. Erika Mann reported that her father, exiled Nobel laureate Thomas Mann, heard daily from distinguished figures in the European world of arts and letters who were piled up in the south of France, desperate, their backs to the sea. The sentiment emerged that a new organization should be created, to save a wider range of fugitives. Thus was born the Emergency Rescue Committee (ERC).

Dr. Frank Kingdon, a prominent Methodist churchman (and former student of Niebuhr's), now president of the University of Newark, assumed the chair. Harold Oram, a militant socialist who had raised money for the Loyalists, took on fundraising. Ingrid Warburg, anti-Nazi activist and niece of banker Felix Warburg, hosted initial meetings at her West 54th Street apartment overlooking the Museum of Modern Art's garden. Soon the ERC established an office in the Chanin Building, across from Grand Central, staffed by

AFGF personnel loaned by Karl Frank. High-profile members signed on from the worlds of New York politics, arts, education, religion, labor, and the media, among them Norman Thomas, New School president Alvin Johnson, Hunter College chief (and former *Commonweal* editor) George Shuster, journalist Dorothy Thompson, writers John Dos Passos, Upton Sinclair, and Elmer Rice.

In July 1940, the ERC set to work compiling lists of endangered refugees, many of them members of Europe's cultural elite. Thomas Mann's candidates included publishers Kurt and Helen Wolff and Jacques Schiffrin, film critic Siegfried Kracauer, philosopher Hannah Arendt, and writer Lion Feuchtwanger (on Hitler's personal hit list for his scalding treatment of der Führer in a 1934 anti-Nazi novel). Alfred Barr, director of the Museum of Modern Art, proposed preeminent visual artists like Picasso, Matisse, Chagall, Breton, Duchamp, Kandinsky, Max Ernst, and Jacques Lipchitz.

Suggestions for antifascist political activists were gathered from exiles resident in Gotham. Frank favored his *Neu Beginnen* comrades. Austrian names were provided by Viennese socialist Joseph Buttinger, who had led the underground there until Hitler's legions marched in, after which he'd escaped to New York with his American-born wife, heiress Muriel Gardiner, who had worked with the Viennese resistance. French candidates were supplied by philosopher Jacques Maritain; Spaniards by J. Alvarez del Vayo, former official of the Republic; Italians by journalist and New School professor Max Ascoli.

At the same time, the Jewish Labor Committee was developing its own list of labor union and social democratic activists—Polish Bundists, Russian Mensheviks, German, Austrian, and Italian socialists, Yiddish writers—with whom Gotham's garment union leaders had longstanding personal and ideological ties. The JLC hoped to provide a haven in New York wherein the leadership cadre could survive the Nazi nightmare, then return home to help rebuild their countries.

Both these initiatives—as well as the parallel effort by Williamsburg's Orthodox Jews to save Europe's greatest Torah scholars—faced mounting obstacles. The same Blitzkrieg that galvanized their effort made their task harder to accomplish. FDR's insistence on fencing out Fifth Column spies and saboteurs made it harder for Nazism's victims to gain entry. Roosevelt transferred control over immigration from the Labor Department, run by refugee-friendly Frances Perkins, to the security-obsessed Justice Department and, at the State Department, the untender mercies of Assistant Secretary Breckinridge Long. An anti-Semitic xenophobe, Long was opposed in general to letting in Polish and Russian Jews, believing them (in words he quoted approvingly from America's ambassador to the Soviet Union) to be "lawless, scheming, defiant—and in many ways unassimilable," just like "the criminal Jews who crowd our police court dockets in New York." Long ratcheted up restrictions until by June 1940 he had managed to halve the flow of imperiled refugees from Germany and Eastern/Central Europe. That same month witnessed the Smith Act's legalizing of deportation of "subversive" foreigners. All in all, it was not the ideal moment to seek admission for a substantial number of exiles, many with socialist (though not communist) backgrounds.

There were, however, ways to circumvent (or plow through) these roadblocks—avenues of influence that ran along the NY/DC corridor. Thus, Joe Lash, former Socialist Party activist, introduced fellow socialist Karl Frank to his good friend Eleanor Roosevelt, who then sent the Emergency Rescue Committee's list along to Sumner Welles, her sympathetic ally in State. ER also talked to Franklin, who ordered State to issue Emergency Visitor's Visas to "persons of exceptional merit, those of superior intellectual attainment, of indomitable spirit, experienced in vigorous support of Liberal government and who [are] in danger of persecution or death at the hands of autocracy." Getting these visas required considerable hoop-jumping. Applications had to be approved by the President's Advisory Committee on Political Refugees (established in 1938), then by Justice, and then by State, which notoriously dragged its heels. By September 1940, 576 names had been certified by the presidential committee, yet only forty visas were issued. So the First Lady, who kept on the case, went back to the president and threatened that refugee leaders and "American friends" would rent a ship, load it up with endangered refugees in France, then cruise up and down the US eastern seaboard until allowed to land. The visas were forthcoming.

A second current of influence flowed from David Dubinsky in New York to AFL president William Green in Washington. On July 2, 1940, the two men headed a delegation that asked Secretary of State Hull to authorize "temporary haven" for refugees prominent "in the democratic and labor movements in Europe." Their list of approximately 400 names included "world-famous writers, editors, labor leaders, former government officials and ministers" who were endangered either by Nazis or Stalinists, and whose "loss would be irreparable for the civilized world." Hull and Long bowed to Green's clout and accepted the "Dubinsky list" as well.

In addition to providing visas, money, and transatlantic tickets, both groups decided to dispatch a representative to give on-site assistance to the refugees.

The labor crowd picked Dr. Frank Bohn, economist, author, and chair of the German American Congress for Democracy, an amalgam of a dozen New York anti-Nazi and anti-Bundist organizations. Bohn left from New York Municipal Airport–La Guardia Field for Lisbon on Pan American Airways' Dixie Clipper on July 22, 1940, and finally arrived on August 2 in Marseille, the last French port not in Nazi hands, jammed with penniless exiles from all of Europe. Bohn collected his visas from the American consulate, contacted persons on his list, provided them with money, and helped organize their departure.

The more culturally oriented crowd at the ERC, meanwhile, chose as its agent a thirty-two-year-old, Gotham-born journalist named Varian Fry. Son of an affluent stockbroker of liberal Protestant background, Fry had attended Hotchkiss and Taft, then studied classics at Harvard, where with classmate Lincoln Kirstein he founded a literary magazine called the *Hound & Horn*. After graduating in May 1931 he settled in Manhattan, worked on liberal journals (like *The Living Age*) that concentrated on foreign affairs, and was soon on first-name terms with people like Roger Baldwin and Norman Thomas. In May 1935, on a trip to Berlin, Fry saw storm troopers beat Jews in the streets. He watched in horror as two Nazi thugs approached a Jewish-looking man in a Kurfürstendamm café and, when he reached for his mug of beer, nailed his hand to the table with a dagger. Upon his return, Fry wrote of what he'd seen for the *New York Times*. Karl Frank read the piece and recruited the young journalist for the American Friends of German Freedom. In 1940 Fry helped organize the Commodore event, then segued into the ERC, and decided to offer his services.

"What is urgently needed now," Fry wrote Mrs. Roosevelt on June 27, "is a new Scarlet Pimpernel who will go to France and risk his life, perhaps many times over, in an attempt to find the intended victims of Hitler's chopping block, and either provide them with means to keep alive in hiding or, if [this] is possible, to get them out of France before the French authorities reach them." (Fry was remembering the film *Scarlet Pimpernel*—based on the novel about a fictional English aristocrat, played in the film by Leslie Howard, who had helped French aristocrats escape the guillotine—that had been a big hit at Radio City Music Hall back in 1935). "I have volunteered to go myself," he told the First Lady, "and shall do so if no more suitable person can be found."

Frank indeed hesitated to send such a novice, but Fry spoke good French and had some German, possessed cultural credentials and New York connections, and looked presentably scholarly, in a horn-rim-glasses sort of way; in the end he got the job. On August 4, 1940, he boarded a Dixie Clipper, impeccably dressed as always, carrying $3,000 strapped to his belt, a list of 200 luminaries taped to his leg, and a return ticket dated August 29 (they all assumed his visit would be a flying one). After stops in neutral Portugal and Spain, he arrived in Marseille on August 15 and quickly discovered the magnitude of his task.

The Vichy authorities were not issuing the "exit visas" that would allow refugees to leave French territory. Escapees would have to cross the border into Spain illegally and then make their way to Lisbon (the Franco government was still issuing transit visas through Spanish territory to those holding valid US visas). Fry quickly set up an operation to smuggle his charges over the Pyrenees, with the help of peasant mountain guides, Marseille forgers (who confected the requisite papers), and various visiting Americans, among them heiress Peggy Guggenheim, in France buying up paintings from cash-strapped artists. To each embarking on the perilous journey (some of whom, like Walter Benjamin, would never make it through), Fry would say, in a spirit-lifting way: "See you in New York!"

Fry quickly attracted the attention of the secret police, who detained him for questioning on several occasions, and Vichy authorities, with growing vehemence, sought his removal from the country. They had a stout ally in Breckinridge Long, who, by the fall of 1940 was telling FDR that too many of the refugees were "not of the desirable element" and urging that exemption lists be shut down. In October 1940, he succeeded in pressuring the AFL into recalling Bohn and closing his operation. The ERC in New York passed along State Department wishes to Fry, but he refused to budge.

Besieged by surging numbers of frightened men and women, he had grown increasingly uncomfortable with the grim triage he was forced to practice. The shopping expedition aspect of the enterprise distressed him (an American official in Lisbon had told him that "there is a fire sale on brains going on here, and we aren't taking full advantage of it"). Nor, he discovered, were the superstars on his list necessarily the most endangered; indeed, many of them—Picasso, Matisse, Kandinsky, Pablo Casals, André Gide, André Malraux—declined his offer of asylum in America. So Fry began expanding his list to include antifascist activists (though continuing to draw the line at communists) and Jews, who were increasingly imperiled as Vichy imposed its own anti-Semitic statutes. When Bohn returned home, Fry added his people to his own list, which by winter had swelled to many hundreds and would soon number in the thousands.

Back in New York, ERC leaders signaled their growing dismay and pushed Fry to hew to more selective criteria—partly to avoid angering the increasingly antsy State Department, partly because, in harsh truth, it was far easier to fish for money if there were big names to use as bait. "If Albert Einstein could be brought to America today," Oram wrote Fry, "we could raise one million within a short time by exhibiting him throughout the country. Casals is probably worth one hundred thousand, Picasso fifty thousand." Oram admitted, "Your trio [Heinrich Mann, Franz Werfel, Lion Feuchtwanger] brought in thirty-five thousand," but "since their arrival we have had nothing good to offer to the public and they are pretty shopworn by this time."

Still, Fry didn't do badly by any criteria. In the end—before being forcibly escorted to the Spanish border and summarily ejected in August 1941—he helped save as many as 2,000 people. While most were not household names, a remarkable percentage were. Picasso passed, but world-class painters like André Breton and Max Ernst (their passage paid by Peggy),

Marc Chagall, Jacques Lipchitz, and Marcel Duchamp crossed the Atlantic, as did an astonishing number of other accomplished Europeans. As Victor Serge, one of their number, wrote: "In our ranks are enough doctors, psychologists, engineers, educators, poets, painters, writers, musicians, economists and public men to vitalize a whole great country." (He might well have added physicists, filmmakers, anthropologists, linguists, and architects, among innumerable other categories.) New York would be the preeminent beneficiary of this colossal transfer of intellectual and artistic capital—though by no means exclusively so. Chagall, Fry wrote, "has a horror of New York and wants to get out of it as fast as possible, and into a quiet place"; others opted for Hollywood and university towns across the continent. But it was Gotham that had reached out across the Atlantic and snatched these human brands from the burning, and it was in Gotham that many would stay, some for the moment, others forever; and their consequent interactions with New Yorkers would have world-class consequences, for the city and the world.

The initiative also provided a significant bonding experience for the congeries of fighting liberals who engaged in it, strengthening their determination to push for American intervention against fascism. Ironically, these New Yorkers could not help but notice another constellation of Gothamites, clustered down in Wall Street, who, though distinctly to their right, and indeed for the past decade their inveterate enemies, seemed to be pushing in the same direction.

WALL STREET WARRIORS

The New York Stock Exchange on September 7, 1939. (Photo by Popperfoto via Getty Images/Getty Images)

61

Let's Make a Deal

On June 26, 1940, four days after France surrendered, Dr. Gerhardt Westrick threw a private party at the Waldorf Astoria to celebrate the Nazis' victory. The guest list included such corporate chieftains as Colonel Sosthenes Behn, chief executive of International Telephone and Telegraph (ITT); James D. Mooney, head of General Motor's overseas operations; Edsel Ford of the Ford Motor Company; and Torkild Rieber of the Texas Company (Texaco). Westrick was an elegant host—faultless manners, flawless English—but it wasn't charm alone that drew such a distinguished company. Officially, he was in New York to talk about the business opportunities that would blossom in Europe after the Allies were crushed: "We in Germany are expecting a short war," Westrick had told an interviewer back in April, when he'd arrived to assume his duties as a "Commercial Counselor." His goal was "bettering trade relations with all nations during the coming peace."

There was, however, a secretive air to Westrick's activities that seemed suspicious. He had first established himself at the Plaza; then, to escape unwelcome press attention, had slipped away to the Carlyle (on Madison and 76th), registering under an assumed name; then segued to the Waldorf. He'd also leased an estate up in Scarsdale whose driveway "fairly buzzed with streams of automobile visitors," so a *Herald Tribune* reporter discovered (having been tipped off by a mysterious source)—visitors the newsman soon revealed, by tracing their license plates, to be American industrialists and oil executives.

When the story broke in July, Westrick was portrayed as no mere commercial counselor but rather an emissary of Foreign Minister von Ribbentrop, dispatched by Hitler himself to lure American corporations into an emerging Nazi empire. These charges received high-decibel amplification from Walter Winchell and other columnists, replete with lurid suggestions that the German was something of a one-man Trojan Horse. In the ensuing uproar, Westrick—evicted from his Scarsdale quarters and hounded by reporters—packed up his Waldorf operation, fled west with his entourage to San Francisco, and sailed away to Japan.

Westrick hadn't come to spy. He *had* engaged in espionage in New York, back during the First World War, in tandem with Heinrich Albert, the commercial attaché and German agent who had accidentally left behind, on the Sixth Avenue El, a briefcase full of incriminating documents, which were soon splashed across the pages of the *World*. Albert had survived that embarrassment, however, and after the war had served in the Reich Chancellery, and later as finance minister. He'd also teamed up with Westrick—both were lawyers—to establish Albert & Westrick. Their firm, thanks to Albert's connections, had become the preeminent legal agent of the many American enterprises, chiefly headquartered in New York, that would invest millions of dollars in Deutschland. By 1940, Westrick had been shuttling between Gotham and Germany for many years, and his return mid-Blitzkrieg was aimed at mending commercial relations badly frayed by a division on Wall Street over whether to do business with Nazis at all.

Many in the camp prepared to deal with Hitler—well represented at Westrick's party—had been heavily invested in Germany since the twenties, when US corporations, given the crumpled mark, had picked up firms for a song. General Motors had taken over Germany's largest car manufacturer, Adam Opel. Ford established Ford-Werke in Cologne. ITT gained control of several German manufacturers and, together with GE, challenged the electrical giant Siemens on its own turf. IBM, in 1922, bought a 90 percent share in Dehomag, the leading business machine company. Other US firms established cartels with their German competitors to divide markets, fix prices, and share patents and research. In 1927, Standard Oil of New Jersey agreed with the chemical combine I. G. Farben that Standard would stay out of chemicals if Farben stayed out of oil—rather as Spain and Portugal had divvied up the newly expanded globe in the Treaty of Tordesillas in 1493.

The 1920s surge of capital into Germany had been channeled by New York investment banks. The House of Morgan had supplied the lion's share of the massive Dawes Plan and Young Plan loans to the German state, enabling it to keep paying First World War reparations. US firms acquiring German companies, and German firms seeking funds for expansion, had gotten their capital from Wall Street old-timers like the National City Bank, or more recent arrivals like Dillon, Read (where James Forrestal and Ferdinand Eberstadt were principal deal makers) and Averell Harriman's investment arm, W. A. Harriman & Company (overseen by George Herbert Walker and his son-in-law Prescott Bush).

Hitler's arrival threatened these arrangements. The Nazis repudiated governmental and private debts. They also refused to let US German subsidiaries repatriate profits. Given the choice of quitting the German market or investing their blocked capital in Hitler's highly profitable rearmament program, many US corporations and banks chose to stay. American investment in Germany zoomed by nearly 49 percent during the 1930s, while inching up only 2.5 percent in Britain and falling elsewhere in continental Europe.

Some New York firms, notably IBM, became especially embedded with the Third Reich. Germany became the company's best customer outside the US. Its Dehomag subsidiary supplied the custom-built Hollerith machines that inventoried spare parts for the Luftwaffe, tracked railroad schedules for the Reichsbahn, and tabulated ethnic-coded census results, facilitating enforcement of racial decrees. Despite the ban on repatriating profits, skilled IBM accountants and lawyers (Heinrich Albert was on the legal team) developed ways of clandestinely shipping millions in Dehomag dividends to corporate headquarters at 270 Broadway, across from City Hall Park. Overseas profits allowed the company to boost wages at the depth of the Depression, starting at the top: Thomas Watson became the country's highest-paid executive. They also aided IBM in erecting a grand new World Headquarters Building at Madison and 57th Street, dedicated with great fanfare, in January 1938. Watson drummed up additional business for the Reich in his capacity as president of the International

Chamber of Commerce (ICC). The IBM chief led a delegation of ninety-five American executives to the ICC's 1937 meeting in Berlin, where they heiled Hitler on his arrival at the Opera House and Watson was awarded the Merit Cross of the German Eagle with Star, the highest honor that could be bestowed on a non-German.

Henry Ford and James Mooney of GM were also be-medaled by Hitler, no surprise, given the amount of military hardware churned out by GM and Ford subsidiaries linked, respectively, to the General Motors Building at Broadway and 57th Street, and the Ford Building three blocks farther south at 54th Street. Ford supplied trucks and personnel carriers to the Wehrmacht; GM built bombers for the Luftwaffe; and together GM and Ford produced half of Germany's tanks. Albert & Westrick served as Ford's attorneys. In 1936 Albert became board chair of all Ford's Third Reich operations.

General Electric's German affairs were handled by Westrick, who reported to the firm's New York headquarters, which also moved uptown during the Depression. In a musical-chairs arrangement, GE abandoned the old Equitable Building at 120 Broadway and relocated to recently built (1931) RCA Building at Lexington and 51st Street, when RCA jumped to the even-newer Rockefeller Center. Renamed the GE Building, its Art Deco iconography—a crown of radio-waves and a lobby festooned with electric bolts—proved happily in tune with its new owner's high-voltage business.

Similarly, Westrick connected ITT's German companies with the 33-story Gothic skyscraper at 67 Broad Street, replete with its own lightning-bolt mosaic, from which Sosthenes Behn ran his increasingly overstretched international empire. ITT had been hard hit by the crash, leaving it desperately dependent on income from overseas subsidiaries. In Spain, Behn backed Franco and provided communication facilities to Falangist forces, partly out of conviction but largely out of fear the Popular Front government would nationalize ITT's extensive telephone holdings. (Later he tried to hedge his bets by opening lines to the Republicans but only managed to alienate both sides.) In Germany, equally eager to protect his holdings, Behn arranged a tête-à-tête with Hitler at Berchtesgaden in 1933—the dictator's first-ever meeting with an American financier. Behn played ball with the Nazis throughout the decade, putting Party members on his boards, making financial contributions, dismissing Jews from management positions (as did many German affiliates of American corporations), and plowing blocked profits back into German arms companies, notably the aircraft manufacturer Focke-Wolfe.

ITT/Focke-Wolfe fighter planes, soon swooping over southern England, needed tetraethyl lead for their hi-octane fuels, and Westrick clients Standard Oil and General Motors supplied it. In 1924 the two had formed the Ethyl Gasoline Corporation in New York; in 1935 Ethyl teamed up with I. G. Farben to begin production in Germany, ignoring protests by the US Army Air Corps.

Germany needed oil, too, some of which it imported and stockpiled from companies like Texaco (domiciled in the Chrysler Building). Westrick brokered a deal with Texaco chairman Torkild Rieber, an admirer of Hitler, to ship diesel fuel to the German navy from neutral South America via the ports of an accommodating Spain (Rieber having delivered large shipments to Franco's forces during the Civil War).

Synthetic fuel was also made available to the German military machine, by Standard Oil of New Jersey—despite its name, still resident in Manhattan. (Though it, too, joined the parade Uptown, transferring corporate offices, and those of John D. Rockefeller Jr., from 26 Broadway to Rockefeller Center in 1933, leaving the Downtown tower to Standard Oil of New York.) The Standard held fast to its cartel agreements with the clearly Nazi-dominated

I. G. Farben. They were not alone in doing so—fifty-three US companies were connected with Farben during the 1930s—nor was it illegal. Still, Jersey Standard was particularly helpful, assisting its German partner in developing the synthetic fuel without which, Hitler's armament minister Albert Speer said, the Führer "would never have considered invading Poland." The oil firm was equally obliging in providing Farben with patents for their new synthetic substitute for natural rubber, of which Germany had none and on which the Wehrmacht depended.

With the outbreak of war in 1939, US subsidiaries came under fire in Germany from nationalists who considered them American Trojan Horses. For all Behn's kowtowing, some Nazi leaders urged ITT's subsidiaries be seized. To forestall this, Behn placed the ubiquitous Westrick in charge of all ITT's German operations, as a "conservator" of New York's interests. It worked, in the sense that the regime settled for administering ITT's shares rather than confiscating them, but de facto control of ITT plants, like those of most other US companies, passed to managers who were German nationals and Party faithfuls.

Reich-related companies also took heat in the US in 1939. As the tide of public opinion turned more sharply against the Axis powers, such businesses increasingly felt compelled to justify their Nazi entanglements. The chief weapon in their intellectual armory proved to be that old chestnut of merchant capitalism—that free trade amongst nations was a force for peace. Not for nothing did Watson emblaze on IBM's new headquarters the motto "World Peace through World Trade," a proposition that served to legitimate a kind of moral blindness about deal-making with unsavory partners. As Watson cheerily put it: "We do business in 78 countries and they all look alike to me—every one of them." This quickly became the stock response of beleaguered businessmen. In April 1939, GM board chairman Alfred P. Sloan Jr. declared that "an international business operating throughout the world, should conduct its operations in strictly business terms, without regard to the political beliefs of its management, or the political beliefs of the country in which it is operating." A spokesman for Dow Chemical put it somewhat more candidly: "We do not inquire into the uses of the products. We are interested in selling them."

The problem with this tack was its transparent cupidity. Fortunately, less self-serving justifications were available, based more in geo-strategic than commercial considerations, and provided by one of Wall Street's own—John Foster Dulles, senior partner of Sullivan & Cromwell, the largest law firm in the world.

62

Change Agent

Since the 1920s, when he had become Sullivan & Cromwell's point man in the Weimar Republic, Dulles had been stationed at the New York end of the capital pipeline running from the US to Germany. As Gotham's counterpart to (and ofttimes associate of) Heinrich Albert and Gerhardt Westrick, Dulles had represented US corporations interested in buying up German firms or allying with them in cartels. He'd also worked with German businesses (or governmental entities) interested in selling their securities in New York, matching them up with investment bank clients of his—like Dillon, Read; Kuhn, Loeb; Goldman Sachs; Brown Brothers Harriman; and W. A. Harriman—who bought German bonds wholesale, resold them in the US retail market, and paid Dulles a percentage of their profit.

Then the Depression further devastated the German economy and put a billion dollars of Dulles-arranged debt at risk of default. In 1934, the axe fell. A delegation of American creditors was summoned to Berlin. They chose Dulles as their tribune. On arrival, they met with the head of Hitler's Reichsbank, Dr. Hjalmar Horace Greeley Schacht—so-named because his parents had lived in Brooklyn where his brewery-worker father had read the *Tribune* and admired its publisher. Schacht informed them that Germany would no longer pay either reparations or the interest on private loans. Dulles warned Schacht of irreversible damage to Germany's credit rating, but to no avail. His clients took a massive hit.

Dulles, undaunted, continued to ply the German–American capital highway. He handled more bond issues. He arranged new cartel agreements between US firms and the likes of I. G. Farben. He continued his association with Albert & Westrick; indeed, Albert's son clerked at Sullivan & Cromwell in the mid-1930s. All this business was lucrative for the firm, and for Dulles himself, who in 1936 received the stupendous sum of $377,000, making him (it was rumored) the highest-paid lawyer on Wall Street.

But Foster Dulles's dealings with the Third Reich made his partners—including his younger brother, Allen Dulles—uneasy. They seemed distasteful; politically unwise. The firm was getting a reputation for being pro-Nazi. This seemed particularly inappropriate for a house that, unlike most white-shoe competitors, had taken on Jewish partners, such as

Eustace Seligman. At a showdown meeting in June 1935, Allen and the others demanded Foster Dulles close the Berlin office. Angry and adamant, he protested the potential loss of profits. They insisted, threatening mass resignations. Hurt, bewildered, and isolated in the boardroom, Foster Dulles capitulated ("in tears," Allen recalled). Though the German office was shuttered, the elder Dulles continued to do deals, if at a reduced pace, on trips to the Reich in 1936, 1937, and 1939.

Foster Dulles also began arguing in public venues that it was important to *understand* the fascist regime. He had long believed—a not-uncommon assessment—that Britain and France (and the US) had committed enormous blunders at Versailles, blunders "so colossal that they must be paid for." At the 1919 Paris Peace Conference, where he'd been a young legal adviser, Dulles had argued for imposing only modest reparations, the better to quickly re-integrate Germany into the circuits of international trade. Instead, the victors had laid on a crushing burden and sown the seeds of another war. Hitler's aggressions were a predictable and to some degree legitimate reaction to Franco-British shortsighted greed.

Dulles went farther. Shifting the analysis to a more abstract plane, he argued that Germany—and Italy and Japan as well—represented "change." Change was inevitable, so Henri Bergson had taught him at the Sorbonne. Nonetheless, "static" countries like Britain and France (and the United States) had refused to accommodate the rising energies of the more "dynamic" nations, leading the latter to "feel within themselves potentialities which are repressed." This, Dulles believed, was a recipe for war, as dammed-up forces of change inevitably broke through constraints, often violently. Mussolini had intervened in Spain, Dulles proposed, because the democracies had failed to recognize Italy's conquest of Ethiopia in a timely manner, and his Ethiopian invasion, in turn, had stemmed from Italy's legitimate desire for imperial parity with Britain and France.

The way to avoid war, Dulles suggested, was by circumventing rigid barriers to change, or cutting sluiceways through them to provide the global system with fluidity. International businessmen were good at this, especially those (like Dulles's clients) who created cartels. Cartels transcended parochial boundaries, which was why they drew fire from country-bound politicians who were "insular and nationalistic," addicted to border defense, and prone to war. Businessmen were more sensible, more inclined to peace. As "people who have had to cope realistically with international problems," they "have had to find ways for getting through and around stupid political barriers."

Dulles was also impressed with the theologians who were advancing a similar call to transcend archaic nationalism. This was something of a new departure for him. Though Dulles had grown up in a liberal Protestant household, as an adult he'd been only a nominal practitioner. At the Park Avenue Presbyterian Church, he served as elder, though focused mainly on administrative and financial matters. Yet his interest had been piqued by the Federal Council of Churches' international initiatives, and he'd attended the 1937 Oxford conclave. There he'd been greatly impressed by the assembled churchmen, especially Reinhold Niebuhr and Henry Van Dusen (he'd represented Van Dusen during his heresy trial back in 1924). Dulles found that their ecumenical vision—of a world in which narrow national interests were subsumed in worship of a transcendent god—spoke to contemporary global issues. He also couldn't help noticing the considerable press attention the proceedings garnered, and the man without a political constituency now realized the possibility of developing a faith-based one. Soon enough, Dulles emerged as a leading FCC layperson, whose pronouncements promoting a pan-nationalist ethic—happily in sync with the credo of international businessmen—were regularly aired on radio and reproduced in print.

His lofty ethics didn't descend to addressing more mundane issues, such as Nazi attacks on Jews. This was partly because Dulles shared the country-club anti-Semitism of New York's upper crust, and partly because he thought the phenomenon a temporary (if regrettable) by-product of the process of "change" in Europe. The Munich Agreement, similarly viewed through the lens of his major preoccupation, seemed a step in the right direction: it wasn't appeasement, it was rational accommodation to "change." And when war arrived the following year, Dulles rejected all the pro-British blather about "resisting aggression," which was just "the stock in trade of those who have vested interests which they want to preserve against those in revolt against a rigid system." FDR's denunciation of the (unfortunate) Nazi excesses was needlessly "drumming up mass emotionalism" as, Dulles insisted, "only hysteria entertains the idea that Germany, Italy or Japan contemplates war upon us."

Still, once the Blitzkrieg began, business-as-usual with Hitler's regime became harder to defend. In May 1940, after Holland capitulated, Thomas Watson asked Secretary of State Hull if the government wanted him to return his medal from the Führer. Hull bounced responsibility back to 57th Street. Finally, on June 6, after J. Edgar Hoover had begun scrutinizing the company's Nazi connections, Watson ostentatiously spurned his honor—though IBM New York continued to send Dehomag the punch cards and spare parts it needed to keep functioning, and sub rosa relations would continue, despite the drubbing Watson took in the Nazi press for being a fickle "vulture of profit."

It was at just this juncture that Westrick arrived in Manhattan to argue—given the success of Hitler's armies—that Germany's was the winning side and that those who wanted commercial access to tomorrow's Europe had best make their deals today. However, Westrick offered only tactical enticements, based on momentary military advantage, not geopolitical and ethical arguments that could convince American audiences. And Dulles, who'd painted a bigger picture, began to hedge his bets (he'd recently begun representing the Anglo-French Purchasing Commission). When the storm broke over Westrick's head, Dulles confirmed that yes, in the past they'd had some business dealings; and that yes, the German had visited him soon after his arrival, but only to invite him to a German Red Cross Benefit, which Dulles had declined due to a previous engagement. The voice of Wall Streeters who thought it acceptable to work with the Reich had begun speaking softly, even as spokesmen for a pro-British faction—deeply rooted in the city's financial and legal elite—were vigorously beating the drums of war.

63

The Veriest Roman

Henry Stimson—the anti-Dulles—fiercely believed that the Nazis were not traditional autocrats but rather a novel and deadly menace to "the Caucasian civilization of Europe." He didn't want to cut deals with Germany, he wanted to squeeze the country until it "squirts Hitler and his gang out of their posts in the way you squeeze the pus out of an ulcer."

Like Dulles, Stimson was one of New York's leading corporate attorneys, except where Foster might in another life have become a cleric, Stimson's soul was drawn to soldiery. He gloried—as did his hero and model Teddy Roosevelt—in courage and fitness, duty and honor. "The code of the officer and gentleman was my own code," he said. Also like TR, and his other mentor, Elihu Root, Stimson was a thoroughgoing nationalist, convinced the US had a great role to play on the world stage. He himself, as secretary of war in Taft's Administration, had been instrumental in the country's imperial expansion, and he'd then fought in the Great War as an artillery regiment colonel (the title by which friends addressed him ever after, in the way La Guardia was called "Major"). Stimson even *looked* the part of a gentleman-warrior—a man of stately bearing and dignified countenance, "The veriest Roman of them all," Judge Learned Hand once observed.

After the Armistice, he returned to Winthrop & Stimson at 32 Liberty Street. There his practice focused on domestic cases, unlike Dulles's international ones at Sullivan & Cromwell. His work, though less lucrative, still brought in a very comfortable $50,000 a year during the 1920s. He and his wife moved out of their cramped apartment to a brownstone at 120 East 36th Street, where they stayed when not at Highhold, their country seat in West Hills, Long Island. In 1927, Stimson was called back to government service, first by President Coolidge, to serve as special envoy to Nicaragua and governor-general of the Philippines; then by Herbert Hoover, who made him secretary of state.

As secretary, Stimson had voiced revulsion at the 1931 Mukden Incident, Japan's opening gambit in its invasion of Manchuria. He sought to back strong words with powerful deeds, but President Hoover ruled out a boycott and vetoed using force to halt Japan's infringement of Chinese sovereignty. So did the League of Nations, whose leaders Stimson privately called "damn mushy cowards." Still, neither they, nor he, had the military wherewithal to fight, even had the will been present. Instead, Stimson and Hoover settled for condemning Japan's aggression and refusing to "recognize" its ill-gotten gains—the so-called Stimson Doctrine.

With Roosevelt's election in 1933, Stimson returned to New York to practice his profession. In 1936 he tackled the biggest case of his career, a suit against Standard Oil of Indiana; it was also his longest and most exhausting, dragging on for years, like Jarndyce v. Jarndyce in Charles Dickens's *Bleak House*. In 1937, he was elected president of the New York Bar Association.

Though he was now entering his seventies, the old warhorse remained a public figure, speaking out on foreign affairs and meeting occasionally with FDR, with whom he often found himself in substantial agreement. Stimson detested the Nazis. Their attacks on democracy, covetousness of neighbors' property, rejection of individual freedoms, and "extreme brutality toward helpless groups of people" seemed a "complete reversal of the whole trend of European civilization," to which neutrality seemed a colossally misguided response. He opposed the 1935 Neutrality Act and, in an escalating series of speaking engagements, radio talks, and opinion pieces in the *Times*, denounced the "ostrich-like isolationism which has swept over us." In 1938, irritated by the ships departing the port of New York loaded with scrap iron for Japan, he proposed squelching the trade. In 1939 he called on FDR to lift the embargo on Spain and to support the Republicans' "gallant defense" against Franco and his Fascist friends. In 1940 he championed full-scale rearmament and unlimited aid to the Allies.

All this put Stimson at odds with Dulles. The two were old acquaintances, having traveled in overlapping New York circles. Indeed, they had crossed legal swords in a court case in which Dulles represented the Bank of Spain in an effort to collect (on behalf of Franco's government) $15 million from Stimson's client, the US Federal Reserve Bank—a joust in which Stimson made short work of his opponent. Stimson told Dulles directly that he found his even-handed neutralism "too much detached from certain ethical and psychological factors." And indeed, where Dulles was understanding and accommodating, Stimson was alarmed and pugnacious. Where Dulles saw a clash between "static" Allies and "dynamic" Axis, Stimson saw an epic struggle between fascism and democracy, with civilization itself at stake. Where Dulles focused on the short-term profits to be made in dealing with Nazis, Stimson took the view that a German triumph would, in the long term, be disastrous for American business. Which of these disparate tribunes would Wall Streeters back?

64

Bankers Balked

In the end, most would line up behind Stimson, partly because the city's financial institutions—more so than their industrialist counterparts—discovered the hard way that fascist-controlled countries were problematic business partners.

Consider the House of Morgan's experience. Though intimately associated with England and France before and during the First World War, the bank in the 1920s and 1930s—led by Thomas Lamont and Jack Morgan (Pierpont's son)—had dealings with each of the major fascist powers, which they abandoned only reluctantly.

Japan became an important Morgan client, and the firm supported its incursions into China, a country with which the House did relatively little business. In 1931, Lamont went so far as to act as the regime's press agent, covertly drafting a defense of the very Mukden invasion that Stimson was then denouncing. Not until 1934, after right-wing militarists had assassinated friends of Lamont and made clear their design to subdue all East Asia, did the House of Morgan back steadily away, until by decade's end Lamont was supporting Stimson's call to stop shipping war matériel to Tokyo.

The House of Morgan also lavished loans on Italy in the 1920s and established close connections with Mussolini. The invasion of Ethiopia gave the partners pause—they wrote their Italian agent they were "inexpressibly shocked" by the bombing of villages and slaughtering of women and children—and they cut off short-term credit to the regime. Still, in the end, Lamont pardoned Il Duce's violent excesses—saying he preferred "fascists who make war, to the communists who seek to overthrow our governments"—and again proffered advice on massaging US public opinion, suggesting that Mussolini compare his Ethiopian adventure to America's westward expansion. Not until 1940, when Italy joined Hitler in invading France, did Lamont definitively abandon his old client; and not until 1941 did the bank shut up shop in Rome.

In Germany, the House of Morgan, having arranged the Dawes and Young Plan loans, had been prepared—despite its traditional anti-German animus—to live with Hitler after he acceded to power. Jack, a notorious anti-Semite, had applauded Hitler's "attitude toward the Jews, which I consider wholesome," and had written a friend that he thought the bank and the Nazis "were all going to get along pretty well." Then came the debt moratorium—unmitigated by any possibility of profiting, as could the manufacturing and oil companies, from the Führer's rearmament program. This blow was compounded in 1938 when Hitler, after marching into Vienna, hammered down interest payments on the huge loan a Morgan-led syndicate had made to Austria. Lamont and Morgan now completed their swing to an antifascist stance, and while they supported appeasement at Munich, they also backed Roosevelt's policy of preparedness.

In fact, when legal restrictions on arms sales were eased in 1939—after a campaign in which Lamont had been a prominent player—the House of Morgan hoped to be appointed purchasing agent for England and France, the position it had held (to its great profit) in the first war. But Britain—after FDR warned that Morgan participation would be a major political liability—established their own British Purchasing Commission at 25 Broadway. In January 1940, to avoid competing with France and thus driving up prices, the BPC merged with the French Purchasing Commission; they set up a joint buying operation at 15 Broad Street, just a few frustrating steps away from Morgan headquarters at 23 Wall. The British did, however, turn to Lamont (and the French to Lazard Frères) to handle the sell-off of over a billion dollars in US securities to fund their shopping expedition.

Germany, meanwhile, was being frozen out of international capital markets, as other New York houses involved with the Third Reich grew discouraged at decade's end. Dillon, Read basically decided Germany was no longer an inviting place for US investment, though the company did do refinancing for a few firms, such as the United Steel Works it had helped the Thyssen interests set up in the 1920s. The Union Bank, owned by Brown Brothers & Harriman and run by Prescott Bush, also maintained links with the Nazi-linked Thyssen financial and industrial empire. Chase Bank hung in, too, keeping its Paris branch open under German occupation to run a thriving foreign-exchange business; while in New York the Chase participated in Germany's *Ruckwanderer* ("Re-immigrant") scheme, which sold, at a discount, marks obtained from seized Jewish assets to Americans of German descent who agreed to return to the Reich. On the whole, however, New York financiers opted out because the present was bleak and because a series of strategic assessments suggested the future would be bleaker still should the Axis powers extend their sway.

65

Council Counsel

The principal vehicle for this long-range rethinking was the Council on Foreign Relations (CFR), since the 1920s the primary place where the nation's business elite—its leading bankers, lawyers, corporate executives, media moguls, and commercial chieftains—cloistered with selected academics, journalists, and clerics to assess international affairs. CFR members were overwhelmingly based in and around the metropolis—the rules mandated that at least 50 percent reside in the New York City area—and most were affluent and influential. Many belonged to at least one of Gotham's exclusive men's clubs—officers typically belonged to three—with the Century and Knickerbocker being the most popular. The Council's headquarters—purchased for the Council by a group including Lamont, Rockefeller Jr., Paul Warburg, and Otto Kahn—was a five-story townhouse at 45 East 65th Street (next door to FDR's), so tony that some members listed their CFR affiliation under "club memberships" in "Who's Who."

In 1940 the Council was still heavily influenced by the Morgan men who had chiefly founded it, though it embraced top figures from other firms as well. Lamont was very active, as was Morgan partner Russell Leffingwell (who was also a trustee of the Carnegie Corporation, the CFR's major financial underwriter); Paul Warburg of Kuhn, Loeb, and Frank Altschul of Lazard Frères were also on board. Legal luminaries included John W. Davis and Frank Polk—the senior partners at the Morgan-connected law firm of Davis, Polk, Wardwell, Gardiner and Reed—as well as John Foster Dulles and his brother, Allen, from Sullivan & Cromwell; Henry Stimson from Winthrop & Stimson; and Paul Cravath and John McCloy, from Cravath, de Gersdorff, Swaine & Wood.

While Council members held diverse views—it took a big tent to shelter both Dulles and Stimson—they shared an axiomatic internationalism. For its merchants involved in commerce, expanding global trade was self-evidently desirable. The group's international bankers wanted foreign borrowers to have access to US markets, so they could accumulate dollars and repay their loans. CFR industrialists had been taught by the Depression that domestic markets alone could not absorb their products, so they sought the critical margin of profit that overseas sales could provide. For all these New York–based, internationally oriented businessmen, maintaining a free flow of commodities, capital, and communications was indispensable to a healthy economy; whereas manufacturers were more likely to assume that domestic markets might suffice, if sufficiently protected from foreign competition by high tariff walls.

In the early 1930s, Council members and Wall Streeters in general had convinced the Roosevelt Administration to fight the Depression by promoting exports and expanding world commerce—through scrapping high tariffs, negotiating reciprocal trade agreements, and creating an Export-Import Bank to extend credits to foreign nations so they could buy American goods. Southerners, eager to export their cotton, followed the New Yorkers' lead, as did some Depression-made-desperate Midwestern manufacturers.

The biggest obstacles to untrammeled commerce, Gotham internationalists believed, were countries that maintained imperial trade and currency blocs, with Britain the most egregious offender. By the late 1930s, with England in desperate straits, some saw an opportunity for American business to pry open closed imperial doors. One CFR official thought a European war might even present the US with a "grand opportunity" to replace Britain as "the premier power in the world" (with the corollary possibility of New York's edging out London as the financial center of global capitalism).

Germany—lacking an empire—had not provoked the same concern among open-door internationalists. But now the Reich, along with Italy and Japan, was bidding to carve out its own dominion. More alarmingly, Hitler seemed bent on engorging all Europe—America's chief trading partner—into a Greater German Empire, and an autarchic one at that. How serious this threat was, and how the US should respond to it, were questions that the Council—marshaled by Hamilton ("Ham") Fish Armstrong, CFR's executive director and editor of its quarterly, *Foreign Affairs*—set out to examine in a systematic and disciplined way.

Armstrong had been one of the first Americans to interview Hitler after he became chancellor, in April 1933, and he had returned from Berlin deeply shocked by the Führer's values and goals. To evaluate the danger level and consider possible ripostes, Armstrong organized a series of study groups. In 1933 he started one to examine the pros and cons of America's opting for self-sufficiency. In 1934 he created another—chaired by his old Princeton chum Allen Dulles—to look at the issue of neutrality. In 1936 one was launched on the nature of dictatorships. In each case the conclusions were promulgated via books and *Foreign Affairs* articles which, taken together, advanced a series of propositions.

First, the new collective wisdom swatted down the notion, so appealing to anti-interventionists, that the US could simply ignore the fascist challenge by withdrawing into economic self-sufficiency. It insisted, rather, on what was for New York internationalists a given: the American system of mass production needed open access to world markets to keep from tumbling into crisis. Given Hitler's seeming determination to win control of all Europe and restrict access to US business, a Nazi triumph would imperil US interests.

Council analysts did give serious consideration to the option of the United States forming a rival bloc, big enough to offset the loss of a Nazified Europe, by circling its wagons around the entire Western Hemisphere. They calculated that the resulting resource-and-market catchment would be insufficient to sustain the American economy, unless the US also gained entrée to Europe's Asian colonies, a prospect likely to be forestalled by Japanese overlordship.

US dominance of Latin America, moreover, could not be taken for granted. Germany was a fierce commercial rival there, advantaged by its relatively clean historical slate, free of Yankee-style meddling. US trade with Central and South America had actually been declining in the 1930s, as German commercial houses sold ever more manufactured goods to Brazil, Chile, Mexico and Venezuela, while buying ever more grain, meat, and raw materials from Brazil, Chile, Argentina, and Uruguay. German airlines' 16,500-mile (and growing) network was closing fast on Pan Am's 25,000-mile system, and a German media blitz of shortwave broadcasts and newsreel presentations was reaching ever-larger markets. Brazil's dictator, Getúlio Vargas, was negotiating arms deals with Krupp. In Mexico, Nazis eyed the plentiful oil supply which, in 1938, had been expropriated from American businessmen. Should the Third Reich absorb Europe it would attain even greater leverage over the Southern Cone, particularly in countries that had substantial numbers of German residents. Nearly 1.4 million German-born immigrants lived in South America, along with an even bigger second-generation cohort. Mussolini had a potential base there as well, with Italians constituting nearly 50 percent of the population of Argentina. In a worst-case scenario, Hitler might establish footholds in Latin America with the help of Fifth Columnists and develop the capacity to attack the US directly.

This kind of analysis might have led to the "plague on both your empires" position still popular among anti-interventionists (especially on the left), suggesting there was little to choose from between Germany and England. It did not, because Council analysts, especially those on its dictatorship study group, made the case that Hitler's regime was far, far worse than England's. Armstrong penned a popular summary in 1936—*"We or They": Two Worlds in Conflict*—and *Foreign Affairs* followed up with a drumfire of articles about the dangers of Hitlerism.

Given this assessment, the CFR opposed neutrality early on. Armstrong and Allen Dulles popularized the Council's stance in *Can We Be Neutral?* (brought out by Harper and Brothers under the CFR's imprimatur in 1936) and again in *Can America Stay Neutral?* (1939). Armstrong prevailed on his old friend Walter Lippmann, who'd seen virtues in staying aloof from European struggles, to denounce the Neutrality Act of 1937 in the pages of *Foreign Affairs*. (It would be his last appearance in the CFR journal as the married Lippmann now eloped with Armstrong's wife of almost twenty years, and the doubly betrayed editor barred Lippmann from its pages forever). For the rest of the decade, the Council opposed Axis expansion and favored Roosevelt's formula of all aid to Britain short of war.

66

Anglophiliacs

The tilt toward England by the CFR, and the wider Wall Street community, was based on sentiment as well as strategy. The Council's membership, like much of New York's business elite and patrician upper class, was enamored of England and English culture. Many were of English descent. Many had attended prep schools modeled on British public schools, gone to Oxford on Rhodes scholarships, or lived and worked in England for a time. Gotham's bankers, lawyers, diplomats, and academicians developed strong professional bonds with their British counterparts, crossing paths in settings like London's Middle Temple and New York's Down Town Association. House of Morgan partners—themselves custodians of an Anglo-American institution—were frequent visitors at Lady Astor's weekend parties at Cliveden-on-Thames, the country estate of the British branch of the New York family, the bulk of whose income still flowed from Manhattan real estate. Jack Morgan loved being in England, increasingly a sanctuary from New Dealer denunciations; British royalty lionized him, and he them, entertaining King George VI and Queen Elizabeth at his estate in Scotland, which adjoined that of the Queen's father.

The ties between Gotham's upper crust and that of Great Britain had been steadily strengthening since the Great War had revealed the shifting balance of power between their two countries. After a century of competition, the British elite, newly conscious of England's declining economic and military power, increasingly looked to US counterparts for sympathy and support. And even Americans (like Stimson) who believed the US was destined to inherit England's role as arbiter of world affairs didn't object to the two Anglo-Saxon nations joining forces in the meantime to defend common interests and values. Pilgrim institutions to fortify their special relationship.

In 1930, New Yorker and Standard Oil heir Edward Stephen Harkness founded the Pilgrim Trust, endowing it with a capital of two million pounds, explaining he was "prompted by his admiration for what Great Britain had done in the 1914–18 war, and by his ties of affection for the land from which he drew his descent." Harkness was a member of the Pilgrims Society, the elite Anglo-American dining club, whose English branch had been founded in London in 1902 and whose US branch—in reality, overwhelmingly a New York entity—had followed shortly in 1903. Members—the preeminent figures of business and politics from their respective countries—met two or three times a year for lavish banquets celebrating ties between the British and American establishments. It had been a long-standing custom for American Pilgrims to fête each newly appointed British ambassador, an honor reciprocated by British Pilgrims for each new ambassador to the Court of St. James. On October 25, 1939, a banquet welcoming the Marquess of Lothian, Britain's newest emissary, was held at the Plaza Hotel; its guest list featured John D. Rockefeller Jr., Jack Morgan, Thomas Lamont, and other leading figures in government, diplomacy, politics, finance, banking, shipping, law, industry, and education.

A similar but less exclusive institution, headquartered in New York since its inception in 1920, was the American branch of the English-Speaking Union. Chaired by former ambassador to London (and Morgan attorney) John W. Davis, it had as its avowed purpose the drawing together "in the bond of comradeship the English-Speaking people of the United States and of the British Empire by disseminating knowledge of each in the other and by reverence for their common institutions."

Some Anglophiles sought a formal merger. In 1939, Clarence K. Streit, a *New York Times* correspondent who had covered the League of Nations and fretted about its failures, came out with a book called *Union Now*. In it Streit proposed a federated union of democratic nations, chiefly (and soon exclusively) the English-speaking ones, that would be modeled on the United States and use the Constitution as its template. In addition to establishing a common currency, communications network, and foreign policy, the Federal Union would also create, as the League had not, a common defense force so clearly capable of defeating any combination of dictatorships that its mere existence would preclude the possibility of war. Streit quit the *Times* and worked full time promoting his proposal, becoming a regular on *Town Meeting of the Air* and other top radio shows, addressing enthusiastic rallies, and winning a large following. Many newspapers endorsed the Federal Union; Henry Luce put Streit on the cover of *Time*; key CFR members found his ideas worth supporting; and President Roosevelt invited him to the White House to discuss the idea.

FDR had his own approach to invigorating the Anglo-American connection, more in keeping with New Deal style populism. In 1938, to boost Britain's stock with the US public, he invited King George VI (only recently ascended to the throne his brother Edward had abdicated) and Queen Elizabeth to add a New York visit to his forthcoming tour of Canada. On June 10, 1939, they arrived at the Battery, the first reigning British monarchs to set foot on American soil. Met there by Mayor La Guardia and Governor Lehman, the shy King and charming Queen were motored up Manhattan, past cheering crowds, at the head of a fifty-car procession. They traveled up the West Side Highway (its downtown lane thronged with pedestrian onlookers, some equipped with portable radios to follow the royal party's progress), then headed east on 72nd Street, through Central Park, and out across 96th Street (acclaimed by cheering West Indian Harlemites), up the East River Drive, across the Triborough Bridge and on, via Grand Central Parkway, to the World's Fair. Later that day it was back to Manhattan, with a stopover at Columbia University's Low Library to inspect the original King's College charter and meet a "select group" of civic leaders, before heading on to Hyde Park, 78 miles to the north, where hot dogs and folksiness awaited.

By early 1940, therefore, when it appeared the British Isles might come under attack, there was a reservoir of goodwill available for the English to tap, particularly among the city's Anglo-elite—though their affinity was seldom depicted as ethnic partiality, much less fifth columnism, characterizations reserved for German or Italian national loyalties. In January, Winthrop Aldrich, chairman of Chase Bank, organized the Allied Relief Fund as a "rallying point for American friends of France and Great Britain in this hour of great need." The same month brought the birth of Bundles for Britain, a group found by New York society matron Natalie Wales Latham (John W. Davis was among the sponsors) that organized "Knittin' for Britain" circles that turned out gloves, socks, and knitted helmets for British sailors patrolling the North Sea and collected bales of used clothing for refugees; in short order, chapters sprang up nationwide. In June, Aldrich helped organize a British American Ambulance Corps. And plans were set on foot to evacuate British children should an attack come, an effort in which Jack Morgan was heavily involved.

However, England, grateful though it was, wanted far more than ambulances and knitwear from its Anglophile friends.

67

Intrepid

Early one morning in May 1940, Randolph Churchill was visiting his father, who was in the midst of shaving with his old-fashioned Valet razor, and was surprised to hear him say of Hitler's Blitzkrieg that he was confident England would yet "beat the bastards." The son replied that he couldn't see how it could be done. "By this time," Randolph recalled, "he had dried and sponged his face and turning round to me said with great intensity: 'I Shall drag the United States in.'"

If anyone was well situated to effect such a trans-Atlantic alliance it was Winston Churchill, himself the fruit of an Anglo-American marriage between monied New York and aristocratic England. His socialite mother, Jennie Jerome—Brooklyn-born daughter of millionaire speculator and sportsman Leonard Jerome—had married Lord Randolph Churchill in 1874, the same year Winston was born, and the very year (or so the story goes) in which she invented a quintessential New York cocktail—the Manhattan, no less. Winston had made his first visit to the US in 1895, been back repeatedly, and had long wanted to work on Wall Street.

Churchill would indeed be indefatigable in his efforts to get the US into the war but knew he couldn't afford to be seen doing so. Americans were convinced they had been propagandized into the last war and were determined not to be inveigled again. The English were extremely sensitive to this. Lord Lothian told the banqueting American Pilgrims in October 1939 he was well aware that "you are quite rightly suspicious of propaganda," and he ardently forswore its use. In fact, however, the British at that very moment were on the verge of mounting an enormous and organized propaganda operation to draw Americans to their side. It would be headquartered scant blocks from the Hotel Plaza, where Lothian's audience sat, and it would be a far more subtle campaign than the retailing of tales about skewered Belgian babies that had preceded the Great War.

During the 1920s and 1930s, Britain's Secret Intelligence Service (SIS) had maintained a minimal undercover presence in the Passport Control Office, located in the Cunard Building (25 Broadway), which also housed the British Consul General's office. A sizable espionage operation seemed unnecessary, as the FBI kept British intelligence up to date. In September

1939, however, with England now a combatant, the State Department ordered Director J. Edgar Hoover to cut off collaboration, lest it compromise American neutrality. In November, the British opened their Purchasing Commission, and His Majesty's SIS grew increasingly anxious to reestablish its FBI liaison, worried that German agents might try to sabotage the flow of war matériel from New York to England as they had in the First World War, most notoriously at Black Tom, the munitions depot in New Jersey. Finally, in April 1940, it dispatched William Stephenson, a forty-four-year-old Canadian-born millionaire, to parlay with Hoover.

Stephenson seemed a good choice. A Royal Flying Corps ace during the First World War, he had become a hugely successful industrialist, with big holdings in steel. Learning that the Germans were diverting large amounts of steel into arms production, he had passed the information on to SIS. Stephenson also had a link to Hoover via a mutual friend, boxer Gene Tunney. A sit-down was arranged. Hoover, never keen on sharing, said he would work with Stephenson only if FDR so decreed. Stephenson now turned to another friend, Ernest Cuneo, who arranged a meeting with the president. FDR said he wanted the "closest possible marriage" between American and British intelligence, and the reluctant FBI was ordered back into joint harness.

Mission accomplished, Stephenson returned to England, just as Churchill came to power. The new prime minister asked Stephenson to go back to New York. He wanted him not only to oversee the physical security of British purchases but to establish in Gotham—the hub of American commerce and communications—a base from which to wage clandestine war against the Nazis anywhere in the Western Hemisphere, and perhaps, should the worst happen, to direct guerilla operations against the Wehrmacht inside a German-occupied England.

Stephenson returned on June 21, 1940, on the RMS *Britannic*, and quickly set up the British Security Coordination (BSC) on the 36th floor of Rockefeller Center's International Building, behind a door marked "Rough Diamonds, Ltd." (Its cable address was INTREPID, NEW YORK, a handle that stuck to Stephenson.) That same month, Roosevelt established an American Special Intelligence Service within the FBI and charged it with monitoring German agents in the US and Latin America. It was housed eight floors above Stephenson's operation, on the 44th floor, with a functioning wood-paneled law firm as front-office cover.

The BSC rapidly expanded its activities, becoming the New York umbrella for MI-6 (in charge of intelligence operations outside Britain and the Commonwealth), MI-5 (covering internal security for Britain and its empire), and Scotland Yard's Special Branch (specializing in potential "subversives," like fascists, communists, and Irish or Indian nationalists). Making the fullest use of the president's grant of remarkable freedom to operate on US soil, Stephenson had secret operatives flown in by the hundreds (much to Hoover's annoyance). They were put to work running espionage operations from Halifax to Trinidad—planting agents, opening mail, tapping phones, tracking down Nazi radios, and keeping London informed, courtesy of FDR, via State Department transmitters.

Stephenson's brief included something even higher on Churchill's agenda than countering Nazi operations. "Intrepid" was to help create a popular mood favorable to US aid—better yet, intervention—without getting caught committing propaganda. Stephenson's approach was to work through sympathetic New York media, planting rumors and feeding facts—whatever would best stoke antifascist sentiment and discredit anti-interventionists—to a host of print reporters and radio commentators. Walter Winchell was a prime conduit. Stephenson, via Cuneo, passed along intelligence items and propaganda bits that helped, as

Cuneo put it, "clear the way for the President and the preparation of war." The BSC also worked with the staff and publishers of *PM*, the *Nation*, the *New Republic*, the *New York Times*, and the *New York Herald Tribune*—leaking, for example, the information about Nazi fifth columnists that journalist Edgar Ansel Mowrer deployed in his *Tribune* series and serving as the mysterious source who alerted the same paper to Dr. Westrick's doings in the Waldorf-Astoria.

Working alongside Stephenson's operation was the British Press Service (BPS)—situated conveniently nearby in an RCA Building office aerie. The BPS funneled images and exclusives more openly to US press and radio contacts, and to labor, church, and business groups, but its goal was the same: as Isaiah Berlin (a young Oxford philosopher assigned to the operation) recalled: "My brief was to drag the Americans into the war." The British Library of Information (BLI), also housed in a Rockefeller Center tower, monitored US public opinion on a daily basis and arranged for speakers and literature to be dispatched to friendly institutions like the English-Speaking Union. The Ministry of Information (MOI) established an improved London-Lisbon-New York air link to rush film footage to newsreel companies like the March of Time, and thence to American screens.

Anti-interventionists cried foul. Senator Burton Wheeler, Winchell's great antagonist, accused him of being in the pay of the British, and though no money changed hands, he wasn't entirely off base. For all the hue and cry raised about German and Italian fifth columnists, and for all the investigations launched into Russian, German, and Japanese espionage, the spies and sympathizers of fascist or communist persuasion were utter pikers and bumblers when compared to the legions of British agents, perhaps a thousand or more, who ran their immensely effective espionage and un-propaganda campaign out of midtown Manhattan. They had the advantage, naturally, of doing so with the full approbation of the American government and Anglophile Wall Street. Ernest Cuneo, a man in the middle of these machinations, noted that "Of course the British were trying to push the US into war," but added, "We were indeed a pushover." In fact, the New Yorkers were far more active agents in promoting intervention than such a passive term implies.

68

Aid the Allies!

When war arrived in 1939, the Wall Street Warriors on the Council on Foreign Relations moved immediately in two directions—one clandestine, the other hyper-public.

Days after the invasion of Poland, Hamilton Fish Armstrong went down to DC to meet with State Department officials. Well aware that the still-minuscule federal bureaucracy had few resources available for policy planning and research, and that it would have to turn to outside experts as it had, extremely belatedly, in the First World War, Armstrong made them an offer they didn't refuse. The Council on Foreign Relations would assemble "the best brains in international relations" and establish a "War and Peace Studies Project," to be privately run and funded from New York—secretly so, lest anti-interventionists charge Wall Street with pushing the government toward war. By December, the Rockefeller Foundation had provided start-up funds (and over the next six years would give $300,000 more).

The enterprise was kept so tightly under wraps that even Council members who were not directly involved (the great majority) were unaware of it—though it must have been hard not to notice the tremendous expansion in staff and activities at East 65th Street. Almost a hundred Project participants, organized into four working groups, met in hundreds of sessions, usually held over dinner and on into the night. War and Peace people prepared hundreds of memos for the president and his foreign policy advisers, not only on what should be done in the immediate circumstances but on what America's postwar goals should be. Remembering the disastrous fate of Wilson's postwar proposals in 1919, and determined to avoid that this time around, CFR members refused to wait for the peace conference before tackling the big issues; they didn't even wait for the war.

Gotham's internationalists argued it was imperative to use the coming victory to establish a new world order, one that would put paid to the bellicose rivalries between European empires that had repeatedly dragged the planet into war. Project members wanted a stable, predictable, orderly world—an improved version of the Pax Britannica that had broken down in 1914—which the United States would ultimately oversee, though not in a unilateral way. What was needed was a set of international institutions, including a political body that could (as the League of Nations had not) bring collective power to bear on nations that threatened world peace; and a group of economic institutions that would underwrite a free trade global marketplace, provide short-term loans to ease currency crises, and offer long-term loans to promote economic development. These programmatic ideas, evolving quietly and invisibly in New York, would in the not-too-distant future emerge to the global limelight and reshape the international order.

But first, there was a war to be gotten into, and this demanded a very different kind of intervention—noisy and visible.

The first such initiative came in October 1939, when a group of CFR members took the lead in forming a Non-Partisan Committee for Peace through the Revision of the Neutrality Law. Clark M. Eichelberger—Council member and head of the League of Nations Association—consulted with FDR, who backed the idea of a private effort to rally public support for his battle to loosen the law's constraints. To head this committee, at least nominally, Eichelberger turned to William Allen White, editor of the *Emporia Gazette* (published in Emporia, Kansas). White was a soothing choice, being a widely respected Midwestern Republican and a former pacifist who had strongly backed neutrality yet had reluctantly concluded that the best way for Americans to stay out of war was to help the British fight it on their behalf. The cautious White wanted to be convinced that the organization would not be funded by "international banking and munitions money" and was duly given such assurances, though Thomas Lamont, the ur-international banker, was a key behind-the-scenes player in the initiative; then again, Lamont was a close friend of White's. The Midwesterner would not be a mere figurehead, but the Committee's central figure would be New York's Eichelberger, operating from the bustling headquarters at 8 West 40th Street, where his League of Nations Association was housed.

The "Non-Partisan" in the Committee's mouth-filling name captured more than the commingling of Democrats and Republicans. By the end of the month, among the over 350 prominent Americans that joined the core group of Wall Street Warriors was a contingent of Fighting Liberals, including David Dubinsky, Fiorello La Guardia, Herbert Lehman, Lewis Mumford, Reinhold Niebuhr, and Robert Sherwood. They'd been willing to set aside differences with the businessmen over domestic concerns, given the Committee's resolute focus on foreign policy, and a single issue at that. This first joint foray was a brief one, however, and without significant aftermath, as the goal was attained quickly—the law was revised in November—and the Committee disbanded immediately.

Many of the same players reassembled in May 1940, days after the Battle of France began, when Eichelberger and White set up the Committee to Defend America by Aiding the Allies (CDAAA), with White as chair and Eichelberger as executive director. This organization made no pretense of even-handedness. It stoutly championed England as the upholder of international morality and excoriated Hitler, calling for his defeat. As CDAAA member A. Philip Randolph argued, in justifying the jettisoning of his "plague on both your empires" position: "By every standard of decency and civilization, democratic England is as different from totalitarian Germany and Italy as New York is from Georgia."

The Committee's goal was to mobilize the widest possible popular support for aiding the Allies, and its membership reflected that goal. Strict attention to foreign affairs and avoidance of divisive internal issues made feasible a grand coalition, with New Yorkers still at the center of the action. Wall Street Warriors were much in evidence, including the Council on Foreign Relations' top brass—Executive Director Hamilton Fish Armstrong, Treasurer Whitney Shepardson, and Organizational Director Francis P. Miller—along with such exalted Wall Street personages as Lamont, Stimson, Winthrop Aldrich, John J. McCloy, and Lewis Douglas, president of New York's Mutual Life Insurance Company. Fighting Liberals on hand included politicians La Guardia and Lehman, theologians Niebuhr and Van Dusen, intellectuals and playwrights Mumford and Sherwood, labor leaders Randolph and Dubinsky. Their intermingling at CDAAA meetings produced some strange tableaux. At one affair, a quartet composed of Dubinsky, Lamont, Rockefeller Jr., and Aldrich was spotted deep in conversation, assessing the quality of Aldrich's cashmere. Even stranger, perhaps, Jay Lovestone, former head of the American Communist Party, was appointed (through Dubinsky's intervention) the Committee's labor secretary.

The Committee's mass-mobilization campaign was jump-started on June 10, when Sherwood penned a full-page thousand-word ad for CDAAA, headed STOP HITLER NOW!, which ran in seven New York papers and a dozen out-of-town sheets, with the costs largely picked up by the playwright. The copy argued for supporting the Allies on the grounds that if Hitler won, the US "will find itself alone in a barbaric world." Indeed, barbarians were already inside the gates—"Trojan horses are grazing in all the fertile fields of North and South America," Sherwood declared, adding that "anyone who argues that the Nazis will considerately wait until we are ready to go to war is either an imbecile or a traitor." Displayed in the windows of CDAAA national headquarters (again at 8 West 40th Street, across from the New York Public Library), the ad drew crowds. FDR, asked about it the next day, called it a "great piece of work," and hailed "Bill White and his committee." In truth, White was alarmed at Sherwood's overheated rhetoric about "traitors"; CDAAA New Yorkers, for their part, bridled at White's caution.

Sherwood's broadside helped galvanize growth. On June 9, the Committee claimed 125 local chapters. By July 1, there were 300 chapters nationwide. By the fall, there were 750, with an aggregate of hundreds of thousands of members. Ten thousand active workers stoked the national propaganda campaign, directed by eighty-nine staffers at national headquarters. Between June and October 1940 alone, two million copies of printed materials were distributed—pamphlets, posters, press releases, broadsides, and reprints of speeches and articles. The CDAAA held literally thousands of rallies and collected two million signatures on petitions it sent to the White House. All of this was aimed (with FDR's full if behind-the-scenes connivance) at pressing the president to do what he wanted to do already.

Some New Yorkers, however, wanted to push him still further. With Hitler's legions sweeping westward, a group of CDAAAers decided that only direct American intervention would truly stop him. The same day Sherwood issued his blast, they offered a manifesto of their own, "A Summons to Speak Out." Written by CFR official Whitney Shepardson, it asserted that the United States should immediately declare that "a state of war exists between this country and Germany." Formally ending neutrality would cut the Gordian legislative knot and free the government to extend credits and export arms. Over the summer they began holding a series of biweekly dinner meetings in a private room on the top floor of the Century Association (at 7 West 43rd Street, a few blocks up Fifth Avenue from CDAAA's HQ). Soon known as the Century Group, they hammered out a program that would make midtown Manhattan the national headquarters of interventionist activity. They called for the use of US warships not only to convoy food and ammunition but to defend England itself against the threatened German invasion, and they urged Roosevelt to introduce conscription as well.

Where the CDAAA opted for accessibility, Centurions hewed to a narrower demographic. They were, in the main, white, Republican, Protestant, well-educated Anglophiles from New York and vicinity. Core activists included corporate executive Lewis Douglas, banker James Warburg, lawyers Allen Dulles and Dean Acheson (who had offices in New York and DC), clerics Van Dusen and Coffin, and Council on Foreign Relations leaders Armstrong, Eichelberger, and Francis Miller, the latter of whom took a leave from the Council to serve as executive director. Most crucially, the Century Group was top heavy with writers, editors, publishers, journalists, and playwrights who were members in good standing of the New York media complex, the kind of people who could arrange for an editorial, a column, a speech, a radio show—people like Robert Sherwood, Harold Guinzburg (president of Viking Press), Elmer Davis (CBS commentator), Joseph Alsop (*Herald Tribune* columnist), and above all, the country's virtual minister of information, Henry Luce, whose media empire of magazines and newsreels—newly relocated from the Chrysler Building to Rockefeller Center (the top seven floors of the brand-new, 36-story Time-Life Building, on Sixth Avenue between 48th and 49th Streets)—regularly reached 40 million of the country's 132 million citizens.

Luce's presence in the Century Group's inner sanctum capped a rapid glissando across the political keyboard. As late as 1938, the bushy-browed mass communicator had been still on the fence about fascism, his ambivalence reflected in the varying editorial stances of his different magazines. At *Time*, Luce let foreign editor Goldsborough promote what was probably his own position—the world was moving toward a division between communism and fascism, and between the two he preferred the latter. Thus, *Time* backed Franco, flirted with anti-Semitism, accepted the Anschluss, and supported Munich. At *Life*, however, the 1937 Yuletide issue ran a "Christmas in Naziland" spread that depicted German children playing with toy tanks under trees bedecked with hanging Jews; and the magazine responded to the Anschluss with a sixteen-page disapproving review of Hitler's rise to power. The *March of Time*, run by the pro-British, pro-interventionist Roy Edward Larsen, with virtually no input from Luce, was farthest from his position. In January 1938, the newsreel released a sixteen-minute examination of Hitler's racial purification program called *Inside Nazi Germany*. It supplemented smuggled-out footage from the Reich, with reenactments staged in New York, using antifascist German Americans to play the bad guys and Manhattan East Side charwomen (wearing habits rented from the Eaves Costume Company) acting the part of persecuted nuns.

In May 1938 Luce had gone to Europe to assess the situation firsthand. After talking mainly to Nazi apologists—wealthy Berliner and resident American businessmen—he came out with a mainly apologistic assessment—lauding Hitler for having "suspended the class war" and declaring that "National Socialism is thoroughly misunderstood in the U.S." Japanese attacks on China, where the old missionary's son had a personal stake, helped galvanize his subsequent change of heart—by the autumn of 1938 *Time* was characterizing the Japanese as sadists—and Kristallnacht pushed him farther along. Not only did *March of Time* reenact the German pogrom for newsreel audiences, *Time* and *Life* denounced it as well. Shortly thereafter Goldsborough was deep-sixed, and the Foreign News section began depicting the dictators through a darker glass. In 1939 *Time* began talking up rearmament, and, in *Life*, Luce gave Walter Lippmann a platform from which to expound his now full-throated interventionism. Lippmann's "The American Destiny," in the June 5 issue, warned (as had Roosevelt and the Council on Foreign Relations) that if Germany came to dominate Western Europe and the Atlantic sea lanes, it would threaten America's military, economic, and political interests. More grandly, he argued that the nation had to accept its responsibility—its destiny—to play a leading role on the world stage. "The controlling power in western civilization has crossed the Atlantic," Lippmann announced. "What Rome was to the ancient world, what Great Britain has been to the modern world, America is to the world of tomorrow."

Luce found this argument compelling. In April 1940, on his way to Europe for another personal inspection tour, he wrote a colleague that he himself, like the USA, had been reluctant to utilize his power—in his case, the enormous influence his magazines exerted—and now realized he'd been wrong. America's ideals of freedom and individualism could not be secured if the US was forced to be "self-contained either economically or ideologically"; they must be exported abroad to be sustained at home. Americans had to understand—and he would help them—that fighting Hitler was a fight to defend the democratic faith and that armed intervention to save civilization was now "inevitable." Luce's determination was given added spur when, on May 9, shortly after this epiphany, he and his wife were dining at the American Embassy in Brussels when a German bombing raid blew up a house across the street. Soon Luce was winging urgent cables home saying the US must start churning out airplanes, whatever the cost. After returning to New York, he instructed his editors to "cultivate the Martial Spirit," and he himself enlisted with the Wall Street Warriors of the Century Group. Il Luce had seen the light.

For all his new enthusiasm about Rooseveltian rearmament, Luce remained at odds with the president's domestic agenda and deeply opposed to a third term. He had long criticized what he saw as FDR's authoritarianism, and in a November 1938 *Life* photo montage—labeled "Speaking of Dictators"—the magazine had juxtaposed a series of pictures, each capturing an identical pose (giving a speech, pinning a medal, swimming)—of Hitler, Mussolini, Stalin... and FDR. As late as July 29, 1940, a *Life* article compared FDR to the Führer, and the Chicago convention that had nominated him, to a Nazi conclave.

Luce's dilemma—how to back the president's antifascism without supporting his New Dealism—was widespread among Gotham Republicans and perhaps best embodied by one of their number who was not a member of the Century Group—despite being more militant than most of them—because she happened to be the wrong gender.

69

Fifth Columnist

Dorothy Thompson, daughter of an English-born Methodist minister and an Anglo-Irish mother, had grown up in western New York State and attended Syracuse University, a Methodist institution, which gave ministerial discounts. Graduating in 1914, having been an active member of the Equal Suffrage Club, she moved to Gotham, worked as a publicist and journalist, then spent much of the 1920s as a foreign correspondent, sending back copy from Vienna, Berlin, Budapest, and Moscow to the New York *Evening Post* and other papers. She married a writer who turned out to be a serial philanderer, divorced him in 1927, then married another writer-philanderer (and heavy drinker, to boot), only this one was Sinclair Lewis, already famed for *Main Street*, *Babbitt*, and *Arrowsmith* and about to win the Nobel Prize for Literature. The couple took an apartment on West 10th Street in 1928, and after a short and stormy period of domesticity, Thompson resumed her reporting from Europe with a November 1931 interview with Adolf Hitler.

Her assessment—not the most astute of her career—was that the man who had "set the whole world agog" was in fact someone of "startling insignificance" and would not likely amount to much, a take she carried over into a book (*I Saw Hitler!*) that came out not long before he assumed command of Germany in 1933. Her subsequent reports on Hitler's doings did not make the same mistake, and indeed she penned some of the first condemnations of Nazi anti-Semitism. Thompson soon became such a thorn in the dictator's side that in 1934 he personally banned her from Germany forever. Her expulsion—front page news across the US—made her a celebrity in her own right, not only as Mrs. Sinclair Lewis. She was deluged with speaking invitations, particularly from Jewish groups eager to hear their Christian champion, but the career-transforming request—for a talk at the *Herald Tribune* Conference in October 1934—came from Helen Rodgers Reid.

Reid, wife of Ogden Reid, publisher of the *Herald Tribune*, was in fact that paper's captain, because her husband, an often-hospitalized alcoholic, was incapable of steering it. Helen, a former suffrage activist, was a zealous advocate of women in journalism and had placed more female staffers on her paper than were on any other in the country. She took a shine to Thompson and, in 1936, decided to make her a political columnist, up till then a male monopoly (apart from Eleanor Roosevelt, whose *My Day* column had started up the year before).

Thompson's *On the Record* began running three times a week, alternating with Walter Lippmann's *Today and Tomorrow*, and was in short order a spectacular success. By 1937 it was syndicated to seventy papers, soon to another 100, and by decade's end she was reaching between eight and ten million readers. Another five million tuned in to her weekly radio broadcast of commentary on the news, which NBC launched in 1937 (the same year her second marriage in effect ended—Lewis couldn't handle her success—and she set up separate quarters in 88 Central Park West at 69th Street). As a media phenomenon, Thompson was second only to Walter Winchell. As a woman journalist her only rivals were ER and Anne O'Hare McCormick, to whom the *Times* gave an (unsyndicated) column a year after Thompson had blazed the trail; McCormick, who had made her name chronicling Mussolini's rise to power, won a Pulitzer for Foreign Correspondent in 1937, the first woman to do so.

Thompson captured a different kind of gender first, becoming the only woman ever asked to address the Union League Club and the first, as well, to speak to the New York State Chamber of Commerce in all its 169-year history. Her popularity with businessmen and financiers stemmed from her opposition to Roosevelt and his New Deal, nearly as ardent as her opposition to fascism. Reid, whose paper was an East Coast Republican flagship, had seen in Thompson a foil to Eleanor and billed her as an advocate of "liberal conservativism." *On the Record* routinely excoriated public works projects, welfare, the Federal Writers Project, organized labor, and Social Security (one column hailed "The Right to Insecurity"). Hers was the conservatism of a self-made woman, mildly contemptuous of those less successful, and she took her cues on domestic policy from New York financial eminences like Alexander Sachs of Lehman Brothers and Frank Altschul at Lazard Frères. FDR thought her "the oracle of Wall Street." She thought Roosevelt frighteningly charismatic, almost dictatorial in style, and she worried about the emergence of an American fascism (as had Lewis in *It Can't Happen Here*).

Still, Thompson worried far more about Hitler, and her ferocious opposition escalated rapidly. Between 1938 and 1940, she devoted nearly 60 percent of her column words to furious attacks on the Nazi regime and the cowardice of the West in dealing with him. She worked closely with Council on Foreign Relations chief Ham Armstrong and wrote blistering pieces for his *Foreign Affairs*. She was apoplectic over Munich. She became the only journalist of her stature to take up the cause of European Jews, saying: "We who are not Jews must speak, speak our sorrow and indignation and disgust." In 1939, as president of American PEN, she organized a conference to draw attention to the plight of refugees. She personally sponsored many German Jewish refugees and was an officer of the Emergency Rescue Committee that dispatched Varian Fry. (By contrast her *Herald Tribune* colleague Walter Lippmann wrote virtually nothing on the issue, though in November 1938 he did offer two articles on Europe's "over-population" problem, suggesting the excess be sent to Africa.)

Thompson was also vigorously anti–fifth columnist, though on one famous occasion she made herself a Trojan Horse. In February 1939, she made her way into Madison Square Garden, where the German American Bund's George Washington's Birthday rally was in full swing. When Bundesführer Fritz Kuhn addressed the throng and attributed the moral superiority of those assembled to the purity of their white Christian lineage, Thompson broke into loud and raucous laughter, and, as be-swastikaed storm troopers manhandled her out the door, she bellowed "Bunk, bunk, bunk!" all the while.

Yet even as Thompson joined the fight to revise the Neutrality Act, gave Churchillian addresses to CDAAA rallies, came out for conscription, and more than matched Century Group members in ardent antifascism, she maintained her opposition to Roosevelt, with whose overseas views hers were fast converging, on grounds of their domestic differences.

70

Fighting Liberals v. Wall Street Warriors

From his side of that divide, FDR faced a similar dilemma. The New York business world was now studded with potential allies who were also political opponents. Indeed, he and his New Dealers had recently renewed their antagonism to Wall Street. During the 1937–38 recession, which he and his advisers largely blamed on a capital strike by monopolists, Roosevelt had sent Congress a message concerning the concentration of economic power, in which he cited some disturbing statistics. Less than 5 percent of all US corporations now owned 87 percent of all corporate assets, and stock ownership was similarly clustered in a tiny number of hands. In the light of developments overseas, this accumulation of power appeared newly ominous. "Unhappy events abroad," Roosevelt said in 1938, show that "liberty is not safe if the people tolerate the growth of private power to the point where it becomes stronger than that of their democratic state itself. That, in its essence is Fascism." The president called for a "thorough study of the concentration of economic power," and by late 1939, a joint legislative and executive body—the Temporary National Economic Committee (TNEC)—had been established and begun holding hearings, reminiscent of those by the Pujo Committee, into the growth of monopoly in banking. That December, House of Morgan partners were called to the stand and grilled. The investigations were still going on in early 1940, with every sign that their findings would likely become part of the arsenal of the Democratic candidate for the White House.

At the same time, a skirmish broke out on a different part of the field—the first clash over the question of who would actually *run* a war, should the US get into one. In August 1939, as TNEC was gearing up, FDR, at the War Department's urging, convened a War Resources Board (WRB) and mandated it to come up with recommendations about how a military mobilization should be carried out. The primary extant model was the First World War's War Industry Board (WIB), whose director, Bernard Baruch, though now nearing seventy, was very much alive and kicking. Baruch contacted Roosevelt and urged him to redeploy the WIB approach (and perhaps Baruch himself) in his preparedness campaign.

FDR had no intention of delegating power to Baruch, though he did agree to appoint Edward R. Stettinius Jr. as WRB head. Since 1938 Stettinius had been chairman of the board of United States Steel. A denizen of New York society's upper echelon—he besported himself at the Piping Rock Club and other such exclusive venues—Stettinius was, like Harriman, one of the small contingent of Wall Streeters for Roosevelt. A pleasant man who'd nearly gone into the ministry and instead opted for running General Motors' welfare programs, he rose through the ranks there, not unaided by being the son of a Morgan partner. Even so, under his aegis the nascent WRB proposed a Baruchian approach—letting "patriotic business leaders" supervise any mobilization, while proposing that some laws protecting workers be laid aside.

FDR's liberal subordinates smelled extreme danger. Already convinced that economic royalists were champing to use militarization as a way to undermine New Deal social and economic reforms, Harold Ickes wondered how far Roosevelt would go toward "abdicating in favor of big business, as Wilson did at the time of the First World War," when they seized the opportunity to reverse reform. Frances Perkins wondered aloud why organized labor was not on the WRB. Antiwar, agricultural, and Midwest business interests antagonistic to Morgan influence added to the clamor. FDR himself had no interest in turning the economy over to businessmen who had fought the New Deal tooth and nail and remained myopic about the public interest. So he abruptly changed course and disbanded the Board, which expired in November 1939. As New Deal opponent Hugh Johnson asked a somewhat stunned Stettinius: "Do you suppose the present pack of semi-Communist wolves intend to let Morgan and Dupont men run a war?"

Then came the Blitzkrieg, and the Administration's Fighting Liberals, and Wall Street's like-minded Warriors—each with an enormous power base (one in command of the state, the other in command of the economy), each possessing access to powerful mass media, and each, to an astonishing degree, rooted in New York—would fashion a de facto foreign policy detente that opened the way to war, while continuing to do domestic battle—fittingly enough through the mechanism of a Subway Series Presidential election.

71

We Want Willkie!

As the June 1940 Republican National Convention approached, Wall Street Warriors grew ever more dissatisfied with the leading would-be nominees.

Ohio Senator Robert Taft was clearly out of the question. Not only was he utterly opposed to aiding England, but he even argued a German victory would be preferable to US participation in a war. Rearming to build a "Fortress America" was okay with him, but the real menace, Taft told a Kansas audience, was domestic rather than foreign. "There is a good deal more danger of the infiltration of totalitarian ideas from the New Deal circles in Washington," he declared, "than there ever will be from activities of the communists or the Nazis." New York Republicans, while hardly fans of the New Deal, thought Taft's assessment absurd, especially now that further social democratic initiatives had been checked in Congress. Besides, running against Roosevelt's enormously popular programs seemed suicidal.

From this perspective, Thomas Dewey seemed a far more formidable champion, and a home-town boy to boot. Dewey was well to the left of Taft. He even called himself a "New Deal Republican." When he critiqued Democratic programs, he did so on grounds of execution rather than conception: they hadn't solved unemployment, they'd shifted too much power from the states to the feds, and their hiring practices smacked of political corruption. And Dewey could stress his accomplishments on another front altogether: as district attorney he had cleaned up Gotham; now he'd clean up Washington. Until the spring of 1940 this strategy had made him the favorite of nearly two-thirds of the Republican rank and file and won him substantial support from the likes of Rockefeller, Lamont, and Luce.

Dewey had his drawbacks. He was relatively young—only thirty-seven when he announced his candidacy ("He threw his diaper into the ring," Ickes cackled). He had no national or even state-level record: he had run well against Lehman in his 1938 try for the New York governorship, but he'd lost. Dewey's reputation rested almost entirely on well-publicized convictions of New York racketeers—Bogart had played him in the movies—and even that record was marred by over-zealousness. He was, moreover, an uptight campaigner, too prickly and punctilious for the requisite donning of war bonnets and ten-gallon hats.

The Blitzkrieg highlighted these limitations and foregrounded others. Dewey had no foreign policy credentials whatever: his overseas experience, it was said, consisted of a bike tour of France fifteen years earlier. Worse, from the point of view of his wealthy interventionist backers: such ideas as Dewey *did* have were those of Foster Dulles. The Sullivan and Cromwell chief had known and admired Dewey since the early 1930s. He had even offered him a partnership in 1937, which Dewey had accepted but then declined (with Dulles's blessing) when pressed to run for district attorney. Now, having made Dulles his foreign policy counselor (and, it was rumored, his secretary of state-in-waiting), he dutifully read off Dulles-drafted speeches staunchly opposing US involvement in what his mentor still characterized as a "struggle between the dynamic [Axis] and the static [Allied] forces of the world." After the Nazi invasion of the Low Countries in May 1940, Dewey did underscore his tough guy credentials—it had become "a gangster world," he growled, and "I know something about gangsters." Yet to Wall Street Warriors the conviction of Lucky Luciano seemed quaintly irrelevant now that Hitler was Public Enemy Number One—especially as Dewey/Dulles continued to rule out US intervention of any kind.

At this point they turned their full attention to a dark horse who'd been spotted amidst their own herd.

The Indiana-born Wendell Willkie had been a New Yorker since 1929. A power company executive whose office overlooked Wall and Broad, he had spent much of the 1930s in tight alliance with the Morgan interests, fighting Franklin Roosevelt's electric utilities reforms. In particular he opposed the TVA, which threatened public provision of cheap energy, and cast himself as a free enterprise David against a big-government Goliath. By decade's end Willkie had extended his critique to much of the New Deal's domestic policy, denouncing excessive federal spending, arrogant bureaucrats, and an overweening state. He did not, however, call for reviving laissez-faire. Instead, Willkie frankly admitted there had been serious corporate abuses under the ancien régime, and he accepted the core New Deal social, labor, and financial remedies, drawing the line only at direct (TVA-style) competition with corporations. This modulated domestic stance, though anathema to the Republican right, was one that more liberal New York Republicans could live with. But it was Willkie's position on foreign affairs—pro free trade, pro Allied aid—that endeared him to Gotham's internationalist and Anglophile elite, with whom he mingled at the Century, University, and Downtown clubs.

In addition, Willkie had a winning personality. His bubbling buoyancy, broad open face, big grin, and Hoosier twang offered a warm and welcome contrast to the prosecutorial Dewey who, as even an aide admitted, "was cold—cold as a February iceberg." Though Willkie had never held *any* office, his folksy unpretentiousness, on a par with that of Will Rogers (or even honest Abe, according to *Fortune*); his easy bantering relationship with the press; and his proven PR ability to advance the corporate cause without seeming to shill for the rich (a "homespun, rail-splitting, cracker-barrel simplifier of national issues," *Fortune* opined)—all bode well for his electoral chances. Still, Willkie might never have entered the political arena had not those same infectious qualities afforded him access, via an affair of the heart, and the city's social circuitry, to Gotham's intellectual and media elite.

All was not well in the luxurious 1010 Fifth Avenue apartment (across from the Met) where the rail-splitter and his wife, Edith, dwelt. Edith was shy and home bodied; Wendell was restless and full of driving energy. She was uncomfortable with his predilection for public affairs and still more so with his fondness for private ones. Willkie's rumpled vitality appealed to many women—"he has the well-organized bulkiness of a healthy bear, and singularly brilliant eyes," noted writer Rebecca West—and in the winter of 1937–38 his wandering eye caught the attention of Irita Van Doren, editor of the book review section of the New York *Herald Tribune*.

A protegée and confidante of publisher Helen Reid, Van Doren was one of the nation's most influential literary figures. The Birmingham-born Alabamian Irita Bradford had come to New York to work on an English PhD at Columbia and in 1912 had married fellow graduate student Carl Van Doren. In 1920 she joined the staff of the *Nation*, where Carl was literary editor, and three years later succeeded him in that position. In 1924, she moved to the *Herald Tribune* and in 1926 took charge of its literary section, commencing a long and brilliant editorial career. After she and Carl divorced in 1935, Irita continued her bohemian life in the West Village, hostessing a salon at her 123 West 11th Street apartment that attracted luminaries from Gotham's academic and literary circles and one adventurous Wall Street executive, Wendell Willkie.

The two commenced an indiscreet affair (though it was never reported in the press). Editor Van Doren not only helped him frame his ideas and hone his communication skills, she afforded him entrée to the city's intellectual and journalistic worlds—"Irita opened enormous doors to Willkie and he loved it," said one friend. The most important door was that of her employers—the couple often dined at the Reids' table—and it was a letter to the editor from Helen's brother, published in the *Herald Tribune* in March 1939, in which the first trial balloon for a Willkie nomination was sent aloft, a proposal propelled along by the influential Arthur Krock, DC bureau chief and political columnist of the *New York Times*. In August 1939, at another fashionable East Side dinner party, Willkie captivated Russell Davenport, *Fortune*'s managing editor, who offered (and was authorized) to make a Willkie candidacy happen. Each week that summer Davenport arranged informal dinners with small clusters of leading lights from Gotham's business, political, and journalistic worlds—the most crucial introduction being the one to his boss, Henry Luce. The media mogul saw in Willkie a man who could forge a modern, progressive, internationalist Republican Party—and in the process afford Luce himself access to the wellsprings of national power in Washington, from whose Democratic-dominated precincts he'd long been kept at bay.

Other powerful supporters began to gather around Willkie. Frank Altschul, the wealthy and influential head of Lazard Frères, and a Council on Foreign Relations director, was a leading Republican donor (he'd been chairman of the party's National Finance Committee); he now set about recruiting angels from Wall Street, with the Cravath law firm hosting the fundraising operation. Thomas Lamont pitched in as well, arranging dinners in his 70th Street residence at which Willkie gave "I'd-aid-the-British" talks to Wall Street luminaries assembled by the Morgan chief.

None of these Republicans were overly troubled by the fact that Willkie was a longtime Democrat. Back in 1924 he'd been an Al Smith delegate at the donnybrook in Madison Square Garden; in 1935 he'd been selected—by Tammany Hall, no less—to serve on a County Committee; and in 1938 he'd backed Lehman for the governorship over Dewey. Only in late 1939 did he quietly switch his registration. Conservative Democrats like Smith were not affronted by this apostasy; indeed, Smith endorsed the new-minted Republican, and Century Group founder Lewis Douglas established "Democrats for Willkie."

In March 1940, Davenport established a Willkie headquarters in the sedate Murray Hill Hotel on lower Park Avenue and set about mobilizing influential shapers of public opinion. Freely acknowledging that "Mr. Willkie is not a political reality"—a Gallup survey had just shown his man to be the first choice of fewer than 1 percent of Republican voters—Davenport baldly asked, "Why in the hell don't we make him one?" It was, he wrote privately, "up to the progressives in the Republican Party, the people, the columnists, and the editors to make Wendell Willkie a political figure."

New York City Republican publications leapt on the bandwagon, starting with those of Henry Luce. Davenport helped draft "We the People"—a declaration of Willkiean principles replete with Lucean ideas—and ran it in *Fortune*'s April 1940 issue. *Life* followed up on May 13 with eleven pages of puffery on W.W. as "by far the ablest man the Republicans could nominate." And *Time*'s June 24 issue completed the trifecta with the inspirational "Story of Wendell Willkie." The Reids of course plumped for Willkie in their *Herald Tribune*, as did their prize pundits Lippmann and Thompson. And the *New York Times*, which had backed FDR in 1932 and 1936, came out for Willkie in 1940. So did nearly 700 papers across the country.

New York's advertising and public relations industries piled on as well. Bruce Barton joined up to sell the Willkie product, though he had retired from Batten, Barton, Durstine and Osborne and was serving as Republican congressman from New York's Silk-Stocking District on the Upper East Side. So did John Orr Young, cofounder of Young and Rubicam. These Madison Avenue eminences helped Davenport recruit a crew of over twenty experts for what Hearst columnist George Sokolsky whimsically labeled "an advertising man's holiday." The professionals arranged countless publicity ops for Willkie, snaring a much-coveted invite to *Information Please*, the radio quiz show moderated by Clifton Fadiman of the *New Yorker*, on which their man displayed erudition on such subjects as Matthew Arnold and *Nicholas Nickleby*. To underscore Willkie's accessibility to the press, they even arranged to have him interviewed while taking a bath. All in all, as one flack recalled proudly: "It should never be forgotten that the 'Willkie boom' was one of the best engineered jobs in history."

One goal of the image engineers was to efface the inconvenient truth that Willkie's day job was on Wall Street. The admen constructed a replacement persona—suggesting he was a rustic, homespun, small-town, "good ol' boy" from Indiana. (Just a "simple, barefoot Wall Street lawyer," Ickes snorted.) They cast him, too, in the role of un-politician, a real-life version of the Jimmy Stewart character in Frank Capra's *Mr. Smith Goes to Washington*, which had opened to boffo box office the previous October at Radio City Music Hall. (In a life-follows-art twist, the breakthrough that solidified Willkie's Capraesque credentials came not from the professionals, however, but from an eager amateur. In April 1940, Oren Root Jr., the twenty-nine-year-old grandnephew of Elihu Root and a fledgling lawyer at the Wall Street firm of Davis, Polk, sent to Thomas Lamont, the head of J. P. Morgan and one of Willkie's principal Wall Street backers, the seemingly irony-free suggestion that if their candidate were to be put over successfully, "somehow we must get rid of the 'Wall Street stigma.'" Root volunteered to do this by organizing a popular movement on Willkie's behalf.

He accordingly wrote up a petition calling on the Republican Party to nominate Willkie, printed up 800 at his own expense, and sent off a test mailing to the Princeton class of '24 and the Yale class of '25. On receiving a gratifying response, he ordered 20,000 more and put an ad in the *Herald Tribune* seeking contributions and help in drumming up signatories. Soon petitions bearing 200,000 signatures arrived, and the firm's switchboard was jammed with calls from would-be Willkie volunteers ready to sign up still others. (His superior at Davis, Polk, irked at Root's running such an operation on the firm's time and premises, called him on the carpet, only to turn ingratiatingly supportive after receiving a phone call from Lamont—the House of Morgan being Davis, Polk's principal client.)

Thus encouraged, Root organized his young, affluent, suburban, Republican, college-educated, white-collar professionals into Willkie Clubs, which gathered still more signatures. When one columnist suggested to the acerbic Alice Roosevelt Longworth, a Taft supporter, that all this ferment demonstrated Willkie's support at the grass roots, she said yes, "the grass roots of ten thousand country clubs." (In truth, the Murray Hill Hotel professionals gave the amateurs a boost by arranging for local utilities companies across the nation, linked through their trade association, the Edison Electric Institute, to form "grass roots" committees of their employees, who were instructed to get behind Root's campaign.)

The crusade now began to gather momentum. Willkie's poll numbers, still only 3 percent of Republicans in April, began to move in May—in almost direct proportion to the success of Hitler's troops. By May 16, Willkie was up to 5 percent, Dewey down to 62 percent. Two weeks later Willkie was up to 10 percent. Two weeks farther on—in a June 12 survey—he had passed Taft and seized second place (Dewey 52 percent, Willkie 17 percent, and Taft 13 percent). By June 19, with the Germans ensconced in Paris, the dark horse was closing fast on the front runner (Dewey 47 percent, Willkie 29 percent).

Then, on June 20, Roosevelt announced he had chosen Henry Stimson to be the new secretary of war. Coming as it did four days before the Philadelphia convention, the news landed like a bombshell in Republican ranks, leading enraged Midwesterners to bitterly denounce Stimson's "treachery" with FDR and read him out of the party. The timing seemed exquisite, though Roosevelt had hesitated till the last and had had to be nudged into taking the step by Gotham GOPers.

Roosevelt and Stimson had long seen eye to eye on many aspects of foreign policy; and, conversely, the president had grown increasingly unhappy with Harry Woodring, his anti-interventionist secretary of war, yet been unwilling to remove him. The crucial push came from Grenville Clark, senior partner in the prestigious and powerful Wall Street law firm of Root, Clark, Buckner and Ballantine. Back in 1907–10, Clark had been the fellow law clerk of Franklin Roosevelt at Carter, Ledyard, and Milburn; FDR still called him "Grenny." Clark had been the moving spirit in the old Plattsburgh Preparedness Movement of 1916; he had become equally ardent about preparedness in 1940; and he saw Woodring as an obstacle to his plans. So, together with Altschul, Lamont, and Felix Frankfurter, Clark urged FDR to oust Woodring and replace him with Stimson. At Roosevelt's request, Clark had his partner Elihu Root Jr. prepare background information on the state of the seventy-two-year-old Stimson's health. Finally, on June 19, a day after Stimson made a strong radio speech calling for all-out aid to Britain, Roosevelt obtained Woodring's resignation (the ex-secretary told friends his excision had been sought by "a clique of international financiers") and phoned Stimson at his New York office with the offer.

On June 24, Republican convention delegates in Philadelphia cheered an opening-day rendition of the Robinson/Latouche *Ballad for Americans*, unaware, perhaps, of its Federal Theater Project origins. (In July, at Chicago, the Democrats would counter with *God Bless America*, a song Irving Berlin had written back in 1918, then set aside as too jingoistic even for that era. In 1938 he'd touched it up for songstress Kate Smith, and by fall 1940 her rendition had swept the nation.)

On the second day, the AP reported Hitler as declaring, "We will sail against England"—news reports from Europe were avidly followed by the conventioneers—and Dewey continued to lose support. Meanwhile, delegates were being deluged by telegrams and phone calls demanding Willkie's nomination. The chair of the New York delegation, a strong Deweyite, received 7,500 telegrams at his hotel and 20,000 more at his White Plains home, part of the torrent of perhaps a million messages that inundated conventioneers by week's end. Many were genuine, but many were the work of the utility companies—"The Charge of the Electric Light Brigade," snickered those in the know. Philadelphia was also flooded with employees of local and New York banks and law firms—attractive young men and pretty receptionists, who had been dispatched, all expenses paid, to hand out literature and bellow "We want Willkie" from the galleries. Lamont kept a low profile at the convention, but his presence did not go undenounced: one North Dakota congressman protested the "machinations and attempts of J. P. Morgan and other New York City bankers in forcing Wendell Willkie on the Republican Party," and the *Brooklyn Eagle* concurred that "Wall Street has invaded Philadelphia in force to sweep Mr. Willkie over the top." In the end, thanks to events in Europe and the brilliant campaign directed from Gotham, Willkie got the nod. An enraged Taft denounced his opponent's triumph as "engineered from Wall Street." Still, the deed was done.

72

War Hawks at Work

During the ensuing months of presidential campaigning New York interventionists took the lead in winning adoption of two key initiatives that ratcheted up US involvement in the European war.

In June 1940, Britain faced Hitler's threatened invasion with its fleet drastically diminished: U-boat attacks had scuttled 108 of its 176 destroyers. Churchill pleaded with FDR to offset these losses by sending fifty of the 172 obsolete destroyers recently recommissioned by the US as a stopgap defense measure. FDR was sympathetic to the PM's argument that, should Hitler triumph, his booty might well include the British fleet as well as the British Isles, enhancing the Nazis' ability to menace the Americas. Roosevelt refused nevertheless, doubting the lawfulness of such a transfer under remaining neutrality legislation and convinced that anti-interventionists in Congress would block any change in the legal status quo.

In New York—the central beehive of British supporters—influential members of the Committee to Defend America by Aiding the Allies, and its more militant offspring, the Century Group, set to work fashioning a solution and engineering its realization. In July, they came up with a potentially viable strategy, suggesting that sending destroyers might be made more politically palatable if the US got something in return. Their proposed quid pro quo involved England's handing over nine strategic naval bases in Newfoundland, Bermuda, and the British West Indies. Those New Yorkers with access to the president ran the idea past FDR, who expressed interest but wanted a guarantee that Willkie would not attack him on the issue. Gothamites with access to the Republican candidate got Willkie's private agreement, though not his public endorsement.

On July 25, Henry Luce flew down to Washington and visited Roosevelt in the White House, ostensibly to screen the *March of Time*'s new "The Ramparts We Watch," in fact to discuss progress on the destroyers-for-bases swap as emissary of the Century Group. Roosevelt, still concerned about congressional resistance, made clear he wanted help from the New Yorkers—starting with Luce himself—in mobilizing popular support: "Harry," the president said, "I can't come out in favor of such a deal unless I can count on the support of the entire *Time-Life* organization for my foreign policy." In short order *Time* served up its 4–5 million readers an essay, complete with maps, called "Strategic Geography of the Caribbean Sea," which laid out the case for securing the bases. Other Gotham hawks flew into action as well. Clark Eichelberger had the CDAAA staff launch a major promotional campaign, and the Century Group persuaded General John J. "Black Jack" Pershing, great hero of the Great War, to back the deal in a speech (that Lippmann helped write) over the Mutual network on Sunday evening, August 4, which duly received front page attention in the *Herald Tribune* and *Times*.

Anti-interventionists fought back—arguing the deal would be a de facto act of war—and Roosevelt remained reluctant to put the matter before a divided Congress. So the New Yorkers suggested circumventing the legislature altogether. Dean Acheson, after canvassing lawyer-members of the Century and CDAAA, argued that the president could use executive authority to make the swap. Acheson laid out the case publicly in a letter to the *Times* cosigned by three eminent leaders of the New York Bar, C. C. Burlingham, Thomas Thatcher, and George Rublee. (Acheson had asked Allen Dulles to sign as well, but Allen demurred, given his brother Foster's opposition, which Acheson thought unforgivable and rooted in Foster's excessive coziness with German clients.) The attorney general then ratified the legal reasoning.

With public opinion polls demonstrating broad support for acquiring the bases—even Fortress America proponents applauded extending the country's defense perimeter—FDR took the plunge and announced the swap on September 3. Luce publications hailed the transaction, of course, calling it a "brilliant bargain for the US," but there was widespread approval in the heartland as well for this shrewd Yankee deal: "We haven't had a better bargain," exulted the Louisville *Courier Journal*, "since the Indians sold Manhattan Island for $24 in wampum and a demi john of hard liquor."

This giant step toward shedding neutrality—well understood as such in Berlin and Rome—was followed two weeks later when another campaign, led by war hawks in Gotham, with a critical assist from Wendell Willkie, climaxed in Roosevelt's signing the Selective Service Act into law.

In the spring of 1940 the US Regular Army had a mere 245,000 men; it could muster only five fully equipped divisions (for comparison, the Germans had deployed 141 divisions in their western campaign); and many of its weapons were First World War relics. All in all, the US military ranked twentieth in the world, just below Holland's.

Grenville Clark, the point man in Stimson's elevation to secretary of war, set out to mobilize American manpower en masse by getting Congress to enact the nation's first peacetime draft. Clark, though a civilian, had been deeply involved with military affairs since he'd spearheaded the formation, in 1916, of the Military Instruction Camps for Business and Professional Men at Plattsburgh, New York. After the Armistice, he'd helped the Army recruit candidates for an ongoing training camp program, held each summer. On May 8, 1940, he and other Plattsburgh veterans gathered at the Harvard Club in New York to commemorate the founding there of the original movement. Clark persuaded his assembled comrades to think of the future as well as the past and to launch a new preparedness campaign. FDR gave private encouragement to Grenny's plan, while publicly keeping his distance from it. On May 22, again at the Harvard Club, Clark gathered a hundred elite New Yorkers, among them Stimson, William Donovan, and Lewis Douglas, who together set in motion a nationwide agitation for a conscription law. Clark also enlisted Howard C. Petersen of Cravath to help draw up enabling legislation, and on June 20 the Burke-Wadsworth Bill was submitted to the Senate. The crucial question, once again, was whether Willkie would back the initiative. He would, and did, endorsing it publicly on August 17. Swiftly passed by House and Senate, it was signed September 16.

Almost immediately preparations got under way for registering sixteen million young men between twenty-one and thirty-six. Of these, one million lived in New York City. Posters went up all around Gotham—in windows of subways, buses, ferries, city vehicles, hotels, restaurants, etc.—directing them to go, on October 16, to the nearest of 712 designated public schools. There, volunteer teachers and election officials would be waiting to take down the answers to questions about age, place of birth, and current whereabouts, and then issue draft cards. The process proceeded smoothly—spurred along by provisions making failure to register grounds for arrest, with possible penalties (if convicted) of five years in prison and a $10,000 fine (though manhunts like those of 1917–18 were forbidden).

There was one exception to the universal acquiescence (and occasional eagerness). Eight divinity students at the Union Theological Seminary refused to register—a matter of principle, not self-interest, as divinity students were specifically exempt under the law. Nor would they follow the procedures for conscientious objection that had been inserted into the legislation at the urging of UTS president Henry Sloane Coffin, a close friend of Stimson's. Rather, the students denounced the law's "totalitarian nature," to which registering would make them a party. Coffin refused to expel the nonregistrants, and faculty members Niebuhr and Van Dusen were supportive, though urging the students to obey the law and not court martyrdom. Nonetheless, George Houser (son of a Methodist minister, a social gospel pacifist, a supporter of labor, and an opponent of racial discrimination) refused; so did David Dellinger (a pacifist who had left college to work with the unemployed and was living in Harlem); and so did their comrades. They were all sentenced to a year in Danbury prison. By November, the first draftees began showing up at Camp Upton in Yaphank, Long Island, and Fort Dix near Wrightston, New Jersey (not far from where Welles's Martians had landed at Grovers Mill).

73

Martin, Barton, and Fish

Even as Willkie provided essential cover to the interventionist cause, his campaign had begun to flounder. Some of this was his own fault (he was a notoriously undisciplined candidate) and some the fault of his amateur campaign team (winning nominations was one thing, winning elections quite another). Larger currents were trending against him, too. Signs of returning prosperity were poking up nearly everywhere through the melting Depression snows, thanks in large part to British weapons purchases; this seeming renaissance undermined Republican claims that only a businessman could restart the economy.

Willkie's main difficulty was the war news. The Battle of Britain had gotten under way in July when Hitler authorized air attacks to soften up resistance to—and establish aerial superiority for—the invasion he planned for mid-September. Through July and August, the Luftwaffe bombed fighter airfields and aircraft plants. Then, on September 5, the Führer ordered "disruptive attacks on the population and air defences of major British cities, including London, by day and night." The Blitz began late on the afternoon of September 7, when 300 bombers from airfields in Belgium and northern France, escorted by 600 fighters, struck the capital; another 180 pounded the city that evening. Between mid-September and mid-November—the peak weeks of the presidential campaign—between 100 and 200 planes attacked London virtually every night.

This terrible pummeling was transmitted directly into American living rooms by the grave and gravelly voice of Edward R. Murrow—accompanied by his signature theatrical pauses ("THIS...is London") and brilliant aural renderings. By the fall of '40 the CBS radio correspondent had mastered the art of reportage for the ear, his mike catching and passing along the sounds of air raid sirens, exploding bombs, ack-ack fire, and the footfalls of Londoners as they descended into air raid shelters. Murrow had also abandoned any remaining pretense of neutrality, and his bone-deep antifascism and pro-interventionism came through clearly. "A thousand years of history and civilization are being smashed," he intoned that September 7, as bombs crashed down on London.

Nor did CBS chief William Paley try any longer to rein him in, despite outcries from anti-interventionist congressmen. In part this was because the movers and shakers in his

New York social circle were now—as was the Administration that controlled his license—unequivocally up in arms. Indeed, Paley lionized Murrow for his partisan outspokenness, even threw him a banquet at the Waldorf Astoria when he returned to New York for a breather in the fall of 1941. Eleven hundred guests were in attendance, and millions more listened in via a national broadcast to hear Archibald MacLeish tell Murrow: "You burned the city of London in our houses and we felt the flames that burned it."

With war looming—and putting a premium on experience in office—Willkie's standing sagged. In September, turning desperate, he yielded to calls from the Taft wing and Republican professionals and began to decry Roosevelt's interventionist moves as warmongering and "dictatorial" (even while accepting them in substance). Republicans churned out campaign buttons reading: "Third Reich. Third International. Third Term."

Willkie's weakening infuriated his interventionist supporters. Some complained but stayed with him—Douglas continued to stump, Luce kept writing speeches and raising money—but others jumped ship. In October, Dorothy Thompson wrote a column switching her support to FDR. Appalled, Helen Reid made clear that Thompson's job was in jeopardy. Undeterred, the doughty Dorothy began working for Roosevelt as an adviser on Germany and writing in *PM* the columns she was forbidden to publish in the *Herald Tribune*. This made her a clandestine colleague of Walter Winchell, who sent his pseudonymous pro-FDR pieces to *PM* when Hearst banned them from the *Mirror*, the press magnate being less than keen on Winchell's favorite slogan: "Willkie for the millionaires; Roosevelt for the millions!" Thompson's other colleague, Walter Lippmann, didn't go as far as she did, but having become certain the Nazis were hoping for Roosevelt's defeat, he opted for neutrality. The Reids refused to publish Lippmann's column offering his rationale for not endorsing either candidate, but they let him keep his job. Whereas Thompson, telling Helen Reid, "I feel an unbridgeable hostility to me in the *Tribune*," moved to the *Post* when her contract expired the following March.

Ship jumpers in abundance could also be spotted abandoning yet another presidential vessel, that of Norman Thomas, the third New York candidate in the race. Thomas had urged his Socialist Party to run him again in the hope of galvanizing a strong protest vote against American intervention in the war. He continued to see that conflict—for all Hitler's admitted hyper-brutality—as yet another iteration of Old Europe's incurable imperial impulse, with the combatants clashing over access to markets, raw materials, investment opportunities, and cheap labor. Those who argued England represented "democracy" and "civilization" against German "totalitarianism" and "barbarism" were (Thomas believed) "bound up, subconsciously, with British or English-speaking supremacy." Willkie was no better than Roosevelt on this score, Thomas thought, as both were beholden to "Wall Street and other interventionists who would stake everything on the preservation of the British Empire." For him, the simple truth was that unlike the English (or their US fellow-travelers), ordinary Americans didn't need a war: "We still have two oceans to guard our ramparts."

The Socialist Party campaign was forced to rely heavily on cadre from the Keep America Out of War Congress—indeed the two organizations all but merged—because apart from a handful of intellectuals, including John Dewey, John Haynes Holmes, A. J. Muste, John Sloan, and V. F. Calverton, large numbers of Socialists refused to back Thomas's stance or candidacy. Many bailed out of the Party altogether. In New York, the Socialists' last redoubt, some members (led by Reinhold Niebuhr) decamped to the Democrats, others left for the American Labor Party. The entire Italian Socialist Federation opted for intervention. And Jewish socialists, whose access to sources in the Polish underground and Polish Bund gave them a very different perspective on the war, pulled out en masse. By the time the stampede to the exits slowed, national membership had shrunk to under 1,200.

FDR's campaign had its own problems. Boss Flynn ran a feisty Democratic headquarters operation out of the Biltmore Hotel but reported to Roosevelt that the organization's rank and file were surly and listless; they resented (as did Flynn) the flow of federal patronage to their enemies, the New Deal Democrats and La Guardia Republicans. This was especially true at Manhattan's Tammany Hall, against which FDR and La Guardia had waged war for a decade. But even the borough machines had been losing organizational edge; their ability to generate election-day turnout via house-to-house canvasses could no longer be taken for granted. And looming over the campaign was the question of how New York's ethnics might vote: would the Irish, German, and Italian opposition to intervention translate into opposition to Roosevelt?

There were, however, potentially powerful countervailing forces—Jews, Blacks, and labor unions—that could offset any such apostasy. And a vehicle existed—the American Labor Party—that could mobilize such supporters should the Democratic machines falter. The ALP was itself divided between liberals and (the currently anti-interventionist) leftists. However, La Guardia—vicious as a pit bull in his own attacks on Willkie—managed to patch up a truce within the ALP, and both factions worked together more closely than they ever had before, channeling money and manpower into the race from Sidney Hillman's ACWA and Dubinsky's ILGWU.

FDR himself, though increasingly irked by Republican attacks, largely forbore from returning fire until October 28, ten days before the election, when he traveled up to Gotham to mobilize his base with a massive display of organizational and oratorical skill. Entering Staten Island early that morning via the Bayonne Bridge, the president—battered hat and jaunty cigarette holder in place—took his place in the lead car of a forty-auto motorcade that would, by day's end, display the candidate to two million people along a 58-mile, five-borough route.

On reaching Staten Island's St. George ferry, the party transferred to a vessel that—accompanied by P-98s and P-10s, the latest-model torpedo boats—ferried them across to 39th Street in Brooklyn. The column then proceeded north and made a stop at Hamilton Avenue and Van Brunt Street, where FDR participated in a ground-breaking ceremony for the Brooklyn-Battery Tunnel. Robert Moses was notably absent; just as well, given that two weeks earlier *Life* had published a Moses article entitled "The Case against Roosevelt."

Then, via the Manhattan Bridge, it was on to a stop at the Lower East Side's Roosevelt Park at Christie and Canal; up Essex to Houston; over to Second Avenue, and up to 23rd Street, then west to Seventh Avenue, where a right turn sent the cavalcade into the heart of the Garment District, passing immense crowds between 24th and 41st Streets, as a storm of colorful cloth confetti rained down from factory windows above. Proceeding through Times Square, Roosevelt & Co. made their way to Hunter College's new home at 68th and Lexington (which, like all the other projects visited that day, was a New Deal contribution to the city's landscape).

Then it was on to Queens, via the new midtown tunnel; up 21st Street to a stop at the Queens Bridge Housing Development; then out to La Guardia Field, where the procession looped around the terminals of various airlines.

Now it was off to the Bronx, past cheering throngs along East 138th Street and the Grand Concourse all the way up to Fordham University, where he was greeted by President Gannon and Archbishop Spellman, thus offsetting Wendell Willkie's appearance at the

Fordham–St. Mary's football game the previous Saturday. At 5:15, almost precisely on schedule, the president arrived at the Mott Haven yards of the New York Central and took a dinner break before his 9:45 speech at Madison Square Garden.

At the appointed hour, before a capacity crowd, the president lit into Republican congressmen, particularly Joe Martin, the house minority leader; Bruce Barton, Willkie backer and Silk-Stocking representative; and longtime nemesis Hamilton Fish. Contrasting their votes against preparedness with the stance of their candidate Wendell Willkie, FDR led the crowd in a derisory chant of "Martin, Barton, and Fish." His masterly campaign speech was the first to be carried live by the still-experimental medium of television. The signal was carried by a novel "television 'pipe' " (coaxial cable), provided by engineers of Bell Telephone Laboratories, to a control room at Radio City, whence it was relayed to the NBC transmitter atop the Empire State Building and beamed to roughly 40,000 viewers gathered at 4,000 locations in the metropolitan area where "sight-sound receivers" had been set up. Reception was poor—the images dark and fuzzy—but at least the DNC wasn't out of pocket, as this was an FCC-authorized test.

So was the broadcast of Willkie's windup campaign speech at the Garden that Saturday night, November 2, before another overflow crowd, with another 50,000 surrounding the building chanting "We Want Willkie."

They didn't get him. Though it was remarkably close. Nationally FDR garnered 54.7 percent to Wilkie's 44.8 percent—his plurality of a little over 5,000,000 votes being the smallest since 1916. In the Electoral College the results were more decisive, with Willkie's 82 electoral votes dwarfed by Roosevelt's 449, of which 47 were New York State's, put in the president's column by his overwhelming triumph in New York City—more precisely, Brooklyn.

Willkie lost the state by 224,440 out of the total vote of roughly 6.3 million. He led FDR by 175,000 in Westchester, Nassau, and Suffolk, which, when added to his other suburban and upstate pluralities, gave him a total basket of 494,019 votes. Roosevelt, however, carried New York City by 718,459 votes, giving him his winning quarter-million margin.

The president's Gothamic constituency, however, was not evenly distributed. He didn't capture Queens or Staten Island, and he suffered serious defections in parts of Brooklyn and Manhattan as well. Democratic bailouts, not surprisingly, hailed from anti-interventionist communities. German Americans in Yorkville and Ridgewood parted company with Roosevelt, following the lead of the Steuben Society, which had come out for Willkie, and against a third term that might mean "erecting a dictatorship here." Italian Americans— furious at FDR's stereotype-wielding stab-in-the-back speech, and fearful of the fifth column frenzy he'd helped stoke—refused to follow Generoso Pope, who had endorsed a third term: where 79 percent had voted for Roosevelt in 1936, only 42 percent did so in 1940. Irish Catholic Democrats similarly voted their anti-interventionist and increasingly conservative convictions; of Brooklyn's twenty-three wards, the three that were predominantly Irish Catholic each went Republican for the first time in the history of the city.

All these defections, however, were offset by Roosevelt's ability either to hold his own—as was the case with African Americans—or to attract new supporters, like the city's Polish Americans—or, most critically, to galvanize near unanimous support from the biggest electoral bloc in the United States, New York's/Brooklyn's 1.1 million Jews. It was their tidal turnout that gave Roosevelt his whopping 350,000-vote margin in Brooklyn. Many of these Jewish supporters (including a large body of defectors from the Socialist Party, which suffered a grievous electoral falloff) voted the Democratic ticket. But many, mobilized by the needle trades unions, pulled the lever for Roosevelt on the American Labor Party line, and the 317,318 votes the ALP delivered the president gave substance to the party's claim that it had handed him his triumph.

Safely re-ensconced in power, Roosevelt—working in tandem with the New York bankers, publishers, lawyers, and intellectuals who had in effect seized control of the Republican Party—now took another decisive step toward war.

74

Arsenal of Democracy

On November 22, 1940, Lord Lothian, England's ambassador to the US, returned to New York after a brief visit to London. Alighting at La Guardia, he startled the assembled press corps by baldly declaring: "Well, boys, Britain's broke. It's your money we want." Roosevelt had heard the same directly from Churchill right after the election: England was running out of dollars to pay for the ships, bombers, and munitions on its shopping list and wanted to borrow the wherewithal to keep buying. The Administration favored the idea—it would allow England to keep fighting and keep revitalizing the US economy—but such loans were still precluded under US law. In early December FDR came up with a way to finesse the restrictions—by lending or leasing Britain the necessary war matériel rather than selling it. He explained his idea at a December 17 press conference, using the homely metaphor of lending one's garden hose to a neighbor whose house was on fire and getting it back when the crisis was over. He elaborated on the proposal in a December 29 fireside chat, in which he said: "We must be the great arsenal of democracy." And on January 10, 1941, he sent a Lend Lease bill to Congress, patriotically packaged as H.R. 1776, and set about mobilizing support.

His Republican troops were ready to roll. Titular leader Wendell Willkie—newly liberated from campaign kowtowing to the party's right wing—was an ardent and active supporter of Lend Lease. Representatives of leading Wall Street clans were similarly on board. Winthrop Aldrich, chairman of the Rockefeller-affiliated Chase Bank (and Rockefeller Jr.'s brother-in-law), had already gone on record in favor of opening up America's vaults: "We can no more afford to have England break down financially than we can contemplate her defeat in this war," said Aldrich. "In both cases our own interests are vitally involved." And Morgan partner Russell Leffingwell had signaled the firm's concurrence directly to the president in a December 24 letter, writing that "whatever differences there may have been about domestic affairs, I and my colleagues are heart and soul with you for unlimited material aid to Britain and for national defense."

It was Roosevelt's left flank—and the mass of the citizenry—to whom he devoted most attention. In his Annual Message to Congress on January 6, he put an unmistakably liberal stamp on the meaning of any such financial support to England—and of any future military intervention—by stressing "democracy" as much as "arsenal." In committing the nation to "full support of all those resolute people everywhere who are resisting aggression," Roosevelt was not only acting defensively ("keeping war away from our hemisphere") but expansively, demonstrating "our determination that the democratic cause shall prevail." Democracy, however, could not prevail if it was not universal (any more than Lincoln's "house divided" could withstand being half slave and half free). The justification of war, should it come, would be in the extension of "essential human freedoms"—four in particular—to the entire planet.

"The first," Roosevelt affirmed, was "freedom of speech and expression—everywhere in the world." The second was the "freedom of every person to worship God in his own way—everywhere in the world." The third was "freedom from want, which, translated into world terms, means economic understandings which will secure to every nation a healthy peacetime life for its inhabitants—everywhere in the world." And the fourth was "freedom from fear, which, translated into world terms, means a worldwide reduction of armaments to such a point and in such a thorough fashion that no nation will be in a position to commit an act of physical aggression against any neighbor—anywhere in the world." This was, FDR insisted, "no vision of a distant millennium" but rather "a definite basis for a kind of world attainable in our own time and generation," and one, moreover, that was "the very antithesis of the so called 'new order' of tyranny which the dictators seek to create with the crash of a bomb."

Lest anyone miss the point that his sweeping definition of democracy contained a crucial social component, Roosevelt ran through a checklist of the "basic things" people expected of their "political and economic systems": "Equality of opportunity for youth and for others. Jobs for those who can work. Security for those who need it. The ending of special privilege for the few. The preservation of civil liberties for all. The enjoyment of the fruits of scientific progress in a wider and constantly rising standard of living."

The president did not claim that the US had itself attained these goals, though the country could take "great satisfaction and much strength from the things which have been done to make its people conscious of their individual stake in the preservation of democratic life in America." There was still work to be done: "We should bring more citizens under the coverage of old age pensions and unemployment insurance. We should widen the opportunities for adequate medical care. We should plan a better system by which persons deserving or needing gainful employment may obtain it."

Roosevelt was calling for expanding New Deal–style social democracy at home and extending it on a global scale—for launching a simultaneous and mutually reinforcing crusade against domestic illiberalism and international fascism. Any auditors unclear about this would have been vigorously set straight had they been able to read a verbosely entitled memorandum privately penned that April 12 by Harry Hopkins, the president's right-hand man. In "The New Deal of Mr. Roosevelt Is the Designate and Invincible Adversary of the New Order of Hitler," Hopkins argued that fascism could "never be conclusively defeated by the old order of democracy, which is the status quo," as who would fight to preserve an order marred by, among other things, "want and unemployment." It would, rather, take a "new order of democracy, which is the New Deal, universally extended and applied," to do the job of rallying popular support by holding out hope that winning would actually *improve* their situation, not simply sustain it. "Universally extended and applied," moreover, meant exactly that, Hopkins added in a messianic aperçu: "The world is now a unit. If the New Deal is to rule America, it must rule the world."

A poster distributed by the Roosevelt Administration advertising their plan to build war planes. (Hoover Institution Library & Archives)

The Wall Street wing was drawn to a similarly messianic vision, most gleamingly expressed in an essay entitled "The American Century," written by Henry Luce and published by Henry Luce in a February 1941 issue of his *Life* magazine. Like Roosevelt's Four Freedoms speech the previous month, "The American Century" was designed to rouse the citizenry to aid Britain and defeat fascism, but it replaced presidential invocations of social justice and economic equity with paeans to opportunities for commercial and spiritual profit.

Expanding on Walter Lippmann's essay "The American Destiny" that he'd published back in 1939, Luce stressed that the burdens and opportunities of global leadership were passing from England to America, if the latter would but seize them. The time had come to "accept wholeheartedly our duty and our opportunity as the most powerful and vital nation in the world and in consequence to exert upon the world the full impact of our influence, for such purposes as we see fit and by such means as we see fit." As Britain had once ruled the waves and guaranteed freedom of the seas, so now should the United States, especially as underwriting the flow of global commerce could be highly profitable, particularly in Asia (the missionary son's old fixation), where it might "be worth to us four, five, ten billions of dollars a year." But money wasn't everything: America was also a repository of ideals and values—its own, and those of Western civilization—and "it now becomes our time to be the powerhouse from which the ideals spread throughout the world and do their mysterious work of lifting the life of mankind from the level of the beasts to what the Psalmist called a little lower than the angels."

The justifications advanced by New York's social democratic and corporate elites, of an interventionist foreign policy in general and Lend Lease in particular, by no means swept the metropolitan (much less the national) board. Opposition to Four Freedom and American Century perspectives came not only from the continental heartland but from Gotham's five boroughs as well, where a wildly variegated collection of individuals, of profoundly differing political persuasions, gathered for a last ditch stand on behalf of an anti-interventionist and nationalist alternative to war.

75

America First

In the spring of 1940, two Yale students, Kingman Brewster Jr. and Douglas Stuart Jr., organized a campus campaign to keep the US out of the European conflict. That summer the idea was picked up by some rich and conservative Midwestern businessmen who were furious that New Yorkers had walked off with the Republican nomination, leaving them bereft of a horse in the presidential sweepstakes. They decided to set up a national membership and lobbying organization—the America First Committee (AFC)—that could grapple with Gotham-based groups like the CDAAA and Century, whose ill-advised interventionism, they were sure, would ruin American capitalism.

The leading AFC figures had differing positions on domestic policy—Robert E. Wood, a retired US Army brigadier general and board chairman of Sears, Roebuck, had backed many of Roosevelt's initiatives, while *Chicago Tribune* publisher Colonel Robert McCormick was a New Deal nemesis. They did see eye to eye on staying out of the war and made the fight against Lend Lease their first great campaign.

Because the entire AFC National Committee hailed from the Midwest, and the vast majority of chapters and members were within 200 miles of Chicago headquarters, the organization's high command believed it was essential to open up a second front inside Gotham, which they regarded as the "citadel of interventionism." Indeed, a national committeeman argued, the new movement could not succeed if "whipped on this strategic Eastern battleground."

But who could undertake such a mobilization? No first-rank New York businessman was willing to buck Wall Street's dominant interventionism. There was Captain Joseph Patterson—Colonel McCormick's cousin and publisher of the *New York Daily News*—who had broken with FDR over Lend Lease and whose powerhouse paper was now fulminating against the "Dictator Bill"; but Patterson was not prepared to be the AFC's New York point man. Nor was Herbert Hoover, ensconced in his Waldorf Astoria Tower suite, though he would profess "profound admiration for the battle" waged by America Firsters. John Foster Dulles proved helpful in getting legal papers drawn up for a New York wing. However, though he applauded AFC tactics, he could not, being a staunch internationalist, approve its principles. The best business-class candidate Chicagoans could come up with was the cranky Edwin Sibley Webster Jr., senior partner in the Wall Street investment firm of Kidder, Peabody. An extreme opponent of government regulation, Webster was the sort who described Nazis as German New Dealers. The AFC would get nowhere in New York with Webster at the helm.

Yale's Kingman Brewster suggested a very different strategy: to look for leadership not on Wall Street, which was hopelessly locked up by interventionists, but among the city's disaffected liberals. And he knew just the person: John Thomas Flynn.

Born in a Washington, DC, suburb, Flynn had studied to be a lawyer at Georgetown but in 1916 decided to assay a journalistic career in Gotham. During the late 1920s and early 1930s, Flynn had made a name for himself with books like *Investment Trusts Gone Wrong!* and *Graft in Business* that criticized Wall Street corruption and pinned the Depression on the city's brokers and bankers. In 1933 he began writing a weekly column ("Other People's Money") for the *New Republic*.

Flynn welcomed FDR's 1932 election then soon grew disaffected, deeming the Securities Exchange Act of 1934 a toothless compromise with Wall Street. Flynn was also an antimilitarist, and he believed FDR was confecting war scares to revive the economy and win reelection. In the 1940 campaign he claimed Roosevelt's defense plans were an "excuse to spend another ten or fifteen billion dollars to return his party to power."

Flynn (an Irishman) was no Anglophile. It galled him that those promoting aid to England were deemed patriotic, while antiwar Americans got labeled fifth columnists or Nazis. Nor did he see the European war as a struggle between democracy and dictatorship, given England's overlordship of colonial peoples. He thought, too, that fears of a Nazi invasion were seriously over-hyped: if the fascists did jump the South Pacific from Dakar to Brazil (a popular interventionist scenario) they'd wind up farther from the US than they'd been in Germany. The economic peril seemed similarly oversold: even if the Third Reich grabbed all Europe it would still need to import food and export products and be in no position to opt for autarchy or dictate terms of trade. Finally, he was convinced that if Americans set out "on a fool's errand to remodel the world" they would end up losing democracy at home.

Anti-interventionists on the right agreed with much of Flynn's perspective, as did many on the left, such as Socialist Norman Thomas, liberals like John Haynes Holmes, and pacifists like Oswald Garrison Villard. Indeed, in 1938 Flynn had joined with these and other New York anti-interventionists to found the Keep America out of War Congress (KAOWC) and even served as its national chair. It was only at the end of 1940, after Thomas's presidential campaign flamed out, that he accepted the chairmanship of the local America First Committee in the belief that, being neither leftist nor pacifist, it might attract wider support. In this he proved more correct than he bargained for.

The New York operation grew rapidly. By August 1941 it claimed a membership of more than 135,000. By year's end it was the AFC's most highly organized branch, with eighty-four chapters and units in Gotham, all tightly controlled by Flynn from his headquarters at 49 East 53rd Street (off Madison Avenue). The office was jammed with volunteers, many of them peace movement veterans, who organized lecture series and street speakers, set up twenty-eight storefront offices, and raised enough money, most of it from small contributors, to make it the richest AFC operation in the US—four times as affluent as Chicago's.

The organization's growth was a function of its having become a catchment for antiwarriors from all bands on the political spectrum. Norman Thomas was not a member of the

A crowd gathers in front of the Manhattan Center, where Charles Lindbergh, among others, spoke at an America First Committee rally. (Everett Collection Historical/Alamy Stock Photo)

board of directors, though he was invited to serve, but he did speak under AFC auspices at rallies in Brooklyn and Manhattan, some of them cosponsored by the KAOWC, and was denounced by Dorothy Thompson for consorting with bigots. Liberals like Villard and Chester Bowles signed on as advisers and associates. Though many clerical pacifist colleagues had repaired to the interventionist standard raised by Niebuhr, Coffin, and Van Dusen up at Union Theological, Harry Emerson Fosdick continued to insist that an escalated US involvement "would be a colossal and futile disaster." While Fosdick declined to join the national committee, he accepted AFC funds so his Ministers No War Committee could mail literature to clerics. Assorted ethnic organizations also urged support of America First: the Steuben Society was sympathetic; AFC officers were well received at rallies in Italian neighborhoods; and Patrick Scanlan's *Tablet* responded favorably as well. Working-class New Yorkers were attracted by the argument that Anglophile interventionists were particularly thick on the ground among the city's upper strata: "This Is a Park Avenue War," ran one AFC slogan.

Communists were barred from AFC membership, but as the Party was still in Pactmode, its "Yanks Are Not Coming" members were in effect fellow travelers. Nazis and Bundists were barred, too, but they wanted in, and at times gained a foothold, along with Coughlinites, Christian Fronters, and Handsome Joe McNazi's Christian Mobilizers. Flynn disavowed and repelled such support, but enough far-rightists clambered aboard the AFC vessel to allow opponents to tag it as subversive.

Both sides squared off over Lend Lease. La Guardia led a campaign to push the legislation. (The mayor had replaced William Allen White as chair of the New York CDAAA in January, when White resigned, complaining that warmongers had taken over.) In February,

La Guardia testified in Congress on behalf of H.R. 1776, pooh-poohing predictions that passage would inflame ethnic hatreds in New York to the point of civil war.

Flynn launched a campaign decrying the "War Dictatorship Bill" with an ad in the *New York Times* on January 28. On February 20 an AFC/KAOWC rally drew 3,500 to the Mecca Temple to hear Flynn, Thomas, and others lambaste the bill for allowing the US to lend England money, guns, and the use of American ports.

Critics also claimed England still had billions in assets and was only faking poverty (as did the "unworthy poor") in order to get a handout. This charge struck home, and the Roosevelt Administration moved to rebut it, by forcing Great Britain to liquidate their American securities. In January, British treasury agents in New York began dumping such holdings at the rate of ten million dollars per week. In March, England was required to disgorge their largest US industrial holding, the American Viscose Company, perhaps the world's largest rayon producer. (Churchill grumbled, in private, that "we are not only to be skinned, but flayed to the bone.") A syndicate headed by Morgan Stanley and Dillon, Read bought Viscose shares for $54 million (with J. P. Morgan providing the necessary loans), resold them for $62 million, and pocketed the difference. Churchill thought he'd been fleeced by the bankers, but the spectacle of forced sales did help win final passage of Lend Lease, and on March 11, 1941, FDR signed it into law. Congress immediately approved seven billion dollars of aid—the first of an eventual fifty billion—and vessels (mostly British) began hauling munitions, foodstuffs, and other vital supplies from New York and other ports.

76

Second Platoon

As the United States moved closer to war, a small contingent of New Yorkers readied themselves to run it. Trailing Henry Stimson, an advance guard of Wall Street Warriors moved down to DC and settled into the topmost echelons of its civilian-military establishment. Then they summoned to their aid a platoon of friends and associates from Gotham's interlocking worlds of big business and high society—altogether a very different breed of New Yorker from the social workers and labor leaders who had trooped down to Washington a decade before to run the New Deal.

Joining Stimson at the War Department as his second-in-command was Judge Robert Patterson. His appointment had been part of the deal brokered by Grenville Clark, as everyone had agreed the elderly Stimson would need a younger but seasoned assistant. Patterson had worked for Clark back in 1915 when he joined Root, Clark, Buckner and Ballantine right out of Harvard Law. He had also enlisted in the fashionable old Seventh Regiment of the New York National Guard; volunteered for officer training at Clark's Plattsburgh barracks in 1917; and served during the war as a company commander in New York's 77th "Statue of Liberty" Infantry Division. In the 1920s Patterson became one of Wall Street's best-known lawyers. In 1930, Hoover made him a federal judge. In 1939, Roosevelt promoted him to the Second Circuit Court of Appeals, where he sat with Learned and Augustus Hand. In 1940, obsessed by the looming war, he volunteered to resign his lifetime judgeship and return to active duty, as a private if need be, and even went back to Plattsburgh for training. It was there, while doing KP duty, that the camp commander informed him he'd been nominated to help Stimson run the War Department, overseeing industrial mobilization.

Banker Robert A. Lovett, another War Department recruit, was the son of Judge Robert S. Lovett, E. H. Harriman's chief counsel at Union Pacific. When the old railroad magnate died in 1909, Judge Lovett succeeded him and set about grooming young Averell Harriman to take over the line. In and out of the Lovett home on Central Park West, young Robert and Averell grew up as friends; both became avid members of the Knickerbocker Greys, both went to Yale (and were tapped for Skull and Bones). During the First World War, while his father served on the War Industries Board with Bernard Baruch, Lovett commanded a naval air squadron. After the war he finished up at Harvard Law, married Adele Brown, and joined Brown Brothers (headed by his father-in-law), becoming a full partner in 1926. The couple lived in a town house on East 83rd Street that commanded a panoramic view of the East River, were avid fans of jazz and movies, and participated in Café Society, rubbing elbows with the likes of Archibald MacLeish, Robert Benchley, Robert Sherwood, Lillian Hellman, and Dorothy Parker, many of whom were also friends of Averell and Marie Harriman.

At the outset of the Depression, Lovett helped merge the Harriman banking interests with those of Brown Brothers, and it was on a working trip to Europe for Brown Brothers Harriman in May 1940 that he became impressed with, and alarmed by, Hitler's Luftwaffe. On his return he set off on a survey tour, ostensibly of Union Pacific operations, actually of US aircraft factories, which he found drowsing in horse-and-buggy days—inadequately capitalized and technologically backward. He wrote up a report arguing that manufacturers should retool their plants by adapting assembly-line techniques from the auto industry. Lovett showed his findings to James Forrestal, a neighbor of his in Locust Valley (in the middle of Long Island's Gold Coast), who himself had just been called down to Washington. In November 1940 Forrestal shared Lovett's report with Stimson, who hired Lovett on the spot as an adviser, and soon elevated him to assistant secretary of war, with responsibility for overseeing the US Army Air Corps.

John J. McCloy, unlike his friend Lovett, had not been to the manor born but had moved in nevertheless. McCloy, as a scholarship student at Amherst, had knocked on the doors of the great estates of Maine and Adirondacks, offering his services to the rich as a tennis coach, which is how he first met the Rockefellers. McCloy served in Clark's camp at Plattsburgh, fought in France, graduated Harvard Law, went to Wall Street, became a Cravath partner, and did exceedingly well in the Depression, especially after Rockefeller Jr. began consulting him on business and philanthropic matters, leading much of Wall Street to do the same. He and his wife lived on Beekman Place. He joined the University, Grolier, Broad Street, and Anglers' Clubs.

McCloy saw himself as the latest in a Wall Street lineage; as he told his diary, "I felt a direct current running from Root through Stimson to me." Stimson, for his part, was impressed by his would-be heir, particularly McCloy's near-legendary handling of one case in particular. Arms manufacturer Bethlehem Steel had lost a small fortune when the Black Tom munitions depot, across the Hudson from Lower Manhattan, had been blown up by German saboteurs in 1916. After new evidence of German responsibility emerged in 1928, the company hired McCloy to collect damages from German funds held in the US. McCloy brought suit before the German American Mixed Claims Commission at The Hague but lost, the evidence being deemed insufficient. McCloy got a rehearing and lost again. Over the next decade, with dogged persistence, he scoured Europe for satisfactory proof, repeatedly suing and losing, until 1939, when he won, and the claimants were awarded $50 million. In September 1940, shortly after a terrific explosion of undetermined origin at a New Jersey powder plant killed over fifty people and blew up a load of ammunition bound for England, Stimson brought McCloy down to the War Department as a consultant on German espionage. Several months later he was elevated to assistant secretary-hood.

Another flock of New Yorkers migrated south to staff the Navy Department, whose top slot FDR had awarded to *Chicago Daily News* publisher Frank Knox. James Vincent Forrestal, picked by Roosevelt for the number two position, was, like McCloy, in, but not of, the metropolitan elite. He had been born in New York's Dutchess County (in 1892) to a family of Irish immigrants—his mother a Catholic school teacher, his father a successful construction contractor who was also a local Democratic Party boss and a friend and supporter of neighbor Frank Roosevelt. Forrestal attended Princeton, though he left in 1915 just before graduating, and briefly became a reporter on Swope's *New York World*, before signing on, in 1916, as a bond salesman for William Read and Company. He did most of his Great War service in Washington, working on unglamorous supply issues at the Office of Naval Operations but also getting closer to his father's old ally, Assistant Secretary of the Navy Franklin Roosevelt.

On returning to (the now renamed) Dillon, Read, he enjoyed a spectacular Wall Street career during the glory days of the 1920s, and—assiduously distancing himself from his plebeian origins—he partied in the city's Café Society where (in 1926) he met and married Josephine Ogden, *Vogue Magazine* editor and former Ziegfeld Girl. During the Depression, Forrestal, unlike most Wall Streeters, not only supported Roosevelt but backed his financial and social reforms as well. In 1938 he succeeded Clarence Dillon as head of the firm. In 1940, he told Harry Hopkins he was interested in a government post, which dovetailed with FDR's need for a Democratic financier to strengthen his newly mended links with Wall Street. On June 22, 1940, the day France fell, Roosevelt took him on as an assistant, then bumped him up (in August) to undersecretary of the Navy, with authority over economic planning.

To assist him in remaking a calcified naval establishment, Forrestal called in two old Dillon, Read associates, Ferdinand Eberstadt and Paul Nitze, both of German descent.

Eberstadt's father, an affluent Gotham import-export merchant, sent his son (born in 1890) to Princeton's class of 1913, where he befriended Forrestal, and then to Columbia Law, where his studies were interrupted by the First World War. Eberstadt joined the Plattsburgh contingent and the Statue of Liberty Division, meeting John McCloy and Robert Patterson (with whom he became close), and serving under Colonel Stimson. After the Armistice he worked in corporate law, then in 1923 switched to investment banking, joining Forrestal at Dillon, Read, where he specialized in German finance and corporate mergers (helping arrange the marriage of Chrysler and Dodge). Eberstadt did well for the firm, and vice versa, which allowed him to join elite clubs and buy elegant homes (together with and near his college chum Forrestal). After the crash he backed the New Deal for a time, convinced of the need for direct federal intervention, but shifted toward advocating business preeminence in such public-private initiatives. In 1941 Forrestal brought Eberstadt to Washington to hammer out a productive relationship between the various (and competing) military services, and industry and finance, and labor and government, and New York and Washington. As a Baruch disciple, he urged that a War Industry Board–type institution coordinate these disparate interests. Forrestal and Patterson agreed, and soon Eberstadt would be exercising his tough managerial style (he became known as "The Prussian") as chair of the Army Navy Munitions Board, a crucial synapse in an emerging military-industrial network.

The much younger Paul Nitze (born 1907) was a '20s whiz kid who leapt into investment banking immediately on graduating Harvard in 1928. Asked by his Chicago employer to analyze the German investment scene, the brash young Nitze went directly to Clarence Dillon in New York and asked for and got letters of introduction to important Weimar figures. Nitze returned to report that further German growth depended on further loans, and if the flow slowed, the economy would likely collapse. Dillon was himself convinced a crash was coming and, indeed, laid off most of his staff in 1929; but he was so impressed by Nitze's analysis that he hired the twenty-two-year-old, who set up shop in Gotham. In 1932 Nitze married Standard Oil heiress Phyllis Pratt; the couple settled into a spacious Upper East Side apartment, and he entered the rarefied world of New York's social and business elite.

Despite his new status, Nitze voted for Roosevelt in 1932 and 1936, only parting political company with the president after FDR's court-packing episode, when he became a Republican like most of his Wall Street colleagues.

In 1937 Nitze took a vacation trip to Germany, was awed by the turnaround of the German economy, and decided Hitler's rule had redeeming social value. Nor could the German American banker see any outstanding moral virtue in Britain or France. After the invasion of Poland, at a dinner party with Vincent Astor he startled the guests by saying he would rather see the US under Hitler's dictatorship than England's Empire. Yet when Germany smashed into France in 1940, his commitment to neutrality evaporated, and he answered Forrestal's call with alacrity (not so the FBI, whose background check into Nitze's Nazi sympathies proved prolonged, though in the end not disqualifying).

In addition to the War and Navy Departments, New Yorkers assumed key positions in the civilian war planning machinery that Roosevelt set up to replace the War Resources Board (WRB), which had been shot down in 1939. This time he took care to include New Dealers as well as businessmen, pledging, in a fireside chat, that "I can assure you that labor will be adequately represented" in the new defense setup. At the end of May 1940, he revived an organization that had been hibernating since the First World War—the Council of National Defense, a collection of six cabinet officers—and placed alongside it a seven-man National Defense Advisory Commission (NDAC). Like the WRB, the NDAC gave oversight of industrial mobilization to big business leaders, notably New York's Edward Stettinius (US Steel) and Detroit's William Knudsen (General Motors). Now, however, FDR included a labor division, and appointed CIO vice president and Amalgamated chief Sidney Hillman to run it. Not satisfied with this arrangement, in December he scrapped the NDAC and replaced it with the Office of Production Management (OPM), now under two co-equal heads, Knudsen and Hillman; Stettinius would later be transferred to head Lend Lease.

The Lend Lease program was where Averell Harriman finally came to roost, after a long and arduous pursuit of a major position in the defense effort. Harriman, a Roosevelt ally since National Relief Association days, had been repeatedly passed over and had had to settle for advising Stettinius at OPM on railroad issues. In part this was because, for all his achievements in banking and transport, Harriman was widely seen as a lightweight, with his business accomplishments overshadowed by his prowess at polo and croquet, his creation of the star-studded ski resort at Sun Valley, and the glittery parties he threw for friends at his 20,000-acre estate up at Arden, forty miles north of New York. One of those friends was Harry Hopkins, whom Harriman had come to know at croquet parties at Swope's Sands Point estate, and Hopkins—devoted to the poor but attracted to the rich—had cultivated the relationship. And so it was that in 1941, at Hopkins's behest, the forty-nine-year-old Harriman was appointed as Defense Expediter of Lend Lease to Great Britain (soon with the rank of ambassador attached). In short order he became Roosevelt's personal liaison to Churchill (and shortly to Stalin), ascending to a position of considerable power.

This advance guard of Wall Streeters—Stimson, Patterson, Lovett, McCloy, Forrestal, Eberstadt, Nitze, Stettinius, Harriman—was quickly followed by an armada of dollar-a-year men, loaned to Washington by the wider corporate world. An amazing number of those who agreed to fill second- and third-rung posts were drawn from New York's Bar and boardrooms.

Many were preselected, as it were, by virtue of membership in institutions like the Council on Foreign Relations. As the CFR's John McCloy would later recall: "Whenever we needed a man we thumbed through the roll of Council members and put through a call to New York."

Another talent pool was Ferdinand Eberstadt's "Good Man List," an elaborate inventory he had compiled over four decades of "conscientious high class men" in law, business, industry, education, government, and the professions. One analysis of the "Good Man List" found that nearly 75 percent were Wall Street lawyers and bankers who served the nation's biggest corporations as advisers, planners, organizers, and publicists; most of the remaining 25 percent were top managers in those same companies. Sixty percent of the List had attended Harvard, Princeton, Yale, or Columbia, though ethnically and politically Eberstadt's picks were more promiscuous and meritocratic: while over half were Anglo-Protestants, German Jews and Irish Catholics were also well represented; and there were comparable numbers of Republicans and Democrats.

Apart from mining these particular lodes, the initial Wall Street appointees reached back along lines of consanguinity and geography—rather as did the pioneering first arrivals of any in-migration stream—and drew to their side those of their relations, friends, neighbors, and associates who (ideally) had the skillsets needed for building a military-industrial machine. New York bankers and lawyers and corporate directors were in demand either for their specific expertise (Artemus Gates, a director of Pan Am and president of the New York Trust Company, became assistant secretary of the Navy for air), or for their general managerial capabilities (Lewis Strauss of Kuhn, Loeb was brought in to review the Navy's inspection system; Goldman, Sachs partner Sidney J. Weinberg to coordinate thirty OPM commodity procurement committees).

The march of talent from New York's Birnam Wood to Washington's Dunsinane was not limited to managerial and legal wizards; it embraced a vast variety of urban-nurtured experts. When James Forrestal found the Quartermaster Generals' Construction Division not up to snuff, he called in Michael J. Madigan, partner in Madigan and Hyland, the experienced engineering firm that had helped build many of Gotham's parks and highways. Other top officials found they needed plant superintendents, research experts, division managers, accountants, insurance underwriters, security experts, firefighters, chefs, marketing specialists, etc.—and they called home to get them from the city that had everything; when a contingent of six accident-prevention authorities was required, they were provided by Gotham's Sheffield's Milk and SS White Dental.

These mid-level appointees were in turn part of a still wider tidal flow of would-be federal employees, flooding into the capital from around the country to meet the military-industrial bureaucracy's voracious demand for labor. The staff of Robert Patterson's Office of the Under Secretary of War, alone, surged from the 181 in place when he arrived in July 1940 to 1,200 by the end of 1941. Mushrooming Washington had begun a boomtown explosion that would deepen, then dwarf, the one generated during the New Deal era. Then DC's population had jumped from 486,869 (in 1930) to 663,153 (in 1940), but over the next *two* years it would leap to over a million.

While the bulk of NY/DC train and plane travelers headed southward, there were some arenas—notably espionage and propaganda—in which New Yorkers summoned to defense work didn't have to leave home at all.

77

007 and the Stork Club Detective

By the late 1930s it was not clear exactly where "Wild Bill" Donovan had earned his nickname—whether on the Columbia football field, in Mexico with Pershing fighting Pancho Villa, in France where as a major in the Fighting 69th he'd charged German machine-gun nests (winning the Medal of Honor), or in New York, where as assistant attorney general he'd raided his own social club for violating Prohibition and as Republican gubernatorial candidate in 1932 had taken on and been trounced by Herbert Lehman. What *was* clear—particularly to Franklin Roosevelt—was that Donovan, while perhaps pugnacious, was anything but wild, having founded (in 1929) and built one of Wall Street's most successful corporate law firms, which in mid-Depression was earning him a half a million a year. This, plus his strong advocacy of preparedness and his careful studies of 1930s military operations in Ethiopia and Spain, led FDR, on the recommendation of Frank Knox, to send Donovan in the summer of 1940 on a secret mission to imperiled London.

Roosevelt didn't trust the reports coming from another Gotham-based Irishman, Ambassador Joe Kennedy, who rated Britain's chances of holding out against Hitler somewhere between dismal and hopeless. Donovan met with King George and Churchill, journalists and businessmen, US military attachés and RAF pilots, and on his return in early August presented FDR a more optimistic assessment, though stressing the need for additional US support. As a member of New York's Century Group, he added his voice to those pushing to swap destroyers for bases.

Donovan also collaborated (at FDR's urging) with journalist Edgar Mowrer in producing *Fifth Column Lessons for America*, a pamphlet that claimed millions of German Americans would happily aid the Gestapo should war come. Much of the "data" for this canard had been supplied by William Stephenson, head of British Security Coordination, who had befriended Donovan and developed big plans for him. "I have been attempting," the secret service chief cabled London, "to maneuver Donovan into the job of coordinating all United States Intelligence."

US intelligence was badly in need of coordination, and nowhere more so than in New York. Gotham was spy-versus-spy central—with competition or mutual surveillance the norm among the FBI, the FBI's Secret Intelligence Service (SIS), the Army's Military Intelligence Division (MID), the Navy's Office of Naval Intelligence (ONI) and Third Naval District Intelligence office, the New York Police Department's Sabotage Squad, the Department of State's Bureau of Intelligence, and the Treasury's Secret Service, plus the various branches of German, Russian, and British espionage and propaganda agencies.

On paper Hoover's FBI had pride of place. Since the early 1920s, the Bureau's domestic spying and counterintelligence operations had been tightly bridled, but in 1936 Roosevelt had given the agency its head, asking Hoover to survey the impact of "subversive activities" on the life of the nation. Bit in teeth, the director galloped forward. By 1938 he had revived the General Intelligence Division (GID) which, during the Red Scare, under his supervision, had assembled dossiers on over 100,000 dissidents before being shut down in 1924. Now it busily compiled extensive files on radicals, nationalists, fascists, Christian Fronters, communists—and Jews: Hoover sent FDR memos warning that Nazis and Soviets had planted agents among Jewish refugees and cautioned against relaxing immigration quotas. In November 1939, shortly after war broke out, the director established a Custodial Detention List of persons to be rounded up and put in concentration camps should the need arise, including aliens and citizens of "German, Italian and Communist sympathies," radical labor leaders, journalists critical of the administration, writers critical of the FBI, and even a member of Congress.

To demonstrate his efficacy and political even-handedness, Hoover staged two highly publicized back-to-back raids in New York. On January 14, 1940, newsmen were summoned to the FBI's Gotham field office in the Federal Courthouse, to hear Hoover announce the arrest of seventeen men engaged in a "vast plot" to overthrow the government and establish a fascist dictatorship. Then, on February 6, in a series of 5:00 a.m. raids, G-men arrested twelve veterans of the Abraham Lincoln Brigade and charged them with having violated—back in 1937—a federal law prohibiting recruitment of foreign armies on US soil. Both cases quickly crumbled; the attorney general dismissed the Loyalist cases out of hand; and the Christian Fronters were acquitted or dismissed (in part because it came out that a key informer-participant had purchased ammo and liquor with FBI funds).

Overplaying his hand brought down on Hoover widespread denunciations for running an "American OGPU" (the forerunner of the KGB). Even the American Civil Liberties Union criticized the director, despite General Counsel Morris Ernst's being a closet Hoover champion. "Dear Edgar," Ernst wrote in one letter of a decades-long secret interchange: Ernst affirmed this ACLU seal of approval to Adolf Berle, the State Department's liaison with the FBI, saying Hoover "has run a secret police with a minimum of collision with civil liberties, and that is all you can expect of any chief of secret police." Ernst's left-wing opponents in the National Lawyers Guild (NLG) were less forgiving. They criticized the FBI's "gestapo activities" and demanded Hoover's removal. The FBI riposted by adding the NLG to its surveillance list, and apparently, by breaking into its Washington office to photograph its membership list, minutes, and correspondence.

Congressman Vito Marcantonio also denounced the revived subversives list, calling it a "system of terror by index cards." Hoover responded by adding him to the list of candidates for possible "custodial detention." Marcantonio had already been on Hoover's personal non grata list for having scored a palpable hit in the director's most vulnerable spot, his public image. Since his mother had died in 1938, Hoover, accompanied by Clyde Tolson (the Bureau's #2), had been spending most weekends up in Gotham. Though the justification was that New York was home to the Bureau's largest field unit, the duo rarely dropped by the office. Arriving by train on Friday night, the pair would breakfast in their complimentary Waldorf suite on Saturday morning, host friends, then head to the track. Saturday nights they dined at Souls or Maxim's or Gallagher's; visited 21 or Toots Shor's; and ended the night at Winchell's table at the Stork Club. In March 1940, a month after the Abraham Lincoln Brigade arrests, Marcantonio blasted the director as a "Stork Club detective," and the *Daily News* ran an old photo of a nightclubbing, tipsy-seeming Hoover wearing a silly party hat and hoisting a toy machine gun. Henceforth the FBI chief, though he continued his trips to New York, would cut down on clubbing, and when he did indulge, he'd insist all drinks be removed from his table before the photogs brought out their Speed Graphics.

In truth, Hoover was untouchable by such critics, as the president was in his corner. Roosevelt backed Hoover's raids and lists and wiretaps, partly out of real concern about possible subversion, partly because he was an espionage junkie, and partly because the director provided similar services to the White House on a clandestine basis, allowing FDR to keep tabs on his opponents. During the campaign year of 1940 alone, Hoover ran background checks on 131 Roosevelt critics, including many America Firsters—though the director drew the line at bugging Wendell Willkie.

Still, FDR was annoyed and disturbed by interagency squabbles over spying rights. In 1939, to delimit the field, he'd issued a secret directive expressing his desire that "the investigation of all espionage, counterespionage, and sabotage matters" be centered in the FBI, MID, and ONI alone. Hoover used this presidential backing to swat away lesser competitors. When Police Commissioner Lewis Valentine, an old enemy, set up a fifty-detectives-strong

J. Edgar Hoover wears a Mickey Mouse mask at a New Year's Eve party at the Stork Club, 1937. Walter Winchell is seated next to him. (Photo by NY Daily News Archive via Getty Images)

New York City Sabotage Squad, Hoover got the president to issue a press release to "all police officials in the United States" instructing them "promptly to turn over to the nearest representative of the Federal Bureau of Investigation any information obtained by them relating to espionage, counter-espionage, sabotage, subversive activities and violations of the neutrality laws."

Stimson proved a tougher opponent. In 1940 the secretary of war backed MID's decision to keep its own office in Gotham. Army intelligence, concerned about German penetration of Latin America, wanted to gather information about hemispheric affairs by debriefing returning New York businessmen as they debarked from planes and boats. But the FBI, which interviewed the same traders, was not happy when companies began complaining about the duplication. Hoover—an Anglophobe—was also irked by Stephenson's burgeoning British operation, which wiretapped US citizens and transmitted intelligence back to Britain in a code the Bureau couldn't crack. The director protested to his State Department ally Adolf Berle, who investigated and reported with dismay that Stephenson was running "a full size secret police and intelligence service" out of Rockefeller Center.

To overcome interagency and international competition, FDR had initially turned to a most unorthodox assistant, his boyhood friend Vincent Astor. Since 1927, Astor had been running an amateur spy operation—which he called The Room—out of an East Side townhouse (34 East 62nd Street) complete with mail drop and unlisted phone. The dozen or so members who met monthly, in secret, to trade informal intelligence tidbits, included banker Winthrop Aldrich, publisher Nelson Doubleday, philanthropist William Rhinelander Stewart, and assorted brokers and lawyers. Most had worked for Allied intelligence in the First World War, and most had familial, educational, and emotional ties to England. Most were also close to Roosevelt—sailing buddies on Astor's 264-foot yacht, or relatives like Teddy's sons Kermit and Theodore Jr.—and after becoming president he turned to them (via Astor) for inside info about international affairs.

With war in 1939, his requests to Astor became more focused, more urgent. When FDR worried that Soviet purchases of American molybdenum (used for specialty steels) might be helping their Pact-partner Germany build tanks and aircraft, Astor had Aldrich track the procurement agency Amtorg's account at Chase National Bank. Astor himself—a director of Western Union—perused and passed along cable traffic from Japan.

For a time, FDR also relied on Astor to help out with spy traffic control: a June 26, 1940, presidential directive gave Astor authority "to coordinate the Intelligence work in the New York Area." In 1941, however, as the likelihood of US involvement increased, a more professional and institutionalized approach seemed necessary, something more akin to what Donovan (at Stephenson's urging) was proposing: establishment of an independent coordinating body. FDR asked Donovan to write up a specific proposal. Donovan consulted Stephenson. And Stephenson called in an expert from England.

On May 25, 1941, Lieutenant Commander Ian Fleming, personal assistant to the director of British Naval Intelligence, Rear Admiral John H. Godfrey, arrived at La Guardia and went directly to BSC headquarters in Rockefeller Center to assess the situation. He quickly decided (after a trip to DC to interview Hoover) that the key to success lay in transcending the FBI and its parochial culture. The Bureau, Fleming found, "has no conception of offensive intelligence and is incapable of a strategic mentality." Its bureaucratized, strait-laced, mostly Catholic G-men (Fleming argued) were taught to look, but not to see; to gather data, but not to analyze it. The FBI was a collection of clerks.

Fleming wrote out in longhand a suggested charter for a centralized intelligence agency. His text informed the proposal Donovan presented to FDR on June 10. Admiral Godfrey himself met with FDR, supported the plan, and pushed Wild Bill's qualifications. FDR, easily convinced, overrode Hoover's protests and opted for the Hero over the Clerk. On July 11 he announced the appointment of Donovan as Coordinator of Information (COI), enjoined officially with the task of analyzing all information "bearing on national security" gathered from existing departments and agencies. Unofficially, his brief included the establishment of a world-wide propaganda arm to counteract Axis operations.

Fleming cabled the news to Rockefeller Center, and Stephenson relayed it to Churchill: "You can imagine how relieved I am after three months of battle and jockeying for position in Washington that our man is in a position of such importance to our efforts." Given its Anglo-American origins, it's perhaps not surprising that when Donovan opened the COI's Gotham office six months later (putting Allen Dulles in charge), he installed it on the 36th floor of 630 Fifth Avenue, just down the hall from Stephenson's shop.

By that time another wing of Donovan's operation—the opaquely named Foreign Information Service (FIS)—was already flourishing in New York. The day after COI was established, Robert Sherwood wrote Donovan about the appalling absence of an American governmental shortwave apparatus capable of countering the aggressive agitprop Hitler was beaming across the Atlantic 21 hours a day. New York congressman Emanuel Celler had introduced bills in 1937, 1938, and 1939 to create a government operation that, on defense, could respond to German propaganda, and, on offense, undermine the enemy's will to fight. Yet the private networks objected to a government-run competitor, and FDR, who himself remembered Creel's First World War's excesses, balked at the idea. The country's shortwave resources remained limited to roughly a dozen low-powered, commercially owned and operated transmitters.

By 1941, however, FDR and the military high command were convinced a propaganda operation was essential, and Donovan and Sherwood were authorized to create one. The playwright wanted it situated not at COI headquarters in Washington, but in New York, close to radio networks, wire services, organizations like Sherwood's Century Group that were already engaged in influencing American public opinion, and the city's huge pool of artistic, journalistic, technological, and advertising talent. In August, Sherwood set up an office in 270 Madison (between 39th and 40th) and appointed Joseph F. Barnes, foreign news editor of the *Herald Tribune*, to run it; together they began recruiting an impressive group of writers, journalists, and political activists. As always, the English were eager to help: the New York office of the BBC, established in 1935 in Rockefeller Center's British Empire Building, offered advice and arranged for Sherwood and Donovan to visit Broadcasting House in London.

It soon became apparent that Sherwood and the New Yorkers understood their mission differently than did Donovan and his Washington colleagues. The New York crowd, overwhelmingly Fighting Liberals, were as intent on promoting a war *for* democracy (i.e., the Four Freedoms and a globalized New Deal) as one *against* fascism. Methodologically, they believed presenting truthful information and stirring ideals was the way to win support. The DC people—Wall Street Warriors and their military allies—were more focused on beating back the German menace. They considered propaganda a branch of psywar and were prepared to tell whatever tales would wear down enemy morale and strengthen anti-Nazi resistance, with veracity a secondary consideration.

For the moment, Donovan would let the New Yorkers go their own way, in part because Sherwood's still-tiny operation was of less concern to him then another recently established, far bigger, and more competitive operation, also run out of Gotham, and headed by yet another formidable New Yorker, Nelson Aldrich Rockefeller.

78

Down South America Way

In 1933—still under the spell of Mexican muralists, despite the brouhaha over Diego Rivera's Lenin-headed contribution—Nelson Rockefeller had made his first visit to Latin America, spending a month in Mexico buying pieces for MOMA and exploring pre-Columbiana. In 1937 he was again drawn south of the border, this time as much by oil as art. He had recently purchased an interest in, and joined the board of, Creole Petroleum—Jersey Standard's Venezuelan subsidiary, whose Lake Maracaibo fields had made that country the second-biggest oil producer on earth. Now he, his wife, and a substantial entourage of New Yorkers embarked on a grand tour of Creole properties and the wider continent, taking in Venezuela, Brazil, Argentina, Chile, and Peru, among other countries. Rockefeller fell in love with the people and their culture—its *abrazo* exuberance resonated with his own—but found himself appalled by some of his fellow Americans, notably oil executives, who aped the most arrogant of British colonialists. Living inside barbed wire compounds, aloof from all but the richest locals and seldom bothering to learn Spanish, they treated with supercilious disdain their workers who lived in filthy and disease-ridden oil towns, bereft of sewers, clinics, or schools.

Back in New York, the idealistic young man lectured some three hundred Standard executives, gathered in annual conference, on "The Social Responsibility of Corporations." Companies, he explained, had an obligation to improve local conditions for "the people in the host country," adding that, ethics aside, if better relations weren't cultivated "they will take away our ownership." Oil officials were unmoved, until Mexican president Lázaro Cárdenas in 1938 nationalized US holdings (and those of Great Britain), promising compensation. In a fury, the oil men demanded Roosevelt roll back the expropriation, but the president refused to intervene, his larger priority being the cultivation of hemispheric support against the Nazis. Balked, Big Oil organized a boycott, though it was quickly scuppered when Germans, Italians, and Japanese lined up to buy Mexican crude.

In Venezuela, to forestall a similar fate, Creole let Rockefeller have his reforms. Returning in 1939 with twelve New York Berlitz teachers in tow, he introduced mandatory Spanish lessons (having himself developed a passable facility); had the barbed wire removed; phased out job discrimination against Venezuelans; and introduced some schools and public health clinics modeled on those established by the Rockefeller Foundation's International Division. He also launched the Compañía de Fomento Venezolano (Company for Venezuelan Development) to mobilize venture funding for physical and social infrastructure projects (from water drilling to low-cost housing) that would demonstrate the benignity of capitalism, the compatibility of profit and progress. The only venture that got airborne, however, before war-spawned economic crisis grounded such visionary flights, was the luxury-class Hotel *Avila* for the Caracas elite and visiting American businessmen.

Britain's blockade of Europe throttled the export trade of Venezuela and all Latin America. As agricultural and mineral surpluses piled up, their economies grew ever more parlous. Rockefeller saw an opportunity here "to lessen the dependency of Latin America upon Europe as a market for raw materials and a source of manufactured articles," and a concomitant chance for the United States to replace Britain as the hemisphere's dominant trading partner. He also understood that British firms might be superseded not by US but by German interests, which were strongly ensconced and well positioned for expansion should the Third Reich win the war, as seemed decidedly possible.

Rockefeller and a group of advisers—the jocularly named "Junta"—began meeting at his Fifth Avenue apartment to plan a commercial and cultural assault on Axis influence in Latin America. The public-private strategy they mapped out called for having the US buy up the vast surplus of Latin American commodities for its own emergency stockpiles; increase inter-American trade by reducing or eliminating tariffs; reshape southern production to meet the needs of northern industry; refinance external debts; subsidize US investment; and launch a vigorous program of cultural, educational, and scientific exchange. All this, the plan suggested, should be run by an independent government agency, advised by private industry and headed by a coordinator directly responsible to the president. Nelson Rockefeller was designing himself a job.

At first neither the program nor its progenitor could gain traction. In September 1939, when Treasury Secretary Morgenthau had recommended Rockefeller for another important position, FDR had squelched the idea, saying, "You don't want to get too many of these kinds of people in." Germany's conquest of France instantly notched Latin America up on the presidential priority list, and Stimson's appointment opened the door to Rockefeller's "kind of people." Junta member Beardsley Ruml took the program, distilled to a memo, to Harry Hopkins on June 15; Ruml and Anna Rosenberg arranged a White House meeting with Hopkins for Rockefeller; and on August 16, after the details had been hammered out by James Forrestal, FDR announced creation of the Office of the Coordinator of Commercial and Cultural Relations between the American Republics, and Nelson's appointment to run it; the following July his title was shortened to the more bite-size Coordinator of Inter-American Affairs (CIAA).

In the new position, to his disappointment, Rockefeller would have only a marginal hand in promoting the big structural remedies he'd proposed. Instead, he was told to wage an anti-Nazi Kulturkampf—winning over fascist-leaning Latin American hearts and minds by enhancing the USA's image (or, if need be, by applying a judicious amount of economic muscle). Though Nelson hadn't much training in PR per se—apart from touting the virtues of Rockefeller Center to prospective tenants—his Venezuelan ventures and his connections in New York's media and museum worlds had left him well prepared for the task.

Rockefeller quickly established an OCIAA Communication Division, operating out of Gotham, and persuaded James W. Young, former top executive at J. Walter Thompson, to head it. The Division had three units, corresponding to the OCIAA's major media initiatives—Press, Movies, and Radio.

Young's first goal was to counter or eliminate the Nazis' easy and extensive access to Latin America's press, which had been facilitated by the German Transocean Agency's willingness to provide—cut rate or free of charge—ready-to-print features and photos. Young's Press Section began buying huge amounts of ad space in Latin American papers, and, as well, subsidizing shipments of scarce and vital newsprint. Hundreds of beholden publishers now declined Nazi offerings and ran instead the pro-American news, features, photographs, and cartoons that the Press Section turned out in abundance. In 1941 the OCIAA went a step further and began producing its own high-quality glossy newsmagazine, *En Guardia*. Blatantly propagandistic but free of charge, and far slicker than any competing local or Axis product, its initial print run of 80,000 was snapped up, and its circulation would soon soar to 550,000.

Any similarity between *En Guardia*'s look and that of *Life* was purely uncoincidental: Henry Luce, a member of the OCIAA's Advisory Committee, had lent Rockefeller his editors. The two men had been engaged in mutual back scratching for some time, with Harry, an ambitious social climber, having put Nelson on the cover of *Time*, and Nelson, keen on publicity, having put Harry on the board of MOMA. Luce had pecuniary as well as status-based reasons for pursuing Rockefeller. He had long wanted to expand his New York empire southward and now could do so with the coordinator's assistance.

In 1941 Luce produced an Air-Express edition of *Time* (in English) and sent 20,000 copies winging down to Mexico, Colombia, and Peru in Juan Trippe's Pan Am planes. *Time* also started a syndication service (in Spanish) that generated each week an 8,000-word summary of the current issue that was then printed in twenty Latin American papers with a collective circulation of one million. Up in Pleasantville, Dewitt and Lila Acheson Wallace had made a more daring bet when they decided, in 1940, to publish *Reader's Digest*'s first foreign-language edition. It paid off handsomely: within a year *Selecciones del Reader's Digest*—circulation 350,000—had become the largest-selling Spanish-language magazine in the world.

Trippe's planes also airlifted south reels of *La Marcha del Tiempo*, and soon the Spanish (and OCIAA subsidized) version of *The March of Time* was playing in 500 Latin American movie houses. Then the OCIAA began producing its own newsreels, along with cartoons, documentaries, and features (short and long) on the sunnier side of North American life, and heroic episodes from South American history (*The Life of Simón Bolívar*). Much of the production was handled in conjunction with MOMA'S Film Library, whose president, John Hay Whitney, had been appointed by Rockefeller to take charge of the Communication Division's Motion Picture unit. The Film Library supplied not only raw footage but the services of translators—including refugee movie professionals like Luis Buñuel—to subtitle or dub US productions into Spanish. Whitney, who as a producer had pioneered Technicolor and backed *Gone with the Wind*, was also tasked with getting Hollywood to lighten up on its racist Latino stereotypes and getting Walt Disney into OCIAA harness. As distribution of American films was denied to any Latin American theater projecting Nazi product, the Germans found themselves being driven from the screens.

The Radio Division—which drew on the services of New York industry heavyweights—generated Spanish-language programming that was shortwaved south over the same network of private transmitters used by Sherwood's operation. Reception was poor, however, and receivers few, so attention was devoted to arranging rebroadcasts of material over chains of local stations. These, in turn, were established in cooperation with New York's private networks, with whose chieftains Rockefeller was well acquainted (he knew David Sarnoff through Radio City dealings and had put William Paley, another social aspirant, on the board of MOMA). In November 1940, after meeting with the coordinator, Paley set off on a tour of Latin America to sign up affiliates and returned with sixty-four of them; in July 1941, John Royal, vice president of NBC, made a similar trip, with better results, garnering 125 stations for his network. Working with CBS and NBC facilities, OCIAA personnel also produced newscasts, features, and musical performances—in the process greatly expanding Gotham's hemispheric reach.

The OCIAA's Cultural Relations Division also arranged for face-to-face encounters, which ranged from bringing students from each of the twenty republics to Gotham for a year on "New York City Scholarships," to sponsoring tours by major cultural institutions.

In 1941 Rockefeller asked his old friend Lincoln Kirstein to work up a six-month-long visit to Latin America of his new American Ballet Caravan. With George Balanchine, the company's artistic director, Kirstein selected ballets (Balanchine would create four new ones for the trip); chose thirty-five dancers (many from the defunct Ballet Caravan); drew up a budget (of $95,000); held rehearsals (in the Hunter College auditorium); and sailed for Rio on June 6 (on the *Argentina*). Despite the modernist company's lukewarm reception from conservative US Embassy personnel and ultraconservative American colonies of businessmen and expats, local press reception was overwhelmingly positive, especially in Caracas, Bogotá, and Lima, where Copland came down to conduct *Billy the Kid*. The grudging willingness of elite South Americans to admit what they'd long doubted—that the US could contribute something to the arts—received additional affirmation that same summer when the Museum of Modern Art, in cooperation with the OCIAA, arranged a traveling exhibition—*Exposition of Contemporary North American Painting*—put together from holdings of the Met, MOMA, Whitney, and Brooklyn Museum.

In October 1941, after a feverish year's work in which Rockefeller's operation, staff, and appropriations had grown imposingly, the Coordinator of Inter-American Affairs was challenged by the newly designated Coordinator of Information. Donovan told Rockefeller that as he had been assigned the task of disseminating news and information abroad (Sherwood's operation was already up and running in New York), and as this task had to be done in a unified manner, Rockefeller's responsibilities in this area should be transferred to Donovan's domain. This meant war. In the ensuing struggle for Roosevelt's backing, Donovan, it turned out, was seriously overmatched. Though he enlisted James Roosevelt as liaison to the White House, Rockefeller countermobilized key people in FDR's inner circle—among them Harry Hopkins, Anna Rosenberg, and Adolf Berle—and Donovan, outmaneuvered, was informed by Roosevelt that his writ would not run in Latin America.

79

You Go to War with the Capitalists You've Got

In empowering this array of Wall Street Warriors, Roosevelt alarmed his Fighting Liberal allies. The appointment of Dillon, Read chief James Forrestal provoked a typically angry query from *The New Republic*: "Just how chummy can the New Deal be with Wall Street," the editors demanded, "and continue to be the New Deal?"

For a time, the divisions between these two sets of powerful New Yorkers were papered over by their mutual annoyance at the many private-sector industrialists who, during 1940 and 1941, refused to step up production of war matériel. This reluctance was motivated partly by caution—what if they invested in a new plant and the war ended quickly?—but mainly by the scent of profit in the air. With the economy turning up, the auto industry anticipated sales of some four million cars in 1941; this was not the moment to stop churning out Cadillacs and start turning out tanks. It was much the same in the aircraft industry, which kept its focus on civilian planes; and in the steel business, which shipped its product to civilian construction sites; and in the railroad, oil, and electric power industries, whose owners and managers proved similarly averse to switching priorities.

With civilian production hogging raw materials, the fledgling military economy was deprived of desperately needed resources. In 1941, accordingly, a donnybrook broke out between Wall Street Warrior and Fighting Liberal "all-outers," on one side, and "business-as-usual" corporations on the other. Stimson, Patterson, Forrestal, Eberstadt, and other civilian-military leaders were furious at profit-centric industrialists and at their dollar-a-year enablers in the defense agencies, men like Office of Production Management chief Knudsen (of General Motors), whom Stimson thought "too soft and slow because of his connection with the auto industry." FDR joined in denouncing industrialists who refused conversion from civilian to military production, and *PM*'s I. F. Stone echoed the point when he wrote: "We cannot fight a war with convertible coupes."

With corporate reluctance bordering on resistance, the sense that a de facto "capital strike" was under way was strengthened by the *Wall Street Journal*'s declaration that "Industry will demand many concessions in the way of tax exemptions, amortization policies, relaxation of labor laws, et cetera" in return for rapid expansion of military production. The "all-out" camp, for its part, called for aggressive government action, with Wall Streeters as well as New Dealers floating proposals that urged seizing companies that refused defense work—drafting capital as well as labor. This was a wildly popular idea among the citizenry—it garnered an over 70 percent approval rating in the polls—and provoked frenzied resistance from business groups.

In the end, the Wall Street Warriors—whose perspectives had been shaped in the very corporate world they were chastising—opted for concession rather than confrontation. As Stimson said: "If you are going to try to go to war, or to prepare for war, in a capitalist country, you have got to let business make money out of the process or business won't work."

Patterson agreed—"We had to take industrial America as we found it," he said—and he came up with an offer that business wouldn't refuse: government would guarantee the corporations a profit while assuming all the risk. Starting with the aircraft industry, Patterson designed a "cost-plus-fixed-fee" contract system which gave suppliers a percentage of their development and production costs for defense-related plant and equipment. Companies could also amortize all their capital expenses within five years (deducting 20 percent of the total each year from their gross income, thus lowering the net figure on which taxes were to be paid). Better still, much of the requisite capital would come from the government itself: the Defense Plant Corporation (DPC)—a new subsidiary of the 1932 Reconstruction Finance Corporation—would foot the bill for expanding old facilities, or pay to erect new ones from scratch with the assurance that such arsenals of democracy would eventually be turned over to the companies that ran them, at bargain basement prices. The "cost-plus" system would prove to be wildly expensive and wasteful as well (why search for efficiencies when the higher a product cost, the more profit accrued to its maker?). But it worked.

Another price corporations demanded—and got—for revving up their military-industrial engines was the "relaxation" of antitrust laws. It would not do, Secretary Stimson and his colleagues agreed, for Justice to be prosecuting giant corporations for collusion at the same time that War and Navy were relying on them for production. Congress agreed, and authorized defense officials to substitute negotiation for competitive bidding. The Temporary National Economic Committee antimonopoly project was shelved—literally—with all thirty-one volumes of testimony and forty-three accompanying monographs dispatched to the archives. Similarly discarded were its findings that monopolies were responsible for many of the nation's economic and social woes, and its conclusion that New Deal social democratic programs should be vastly expanded (though this, too, had overwhelming popular approval).

Corporate cartel arrangements with potential enemies were, like monopolies, to be overlooked in the new dispensation. I. F. Stone and others demonstrated the degree to which some of the industrial giants' unwillingness to enroll in the antifascist struggle was a byproduct of their collaborative connections with Nazi enterprises like I. G. Farben. Critics pointed, too, to the ongoing shipments of steel and oil to Axis powers, exports that further exacerbated shortages at home. Missouri senator Harry S. Truman opened an investigation into these charges and would find many of them well founded.

Corporations wanted labor laws "relaxed" as well, but this met with resistance from organized labor, which on paper, and in the person of Sidney Hillman, was a coequal partner in preparedness. Officially, defense contractors had to adhere to National Labor Relations Act provisions and obey National Labor Relations Board decisions or face loss of their contracts. When the Army gave a handsome assignment to the Ford Motor Company—notoriously contemptuous of labor and labor law alike—OPM's Hillman managed to get the contract reassigned to Chrysler. Yet with many corporate leaders intent on rolling back gains unions had made under the New Deal—as Hillman's "partner," GM's Knudsen, put it: "We don't want any part of that Russian system over here"—all-outers like Patterson acquiesced in refusing to require that contractors obey the law.

With legal redress denied, strikes broke out in defense plants as workers sought to maintain (or enhance) union power or share in exploding corporate profits. Nineteen forty-one witnessed more strikes than any year in US history except 1919 and 1937. In New York thousands of members of the CIO's Industrial Union of Marine and Shipbuilding Workers walked off work, or threatened to do so, at Crane Shipbuilding and Morse Shipbuilding (Brooklyn's Bethlehem Steel subsidiaries at the foot of 27th Street and 56th Street respectively); at the yards of the Federal Shipbuilding and Drydock Corporation (US Steel's subsidiary in Kearny, New Jersey); and at Brooklyn's huge Robins Dry Dock and Repair company (owned by the Todd Shipyards Corporation).

Knox and Stimson opted for a tough response, claiming these strikes were a species of sabotage meriting military intervention. Hillman, too, condemned strikes, but while this won him credibility with his Wall Street colleagues—"Hillman is a pretty good little fellow," said Stimson with inbred patrician condescension, "and I think on the whole it is wise to give him a chance"—it cost him the support of rank-and-file unionists. Undermined by his fellow bureaucrats, sabotaged by Army and Navy directives, targeted by businessmen out to restore their power, and vilified by congressional rightists, Hillman found himself increasingly isolated.

Gleeful Wall Streeters believed their restoration to power was all but assured. As Knudsen's Wall Street attorney Fred Eaton boasted: "When the New Dealers were in power they didn't include us; now that we are in power we won't include them." Harry Hopkins, for one, was alive to the threat. "There is a danger here," he warned, that the "old order" of "big business, high finance, [and] the Republican Party" will use its new authority to reverse all the social democratic accomplishments of the last decade. Though it "doubtless wants to beat Hitler," the "old order" will insist on beating Hitler in its own way, Hopkins feared, but "the New Deal must insist on beating Hitler in its own way. Or we will end just where we began."

Eaton's "mission accomplished" declaration would prove premature—the battle between Wall Street Warriors and Fighting Liberals was far from over—but a significant restoration had indeed been achieved. The consequences for New York of the rise of a Washington-based military-industrial complex, and the attendant shift in the balance of national power between corporate and social democratic forces, would, in time, be enormous and profound. The most immediate upshot of this changing of the guard was a relative decline in the flow of federal resources to the city.

As Wall Street professionals and managers gained greater control over the preparedness program, they funneled the billions of dollars Congress was making available to the giant corporations with (and for) whom they had worked all their professional lives. By the summer of 1941, after a year of mobilization, almost three-quarters of Army and Navy prime contracts had gone to fifty-six large companies, with six of the biggest garnering almost a third of these. This was in many ways a sensible strategy: big business had the big factories and experienced managers who could handle enormous and time-sensitive orders. But as few of these industrial behemoths were in Gotham, much of the vast flow of federal funds went elsewhere. As a direct result, in late 1941, prosperity could be spotted peeking around the next corner in many parts of the country. In New York City, however, the end of the Depression was still nowhere in sight.

GOTHAM GIRDS FOR WAR

A crewman photographer of the 2nd Air Base Squadron stands in the cockpit to demonstrate the use of a Keystone F8 aerial reconnaissance and map making camera at Mitchel Air Force Base in Long Island. December 1939. (US Army Air Force Official Photo / Photo by Keystone/Hulton Archive/Getty Images)

80

Cash and Carry

New York's harbor was thronged with maritime traffic in the fall of '41 as food and war matériel poured into Gotham for trans-shipment to Britain. Wheat from the Midwest—barged across the Erie Canal and down the Hudson—was transferred directly to oceangoing vessels by floating grain elevators that could offload tons in minutes flat or piled high in the immense grain terminal adjacent to the Erie Basin and Gowanus Canal. Oil was pipelined in from Pennsylvania to area refineries and storage tanks (like the vast cluster at Bayonne), where it was picked up by an endless stream of tankers, lined up like cabs at a taxi stand (off Staten Island between Tompkinsville and Fort Wadsworth), waiting to fill up and carry their cargo out into the North Atlantic to fuel England's bombers and warships. Munitions and manufactured goods rolled in on the national rail network, were transferred to freight-car lighters (there were 2,000 available, each could carry 24 boxcars), then towed by tugs to one or another of the port's roughly 900 piers, where they were transferred to deep sea transports. (There was more freight-handling machinery in New York than in any port in the world.) All night long the bustle continued, as shadowy hulls, barges, lighters, and tugs crisscrossed the great bowl of the Upper Bay, its dark waters rimmed with shore lights, dotted with winking gas buoys, and pierced by beams from fixed and revolving lighthouses.

This surge in traffic—the volume of foreign trade through the port rose 44.5 percent in 1941—was underwritten by a torrent of money, first largely British, then increasingly American, as US government preparedness expenditures climbed from $6.8 billion in 1938, to $8.9 billion in 1939, to $13 billion in 1940, and in 1941—after Lend Lease kicked in in March—to $34 billion. These funds underwrote a host of collateral naval enterprises in Gotham.

Lend Lease authorized payment for ship repairs to damaged vessels of nations whose defense the president had deemed vital. England's first wounded warship steamed into New York harbor on March 19, 1941, where it could take its pick among commercial dry docks, floating docks for making repairs above the waterline, and the unrivaled facilities of the Brooklyn Navy Yard.

Government funding also put shipbuilding back on the city's agenda big time, the long doldrums of the 1920s and 1930s having been terminated by Japan's abrogation of the Naval Limitation Treaty in 1936, which triggered a naval arms race. Almost immediately, FDR had launched a construction program, in which Brooklyn's facilities figured prominently, especially the Navy Yard. In 1937, the keel had been laid there for the *North Carolina*, a new generation of battleship: 35,000 tons, 704 feet long, capable of making 28–30 knots, and replete with 16-inch guns and airplane catapults. It slid down the ways (aided by 54,000 pounds of grease) in June 1940, to the accompaniment of shrieking tugboat whistles and cheers from the 50,000 who had gathered to witness the advent of the world's greatest battleship. Then, two weeks later, the Yard set about superseding it, laying the keel for the *Iowa*—which, at 45,000 tons, 880 feet, and likely capacity for making 38 knots, was expected to be the largest man-of-war ever. Until June 1941, when it was announced that the Navy Yard had been assigned construction of two even more colossal (58,000-ton) super-dreadnoughts, the *New Hampshire* and the *Maine* (the latter a replacement for the unfortunate Brooklyn-built vessel that had blown up in Havana's harbor in 1898)—with work expected to begin in December 1942.

All this activity generated jobs—by 1939 there were 9,000 men employed at the Yard, by mid-1941, over 20,000. It also demanded new equipment and additional space, and in 1941 Navy Yard commandant Rear Admiral Clark Woodward launched a massive overhaul and expansion of the entire physical plant. All older factories (many dating back to the Civil War) were remodeled and repaired. A huge new turret shop was built; a mammoth Hammerhead crane, capable of lifting 350 tons, was constructed to enable battleship fabrication; and contracts were let for two 1100-foot construction dry docks for building super battleships. To make room for all this, La Guardia agreed to Woodward's request that the city use eminent domain to take over the fifty-six-year-old Wallabout Market, abutting the Yard to the east, and give its four city blocks worth of land to the Navy, effectively doubling capacity. This was done with dispatch: by June the Wallabout had shut down, packed up, and moved to a new Brooklyn Terminal Market in Canarsie; twenty-five construction projects had gotten under way; miles of roads and railroad tracks were being laid to integrate the two territories; and the employment level had risen to 22,000, with the possibility being bruited about that it might rise to 40,000.

The Navy Yard wasn't the only Brooklyn shipyard undergoing dramatic expansion under the spur of American and British orders. In July 1941, the borough's maritime manufactories—including Todd Shipyards' huge Robins operation and Bethlehem Steel's Crane and Morse subsidiaries—employed nearly 33,000 workers. Bethlehem was building on Staten Island, too: in 1938 it took over the United Drydocks Company, at Richmond Terrace in Mariners Harbor, just below Shooters Island (the old First World War shipbuilding complex), and expanded its capacity with a $6 million assist from the Navy. The Kill van Kull soon filled with hulls. New Jersey operations were growing as well—notably Todd Shipyard's Tietjen and the Lang plant on the Hudson at Hoboken, as well as the yard of US Steel's subsidiary, Federal Shipbuilding, in Kearny Meadows at the confluence of the Passaic and Hackensack Rivers.

These shipbuilding projects, in turn, summoned up other jobs. The New York Navy Purchasing Office (itself expanding inside the Federal Office Building at 90 Church Street in lower Manhattan) issued orders to local machine shops for making parts and equipment for the new battleships. Local contractors got multimillion-dollar orders for building the new dry docks. And the city's building trades were set to housing the swelling work force of civilian and naval personnel—constructing such complexes as the Wallabout Houses near the Navy Yard, and the Edward Markham Houses on Richmond Terrace in West New Brighton.

Beyond these boatbuilding-related jobs were those created by federal contracts for the plethora of goods demanded by the broader military buildup. Week after week the *Times* carried announcements—headlined: "Defense Contracts in Day"—which disclosed the total number of government dollars disbursed nationwide in the previous twenty-four hours and provided a detailed roster of which New York businesses had been among the fortunate recipients. In the spring of 1941, the daily totals tended to be relatively modest: $9,130,272 on April 11; $25,521,033 on April 17; $7,244,433 on April 22; $36,265,631 on April 26. By fall the orders were more jumbo, with typical one-day October payouts weighing in at $154,440,241, $167,403,208, and $302,894,413.

In Gotham, some of the most substantial contracts went to the cluster of high-tech firms that had, since the First World War, dominated the nation's output of gyroscopic and mechanical analog computer equipment—bombsights, compasses, fire-control systems, automatic pilots. The Big Four companies, whose genealogies were intricately intertangled, were Sperry Gyroscope (whose three plants in Brooklyn and one in Long Island City expanded employment from 5,500 in 1940 to 8,000 in 1941); Ford Instruments (whose William H. Newell, having mastered engineering at CCNY in the evenings, was now producing scores of inventions critical to naval gunnery); Carl L. Norden, Inc. (whose famous bombsight, produced at 80 Lafayette Street in Manhattan, was reserved for US planes, the British having to settle for Sperry's not-quite-as-good version); and Arma Corporation (whose gyrocompass, produced since 1924 in Brooklyn at 254 36th Street, was the preferred device for navigation and fire control on US submarines and battleships, with Sperry's favored for smaller surface ships).

City manufacturers also received contracts for more conventional arms or accessories like gun mounts, searchlights, anti-aircraft apparatus, and artillery material. Hoe and Company—the venerable printing firm—received one of the latter. New York businesses were also showered with orders for noncombat-related items, notably clothing. Some of this was done under direct military supervision at the United States Naval Clothing Depot, at Third Avenue and 29th Street in Brooklyn—one of the biggest and most efficient clothing plants in the world. There, over a thousand Civil Service employees made, packed, stored, and distributed the white twill and blue flannel uniforms, trousers, pea jackets, and dress jumpers worn by all the sailors in the entire US Navy. Some of this production was farmed out to local manufacturers when the Depot was overloaded, and separate contracts were issued as well, such as one for olive-drab Army wool overcoats, to Garment District companies. In addition to orders for arms and clothing, contracts were issued for a vast panoply of miscellaneous items, including dental operating chairs, paint, feather pillows, rope, goggles, trunk lockers, engineers' wrenches, printing equipment, surgical instruments, hairbrushes, cotton sheeting, flashlight batteries, drugs, aero-photo enlargers, electrical capstans, canteen covers, blood lancets, cap insignia, mixing bowls, stopwatches, nails, cable, tar oil, gages, optical goods, machine parts, tool kits, chemicals, and canned spinach (for which Kemp, Day & Company, at 73 Hudson Street, received a contract in 1941 valued at $191,602.30).

For all this, New Yorkers did not benefit nearly as much from defense spending as did other industrial areas. When the fifteen largest recipient cities were ranked by the dollar volume per capita of contracts awarded between June 1940 and March 1942, New York came in dead last, with Newark, San Francisco, Cleveland, and Los Angeles each garnering roughly four times what Gotham did, and Detroit pulling down approximately six times New York's take.

In part this was because Gotham, though long the nation's manufacturing powerhouse, seemed too geared (in the estimation of defense chiefs in Washington) toward small-scale production of consumer goods by small-scale outfits. And it was true that of the 27,174 factories in the city in 1940, the average workforce was twenty employees, in sharp contrast to the average of 113 in Detroit plants, home to the big auto companies now converting (albeit reluctantly) from coupes to tanks.

In part, New York's last place finish was because politics affected the allocation of funds. Contracts from agencies like the Defense Plant Corporation, which channeled vast sums into building shipyards or airplane factories from scratch, became the new pork barrel, and senators and congressmen deluged the White House in 1941 with pleas to build something military in their states and districts. Southern clout helped ensure that by May 1941, the Gulf Coast from Tampa to Galveston, where oceangoing ships had not previously been built, now boasted four shipyards working 'round the clock, with another four under construction.

The Sunbelt southern and western states, moreover, had been beneficiaries, during the 1930s, of vast New Deal programs that had developed the up-to-date infrastructure that now enabled them to seize the opportunities afforded by rearmament. Some of the Depression-era builders, moreover, found that the close connections they had developed with government funders now stood them in good stead for preparing to fight fascism. California contractor Henry J. Kaiser had worked on the Hoover, Bonneville, and Grand Coulee dams, gotten canny about getting federal subsidies, and was now reaping remittances for colossal shipbuilding and other enterprises. Gothamites were also up against operators who had no particular (or no exclusive) ties to the city. During the last war, Todd Shipbuilding, though long based in New York, had developed subsidiaries in Seattle and Galveston, and when British purchasing agents wanted sixty cargo ships built, Todd teamed up with Steven Bechtel's Six Companies to build them—not in Gotham but on the West and Maine coasts, with the Navy and Maritime Commission providing financing.

The availability of such financing was yet another reason New York was less nourished by the military buildup than it might have been. Congress had authorized the Reconstruction Finance Corporation (and subsidiaries like the Defense Plant Corporation) to make long-term, low-interest loans to companies that enhanced old facilities or created new ones. The government expanded the RFC's lending capacity accordingly and, by February 1941, almost 800 defense plants had been budgeted on the RFC's books for over two billion dollars of aid—two billion that corporations did not have to raise by floating stocks or bonds in New York's financial complex.

William McChesney Martin Jr., president of the New York Stock Exchange (NYSE), complained about this unfair competition in a December 1940 speech. He argued that the private sector could and should take a bigger part in the mobilization effort. (He also called for blocking any increase in federal taxes, hoping to deprive FDR of the funds needed to finance the defense program directly.) In truth, Wall Street in early 1941 was in no shape to handle the massive financings needed by American industry. Big institutional and individual investors alike had fled from stocks; war news had driven both prices and volume on the Exchange down to their lowest levels since 1918; and underwriting houses were consequently reluctant to take on the task of selling millions of dollars of securities to an almost nonexistent community of investors—and, increasingly, when they did try, they failed. Even in November 1941, with the national economy surging and dividends fattening, the market continued trending down.

As a result, the brokerage business was moribund. Where the NYSE had had 2,336 employees at the end of 1937, in mid Depression, by late 1940 it was down to 1,665; and in

1941 dozens more brokerages folded or merged, even as the economy boomed along without them. Many of the remaining NYSE specialists had no trades at all. The floor was so quiet that brokers sat in their offices reading the papers, passing the time of day. This somnolence at the center of the financial sector had wider ramifications. At the height of the bull market in 1929, the securities industry as a whole had employed 125,000; by late 1941, the figure was down to 33,000, and their salaries had dropped considerably. Wall Street had stopped attracting talent: where in 1928 17 percent of the Harvard Business School's graduates had entered the investment field, in 1941 fewer than 2 percent did. By the beginning of the following year, a NYSE seat sold for $20,000. A figure that low hadn't been seen since 1898.

Astonishingly, the financial industry found itself being squeezed out of lower Manhattan. During the Depression, when hundreds of brokerages had gone out of business, office buildings had often been left a quarter to a third empty. By 1941, the percentage of downtown office space occupied by NYSE firms had fallen 60 percent since 1933. At the same time, the federal government's presence had expanded as Gotham became the second-largest administrative center of national programs after Washington. By 1941, the four-year-old, fifteen-story Federal Office Building at 90 Church was crammed full. Government agencies, most connected with the mobilization effort, were leasing entire floors elsewhere in the district, many of them formerly occupied by financial firms (the Army Quartermaster's Department now occupied a considerable chunk of 120 Wall). Federal employees were coming close to outnumbering financial workers on their home turf. Little wonder that William McChesney Martin Jr. was frustrated and gloomy—"We have Hitler to one side of us and the government to the other," he declaimed in March, "and we are fighting to preserve our way of life."

From the perspective of the wider city, however, the deeper problem was that the government wasn't doing enough. The enormous amount of federal funds flowing into the country's economic arteries was, with amazing dispatch, erasing the Depression across the continent. National income had shot from $69 billion in 1939 to $92 billion in 1941 and was rising fast. In 1939, 17.2 percent of the US workforce had been unemployed; by 1941 that had been cut in half. Real earnings were up 30 percent and people were shopping again. By mid-1941, national retail sales were up 16 percent over the previous year; by autumn, sales had jumped 40 percent, with radios, refrigerators, washing machines, and furniture flying out the door.

But in New York, overall, the Depression dragged on. A year after the Crash, 46 percent of the total population had been gainfully employed; by 1940, the figure had dropped to 38 percent; and in 1941, unemployment actually increased in Gotham, even as it was evaporating elsewhere. Over 10 percent of the population still received some form of government assistance that year: approximately 159,000 families remained on the home-relief rolls (only 27,000 fewer than in 1937), and in November, 63,500 were holding WPA jobs. An estimated 6,000 panhandlers walked the street, undeterred by a La Guardia message posted in the subway saying: "BEGGING IS UNNECESSARY. The City Provides for Its Destitute and Homeless. DO NOT GIVE TO BEGGARS! Refer Begging Men and Women to the Department of Welfare."

As always, how you made out depended largely on who you were. Some New Yorkers—by skill and experience and connections—benefitted from the defense program, and many more would have, had it been larger in scope. Others were precluded from participation by law and/or custom. In 1940, Congress, feverish with concern about possible Fifth Columnist spies and saboteurs, had barred resident aliens from holding certain defense jobs. The exclusion was based solely on their country of origin, not their politics: all German aliens were verboten, whether Nazis or antifascist refugees. Many businesses, moreover, wishing to take no chances on violating federal guidelines, went farther and banned not only aliens but Americans with "alien" (e.g., Italian) names. The Carl L. Norden Company sought "Christian, not Italian" applicants; the personnel director explained that a large number of the firm's employees were Germans who didn't like to work with Italians (or Jews). Help wanted ads were festooned with qualifiers like "American parents" or "Native (or American) born," though some stipulated more broadly that "Nordic" would be O.K.

There was yet another constellation of New Yorkers in the "need not apply" category—men and women who though in fact citizens, often of very long standing, nevertheless confronted their own exclusionary qualifiers on the Help Wanted page, terms like "White Only" or "Anglo-Saxon." Now, with the looming likelihood of war against racial supremacists abroad, Gotham's African Americans would take unprecedentedly dramatic steps toward overcoming local varieties at home.

81

Black Power

In the winter of 1941, more than 120,000 New Yorkers held defense-related jobs. Fewer than 3 percent of them were Black—the lowest rate of any of the major defense-production regions—and the jobs they held were the least attractive, worst paid, most dead-end. The ranks of reluctant employers included leading high-tech, naval, and aeronautic companies. Sperry Gyroscope refused to employ Blacks, Arma Corporation hired them only in menial capacities. At Bethlehem Steel's two Brooklyn shipyards, there were 6,552 employees, 180 of whom were Black. The National Urban League protested discrimination at Brewster Aeronautic, Grumman Aircraft Engineering, and Republic Aviation. A 1941 survey of 202 New York City defense firms found 32.7 percent of their positions classified as "white required," 36.6 percent as "white preferred," and 30.7 percent as "open." Another study that year—a detailed scrutiny of ten New York-area defense plants—discovered that African Americans held 142 of the 29,215 positions.

Black applicants found themselves up against an interlocking and all-but-impervious system of discrimination, comprising employers, skilled-trade unions, and training schools, each of whom shifted responsibility to the other. Businesses with closed shop agreements turned down Black applicants on the grounds they were not in a union, a Catch-22 situation, as many unions refused to admit Blacks, notably the Boilermakers and the International Association of Machinists (both AFL), which dominated the shipyard and aircraft industries. Employers also rejected Black job seekers as unqualified, but industrial training schools restricted their intake of Black candidates to less than 5 percent, arguing it was pointless to train them as they had no job prospects.

When it came to the military—an escape route from unemployment open to whites of whatever background—Blacks faced a similar set of barriers. New York's Senator Wagner had won an amendment to the 1940 Selective Service Act that forbade racial discrimination in drafting men into the armed forces, but the law did not bar the armed forces from segregating their ranks. The Army had four separate Negro units, only one of which trained its members for combat, with the others assigned to support duties—digging ditches, building roads, cooking and serving meals. Draft picks were indeed made on a de jure nondiscriminatory basis: names were selected by a color-blind lottery and assigned a number. Inductions proceeded on a de facto racial basis, skipping over the next draftee in line if he was Black, when filling white units, and reaching into the Black community only when necessary to bring one of the four Black outfits up to strength. This meant that some 300,000 single Black men who were in the 1-A (prime) eligibility pool went undrafted, even though this forced draft boards to call up married white men to meet their overall quotas. As a result, by fall 1941, an Army of one-half million included only 4,700 African Americans. This was a better percentage than the Navy attained—it accepted Blacks only as mess men (to cook, make up officers' beds, shine their shoes)—much less the Marines, which refused Black enlistments altogether. As one Harlemite summed up the situation: "We can become no more than flunkies in the army and kitchen boys in the navy."

These limits on access to defense jobs and to the military—coupled with ongoing everyday civilian racism—were one reason that in November 1941 Welfare Department statistics showed Blacks constituting 26 percent of New York's total relief roll. They also accounted for 20–23 percent of the 63,500 still in WPA positions, though in 1937 they'd been only 13 percent: their percentage had risen as whites had left to fill positions from which Blacks were barred.

Faced with such Jim Crow practices, the country's Black leadership began to protest. In June 1940, the annual convention of the National Association for the Advancement of Colored People (NAACP) resolved to campaign against racial exclusions, and in September 1940, the Brotherhood of Sleeping Car Porters (BSCP), assembled at the Harlem YMCA, argued for the same strategy. When BSCP leader A. Philip Randolph and NAACP leader William White asked for an appointment with FDR to argue their case, they were turned aside by his deeply racist secretary, Steve Early. When Eleanor Roosevelt learned of this snub—she'd been a guest at the BSCP's Harlem gathering—the First Lady wrote her husband a letter advising him to take the meeting and address the issues; not to do so, she added pointedly (the presidential election being in full swing) would be "bad politically besides being intrinsically wrong."

Thus began a remarkable dialogue/confrontation between the nation's Black leadership—almost without exception from New York City—and the nation's highest elected and appointed military command—almost without exception from New York City.

On September 27, the president, Assistant Secretary of War Patterson, and Secretary of the Navy Frank Knox met with White, Randolph, and T. Arnold Hill of the National Urban League. The visitors related the rebuffs their people were experiencing in trying to get jobs, enter unions, and join the military. Roosevelt was cordial, listened intently, asked questions. When Knox explained that integrating the Navy was almost impossible because the different races would be confined together on a ship, Roosevelt suggested—without irony or intended disrespect—that perhaps Negro bands might be put on board so white sailors could get accustomed to a Black presence. At meeting's end, he thanked the leaders for coming and promised to confer with other officials about the issue.

Secretary of War Stimson wasn't into conferring. Indeed, he groused in his diary about "Mrs. Roosevelt's intrusive and impulsive folly" and deplored the "tremendous drive going on by the Negroes" to take "advantage of the last weeks of the campaign in order to force the Army and the Navy into doing things for their race which would not otherwise be done and which are certainly not in the interest of sound national defense." Were the Army to "mix the white and the colored troops together in the same units," Stimson insisted, then "we shall certainly have trouble," and he flatly opposed any concessions "to satisfy the Negro politicians."

Stimson's obduracy was partly pragmatic—a response to the racial battles already under way between Black and white recruits in southern training camps—but may have gained extra force from the gulf between the patrician New Yorker and the representatives of those he normally encountered as servants—Randolph was, after all, the spokesman for Pullman porters. It was also grounded in the received wisdom of many who had been junior officers during the Great War. In Stimson's recollection, when Wilson appointed colored officers to divisions in France "the poor fellows made perfect fools of themselves," and this in turn justified to the secretary his conviction that "leadership is not imbedded in the negro race yet and to try to make commissioned officers to lead men into battle—colored men—is only to work a disaster to both." Colored troops, he did acknowledge, could "do very well under white officers but every time we try to lift them a little bit beyond where they can go, disaster and confusion follows." This position was marginally more liberal than the widely held dogma, codified in a 1925 Army War College study, that "the black man was physically unqualified for combat duty; was by nature subservient, mentally inferior, and believed himself to be inferior to the white man; was susceptible to the influence of crowd psychology; could not control himself in the face of danger; and did not have the initiative and resourcefulness of the white man."

Patterson, though less prejudiced than Stimson, believed radical shifts in the Army's racial policies would impede preparedness and weaken public [white] support for the military. He accordingly drafted an official statement of War Department policy for Roosevelt's consideration, which proclaimed that refusing "to intermingle colored and white enlisted personnel in the same regimental organizations" had "been proved satisfactory over a long period of years, and to make changes now would produce situations destructive to morale and detrimental to the preparation for national defense"—a statement Roosevelt approved on October 9. Steve Early (being press secretary was part of his duties) not only promulgated this document to the public—a slap in the face to the leaders who had been awaiting FDR's response—but managed to convey the utterly false impression that they had agreed to this perpetuation of segregation.

Randolph was stunned. Harlem was enraged; thousands attended a mass protest meeting. FDR—having noted polls showing Willkie gaining ground (the Republican was far stronger on civil rights)—publicly regretted Early's remarks and insisted Blacks would be treated on a "nondiscriminatory basis." On October 25, three days before his final campaign swing through Gotham, the president announced he was promoting, to Brigadier General, Colonel Benjamin Davis, commander of New York State's 369th National Guard Infantry Regiment (the old Harlem Hellfighters who had so distinguished themselves in the Great War, *pace* Stimson's memory). Privately, Stimson snickered with Knox about his "colored Brigadier General," and ribbed the Navy Secretary, saying he would now have to come up with a matching "colored Admiral."

Three days later, up in New York, Secretary Early managed to pour accelerant on the flames Roosevelt had tried to douse. After FDR's Madison Square Garden speech winding up his Gotham visit, the presidential party was boarding a train back to DC when James Sloan, a Black New York Police Department officer, unwittingly blocked Early's access to the presidential compartment. The choleric Early hauled off and kicked Sloan in the cojones. This triggered headlines across the country, massive outrage from Blacks, and yet another apology from FDR. Once the election was safely past, and Black leaders asked for another conference with the president, they were once again rebuffed.

Randolph now concluded that African Americans were up against a system that could not be changed politely from within but had to be frontally assaulted from without. He decided, accordingly, on a drastic change in tactics. In early January 1941 Randolph published an article in the Black press arguing that "only power can effect the enforcement and adoption of a given policy." The requisite degree of power, moreover, could never be mustered by quiet backstage diplomacy but only by mobilizing the Negro masses for direct and highly public action. "I think we ought to get 10,000 Negroes and march down Pennsylvania Avenue asking for jobs in defense plants and integration of the armed forces," he declared. Only this "would shake up Washington" and embarrass the administration into reversing discriminatory policies that Randolph branded as "undemocratic, un-American, and pro-Hitler." On January 15, he formally issued a press release calling for a March on Washington, under the slogan: "WE LOYAL NEGRO AMERICAN CITIZENS DEMAND THE RIGHT TO WORK AND FIGHT FOR OUR COUNTRY." If Blacks were to get anything out of the federal government, he asserted, "WE MUST FIGHT FOR IT AND FIGHT FOR IT WITH THE GLOVES OFF."

Randolph's unabashed militancy attracted rapid and widespread support from Blacks in New York. Some were already well versed in direct action—notably the members of his union, the largest organization of Black workers in the United States, for whom picket lines were a modus operandi of labor struggle. Activist Adam Clayton Powell's "Don't Buy Where You Can't Work" campaign had accustomed thousands of Harlemites to taking to the streets to overcome discrimination. But even middle-class moderates like William White and the NAACP's rank and file had been impressed by the tangible benefits of New Deal interventions and were now prepared to push for federal political action to increase local economic opportunity. The notion that fighting for jobs and expanding civil rights were complementary projects was born, like the New Deal itself, on the sidewalks of New York.

The unprecedented unity of African Americans across the political spectrum became apparent when a conclave at Harlem's Hotel Theresa issued the official call for a March on Washington, to be held on July 1, 1941. It would be followed by a rally at the Lincoln Memorial, site of Marian Anderson's open-air concert back in 1939, when the Daughters of the American Revolution had refused her the use of their Constitution Hall, and DAR member Eleanor Roosevelt, after resigning, had arranged for the event that drew 75,000 listeners. The call was signed by Randolph, White, Powell, Lester Granger of the National Urban League, Layle Lane of the American Federation of Teachers, Frank Crosswaith of the Harlem Labor Committee, and Channing Tobias of the YMCA, among others.

This alliance managed to survive even Randolph's insistence that the March exclude whites. When the interracial NAACP complained about this, Randolph's first justification was that if whites weren't barred "we would be swamped with Communists who would use the March for ulterior purposes." When the NAACP noted that, given the plenitude of Black communists, racial exclusion would not have the suggested effect, Randolph shifted to a different rationale, arguing that while the goal of the March was integrationist, its means must be separatist, as "there are some things the Negro must do alone." African Americans, he said, "possess power, great power," but they had to manifest it, to demonstrate to themselves and others that "Negroes can build a mammoth machine of mass action with a terrific and tremendous driving and striking power that can shatter and crush the evil fortress of race prejudice and hate, if they will only resolve to do so and never stop, until victory comes."

One victory came almost immediately, when in March 1941 Governor Lehman appointed a Temporary Committee on Discrimination in Employment—the first in the United States—and gave it the task of exposing job discrimination and encouraging its voluntary elimination via persuasion and conciliation. A month later the New York State

Eleanor Roosevelt greeting contralto Marian Anderson in Japan. (National Archives and Records Administration, Franklin D. Roosevelt Library Public Domain Photographs)

Legislature gave the Committee some teeth, when it made discrimination by public officials or defense contractors on grounds of race, color, or creed a misdemeanor, punishable by fines of up to $500—hardly a crippling sum, but still a step toward enforceability.

Meanwhile, Randolph pushed ahead on the federal front, indeed raised the stakes by deciding to summon not 10,000 but 100,000 Blacks to DC. Pullman porters carried the word to Black communities throughout the country. The March on Washington Committee (MOWC) opened headquarters—two in Gotham (Brooklyn, Harlem) and one each in eighteen other cities. Randolph himself pounded the pavement in New York, talking up the project in beauty parlors and taverns and barber shops. Thousands of "March on Washington" buttons were sold. Buses were hired, trains chartered.

Randolph sent a letter to Roosevelt, Knudsen, Stimson, Hillman, and Eleanor, inviting each to address the hundred thousand Blacks who would arrive on July 1. The MOWC asked Black churches and schools in the capital to help feed and house the marchers, though when asked publicly where the assembled thousands would sleep and eat, Randolph replied they would stay in Washington's hotels and eat in its restaurants. The notion of a massive Black invasion of the capital's lily-white establishments ratcheted up the anxiety levels of government officials already deeply nervous about the proposed march.

FDR's placid facade began to crack. "I want you to go to New York," he commanded Aubrey Williams (National Youth Administration head), "and get White and Randolph to call off the march.... Get the missus and Fiorello and Anna [Rosenberg, regional director of New York City's Social Security Board] and get it stopped."

On June 10, accordingly, Eleanor told Randolph his plan was a "grave mistake" and might do more harm than good if, as seemed likely, it led to violence. On June 13, La Guardia, who Steve Early thought had "great influence with the New York negroes," dutifully tried to wield it at a meeting in City Hall. A hyperventilating Archibald MacLeish chimed in that perhaps "American Fascists" out to "incite the Negro population" were behind the March, another reason for curtailing it. Under this pressure, some moderate Blacks wavered, suggesting that perhaps FDR should just be trusted to do the right thing. Nonsense, White replied, noting astutely that "the President's promises are not more than water, and soon forgotten because it is politically expedient." Randolph never budged an inch.

Finally, on June 18, FDR summoned White, Randolph, and others to a White House sit-down. Roosevelt turned on the charm, but Randolph, in no mood for banter, bluntly told the president: "Our people are being turned away at factory gates because they are colored. They can't live with this thing. Now, what are you going to do about it?" Roosevelt offered to call up the heads of those plants and ask for equal opportunity. "We want you to do more than that," Randolph replied. "We want something concrete, something tangible, definite, positive, and affirmative." Specifically, "we want you to issue an executive order making it mandatory that Negroes be permitted to work in these plants." Roosevelt insisted nothing could be done until the march was called off. Randolph, equally insistent: "I'm sorry, Mr. President, the march cannot be called off." Roosevelt, probing: "How many people do you plan to bring?" Randolph, steely: "One hundred thousand, Mr. President." Roosevelt, turning to White, hoping for a better number: "Walter, how many people will really march?" White, steadfast: "One hundred thousand, Mr. President."

At which point La Guardia piped up: "Gentleman, it is clear that Mr. Randolph is not going to call off the march, and I suggest we all begin to seek a formula." FDR concurred, charged the mayor with hammering out an agreement, and the meeting adjourned. Five days later La Guardia proposed that FDR establish by executive order a Fair Employment Practice Committee (FEPC) that would have the power to withhold defense contracts from manufacturers that discriminated in hiring, and even to seize a plant should its owner prove refractory. Stimson, Patterson, and Forrestal objected; FDR overruled them; and Executive Order 8802 was issued the following day, June 25. It required all defense industries and training programs receiving government contracts to "provide for the full and equitable participation of all workers...without discrimination because of race, creed, color or national origin." A watchdog FEPC was authorized to investigate and act on reports of discrimination—the first federal agency since Reconstruction mandated to promote equal opportunity for African Americans.

The executive order, however, did not apply to the armed forces—Stimson had drawn the line at desegregation—but Randolph, calculating he'd gotten as much as he was going to get, called off the March, scant days before it was scheduled to get under way.

There was considerable grumbling about this among Randolph's troops, not only about the failure to win changes in military policy, but the limits on the FEPC's ability to alter industrial practice. On paper, the Committee had tremendous power—it could cancel the contract of any firm that discriminated—yet that very power was its greatest weakness. The FEPC had no small arms in its enforcement arsenal; it could not fine recalcitrant companies, or reduce their profits, or send their executives to jail; it was the big gun of termination, or nothing; and given the tremendous push for preparedness, cancellation of a major rearmament order was simply not in the political cards.

One of loudest grumblers was Bayard Rustin, a young Black man who had joined the March movement shortly before it was aborted. Rustin, whose clipped quasi-British accent gave some people the impression he hailed from the West Indies, came in fact from West Chester, Pennsylvania, where he'd been born into a Black family of genteel aspirations (his accent was the product of elocution lessons). Rustin was raised by his grandmother Julia, a nurse, a Quaker-influenced African Methodist, and an early member of the NAACP (W.E.B. Du Bois and James Weldon Johnson stayed with the Rustins whenever they came through town). Bayard attended Wilberforce University, the first college founded by and for Blacks, and then, in 1934, shifted to Cheyney State Teachers College, a Quaker-created institution for African Americans. There he formally joined the Society of Friends and enlisted in the surging student peace movement and the Emergency Peace Campaign. There he also discovered the risks attendant to being gay, when he was caught having sex, in a public park, with the son of one of the town's leading white families, which probably accounted for his departing West Chester before graduating and relocating in 1937 to New York.

Rustin plunged with gusto into Gotham's diverse communities. He got a WPA job teaching English to immigrants at Benjamin Franklin High School in East Harlem. He attended Quaker meetings. He explored the thriving gay subculture. He sang in church choirs in Harlem, and, briefly, on Broadway: Rustin's great tenor voice had won him a music scholarship to Wilberforce, and in 1939 it got him a spot in the chorus of *John Henry*, the all-Black musical starring Paul Robeson that closed after five performances, time enough for Rustin to befriend blues singer Josh White, with whom he joined in recording an album for Columbia and in performing regularly at Café Society Downtown. He also joined the Young Communist League (YCL), attracted by the Party's racial stance (where socialists and Trotskyists promised gains only after the Revolution, the communists defended the Scottsboro Boys in the difficult present). He registered as an evening student at City College, agitated for YCL on campus, volunteered in Congressman Marcantonio's district office, and in 1941 accepted the task of organizing a campaign against segregation in the armed forces. However, in June 1941, when the Nazis invaded Russia, the Party shut down his operation, putting Soviet interests above those of American Blacks. Rustin promptly broke with the Communists, dropped out of CCNY, and headed downtown to the West 12th Street office of the Brotherhood of Sleeping Car Porters, where Randolph assigned him to the Youth Division of the March on Washington Committee, the group which most strongly objected to calling off the March.

Randolph reprimanded Rustin and his youthful colleagues as naive romantics, though he also promised he would maintain the organization as a "watchdog" and use the threat of reviving the March as an "ace in the hole" to keep the government from backsliding. Rustin nevertheless decided to move on once again. In September he traveled back uptown to the offices of the Fellowship of Reconciliation (FOR). There he offered his services to Chairman A. J. Muste, whom he'd met at a Quaker meeting. Muste appointed him along with James Farmer (a recent Howard University School of Religion graduate) and George Houser (one of the eight Union Theological Seminary students who'd been jailed for resisting the draft) to key positions as national organizers for the pacifist organization.

Rustin also began visiting the Gandhian ashram that had been established in 1940 (under FOR auspices) on Fifth Avenue near 125th Street, opposite a saloon called the Bucket of Blood, and only a few blocks from the FOR office where Rustin worked. Muste had urged FOR members to explore the implications of nonviolence for transforming both the political status quo and their daily lives. The ashram project appealed to Rustin partly because its progenitors considered "the problem of racial justice as America's No. 1 problem" and actively did something about it. In Harlem, its Black and white members helped southern migrants find housing, investigated police violence, established a Black- and Puerto Rican–run credit union and a cooperative buying club. The ashram was also a retreat where peace radicals collectively studied texts like *War Without Violence* (1939), an account of Gandhi's methods and accomplishments written originally as a Columbia doctoral dissertation by Krishnalal Shridharani, an Indian national who had worked with the Mahatma before coming to New York in 1934. These ashram discussions would lead to the founding of a "Nonviolence Direct Action Committee."

By opting—in late 1941—to become a professional pacifist, Bayard Rustin situated himself at the farthest possible remove from the powerful currents of thought and feeling then surging through the city, as a mighty confluence of opinion-makers demanded America's immediate entry into the world war now two years old. These proponents, moreover, were growing increasingly less tolerant of opposing views, more inclined to brand those who resisted intervention on Britain's behalf as little short of fascists themselves, whose perspectives (and perhaps persons) might best be suppressed, if democracy itself was to survive.

82

Illiberal Liberals

In April 1941, the elite, by-invitation-only Century Group morphed into the inclusive, mass-membership, and high-profile Fight for Freedom Committee (FFC), the better to mobilize support for war. Headquartered in Rockefeller Center, the FFC formed hundreds of chapters, in scores of cities. Most who joined the Gotham chapter were white, Anglo-Saxon Protestants from the middling or upper ranks of New York society, with businessmen, churchmen, academics, and writers heavily represented. The Freedom Fighters who would be most in the public eye were Hamilton Fish Armstrong, James P. Warburg, and mystery writer Rex Stout (creator of Nero Wolfe, the Falstaffian detective who fictionally resided on West 35th Street).

Fight For Freedom launched a press operation that sent prowar messages out to more than 600 newspapers serving small town and rural America, but their most spectacular propaganda initiatives were generated by the Theater, Radio, and Arts Division, established in August 1941, cochaired by actors Burgess Meredith and Helen Hayes. On October 5, the FFC presented a "Fun to Be Free" spectacular at Madison Square Garden. The evening featured a musical revue written by Irving Berlin and narrated by Lynn Fontanne. It offered a patriotic pageant with music by Kurt Weill and a script by Ben Hecht and Charles MacArthur, narrated by Tallulah Bankhead and Claude Rains. It had a variety show organized by showman Billy Rose, featuring turns by Eddie Cantor, Jack Benny, Carmen Miranda, Ethel Merman, Eddy Duchin, Dodgers manager Leo Durocher, and Bill "Bojangles" Robinson, who tap danced atop "Hitler's coffin" as the band played "When That Man Is Dead and Gone." The most dramatic segment was a Wellesian one, which commenced with the loudspeakers cutting to "radio announcers" who warned that an enemy air armada had been spotted approaching New York, indeed was closing fast on the Garden itself. At this point the lights went out, searchlights began sweeping the giant amphitheater, a deafening soundtrack simulated a bombing raid, and from high up in the catwalks thousands of Nazi parachutists came cascading down upon the audience (quickly revealed as five-inch cardboard figures dangling from eight-inch-wide chutes). On the way out, the attendees (some of whom said they'd been scared witless) were handed a Fight for Freedom statement demanding an immediate declaration of war against Germany.

A similarly bellicose organization, the Council for Democracy, was formed at the instigation of Henry Luce to lobby for the defense buildup, and to instill in the American people a conviction that democracy was worth fighting for. The Council was organized by Luce's righthand man, C. D. Jackson, since 1937 the general manager of *Life*, and since 1940, vice-president in charge of public relations. Jackson recruited a board of over 100 distinguished figures—including David Dubinsky, A. Philip Randolph, Freda Kirchwey, Ham Armstrong, Dorothy Thompson, and Raymond Gram Swing, who served as chair. Then, from offices at 285 Madison, he launched a nationwide, multimedia promotional campaign that, among other things, placed anti-Hitler editorials and articles in 1,100 newspapers around the country, and broadcast a radio series—"Speaking of Liberty"—that its producers proudly characterized as just short of "warmongering."

A third entrant in the pro-intervention lists arrived in April 1941, with the formation of the Union for Democratic Action (UDA). Chaired by Reinhold Niebuhr, with Freda Kirchwey as Treasurer, the UDA was dominated by Fighting Liberals. It included former members of the Socialist Party; former pacifists who had come to believe in the war's necessity; and active members of the union movement and the American Labor Party's right wing; communists were refused admission. The UDA had more expansive war goals than the other associations. Defeating fascism was a main aim, but so, too, was ending colonialism: while the UDA considered it "criminal folly to assume that there is nothing to choose between a British and a German victory," it was not prepared to forget that Great Britain was an imperialist power, and they supported freedom for India. Nor did they target only overseas foes. Like Harry Hopkins, Niebuhr and his colleagues believed that mobilizing Americans to fight would require convincing them that victory would produce a better world for themselves as well as foreigners. Fighting for freedom required tackling racism, unemployment, intolerance, and economic inequality by inaugurating "basic economic changes and new social arrangements" that ranged from democratic planning to the socialization of big banks and large industries. The UDA was also prepared to fight "reactionaries" who would use the war "to destroy social gains" won by the New Deal; it defended labor's right to strike in wartime; and it urged the war be financed by taxing profits and luxury goods. All these planks, most of them notably absent from other prowar platforms, were talked up by UDA speakers at street-corner rallies around the city in the fall of '41.

For all their differences, there was substantial overlap in principles and personnel among the interventionist organizations, a conjunction which Fiorello La Guardia took it upon himself to underscore. The mayor decided to involve all these groups, and the city's entire elite, in orchestrating a gigantic rally, far vaster than any mere Madison Square Garden gathering, something so big it would demonstrate definitively that Gotham, heretofore noted as much for its opposition to war as support of it, would henceforth be considered firmly in the war hawk camp.

La Guardia announced the city would sponsor an "I-Am-An-American Day" rally on the Central Park Mall and created a committee of 1,200 New York luminaries to sponsor it. This committee included the City Council, the Board of Estimate, the heads of all municipal departments, the city's State Legislators, its Congressional delegation, virtually all its judges, and regiments of representatives from banking, industry, commerce, the legal and other professions, social welfare groups, civic organizations, and on and on. He appointed twenty-four vice presidents—on the order of Al Smith, John Davis, and Wendell Willkie—and a slew of vice chairmen from the spiritual side—including Archbishop Spellman, Bishop Manning, and Rabbi Wise. To plan the event, he enlisted the general manager of the Metropolitan Opera, the director of the Philharmonic, David Sarnoff of RCA, showman Billy Rose and impresario Sol Hurok, and threw in Robert Sherwood, Eddie Cantor, and George M. Cohan for good measure. It was, on paper, a mid-twentieth-century version of the early-nineteenth-century practice of municipal *prominenti* parading through the streets, organized into ranks and occupations, to demonstrate civic unity on great occasions like the completion of the Erie Canal.

The turnout on May 18 was immense. Seven hundred fifty thousand people, a larger number (it was noted) than lived in Munich, overflowed the Mall and filled the Sheep Meadow, to hear speeches and entertainment: Bill Robinson tapped, Eddie Cantor joked, Kate Smith and Marian Anderson sang, and Irving Berlin led the gathering in a rendition of "God Bless America" with the mayor conducting a 225-piece ensemble that combined the Police, Fire, Sanitation, and Park Department Bands. In the end there was a mass pledge of loyalty to the nation by the entire assemblage, broadcast coast to coast and fed by the new networks to Latin America.

What did it all mean? La Guardia explained. First, New York was a peaceable kingdom: "We have demonstrated that it is possible for people coming from all lands and climes of the world, or their descendants, to live together as good neighbors, in peace and in harmony," said Fiorello, adding, "If we can do it here, it can be done elsewhere." Second, New York had to be vigilant: "Here in New York City, the world's largest metropolis in freedom, we must present visible evidence that America is awake and prepared." Third, New York was sending a message to "Adolf, Benito and Joe that 'We are not afraid to defend our institutions!'"

What that defense might entail had been made clear the evening before the great assembly in the park, when thousands of other New Yorkers, who hailed from parts of town still stubbornly unwilling to join the Great Consensus that La Guardia was fashioning, found themselves on the receiving end of official raiding parties. Squadrons of police piled into Yorkville, Ridgewood, Williamsburg, Red Hook, Bath Beach, and other areas where large concentrations of Germans and Italians had their homes and began making random interrogations (800 were questioned in Ridgewood alone). People were required to prove they were citizens, and if they were not, to produce alien registration cards that showed they had complied with the Smith Act. If they could not, they were held for further questioning or taken forthwith to Ellis Island. In some instances, police had more precise targets in mind, raiding the kitchens of hotels and nightclubs where there was a higher likelihood of catching unregistered aliens; sure enough, two Italian busboys were arrested at El Morocco and two more netted at the Ritz-Carlton.

This wasn't the first such sweep. Only two weeks before, the FBI had pounced on German merchant seamen and Italian waiters who had worked at the World's Fair but opted to stay rather than go home to serve in Hitler's or Mussolini's legions. Some had been taken to Ellis and deported; others were sent to internment camps at Fort Stanton, New Mexico, Fort Lincoln, North Dakota, or Fort Missoula, Montana.

Vito Marcantonio denounced such raids as Gestapo tactics, but after June, when a real espionage network was uncovered, it became harder to contest the argument that these sweeps were merely prudent efforts to nab potential spies and saboteurs. The FBI announced the arrest of thirty-three German spies in New York in what J. Edgar Hoover called, on Walter Winchell's broadcast that evening, "the greatest spy roundup in U.S. history." The ring had been put together by Nikolaus Ritter, head of US operations for the Abwehr (German military intelligence), and unlike some of the Third Reich's earlier clownish endeavors, had actually succeeded in stealing secrets, most notably when Hermann Lang, an engineer who worked on the Norden bombsight, passed along blueprints in 1938.

The operation began to come undone in February 1939, when one William Sebold, a naturalized American citizen, visited his mother in Frankfurt, was picked up by the Abwehr, and told to become a spy or his mother would suffer. Sebold managed to inform the American Consulate in Cologne and was told to play along. Sebold was sent to spy school and trained in radio work, because the Germans wanted to replace the now-defunct communications system, which had relied on ocean liner crewmen as couriers, with a shortwave radio link. The idea—egregiously sloppy spycraft—was to have all intelligence brought to one central spot in New York and then beamed across the Atlantic. Sebold returned to Gotham in 1940, when the Nazis had set up an "office" for him in Times Square, at Broadway and 42nd Street. Ritter's agents now came by the "Diesel Research Company," dropped off purloined secrets, and were secretly filmed and taped by hidden FBI agents. The Bureau then substituted bogus secrets, which Sebold delivered to the Nazis' transmitter at Centerport, Long Island.

Having established a perfect counterintelligence operation, the FBI busted it up with the arrests, apparently because Assistant Secretary of War McCloy wanted Congress to legalize the wiretapping of suspected subversives, and he thought that exposing some spies on the eve of the vote would gain support. Hoover rolled up the operation, but the House defeated the bill. Still, the spectacular trial held that September at Brooklyn's Federal Courthouse (Sebold's testimony convicted all the accused), gave leverage to prowar campaigners seeking to discredit anti-interventionism by equating it with disloyalty.

So did the indictment, conviction, and imprisonment of George Sylvester Viereck for failing to comply with the Foreign Agents Registration Act. The longtime German propagandist, active since the First World War, had been hired in 1939 by New York's German Library of Information to counter anti-Nazi sentiment by publishing a slick magazine. Viereck got anti-interventionist congressman Hamilton Fish to contribute to the first issue, and when it was revealed that Viereck was on the Third Reich payroll, it allowed war hawks to suggest that all Roosevelt's critics were controlled by Berlin.

The pro-warriors' chief target remained the America First Committee. The FFC circulated a broadside—*America First: The Nazi Transmission Belt*—that denounced the Committee as a means by which "the apostles of Nazism are spreading their antidemocratic ideas into millions of American homes." *Life*, *PM*, and the *New Republic* denounced the AFCers as potential fascists. Winchell assailed the "Hitler First–America Last Committee." Dorothy Thompson told a meeting of 1,200 New York clubwomen at the Hotel Plaza, gathered by the Council Against Intolerance to celebrate the 150th anniversary of the Bill of Rights, that freedom of speech and assembly had doomed the Weimar Republic, and she clearly implied, to vigorous applause, that such freedoms should be allowed only to friends of democracy." Frank Kingdon of the CDAAA put it more bluntly: leading AFC spokesmen "should be muzzled."

Aware of the campaign to tar the AFC by associating it with pro-fascist outfits like the German American Bund and Father Coughlin's National Union for Social Justice, New York AFC leader John Flynn tried keep Nazi wannabes at a distance. It proved impossible to stop some from showing up at mass meetings. The real problem for Flynn was the man on the speakers stand who the McNazis were flocking to hear, Charles Augustus Lindbergh.

Even before April 1941, when he officially enlisted in America First, and even before September 1939, when war broke out, Lindbergh had been arguing it was foolish for the English and Germans to fight among themselves. Instead, faced with what he called—borrowing Lothrop Stoddard's terminology—a "rising tide of color," whites should work together to "defend the white race against foreign invasion," forming "a Western wall of race and arms which can hold back either a Genghis Khan or the infiltration of inferior blood." Besides, he argued—borrowing John Foster Dulles's argument—the Germans were only claiming their just due, the "right of an able and virile nation to expand."

Such talk drew big crowds in New York, fans and foes alike. On April 22, 1941, 35,000 turned up at the Manhattan Center on 34th Street to hear Lindbergh say that while "a minority" possessed of "power" and "influence" was trying to lead the country into war, Americans should oppose sending any new American Expeditionary Force to aid the British. This message was greeted with wild cheers from those assembled, many of whom were German, some of whom were Bundists or Christian Mobilizers. The national networks refused to carry the speech. WMCA broadcast it locally, adding a rebuttal by FFC stalwarts Rex Stout and James Warburg.

A month later, a boisterous crowd filled and overflowed Madison Square Garden, applauding Lindbergh (and Norman Thomas), while booing any mention of Roosevelt, Willkie, Stimson, or the British Empire, and refusing to sing "God Bless America," considered an interventionist anthem. City Council president Newbold Morris charged that 60 percent at the rally were Nazi or Bundist supporters, and Dorothy Thompson was one of many (including FDR himself) who accused Lindbergh himself of being at least a Nazi fellow traveler.

Lindbergh struck back on September 11, in Des Moines, Iowa, when he denounced the "smear campaign" in which "the terms 'fifth columnist,' 'traitor,' 'Nazi,' 'anti-Semitic' were thrown ceaselessly at anyone who dared to suggest that it was not to the best interests of the United States to enter the war." Many "dared no longer speak," but Lindbergh was not among them. Instead, he named names. The "three most important groups who have been pressing this country toward war are the British, the Jewish and the Roosevelt administration," he declared. Behind these, though of lesser importance, were "a number of capitalists, Anglophiles, and intellectuals who believe that the future of mankind depends upon the domination of the British empire"; and, since June 22, the Communist Party.

Some of Lindbergh's charges were accurate enough. The British and the latter-day communists were unquestionably pushing the US to enter the war. And Roosevelt, for all his caution, was pressing step by step toward deeper involvement (though Lindbergh attributed this solely to FDR's political opportunism). In the case of the other accused warmongers, Lindbergh either pulled his punches or swung wildly.

The notion that Wall Street Warriors were Anglophile capitalists who wanted to be dominated by the British Empire—rather than establish their own imperium—was as ludicrous as the suggestion they were second-rank interventionists. Lindbergh had married into that movement's innermost circle (Anne Morrow Lindbergh being the daughter of Dwight Morrow, a leading Morgan partner); he knew precisely where the New York financial world stood; indeed he'd been socially ostracized in Gotham and out on Lloyd's Neck by his former Wall Street friends and publicly attacked by his mother-in-law; yet he gave the Money Power, against which his Midwestern populist father had railed, virtually a free pass.

As he downplayed the power of Wall Street, he wildly inflated that of "the Jews." Lindbergh insisted he understood and sympathized with Jewish hatred of the Nazis—"no person with a sense of the dignity of mankind can condone the persecution of the Jewish race in Germany." Yet while their "wish to involve us in the war" was "understandable from their viewpoint," it was "inadvisable from ours," he said, neatly positing an us and them. "We cannot allow the natural passions and prejudices of other peoples to lead our country to destruction." And the Jews had the potential capacity to pied piper us—were thus a "danger" to "our" country—because of "their large ownership and influence in our motion pictures, our press, our radio and our government."

Lindbergh was right enough about the media's bias, though off base as to who controlled it. He correctly pointed to the prevalence of "plays portraying the glory of war," and it was true that Lillian Hellman was writing interventionist dramas, though so, too, were Robert Sherwood, Archibald MacLeish, and Orson Welles. He was right that newsreels had "lost all semblance of objectivity." Yet *The March of Time* came from the camp of Henry Luce, the missionary's son. Newspapers and magazines were, indeed, overwhelmingly pro-British in 1941, though the vast bulk of them—even *PM*—were not Jewish-run or Jewish-owned. Jewish Hollywood moguls in 1940–41 were deeply reluctant to beat the drums for war, precisely because they feared Jews would be blamed for starting it. The radio networks, headquartered in Gotham, were unquestionably throttling anti-interventionist voices (Norman Thomas couldn't even buy time on local New York stations), and the airwaves were in fact flooded with newscasts, public service spots, and dramatic series that bolstered the Administration's position—like the sequence of original plays on the meaning of freedom produced for CBS by The Free Company, whose member/writers included Orson Welles, Sherwood Anderson, William Saroyan, Stephen Vincent Benet, Archibald MacLeish, and George M. Cohan. And Paley and Sarnoff, whatever their personal persuasions, were only too aware that FDR and the FCC were watching them closely. FDR, who monitored the airwaves like a hawk, ordered up a survey of July 1941's programming and was pleased to learn its eight hours of unfriendly chatter had been far offset by forty-two hours of fandom. And Roosevelt's government, which Lindbergh placed in the Jewish-influenced camp, was more than ever headed up by old-line Wall Street Protestants.

Lindbergh's skewed assessment of who held cultural and political power—coupled with his eugenicist proclivities, his blather about inferior breeds, his coziness with Goering, his acceptance of Hitler's Order of the German Eagle with Star—gave the menacing air to his putatively well-meaning advice to Jews that they should oppose war "for they will be among the first to feel its consequences." People sensed his anti-Semitism, even without knowing of his private ruminations, like a 1939 journal entry complaining that "A few Jews add strength and character to a country, but too many create chaos. And we are getting too many," he believed, especially "in places like New York." This was perhaps why the ensuing hurricane of protest came not only from Jews and liberals, but from right across the political spectrum. Hearst's papers disassociated themselves from speech and speaker, with the *New York Journal-American* giving over almost three pages to denunciations from Protestant and Catholic leaders. The Brooklyn *Tablet* followed suit. And conservative Republican Robert Taft called Lindbergh's reference to "the Jews, as if they were a foreign race, and not Americans at all, a grossly unjust attitude."

A few weeks later, in responding to Arthur Schlesinger Jr., a young historian in the UDA circle who had cast the Republicans and big business as appeasers, whereas Democrats and liberals were antifascists, Senator Taft suggested the kind of populist critique Lindbergh might have mustered, had he foresworn his obsession with Jews. Schlesinger had gotten it backward, Taft argued: "The Wall Street bankers, the society group, nine-tenths of the plutocratic newspapers, and most of the party's financial contributors—are the ones who favor intervention in Europe," and it is "the average man and woman—the farmer, the workman, except for a few pro-British labor leaders, and the small business man—who are opposed to the war." The war party, Taft summed up, "is made up of the business community of the cities, the newspaper and magazine writers, the radio and movie commentators, the Communists, and the university intelligentsia."

Had Lindbergh argued this way he might have rallied his troops; instead, he'd thrown a stink bomb in their ranks. Oswald Garrison Villard resigned from America First. Norman Thomas, who had been holding out against critics like the Spanish branch of the Socialist Party, which accused Lindbergh of "open collaboration with American reactionary forces and sympathizers of Nazi and fascist dictators," now finally pulled back; though he doubted Lindbergh was really an anti-Semite, he had certainly proven himself "a great idiot." Even Flynn was furious, though he also resented efforts "to brand everyone opposed to war as anti-Semitic and pro-Nazi," yet he had nowhere to go but forward. Lindbergh could still turn out a crowd in New York—he filled the Garden on October 30, for a talk free of allusions to race or religion. Still, the Des Moines speech was a blow from which America First never fully recovered.

Even independent anti-interventionist holdouts like *Il Progresso*'s publisher Generoso Pope buckled in the aftermath. FDR had personally warned Pope of the perils of supporting Mussolini, and in early 1941 the FBI launched an investigation of his activities, but Pope hewed to his fascist-friendly line. Not until September 12, the day after Des Moines, did he finally make a statement urging destruction of the Axis powers, including Mussolini. He thus swung into the ranks of ethnic interventionists—like Assemblyman Robert F. Wagner Jr. (the senator's son) and Dr. George N. Shuster (president of Hunter College), who had together launched the Loyal Americans of German Descent back in July; and Al Smith, who had put aside his bitter animosity to Roosevelt, visited the White House in June, and called on the Friendly Sons of St. Patrick and other Irish American groups to join Roosevelt's side.

Despite the growing numbers of interventionist opinion makers, and the tarnishing of influentials who opposed involvement, the overwhelming majority of polled Americans continued to reject declaring war on the Axis powers. On the other hand, each passing day seemed to bring Axis power closer to American shores, provoking anxieties that whittled away resistance.

83

Battle of the Atlantic

In March 1941, Hitler riposted to the passage of Lend Lease by extending military operations westward, to the eastern coast of Greenland, and the Battle of Britain segued into the Battle of the Atlantic. From pens on the Nazi-occupied French Atlantic coast, Admiral Karl Dönitz's U-boats swarmed into mid-ocean, where British air cover was thinnest, looking for English merchantmen to sink. Where once lone submarines had lurked outside harbors, waiting to ambush departing freighters, now wolf packs attacked entire convoys, first torpedoing a straggler to draw off armed escorts, then savaging the defenseless main body at will. In April alone, subs claimed over 650,000 tons of shipping. With boats being destroyed at nearly five times the rate new ones could replace them, England's merchant marine was dwindling away; and with oil tankers a favorite target, so were the fuel reserves of the Royal Navy.

The German Navy's chief, Admiral Erich Raeder, wanted the Führer to push still farther west, into the 300-mile-wide offshore "neutrality zone" FDR had proclaimed. Hitler, preparing to invade the Soviet Union, insisted on avoiding any such challenge. New York war hawks, meanwhile, pushed in the opposite direction, urging FDR to abandon what remained of neutrality and provide military escorts for ships carrying Lend Lease goods to Britain. At a May 7 Madison Square Garden Committee to Defend America by Aiding the Allies rally, after British music hall star Gracie Fields had opened the proceedings by singing "There'll Always Be an England," some speakers wondered if, without US intervention, such a sentiment wasn't overly optimistic. La Guardia asked the huge crowd if it made sense for American workmen to manufacture tanks, planes, and artillery, load them on a Britain-bound boat, and then tell the Nazis: "Come on and sink it"? The thunderous cries of "No!" were echoed in a rising level of public support for instituting convoys—41 percent of those polled were in favor as of April, 52 percent in May. But Roosevelt limited himself to verbal bellicosity, mindful that shepherding military supplies through hostile waters might lead to armed clashes with German forces, perhaps triggering the war to which nearly 80 percent of the population remained opposed. On May 27 he proclaimed an Unlimited National Emergency and promised to "give every possible assistance to Britain," but in fact he authorized only extended reconnaissance "patrols."

Into this breach sailed the Royal Canadian Navy, whose warships protected convoys from Newfoundland as far as Iceland (which England had occupied), from where the Royal Navy ushered them on to the British Isles. Not until September, well after Hitler's invasion of Russia in June had drawn off some German forces (reducing the risk) and added the Soviets to the list of Lend Lease recipients (increasing the need), did Roosevelt authorize the Navy to begin escorting both American and British ships to Iceland, whose defense the US had taken upon itself. In a proposed tit for tat, Dönitz urged the now nearly 200-strong U-boat fleet be deployed in American waters. Hitler banned intentional sinking of US warships, though doing so in self-defense was acceptable.

On September 4, the inevitable clash occurred. The US destroyer *Greer*, informed by a British bomber of a sub ahead, engaged in hostile pursuit. The bomber dropped depth charges; the U-652 fired off two torpedoes at the *Greer* (both missed); the *Greer* dropped its own depth charges (which also missed); and the engagement was broken off. Roosevelt seized on the confrontation, presenting it as a treacherous and unprovoked attack, and declared German submarines "the rattlesnakes of the Atlantic." Noting that one didn't wait for a rattlesnake to strike before crushing it, he ordered a policy of "active defense," authorizing preemptive strikes on any sub that entered US-protected waters, which he now defined as extending to within 400 miles of Scotland. Sixty-two percent of the Gallup polled approved the policy.

The Berlin high command considered this a limited declaration of war. On September 17, Raeder urged a vigorous response. Hitler, still concentrated on Russia, again forbade offensive measures but again accepted defensive ones. On October 17, the USS *Kearny* was torpedoed while resisting a wolf pack attack on a Canadian convoy. It limped into Iceland with eleven dead sailors.

On October 27, Roosevelt called for arming American merchant ships and letting them carry cargoes into combat zones. This would require repealing the 1939 Neutrality Act, a move vigorously resisted by America First and many in Congress—until October 31, when the destroyer USS *Reuben James*, part of a patrol shepherding a merchant convoy, was torpedoed without warning by U-552. Its forward magazine exploded, and the ship broke in two, sinking almost instantly, killing at least 100 seamen. (In November, Woody Guthrie wove the names of all one hundred, as printed in the *New York Times*, into an ungainly song; after revision by his Almanac partners—Pete Seeger suggested citing only some victims and including the refrain "Tell me what were their names"—it became a rousing ballad, "The Sinking of the Reuben James.") The disaster helped win congressional approval for putting an end to neutrality legislation—though just barely, the House accepting repeal by a margin of only eighteen votes.

The Navy moved immediately to begin fitting out merchant vessels with 3-, 4-, or 5-inch deck guns and .50 caliber anti-aircraft machine guns and providing trained crews to man them. The nation's first armed freighter—the *West Nohno*—was readied on November 26 at the Todd Shipyard's Tietjen & Lang Dry Dock, at the foot of 17th Street in Hoboken.

With New York now emerging as the prime point of departure for armed convoys funneling war matériel to Britain and Russia—and an ever more likely candidate for Nazi reprisals—the US military redoubled its efforts, under way for some time, to build up the city's defenses against possible assault.

In March 1941 Rear Admiral Adolphus Andrews ("Dolly" to his friends) had arrived in Gotham to assume his duties as commandant of the US Third Naval District, which covered Connecticut, New Jersey, and southern New York; and his even vaster responsibilities as commander of the North Atlantic Naval Coastal Frontier, charged with protecting virtually the entire eastern seaboard, from Maine through North Carolina.

Andrews, a sixty-two-year-old Texan and one of the best-known flag officers in the Navy, established his personal headquarters on the top (15th) floor of the Federal Building at 90 Church Street, between Vesey and Barclay in Lower Manhattan. One floor below, he installed the Coastal Frontier's communications center (with telephone switchboard and teletype room), offices, and a large "Operations" room walled with charts of the Atlantic coastal area whose defense he planned to manage. Harbor traffic control—and indeed oversight of all shipping in the Port of New York—was to be handled, in the event of war, by the Navy's port director, Captain F. G. Reinicke. The port director reported to Andrews, but Reinicke and his staff (which at this point consisted of one assistant and one secretary) were quartered a few blocks farther south, in the Whitehall Building, long a hive of Gotham shipping companies attracted by its location overlooking the Battery and Upper Bay.

Admiral Andrews also took under his wing the Atlantic Fleet's air arm, soon to be housed at Floyd Bennett Field on Jamaica Bay. The Navy had run flight-training programs at Bennett ever since it had opened as New York's municipal airport in 1931. By 1941 the military's expanded defense duties, and the departure of most civilian operators to La Guardia Field in North Beach, Queens, after it came on line in '39, had led the city to transfer to the Navy all of Floyd Bennett's 387 acres, along with its Art Deco control tower, eight hangars, modern communication equipment, and newly built seaplane base on the bayfront, adjacent to the Coast Guard's Air Station. On June 2, 1941, the field was formally commissioned as the United States Naval Air Station, New York. Its seaplane squadron of twelve Consolidated PBY patrol bombers would undertake long-distance sea-scanning (the PBYs could fly 2,500 miles without refueling and they carried depth charges), complementing the closer-in surveillance performed by a small fleet of observation scouts (Grumman J2F-5 "Ducks" and Vought-Sikorsky OS2U-3 "Kingfishers").

The Army, too, had upgraded its presence in New York. Its venerable home base on Governors Island—an Army post since the eighteenth century, and a major Army administrative center since 1878—had in 1933 been designated as headquarters of the United States First Army (the neo-Georgian Pershing Hall was erected for its use in 1934.) In 1938—in testimony to Gotham's importance in military eyes—the position of commander was assigned to Major General Hugh A. Drum, the Army's third-highest ranking officer and one of its most distinguished, having served as the AEF's chief of staff during the Great War. When Ulysses S. Grant's old rank of lieutenant general was reauthorized in 1939, Drum assumed that title (though George Marshall, not he, was made chief of staff). In addition to overseeing the rebuilding and training of the national Army (through field maneuvers of increasing size, scale, cost, and complexity), and expanding the First Army's ground presence in the city (new barracks went up on Governors Island in 1940), Drum was also in charge of the Northeast Defense Command and its air wing, the First Air Force, activated in December 1940 at Mitchel Field near Hempstead on Long Island. In the US Army Air Corps' latest reorganization, the country was divided into four districts, each with its own Air Force, with the First covering the Northeast, deemed the most vulnerable. Each in turn was divided into a Bomber Command and an Interceptor Command, the former to attack enemy bases established or seized in the Western Hemisphere (for which Mitchel had B-17s), the latter to shoot down enemy bombers (P-39s and P-40s were the planes of choice). To remain in tandem with the Navy's coastal defense operations, the two branches set up a Joint Control and Information Center at the Federal Office Building, where the Army was also given space for its Northeast Defense Command and First Air Force. Together they held joint air maneuvers, as on October 12, 1941, when "enemy" bombers and "American" pursuit planes roared back and forth above Manhattan, jousting high in the sky over Union Square.

Sea defense was also a joint affair. The Army's Coast Artillery Corps set about remanning and refurbishing the city's somnolent harbor forts, whose troop strength had been diminished, and some batteries abandoned, during the belt-tightened 1920s and 1930s. After the fall of France, the WPA undertook a crash program to build or rehabilitate barracks, install gas and electrical lines, and run sewers and waterpipes at the installations guarding water routes to the city. The inner-ring southern gatekeepers were stationed on either side of the Narrows—Fort Hamilton in Brooklyn and Fort Wadsworth on Staten Island—and were supported by an outer ring consisting of Fort Tilden at Rockaway Point, Queens, and, on the Jersey side, Fort Hancock at Sandy Hook and Battery Lewis at Navesink Highlands. Battery Lewis and Fort Tilden's Battery Harris commanded the heaviest firepower, each possessed of battleship-class sixteen-inch guns that could rifle one-ton shells against an offshore target twenty miles away. Protecting the near-in northern approach, where the Long Island Sound flowed into the East River, was Fort Totten, at Willets Point, Queens, and, on the opposite (Bronx) shore, Fort Schuyler on Throgs Neck, with the outlying defenders consisting of Fort Slocum on Davids Island and Fort Wright on Fishers Island.

Inner-ring Army gunners were prepared to fire hove-to shots across the bow of (or if need be, blow out of the water) any boat identified as suspicious by outer-ring spotters. On the southern side, an advance Harbor Entrance Control Post (HECP) at Fort Hancock could radio information to the HECP at Fort Wadsworth, located in the high bastion—a remnant of the 1861 Fort Tompkins, itself on the site of Staten Island's original 1663 blockhouse—overlooking the Ambrose and secondary channels approaching the inner harbor. The Long Island Sound approach way was supervised by the Fort Schuyler HECP, in constant touch with its counterpart at Fort Wright; like Wadsworth, it could dispatch Coast Guard patrol boats to board and inspect vessels of doubtful provenance.

All this fortified firepower, intended to ward off naval armadas, was supplemented by three-inch anti-aircraft guns, intended to ward off air armadas (thus the 62nd Coast Artillery Regiment at Fort Totten had primary responsibility for protecting the Navy Yard). In 1940–41, with the Battle of the Atlantic drifting ever closer, the more fearsome possibility was an assault by U-boats, which might not simply wreak havoc on outbound ships laden with Lend Lease munitions, though by sinking some of them in the Ambrose Channel, shut down the port altogether. Forestalling this was the Navy's job, which it hoped to do by laying submarine nets, as had been done during the First World War. This proved difficult—the previous war's nets were still on hand though obsolete—until the British, who had continued to develop netting technology during the 1920s and 1930s, donated their expertise to the Navy in 1939. To manufacture the requisite steel cable, the kind used nearly seventy years earlier in the Brooklyn Bridge, the Navy turned to the corporate descendent of the man who had invented it—John A. Roebling's Sons—still going strong in Trenton, New Jersey. By November 1941, a net had been drawn across the Narrows, from Norton's Point in Coney Island to Hoffman Island, the old quarantine station, since 1938 a training base for merchant seamen, run by the US Maritime Service. The underwater barrier came equipped with a gate that could be opened and closed by a net-tender vessel (itself pulled by tugs), at the command of HECP Fort Wadsworth. It afforded only a 900-foot passage—a tight squeeze for convoys of fifty or more ships being buffeted by currents of four or more knots.

This multilayered defense structure looked more impressive on paper than it was in reality, according to responsible officials. The Army Air Force bomber crews at Mitchel weren't trained for antisubmarine work. Three-quarters of the Navy's available aircraft at Floyd Bennett were useless as sub-killers, and the remainder had over 1,500 miles of coastline to cover, a mighty big haystack in which to spot U-boat needles. At sea, Admiral Andrews commanded only 20 small vessels—7 Coast Guard cutters, 4 converted yachts, 4 wooden submarine chasers, 3 First World War–vintage patrol boats, and 2 gunboats dating to 1905, with a good proportion of them in the repair shop at any given time. Andrews asked the new commander-in-chief of the US Fleet, Admiral Ernest J. King, to send up support from the massive fleet assembled in Virginia, noting that among his pathetic armada there was not one "that an enemy submarine could not outdistance when operating on the surface," and, worse, in most cases their guns "would be outranged by those of the submarines." Given King's insistence on keeping his ships at the ready for possible battle with the German or Japanese fleets, Andrews was forced to declare for the record that "should enemy submarines operate off this coast, this Command has no forces available to take adequate action against them, either offensive or defensive."

Nor were the land-based operations as formidable as they appeared. During war games testing the city's defenses on October 11, 1941, an "enemy" raiding party (soldiers from Fort Hancock), attacked "Americans" (soldiers at Fort Tilden). With embarrassing ease, they "captured" the big sixteen-inch guns of Battery Harris, turned them in the direction of Manhattan, and fired off an imaginary barrage of thirty to forty rounds of 2,300-pound shells, theoretically blowing Midtown to smithereens. Admiral Dönitz was so underwhelmed by what he understood to be the effectiveness of Gotham's nets and shore batteries that he believed "a U-boat could steam directly into the throat of New York Harbor, on the surface, at night, without being challenged."

Little wonder that Mayor La Guardia wondered "if the Republic could even guarantee the defense of Coney Island."

84

Civilian Defender

La Guardia's concern about the military's ability to protect the city was one reason he so fervently advocated building up New York's capacity to cope with an enemy strike. That, and the ongoing horrible example of the devastation German forces visited on London. At the beginning of 1941, the British capital had already been subjected to well over a hundred air raids, some of tremendous dimension. Even more catastrophic ones rained down on the city through the winter and spring. On April 16 and 19, wave after wave of German bombers dropped hundreds upon hundreds of heavy explosives and thousands of incendiaries, filling morgues and hospitals with dead and wounded. On May 10, 541 Luftwaffe bombers set grim new records, killing 1,436 and seriously wounding 1,800 while damaging or destroying the British Museum, the House of Commons, St. James's Palace, and Westminster Abbey.

On May 21, La Guardia declared that because "New York City is the logical and most attractive and tempting target for a foreign enemy" it was imperative to assume the worst might happen. The odds were overwhelming—95 percent, he reckoned—that Gotham would remain inviolate, but "in the light of what is going on in Europe, of what we read day after day of the death and destruction and hardship and suffering of the civilian population, no prudent government, interested in the welfare of its people, could possibly fail to appreciate its responsibility to prepare accordingly and to take no chance."

By that point La Guardia had been at work for months developing a comprehensive emergency plan. He had begun by establishing a City Defense Council of 100 members drawn from top municipal officials—heads of the Police, Fire, Health, Dock, and Water Supply Departments and chiefs of the Tunnel Authority and Board of Education—and from the private sector: bankers, business executives, hospital administrators, newspaper publishers. At their first meeting, held in City Hall on January 15, 1941, Council members heard a report from three firemen just back from a two-month study of how London's firefighters worked under bombardment, and another on the pros and cons of using the subways as air raid shelters. All received a four-page pamphlet entitled *If it Comes*, whose front cover displayed the Empire State with nineteen bombers zooming toward it. (That same day, in

Midtown, civil engineers were pondering how to protect New York skyscrapers, perhaps by vacating upper floors and strengthening lower ones against bomb impact.)

The City Defense Council exemplified, in microcosm, La Guardia's proposed architecture of defense, one that harnessed together city workers and civilians. Much the same approach was being taken by the military, which had decided to augment its forces by summoning volunteers. On January 20, 1941, a vast air-raid test organized by the First Air Force got under way when 14 twin-engined bombers took off from Mitchel Field to "attack" the New York metropolitan area. Throughout a four-state region, 10,000 civilian volunteers waited and watched at over 650 observation stations—on the ground, on housetops, on skyscraper towers (the Empire State among them). When spotters sighted "enemy" planes they phoned in to an "information center" at Mitchel Field, where other volunteers, men and women, plotted the trajectories of incoming "hostiles," and pursuit planes were dispatched to repel them. Lieutenant General Drum judged the experiment a success, and in May it was institutionalized; soon thousands of volunteers had signed up to work under Army direction as spotters and plotters.

La Guardia created a municipal version of that structure. In early June, two weeks after Roosevelt proclaimed the Unlimited National Emergency, the mayor appointed Commissioner Valentine as police defense coordinator and directed him to set up an air raid warden operation. The city's 82 police precincts were subdivided into 152 "zones," each comprising fifty thousand residents, and precinct commanders selected a zone warden from among their locality's "outstanding citizens." The 152 zones, in turn, were divided into 1,515 "sectors" of five thousand inhabitants each; and these, in turn, were broken down into 15,086 "posts," each encompassing five hundred residents. Enrollment of volunteers for zone, sector and post warden positions began on June 20, 1941. By July 8, 43,005 had signed up. By year's end, 115,433 were on board.

Also in early June, La Guardia directed the fire commissioner to establish an analogous network of auxiliary firemen, fire watchers, and fire wardens. Training programs in the city's 531 fire houses offered sixty hours of instruction over a fifteen-week period in how to handle incendiary explosives and fight fires until the professionals arrived. Thirty-two thousand volunteered in the first two months. Of these—unlike the all-male air warden service—12,000 were women, drawn particularly from the American Women's Voluntary Services (AWVS), headquartered at 7 East 51st Street. The AWVS had been founded by a group of upper-class New York women, inspired by Britain's quasi-official Women's Voluntary Service for Civil Defence, which since 1938 had recruited over a million British women to serve in defense and rescue operations. The Gotham group had taken an early role on the fire-fighting front when it embarked, under Fire Department supervision, on a district-by-district analysis of the metropolitan area's vulnerability to incendiary attacks.

Other municipal departments established similar mechanisms for responding to enemy assaults. The Health Department stockpiled vaccines and antitoxins against poison gas attack; set up a medical emergency division that included 8,000 doctors and 14,000 nurses and nurses' aides from the city's twenty-one municipal and private hospitals; and worked with the Red Cross and AWVS to instruct volunteers in first aid, home nursing, motor-pool duties, and the staffing of 550 casualty stations (in 1941, 19,034 were trained in Manhattan and the Bronx alone). The Public Works Department set up an Emergency Division responsible for demolishing bombed buildings, decontaminating gassed areas, and restoring utility services; it drew volunteers from the building trades unions. The Welfare Department planned for 800 crisis centers to dispense emergency relief. And the Board of Education worked out plans for evacuating schoolchildren in air raids, with the elementary through junior high students escorted to their homes. The system was tested on November 13 in a simultaneous citywide drill involving 1.1 million pupils. It went off in disciplined fashion, though some critics questioned why children were being sent into the streets when adults were ordered off them; and in future drills they were directed instead to the hallways of their school buildings.

On September 24, La Guardia showed off the results of months of preparation at a mock air raid staged in Madison Square Garden. Accompanied by the amplified din of an actual air raid recorded in London, "incendiary bombs" were set off in the arena, giving auxiliary firefighters a chance to extinguish them; "gassed" areas were chemically treated by the Decontamination Squad geared in rubber outfits; fake bombs were excavated by the Bomb Removal Squad; a "wrecked building" was cut open by police auxiliaries who carried the "wounded" out on stretchers to be aided by doctors and nurses on the scene; and the newly "homeless" were fed at a Mobile Canteen—with all this action carried live on a coast-to-coast radio hookup.

The combined national and local coverage was particularly appropriate because by then La Guardia was preparing the country as he had the city. On May 18, he had been appointed as director of the newly created US Office of Civilian Defense (OCD), while keeping his job as Gotham's mayor. He now traveled down to DC on Tuesday mornings and returned on Thursday nights, at least during weeks he wasn't dashing about the country, helping the states develop their own emergency programs. Fiorello threw himself into the work with his customary energy and penchant for micromanaging—one day writing booklets on the duties of air raid wardens, the next arranging round-the-clock protection for defense plants, railroad beds, and reservoirs to ward off saboteurs.

Though a firm believer in panic control—having seen from close up the impact of Orson Welles's Martian chronicle—La Guardia drummed up support for civilian defense by warning of imminent peril: "The war," he told an NBC national audience on January 1, 1942, "will come right to our cities and residential districts." Many thought his defense-mongering overwrought, and his wolf-cries irritating.

Eleanor Roosevelt was irritated too, but for a different reason. She had pushed Franklin to establish the Office of Civilian Defense because she'd been impressed with England's Women's Voluntary Services for Civil Defense, directed by her good friend Lady Stella Reading. The WVS believed preparedness had a social dimension as well as a protective one. As ER believed—with FDR, Hopkins, and Niebuhr's Union for Democratic Action (UDA)—that "we must continue with the progressive social legislation as part of national defense," she took Lady Stella's program as a model. Working with Florence Kerr, the head of WPA Community Service Projects, Eleanor produced a blueprint for the Office of Civilian Defense (OCD), which FDR adopted, that mandated it promote volunteer community service work in health, housing, welfare, and childcare, as well as protecting the civilian population.

La Guardia showed little interest in what he dismissed as "sissy stuff," until the Bureau of the Budget told him they would withhold OCD funds unless he complied with the terms of the Executive Order. So on September 13 he created a Civilian Defense Volunteer Division "to better the health, economic security, and well-being of our people," and announced that he was appointing ER as assistant director in charge of voluntary participation. Within weeks she was promoting programs ranging from day care and housing for defense workers to venereal disease prevention for prostitutes near military camps.

In October, La Guardia, wearing his mayoral hat, established a municipal version of ER's division, the Civilian Defense Volunteer Office (CDVO), chaired by Winthrop Aldrich, wife of the chairman of Chase Bank. The CDVO was charged with recruiting, training, and placing volunteers for the protective agencies and social agencies dealing with health, child-care, education, and welfare. The mayor also added to the City Defense Council fifty-three women who were active in welfare work and charitable endeavors—among them prominent figures like Anna Lord Strauss, Rose Schneiderman, Dean Virginia Gildersleeve, Mrs. David Sarnoff, Mrs. Julius Ochs Adler, Miss Louise Iselin, Mrs. Albert Lasker, and Mrs. David de Sola Pool.

People marveled at La Guardia's ability to (more or less) handle *two* enormous jobs at the same time. After July 1941, he was juggling *three* jobs— running City Hall, running civilian defense, and running for reelection. And before July 1941, he'd been dreaming of holding only *one* job, and it was none of the above.

85

La Guardia Third Term?

As early as 1940, Fiorello La Guardia had had it with being mayor of New York. Partly this was because he believed that much of what he'd set out to do, he'd done; and it seemed unlikely he'd be able to do much more. Out at La Guardia Field one day he'd been chatting with Adolf Berle, and they agreed that the airport was perhaps the last big public project that would get done in Gotham, given the city's limited tax base. The next mayor would be a manager not a builder—"a glorified janitor," Fiorello said.

Also, La Guardia desperately wanted to get in on the war. "Rex," he'd told Rexford Tugwell in June 1940, "what shall we do? I can't stay here with the world falling to pieces." He yearned to vault out of Gotham down to DC, where so much of the action was.

As well, it was by no means clear that if he ran for a third term he could win. Fiorello had fallen out with key leaders of the Fusion Movement, in particular Judge Seabury, who was annoyed that La Guardia had supported Roosevelt and furious that he'd given former mayor Jimmy Walker a job. Seabury's old nemesis had fallen on hard times and been ill and all but penniless when La Guardia had appointed him a labor mediator for the women's coat and suit business—partly out of decency, partly (as Seabury figured) to curry favor with FDR and Tammany. The mayor's quondam Republican backers were equally out of sorts with him, not so much because he'd backed FDR against Willkie (who wasn't one of their own), but because in the gubernatorial race of 1938 he'd backed Lehman against Dewey (who *was*). And La Guardia's American Labor Party supporters, who'd been crucial in 1937, were now split between Left and Right, with the Communist-affiliated (and at that point "Yanks are not coming") faction threatening to run Marcantonio against the city's leading interventionist.

So Fiorello's fancy turned to thoughts of higher office. In early 1940, when FDR was thinking of stepping down after his second term and promoting a liberal successor, La Guardia, like Hopkins, briefly envisioned himself in that role. Slightly more plausibly, he entertained the possibility of being someone else's vice-presidential running mate, especially after Berle queried him about his availability, though on more sober days he reasoned that "the son of a wop who lives in a tenement doesn't become vice-president."

Once Roosevelt announced for a third term, La Guardia began hoping for a cabinet post, a much less improbable dream. FDR told Harold Ickes he was considering La Guardia for secretary of war, and even after that post went to Stimson, Roosevelt continued to ponder a possible slot in the third term's inner circle for his longtime ally, though the notion proved controversial. Leading New Deal liberals, including many of Fiorello's friends, warned the president that if the mayor did not run again, Tammany would surely recapture City Hall. Governor Lehman argued that in the event of war La Guardia would be the best man to have at Gotham's helm, someone who could deal with fifth columnists, spies, and local antiwar types. Some suggested the mercurial La Guardia was temperamentally unsuited for a cabinet post. Then, at the end of 1940, FDR indicated he would make La Guardia his chief liaison with the defense establishment. This met with the unanimous opposition of Stimson, Knox, Knudsen, and Hillman—on the grounds that La Guardia was not a team player—and he dropped the idea. Finally, he offered Fiorello a position as coordinator of civilian defense, which he refused, as it wasn't of cabinet rank.

La Guardia's old friend and adviser C. C. Burlingham tried to convince him that the mayoralty of New York was, after the presidency, "the most important office in the USA—certainly far more important than any Cabinet post, even the highest." Fiorello wasn't having any; he was angry and disconsolate and a terror to his underlings. Nor was his disposition improved by the emergence of a Citizens Non-Partisan Movement to Draft La Guardia for Mayor. On April 19 he said publicly he would "prefer not to run again for Mayor," and privately, he began reappraising the civilian defense job he'd spurned. Since then, he'd become an expert on preparedness and had realized that, if war came, the position would be nothing to sneeze at: in England, the minister of home defense was a leading figure in the Cabinet. On April 25, he sent off a memo to FDR laying out how he'd run the operation and signaled via Anna Rosenberg that he would forgo cabinet status if he could sit in on meetings. FDR agreed, and on May 18, hard on the heels of his triumphal "I Am an American Day," he flew to Washington to start his second job.

In his first radio address as OCD director, he did refer to the impending New York election, saying it was hard to plan ahead given the unsettled world situation but that he expected to clarify his position on running again in the next few months. Through this door, left slightly ajar, the Draft La Guardia forces plunged. Thousands signed petitions exhorting him to run. And disaffected former supporters began returning to the fold.

In June the American Labor Party's right wing, as expected, officially endorsed a third term. Unexpectedly, the left wing followed suit, their attitude toward La Guardia, as to much else, having been transformed by Germany's invasion of the Soviet Union.

In July, Seabury and his colleagues got Fusion back up on its feet again and marched it into La Guardia's camp.

At this point the mayor threw his fedora in the ring and said he would seek Republican backing as well. Liberal Republicans were amenable: Willkie, whom La Guardia had denounced during the 1940 campaign as both a "pimp" *and* a "whore," now endorsed the Little Flower, a move the mayor pronounced "generous and sporting." Conservatives were *not* amenable: John R. Davies, an elderly and respected opponent of intervention who also loathed the New Deal, said Gotham needed a *real* Republican in City Hall, someone who supported Republican candidates and was not a de facto member of FDR's cabinet. Davies announced he would challenge La Guardia for the nomination in the upcoming September 16 Republican primary.

Regular Republicans and party officials feared a Tammany resurgence above all else. They did not buy Davies's argument that Democratic bosses were far less a menace than the left-wingers who had flourished under Fiorello. Most waited to see what Dewey would do. In July the Manhattan district attorney had announced he would not seek another term; he clearly intended to devote himself full time to the 1942 gubernatorial race. Dewey calculated that if Davies won and ran on the Republican line, splitting La Guardia's forces, it would not only guarantee Tammany's recapture of City Hall but also strengthen the Democrats and weaken his ability to recapture the Governor's Mansion. Accordingly, when Burlingham sought his support for the mayor, Dewey told him: "C.C., I shouldn't do this for the son-of-a-bitch, but we're going to give him the endorsement again!" Which Dewey did, three days before the primary. Which La Guardia won handily—but not overwhelmingly (63,246 to 43,426), with Davies capturing the Bronx and Queens, a startling indicator of conservative strength.

Still, La Guardia now had the backing of his old Fusion-ALP-Republican triumvirate. He also had the support of most of the press—including the *Times*, *Herald-Tribune*, *PM*, *World-Telegram*, and *Daily News*—and of a newly organized consortium of 500 civic worthies that included such variegated boosters as Winthrop Aldrich and David Dubinsky, Nicholas Murray Butler and Eddie Cantor, Sidney Hillman and Frank Polk, Victor Ridder and John Haynes Holmes.

To do battle with this coalition, the Democrats picked William O'Dwyer, the feisty district attorney from Brooklyn who had been mowing down members of Murder Incorporated at a fearsome and publicity-garnering rate. The Irish-born O'Dwyer, one of eleven children born to two impoverished schoolteachers, had emigrated in 1910 to New York, where he'd worked as a deck hand on an ocean freighter, a stoker on a Hudson River boat, a longshoreman, a hod carrier, a plasterer's apprentice, and a bartender at the Plaza Hotel. In 1917 he joined the New York Police Department and for seven of his eight years as a cop he studied nights at Fordham Law, winning his degree in 1924. After working as a lawyer for seven years—the broguish O'Dwyer proved to have a way with words—he was picked (in 1931) for the Brooklyn Magistrate's Court and elected (in 1938) to the Brooklyn County Court. In 1939, when Judge O'Dwyer was tapped by Brooklyn boss Frank Kelley to run for district attorney, he agreed, won, and took office on New Year's Day 1940.

O'Dwyer immediately declared war on Brooklyn's criminals. Using a recent vagrancy law, the DA had hundreds of suspected mobsters picked up, particularly from places like Brownsville and Ocean Hill. One sweep netted Abe "Kid Twist" Reles, against whom O'Dwyer brought a murder case so airtight that Reles, to escape the chair, offered (in March 1940) to become a canary. He would, however, only start singing about the misdeeds of former colleagues and bosses—up to and including Albert Anastasia and Lepke Buchalter—if he could be guaranteed total protection from these utterly ruthless killers. O'Dwyer obliged by ensconcing Reles and some other informants in their own wing of Coney Island's Half Moon Hotel, sealed off with a stout steel barrier, and protected on a 24/7 basis by an entire squad of detectives. From this "impregnable fortress," Reles, for more than a year, was transported repeatedly to the courtroom where he spilled the details of eighty-five murders committed in Brooklyn and around the country by the Jewish and Italian contract killers who styled themselves the "Combination." (Early in the trials, Harry Feeney, longtime crime reporter at the *World-Telegram*, applied the more descriptive moniker "Murder, Incorporated," which stuck.) Thanks to Reles and other squealers like Tick Tock Tannenbaum and Blue Jaw Magoon, one hitman after another was arrested and convicted.

Sensational story followed sensational story. On February 6, 1941, O'Dwyer announced that his men had unearthed the rope-trussed remains of Peter Panto, the long-missing-in-action insurgent longshoreman, from a lime-lined grave in a desolate meadow near

A political cartoon from the 1941 mayoral race. (Artist unknown)

Lyndhurst, New Jersey. The DA added he had first-rate information that pointed to Lepke associates Albert Anastasia and Emanuel (Mendy) Weiss—both currently fugitives—as being the killers. On April 7, Weiss was arrested in Kansas City. On April 11, O'Dwyer arranged with the Feds to have Lepke, then serving fourteen years in Leavenworth on a narcotics charge, brought to Brooklyn to stand trial for the murder of Joseph Rosen, a candy store owner whose death in 1936 had neatly eliminated any possibility he might testify against Lepke before Thomas Dewey's then ongoing investigation. On May 9, Lepke was arraigned for murder. On May 16, Kid Twist, carted over once again from the Half Moon Hotel, recounted how he and Lepke and Mendy Weiss had planned the killing of Rosen in Lepke's hideaway, Lepke then being on the lam. In June, Pittsburgh Phil Strauss was electrocuted in Sing Sing, the first of Murder, Inc.'s employees to die. In July, William O'Dwyer received the Democratic nomination to be mayor of New York. In October, Lepke's high-profile trial commenced; it would make headlines throughout the election campaign.

The campaign itself proved to be a gloves-off affair. Knowing that a tough-on-crime rep was not enough to beat La Guardia (who had his own crime-busting credentials), O'Dwyer and the Democratic bosses tried hard to detach various of his constituencies from their allegiance to the mayor.

Playing to conservative Democrats and disaffected Republicans, State Democratic Chair James Farley said Fiorello was "completely dominated by Communists, reds, and promoters of subversive activities"; he was, no less, the "favorite son of Stalin." O'Dwyer joined in the red-baiting, though more circumspectly—partly because he knew the claim was absurd; partly because Paul O'Dwyer, his brother and campaign manager, was a liberal attorney who represented left-wing labor leaders; and partly because the candidate, who boasted (accurately) that he'd been a friend of labor on the bench, was trying to persuade some of the city's powerful unions, notably the communist-led Transport Workers Union, to come over to his camp.

La Guardia had a longstanding and unimpeachable record as a friend of labor. But his support for employee organizing in the private sector did not extend to the public realm, wherein he, as mayor, was the employer. In March 1941, Mike Quill led the TWU out on strike against the city's leading private bus lines—the Fifth Avenue Coach Company and the New York City Omnibus Corporation—shutting down 95 percent of Gotham's surface transit. Where normally La Guardia might have been sympathetic, he saw the bus strike as the opening gambit of a TWU drive to unionize the reorganized municipal subways and therefore opposed it as "bullheaded, obstinate and stupid." This was, to be sure, a mild-mannered response compared to the suggestion by Hearst's *Daily Mirror* that the bus strike was a "brazen demonstration of Communist tactics," intended to create chaos in the city, so a "well organized knot of Reds can step in and take over." When coupled with the mayor's opposition to unionization efforts by city sanitation and welfare workers, however, it created some disaffection in labor's ranks, on which the O'Dwyer brothers tried to capitalize. In the end, however, the AFL's New York State Federation of Labor, the CIO's Greater New York Industrial Union Council, the city's Central Trades and Labor Council, and even Mike Quill's TWU endorsed La Guardia for a third term (though not without considerable grumbling among the Irish rank-and-file who were decidedly cool to pro-British warmongers).

The O'Dwyer team made even less headway winning over Jews. There was some Jewish dissatisfaction with La Guardia's refusal, on free-speech grounds, to simply ban anti-Semitic speakers from the public streets. O'Dwyer seized on this, declaring he would take a tougher line against Christian Fronters than had the mayor. But La Guardia's pro-Jewish and anti-Fascist credentials—quite apart from his being half-Jewish himself—made him utterly unassailable (certainly by an Irish Catholic).

O'Dwyer thought he might have a better shot at winning African American support, given Harlem's ongoing unhappiness with what they thought was La Guardia's insufficient response to their plight. The Democrat told a rally at 136th Street that he understood the problem of discrimination in the job market and, as mayor, would do all in his power to solve it. One difficulty here was that La Guardia had supporters Uptown as well as critics— he'd won kudos for mediating the Randolph/Roosevelt talks that produced the Fair

Employment Practice Committee. More important was the fact that the city's African Americans, long unhappy with their political marginalization, chose this particular campaign cycle to launch a bid for independent power, under the leadership of Adam Clayton Powell Jr.

Powell was on a roll in the fall of '41. Back in March he had displayed great skill and shrewdness in winning a major victory for his "Jobs for Negroes" campaign. Among the many institutions that relied on the patronage of Harlemites while refusing to give them jobs were the very same bus companies struck by the TWU: out of 3,202 bus employees, there were fourteen Blacks, all porters. Powell knew that the TWU's leftist leaders had long talked the talk on antidiscrimination, even if they had refused to walk the walk. He also knew they needed support in their struggle. So before the strike, Powell went to Quill and offered a deal. Blacks would back the TWU's walkout, if the TWU would then support the hiring of Black drivers and mechanics. Quill agreed.

Five hours after the TWU declared victory, Powell's Greater New York Coordinating Committee for Employment, leagued with other militant groups in a United Negro Bus Strike Committee, announced that thousands of African Americans would refuse to ride the coaches that had barely begun to run again. The well-organized bus boycott was spectacularly effective, the companies lost revenue and reaped adverse publicity, and on April 19 they capitulated. A remarkable and unprecedented agreement was now signed, not only by Powell's Strike Committee and the employers (Fifth Avenue Coach and New York City Omnibus), but by the TWU as well. The union—waiving seniority rights—agreed that the next 100 driver slots and the next seventy maintenance jobs would be given to Blacks, after which whites and Blacks would be hired alternately until 17 percent of the companies' employees were African American.

Powell's stock soared in Harlem and was boosted further in May and June by his active supporting role in the March on Washington movement. It really took off on the September Sunday he announced from the pulpit of Abyssinian Baptist that he was going run for the City Council. This announcement of a bid to become the first African American in the history of New York to occupy a seat in the municipal legislature triggered a twenty-minute bedlam of amens and hallelujahs. Enthusiasm was quickly channeled into organization. A People's Committee chaired by Powell, with *Amsterdam News* journalist Roi Ottley handling public relations, was run out of Abyssinian. Most of the 1,800 campaign workers who held street-corner rallies and set up storefront headquarters in Black neighborhoods were members of Powell's flock, fast morphing into Powell's machine. And this machine was beholden to no party: "I always liked the guy," he said on announcing his candidacy, "who was nationally a Democrat, locally a Republican, theoretically a Socialist, but practically a Communist." The American Labor Party picked Max Yergan to run against him. Powell persuaded Yergan to drop out; he got Channing Tobias, whom the Republicans put forward, to do the same thing. Tammany, however, ran a Black Democrat and refused to withdraw him, which by itself probably finished off whatever slim chance O'Dwyer might have had for getting substantial Black support.

What gave Powell a real shot at winning without major party backing was the city's new proportional representation system, though that same process required him to come up with white allies. Voting was not done by district, but by borough—in this case Manhattan. All candidates (anyone who came up with 2,000 signatures) were listed on the ballot in alphabetical order. Voters then ranked them in order of preference. Whenever a Council candidate received 75,000 votes, he or she was declared elected, and additional ballots on which the winner had been selected as first choice were transferred to the second-choice candidate and thus were not "wasted." Even if someone fell short on the first round, if they'd gotten enough votes to stay in the running (those at the bottom were removed), they still had a chance to win if enough voters had opted for them as their second choice. This put a premium on making alliances in which candidates would agree to urge their supporters to put their ally in the second position. Powell thus needed someone with clout among liberal white Manhattanites, and there was no one who better fit that bill than La Guardia, whom he had denounced in the past. La Guardia, for his part, was heavily courting African American voters throughout the city and aware of Powell's popularity in Black precincts. So the duo buried the hatchet. Powell endorsed La Guardia and vice versa. La Guardia's endorsement of Powell brought in its wake a host of others, and the Abyssinian activist now became the first or second choice of the American Labor Party, Fusion, United City, many CIO and AFL unions, several civic organizations, and a slew of newspapers including the *Daily News*, *World-Telegram*, *Herald-Tribune*, *Daily Mirror*, *Times*, *PM*, and *Sunday Worker*.

O'Dwyer's detachment strategy, clearly, had not worked with labor, Jews, or Blacks, but as a Democrat he still possessed a high card, the endorsement of the president, which the political chiefs had promised him when he signed on. O'Dwyer made a point of backing FDR's domestic and foreign policy stands on the campaign trail, but so did La Guardia, and he had done so for much longer. On October 24, therefore, when Roosevelt announced he would remain neutral in the mayoral race, he added in a casual, almost parenthetical way, that he thought Fiorello La Guardia had given Gotham the "most honest and, I believe, the most efficient municipal government of any within my recollection." The following day Fiorello sent a one-word telegram winging southward that read: "MERCI."

This left the Democrats with just three arguments. First, the mayor's civilian defense work was shortchanging New York. As one Democratic official put it, "would you want a doctor who is out of the city every other day?" This slogan cut little ice.

Second, there was the matter of Fiorello's "unbridled tongue": when Governor Lehman, unlike FDR, dutifully (if tepidly) endorsed the Democratic candidate, La Guardia went berserk. His vituperative attack on the extremely popular Lehman dominated headlines in the final weeks, giving O'Dwyer another issue—the mayor's temper. Yet while his outburst clearly cost him votes, it was hardly enough to sway the election.

The third argument was one virtually never made out loud—that knocking La Guardia out of City Hall was one of the few ways left (in the aftermath of the Lindbergh debacle) that people opposed to entering the war could register their dissent from interventionism without being denounced as traitors. William O'Dwyer was no America Firster (much less a Christian Fronter, as a whispering campaign had it). He became the candidate of choice for antiwar voters, and there were nearly enough of those in New York City to topple La Guardia.

The mayor won his third term, yet the victory was a squeaker. He got 1,186,630 votes; O'Dwyer got 1,054,175. La Guardia's margin of 52.3 percent (compared to the 60.1 percent he had gotten in 1937) made the 1941 race the closest since 1904.

The sources of the falloff were clear enough: La Guardia's backing in New York's Irish, German, and Italian quarters had dropped substantially since his last electoral outing. In 1937 he had gotten 36.8 percent of the Irish vote; he received only 23.9 percent in 1941. Gotham's Germans had given him 46.4 percent then, 28.3 percent now. Italians—Italians!—had gone from 62.6 percent to 46.1 percent. And the boroughs where these groups were strongest—Queens and Staten Island—O'Dwyer carried.

The sources of the mayor's support were equally clear: Jews provided him with 72.8 percent of their vote, and as they were the biggest ethnic group in the city, their backing (much of it included in the American Labor Party's 435,374 votes) was decisive. Republicans, among whom the prowar business and professional classes were well represented, provided his biggest block of votes, 668,485. Blacks turned out in droves—90 percent of Harlem's registered voters went to the polls on November 4—swelling La Guardia's total and sending Powell to

Police gather around the body of Abe "Kid Twist" Reles on the rooftop of the Half Moon Hotel, November 12, 1941. (Photo by Irving Haberman/IH Images/Getty Images)

the City Council. He came in third among the Manhattan candidates, an astonishing showing from a historical perspective and one clearly facilitated by proportional representation, which allowed voices to be heard that had heretofore been muffled by the political machinery. The new City Council, though dominated by Democrats (17), also included three women, two Republicans, two ALPers, and one Communist, Pete Cacchione of Brooklyn.

O'Dwyer went back to prosecuting Brooklyn mobsters, though one of his biggest cases, against the still-at-large Albert Anastasia, went out the window—all too literally—when on November 12, Abe Reles was found dead, sprawled broken-backed on the roof of a kitchen extension, forty-two feet below his room at the Half Moon Hotel. According to the authorities, all six of his full-time bodyguards having fallen asleep, Kid Twist had seized the moment to twist together two bedsheets and a length of wire, wrap the wire around a radiator pipe, flip the homemade rope out his window, and slide down it to the window of the room below, which he was trying to enter when the wire came loose, precipitating the fatal fall, and immortalizing Reles as "the canary who could sing, but could not fly."

Eyebrows were raised at the official line that this was a botched escape attempt: Reles had lived in total terror of Anastasia, and the idea that he would trade life in his fortress for certain (and likely excruciating) death on the streets seemed highly improbable. Tongues wagged, too, about O'Dwyer's role in the business. The most voluble commentator was Burton Turkus, O'Dwyer's number two. As assistant district attorney, chief prosecutor, and head of the Homicide Division, Turkus was furious that the case against Anastasia had fallen apart. He wondered aloud if Reles hadn't been sent sailing out that window by his police guards—photos of the body showed it twenty feet out, a location more compatible with having been hurled rather than having fallen—perhaps bribed by Mafiosi, perhaps at the behest of the DA himself.

86

Pearl Harbor

On the chilly Sunday afternoon of December 7, 1941, 55,000 NFL fans were at the Polo Grounds in Upper Manhattan, watching the football Dodgers hammer the football Giants, when an "urgent message" came over the public address system asking Colonel William J. Donovan "to call Operator 19 in Washington immediately." Later came an equally cryptic announcement that all military personnel were to report to their respective posts forthwith. What puzzled the crowd was clarified for those listening to the game on the Mutual Broadcasting Network when at 2:26 p.m. the network interrupted its broadcast with the news that Japan had attacked Pearl Harbor.

Other stations quickly followed suit; at 2:31 CBS anchorman John Daly kicked off *The World Today* program with a bulletin from the Pacific. Mayor La Guardia heard the word at home, summoned a patrol car, and dashed downtown from 108th Street to City Hall. Throughout the late afternoon he and his staff, in conjunction with federal officials, activated contingency plans set in place over the preceding year.

The mayor dispatched guards to the city's bridges, tunnels, reservoirs, shipyards, power plants, war factories, public buildings, docks, and railroad stations. The Port of New York Authority canceled vacations and leaves and sent security to its bridges and tunnels. Bayonne officials ringed oil refineries and storage tanks. The FBI secured the Kensico and Croton dams, as well as the Brooklyn Navy Yard, where the battleships *Iowa* and *Missouri* were under construction. Police Commissioner Valentine mobilized the volunteer air-raid wardens, and by midnight a significant percentage of the 15,086 posts were covered.

Squads of city detectives and FBI agents went to the homes of about 200 of the 2,000 to 2,500 Japanese nationals who resided in New York and its suburbs. Told to pack a suitcase with travel essentials, they were taken to station houses, booked as prisoners of federal authorities, removed to the federal courthouse at Foley Square, then transferred to the Barge Office at the Battery and ferried to Ellis Island for detention. The mayor ordered Japanese subjects to remain in their homes until their status was determined by the federal government. To hamper congregating, he closed the Nippon Club (on West 93rd between

Amsterdam and Columbus) and shuttered the city's Japanese restaurants. Japanese nationals who tried to leave the city by plane or boat were turned back by police.

La Guardia also conferred with local military commanders General Hugh Drum and Admiral Andrews. The latter held a press conference at 90 Church to reassure the citizenry that no Japanese ships were in the harbor and to announce that his North Atlantic Naval Coastal Frontier (soon to be renamed the Eastern Sea Frontier) was putting the port on a war footing. City police were dispatched to help round up seamen and soldiers from weekend liberty, and soon Grand Central, Penn Station, and New York's subways and buses were crowded with men in uniform hurrying to ships, camps, and shore stations.

The Army's First Interceptor command at Mitchel Field—which had already sent fighters aloft, in conjunction with Navy patrol planes, to guard against surprise attack—issued a call through local radio stations for all civilian aircraft spotters to report to their posts. The 62nd Coast Artillery dispatched anti-aircraft guns and searchlights from Fort Totten to various strategic points around the city, including (appropriately enough) Lookout Hill in Prospect Park and (somewhat more discordantly) Bryant Park, behind the New York Public Library.

At 5:15, the mayor held his own press conference and immediately afterward took to the airwaves. New Yorkers, he told his WNYC audience, should have no false sense of security because they lived on the East Coast, as "Nazi thugs and gangsters" were the "masterminds" behind the Japanese offensive. In an acerbic aside directed to all who had dismissed him as a Chicken Little, prone to exaggerating the likelihood of war—La Guardia added: "I want to assure all persons who have been sneering and jeering at defense activities...that we will protect them now. But we expect their cooperation and there will be no fooling."

Early the next morning, Monday, December 8, La Guardia put on his Office of Civilian Defense (OCD) director's hat and flew down to Washington, leaving Gotham in the charge of City Council President Newbold Morris. At 12:30 the president addressed Congress. Seventy-nine percent of all American homes were tuned in to his "date which will live in infamy" speech, in which he asked for a declaration of war (and got it thirty-three minutes later). La Guardia made his own nationwide address; met with Roosevelt; then flew with the First Lady to Los Angeles to inspect West Coast defenses.

In New York much of the city had shut down to listen to the president; thousands had gathered in City Hall Park where WNYC had set up loudspeakers to relay the message. All day long, citizens had also been lining up to enlist. By 3:30 p.m., 1,800 men had swamped 90 Church Street seeking to join the Navy (only 700 were interviewed, the rest were told to return later) or the Marines (500 applications were processed). Three hundred were examined by the Coast Guard at 1 State Street, and 400 checked through the Army Building at 39 Whitehall. The Civilian Defense Volunteer Office's sixty-eight branches were deluged by would-be air raid wardens: 3,581 signed on (the next day another 5,992 would, bringing the pre–Pearl Harbor total of 115,000 to over 125,000).

Acting Mayor Morris warned that a "token visit" from Axis bombers could come at any time.

On Tuesday, December 9, as if on cue, sirens sounded from 1:30 till 1:47 p.m.—alternating long and short blasts—and then a second round wailed out from 2:04 to 2:41. These wails were not emitted by dedicated air-raid equipment (none existed) but by police cars driving about the streets and fire trucks rolling out from firehouses. They could only be heard a short distance away, and most who did hear them assumed they signified some merely everyday emergency.

Those who did figure out that a Pearl Harbor–style attack might be in the offing did the opposite of what the well-laid plans called for: instead of rushing to shelter, they ran to the streets, milled about in crowds, gawked at the sky. In short order one million schoolchildren swelled these throngs when—in this instance according to plan—they were dismissed from class and sent to the streets. In Seattle, shown a wirephoto, La Guardia fumed: "Am I embarrassed? Am I humiliated? Here I go around the country telling people they must stay inside during air raid alarms. And right in my own city this happens—this!"

Adding to the confusion were conflicting signals from authorities about whether enemy planes had in fact been spotted. Early on, some reporters relayed word that they'd been told in confidence that the "air raid" was really a "full dress rehearsal." Later in the day the War Department denied this, insisting the military had acted on a "phony" tip from an unidentified but supposedly credentialed man. Most New Yorkers figured "dress rehearsal" was the more plausible explanation and took the disruption in stride, though hotel operators complained about cancelled bookings, and the test had triggered panic selling on the New York Stock Exchange.

In Seattle, La Guardia had said of the city's response that somebody was going to "catch hell about this when I get home," but when he returned on December 13—two days after Germany had declared war on the US—it was he who found himself on the firing line. Already the *Times* had editorialized that while the mayor had more energy than ten ordinary people, "the time has come when civilian defense can no longer be a part-time job"; others chimed in with complaints that the "Mayor has tried to do too many things all at once." And on December 19, William Jay Schieffelin, distinguished retiring chairman of the Citizens Union and long-time La Guardia backer, called on the mayor to turn over his civilian defense duties to someone better fitted to perform them.

In a blistering New Year's Day address over WNYC Fiorello blasted critics as "Japs" or "friends of Japs"; warned starkly that "we will be attacked," that indeed "the war will come right to our streets and residential districts"; and suggested he had made "great preparations" to deal with the coming crisis, even if some sought to "belittle the effort." The mayor insisted he could handle more than one job, pointing to others who were doing so, and argued that in New York's City councilmen, borough presidents, and commissioners he had a bench of capable pinch-hitters. Nor, he added with some asperity, was it "an indictable offense for anyone to work overtime for his own country." FDR agreed with the critics and told La Guardia that, as of January 9, 1942, he was appointing Harvard Law School dean James M. Landis as the OCD's full-time administrator. As a face-saving gesture, FDR let La Guardia keep his title for a time; in February he'd be eased out altogether.

La Guardia was right about war being on its way to New York, just wrong about the altitude at which it would arrive. The mayor's attention, like that of most people, was fixated on the sky: the aerial attacks on London, and now Pearl Harbor, seemed the likeliest template for an assault. The real menace emerged from beneath the sea—on January 14, 1942, in the dead of night—when U-Boat *Eins Zwei Drei* (One Two Three) surfaced silently just off Coney Island, and Captain Reinhard Hardegen became the first German military officer to gaze on the US in wartime.

The Nazi wolf was at the city's throat.

UNDER THE GUN

Tugboats help the French battleship Richelieu up the East River for refitting and repair at the Brooklyn Navy Yard. February 1943. (US Official Photo 7570- P / Photo by Keystone/Hulton Archive/Getty Images)

87

Turkey Shoot

When the news of Japan's assault on the US in the Pacific had reached U-boat commander Admiral Karl Dönitz, he had immediately set about planning a devastating Atlantic counterpart. He would launch a surprise submarine attack against merchant ships sailing north or south along the North American coast, rather than waiting for east- or westbound convoys to reach mid-ocean. He would seek to sever the flow of supplies—food, guns, oil—that had enabled Britain to fight on since 1939, while humiliating the United States and revealing its vulnerability. Dönitz calculated that his new, larger U-boats (Types IXB and IXC) would be able to cross the Atlantic and still have sufficient diesel fuel to spend a week or two along the seaboard, torpedoing cargo ships and tankers. The day after Germany declared war on the US, Hitler and his naval commander Grand Admiral Erich Raeder authorized the unleashing of six of Dönitz's top U-boat aces (Hardegen among them). This initiative to carry the war to America's doorstep was portentously code-named Operation *Paukenschlag* ("Roll of the Drums").

As Japan had not given its Axis ally advance notice of Pearl Harbor—much less, *pace* La Guardia, been working under Nazi direction—Dönitz and his staff worked in great haste to ready the initial strike force in a timely fashion. On Christmas Eve, 1941, *U-123* left the German-occupied port of Lorient under sealed orders, to be opened only after reaching twenty degrees longitude. While plowing west, the crew in the forward torpedo room laid wagers as to their destination, with the smart money riding on Halifax, where most enemy convoys formed up. But on December 27, when Hardegen assembled his officers and opened the big blue envelope, their instructions read: "make attacks at and around New York Harbor"—a better bet, really, given the scores of unescorted vessels to-ing and fro-ing from Gotham each day.

A bemused Hardegen observed that the high command had been unable, on such short notice, to assemble proper marine maps and operational charts for the target area. "Flotilla did not leave us totally empty-handed, gentlemen," he added dryly, passing around a tourist guidebook someone had picked up at the 1939 World's Fair. Its garish front cover featured three emerald skyscrapers, a golden Statue of Liberty, and a depiction of the sale of Manhattan to Minuit; though tucked away in an inside back cover pocket was a large map showing all the ports and bays, including the main ship channel into the harbor, its point of entry marked by the Ambrose Lightship.

Days later, cruising west past Montauk's lighthouse, sixty miles off Long Island's southern shore, *U-123* encountered the *Norness*, a sizeable (nearly ten-thousand-ton) tanker owned by a Norwegian company that had moved to New York after the Nazis conquered their country. At 1:37 a.m. on Wednesday, January 14, 1942, Hardegen released two "eels" (as torpedoes were known). Their violent detonations stopped the target; a third eel sank it.

Carrying on, *U-123* approached New York's harbor on the surface in the last predawn hours of January 14. With the water getting ever shallower, and the bright red morning sun silhouetting the sub's tower for any alert lookout, Hardegen submerged at 7:30 a.m. and began to prowl for targets. He spotted a promising merchantman, but it proved to be a neutral Spanish vessel, so he aborted the attack. Finally he decided to bottom out thirty meters down and rest on the mud till the evening, when he hoped to find fresh victims entering or exiting the port. During the day, the crew ate, slept, and surfed the radio, puzzling over *The Goldbergs* on WOR, and *Missus Goes A-Shopping* on WABC, before settling on WNYC's *Gramercy Chamber Trio*.

At nightfall Hardegen surfaced again and crept closer to the city, looking for but failing to find the lightship (it had been temporarily removed); at one point he nearly ran aground on the Rockaways. At 10:00 p.m., just below Coney Island, he paused on the city's very doorstep, gazing in amazement at the Ferris Wheel and Parachute Jump highlighted against the blazing backdrop of light thrown up from incandescent Manhattan. The captain was mesmerized, and also irritated at the arrogance implicit in the luminous spectacle. Recalling blacked-out Europe, he jotted in his war diary: "Don't they know there's a war on?"

U-123 submerged again, scouting for targets, though only minnows passed overhead—tugs, pilot boats—no big fish. Hardegen was nothing if not audacious, though he didn't know the traffic lanes, could no longer dive deeply enough to escape depth charges, and couldn't believe the US Navy wasn't about to pounce on him. (The lookouts in the 100-foot-tall towers at Fort Tilden and Arverne never spotted him, and no action was taken by shore defenses or patrol aircraft.) Reluctantly, he turned his U-boat away and steered east, leaving the city behind, until finally, at 1:40 a.m. on Thursday, January 15, 60 miles out, he sighted the British tanker *Coimbra*. A torpedo to its stern ignited its cargo of oil, sending a 600-foot pillar of fire into the night sky (all too visible to horrified residents of the Hamptons, 27 miles to the north); a second one sent it to the bottom, with only nine of the forty-six crewmen surviving.

Thus began what the Germans called the "happy time"—*Die Glückliche Zeit*—or the great "American turkey-shoot." Within two weeks, Hardegen and his handful of colleagues—spread out between Newfoundland and Bermuda—sank thirty-five ships, with the *U-123* alone accounting for seven of them before it ran out of torpedoes. By early February, when the initial deadly cohort returned to the Bay of Biscay to reload and refuel, it had already been replaced by a new and larger wave of U-boats that took up the slaughter where the initial *Paukenschlag* force had left off.

It was all too easy: approach a shipping lane at periscope depth, surface at night, then torpedo from seaward the vessels starkly silhouetted against the blazing shore lights, which coastal cities and resorts refused to extinguish. Oil tankers lumbering up from Gulf Coast ports to northeastern refineries and storage depots were particularly prized and easily dispatched: in the first three months of 1942 almost four times as many tankers were sunk as were built.

By February, the extent of the carnage was becoming widely known, despite efforts by the military to censor information about the sinkings. Dead bodies, debris, and vast slicks of oil were washing ashore on East Coast beaches. Six cargo ships in New York harbor refused to sail until they were given adequate protection, and didn't get it. Merchantmen had to be content with extinguishing their lights, muting their radios, and praying for the best.

Even more than Dönitz had hoped, the U-boat offensive was shaping up to be a greater strategic setback than Pearl Harbor, as the sinkings threatened to shut down the war against Hitler before it started. At the end of February, Brigadier General Dwight Eisenhower told Army Chief of Staff General George Marshall that securing the "maximum safety of these lines of communication is a 'must' in our military effort."

The Army and Navy seemed helpless to repel the attackers. As Andrews had predicted, his puny fleet was all but useless. Efforts at bolstering it with a Coastal Picket Patrol organized by private yachtsmen proved counterproductive when the amateurs, having established a patrol line 50 miles offshore, proceeded to relay countless false submarine sightings, dissipating the Eastern Sea Frontier's scant resources in wild U-goose chases. Navy patrol planes and Army Air Force bombers proved equally ineffective: spotting subs in all that ocean was inherently difficult, few pilots were properly trained, and fewer planes were equipped with even the rudimentary ASV (Air to Surface Vessel) radar then available. In the sky, too, civilians joined the hunt. A Civil Air Patrol welcomed pilots willing to fly missions in their own light planes, but sightings of subs proved far fewer than sightings of sub victims: sinking ships, life rafts, or merely slicks of oil.

Gotham's inner harbor security was tightened. The antisubmarine net at the Narrows had been supplemented on December 10, 1941, when mariners received notice that "a mined area covering the approaches to New York Harbor has been established" and that incoming vessels should "secure directions for safe navigation from patrol vessels stationed off Ambrose Channel Entrance." These buoyant mines proved to have drawbacks, however—they often broke loose in bad weather and drifted ashore at places like Asbury Park—and were replaced by ocean bottom mines, hardwired to Harbor Entrance Control Posts, which could trigger them from shore.

Other new technologies were rushed into service to bolster harbor defenses, not always to good effect. Underwater listening devices called "hydrophones" proved unable to distinguish friend from foe amid the tremendous volume of harbor traffic. Magnetic detection loops were laid along the bottom of the Ambrose Channel, but these failed to detect vessels smaller than tankers and tended to get snared by anchors (as had Morse's pioneering telegraph wire to Governors Island a century earlier). A Radio Direction Finding set (RDF) was put in place at Jones Beach, hoping to triangulate on the encrypted radio signals sent by the German U-boats. Mostly, however, the RDF picked up the "send help" signals from U-boats' victims—the "SSS" variant of "SOS" used when a ship had been torpedoed. More promisingly, SCR-582s (an improved form of harbor-surveillance radar) could detect incoming enemy airbornes at night and in bad weather, though they couldn't see beneath the sea.

Given limited harbor defenses and the ongoing offshore devastation, the security of the city itself could not be guaranteed. As the president himself warned, in a press conference held on February 17, 1942: "Enemy ships could come in and shell New York tomorrow night, under certain conditions."

FDR had an even keener concern about land-based dangers—sabotage—a concern that had spiked sharply since the calamity on the Hudson that had taken place little more than a week before.

88

Sabotage?

On February 9, 1942, the *Normandie*—the world's most glamorous ocean liner—had been the site of feverish activity, as 1,750 workers from the Robins Dry Dock & Repair Company, and 675 other laborers from sixty assorted subcontractors, worked to convert the rakish, Art Deco, red-and-black vessel—whose elegant staterooms had hosted the likes of Marlene Dietrich, Cole Porter, and Ernest Hemingway—into a drabbed-down, bunk-laden troopship.

The *Normandie* had been tied up at Pier 88 (at the foot of West 48th Street) since arriving from Le Havre on August 28, 1939, four days before Germany invaded Poland. Rather than have its crown jewel brave torpedoes at sea, or bombs back in France, the French Line, *Compagnie Générale Transatlantique* (CGT), laid up its vessel indefinitely on September 6, leaving on board only a skeleton crew of 113 (out of 1,227) to keep it shipshape. There it stayed, through the fall of France, while other sea queens came and went (at one point, in March 1940, the gray-camouflaged sisters *Elizabeth* and *Mary* were berthed in adjacent piers).

On May 15, 1941, the US government took the *Normandie* into protective custody, leaving French ownership intact but housing a contingent of armed Coast Guardsmen on board to forestall possible sabotage by crew members loyal to the Vichy government. (The Pétain regime was getting increasingly cozy with Germany: Vice Premier Admiral François Darlan had just visited Hitler on May 11.) American thoughts turned to possible uses of the giant ship, in the event of an actual confiscation, and proposals were floated to use it as a dockside super-barracks, or to move it to Brooklyn, where it could serve as a backup power supply for the entire city, capable as it was of generating 150,000 kilowatts. When the *Normandie* was seized, on December 12, the day after war with Germany broke out, the troopship option won out. The vessel was transferred to the Navy, renamed the USS *Lafayette*, and turned over to contractors who began carting off the legendary artwork and sumptuous furniture to the Chelsea Warehouse and converting the staterooms, which had housed 1,972 First, Tourist, and Third-Class passengers, into bunkrooms that would carry 14,800 soldiers to war.

With nearly 2,500 workmen (plus Coast Guardsmen and crew) constantly coming and going, the noise, confusion and disorder on the ship attracted the attention of Ralph Ingersoll, editor of *PM*. Security seemed dangerously casual to him, so Ingersoll assigned reporter

Edmund Scott to find out how easily a potential saboteur might penetrate the *Normandie*'s defenses. It proved to be a snap. Scott joined Local 284 of the International Longshoremen's Association (ILA) and got a job lugging furniture aboard. Once on deck, it proved easy to wander about as he pleased, and he was struck by how simple it would be to set a fire. On January 3, 1942, he filed his story, which Ingersoll decided not to run—it being, in effect, a blueprint for sabotage—and instead got in touch with the authorities, who seemed uninterested.

When a fire broke out at 2:34 on the afternoon of February 9, crewmen discovered to their horror that the fire hoses could not connect to the standpipes, as the latter had been converted to American fittings, while the former still spoke French. Efforts to sound the fire alarm also failed—it had been disconnected a few days earlier, along with the ship's link to the city's fire department, by a subcontractor who had forgotten to tell anyone. In the meantime—it was a blustery winter day—the wind whipped through the corridors, spreading the blaze until it was beyond control, with great sheets of flame leaping skyward. Most of the nearly 3,000 on board dashed down the gangplanks and joined the thirty thousand New Yorkers who choked Twelfth Avenue. Fire trucks now combined forces with fire boats to inundate the upper decks: over the next four hours, they poured on 3,000 tons of water. The ship began to list. The French officers who had rushed to the pier realized the danger; their calls to refill the ballast tanks to ground the ship on the slip bottom were rejected, as were their urgings to close the portholes.

The inundation continued, as La Guardia, who had rushed to the pier, said it was out of the question to let a fire rage unchecked in midtown Manhattan. Even after the inferno seemed contained, around 8:00 p.m., the fireboats—ordered by Commissioner Walsh to stop

The US Coast Guard flies over the wreckage of the USS *Lafayette* (previously known as the SS *Normandie*) at Pier 88, August 12, 1943. (U.S. Navy Photograph)

pumping—didn't get his radioed message; and having gotten dark, his semaphore signals went similarly unheeded. By the time a cutoff was accomplished, the *Normandie* had taken on 16,000 tons of water, most trapped on the port side, a burden no ship could have borne. At 12:30 a.m., Admiral Andrews gave the order to evacuate. At 2:32 a.m., it rolled over in the gray Hudson ice and came to rest, its funnels just barely above the waterline, slumped ignominiously in the mud.

Rumors of sabotage flew, starting at the top. FDR asked Navy Secretary Knox the next morning if any enemy aliens had been permitted to work at the site. The truth flew almost as quickly yet had difficulty catching up. The first press reports carried District Attorney Frank Hogan's statement—"There is no evidence of sabotage"—and Admiral Andrews's concurrence, along with the facts they had ferreted out. The fire, they said, had been an accident, caused by carelessness. One worker had been using an acetylene torch to cut down a metal stanchion in the Grand Salon, the resulting sparks contained by an asbestos board held up by another laborer. When the second man put down his board for a minute to help a colleague, a spark leapt toward a pile of 1,140 life jackets, each filled with flammable kapok, each wrapped in even more flammable burlap. Up they went, in turn igniting a nearby mass of bunk-bound mattresses. On February 12, the FBI staged a re-creation at the Brooklyn Navy Yard; followed up with a full-dress investigation in which they interviewed 760 people, and came to the same conclusion. So did two congressional committees. No sabotage.

Nonetheless, doubts continued. Many refused to buy the verdict, especially after *PM* published Scott's original story. The notion that Nazi saboteurs had done the deed was further nurtured by Alfred Hitchcock, then shooting and editing *Saboteur* (1942). The director inserted a sequence that showed his weaselly Nazi villain (played by Norman Lloyd) being taxied down the West Side past the capsized *Normandie* (shown in actual newsreel footage). As he surveyed the wreckage, Lloyd gave a perfectly calibrated, wickedly knowing half smile, as if to say: "Ah, our handiwork." The Navy tried hard to muscle Hitchcock into excising the bit; it failed, and the ranks of doubters grew.

There was one person who did more than doubt—he was utterly certain the *Normandie* was the victim of foul play, because he himself had ordered the hit. No Nazi, he was the nation's most celebrated jailbird, languishing up in Dannemora Prison (known as "New York's Siberia"), doing a thirty-to-fifty-year stretch.

89

The Mob and the Military

Lucky Luciano saw Pearl Harbor as a potential "Get Out of Jail Free" card, if he could figure out how to play it right. In early 1942—as he later recounted the story—Luciano and the visiting Frank Costello and Meyer Lansky concocted a plan to win him a pardon. The idea was to undertake some spectacular act of sabotage on the waterfront—it "hadda be front-page stuff"—something that would cause the government to panic and turn to the Mob to prevent future incidents. Luciano would broker this deal, in exchange for his own release. Costello conveyed Luciano's thoughts to Tough Tony Anastasio, a power in the International Longshoremen's Association, and his even tougher brother, Albert Anastasia of Murder, Incorporated. Albert suggested that dispatching the *Normandie* would be just the thing, "a real big hunk of sabotage, something so big it would scare the shit out of the whole fuckin' Navy." Luciano (in his retelling) gave the go ahead. When shortly thereafter the ship went up in flames, Luciano commented admiringly: "That god-damn Anastasia—he really done a job." Luciano would ever after remain convinced he had been responsible, especially given that later he was sprung from prison.

This preposterous narrative might be chalked up to what the intake psychiatrist at Sing Sing had deemed Luciano's "borderline intelligence," or perhaps the effects of having been confined to his own cell for fourteen to sixteen hours a day since he'd been sent up by Dewey in '36. In truth Luciano's recollections were just a badly garbled version of an equally bizarre reality.

By early February 1942, when the *Normandie* went down—with no help from Tony or Albert—the US had lost seventy-one merchant ships at sea since Pearl Harbor. In March, another fifty were sunk, six on one day alone (March 29), among them the *City of New York*, torpedoed by *U-160* off Cape Hatteras. As the toll mounted, and the pace accelerated, the Third Naval District (TND)'s Intelligence Office (aka B-3) struggled to understand the U-boats' success. Perhaps, they thought, Italian American Fifth Columnist longshoremen and fishermen were supplying the raiders with info and fuel; how else could they get word on their targets' whereabouts, and how could they travel such distances without aid? The former query was all too easy (and too embarrassing) to answer—U-boats didn't need to be tipped off, with the blazing coastline providing them a backlit shooting gallery. The second was also readily explicable, though the answer was top secret, hence unavailable. Top brass at the Chief of Naval Operations level knew from transcripts of deciphered German codes that Dönitz's improved model subs could reach New York from Lorient without refueling, hence they couldn't broadcast this information without alerting Germany their codes had been cracked.

Had TND officials known this, they might never have sent two intelligence officers to District Attorney Hogan's Leonard Street office on March 7 with a request to help enlist the Mob in garnering information from stonily uncooperative Italian longshoremen and fishermen. Hogan knew the underworld well, having been Dewey's deputy in the Luciano investigation. So did Assistant DA Murray Gurfein, head of the Rackets Bureau, who was investigating crime on the waterfront. They suggested contacting one of their targets, Joseph "Socks" Lanza, head of Local 16,975 of the United Seafood Workers Union. Better known as the boss of the Fulton Fish Market, Socks ran the "union" in classic fashion. From his office in the rundown Meyer's Hotel, he'd negotiate pay raises for members, take payoffs from employers to keep those raises modest, then demand kickbacks from the workers (and have them goon-stomped if they refused); he also threatened wholesalers with costly delays in loading or unloading hyper-perishable fish if they didn't come across with cash. Facing an extortion indictment and having no desire to repeat the two years he'd spent in stir (1937–39), Socks was prepared to cooperate. Besides, mobsters like Lanza had no love lost for Mussolini—Hitler's ally was the Mafia's foremost enemy—and many professed a patriotic love for their adopted country, which had given them so many opportunities.

A meeting was arranged between Lanza and Lieutenant Commander Charles Haffenden, who presided over B-3 as it swelled to 131 officers, enlisted men, and civilians, forcing a move to more spacious quarters in nearby 50 Church. The bluff and hearty Haffenden, who puffed on a Holmes-style pipe, enjoyed the cloak-and-dagger aspects of Operation Underworld, and so did Socks. They struck their initial deal in neutral territory—a park bench along Riverside Drive—then held regular clandestine conversations at a secret mezzanine office the Navy maintained in the Astor Hotel, or in fishier venues, like Meyer's Hotel (at South Street and Peck Slip) or Sweet's Restaurant (at South and Fulton).

Lanza was as good as his word. He gave Navy spooks union cards and work assignments on suspect fishing smacks. He himself canvassed crews along the docks about subversive activities. More broadly, Socks had vending machine collectors, numbers runners, and checkroom attendants report on suspicious conversations overheard around town. And he helped Haffenden get agents inside Downtown office buildings, to make after-hours surreptitious searches seeking evidence of espionage—aided by office cleaners, elevator operators, and porters, courtesy of Local 32B of the Building Service Employees Union.

Yet there were large and crucial areas where Lanza's writ did not run. The boss of the Fulton Fish Market had little influence over International Longshoremen's Association (ILA) overlords like Joe Ryan, or Johnny "Cockeye" Dunn on the Hudson docks, or the Camarda Brothers on the Brooklyn waterfront, much less potentates like Joe Adonis, a power in Brooklyn, or Frank Costello, who handled politics. Lanza told the Navy that getting broader cooperation would require bringing in the man who, though incarcerated, could still "snap the whip in the entire underworld."

South Street, near Peck Slip, October 1938. WPA Art Project Photograph by Sol Libsohn. (WPA FWP Collection, Municipal Archives)

Gurfein contacted Luciano's attorney, Moses Polakoff, a highly respected member of the Bar, who in turn set up a meeting at Longchamps Restaurant on West 58th Street between Racket Bureau chief Gurfein and racketeer chief Meyer Lansky. Jewish and stoutly antifascist, Lansky agreed to take time out from building his jukebox empire to make the link to Luciano. Polakoff arranged to get his client transferred from Siberia down to the far more convenient Great Meadow Prison, not far from Albany, and on May 15, Lansky and Luciano (to the latter's astonishment, having been given no clue of what was afoot) were allowed a private confab. Luciano signed on, and on June 4, Socks was brought up to receive Luciano's benediction: "I will have word out," said Lucky, "and you won't have no difficulties."

He was right. Doors swung open. Cockeye Dunn, for instance, began his own tête-à-têtes with Haffenden, and soon Navy personnel covered the waterfront. Dunn also had major clout in the hotel and restaurant trades, and soon an auxiliary army was at work in establishments throughout the city—waiters listening to table talk, bellboys eavesdropping on conversations in hotel lounges—to scout out fifth columnists and Nazi spies.

It would never be clear whether this Runyonesque collaboration had any effect whatever—though the Navy was grateful enough for services rendered to arrange a pardon for Luciano (from Governor Tom Dewey, no less). It certainly had no impact on the Battle of the Atlantic—which would respond only to quite different and far more powerful forces. Nor is there any evidence that it uncovered or thwarted efforts by Axis agents to disrupt the port. Indeed, when it came to dealing with the one known instance of a serious (if astonishingly incompetent) plot against the city and the nation, the gangsters were sitting on the sidelines.

90

Sabotage!

Shortly after midnight on the morning of June 13, 1942, just off the southern coast of Long Island, near Amagansett, the submarine *U-202* disgorged a quartet of Nazi saboteurs. The four men, dressed in German naval uniforms so they wouldn't be shot as spies if captured, were paddled to the beach on a rubber dinghy, under cover of a heavy fog, by two crewmen armed with submachine guns. Once ashore, they unloaded their supplies and began scrabbling in the sand, preparing to bury them.

Suddenly out of the fog appeared a twenty-one-year-old Coast Guardsman named John Cullen. He spotted George John Dasch, the group's leader, and asked who they were. Dasch responded: "We're fishermen from Southampton and ran aground here." Cullen offered to put them up at the Coast Guard Station, a mile down the beach, until the morning. Dasch was declining when one of the others came up and asked—in German—what was happening. Dasch hissed at him: "Shut up, you damn fool—go back to the boys and stay with them!" Dasch now offered Cullen $260 to forget he'd ever seen them. Armed with only a flashlight, Cullen accepted the cash, raced to his station, and returned with a patrol less than an hour later. The four had disappeared—having caught the Long Island Rail Road's 6:57 train to Manhattan (via Jamaica)—but a search of the beach soon uncovered four waterproof cases containing TNT, timing devices, detonators, German cigarettes, and four German uniforms (their owners having switched to civvies).

The saboteurs had been badly freaked by the incident at Amagansett and, fearing imminent arrest, went to ground in New York. None were hardened professionals. Most had been civilian workingmen, selected by the Abwehr largely because each had lived in the US and spoke fluent English. The New York four, with another team to be set ashore in Florida, had been given special training at a school for saboteurs near Berlin where they were taught to use explosives, drilled in American culture and customs, and given false life histories and fake documents. Then they were instructed to embark on a two-year cross-country campaign, blowing up bridges (including Hell Gate), railroad stations, power plants, waterworks (including New York's), Jewish-owned businesses, and, especially, aluminum plants (including one in Queens) in order to slow up American aircraft production.

Out on Long Island, the FBI hadn't a clue who they were after or where they'd gone. But at that very moment Dasch was crumpling under the strain. On June 15 he called the local FBI office, saying he'd just arrived from Germany, had vital information, and was coming to Washington to speak with J. Edgar Hoover; the call was filed with the day's other nutjob messages. Dasch did show up in DC and finally got them to listen to the story. Using his information, agents quickly rounded up the others, in Florida as well as New York.

On June 27, Hoover announced the arrests, deleting Dasch's part in them, leaving the distinct impression that the FBI, by dint of brilliant detective work, had stopped the Nazis before they could do any damage. Apart from displaying his usual concern for the Bureau's public relations, Hoover did not want the country to know how easily the conspirators had been landed, and how close they'd come to succeeding. Nor did he want the Nazis to know, lest they be encouraged to try again. Neither did Roosevelt, which was one reason that on July 2 the president authorized the prisoners be tried by a secret military tribunal, whose proceedings would be closed to press and public and whose decision would not be subject to judicial review. The military, moreover, could impose the death penalty, while a civilian court could only charge attempted sabotage (no act had been committed), and even that would be hard to make stick, as they hadn't even gotten around to trying. The only remaining civilian options were to accuse them of violating the customs laws (bringing in TNT without a license), illegal immigration, or conspiracy; none of which brought more than three years in prison.

One defense counsel, at considerable risk to his military career, challenged the president's authority to bypass civilian courts; on July 31, the nine justices of the Supreme Court refused to interfere with the Executive Branch during wartime. On August 3, all eight defendants were convicted and condemned to death; Dasch's sentence was reduced to thirty years, one of his confederates got life; and on August 8 the other six were electrocuted.

91

Aliens

In this period of high anxiety, with many New Yorkers feeling besieged from without and within, tensions were ratcheted higher still when a substantial number of residents were branded "enemy aliens." On December 8, 1941, invoking the Alien Enemy Act of 1798, FDR issued three identical presidential proclamations, assigning that status to Japanese, German, and Italian nationals. On January 15, 1942, all such aliens aged fourteen or older were ordered to register with federal authorities, even if they had already done so back in 1940, under the Smith Act. Of the 2,319 Japanese, 128,845 Germans, and 246,134 Italians covered by the proclamations who were living in New York State, roughly a quarter million—two-thirds—resided in Gotham.

Starting February 1, they began lining up at post offices to fill in a questionnaire about themselves and their overseas kin, hand in three photographs, and have their fingerprints taken. If found to be above suspicion, each would be sent a Certificate of Identification, which they had to carry at all times. In addition, their movements were proscribed—they could not cross state lines after 8:00 p.m., take long trips without permission, or possess cameras, flashlights, firearms, or radio communication equipment (receivers as well as transmitters). Being found with forbidden items was—like failure to register—punishable by internment for the duration of the war.

Soon a new and frightening possibility emerged—that aliens might be interned solely on grounds of their nationality. On February 19, Roosevelt signed Executive Order No. 9066, giving the War Department authority to designate military zones "from which any or all persons may be excluded." In February and March, as one Japanese victory followed another in the Pacific, and a Japanese submarine brazenly shelled a California oil refinery, rising rage and growing panic led to calls for excluding all Japanese from the continent's western coast. In April, orders were posted directing all of Japanese ancestry—aliens and US-born alike—to report to assembly points. Given only days to prepare, they were forced to sell their farms, businesses, homes, and cars—at tremendous loss—to eager and envious neighbors. By the beginning of June, over 120,000 people living in California, Oregon, and Washington, most of them citizens of the United States, had been evacuated and taken to barbed wire- and watchtower-ringed concentration camps.

If New York's Japanese could take comfort in not having been rounded up, they couldn't help but notice how enthusiastically key New Yorkers had supported locking up their kinfolk. Highly placed Wall Street Warriors presided over the enterprise, with Secretary of War Stimson uncritically accepting charges that Japanese were generically and genetically potential saboteurs. "Their racial characteristics are such that we cannot...trust even the citizen Japanese," Stimson argued, evidencing a habit of mind akin to that he'd displayed in dealing with Blacks in the military. His decision—executed with alacrity by his security-obsessed deputy John McCloy—was backed by FDR on February 12, 1942, qualified only by a suggestion that Stimson be "as reasonable as you can" with the Japanese Americans.

Roosevelt had been egged on, as well, by Gotham's Fighting Liberals. Walter Lippmann demanded internment of Issei and Nisei alike and even came up with a rebuttal to those who caviled that not a single Japanese had engaged in sabotage. Precisely, said Lippmann; such innocence proved their guilt. That they had not committed overt acts meant simply they were awaiting the occasion—a Japanese invasion—when their efforts would be more productive. The powerful pundit thus intensified the panic and gave cover to those like Lieutenant General John L. DeWitt, head of the Western Defense Command, who declared "that no sabotage has taken place to date is a disturbing and confirming indication that such action will be taken."

Others, like *PM*'s cartoonist, Theodor Seuss Geisel, stoked the fires of suspicion. The Massachusetts-born Geisel had been cartooning since he'd arrived in New York in 1927 after study at Dartmouth and Oxford. When one drawing—of a character using the bug spray Flit—caught the eye of an ad exec handling the account of Standard Oil, which manufactured Flit, Geisel found himself on the Esso payroll for the next seventeen years. This, plus other corporate advertising work, allowed him to ride out the Depression comfortably in a Park Avenue apartment and to begin publishing, as "Dr. Seuss," a series of children's books including *And to Think That I Saw it on Mulberry Street* (1937), *The 500 Hats of Bartholomew Cubbins* (1938), and *Horton Hatches the Egg* (1940). A strong antifascist, Geisel also crafted some cartoons excoriating Mussolini's regime. A friend who worked on *PM* showed them to Ingersoll, who ran one in January 1941, and soon Dr. Seuss cartoons were a regular feature, three or more per week. Before Pearl Harbor, Geisel focused on eviscerating anti-interventionists, lashing the likes of Lindbergh as "Enemies of Democracy." Afterward he switched his attention to enemies and aliens, with one cartoon—"Waiting for the Signal from Home"—depicting a long column of smiling Japanese lining up to collect TNT at a house labeled "Honorable 5th Column."

When internment got rolling, some New York liberals did protest. Norman Thomas, seeing it as a harbinger of the fascism he'd long feared would be ushered in by war, penned an open letter condemning the practice; W.E.B. Du Bois was among the signers. Many individuals, groups, and journals committed to fighting discrimination, from Mayor La Guardia to the NAACP to the Communist Party to the American Jewish Committee, either remained silent about internment or defended it, with La Guardia particularly wholehearted in his advocacy. The ACLU did deplore the "invasion of the liberties of American citizens on the basis of racial origin," yet it voted 2–1 against challenging its legality; ACLU head Roger Baldwin, in the minority, remained a very public dissenter.

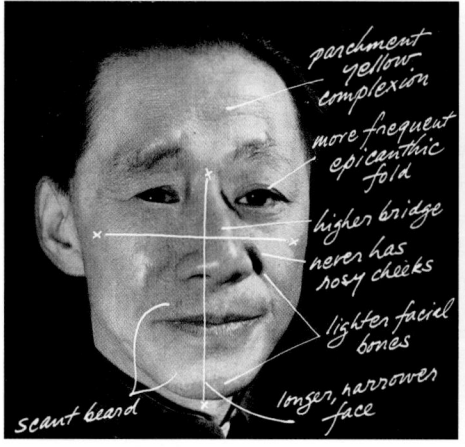 

"How to Tell Japs From the Chinese," *Life* magazine, December 22, 1941. (Carl Mydans/The LIFE Picture Collection/Shutterstock)

While much of the anti-Japanese animosity was a response to being attacked, some was rooted in residual racism, as long-standing anxieties about the Yellow Peril enjoyed a resurgence after Pearl Harbor. A poster depicting a lustful Japanese soldier carrying off a naked white woman was among the thousands submitted to a "This Is the Enemy" contest, organized in 1942 by Artists for Victory; it was selected to be one of 200 displayed in a MOMA exhibition that autumn, and singled out again for reproduction in *Life*'s December 21, 1942, photo spread on the event. Though Nazis were depicted as nasty pieces of work, Japanese were routinely portrayed in a simian subhuman manner, all fangs and claws.

Yet anyone tempted to wallow in anti-Asian racism quickly ran up against the ongoing and widespread support in the city for the cause of the Chinese. Indeed, careful efforts at ethnic differentiation began almost immediately. On December 22, 1941, *Life* ran a "How to tell Japs from the Chinese" article, which while acknowledging the Boasian debunking of "race myths," nevertheless microanalyzed two male facial photos, pointing out the "anthropometric conformations" that could help readers distinguish "friendly Chinese" from "alien Japs." Gotham's Chinese themselves took pains to distance themselves from the Japanese: beginning December 17, 1941, New York's Chinese Consolidated Benevolent Association (CCBA) distributed buttons to Chinese nationals and Chinese Americans bearing the crossed flags of China and the US. Some opted for handwritten notes tacked to their jackets reading: "NOT JAPANESE PLEASE."

The fate they were seeking to avoid was the one visited on New York's tiny Japanese community—estimated as numbering around 1,500. Wholesale arrests weren't the issue, though the initial roundup after Pearl Harbor had seemed indiscriminate, netting not only plausible espionage suspects but also the likes of Dr. Sabro Emy, who had come to Gotham in 1906, fought in the First World War, gotten his medical degree from Bellevue in 1922, and opened a practice on Park Avenue—from where he was arrested, only to be eventually released, uncharged. Nor was vigilante violence a concern: New Yorkers heeded Attorney General Biddle and J. Edgar Hoover's insistence that citizens not take "direct action" against noncitizens (though Robert Moses did wreak some symbolic mayhem in ordering the demolition of the Japanese Pavilion in Flushing Meadow Park, given to Gotham by the City

A spread from *Life* magazine of the posters on display at the National War Posters exhibition at the Museum of Modern Art, 1942. (LIFE Magazine; Patti McConville/Alamy Stock Photo)

of Tokyo as a "monument for peace and goodwill"). Nor were local Japanese subjected to Western-style relocation, partly because they constituted such a tiny sliver of the population and owned nothing that others coveted.

Nevertheless, life became very difficult for that sliver. Other New Yorkers made very clear how unwelcome the Japanese were, starting with Mayor La Guardia, who warned them to stay off the streets and subways. Those in business were soon bankrupt, those with jobs soon fired. Most were reduced to dependence on religious charities. A Church Committee for Japanese Work was constituted in March 1942 by Presbyterian, Episcopalian, Methodist, Quaker, Reformed, Baptist, and Buddhist clergymen; in April 1942, one minister found "almost total unemployment" among the city's Japanese.

The little community—overwhelmingly horrified by Pearl Harbor and the subsequent war—struggled to prove its loyalty. A Japanese American Committee for Democracy (with 300 members in the spring of 1942) sponsored victory rallies, organized blood donor units, raised money for the National War Fund, and denounced Japanese atrocities (while also protesting internment). None of this mitigated their plight a whit.

Gotham's Germans and Italians, meanwhile, faced their own forms of discrimination, though mass internment was never in the cards. There were far too many Euro-aliens, and they were far too white: it would have been a logistical and political nightmare. Most of the country's 264,000 German and 599,000 Italian nationals had children who were US citizens. These could, and did, petition their representatives, who in turn bombarded FDR's office with complaints about the terrible effect the threat of internment was having on the morale of their—and his—constituents. The president ordered Secretary Stimson to take no action against Italian or German aliens on the East Coast without his express and prior approval. Then, on April 26, 1942, just as internment was getting into gear in General DeWitt's Western Defense Command, General Drum declared flatly that in his Eastern Defense Command "mass evacuation is not contemplated." Anyone who gave aid and comfort to the enemy—be they aliens or disloyal citizens—would be dealt with, Drum made clear, on a case-by-case basis only.

There proved to be many such cases. The first year of war brought repeated raids and dragnets in New York, overwhelmingly in German areas. Though the German American Bund officially dissolved itself the day after Pearl Harbor, the FBI raided its headquarters on December 11, seized its records, and proceeded in coming months to arrest, indict, and convict its former officials. Charged with conspiracy to violate the Selective Service Act by supposedly counseling German youth to resist the draft, Bundists were incarcerated in Fort Lincoln, North Dakota—from which they would be released, in 1945, when the Supreme Court overturned their convictions.

Other crackdowns followed, sometimes based on tips, sometimes on a random basis—like the March 4, 1942, raids, on 350 locations, which netted thirty-three aliens (thirty Germans, three Italians) along with contraband material. By that point, 675 people had been taken into custody in New York—317 Japanese, 262 Germans, and 96 Italians. This represented about one-tenth the US total: as of March 18, 1942, the national count stood at 6,731, including 3,935 Japanese, 2,026 Germans, and 770 Italians; of the first 2,000 whose cases were reviewed, about half were put in camps for the duration.

Dragnets continued, even expanded in scope, during the succeeding high-tension, sub-menaced months. On April 11, 1942, eighty-five simultaneous raids in Yorkville and parts of Brooklyn led to the arrest of sixty-four members of the Kyffhaeuser Bund, an officially dissolved German war veterans' group, whose members—butchers, machine tool operators, musicians, mechanics, waiters, janitors, and truckers—the FBI charged, none too convincingly, with plotting at surreptitious meetings in bowling alleys and restaurants to disseminate Nazi propaganda. Another round of raids followed the June capture of the real Nazi saboteurs. On July 11, 158 people were seized in their homes in Brooklyn, Queens, Nassau, and Suffolk. They were mostly members of the German American Vocational League (headquartered on East 86th Street), a group linked—it was tenuously claimed—to one of the Amagansett Four. They were, however, undeniably pro-Nazi, and possessed cameras, shortwave receivers, and home movies of themselves doing rifle practice.

On July 23, twenty-nine assorted philo-fascists around the country were indicted for sedition and for plotting to impair the loyalty, morale, and discipline of the armed forces. Behind these grand charges lay small beer particulars: the defendants were accused of "personal vilification and defamation" of public officials; of asserting that the United States "was safe from attack"; and of making boilerplate suggestions that the war was being fought for the benefit of "International Jewry-organized finance" and "British-American capitalists." The case limped along, unable to prove treasonable connections, until it finally collapsed. By 1943, when the crackdown campaign ran out of steam, the number arrested since Pearl Harbor, in New York alone, had mounted to 1,800.

The government waged war on presses as well as persons. As early as January 1942, referring to right-wing vehicles, Roosevelt wrote J. Edgar Hoover that it "looks like a good chance to clean up a number of these vile publications." Father Coughlin's *Social Justice*—in Roosevelt's cross hairs for years—was an early target. In April 1942, Attorney General Biddle, as bidden, ordered a federal grand jury investigation of the paper's allegedly pro-Axis propaganda; three weeks later, the US Post Office suspended its second-class mailing privileges; and the real coup de grâce was given by the Archbishop of Detroit, who finally forbade his priests from having any ties with *Social Justice*, or any other publication. Domenico Trombetta, another long-pricking thorn, shut down his weekly *Il Grido Della Stirpe* a week after Pearl, though it didn't stop the government from interning him as a dangerous enemy alien, winning a denaturalization case against him in September 1942 and later indicting him for failure to register as an agent of the Italian government. And among the group accused of sedition in July 1942 was William Griffin, professional Irishman, Tammanyite, and publisher of the city's only Sunday afternoon paper, the *New York Enquirer*, which he'd launched in 1926; Griffin had long been wildly anti–New Deal, wildly pro-Hearst, and wildly anti-intervention (he'd boomed Ham Fish for president). Roosevelt even suggested to Biddle (in May 1942) that some editorials in the *New York Daily News* might be actionably seditious, but no prosecution ensued—the president stuck to marginal presses—and FDR settled (that December) for presenting John O'Donnell, the paper's Washington bureau chief (who despised Roosevelt and the New Deal), with a mock Iron Cross for services rendered to Hitler.

While a few of the over 100 publications suppressed in 1942 were of the left, like the Trotskyist Socialist Workers Party's *The Militant*, and two—the *Police Gazette* and *Esquire*—were banned in the name of morality, most were from the far right, a provenance that helps explain why New York liberals hailed their suppression. They were integral parts of the "fascist offensive," thundered *Nation* editor Freda Kirchwey, and they "should be exterminated exactly as if they were enemy-machine-gun nests in the Bataan jungle." The *New Republic* agreed that "muzzling the fascists" was "wise and proper," and Reinhold Niebuhr argued that "freedom of speech should be withheld from those political groups which intend to destroy liberty." Norman Thomas again stood against the current—denouncing liberals for betraying their principles and suggesting that the next knock in the night might be upon their door. "In the inevitable post war reaction," Thomas warned Kirchwey, "the principles you seem to advocate...will be turned with a vengeance against *The Nation* and every other liberal paper or person."

The federal government and private organizations monitored the airwaves as well as print-and-ink media. The Justice Department, the Office of War Information, the Office of

Radio Research, and various refugee groups all tuned in to stations featuring foreign-language programming—notably New York's WBNX, WOV, and WHOM. Word of any on-air philo-fascist leanings was relayed to the Federal Communications Commission (which threatened to suspend licenses) and to advertisers (who threatened to stop underwriting) unless particular broadcasters or programs were removed from the air. Some stations preemptively began prohibiting any use of "enemy" languages, no matter how innocuous.

Ethnic groups responded to all this surveillance with repeated affirmations of loyalty. On March 1, 1942, sixty German American organizations gathered at Webster Hall on East 11th Street and pledged their allegiance. German New Yorkers participated in bond drives and provided air raid wardens. The *Staats-Zeitung* called for an Allied victory. Still, pockets of sullen resistance could be detected in Yorkville and other neighborhoods, one reason, perhaps, they were subjected to repeat raiding.

The Irish, though not enemy aliens, remained under a cloud for their prewar anti-interventionism, which the community's leadership now sought to dissipate by fervent recantations. After Pearl, the *Gaelic American*, the *Tablet*, and the *Irish World* pledged their support to FDR, as did the Catholic bishops (and even Father Curran). Fordham's president, the Rev. Robert I. Gannon, repudiated his former resistance, saying: "It is humiliating, but many of us are ready to stand up and confess that we were wrong and [the President] was right. It was our war from the first." Despite this, unrepentant Christian Frontism simmered in several Irish working-class neighborhoods.

The Italian response was more complex. For all its former flirtation with Mussolini, the community was horrified by Italy's declaring war on the US. Within days of Pearl Harbor, local *prominenti* burned their Fascist Party membership cards, severed ties with suspect clubs and lodges, and began returning the medals and decorations heaped upon them by Mussolini's government. On Mulberry Street, storefronts replaced Il Duce's portrait with that of FDR. Other shops and clubs, sensing a need to demonstrate linguistic loyalty, placed signs in their windows declaring "No Italian Spoken for the Duration of the War."

Italian New Yorkers also deeply resented the stigma of being labeled enemy aliens (or children thereof). They resented the presumption of disloyalty, the humiliating accommodations they had to make, and the unjust detentions—which, though far fewer in number than those suffered by the Germans, could be equally capricious. When opera singer Ezio Pinza was seized on March 12, confined on Ellis for three months, and threatened with duration detention without being told the charges against him, pressure from fans won his release. The community complained, too, as had the city's African Americans, of discrimination in defense plant hiring, where contractors often barred not only Italian aliens but Americans with Italian names.

Italians set out to regain full incorporation in the body politic. In doing so they had significant political and cultural assets. Powerful figures like Congressman Marcantonio spoke up for the community, and La Guardia, already a nationally known superpatriot, underscored the difference between Italian Americans and Italian fascists when in 1942 he began beaming a weekly shortwave program—"Mayor La Guardia Calling Rome"—dedicated to blasting Mussolini. The community could draw, as well, on the cultural potency of superstar Joe DiMaggio, to whom the hero-hungry nation had turned its eyes in the summer of 1941, when he had hit successfully in fifty-six straight games. Joltin' Joe's streak not only established a new record in a mad-for-statistics sport, but his exhibition of skill and grace under pressure, at a time when the world was descending into chaos, drew applause from all but the most die-hard of anti-dago bigots. After Pearl, his status as the "Yankee

Clipper" was sorely tested when he refused to enlist—as a married father he was exempt from the draft. As a result, he was jeered on the field during the 1942 season—batting .258 didn't help—and received letters asking, "Why didn't he go back to Italy with the rest of the coward wops?" DiMaggio, and his countrymen, were restored to fandom's good graces when he (reluctantly) signed up in February 1943.

Italian Gotham's collective clout rested on even sturdier foundations, notably their proven ability to raise money and mobilize votes. By early 1942, *prominenti* like Generoso Pope, so recently in bad odor, had become a decided asset to the Treasury, raising cash for war bonds as he had once raised money for Mussolini. On the political front, Governor Lehman wrote Roosevelt in March 1942 pointing out that the gubernatorial election was coming up, and that Democratic success against Tom Dewey (the certain Republican candidate) might well hinge on regaining the affection of alienated ethnic voters. Roosevelt well recalled the massive Italian defections from the Democratic camp in 1940 and was only too aware that a 1942 victory in New York would put Dewey in a strong position to challenge him in 1944. Accordingly, FDR decided on a dramatic peace offering. On Columbus Day, October 12, 1942, three weeks before the elections, Attorney General Biddle announced that henceforth resident Italian citizens would no longer be classified as "aliens of enemy nationality"—an offer pointedly not extended to the Germans, much less the Japanese.

The old *prominenti*—Pope foremost among them—were now welcomed into the all-American fold, even by such former opponents as Luigi Antonini of the ILGWU and Congressman Vito Marcantonio. Nonetheless, one obstacle still remained to their complete rehabilitation. Anti-Fascist Italian refugees like Max Ascoli, president of the Mazzini Society, had developed strong influence and connections in Washington, and some liberals in the Administration had backed their efforts to oust conservative (and recently pro-Fascist) *prominenti* from leadership positions in the Italian community. That support waned when it became clear that Roosevelt was prepared to deal with Pope and that the Italian American masses—deeply suspicious of having refugees imposed on them—preferred to stick with established leaders.

One figure, however—the well-liked Carlo Tresca, editor of *Il Martello*—had for over a decade been hammering away at Pope's connections to Mussolini and to local mafiosi as well, and he refused to accept the new detente. On September 10, 1942, Tresca was invited to an Italian American War Bond banquet at the Manhattan Club and came only when assured that Pope would not be in attendance. In fact, Pope showed up, accompanied by his bodyguard and factotum Frank Garofalo, a ranking Mafia man, with close ties to Luciano, who had physically threatened Tresca and other anti-Pope-ists back in the 1930s. An indignant Tresca loudly denounced the "the fascist Pope" and "his gangster" Garofalo and stormed out after a verbal altercation with the latter.

Four months later, at 9:40 p.m. on January 11, 1943, Tresca emerged from the *Martello*'s 96 Fifth Avenue office, through the side door on 15th Street, attired as usual in his signature big black hat and flowing cloak, when a dark sedan pulled up at the curb. A man jumped out, pumped three bullets into Tresca's head at close range, then sped off, leaving the editor slumped in the gutter; he was pronounced dead on arrival at nearby St. Vincent's hospital. A major manhunt ensued—Tresca being a friend of La Guardia's among many others—and mobster Carmine Galante was soon captured. Though he was almost certainly the triggerman, the case couldn't be proved, and after being held eight months, Galante was released. Nor was the person who ordered the hit ever uncovered, though Garafolo—Galante's superior in the Bonnano family—was always the prime suspect. Nor was it ever possible to connect

Pope with the assassination, and though he probably rejoiced at the death of his old enemy, it was never clear why he would have chosen this moment to order an execution.

In any event, the Italian community was rehabilitated, and Pope was back on top—he would serve as Grand Marshal of the Columbus Day celebrations in October 1943. And so were the underworld *prominenti*—especially when their recently established alliance with the US Navy was further strengthened by their role in the 1943 invasion of Sicily. Not being in possession of detailed information about the planned landing site and adjacent interior, the Office of Naval Intelligence again turned to Luciano & company. In this case, the imprisoned *capo* got Joe Adonis on the case, who, to Commander Haffenden's delight, began shepherding recent Sicilian immigrants to 90 Church Street, bearing photographs, postcards, letters, and documents—mementos of their respective hometowns. These items, when affixed to a plastic overlay of a huge map of Italy, collectively constituted a helpful micro-guide to those planning the successful landings of July 10.

92

Dissenters

Of the once-mighty antiwar movement almost nothing remained. "We are still pacifists," wrote Dorothy Day in the first post–Pearl Harbor issue of the *Catholic Worker* (January 7, 1942), and "we will try to be peacemakers." She and her followers "love our country and we love our President," Day declared, but "we will not participate in armed warfare or in making munitions, or by buying government bonds to prosecute the war, or in urging others to these efforts." As Day would acknowledge, however, a good 80 percent of her troops refused to follow her in this commitment. By the end of 1942, half the Catholic Worker Houses had closed, and the paper's circulation had tumbled into free fall (it would dive from 130,000 copies a month in 1939 to 50,500 in 1944). Even cofounder Peter Maurin thought silence better than opposition, and by 1943 Day herself had throttled back, staying away from the *CW* offices for months at a time (even taking an official leave of absence), and spending time on retreats. The FBI tracked her movements as a suspected subversive but basically left her alone, probably because she was still under Spellman's protection and her movement was in obvious decline.

Some pacifist organizations did grow stronger during the war years—the membership of A. J. Muste's Fellowship of Reconciliation (FOR) and Jesse Hughan's War Resisters League (WRL) actually swelled—though they did so by maintaining their commitment to absolute pacifism while refraining from challenging the war frontally. Instead, they concentrated on working with Conscientious Objectors (COs) and on overseeing the 150 Civilian Public Service (CPS) camps that had been set up under the Selective Service Act as places where drafted COs could do "work of national importance under civilian direction." Increasingly, however, numerous COs found themselves sequestered in Civilian Conservation Corps–style camps in rural areas, doing nothing whatever of "national importance," and doing it under de facto military authority. Deciding they had been coopted into the "war machine," thousands decided to opt out, sometimes simply walking away from the camps, sometimes engaging in direct civil disobedience, knowing in either case they were opting for jail.

Bayard Rustin was one of them. In 1940 he had been granted CO status by his Harlem draft board, chiefly because he was a Quaker. Rustin spent the early war years traveling around the country on Muste's behalf, organizing for FOR, holding workshops on Gandhian nonviolent direct action, visiting the CPS camps, and interceding on behalf of Japanese American families. In November 1943, he was told by his draft board to report for assignment to a camp. He decided to refuse—not without qualms, as the likely fate of a Black, gay war resister in a heartland prison was not pretty to contemplate. He did so partly because John Haynes Holmes—the still staunchly antiwar preacher of New York's Community Church—had convincingly argued that CO status should not be reserved for religious war objectors but also awarded to secular war opponents. So Rustin rejected his own privilege, refused cooperation, and was arrested (in January 1944). Pleading guilty, he received a three-year term—higher than the conventional year-and-a-day sentence, probably because of his public agitation against war. His first ten days were spent in West Street Jail—the Federal House of Detention at West and Eleventh Streets—which shortly before his arrival had hosted a celebrated confabulation between Lepke Buchalter, then awaiting execution, and several war resisters, including the fledgling poet Robert Lowell, in which the Murder, Incorporated capo first learned, and found hilarious, that people could be jailed for *not* killing.

As in all Federal prisons, West Street's inmate facilities were segregated. Rustin refused to sit at a designated Negro table in the dining hall. He was promptly thrown into solitary and branded a "troublemaker" by authorities. Rustin continued making trouble—demanding desegregation—at the penitentiary in Ashland, Kentucky, where he teamed up with the many civil disobedience–oriented COs then flocking from camps to jails.

Ashland was home, as well, to a large number of Jehovah's Witnesses, whose adherents refused to serve in the military, or buy war bonds, or salute the flag, or vote. While not strictly speaking pacifists, members of the Brooklyn-headquartered Watchtower Bible and Tract Society (122–124 Columbia Heights) considered themselves soldiers in the army of Jehovah, hence unable to give allegiance to a civil power as that would mean exalting the State over God. Perhaps 75 percent of those jailed nationally for refusing war service were Witnesses. Already widely reviled for their opposition to the war—and for their vitriolic attacks on other clerics ("scum" and "harlot" were among the milder brickbats hurled at theological rivals, especially Catholics, by their leader J. F. Rutherford)—Witnesses won additional enemies by not letting their children recite the Pledge of Allegiance at school. After a 1940 Supreme Court decision ruled that school boards could expel such recalcitrants, Witnesses were subjected to a wave of hysterical and often violent attacks (by American Legionnaires and others)—the persecution was nothing compared to what they received at Nazi hands—until the high court reversed itself in 1943.

For all Holmes's and Rustin's arguments, strictly secular opposition to the war was all but nonexistent. The shriveled Socialist Party, which had lost so many followers for its stand *against* intervention, now lost others (of the few remaining) who thought Norman Thomas had sold out when he offered "critical support" to the war effort after Pearl Harbor. In early 1942, Thomas liquidated the Keep America Out of War Congress—the America First Committee (AFC) had similarly dismantled itself—and immediately established a Post War World Council, with the same chairperson (himself) in the same office (112 East 19th Street), adding only some noted pacifists like Holmes and Muste. While Thomas backed the war, he hoped to mitigate its negative domestic consequences by striving to protect civil liberties (most notably those of the interned Japanese) and to ensure that economic burdens were distributed equitably. Thomas also struggled to broaden the war's overseas goals. He tried to keep the anti-imperialist perspective alive by underscoring the gap between FDR's promotion of Four-Freedom democracy while acquiescing in the imperial ambitions of English,

Russian, and French allies. Thomas fought to keep the fate of Algerians and Indochinese on the table, and he supported the independence struggle of the India League of America, led in New York by Jagjit Singh, a Sikh importer with a store on East 56th Street.

Though long on moral authority, Thomas was short on followers, a situation George Wilfried Hartmann set out to correct. Hartmann, a Teachers College professor and the Socialist Party's candidate for mayor of New York City in 1941, was director of the Jane Addams Peace School, which had been set up to train peace workers at the Labor Temple on 14th Street and Second Avenue. Though a Methodist with Quaker leanings, Hartmann wanted to establish a secular pacifist operation, and in 1943 he and others created Peace Now. Focused on war aims, Peace Now proposed that in the interest of gaining a lasting settlement, the US should abandon unconditional surrender (which would only lead to another Versailles Treaty disaster) and instead seek a negotiated peace. He also urged the British to renounce their prewar empire; and the Russians to assure Eastern Europeans that Soviet troops would be withdrawn at war's end. A Carnegie Hall rally endorsed this sweeping but breathtakingly naive program on December 30, 1943, after which a perfect storm of criticism broke over him. The religious pacifists refused to support a purely secular initiative (and condemned Hartmann for having hired some dubious staff people, including a suspected Nazi plant and some former America Firsters). The press lobbed vicious and unfounded attacks on his patriotism with ecumenical ardor—Hartmann had the distinction of being pilloried by the *Post* and *PM*, *The New Republic* and *The Nation*, Walter Winchell, *Life* magazine, and the Communist Party. The Dies Committee invaded his office in February 1944 but failed to find the slightest hint of Nazi connections. After this onslaught, Peace Now managed one more public meeting, then collapsed. The policy of unconditional surrender would henceforth go virtually uncontested.

The last redoubt of doubt lay on the outer margins of the anti-Stalinist left, though even here there were defections. The January 1942 issue of *Partisan Review*, the first published after Pearl Harbor, informed readers that its editors were divided on the war. Philip Rahv and William Phillips were moving toward offering "critical support," while Dwight Macdonald, at the editorial helm, hewed to his antiwar course. Macdonald dismissed the Four Freedoms as hypocritical propaganda, mere rhetorical cover for a war stripped of political purpose. The administration had, he charged, acquiesced in enormous profits for big business, frozen wages and instituted regressive taxes, accepted repression of Gandhi's liberation movement, and segregation in the military. In February, spurred by calls to take Randolph Bourne's boldness as his model—calls made most vigorously by Trotskyist Irving Howe, an antiwar firebrand and recent City College graduate—Macdonald solicited a bold antiwar manifesto for the July–August issue from the anarcho-pacifist writer Paul Goodman. Goodman sent in a Bournean blast that urged intellectuals and artists to refuse to register for the draft and to commit other acts of antiwar civil disobedience. Phillips and Rahv wanted the piece spiked, in part because they feared the government would shut down *PR* as it was then shuttering scores of other publications, but mainly because they were now prepared to break completely from what they saw as Macdonald's utopian and "morally absolutist" position (Sidney Hook called it "infantile leftist"). They would back the Allied war effort, for all its admitted imperfections, because the bottom line was this: if Hitler won, democratic socialism had no future; if he was defeated, it might yet have a chance.

93

"As Dark as Hitler's Heart"

By the late spring of 1942, the city was beginning to breathe easier. Not that the submarine menace had slackened. Quite the opposite: the toll in ships sunk and lives lost had grown steadily greater as German shipyards turned out newer, bigger, and better behemoths and javelined them into action. In January there had been a daily average of nineteen U-boats working the western Atlantic; in February there had been twenty-eight; by June there were forty. But Gotham had greatly improved its capability of responding to assault by sea or air. And the participation of an enormous number of its citizens in an astonishingly comprehensive defense system—the most highly organized in the United States—itself had a calming effect.

To begin with, an elaborate network had been set in place for alerting the city to an impending attack (with state-of-the-art assistance from the Technical Communications Group for the City of New York, organized by media magnate David Sarnoff). Should the Army Information Center get word of incoming hostiles, it would inform the Bureau of War Operations of the New York Police Department (NYPD), using dedicated phone lines. NYPD headquarters would then relay the alert by a teletypewriter network to Fire Department Headquarters (which would pass on the word by telegraph to all firehouses), and to all police station houses (which would in turn notify patrol cars via radio and contact nearby schools, hospitals, public utilities, and defense plants by means of a push-button-activated wire network furnished by the telephone company).

At the same time, the alert would be passed down another chain of command, from the New York City Control Center, to the Borough Control Centers, to the 71 local Report Centers (located in precinct houses), each of which in turn would call the local Warden Zone headquarters, whose staff would then alert individual wardens by ringing their doorbells. There were a lot of bells to ring. At its peak in September 1943, the Air Warden Service contained approximately 290,000 volunteers, but the high and constant turnover brought total enrollment over the war's duration to about 400,000, 80 percent of them men. To mechanize the training process, still-scarce television sets were rounded up and, with NBC's cooperation, installed in each station house, where each new crop of volunteers would watch civil defense training films that incorporated footage of Luftwaffe raids over England.

Finally, the public at large was alerted, via 454 dedicated air raid sirens installed on the roofs of station houses, firehouses, El stations, and tall buildings (one was perched atop the RCA tower), each activated from local police and fire houses. After the initial Rube Goldberg system deploying police cars and fire trucks had failed so signally, Bell Labs had been brought in to design an alternative. Their new Victory Siren was first tested (on March 4, 1942) from the Manhattan Bridge and declared a success when its piercing wails were easily heard below Canal Street. By November an improved version, rated the loudest howler in the world, could be heard over nine square miles in residential areas.

On hearing an alert, the now-better-instructed citizenry knew they were stay off the streets. There'd been a debate about sending people into the subways, where Londoners went, but New York's cut-and-cover system was deemed too shallow to withstand bombing, and the idea was dropped. Schoolchildren, too, would now be kept indoors, crouched in corridors, attended by teachers, 6,500 of whom were trained in first aid. By July, at the initiative of the School Defense Council (which included public, private, and parochial systems), 1,600,000 children had been given 3.5-inch-long stainless-steel identification tags to wear around their neck, each embossed with their name, date of birth, school district, and assigned serial number.

In the event of an alert, moreover, the city was now capable of turning off its lights, though the learning curve had been excruciatingly lengthy, and, in the end, it had required a mighty nudge from the military to make them switch off. La Guardia's initial strategy had been to leave the lights blazing and to practice shuttering them on a street-by-street, then area-by-area basis. The first "dim-outs" of streetlamps came on January 5, 1942, along stretches of Fifth and Eighth Avenues in Manhattan and Union Turnpike in Queens, as wardens walked about turning off most lamps in mid-block and two at each intersection—a laborious business that required unscrewing each pole's metal plate. Next, on January 28, just before 8:00 p.m., all street and apartment lights got doused along the entire south side of 86th Street between Central Park West and Riverside Drive. On hearing a test signal broadcast over WMCA, wardens directed autos to pull over to the curbs and hurried pedestrians into hallways. Whenever they spotted a still-illuminated window, wardens entered the offending building, loudly blowing their whistles. (In those early days, they had to provide their own dime-store whistles, which, embarrassingly, often bore the legend "Made in Japan.")

From blacking out blocks the city proceeded to darkening whole areas. Each test began at 9:00 p.m. and lasted twenty minutes. The first took place on March 19, 1942, along the twelve-mile strip of coastline bordering the Atlantic—from Seagate at the western end of Coney Island, to the Nassau County border at Far Rockaway—past which *U-Boat 123* had cruised just two months before. Four days later it was all of Staten Island's turn, followed two days later by all of Lower Manhattan (everything south of 14th Street). On April 9, the upper four-fifths of the Bronx, an area home to 885,000 residents (including the prisoners on Rikers Island), went dark for the prescribed twenty minutes. On April 13, a 54-square-mile chunk of Brooklyn followed suit, its de-illumination overseen by 57,663 wardens. Subways continued to run, with their entryway and car lights dimmed, making it impossible to read while traveling. On the darkened streets above the only thing lighted that moved was La Guardia's improvised Mayormobile—a black coupe, with faintly phosphorescent front and rear bumpers, crowned by a taxi-type sign reading: MAYOR.

Commercial centers for whom lighting was lifeblood—Times Square, Coney Island—kept their illumination going full blast but developed specialized strategies for rapid reaction shutdowns. Each Times Square spectacular kept an electrician on duty, ready to pull the requisite switches, while Broadway theater union men were deputed to extinguish marquee names-in-lights. Local businessmen claimed the Square could be blacked out in five minutes flat. At Coney—visited during 1941 by 50 million people—Luna and Steeplechase Parks installed central switches that could be pulled in case of raid. The iconic Statue of Liberty, by contrast, went into 24/7 dimout, shutting off the powerful electric lamps in the Lady's torch and the floodlights on her garments, leaving only a couple of 200-watt bulbs aloft as a marker for domestic pilots.

Andreas Feininger, *Times Square*. Gelatin silver print. (Collection of University Art Museum, University at Albany, State University of New York on behalf of The University at Albany Foundation, gift of Marvin and Carol Brown. Copyright © Andreas Feininger)

On April 1, La Guardia swore that if an attack came, the "city will be as dark as Hitler's heart."

This was all fine and well, yet it did absolutely nothing to address the fundamental problem, which was that, in the here and now, the city's undimmed lights, left to blaze all night, were creating a mammoth dome of light, whose glow, bounced off low-drifting clouds, could be plainly seen 10 to 30 miles out to sea—out where the U-boats gathered, in growing numbers, to sink the hapless vessels so starkly outlined against this urban luminescence, taking their crews with them to the bottom.

Finally, the military had had enough. On April 26, 1942, General Drum announced the Army was taking control of the city's lights to "prevent the silhouetting of ships." Henceforth every light in New York 15 or more stories above the ground was to be shut off or shaded after dark. (This set off a rush to buy blackout materials—the sateen and pyroxylin coated cloths that farsighted manufacturers had introduced at the New York Curtain and Drapery Show in January, along with the transverse tracks that permitted a complete overlapping of draperies, and a "blackout glue" for affixing heavy paper to windows, which equally entrepreneurial hardware companies had swiftly brought to market.) Streets and parkways along the coast were to be permanently dimmed down, to the degree compatible with safe driving. Exterior lights along the shoreline—boardwalks, places of amusement, hotels, and commercial establishments—were to be completely extinguished between sundown and sunup: Coney Island had gone dark for the duration.

So did Times Square, when the dimout was extended to include its signage. On April 29, at 10:30 p.m., the great spectaculars were lowered 95 percent or switched off altogether, and

Headlights illuminate Broadway during a brownout, November 1, 1943. (Photo by Fox Photos/Getty Images)

theater marquees were limited to under-canopy lighting (though the *Times* "zipper" was allowed to continue its rounds). Spectacle-meister Douglas Leigh said the Square had offed 265,000 bulbs and 65 miles of neon, wiping out 8,582,200 watts of luminescence. Leigh, despite having switched off all sixteen of his signs, was the blackout's big winner, because while he and his competitors had been equally erased from the nightscape, Leigh had taken virtually sole possession of the daytime scene. In June 1941 he had erected the only sunshine-oriented, unilluminated spectacular on Broadway, which now became its premier sign. An ad for Camel cigarettes, mounted on a billboard on the Claridge Hotel (between 43rd and 44th Streets), it featured a man who puffed perfect smoke rings—steam rings—out of a two-foot-wide circular opening in his lips, emitting one every four seconds. Its success at gathering crowds was boosted by Leigh's putting his smoker in uniform, with the original soldier alternating, at four-month intervals, with a sailor, marine, and airman.

With Broadway now the Great Dim Way, and Gotham drained of most of its incandescence, the city moved on to practicing total blackouts. On June 5, New York held its first five-borough, citywide test, which Mayor La Guardia reviewed from the tippy top of the Empire State Building, where he was thrilled to see the great grid of lights snuffed out with startling speed and efficiency, in districts slum and posh, leaving only some ruby glows from a few drill-exempt defense plants, notably the Navy Yard. Thousands lined the Jersey Palisades to marvel at the sight of giant Gotham winking out.

As the city, by June, had mastered the art of obscuring itself in case of enemy attack, so, too, had it organized to deal with the consequences of an enemy getting through its defenses.

Camel Cigarettes billboard on the Claridge Hotel, Times Square, c. 1944. (Photo by Anthony Potter Collection/Getty Images)

In essence, first responders would send information rolling backward up the great chain of communications that had earlier funneled a warning down to the street. In the event of bomb damage, wardens close to the scene would head to the nearest phone, either in their sector headquarters (where 1,560 coin phones had been installed for the duration), or to one of the over 4,500 phones at auxiliary communication points, usually situated in the lobbies of office buildings, restaurants, garages, and residences. From there the warden would call in a situation assessment to the nearest Report Center, which would in turn pass the word up to its Borough Control Center, where the emergency response commands (Police, Fire, Public Works, Medical, and Welfare) each maintained an office, stocked with the "latest scientific canned foods." While Control Center personnel charted incidents on a borough-wide map and forwarded a situational overview to the citywide Control Center, they also sent out calls directing appropriate agencies to head to the scene. In case phone lines went down, two backup communication systems were in place—an Air Warden Messenger Service, which consisted of over 20,000 volunteer boys aged sixteen to eighteen, and a War Emergency Radio Service, whose 324 sending and receiving units (some in cars, others in portable packs) were manned by 600 licensed ham radio operators.

Standing by was a small army of potential responders, each of them mobilized in large and complex organizations. There were, for instance, the 2,148 nurses and doctors of the Emergency Medical Service (EMS), divided into 204 squads, based at eighty-five hospitals (twenty-one municipal and sixty-four private), who could draw as needed on Borough Medical Storage Depots, each stocked with 6,000 stretchers, 18,000 folding cots, and 48,000 blankets; and the EMS could refer less critical cases to one of the 800 Rest Centers maintained by the Red Cross to dispense first aid relief; or they could send bombed-out but medically OK survivors to one of the seventy-three Emergency Welfare Centers staffed by private charities and the Welfare Department; each was ready with emergency housing, clothing, food, or cash money for victims of an air raid or other enemy action.

Never had the city been so well organized, so *wired*. The immense and intricate defense-and-response apparatus was a thing of bureaucratic beauty. It no doubt offered the anxious citizenry comfort and reassurance. What it did not do is have the slightest impact on the root of their anxiety, the wolf packs prowling off their shore. There, too, relief was on the way.

94

Convoys

The appearance of U-boats off the East Coast in January 1942 had come as no surprise to Navy officials. They had, after all, been fighting the Battle of the Atlantic for over a year. Admiral Ernest J. King—since February 1, 1941, commander in chief of the Atlantic Fleet—had warned in December 1941, after Germany's declaration of war, that enemy submarines would soon appear off the Atlantic seaboard. When Dönitz's U-boats did open their second front, attacking coastal as well as transoceanic shipping, King knew that Admiral Andrews's Eastern Sea Frontier couldn't protect coastwise cargos. The only effective response to *Paukenschlag* would be naval escorts. English and Canadian navies had been shepherding transatlantic convoys since 1939. In May 1941, the (then-neutral) US Navy had begun playing an auxiliary role. And in September 1941, it had started accompanying convoys from Halifax to Iceland and escorting ships filled with Russia-bound Lend Lease goods from Iceland to Murmansk.

So the Navy would have liked to dispatch destroyers to beat back Dönitz's attacks. There simply weren't enough boats to go around. After Pearl Harbor, King had been elevated to commander in chief of the entire United States Fleet; in March 1942 he also assumed the post of chief of naval operations. His responsibilities during *Paukenschlag* were therefore worldwide. They included responding to the ongoing debacle in the Pacific; keeping the German surface fleet bottled up in Europe; protecting the American coastline from Newfoundland to Brazil; escorting transatlantic convoys; and, at the top of his agenda, getting US Army and Army Air Force troops and equipment safely across to Iceland and Northern Ireland, given that Roosevelt and Churchill had agreed on a Germany-first strategy. Scarce destroyers were thus directed to protect convoys like the one that left Gotham in February 1942 for Londonderry by way of Halifax, escorted by the battleship *New York*, the light cruiser *Brooklyn*, and twelve destroyers. (Aircraft, too, were subject to diversion: in April 1942, when the Eastern Sea Frontier had only two antisubmarine patrol planes equipped with ASV radar, a squadron of ASV-equipped B-24 Liberators was dispatched not to Gotham, but to the Indian Ocean.) Building more boats was the mid-range solution, and the

Navy did have a crash Destroyer Escort program under way, but Roosevelt had assigned a higher priority to building merchant vessels, and the DE program had fallen far behind schedule.

Admiral Andrews had considered—as a stop-gap measure—instituting a coastal convoy system with an understrength escort component. However, he, King, and US naval strategists in general believed that in the case of seaboard convoys—which had to groove along in established shipping lanes and thus lacked the searoom for evasive routing—assembling large and weakly defended groups of vessels would only provide the enemy with more inviting targets.

Still, something had to be done. Sinkings in March took a fearful toll. Stimson was told by the heads of major US oil companies that their tankers, coming up from oil ports in Mexico, Venezuela, and Texas, were being destroyed far faster than they could be replaced and that within a few months the entire fleet might cease to exist. Chief of Staff George Marshall agreed that any more of this carnage could cripple the war effort. Admiral Pound, England's First Sea Lord, offered to lend the Navy some older coal-burning trawlers, fitted out for limited antisubmarine service, and some arrived in April. Andrews, desperate, inaugurated a "bucket brigade" operation that month, ordering ships to hop their way down the coast, scurrying from harbor to harbor by day, using available air and sea cover, then holing up by night. For all this, forty-seven more merchantmen were torpedoed along the coast in April and May.

Meanwhile the outline of a possible solution was emerging, which was to spread out the transatlantic convoy cycle—lengthen the time between sailings. Going from six to seven days would free up twenty-eight Atlantic Fleet destroyers and thirty-nine smaller escort craft. London and Moscow were not happy, as this would crimp their flow of critically needed supplies. Tough negotiations ensued, during which King ordered Andrews to assume the best and proceed with planning. Finally, in May 1942, an agreement was reached, and the Interlocking Convoy System went into effect.

It started slowly, on May 14, with escorted convoys sailing daily from New York to the Delaware capes, and then on to Chesapeake Bay. By August, more reinforcements had arrived from the Pacific: the defeat of the Japanese fleet at the Battle of Midway in early June had reduced the need for destroyers to escort shipping between the west coast and Hawaii. Service was soon extended to Guantanamo and Key West. These harbors in turn became the assembly points for convoys coming up from the Venezuelan oil fields via Aruba, or from the Gulf of Mexico, or eventually from all South America (by year's end escorts were available for service to and from Brazil). At Guantanamo or Key West, local convoys from the south would join the next express convoy heading north. These left once a week, with the clockwork regularity of scheduled rail service, courtesy of the Third Naval District's routers up in 90 Church. After September 1942, their arrivals in Gotham were timed to allow them to join convoys departing for Londonderry, as the Port of New York now replaced Halifax as the great transatlantic terminus and thus became the hub of the entire hemispheric system, the critical interlink between Europe and all the Americas—eerily echoing its lynchpin role in the trading pattern of the eighteenth century.

The new system was instantly effective. From June on, U-boats were denied their profitable hunting grounds in shallow coastal waters and found it harder to locate unescorted ships even in deeper waters. Dönitz savvily withdrew his U-boats immediately and sent them south to seek easier pickings in the Gulf of Mexico, where losses correspondingly soared to 121 in June. By August, Navy Secretary Knox could say that "at long last, we seem to have made considerable progress in the antisubmarine fight." By September 1942, U-boat sinkings of merchant ships off the US coast, from Maine to Florida, had dropped to almost zero.

By June 1942, therefore, the noose around New York's neck had loosened considerably: the U-boats had been swept away; there had been not a single air attack, nor a single significant act of sabotage; and an elaborate civilian and military defense machinery had been set in place. As a consequence, the coiled-spring city began to unwind just a bit, even while remaining tautly on guard. It was at just this moment—a week after the great victory at Midway—that Gotham mounted a lollapalooza of a parade, the most colossal and spectacular of its entire 300+ year history.

95

"New York at War"

At 9:15 a.m. on Saturday morning, June 13, 1942, the first of 500,000 marchers set off from Washington Square on a 3.5-mile trip up flag-bedecked Fifth Avenue, past the reviewing stand at the New York Public Library, on to the mustering out area above 72nd Street. They would be accompanied by scores of bands, hundreds of floats, thousands of flags and banners, masses of tanks and jeeps, and an overhead escort of fighter planes, dive bombers, and Flying Fortresses. Along the way they'd be cheered by a mammoth throng packed deep along the sidewalks from the curbs to the boarded-up windows of shops and department stores, while thousands more hung out of windows tossing down a snowstorm of torn paper. The crowd—in great good humor despite the sweltering heat—was estimated at two and one half million people, one-third of Gotham's population, a gathering bigger than the entire citizenry of Philadelphia, Los Angeles, or Detroit.

This extravaganza—called "New York at War"—was far more than the usual ethnic-day potpourri of bands and majorettes. Thanks to the Mayor's Committee for Mobilization, New York at War, Inc., chaired by Grover Whalen, it was as thoroughly planned and as meticulously organized as the lengthy preparedness movement of which it was the culmination and prideful demonstration. But "New York at War" afforded more than just an opportunity for a mighty gathering of the metropolitan clan to grasp (and marvel at) the magnitude of the defense system it had collectively wrought. This pageant in motion embodied a narrative—a history of the war to date—and offered a rationale for why it should be fought. Part of that rationale was about transcending Nazi-style nationalism in favor of pluralism—represented by the incredible diversity (very much on display that day) of the coalition of Allies that had come together to battle the Axis, and by the spectacular variety of Gotham itself (as evidenced by both watchers and walkers): the parade, like the city that mounted it, embodied a vision of the kind of postwar world that the war, it was hoped, might foster. It did all this by using a form of street theater that, like the convoy system, harked back to the eighteenth century in being the kind of urban processional one might have thought passé in the era of mass communications; yet it also drew on the immediacy of contemporary media, borrowing from the radio and WPA's Living Newspaper the ability to comment on virtually up-to-the minute events.

Its story began, appropriately enough, with a Prologue, which recounted the war's beginning, and pinned it squarely on the enemy. The first sequence of the Prologue, as listed in the official line of march, was entitled "Hitler Unlooses War." It was led off by "Death on Horseback," a float, draped in black crepe, bearing an ancient-looking cloaked skeleton, its skull graced with mustache and shock of hair. Seated astride a decrepit horse, Death's towering arms rose and fell (thanks to two hidden puppeteers) on two blood-red be-swastikaed kettledrums hanging from its mount's flanks, while behind it a band dirged the "Dead March" from Handel's *Saul*. Next came a depiction of Hitler's earliest victims—a float depicting starving, beaten, half-clad men, women, and children lying behind the barbed wire of concentration camps, and then tattered refugees pulling carts piled high with their household goods. Close on their fleeing heels came a 55-foot long, 3-story-tall, mechanical "Axis War Monster" that belched real smoke from its nostrils and sides while blaring militaristic trumpet blasts, mingled with loudspeaker barks of "Heil Hitler" and "Il Duce." All around it lay the bodies of those who had not escaped its wrath and been trampled under foot.

Then it was off to the Pacific. Floats recounted Japanese treachery at Pearl Harbor—one featured a prone figure of an American soldier with a knife sticking out of his back. The heroic defense of Bataan and Corregidor was represented with the aid of actual Philippine

A float titled "Hitler the Axis War Monster" rolls down Fifth Avenue during the New York at War parade, June 13, 1942. (AP Photo/Joe Caneva)

allies: Igorot natives in loin cloths, flown in from the mountains of Luzon, duplicated their MacArthur-hailed feat of riding US tanks, knives and spears in hand, as they annihilated a Japanese infantry regiment. They were joined by smartly turned-out Filipino Scouts, and unshaven American troops in battle dress and helmets, and Death March reenactors—emaciated and bandaged men and women barely dragging themselves along. Behind these, in an auto, rode Philippine president Manuel L. Quezon, who had just arrived in the US to set up a government-in-exile.

Now other allies strode by, constituting a parade within a parade. There were fighters from Great Britain and its empire (the Royal Air Force and Royal Canadian Air Force in light blue, Australians in khaki shorts, South African sailors in white uniforms). And there were guerillas or citizens from the fallen countries: daredevil Polish fighter pilots in the RAF; Free French marching behind the Cross of Lorraine; Hollanders with a float showing a Gestapo firing squad in action; Yugoslavs armed with mountain rifles shooting at a Nazi tank. A Czechoslovak hearse rolled by, drawn by four white horses, marked "The Crime of Lidice"; it commemorated the village in which, a scant three days earlier, Nazis had shot all the men and sent all the women to concentration camps, in reprisal for the assassination of Gestapo "hangman" Reinhard Heydrich. There were Belgians, Greeks (the King himself was on hand), a Chinese contingent, and Soviet sailors carrying the red flag with hammer and sickle alongside the Stars and Stripes (these last two got an ovation from the crowd). Another float extolled Pan American democracy and hemispheric solidarity.

Father Knickerbocker merited a sequence of his own. He was depicted as rolling up his sleeves while New Yorkers of all races and nationalities came to his aid, including Indians, Negroes, Filipinos, Puerto Ricans, and—strikingly—loyal Italian American and German American delegations (the American-German Trade Unionists' float featured a heroic figure of a laboring man taking a sledge hammer to a swastika held in a workbench vise). Tolerance stopped at the Pacific's edge, however: there was no contingent of loyal Japanese Americans, an exclusion four members of the American Civilian Liberties Union had protested the day before, telling Mayor La Guardia it constituted "discrimination on purely racial grounds." Instead, the Prologue's final component—"Tokyo, We Are Coming!"—diverged from the careful distinction elsewhere made between the German or Italian *peoples* and their fascist *regimes* and reached instead for a verminous metaphor that branded all Japanese as evildoers. The float depicted an American eagle, followed by bomber planes, swooping down and driving a swarm of yellow rats into the sea.

All this was just for openers.

The remainder of the parade, organized into six divisions—Army, Navy, Reserves, War Industry, Protective Services, and Home Front—suggested what the US and New York were doing about the Axis challenge.

The First Division, led by Lieutenant General Drum, featured an actual division of infantrymen, also tank groups, armored personnel carriers, field artillery, howitzer batteries, mobile anti-aircraft guns, the signal corps (replete with mobile cotes for carrier pigeons), a pontoon company (with ten-ton pontoons), assault boats, and a trailer bearing an Army Air Corps Curtis P-40 Warhawk. As the mechanized legions passed the reviewing stand, bristling with their brand-new paraphernalia of modern warfare, Army combat planes from Mitchel Field roared by overhead. Next up, under the command of Admiral Andrews, marched the Navy—midshipmen, marines, sailors, coast guardsmen, and a Navy fighter plane. Third came the New York Guard (mostly middle-aged veterans) whose regimental bands—the 23rd, the 7th—played Great War tunes ("Over There," "Tipperary"); they were followed by the Red Cross, Naval Militia, Jewish War Veterans, Veterans of Foreign Wars, and American Legionnaires, among others. (Smuggled in at this point was a gigantic bust of Franklin Roosevelt, 25 feet high, which had missed its place in the Prologue and was playing catch-up.)

Sixty thousand industrial workers dominated the Fourth Division, arrayed by unions: first the AFL outfits—Teamsters, Butchers, Seafarers International (SIU), Dubinsky's ILGWU, etc.—then the CIO's—Newspaper Guild, Auto Workers, National Maritime (NMU), Hillman's Amalgamated, etc. The loudest cheers went up for the seamen whose ships had been torpedoed but had lived to tell the tale: fifty survivors marched with the SIU contingent and another 150 with the NMU; the latter's float, befitting its interracial politics, featuring a lifeboat crowded with white and Black seamen. Another favorite was the float of the Union Parts Manufacturing Company of Brooklyn on which six lathe operators turned out 3-inch shells as they rolled up the avenue. District Council 9 of the Painters, Decorators and Paperhangers (AFL) had one dedicated "To A. Shickelgruber, Paperhanger, Berchtesgaden," on which members painted over a map labeled "New World Order" with pictures of Allied bombers, tanks, and warships. The United Electrical, Radio and Machine Workers Union, CIO, showed a giant Hitler head being squeezed between massive pincers, one labeled "west front," the other "east front" (many in the laboring contingent wore red-white-and-blue paper caps embossed with "Second Front").

The Fifth Division gave Gotham's protective forces a chance to strut their stuff—air raid wardens, auxiliary firemen, nurses' aides, City Patrol Corps, etc.; Mayor La Guardia came down from the reviewing stand to march at the head of his civilian army, the old soldier's arms swinging vigorously back and forth. The Sixth (Home Front) Division was given over to women with sons in service, women's volunteer organizations, war relief groups, religious organizations, athletic groups, actors, the ASPCA, Brooklyn Union Gas, IBM—seventy-five entities in all. The New York Public Library's float paired books sheltered under the wings of an American eagle, with books going up in flames, under the slogan: "Fascism BURNS books: Democracy READS Books."

Just before dark the torches were lit for the last 15,000 leaving Washington Square—all carefully shielded so as not to emit a submarine-attracting glow—and slowly Fifth Avenue grew tremulous with smoke and light. Most of these later-in-the-day marchers were members of the "Conquered Countries Arisen" contingent—yet another multinational array of nations under Axis attack: folk-garbed Ukrainians singing "The Star-Spangled Banner," drum-pounding Chinese behind a twenty-foot-long lion-dragon, bereted Frenchmen and bonneted Bretagnards, and accordion-playing Russians led, curiously, by an American Indian in full feather. Finally came floats hailing the Atlantic Charter (Roosevelt and Churchill were displayed signing it on shipboard), and others depicting specific war aims—"International Justice," "Freedom from Aggression," each of FDR's Four Freedoms, and "The Triumph of the Democratic Ideal." Finally, courtesy of RCA Victor, came a float labeled "Fort McHenry," atop which the soprano Lucy Monroe, star of stage, radio, and the Metropolitan Opera, sang patriotic songs, ending with the national anthem. By 8:16, nearly eleven hours after it started, it was over.

THE WAR, HOWEVER, HAD ONLY just begun. There were many dark hours just ahead, on land—*Generalfeldmarschall* Erwin Rommel would capture Tobruk within days, the Germans launch their drive on Stalingrad within weeks—and at sea. Dönitz, driven from western waters, had regrouped brilliantly in the mid-ocean gap, southeast of Greenland, still beyond the reach of Allied air power, through which all convoys to Britain and Russia had to pass. His U-force, augmented at a terrifying rate—by early 1943 he had 100 working this territory, most of them new-and-improved models—was able to wreak terrible damage on convoys, escorted or not. Between July and December 1942, 480 Allied ships were sunk in the North Atlantic, four-fifths by U-boats. By year's end Britain's civilian oil reserve was down to a three-month supply. Things worsened in 1943: in March alone 108 ships went down, and the Battle of the Atlantic was within an ace of being lost.

Then, with astonishing speed, the scales tipped. The Allies broke new U-boat codes. Improved radar was rushed to the aquatic front. Sixty B-24 long-range Liberators were transferred in from the Pacific to cover the gap. US shipyards delivered "escort carriers" (aka "baby flat-tops"), each capable of carrying two dozen aircraft. High Frequency Direction Finding ("Huff-Duff") equipment pinpointed U-boat radio transmissions. Thus equipped, naval escorts began sinking subs. In May, 30 percent of the U-boats were lost; the average sub now survived less than three months; the German submarine service casualty rate soared to 75 percent; and on May 24, Dönitz ordered all but a handful out of the North Atlantic. In the next four months, sixty-two convoys of 3,546 merchant vessels crossed over without the loss of a single ship. That summer Dönitz was forced to admit that "the methods of radio-location [radar] which the Allies have introduced have conquered the U-boat menace."

Once in control of the Atlantic, the Allies could and did quickly take the offensive; on the night of July 9–10, the US Seventh Army and Britain's Eighth Army invaded Sicily, conquered it in five weeks, and in September the invasion of Italy got under way. The fighting had moved far from New York, and it would not return. There would be occasional scares, from sea and air. On November 13, mines laid by *U-Boat 608* were spotted beyond the Narrows, two miles southeast of the Ambrose Lightship; the net gate was closed and the port shut down; but within thirty hours minesweepers had done their job, and Gotham was back in business. And on May 11, 1943, a *PM* story, headlined "Bombing of New York a Real Possibility," quoted Office of Civilian Defense chief James Landis as saying that seaplane bombers—refueled by subs spaced across the ocean—might hit the coast, but such speculations seemed increasingly farfetched.

With its coast cleared, New York, too, shifted from defense to offense. It was about to become the most spectacular war port in the world.

WAR PORT

Ships docked in the Gowanus Canal, 1938. (Photo by James Suydam for the Federal Writers' Project. New York City Municipal Archives.)

96

Anchors Aweigh

Once again, in a reversion to its most basic and enduring of roles, New York was first and foremost a maritime city. As the critical link between the industrial might of the American continent and the immense armies assaulting Hitler's Europe, Gotham shipped out more goods and people than did any port in the wartime world, more than at any point in its own history.

The contrast with the clogged harbor of the First World War was stark, but not surprising: since that debacle, much work had gone into ensuring that things would flow in and out of the city—whether by rail or road or air or sea—with vastly greater efficiency in any future conflict. The winning strategy had been to replace free-market competition and chaos with government-arranged cooperation and coordination between corporate rivals, between capital and labor, and between harbor and hinterland.

Nowhere was the beneficial impact of this advance planning more evident than on the railroad front. In 1917–18 the city's train network had been hopelessly snarled by corporate catfights, which had also defeated the Port Authority's efforts at rail rationalization in the 1920s. In the 1930s, under New Deal prodding, and pressure from the growing trucking industry, the member companies of the Association of American Railroads (AAR) had finally agreed to an unprecedented pooling of resources and information in the event of war. Though not under National Recovery Administration (NRA) jurisdiction, the carriers were allowed to work out their own collective arrangements, just as the NRA let each industry organize itself. But Roosevelt made clear that if they bollixed things up the government would step in, a message underscored two weeks after Pearl Harbor by his creating an Office of Defense Transportation to provide oversight and guidance. Once harnessed, the railroads turned in an impressive performance, moving 200 million tons of military freight between 1942 and 1945 far more dexterously than they had 11.2 million tons between 1917 and 1918. Some of this was due to general improvements in operational efficiency—larger cars, more powerful locomotives, greater electrification, superior traffic control; and, locally, the rebuilding and relocation of Manhattan's West Side tracks. However, it was chiefly coordinated planning that enabled the port to handle 200–300 freight trains a day without track-lock.

Passenger volume soared as well, as millions of draftees were sluiced into town and war-related commuting exploded. Traffic at Pennsylvania Station shot up 80 percent between 1941 and 1942, with the Long Island Rail Road connection helping push its numbers ahead of Grand Central's. In 1945 nearly 110,000,000 soldiers and civilians passed through its gates and concourses, with daily volume surging to 500,000—more people than lived in either New Orleans or Minneapolis—when big contingents of servicemen passed through. Little wonder that Penn Station loomed large in the national imagination, spurred by movies such as Vincente Minnelli's *The Clock* (1945), in which Joe (Robert Walker), a soldier arriving on a brief leave, meets Alice (Judy Garland) inside the station. They commence a whirlwind romance on a bus ride up Fifth Avenue; get separated in the subway when the platform crowd sweeps her onto a downtown local and he unwittingly pursues her on an express; are later reunited in the great terminal; rush off to get married; and finally return to Penn Station, where they part, amid a throng of other separating lovers, perhaps never to meet again—helping brand the wartime station, and its city, as a place of comings together and wrenchings apart.

The resurgence of rails was due, too, to wartime constraints on cars. In response to the Japanese seizure of Southeast Asian rubber plantations and the sinking of coastal oil tankers by German U-boats, Washington rationed rubber and gas and halted production of automobiles for the civilian market. This gave coal-fired steam locomotives a tremendous advantage (the War Production Board even throttled back on diesels to save fuel oil). Where in 1939 wheeled transport had accounted for over 90 percent of intercity passenger miles, by 1944 that had sagged to 63.8 percent, while rail had increased its share from 8.6 percent to 34.6 percent,

A central atrium of the original Penn Station. (Bettmann / Contributor / Getty Images)

restoring nearly half the losses of the previous twenty years. Freight service followed a similar if less dramatic pattern: railroads had carried 76 percent of the nation's ton-miles in 1926; this had dropped to 63 percent by 1940, then rebounded to 73 percent by 1943. By war's end, railroad profit margins had reached levels not seen since early in the century.

Unhappy highwaymen were battered, as well, by the government's virtual shutdown of new roadway construction, apart from strategic projects like the Alaskan Highway. None were more miserable than New York's Mr. Auto, Robert Moses. Not only had the federal parkway pump gone dry; not only had Mayor La Guardia slashed the city's capital budget (preventing him from completing his Belt System arterial tapestry); but the rationing-induced 56 percent drop-off in 1942 traffic over his Triborough Bridge Authority's (TBA) five spans—and the attendant slump in toll revenues—had by 1943 brought his beloved agency close to defaulting on its bonds.

Moses's misery was compounded by the war-enhanced power of his great enemy, President—and Commander-in-Chief—Franklin Roosevelt. Moses had gotten a glimpse of what lay in store for him back in 1939, when FDR had used the mere possibility of American military involvement to balk Moses's dream of building a massive bridge between Lower Manhattan and Brooklyn. Protests had erupted at his plan to send an off-ramp barreling over bucolic Battery Park, replacing downtown's glorious harbor views with a forest of pillars and the underside of an elevated highway. Opponents advocated a tunnel, but Moses tried to bulldoze them aside by arguing (falsely) that a tunnel would cost more and earn less than a bridge, when his real beef was that a tunnel would be built (and its tolls collected) by a rival agency. He was on the point of triumph when C. C. Burlingham penned a note (in "graveyard confidence") to Franklin Roosevelt. "Nobody fit to have an opinion wants the Battery Bridge except Bob Moses," said CCB, adding helpfully that "The War Department can stop it...." A word to the wise was indeed sufficient, and on May 18, 1939, the secretary of war rejected a bridge on the (spurious) ground that war bombs might knock it down and thus block access to the Navy Yard, as if there weren't already two bridges seaward of the Yard that could serve that nefarious purpose. In addition, federal funds were suddenly located and made available to La Guardia—for building a Brooklyn-Battery *Tunnel*, over whose groundbreaking FDR happily presided on his campaign swing in 1940.

Incandescent with fury, but unable to contest a "military" judgment without seeming unpatriotic, Moses had a tantrum. Declaring in 1941 that Castle Clinton's much beloved and heavily patronized Aquarium (over two million visits that year) was "obsolete" and "unsuitable," he summarily shut it down. He then tried to tear down the old fort itself—claiming (falsely) that the *tunnel's* construction required this—but no demolition company could tackle the massive stone walls, as most of the city's heavy construction equipment was engaged in defense work. Moses settled for removing its roof, rendering it useless, and closing off Battery Park to the public altogether, blaming closure on the *tunnel*. Then he pushed the city to adopt a proposed fort-free park design that would allow him to get on with demolition, while opponents like George McAneny, president of the Regional Plan Association, maneuvered to get the National Park Service to save a structure so "steeped in historical association."

In the meantime, the master builder set out to spike work on the tunnel itself, which the War Production Board (WPB) had quietly allowed to go forward, despite the general ban on big civilian projects, because there was no other work in their field for the 1,200 sandhogs (most too old for military service), and because the tunnel tubes on which $15 million had already been expended might get ruined by water seepage unless lined with the metal sheathing already purchased. Moses made a big public to-do about how the lining material—"28,000 tons of steel"—should instead be melted down and used, patriotically, for the war effort. This was yet another lie—the metal was cast iron, not steel, hence useless for war production—but a skittish WPB, the issue now spotlighted, suspended all further tunnel work for the duration.

Franklin Roosevelt would have the last spiteful laugh. It is said—perhaps apocryphally— that the president told an associate of Moses: "This war is going to be fought on two oceans, on several continents, and in a dozen countries. It will be fought in towns and cities across the world. And there is no place in this war for Robert Moses." Accurate or not, no important position was ever forthcoming for this difficult but talented man who might have contributed much to the national effort. Moses (like highwaymen in general) had to content himself with spinning plans for postwar projects—in Gotham, and in cities (like Portland) that sought him out as a consultant—plans that all revolved around constructing gigantic highways. And *bridges*.

FOR NOW, PEOPLE AND GOODS heading for the European Theater of Operations, whether they arrived in New York by rail or by road, had to be transferred to a transoceanic mode of transport.

In this war, unlike the last, they could travel by air as well as by sea, and Fiorello La Guardia's airport became a crucial transit hub. People were easiest to carry, and diplomats, generals, admirals, Roosevelt, and Churchill were among the many shuttled back and forth across the Atlantic via Pan Am Clippers (the great flying boats drabbed down by sea-gray camouflage paint), or Transcontinental & Western Air (T&WA) Stratoliners (the four-engined land planes whose pressurized cabins allowed for above-the-weather altitudes). In 1945, two million passengers arrived in Gotham by air.

Increasingly, freight flew, too: passenger planes like the Douglas DC-3 and DC-4 were converted into C-for-cargo versions—transmuted into C-47 Skytrains and C-54 Skymasters—which airlifted thousands of tons of war supplies from La Guardia Field to battlefields in Europe, Africa, and Asia. As in the rail sector, competing airline companies were brought together under federal aegis. At first, various Washington government agencies simply signed contracts with Pan Am or Eastern or T&WA to provide transport services on a need-to-fly basis. The profusion of deals, however, led to growing confusion, and in June 1942, the Army Air Force established the Air Transport Command (ATC), which put all airline operations under unified management. Though a military entity, the ATC was largely run by senior executives drawn from commercial companies and commissioned as officers. They, in turn, purchased airplanes from their own companies and also contracted with them to supply civilian pilots, navigators, and ground crews to fly and service the aircraft. In effect, the ATC became a consortium of commercial airlines whose now-coordinated operations became as efficient as those of the rail consortium, capable of delivering virtually anything from Gotham, to anywhere on earth, within sixty-six hours. The quantum leap in demand and degree of organization—supplemented also by wartime advances in air traffic control and a municipal-fostered growth in trained support crews—left New York's aviation industry well positioned to sustain its primacy into what promised to be an emerging air age.

For now, however, nautical trumped aeronautical, and the great bulk of people and goods arriving in wartime Gotham were switched to outbound boats—though only after a transitional period, of varying length, during which they were parked and processed in the metropolitan area.

The over three million troops who sailed from New York between 1941 and 1945 were sent first to giant staging areas like Camp Kilmer (near New Brunswick, New Jersey) and

Camp Shanks (at Orangeburg, New York), or the more modestly scaled Fort Hamilton in Brooklyn. After about a week—in which equipment was inspected, arms injected, lifeboat drills practiced, and the twelve-hour passes to Gotham enjoyed—they were transported to their vessels. Those from the out-of-town camps came in by rail and/or ferry. Those from Fort Hamilton were rumbled through the night on convoys of one-and-a-half ton army trucks that nosed onto the Belt Parkway and drove north along Shore Drive, up the Gowanus Parkway over the canal, up Henry Street and across the Manhattan Bridge, and thence to the North River Terminal on the Hudson—the series of 1,100-foot-long piers (#84 to #92) between 44th and 52nd Streets, part of the famous prewar "Ocean Liner Row." Here soldiers clambered aboard some of those same liners, notably the *Queen Mary*, now painted battleship gray, up whose Pier 90 gangplank, on July 23, 1943, clumped 15,740 khaki-clad GIs, an entire infantry division, packs on backs, duffel bag in one hand and rifle in the other, so burdening the boat that only a foot of water remained under its keel as it slid past the top of the Lincoln Tunnel between 34th Street and Weehawken. These giants—the *Mary* and her sister *Elizabeth*, the *Aquitania* and *Mauretania II*, the *Ile de France*, *Pasteur*, and *Nieuw Amsterdam*—were fast, capable of 20 knots or better (the *Queen Mary* and the now dead-in-the-water *Normandie* had topped 30 in winning their respective Blue Ribands). Far faster than any U-boat, so fast no escort could keep up with them, they often sailed alone, relying only on their speed for protection; not a single one was ever caught.

As for freight, the staggering quantities pouring into the city were received at the Army-run New York Port of Embarkation (NYPE)—not one place but congeries of coordinated terminals spaced around the vast harbor, employing among them an average of 55,000 men and women. The heart and headquarters of the NYPE was the colossal Brooklyn Army Base at First Avenue and 58th Street, designed by Cass Gilbert and built in the waning months of the First World War. Embodying the distilled wisdom of New York's three hundred years of experience with the unglamorous but vital skill of warehousing, it sprawled over 48 acres, its key structures consisting of two immense 8-story structures, and four massive, covered piers—the land and sea complexes linked by an intricate network of rails. Lighters coming from the Jersey railheads would offload freight-laden railcars, which were then rolled into one of the cavernous warehouses and onto one of the ninety-six centrally controlled elevators (the largest such installation in the world), then hoisted to a floor above; 450 freight cars could be stored in the base's nearly four million square feet. Conversely, troops could be assembled there, marched to the pierheads, and onloaded to ships like the *Queen Mary*.

Up the Brooklyn waterfront a bit, Bush Terminal, dominating Sunset Park at First Avenue and 46th Street, contributed to the NYPE another eight piers on the Upper Bay, another million and a half square feet of storage space, and trackage for an additional 150 freight cars. On the far opposite side of the harbor, in Jersey City, lay the Claremont Terminal at Caven Point. Originally built by the Lehigh Valley Railroad as its freight handling facility, it had been taken over by the Army, which added a 3,600-foot pier for shipping matériel (especially ammunition) and troops trained in from Camp Kilmer. Farther south down the Jersey shore, at Bayonne, the Port Johnson Terminal specialized in receiving and assembling combat vehicles—trucks, trailers, ambulances, tanks—then sending them off on lighters to other terminals in the NYPE network.

Heading west along Staten Island's northern shore from Port Johnson, sailing on the Kill Van Kull to where it merged with the Arthur Kill, one came to Port Ivory, where Procter & Gamble was still turning out the "soap that floats," and, right next door, to Howland Hook. Here oil products were stored and shipped, perhaps the most critical war matériel handled by the New York Port of Embarkation: "This is a war of engines and octanes," ran a famous Stalin toast to the "American auto industry and the American oil industry." In 1942, with U-boats methodically sinking the oil companies' tanker fleet, new methods were required to ensure the flow of petroleum to Howland Hook's storage tanks and to Jersey Standard's nearby refineries at Bayonne, Elizabeth, and Jersey City. As a stopgap measure, railroad tank cars were rushed into service. For a long-term solution, the War Production Board authorized one of the war's most astonishing engineering feats—the construction of a pipeline all the way from the East Texas oil fields to the harbor of New York.

Work got under way August 3, 1942, on the Big Inch—"big inch" in oilspeak being any pipe over 12 inches in diameter, and this one was twice that. The construction tab was picked up by the government's Defense Plant Corporation, but the job itself was contracted out to another government-arranged private consortium, composed of eleven leading oil companies. Crews dug a ditch 4 feet deep, 3 feet wide, and 1,254 miles long. It ran from Longview, Texas, under the Mississippi River and up to Southern Illinois, then east to Linden, New Jersey, and on via feeder pipelines across the Arthur Kill to Staten Island and Bayonne, with lines branching off to local refineries. All this was done in one year flat, and soon after completion on August 14, 1943, the Big Inch's twenty-six pumping stations were boosting 335,000 barrels-worth of oil on its way each day. By then a second line was under construction—the Little Big Inch, "little" referring to its relative width (20 inches), not its longer length (1,475 miles). Authorized in April 1943, it was completed on March 2, 1944, and began carrying gas and other products (including heating oil for Gotham) from the refinery complex between Houston and Port Arthur to New York's harbor.

Doubling back from Howland Hook, a vessel sailing east on the Kill van Kull along Staten Island's northern shore would soon have come to the NYPE's Staten Island Terminal at Stapleton, which provided another four million square feet of storage, another ten piers, and trackage for another 235 freight cars. And if the boat had carried on down through the Narrows and struck out south across Raritan Bay and on into Sandy Hook Bay, it would have arrived at the NYPE's farthest-flung installation—the Earle Naval Ammunition Depot. Built in 1943 after the volume of explosives passing through the port warranted finding a spot at safer remove from homes, offices, bridges, and factories, Earle consisted of pierheads near Leonardo that were connected to an 8,000-plus-acre storage site 12 miles farther inland, built on a wooded swampy tract. Here explosives awaiting transit—enough to have blown a considerable chunk of New Jersey off the map—were sheltered from enemy shelling.

The vast and varied cargos assembled at the Port of Embarkation, once ready to sail, were loaded onto a vast and varied merchant fleet, under the domain of yet another federal agency tasked with coordinating the work of private capital: the War Shipping Administration (WSA), created by FDR in February 1942. The WSA assumed many of the functions of the US Maritime Commission (USMC), a New Deal entity established in 1936 to build, own, and oversee the operation of a fleet of 500 modern cargo ships that would replace the First World War–vintage vessels making up the bulk of the US Merchant Marine. The Maritime Commission had been building boats at a fast clip, but after Pearl Harbor, with U-boats sinking them at a still faster pace, Roosevelt and Congress went into hyperdrive, allocating nearly four billion dollars for a crash construction program. By war's end, shipyards working under USMC contracts had built a total of 5,777 vessels, the largest fleet of merchant ships in history.

The War Shipping administrator—Rear Admiral Emory Scott Land, who also retained his position as head of the Maritime Commission—assumed responsibility for operating

Poster for the New York Department of Docks by Martin Weitzman, c. 1937–1939. (WPA Federal Arts Project. Library of Congress, Prints and Photographs Division)

these new-built vessels, and the many others that the WSA requisitioned from the nation's 131 private shipping firms (heavily headquartered at the bottom of Manhattan Island). The entire fleet was treated as a collective pool from which boats were drawn and allocated to the armed services, federal agencies, or allied governments, as dictated by military exigencies. The WSA did not, however, operate the vessels itself, rather it contracted the job out to the steamship companies (often leasing a boat back to the same firm from which it been requisitioned in the first place). Shippers, even industry giants like New York's Grace, Moore-McCormack, and American President, became "general agents" of the government: they crewed,

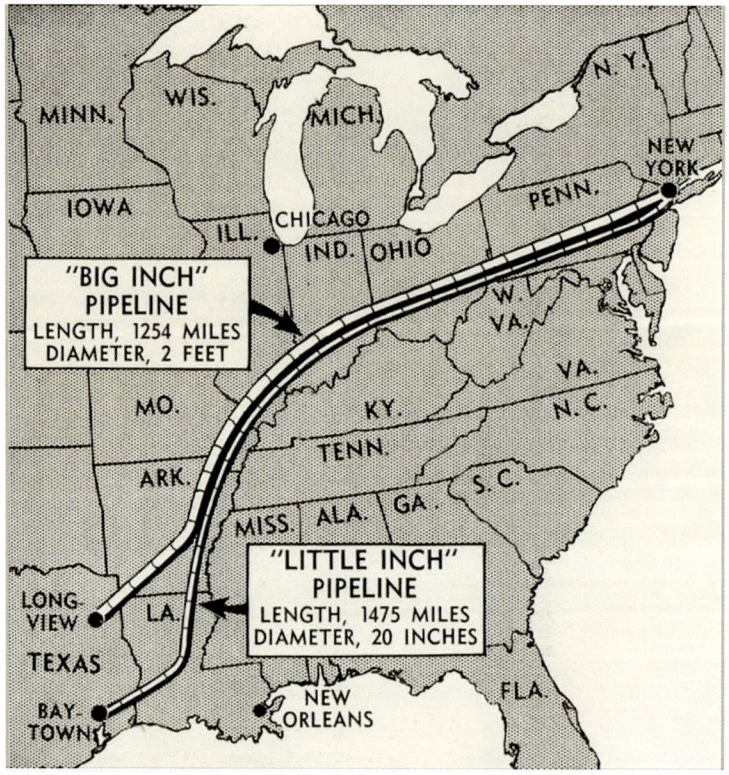

Map of the Big Inch and Little Inch Pipelines, c. 1942. (Copyright Enbridge Inc.)

chandlered, fueled, and repaired WSA vessels and carried WSA-assigned cargos on WSA-assigned routes. Like their corporate rail and aviation counterparts, they were compensated handsomely (some said extravagantly); shipping industry profits rose dramatically, boosted by the government's covering of insurance costs. The city's shippers also gained valuable experience dealing, on a global scale, with far more traffic than they ever had before: Grace Lines as general agent handled eight times the ships it had on its own steam in peacetime, and Moore-McCormack operated 150 vessels, which collectively carried over thirty million tons of cargo. This was one reason that, as the president of the Foreign Commerce Club enthused in March 1944, "the port's position in international commerce is stronger today than ever before."

Again, coordination enabled efficiency. Between 1939 and 1943, the volume of export freight dispatched from the harbor more than tripled, yet the turnaround time was faster than ever. The WSA (whose Atlantic Coast director's office was at 45 Broadway) worked closely with the Maritime Association of the Port of New York (housed steps away in its Maritime Exchange Building at 80 Broad Street), which in turned established a Joint Steamship and Railroad Committee to ensure a smooth interface between trains and boats. But when it came to hoisting anchor and heading out to sea, all these answered to a higher power, for at this point the US Navy assumed command.

The manager of the world's biggest marine traffic job was Port Director Captain F. G. Reinicke (Commodore Reinicke after May 1943), who reported to Admiral Andrews, Commander of the Eastern Sea Frontier. Reinicke was still perched high up in the Whitehall

Building, overlooking the harbor at 17 Battery Place. His 1939 staff of two, housed in a single room, had now swollen to 1,200, spread over four floors. It was their task to coordinate the movement of all merchant ships from the time they entered the port until they cleared the antisubmarine net on the way out.

To achieve this, the Whitehall office employed a state-of-the-art communications system. It connected the port director by teletype circuits to Washington, to the four major cable and telegraph companies in New York (Western Union, All-American Cables, RCA, and Mackay), to eight locations around the harbor, and to merchant vessels at sea. Messages were decrypted and encrypted in the Code Room. All this data was assembled and pieced together in the Joint (Army and Navy) Operations Office, where the positions of ships, aircraft, icebergs, and enemy subs throughout the Atlantic were constantly plotted by air and surface controllers on a 28-foot-long Main Situation Board, with the Caribbean situation monitored on the linoleum floor below.

In the adjacent Plotting Annex, the Merchant Marine Section (Convoy and Routing) oversaw the forming up of the large armadas, sometimes more than a hundred ships, that assembled in the Hudson River and moved out during darkness. The resulting volume of traffic was tremendous, especially after September 1942, when New York replaced Halifax as the assembly point for fast convoys, and it swelled again as the Allies began mounting invasions. At the end of 1942 roughly 900 ships were arriving or departing each month; by early 1944, over 1,200. Over the 3-year-and-9-month span ending May 30, 1945, 1,462 convoys comprising 21,459 ships left the Port of New York,

The harbor could get terrifically crowded—on one peak day in 1943, 543 oceangoing merchant vessels rode at anchor, quite apart from the hundreds of other vessels out on the water, such as lighters, warships, ferries, coal barges, scows, carfloats, and tugs. Not surprisingly this led to costly mishaps, as when in February 1943—with four military and twelve mercantile convoys entering and departing in a ten-day stretch—there were thirty-one ship collisions; or on April Fool's Day that same year, when 114 vessels, sent off at three-minute intervals, got hopelessly entangled in a pea-soupy fog, and a dozen crashes ensued. Yet the port never seized up, nor did the backlog of cargo ever surpass seven days (whereas in the last war ninety-day lags had been common).

In considerable measure this was because the Navy worked in close conjunction with Gotham's highly skilled maritime veterans—like the New York and New Jersey Sandy Hook Pilots Association, which traced its beginnings to 1694. It was the pilots who helped departing convoys thread their way past the harbor's hidden reefs, shoals, and bars, and who met arriving battle-damaged boats or giant liners at the Narrows, went aboard, and guided them to their berths. Travel in and out through the harbor's back door was overseen by the Hell Gate Pilots' Association, whose men between 1942 and 1945 guided thousands of vessels through the East River to Long Island Sound without incident.

The Navy and Army could rely, too, on highly professional tugboat operators to haul barges and lighters about the harbor. Edmond J. Moran, current head of the family business founded in 1863, oversaw a fleet of 112 tugs, fifty-three of them government-owned (having been built by the Maritime Commission). After 1942, Moran became director of the War Shipping Administration's barge and towboat service. In that capacity he set hundreds of tugs, commandeered from his and other companies, to hauling barges, drydocks, dredges, derricks, and landing craft to far distant fronts—from the South Pacific and the Aleutians (via the Panama Canal) to Normandy, where Moran personally oversaw "Operation

Mulberry," the dragging by a massive tugboat fleet of the components of two gigantic artificial harbors, each the size of Dover, which were assembled off Utah and Omaha beaches.

THE MILITARY'S RELATIONS WITH NEW York's longshoremen were far more complicated, and contradictory in their consequences. The Army and the War Shipping Administration sought above all else stability and efficiency on the docks. From their perspective, the port's established way of doing business was chaotic and inefficient. In particular, Admiral Land strongly criticized the shape-up—the picking of workers by hiring bosses from among whoever turned up at the pier, with the gang thus assembled laboring anywhere from a few hours to a few days, as long as it took to load or unload a vessel, after which its members went back into the general pool and on their next job might well work with a different crew on a different pier. After a congressional investigation echoed Land's complaint, some called for drafting longshoremen into the Army, or simpler still, sending in the Army to do the work. This was disapproved at the highest levels of the administration, where social democratic ideals and political realities militated against it. Instead, the Brooklyn Army Base pioneered the use of "steady gangs," organizing men into groups that remained intact and worked the same pier; this procedure spread throughout the port, and by 1945 roughly two-thirds of the work force belonged to a steady gang.

Decasualization encouraged a more solidaristic culture—at the very same time a flight of longshoremen from the docks to war plants and the military was creating a labor shortage, enhancing the leverage of those who remained. Together these developments helped reignite the rank-and-file insurgency against the mob-backed International Longshoremen's Union (ILA) that had been snuffed out by the murder of Pete Panto back in 1939. The rank and file had plenty to complain about beyond the "pistol union's" reign of terror. The unprecedented tonnages of cargo moving through the port, the pressure to get supplies to the front fast, and management's omnipresent desire to lower turnaround time and increase profits, all generated a speedup on the docks. Sling loads—once limited to a single ton (and still that on the West Coast docks)—grew to the point that drafts of 6,000 pounds became common, forcing a faster work pace on dock gangs and hold gangs, while making the workplace more dangerous. A series of wildcat strikes broke out, and by the end of 1942 thousands were openly defying ILA boss Joe Ryan.

If the Army had (unwittingly) fostered a dockside insurrection against the gangster-ridden union, the Navy was in bed with the mob. Everyone on the waterfront knew about Commander Haffenden's clandestine meetings with Cockeye Dunn, rackets boss of the Lower West Side docks and close ally of Ryan—a coziness that signaled tacit acceptance of underworld overlordship of the piers. More overtly, the Navy enlisted gangster help in dealing with Harry Bridges, leader of the International Longshore and Warehouse Union (ILWU), the ILA's leftist, mob-free, CIO-affiliated, West Coast counterpart. In 1942 Bridges came east to support rank-and-file protests and to promote the use of centralized hiring halls, which worked well out west. This alarmed Ryan and the ship owners. It also worried Naval Intelligence, which feared port disruption, even though Bridges, like the communists, was well known to be gung-ho about the war. Haffenden passed the word that the Navy didn't "want any trouble on the waterfront," and goons obligingly disrupted Bridges' meeting at Webster Hall, after which Haffenden enthused to Meyer Lansky: "Gee, you did a swell job." The insurgents fared no better when, in early 1943, they turned to the Communist Party for help in breaking the ILA grip on the waterfront; Earl Browder refused to fight Ryan and the war at the same time. Bereft of powerful allies, the rank-and-filers were (for the moment) crushed by Ryan who, in 1943, had himself declared ILA "President for life."

The Navy and WSA were, however, prepared to work with the National Maritime Union (NMU)—a left-wing CIO outfit whose head, Joe Curran, was a close ally of the much-feared Harry Bridges—in part precisely because it *was* a red union, and thus, like the communists, 1,000 percent for labor productivity. Right after Pearl Harbor, Curran called an emergency meeting at the new NMU headquarters at 346 West 17th Street, during which over 2,000 mariners backed a no-strike pledge for the duration policy. The NMU, moreover, joined its AFL rival, the Seafarers International Union (SIU), in sitting down with government and shipowners to hammer out a war policy for the merchant marine. Collective bargaining remained in place. So did the use of union hiring halls to fill ship rosters: companies with NMU contracts contacted the 17th Street headquarters, where hundreds of members congregated night and day on a floor as large and crowded as the Stock Exchange. Dispatchers read out job openings as they came in; sailors who were interested presented their registration card; those who'd been longest ashore got first crack.

The sailors' unions also worked hard to improve working conditions. "Liberty" Ships—first fruits of the Maritime Commission's big production push—were easy to mass produce but dangerous to work in: their lumbering pace left them easy prey for U-boats, and if torpedoed, their thin hulls and poorly designed escape routes led to many needless and horrible deaths. The NMU accepted the Liberties as an emergency response but argued for design changes, using sworn affidavits collected from survivors to make their points, and they helped shift production to an improved successor line of "Victory" Ships.

To help provide crews for the burgeoning fleet—1,800 merchant vessels came down the ways in 1943, where only eighteen had been built during 1937—the unions sent "Keep 'Em Sailing" posters to union halls and factories, asking able-bodied seamen laid off during the Depression to return to the sea. The NMU offered upgrade courses at 17th Street, graduating 6,841 by war's end. And when the government authorized recruitment of refugees from countries overrun by the Nazis, the NMU organized a Committee of European Seamen that assembled over a thousand Norwegian, Danish, Dutch, Belgian, French, Greek, and Yugoslav sailors.

Still, demand far outstripped this limited source of supply, and the government set about training a new generation of mariners, nowhere more intensively than in New York. In the spring of 1942, the Coast Guard purchased 118 acres of property at Manhattan Beach—site of a former amusement park at the eastern end of Coney Island, fronting on Sheepshead Bay—and here built the service's largest training station. It also set aside 76 acres for the United States Maritime Service Training Station, which, by December 1942, had 10,000 apprentice sailors in residence learning the ropes of their trade. By August 1945, Sheepshead Bay had graduated 115,000 of these as merchant seamen, who collectively constituted two-thirds of those who crewed Liberties and Victories for the War Shipping Administration.

Officers, meanwhile, were being turned out on Long Island's northern shore. The Maritime Commission in 1938 had founded a new US Merchant Marine Academy, and in 1943 Admiral Land purchased a home for it, the former Walter Chrysler estate at Kings Point (in Great Neck); dedicated in September, by war's end it had graduated 6,634 officers. At the same time, just across Long Island Sound on Throgs Neck in the Bronx, the long-established New York State Merchant Marine Academy continued to produce officers in the de-garrisoned and WPA-spiffed-up Fort Schuyler.

Despite its contributions to the war effort, the NMU came under fire from the WSA, which was unhappy at the degree of autonomy the union preserved for the workforce. Ship's crews elected committees on each voyage, which negotiated with ship's officers, arranged on-board classes, and passed political resolutions (from condemning Franco's Spain to protesting

Japanese internment). It wasn't surprising that right-wing columnists like Westbrook Pegler excoriated the NMU.

It *was* surprising that Pegler sniped at the entire Merchant Marine and was joined in this by the likes of Walter Winchell and *Time* magazine. The civilian sailors were denounced as draft dodgers—they were exempt from military service, though so were many others who worked in essential war industries—and as overpaid profiteers, this because before the war, during the hyper-dangerous Lend Lease forays to England and Russia, union protests (led primarily by the AFL-affiliated SIU rather than the CIO's NMU) had won government provision of cash bonuses for war-zone service (double pay for the most dangerous runs) and a $5,000 life insurance policy.

The denigration was bizarre, even grotesque, given that by early 1942 more than 1,000 merchant seamen had lost their lives, many of them on boats that went down just off the continental coast in plain sight of civilians (and columnists). Over the course of the war 8,380 of the 215,000 active merchant seamen died—burned alive in exploding oil tankers or frozen alive when their boats went down in arctic waters—a death/life ratio higher than that of any branch of the military other than the Marines. The seamen were vigorously defended by the WSA, by President Roosevelt (who in 1943 organized a White House reception for torpedoed sailors, and included Joe Curran), and by military men of the highest rank: "They brought us our lifeblood," General Douglas MacArthur recalled, "and paid for it with their own."

97

Smaller War Plants

More than a shipping center for the products of heartland manufacturing, New York became an arsenal itself, though only well after the rest of the country had gone into high gear. The time lag was largely a function of the government's reluctance to send war contracts Gotham's way, and that, in turn, was a function of how Wall Street Warriors had restructured the national economy.

No sooner had Stimson, Patterson, Lovett, McCloy, and Forrestal, et al., finally forced the corporate world to shift from civilian to military production, than frenzied competition broke out to snare defense contracts and the scarce raw materials—particularly steel, copper, and aluminum—needed to fulfill them. This led to hoarding, over-ordering, bottlenecks, logjams, and general chaos. With manufacturing approaching paralysis, Roosevelt and his civilian high command set out to impose order on the private sector, without superseding it—the same approach employed in harnessing transportation companies.

In January 1942, FDR created the War Production Board (WPB) and put Donald Nelson in charge. Nelson, a former Sears, Roebuck executive, had liberal inclinations but nevertheless relied on dollar-a-year men—corporate executives, lawyers, and financiers—to run his agency. The key player proved to be New York investment banker Ferdinand Eberstadt, who immediately after Pearl Harbor had been summoned back down to DC by his old friends James Forrestal, undersecretary of the Navy, and Robert Patterson, undersecretary of war. Eberstadt was given command of the Army and Navy Munitions Board (ANMB), where he devised a way for the warring military services to plan and prioritize their matériel requirements. Then he was brought over by Nelson—at the urging of Bernard Baruch, among others—to be vice chairman of the War Production Board. There, in the fall of 1942, he formed the Controlled Materials Plan (CMP). Eberstadt's ingenious system rearranged the way the WPB distributed precious metals—not directly to each of the thousands of war plants ("horizontally"), but "vertically," allocating copper, steel, and aluminum only to prime contractors (chiefly big corporations and the military services themselves), which in turn passed "controlled" substances, as needed, down to subcontractors. This allowed the WPB to retain ultimate control of the flow of essential metals—and thus, indirectly, of the economy itself—while decentralizing day-to-day administration. Eberstadt's CMP worked: in conjunction with his revamped ANMB procedures, it broke logjams, ended bottlenecks, and minimized (though did not eliminate) corporate quarreling.

The CMP only exacerbated the battle between big businesses and smaller ones. WPB's dollar-a-year men tended to give prime contracts (and raw materials) to the industrial giants they had run or counseled. These primes were then allowed to pick—or *not* pick—their own subcontractors: many preferred to centralize production in their own plants, or in new ones the government was building for them, rather than outsource the work. Smaller companies, deprived of access to capital and materials, began to fail; by 1943, there were 500,000 fewer businesses in operation nationwide than in 1941.

New York suffered most from the new arrangements. Despite being by far the largest manufacturing center in the nation, it was relentlessly bypassed when it came to handing out war contracts. At the end of October 1942, Detroit's share of such expenditures amounted to $2,750 per capita. Gotham's was $198, lowest of any leading urban area in the country.

Why? Partly because New York was subcontractor country: apart from shipyards, it had few giant Detroit-style plants run by giant corporations, the kind WPB officials favored. Then, too, the high command (civilian and military) worried about the coastal city's vulnerability to enemy submarines or bombers; its high concentration of citizens who'd opposed the war; and its elevated (and union-defended) wage scales. As a result, even in areas like garment manufacture, where the city was patently in the forefront, the government gave the great bulk of trouser orders to southern companies, saving 10 percent per pair but requiring (as critics like Brooklyn congressman Emanuel Celler pointed out) construction of expensive new plants and installation of expensive new equipment.

At first, Gotham's garment manufacturers were relatively indifferent to this shortfall in contracts, because civilian production remained highly profitable. With customers being drafted and raw materials getting scarcer, however, a growing number of enterprises were driven out of business. By war's end 100,000 of New York State's small businesses (of all descriptions) had folded.

Labor, too, suffered from contract deficiency, though again, not at first, as jobs in consumer-goods production paid better than war work (Gotham was exceptional in this). But when demand fell off and rationing kicked in, unemployment grew and was not offset by government work. By June 1942, 300,000 New Yorkers were registered as unemployed; by October the figure had risen to 369,000 (some said 400,000), higher than it had been in 1939.

At the same time Gotham's labor surplus was swelling, other areas were experiencing labor deficits—war contracts having been awarded without regard for the local labor supply. Some government officials accordingly advised job-seeking New Yorkers to leave the city. Trainloads of men and women, chiefly small manufacturing workers, left town for the centers of war production, an exodus that averaged one thousand per week, surging to as many as ten thousand a month. The West Coast was a major destination for New Yorkers and other easterners: as the Empire State lost 223,000 residents between April 1940 and November 1943, California grew by 1,368,600. This was the demographic context in which the NBC Blue network, during the summer of 1943, began airing *The Life of Riley*, a sitcom that focused on an amiable Brooklynite (played by William Bendix) who had moved to California to work as a riveter in the Stevenson Aircraft factory. This population shift, moreover, wrought collateral damage in New York: where elsewhere the influx of war workers triggered building booms, Gotham in 1942 had 75,000 apartments empty and many homes for sale, and with the market thus glutted, the construction industries slowed to a near halt. In August 1942, the building trades sector contributed 60,000 to the jobless pool.

Small businesses throughout the city and country, and their allies in Congress, protested these procurement policies as socially inefficient, arguing they should be revamped to take advantage of unused capacity in plant and personnel. Critics also denounced the use of taxpayers' money to extinguish small industry and promote monopolization. New Dealers led by Senator Wagner got Congress (in June 1942) to mandate creation of the Smaller War Plants Corporation (SWPC), placing it under the aegis of the War Production Board, whose chief, Donald Nelson, was sympathetic to its mission of redirecting contracts to smaller firms. Yet Nelson also went along with Eberstadt's Controlled Materials Plan even though, he admitted, it would reduce small companies to "semi-feudal dependence upon big and middle-sized business, because of the necessity for subcontracting." In the end, the SWPC lacked the muscle to do much more than sweep a bigger pile of crumbs toward the littler operators.

New York, however, *did* have the requisite muscle—it bulged with political clout—and taking a leaf from A. Philip Randolph's book, the city (and state) demanded a fairer and more intelligent allocation of defense contracts. In the summer of 1942, Mayor La Guardia and Governor Lehman seized FDR's attention by warning him that Thomas Dewey was raising the unemployment issue on the gubernatorial campaign trail. They did not have to underscore the point that if Dewey won the governorship it would serve as springboard from which to challenge Roosevelt himself in 1944. The president ordered the War Production Board to rethink "the use of plant and manpower facilities in New York City," and the military, too, was given its marching orders: Forrestal told La Guardia the Navy intended "to deal positively with what we all recognize to be a serious unemployment situation in the New York City area." A substantial affirmative action program followed. As one component, 12 percent of all Navy contracts distributed between July and October 1942 went to firms in Gotham. By the November election, Roosevelt proclaimed a reduction in joblessness from 400,000 to 280,000. Republican Dewey won anyway, his path to the Governor's Mansion smoothed by divisions among conservative and liberal Democrats.

Governor-elect Dewey kept up the pressure to bolster New York's economy. He appointed a committee to study the unemployment problem—headed by John W. Hanes, former undersecretary of the treasury—which included powerful labor representatives like David Dubinsky; the results of its survey of 1,000 distressed plants in the metropolitan area helped spur further federal action. Sidney Hillman, the War Production Board's labor director (a comedown from his status as cohead of the WPB's predecessor, though not without influence), arranged for big Army and Navy uniform contracts to come to Gotham's union shops (and those in other cities as well). He called his program a "model for 100 per cent utilization of existing facilities and manpower." It certainly went a long way toward reviving the garment industry's sagging fortunes.

Finally, by mid-1943, the Depression was laid to rest in New York. Business failures were down 47.1 percent over those of mid-1942; the average number receiving unemployment insurance benefits had declined 62.7 percent in the same period; home relief cases were down 51 percent. The number of homeless men seeking temporary lodging had cascaded down from its Depression peak of 17,000 to below 2,000, and the number of homeless women had dropped to the point that in June 1943 the Welfare Department closed the Women's Shelter at 630 East Sixth Street and moved its remaining twenty-five occupants to the second floor of the Municipal Lodging House at 438 East 25th Street—itself housing only 400 transients a night in its thousand-bed quarters. La Guardia even set out to "clean up" remaining pockets of poverty, like Skid Row. He dispatched a police squad, which rounded up Bowery vagrants, brought them to station houses for decontaminating and sobering up, then transported them to the Essex Market Court, where the 513 men considered able-bodied were directed to jobs in war plants and other venues; four months later, 284 of these were still employed.

The range of jobs that now opened up validated the claims of those who had argued that New York's manufacturing system was not inferior to the Ford-style mass production favored in the Midwest—just different. Gotham's matrix of more modestly scaled concerns, linked to a dense concentration of skilled workers and engineers, had long been capable of responding rapidly to changes in design, technology, and market demand. Now properly capitalized, the city's myriad workshops—large and small—were quickly converted to turning out war matériel, in each of the five boroughs.

In the Bronx, the 254 employees of American Cystoscope, at 1241 Lafayette Avenue, switched from making medical instruments to producing reflection sights for rocket launchers; and the century-old Hoe and Co., the leading US manufacturer of printing presses, set its huge plant on the East River at 139th Street to fabricating recoil mechanisms.

Staten Island's S. S. White Dental Manufacturing Company at Prince's Bay, famous for its toothpaste, now turned out tachometer drives for airplanes.

Manhattan's Horni Manufacturing Company at 420 West 45th Street redirected its focus from traffic signals to anti-tank mine locators; Treitel-Gratz Industries, a precision sheet metal workshop (at 32nd off Lexington), which had produced architectural metal elements and custom furniture for Radio City Music Hall, now made chairs for the Navy and chassis for electronic equipment. The identification tags given schoolchildren by civilian defense authorities came from the Addressograph Corporation at 329 Fifth Avenue. Manhattan also featured food producers, from Katz's Delicatessen at East Houston and Ludlow (whose slogan was "Send a Salami To Your Boy In The Army"), to the National Biscuit Company's plant at 425 West 15th Street (the island's largest manufacturing unit), which furnished emergency field rations for paratroopers and dog biscuits for the K-9 Corps.

Brooklyn's roughly eight hundred plants churned out war supplies of an astonishing variety, valued in the aggregate (in 1945) at over $3.5 billion. The Hills Brothers fruit-packing plant sent off Dromedary dates and energy nut bars to GIs. The Rheem Manufacturing Company, which normally dealt in gas water heaters and steel barrels, shifted to artillery shells. The S. and S. Corrugated Paper Machine Company sold depth charge release tracks. The Kollmorgen Optical Corporation segued from optical instruments to submarine periscopes. E. W. Bliss at 54th Street and 2nd Avenue continued to manufacture machine tools, but on a grander scale for newer markets, like the enormous mechanical presses dispatched to Russia under Lend Lease, including one of 1.5 million pounds, larger than most used in auto plants. The borough's chemical firms dealt in both life and death, with Charles Pfizer & Co., manufacturing chemists at 11 Bartlett Street, producing well over 50 percent of the country's wartime supply of penicillin, while J. S. & W. R. Eakins, which normally manufactured color pigments at 12 Wallabout Street, now produced a thickener of naphthalene and palmitate (hence: "napalm")—invented by a Harvard chemist in 1942—which when added to gasoline produced a gel used in flame throwers and incendiary bombs.

Queens' industrial complex blossomed under the rain of contracts. General Register Corporation moved from office machines to target-practice devices, and General Bronze from Art Deco architectural art to machine-gun mountings. Waldes Koh-i-Noor, Inc., went from manufacturing pins and needles to making bomb tail fuses in such numbers that it had to build new factories along 27th Street at Austel Place. In Maspeth, a $33 million, 101-acre aluminum plant, one of the largest in the United States, went up in 1942 on the Queens side of Newtown Creek; financed with federal funds and operated by the Aluminum Company of America, it employed 10,000 workers and required so much power that Con Ed had to run it a 132kv transmission line.

Also in 1942, Astoria's General Aircraft Corporation (GAC) got an Army Air Force contract to build behemoth gliders, their steel fuselages lifted aloft on wings made of plywood, which new technology could make as strong as steel, thus reserving scarce metals for combat planes and bombers. General Aircraft, in turn, subcontracted wing production to woodmeisters Steinway & Sons, who had shut down piano production when the War Production Board denied them steel and copper. Steinway's workers turned to glueing together the 84-foot-long wingspans in an old foundry building, which were then paraded through the streets of Queens to the GAC plant nearby. Alas for all concerned, the gliders' design proved flawed—they became known as "flying coffins"—and the firm, casting about for wood-based alternatives, turned to making *actual* coffins, for the National Casket Company in Long Island City. Somewhat farther afield, though a musical entertainment venture of sorts, Steinway sought to boost the productivity and morale of home front industrial workers with its "Operatic Plant Broadcaster," a rival to Muzak. Alas, Muzak was still flourishing mightily in its studios at 229 Fourth Avenue and had pretty much cornered the market, with over a thousand accounts in New York alone, including war plants and civilian venues (bars, clubs, hotels, restaurants, and department stores). Fortunately, Steinway managed to segue back to its core business when, in June 1943, it got its first order for 405 olive-drabbed Victory model uprights for entertaining the troops. Each came in an olive-green packing case, equipped with handles so that four soldiers could carry it, and cost $486, complete with tuning kit. By the end of the war, Steinway had shipped 5,000 of these pianos, roughly half to the armed forces, the rest to churches, educational institutions, and hotels.

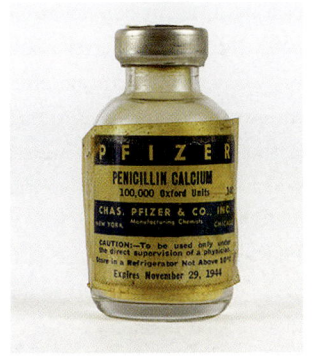

Charles Pfizer & Co., Inc., Penicillin bottle, 1944. (Center for Brooklyn History)

One Queens airplane manufacturer had deep roots in the borough. The Brewster Aeronautical Corporation (organized in 1932) was a descendant of the old Brewster & Company carriage-maker firm, which itself had evolved into Brewster Auto. Brewster Aeronautical rented space in Brewster Auto's 1910 red-brick factory in Long Island City, facing Queens Plaza at the end of the Queensboro Bridge. Here—and in space leased in the nearby Pierce-Arrow and Ford buildings—Brewster built dive bombers and carrier-based fighters, trucking the finished products, in sections, out to Roosevelt Field for final assembly.

The future of the aviation industry, however, did not lie in the city's crowded streets. Rather, its dramatic wartime expansion took place out in the suburbs, notably Nassau County, part of an industrial migration that would have potent long-term consequences for the five boroughs.

Grumman Aircraft Engineering Corporation had opened for business in 1930 in an abandoned auto showroom-garage in Baldwin, a Nassau County village about twenty miles east of Manhattan, on Long Island's southern shore. There, twenty-one employees repaired flying boats and built replacement parts until, in 1931, Leroy Grumman got a Navy contract to build a prototype carrier-based fighter plane, the FF, which led to a move 8 miles farther east, to a vacant hangar at Curtiss Field in Valley Stream. When the XFF-1 tested successfully, the Navy ordered a squadron's-worth, and, with more contracts on the way, the company was off to Farmingdale, 16 miles farther east, and then finally, in 1936, it settled in a few miles to the north at Bethpage, where it began to grow in place. In 1937 Grumman came up with an experimental single-wing fighter that by 1939 had evolved into the stubby but rugged F4F Wildcat, just as war broke out in Europe. Mass orders by England and France in 1940 sent the company into overdrive—the payroll leapt from 700 in 1939 to 6,500 by Pearl Harbor—and catapulted it to the front rank of military provisioners. Over the next three years employees soared to 25,000 (none of them unionized), while the Bethpage plant doubled in size, courtesy of the Navy, using columns of steel salvaged from the World's Fair site. Over the course of the war Grumman turned out 17,000 planes—the 330 m.p.h. Wildcats, which were on board all Pacific Fleet carriers by the Battle of Midway in June 1942, and the successor 400 m.p.h. F6F Hellcats, which were developed to do battle with the Japanese Zero, and did, becoming the most successful aircraft in naval history.

The other major-league Nassau County firm, Republic Aviation, had a somewhat more exotic backstory, its roots traceable to the Seversky Aircraft Corporation, founded in 1931 by Russian expatriate Alexander de Seversky. An ace in the Imperial forces during the First World War, and designer of a widely adopted bombsight, Seversky built his company around Russian engineers who had escaped Stalin's purges. Headquartered in Manhattan, he set up production near Farmingdale in 1934 and won his first Army contract the following year, for a land-plane version of a streamlined amphibious he'd designed in 1933. After this auspicious takeoff, Seversky Aircraft ran into financial headwinds, was kept aloft for a time by Wall Street investors, but crashed in 1939, when it was reorganized as Republic Aviation, and Seversky was ousted from the firm he'd founded. Shortly thereafter came the military buildup, and major orders flowed in. Government loans financed a quadrupling of Republic's factory space and the building of three new runways on its 560-acre Farmingdale site. The workforce, which shot up to 25,000, would turn out 9,000 P-47 Thunderbolts for the Army Air Force, which sent it into action against the Luftwaffe and by 1944 was deploying it also as a fighter-bomber.

While some housing for defense workers sprang up around these giants, and near the new Sperry Gyroscope plant (also in Nassau), the great bulk of the labor force commuted out from the city on special Long Island Rail Road trains. Still, war contracts had clearly created the potential economic and demographic nucleus for a major suburban development, once the freeze on new housing construction was lifted, and this vision would be pursued by J. Russell Sprague, the county executive, Republican Party boss, and stalwart supporter (and beneficiary) of the rise of Tom Dewey.

Another metropolitan area commuting complex boosted by the war lay on the city's western flank—the towns and cities of northern New Jersey. Existing factories expanded and new ones flowered in Bayonne, Bloomfield, Clifton, Edgewater, Elizabeth, Harrison, Hoboken, Jersey City, Kearny, Linden, Newark, North Bergen, Perth Amboy, Port Newark, Rahway, Teterboro, and Woodbridge. Quickly exhausting the local labor supply, war plants imported workers. The small town of Harrison, population 14,000, soon had more than 90,000 workers commuting to it on a daily basis, many via the Hudson and Manhattan Railroad, direct from lower Manhattan. Employees headed to and from Federal Shipbuilding and Drydock's yard in Port Newark could take dedicated Central Railroad of New Jersey trains (accessible from New York via the Liberty Street ferry) straight to the door, at starting and quitting time. Bendix Aviation Corporation's subsidiary, Pioneer Instrument Company, which Bendix relocated from Brooklyn to Teterboro, hired heavily to meet the demand for aircraft instrumentation and was reachable by train from Manhattan (via Hoboken). The old (1915) Aluminum Company of America plant in Edgewater, directly across the Hudson from Harlem via the 125th Street Ferry, dramatically expanded its rolling mill operations (becoming the second largest in the US) as it switched from making toothpaste tubes to aircraft parts.

For the moment this surge of war-induced (and possibly only temporary) industrial plants in the greater metropolitan region seemed less like suburban competition than providential job provision for underemployed central city dwellers. More worrisome was the ongoing flow of contracts to the South, Midwest, and West, which continued to build up rival centers of production, eroding the city's quondam preeminence even in some of its historically strongest suits, like shipbuilding. The Brooklyn Navy Yard nonetheless remained the largest boat-builder in the country, perhaps in the world. At its peak, 75,000 civilian and naval personnel labored (in three shifts) around the clock—the yard a mountain of light at night—building battleships and carriers and repairing over 5,000 wounded vessels, amid the thundering clang of foundries and incessant hammering of riveters. And it was only one of forty active shipyards in the Port of New York—both immense ones, like Bethlehem Steel's operation at Mariner's Harbor on Staten Island, and the more boutique-scaled Consolidated Shipbuilding Corporation at Morris Heights in the Bronx (on the Harlem River at 177th Street), which specialized in sub chasers. All grew rapidly during the war years—Brooklyn's ship works (not including the Navy Yard) had 60,548 laborers between them in 1942; by the summer of 1943, 96,090 were at work, mainly producing or repairing military vessels.

Cargo ship production, however, was largely done elsewhere. The nearly 600,000 strong workforce employed by the Maritime Commission labored predominantly on the Pacific or Gulf coasts, or at other eastern seaboard ports. US Steel's Federal Shipyards in Kearny, New Jersey, did construct some cargo boats for Admiral Land, but they were a relatively small percentage of the 400 ships it built during the war. When the Maritime Commission issued "M" pennants for outfits with superior construction records, New York yards were seldom on the list. The Commission—taken to task for failure to erect one of its new yards on Staten Island—argued it was hard to find unoccupied land, and that, plus the higher cost of such metropolitan real estate as was available, does provide some of the explanation. Nevertheless, it was also due to a technological revolution in shipbuilding, in which New York, unusually, was not in the forefront.

Traditional construction technique worked from the keel up, with the vessel being completely constructed on its way, each new piece being riveted in place. Newer yards prefabricated and preassembled a ship's sections, then welded them together, which was considerably less labor intensive (hence cheaper) and produced a smoother more frictionless hull. The advantages of this approach had long been known to New York shipbuilders. In 1912, Wallace Downey, head of the Downey Shipbuilding Corporation of Mariner's Harbor, Staten Island, had called for building standardized ships, and Averell Harriman's Chester, Pennsylvania, yard had used welding extensively during the First World War. But converting to new techniques required reconstructing shipyards to accommodate them, an expensive business for long-established firms. Those who trailblazed were those who were building from scratch, with federal money, notably Henry Kaiser, who himself had no shipbuilding experience, nor did Portland, Oregon, where he constructed facilities. His attendant unconventionality helped him cut the time it took to build a Liberty Ship from a year to 196 days, and then to slash it again to twenty-seven days by 1943. Similarly, Richmond, California, which hadn't had a shipyard before the Second World War, produced more merchant vessels than any city in the country. Little wonder New Yorkers went west to such centers—by July 1943 roughly 2,500 New Yorkers had gone to work in Kaiser's Portland yard.

There was, however, one manufacturing sector in which New York was able to build upon established strengths rather than being constrained by them—the new and rapidly expanding "electronics" industry. A vague term, used only fleetingly in the 1920s, it became suddenly fashionable around 1930, employed to refer to that sector of the "electrical" industry which dealt with the production and use of vacuum tubes. These devices—traceable to Edison's discovery in 1883 that a current of electrons will flow, inside a vacuumed bulb, from a negatively charged filament to a positively charged metal plate, and Lee de Forest's discovery in 1906 that adding a metal grid between the other two elements (creating a "triode"), allowed this flow to be controlled and amplified. The "tube" had become widely known, and hailed, for its centrality to radio and talking pictures. It was in the early Depression years that attention was suddenly paid to the host of other marvelous developments—previously overshadowed by broadcasting and talkies—that the tube, in its now hundreds of specialized varieties, had made possible.

"A New Industry Springs up from Tiny Speck of Electricity," bannered a *New York Times* story of March 23, 1930, describing the "new industry called electronics." A leader of the Electrical Association of New York explained that "without anybody noticing it particularly"—outside of engineering circles—a "new science and industry has developed within our world of electricity." It "has been given the name electronics, indicating the new realm of the vacuum tube," a realm, he noted, which had now expanded far beyond "radio, telephone, sound pictures and broadcasting." In April 1930 a new magazine brought out by McGraw-Hill, called *Electronics*, devoted itself to be-wondered explorations of these new applications, including facsimiles, medical x-rays, musical instruments, phonographs, amplifiers, and lie detectors; and devices that controlled giant industrial machines, tracked stars, leveled elevators at each stop, and located underground oil. For many, the most dazzling inventions were those using photoelectric cells—automatic traffic lights, safety devices on dangerous machines, burglar alarms, and lights that switched on when one entered the room.

New York had been at the center of the electronics revolution, not only because of resident inventors like Edison and de Forest, but because the city had long been a junction point between the electrical and the communications/entertainment industries, each feeding on and sustaining the other. The city had also repeatedly been able to roll over a preeminence established in one era on into the next one when a new technology emerged, which is why it figured so prominently in the sequential crucibling of the telegraph, Atlantic cable, telephone, light bulb, movies, sound movies, and the still-in-the-works television.

So it was with electronic devices. Their invention and manufacture were nurtured in the New York metropolitan region because their rapidly involving technology thrived on interaction with the city's deep pools of researchers, designers, scientists, engineers, technicians, skilled craftsmen, capitalists, other manufacturers, and markets. The Radio Corporation of America, headquartered in Rockefeller Center, had at first purchased its tubes from other suppliers and inspected them in the Technical and Test Laboratory it built opposite Van Cortlandt Park in the Bronx in 1924. When in 1930 David Sarnoff decided to manufacture electronics as well as marketing them, he bought up and expanded the old Edison Light Works in Harrison, New Jersey, just across the Passaic River from Newark. Similarly, Western Electric—the AT&T-owned manufacturing arm for the Bell Telephone system—though it had its major plant in suburban Chicago's Hawthorne Works (1905), because its corporate roots were in that city, also established early on an eastern base in New York at 363 West

Street. In 1925 it transferred manufacturing and distribution functions to a new 11-story behemoth at 395 Hudson Street, the largest concrete structure on Manhattan Island. The Western Electric Tube Shop as it became known filled the entire block bounded by Hudson, West Houston, Greenwich, and Clarkson, and combined factory, warehouse, and office functions. (The same year, Western Electric opened a large plant in Kearny, New Jersey, just north of RCA's operations in Harrison.) Around these giant tube suppliers clustered an array of large and small manufacturers of radio sets, along with parts suppliers and the secondhand stores on Radio Row. By the late thirties, Gotham appeared to be not only a Radio City but an Electronic City.

The war seemed, at first, to menace this consumer electronics complex. Soon after Pearl Harbor, production of radio (and experimental television) sets for the civilian market was quashed for the duration. This cessation of sales was followed immediately by a torrent of orders from the federal government and armed forces—customers who also supplied the capital that enabled electronics makers to expand and retool their plants.

Military demand also summoned forth a constant flow of new inventions, too, most spectacularly radar and the atomic bomb. New York played a significant role in their respective developments, contributing crucial financial, political, experimental, and theoretical inputs. Gotham did not dominate the two breakthroughs, though, as it had previous ones. The wartime mega-projects required stupendous financial resources, which only the federal government could provide, and an assemblage of intellectual resources, on which Gotham held no monopoly. Still, New Yorkers, and the European exiles they made welcome, proved indispensable to the nick-of-time creation of the radar defenses that drove the U-boats from their own shores, and to the design and production of the ultimate offensive weapon.

SCIENCE IN THE CITY

Two men work on a cyclotron in Columbia University's Nevis Laboratories. (University Archives, Rare Book & Manuscript Library, Columbia University Libraries)

98

R&D: Radar

It was in 1908 that ten-year-old Isidor Isaac Rabi first learned, to his astonishment, that the earth went around the sun. This was not something he'd heard around the dinner table of his orthodox Jewish family, who had come from a small village in Galicia to 91 Willett Street on the Lower East Side shortly after he was born. His father worked in a sweatshop, saved enough to start a grocery store, then in 1907 moved the family to Brownsville, where he opened a larger shop (which doubled as house) at 481 Hopkinson Avenue, near Pitkin Avenue. It was here that Isidor discovered the Carnegie Library, six blocks away, and began methodically going through its science collection, in alphabetical order, starting with astronomy, which is how he came across a book about Copernicus, with its revelation about the structure of the universe. Soon, with other neighborhood kids, he got immersed in telegraphy, strung wires across streets, learned Morse code. He plunged ahead into wireless, built himself a tuner, transmitter, and coupler, designed a condenser to store electric energy, and put up big antennas that allowed him, Sarnoff-style, to pick up dispatches from ships. While still in elementary school, he published his first scientific paper in Hugo Gernsback's *Modern Electrics*, of which he was a devout fan.

Perhaps his practical bent influenced Rabi's decision not to attend Boys High (at Marcy and Madison in nearby Bedford-Stuyvesant), where all the smart Jewish kids went, but rather the predominantly Gentile Manual Training High School (farther away at Seventh Avenue and Fourth Street in Park Slope). Manual offered carpentry, machine shop, and foundry work, but getting there meant traversing three miles of hostile gang-controlled streets. In 1916 Rabi won a New York State Regents College Scholarship (a public program established in 1913), thanks to which he attended Cornell, studying electrical engineering and chemistry and encountering the gentlemanly anti-Semitism that permeated academic science departments in those years. He was told such prejudice extended to the hiring practices of scientific institutions, something he verified after graduating in 1919, though he did hold a job for a time in the Lederle Laboratories analyzing furniture polish. Mostly he hung out with Jewish friends, arguing science and philosophy and reading in both fields at the main New York Public Library on Fifth Avenue.

In April 1921 Albert Einstein—spectacularly famous since 1919, when his general theory of relativity had received experimental support during a solar eclipse—made his first visit to the US. He arrived in Hoboken, was ferried to the Battery where he was welcomed by thousands (many of them fellow Jews), and later was received at City Hall by Mayor John Francis Hylan before another throng of well-wishers. The welcoming process was not without its hiccups, however, as when one Bruce M. Falconer, a member of the Board of Aldermen, blocked an otherwise unanimous vote to extend Einstein the "freedom of the city." Denunciations showered down on the alderman's "narrowness and bigotry," but Falconer held his ground. He denied he was anti-Semitic, noting that his private physician (and some of his best friends) were Jewish, insisted that the city's "freedom" had been handed out all too promiscuously, and maintained that he, as a descendant of the Secretary of Lord Cornbury, the first to be so honored (in 1702), had a special responsibility to uphold standards. Up in Albany, the Senate, calling the aldermanic failure "a disgrace," extended Einstein the freedom of the entire *state*.

Overflow crowds turned out to hear the physicist lecture, first at Columbia on April 15 (escorted by Professors M. I. Pupin and G. B. Pegram), then on April 20 and 21 at City College, where Einstein's auditors included I. I. Rabi. Whether or not the startling degree of hyper-glamour attached to a Jewish physicist was part of his motivation, Rabi returned to Cornell in 1922 for graduate work, shifting from chemistry to physics. When he didn't get a fellowship, he moved back to Gotham and, in 1923, entered Columbia, which he found somewhat less anti-Semitic than Cornell, though no more generous as to funding; after 1924, a teaching assistantship at nearby CCNY helped pay the bills. More troubling, there was no one at Columbia, or in virtually any US university, capable of teaching quantum mechanics, the new theoretical development emerging in Europe between 1925 and 1927.

Theory had never been American (or New York) science's strong suit. Some of its greatest names—Morse, Edison, Lee de Forest—knew just enough to make their breakthroughs, but not enough to push the theoretical envelope. Physicists were especially thin on the ground, and (with some notable exceptions) their contributions to the field were even thinner. The *Physical Review*, founded in 1893, had been edited out of Cornell until 1913, when it became the responsibility of the American Physical Society (APS). This body, created in 1899 at a Columbia conference, made New York its home (though it didn't get its own headquarters until 1943, when it bought a 5-story building at 57–59 East 55th Street). The change in venue from Upstate to Downstate didn't make the journal any more compelling, and as late as 1927, when Rabi got his PhD, the Göttingen physics department, confident it wouldn't miss much, didn't bother having current issues of *Physical Review* delivered; it saved on trans-Atlantic postage and had a year's worth delivered at a time.

Rabi's generation of American physicists—which had grown in numbers as more and more PhDs got turned out by Columbia, Cornell, Harvard, Johns Hopkins, Chicago, and California, among others—wanted desperately to catch up. Fortunately, an unprecedented amount of money became available for postdoctoral fellowships, critically from two New York–based institutions, the International Education Board (IEB) created by John D. Rockefeller Jr. in 1923, and the John Simon Guggenheim Memorial Foundation, established in 1925 by Simon Guggenheim. Rabi was among the roughly fifty scientists sent off to Europe at the end of the 1920s—he went to Hamburg in 1928, and in 1929 (on an IEB fellowship) to Leipzig, where he worked with Werner Heisenberg. Rabi met many other leading European physicists—established elder figures like Niels Bohr, and members of his own generation like

Edward Teller, Hans Bethe, Enrico Fermi—and other young Americans, too, notably J. Robert Oppenheimer, a fellow New Yorker, though from a different part of town. Born in 1904 to a prosperous and highly cultured German Jewish family, Oppenheimer grew up on Riverside Drive and 88th Street and was schooled at Ethical Culture (on Central Park West), Harvard, and Cambridge. Though Oppenheimer was extremely assimilated, while Rabi remained far more comfortable with his Jewishness, the two got on famously and traveled together during their European sojourn.

In 1929, Oppenheimer went to Pasadena to accept a joint appointment at California Institute of Technology and the University of California at Berkeley. The same year, Rabi moved back to New York and accepted a lectureship at Columbia. These and other Jewish hirings represented both a larger cultural opening and a specific need for faculty to teach the new quantum mechanics. Columbia's Physics Department chairman George Pegram wanted a "hotshot" physicist, Werner Heisenberg highly recommended Rabi, and voilá! Columbia's first Jewish physics professor was on board, teaching flocks of graduate students, many of them Jewish graduates of City College. Nationwide, too, graduate physics programs exploded; between 1933 and 1941 nearly 1,300 newly minted physicists entered the profession. The surge of new talent quickly eliminated the gap between the quality of European and American research, and current issues of *Physical Review* became required reading in Göttingen and all Europe.

At the same time that US physics was opening up, Hitler was shutting German physics down. By April 1936 over 1,600 scholars, roughly one-third of them scientists, had been dismissed from German universities and scientific institutions. Between 1933 and 1941 over 100 émigré physicists (including eight past and future Nobel winners) found academic posts in the US, often with help from the Rockefeller Foundation, whose goal was to disperse them throughout the country. Some did come to Gotham, but more settled in its hinterland—if defined broadly enough to include Princeton, an hour's train ride away—notably Einstein himself, who in 1933 accepted a position at the recently established Institute of Advanced Studies (modeled on Berlin's Kaiser Wilhelm Institute).

In general, the European émigrés melded well with their American colleagues, appreciating the closer collaboration between theoreticians and experimentalists and the assembling of large teams grouped around big machines, notably cyclotrons. Invented in 1930 by Ernest Lawrence and his Berkeley colleagues, cyclotrons allowed researchers to transcend the limits of natural radioactive substances, like radium, as sources of high-energy particles with which to bombard neutrons. By 1934 the Berkeley cyclotron, popularly known as "merry-go-round atom-gun," was using an 85-ton magnet to whirl and send particles smashing into targets at 25,000 miles per second. It also helped California emerge as an R&D rival to older established centers back East. The money came in part from local energy utilities, which had no intrinsic interest in basic physics but were extremely interested in funding anything that might lead to improved high-voltage transmission of hydroelectric power.

In New York, Columbia's efforts to catch up were constrained by its Depression-strained finances, but physicist John R. Dunning scavenged some salvageable equipment. In December 1935 he located a 65-ton Navy-surplus magnet and had it hauled up from Annapolis, in sixty-five pieces, on a thirteen-truck caravan, and delivered to the basement of Pupin Hall at Broadway and 120th Street.

By then, upstairs on Pupin's fifth floor, I. I. Rabi had his molecular beam laboratory up and running, using the resonance method he'd devised to measure the magnetic properties of atomic nuclei and thus reveal their secrets. Funding came, not from cash-strapped

Columbia, but from his colleague Harold Urey, who had joined the Chemistry Department in 1929 and in 1932 discovered deuterium, the heavy isotope of hydrogen. Even before Urey got the Nobel Prize in 1934 for this crucial breakthrough, he received a cash grant of $7,600 from the Carnegie Foundation, half of which he gave, in an act of remarkable generosity, to the young and seemingly promising Rabi. Urey's assessment proved correct; a series of first-rate papers from Rabi and his graduate students began appearing in *Physical Review*. And long before Rabi's work was recognized with its own Nobel, in 1944, Columbia in general and Rabi's lab in particular had moved to the forefront of the profession and become a must-see stopping-off place for visiting European physicists.

It was not the only one in town. By the mid-1930s a *second* center of cutting-edge physics had emerged in New York. This one, in dramatic contrast to the constellation of university-trained and university-employed professionals, revolved around just one man, and that man, Alfred Lee Loomis, was an amateur, probably the last great amateur of science. Loomis was also, in addition to being a brilliant experimenter and inventor, a staggeringly *rich* amateur, and well wired into the social circuitry of New York's upper class; as a result, his research projects would have outsized impact.

Loomis emerged from prosperous Episcopalian Manhattan—a very different Gotham from Rabi's Jewish Brownsville. His grandfather was a famous medical man who specialized in the treatment of tuberculosis and accumulated a substantial estate; his father was a highly regarded physician and professor; and his maternal uncle, also a doctor, sired Henry Stimson. After studying math at Yale, Loomis went to Harvard Law School and, on graduating in 1912, started a clerkship at Winthrop & Stimson, cousin Henry's law firm. In 1917, he attended the Plattsburgh training camp with Stimson, who looked after Loomis's military service as he had his legal career. Given Loomis's math skills and obsession with the history of artillery, he was commissioned as a captain and posted to the Army Proving Ground at Aberdeen, where, placed in charge of research and development, he invented an ingenious device to measure the velocity of shells.

After the Armistice, bored with law, Loomis switched to finance. With his brother-in-law, Landon Thorne, he took over a sagging investment firm, Bonbright & Company. During the 1920s they turned it into a powerhouse—literally so, in that it became the leader at raising capital for the fast-growing electrical industry. Bonbright & Co. also arranged mergers that produced huge power utilities like Consolidated Gas of New York and Commonwealth and Southern, whose president, Wendell Willkie, was a Loomis appointee. By February 1930, *Fortune* described the Loomis and Thorne duo as "the most potent force in shaping the present and future organization of America's huge, complex power and light business." They had also become multimillionaires. Loomis had a luxurious penthouse off Central Park at 21 East 79th Street; a house in hyper-exclusive Tuxedo Park (the 3,000-acre barbed-wired enclave for New York's superrich in the Ramapo foothills, less than an hour's drive from the city); and a summer place in East Hampton. He and Thorne also bought the entire island of Hilton Head off South Carolina for riding and hunting with friends, and together they designed and had built a racing sloop for the America's Cup competition.

But Loomis had another life. At Aberdeen he'd struck up a friendship with Robert W. Wood of Johns Hopkins, a brilliant experimental physicist and prolific inventor, and in 1924 the two became collaborators. Loomis set up research facilities in his Tuxedo Park garage, and Wood picked out projects and tutored Loomis in physics. In 1926 the two went on a high-end version of the European scientific grand tour that academics were taking, with Wood providing introductions to leading physicists and Loomis footing the bill. In 1927, needing more research space, Loomis purchased the Trask mansion in Tuxedo Park, a massive stone structure with a medieval-style tower and battlements, and outfitted it as a world-class scientific facility.

In 1929, chary of the speculative fever sweeping the market, Loomis converted his securities into bonds and cash, just before the Crash. Then he and Thorne plowed their funds into mainstream banking, becoming dominant powers in Bankers Trust and First National, and by 1932 they were towering figures on Wall Street. Loomis made roughly fifty million dollars during those first years of the Depression, and he raked in a lot of money for Henry Stimson, too, providing the financial underpinnings of his cousin's political career. Then, as public outrage at Gotham's banking elite reached feverish heights, Loomis quit the Street altogether and retired to his crenelated stone tower.

During the Depression, Loomis funded significant research at Tuxedo Park. He also sponsored dozens of scientific conferences and invited eminent scientists to spend time there. Visiting Europeans were met at their boats and swept up to Tuxedo by limo or private train. Bohr, Heisenberg, and Einstein were among the guests. (Loomis's welcoming of Jews was definitely a no-no in that Protestant citadel, but with so many residents ruined by the Crash, the community had other things to worry about.) Loomis also invited impecunious young scientists for long-term stays and gave them stipends to live on while working as researchers in his lab.

Loomis threw a financial lifeline to Depression-strapped universities, whose research budgets had been wiped out, and when the *Physical Review*, like many academic journals, was on the brink of bankruptcy he anonymously covered some of its bills. He was particularly generous with MIT, having helped his friend Karl Compton become its president in 1933 and having himself been made a trustee.

So in 1939 he immediately agreed to Compton's war-related request for help investigating the use of radio waves as detection devices.

It had been known since 1888 that radio waves got reflected back from solid objects. In 1922 Marconi had suggested using them on boats to detect obstacles ahead in the fog or dark. With the German bombing of cities during the Spanish Civil War, finding a way to sniff out planes at a distance (and soon submarines as well) became an urgent priority. The British developed the first practical system of radio detection and by mid-1938 had installed sets atop wooden towers along England's southern and eastern shores. In 1940 this Chain Home Network proved capable of picking up German bomber armadas before they were halfway across the North Sea, allowing the dispatch of RAF fighters to meet them. However, the Network could only generate *long* wavelengths—ten meters or more—which couldn't pick out small targets such as individual aircraft, much less submarine periscopes.

MIT had been studying how to generate very *short* wavelengths—*micro*-waves, ten centimeters or less—and in the summer of 1939, on receiving Compton's request for help, Loomis dropped all other research projects and welcomed a team of MIT physicists to Tuxedo Park. By the following summer they and Loomis had developed a crude device, which they tested by tracking cars on a nearby highway. It worked so well at spotting speeders that one said, "For the Lord's sake, don't let the cops know about this."

In the meantime, radio detection had emerged as a major priority at a third site of Gothamic physics—the business-based invention factory, Bell Telephone Laboratories. As a wholly owned subsidiary of AT&T and Western Electric, Bell Labs' research had at first been strictly instrumental, firmly focused on improving telephone technology. Over time it had embraced basic research as being essential to that goal, even research that didn't promise any immediate payoff. Adopting a long-range planning horizon was something the giant and supremely profitable monopoly had the luxury to afford.

That it did so was in large measure due to Frank B. Jewett. The son of a California businessman, Jewett got a PhD in physics from the University of Chicago in 1902, having studied with Albert A. Michelson, who became the country's first Nobel Laureate in 1907. That was also the year Jewett moved to Gotham to work in the research department of Western Electric, AT&T's manufacturing subsidiary, newly consolidated at 463 West Street (at Bethune). Jewett took on the task of improving long-distance service. At the time, New Yorkers could call no farther than Chicago, as there was no satisfactory way to amplify signals that weakened as they went. In seeking a solution, Jewett included a small group of talented physicists in his West Street team. By 1915 they had cracked the problem, with the indispensable aid of de Forest's triode amplifier, whose patent AT&T purchased in 1913. The first transcontinental telephone line was showily introduced when Alexander Graham Bell picked up a phone in New York and called his old associate, Thomas Watson, telling him what he'd famously told him nearly forty years before—"Mr. Watson, come here, I want you"—to which Watson replied, from San Francisco: "It would take me a week to get there now!"

Jewett urged AT&T to explore the fundamental characteristics of electrons, in tandem with university-based physicists, in a structured and ongoing way. In 1925 the company agreed, setting up Bell Labs (in its West Street building) with a staff of 3,600, and put Jewett in charge, freed from any pressure to obtain short-term results. Convinced that academic and industrial research labs were "very closely associated and must grow together," Jewett had staff members take courses in Rabi country—Columbia University was a straight shot uptown on the I.R.T.—and he encouraged Bell researchers to present and publish professional papers about their work. In 1927, Clinton Davisson, a staff physicist, showed by experiment that electrons could behave as waves as well as particles, work that would win him a Nobel in physics, the first such prize to go to a scientist in an American industrial laboratory. With the West Street complex conveniently handy to the Hudson River piers—the New York Central's elevated freight line ran through the building's third floor—Europe's leading physicists often stopped by to give seminars when visiting the United States. It was a measure of how closely industrial and university research had become intertwined that Jewett himself was chosen president of the National Academy of Sciences in 1939.

At the same time, industrial and academic labs were being drawn into military research. In 1937, Bell Labs was contacted by both Army and Navy to help in further developing radio-detection devices, a project on which military researchers had been working since 1934. By July 1939, Bell engineers were able to demonstrate a working prototype to armed forces representatives: set atop an 80-foot-high bluff overlooking Sandy Hook Bay, at Atlantic Highlands, New Jersey, it proved able to accurately plot the movement of ships in and out of the Ambrose Channel, picking up targets as far as 15 kilometers away.

In 1940, the Blitzkrieg galvanized the federal government into organizing an agency to mobilize and coordinate the work of all three kinds of scientists, in New York and throughout the country. On June 27, ten days after the fall of France, Roosevelt created a twelve-man National Defense Research Committee (NDRC), to be run by Dr. Vannevar Bush, who had proposed it to FDR two weeks earlier. Bush, the MIT dean of engineering who in 1938 had become president of the Carnegie Institution of Washington, quickly assembled his dozen members, including MIT's Compton and Bell Labs' Frank Jewett. The group decided not to build a consolidated research entity from scratch and instead to contract projects out to existing institutions. After surveying 775 universities, industrial labs, nonprofits, and military research centers to find out who was doing what, and what resources were available, the NDRC set up a series of project-oriented committees.

To head the all-important Microwave Committee, Bush chose Loomis, who as a gentleman amateur fit none of the three categories; but he had done significant radio wave research on his own and with MIT physicists, and it didn't hurt that he was immensely rich, or that his first cousin had just been appointed secretary of war. Indeed, Stimson would give high priority attention to his cousin's work on what Stimson liked to call the "radio eye" but which now, in 1940, became officially known as "radar"—an acronym, selected by a US Navy officer, for RAdio Detection And Range.

No one, however, had developed a transmitter capable of generating sufficiently short wavelengths, until September, when a delegation of British physicists arrived bearing the solution. Hot from the lab, it was a radio transmitter called a magnetron, capable of producing microwaves a thousand times stronger than any American equipment. Only twelve existed. The Brits—preoccupied with German air raids—needed US scientific expertise to develop radar units small enough to fit in planes and US industrial might to churn them out in mass quantities. Loomis arranged a meeting between British and American scientists at Tuxedo Park, then brought the device down to Bell Labs for technical conversations. On October 14, at his Manhattan penthouse, Loomis handed out contracts to Bell, Sperry, GE, RCA, and other New York industrial producers, for the production, in thirty days, of magnetrons for use in a crash research project to come.

For that project itself Loomis decided a central laboratory would have the best chance of coming up with the workable radar sets desperately needed for land, sea, and air defenses. His committee agreed that a civilian-run entity, modeled on his Tuxedo Park operation, was the way to go, but where to put it? Loomis, Compton, and Bush pushed for MIT. Jewett held out for Manhattan, noting that Bell, having run a similar effort during the First World War, had the managerial expertise to handle a colossal enterprise. The MIT boosters argued that Cambridge would provide better cover for a large assemblage of scientists, whose true mission had to remain secret, as the US was still neutral and many Americans (particularly numerous in New York) were unwilling to risk further involvement by aiding the British.

In October the contract went to MIT, which established the Radiation Laboratory (aka the Rad Lab). Loomis shut down Tuxedo Park and moved to Cambridge. So did Isidor Rabi, who arrived on November 6 to accept the position of associate director, in charge of developing the magnetron. The project grew quickly, eventually employing 4,000 people, 500 of them physicists. It developed about 100 specialized radar systems, which were rushed into service, including the superb SCR-584, which could direct anti-aircraft fire, and the microwave Air to Surface Vessel radar SCR-517, which was installed on Army Air Force Liberators and sent into action in spring 1942.

By the summer of 1943, U-boat chief Dönitz was deeply worried about "the methods of radio-location which the Allies have introduced"; by December he was forced to admit that the enemy, through "his superiority in the field of science," has "torn our sole offensive weapon in the war against the Anglo-Saxons from our hands."

By this point, New Yorkers—newly minted and long established—were deeply involved in developing a very different kind of offensive weapon, the most powerful the world had ever known.

99

R&D: Manhattan Project

In 1938 nuclear physicist Leo Szilárd arrived in New York and settled into the King's Crown Hotel, at 420 West 116th Street, steps from Columbia University. Having no actual affiliation there, Szilárd had to content himself with poking around Isidor Rabi's lab and suggesting experiments, to the latter's great annoyance. ("You have too many ideas," Rabi said.) Szilárd was indeed buzzing with ideas, but one was overwhelmingly predominant.

In 1933, days after the Reichstag fire, the Budapest-born agnostic Jew had left his position at the University of Berlin and fled the fascists, eventually making his way to London. There he came up with his immense idea, inspired by a reading of H. G. Wells's fantasy, *The World Set Free* (1914), in which the planet's metropoles are destroyed by atomic bombs, and by James Chadwick's discovery of the neutron the previous year (1932). Szilárd had immediately hypothesized that as a neutron had no electrical charge and would not be repelled by similarly charged particles, it could be fired straight into an atom's nucleus. While crossing a London street in October 1933, it came to him that if he could find an element that would emit two neutrons for each one it absorbed, it might be possible to sustain a nuclear chain reaction, which in turn might make it conceivable "to liberate energy on an industrial scale and construct atomic bombs." Beryllium seemed the likeliest candidate, though he also mentioned uranium in the patent for chain reactions he filed in 1934, and then assigned to the British Admiralty, to keep it out of Hitler's hands. Next, he set to work (on a refugee fellowship) exploring beryllium's possibilities in Oxford's Clarendon Laboratory.

In 1935, convinced that war was coming, Szilárd announced he would leave England one year *before* it broke out, "at which time I would shift my residence to New York City," where he "would be a free human being and very soon would not even be a 'stranger.'" The Munich Agreement of September 1938 triggered his move, and he arrived at the King's Crown in November, roughly a year before the conflagration started. It was there, in the lobby, that in January 1939 he ran into Enrico Fermi, also in flight from fascists, in his case the Italian variety.

Fermi, from 1927 professor of theoretical physics at the University of Rome, had been experimenting since 1934 with shooting "slow neutrons" into nuclei. He had also been growing more concerned about the fate of his Jewish wife, Laura. In 1938, with the passage of

Mussolini's racial laws, the couple decided to emigrate to the US. Fermi had taught a summer course at Columbia in 1936 and been attracted by the city, the country, and American physicists, who'd given him a cordial reception. As Italian citizens could only take $50 with them into exile, Fermi declared he was going to lecture again at Columbia only for some months and would then return. Still, he couldn't sell his household goods nor empty his savings account without alerting the fascisti. A solution emerged on November 10, when the same radio broadcast that announced more anti-Jewish laws carried word that Enrico Fermi had won the Nobel Prize. The couple went to Stockholm, picked up the prize money, and exchanged their tickets back to Italy for berths on the Gotham-bound *Franconia*. On January 2, 1939, they were met at the pier by Columbia Physics Department chairman Pegram, who escorted them up to the King's Crown Hotel.

The Italian and Hungarian were thus in town when the Dane Niels Bohr arrived on January 16, not a refugee but a visitor, come to argue quantum theory with Einstein and lecture at Princeton. Bohr was also bearing remarkable (and secret) news. Just weeks before, when German chemists Otto Hahn and Fritz Strassmann in Berlin had bombarded uranium with neutrons, they had discovered barium amidst the debris, its weight only about half that of the "mother atom," a result they couldn't explain, as no previous experiment had knocked off more than a particle or two. They consulted their colleague Lise Meitner, who, a Jew, had fled Berlin in 1938 and settled in Stockholm, from where she kept in touch with Hahn in Germany and Bohr in Copenhagen. Meitner and her physicist nephew and coresearcher Otto Robert Frisch believed the uranium nucleus had undergone "fission" (a term borrowed from biology), splitting into pieces with attendant loss of mass and liberation of energy, in the ratio Einstein had predicted. Meitner and Frisch devised and successfully executed an experiment that verified this hypothesis, a result they reported to Bohr just as he was embarking for New York. Bohr promised not to spread the news until they had published their nearly completed paper. He did, however, tell Leon Rosenfeld, the associate with whom he was sailing, though he neglected to swear him to silence. When the Swedish American liner *Drottningholm* docked at West 57th Street, Enrico and Laura Fermi met Bohr at the pier and took him off for a day on the town, while Rosenfeld went on ahead to Princeton, where the beans were spilled to physicists there, including the visiting Rabi.

When word got back to Fermi in New York (whom Bohr had not told), he proposed to John R. Dunning, the Columbia physicist who had built the cyclotron in Pupin's basement, an experiment (similar to that of Meitner and Frisch, of which he was unaware) to confirm that splitting uranium released a great deal of energy. On January 25, Fermi helped Dunning to start the experiment, then left for a conference in Washington, where he and Bohr would publicly announce the arrival of fission. That evening, when huge green lines shot up on the oscilloscope screen, Dunning calculated 200 million electric volts were being generated. At that rate, he calculated, one pound of fissionable uranium could yield as much energy as five million pounds of coal.

When Szilárd heard the news, his immediate thought was to suppress it, because it clearly meant his chain reaction, and hence a Wellsian bomb, were distinct possibilities. As he wrote a friend that day, if the Germans figured this out, "Hitler's success could depend on it." But when he urged Fermi and Rabi to keep the news secret, Fermi's (idiomatically up-to-date) response was: "Nuts." It wasn't that he disagreed about the danger—indeed, soon after the test he had looked out at Manhattan from his Pupin office, cupped his hands as if holding a ball, and said, "A little bomb like that and it would all disappear." But he believed the bomb a "remote possibility." When Rabi asked what that meant, Fermi replied, "10 percent," to

Dana P. Mitchell, Enrico Fermi, and John R. Dunning stand in front of the Pupin cyclotron. (University Archives, Rare Book & Manuscript Library, Columbia University Libraries/AIP Emilio Serge Visual Archives)

which Rabi harrumphed: "If I have pneumonia and the doctor tells me that there is a remote possibility that I might die, and it's ten percent, I get excited about it."

All agreed the next step was to measure the likelihood that enough neutrons would be emitted by fissioning uranium to start a chain reaction. Fermi, Dunning, and Szilárd each ran different experiments, and by March it seemed clear that chances of a reaction happening were above 50 percent, high enough, they thought, to warrant informing the US government. Pegram knew the undersecretary of the Navy (Thomas Edison's son), who arranged a meeting between Nobel Laureate Fermi and naval officers and scientists. Little came of this, partly because Fermi's presentation was itself full of question marks. Yet the horrific possibilities of nuclear fission were seeping into the wider culture. In May 1939 a *New York Times* science reporter suggested, with scary specificity, that a uranium bomb "would wipe out the entire City of New York, leaving a deep crater half way to Philadelphia and a third of the way to Albany and out to Long Island as far as Patchogue."

By July, Szilárd was convinced the physicists must do more, perhaps tell Belgium to make sure the Belgian Congo's stockpile of uranium ore did not fall into Nazi hands. He knew that his old friend Einstein had a line to the royal family and that he was then summering out in Nassau Point at Peconic Bay, on the southern shore of Long Island's northern fork. So, on Sunday, July 16, Szilárd (a nondriver) had Eugene Wigner, an émigré physicist at Princeton, chauffeur him out. Einstein agreed to act on the uranium front, though the three refugees thought it behooved them to first check with the US government, and they decided to query the State Department. Worried about getting lost in the bureaucracy, Szilárd asked economist Gustave Stolper, a former member of the Reichstag now resettled in Gotham, if there wasn't a better way to proceed. It turned out there was a much better go-to person, two degrees of separation further up New York's social circuitry.

Stolper suggested consulting Dr. Alexander Sachs, like Stolper and Szilárd a Jewish refugee, though of a much earlier vintage. Born in Lithuania in 1893, Sachs and his family had come to New York in 1904. Here he attended Townsend Harris High School, shot through Columbia in three years, got a PhD from Harvard, and then went to work on Wall Street, first as a bond salesman, then as an economist. In 1929 he became chief economist for the Lehman Corporation (Lehman Brothers' investment trust subsidiary), whose bacon he saved by predicting the Crash and shifting to cash. Though Sachs was a pillar of the private sector, he rejected laissez-faire responses to the Depression; backed and advised FDR during his 1933 campaign; and, though wary of the NRA, signed on as its chief economist. Sachs suggested the scientists go straight to the top and offered to hand-deliver an Einstein letter to Franklin Roosevelt.

Einstein agreed, drafts were worked on, another meeting was held out on Long Island (this time with physicist Edward Teller as Szilárd's driver), and finally Sachs was given a letter, dated August 2, in which Einstein explained that "recent work by E. Fermi and L. Szilard"—"in America," he added, referring to the New York experiments—suggested the possibility, though not the surety, that chain reactions might enable the building of bombs. "A single bomb of this type," he warned, "carried by boat and exploded in a port, might very well destroy the whole port together with some of the surrounding territory."

Before Sachs could snare an appointment, war broke out on September 1, and Roosevelt became otherwise occupied. Finally, on October 11, Sachs went to the White House where, rather than plunging into Einstein's letter, he cannily told FDR a story. A young American inventor once wrote a letter to Napoleon proposing to build a fleet of ships that had no sails, and thus, regardless of wind or storm, could transport Napoleon's armies to England in a few hours; to which Napoleon scoffed: "Bah! Away with your visionists!" The inventor, Sachs reminded the president, was Robert Fulton, adding that his own presentation involved an invention far more portentous than the steamboat. This was a pitch perfectly calculated to appeal to a Hudson River Lord with a highly developed sense of New York history; and, indeed, after hearing it, FDR called for a bottle of Napoleon brandy and two glasses, then gave Sachs his full attention. The economist summarized Einstein's letter, explained fission in layman's language, and noted that the Reich had blocked the sale of uranium from Czech mines it now controlled. Roosevelt's immediate response—"Alex, what you are after is to see that the Nazis don't blow us up"—was followed by his summoning aide General Edwin ("Pa") Watson and saying: "Pa! This requires action!"

The action proved sluggish. Roosevelt did appoint an Advisory Committee on Uranium that fall, but by the spring of 1940 it had approved only $6,000—to underwrite an attempt by Szilárd and Fermi to generate a chain reaction at Columbia. Their first hurdle was finding a material to slow the neutrons, emitted at tremendous speed upon fission, sufficiently so that they could split other nuclei. Carbon in the form of graphite (as in pencils) was their first candidate, and Szilárd visited the National Carbon Company of New York to find graphite blocks of sufficient purity, eventually purchasing fifty tons, in which they planned to embed five tons of uranium oxide. Actual construction proceeded very slowly, speeding up a bit only after the Committee on Uranium was incorporated into Vannevar Bush's newly established National Defense Research Committee (NDRC), which in November 1940 gave Columbia a contract to move forward. The pace accelerated again in June 1941, when Roosevelt created the Office of Scientific Research and Development (OSRD), which absorbed the NDRC's powers and added the ability to move experimental prototypes from conception to production; Vannevar Bush remained in overall control.

During the summer of 1941 Fermi, Szilárd, and their colleagues began piling up their uranium-graphite lattice on a Pupin floor (Fermi called it a "pile"). Their backs soon ached from lugging 50- and 100-pound cans of uranium oxide and sooty graphite bricks, which made them look like coal miners. Worse, when they ran out of room, they had to move the growing reactor across campus to the basement of Schermerhorn Hall. Pegram suggested hiring Columbia College football players by the hour, and soon a dozen husky youths were schlepping the cans, clueless at to what they were carrying.

At the same time, Bush's OSRD established another program at Columbia, under Harold Urey, assisted by John Dunning, to figure out how to separate from one another the two isotopes of uranium—U-235 (which was fissionable) from U-238 (which was not). They applied a method called gaseous diffusion, which made use of the different rate at which isotopes of different weights diffused—once vaporized—through a porous barrier, in a mechanism set up in the basement of Pupin.

After Pearl Harbor, Roosevelt authorized an all-out effort, and Vannevar Bush set up a chain reaction task force. On security grounds, only citizens were deemed eligible for chairmanship, so Fermi was passed over: as of December 8, he'd become an enemy alien, unable even to take the ferry home to New Jersey after 8:00 p.m., the hour after which enemy aliens were barred from crossing state lines without special permission. The fission program was put in charge of Arthur H. Compton, a Nobel physicist, the younger brother of Karl Compton and a professor at the University of Chicago. Compton decided that fission research should be consolidated in one location and proposed his own campus as the site. Szilárd and Fermi, having assembled their multi-ton pile in New York, wanted to stay put. Gotham had its drawbacks, however: the researchers were outgrowing their Columbia basement—they'd been scouting new off-campus locations, including the Polo Grounds—and the seaboard city did seem dangerously vulnerable, especially in early 1942, when U-boats were on the prowl. Over the next six months, therefore, their operation was dismantled and transferred to Chicago, where, in December 1942, Fermi and Szilárd (in de facto if not de jure charge) produced the world's first self-sustaining nuclear reactor.

Ironically, just as New York lost a core component of the bomb project, it nominally became headquarters for the entire enterprise. When Vannevar Bush started up production in June 1942, he called in the Army Corps of Engineers (ACE) to take charge. ACE colonel James C. Marshall set up his command post in Gotham, at 270 Broadway, which housed the Corps' North Atlantic Division. At first the supersecret project was called the Laboratory for the Development of Substitute Materials, but the unusual moniker was thought more likely to attract than deflect attention. In choosing a blander alternative they went by the (Corps') book—which dictated naming a big construction project after the ACE District—districts being subsets of divisions—in which the project was located. The atomic program would have many different locations, all of them top secret, but its head office, for the moment, was in New York. Hence, on August 13, 1942, the Corps established the Manhattan Engineer District—a handle quickly and popularly shortened to Manhattan Project. When Brigadier General Leslie R. Groves—then overseeing construction of the Pentagon—was chosen to direct the enterprise in September, he quickly whisked the headquarters to Washington, and later to Oak Ridge, Tennessee. But the "Manhattan Project" brand was left in place, deliberately so, to provide the A-bomb program with a false front: Gotham had become the project's "beard."

Individual New Yorkers continued to play important roles in the atomic drama, notably Isidor Rabi. When Groves appointed J. Robert Oppenheimer to head bomb development at Los Alamos, New Mexico, in November 1942, Oppenheimer asked his old friend to become the project's associate director. Rabi declined, because he was convinced radar was more important and because he opposed military control of the invention process. He particularly objected to Groves's limiting of communication between the scientists, which stifled intellectual interchange. Rabi understood the need for secrecy to defend against espionage but found such compartmentalization self-defeating. Groves grudgingly acquiesced in internal civilian control, while strictly isolating the camp from outsiders.

The Army and FBI succeeded in keeping German spies and saboteurs out of Los Alamos, yet failed to prevent its infiltration by agents of the Russians, who, though now allies, had been kept at arm's length. Ironically, the Soviets had been alerted to the bomb enterprise by the sudden cessation—largely Szilárd's doing—of publications on uranium research in scientific journals like *Physical Review*, an absence first noted by Leonid Kvasnikov in the

Fat Man in the lab. (Los Alamos Scientific Laboratory/National Archives and Records Administration, Photograph Collection. Transferred to the Photographs from the Robert A. Lovett Papers)

KGB's scientific intelligence section in Moscow and confirmed by Soviet agents in England like Donald Maclean.

In 1943 Kvasnikov himself was dispatched to New York to take charge of scientific and technical espionage, especially regarding *Enormoz*, as the Soviets had code named the Manhattan Project. Kvasnikov's initiative was part of a reconstitution of Gotham's KGB presence, which had fallen into disarray before the war, partly due to Stalin's purges, partly to FBI arrests (notably that of Gaik Ovakimian in May 1941). Now, under Rezident Vassily Zarubin, some top-flight agents were installed on the third floor of the Soviet Consulate General at 7 East 61st Street, including Kvasnikov, Anatoli Yakovlev (real name Yatskov), and a young case officer, Aleksandr Feklisov, whose first assignment was to set up a transmitter atop the building to keep Manhattan in contact with Moscow Central. Another KGB heavyweight, agent Semyon Semenov, made his headquarters at Amtorg, where he was ostensibly head of the Engineering Department.

The Soviet spy team had little luck in penetrating *Enormoz* until the arrival in New York of Klaus Fuchs, a German-born scientist who had fought Hitler first as a Social Democrat, then as a Communist, before fleeing to England. Briefly interned at the start of the war, Fuchs—a brilliant theoretical physicist—was released and recruited for England's atomic bomb project. The British were unaware that Fuchs had agreed in 1941, after Hitler invaded Russia, to transmit military secrets to Moscow, believing it was not right to deprive Britain's new ally of such information, especially as it was bearing the brunt of the fighting.

In December 1943, Fuchs was sent to Columbia to work on Harold Urey's uranium isotope separation project, at which time his control was transferred from the GRU to the KGB. In subsequent months Fuchs kept the Soviets informed of developments through a courier named Harry Gold, dispatched by Semenov. Gold and Fuchs met at places like the entrance to the Henry Street Settlement, a ramp onto the Queensboro Bridge, a movie theater on the Grand Concourse, and a subway entrance near the Museum of Natural History, until August 1944, when Fuchs was assigned to Los Alamos as part of a British contingent of scientists. He continued to send information east via Gold.

Unbeknownst to Fuchs, Gold was also carrying information, albeit of lesser caliber, obtained by one David Greenglass, an Army machinist from New York. Greenglass, a 1940 graduate of Haaren High, had dropped out of Brooklyn Polytechnic, and was working as a machinist at Peerless Laboratories on East 23rd Street, when he was drafted in April 1943. After training at Aberdeen and service in California and Mississippi, he was transferred, in August 1944, to Los Alamos. Greenglass was not a Communist Party member, though, encouraged by his sister, Ethel, and her husband, Julius Rosenberg, he had joined the neighborhood Young Communist League (YCL) in 1938 but was never as ardent as they were.

Ethel Greenglass, a Seward Park High School graduate and amateur choral singer, had gotten involved in union organizing at her clerical job in the garment center and then entered radical politics, joining the Young Communist League, where in 1936 she met Julius Rosenberg.

Born in 1918 in East Harlem to Polish immigrants, Julius became a torah student, a pupil at Seward Park, a union and political organizer, and an engineering student at CCNY's School of Technology, where he organized a YCL affiliate, the Steinmetz Society (named after the socialist electrical engineer). Rosenberg became a full Party member in 1939, the year he graduated from City with a BS in electrical engineering, and he and Ethel married. In 1940 Julius got a job as a civilian engineer with the Army Signal Corps, inspecting equipment that defense contractors were manufacturing in New York. Driven by his desire to help Russians fight fascists, he offered to pass along information gleaned on his inspections to the

CPUSA's Jacob Golos, who had assembled a network of party members that gathered material for the Party's top brass, some of which he also passed on to the Russians.

The KGB thought Golos's spycraft, and that of his informants, hopelessly sloppy. In 1942 Semenov peeled Julius—who he considered "absolutely unripe" as an agent—away from the CPUSA "compatriots" to direct KGB control. Rosenberg received a crash course in *konspiratsia*, including the art of handing off information (best done in rush hour subways or Friday night fight crowds outside Madison Square Garden). He also recruited others—some of them fellow CCNY electrical engineering alumni—who got access to many of the city's war plants, including Western Electric, Bell Labs, Sperry Gyroscope, and Republic Aviation, as well as the Army Signal Corps Lab at Fort Monmouth, and there photographed 9,000 pages of secret documents relating to more than 100 weapons programs, including such major technological breakthroughs as the SCR-584. On Christmas Eve 1944, Rosenberg met agent Feklisov at the Times Square Horn and Hardart Automat and presented him with a gift-wrapped "present for the Russian people"—a top-secret proximity fuse he had smuggled out of Emerson Radio and Phonograph's factory in the Port Authority Commerce Building at 111 Eighth Avenue.

Julius had not been involved in atomic espionage, but when he learned in September 1944 that his brother-in-law had been sent to Los Alamos, he asked permission to recruit him. Feklisov was dubious about the reliability of a twenty-two-year-old dropout, but his superior, Kvasnikov, overruled him, and soon Greenglass was funneling information back to New York, via Julius and Harry Gold, who passed it on to Yakovlev, whence to Moscow, where its chief value lay in backing up Fuchs's material.

Below these high-peaked dramas of scientists and spies lay the longer-termed transformations wrought in the city by the flood of federal money to Gotham's universities, industrial labs, and manufacturing companies.

The effects were particularly remarkable at the Columbia campus which, before the war, had received virtually nothing from Washington. Though Fermi and Szilárd's reactor had left town, Urey's isotope project remained, indeed grew rapidly, until by 1943, he was overseeing more than 1,500 scientists, soldiers, and office workers. Rabi had moved to MIT for the duration, but Columbia's Rad Lab branch employed another 1,200 people. Many other parts of the university were also fertilized by federal funding: by war's end, fourteen government agencies had negotiated over 200 contracts with Columbia, totaling $43 million.

NYU underwent a similar government-induced muscling up, with émigré Richard Courant an important beneficiary of the transformation. Expelled by the Nazis from the Mathematical Institute at the University of Göttingen—guilty of being Jewish—Courant received a visiting appointment at NYU in 1934, his salary underwritten by the Rockefeller Foundation and the Committee in Aid of Displaced German Scholars. Courant wasn't altogether pleased with his new situation. There was, he said, "really nothing scientifically at NYU"; the students at Washington Square were "extraordinarily poorly prepared"; and by September 1941 after seven years of effort, the Graduate Center for Mathematics he'd established had a total faculty of three (and no staff). Then came the war, and with it the Office of Scientific Research and Development grants to work on mathematical problems ranging from underwater acoustics to explosion theory. With money in hand, faculty were hired, and interesting students appeared. OSRD contracts flowed to other parts of NYU, too, stimulating specialized research in chemotherapy, tropical diseases, neuropsychiatry, and syphilis, 1,943 separate contracts in all, totaling $2.8 million.

Washington strengthened New York's higher education complex in other ways as well. Given the staggering growth in demand for engineers, particularly experts in electronics and communication, the United States Office of Education helped underwrite an expansion of resources. And, as in other industries, normally competitive institutions—Cooper Union, Columbia, NYU, CCNY, Brooklyn Polytech, Pratt Institute, Manhattan College, Long Island University, and Stevens Institute of Technology, among others—banded together, setting up a Defense Training Institute to enhance the supply of technically competent men (and increasingly women).

The war fostered more direct links between industries and universities. At Columbia, Astronomy Professor Wallace J. Eckert had forged a relationship with IBM in the 1930s, when the Thomas J. Watson Astronomical Computing Bureau was set up in the attic of Pupin Hall as a nonprofit resource for sky-searchers. In 1942, it was turned over to military uses, and its IBM 601 Multiplier was set to working out not celestial mechanics but fire-control calculations for B-29s. Eckert and others also constructed nautical almanacs that cut the amount of time needed—from thirty minutes to one—for an airplane to attack a sub. In February 1945 Watson and Eckert opened the Thomas J. Watson Scientific Computing Laboratory, also in Pupin, though it soon moved to an abandoned fraternity house at 612 West 116th Street. Its mission was to provide free access to state-of-the-art calculating machines to academic researchers in any field, and it would pull visiting scientists to New York from all over the world. In 1945, however, its major role was tackling problems—like shockwave calculations—brought in by Manhattan Project scientists such as mathematician John von Neumann.

Gotham's industrial research laboratories were similarly given a tremendous boost by the war, sometimes boosting them right out of the city. In September 1942, Bell Labs—the world's largest—had 5,875 people working in its West Street complex on 180 projects for the Army, 120 for the Navy, and 1,930 for the OSRD. These included the development of over a hundred different types of radar; antisubmarine acoustic homing torpedoes and echo-ranging sonar devices; and the high-powered air raid siren for New York. In 1941, anticipating such growth, Bell had opened a branch facility in Murray Hill, New Jersey, in the north-central part of the state, where open land was plentiful and cheap. By war's end almost 1,000 employees had been transferred there, and it was becoming a question as to which would be the branch and which the tree.

RCA's research operations jumped to the suburbs more decisively, also in 1941, when rising military demands and the desire to consolidate scattered operations led Sarnoff to dictate a relocation. The company moved to a 260-acre swath of farmland on Route 1 in Princeton, equidistant from RCA manufacturing operations in Camden and corporate headquarters in Rockefeller Center. It opened on September 27, 1942, setting 1,300 scientists and technicians to working on, among other things, streamlining radar and radio antennas to fit into hulls of high-speed airplanes, and improving acoustical depth charges. Sarnoff presided over a total conversion of RCA manufacturing to war work, too, and in spring 1944 went to London, at Eisenhower's behest, to help rationalize the communications infrastructure for D-Day; he reached Paris a day before de Gaulle and restored the radio-telegraph link between Paris and New York, severed since the Nazi occupation.

Perhaps the most immediate impact of wartime government spending was in consolidating and strengthening Gotham's nascent electronics industry, even though some of the larger firms overflowed the city's boundaries. Sperry Gyroscope's plant at 40 Flatbush Avenue Extension, where the Manhattan Bridge debouched into Brooklyn, continued as a major production center through most of the war, but much of the company's tenfold expansion would take place on its 26-acre site at Lake Success, just across the Queens border in Nassau County, in a factory which the Defense Plant Corporation built for it. It opened for business in the summer of '42 with over 8,000 employees; in 1944, the Brooklyn plant was sold to Howard Clothes, a manufacturer. Western Electric's Hudson Street megalith still had a substantial force working around the clock in 1944—1,000 on the night shift alone (700 of them women)—making vacuum tubes and turning out radar sets designed at Bell Labs ten blocks farther north. However, what enabled Western Electric to produce over half the wartime radars made in the USA were the supersized plants in Jersey, at Kearny and Hawthorne.

New York's special strength, once again, lay in its flexible small manufacturers, with radio assembly shops swiftly converting to production sites for walkie-talkies, specialized tubes, batteries, capacitors, resistors, transformers, filters, and the innumerable other electronic paraphernalia that were essential to modern warfare communication systems. Little companies like Emerson Radio and Phonograph on 16th Street retooled themselves to meet Army/Navy demand for electronic equipment (like the proximity fuse with which Julius Rosenberg walked off), and they saw sales soar—doubling the order volume from twelve to twenty-three million dollars' worth between 1943 and 1944. Similar feats marked outfits like Freed Radio Corporation of New York (on Hudson Street), United Scientific Laboratories (436 Lafayette Street below Astor Place), Pilot Radio (in Long Island City), and Amperex Electronics (at 79 Washington Street, down under the Manhattan and Brooklyn Bridge overpasses). These concerns were small enough to squeeze into expansion niches in the most built up of areas. The Hudson-American Corporation, at 25 West 43rd Street, which had been assembling radar equipment, announced in January 1944 that the company now had five war plants in the Times Square area, making items like crystal oscillators for bomber radios, on contract to the Army Signal Corps. N. K. Hoskins, Hudson-American's executive vice-president, said the company's policy of establishing plants in the middle of the metropolis was a "sound" one, due to the availability of women workers "within a five cent fare." On August 2, 1944—in a sure sign of a stabilizing industry—many such companies decided to act in concert, as well as competition, as representatives from metropolitan area firms like the Electronics Corporation of America, United Scientific, Freed Radio, Fada Radio, Hamilton Radio, and Espey Manufacturing gathered at the Waldorf Astoria to form the Electronics Manufacturers Association.

New York even attracted electronics plants from out of town. In June 1943, Standard Aircraft Products of Dayton, Ohio, faced with Army war orders that made expansion imperative, opted to set up a plant in Gotham because (explained Vice President E. A. Lotti) it afforded a "happy combination" of labor, materials, and transportation. His company had just leased 50,000 square feet for its 450 employees in 345 Hudson 17-story structure built around 1929. Lotti liked being in the Lower West Side industrial cluster, a few blocks south of Western Electric and Bell Labs. He liked the building space as it was light, airy, and spacious enough to include a laboratory dedicated to research in electronics—"a field that will have a great post-war development"; and he liked that "scientists on the faculties of the city's many universities and colleges are available for such experimental research." The plant was right next door to St. John's Freight Terminal and thus offered great rail connections to "all parts of the country"—there was good airplane service, too—and an alternative to trucking was particularly helpful given gasoline shortages. Yes, labor costs were a "little higher" here, but these were offset by the greater productivity of Gotham's skilled workforce. And yes, rents were "much higher" here, but these were offset by being in the center of things, near their sales headquarters, markets, and a myriad of subcontractors (whom the Smaller War Plants Corporation proved helpful in contacting).

It had taken a long time for the war to become a source of fructification rather than frustration for the city's manufacturing sector, but in the end the conflict revitalized New York's industrial base, as it had the city's shipping and railroads and research sectors.

100

The Anthropology of New York City

The fertile interaction of émigré and New York physicists—between Fermi and Rabi and Szilárd and Dunning—had its counterpart in the city's social as well as its physical sciences. Here, too, arriving Europeans encountered accomplished local practitioners who were comfortable enough to welcome sophisticated exiles and engage them in dialogue. This was true in many fields—interactions in psychology and art history were particularly productive—but perhaps the most generative conversations took place in anthropology, a field in which the city's scholars had attained unmatched preeminence in the US and a distinguished reputation abroad.

Indeed, Claude Lévi-Strauss, while a philosophy student in Paris in the early 1930s, was converted to ethnology by his reading of New Yorker Robert Lowie's *Primitive Society* (1920). The Viennese-born Lowie had been brought to Gotham by his family in 1893 at the age of ten. After graduating from City College in 1901, he studied at Columbia under Franz Boas and Professor Clark Wissler—also curator of the Department of Anthropology at the American Museum of Natural History—who guided his field work among the Shoshoni and Crow. Lowie became a leading expert on Plains Indian peoples, practicing a form of "salvage ethnology," collecting information about cultures in imminent danger of obliteration. In 1921 Lowie joined the anthropology faculty at the University of California, Berkeley, which he helped shape into a bastion of Boasian antipathy to Victorian-era evolutionism. Young Lévi-Strauss—bored with Parisian hyper-intellectualism—was attracted to Lowie's mixing field work and theoretical labor; and in 1933, at the age of twenty-five, he opted out of philosophy and into a social science that could legitimize his adventurous proclivities.

In 1935 he sailed to Brazil, having accepted an offer from the University of São Paulo to teach sociology, with the right to do field work in the interior between semesters. He spent time with various peoples in the western state of Mato Grosso and published his first article on the Bororos in 1936, in the *Journal de la société des Américanistes*. His study attracted the attention of Lowie and other American ethnologists who (as Lévi-Strauss came to believe) "had begun to think that they knew enough about the Indians of North America and were looking towards the southern hemisphere. My work was coming at the right time." He returned to France in 1939, at just the wrong time, and was drafted into the French army. After defeat and demobilization in June 1940, he landed a teaching post, but in October the Vichy government excluded Jews from public office, and Lévi-Strauss—a rabbi's grandson—was stripped of his position.

Luckily, Lowie helped arrange an invitation to join the New School, with assistance from the Rockefeller Foundation. More luckily still, with papers in hand, he got passage in February 1941 on a converted cargo ship, the *Capitaine Paul Lemerle*, that was leaving directly from Marseille for Martinique. A combined expulsionist/emigrationist project on the part of some Vichy officials, it was the last legal avenue out of France. Still on a roll, he was granted a bunk in a private cabin—one only of four men so privileged—as the vessel was run by same shipping line that had taken him to Brazil and an official remembered him. The rest, over two hundred desperate refugees, were packed below decks, among them André Breton, the apostle of Surrealism, who had been steered to the *Paul Lemerle* by Varian Fry; Lévi-Strauss met and befriended Breton on board, and, after some rough handling on arrival in Martinique, made his way, via Puerto Rico, to New York.

Lévi-Strauss settled into a rented studio in a brownstone at 51 West 11th Street, near Sixth Avenue. His old Italian landlord was then renting another room to Claude Shannon, an electrical engineer and mathematician at the Institute for Advanced Study, who had come to New York to work at Bell Labs on fire-control systems and cryptography, under a contract from the National Defense Research Committee, all the while continuing to create the field of cybernetics. Though the two had a coresident friend in common, who told Lévi-Strauss, "I know someone in our house who works on artificial brains," this was one wartime encounter that never happened. But others quickly did, not surprisingly, given the number of world-class intellectuals—Americans and exiles—who saturated wartime New York.

At the New School, Lévi-Strauss was asked to teach a class on the sociology of contemporary Latin America, in English. (He was also asked not to use his own surname as "the students would find it funny, because of the blue jeans"—"here," he was told, "your name shall be Claude L. Strauss.") As he "knew nothing at all" about the subject, Mr. Strauss tutored himself at the 42nd Street branch of the New York Public Library, where he discovered a vast collection of material, particularly rich on Peru and Argentina. "Everything I know about ethnology," he would later admit, "I learned there."

His benefactor Robert Lowie was in Berkeley, but Lowie's teacher, and the titan of American anthropology, was in Gotham, and Lévi-Strauss went to introduce himself. Boas was very gracious, invited him to dinner at his home, and the visitor was swiftly and warmly admitted to a circle that included Margaret Mead, Ruth Benedict, and Ralph Linton (the latter two saw him separately as they hated each other). The free interaction with acclaimed academics, unhindered by hierarchical barriers, was a refreshing change from Parisian practice. And it was more than just socially pleasing. Lévi-Strauss found Boas's work essential to his own development. He was particularly entranced by the Northwest Coast Hall at the American Museum of Natural History, in whose construction Boas had been instrumental—especially its totem poles: "There is in New York," he wrote the Parisian *Gazette des Beaux-Arts*, "a magic place where all the dreams of childhood hold a rendezvous, where century old tree trunks sing or speak."

Lévi-Strauss's relation with Boas was not destined to be a lengthy one. On a freezing day in December 1942, Boas held a luncheon at the Columbia Men's Faculty Club in honor of an old friend, the French ethnologist and linguist Paul Rivet. Founder of the Musée de l'Homme, Rivet's antifascist activities had forced him to flee Paris, and he was passing through New York on his way to Colombia, by way of Mexico. Boas, aged eighty-four, was wearing an old fur hat, perhaps picked up during his stay with the Eskimos sixty years earlier, and was in jovial spirits. Suddenly, in mid-conversation, he suffered an instantly fatal heart attack, during which he shoved himself violently away from the table, and as he fell backward it was Lévi-Strauss, seated next to him, who bent down to lift Boas up—a symbolic passing of the anthropological torch.

Lévi-Strauss also developed connections with fellow European exiles, linkages facilitated by the New School's Alvin Johnson. In September 1941, Johnson, with Rockefeller Foundation assistance, agreed to a proposal by several Vichy refugee scholars to launch a counterpart of the German University in Exile. The resulting École Libre des Hautes Études, which opened its doors in February 1942, was different from the German University in that nearly all its faculty saw themselves as temporary sojourners in New York. Many also considered it a base from which to oppose the Vichy regime—General de Gaulle cabled congratulations on its opening and authorized it to grant degrees in the name of Free France, though by no means all of the faculty were Gaullists (Lévi-Strauss was). The École Libre quickly emerged as a prominent feature on Gotham's cultural landscape. Within a few months it had mustered a faculty of over sixty instructors and was offering some two hundred courses to nearly 1,000 students, mostly adults.

Lévi-Strauss was delighted at the opportunity to teach in his own language, and to be part of a Francophone community, but the most critical bond he formed at the École was with a scholar whose native tongue was Russian. The Moscow-born Roman Jakobson had relocated to Czechoslovakia, lived there from 1920 to 1939, and when the Germans entered Prague fled to Norway, then Sweden, then New York, arriving in June 1941. Though Jakobson was considered by many the world's preeminent linguist, with an impact on his field the equivalent of Einstein's in physics, Lévi-Strauss had never heard of him and knew almost nothing about linguistics. Boas certainly did, having written dozens of grammars of indigenous languages, proving they were not simply Indo-European derivatives, as many had believed. As early as 1911 Boas had argued that the laws of language functioned on an unconscious level, beyond the control of speaking subjects, a notion he explored in discussions with Jakobson, who similarly proposed the existence of universal laws of human language, and posited that a foundational linguistic structure underlay everyday speech.

Lévi-Strauss first went to Jakobson hoping simply to learn more about the languages he had encountered in Brazil. The meeting proved far more transformative. What the anthropologist called Jakobson's "revelation of structural linguistics" resonated profoundly with his own effort to uncover the universal rules underlying diverse social norms and customs. He was particularly struck by the possibility that the methods of linguistic theory could be applied to the analysis of kinship systems.

It was the beginning of a great friendship. Lévi-Strauss attended Jakobson's École course, "Linguistique générale." Jakobson sat in on Lévi-Strauss's "Ethnographie générale." And the Russian encouraged the Frenchman to write up his lectures about "kinship structure" in cultures ranging from the Kwakiutl to the Chinese. Lévi-Strauss now settled down to researching what would become *Les structures élémentaires de la parenté* (*The Elementary Structures of Kinship*), via daily visits to the New York Public Library, mining each morning its vast resources—"sleeping treasures"—then heading home to write.

Or to walk: for at the same time that he was doing virtual field work in the library, he was exercising his penchant for actually-in-the-field work by taking Gotham itself as a site for investigation. Some of his earliest saunterings were undertaken not with Jakobson but with his former shipmate André Breton and others of the Surrealist set who had escaped to New York, notably Max Ernst. They particularly liked antiquing in the small shops along Third Avenue, especially after they discovered the gallery of Julius Carlebach, at 943 Third Avenue (near 57th), a dealer who was always well stocked with pieces of the "primitive art" prized by anthropologists and surrealists alike—stone masks from Teotihuacan, wood carvings from the Northwest Pacific coast. It turned out that Carlebach was channeling items being deaccessioned by George Heye, founder and director of Museum of the American Indian; in fact, Lévi-Strauss and company were soon allowed to go up to Heye's warehouse in the Bronx and pick out pieces, which then made their way down to Third Avenue, where they were bought up at bargain basement prices.

Though astonished that it seemed "all the essentials of humanity's artistic treasures could be found in New York, where samples were constantly bought and sold," what really amazed Lévi-Strauss was that it seemed all of humanity's *cultures* were on display in the astonishingly heterogeneous wartime city. The anthropologist had long been worried about industrial civilization's steamrollering of the planet's disparate societies—those Lowie had been salvaging, the imperiled ones he'd seen in Brazil, those of Central and Eastern Europe whose remote countrysides had been combed by folklorist colleagues of his, searching for remnants and surviving storytellers. Yet here was New York, chock-full of immigrant communities that had preserved customs and tales which had vanished without a trace in the old countries. Indeed, Gotham seemed a vast collection of remnants and survivals from many continents and different eras, a palette of cultural possibilities, an anthropologist's dream.

Lévi-Strauss had expected an "ultramodern metropolis" but found an "aggregation of villages"—"an immense horizontal and vertical disorder attributable to some spontaneous upheaval of the urban crust rather than to the deliberate plans of builders." He flaneured the city, reveling in its juxtapositions, from the "syndicalist" atmosphere of Greenwich Village (which reminded him of Balzac's Paris), to the Upper East Side lairs of the "New York aristocracy." He loved "the incredibly complex image of modern lifestyles next to almost archaic ones," from the "towers of Wall Street," to the performances of Chinese opera held under the first arch of the Brooklyn bridge. Gotham's streets were lined with doorways to other times and places: "Like the urban fabric, the social and cultural fabric was riddled with holes. All you had to do was pick one and slip through it if, like Alice, you wanted to get to the other side of the looking glass and find worlds so enchanting that they seemed unreal."

As the city for Lévi-Strauss was diversity defined—its preexisting jumble of shards and fragments only enhanced by the tumbling in of refugees seeking shelter from the storm of war—it seemed only fitting that out of his struggle to grasp the totality of its being, an effort aided by the intellectual collisions fostered by its hothouse atmosphere, would emerge a system of thought—structural anthropology—which took as its goal "to reveal the *unvarying* through variety."

SELLING THE WAR

Partygoers on 52nd Street buy defense stamps from the American Women's Voluntary Services, July 22, 1942. (Bettmann / Contributor / Getty Images)

101

"Any Bonds Today?"

The New York money market—at the heart of war finance since John Jacob Astor helped underwrite the War of 1812—was in this conflict shouldered aside by the federal government and relegated to an ancillary role. The greatest economic expansion in American history was overwhelmingly underwritten not by Wall Street but by Washington.

In the months after Pearl Harbor, as factories revved up, the New York Stock Exchange revved down. By March 1942, the turnover of stocks had dropped to levels not seen since 1918. By April the trading floor was almost deserted. Between 1942 and 1945 those working in Lower Manhattan's financial shops were outnumbered by those laboring in its bulked-up federal offices. The brokers and clerks who trooped off to war were uncertain whether, after the conflict, there would be a financial district to return to. Individual and institutional investors did begin to jump back into the market as war news improved: volume recovered in 1943 and advanced modestly the following year. But stock prices never reflected the surge in corporate profits. Even when the war economy hit its peak in 1944, market values failed to regain their 1939 levels.

Banks were bypassed, too. Many major corporations preferred to deal with the government's Defense Plant Corporation (DPC). When four of New York's biggest financial institutions—Chase, National City, Guaranty Trust, and Bankers Trust—proposed setting up as a clearing house for defense contracts, businessmen balked at placing Gotham's giants athwart their funding stream. The president of the American Bankers Association chided contractors for shortsightedness, warning that the "future independence of business" was at stake: if companies relied on the state during wartime, they would be dependent on it ever after. Yet large industrial firms *liked* a system that allowed them to expand vigorously while shaking off investment banker controls dating back to Morgan's day. This was especially true in emerging regions. East Texans, hungry to get in on mobilization-driven development, petitioned Wall Street bankers for loans to fabricate pipelines for the booming oil industry. New York refused. The DPC, on the other hand, approved, enabling the Texans to circumvent Gotham's stranglehold on credit.

This is not to say New York banks weren't involved in war finance, just that their participation was circumscribed and indirect—limited to loaning Washington the funds it needed to finance corporate expansion. The Federal Reserve, moreover, in effect capped what banks could charge for their loans. Throughout the war, whenever market pressures threatened to push interest rates on the government's longest-term bonds above 2.5 percent, the central bank simply bought the issues itself.

Even so, Roosevelt preferred to avoid borrowing from the capital markets and to pay for the war out of tax revenues instead. The president got Congress to raise levies on big business—boosting the maximum corporate rate from 19 percent to 40 percent and imposing an excess-profits tax, whose top rate was ratcheted up from 50 percent to 95 percent. But the increasingly conservative legislators, responding to corporate outcries, also passed regressive levies, sending the burden back down the social scale. The Victory Tax, part of the Revenue Act of 1942, slapped a flat 5 percent charge on all Americans with incomes above $624. It fell heavily on low- and moderate-income workers, thirteen million of whom were now required to pay taxes for the first time. In 1943, Congress brought even more people into the tax system (and culture) by establishing a vast pay-as-you-go withholding system, with employers deducting taxes from wages and salaries as they were paid. By war's end, individuals, in the aggregate, were contributing more than corporations.

Washington had created a mighty revenue river of tax-generated income for the federal government, but the current wasn't powerful enough to pay for all of the Second World War, which was astronomically expensive. Cost estimates vary wildly—from $260 to $360 billion, in part because they measure different things—but it seems clear that the national government spent at least twice as much between 1940 and 1945 as it had during the preceding 150 years. Given the magnitude of this wartime tab, taxes covered only 46 percent of it (up from 30 percent in the First World War). To gather the remaining 54 percent, the government was forced to borrow.

The Treasury floated bonds, with administration New Dealers, led by Treasury Secretary Henry Morgenthau Jr., seeking to minimize bank involvement by maximizing popular purchases. Even before Pearl Harbor, Morgenthau had tried to finance rearmament and Lend Lease programs by selling Defense Savings Bonds directly to the public. This was more democratic than relying on banks, he argued, and it would have the added benefit of dampening inflation, by directing swelling incomes into savings rather than consumption. On May 1, 1941, the newly created Series "E" Savings Bonds went on sale. Everything about them was aimed at ensuring popular palatability. They were available in low denominations: 25, 50, 100, 500, and 1,000 dollars. Even children could afford them, by purchasing "stamps" for 10¢, 25¢, 50¢, $1, or $5, then bundling them in "pocket albums," which could be exchanged for bonds. They were easy to buy, being available at commercial and savings banks, post offices, and department stores, or through payroll deduction plans at work. They were easy to understand: priced at 75 percent of their face value—$18.75 bought a $25 bond—they were redeemable at full value after ten years. They were safe: registered in their owner's name, they could be replaced if lost or stolen, and they were backed by the Treasury, an essential guarantee for a generation scarred by the collapse of the banking system. They were steady, too: unlike the First World War's Liberty Bonds, which had fluctuated with the bond market, they were nonnegotiable, preventing professional traders from scooping them up when prices dipped and reselling them when prices recovered, thus scoring handsome profits— a First World War practice that had soured citizens on government issues. Bottom line, they were a good investment: the 2.9 percent return was not extravagant, but few vehicles and virtually no savings banks paid better.

For big investors and commercial banks, the Treasury offered Series F and G bonds, in denominations up to $10,000. To prevent such buyers from monopolizing the market, these instruments were offered at a slightly lower rate (2.5 percent), and total purchases were limited to $100,000. Nevertheless, as this return was higher than the 1.5–2.0 percent obtainable from other government securities, the Fs and Gs proved attractive to banks, corporations, and labor unions.

There would be no special drives or campaigns, Morgenthau decreed, no quotas assigned, no hoopla or hysteria, no appeals to hate or fear—all characteristic of the Liberty Loan era. However, publicity was acceptable, indeed requisite, and Morgenthau plunged in with gusto. He closed his first sale—to Franklin Roosevelt—on a national radio hookup. In July 1941 the *Treasury Hour* was launched, a weekly radio show produced in New York by well-known writers and actors who volunteered time and talent to help sell securities. And at the secretary's request Irving Berlin confected a song—"Any Bonds Today?"—crooned by Bugs Bunny (wearing Al Jolson blackface) in a cartoon that pitched bonds for "Uncle Sammy" in movie theaters. Primarily, however, this pre–Pearl Harbor preparedness effort had relied heavily on volunteers—from clubs, civic organizations, and local businesses.

This amateur approach had succeeded in creating broad public awareness of the bond program, but actual sales had been anemic, and most bonds had been bought by large investors rather than the targeted popular audience. Pearl Harbor sent sales soaring—New York's demand jumped 800 percent—but they soon began to slump again. With war expenditures exploding, Morgenthau was criticized even by fellow New Dealers for not generating the revenue to meet them.

Needing help, Morgenthau turned to Madison Avenue, itself desperately in need of assistance.

The advertising industry—overwhelmingly centered in New York—was still in the New Deal's dog house, still under assault from consumer activists who decried its hucksterism and denied its necessity. Ad men had been fighting back since the late 1930s, denouncing consumerists as reds or pinks intent on bringing down the capitalist system of which Madison Avenue was an essential component and defender. But they had proved unable to block passage of the reformers' Wheeler-Lea Act in 1938, which had given the Federal Trade Commission (FTC) modest regulatory powers, and in 1940 the FTC was proposing an investigation of the industry. Antitrusters were another menace—convinced as they were that advertising bolstered large corporations and fostered monopolization—and Justice Department prosecution seemed another alarming possibility.

During 1941, such threats paled before those posed by imminent war. If the US got directly involved, production of civilian commodities would surely be curtailed, depriving ad men of products to sell. Worse, a wartime spirit of self-denial would imperil an enterprise so geared to stimulating self-indulgence. Indeed, an outbreak of hostilities might provide their domestic enemies a long-sought opportunity to kill the industry.

A siege mentality took hold. "Advertising is threatened today as it has never been threatened before," warned *Printer's Ink* in October 1941. In November, 700 industry executives gathered at a special conclave to plan a course of action. The air rang with hysterical attacks on their critics, whom they accused of backing "the totalitarian idea, with people as the vassals of the state," in opposition to "the American philosophy of free enterprise," of which they were a bulwark. A massive public relations offensive was proposed, on behalf of the ad industry and its corporate clients, "to regain for business the leadership of our economy." James Webb Young of J. Walter Thompson argued that "we have within our hands the greatest aggregate means of mass education and persuasion the world has ever seen—namely, the channels of advertising communication"; moreover, "we have the masters of the technique of using these channels." "We have power," Young summed up bluntly: "Why do we not use it?"

Then came Pearl Harbor. As feared, a new spirit was instantly abroad in the land. Donald Nelson of the War Production Board declared "this nation must be converted from peacetime habits and customs to an all-out war basis calling for conservation, saving and doing without luxuries"—a chilling pronouncement, from an adman's perspective. As expected, the production and sale of most consumer goods was soon snuffed out. With no cars, refrigerators, or radios to sell, Madison Avenue accountants were projecting an 80 percent falloff in business, with shortages of paper, ink, and copper (for halftones) menacing the remainder.

The ad men's standing wasn't helped by an efflorescence of tasteless hucksterism, as those with goods to sell scrambled to give them a "war angle." GE boasted that its light bulbs had survived the sinking of the *Oklahoma* at Pearl Harbor; and a New York cemetery firm sponsored a news program which, after reeling off casualty figures, segued to a spot that reminded listeners: "You never know when to expect bad news. So be prepared. Buy a family plot."

G.I. and civilian outrage at such tawdriness was echoed at several of the bigger agencies, where executives found the carnival barking not only offensive but dangerously foolish. Shrewder industry strategists also questioned the wisdom of waging a private war against the New Deal and its consumerist allies and began suggesting instead (as *Advertising Age* put it) that Madison Avenue "would do better to impress the public with efforts in behalf of the country, rather than efforts on behalf of itself." To one of the smartest such analysts—Walter Weir of the Lord and Thomas Agency—the war was in fact "the greatest, the most golden, the most challenging opportunity ever to face American advertising." It gave practitioners a chance, Weir argued, to "demonstrate the power of advertising as it has never been demonstrated before" and to "justify its existence as it has never been justified before." Madison Avenue, Weir suggested, could win its war for survival by launching an offensive not against the Administration and *Consumers Union*, but against Germany and Japan. "If we make advertising fight today," Weir declared, "we'll never again have to defend its place in our economy."

Almost immediately, this became the new mantra and guide to action. In February 1942 industry leaders launched the Advertising Council to mobilize support for the war effort. Dominated by the large agencies and headed by Chester (Chet) J. LaRoche (chairman of Young & Rubicam), its sponsors included allies like the associations of newspaper publishers and radio broadcasters, whose members' incomes were heavily dependent on ad revenues; and the typographers, lithographers, and photoengravers, whose livelihood depended on having ads to produce. Behind this phalanx stood the innumerable companies—including the country's biggest corporations—that were desperate to advertise, whether or not they had products to sell, in order to keep their brand names before the public, positioned for postwar sales.

So it was that just as Morgenthau was reaching out to ad men, they were reaching out to him. In short order, another detente was arranged between New Dealers and quondam adversaries, one of many forged in the heat of war.

The first collaboration came almost immediately, when in February 1942 the Advertising Council undertook to promote a Treasury-designed tithing proposal—urging workers to accept 10 percent of their salaries in bonds by signing on to a payroll deduction plan. By the end of the year, 24 million workers were enrolled, and their collective purchases were funneling $365 million into federal coffers each month.

For his part, Morgenthau announced in May that a "reasonable amount" of good will and institutional advertising—promoting a brand but not a product—would be deductible as a business expense. This meant that eligible companies could write off up to 80 percent of the cost of ads, a bargain they couldn't (and didn't want to) refuse, especially as the money would otherwise go to the government. Morgenthau would complete his peace offering to Madison Avenue in September 1942 when he had the Bureau of Internal Revenue declare that virtually any amount of advertising would be declared "reasonable," especially if was connected to "the promotion of government objectives in war time, such as conservation, salvage or the sale of war bonds."

Though Morgenthau began to incorporate some professional advice in 1942, he also continued to rely on volunteer activities. May and June saw a succession of neighborhood war-bond rallies in New York—one on Wall Street featuring tanks, another in Times Square featuring Jimmy Walker—and these proved mere preludes to an initiative as colossal as La Guardia's *levée en masse* of air raid wardens. A Greater New York War Bond Pledge Campaign was set up to recruit and train 200,000 Minute Men and Minute Women to make door-to-door house calls (June 14–24) on more than a million Gotham families (over 60 percent of the city's homes), soliciting written pledges to make regular future bond purchases ("Listen for the Victory Knock on the Door" was the slogan). With the aid of volunteer businessmen, Boy Scouts, labor leaders, and the American Women's Volunteer Service, Minute People were enrolled and given crash courses in sales technique, while another crowd of volunteers was enlisted to staff over 1,000 bond booths throughout the five boroughs where people could come make pledges. (Morgenthau remained choosy about would-be purchasers: when he heard a booth had been set up in Rockefeller Plaza, near shops that sold jewels and furs to "people on Fifth Avenue," he groused that "those aren't the kind of people I want to reach.") In the end nearly two million pledges were made, with an average annual promise-to-pay of $175—a seeming triumph of volunteerism.

Still, promises weren't purchases, and sales failed to keep pace with needs. Morgenthau therefore called on the Advertising Council to take a bigger role. A Council leader told the Advertising Federation of America, assembled in annual convention at the Hotel Commodore, that on July 1, 1942, his group would launch a sales campaign that would be "one of the most intensive ever imagined." This time, relying more on media than manpower, it would be a "high powered" drive, rather than (he sniffed) the "low powered" effort the Minute Men and Women had just concluded. It would draw upon (and demonstrate) advertising's "capacity to mold the thinking, the feeling and the habits of the American people."

Alas, by August, this approach too had proven insufficient, leading Roosevelt to ask: "Henry, now that your War Bonds are not going so well, what are you going to do about it?" In October, Congress offered its own answer by enacting the Victory Tax, opting for compulsion over cajolery.

Morgenthau rallied for one last effort, a Victory Fund Drive, which would mix and match armies of volunteers with legions of professionals. Between November 30 and December 23, 1942, he planned to raise no less than nine billion dollars, the largest government borrowing in history. National in scope, the drive would take New York as a prime target (since that's where so much of the money was) and its principal source of sales expertise (notably in Gotham's advertising, entertainment, and financial sectors). A Victory Fund Committee, headed by an executive manager from Morgan Stanley, assembled 50,000 volunteer bankers, brokers, and insurance agents, and divided them into fifteen sales teams, each headed by one of the largest banks in the city. These pros knew how to reach deep-pocketed investors—the clients they'd long worked with. The Advertising Council, for its part, coordinated ad agency professionals in preparing copy and images aimed at a wider audience, which large advertisers then paid to have inserted in newspapers, magazines, and radio spots.

This time it all came together. The New York Victory Fund Committee raised two billion dollars in the drive's first two days and eventually piled up over five billion in the allotted three weeks. Nationally, sales totaled $13 billion, oversubscribing the goal by $4 billion. Morgenthau was ecstatic—he thanked the Ad Council "for the truly wonderful help you have been giving the Treasury in our war financing campaigns"—with the only downside, from his perspective, being that a mere $1.6 billion of the total got purchased by individuals. Corporations, banks, and insurance firms took the lion's share—the Bowery Savings Bank plunking down $53 million, Equitable Life anteing up $50 million—though nonfinancial entities bought in as well, with the City of New York signing on for $10 million.

The Second War Loan Drive in April 1943 did even better—both in total sales and increased individual subscriptions. In part this was because of an Ad Council–orchestrated torrent of full-page ads and outdoor posters that Morgenthau proclaimed "the greatest advertising operation in the history of the world."

Entertainers of every stripe were especially prominent. Arturo Toscanini led the NBC Symphony Orchestra in live concerts (heavy on Beethoven) with seats available only by purchasing war bonds; often they featured his own arrangement of "The Star-Spangled Banner," which he conducted facing the audience, eyes ablaze, singing along with them in hoarse baritone; the concerts racked up over ten million in sales. The powerhouse contralto Kate Smith sang and spoke to twenty million CBS listeners on War Bond Day (September 21, 1943), in a radiothon that lasted from 8:00 a.m. until 2:00 a.m. the following day, selling thirty-nine million worth in the process—a feat so astounding that Robert K. Merton, of Columbia's Bureau of Applied Research, devoted an entire book to its analysis (*Mass Persuasion: The Social Psychology of a War Bond Drive*).

Special football and baseball games were arranged, again with a war bond the price of admission. On August 26, 1943, an All-Star team composed of Yankees, Giants, and Dodgers beat a crack servicemen's team at the Polo Grounds, 5–2, with one of the winning runs a homer belted into the upper-right-field stand by Babe Ruth, out of retirement for the occasion.

Small businesses stepped up to the plate in profusion—like the Manhattan Tavern Owners' Fourth War Loan Drive Committee, which enlisted 7,500 bartenders to sell bonds; or the alliance of 120 cigar stores, which set up as sales locations; or the Society of Restaurateurs, whose 200-member dining establishments, during the Second War Loan, offered a free lunch to bond buyers. Larger industries joined in, too, like the publishing trade, as evidenced by the efforts of the Books and Authors War Bond Committee chaired by Mark Van Doren.

Labor was particularly active. In June 1942, CIO barbers in Brooklyn sold bonds while cutting hair. In September 1943, as part of the Third War Loan drive, the Amalgamated (CIO) ran a "Clothe the Army" campaign whose goal was $2.5 million in monthly bond purchases. (The Amalgamated also put 75 percent of its financial assets into Series F and G bonds and Canadian offerings.) Not to be outdone, the Cloak, Suit, Skirt and Reefer Makers Union (ILGWU, AFL), pledged $5 million toward the Fourth War Loan.

Most remarkable was the degree to which national origin became the basis around which bond sales were organized, in sharp contrast to the First World War's effort to efface ethnicity. There was a German American War Bond Committee, a Polish War Bond Committee, a Chinese War Bond Committee, a French American War Bond Committee, a Bronx Zionist War Bond Committee. And these groups mounted a plethora of community events—bazaars, rallies, marches, fairs, dinners, conclaves, picnics, performances—at which the leitmotif of America as a place that accommodated and fostered diversity was endlessly in evidence. On September 29, 1942, a Spanish American War Bond Committee held a rally at Broadway and 136th Street for local Hispanic residents, the proceedings of which were broadcast to Latin America by Rockefeller's Office of the Coordinator of Inter-American Affairs. On September 4, 1943, 3,500 people, mostly Mexican and Central American residents of New York, held a war bond rally at the Beacon Theater at 74th and Broadway under the auspices of the Good Neighbors Center of New York. Generoso Pope, having landed firmly on his feet, chaired the War Savings Committee of Americans of Italian Extraction; a banquet he threw for 250 guests at the Hotel Biltmore generated two million dollars in pledges.

Yet in the end, though the eight drives raised a total of $185.7 billion, and over 85 million individual Americans participated, the aggregate investment of individuals—a major Morgenthau priority—constituted only 27 percent of the total. For all the incessant ballyhoo, the quota for individuals was seldom filled, leaving banks (52 percent), corporations/associations (11 percent), and insurance companies (9 percent) to take up the slack. This distribution pattern underscored New York's centrality to the money-harvesting. In drive after drive, Gotham, with 6 percent of the population, was assigned dollar quotas amounting to 25–30 percent of the national sales target and invariably met them, given that the city was home to so many of the country's richest individuals and headquarters to so many of its biggest corporations. The size of some local purchases was simply staggering. Metropolitan Life alone accumulated $3.7 billion worth, and by war's end these government securities constituted half the company's total assets, seven times the amount it held in railroad bonds, long its premier investment.

Much of this purchasing was driven by patriotism, but it was highly lucrative as well, especially for banks, whose profits more than doubled between 1940 and 1946. Much of the gain was accrued simply by passively collecting interest on government securities. The total, however, was boosted by super profits garnered through more activist approaches. Banks nimbly sold off their negotiable bonds in the marketplace and used the proceeds to buy newer higher-interest offerings, reaping quick gains without adding to the stock of bombs or tanks. In similar fashion, banks purchased from big investors securities they'd bought in earlier drives and resold them; this fruitless speculative churning (involving billions of dollars) smacked, said Morgenthau, more of "greed" than "patriotism." Banks also loaned to speculators known as "free riders" or "quota riders," traders who bought and sold bonds at a profit without putting up any of their own money. They would subscribe on 10 percent margin to more of a limited offering than they could pay for and then resell the bonds they'd been allotted to others who hadn't gotten all they wanted (given the ceiling on purchases) and were forced to pay a premium in the marketplace.

A deeper source of bank super-profitability stemmed from the way the Fed carried out its Treasury-assigned task of keeping interest rates low. It bought up outstanding government securities from banks that held them. The banks then loaned this fresh crop of capital to customers who, in turn, lent it back to the government by buying the newest treasury issues. Then the customers sold these new securities to the banks, which eventually resold them to the Fed the next time it needed to expand the money supply. The government, in effect, was borrowing its own money and paying fees to middlemen bankers and investors for the privilege. Federal Reserve Board Chairman Marriner Eccles, who thought the process "outrageous," noted that bankers and bond dealers were delighted by these sales and resales, which "ensured them a windfall of profits, as they did to countless corporations and insurance companies."

The bottom line was that Wall Street had an exceedingly good war, even if its power to control the economy waned; and Washington obtained the wherewithal to wage and win that war, even as (given its mammoth borrowings) the national debt quintupled, rocketing from $48 billion in 1941 to $260 billion in 1945.

Morgenthau was of course disappointed that individual bond sales had failed to keep pace with corporate ones, but in truth raising revenue had not been his sole concern. Especially before Pearl Harbor, he envisaged the fundraising program as a way to mobilize support for preparedness and afterward to help unite the country behind the conflict. One of Morgenthau's chief advisers—an academic public opinion expert named Peter Odegard—argued that "the experience of participation in a joint effort breeds community of purpose, conveys a sense of national direction, creates what is commonly referred to as morale." A bond drive, Odegard counseled, could be "the spearhead for getting people interested in the war."

Morgenthau agreed. The government, he decided, would "use bonds to sell the war, rather than vice-versa." From this perspective, involving Madison Avenue in the process seemed an unambiguously good idea. But from the perspective of others in the Administration, giving the ad industry a say in defining the nation's war aims seemed a deeply dubious decision. In short order, this division of opinion opened up yet another front in the war between the New York–dominated camps of Fighting Liberals and Wall Street Warriors—this one about the very meaning of the global conflict.

102

"What This War Is All About"

Before Pearl Harbor, several of Roosevelt's closest advisers had urged him to set up a government apparatus to push for preparedness, rather than leave the job to private entities like the Century Group and the Fight for Freedom Committee. This Roosevelt was deeply reluctant to do. He was well aware the American public believed it had been propagandized into the First World War; he had terrible memories of the Creel Committee's behavior during the war itself; and he half hoped the deteriorating global situation would convince people that intervention was a self-evident necessity. Hopkins, Rosenman, Sherwood, MacLeish, and Stimson argued strongly for creating a vehicle to overcome public apathy and outright resistance.

Roosevelt cautiously acquiesced in May 1941 when he added a "morale-building" function to La Guardia's Office of Civilian Defense portfolio. La Guardia had no interest in this aspect of war-readiness, and he spurned PR people's offers to help with a curt "We don't believe in this country in artificially stimulated high-pressure, doctored nonsense."

Advisers again pressed the president, pointing out that, at the least, the flow of information from government offices to the pubic badly needed coordination. In October of 1941, FDR agreed to set up the Office of Facts and Figures (OFF) under poet Archibald MacLeish. The name suggested it would distribute information in a value-free, un-hortatory way. But the staff MacLeish assembled—writers, journalists, and radio people, almost all of whom were Fighting Liberals—marshaled facts in support of values and argued that Americans should support preparedness, even war, if necessary, to defend those values.

That fall, FDR himself proposed using the 150th anniversary of the ratification of the Bill of Rights—coming up on December 15, 1941—to affirm key American values. William B. Lewis, former program chief at CBS and now director of OFF's Radio Division, asked Norman Corwin, the veteran CBS radio dramatist, to develop a special broadcast. Corwin—who in 1939 had aired Paul Robeson singing the *Ballad for Americans*—created a script ("We Hold These Truths"); assembled a "million-dollar cast" of major stars, including James Stewart, Orson Welles, Lionel Barrymore, Walter Huston, Edward G. Robinson, Walter Brennan, and Rudy Vallee; and commissioned an original score for the New York

Philharmonic Orchestra, led by Leopold Stokowski. Planned before Pearl Harbor, it aired eight days after, with FDR himself offering a vigorous postscript. Sixty-three million people tuned in, half the country's population, and the program was acclaimed from coast to coast as a brilliant exposition of the principles on which the United States was founded.

With the country now in the fight, the Office of Facts and Figures took up the task of explaining the conflict's meaning. MacLeish quickly authorized production of *This Is War!*, a thirteen-part series of half-hour programs to be aired on Saturday evenings by all four networks, beginning in February 1942. Each series segment was written by Corwin or under his supervision, with contributions from the likes of playwright Maxwell Anderson and author Stephen Vincent Benét. The opening show featured the Almanac Singers' rousing performance of "Round and Round Hitler's Grave"—Pete Seeger's wartime spin on "Old Joe Clark," with Woody Guthrie supplying a verse on Mussolini.

This Is War! hammered away on the proposition that the conflict pitted liberal democracy against illiberal fascism, though occasionally it deployed a more melodramatic, Brownsville-gangster metaphor: "The enemy is Murder International, Murder Unlimited." The analysis was staunchly internationalist. It was also pluralist—the "race-against-race line is old Nazi stuff"—and it challenged discrimination against African Americans in defense industries and unions. (Despite such tolerance talk, the program labeled anyone who challenged US war policies an Axis stooge and urged reporting any such critic to the FBI to be sure "that termite will be taken care of.") The broadcasts included many kind words for Franklin Roosevelt, who was compared to George Washington and Abraham Lincoln, and for his domestic policies, described as "trying to see the hungry got fed and the jobless got work, trying to remember the forgotten man, trying to deal out a better deal around the table." Twenty million listened to *This Is War!* Nelson Rockefeller's Inter-American Affairs office rebroadcast the programs to Latin America; and critics raved, with *Variety* praising its "tough talking, spade-calling, spine-walloping propaganda of pugnacity."

The Hearst papers, of different mind, attacked OFF as an agitproperator for Roosevelt. Such assaults may have hastened the end of OFF, in June 1942, but the agency's demise had more to do with FDR's unhappiness at the inefficient way it managed the now-immense flow of information out of the war agencies. The president replaced OFF with OWI, the Office of War Information. Headquartered in Washington, it also set up shop in Gotham, the nation's media capital, where its midtown offices—in the old General Motors Building (224 West 57th Street, just off Broadway)—afforded easy interface with the city's radio, newspaper, magazine, book, theatrical, recording, and songwriting industries.

To direct the operation, Roosevelt chose Elmer Davis, a journalist, writer, and radio professional. Davis had done a ten-year stint as a *New York Times* reporter, then tried his hand at freelance writing. In the fall of 1939, he'd been asked by CBS to pinch hit for news analyst H. V. Kaltenborn, then on location in Europe—"a little like trying to play center field in place of Joe DiMaggio," as Davis put it. An instant success, thanks in part to his engaging persona and trust-inducing Hoosier accent, Davis got his own regular slot doing five-minute commentaries which by 1941 were drawing over twelve million listeners nightly. As OWI chief he adopted the slogan: "This is a people's war, and the people are entitled to know as much as possible about it."

The entity Roosevelt handed Davis was divided between media and advertising executives, and New Deal liberals, with the first group largely in charge of national broadcasting, the latter in control of messages beamed overseas.

The OWI's Domestic Branch was placed under Gardner ("Mike") Cowles Jr., a midwestern Willkie Republican businessman who owned a small newspaper chain, a radio station,

Poster for "Sing for Your Supper," a musical revue put on by the WPA Federal Theatre. (WPA Federal Arts Project, Library of Congress, Prints and Photographs Division)

and *Look* magazine. Cowles staffed his wing with media and ad execs and happily joined forces with the Advertising Council.

Each of the OWI Domestic divisions—Campaigns, Radio, News, Motion Pictures, and Publications and Graphics—established a close working relationship with its counterpart in the media world. Standard operating procedure at the Bureau of Campaigns, for example, was that any federal agency with something to promote should get in touch with the OWI, which would then link them up with an executive assigned by the Advertising Council to run their campaign. This coordinator would pick an agency to work up copy, which was then given to a thematically related advertiser: if it was a scrap-metal campaign, a steel or auto company would include the material in its advertising; if it was to promote nutrition, the OWI might turn to Sheffield Farms, a dairy based in New York's Orange County, to be the bearer of good news about milk.

Though the Domestic Branch did house some New Deal liberals, it was staffed mainly by industry executives. The opposite was true at the Overseas Branch, which had begun life as Robert Sherwood's Foreign Information Service (FIS), a wing of Wild Bill Donovan's Coordinator of Information (COI) operation created in July 1941. Sherwood had recruited an impressive group of liberal writers, journalists, and political activists to the FIS and housed them at 270 Madison.

Sherwood now gave command of what soon became known as the Voice of America to producer-director John Houseman, who was superbly qualified for the position of top overseas propagandist. A multilingual Euroamerican, Houseman had been born in Bucharest to a British mother of Welsh and Irish descent and an Alsatian Jewish father, then raised in France and England. Professionally he brought to the task an extensive background in theater (including his work with Welles on *Negro Macbeth* and *The Cradle Will Rock*), and in radio (again collaborating with Welles, notably on the *War of the Worlds*). Houseman immediately ramped up the dramatic level of Foreign Information Service broadcasts. After the intro—"This is New York, the United States of America, calling the people of Europe"—presentations would employ multiple high-energy voices, of differing quality and pitch, along the lines of the *March of Time*, rather than the uni-vocal low-key sound of the BBC and commercial US networks. Speakers would recount high-level military and diplomatic developments but also relate war stories about ordinary participants. On February 24, 1942, the FIS began beaming its first programming to England—three fifteen-minute broadcasts daily, in German, French, and Italian—which were then relayed to the continent via BBC transmitters. By March it was sending out over six hours' worth each day, in four languages, and the number of hours and languages multiplied rapidly through April and May.

By then, however, it had become apparent that the office of Coordinator of Information (COI) wasn't big enough for both Sherwood and Donovan, their approach to propaganda and politics being so dissimilar. In June 1942 Roosevelt dissolved the COI and divided its functions between two new agencies. Donovan's Office of Strategic Services (OSS) was tasked with overseas espionage, and a New York branch, under Allen Dulles, was installed in Rockefeller Center, where a burgeoning staff of businessmen, bankers, lawyers, intellectuals, and office workers soon made it the complex's second-largest tenant after the Rockefeller interests.

At the same time, Sherwood's shop was transferred to the Office of War Information, becoming its Overseas Branch. Sherwood and company continued doing what they'd done before—disseminating information abroad about US war aims and activities.

The Overseas Branch now grew dramatically: by October 1942, 1,800 people worked in the New York office and eighteen outposts overseas. While it did produce movies, books, and photos for foreign distribution, radio remained the heart of the operation, if for no other reason than it was far more difficult to smuggle physical objects into enemy-occupied territories than to airlift programs. Once it reached full-throatedness, the Voice of America was on the air virtually continuously, broadcasting 6,000 transmissions weekly out of sixteen studios at 57th Street to every part of the world, in more than forty languages.

Émigré-drenched New York was the perfect place to recruit a multilingual staff. The French desk, biggest and most politically crucial, was headed by Pierre Lazareff, who had edited *Paris-Midi* and then *Paris-Soir* until the day the Nazis took the city, whereupon he fled to New York. Lazareff was easily able to hire a stellar crew of Francophones, including philosopher Jacques Maritain, writer Denis De Rougemont, actor Yul Brynner, surrealist André Breton, and anthropologist Claude Lévi-Strauss, who presented the news two or three times a week and was often picked to read FDR's speeches on air as his voice proved the easiest to hear over enemy jamming.

The only tongues outside OWI domain were Spanish and Portuguese—Nelson Rockefeller's Office of Inter-American Affairs (OIAA) having maintained its lock on propaganda aimed at Latin America. Hundreds of Spanish-speaking émigrés and local Hispanics (along with some Portuguese and Brazilians) worked as writers, translators, announcers, actors, singers, and commentators out of the Newsweek Building (the former Hotel Knickerbocker) on the southeast corner of Broadway and 42nd Street. The OIAA's most popular production was *Americanos Todos* (*Americans All*), a half-hour show broadcast five nights a week, that combined news and entertainment with dubious assertions about North and South America being as one in their common love of freedom and individualism.

Rockefeller—like Davis and Cowles—worked closely with New York commercial station and ad agency elites, whom he lured away from the private sector. Sylvester "Pat" Weaver, who had been director of radio programming at Young & Rubicam before moving to American Tobacco as advertising manager in charge of the Lucky Strike account, came to the OIAA when tapped by Rockefeller, his friend and fellow Dartmouth alum. At the *Newsweek* shop Weaver beavered away with a crack team of advertising and radio professionals, including James Webb Young, a top executive at J. Walter Thompson, and Don Francisco, president of Lord and Thomas.

These two giants—the OWI and the OIAA—dominated all propaganda coming out of New York, with the exception of that generated by a lone radio ranger, Fiorello La Guardia. In 1942, the mayor worked out a private arrangement with NBC to use its New York shortwave stations WRCA and WNBI (with transmitters in Bound Brook, New Jersey) to broadcast a fifteen-minute show to Italy on Sunday afternoons. Entitled "Mayor La Guardia Calling Rome," it featured Fiorello urging Italians to break with their Nazi allies. Fascist officials denounced him as a "false Italian and authenticated Jew" and ridiculed his "American accent" and "bad Italian language." This latter assertion was verified by American undercover agents who, *Time* magazine reported, claimed that even local anti-Fascists found his Italian comical. The OWI noted in October 1943 that La Guardia's talks topped all US broadcasts to Italy. Anti-Fascists—heartened by the sense he conveyed that America was supporting them—listened to him regularly even though some were jailed for doing so. As to his command of the language, the mayor noted drily that, given the furious calumnies coming his way from the Fascist regime, they did "seem to understand my bad Italian."

103

Clashing Visions of Victory

Taking Sherwood's operation out from under Donovan's jurisdiction ended one battle but provoked a new one, a fracas between the OWI's writers and artists, and its advertising and media executives.

The liberals defined the agency's mission as articulating the war's meaning, something deemed critical in light of an OWI-commissioned spring 1942 poll, which found that half the respondents didn't have "a clear idea of what the war is all about." More troubling was that one-third of the respondents in a summertime survey saw no US stake in the European war, mistrusted our Anglo-Russian allies, and were prepared to make a separate peace with Germany.

To demonstrate to doubtful Americans why they *did* have a stake, OWI argued the enemy was not just the Axis armies but their pernicious social and economic orders. Victory entailed more than crushing the Axis. It required establishing the Four Freedoms in the conquered countries and, as FDR had said, "everywhere in the world." OWI liberals envisioned New Deal–style social democratic reforms sweeping the postwar planet, ushering in government-guaranteed rights to a job at fair pay, and to adequate food, clothing, shelter, and medical care. Victory would hopefully bring, as well, the rejection of colonialism, imperialism, discrimination, and undemocratic rule by big business and the military.

In 1942 the premier spokesman for this perspective was Vice President Henry Wallace. In a May 8 address ("The Price of Free World Victory") to the Free World Association at the Hotel Commodore, he gave the new global vision its definitive formulation. The war, he hoped and believed, would see the beginning not of Henry Luce's "American Century" but rather a "Century of the Common Man." It would be achieved through a dismantling of the old colonial order and a global extension of the New Deal. The former would unfetter the world economy by scrapping imperial blocs and outlawing international cartels, thus establishing free trade and equal access to markets and raw materials. The latter would create a global investment fund (akin to the Reconstruction Finance Corporation) to reconstruct postwar Europe and develop post-colonial countries through a vast network of Tennessee Valley Authorities and Rural Electrification Administrations. It would also guarantee workers' rights and ensure a decent standard of living worldwide, which would in turn enhance mass purchasing power and keep depressions at bay.

Wallace's vision of a new world order combining reformed capitalism with social democracy was hailed by the wider liberal community. Kudoed in *PM*, *The Nation*, *The New Republic*, and *Common Sense*, it was taken up as well by the Union for Democratic Action, the leftist (but anticommunist) activist group headquartered at 120 East 16th Street, whose luminaries included Reinhold Niebuhr, Freda Kirchwey, and A. Philip Randolph. Wallace's speech, printed up as a pamphlet, was also distributed—in the hundreds of thousands—by its fans in the federal propaganda establishment, of whom OWI director Elmer Davis was one of the most ardent.

Not all on the left were swept away by Wallace's rhetoric. In a perceptive 1942 *Partisan Review* essay—"The (American) People's Century"—Dwight Macdonald noted that the vice president's exhilarating vision of worldwide economic reconstruction cum social security had more in common with Luce's formulation than either would admit. In both instances, private enterprise was to be preserved, and the US (with Britain) was to police the postwar world and refashion it in the image of the US. Wallace failed to recognize that in practice the workings of the profit-based system grossly contradicted its principles and didn't realize it was hardly likely that expanding a capitalist economy would usher in a cooperative commonwealth, something only democratic socialism could achieve.

Macdonald shrewdly situated Wallace's (and liberals') wishful bridging of this divide in the larger detente between Fighting Liberals and Wall Street Warriors. FDR, he suggested, had figured out long before the business community that the problems of US capitalism could best be solved on a world scale. Republicans had provincially shied away from accepting an imperial role, with Macdonald's former boss, Henry Luce, being among the recalcitrant. However, the 1937–38 relapse into depression had convinced Luce, and the House of Morgan, that isolationism was not a viable foreign policy. The New York international bankers and media moguls, overcoming resistance from industrialists, farmers, small businessmen, and parochial politicians, had seized the Republican Party during the Willkie campaign and struck up an alliance with FDR on foreign policy. Though there were, Macdonald admitted, real differences between the Luce and Wallace visions, for the moment both fit comfortably within the wartime consensus.

OWI ad men were uncomfortable with their liberal colleagues' approach to the common mission. Copywriters were trained to sell products, not principles. They were accustomed to appealing to private motivations rather than civic obligations, especially when the latter involved touting the New Deal, their industry's bête noire. Ad men tended to equate democracy with consumer choice, freedom with the right to buy commodities, and making the world safe for democracy with making it safe for shopping. "WHAT THIS WAR IS ALL ABOUT," an ad for Royal Typewriters trumpeted, was hastening the day when you "can once more walk into any store in the land and buy anything you want!"

Ad men had a matching vision of the postwar world. Copywriters, artists, and creative directors generated ad copy that promised a "better, brighter World of Tomorrow," a fantastic world of superhighways, glass cities, streamlined autos, a helicopter in every garage, and suburban homes in which consumers could surround themselves with creature comforts made by their advertisers. "Look . . . the Smiths are building a new home!" ran one ad from General Electric. By buying war bonds, it said, readers could bring victory nearer; and with it "the fruits of victory"—"THE HOME YOU HAVE ALWAYS WANTED!" and "*with everything in it that makes it a real home.*" Such were the blessings of democracy, explained another ad: Americans owned things "that belong only to a free people," things like "warm comfortable homes," and "electrical machines to keep and cook our food; to wash and clean for us," while "those who live under dictators merely dream of such possessions."

This approach drove OWI liberals nuts. As one writer derided it in doggerel: "Oh boy, but there's an ocean / Of joy in promotion, / Answering the question / "What's in it for me?" Also grating was the ad men's conviction that the best way to sell a commodity—in this case, the war—was to skip tedious explanations about the product in favor of pitching it through simple slogans, endlessly reiterated, or, better still, associating it with positive emotions. "Try this delicious health-building War!" penned another parodist: "Buy all you need—then buy some more! Never mind what we're fighting for!" To ad men it seemed Best Practice professionalism to appeal to the man on the street in terms they believed he would understand. To liberals intent on explicating grand policy, Madison Avenue's approach seemed like condescension, manipulation, treating people as "if they were twelve years old." They were offended at having to share power with those they deemed hucksters and con men, especially after the autonomy they had enjoyed in OFF.

For their part, the media executives thought the writers self-righteous, impractical, and expendable. Cowles thought the OWI should stick to developing narrowly framed ad campaigns for other government agencies, rather than initiating projects, much less attempting to make public policy, something not in the OWI's purview. In this they were heartily seconded by the Departments of State and War, which objected to OWI interventions against anything that undermined the stalwart antifascism they had proclaimed the nation's premier war goal. Thus Sherwood, James Warburg, Joseph Barnes, and Houseman decried US recognition of the Nazi-collaborationist Vichy regime of Phillipe Pétain, Pierre Laval, and Admiral Jean Darlan. They did believe that FDR—unlike State and War—was on their side in this. Which is why they were brought up short in November 1942 when, during the American-led invasion of North Africa, General Eisenhower cut a deal with Darlan to accept continued local Vichy rule (with its anti-Semitic campaigns and concentration camps) in exchange for a French cease fire that would minimize American casualties. Roosevelt further dismayed liberals by opposing General de Gaulle and his Free French forces, who thirsted to overthrow Vichy. Their outrage was reflected in VOA programming, to FDR's annoyance, though as he needed liberal support, the president soft-pedaled his response.

Not so Congress, which in the elections of fall 1942 had been decisively captured by a coalition of conservative Republicans and Southern Democrats. They considered the OWI Domestic Branch a New Deal propaganda mill. Southern congressmen were particularly irate that the federal agency published antiracist tracts like Chandler Owen's pamphlet "Negroes and the War," and they began to let fly wild accusations of communist infiltration.

In 1943, after Roosevelt warned Elmer Davis that Congress was considering slashing OWI's appropriation, Davis gave Cowles the go-ahead to rein in the Domestic Branch. Writers were ordered to write only to specification, and a former ad manager for Coca-Cola was put in charge of artists. One of the latter was Ben Shahn, whose proposed posters got routinely scuttled. Shahn now drew and circulated in-house a mock poster illustrating his contempt for the new regime. It featured the Statue of Liberty holding aloft a frosty bottle of Coke, with three more bottles tucked under its arm, under which ran the caption: "Try the Four Delicious Freedoms—the War that Refreshes." Finally, in April 1943, a group of writers resigned en masse and issued a press statement charging the OWI was now controlled by "high-pressure promoters who prefer slick salesmanship to honest information."

Two war-time Coca-Cola ads, 1942. These appeared in most major publications, notably *Life* magazine and the *Saturday Evening Post*. (Left: Courtesy of the Coca-Cola Company. Right: Patti McConville / Alamy Stock Photo)

Congress, unpacified, nearly shut down the Domestic Branch altogether but settled for slashing its budget by 90 percent and prohibiting it from publishing pamphlets or producing radio series.

Next the Congressional crosshairs focused on the Overseas Branch. Calls came for curtailing New York's independence. Sherwood, who retained Roosevelt's support, fought back. One congressional investigation followed another, making liberals' lives miserable (Houseman quit in 1943). Internally, Davis brought in CBS executive Edward Klauber—a Roosevelt supporter but also a ruthless administrator—to bring the Gotham office to heel. In February 1944, Sherwood abandoned the struggle, moving to London to direct OWI operations there; the unprotected Warburg and Barnes were axed. In September 1944, when FDR summoned Sherwood back to speechwriting duties for his fourth-term campaign, Congress complained about the conflict of interest, and the playwright resigned altogether.

This completed OWI's capture by New York's media and promotional industries. The executives now in charge of the government's public relations apparatus, in tandem with their colleagues in the War Advertising Council (or WAC, as the AC renamed itself in June 1943), concentrated, as promised, on public service campaigns. Yet the Madison Avenuers soon found, as had Stimson in dealing with General Motors, that many headstrong businesses preferred to stick to servicing their own interests. In November 1943 one dismayed WAC director disclosed that a survey of ads in large circulation magazines demonstrated that only 10 percent purveyed the desired message about war bonds or victory gardens. Fifty percent of the ads didn't mention the war at all. The other 40 percent did include WAC copy, as much as anything as a device to draw attention to their own pitches and logos, or to envelop their products in an aura of patriotism. Firms without commodities to sell often suggested their enforced hiatus from the marketplace was a blessing in disguise, as wartime research meant improved consumer goods were in the offing: "From Textron's war laboratories of today will come fabulous, fantastic fabrics to adorn you and your home tomorrow."

James Young of J. Walter Thompson—a prewar industry booster and a wartime head of the WAC—complained that too many ads just "slop bilge water over the decks," thus providing an opening for critics to again bring Madison Avenue into disrepute. Consumers' Union did indeed caustically attack the use of home front campaigns to boost corporate commodities and brand names, especially as taxpayers were subsidizing them. Smarter businesses—usually those that could afford to take a longer view—garnered points with the public by running counterintuitive ads that called for *restraint* in the use of their products, thus making a virtue out of government-imposed rationing or outright bans. One Esso ad advised: "Oil is Ammunition, Use it Wisely." Another from Texaco urged saving fuel oil by lowering thermostats—you'll live in a colder home but "with a warmer heart."

Walter Weir, the creative director at Lord & Thomas, took this a giant step farther, arguing that advertisers should induce guilt in civilians who spent their money on themselves rather than on war bonds. Copywriters, Weir proposed, could use powerful language and affective imagery to bring home to the home front the harsh realities of distant war, reminding them that "soldiers get wounded and die and that the enemy is a hateful, despicable creature." Weir's staff blazed the way, putting out revolutionary ads that—with unprecedented verve and vigor—addressed, indeed bludgeoned, the inner selves of their audiences. One relatively mild entry, addressed "To the Girl with a Soldier Overseas," asked her baldly: "How much do you really want him back?" Enough to buy a bond and "pass up that jeweled bracelet you've had your heart set on?" Others were tougher still. One argued that if you failed to buy a war bond, there would not be enough money to buy the torpedoes that could smash the Japanese carrier that could now with impunity assault a beach filled with our fighting men, sending "battery after battery of death and destruction against your brothers or your sons." By the Fifth War Bond Drive, an explicitly drawn dead soldier, a bullet hole in his helmet, blood trickling down his face, eyes open in glassy stare, "spoke" directly to the viewer: "I died today...what did *you* do?"

If guilt didn't do the trick, fear waited in the on-deck circle. One ad addressed to mothers, featuring the picture of a sleeping baby, asked them to urge their husbands to join a Payroll Savings Plan to "help protect that child—from fear, from starvation, from death—the fate that has befallen millions of children under the rule of Nazi and Jap tyrants." Another, aimed at husbands, deployed the image of a Japanese soldier breaking into a house and menacing the woman within, then noted: "Of course, you've never pictured *your* wife in the hands of an Axis soldier. . . . But. . . ." One directed to fathers, called "A High Honor for Your Daughter," showed a lineup of American beauties being reviewed by enemy procurement officers and explained that as the Nazis were big on selective breeding, if your daughter was "young and healthy and strong, a Gauleiter with an eye for beauty may decide she is a perfect specimen for one of their experimental camps." Perhaps the most famous ad—"Ever Face a Firing Squad?"—was addressed to you, yourself. It showed an array of converging gun barrels pointed at your head, beyond which lay your last view—of the Rising Sun flapping over the Capitol dome.

Weir's style was quickly and widely imitated, though in other hands veered rapidly from his intended usage—injecting a gritty realism and tragic sensibility into appeals to support the war effort—and instead became a melodramatic device for attracting attention to a brand or commodity. Some variants wallowed in mawkish sentimentality, others drummed up a sense of adventure by setting swashbuckling soldiers (resembling comic book heroes) to lay effortless waste to the enemy; in either case, war became a backdrop for product placement.

War bonds advertisement from Bourjois, Inc., 1943, in *Glamour*. (Duke University Libraries)

Weir criticized this degeneration—dismayed his tactical suggestions had gone awry—but his strategic plan for restoring Madison Avenue to the country's and the administration's good graces worked perfectly. The ad industry was widely deemed rehabilitated by its public-spirited contributions to the war effort. And *Broadcasting*, a trade journal, noted that an atmosphere of "mutual confidence" had grown up between promoters and politicians, a bond "strengthened by the influx of business and advertising men into war agencies." Indeed in 1944, FDR invited over a hundred advertisers, ad agency reps, media leaders, and War Advertising Council board members to dine with key government officials and lavishly praised their contribution.

More broadly, Madison Avenue's approach to selling the war came to overshadow the Fighting Liberals' call for making it a crusade against fascism. While many in Britain continued to cast the conflict as a "people's war," a fight for a social democratic future, here many fought to preserve the "American way of life," a term that managed to embrace both a defense of freedom and a defense of advertising. As Walter D. Fuller put it in *Printers Ink*: "Our enemies"—a term capacious enough to include fascists and consumer activists alike—"are warring upon our 'selling way of life' as surely as they are warring upon democracy itself."

Perhaps best of all, Madison Avenue discovered that, as one practitioner put it, "social responsibility" on the part of business and advertising "*brings rich returns to those who act on it*." Surfing on taxpayer subsidies, New York's ad industry entered its golden age. Print media lineage bottomed out in June 1942, then grew through the war, until by 1945 it had drawn abreast of its 1929 peak. Revenues jumped 85 percent during the conflict, and pretax profits soared 120 percent from those of 1940. As one Advertising Council president would advise the next generation of ad men about the boons that accrued to public service: "True, you are casting your bread upon the waters—but it will return to you well buttered."

Radio advertising did equally well, with volume almost doubling and budgets bulging from $195 million in 1942 to $390 million in 1944. Income from this torrent of on-air ads in turn provided CBS and NBC with healthy wartime profit margins, even as they relinquished remaining control over programming to Madison Avenue agencies, which decided on stars, scripts, formats, and show placement in network schedules.

Thanks to the industry's increase in power and profitability, New York's advertising fraternity took on a glamorous patina during the war. Account executives had lots of money to spend on entertaining clients or themselves, and ad men and media mavens alike became well-known frequenters of such midtown hangouts as 21, Toots Shor's, the Cub Room, Au Cheval Pie, and Joe and Rose's steak place on Third Avenue and 46th Street (particularly popular with Young and Rubicam or J. Walter Thompson people). But these were the officer corps of the city's symbol mongers; the ordinary troops—the rank-and-file wordsmiths and songwriters who enlisted in the war effort—led much more humdrum (and occasionally desperate) lives.

104

Writers on Demand

One reason the OWI brass easily weathered the walkout by their top writers was that they had a small army of other pen wielders at their service. Shortly after Pearl Harbor, the head of the Treasury Department's writing staff had asked Broadway playwright and producer Howard Lindsay how to find professional scribes to help sell war bonds. Lindsay recommended asking Rex Stout to put together a writer's organization. Stout agreed and on January 6, 1942, chaired the first meeting of the Writers' War Board (WWB), in the 6 East 39th Street offices of the Authors' League (of which Lindsay was president).

Stout was tailor-made for the job. Well known as the creator of the stout ("seventh of a ton") detective Nero Wolfe, he was equally familiar as an early and vociferous antifascist and pro-interventionist. A stalwart of the prewar Fight for Freedom Committee, Stout had been one of its most popular speakers, frequently debating anti-interventionists on radio. He couldn't abide Charles Lindbergh and predicted in one radio talk that if the Nazis ever conquered the world, Lindbergh would serve as collaborationist president of the United States.

Stout gathered around himself a committee of twenty or so like-minded members, a group small enough to meet at least once a week; all lived in or around New York. His number two in overseeing writing for print media was Clifton Fadiman, book review editor of the *New Yorker* and witty master of ceremonies of *Information Please*, the popular radio quiz show. Writing for broadcast was the domain of a Radio Committee in which Erik Barnouw, Dutch-born script editor for NBC, played a major role; and creation of song lyrics was the bailiwick of board member Oscar Hammerstein II (famed for *Show Boat*, his 1927 collaboration with Jerome Kern, and about to be famed for *Oklahoma!*, his 1943 collaboration with Richard Rodgers).

In the spring of 1942, WWB leaders sent out a questionnaire to 3,000 professional writers across the country, whose names were drawn from Authors' League files; 2,200 responded; and from these were drawn the initial corps of volunteers—it would eventually grow to 5,000—who offered their services, through the WWB, to a variety of federal agencies. Bureaucrats submitted requests for texts via the OWI, with which the WWB established a quasi-official affiliation in October 1942. Though remaining formally independent, Stout's group would receive a very modest subsidy of $34,000 per annum, which mostly went to cover the expense of running an office in the Chanin Building at 122 East 42nd Street.

To support a particular campaign—getting housewives, say, to pledge they'd abide by rationing rules—WWB propagandists might bang out magazine articles on the theme, or embed the desired message in radio scripts, or in newspaper stories, or stage shows, dramatic sketches, slogans, jingles, catch phrases, wisecracks, radio plugs, newspaper fillers, scripts for school performances, or pieces for industrial house organs. Émigré writers signed on, too, churning out material for distribution abroad: translated articles from US sources, written-to-order pieces for the presses of fifty nations, scripts for broadcast over OWI shortwave, leaflets to drop over enemy territory. Most writers were paid nothing, and though there was compensation in the fact that the words they assembled might reach millions of eyes and ears, their messages did not, alas, always have the maker's name attached; on occasion their prose might even be sent out under a more famous writer's (or celebrity's) name, the better to garner attention; thus "Gypsy Rose Lee" held forth on war bonds, "J. Edgar Hoover" on security matters, and ventriloquist's dummy Charlie McCarthy on the income tax.

Not every text was tailored to government order. The board's independence allowed it to promote causes not officially sanctioned, or even frowned upon by Congressional overseers. Reflecting one of Stout's passions, the WWB established a Committee to Combat Race Hatred, which touted tolerance and racial equality. Reflecting another, the WWB argued for international cooperation, even global governance—Stout being president of the Society for the Prevention of World War III, a pro–world government group.

Still, most of their prose, and poetry, was bespoke, and little of it imperishable. Edna St. Vincent Millay produced a made-to-order poem for the WWB entitled "The Murder of Lidice." Intended to arouse horror and fury, it was aired nationwide with great fanfare on October 19, 1942, and widely hailed. She knew better. It was, she thought, "merely propaganda," and she very much hoped that it "would be allowed to die along with the war that provoked it."

105

War Songs

As magazine and radio writers were given marching orders, so, too, were lyricists and composers of popular music: their orders were to write a march. More precisely, an infectiously martial song on the order of George M. Cohan's "Over There." The Office of War Information remembered that Americans had gone off to war in 1917–18 with stirring songs on their lips, and it wanted some contemporary rousers drummed up. In the summer of 1942 OWI's William B. Lewis, arguing that good war songs were essential to American morale, set about encouraging professional and amateur songsmiths alike to turn some out. The OWI set up a National Wartime Music Committee, which outlined what was wanted: brisk and bouncy marching tunes for soldiers, and also "Victory Dances with spirited, military steps" that they and civilians could dance to. Federal officials assumed Gotham's Tin Pan Alley's assembly lines could be retooled from turning out love songs to churning out war songs, the way General Motors had switched production from autos to tanks.

Tin Pan Alley thought so, too. Publishers came together to form a Music Industries War Council. Writers and composers fashioned a Music War Committee (Hammerstein chaired; members included Rodgers and Kern, Berlin and Ira Gershwin, Johnny Mercer and Billy Rose). Both groups pledged to provide and promote a Great American War Song. So did ASCAP, the American Society of Composers, Authors, and Publishers, of which Hammerstein was also head (and whose headquarters were in Rockefeller Center). ASCAP wanted to help the war effort, and—as the key licensing agency that collected performance royalties on behalf of members—also to keep at least one eye on the potentially enormous profits that might follow in a war song's wake.

The Brill Building began to buzz. As the epicenter of New York's popular music industry—over forty ASCAP publishers had their offices at 1619 Broadway (corner of 49th Street)—it was the site of innumerable brainstorming sessions. Would-be Cohans gathered in groups of two and three, came up with lyrics, grabbed a composer to fashion a tune, cornered a publisher and pounded it out for him on a house piano. Other candidate war songs poured in from producers of pop music for records and radio elsewhere in the city, from songsmiths who wrote for Broadway and Hollywood, and from amateurs around the country responding to an OWI-announced competition. The vast majority didn't survive their initial audition, but about 1,700 (produced by a core of 700 Alleyites) were sent off into circulation.

And promptly sank. Some stayed afloat awhile. "Remember Pearl Harbor," which appeared ten days after the Japanese attack, got a few weeks of play before vanishing. Frank Loesser, a journeyman lyricist working out of New York and Hollywood, scored with "Praise the Lord and Pass the Ammunition," making the CBS Hit Parade in 1942, then faded away.

Hundreds of other TPA efforts seeking to navigate from croon-moon-June to mama-Yokohama ran on the rocks more quickly. The wannabe classic "You're a Sap, Mister Jap" went nowhere even when its lyrics—"You're a sap, Mister Jap, / To make a Yankee cranky. / You're a sap, Mister Jap, / Uncle Sam is gonna spanky"—were deployed as the soundtrack of a Popeye cartoon. "We're Gonna Find a Fellow Who Is Yellow, and Beat Him Red, White, and Blue" and "When Those Little Yellow Bellies Meet the Cohens and the Kelleys" met similar fates. It's not that they didn't get put in play, rather that no one would play them. The jukebox boom, begun during the Depression, exploded during the war, with Wurlitzers, Rock-Olas, and Seeburgs getting heavy use in taverns and cafes, especially around military bases and defense plants, even as production of new machines was halted for the duration. Jukebox operators accepted war-song platters—beginning with Berlin's bond-hawking number—in order to demonstrate their commitment to the war effort, but customers refused to plunk in their nickels. One music publisher noted that "jukeboxes carry songs exclusively from the Hit Parade instead of from the 'Hate Parade,' even though the Government has expressed its desire for more of the latter."

Live venues were equally inhospitable. Bandleaders wouldn't play these "cheesy songs," *Down Beat* reported, unless commanded to by the public, which didn't. Managers of lite entertainments at nightclubs and theaters reported an equivalent hostility to overtly military music. The record and radio industries followed suit, with the former reluctant to press records (especially given the scarcity of shellac, as imports of resin from India were interrupted by the war) of songs with no staying power, and sponsors of on-air musical entertainments shied away from martial material that they believed alienated housewives and teenage girls, a mushrooming market.

As production of war songs slowed to a trickle by 1943, analysts offered assessments of why the government campaign had failed. *Variety* thought it was simple: most of the entries stank, had bad tunes and worse rhymes. By 1944 Hammerstein himself admitted this, noting that patriotic intentions weren't sufficient, that success required a "really good *song*." Others stressed their patently made-to-order quality. One D.J. found them "cheap and insincere," reeking of "synthetic patriotism." Soldiers were insulted by the notion they wouldn't fight unless galvanized by a song. Civilians complained they weren't danceable, which they weren't: tin-eared officials had insisted a proper war song must be march-tempoed, but while that beat had worked back in the First World War, when one-steps and two-steps were popular, it was out of step in an era when swing was king: jitterbuggers wanted jive ditties like the Andrews Sisters' "Boogie Woogie Bugle Boy of Company B."

Officials were also locked into a time-bound definition of what a war song *was;* they were so enslaved to a Maginot musical line that when hit war songs did emerge—albeit songs of a different color—they were declared to have become successful for the wrong reasons.

Thus the Spike Jones and his City Slickers version of "Der Fuehrer's Face"—written originally for a Disney cartoon starring Donald Duck—became wildly popular. However, its lyrics—"Are we not the supermen / Aryan pure supermen / Ja we ist der supermen / Super-duper supermen / Ist this Nutzi land not good? / Would you leave it if you could? / Ja this

Nutzi land is good! / Vee would leave it if we could"—were definitely not the high-minded inspiration the OWI had in mind. To say nothing of its chorus: "When Der Fuehrer says, 'We ist der master race' / We HEIL! [Bronx cheer] HEIL! [Bronx cheer] Right in Der Fuehrer's face"—with the fart sounds produced not by derisive fans in Yankee Stadium but by a Jones-invented rubber "razzer." (Other Spike Jones novelties—like "Little Bo-Peep Has Lost Her Jeep"—did nothing to redeem him with officialdom.)

Other winners had the right sentiments but the wrong style—notably the 1942 hillbilly hit "There's a Star-Spangled Banner Waving Somewhere." It sold 800,000 copies in sheet music, topping a 1943 *Variety* listing of the top post–Pearl Harbor war tunes, and 1,100,000 records, coming fourth on the same survey. The problem here was its "country" genre, particularly troubling to musical mandarins at ASCAP. The Society had long considered itself the arbiter of good taste and had enforced its Broadway/Hollywood cultural predilections by refusing membership to cowboy warblers (like Gene Autry), and relegating country music to the commercial periphery, along with "race music." The ascension of "Star-Spangled Banner" to such spectacular heights was a disturbing sign that the New York establishment's ability to impose its preferences was slipping. It also provided alarming evidence of the growing power of its recently arrived rival, Broadcast Music, Inc. (BMI), set up in 1939 (at 23 West 47th Street) by radio broadcasters to challenge ASCAP's near monopoly on what could and could not be heard on the air. When ASCAP sidelined itself in 1941 during a struggle with the networks—banning the use of its artists' music—BMI, seeking to capitalize on the opportunity, discovered a big emerging market for Appalachian hillbilly songs among the displaced Midwesterners and Southerners who had come to work in Eastern and Western defense plants and were seeking some Southern comfort.

But the songs that really blindsided officialdom, by becoming far and away the overwhelming wartime favorites, were the sentimental/romantic love ballads that spoke to the separation of servicemen and their sweethearts, sometimes explicitly, as in Glenn Miller's "Don't Sit Under the Apple Tree (With Anyone Else But Me)"—but often as not with no direct mention of the war at all, as in Cole Porter's "You'd Be So Nice to Come Home To," or Bob Russell's lyrics for Duke Ellington's tune "Don't Get Around Much Anymore" ("Been invited on dates / Could have gone, but what for? / Awfully diff'rent without you / Don't get around much anymore"). These songs hardly struck the right martial tone, the OWI worried, and by stoking loneliness and anxiety might even undercut battlefield efficiency.

Even more problematic were songs that looked longingly ahead to the end of the war, or nostalgically back to prewar days, rather than fixing the listener's attention on the present-day business at hand, thus perhaps softening resolve, weakening the will to fight. Unfortunately (from this perspective) these were often chart-toppers—like "The White Cliffs of Dover," which sold over 2,000,000 records, or "When the Lights Go On Again," which sold 1,250,000, or the monster hit of them all, "White Christmas," which Irving Berlin hadn't intended to have anything to do with the war, and whose success he considered something of a fluke. Written in 1940, aired by Bing Crosby on his NBC show *The Kraft Music Hall* on Christmas Day of 1941, its nostalgic evocation of a simpler time caught the imagination of GIs abroad (Armed Forces Radio was flooded with requests) and civilians on the home front, and together they lofted it to legendary status (Crosby's recording for New York's Decca in 1942 would sell over 24 million copies before the decade was out). The OWI, however, thought it overly sentimental: clarinetist–band leader Woody Herman reported being asked to not play "White Christmas" as it "makes the boys too nostalgic." And USO (United Service Organizations) recreational facilities for servicemen, like the Stage Door Canteen in Times

Square, actually banned "slush" music—anything that might make soldiers homesick or lovelorn—forcing those who wanted to hear about bluebirds over Dover to seek out the nearest jukebox.

In the end the OWI and Gotham's various music committees admitted failure on the war song front and turned to other tasks, like composing tunes to order for branches of the armed forces, or arranging patriotic concerts for community groups, war plants, and bond drives. Tin Pan Alley, nevertheless, had a great war. All that slush generated handsome profits for New York's publishers, composers, and performers, and for the city's radio broadcasters, recording studios, and jukebox operators. Even the stepped-up rationing of shellac and of paper (thus crimping sheet-music production) didn't slow sales. ASCAP reported a hefty increase in royalties; and some declared the music biz had in general risen 50 percent over its fin-de-Thirties standing.

106

"Smashing Thru, Captain America Came Face to Face with Hitler…"

Over the course of the war the Army Postal Terminal at 464 Lexington, part of the New York Port of Embarkation, handled over three billion pieces of first-class mail (sent and received). It was able to do so because the millions of magazines shipped off to the fronts each month were channeled through other facilities—special terminals set up at 50 Jay Street in Brooklyn and 123 East 22nd in Manhattan. By the end of 1942 over 30 percent of this armada of printed matter consisted of comic books. That same year the Navy Department insisted that *Superman* comics be placed on the list of essential supplies destined for the Marine garrison at Midway.

For all Superman's popularity with the US Armed Forces, Pearl Harbor had put the Man of Steel—and his creators, Jerry Siegel and Joe Shuster—in something of a quandary. Shouldn't he enlist? If he did, couldn't he lick the Nazis and Japs in a week or so, at most, given the ever-greater powers with which he'd been endowed? If he didn't, what would people, especially soldiers, say about his patriotic credentials? Mightn't some snoopy congressional committee raise questions about his pacifist leanings, pointing to his now-embarrassing intervention—as chronicled, unimpeachably, in *Action Comics* #2 (July 1938)—to end a war between Latin American countries that had been duped into combat by a nefarious arms merchant? ["Superman: Then why are your armies battling? Army head: I don't know! Can you tell me? Other army head: No, can you? Superman: Gentlemen, it's obvious you've been fighting only to promote the sale of munitions—why not shake hands and make up?"]

Scriptwriter Siegel decided to have it both ways. Clark Kent enlisted enthusiastically, but *so* enthusiastically that when he took his physical, he mistakenly used his X-ray vision for the eye test, read off letters from the chart in an adjoining room, and was declared 4-F, much to Lois Lane's disgust. Superman, however, went before a Joint Session of Congress to explain himself—as recounted in the DC Comics strip in the *Washington Post* on March 10,

472   SELLING THE WAR

1942. "Like every other patriotic American I want to aid in the downfall of these fascist vultures," the Man of Steel told the assembled legislators, "but the American Armed Fores are powerful enough to smash these treacherous foes without the aid of a Superman." Accordingly, he declared, "I believe I can best serve the nation on the home front, battling our most insidious foes," those "hidden maggots—the traitors, the fifth columnists." (Good as his word, he immediately foiled a German plot to blow up Congress itself.) Being a Fighting *Liberal*, he also promised to remain "on the alert for the old totalitarian trick of creating disunity by

Cover of *Action Comics* #86, July 10, 1945.   (Auction photo)

Interior of *All-Star Comics* #8, October 21, 1941. (Auction photo)

spreading race hatreds." Meanwhile, the struggle overseas would be safely left to "the greatest of all heroes, the American fighting man."

So Superman sat out the war, watching for spies and hawking war bonds, always modestly underscoring his subordinate status. Even when he mightily aided the Seventh War Loan by burying a passel of Japs under a blizzard of bonds (on the cover of *Action Comics* #86, July 1945), he insisted: "And it isn't Superman who's doing this, it's the American People!" Unfortunately, all this self-effacement—rooted, ironically, in his excess of power—had its downside. It opened the door to rival heroes who were a little less super, and to would-be publishers like Martin Goodman, a younger and hungrier version of Harry Donenfeld, the Detective Comics magnate who was now flying complacently high on the back of his red-caped crusader but was about to receive a comedownance.

The Brooklyn-born Goodman had dreamt of publishing since he was a kid. After apprenticing in sales, he worked his way into pulp magazine production, finally founding his own company—soon-to-be empire—in 1932. Focusing first on westerns, Goodman branched out into mysteries, sports, jungle adventures, and science fiction until, by 1938, he was producing twenty-seven pulps out of his offices in the McGraw-Hill Building at 330 West 42nd. In 1939, discerning the huge popularity of comic books in general, and Superman in particular, he opened up a comics division, dubbed it Timely Publications, and went shopping for a superhero. Rather than hire his own staff, he subcontracted the task to one of the Midtown comic-book "packagers"—outfits that hired freelance artists to whip up material for publishers who, like Goodman, were toeing the comic book waters. This one, Funnies, Inc., had just been set up by comic industry veteran Lloyd Jacquet in a rundown office building off Times Square at 45 West 45th Street. Thanks to some very talented young artists on his payroll, Jacquet was able to hand Goodman a collection of tales that Timely brought out as *Marvel Comics* #1, cover-dated October 1939. It featured two instant-smash-hit characters—the Sub-Mariner, mutant king of an undersea race who hated surface people for exploiting the ocean (he invaded New York to get us to lay off); and the Human Torch, an android created in a Brooklyn lab, who at first burst uncontrollably into flames, spreading terror, before learning how to get a grip on his incendiary capabilities, after which he used them to help save Gotham from the Sub-Mariner's depredations. The initial *Marvel* immediately sold 80,000 copies. Doubling down, Goodman ordered a mammoth second printing, cover-dated November 1939. It sold 800,000 copies. With a hit on his hands, Goodman, in early 1940, now began assembling an in-house staff, starting with one of those talented freelancers at Funnies, Inc., the twenty-seven-year-old Joe Simon.

Simon, a Rochester native, after doing newspaper artwork in his hometown and then Syracuse, moved down to Gotham in the mid-1930s, where he worked for Paramount Pictures (retouching the movie studio's publicity photos) and McFadden Publications (doing illustrations for *True Story*). At decade's end Simon was deep into cartooning, freelancing for various packagers like Jacquet's Funnies and Victor Fox's Fox Publications. When Goodman offered to pay him $12 a page compared to the $7 he'd been getting, Simon, who had ambitions of his own, insisted on a titled position (editor-in-chief of the Timely division) and a percentage. He also brought along a twenty-three-year-old budding cartoon genius he'd recently met at Fox, with whom he'd struck up an informal collaboration.

Jacob Kurtzberg, son of Jewish Austrian immigrants (father: garment worker, mother: seamstress), grew up poor in a tiny tenement apartment on Suffolk Street. Young Jake longed to transcend the Lower East Side, where Jewish gangs constantly had to battle the Irish gangs who wandered over from the waterfront equipped with rocks, bottles, and clubs, but he was temperamentally unsuited for the usual avenues of mobility, like politics or crime. Then he discovered comics. He devoured the strips by Alex Raymond (*Flash Gordon*) and Milton Caniff (who was doing *Terry and the Pirates* for the *Daily News*) and began to draw his own. He even found an outlet for his work at the Boys Brotherhood Republic, on East 3rd Street, a "miniature city" established by philanthropists and social welfare workers in the early 1930s, where street kids ran their own "government" and published their own paper, for which Jake drew cartoons. Plans for professional training collapsed when his father, who had saved enough to allow him to enter Pratt, lost his job when the Depression hit bottom, and soon his son was back on the streets.

So Kurtzburg turned to on-the-job training. He worked at the Max Fleischer studio at 1600 Broadway (between 48th and 49th) as an "in-betweener" doing Popeye cartoons— filling in the action between major-movement frames—an operation Kurtzburg would describe as "a factory in a sense, like my father's factory. They were manufacturing pictures." He worked as well for the Lincoln Newspaper Syndicate, where artists pseudonymously inked newspaper strips and single-panel advice cartoons; Kurtzburg took the pen name Jack Kirby, as it reminded him of Jimmy Cagney, a hometown movie hero; later he changed it legally. He worked at the packaging shop of Will Eisner and Jerry Iger—a two-room office across from the *Daily News* building on 42nd Street—where, in the back room, he and other artists toiled on comic books for $3.50 to $5.50 a page. And in 1940, he had just gotten a salaried staff position at Fox ($15 a week), and was sitting among rows of artists, churning out his first super-hero work (the *Blue Beetle*), when the dapperly dressed Joe Simon showed up and joined Fox in an editorial capacity (at $85 a week). Taken with Simon's creative capabilities, and awed by his sartorial splendor, Kirby asked if he could do some freelancing with him; Simon, impressed with Kirby's artwork, agreed; and, without either telling Fox, they moonlighted together for Funnies, Inc., on *Blue Bolt*, a science fiction title Simon had created. And when Simon cut his deal with Martin Goodman in early 1940, Kirby came on board as part of the package, soon becoming Timely's art director.

Simon and Kirby were hired to work on Goodman's existing properties, as well as to develop new ones. They accordingly set out to fashion a superhero who would be in touch with the fast-changing 1940 Zeitgeist (the Germans blitzkrieging France, the FDR–Willkie campaign getting under way). And as both were Fighting Liberals and staunchly antifascist, they wanted a character who would take on Hitler directly. They had already nudged the Human Torch and Sub-Mariner in this direction, making the old enemies allies against the Nazis, but wanted to go still further: "The opponents to the war were all quite well organized," Simon recalled. "We wanted to have our say too." In particular they wanted a hero with superpowers, though not *too* super to be a member of the Armed Forces. After a few failures they came up with a winning formula, featuring an anti-Nazi character drawn straight from the city's streets.

According to *Captain America Comics* #1 (cover-dated March 1941 but on sale from December 1940), President Roosevelt, determined to counter "a wave of sabotage and treason" by foreign agents and Fifth Columnists, had authorized a top-secret defense plan. Federal officials had enlisted the aid of a brilliant scientist, Dr. Reinstein, who had developed a secret formula that could create a "corps of super-agents" that would be "a terror to spies and saboteurs." A volunteer was needed to test Reinstein's serum, and the opportunity was offered to one Steve Rogers, a young man from the Lower East Side. Patriotic but poor, hence underfed and scrawny, Rogers, to his great disappointment, had been declared 4-F, and he jumped when given this secret opportunity to serve. Once injected, Rogers grew in height, muscle mass, and mental capability, becoming, said a satisfied Reinstein, the first of an army of super soldiers. Alas, Rogers proved the last of his line, as a Nazi saboteur popped up, shot and killed Reinstein (who'd kept the formula in his head), leaving Rogers a one-of-a-kind chemically enhanced human. Making the best of things, the government set him up as a special agent—code named Captain America—and provided him with a cover identity by inducting his nebbishy alter ego into the Army. Private First Class Steve Rogers revealed his true powers only when he doffed his fatigues and donned his red-white-and-blue fighting togs and indestructible shield— powers revealed spectacularly on that initial cover when Captain America leapt over the walls of

Berchtesgaden, smashed through legions of jackbooted fascists, and belted Hitler himself in the kisser—a full year before Pearl Harbor.

That issue sold a million copies, instantly vaulting Martin Goodman's operation into the big leagues, his trio of Captain America, Sub-Mariner, and Human Torch now able to go toe to toe with Superman and Batman over at Harry Donenfeld and Jack Liebowitz's DC shop. The vigor of Joe Simon's anti-Nazi story line accounts for much of the mag's instant popularity, but so, too, did Jack Kirby's artwork. Light years away from the somewhat wooden panels of *Superman* and most of its competitors, *Captain America Comics* #1 featured ripplingly muscular figures with faces contorted in passion hurtling through space, cascading across panels, threatening to burst off the page into the readers lap—a cinematic sensibility that immediately rewrote the rules of comic-book art.

Cover of *Headline Comics* #8, 1944. (Auction photo)

Not everyone was enthralled with the new hero. *Captain America* Comics #5's "Killers of the Bund" generated lots of hate mail and phoned-in death threats aimed at the largely Jewish staff—but it also won them friends in high places, when Mayor La Guardia himself called Goodman's office (or so Simon would tell the tale) and informed Joe: "You boys over there are doing a good job! The city of New York will see that no harm will come to you."

La Guardia couldn't protect the boys from their boss. Simon had worked out his percentage deal, 25 percent of the take from *Captain America*, which as million-monthly sales continued throughout the war, generated staggering amounts of money. Goodman lied about the intake and didn't even pay what he said he owed. As it had just been a handshake deal, there could be no real recourse to law. So, after producing ten issues, Simon & Kirby—now on a par with Siegel & Shuster—walked over to DC offices at 480 Lexington (at 46th) and defected. Goodman handed *Captain America* et al. to the only person left in the office, his wife's cousin, a nineteen-year-old kid named Stanley Martin Lieber, who jumped into the breach wielding the pen name Stan Lee.

Over at DC it took the dynamic duo awhile to find their footing, but they eventually clicked with a new genre, "kid gang" comics (shades of Suffolk Street), of which the biggest hit was *Boy Commandos*. Each of the four youthful heroes hailed from a different Allied country—France, England, Holland, and the USA, with the latter represented by a kid named "Brooklyn," a violent Kirby stand-in who sported a derby hat and a tommy gun (carried gangster-style in a violin case). On and after its July 1942 premiere, *Boy Commandos*' sales consistently topped a million a month, elevating it to the DC Olympus whereon dwelt Superman and Batman.

Comic book sales simply exploded during the war—no branch of New York's publishing industry could touch them—with competitors pouring into the superhero fray, like Fawcett Publication's Captain Marvel (in whose creation Simon & Kirby had had a hand but had retained no rights), who soared past Superman into the *two* million a month empyrean. A dozen new publishers popped up in Midtown, then two dozen, then more, as pulp houses, printing companies, small time distributors, script writers, and art school dropouts alike started up operations in rented lofts, from which tumbled out new titles on what seemed a daily basis—many of them blood-racingly monosyllabic: *Crack*, *Pep*, *Zip*, *Flash*, *Speed*—and most of them hell-bent on bashing fascists. Lev Gleason, printing salesman turned publisher, came up with *Daredevil*, whose debut cover in 1941 also took on Hitler directly—"DAREDEVIL deals the ACE OF DEATH to the MAD MERCHANT OF HATE!"—and Will Eisner helped create the more esoteric *Blackhawk*, in which a multinational group of paramilitary aviators, led by a Polish pilot, sets out to overthrow the Nazis. Soon homegrown villains (greedy businessmen, corrupt politicians, thuggish gangsters) had been swept off the board, replaced by butch-haircutted Nazis and buck-toothed Japanese, with heroes fighting fascism as a species of international crime.

This juggernaut was barely slowed by the induction of nearly all of the writers and artists and editors into the military, or the growing shortages of paper, as these were offset by tidal demand from two crucial demographics—teens and preteens, many of whom had wartime jobs hence nickels to spend, and soldiers, whose addiction to comics was fed by government suppliers (at PXs, comics outsold *Saturday Evening Post*, *Life*, and *Reader's Digest* combined, by 10–1).

Once again, for yet another sector of New York's economy, the war had provided an opportunity to do well by doing good.

HOME FRONT

A riveter at work at the Federal Shipbuilding and Drydock Corporation in Kearny, NJ. May, 1942. (Library of Congress, Prints & Photographs Division, Farm Security Administration-Office of War Information Black-and-White Negatives)

107

Women at Work

"Of all sad words of tongue or pen / The saddest are these: there are no men."

Or so ran a popular wartime rewrite of John Greenleaf Whittier's famous stanza. An overstatement, to be sure. Still, in Gotham, as across the nation, the draft made significant withdrawals from the male side of the demographic ledger. In October 1944, according to the city's Selective Service chief, an estimated 763,000 local residents were serving in the armed forces. As perhaps 11,000 of these were female, which meant three-quarters of a million New York men were off fighting on foreign fronts, at a time when the city's male population of *all* ages—post-cradle to pre-grave—totaled roughly 3.7 million.

The deficit of eligible lads was much lamented by local lasses—as evidenced by 1943's plaintive hit song "They're Either Too Young or Too Old"—but it was also a problem for government officials and private employers who were facing a sharp falloff in the male labor supply just as demand was rising rapidly. Their solution? Recruit women.

In New York, most females who answered the call were volunteers. The leading mobilizers of unrecompensed womanpower were two defense organizations—created in 1940–41 to cope with then-feared Nazi air raids—that had morphed into war agencies after Pearl Harbor. The American Women's Voluntary Services (AWVS) had at first, like its British forerunner, trained women as rapid responders to bombed-out sites. Now it assembled an army of females—115,000 in 1943—to undertake a myriad of more mundane tasks. Operating out of headquarters at 11 East 58th Street, the AWVS set up 126 branch offices throughout the city, staffed by 18,000 women. They in turn recruited volunteers who aided draft boards, sold war bonds, worked as hostesses in canteens and USO clubs, ran telephone switchboards, staffed typing pools, offered courses, organized a Motor Transport Service and an Ambulance Corps, and joined sewing and knitting workshops that churned out sweaters, scarves, socks, helmets, and gloves for front line troops and local charity recipients. Women also replaced departing males in welfare and war service agencies throughout the five boroughs: the 1943 annual report tallied 57,000 volunteers so placed in the previous year. The AWVS also assisted specialized entities like the New York City Defense Recreation Committee, which worked out of a city-owned building—the former Uptown headquarters of the Henry Street Settlement, at 99 Park Avenue (corner of 40th Street)—that La Guardia had loaned for the duration. Here volunteers helped visiting American and Allied servicemen sort out personal problems—how to locate distant relatives who lived in New York; how to marry their sweethearts "right away"—and handed out free tickets to plays, sports events, dances, parties, concerts, and movies, all provided gratis by local organizations.

An even bigger entity, the Civilian Defense Volunteer Office (CDVO), had been created by La Guardia in 1941, largely in response to Eleanor Roosevelt's insistence that "defense" be redefined to include social welfare concerns—housing, education, nutrition, recreation, health care, and protection of children—and that women volunteers be mobilized to tackle them. After Pearl Harbor, the CDVO became the city's official agency for channeling voluntary labor power into agencies losing personnel to the military. Its 260,000 volunteers, organized in sixty-eight branches, constituted a labor force bigger than the one assembled by the WPA during the Depression. The women worked in municipal bureaus; ran the Pershing Square Information and War Services Center (across from Grand Central); and set up a network of 20,000 block leaders ("Neighborhood Representatives") who transmitted local needs and complaints up to higher authorities and passed down information about citywide and national campaigns to their communities. The organization also engaged in many of the same activities undertaken by the privately run AWVS, triggering occasional jurisdictional conflicts which, on the whole, were negotiated amicably.

Whatever their differences, the CDVO and AWVS joined in aiding the city's third large-scale mobilizer, the American Red Cross. Before Pearl Harbor its five borough-wide chapters had taught first aid to hundreds of thousands of New Yorkers so they could help bomb-victims; now the Red Cross turned its attention (with help from 100,000 volunteers) to raising funds for wartime activities (like stocking blood banks).

The Red Cross volunteers also responded to a looming shortage of metropolitan health-care providers. Early in 1942 the city's medical institutions began rapidly losing personnel. By year's end the seventy-six private hospitals grouped in the United Hospital Fund had released roughly 10,000 doctors, nurses, and other health-care workers to the Armed Forces, and there had been losses as well at the municipal public hospitals and district health centers. Volunteers were needed to shore up these shrinking institutions—and also to augment an expanding military medical network.

The US Naval Hospital adjoining the Brooklyn Navy Yard, commissioned in 1838 as a single building, had grown over the subsequent war-drenched century to an ensemble of thirty-seven structures. With further expansion physically foreclosed, the US used eminent domain to seize the 122-acre St. Albans Golf Club (conveniently situated, in Queens, on the main line of the Long Island Rail Road), and in April 1942 began construction of a United States Naval Base Hospital; in six months its wooden barracks-style buildings were ready to use. That same year the Army took control of a complex that New York State had just built in Willowbrook, Staten Island, for the care of mentally disabled children. Rechristened Halloran General Hospital, it became the nation's largest treatment center for returning war casualties; in January 1945 alone 16,675 disembarking wounded were sent to Halloran. In addition, in 1944 the Navy took over and renovated the 15-story Half Moon Hotel (from which the unfortunate Abe Reles had fallen, or been defenestrated), thus providing recovering sailors with a Coney Island beachfront facility: the United States Naval Convalescent Hospital.

The women who joined the Volunteer Nurses' Aide Corps of the American Red Cross helped fill personnel gaps at these military and civilian institutions—by summer 1943 over 4,000 had taken crash training courses and worked in New York hospitals. Other women signed on to roll bandages at Red Cross stations around town, or logged time at the Red Cross packaging center (39 Chambers Street) filling thousands of cartons with powdered coffee, condensed milk, and cigarettes, for sending on to prisoner-of-war camps in Europe.

Female Gothamites also enlisted in the military, as they had during the First World War, when the Yeomenettes had done yeoman service. In May 1942 the Women's Army Auxiliary Corps (WAAC) was established, after Army Chief of Staff General George Marshall helped overcome staunch congressional (and Army) opposition, though it was not until July 1943 that the organization was given full military status and the Adam's-rib term "Auxiliary" deleted from its title. The Navy quickly followed suit and established the WAVES; the Coast Guard set up the SPARS (from their motto "Semper Paratus—Always Ready"); and the Marine Corps created the Women's Reserve. No sooner had the WAAC been authorized than women in New York, married and single, surged into the Army Recruiting Headquarters at 39 Whitehall Street, shouldering aside would-be male Army recruits in their eagerness to sign up for officer or rank-and-file slots, telling on-scene journalists of motivations ranging from patriotism to desire for adventure. By early June 1942, 6,000 had applied. By 1944, roughly 11,000 Gotham women were serving in all the women's branches, and another 1,700 had donned the khaki-colored skirts and coats of the "woman's division" of La Guardia's City Patrol Corps.

The city became a major training center as well as applicant pool when in 1943 the Navy commandeered Hunter College's Bronx campus; colloquially renamed "U.S.S. Hunter," it would train over 80,000 WAVES, 3,000 women Marines, and 2,000 SPARS. Their lessons, however, did not include preparation for combat, from which women were barred. Rather, WAACs and WAVES were taken on to do jobs located overwhelmingly in the clerical, communications, or cookery spheres. Given the armed services' thitherto all-male status, men had been obliged to learn and undertake such "feminine" duties. Now top brass could draw on civilian women—already highly skilled as stenographers, typists, telephone operators, bakers, photographers, and clerks—and release men-working-as-women for male-only combat. In short order the new gender arrangements became apparent in military installations across the city, nowhere more dramatically than in the burgeoning lower Manhattan administrative offices of the Eastern Sea Frontier.

New York women also poured into the paid civilian workforce, with their presence and impact varying significantly by economic sector.

Much of the flow went into white-collar workplaces where females had previously established a strong presence. By 1940, women had already reached parity with men in Gotham's offices, holding down roughly half the typing, stenography, and secretarial jobs, and their wartime en masse takeover of such posts simply completed a gender recomposition long in progress. At moments the transformation could seem more epochal, as when particularly crusty holdouts like the New York Stock Exchange swung open their doors: in 1943 Helen Hanzelin, a Merrill, Lynch, Pierce, Fenner & Beane telephone clerk, became the first female employee of a member firm to work on the floor of the Exchange in its entire 126-year history, and she was soon joined by squadrons of quotation clerks and carrier pages. Banks followed suit, switching to page girls, even taking on women tellers. Corporate headquarters also shifted gender ground, as at IBM, where male secretaries had been the invariable rule, a rigidity abandoned after Pearl Harbor. Government bureaucracies, too, opted for females, as at the Office of War Information's Overseas Branch—New York's bustling propaganda central—which was manned by women stenographers, administrators, teletype operators, translators, analysts, and writers.

Women similarly expanded their presence in the professions—both those they had long dominated, like teaching and nursing, and others where they had been only marginally represented, notably journalism, music, and art. In 1944, Gotham's *Editor and Publisher* (the newspaper industry's leading trade journal) estimated that the 8,000 editors and reporters in uniform had largely been replaced by women; even as city radio stations upped the number of female on-air announcers and control room engineers. Also in 1944, when Leopold Stokowski created the New York Symphony Orchestra, fully one-third of the musicians he hired were women, a startling statistic in that male-dominated field. (The war-driven willingness to accept female musicians wreaked some collateral damage, however, as when New York's all-woman Orchestrette Classique was forced to disband after too many members decamped to the mainstream.) In the art world, members of the New York Society of Women Artists were active in Artists for Victory; many found employment doing camouflage work or making posters for the Civilian Defense Volunteer Office; and in 1943 Peggy Guggenheim mounted a trend-setting *Exhibition by 31 Women*, including Frida Kahlo and Louise Nevelson.

Change came more grudgingly in higher status and better-paid professions like law and medicine, male preserves on whose doors women had been knocking for a century. The New York Woman's Bar Association (NYWBA)—founded in 1935 by Hilda G. Schwartz and other lawyers after they'd been refused membership in the Association of the Bar of the City of New York (ABCNY)—had wrung access from ABCNY back in 1937, and in 1940 the Brooklyn Bar Association had elected its first women. However, female attorneys had had trouble following up such victories. With senior partners at corporate law firms facing the wholesale loss of their junior associates, some did open their doors a crack to replenish the lower ranks—and sometimes even those higher up, as when Emmet, Marvin & Martin accepted its first woman partner in 1944—but the number of female attorneys in white-shoe offices remained minuscule (as did the number of admissions to Columbia Law School, where Hunter College graduate Bella Abzug was one of only a handful of females in the Class of '45). And while droves of New York's male attorneys went down to Washington to help run the war as dollar-a-year men, the energies and talents of Gotham's female attorneys were channeled into zero-a-year and less-momentous contributions, as when in 1942 the NYWPBA set up a legal advice bureau in the American Women's Voluntary Services headquarters for servicemen who couldn't afford a lawyer.

Organized women doctors did leverage wartime exigencies into small victories, notably in winning reversal of a ban on allowing female physicians to serve as commissioned officers in the Army and Navy medical corps. The point woman on this campaign, Dr. Emily Dunning Barringer, had battled her way back in 1902 into becoming the first female resident at Gouverneur Hospital, with help from Dr. Mary Putnam Jacobi, the distinguished survivor of an even earlier generation of determined female physicians. In 1941, when Barringer assumed the presidency of the American Medical Women's Association (AMWA), she launched a two-year lobbying campaign that finally won congressional permission for women doctors to tend wounded soldiers.

The vigorous wartime activities of Gotham's women's colleges suggested that *future* female access to professional positions might yet be enhanced. In 1942, Barnard's dean, Virginia C. Guildersleeve, arguing that the nation needed "trained brains," introduced a "War Minor." And Hunter similarly laid on courses in bacteriology, cartography, meteorology, blood chemistry, nutrition, physics, radio technology, drafting, basic engineering, navigation, and the economics of war. Co-ed universities, too, pried open some preprofessional programs, less from feminist conviction than a desire to stay solvent. When NYU's student population plummeted 30 percent between 1938/39 and 1943/44, it responded by taking on a greater number of women, driving the 1944/45 percentage of females to over 50 percent of total enrollment. And the city's eight engineering schools, with federal help, jointly set up a Defense Training Institute (at 375 Pearl Street in Brooklyn) to offer female college graduates a ten-week, full-time, tuition-free course in engineering that paved the way to civil service jobs, albeit mainly in marginal positions as testers, inspectors, draftsmen, lab assistants, and engineering aides.

The glass ceiling for women professionals proved most impenetrable at the apex of the national war machinery. In 1942, thirteen women's organizations, many of them headquartered in New York, wrote the War Manpower Commission (WMC) demanding appointments to government policy-making boards. The group included such diverse entities as the National Federation of Business and Professional Women's Clubs, the National Association of Women Lawyers, the National Council of Jewish Women, the National Association of Negro Business and Professional Women's Clubs, the YWCA, and the American Library Association. They got nowhere—not a total surprise, given that members of the all-male WMC itself threatened to resign if women were added to their ranks. FDR "solved" the problem by creating a toothless Women's Advisory Committee as a WMC adjunct: it had no staff, and its recommendations, seldom sought, were invariably ignored.

Most female war workers wore blue collars. Some of these made something of a media splash because they were in jobs where they interfaced with the public. The press remarked regularly on the novelty of women running elevators in the city's office buildings and hotels (the Astor and Waldorf Astoria were among the first to switch); their ubiquity was a consequence of draft regulations that granted limited deferments to building maintenance and operating employees (engineers, electricians, plumbers, carpenters) but withheld them from elevator operators. Female cabbies particularly tickled the popular imagination; *On the Town*'s scriptwriters played to this cultural resonance in crafting their taxi driver character, Brunhilde Esterhazy. In truth there were not many Hildys: in 1944 only sixty-eight women held hack licenses. Similarly, female bus and trolley conductors garnered a lot of attention, but the real news was that the New York City Transit System, with the full support of the Transport Workers Union, preferred to leave 3,000 positions vacant rather than fill them, even temporarily, with women.

Even more newsworthy was a set of females driven *out* of work—the women of the merchant marine, who had been banned, after Pearl Harbor, from the perilous seas. In 1943, 300–400 female sailors who had been ousted from Grace Line and other companies' vessels, where they'd served as stewardesses, ships nurses, and radio operators, formed an American Seafaring Women's Committee. The group lobbied for permission to return to duty, especially on the many Liberty ships then being built, so that men could be released for more arduous tasks. The ladies made clear they were prepared to brave the very real dangers—one of their number, a Miss Carmen Quiñonez of 162 Sands Street, Brooklyn, had already been torpedoed at sea and acclaimed a hero by Mayor La Guardia for having helped rescue others—and they pointed to the example of England's Wrens and Soviet women sailors, who even served in gun crews. They also wanted the right to train at Maritime Service Schools, then open only to men, so they could win ratings as radio operators, messmen, cooks, and pursers, thus making postwar positions attainable. While the National Maritime Union was sympathetic, the Navy, Coast Guard, and War Shipping Administration remained adamant, so in 1944 nineteen of their number shipped out of New York on Norwegian freighters of the Allied Merchant Marine.

THE BIGGEST BLUE-COLLAR BATTALIONS WERE those in production work. Some labored in sectors where women had long been employed, like electrical manufacturing; others trooped into airplane and ship building, where their arrival seemed a striking break with gender conventions.

Prewar electrical plants had long considered putatively "feminine" attributes like nimble fingers, superior concentration, and attention to detail as assets (along with lower wages) for people doing coil winding and other light assembly work. To fulfill immensely expanded military orders, however, women were taken on board in great numbers—at peak they constituted half the production force—and were increasingly assigned to "male" jobs like operating turret lathes, drill presses, or milling, gear-cutting, and grinding machines. Much the same happened in instrument making: Sperry Gyroscope's Brooklyn plant had 5 percent women just before Pearl Harbor, but 20 percent a year later, with many running engraving machines, drill presses, and bench lathes.

In March 1942, Grumman Aircraft Engineering Corporation's Bethpage works became the first aviation plant in the east to hire women welders. More boldly still, Grumman hired three women as dive bomber test pilots, reputedly the first ever in the US. In 1944, Wright

A woman operates a hand drill at a Vultee Aircraft plant in Nashville, 1943. (Farm Security Administration – Office of War Information photograph collection, Library of Congress, Prints and Photographs Division)

Aeronautical Corporation, the aircraft engine manufacturing division of Curtiss-Wright Corporation, had 11,000 women working at its Paterson plant, women they had actively pursued, having hired broadcaster Lowell Thomas to make short company recruitment films and having proudly displayed a women-built Curtiss-Wright Cyclone engine, destined for a B-17 Flying Fortress, at a 1943 *Women-in-the-War* exposition in Hearn's Department Store (5th Avenue and 14th Street).

The arrival of women at New York area shipyards was even more startling. When the Todd Erie Basin Dry Docks hired a female production worker, she became the first to set foot on the yard's soil since it had opened back in 1869. And when the Navy Yard employed them in 1942 it shattered an exclusion policy in place for 141 years (apart from women who labored in the flag loft, manufacturing the pennants flown on navy ships and stitching linens for the officers' dining tables). Making up for lost time, the Third Naval District Command aggressively recruited trainees. By January 1945, 4,657 women wage earners were occupying positions (for the "duration plus six months") formerly defined as male-only: pipefitters, electricians, welders, crane operators, truck drivers, sheet metal workers, riveters, ship fitters, and machinists.

On the other hand, gender inequalities survived: women at the Navy Yard were never allowed to supervise male workers (even the flag loft, which by 1943 encompassed 680 women, was overseen by men). Women, moreover, almost never worked on the ships directly; they

Welders at the Todd Erie Basin dry dock in Red Hook, Brooklyn, 1943. (Farm Security Administration – Office of War Information photograph collection, Library of Congress, Prints and Photographs Division)

Anne Moses poses with a journalist at Todd Shipyards. (Collection of Michael Levine)

were dispatched to the ship fitters' shop, where hulls were preassembled before being delivered to the ways. This was not wholly unreasonable: the Brooklyn Navy Yard specialized in highly skilled custom work—the building and repairing of fighting ships—that required workers who had undergone the kind of lengthy craft apprenticeship theretofore open only to males. Sub-assembly work was less demanding and needed less rigorous training, one reason that Pacific coast yards, which mass-produced single design cargo ships, employed far more women. At the Brooklyn Navy Yard, females never constituted more than 7.7 percent of the production staff, and when, in June 1944, women were for the first time assigned to hull work on huge *Essex*-class carriers for the Pacific war, their numbers were tiny: of the crew of 12,000 that labored on the USS *Kearsage*, only 400 were women. And women continued to be excluded from the craft apprenticeship program itself—the prerequisite to a career in the skilled maritime trades. Females could get further training, but only *after* working hours, at times when wives and mothers had other obligations. The end result was that female hires were relegated to the bottom of the skilled worker totem pole, or stuck in lower-paid semi-skilled or unskilled positions.

Still, these women played an indispensable role in the clangorous Arsenal of Democracy, and if their percentage was low, their absolute numbers were high: a January 1944 survey of the 341 major war plants in New York City found that 134,000 of the entire workforce (27.9 percent) were women. This was somewhat below the female average of 38 percent for all US industrial jobs, but it nevertheless constituted a massive fact-on-the-ground, one that had altered the workplace landscape. Whether women's movement into war plants, volunteer brigades, and military services had rearranged the *mental* landscape—much less effected a transformation in the social relations between men and women—was another matter, one that quickly became the subject of a massive national debate, with New Yorkers in the forefront of the conversation.

108

Rosie and Charlie

Women volunteering was considered eminently respectable. Indeed, its practitioners were honored by the municipality, beginning with a Women's Parade on April 11, 1942—the city's first all-women march since the First World War. Fifteen thousand volunteers, many garbed in their respective organization's quasi-military uniform, strode down Fifth Avenue from 86th to 68th Street accompanied by a score of bands and led by Grand Marshal Harriet Aldrich (Civilian Defense Volunteer Office chief and wife of the head of Chase Bank) and Helen Lippmann (national director of the Nurses' Aide Corps and wife of the celebrated columnist). Pride of place went to the Civilian Defense Volunteer Office (CDVO), the American Women's Voluntary Services (AWVS), and the Red Cross, but also on hand were air raid wardens, City Patrol Corpswomen, Girl Scouts, YWCA and YWHA members, and representatives from many New York women's organizations.

Such celebrations of womanpower came easily to city officials because—in addition to being well merited—female brigades raised no troubling challenges to the gender order itself. Their efforts were entirely consonant with traditional wartime practices: New York women had knitted for troops in the Revolution, served as hospital auxiliaries during the Civil War, and entertained soldiers in the First World War. The volunteer operations were also reassuringly hierarchical in nature, with upper-class women occupying the upper rungs. Setting aside the fact that the organizations themselves were enormous, powerful, and run almost entirely by women, the things they *did* required no reflection on, much less reconsideration of, the proper role of women in public.

The arrival of women in the military, on the other hand, touched off a tremendous rumpus. The notion of women defending men, or female officers issuing orders to male GIs, turned the gender world upside down. Soldiers and civilian males responded with a torrent of ridicule and abuse of WAACs and WAVES, much of it centered on their sexuality: any woman who volunteered for military service, it was argued, must be ipso facto either a lesbian or loosely moraled. The *Brooklyn Tablet*'s Patrick Scanlan declared cholerically (and somewhat incoherently) that the WAAC was "an opening wedge, intended to break down the traditional American and Christian opposition to removing women from the home and to degrade her by bringing back the pagan female goddess of de-sexed, lustful sterility." Rumors flew that the Army was supplying WAACs with condoms or (somewhat contradictorily) that boatloads of pregnant WAACs were being shipped back home; both were false yet attained folkloric status.

Anxieties abated after the military refuted the condom story, scuttled rumors of mass pregnancies, and made clear that military women were precluded from combat (hence weren't protectors); women officers were forbidden to issue orders to any male serviceman (hence weren't bosses); and women weren't taking "men's jobs" (hence weren't competitors). They were, however, liberating men from doing "women's work." Some of the soldiers thus liberated were perhaps less than pleased at being freed to face death on the battlefield, and hostility toward females continued inside the services. But the tightly circumscribed nature of women's military status won grudging acquiescence in the public arena: by 1945 the New York Archdiocese had created a special medal for Catholic members of the Women's Army Corps, and SPARs were being honored with special masses at St. Patrick's.

It was the movement of women into the paid civilian labor force that roused most opposition, especially when it breached the line between "men's work" and "women's work." Criticism grew especially voluble when, as the war dragged on, more of these trespassers were wives and mothers, rather than single girls, the customary pool from which working women had been drawn. Male opponents could now cast their resistance not as a narrow defense of gender privilege but rather a well-warranted concern about the deleterious effects of such employment on the wider society. Many fretted that female factory workers might be drawn (or leap) into adulterous activities on the night shift, or simply neglect their wifely and maternal duties. Churchmen especially believed that "women who maintain jobs outside their homes weaken family life, endanger their own marital happiness, [and] rob themselves of man's protective capabilities," as the conservative Paulist Fathers' *Catholic World* put it in April 1943. The liberal Catholic *Commonweal* concurred, protesting that "if the home is thought of impatiently as that which keeps the wife and mother from war work, the amount of war work which she might do no longer signifies, for the soul of our society will already be lost."

Protestant prelates could be equally forceful. The Reverend Dr. William Ward Ayer, pastor of Calvary Baptist Church at 123 West 57th Street, warned in February 1944 of the "unspeakable and irretrievable damage done to the nation by emptying the home of its mothers"; the US was undermining "the morally stable life which has made it great." And *despite* all the talk about working wives and mothers being activated by patriotism, Reverend Ayer suggested acerbically that their motives were "not without mercenary qualities," given their attraction to war plants "where there are abnormally high wages."

For most of the war, however, such reservations were blown to the sidelines by a hurricane of propaganda issuing from the highest civilian and military circles, which insisted that patriotism, indeed victory itself, demanded setting aside gender-business as usual, at least for the duration of the war. President Roosevelt set the pace when he stated firmly on Columbus Day of 1942 that while "in some communities employers dislike to hire women" and "in others, they are reluctant to hire Negroes," given wartime exigencies "we can no longer afford to indulge such prejudice." The War Manpower Commission and Joint Army-Navy Personnel Board—similarly convinced that defeating fascism required homemakers to enter industry and the military—directed the War Advertising Council, Office of War Information, and Writers' War Board—Gotham's triadic propaganda apparatus—to rev up another social engineering initiative, akin to war bond drives, to overcome such "prejudice."

The OWI's Bureau of Campaigns accordingly launched a *Women in the War* initiative to create awareness that "women must work as men must fight." Its Magazine Bureau laid out storylines that would promote this theme; and journals were urged to put women workers on their front covers (the best depictions to be displayed in a MOMA exhibition). OWI statisticians reported their campaign had instigated the publication of 2,135 stories and articles, in 146 magazines, with a total circulation of 87 million. The Radio Bureau chimed in with spot announcements and worked with CBS to launch a dramatic series; the Motion Picture

Spread from *Life* magazine, October 26, 1942, depicting women at manufacturing plants in wartime. (Courtesy of LIFE)

Bureau generated womanpower shorts for neighborhood theaters; and the News Bureau distributed women-worker human-interest pieces to press syndicates and dispatched custom-written stories to the rural, labor, Black, and foreign language press.

This barrage of publicity—on its face intended to cajole reluctant women out of their domestic cocoons—addressed presumed female anxieties about their ability to do male work. Propagandists suggested reassuringly that welding and riveting were not all that different from conventional household tasks. "Note the similarity between squeezing orange juice and the operation of a small drill press," said one recruitment pamphlet. "Millions of women find war work pleasant and as easy as running a sewing machine, or using a vacuum cleaner," said another. Almost any job could be relabeled as "woman's work" except for those demanding heavy lifting, and modern electrical machinery had mitigated or eliminated most such tasks. As Paul McNutt of the War Manpower Commission summed up: "Women have shown that they can do or learn to do almost any kind of work."

Women who did their part were therefore—*pace* the clergymen—not to be condemned as subverters of the natural order but hailed as home-front heroines, in print and poster and cinema and song. Tin Pan Alley led the way here when in 1942 the Paramount Music Corporation (housed in the Brill Building) published a ditty called "Rosie the Riveter." Written by Redd Evans and John Jacob Loeb, and quickly recorded by Big Band leader Kay Kyser, the lyrics noted approvingly that "All the day long, whether rain or shine, she's a part of the assembly line. She's making history, working for victory, Rosie...[imitate noise of riveting machine]...the Riveter." The ditty insisted, moreover, that "she's never twittery, nervous or jittery," and indeed claimed that "that little frail can do, more than a male can do." "Rosie" posters soon flowered everywhere, most depicting her as a superconfident, supercompetent worker who yet retained a delicate air of middle-class femininity. Norman Rockwell—whose *Saturday Evening Post* cover of May 29, 1943, was far and away the most famous version—was more honest than the official agitpropers in depicting Rosie as a working-class figure, obviously Irish (like his real-life model), whose rolled-up sleeves revealed well-developed shoulders and massive arms. Rockwell's Rosie, too, sported lipstick, rouge, and a dainty lace hanky peeking from her pocket. Indeed, Rosie was generally presented as having a husband or sweetheart whom she was backing up by doing war plant labor. As Evans and Loeb's lyrics had it: "Rosie's got a boyfriend, Charlie; Charlie, he's a Marine. Rosie is protecting Charlie, working overtime on the riveting machine."

To Rosies without Charlies, officials and ad men promised romance as well as kudos. The Magazine Bureau provided plots that pulp-fiction writers could repackage using their publication's formula. Thus *True Story*—still being cranked out at the East 42nd Street headquarters of the Macfadden Publishing Company—fitted government-confected storylines into their signature redemption narrative: a twenty-year-old woman, shunned by her community because her family is disreputable, finds her true value recognized when she takes a job making precision instruments at a war plant where, for good measure, the boss's son falls in love with her. Military-recruitment ads, analogously, paired images of servicewomen in fatigues with depictions of them off-duty, glamorously gowned and in the arms of officers.

As demand for women's labor began to outstrip the traditional supply of unmarried girls and childless wives, propagandists began to scold and hector women who hewed to domesticity, belaboring "Mrs. Stay-at-Home" as a shirker. "Women have been allowed to fall into habits of extraordinary leisure," said the War Manpower Commission and were "getting by just by being 'a good wife and mother.'" Rex Stout of the War Writers Board penned an acerbic piece in *Glamour* suggesting that women who clung to their homes when their country

Rosie the Riveter poster from Paramount Music, 1942. (Universal Images Group North America LLC/Alamy Stock Photo)

called were "slackers," whose "flimsy alibis" masked the deeper truth that they did "not care that much about winning the war." Some, like Philip Wylie in his bilious bestseller *Generation of Vipers* (1942), went so far as to claim that American mothers had over-parented their kids, that "momism" accounted for the failure of so many Army inductees to meet basic physical and mental standards.

In general, however, the pitch remained positive and the cultural marketplace flooded with images of competent and confident (and white and middle-class) women happily doing their share. Hollywood carried much of this load, with films like *Rosie the Riveter* (1944) and *Swing Shift Maisie* (1943), in which Ann Sothern as a Brooklyn-vaudevillian-turned-airplane-riveter belts out "There's a Girl Behind the Boy Behind the Gun." New York's comic book industry also got into the act—Tillie the Toiler became a WAC, Winnie Winkle married

a GI—in no small part because as male artists trooped off to war, female artists often took their place: in 1942 alone the number of women in the funny business tripled. Yet the comic world's *ultimate* female hero—the female counterpart to Captain America himself—was a woman concocted by a man.

In 1928, Dr. William Moulton Marston, a psychologist with a Harvard PhD then teaching at Tufts, published a popular book promoting some unconventional ideas on sex and gender and was shown the academic door (his exit perhaps spurred by a louche living arrangement involving his wife and a former student). Marston continued writing popular psychology and in a 1940 interview for *Family Circle* suggested that comic books had serious educational possibilities. Pleased by this sentiment, Maxwell Charles ("Max") Gaines, the All-American Comics publisher, hired Marston as an educational consultant, seeking to enhance his firm's respectability. Max was even more pleased when Marston proposed designing a female superhero who would increase market share among girls.

Wonder Woman, their collaborative creation, made her debut in All-American's *All Star Comics* #8 (December 1941–January 1942). Her foundation story involved an Army intelligence officer, Steve Trevor, who crash-lands his plane on Paradise Island, home of the Amazons, ruled by Queen Hippolyta. Trevor is nursed back to health by the Queen's daughter, Princess Diana, who is dispatched to escort Trevor back to the USA and charged with championing "America, the last citadel of democracy, and of equal rights for women" against the fascists with whom they are at war. Not utterly super, the Amazon princess relies on bullet-deflecting bracelets and a magic lasso that compels those she snares to obey her every command (and to tell her the truth as well, Marston having had a hand in inventing the lie detector). Princess Di becomes Diana Prince, an Army nurse who serves as alter ego to Wonder Woman, the red-white-and-blue-spangled battler against spies and saboteurs, who even leads Marines into battle against Japs and Nazis.

Marston couldn't resist investing *Wonder Woman* with his psychological theories. In an old-fashioned Victorian way, he believed that women, being creatures of superior virtue, had the capability and duty of restraining men, whose nature was inherently aggressive and warlike; similar sentiments had animated some in the feminist-pacifist movement. Marston put a kinkier spin on things, however, by arguing that men—subconsciously—were eager "to be mastered by a woman who loves them." Full of unbound force, men enjoyed being bound if the context was erotic, hence were always on the lookout "for an exciting, beautiful girl stronger than they are." Girls too, including Wonder Woman herself, were drawn to the pleasures of submission. Enter the magic lasso: virtually every issue was replete with WW and bevies of girls tying and being tied up. Indeed, panels were festooned with bodies trussed, chained, manacled to walls, shackled to beds, with many featuring—as an added bonus—girls being stripped to camisoles, panties, and garter belts. The book featured discipline as well as bondage; in one panel sorority girls chase a bad guy, yelling "Paddles up, sisters. Give him the works!"

Marston and Gaines, it quickly transpired, had hit the psychic jackpot. *Wonder Woman* was an immediate and astonishing success—the princess got her own book in the summer of '42—and often outsold *Batman*, even *Superman*. Only one element of their best-laid plans went awry: though they had aimed at the girl market, 90 percent of the avid readership turned out to be preteen and teenage boys. Girls, it seemed, favored *Superman* far more than the heroine they'd been offered.

In a way, the government's propaganda campaign, aimed at cajoling or browbeating women into the workforce, similarly missed its intended target. Or perhaps—subconsciously?—it had been aimed at men all along, its goal being to assuage *male* anxieties, not female ones. Surveys showed, after all, that men were more wedded to the notion that a woman's place was in the home than were female respondents, who were more prone to favor the entry of married women into war plants. More to the point, women didn't *have* to be seduced or guilted into working in factories or shipyards, because most of them saw such work as either an opportunity or a necessity.

The propagandists had assumed they were talking to white middle-class stay-at-home housewives who didn't want or need to work. In fact, the vast bulk of female recruits were already *in* the labor force, or had been before the war, and had withdrawn only in the face of fierce Depression-era pressures not to compete with men. Most worked in low-wage jobs—as teachers, clerks, stenographers, secretaries, waitresses, laundry workers, telephone operators, garment workers, or domestics—and when offered higher wages and better working conditions, in industries from which they'd been excluded before 1940, they leapt at the chance. No sooner had the Navy Yard announced it was hiring than over 20,000 applications began rolling in.

As the war wore on, more full-time homemakers began entering the remunerated workforce, though most weren't hieing after pin money; they *needed* jobs to support themselves or their families. Many servicemen's wives were having a hard time—given the escalating cost of living—making ends meet on a fixed allotment of $50 a month. Economic travails obliged many GI brides and young mothers to take in boarders, move in with other war-wives (or back with their parents), or take war jobs. There were also the Gold Star wives whose husbands would never be coming back—many of the roughly 18,000 New Yorkers who died in the war left widows behind—and there was the soaring divorce rate, as well, with the ever-present possibility of a Dear Jane letter arriving in the mail.

OWI's reassurances that wage work was compatible with traditional gender arrangements were similarly off target (though perhaps comforting to men): many women entered war work precisely because they were dissatisfied with housewifery. When women in war industries were asked if they preferred working or staying at home, an eye-opening 79 percent opted for work, and of this number 70 percent were married with children. They liked the sociability of the workplace versus the isolation of the household; they liked the ability to contribute financially to the family economy; they liked learning new skills and having the satisfaction of doing a valued job well; and they enjoyed the heightened sense of independence and self-respect. Surveys of women who joined the military revealed similar attitudes: one 1943 study of WAC enlistee motivation found over 40 percent citing a desire to escape unhappy homes, leave boring jobs, and embark on a search for adventure; 25 percent wanted to improve their economic or social status; fewer than 20 percent cited patriotism.

No single group responded with more alacrity to the inducements of improved wages and working conditions than did New York's African American women who, though unaddressed by white-focused blandishments, were much in evidence at factory gates and in office lobbies. Long resigned to laboring outside their homes after marriage—overwhelmingly in white women's households—they had been scrabbling for a decade to underbid one another for demanding and demeaning day jobs at outdoor "slave markets" like those at the Grand Concourse and Highbridge Road in the Bronx, or Prospect Avenue near Prospect Park in Brooklyn. Conditions had improved slightly in 1941 in response to a two-year-long campaign by the New York City Committee on Street Corner Markets aimed at shutting down such embarrassing venues. This formidable reform coalition, spearheaded by the maids' own Domestic Workers Union (Dora Jones, president), included the Harlem YWCA (mobilized by Dorothy Height), the Urban League, the Rabbinical Association of America, the Women's Trade Union League, the Women's City Club, the YWCA, the NAACP, and the *New York Times*, which now joined *PM* in running exposés of the markets and calling editorially for their abolition. Finally, the city and state intervened. On May 1, 1941, La Guardia presided over the opening of the Simpson Street Day Work Office, just off Westchester Avenue in the East Bronx. Free to would-be employees and employers, the indoor hiring hall allowed housewives and day workers to conduct their negotiations in a more dignified manner. Comfortable quarters didn't change the fact that mistresses held the upper hand in bargaining with maids, and indoor venues produced the same miserable results as had deal-making exposed to the elements.

The war, however, altered the balance of power by enabling an epochal shift out of domestic service into industry, office work, and the military. Where in 1940 64 percent of New York's employed Black women had been domestics (77 percent in Queens), only 36 percent were so situated two years after the war. (Black men, too, shed personal service, their percentage dropping from 40 percent to 23 percent over the same period.) As the number of domestic servants in Gotham plunged by roughly a third, housekeepers who did remain in service found that thinned-out ranks enhanced their leverage for extracting higher wages. That in turn meant that hiring help—long a perquisite (and to some degree a prerequisite) of middle-class life—now receded beyond the reach of many families, leaving relatively well-off women to do their own housework. The new scarcity allowed maids to win better working conditions, too. Those who could still afford to hire household staff complained bitterly about the "servant problem," with some irate employers convinced that Black cooks and maids had joined "Eleanor Clubs" organized by the ever-subversive First Lady to disrupt the racial status quo. Obstreperous Eleanorians—ran this conspiracy theory—had pledged to refuse to undertake certain tasks and would soon, rumor had it, demand that white mistresses cook dinner for their maids' families!

These paranoid fantasies of pending misrule were based to some degree in the real-world efforts of organized NYC domestics—in conjunction with the Women's Trade Union League, YWCA, unions, and local interracial coalitions—to win coverage by federal and state programs (Social Security, Workmen's Compensation, and the Fair Labor Standards Act) from which they had been excluded. These efforts failed, and at war's end housekeepers-for-hire remained outside the law's protection. Nonetheless, this same coalition made headway on other home fronts, from raising novel demands for rearranging "male" workplaces to suit "female" labor, to challenging the very notion that some kinds of work—be they in or out of the household—were inherently the province of one gender or the other.

109

"Wenches with Wrenches"

As women entered the labor force they entered unions, too. In many cases this happened automatically, a function of the War Labor Board's "maintenance of membership" decision that workers hired by a company covered by a union contract became dues-paying members forthwith (unless they actively chose in the first weeks on the job not to join—an escape hatch that the War Labor Board had provided to placate opponents of union shops). In addition, some unions launched their own campaigns to recruit women, and none more energetically than the communist-inflected United Electrical, Radio and Machine Workers of America (UE). By war's end the UE had become the CIO's third-largest union, with 700,000 members, 40 percent of whom were women. The union's leadership reflected this demographic—and helped produce it. The UE's national staff (headquartered in the old Vanderbilt townhouse at 11 East 51st Street, across from St. Patrick's Cathedral), which had been only 2 percent female in 1942, shot to 17 percent within a year. By the end of 1944, more than a third of its full-time organizers were women.

Some, like Ruth Young, rose to still higher pinnacles of power. Young, daughter of Jewish immigrants from Ukraine, grew up in Chicago, worked in factories, and became a union activist, first in the communist-led Trade Union Unity League (she joined the Party in 1937), and then in the UE. Elected the second-ranking officer of the union's huge District 4 (New York and New Jersey), Young went on to become the only woman to sit on the national Executive Board, making her the highest-ranking female labor union official in the United States.

One thing that galvanized these women into action was the shock of discovering that when a woman replaced a departing male worker, she received only 50–80 percent of the wage he'd received for doing the identical job. This led labor feminists—notably women activists in the UE—to begin demanding equal pay for equal work. Remarkably, they found their male UE colleagues in complete agreement. Indeed, other unions swiftly took up the call, not only left-wing ones like the furriers, who were ideologically predisposed to do so, but also conservatively inclined organizations like the AFL. The reason was simple. Men realized that if businesses could get away with paying less for some jobs, in effect redefining them as "women's work," it might not be so easy to get them re-masculinized (and their original wage

Black laundromat workers of the Laundry Workers International Union, Local 135 (AFL affiliate), on strike in Brooklyn. Possibly January 23, 1934. (Library of Congress Prints and Photographs Division)

level restored) when the troops came home. Only if the tasks were locked in as being "male"—albeit occupied temporarily by females being paid at male rates—could men be sure their jobs would be intact on return.

Eliminating discriminatory pay differentials could be done through collective bargaining, and the UE and many unions won such contractual guarantees on a company-by-company basis. Nonetheless, making discrimination *illegal* across-the-board seemed an even surer bet. So, when Jane Todd, a New York State Assemblywoman from Westchester, put an "equal pay" bill in the legislative hopper, she was able to win backing from the AFL, the CIO, the Women's Trade Union League, the Women's City Club, and the National Federation of Business and Professional Women's Clubs.

This coalition soon found it was pushing on an (almost-) open door. Businessmen opponents still beat back the bill on its first outing. But more far-seeing employers realized that if they wanted to guarantee the steady flow of labor power needed to fulfill their war contracts, they had best avoid tangling with alarmed male unionists and risking disruptions. Better to save the *structure* of "men's work/women's work," even if it meant forgoing, for the duration, the hyper-profits they routinely culled from female labor. Accordingly in 1944, the State Legislature passed the Equal Pay Law. which stated—in language broader than that adopted by other states passing similar laws—that "no employee shall, because of sex, be subjected to any discrimination in the rate of her or his pay." (As usual, the law did not apply to domestic servants; nor did it cover public employees.)

The State Department of Labor asserted forthrightly that the law was intended, narrowly, "to assure that where women replace men in a specific job, where the duties and responsibilities are unchanged, the same rate or rates of pay shall be applicable regardless of sex." Sharp-eyed observers noted that the language of the law itself was open to a more revolutionary interpretation. Mightn't the ban on discrimination apply to jobs historically performed only by women, if, on evaluation, they proved to require a quality and quantity of labor equal to jobs performed by men? More broadly still, the entire episode invited reflection on whether the gender-typing of work made any sense at all—apart from being an iniquitous device allowing employers to pay women less for doing essentially the same work as men. Few labor feminists nonetheless chose to press such a case in the midst of war. They did, however, tackle the more immediately pressing issue of how (and how much) to restructure social arrangements to accommodate women's en masse arrival in the workplace.

The UE's Ruth Young was among the many activists who noted that the root of the problem lay in women's having to do double duty, as war workers and homemakers. After hours, they still had to feed their family. As Grumman's PR office noted approvingly, their pilot Teddy Kenyon, after a hard day's testing dive bombers, drove home each evening "in time for her to cook supper" for her husband, a Grumman research engineer. At what hour were Kenyon and other female employees to shop? If they waited till evening (assuming a day shift), they would find the groceries emptied by stay-at-home housewives. And what if a husband got sick? Or the kids were having problems at school?

Businesses had long professed the impossibility of hiring women because there were no bathrooms for them. But women in war plants, Young and others insisted, needed a great deal more than merely facilities (not only bathrooms, but lockers, washrooms, recreation rooms, first aid equipment, medical and sanitary supplies, stools, chairs, tables, and feeding facilities). They needed a social support system that helped them lead their double lives. Unions could do some of this—Young's District 4 hired social workers to staff a "Union Personal Service Department" that assisted women members in handling "personal and family problems." So could businesses. Some factories, to diminish absenteeism, allowed food stores to take orders from women workers at the beginning of their shift and deliver groceries at the end of it. Sperry Gyroscope invited Bloomingdale's to establish a pioneering branch at their Long Island plant, enabling women to shop without going AWOL.

What women needed far more than assistance with shopping and transportation was help in arranging for childcare. Businesses (and unions) were of virtually no use on this score. In 1943, Grumman was running three-day nurseries for female employees, but together they accommodated a mere 110 children (aged two to five), and this paltry program, according to the War Production Board, was among the largest of the only twelve employer-run programs in the entire country. It was clear that launching a large-scale initiative would require resources that only governments—municipal, state, and federal—could bring to bear, and an alliance between New York's labor union activists and middle-class feminists set out to make it happen.

In 1942, Elinor S. Gimbel, of the wealthy department store family, helped organize and assumed leadership of the Committee for the Care of Young Children in Wartime (CCYCW). Gimbel had been involved in progressive education, as vice president of the Lincoln School's parents' association, and in Popular Front politics, as an investor in *PM*. Now she put together an alliance of liberal and leftist women, including CIO and AFL officials, professionals, philanthropists, parents' groups, neighborhood organizers, unionists, reformers working on health, education, welfare and housing issues, club women, the Red Cross, the YWCA, and assorted politicians. The group's executive secretary, Annette T. Rubinstein, was both a progressive educator—headmistress of the Robert Louis Stevenson School—and an American Labor Party stalwart and associate of Vito Marcantonio. One of the CCYCW's most active (and best-known) organizers was Elizabeth Hawes, who in 1940 had shuttered her highly successful dress design business to become editor of the "News for Living" section of *PM* and was also a consumer activist in the League of Women Shoppers.

In June 1942, by which time Gimbel claimed her committee represented 850,000 New Yorkers, she began a drive to win government backing for daycare centers. She noted that England had over 5,000 nurseries, whose costs were entirely borne by the state, and that the Soviets had a similar system. To demonstrate that popular support existed in Gotham, and to bolster their claim that childcare availability would free many more mothers to undertake volunteer service or war work, the CCYCW sent canvassers to poll women in Chelsea, Brooklyn, Harlem, Flushing, and Inwood; 73 percent of those questioned declared they would be glad to get more involved if quality childcare was provided. The Committee then drew up a master plan for a citywide system of wartime nursery schools, to be underwritten by federal and municipal agencies and private groups, and presented it to La Guardia. Impressed with the size and strength of the coalition, La Guardia appointed a Mayor's Committee on Wartime Care of Children to work with Gimbel's committee in assessing where in the city such centers were most needed. La Guardia also asked Dr. Leona Baumgartner, director (since 1941) of the Bureau of Child Hygiene, to find out how many units were already in operation.

Next the coalition turned to Washington for funding. The precedent for such assistance was the WPA Nursery School Program that hired unemployed teachers to look after children of families on "home relief." In July 1942, Congress—pushed by the New York CCYCW and the Congress of Women's Auxiliaries of the CIO—authorized using $6 million of the WPA's appropriation to support facilities for children of war-working mothers, not only those on welfare. In 1943, however, the twenty-eight play schools serving 950 children (aged two to five) run by the New York City WPA in cooperation with the Board of Education, were facing (like the WPA itself) imminent liquidation. The labor feminists accordingly sought to tap another federal funding stream—the 1941 Lanham Act, which authorized the Federal Works Administration to spend money building community facilities (schools, hospitals, roads, sewers) in heavily war-impacted areas. Nudged by Eleanor Roosevelt—Ruth Young met with the First Lady in her apartment at 29 Washington Square (where ER regularly spent a day or two each week) to enlist her help—FDR ruled that Lanham funds could be spent on childcare, and the first such center was approved that summer. Unfortunately, Gotham was declared ineligible to receive such Lanham aid, because it was deemed insufficiently "war-impacted."

Gimbel & company shifted their lobbying pressure to Albany. In March 1943 Governor Dewey agreed to set up a state program, and in April he signed enabling legislation. Uniquely in the nation, New York State appropriated direct funding ($2.5 million) to fund one-third the cost of nurseries and play centers for New York City children whose parents worked in war plants. The municipality would have to come up with another third, and the centers themselves the final third, by charging parents tuition or fundraising on their own.

La Guardia at this point dragged his heels a bit. Gimbel's operation had run into opposition, notably from the National Catholic Welfare Conference (NCWC), itself a major provider of (faith-based) childcare. The NCWC feared the Federal Government might use wartime exigencies as "a means of fixing a national pattern on American community life." If it was truly essential for mothers to work, then at least, said the NCWC, "the fullest use should be made of the religious resources of the community" when arranging for "children needing care away from their own families." The mayor, perhaps with his eye on this constituency (as it had been so often in recent years), began putting some daylight between himself and the Gimbel committee. "Certain groups" of "society ladies" and "old maiden ladies," he said, were "trying to exploit the war for their own private purposes," but he, for one, did not believe in making the state the "father and mother of a child," adding that "the worst mother is better than the best institution."

Still, his Mayor's Committee set to work. First it found sponsors for seventeen of the WPA nursery schools facing extinction, then it raised private funds to match state and municipal aid for another fifty or so. Many were situated in parish houses, schools, social agencies, housing projects, and specially rented buildings. Many provided their charges—with help from AWVS and CDVO volunteers—with a variety of novel services: recreation, athletics, dramatics, snacks, regular medical exams, vaccinations (often their first), and a hot midday meal (gains of five to twenty-five pounds over the first 2–3 months were recorded routinely). In addition, Dr. Baumgartner's Bureau set up a Day Care Unit to inspect each of the roughly 400 independent centers—which collectively looked after 12,000 children—and discovered that many of these for-profit ventures exhibited a Dickensian disdain for health regulations. Only half met minimum standards, which was one reason—together with the Depression-era association of daycare with charity—that many working women preferred, if possible, to make their own arrangements with family or neighbors.

Above and beyond these tactical battles for equal pay and day care, some activists formulated broader challenges to the established gender order, addressing the kinds of issues that had not been raised forcefully since the feminist movement had gone into remission—the consequence, in part, of having backed prewar pacifism, and in part of wartime hyper-masculinization. Some of these women advocates had been long in the field, others were agitating newcomers, and together they helped keep the feminist pot a-simmer.

Elizabeth Gurley Flynn was not a feminist, exactly. Nor was the Communist Party—which she had joined in 1937 on returning to New York, and into whose highest circles she had since ascended—into women's rights, which male leaders continued to characterize as a bourgeois concern. Flynn emerged as the Party's foremost spokesperson on such matters during the war years—she chaired its Women's Commission and wrote a thrice-weekly *Daily Worker* column called "The Feminine Ferment"—and grew steadily more critical of sexism in the workplace, the unions, the Party, and the larger culture. In 1942 Flynn penned a popular pamphlet, *Women in the War*, in which she noted that every day brought a thrilling account of some new job mastered by a woman, or word of yet another sexist stereotype exploded. This led her not to complacent celebration but to a strong attack on the whole notion of gendered labor. "Work is not *man's* versus women's," Flynn argued, "any more than it is *white's* versus Negro's or *native born's* versus foreign-born's, or *Christian's* versus Jews." That mode of thought and practice was "typically Nazi," and "repugnant to American concepts of democracy." In reality, "work is the right of all, regardless of sex, color, creed, or language," and a thorough "scrapping of past prejudices, underestimation, and antagonism to women workers is imperative."

Where Flynn had been in the political trenches for a generation, Betty Goldstein was a newcomer. The Peoria-born Goldstein graduated Smith College in 1942, spent a year at Berkeley studying psychology, and in 1943, aged twenty-two, moved to Greenwich Village. There she shared a Waverly Place apartment with recent Smith and Vassar grads and worked as a staff writer for the Federated Press (FP), the left-wing news service. Launched in 1919 by socialists and militant trade unionists, the FP was still going strong during the war. Under the editorship of Marc Stone (I. F. Stone's brother), it served 250 clients across the country, many of them union papers.

One of Goldstein's first assignments was to interview the UE's Ruth Young. The youthful journalist gave an enthusiastic account of the union leader's assessment that the government would never reduce female turnover "merely by pinning up thousands of glamorous posters"; it had to face the fact that "women still have two jobs to do" and provide childcare, a goal Goldstein endorsed. She also wrote an article on the new book just out from Elizabeth Hawes who, having helped win childcare in New York, had decided to see for herself what war work was like for women. Her *Why Women Cry; or Wenches with Wrenches* (1943), was a report from the factory floor of the Wright Aeronautical Corporation in Paterson, New Jersey, where she worked the swing shift (11 p.m. to 7 a.m.) on a grinding machine. For all the difficulties women faced there—Hawes continued to bang the drum for childcare—she thought the experience positive on the whole, and she urged that every woman should "have the chance to work outside her own home." This thought was paired with a harsh critique of housekeeping, especially when not mitigated by a maid. Given the mass defection of hired help, middle-class women were now being forced to confront "how ridiculous it is to attempt running a house along eighteenth century lines while being a modern woman." Housework was solitary, boring, and it condemned wives to a species of "economic slavery for their husbands." Hawes urged women to overturn "the Hitlerian routine of children-kitchen-church for the next generation" and to insist that "females, as well as males, are human beings."

Energized by Hawes, Goldstein perorated along similar lines in her review, declaring: "Men, there's a revolution cooking in your own kitchens—revolutions of the forgotten female, who is finally waking up to the fact that she can produce other things besides babies." Goldstein went on to become an accomplished Popular Front journalist, writing stories that denounced sexism and racism, advocated daycare and equal pay, promoted unions and opposed corporate exploitation. At war's end she became a staff reporter for *UE News* and, notwithstanding her reservations about housekeeping, entered into wedlock with one Carl Friedan; her future writings would appear under the name Betty Friedan.

During the war, Friedan, Hawes, Young, Flynn, Gimbel, Rubinstein, and countless other labor feminists thought they were swimming with the wave of history. Then, after D-Day augured the end of Nazism, they found themselves caught in a rip tide. In late 1944 the War Manpower Commission asked the OWI to end its womanpower campaign, and far more than simple cessation was in the offing. Rather, a whole new line on Rosiesque riveting was adopted, and a volte-face executed, which in abruptness matched any turnabout committed by the CPUSA. The federal government—hitherto laboring women's strongest ally—proceeded to throw the great clanking machinery of its war agencies and propaganda apparatus into full reverse. Now magazines and newspapers and radios and movies and advertisements began to bray, with one voice, that the nation's children were going to hell and that it was all their mothers' fault.

110

Bad Moms

Worrying about momism (over-mothering) was over; under-mothering the concern du jour. Spotlights were trained on the emotional and behavioral problems of adolescents and the younger "latchkey children" who (it was claimed) had been left unsupervised by errant absent moms. And a charge was leveled: mothers who'd left the home and gone to work had birthed a "new national problem"—juvenile delinquency.

The term—a nineteenth-century hand-me-down—was now applied to so-called Victory Girls having sex with servicemen, a phenomenon that shocked many, and one with epidemiological consequences: the syphilis rate among young women aged fifteen to nineteen in New York City was said to have soared 204 percent between 1941 and 1944. Though the sex was consensual, not commercial, the response from police was increased incarceration—of the girls, not their male partners—thus generating a rise in the rate of female "delinquency."

The alarums over bad boys were as clangorous as those for bad girls. Particularly disturbing were the male teens who hung out—often attired in gaudy outfits—in poolrooms, juke joints, dance halls, all-night movie houses, and, worst of all, in gangs. Reports began appearing of adolescents forming "commando gangs," some of them highly organized. Up in Harlem, the Chancellors had divisions, organized along age lines, ranging from Tiny Tims through Cubs on up to Juniors and Seniors; many had auxiliary "debutante" contingents too. These wannabe-military outfits initiated raids into enemy territory (adjacent neighborhoods) and did battle with rivals (the Chancellors' great nemesis being the Imperial Lords). Mostly they fought with fists (perhaps enhanced by brass knuckles fashioned out of ashcan or garbage can handles) and crude black jacks. Increasingly, they employed fish knives, switchblades, and the occasional zip gun cobbled together from four-inch pieces of pipe (or tubes from car radio antennas), blocks of wood, and makeshift firing pins which, when propelled by heavy rubber bands, could shoot a .22-caliber bullet as far as two or three blocks.

Some of these gangs were in effect the picket patrols of rival racial, ethnic, or religious communities, whose peacetime divisions had been inflamed by wartime anxieties and animosities. This was particularly evident in Washington Heights, where the longtime resident Irish, feeling besieged by Jewish newcomers, formed gangs like the Shamrocks (inspired, perhaps, by the Shamrock Battalion of the Fighting 69th, deployed in 1943 on the Makin Atoll in the Gilbert Islands). Egged on by Christian Fronters, the Shamrocks (and Amsterdams) assaulted Jewish children and attacked synagogues and Jewish-owned shops with relative impunity, given the Irish composition of the police force. In general, however, the NYPD—driven by hysterical press commentaries and outraged municipal authorities—rushed to reassert control over wayward youths. Arrests and court cases mounted during the war, creating the impression of an explosion of juvenile delinquency.

In truth, actual crime spiraled sharply downward, as attested happily by the watchdog Citizens Committee on the Control of Crime in New York (Harry F. Guggenheim, President). Rates of robbery, burglary. and auto theft all fell steeply, reaching historic lows by war's end. Most strikingly, homicides plummeted to 3.5 per 100,000 people, a rate half the average of the country's thirty-five biggest cities combined, and a twentieth-century nadir.

What really troubled parents was their sense of loss of control over adolescents, a feeling rooted in reality, though not in parental neglect. Most New York women remained homemakers and childminders, after all. Rather, the burgeoning teen independence stemmed from the easy availability of work (hence money) in the superheated economy. Pre-draft-age teens quit school en masse to grab good-paying jobs before they were called up: the New York high school dropout rate averaged 55 percent during the war years. Then they used the money, and the freedom from institutional, familial, and ethnic constraints it could buy, to indulge in commercial cultural pastimes—fashioning their own musical, sartorial, and generational identities. The emergence of a teen culture was an old story by now, but it took a great leap forward during the war years. It had, as well, a new edge to it, stemming from the fact that the youthful partying and clustering was so patently out of sync with the war effort, a drama in which the young had been given no significant part to play. In some, this peripheralization produced mimetic military campaigns; in others it provoked wild attention-getting behavior of the sort sensationalized in Irving Shulman's *The Amboy Dukes*, about a fictitious street gang in Brooklyn, whose protagonist drops out of school to make some "real dough" and comes to a bad end.

Though this overblown surge of "juvenile delinquency" had diverse roots, it was pinned primarily on working mothers, and the antidote (stop working) laid out baldly. In one advertisement the tragic image of a hysterical girl being carted away to a foster home because her mother was away at work was contrasted with an idyllic scene of a mother puttering around the house while the kids played happily under her watchful eye.

Working moms also took the rap for a rising divorce rate. Again, the concern was bottomed in a real social fact—the number of fractured marriages soared from 16/100 in 1940 to 27/100 in 1944—but causation was misattributed to women's attainment of economic (hence psychological and sexual) independence. In fact, the epidemic of GI divorces from 1944 on was the flip side of an o'er hasty rush to the altar during 1940–43. The initial scramble had begun in August 1940, just before passage in September of the Selective Service Act, with many couples wedding so the man could escape or postpone military service (married men being largely exempt from early draft calls). Pearl Harbor brought out record numbers: on December 23, 1941, extra police were assigned to the Brooklyn marriage bureau to maintain order in the line of 1,000 people; the month's final tally for New York was 80 percent higher than that of December 1940.

Draft avoidance was far from being the only motivating factor. Some young women, panicked that a long war would crimp their marital prospects, set out to get a husband while they could, rather than waiting and perhaps losing out to their even younger sisters.

Longstanding sweethearts tied the Depression-delayed knot because the war boom afforded the wherewithal to do so. Newly met couples—like Judy Garland and Robert Walker in *The Clock*—were swept away by war-heightened needs for romance and for someone to hold on to and return home to. Marriage licenses continued to be issued in record numbers, with the City Hall area, wrote one observer in mid-1943, "blurred with running soldiers, sailors, and girls hunting the license bureau, floral shops, ministers, blood-testing laboratories and the Legal Aid Society."

Many of these marriages "were utterly preposterous"—in the contemporary judgment of Columbia sociologist Willard Waller—"contracted by young people because death was whispering in their ears." Resting on flimsy foundations, such unions were soon subjected to tremendous wartime stresses. There was the husband's seemingly unending absence, and the ever-present fear of a War Department telegram ("We regret to inform you..."). Equally dreaded was the "Dear John" letter, the result perhaps of sober second thoughts, or simply wartime loneliness, coupled with a relaxation of traditional constraints and a greater opportunity for on-their-own wives to meet men in their workplaces.

Divorce rates were damped down for a time by a wartime law that gave an overseas GI the option not to answer a divorce summons from his wife, and by the unwillingness of judges to grant women legal separations if the overseas serviceman refused consent. The veterans' return eliminated such restraints and generated many additional separations as hastily arranged alliances cracked under the strain of two strangers belatedly confronting their incompatibility.

Too often this complicated backstory was ignored, and the divorce rate was used (along with juvenile delinquency) to demand that when Johnny came marching home, Jane should too. Propagandists urged women to put aside wartime competencies and concentrate on assuaging male egos: "He's head man again," *House Beautiful* instructed, and "your part in the remaking of this man is to fit his home to him, understanding why he wants it this way, forgetting your own preferences."

Those preferences, as measured in poll after poll, were overwhelmingly in favor of keeping their jobs. There were plenty of war-weary women—emotionally drained by the anxieties of separation and the exhausting labor of double-duty responsibilities—who were more than ready for the comfort and security of a traditional role and who readily embraced the status of "Rosie the Housewife." But a 1945 New York State Department of Labor survey of one thousand women in war plants was not unusual in finding that 93 percent wanted or needed to stay in the same job, or to secure similar factory employment, in order to support themselves and their dependents.

In the end, however, neither preferences nor propaganda determined the outcome. Rather, it was a combination of things—contractual arrangements (many women had been hired for "the duration plus six months"); workplace customs (like seniority); and government policies and laws (the Selective Service and Veterans' Preference Acts granted job-retention rights and preferential hiring to veterans)—that were responsible for great numbers of female workers being driven back to lower-paid women's work or ejected from the labor force altogether.

Anyone who assumed that women dispatched back to hearth and home would settle into quiescent domesticity had not been paying attention to the city's households. If they had, they would have known that from the very beginning of the global conflict, consumption, like production, had been a major battlefield of the home-front war, and its front line ran right through women's kitchens.

111

Controlling Consumption

As a war economy was erected alongside the civilian economy, it swiftly became apparent that the US didn't have the resources to sustain both at full throttle. The war machine's vast maw needed spectacular quantities of raw materials—steel, rubber, tin, aluminum, oil—and the gigantic armies being assembled demanded staggering amounts of food and clothing. Meeting both newer military and older civilian needs was made even more difficult by a loss of access to sources of supply. The Japanese capture of Malaya and Indonesia cut off 90 percent of US rubber imports. The loss of the Philippines, China, and the Indies necessitated replacing 100,000 tons of vital tin and a billion pounds of critical oils and fats. Stocks of sugar and coffee shrank, too, as ships that had carried them up from the Caribbean and South America were redeployed to ferrying troops, and the flow of oil and gasoline was imperiled by sharking Nazi submarines.

Stopgap measures, begun even before the war started, focused on salvaging raw materials from backyards and basements. In July 1941, the Office of Production Management had announced a two-week scrap drive that would gather worn-out aluminum pots and kettles to use in building bombers. It was followed in 1942 and 1943 by a series of mammoth, hortatory, war-bond-style collecting drives—promoted by the War Advertising Council, staffed by vast numbers of Civilian Defense Volunteer Office (CDVO) and American Women's Voluntary Services (AWVS) volunteers, and coordinated by Mayor La Guardia ("Save Some Scrap to Kill a Jap" was one of his favorite slogans). Schoolchildren were set to recycling old toothpaste tubes. Men and boys dragged bed springs, washtubs, and baby carriages to curbside for collection. Housewives collected empty tin cans (critical for alloys and solders), bundled newspapers (for making dynamite caps or packing bullets), and carried their old bacon grease to the butcher's (where AWVS volunteers picked it up for transformation into nitroglycerine). La Guardia kept score and trumpeted results: in late September 1942 he hailed a record-breaking weekly haul of a thousand tons of tin.

Bob Moses was also keeping score, and he not unreasonably pointed out that "without disparaging in any way the collection of loose household and miscellaneous junk by enthusiastic volunteers, it is a fact that a comparatively small amount of heavy ferrous metals will become available in this manner." Appointed by the mayor as local coordinator for *industrial* salvaging, Moses quickly identified 50,000 tons of old breweries, trolley tracks, disused railroad bridges, decrepit warehouses, and obsolete tenements that could be torn down and hauled away. He also fingered, as eminently requisitionable, the 28,000 tons of "steel" lining segments waiting to be installed in the Brooklyn-Battery Tunnel—part of his campaign to disrupt the project of his competitor, the New York City Tunnel Authority. Despite the TA's instant rebuttal (the segments were *not* steel, but cast iron, useless for war production), Moses achieved his main goal, bamboozling the War Production Board into shutting down the BBT for the duration.

Moses resigned his post after seven weeks, claiming (with some justice) that the federal government couldn't get it together to collect the materials he'd identified. And while ferrous drives did help keep the steel mills working, others were more problematic: it turned out that recycled aluminum was useless for bomber production. By the end of 1943, most scrap campaigns had ground to a halt.

On the food front, the stopgap measure of choice involved getting civilians to grow their own, thus allowing farm output to be directed to the troops. In Gotham, Victory Gardens soon sprouted in backyards around town, as women (and men) began raising tomatoes, beans, beets, carrots, lettuce, Swiss chard, and kohlrabi. In their expanding search for more urban acreage, the agricultural legions colonized a wide variety of private and public spaces—rooftops and penthouses, the Bronx Botanical Garden and the Schwab estate on Riverside Drive, Rikers Island and Rockefeller Center's median strips, college campuses and vacant lots (a cornfield bloomed in one on 52nd Street, not far from the jazz clubs). Macy's encouraged branching out into animal husbandry, and the department store hawked ducks, chickens, pullets, and rabbits, along with coops and hutches, everything needed for a Victory Barnyard.

The output was prodigious. In 1942, organizers challenged volunteers to get 250,000 city gardens up-and-growing by the spring of 1943. To many people's amazement, that quota was rapidly and thoroughly oversubscribed, with aid from the CDVO's Pershing Square plant clinic that thousands of urban farmers consulted. By December 1943, the Greater New York Victory Garden Council tallied a total of 400,000 gardens, averaging 25×25 feet, covering in aggregate 6,000 acres. Together they had produced an estimated 200,000,000 pounds of fresh vegetables—3,333 freight cars worth—that would have fetched $30,000,000 had they been sold in metropolitan markets. Prize specimens of this herculean horticulturalism were displayed at what became (for a short time) an annual Harvest Show—the metropolitan equivalent of a county fair—held at the Grand Central Palace on Park and 46th, with outrigger exhibits at RKO theater lobbies in all five boroughs. The CDVO also encouraged women to can their crops by opening community canning centers equipped with modern pressure cookers (seven in Manhattan, eleven in Brooklyn), which were soon jammed with neighborhood women and men putting up produce.

Still, neither sidewalk bed springs nor backyard kohlrabi could long sustain a massive modern army and its coterie of war plants, and volunteerism was soon outstripped by federal edicts. The most obvious way to reserve, say, steel, for tanks and ships was to forbid its use in civilian products, which meant, in practice, shutting down their manufacture. In May 1942, accordingly, the War Production Board began cutting or halting production of over 400 common commodities. One everyday item after another took its leave, banned for the duration: automobiles, refrigerators, vacuum cleaners, sewing machines, electric ranges, washing machines, radios, phonographs, lawn mowers, toasters, stainless steel tableware, bathtubs,

The Big Duck in Flanders, Long Island. (Library of Congress, Prints and Photographs Division, photograph by John Margolies)

pie plates, cash registers, wastebaskets, cigarette lighters, mailboxes, fountain pens, coffee cans, carpet rods, coal chutes, necktie racks, pet cages, hair curlers, hand mirrors, butter knives, bicycles, asparagus tongs, beer steins, spittoons, popcorn poppers, and lobster forks—all these were among the departed, and their leave-taking affected thousands of factories, wholesalers, jobbers, and retailers.

Another way to ensure sufficient supplies of a scarce material—notably rubber—was to ration it on a need-to-use basis. To slash the gigantic civilian demand for rubber tires, automobile driving was restricted, chiefly by rationing gasoline, itself in short supply. East Coast rationing began on May 15, 1942, with auto owners being issued alphabetical stickers for their vehicles' windshields, depending on the driver's duties. The great majority got a basic "A" card, granting the lowest level of allocation, four (later three) gallons a week. A green "B" sticker warranted its holder as an essential war worker entitled to a larger amount, and a red "C" sticker—for doctors, clergy, repairmen, government officials—authorized an unlimited right to buy. "T" truckers and "X" VIPs (notably members of Congress) could also tank up at will. Misrepresenting one's status could lead to trial before a gas-rationing board and a fine of $10,000 or ten years in jail. Taxi companies were required to reduce their fleets by a third, and to limit cruising in favor of taxi stands (reducing gas consumption by ten million gallons a year); cabbies still saw their weekly earnings go up, in part because their ranks had been depleted by the draft.

Overall, Gotham's street traffic declined markedly, with some thoroughfares, like Queens Boulevard, all but deserted at times. Yet despite grumbling, the overall policy was seen as a necessary war measure and overwhelmingly approved—apart from one period when, in an ill-advised burst of zealotry, officials went beyond limiting the *supply* of gas, to decreeing what could be *done* with it. In January 1943, "pleasure driving" was banned. Owners of cars parked in front of New York nightclubs and restaurants found themselves stripped of their ration books by government sleuths, and Sunday drivers taking the family out for a spin got pulled over by investigators. The ensuing uproar brought a policy reversal by September.

A tougher question was how to equitably allocate food, which could not be distributed on a categorical basis, because everybody was equally needy and deserving. Putting distribution on a first-come first-served basis raised the possibility—the likelihood—the certainty—of huge lines at the grocer and butcher (disadvantaging the elderly and women with war jobs), and of hoarding (the snapping up of existing supplies of coffee, sugar, or steak by those with the means to do so). FDR confronted the issue head on in an April 27, 1942, message to Congress. "It is obviously fair," said the president, "that where there is not enough of any essential commodity to meet all civilian demands, those who can afford to pay more for the commodity should not be privileged over others who cannot." Rejecting the free-market dictum that people should be able to buy whatever they could pay for, FDR opted instead for a "democratic, equitable solution": the government would "ration all essential commodities of which there is a scarcity, so that they may be distributed fairly among consumers and not merely in accordance with financial ability to pay high prices for them."

Establishment and oversight of a rationing system was left to the Office of Price Administration (OPA), which had been granted that authority by the Emergency Price Control Act of January 30, 1942, shepherded into law by New York's indispensable Senator Wagner. During 1942, a series of ration booklets, containing stamps, were issued to every man, woman, and child in the city (distributed through neighborhood schools). Each stamp was worth a certain number of points, and so was each controlled commodity—such as a can of peas—with its point value constantly readjusted according to availability and demand. Consumers had to hand retailers the requisite number of points in stamps; retailers would then use those stamps to replenish stocks. At one point in 1943, when individuals were getting fifty points per month to use for canned, dried, or frozen food, an entire month's allotment might net a 1-pound 4-ounce can of peas (16 points), a 1-pound 14-ounce can of pears (21 points), and a 1-pound 2-ounce can of spinach (11 points)—grocers couldn't make change until 1944—meaning no more purchases in that category were possible that month. (This was a serious inducement to Victory Gardening, as one advertisement underscored by depicting a woman rolling up her sleeves and saying: "I'm going to have more fruits & vegetables than my ration book allows.... And I'm going to do it the patriotic way.") Newspapers printed charts explaining the complicated system. AWVS volunteers drove "mobile kitchens" around town describing the point system in various languages and alerted shoppers to new controls as they were introduced—coffee, sugar, and butter in 1942, cheese, processed food, and meats in 1943. They also laid out the program's contingency procedures: if someone entered a hospital, they were to turn over their ration book to administrators; if someone died, their book was to be returned to an OPA office.

Points, however, were not money. Points *allowed* you to buy something but revealed nothing about how much that something *cost*. And costs—which had begun rising sharply even before the war began—were very much on everyone's mind, especially Roosevelt's. In the same April 1942 speech in which he announced rationing, FDR noted that the cost of living had gone up 15 percent since war began in 1939. It was imperative, he said, to stop it from soaring 80–90 percent as it had in the First World War. To accomplish this, the government would impose taxes on individuals and corporations to soak up excessive purchasing power (too many dollars chasing too few goods) and put ceilings on the prices of essential commodities.

The OPA's predecessor organization had begun efforts to stabilize prices in May 1940, but with no power beyond jawboning, it had been ineffective. Since then, the rearmament-driven recovery had pumped billions of dollars to Depression-deprived workers who were itching to spend them. Wagner's Emergency Price Control Act made the OPA an independent agency and gave it power to impose ceilings on consumer items and to fine or imprison those who overcharged. The day after Roosevelt's April 1942 speech, OPA chief Leon Henderson announced a General Maximum Price Regulation—soon known familiarly if not fondly as "General Max"—that restricted retailers, wholesalers, and manufacturers from pricing any commodity any higher than what they'd charged for it in March 1942. In a concession to agricultural interests, prices on most unprocessed agricultural commodities—including eggs, poultry, butter, and cheese—remained unfrozen, while processed items—like sugar, coffee, and canned goods—were fixed. Six months later, butter had shot up 15 percent and eggs 43 percent, while sugar and coffee had actually declined. The Roosevelt administration, pressed hard by urban labor, now won congressional approval (in October 1942) for extending controls to nearly all food products. By war's end nearly 6,000 commodities were covered, 90 percent of all goods sold.

To further forestall a fearsome wage-price spiral—workers, facing higher costs, demanding higher incomes—FDR imposed wage controls as well. The supervising agency was the National War Labor Board (NWLB), composed of representatives of labor, industry, and the public. It was soon supplemented by a series of twelve decentralized "Little War Labor Boards"—the first being the New York–New Jersey area's, established in February 1943 and chaired by Theodore W. Kheel, a Brooklyn-born lawyer and labor mediator. The NWLB and its sidekicks had the power to say yea or nay to virtually any pay increase or cut and to handle disputes between private employers and employees, even those not in war industries. In July 1942, the NWLB announced that wage increases would be limited to 15 percent above what they had been in January 1941, though it did allow labor to bargain for "fringe benefits" such as health insurance.

Many businessmen, especially those operating on tight profit margins, hated being slapped with price controls in such a seller's market, and they went after the OPA hammer and tongs. They saw it as a New Dealer stronghold, and its head, Leon Henderson, as a quintessential representative of that breed. They were correct on both counts.

After working to put New York loan sharks out of business (as head of the Russell Sage Foundation's Department of Remedial Loans and Consumer Credit during 1924–1935), Henderson went on to become a consumer adviser to the National Recovery Administration (NRA) and commissioner of the Securities and Exchange Commission (SEC). At the OPA Henderson not only sought to pound down prices but to promote consumerist policies like standardization and truth-in-advertising. He particularly raised manufacturers' ire by pegging allowable profit margins not to the expense involved in making each product—the cost-plus basis Bernard Baruch advocated—but to the average rate of profit in a company's industry. That meant that if higher-cost producers or retailers failed to increase efficiency, fixed price ceilings might force them out of business. Instead, it was Henderson who was forced out of office, victim of a congressional campaign (stoked by his opponents) to eject New Deal "theorists" from power and replace them with "practical" dollar-a-year businessmen—the same battle being fought out in every branch of the wartime government.

By July 1943, effective power had passed to former New York advertising executive Chester Bowles (he took complete control in October). Despite his business background, and his willingness to relax certain constraints (he thought the ban on pleasure driving a bad idea), Bowles proved an even more formidable antagonist than Henderson. Declaring he would not only decelerate the still-rising cost of living—pursuant to Roosevelt's "Hold the Line" order of April 1943—Bowles announced he would roll it back to where it had been in September 1942. Accomplishing this, however, would require reining in two kinds of black markets that had sprung up to evade OPA constraints—the first a professional operation aimed at end-running gas rationing, and the second an amateur but consequential day-to-day circumvention of price ceilings by retailers.

The entrepreneurial genius behind the professional black market was one Carlo Gambino, hitherto an obscure organized crime capo in Brooklyn. Gambino, a refugee from Mussolini's anti-Mafia campaign, had arrived in New York as a stowaway on an Italian ship in 1921. Like many of his confreres, he became a bootlegger; unlike most, he continued in the business after repeal, which led in 1939 to his receiving a twenty-two-month sentence for conspiracy to defraud the United States of liquor taxes. Eight months later, the conviction having been thrown out as based on illegal wiretaps, Gambino emerged from the slammer into a war economy and soon went into the stamp-collecting business. At first, he and his associates in the Vince Mangano family sent safecrackers to steal gas ration stamps from local boards of the Office of Price Administration. When the OPA responded by parking its stamps in New York bank vaults, Gambino riposted by bribing bank managers and security guards to let his henchmen carry out the goods. The stamps were then sold in bulk to mobster middlemen who, if they were in good standing, were not required to pay up front but could do so later out of profits. These they made by selling the stamps to gas station and garage owners, who in turn handed them over to the government, which then authorized a delivery of gas, which could be sold off the books at a 3–5 cents per gallon markup. It proved a lucrative business. The OPA estimated that 2.5 million gallons were diverted every day for illegal use. One of Gambino's creditworthy go-betweens, a button man named Joe Valachi, cleared about $200,000 between mid-1942 and 1945; Gambino himself made millions.

The feds responded with an agitprop campaign against "chiseling" garage owners and their mobster enablers—aka "criminal scum," who dabbled in gasoline trafficking when not otherwise engaged in white slavery, kidnaping, extortion, and murder. Such hoods were "no better than Nazi saboteurs," potential consumers were informed by OWI-planted editorials, and the public was urged to shun the practice, via media ranging from commissioned posters ("The Racketeers Need You!") to comic books (the OWI Comics Committee got *Popular Comics* to send its "Gang Busters" into action against black marketeers). The agitprop blitz worked. By early 1945 the OPA reported the diversion rate had dropped from 5 percent to less than 1 percent.

The widespread practice of evasion by respectable local store owners demanded a different approach. In New York, many grocers often sold controlled goods only if a shopper paid higher-than-legal prices, and Gotham's butchers engaged in a rich variety of other kinds of under-the-counter finagling. Sellers argued that their competitors were doing it, and so must they, to stay in business. Housewives overwhelmingly supported controls in general but deemed it necessary at times to do what it took to provide their family with essentials. Everyone figured that, whatever the ethics, the odds of getting caught were slim, given that the OPA's limited staff was as overwhelmed as Prohibition enforcers had been back in the 1920s. Two strategies now emerged to alter this status quo—both of which relied on the mobilization of masses of women—though one came from the top down and the other was spurred on from the bottom up.

Fiorello La Guardia, possessed of impeccable gangbusting credentials, quickly declared war on "black markets and chiselers," the new-fashioned racketeers. "That sort of business don't go in New York," he rasped in his best Dick Tracy style. "Not while I'm Mayor. Get me?" But to make good on this promise, La Guardia relied less on macho blustering or police raids than on taking to the airwaves to rally the women of Gotham. Since January 1942 the mayor had been broadcasting a series of half-hour Sunday "Talks to the People" on WNYC; hugely popular, they attracted as many as two million listeners and garnered the city's highest ratings. La Guardia offered everyone his opinions on anything and everything, though spent much of his time addressing the ladies. In full paterfamilial fig, he dispensed advice on what to cook, how to raise children, and when to wear what ("Ladies, I want to ask you a favor, I want you please to wear your rubbers when you go out in this weather").

More strategically, the mayor offered shoppers information of great importance in an era of shortages, leading listeners through the maze of rationing rules and purveying up-to-date data about stocks of food, fuel, and other commodities. These bulletins became springboards to spontaneous mass action, as when—after he hinted at impending shoe rationing—anxious New Yorkers piled into shoe stores to stock up, causing a near riot.

Having discerned this responsiveness, La Guardia began to forge his auditors into a rapid-reaction consumer force he could send into marketplace action. When confronted with what he considered overcharging, he called for and got targeted boycotts. "Hello housewives," he said on one occasion. "Remember what I told you last Sunday about snap beans? Remember? They were asking fifty-four cents a pound and I told you to stop buying snap beans and the price'd come down—and you did, and it did."

While it was true that the female posse comitatus quasi-deputized by Gotham's civic patriarch had its occasional triumphs, it wasn't a patch on the far more organized and far more participatory project launched by Gotham housewives in conjunction with the OPA. By 1943, the New York branch had grown to enormous proportions from its rudimentary beginnings in January 1942 as a three-member "tire-rationing board" (plus three clerks), housed in a corner of the Department of Sanitation garage on West 57th Street, near the West Side Highway. After General Max, it had mushroomed into a citywide network of "War Price and Rationing Boards," deploying great numbers of women volunteers in overseeing gargantuan undertakings such as the issuance, during February 1943, of War Ration Book #2 (covering canned goods) to six million New Yorkers, in three days flat. To pull this off, the OPA mobilized the teachers of the city's 1,100 public, parochial, and private schools to deal with the lines that formed outside their institutions (by surnames—A–F, G–O, P–Z—on each respective day). They had to receive each registrant's prior War Ration Book #1 and a filled-out Consumer's Declaration, which could be clipped out of a newspaper, in which they listed the number of canned items they already owned, after which a corresponding number of stamps were removed from Book #2 before issuance. (AWVS volunteers opened information booths at 124 of their branches, and one at Gimbels, to help people figure out these procedures.) Astonishingly the lines, which could stretch to a thousand or more, remained good humored, if occasionally restless, though even then people reserved their tirades not for OPA bureaucrats and volunteer neighbors but for the faraway Führer: "Hitler started it," stated one housewife queued outside P.S. 217 (at Coney Island and Newkirk Avenues), "and it's up to the American housewife to see it through."

When inflation had continued to rise, nevertheless, the OPA geared up for a more vigorous 1943 enforcement drive to "hold the line." In New York, the Midtown Manhattan War Price and Rationing Board, already the nation's largest, expanded again, relocating to the old

GM showrooms at Broadway and 57th and calling in an army of volunteer clerical aides to help handle interactions with the roughly one million Manhattanites who lived between 14th and 125th Streets (lower Manhattanites dealt with 150 Nassau Street, uppers went to 1130 St. Nicholas Avenue). In September, Bowles launched the Home Front Pledge campaign, an NRA-style program in which 15,000 CDVO block leaders—backed up by mass rallies and radio broadcasts—enlisted housewives as individual foot soldiers in the price-control war. After signing on to the pledge—"I Pay No More than Top Legal Prices. I Accept No Rationed Goods Without Giving Up Ration Stamps"—pledge takers were given an OPA emblem they could affix to their window attesting their commitment—not a Blue Eagle this time but a solemn-looking, aproned, white, blond, middle-class woman, her right arm raised as if taking an oath. Eleanor Roosevelt took the first pledge at the White House, and La Guardia ("Consumer No. 1") kicked off the local campaign at City Hall, declaring on WNYC that if housewives would cooperate, they "would constitute an enforcement corps far more numerous and effective than the combined enforcement agencies of the OPA and the city."

Bowles went a step farther, reaching out to a variety of women's, labor, consumer, and ethnic groups—most of whom had been reaching out to *him*—and arranged for their institutional involvement. He brought dozens of consumer groups, union auxiliaries, African American associations, and civic organizations to meetings at OPA headquarters in the Empire State Building, and he recruited their members—like Helen Hall of the Henry Street Settlement and Ella Baker of the NAACP—to sit on a Consumer Advisory Committee. Then he began adding "price panels" to the War Price and Rationing Boards (whose numbers he doubled), and to these he added the volunteers sent by partner organizations and the CDVO. Thousands of women, armed with OPA authority and a quick training course, fanned out through the city, inspecting stores to see if ceiling prices were posted, "educating" retailers as to their responsibilities, and investigating complaints sent in by shoppers. By early 1944, 4,000 price panelists were regularly canvassing 30,000 stores in the Greater New York area.

In addition to these officially sanctioned surveys, women from middle-class church and civic groups, and others from low-income neighborhood houses, labor unions, and African American organizations, occasionally brought direct action pressure to bear on perceived market miscreants, in ways that recalled the city's long trajectory of consumer protest dating back to the flour riots of 1837, the kosher meat riots of 1902, and the housewives' protests of the 1930s. In the Bronx, women from the Parkchester area set up a Consumer Committee at 1380 Metropolitan Avenue, which in March 1944 not only brought charges against over seventy butchers before the OPA but picketed with signs reading: "Do not stab our boys in the back—it is un-American to pay above ceiling prices." In Brooklyn, civic groups, consumer councils, and women's clubs organized a meat strike against local butchers, which at times got overheated: one woman who crossed the picket line to patronize a meat shop was, on exiting, hit on the head with a chicken.

The campaign was, however, overwhelmingly peaceful, and astonishingly successful. Between 1943 and 1945 consumer prices rose by less than 2 percent, and food costs came down 4 percent. At war's end, the overall inflation rate had been held to 28 percent, far better than the First World War's 62 percent. Polls showed that despite OPA's unpopularity as the enforcer of burdensome regulations, over 90 percent of the public approved of price control and rationing.

This checking of inflation did not mellow the business press or business organizations. The US Chamber of Commerce, the National Association of Manufacturers (NAM), and the National Retail Dry Goods Association poured money into anti-OPA propaganda and lit into what they decried as a "kitchen gestapo." The NAM condemned the campaign as "regimented chaos"—nicely catching their dismay at the twinned intervention, by a powerful state *and* militant consumers, in their affairs and balance sheets. This interference was made worse by the fact that the groups rallying to the aid of the OPA's New Dealish planners themselves hailed overwhelmingly from the left wing of the political spectrum. Even a middle-class outfit like the New York League of Women Shoppers was rife with progressive intellectuals, academics, and artists like Margaret Bourke-White, Lillian Hellman, Dorothy Parker, Mary Beard, Helen Lynd, and Freda Kirchwey.

The protest over price controls was nothing compared to the uproar around labeling. One way businesses skirted OPA regulations was by maintaining price but lowering quality or quantity. "Cotton" shirts morphed into low-grade percale, "wool suits" included rayon waste, "leather" soles turned suspiciously soggy in the rain, breakfast cereal boxes slimmed down an ounce or two. Alternatively, producers issued new putatively higher-quality lines and charged premium prices; in many cases, notably those of canned fruits and vegetables, shoppers had no way of gauging the contents within, which were often decidedly inferior versions and/or present in smaller amounts. To tackle this issue the consumer movement called on the government to inspect foods, grade them, and label the meat or cans accordingly. The consumer movement had been pushing for grade labeling since the 1920s, without success. Now they added the argument that without grade labeling, farmers could sell grade C peas to a packager who could stick them in a can and sell it for a grade A price; for canned peas, they noted, the difference could be 27 percent, for eggs 33 percent. Labeling was thus part of the war on inflation. The OPA agreed, and, in early 1943, committed itself to support the project.

A panoply of business groups promptly went berserk. Labeling was a plot to undermine brand names, they shrieked, and with them the capitalist system (and perhaps Western civilization itself). Grade labeling was "un-American," said the president of the Grocery Manufacturers of America, because imposing A, B and C categorizations would "stultify the free competition which is the essence of the American way of doing business," and instead "substitute government mandate for the free enterprise system." New Deal bureaucrats were thus depriving Americans of "a good slice of the very freedom we are fighting for." Underlying this hysteria were some very calculated concerns. What would happen if consumers had an objective outside basis for deciding between brands? What would they do if they discovered that for all the (very expensive) advertising that had gone into establishing Brand X, it proved on inspection to be more or less identical to Brand Y, which was also cheaper? And mightn't Brand X and Brand Y both find themselves vulnerable to competition, at chain stores and supermarkets, from unbranded generics, but ones the government had certified as being Grade A, even though they cost less than either? An avalanche of lobbying won congressional insistence that the OPA change course, backed by threats to slash its budget, and the agency backed off. A vigorous counterthrust was mounted by a diverse coalition that included the Congress of Women's Auxiliaries of the CIO, the National Council of Catholic Women, National Federation of Settlements, Congregational Christian Churches, League of Women Shoppers, National Council of Jewish Women, National Consumers League, Ladies Auxiliary of the Brotherhood of Sleeping Car Porters, AFL, National Congress of Parents and Teachers, National Federation of Business and Professional Women, General Federation of Women's Clubs, American Association of University Women, American Home Economics Association, and NAACP. The best they could wring from an anti–New Deal Congress was the "compromise" that grades could be included on invoices, and retailers could orally inform individual consumers who specifically requested the information. Meat would continue to be labeled, but the grocers and canners had won another round.

Remarkably, in Gotham, an even more titanic struggle—over rents—would have a very different outcome.

112

Controlling Rents

In April 1942 General Max ordered the imposition of rent controls in 301 newly defined "defense rental areas," one of them being all of metropolitan New York. That designation was quickly rescinded when the Office of Price Administration (OPA) decided that Gotham was not experiencing a housing shortage. In fact, the vacancy rate had been a fairly ample 7.5 percent in 1940, and the rental market had softened further early in the conflict when unemployed workers departed for more promising job markets. Protests over the OPA's decision from consumer organizations and housing activists availed not, though the agency did call for a voluntary limit on rent increases and promised to reassess the situation down the road.

One reason the OPA felt politically able to resist rent-controlling Gotham was that the organizations that had pressed for it during the Depression had been weakened by the war. The neighborhood tenant groups gathered in the Communist Party–affiliated City-Wide Tenants Council had been instrumental in passing the Minkoff Bill of 1938, which prohibited rent increases in old law tenements whose landlords had not complied with the Multiple Dwellings Law; as over 90 percent of these decrepit buildings had racked up major violations, the law had established de facto rent control for low-income tenants. Many of the underemployed lawyers and other professionals who'd been critical in the City-Wide's leadership had, however, volunteered for the military, their patriotism heightened by the CP's gung-ho stance. Talented women replaced them, yet given the host of war-related tasks such females were taking on, tenant advocacy was increasingly relegated to the back burner, especially as wartime unity—even with landlords—seemed of primary importance. The once truly city-wide organization shrank to a few strongholds in public housing projects and in Knickerbocker Village, its point of origin.

Leadership passed to Harlem, where the housing market was truly tight, and getting tighter, as immigrants from the South streamed north only to find their choice of Gotham neighborhoods severely circumscribed by racism. Landlords in Harlem, finding a growing demand for their limited stock, jacked up rents in a way their peers elsewhere in the city were unable to do. In response, City Councilman Adam Clayton Powell Jr. mobilized the People's Committee, which had engineered his 1941 election, and set it to collecting one hundred thousand signatures on a petition to have Harlem declared a "war emergency area," hence subject to immediate controls. The Harlem-based Consolidated Tenants League, born out of the 1934 Harlem rent strike, had remained vigorous, and its lawyers now presented evidence that Harlem landlords had consistently violated the OPA's call for voluntary restraints. Communist Party clubs, left wing unions, and the National Negro Congress joined the drive by collecting petitions among their followers and organizing rent strikes in individual buildings.

Conditions were very much the same in Brooklyn's Bedford-Stuyvesant.

The growing call for rent control was picked up by the left wing of the American Labor Party. Congressman Vito Marcantonio, who had long provided "tenant clinics" as part of his constituency services, pressed the issue on the federal level, and ALP-CP candidates like Mike Quill, Benjamin Davis Jr., and Peter Cacchione made it an issue in their local campaigns. In July 1943 the Women's Trade Union League (WTUL) joined the fray, when Rose Schneiderman presided over a conference of 200 women from AFL and CIO auxiliaries. Denouncing rent gouging in Harlem and Long Island City, conferees called on the OPA to intervene, and their demand was echoed by Mayor La Guardia.

A riot broke out in Harlem days later, on August 1, 1943. It had many roots, but fury at the housing crunch was a deep one. The explosion prompted the OPA to open a branch office on 135th Street and begin monitoring Harlem rents and prices. The Consolidated Tenants League and Adam Clayton Powell's People's Committee flooded the new office with documented hikes in both. At the same time, the city's CIO unions warned the OPA that when leases expired on October 1—which had pretty much replaced May 1 as New York's Moving Day—many landlords intended to institute massive increases. La Guardia, sensitive to the combined clout of the ALP, the Harlem community, the CIO unions, and women consumer activists, escalated his pressure on the OPA during September. The Real Estate Board of New York (REBNY) fought back with equal vigor, claiming rising rents were largely a consequence of high taxes—themselves a function of the mayor's "outrageous" budget—and claimed La Guardia was seeking rent control only to divert attention from his own extravagances.

On September 29, 1943, hours before the mass expiration of leases would take effect, the OPA announced it was instituting rent control in all five boroughs, effective November 1. The new maximum rent for each of the roughly two million covered residential units was set at whatever it had been on March 1, 1943. That was the date (OPA researchers had discovered) since when over 100,000 rent increases had been imposed, a number equivalent to the entire rental housing stock of Buffalo or New Orleans. While the majority of landlords had hewed to the requested moderation, Bowles noted, voluntarism had clearly broken down. Hence all increases that had been imposed since then (or that landlords would require on Moving Day), would be rolled back to the March 1 level.

Even as New York, under pressure from the Left, became the last major city to be moved under the residential rent control umbrella, pressures were mounting from the city's wholesalers and manufacturers for ceilings to be imposed on *commercial* properties, which were not under OPA jurisdiction. What galvanized businessmen into seeking legal relief from the state was the steady upward pressure on loft rentals, particularly manifest in the recent depredations of one buccaneering speculator—Joseph P. Kennedy.

In 1941, just back from the Court of St. James, Ambassador Kennedy had called on Archbishop Spellman to solicit his advice on a real estate matter. Kennedy wanted to sell his Bronxville home and shift his legal residence to Florida, a state blissfully free of income or inheritance taxes; could Spellman recommend a broker? The prelate suggested John J. Reynolds, the savvy Bronx realtor to whom he had entrusted the extensive diocesan holdings and who had parlayed his Catholic connection into major player status. Reynolds not only sold Kennedy's house but explained to Joe that he could make a lot of money in Manhattan commercial real estate, whose values had tanked in the Depression and were only just reviving. Kennedy, who had piled up a nest egg of thirty million dollars in the market, researched the proposed investments and agreed to plunge ahead, using Reynolds as his front man to buy up land and buildings at bargain prices.

In 1943 Reynolds picked up the gigantic old Siegel-Cooper department store building and put it in trust for Joe's children, then proceeded to cut a purchasing swath through Midtown between 42nd and 59th Streets, east of Sixth Avenue. He would buy a building for, say, a million (what Siegel-Cooper reportedly cost), obtaining a mortgage at 4 percent for 80 percent of the price, and then reap 6 percent from rents, rolling the profits over into down payments on other properties. Often he'd flip the buildings—he bought one property at 51st and Lex for $600,000 and sold it for $3,000,000—getting in, and getting out, as Kennedy had no interest in creating a real estate empire. He did, however, need to maximize his revenue stream to keep the game going. When the wartime recovery drove the vacancy rate below 1 percent, Joe was able to put the squeeze on commercial tenants, often doubling their rents.

Almost immediately tenants began to complain. His Siegel-Cooper occupants testified before city authorities about his ruthless exactions and the dubious propriety of such activities during war. Nor was Kennedy the only one denounced as a "greedy landlord"; other loft space speculators were demanding increases of 50 to 200 percent and insisting that renewals be signed six to eight months in advance. Kennedy's high profile put him in the spotlight when his hidden hand was revealed. "J. P. Kennedy Cited as a Rent Gouger," ran a *New York Times* headline on September 29, 1944, over a description of a City Council hearing, jammed with 500 people, mostly businessmen tenants. One of them, a clothing manufacturer who made military uniforms, no less, reported that Kennedy had boosted his rent from $42,500 to $73,000. (The Army and Navy confirmed other cases in which they had had to step in to avert evictions of war contractors who refused to accede to such terms.)

Pressure mounted on Governor Dewey to impose commercial rent control. The American Business Congress said further escalations would lead to a wave of bankruptcies. Union officials like Julius Hochman concurred, saying rising rents would "drive industry from the city, ruin business and ultimately ruin the real estate interests themselves," who had proved they had "no self-control." The mayor agreed. Citing wartime speculators and "chiseling" landlords, La Guardia called on Dewey to act. As the governor hesitated, under pressure from REBNY and Republicans, Senator Wagner announced on October 12, 1944, that he had drawn up a bill for commercial rent control and would introduce it into the US Senate if New York failed to act. When even a "State Legislative Committee Investigating Business Rents" told Dewey action was necessary to prevent "gouging," the governor threw in the towel and told Republicans and realtors alike they had to bite the bullet. On January 24, 1945, loft rentals were limited by law to 15 percent above the levels in effect as of March 1, 1943.

Nor was this the last of it for landlords. The new law explicitly excluded rentals of office space and retail stores. Now doctors, dentists, and lawyers, along with shoe, liquor, and tobacco stores, demanded that they, too, be afforded legal protection. Dewey gave in again, signing enabling legislation on March 30. The Real Estate Board counseled landlords to stick to whatever jumped-up figure they'd last imposed, but when thoroughly respectable professional and commercial tenants threatened massive rent strikes, resistance crumbled, and profiteering halted. Joe Kennedy would walk away from the Manhattan real estate scene a happy man, having tripled his fortune in record time.

BLACKS

Lewis H. Michaux, owner of the African National Memorial Bookstore, sells books outside his store on 125th Street and 7th Avenue. June 1943. (Photo by Roger Smith. Library of Congress, Prints & Photographs Division, Farm Security Administration-Office of War Information Black-and-White Negatives)

113

A White Folks' War?

On January 10, 1942, one month after Pearl Harbor, seventy delegates from eighteen national Negro organizations met in the Harlem branch of the YMCA on 135th Street, to assess Black attitudes to the war. After pondering the situation, they passed a resolution, with only five dissenting votes, stating their opinion that "the colored people are not wholeheartedly and unreservedly all out in support of the present war effort."

The noted African American journalist Roi Ottley, in attendance that day, concurred with their finding in "A White Folks' War?," an article published in *Common Ground* that spring. It didn't seem to Ottley that there would be a repetition of the First World War's rush to the colors, when Blacks had heeded W.E.B. Du Bois's call to "close ranks." Too many remembered such wartime bravery had been rewarded not, as Du Bois had hoped, with a loosening of Jim Crow constraints, but with their tightening, often at the end of a hangman's noose.

This new war, however, was complicated by the color palette of the combatants. European fascism was uniformly condemned. When it came to Far Eastern fascism, some Black New Yorkers had some admiration for the existence of a free and independent nonwhite country— "a country of colored people," as Du Bois put it, "run by colored people for colored people." Back in the 1904–05 Russo-Japanese War, moreover, Japan had punctured the myth of white invincibility, with decisive victories on land and sea. Then at the Versailles Peace Conference in 1919 it had enhanced its standing among the world's darker peoples by insisting on a clause establishing racial equality as an international principle, a proposal scuttled by Woodrow Wilson. Some of Gotham's Black intelligentsia had convinced themselves (without probing too deeply into Japanese racial attitudes) that the land of the Rising Sun could and would champion a coalition of the world's colored peoples—Chinese, Indians, Blacks— against white imperialism. Some even argued that Japanese imperialism was *better* than the Western variant: it wasn't based on racial hatred, and it even had China's long-term interests at heart. "China will yet come to bless the day that she was beaten by Japan," said the *New York Age*; the Japanese would impose order (stomping corrupt Chinese warlords) and develop the country to the point it could resist white aggression on its own. Faith in Japan's liberatory potential survived its aggressive incursions, and a Black New Yorker like curator Arthur Schomburg could declare that "if Japan will help the darker people to gain equal opportunities I am ready to shoulder arms for Japan now."

Imperial Japan had long worked to cultivate Black support, imagining that African Americans might prove useful allies. It had arranged paid visits to Asia by noted Black intellectuals: in 1936 Du Bois traveled through "Manchukuo" and Japan, giving lectures at prestigious universities, praising Japanese accomplishments so highly the *China Weekly Review* denounced him as a hired propagandist.

Most African American New Yorkers, notably those on the left, insisted that Japan was just another fascist power, no better than its allies Germany and Italy, whose Ethiopian conquest Japan had promptly recognized. Adam Clayton Powell Jr., in his *Amsterdam News* columns, argued that Blacks couldn't fight fascism in Ethiopia but not in China, and Paul Robeson said bluntly that Japan's record in China (and Korea) disqualified it from moral leadership of the nonwhite world.

Harlem's predominant voices dismissed as humbug Japan's claim it was fighting to liberate oppressed colored people. "The fact that the Japanese have slapped a few white faces in Hong Kong to the delight of American Negroes who have been maltreated by Jim Crow, does not mean that the Japanese are friends of ours," declared Langston Hughes; "Japanese militarism is a reactionary force," a species of "organized gangsterism."

What worried Black leaders, however, was not whether their people would support the war—thousands had already volunteered for air-raid and other civilian-defense duties—it was whether they would do so "wholeheartedly." Federal officials, wondering if morale in Black Gotham was as low as reported, commissioned Kenneth Bancroft Clark, whose 1940 PhD in psychology was the first ever granted an African American by Columbia University, to get a statistical handle on the depth of the problem.

In April and May of 1942, Clark and his colleagues interviewed 1,008 Blacks and 501 whites in New York and uncovered sharply differing perspectives. His report, "The Negro Looks at the War," found roughly two-thirds of the whites believing the condition and treatment of African Americans would be improved by the war, whereas only 11 percent of the Blacks thought so. When those interviewed were asked, "Would you be better off if America or the Axis won the war?" Blacks displayed no illusions they would gain from a Nazi victory, but 18 percent thought they might come out ahead if Japan triumphed. Most strikingly, 42 percent of the polled African Americans believed it was more important to make democracy work at home than it was to defeat the Axis abroad.

Clark argued that these responses and priorities went hand in hand with the widespread "resentment at Negro discrimination" he'd discerned. He concluded that Black New Yorkers' relatively tepid response to the war effort reflected not sagging patriotism, or obdurate isolationism, but was rather the "direct result of the frustrations they experience in their daily lives."

In truth, America's entering the war against fascism had made the everyday racist barriers Blacks had long faced in jobs and housing seem freshly outrageous and spurred efforts to overcome them.

114

"Checkerboarding" Worksites

While the doors to wartime workplaces did not swing open as Black New Yorkers approached, they did widen somewhat when shoved with sufficient vigor. In no sector was this more the case than in government-funded war plants, because they were subject to regulation by the Fair Employment Practices Commission (FEPC), which A. Philip Randolph had wrung from a reluctant Roosevelt by his threatened march on Washington in 1941. Although its staff was small, its budget petite, and its enforcement capacities limited, the FEPC could and did expose and condemn the discriminatory practices banned by Executive Order 8802. Federal intervention, in turn, emboldened civil rights activists and labor union organizers, much as the Office of Price Administration was then mobilizing consumer activists.

The case of Ford Instrument, a Sperry Gyroscope subsidiary, exemplified the process. In February 1942 the FEPC held public hearings in New York. These demonstrated that Ford, despite having promised to hire young locally trained Black machinists, had in practice refused all such applicants and instead recruited unskilled white workers, from as far away as the South, then trained them on arrival. The resulting negative publicity, coupled with ongoing pressure from local branches and locals of the NAACP, the National Negro Congress, the Communist Party, and the United Electrical, Radio, and Machine Workers of America (UE), won a change in policy, and by spring 1945 Ford had 1,200 Black workers on the payroll.

Expanding on this victory, the UE launched a systematic attack on discrimination in its industry. The union referred Black, Jewish, and immigrant applicants to shop after shop, and when discrimination was uncovered, filed complaints with the FEPC. Federal oversight in turn encouraged shop floor initiatives, helping lift the number of Blacks in forty-one New York electrical plants from 172 in May 1942 to over 1,000 by January 1943.

Equally leveraged were efforts by the National Maritime Union (NMU) to "checkerboard" the merchant marine. The NMU (CIO) militantly rejected Jim Crow. Unlike its boastfully white-supremacist rival, the Seafarers International Union (AFL), 10 percent of the NMU's 50,000 members were Black or Puerto Rican, and its powerful vice president,

Ferdinand Smith, hailed from Jamaica. Within days of Pearl Harbor, the union, relying on 8802, drew a line in the sea. On January 2, 1942, a Swedish luxury liner, which had been converted to a US Lines–run troop ship, asked the NMU hiring hall to send over 140 seamen, which it did. Of these, 115 were accepted (all of them white), while twenty-five were deemed "not acceptable" (all of them Black). NMU president Joe Curran immediately wired FDR himself, protesting the discrimination. Roosevelt took immediate action. The very next morning company officials called the NMU to say the twenty-five had become acceptable.

Roosevelt followed up with a January 14 letter to Curran stating, for public consumption, that "questions of race, creed, and color have no place in determining who are to man our ships." Though not a policy the president was prepared to impose on the Navy, his support helped the NMU win a contract with 125 shipping companies that included an antidiscrimination clause. This led to the hiring of 8,000 Black seamen, the formation of mixed crews, and the appointment of Black ship's officers, including four captains, most famously New Yorker Hugh Mulzac.

The British West Indian–born Mulzac had won (in 1920) the first-ever master's certificate issued an African American and had served as captain of the SS *Yarmouth*, operated by Marcus Garvey's Black Star Line. After the company folded in 1922, however, for the next twenty years Mulzac was able to land only steward's jobs, until NMU lobbying won him the captaincy of an interracially (and multinationally) manned Liberty freighter, the SS *Booker T. Washington*—the first of seventeen Liberty ships to be named after African Americans. Under his command it would successfully make twenty-two round trips and transport 18,000 troops.

Campaigns like these gained new support when Black trade unionists from several Communist Party–inflected outfits like the NMU, UE, Furriers, United Public Workers, and Hotel and Restaurant Employees set up a Negro Labor Victory Committee (NLVC). It drew many CIO and AFL unions into a political campaign to increase Black access to defense jobs and helped win additional muscle for the FEPC.

There remained, nonetheless, powerful resistance to dismantling racial barriers. Metropolitan shipyards were notorious holdouts: the Sullivan Dry Dock's 2,075-strong workforce included only fifty-six Blacks, and every one of the Atlantic Basin Iron Works' 2,035 employees were white. When Blacks finally did win access to the employment ladder, they were usually relegated to the lower rungs. A 1944 Urban League study of New York area war plants found only 8 percent of Blacks in grades above laborer, and some companies fluffed up their interracial credentials by hiring Black janitors. Still, the combined efforts of civil rights groups, labor unions, and federal agencies had a significant impact. In August 1943 the *New York Age* reported that 20,000 Black New Yorkers were holding war jobs, triple the number of the previous year.

In sectors of the economy where the FEPC's writ did *not* run, progress was more halting.

In the city administration itself, given La Guardia's official commitment to equality, outside pressure won occasional triumphs.

In health care, the NAACP succeeded in placing Blacks in several city departments previously closed to them (aided mightily by desperate wartime shortages). In 1942, the commissioner of hospitals announced that all city nursing schools would now accept qualified Black student nurses; by 1943 over 300 Black nurses were serving in the Department of Health, while 1,250 more were working on hospital staffs, giving New York the best Black hiring record in the country.

In welfare, Black social workers were hired in growing numbers, though they were funneled into serving clients in Black communities.

In higher education, Adam Clayton Powell's Greater New York Coordinating Committee for Employment made modest gains in combating racial discrimination in the city colleges. Where in 1942 not one of the 2,282 faculty positions was held by a full-time Black professor, within a year of Powell's assault on discrimination, a handful of Black appointments were in effect or in progress at three of the four institutions.

One of the handful was Kenneth Clark, whose story suggests the obstacles in play. Born in the Panama Canal Zone, Clark had been brought to Harlem in 1918 by his Jamaican mother, a seamstress and ILGWU organizer, to afford her son better educational and employment opportunities. After attending New York's integrated George Washington High School, and getting a BA at Howard University in DC, Clark had been accepted by the Columbia psychology department Boas had built, though as something of an experiment. For all their antiracist progressivism, the Boasian professors were not sure a Negro could cut it in their own bailiwick. Even after he'd done brilliantly, the Columbia faculty assumed he'd teach at some southern Black college, where he could "help his people." Startled to learn Clark wanted the kind of position Columbia PhDs usually got—students far below him in class standing were landing Ivy League slots—they made it clear that Columbia itself was not yet ready for a Black appointment. Only when Professor Gardner Murphy left Columbia to chair the City College Psychology Department did Clark gain his appointment as an instructor in the CCNY evening session; it would take seven years to win an assistant professorship.

Apart from these modest gains, much of the municipal bureaucracy remained resistant to further Black inroads. Still, even these limited openings to Black applicants seemed impressive when set alongside the private civilian sector, most of which remained clamshell shut. Not a single one of New York Telephone's 4,500 phone operators was Black. Metropolitan Life, though it had more than 100,000 policy holders in Harlem alone, refused to hire a single Black to sell them. Slots did open up in the lower level, poorly paid sectors from which whites had fled to war plant opportunities. Blacks filtered into the vacated positions as dishwashers, busboys, launderers, and elevator operators—often in restaurants and hotels that denied them service as customers—and into the garment industry as well.

In the end, despite all the increases in employment, four-fifths of the city's Black workers remained stuck in unskilled, low wage, dead-end jobs, and many had no jobs at all. As a result, poverty levels remained high, and the Black percentage on the WPA rolls rose steadily as whites decamped to superior situations. Having constituted 22 percent of WPA personnel in April 1941, Blacks held almost one-third such positions by October 1942 and would until the agency was shut down in February 1943.

Even more distressing to the city's African Americans was the explicitness with which they were barred from jobs that would force whites to come into contact with them, as if they were bearers of some loathsome disease. When Lord & Taylor and B. Altman first agreed to hire Black salespeople, they did so only in the rug and musical instrument departments, not in those selling "personal" items, like clothing, where their presence might offend white clients. When Chase Manhattan Bank agreed to hire some Blacks, they handed out a few jobs in the mailroom, not teller positions that interfaced with the public; and the new hires were forbidden to eat in the cafeteria with white employees. When white women volunteers were taken along on Sanitation Department collection runs, assisting in salvaging tin cans for the war effort, Black drivers were removed for the day.

If the humiliations encountered by many Blacks in the workplace were somewhat offset by widespread pride in the attainments of the Mulzacs and the Clarks, the obdurate segregation of the city's housing arrangements bred only a mounting outrage.

115

Penned In and Pissed Off

Early in the war, roughly 25,000 Blacks had left town for military service or civilian employment, but soon the population tide reversed its flow, as southern migrants seeking wartime jobs and relief from hyper-racism began trickling, then flooding in. By the end of the war, net in-migration plus natural increase had pushed the Black population of New York from 458,000 (in 1940) to 547,000 (in 1945).

This nearly 20 percent increase was not distributed evenly across the metropolis. Far from it. Given the bristling array of obstacles facing Black newcomers—racial covenants, ongoing FHA redlining, blatant white hostility—the surge was channeled almost completely into already existing encampments, overwhelmingly to Harlem.

The social consequences, as summarized in May 1942 by the City-Wide Citizens Committee on Harlem, were deeply deleterious: "Segregation has confined the Negro people to a black ghetto, shutting them out from normal interchange with their fellow Americans." Inside that ghetto, density levels soared, peaking at 620 per acre—the highest in the city—in the block bounded by 138th, 139th, Lenox, and Seventh. Landlords presented with captive consumers packed tenants in, jacked up rents, and skimped on upkeep. Overcrowding and poverty produced their usual results, including a Black death rate from tuberculosis five times that of the city's whites.

The psychic consequences were equally striking, as captured by Ann Petry in her wartime novel, *The Street*. Petry, a reporter and editor for Adam Clayton Powell's *People's Voice*, and a sometime contributor of short stories to *The Crisis*, described the asphyxiating impact of Harlem life on her fictional character Lutie Johnson: "From the time she had been born, she had been hemmed into an ever-narrowing space, until now she was very nearly walled in and the wall had been built up brick by brick by eager white hands." Lutie and her fellow Harlemites had been "crammed on top of each other—jammed and packed and forced into the smallest possible space until they were completely cut off from light and air."

Petry acknowledged that segregation afforded some benefits. Lutie "never felt really human until she reached Harlem and thus got away from the hostility in the eyes of the white women who stared at her on the downtown streets and in the subway" and "escaped from the openly appraising looks of the white men." Paradoxically, density provided breathing space: "Up here they are no longer creatures labeled simply 'colored' and therefore all alike," but rather, once freed "from the contempt in the eyes of the downtown world, they instantly become individuals."

That such benefits were insufficient to outweigh the indignity of being penned in a ghetto was suggested, in a murky way, by the onset, beginning in the fall of 1941, of a series of what were mislabeled by the larger society as "crime waves."

On November 1, fifteen-year-old James O'Connell was murdered in the course of an attempted robbery by three colored boys (sixteen-year-olds Norman Davis and Clemon Allen, and twelve-year-old Jerome Dore, who wielded the knife). The holdup-killing took place at Fifth Avenue and 99th Street, on the edge of Central Park, where the Irish youth—brilliant and highly devout according to a *Daily News* story—was on his way home to 1518 Madison Avenue (between 103rd and 104th) after confession at St. Cecilia's on 106th between Lexington and Park, since 1883 a center of the East Harlem Irish community.

On November 6, another trio of Black Harlemites, aged seventeen to twenty-one, were arrested in the "mugging" and strangling death in Morningside Park of Joseph Keelan, a thirty-two-year-old laundry worker of 529 West 123rd Street. "Mugging"—the press encapsulating the word in quotes to underscore its novelty—was described by the *Times* as "a favorite method of robbery among Harlem's young criminals" in which the perpetrator crept up behind the victim, threw an arm around his or her throat, stuck a knee in the back, and pulled over backward to the ground; only in this case, Keelan died of a fractured larynx, after which he was stripped of his clothes, which were sold for 25 cents to a fourth person, who pawned them for a dollar.

Several other Black-on-white—but nonfatal—"mugging" attacks were reported in the next few days, one at 99th and 1st Avenue, another at Morningside Avenue and 125th, another at Amsterdam Avenue between 152nd and 153rd. By then the city was in an uproar, touched off by lurid press accounts of what was happening. "Crime Outbreak in Harlem," ran a headline in the *Times*, along with "Youths Running Wild" and "Wave of Terror, Especially in Parks." The *Daily News* spoke of "roving bands of knife-carrying colored youths" and the "terrorism of rape, robbery and murder in the park," and the Hearst tabloids provided similarly inflammatory accounts. Hundreds of police were dispatched to stamp out the "crime wave," with mounted and motor-cycled cops fanning out through lower Harlem and upper Central Park.

This touched off a counter-uproar uptown. The NAACP, Urban League, church groups, and civic organizations held mass meetings and fired off letters to the papers, declaring that the press accounts in effect branded Harlemites—overwhelmingly a "law abiding and decent working people"—as a criminal race. This was a species of racial slander, a virtual "pogrom against the Negroes of New York." They did not deny the incidents had occurred but said their number and novelty and significance had been wildly inflated; and that the white press had ignored the social context of discrimination, segregation, unemployment, poverty, and rising cost of living that gave rise to such criminality. Nor, they insisted, were policemen's clubs the solution, but rather provision of jobs, inexpensive housing, more recreational facilities, better teachers, and increased social services for youths.

What neither side quite focused on was what made the interracial incidents seem so incendiary—less their numbers or nature than their location. The headline events, and similar encounters, mostly took place on the expanding frontier between a bursting-at-the-seams Harlem and its white neighbors. The Black populace sought living space on the periphery of

Police arrest three children caught with stolen nickel bags of tobacco on 145th Street and 8th Avenue, August 16, 1943. (Weegee [Arthur Fellig]/International Center of Photography/Getty Images)

the great ghetto: to the west and northwest (Manhattanville and Washington Heights); to the south (the Italian and Irish territories east of Central Park); and to the east (across the East River into Morrisania and Hunts Point in the Bronx). Each incident blazoned in the headlines was a straightforward criminal encounter. Each became a flashpoint because it was also a de facto skirmish in an ongoing border war.

At times, when individual clashes gave way to collective battles, the larger dimension became more apparent. On Harlem's western flank, where Blacks (and Puerto Ricans) breached the Amsterdam Avenue dividing line and headed toward the Hudson—or on its northern reaches, where pioneers headed into Washington Heights—apartment houses that accepted Black tenants might find themselves daubed with swastikas by gangs of white youths, increasingly egged on by elders to "keep out the colored." Thus challenged, Black families could retreat or fight. If they took the latter path, their children would, perforce, form their own gangs, and their subsequent contests with the pickets defending established turf would redraw the neighborhood lines of demarcation.

To the east, where in 1942 principal Leonard Covello's Benjamin Franklin High School had moved into a grand new building at 116th and Pleasant Avenue (hard up against the East River), the multiracial quality he and Rachel DuBois had worked so hard to achieve with intercultural programming was deeply endangered because the institution was now implanted in solidly Italian territory, a bastion that perceived itself as under siege from expanding Black and Hispanic quarters to the west. White harassment convinced incoming Black students to travel armed, and in 1945 a full-fledged riot erupted with hundreds of Black and Italian youths battling with sticks, stones, bats, clubs, and knives.

Still farther east, across the East River, lay the south Bronx neighborhoods of Morrisania and Hunts Point, which had been occupied by Irish, Italians, and Jews relocating from East Harlem and the Lower East Side. During the war, Black and Puerto Rican families followed suit, attracted by the large apartments, excellent transport, appealing shops, and leafy parks. By 1945 their Bronx outposts contained over 35,000 people. One consequence was a series of turf battles—like those between the Jackson Knights, a white gang, and the all-Black Slicksters, that amazed such onlookers as the priest at Saint Jerome's with their fury and firepower (the contenders deploying Springfield rifles and bayonets).

Similar conditions existed in Bedford-Stuyvesant—"Brooklyn's Harlem"—into whose two square miles 90 percent of the borough's Black population had been concentrated. It, too, faced heavy immigrant inflows, as southerners seeking jobs at the Navy Yard and Long Island City aircraft plants discovered their limited housing options. In addition, many Harlemites, forced out by overcrowding and rising rents, took the A train down to the old Brooklyn brownstone neighborhood. By 1942, its once single-family buildings were being shared by from four to nine families, as landlords packed people in and hiked rents. Some families stuffed in boarders as well, people sleeping five or six to a room in eight-hour shifts. As white building inspectors winked at the violations, the once solidly middle-class community plummeted toward low-rent ghetto status.

White homeowners had been resisting African American arrivals since the 1920s—forming associations to block sales to Black families, creating segregated congregations to curtail contact—but by 1943, with 60,000 colored folks in residence, Bedford-Stuyvesant had turned predominantly Black. The remaining whites felt besieged by crime. In November 1943, 500 of the beleaguered gathered at the Bedford YMCA to protest the "influx of sunburned citizens who come up from the South mistaking liberty for license." They said their streets had turned dangerous, especially after dark, with their school-age children being mugged (the word, now freed of quotes, signified only the threat or use of violence in hold-ups) by groups of young boys armed with penknives. The group pilloried La Guardia for allowing this latest "crime wave" to go unchecked, and while an investigation by Police Commissioner Valentine found the charges overblown, he and the mayor admitted there was fire beneath the smoke. Many of the remaining whites simply packed up and left.

Some of the pressure on housing—for white and Black alike—was due to federal authorities having banned for the duration virtually all new residential construction, private or public, apart from projects specifically designated for war workers (of which, in New York, there were but two, the Wallabout and Markham Houses). The last of the New Deal–backed New York City Housing Authority public projects—the East River Houses in East Harlem, Kingsborough in Bedford-Stuyvesant, and Clason Point Gardens in the East Bronx—were completed and filled by the time of Pearl Harbor; and the growing strength of congressional conservatives, aligned with private housers, suggested there might be no postwar revival for public housing.

Many New Yorkers, therefore, found ground for celebration when in April 1943 Mayor La Guardia announced that the giant Metropolitan Life Insurance Company was planning on building, as soon as the war ended, a giant housing complex on the Lower East Side. Just weeks before, Robert Moses had prevailed on the state legislature to pass a revised Redevelopment Company Law that permitted life-insurance firms and savings banks to invest in limited dividend companies, which would in turn be given generous tax breaks, and granted the power to use eminent domain to acquire and demolish private properties. In this case the targets were some of the 600 buildings in a 72-acre tract bounded by First Avenue and Avenue C, 14th and 20th Streets, the heart of the malodorous old Gas House District.

The project would be called Stuyvesant Town, overlapping as it did Peter Stuyvesant's old bouwerie, and being a scant few blocks from St. Marks-in-the-Bowery (on Second Avenue and 10th) where the bones of the patriarch slumbered. The prospect of a clean, modern, landscaped "suburb within the city" heartened many of Gotham's housing-challenged citizens—though not most of the district's 11,000 soon-to-be-evicted tenants. Met Life would erect thirty-five 13-story buildings, containing 8,755 apartments, capable of housing 24,000 people. And while it was not near any of the major centers of Black population, Stuyvesant Town's arrival, betokening what Moses and others claimed would be a revivifying flood of private capital into a parched housing market, suggested the possibility of broadened housing horizons.

Then, like a colossal slap in the face, came the April 18, 1943, announcement by Met Life president Frederick H. Ecker that Stuyvesant Town would be for whites only. "Negroes and Whites Don't Mix," was Ecker's quoted judgment, as splashed by the *Amsterdam News* across its front page. Reflecting established real-estate industry (and FHA) wisdom, Ecker argued that racially homogenous housing was the safest guarantee of profitability and was in the public interest as well. Allowing Negro tenants into Stuyvesant Town, Ecker explained to a reporter, would be "to the detriment of the city because it would depress all the surrounding property."

Ecker's diktat—in effect declaring that Black New Yorkers, having been walled in, were now to be walled out—triggered a shocked and explosive response.

Though arguably people should have seen it coming. Not only was Met Life itself a notorious non-employer of African Americans (apart from porters and janitors), but in 1941 it had finished building the lily-white Parkchester community—in effect a racial prototype for Stuyvesant Town.

Parkchester, up in the Bronx, was even more gargantuan than Stuyvesant Town would be—its 12,272 apartments housed 42,000 in fifty-one bare-brick, high-rise buildings—and it boasted a large movie theater, a public library, over 100 stores (including the first-ever branch of Macy's). More a "city in the city" than a "suburb in the city" (though it did feature a garage for 3,000 cars), Parkchester's exclusionary policy might have seemed more jarringly at odds with the metropolitan fabric. It was deemed less shocking than Stuyvesant Town because it was entirely a private venture—and the right of private landlords to pick their own tenants was considered unassailable. It helped, too, that its construction hadn't involved mass evictions, much less the use of eminent domain, as Met Life had simply purchased the grounds occupied since 1866 by the immense (and relatively remote) old Catholic Protectory.

Stuyvesant Town was different. It was receiving major public subsidies under the state law Moses had engineered, and Met Life had been relieved of many conventional landlord obligations and restrictions. La Guardia had not only gone along with this, he had failed to inform African American leaders beforehand. Walter White, a close friend of Fiorello's, was deeply hurt; Adam Clayton Powell Jr. was deeply enraged, and called for La Guardia's impeachment. One Harlem parent of a son in the service wrote the mayor he was appalled that his boy and other Black soldiers would come home to find "Hitler's policies right here in dear old New York."

116

GI Jim Crow

For Black Gothamites, though, neither segregation in housing nor segregation at work carried the maddening punch of their treatment by the armed forces. Quite apart from the fundamental outrage—that a war on fascism was being fought with a segregated military—there were a host of infuriating particulars.

In January 1942, with the approval of the secretaries of Navy and War and their respective surgeon generals, the American Red Cross began segregating white and Black blood plasma for transfusions. This was done to placate powerful southern politicians like Congressman John Rankin of Mississippi, who declared that trying to "pump Negro or Japanese blood into the veins of our wounded white boys" was an effort to achieve miscegenation by transfusion, part of the communist plot to "mongrelize America." Protests like the NMU's Ferdinand Smith's—"this policy plays into the hands of those who seek to divide the American people by setting race against race"—got nowhere.

Fred Moore, editor of the *New York Age*, had better luck when he protested the War Department Bureau of Public Relations' (BPR) practice of forcing Black soldiers to pose, eating watermelons, for publicity photos. The BPR retreated on that front but stood fast on censoring photographs of Black men mixing socially with white women. The policy was imposed in 1943 after pictures appeared in the press of African American GIs in England dancing with white women. The military feared a repeat of the brouhaha provoked in 1942 by *Life*'s photo essay on Paul Robeson playing Othello to white actress Uta Hagen's Desdemona in a Cambridge, Massachusetts, production, which had generated such a storm that *Life* banned such imagistic intermingling for the duration. When the BPR followed suit, Black troops mounted a vigorous counterprotest. In 1945 General Eisenhower "compromised," authorizing the ban to continue, lest such photos "unduly inflame racial prejudice in the United States," yet allowing Blacks to send them directly home if stamped "For personal use only—not for publication."

The real firestorms broke out across the American South, in the training camps set up to weld millions of disparate Americans into a unified fighting force. For whites, as dozens of Hollywood movies would soon make clear, the military succeeded in creating the mother of all melting pots, turning out one conscript division after another containing a willy-nilly mixture of old stock Yanks and new immigrants, farmers and factory hands, Protestants, Catholics and Jews, residents from every point on the American compass, whose conjoint experiences on the battlefield would upend old stereotypes and breach longstanding barriers.

Not only were Blacks excluded from the pot—thus deepening the gulf between African and all other Americans—but the rigidly segregated training camps, most of them in the South, became hellholes for Negro inductees as a racist officer corps and all-white-together troops set out to compel a proper respect for Caucasian preeminence. But if degrading harassment was at times successful in overawing southern Blacks, already schooled in subordination by a regime of quotidian terror, it came up against determined resistance from northern recruits—notably the 369th Coast Artillery Regiment (Anti-Aircraft), lineal descendent of the old "Harlem Hellfighters" (the First World War–era 15th New York National Guard Regiment)—whose refusal to put up with business-as-usual helped rewrite the rules of interracial engagement.

The 369th, whose armory overlooked the Harlem River at 142nd, was a beloved and respected Harlem institution. It was composed of various companies—one of men who hailed from the Caribbean, another of South Carolinians, etc.—with the core group, I Company, consisting of volunteers from a ten-block radius in Harlem who had attended the same schools and churches. The regiment had a serious esprit de corps, and it fought to attain combat status. Aided by Congressman Hamilton Fish Jr., a bitter opponent of

Double V for Victory rally and fundraiser on West 119th Street, 1942. (Schomburg Center for Research in Black Culture, New York Public Library. Copyright © The Estate of Austin Hansen.)

Roosevelt's New Deal but an outspoken champion of Black soldiers (having been a company commander of the Hellfighters in the First World War), the 369th succeeded in avoiding the usual designation as a labor force. Though while it was given fighting-status as an artillery unit, in a "compromise" it was also placed in a "special category" that need not be integrated with other (i.e., white) combat units.

The 369th also avoided being sent south for training—the men went to Oswego instead—and after a year of training, under Black command, they were sent, roughly 1,800-strong, to Honolulu to defend Hawaii against further air attack. On arrival, they faced harassment from southern white soldiers who, in addition to spreading rumors amongst the locals that the Black newcomers were subhumans with tails tucked in their trousers, did their best to impose southern-style racial etiquette by demanding that Blacks, even officers, step aside on the street to allow whites, even enlisted men, the right of way. The 369th quickly demonstrated that they (unlike southern Black GIs) would take no shit from the US Marines, and they were backed (albeit reluctantly) by camp commanders who could not excuse such flagrant violations of military protocol.

In 1943, the unit was broken up. Some remained to fight in the Pacific, the others were transferred to Camp Stewart outside Savannah, Georgia, to train other (Black) troops in anti-aircraft skills. White commanders immediately set out to put "the pride of Harlem" back in its place, devising elaborate rituals of degradation—billeting them in a garage with a leaking roof, feeding them scanty rations, keeping them standing in the rain for hours, replacing their Black officers with white ones, and averting their eyes when those who ventured into Savannah were beaten up by white police and civilians. Finally, the volatile atmosphere ignited, leading to a massive interracial firefight in which three soldiers and three MPs were killed and large numbers of troops hospitalized.

All of this was closely watched in Black Gotham. The *New York Age* and other Black papers were deluged with hundreds of letters from the troops themselves and from their friends and relatives, reporting on the "gratuitous insults and beatings and humiliations" suffered at Camp Stewart, which was far from an isolated trouble spot. In 1942–43 bloody clashes at military posts were an almost daily occurrence across the south.

Nor was this entirely a faraway problem. On Staten Island, at Fox Hills, the army set up a "Negro cantonment," a racially segregated army camp with no recreational facilities. When Black troops tried to visit local taverns, they were refused service and harassed by townspeople. Equally irksome was the requirement that the troops had to hike to and from work sites each day, while Italian POWs were driven to the same jobs in trucks. Heated animosities would boil over into violent encounters in 1945, though matters never escalated into gun battles, as happened at New Jersey's Fort Dix, in a shootout between white MPs and Black soldiers.

Galling, too, was the response of high-level military officials to protests against all this. Secretary of War Stimson did appoint Assistant Secretary of War John McCloy to head an Advisory Committee on Negro Troop Policies, partly to deal with low-intensity warfare inside the Army, but his position on the underlying issue was not conducive to vigorous intervention. "Frankly," McCloy wrote, "I do not think that the basic issues of this war are involved in the question of whether Colored troops serve in segregated or mixed units, and I doubt that you can convince the people of the United States that the basic issues of freedom are involved in such a question."

Brigadier General Benjamin O. Davis Sr., who might have been thought sympathetic to the 369th soldiers, having been their commander before attaining his new rank, instead pooh-poohed their complaints, declaring the morale of Black troops excellent and the attitude of camp commanders exemplary (Davis even opposed a proposed ban on post officers using racial epithets against Black troops; on this he was overridden by Stimson). Davis also attacked Black papers for covering the abuse stories, accusing them of "sowing discontent in the minds of the soldiers," though in doing so, the General was but following the example of the nation's civilian leaders.

Franklin Roosevelt, having been forced to make concessions to African Americans before the war, was in no mood to tolerate ongoing protest now that war had come. The president favored the approach of FBI director J. Edgar Hoover, who wanted the African American press to abandon demands for full Black rights until after the war. Hoover dispatched FBI agents to harass editors and reporters and denounced Powell's *People's Voice* as cryptocommunist for articles promoting "the breach and extreme feeling between white and colored races." FDR also called in Walter White and urged the NAACP chief to urge moderation on Black editors, which backfired when White's colleagues denounced him for sycophancy. Postal authorities jumped into the fray as well, leaning on even conservative papers like the *Amsterdam News*, which it called "a hate mongering, vicious instrument of propaganda." In the end, though, all these efforts ran up against the stubborn refusal of Attorney General Biddle—a staunch civil libertarian—to authorize sedition indictments or mail bans, much less outright suppressions, and while Roosevelt chafed for more vigorous action, he remained mindful of the Black vote and allowed himself to be constrained.

Still, government hounding did drive some editors to lower their volume and moderate their tone. Black dismay did not go away; it only deepened. Few caught the malaise better than Langston Hughes, who in January 1943 was drinking at the counter of Patsy's Bar and Grill, in the heart of Harlem at Eighth Avenue and 140th Street (near his home at 634 St. Nicholas Avenue), when the remarks of a fellow customer inspired him to invent Jesse B. Semple, soon better known as Simple, the Black everyman Harlemite character who would offer, in a regular column, his/Hughes's thoughts on issues of the day. And Simple said: "It hurts my soul. To be Jim Crowed hurts my soul. To have on my uniform and have to be Jim Crowed."

Soon, however, the segregationist project would have to answer to more powerful opponents than newspaper publishers and columnists, one of them being the man who had successfully mobilized the Black masses once and was prepared to do so again, now in a novel way and against a larger target.

117

Satyagraha in Madison Square Garden

A Philip Randolph had lived up to his agreement with Roosevelt to call off the march on Washington in exchange for establishing the FEPC, but he was not one to settle for half measures. Now, with the US in the war—which in May 1942 Randolph still characterized as in part a struggle to continue "the subjugation, domination, and exploitation of the peoples of color"—he decided to turn his all-Black March on Washington Movement (MOWM) to tackling the entire system of American apartheid. From his headquarters in Harlem's Hotel Theresa (which itself had only begun admitting Blacks in 1940), Randolph issued a call to scores of Black organizations—churches, fraternal groups, professional organizations, civil rights activists—seeking their help in packing Madison Square Garden for an all-Black rally on June 16, 1942.

Integrated organizations like the NAACP and the Urban League were chary of the union leader's demotic leanings, his radicalism, and the monochromatic nature of the planned event. It was patently clear that Randolph was no racial nationalist. Everyone knew he been an antagonist of Garvey on this score, was a close ally of white socialists and labor leaders, and that his Black-only policy was a way to demonstrate racial self-reliance and declare independence from Republicans, Democrats, and, especially, the Communists, who were now arguing, in synch with Roosevelt, that too militant a defense of Black rights constituted interference with the war effort. Besides, Randolph's standing in the Black community had been unparalleled since the 1941 march—the *Amsterdam News* called him "the nation's No. 1 Negro" and a leader to be "ranked along with the great Frederick Douglass"—so his appeals were hard to resist.

Once again, a massive organizing campaign was set in motion to bring Blacks together—this time not in Washington but in Madison Square Garden, seeking inclusion in the guest book of that house of many protests. Leaflets, stickers, posters were festooned around Harlem and other Black neighborhoods, and the MOWM piggybacked on newly learned war mobilization skills such as civil defense drills. In the end, Randolph pulled it off. A near-capacity crowd of 18,000 turned out—the largest all-Black gathering since Garvey's day. Randolph entered grandly, attended by an honor guard of a hundred uniformed Pullman Porters, touching off five hours of musical pageantry and powerful oratory from speakers like Walter White, Mary McLeod Bethune, Adam Clayton Powell Jr., and Randolph himself, who proceeded to lay out where he thought the Movement should move next.

In his speech, and others in the months to come, Randolph envisioned holding a series of such rallies, in Washington, Chicago, St. Louis, and other cities, that would lead up to a national Black conference. This conclave would propose and discuss, then hopefully ratify and organize, a week-long nationwide campaign of nonviolent civil disobedience against the entire apparatus of segregation (apart from defense plants and the armed forces). "If the national conference adopts this method the Negro people will be called upon to boycott trains, street cars, buses, restaurants, waiting rooms, rest rooms, hotels, schools and institutions that have Jim Crow laws," explained Pauline Myers, one of his key deputies. "The aim," she said, would be "to harness the flow of rising resentment and indignation on the part of Negro Americans that has become intensified due to the war."

At the Garden, and in subsequent speeches into the spring of 1943, Randolph began to explicitly link this MOWM proposal to Gandhi's tactics in India, reflecting on how *satyagraha* might play in the USA. He was aware that it could not be applied without modification, especially as American Blacks were not seeking independence but rather inclusion. Nevertheless, Randolph argued, the spirit and discipline and principles of nonviolence and civil disobedience were transnationally valid.

Yet even as Randolph was crafting a Gandhian strategy for an African American civil rights movement, anger levels at the disjunction between wartime preachment and practice about racial equity were rising to a point that would soon make his pacific approach impossible to consummate.

The anger had been spectacularly evident in the Garden crowd's response to a play starring Canada Lee, a Black actor whose life and career and politics had made him a hero in Harlem. Born in New York in 1907, Lee attended local public schools, then became, seriatim, a concert violinist (at twelve), a jockey, a boxer, a bandleader, and finally an actor, with a boost from Orson Welles and John Houseman, who had cast him as Banquo in the Federal Theatre Project Negro Unit's famous Black *Macbeth* in 1936. In 1941, Welles and Houseman gave Lee the lead role of Bigger Thomas in the Mercury Theatre stage adaptation of Richard Wright's novel *Native Son*, published in 1940. As scripted, the show was potentially incendiary. Not only did it follow the novel in portraying the killing of a white girl by an angry young Black man, it presented a real interracial couple on stage—the first on Broadway since O'Neill's *All God's Chillun* of 1924—as Welles refused to deflect criticism by casting a light-skinned Black woman. The play, moreover, broke with stock Black caricatures and called for a complex reading by Lee. *Native Son* opened to a storm of approval from the critics—Brooks Atkinson called it "most biting drama ever written about a Negro in America"—and unanimous praise for Canada Lee, who Atkinson hailed as both "the best Negro actor of his time" and "one of the best actors in this country."

Lee's rebellious reputation (and arguably those of Richard Wright and Bigger Thomas as well) gave added dimension to his brief performance as a Negro draftee who, called before his draft board, informed them, in the sketch's climactic moment, that "I'll fight Hitler, Mussolini and the Japs all at the same time, but I'm telling you I'll give those crackers down South the same damn medicine!" At this the giant crowd exploded in a bedlam of screams,

The Federal Theatre's Project *Macbeth* opens at the Lafayette Theatre, 1936. (Science History Images/Alamy Stock Photo)

cheers, and claps, and demanded the actor repeat the line, which he did to thunderous applause. It was far and away the evening's high point, though the *New York Times* recapped only the uplifting speeches, and the *Daily Worker* attacked it as "insidious poison." (J. Edgar Hoover seems to have agreed, and when Lee followed up with a speech to CCNY students in which he reportedly told them "I would not fight in an army in which there exists racial segregation," the director put the actor on his "Custodial Detention Index.")

The question remained: would Lee's line register more with a fed-up Black populace than Randolph's call for other-cheek discipline? Signs that it might could be discerned in an unlikely place—among street-level sectors of Black New York that had hitherto been resolutely apolitical.

118

Zoots

In early 1941, fifteen-year-old Malcolm Little arrived in Massachusetts from Michigan to live with his half-sister Ella Collins. His father had died when Malcolm was six; his mother had broken under the strain of raising eight children in mid-Depression and been institutionalized; and the children had been dispersed to foster homes. Collins, who now became his guardian, lived in the upper-middle-class "Hill" section of Roxbury. She hoped to win Malcolm to its ways of respectability and righteousness. The teenager was dazzled by Boston's Black ghetto subculture, with its pool halls, nightclubs, and dance halls, notably Roseland. Collins got him a respectable job there, shining shoes; Malcolm added a shadier sideline, selling the dancers marijuana, and signified his would-be hipster status by buying a Zoot suit on credit.

Zoot suits, the sartorial sensation of 1941, swathed their owners in bright pastel material (Malcolm's was light blue). The outfits featured a three-button jacket that stretched south to the knees and came with bulging shoulders (courtesy of 3 to 6 inches of padding), two breast pockets, slashed side pockets, and (an optional) white doeskin waistcoat. The voluminously pleated trousers ran down from the armpits and ballooned out to 3 feet in diameter at the knees, before narrowing to less than 12 inches at the ankles. Essential accoutrements included pointed shoes (tan calfskin being most popular); string ties; pearl buttons; a yard or two of gold key chain, hung from a belt loop and swung in continuously enlarging and contracting circles; and a colored suede porkpie hat with a 6-inch crown, that sat atop a ducktail (aka duck's ass) haircut—hair "conked" (straightened with a lye-and-potato concoction), greased (preferably with Murray's Pomade), then clipped and combed to a point at the back of the head.

Though there was general agreement on the Zoot suit's components, there were debates over its origin. Some claimed the first one had been ordered up by a Black bus worker—riffing on Rhett Butler's regalia in *Gone with the Wind*—from a tailor's shop in Gainesville, Georgia, from whence it spread north. Most placed its genesis in Harlem's night life, notably the costumes of its jazz band leaders, from whence it spread as far west as the Mexican American pachuco gangs in Los Angeles. Though Irving Shulman's *Amboy Dukes* depicted

Jewish gang members as adopting the costume, Zoots were worn chiefly by working-class Blacks and Latinos who could afford the style's munificence now that the war buildup had put money in formerly empty pockets. Buying a Zoot was thus a flamboyant variant of the larger spending spree on records, magazines, and clothing with which American adolescents joyfully celebrated the end of Depression deprivation.

Wearing a Zoot signified protest as well as playfulness. Many Black and Latino youth, bitter at ongoing discrimination, relished their defiance of reigning styles, their upending of conventional conceptions of symmetry, proportion, and taste. They would not blend in. They would be highly Visible Men.

Ella Collins, trying to pull Malcolm back from this path, extracted him from Roseland and got him a series of respectable day jobs—soda jerk, busboy—all of which he quickly rejected. Then came Pearl Harbor, which did not affect Malcolm directly, he being under the draft age of eighteen, but which did open up jobs on the railroad lines, as employees were called to the military. Hoping to remove him from Boston's bad influence, Collins got him a job with the New Haven Railroad, serving first as dishwasher and then as sandwich boy on the Yankee Clipper's Boston–New York run. This proved a strategic error on her part, as the Clipper deposited him amid a far vaster smorgasbord of temptations.

"New York was heaven to me," Malcolm recalled, "and Harlem was seventh heaven!" At the end of each run he would shed his sandwich peddler uniform and don his blue Zoot, even before the first passenger got off. Then he'd head uptown to the Harlem Y (and later to Mrs. Fisher's rooming house, where many railroad men stayed on layovers). He would hang out in Small's Paradise, impressed by its gambler, con man, pimp, and prostitute habitués. He also spent time around the Braddock Hotel at 126th and 8th Avenue, run-down now, but with a bar still capable of attracting the likes of Dizzy Gillespie and Billie Holiday for a quick drink, given its proximity to the stage door of the Apollo. Best of all was the Savoy Ballroom at Lenox and 140th, whose 250-foot-long hardwood dance floor was Lindy-hopping central.

In 1943, Malcolm moved down to New York, bought himself a way cooler sharkskin gray "Cab Calloway" model Zoot and a 4-inch brimmed pearl-gray hat, and got a job waiting tables at Small's Paradise, supplementing this income with hustles ranging from marijuana peddling to john-walking (steering patrons to prostitutes). When one such patron, who had appeared to be a needy Black GI, proved to be an undercover agent, Malcolm was fired by Small's, lest it be placed off-limits, or even lose its license, for impairing the morals of servicemen. Malcolm now expanded his repertoire of hustles to include pimping; numbers running; being a "traveling reefer peddler" (selling dope to peripatetic jazz bands on the road); assisting Abe Goldstein, aka Hymie, a Midtown latter-day bootlegger; and eventually part-time burgling. When necessary, he would supplement these illegal earnings with stints of legitimate labor, notably, between 1942 and 1944, waiting on tables at Jimmy's Chicken Shack, where Charlie Parker had washed dishes back in 1939.

Little was far from being the only Zoot Suiter who trafficked in illegal operations—one reason the attire had an aura of (minor) criminality as well as rebelliousness. After March 1942, Zoot suits were themselves criminalized, when the War Production Board's fabric rationing regulation L85 forbade their manufacture or sale because of their egregiously wasteful use of material. Now they had to be purchased through informal networks of bootleg tailors, and donning them entailed defying the law. And their gaudy outfits appeared to be mocking sober military uniforms, rather as their ducktails appeared to critique close-cropped military haircuts. As a result, Zoot-clad Blacks and Latinos came to be seen by the authorities, and many white servicemen, as challenging and confrontational, as morally and socially pernicious, and perhaps even politically subversive.

Which was why Malcolm reached into the closet for his "killer-diller" sky-blue Zoot with "shoulders padded like a lunatic's cell"—despite having abandoned it for a more conservative look—when he set out in May 1943 for his appointment with the draft board. Like hundreds of other young men in the Black ghetto who were turning eighteen, he was hoping to hustle his way out of serving in a fight he felt not his. His friend Shorty was ingesting a chemical confection, probably a mix of Benzedrine and coke, that was rumored to make one's heart sound defective to draft board doctors. Shorty, Malcolm recalled, felt about the war the way he and most ghetto Negroes did: "Whitey owns everything. He wants us to go and bleed for him? Let him fight."

Malcolm's dodge was more elaborate. Well aware that undercover Black Army intelligence officers hung around Harlem, sniffing out possible subversives, Little started loudly sounding off in various venues that he was frantic to join the army—the Japanese army. Then he showed up at the draft board togged in his wild Zoot and yellow shoes, running off at the mouth in a mile-a-minute string of street slang, and was soon siphoned off to the psychiatrist. Here he confided in the shrink: "Daddy-o, now you and me, we're from up North here, so don't you tell nobody" that "I want to get sent down South. Organize them nigger soldiers, you dig? Steal us some guns, and kill up crackers!" At which, so Malcolm reported, the interviewer dropped his blue pencil, stared "as if I were a snake's egg hatching," and fumbled for his red pencil. The 4-F card came in the mail.

Little was not the only one who delivered lines reminiscent of Lee's to a draft board. When Dizzy Gillespie was called up in 1943, and the psychiatrist asked his attitude toward fighting, Gillespie recalled replying: "Well, look, at this time, at this stage in my life here in the United States whose foot has been in my ass? The white man's foot has been in my ass hole buried up to his knee in my ass hole!" Then, spelling out the implications, he explained: "You're telling me the German is the enemy. At this point, I can never even remember having met a German. So if you put me out there with a gun in my hand and tell me to shoot at the enemy, I'm liable to create a case of 'mistaken identity,' of who I might shoot." He was promptly reclassified 4-F.

This was the curdling atmosphere in which clashes between Blacks and whites mounted around the city, and concerns about a "crime wave" came again to the fore. As a result, municipal and federal officials began taking measures which, though intended to damp down these conflicts, succeeded only in exacerbating them.

119

Clampdown

Critics of La Guardia, like whites in Bed-Stuy, were scathing about the "appallingly insufficient number of patrolmen" he'd provided, and about the NYPD's failure to adopt "the 'muss em up' attitude that this kind of lawlessness deserves and requires." And when the police department pulled a thousand officers off clerical duty in the spring of 1943 and assigned them to plainclothes work in Bed-Stuy and Harlem, "mussing up" seems to have become the order of the day. Algernon Black, leader of the Ethical Culture Society, reported that station house beatings with baseball bats and rubber hoses were becoming routine (one reason some Harlemites used "slaughter pen" as a synonym for "precinct house"). Adam Clayton Powell's People's Committee was deluged with complaints about police harassment and brutality, and his *People's Voice* published regular examples of what local Black leaders called "Gestapo methods." White officers brought before all-white juries on such charges were invariably cleared.

Another approach to the spiraling disorder was to separate potential white and Black combatants by *escalating* the degree of segregation in the city. Federal and military authorities, alarmed by attacks on white servicemen, put Harlem and other Black areas on the off-limits list, and the Army inaugurated a policy of segregating GIs on their two-week stateside leaves. Whites were sent to top-tier resorts in Miami Beach, Hot Springs, Santa Barbara, and Lake Placid; Blacks were dispatched to Harlem's Hotel Theresa and Chicago's Pershing Hotel. When protests were made to FDR in 1944, Secretary Stimson defended the policy as in keeping with the "War Department's long-standing policy not to force the intermingling of the races but to provide equality of treatment." Besides, said Stimson, Black soldiers at white resorts would no doubt be subjected (as he delicately put it) to conditions unfavorable to their "mental and physical rehabilitation," and FDR let stand the order that spared Blacks such private prejudice, opting for public humiliation instead.

New York police also did their best to discourage white New Yorkers from coming uptown. NAACP official Roy Wilkins complained that cops halted white visitors heading to his house and informed them they were entering a "colored neighborhood"; and one woman trying to visit her mother-in-law in a predominantly Black area of the Bronx was warned she might not leave "nigger" territory alive.

In particular, the police and military did their best to discourage race mixing between the opposite sexes. At several transient hotels, where prostitution or narcotics sales had been discovered, the facilities were declared "raided premises," and a police officer was stationed in the lobby more or less permanently, ostensibly to prevent sexual violations but seemingly fixated on barring Black/white couples. At the Braddock on 126th Street, the cop on duty entered rooms and ejected white persons who had slipped by the front desk.

Of greater moment, on April 21, 1943, authorities shuttered Harlem's largest and most popular dance hall, the Savoy Ballroom, charging it with being a "base for vice" and claiming that 164 servicemen had gotten VD over the past nine months from women they had met there. In fact, the Savoy ran a pretty tight ship where commercial sex was concerned. And prostitution, as Walter White told La Guardia in protesting the closure, was a fact of life all around town, including the Waldorf Astoria, but there had been no padlocking of downtown venues, not even taxi-dance joints. In addition, an NAACP investigation found race mixing rather than sexual solicitation at the root of government concerns. "Cops get purple in the face," Roy Wilkins reported in the *Amsterdam News*, "at the very thought of Negroes and whites enjoying themselves socially together." The Savoy had been told to stop booking white bands, as that encouraged Caucasians to come uptown, and the management even stopped advertising in white papers, but mixed couples continued to take the floor, and the hall was shut down. Adam Powell's response to the shuttering was that "Hitler has scored a Jim-Crow victory in New York."

New York was not the only segregated city; there were others whose racial tensions had been ratcheted up by war and migration; and in the summer of '43 they began to detonate, starting with Los Angeles.

In the first days of June, violent fights broke out there between servicemen on shore leave and gangs of Mexican American youths dressed in Zoot suits and sporting ducktail hairdos. Vigilante-minded (and often drunken) groups of sailors and marines openly cruised the streets searching for pachuco prey, who, when found—in bar rooms, pool halls, or movie theaters—were ritualistically shorn of locks and stripped of attire (the Zoot suits on occasion pissed on) and left stunned and nearly naked in the street. In the ensuing weeks of rioting, Latinos struck back, slashing one sailor, stoning a trainload of others; and street fights broke out daily.

Toward the end of the second week of June, just as the West Coast riots were dying out, the Midwest picked up the torch. Detroit's divisions were more deeply rooted than LA's in that for at least three years, Blacks and whites—the locals and the nearly 300,000 newcomers alike—had been battling over scarce housing, recreational facilities, and jobs, with the Ku Klux Klan undergoing yet another revival, burning crosses and amassing arms. After a confrontation at Belle Isle Park, white crowds roamed the city, stoning, stabbing, and shooting Blacks. White police failed to disperse them, emboldening more rampant attacks, or themselves joined in the beating and killing, with some of the victims being Black soldiers in uniform. In all, thirty-four died, the majority African Americans slain by police, with another 700 injured, and property damage in the millions. A careful assessment of the affair in the August 1943 *Crisis* by Thurgood Marshall—since 1938 the NAACP's chief legal officer—was entitled "The Gestapo in Detroit," and it concluded that "the certainty of Negroes that they will not be protected by police, but instead attacked by them" was something that any group concerned to forestall race riots would do well to address in advance.

La Guardia, who was indeed concerned that the epidemic of violence might next sweep east, began working to prepare for trouble. The mayor sent an interracial group to Detroit on June 28 to study that city's mistakes and dispatched two NYPD officers, one Black, one white, to gather additional information. He also laid down ground rules for police behavior in riot situations: restricting the use of deadly force to defense against physical harm; banning shooting to prevent looting; and directing that large numbers of superior officers be on the scene to control their men. In addition, the mayor promised Black Gothamites they would be protected from white assaults and vowed that anyone, white or Black, who provoked assaults on the other race would be prosecuted. Finally, he asked Langston Hughes to help develop a series of radio plays—"Unity at Home, Victory Abroad"—whose goal would be to show "what New York is, how it came into its present being, and why there is no reason that the peace and neighborliness that does exist should ever be disturbed."

As Malcolm Little remembered, in Harlem during that summer of 1943, "One could almost smell trouble ready to break out."

120

"Get the White Man! Get the White Man!"

On Sunday, August 1, at about 7:00 p.m., near the end of a long hot weekend, rookie patrolman James Collins of the 28th Precinct was on Raided Premises Duty in the lobby of the Braddock Hotel on 126th Street, when Miss Marjorie Polite became obstreperous. It seems she had left a raucous drinking party in one of rooms and gotten into a boisterously inebriated altercation with the desk clerk, who now asked Patrolman Collins to remove her from the premises. When she refused to leave and began verbally abusing the officer (calling him a "mother-fucker" among other things), Collins attempted to arrest her for disorderly conduct.

At this point, Mrs. Florine Roberts intervened. Roberts, a domestic from Middletown, Connecticut, had been staying at the Braddock while visiting her son, twenty-six-year-old Robert Bandy, who was on leave from the 730th Military Police Battalion in Jersey City (the Army's first all-Black MP unit). Mrs. Roberts proceeded to grapple with the officer, trying to loosen his grip on Miss Polite, an effort in which she was joined by her son. In the course of the kerfuffle, Bandy seized Collins's nightstick and struck the officer on the head with it, knocking him to the ground, then attempted to bolt. Collins pulled his revolver and fired one shot, which grazed Bandy's left shoulder. Collins then arrested Bandy and walked him out onto Eighth Avenue and over to Sydenham Hospital three blocks away at 124th Street and Manhattan Avenue.

In the meantime, attracted by the gunshot, a crowd had gathered outside the hotel. As dusk turned to evening, the throng swelled to several thousand and migrated to Sydenham, sullenly awaiting word about the fate of the soldier. When no news was supplied, someone shouted he was probably dead, and bottles began crashing against the wall of the hospital. At the same time, another crowd formed, then mushroomed, outside the Two-Eight station house on West 135th Street, threatening the officer responsible for the alleged killing of Private Bandy, now rumored to have died protecting his mother, an account that seemed all too credible given recent history. Police units were assigned to dispel the false rumors and

A crowd gathers in Harlem at the start of the riots, 1943. (Photo by Weegee (Arthur Fellig) / International Center of Photography/Getty Images)

disperse the gatherings, but as one crowd scattered, another formed elsewhere, and in short order the situation boiled over into a full-scale riot.

Young men began racing through the streets screaming and shouting, "White man kill black soldier! Get the white man! Get the white man! He's to blame!" Roaring crowds swept along 125th Street, overturning and burning cars, setting street fires, smashing windows, and gutting stores—at one clothing shop they dragged white mannequins to the street and tore them limb from limb. From this east-west axis the disorder spread up and down the intersecting north-south avenues, until it encompassed the area from 110th to 145th streets on Eighth Avenue, from 110th to 140th streets on Seventh, and north to 136th Street on Lenox. By 10:30 the "crashing sound of falling plate-glass windows" was loud enough to awaken six-year-old Claude Brown, a child "mascot" of the Buccaneers gang; he assumed that Japanese or Germans were bombing the city.

After the initial rage attack, the crowds turned to looting, ripping protective iron gates from their hinges, squirming through broken panes into grocery shops, furniture stores, haberdasheries, and pawnshops. Children took food and toys, men clothing and liquor, women clothing and household goods and food, carting the items off in bundles and baskets and taxis, if not intercepted by nightstick-flailing police. A carnival atmosphere took hold; the air, as novelist Ralph Ellison remembered it, was filled with screams and laughter, the sounds of people running, and "distant fire trucks, shooting, and in the quiet intervals the steady filtering of shattered glass."

La Guardia, informed around 9:00 p.m. of the riot in progress, rushed up to the 135th station, which he made his emergency command post. After conferring with the police and

An overturned car burns during the Harlem riots, August 2, 1943. (Bettmann/Getty Images)

fire commissioners, he ordered the Braddock and all Harlem taverns closed, imposed a 10:30 curfew, lifted wartime dim-out restrictions, thus flooding the area with light, and flooded it as well with police. By early morning 5,000 were on the scene—a force bigger than Detroit's entire department—and, as planned, the officers, kept on a tight leash but aware of their strength in numbers, proved less prone than their Michigan counterparts to resort to gunfire.

The mayor also called out the civilian defense auxiliary police force, which many Blacks had joined, and deputized still other Negro volunteers, equipping them with batons and helmets, and thus added 1,500 African Americans (including 300 women) to the forces of order. The mayor also requested Army headquarters on Governors Island to send in truckloads of MPs—in equal allotments of Blacks and whites—to remove all African American soldiers and sailors from the area. Governor Dewey, meanwhile, was at the Roosevelt Hotel, ready to order in the 8,000 members of the National Guard, including a Black regiment, who were on standby alert at local armories.

For all the massive show of force, La Guardia spent much of his time attempting to calm the rioters. Cruising the area in a sound truck, accompanied by leftists Ferdinand Smith of the NMU and Max Yergan of the NNC, he explained that Bandy was alive and only slightly wounded and urged the rioters to go home. When the truck was showered with bricks and bottles, the mayor, with Smith and Yergan, took to the airwaves instead, making the first of his five radio broadcasts; these too had minimal immediate results, though his (unusually) uncombative demeanor helped soothe the situation.

As dawn approached, a semblance of order began to return, and by noon on August 2, despite sporadic looting, the riot was over. Now it was time to count costs.

"Get the White Man! Get the White Man!" 549

Orkin's, a discount clothing store on 125th Street, is defaced and plundered during the Harlem riots. (Bettmann/Getty Images)

Six African Americans had been killed, four by the police and two by other Blacks. Estimates of the injured ranged as high as 700, including forty officers. Over 500 had been arrested, most for disorderly conduct, unlawful entry, and burglary; they'd been held at the National Guard Armory at Park and 94th. Nearly 1,500 stores had been vandalized; hundreds of windows had been shattered, crushed glass lay everywhere; and losses were assessed at between three and five million dollars.

There was all but universal praise, even from Powell Jr., for the mayor's "wise and effective" leadership and for the police department's relatively restrained response, though Westbrook Pegler in the *World-Telegram* groused that La Guardia had coddled Negro criminals.

There was less unanimity in summing up exactly what had happened, and what it meant.

One argument was, as per Pegler, that the riot was simply an explosion of criminality, in effect a one-day "crime wave," for which young "hoodlums" (some clad in Zoot suits) were to blame. La Guardia seconded this, as did J. Edgar Hoover, but the characterization also had advocates among the city's respectable Black middle class, conservative and activist alike. The *New York Age* condemned "hoodlums"; A. Philip Randolph pronounced himself "unqualifiedly opposed to all forms of hoodlumism"; and W.E.B. Du Bois said the Black community had "developed a dangerous criminal class." A variation on this theme singled out immigrant southerners, as in the assessment by Claude Barnett, a well-regarded Black journalist, that the rioters were "not the better elements" but rather the "rag tags, the gutter snipes, the vicious," most of whom were "products of the South."

The pure and simple hoodlumism theory ran up against the testimony of many witnesses who reported that while the majority of the rioters were no doubt young and poor, older middle-class Harlemites had also been present, both at the initial protest gathering at Sydenham and as participants in the vandalism. The *Amsterdam News* pointed out that "many good people fed up to the core with the cheating and robbery of the shopkeeper, discrimination in employment, etc., also looted and smashed." And the police acknowledged many "decent citizens" had been on the scene, if not actually looting then aiding and abetting by their presence.

Characterizing the riot as straight-out criminality also seemed an inadequate acknowledgment of the social context of the upheaval. Walter White was inclined to believe the rioters were not "decent folk" and instead "the Bigger Thomases of New York." Still, the event also reminded him of stories he'd heard about the French Revolution, about "starved hordes" who "poured from the sewers and slums of Paris, shouting their hatred of oppression and oppressors." Though he condemned the rioters' actions as "criminal and unforgivable," he was not prepared to ignore the roots of ressentiment in poverty, congested housing, inadequate recreation, exclusion from defense jobs, and the maiming and murder of Negro troops in the South—the kindling which fed the flames. A survey of Harlem residents found similarly that while fewer than one in three thought the riot justified, most believed it a reaction to oppression. The *Amsterdam News* concluded that to avoid future violent outbursts, "Negroes must be made to feel that they are a part of this country." Powell's *People's Voice* similarly read the riot as a wake-up call, a collective assertion that "PEOPLE WANT A NEW HARLEM."

On the issue of what the incident suggested about race relations, thinking was more confused. Many people, on both sides of the criminality versus protest divide, adamantly asserted it had *not* been a "race riot," and in the conventional sense of that term—whites invading Black territories and wreaking havoc (as in Detroit and, for a century, New York)—they were right. There had been no mass assault by whites against Blacks, thanks to relatively few southern whites having moved to Gotham (compared to Detroit); to the relative absence of high-octane race baiters (like Father Coughlin); to the overwhelming and disciplined police presence; but mainly to the immense size and density of the Harlem ghetto, which would have made such a white foray foolhardy, if not suicidal.

Nevertheless, Harlem '43 could legitimately be called a race riot, albeit one of a different color (so to speak), as it fit neatly into the new typology pioneered by Harlem '35. The August upheaval was patently an antiwhite explosion—"Get the white man! He's to blame!"—by penned-in and pent-up Blacks. While safe from incursion from white marauders, they were equally unable to get their hands on perceived oppressors outside their encircling walls, so they had to settle for attacking agents of white authority or commerce *within* their territory—cops and shops—plus any whites unfortunate enough to have been passing through or by.

The racial dimension was manifest, too, in the crowds' attacking stores believed white-owned, while sparing those known to be Black-owned (or which identified themselves as such via hastily drawn signs placed in the front window). Blumstein's and Koch's were wrecked and looted; the *Amsterdam News* office and Elder Michaux's bookshop were left undisturbed. Nor were there any attacks on Black pedestrians, while some whites caught in Harlem or near its border were beaten and some trolley-cars were overturned and the passengers punched. The crowds even discriminated between agents of order: while bottles, ashcans, and bricks rained down from windows and roofs on the all-but-completely-white NYPD, Black volunteers were cheered when they showed up on the same mission.

Local targets, moreover, were often stand-ins for even more unreachable enemies. As community patriarch Adam Clayton Powell Sr. said: "When Bandy hit Collins over the head with that club...he was mad with every white policeman throughout the United States who had constantly beaten, wounded, and often killed colored men and women without provocation." The same held, he believed, for the crowds on 125th: "When they were smashing windows they thought they were breaking the skulls of...race haters and race baiters" around the country.

City College psychologist Kenneth Clark argued the upheaval could be seen as an almost inevitable response to segregation itself. Shortly after the disorder, Clark happened upon a young man who'd been a fervent looter—"R.," a bright, "dark-brown-skinned," eighteen-year-old, New York–born Harlemite. R. consented to an interview, which Clark and a colleague presented verbatim, with accompanying commentary, in an article for the *Journal of Abnormal and Social Psychology* entitled "The Zoot Effect in Personality: A Race Riot Participant."

R. offered such a guilt-free, almost gleeful recounting of the many lootings and beatings he'd observed or participated in (including getting his own "ass whipped"), that Clark cast him as a warped antisocial personality—unable to empathize with others or to respect private property. This, in turn, he thought due to "the impact of racial prejudice and social isolation." Faced with discrimination, rejection, humiliation, and dehumanization, individuals sought "to maintain some ego-security" by adopting "a permeating cynicism and callous indifference" to the larger society's values and ideals, adopting instead a pattern of "generalized defiance"—the "zoot effect"—which "must inevitably manifest itself in societal disturbances." R. expressed the thought more pithily when he concluded his reminiscence saying: "Yea, so it be / I leave this thought with thee / Do not attempt to fuck with me."

Yet not all R.'s resentments were at such a generalized level, nor was he quite as isolated as Clark suggested. R. did live alone in a rooming house, as his mother, separated from his father, hadn't enough room to house him. And he did indeed sport Zooter regalia and was a member of a "cellar club" or gang. He had also been attending vocational high school, if irregularly, until, like many others, he dropped out after receiving word of impending induction and set out to have fun before he went in. Fun included watching movies, reading comic books (especially *Batman*) and newspapers (primarily the *Daily News*). Somewhat more surprisingly, he dropped in at times at the YMCA, and he served as a volunteer civilian defense messenger (which is how Clark encountered him). R., moreover, was not planning on dodging the draft, as had Malcolm—"I will be fighting for Uncle Sam, the bitches"—but he was certainly not "wholehearted" about it: "I do not like it worth a damn. I'm not a spy or a saboteur, but I don't like goin' over there fightin' for the white man—so be it." Among the "Bigger Thomases" themselves, riot motivations were bound up with racial issues.

What did the upheaval accomplish? This question preoccupied budding writer James Baldwin, whose father's funeral had taken place a few hours before the riot broke out. "On the morning of the 3rd of August," Baldwin would recall, "we drove my father to the graveyard through a wilderness of smashed plate glass"—"the spoils of injustice, anarchy, discontent, and hatred were all around us." He couldn't help thinking it was all a colossal waste, that it would do no one any good, that it would have been better to have left the plate glass in the windows and the goods in the stores. Then he reflected: "It would have been better, but it would also have been intolerable, for Harlem had needed something to smash."

The walls that encircled Black Gothamites, being intangible, could not be shattered by such blows. The structures of power that penned them in were impervious to mere violence and so remained intact. And if catharsis provided a fleeting satisfaction, it also left a mess behind. Yet the riot would prove a turning point in galvanizing Black and white New Yorkers behind a radically different approach to righting racial wrongs.

121

Passing the Torch

One consequence of the violent upheaval was its derailing of nonviolence as a civil rights strategy. Moderate and conservative African Americans had been nervous about Randolph's plan to attack American apartheid with a *Satyagraha*-style civil disobedience campaign in mid-war. The riots in Gotham and elsewhere slowed the Gandhian Express long enough for them to jump off en masse and to blame radicals for having engineered the urban train wrecks.

Negro leadership, said Lester B. Granger of the National Urban League, "should return to the more moderate hands in which it was held before 1934 and 1935, when Communists and other extremist advocates [read: Randolph] of 'mass pressure' took over." Walter White, who had cooperated with the sleeping car porter chief, now returned to competitive mode, seeking to recapture movement supremacy for the middle-class NAACP. And the *Amsterdam News* backpedaled away from its touting of Randolph as the new Frederick Douglass.

Their rapidly cooling ardor for a nationwide campaign that would summon Bigger Thomases into the street by the hundreds of thousands frosted over Randolph's project. The direct-action protest was stillborn, and the March on Washington Movement itself withered away, becoming little more than a paper organization.

In the immediate aftermath of the riot, another path opened up, one that unambiguously separated opposition to discrimination from reservations about the war, set aside direct action and embraced legal and political initiatives, and jettisoned all-Black organizing in favor of ardent outreach to other New Yorkers. Galvanized by the events of August, would-be allies now popped up everywhere, and interracial organizations emerged that were dedicated (or rededicated) to achieving the goals for which Black Gothamites had long been struggling, largely on their own.

MEMBERS OF THE BLACK COMMUNITY dedicated to coalition-building would work with virtually any entity that expressed support for their goals. What they particularly sought were partners dedicated to transformation not out of altruistic motives or a desire for "unity" but who were driven by their own analogous needs and who could also bring substantial political and financial resources to the alliance. When African American leaders stuck their heads up from the trenches and looked around they saw nearby, in trenches of their own, the city's Jewish Americans, who were themselves suffering from similar (though less-onerous forms) of city-based discrimination and violence, and whose relatives and coreligionists in Europe were under catastrophic assault, having been walled out of the US and walled inside a colossal charnel house. Despite their problematic prior relations, it would be with those Jewish American New Yorkers that Black Gotham would forge an alliance, under the banners of antifascism and anti-(British) imperialism.

HOLOCAUST

The final scene of *We Will Never Die* at Madison Square Garden. March 9, 1943. (Bettmann / Contributor / Getty Images)

122

Sounds of Distant Slaughter

On September 12, 1940, Arthur Zygielbojm arrived in New York, bearing ominous news. The forty-five-year-old Zygielbojm—factory worker, labor organizer, and a leader of the Polish Bund, a Jewish socialist worker's party—had participated in the September 1939 defense of Warsaw against the German invasion. He'd then helped organize resistance to the Nazi occupation, particularly its plan to wall the city's Jews into a yellow-starred ghetto. Hunted by the Gestapo, Zygielbojm was spirited out of Poland by his comrades in the emerging underground. Using a forged Belgian passport, he made his way across Europe (via Berlin!) to Brussels, where in January 1940, at a meeting of the Labour and Socialist International, he offered one of the first eyewitness accounts, from behind the Nazi iron curtain, of what the Germans had in mind for the Jews.

With the fall of Belgium, Zygielbojm fled to France and then, in September, was brought to the United States by the Jewish Labor Committee (JLC). He thus became one of the first of hundreds of labor and socialist leaders for whom David Dubinsky (himself an old Polish Bundist) secured emergency visas, with the help of Eleanor Roosevelt and the AFL, at the same time Varian Fry was rescuing cultural and intellectual elites in Marseille. On January 17, 1941, the JLC threw a party for 3,000 at Carnegie Hall to celebrate the safe arrival of German, Austrian, French, and Italian refugees, and the sizable Polish contingent categorized by the JLC as the "Arthur Szmuel Zygielbojm Group."

Zygielbojm and his comrades quickly established a Bundist base in Gotham whose mission it was to spread the word about mounting Nazi atrocities in Eastern Europe. He embarked on a countrywide tour in October and November 1940, and in December 1940 and January 1941 he authored a series of articles in the *Jewish Daily Forward*. Dubinsky, a native of Łódź (where Zygielbojm had done much organizing work), arranged jobs for his landsman, as an operator in a New York clothing factory and as administrator of *Di Zukunft* (*The Future*), the Yiddish cultural magazine published by the Forward Association, housed, as was the JLC itself, in the Forward Building at 175 East Broadway, across from Seward Park.

The New York Bundists and the JLC also set about collecting money to assist members trapped in the ghettoes of Polish cities, notably Warsaw and Łódź, into which Jews were being herded. Much of the funding was ultimately provided by the 200,000 members of Dubinsky's ILGWU and was smuggled in to its recipients by couriers of the Polish Underground. The same clandestine circuitry afforded a highway for smuggling out evidence about Nazi activities, which the JLC then publicized via the US labor press to stimulate American sympathy and support.

In March 1942, the Bund transferred Zygielbojm from New York to London to serve as its representative on the National Council of the Polish Government-in-Exile, one of that body's two Jewish members. But the link he had done so much to establish between New York and Eastern Europe would remain solidly in place, and indeed be paralleled by many others, because the thirst for information, and the means to obtain it, were more powerfully conjoined in Gotham than anywhere else.

One reason was straightforwardly demographic. There were 1,785,000 Jews in New York in 1940. Not only did they constitute the largest single ethno-religious group in the city—being 23.9 percent of the total population; not only were they by far the largest gathering of Jews in the United States; they were biggest concentration of Jewry on earth. No other city in the world, ever, had contained a Jewish community of this magnitude.

Nor was this just a raw aggregation; this was an *organized* assemblage. Almost all Judaic denominations and ethno-cultural institutions had their headquarters here. Setting aside the vast multitude of strictly local entities, the authoritative *American Jewish Year Book* (issued annually by the American Jewish Committee) listed 193 Jewish organizations of national or international scope as being run out of New York in the early '40s, and many of these had extensive European connections of their own.

The American Jewish Joint Distribution Committee (JDC) at 270 Madison Avenue between 39th and 40th—chaired by Edward M. Warburg—continued its longstanding practice of funneling funds to victims of anti-Semitism, money which now helped many to survive in or flee from countries under Nazi control. Like the Hebrew Immigrant Aid Society (HIAS), housed since 1921 in the old Astor Library at 425 Lafayette Street, the JDC (or "Joint" as it was generally known) worked through an elaborate network of contact people who both dispensed assistance and kept New York apprised of new developments.

Reform Rabbi Stephen Wise, longtime head of the American Jewish Congress (AJCongress), hung his many hats in the McGraw-Hill Building at 330 West 42nd Street. The blue-green terra-cotta skyscraper also housed a branch of the World Jewish Congress (WJC), which Wise had helped found in 1936 precisely to stitch together far-flung Jewish communities; it had bases in Geneva, Lisbon, Stockholm, London, and Paris, among other cities. With the outbreak of war in September 1939, the Paris office had been moved to Geneva, where, headed up by German refugee Dr. Gerhart Riegner, it became a central receiving station for communiqués from Europe's beleaguered Jewry. Riegner in turn relayed information to WJC world headquarters—which, in June 1940, after the Blitzkrieg, had been shifted to New York, where its work was overseen by Wise and WJC cofounder Nahum Goldmann, who himself had relocated to 42nd Street. The resulting stream of bulletins from Geneva to Gotham gave Wise the informational basis for pronouncements such as one in February 1940 in which he said that "in the matter of the treatment of Jews in Nazi-over-run Poland, we face a spectacle of daily torture and horror such as men have not beheld since the days of Gengis Khan."

Downtown at 132 Nassau Street, where it shared space with the Union of Orthodox Rabbis, its parent body, were the headquarters of the Vaad Hatzalah—the Emergency Committee for War-Torn Yeshivoth—which had been established in November 1939 to help over twenty Talmudic academies flee Poland, first to Vilna in temporarily independent Lithuania, and then farther afield. Their rescue operations were strengthened by the arrival in New York of such leading figures of Eastern European orthodoxy as Rabbi Avraham Kalmanowitz and Rabbi Aharon Kotler, a scholar of such renown that when he detrained at Pennsylvania Station in 1941—having escaped Poland via Vladivostok, Kobe, Japan, and San Francisco—he was greeted by thousands of students, laymen, and prominent rabbis. Both men worked to rescue pupils and teachers of famous schools like the Mirrer Yeshiva, which was relocated from Vilna to Shanghai and eventually to Brooklyn.

Like the WJC, the Vaad had listening posts in Europe, notably in Geneva, where Swiss rescue activists Recha Sternbuch (daughter of Antwerp's chief rabbi) and her husband, Isaac Sternbuch, first helped teachers and students escape to China, then expanded their project by sending aid packages to Jews in Poland, Hungary, and Czechoslovakia and obtaining Latin American papers to facilitate their escape. The Sternbuchs kept close tabs on what was happening throughout occupied Europe and sent their gleanings across the Atlantic in coded messages, arranged by complicit diplomats, to the Polish consulate in New York. This secret line of communication was made available, as well, to the Vaad's close institutional associate, Agudas Israel of America (at 1123 Broadway, just off Madison Square). Itself part of World Agudath Israel, a constellation of worldwide branches, the US Agudas became the operational center of this global network after its head, Jacob Rosenheim, originally from Frankfurt, moved from London to New York in 1941.

In addition to these diverse institutional nerve endings that transmitted reports to the giant ganglion that was Gotham, there were professional news organizations that gathered their own harvest of information on the plight of Europe's Jews. By far the most dedicated and effective was the Jewish Telegraphic Agency (JTA), a wire service established in 1917 by a then-twenty-five-year-old journalist named Jacob Landau. From its office at 106 East 41st Street, Landau's JTA covered events in Europe by collecting dispatches from correspondents in far-flung JTA bureaus, scrutinizing Jewish papers in a myriad of countries and interviewing Jewish leaders, escapees, governments-in-exile, and underground movements.

These items, bundled in the *Jewish Telegraphic Agency Daily News Bulletin*, were then distributed to subscribers—which in New York included Yiddish dailies like *Der Tog* [*The Day*] and the *Forward*, and English-language periodicals like the monthly *Jewish Frontier* (a labor journal edited by Hayim Greenberg), the *Contemporary Jewish Record* (put out by the American Jewish Committee), and the *Congress Weekly* (organ of the American Jewish Congress), each of which had an extensive network of its own.

Coverage by mainstream papers of the unfolding fate of European Jewry was more guarded, more subject to filtration, than was the full-throated treatment afforded by the Jewish press. Nowhere was this more evident than in the *New York Times*, whose coverage was spottier than it might have been, in part because Arthur Hays Sulzberger strenuously sought to minimize the fact that the *Times* was a Jewish-owned paper.

Sulzberger, who had assumed the publishership when his father-in-law, Adolph Ochs, died in 1935, was himself deeply involved in New York Jewish affairs, being a member of three synagogues (Emanu-El, Central, and Shearith Israel) and a director of the Jewish Theological Seminary. Sulzberger defined Jewishness—in accordance with the classic 1885 position adopted by Reform Judaism—as a purely religious phenomenon, a matter of faith and belief, hence something that could be readily doffed by changing one's theological convictions. "As far as I am concerned," Sulzberger avowed in June 1942, "if a Jew were to become a Christian Scientist, he would cease being a Jew and become a Christian Scientist."

From this it followed that a nonreligious Jewish organization (like the Jewish War Veterans) was a contradiction in terms, and Sulzberger had no truck with them. He had refused to join a Jewish fraternity at Columbia, refused to join the American Jewish Committee (which a Sulzberger had been prominent in founding), refused to endorse the Anti-Nazi boycott, refused to donate to the United Jewish Appeal or the American Jewish Joint Distribution Committee.

At a higher level still, in his reading, the Jews as a whole were not a nation, not a people, and, most assuredly, not a "race." Sulzberger was a Boasian. When FDR made a public reference to the "Jewish race," the dismayed publisher wrote his friend Treasury Secretary Henry Morgenthau: "Any anthropologist will, I believe, destroy the theory that there is such a thing as the Jewish race." Sulzberger advised Morgenthau to counsel the president to choose his words more carefully lest "they may all too unwittingly help to play Hitler's game." When Roosevelt shortly afterward spoke of "those of the Jewish faith," Sulzberger happily took credit for the conversion.

Not surprisingly, Sulzberger set out to purge the *Times* itself of such "racial" terminology and to dispel perceptions that his was a "Jewish paper." He was motivated in part by worry that such a label would alienate the Anglo-Protestant establishment that had embraced his paper for its "objectivity," and in part by fear that calling attention to the presence of Jews in the media would aggravate American anti-Semitism. But it was also part and parcel of his principled rejection of anything that suggested Jews were a separate people.

This led him to argue that Jews should not be singled out for special treatment, be it affirmative or negative. He strenuously opposed persecution of Jews but considered most proposed remedies as bad as the disease. Thus Sulzberger never called editorially for lifting immigrant quotas to allow more Jews into the US, and he even barred letters to the editor attacking anti-Semitism in Germany, as running them would require him to offer equal space to *defenders* of anti-Semitism, lest the paper's "objectivity" be called into question.

This at-bottom honorable effort to transcend racial thinking by insisting on Jews' essential humanity evaded direct confrontation with the Nazis' challenge. Hitler, after all, had *not* undergone the Boasian transformation—indeed he'd bonfired Boas's works—and fascists singled out Jews out precisely because they *were* considered a race, a people, a culture apart. Simply insisting it wasn't so did not grapple with the brute fact that most people, and certainly the Nazis, thought that it *was*. And rejecting any course of action that seemed to endorse this perception, as if refusing to acknowledge the problem would make it go away, constituted a species of magical thinking that arguably hindered mounting a more appropriate response.

Sulzberger's effort to avoid anything that smacked of "Jewish journalism" at times led him to avert the paper's reportorial as well as its editorial eye from what was happening, as when, in 1937, he canceled the *Times*'s subscription to the Jewish Telegraph Agency, the single most abundant and trustworthy source of information. As JTA editor Landau explained to his board, the *Times* wanted reports on "controversial" issues to come from "neutral" sources. As Rabbi Wise sized up the situation: "The *Times* seems to consider nothing as news which originates from and through Jews."

In the end, however, Sulzberger was too much a journalist to stick his paper's head in the sand. He surreptitiously asked the JTA for "confidential status reports" on the fate of Europe's Jews, which Landau generously provided, even though the *Times* wouldn't publish his data, as that would require acknowledging its suspect provenance. And there were plenty of more "respectable" sources the paper could and did cite on the subject. Most of the *Times*'s coverage of the emerging catastrophe was buried in its back pages, a decision that arguably constituted a lapse of journalistic—and moral—judgment. The fact remains that from September 1939 to May 1945, the *Times* ran 1,147 articles about the emerging "genocide"—a word that first appeared in its pages in 1944, shortly after being coined by law professor Rafael Lemkin, a Polish Jew who'd escaped to the US in 1941. This averaged out to roughly one story every other day. If the coverage was not as thorough and as highlighted as that of the Jewish press, close readers of the *Times* could keep abreast of events by perusing its pages.

THE EVENTS THEMSELVES, AS REPORTED to New York via these diverse channels, were horrific at the beginning, and got steadily worse.

Hard upon the initial invasion of Poland in September 1939 came word of the work of SS-directed Einsatzgruppen, mobile killing squads that followed in the wake of the Wehrmacht. Their targets were tightly focused at first—they rounded up and shot Polish politicians, professionals, aristocrats, clergy: the infrastructure of leadership—though more wholesale massacres became increasingly common, like one reported by the Jewish Telegraphic Agency on December 8, 1939, in which the SS forced a contingent of Jewish men to dig a large pit, then lined them up and shot them down with machine guns, sending them tumbling into their mass grave. Over the next year, however, most Jews were not murdered outright but rather crammed into ghettos—Warsaw's was sealed off from the outside world by mid-December 1940—where the crowding and confiscations soon triggered typhus epidemics and growing starvation.

In 1941 things changed. The year began with reports of a berserk outburst by Romanian Iron Guards that boggled even storm troopers with its psychopathic excess. Formerly skeptical but now appalled newsmen reported Jews in Bucharest being doused with gas on streets and in their homes and burned alive; Jewish women having their breasts cut off; a "kosher butchering massacre" in which over two hundred men were "ritually" dispatched with knives and axes at a municipal slaughter house.

All this proved mere forerunner. The invasion of the Soviet Union in June 1941 opened the door to Einsatzgruppen on a colossal scale. Machine gunnings of entire communities became an almost daily occurrence as the killing squads pressed east behind the army grinding toward Moscow through Soviet-occupied Poland, Lithuania, Ukraine, and the Baltic States.

In New York the Yiddish and Anglo-Jewish press was ablaze with accounts of the slaughter in Kiev (Ukraine), where in September 33,771 people, virtually the city's entire Jewish population, were executed over two solid days of machine gunning in the nearby Babi Yar ravine (a story the *Times* reported a month later, after it had been announced by Soviet authorities); or the October 1941 murders in Borisov (Belorussia), where 7,000 were shot and thrown into the pit they'd been forced to dig but so botched was the job that when covered over the field was left "heaving like the sea" from the movements of those buried alive; or in Odessa (Ukraine) later that month when about 22,000 Jews were driven inside four large storage buildings into which bullets were fired through pre-drilled holes, after which the buildings were set on fire (the *Times* caught up with this story the following April in a one-sentence reference to a report by a Jewish organization). In addition to outright murders, the stuffing of Jews into Poland's jammed ghettoes proceeded apace, as did the death count within.

Though New York Jews were well aware that a tremendous amount of violence was being perpetrated, the true dimension of the slaughter did not become apparent until May of 1942, and once again Arthur Zygielbojm played a major role in bearing bad tidings. The Jewish underground in Warsaw undertook an accounting of the number of Jews who had by then been murdered—town after town, district after district, month by month—and came up with a total of 700,000. Even more chilling, the report put together by Bundist activist and Cracow lawyer Leon Feiner disclosed a horrible escalation in the technology of homicide. Escapees to Warsaw from the village of Chełmno reported a purpose-built camp had been erected there that was murdering Jews brought in from the nearby Łódź ghetto by cramming them into trucks into which engine exhaust was then pumped; the carbon monoxide methodology proved capable of dispatching people at the rate of a thousand a day.

Feiner's report, which included an appeal for public support to stop the annihilation, was sent by underground courier to Zygielbojm in London, who released its contents to the British press, and on June 2, 1942, broadcast the news over the BBC, along with pleas of "the Jews in the ghettos who day-by-day see their relatives dragged away en masse to their death, knowing only too well that their own turn will come." (The broadcast was picked up in Warsaw itself, and the following morning, recalled Bundist resistance leader Marek Edelman, it was circulated through the ghetto via its various underground papers.)

On June 25, Zygielbojm released the entire report to the press. On June 26, the Jewish Telegraphic Agency published a detailed account. And on June 30, the *New York Times* tardily followed suit with a story headlined "1,000,000 Jews Slain by Nazis, Report Says." It was tucked away on page 7—the *Herald Tribune*, which had maintained its JTA subscription, ran the story on its front page—but regardless of placement, the text, and that of a July 2 (page 6) follow-up, provided a thoroughgoing recap. It discussed the mobile gas chambers of Chełmno; it recounted the mounting death toll in the Warsaw ghetto; it totaled up the 700,000 already dead in Lithuania and Poland and added 125,000 more in Romania, 200,000 in Nazi-occupied Russia, and 100,000 in other countries, to arrive at its one million figure; and it declared flatly that Eastern Europe had become a "vast slaughterhouse of Jews."

The *Times* also quoted Arthur Zygielbojm as saying, "The sources were absolutely reliable, although the story seemed too terrible and the atrocities too inhuman to be true." And indeed many couldn't believe it, not even in the ghettos themselves, much less in faraway New York, where some of the most committed Jewish activists had difficulty registering the unprecedented barbarism. Marie Syrkin, Hayim Greenberg's deputy editor at the *Jewish Frontier*, recalled that when they received word of the mass gassing at Chełmno, they found themselves "unable to assimilate" the news, so they "buried the fearful report in the back page of the September issue in small type, thus indicating that we could not vouch for its accuracy."

In fact, the news as of June 1942 was running six months behind reality. Operation Reinhard, mandating the systematic killing regimen, had been launched in fall 1941. Himmler had ordered immediate construction of secret extermination camps back on October 13, 1941, and gassing of Łódź deportees had commenced at Chełmno the same day Pearl Harbor was bombed. When Joint Distribution Committee headquarters in Gotham began to receive word in early 1942 that massive deportations were under way from Western Europe to "unknown destinations" in the east, these were generally presumed to be forced labor camps. The real terminus points were unknown because they were only just coming online. At Belzec, killing began in March 1942. Sobibór began operating in May. Treblinka (roughly fifty miles northeast of Warsaw) was slated to open in July 1942, with Majdanek to follow along in late autumn. And these malign black holes on the Polish landscape had already been joined by others farther west, as Auschwitz, thitherto a prison and slave-labor camp, had evolved into a death factory. As far back as September 3, 1941, Auschwitz authorities had experimented with new extermination techniques, cramming 600 Russian POWs and 250 sick Polish inmates into a basement where they were gassed with Zyklon B, a highly lethal prussic acid–based pesticide. This piece of diabolic ingenuity paved the way for an Auschwitz gas chamber and crematorium to begin work—from 1941 to 1942 some 60,000 were killed and disposed of therein—and served as a model for Birkenau (four kilometers away but part of the larger Auschwitz facility), which had begun sharing the death-dealing burden in March 1942.

Still, the June 1942 revelations, if not truly up-to-date, were enough to spark the first major protest in New York directed against the killings themselves. On July 21, 1942, 20,000 packed into a Madison Square Garden rally called by the American Jewish Congress, Jewish Labor Committee, and B'nai B'rith (the American Jewish Committee refused to deviate from its ten-year-old policy of opposing public rallies that might exacerbate anti-Semitism, though sent a telegram condemning the "barbarous mass murders" and pledging to cooperate with future endeavors). Speakers at the event—who included Rabbi Wise, Governor Lehman, Mayor La Guardia, and William Green of the AFL—stressed that a speedy victory was the only real hope of preventing further murders, echoing the argument of President Roosevelt, who sent a supportive message to the assembled body, which greeted every mention of FDR's name with an ovation.

No sooner had this first step toward joint action been taken than the city's Jewish community was rocked by another revelation. Around the time Gotham's Jews were assembled in the Garden, Eduard Schulte, a prominent German industrialist and closet anti-Nazi, whose company ran a zinc rolling mill in the town of Auschwitz, was passing a message through several intermediaries to Gerhart Riegner, the World Jewish Congress's man in Geneva. As Riegner summarized Schulte's information in cablese, he had "RECEIVED ALARMING REPORT THAT IN FUHRERS HEADQUARTERS PLAN DISCUSSED AND UNDER CONSIDERATION ALL JEWS IN COUNTRIES OCCUPIED OR CONTROLLED GERMANY NUMBERING 3-1/2 TO 4 MILLION SHOULD AFTER DEPORTATION AND CONCENTRATION IN EAST AT ONE BLOW EXTERMINATED TO RESOLVE ONCE FOR ALL JEWISH QUESTION IN EUROPE STOP." The action was reportedly planned for autumn—scant weeks away— with "METHODS UNDER DISCUSSION INCLUDING PRUSSIC ACID," the active ingredient in Zyklon B. Riegner then asked US diplomats in Switzerland to forward the cable to the State Department, for delivery to Rabbi Wise. Washington received the cable on August 8 but, deeming it utterly fantastic, decided against forwarding it to Wise. Riegner had sent a second copy to British diplomats in Switzerland, for forwarding to the British Foreign Office to pass to Sidney Silverman, WJC's man in London, with a request that he "INFORM AND CONSULT NEW YORK STOP." Given that Silverman was a Member of Parliament, the F.O. did send it along, and Silverman relayed it on to New York; on August 28 Wise had the cable in hand.

On September 1, 1942, he contacted Undersecretary of State Sumner Welles, yet another wealthy and socially prominent New Yorker with close ties to the Roosevelts, and one of Jewry's few friends in a generally anti-Semitic department. Welles asked Wise not to publicize the Riegner cable until State could confirm the information. Meanwhile, through yet another of the data channels flowing into New York, another cable arrived, on September 3, describing yet another part of the genocidal elephant. This one was sent from Recha and Isaac Sternbuch, the Vaad Hatzalah representatives in Geneva, to Jacob Rosenheim (head of World Agudath Israel) and Rabbi Kalmanowitz (of the Vaad Hatzalah) via the Polish government-in-exile's diplomatic pouch, thus evading State Department censorship. In it the Sternbuchs passed along an August 1942 report from the Polish underground that mass deportations of Warsaw Jews to extermination camps had begun. "The German authorities recently evacuated completely the population of the Warsaw ghetto," the Sternbuch cable informed New York. "One hundred thousand Jews were murdered in the most bestial manner. The mass murders still continue. From the corpses, Germans make soap and fertilizer."

In fact, the situation was both worse and better than reported. The Nazis had indeed begun massive deportations on July 22 to the newly opened Treblinka extermination camp, where over the next fifty-two days 300,000 were gassed. This mountain of corpses rose atop the 100,000 ghetto residents who had already died of rampant disease, raging starvation, and random killings, so the Sternbuchs' body count was understated. The soap story, however, was incorrect. Though rumors were then circulating throughout Poland that the Nazis were recycling corpses on an industrial scale, only small-scale experiments would ever be undertaken.

This latter point was at the center of debates among the New York Jewish leadership as to how to respond to Welles's request to maintain public silence. On September 4, immediately after receiving the Sternbuchs' cable, Rabbi Kalmanowitz convinced Wise to call an emergency meeting, and on September 6 representatives from thirty-four major organizations gathered in his midtown office. At the meeting, Wise advised caution and accused the Orthodox rabbis of "spreading atrocity tales." The Jewish Labor Committee delegate berated Wise for inaction, noting that "Zygielbojm, a man who should know, says the Germans are murdering our people wholesale." In the end, however, the group agreed to wait on Welles.

Months passed. More horrific reports came in. The *Times* ran small items, the Jewish press big stories, including a leak, on October 9, 1942, of the Riegner cable by the Jewish Telegraphic Agency. Wise rushed back and forth to Washington, pushing for rescue and relief, with no success. Congressmen Celler—known as Mr. Open-Door—and Dickstein introduced emergency legislation to relax immigration restrictions for those fleeing extermination (even requiring them to leave within six months after the end of the war), but the American Legion and the DAR campaigned against them, State opposed them, FDR didn't back them, and their efforts proved unavailing even before conservative gains in the November elections dimmed prospects even further. Wise, who had to spend much of his time explaining to his people why the government couldn't do what they expected of it, was wracked with self-doubt: "I don't know," he wrote a friend, "whether I am getting to be a Hofjude [court Jew]."

While Welles's investigation ground on through the fall of 1942—the American consul in Berne meeting with Riegner and his colleagues and assembling a dossier of documents—another very public verification of the enfolding catastrophe hit the headlines, with Arthur Zygielbojm again a major player.

At the beginning of October, Jan Karski, a secret courier for the Polish underground, was preparing for another run to London, when he was contacted by two Warsaw ghetto leaders, one of whom was the same Leon Feiner who had written the May memorandum. They asked Karski if they could brief him on the situation of Poland's Jews, for transmittal abroad, and when he agreed, provided him with a meticulously documented statistical account of Jewish fatalities. They also invited him to see the ghetto with his own eyes to become a more credible witness. Karski, himself a Catholic, donned a ragged outfit adorned with the Star of David, and Feiner escorted him into hell through a secret underground passage. There the streets were strewn with naked corpses, catatonic starving survivors sat crumpled against walls, and Hitler Youth perambulated the ghetto making a sport of shooting the living dead. All made a terrible and transformative impression, as did his visit, disguised as a guard, to a nearby "sorting camp" where Jews were held until they could be sent to Belzec or Treblinka, or stuffed into lime-and-chlorine strewn boxcars to die horribly on the spot. When Karski arrived in London on November 15, 1942, he presented his report to the Polish government-in-exile, to various media, and to British and American officials, including the Department of State.

Days later, on November 24, 1942, Welles, now in receipt from Geneva of more than ample verification, cabled Wise to come down from New York and read the documents that "confirm and justify your deepest fears." Wise did; got authorization to release the information; and did so at a press conference that very evening. The Yiddish and English-language Jewish press provided wall-to-wall coverage. Mainstream media coverage was much spottier.

The next day, November 25, the *Times* published a 7½ inch story (on page ten) that nevertheless packed in the essentials, noting that now *two* million Jews were confirmed dead, that the Warsaw Ghetto population had dropped to 40,000 from 433,000 the previous March, and that the Nazis were racing to exterminate by mass gassing the remainder of Polish Jewry by year's end. A dozen other small *Times* accounts followed over the next month, which added up to more coverage than that of most mainstream media combined. The *Herald Tribune* ran a modest number of stories, but *Time*, *Newsweek*, and *Life* maintained a virtually complete silence, and most Protestant and Catholic publications had little or nothing to say. Radio coverage was similarly sparse, though on December 13 Edward R. Murrow told his CBS listeners that "millions of human beings, most of them Jews, are being gathered up with ruthless efficiency and murdered," and that the phrase "concentration camp" was now obsolete, having been replaced by "extermination camp."

Liberal papers did pay serious attention—*PM* and the Jewish-owned *Post*—as did liberal magazines like *The Nation* and *New Republic*. The latter ran a cover story on the "Massacre of the Jews" in its issue of December 21, 1942, by Varian Fry, who after returning in Fall 1941 from his mission to Marseille had joined the magazine as an editor. Fry argued that the "letters, reports, cables all fit together and add up to the most appalling picture of mass murder in all human history." He recognized the events were "so monstrous that the civilized world recoils incredulous before them."

In London, Arthur Zygielbojm did his best to overcome this, throwing himself into a desperate campaign to publicize the material courier Karski had shared with him and Ignacy Schwartzbart, the other Jewish member of the Polish National Council, on December 2, 1942. Schwartzbart had been doubtful about the atrocity stories. After perusing Karski's material, he'd staggered out to cable the New York World Jewish Congress office a semicoherent recitation of horrors that ended "BELIEVE THE UNBELIEVABLE STOP." That same day, Rabbi Wise presided over a memorial service for the dead and dying, carried nationally by NBC, and in Gotham, paced by the needle trades unions, half a million workers lay down tools in solidarity.

On December 8, Wise led a delegation to the White House of six major Jewish leaders: Maurice Wertheim (of the American Jewish Committee [AJC]), Adolph Held (of the JLC), Israel Goldstein (rabbi of Temple B'nai Jeshurun and president of the Synagogue Council of America), Rabbi Israel Rosenberg (chair of the Union of Orthodox Rabbis), and Henry

Monsky of the Chicago-based B'nai B'rith—the only non–New Yorker present. They handed President Roosevelt a twenty-page booklet, "Blue-Print for Extermination," which summarized the recent revelations, and asked him, among other things, to threaten the Nazi high command with at least postwar consequences. To this FDR agreed, and, overriding State Department objections, on December 17, 1942, the United States, Great Britain, the Soviet Union, and eight governments-in-exile issued the Allied War Crimes Declaration, which for the first time formally acknowledged that the "German authorities, not content with denying to persons of the Jewish race in all the territories over which their barbarous rule has been extended the most elementary human rights, are now carrying into effect Hitler's oft-repeated intention to exterminate the Jewish people in Europe." The signatories agreed to "condemn in the strongest possible terms this bestial policy of cold-blooded extermination" and pledged that the perpetrators "shall not escape retribution"—a declaration that made the next day *Times* front page and was widely publicized in the US press.

More than this Roosevelt would not do.

Partly he was all too aware of the anti-immigration and anti-Semitic climate and the obduracy of congressional opposition to relaxing restrictions.

Partly his attention was riveted on the fighting fronts. The ferocious Battle of Stalingrad was still under way, with the Nazis holding most of the city and fatalities mounting toward the million mark. At Churchill's insistence, an Anglo-American force had invaded North Africa in November 1942, to the dismay of American commanders and the Soviet Union, who had pressed for a cross-channel invasion to relieve the beleaguered Russians (a second front that might just possibly have diverted the Nazis from their genocidal rampage). And while the Battle of Midway in June would prove to have been a decisive turning point, there was still heavy fighting in the South Pacific, notably in and around Guadalcanal.

By spring 1943 the military situation had improved. Axis forces at Stalingrad had surrendered after a Soviet counteroffensive had encircled and destroyed the German Sixth Army; the Allies had advanced in North Africa; and Guadalcanal had finally been secured. Nerved by this turn of events, and spurred by never-ending accounts of gassing and burning, Gotham's Jews launched their own counteroffensive on behalf of their European brethren. Rabbi Wise of the AJCongress and Joseph M. Proskauer of the AJC worked with others to hammer out a series of eleven credible rescue plans. The proposals displayed a new militancy in calling for the creation of temporary sanctuaries in Allied and neutral countries for escapees, a liberalization of US immigration restrictions, the formation of a governmental agency to coordinate rescue efforts and exert diplomatic pressure on German satellites (like Bulgaria and Romania) into changing course now that the wind was beginning to blow in an anti-Nazi direction. Those pressures were to include the establishment of a war crimes commission.

The plans were presented to and adopted by the 20,000 attendees at a Madison Square Garden STOP HITLER NOW rally on March 1, 1943 (and hailed by the 75,000 outside in the winter cold listening through amplifiers). Two weeks later, on March 15, 1943, a broad united front of thirty-two organizations pressed their eleven-point program on officials of the American and British governments, which, in response to growing pressure, had agreed to hold a conference in April to discuss how to aid European Jewry. The conference barred all nongovernmental (Jewish) organizations, took discussion of the "final solution" off the table, and was held in inaccessible Bermuda, far from the pressures that could be brought to bear in the streets of New York. The results were worse than expected. Neither government would budge on refusing to accept refugees, none of the proffered plans were adopted, absolutely nothing was accomplished. Bermuda was "not only a failure, but a mockery," declared

Rabbi Goldstein of the Synagogue Council of America, adding bluntly that "the victims are not being rescued because the democracies do not want them."

The disappointment was all the deeper because it coincided with an uprising in the Warsaw Ghetto that went down to disastrous defeat. Pursuant to orders to deport and liquidate the over 50,000 remaining Jews, German SS and police units entered the ghetto on April 19, Passover eve, expecting an orderly roundup, only to be confronted by insurgent Jewish resistance. The stunned German forces suffered some initial setbacks, but soon, possessed of overwhelming numbers and firepower, they set about systematically burning and blowing up the ghetto buildings, block by block, reducing the ghetto to rubble and rounding up or murdering those forced out of hiding. Radio messages went out in the last days to Arthur Zygielbojm, who relayed their anguished calls for assistance to all and sundry. On April 22, 1943, the *Times* ran a short AP story out of Stockholm stating that an underground radio broadcast had been picked up the day before which said: "Warsaw is again echoing to musketry volleys. The people are murdered. Women and children defend themselves with their naked arms. Save us...," and then went dead. Significant resistance ended on April 23, 1943, though the Nazi operation culminated ceremonially with the demolition of the Great Synagogue of Warsaw on May 16, 1943.

On May 12, having learned that the last Jews of Warsaw had been murdered during the uprising—including his wife and sixteen-year-old son—or taken off to camps for extermination, Arthur Zygielbojm turned on the gas in his London flat and committed suicide. He left notes denouncing not only the Nazis but "the passivity with which the world looks on and permits the extermination of the Jewish people," and declared: "My comrades in the Warsaw ghetto died with arms in hand in their last heroic stand. It was not my destiny to perish as they did and with them. But I belong to them and to their mass graves."

After this some of the heart went out of the rescue movement. Efforts would continue, and have some small successes, but it was difficult to escape the sense of impotence. "We have cried out," noted the Jewish Labor Committee, "focused public attention, spoken at meetings, written memoranda, participated in delegations, and—stood before a high wall." Nahum Goldmann captured a widespread feeling when he admitted that "our generation is in the tragic position that one-half of the generation is being slaughtered before our eyes, and the other half has to sit down and cannot prevent this catastrophe."

It is in this context that the seismic and momentous shift in sentiment among New York's Jewry during the war years on the issue of Zionism must be understood.

123

Homeland?

Since Zionism was launched as a political project back at the turn of the century, most New York Jews, like most American Jews, had opposed it. Certainly, there was widespread sympathy for those who had fled the Russian pogroms that followed the assassination of Czar Alexander II back in 1881, many thousands of whom had made their way to Gotham. There was sympathy as well for the much smaller stream, more a rivulet, of Russian émigrés that trickled into Palestine, then part of the Ottoman Turkish empire. The 1897 establishment of a political movement—embodied by the World Zionist Organization—was viewed more dubiously. Its progenitor, the Viennese Jewish journalist Theodor Herzl, believed anti-Semitism universal and inescapable; diasporic Jews could find peace and safety only in a nation of their own, and the First Zionist Congress in Basel decreed that nation belonged in Palestine, the Jewish people's ancestral home.

This did not sit well with the many New York Jews who had found their promised land in the United States. The highly assimilated and wealthy German Jews of the American Jewish Committee rejected the notion. Calling for a homeland in Palestine would expose them, they believed, to a charge of divided loyalty, even disloyalty. It would also undercut their preferred focus on guaranteeing the right of Jews to live as free and equal citizens of any country in which they chose to dwell, rather than huddling in a ghetto-nation, especially one in such a barren and "Oriental" spot. Theologically, moreover, the Reform wing of American Judaism, of which they were prominent members and supporters, had long insisted that Jews were *not* a nation but a religious community. Indeed, the Central Conference of American Rabbis had specifically said back in 1885 it did not expect a return to Palestine or the resurrection of a Jewish state.

Nor did Gotham's Jewish labor movement, centered in the garment trades, see eye to eye with Herzl. Devoted to proletarian internationalism, its members considered Zionism a nationalist diversion from the class struggle. And from yet another direction, many Orthodox Jews dissented from political Zionism, partly from concern at its secular focus, partly because they considered the effort itself borderline sacrilegious, as one Zionist fundraiser learned at an East Side synagogue. "Young man, you are going against God's will," an elderly congregant chided. "If he wanted us to have Zion again, He would restore it again without the help of the so-called Zionists. God doesn't need apprentices. Please go schnorr [wheedle] somewhere else and let us lament in peace, like good Jews."

Nevertheless, it was in New York, amongst the inflooding Russian refugees, that US Zionism took root, and almost immediately. In July 1898, one year after the founding conference in Basel, a group of 100 delegates representing a mix of small, mainly East Side educational societies, synagogue organizations, and fraternal lodges, met at the B'nai Zion Club on Henry Street and formed the Federation of American Zionists (FAZ). As their respectable titular leader they chose Richard Gottheil, a Columbia professor who studied Semitic languages and had authored a *Jewish Encyclopedia* article on Zionism. To do the real work, they drafted, as organizational secretary, a Gottheil student, Rabbi Stephen Wise, who had recently met Herzl and been converted to the cause. Wise would stay on until 1902, when he left for a pulpit in Portland; Jacob de Haas, a protégé of Herzl himself, ran things over the next three years; and when he retired in 1905, Judah Magnes took over until 1908, when he departed to assume the presidency of the New York Kehillah.

Despite this capable leadership, until the beginning of the First World War the FAZ remained a fringe affair, marginal to the city's Jewish life, much less to Jewry's national or international stages. As late as 1914 the Federation had but 12,000 members (out of three million Jews in the US) and an annual budget of $12,150. The members did manage to scrape together a few hundred more dollars and establish *The Maccabean*, an English-language Zionist magazine, which ran stories in the 1910s about strapping young Jews tilling the soil of the Holy Land. These visions of American-style pioneering danced in the heads of FAZ members, particularly those in its new youth auxiliary, Young Judaea; they afforded readers a seeming antidote to the stereotype of urban Jewish weaklings—a Judaic variant of the then-popular Muscular Christianity movement. But few of these New York Zionists actually did "make *aliyah*"—ascend unto Israel; it was a nice place to visit in the imagination, yet not many wanted to live there.

Small as it was, the movement was subdivided into factions. To the left of the "centrist" FAZ was Poale Zion—the Workers of Zion Party—established in Gotham in 1905. Its Eastern European socialist membership defined Zionism as the building of a society free of anti-Semitism and of capitalist exploitation as well. They too put "chalutzim" (pioneers) at the center of their project, conceiving them not as individual homesteaders but participants in a "kibbutz"—a secular communal settlement whose members worked the land collectively and promoted/embodied the ideals of social justice and equality.

To the right of the FAZ was the orthodox Mizrachi Organization of America (1914), an offshoot of the original (founded in Vilna in 1902), which, at the behest of Rabbi Zev Wolf Gold, a Polish-born cleric working in Williamsburg, had sent over someone to organize Americans. The Mizrachi saw Jewish nationalism as a tool for achieving religious objectives— a state centered on the Torah—and believed Palestine belonged to the Jewish people by "tradition" and "right."

Somewhat apart from this founding trinity was Hadassah, a more Uptown organization, founded in 1912 by Henrietta Szold, a Baltimorean who had moved to New York in 1903. Daughter (and prize student) of a Hungarian-born rabbi, the erudite Szold ran the Jewish Publication Society, studied at the Jewish Theological Seminary (on condition of foreswearing any notion of seeking ordination as a rabbi), participated in a study circle of young college-educated women (the Daughters of Zion), and worked for the FAZ, on whose Executive Committee she was the only female member. She and her mother first visited

Palestine in 1909 at the suggestion of her friend Rabbi Magnes. Appalled by the poverty and ill health of the locals (both established Arabs and Jewish newcomers) and inspired by the work of Lillian Wald's Henry Street Settlement (particularly its Visiting Nurse Service), Szold convinced her study circle, at a 1912 meeting in Temple Emanu-El, to embrace "practical Zionism" by undertaking a campaign to meet the health needs of Palestine's people, Arabs and Jews alike. Having met on the holiday of Purim, they adopted the name "Hadassah" (the original name of Queen Esther, heroine of the Purim story) and chose Szold as president. The FAZ considered Hadassah its women's auxiliary, but it quickly developed considerable autonomy. In 1913, with a financial assist from philanthropist, health activist, and Macy's owner Nathan Straus, a two-nurse operation was established in Jerusalem that treated 5,000 patients its first year.

A year later the Great War broke out. It would utterly transform the Zionist enterprise—in the Middle East, in Europe, and in New York.

A nightmare on all fronts, the war was disastrous for the "Yishuv"—the roughly 85,000 Jewish settlers in Palestine—who in 1914 were still largely dependent for their survival on links to Europe. When fighting severed the flow of funds and access to markets, they quickly faced destitution. Henry Morgenthau Sr., then US ambassador to the Ottoman Empire, appalled by the misery, cabled Jacob Schiff on August 31, who in turn rallied fellow New York German Jewish philanthropists in the American Jewish Committee to supply an immediate cash infusion.

At virtually the same moment Morgenthau was mobilizing non-Zionists, Zionists were assembling, on August 30, at the Hotel Marseilles (Broadway and 103rd Street). They planned to set up an emergency body to take charge of supporting Palestine, and perhaps to assume direction of the global movement as a whole, given that the World Zionist Organization, headquartered in Berlin, seemed likely to be hors de combat for the duration. Chairmanship of the meeting was offered to Bostonian Louis Dembitz Brandeis. A close adviser to President Woodrow Wilson, Brandeis was a famous and distinguished American Jew (the "People's Attorney"), and far and away the best-known American Zionist. Himself an affluent German Jew, Brandeis had had little contact with immigrant Jewish life until he'd come to New York in 1910 to mediate the great garment strike. Enormously impressed by the Eastern European Jews with whom he worked there, Brandeis was also won to the Zionist cause by Herzl disciple De Haas, and he joined the FAZ in 1912. In August 1914 he agreed to chair the Hotel Marseilles meeting, as well as to run the Provisional Executive Committee for General Zionist Affairs (PEC) it established.

Brandeis launched a major fundraising initiative that was quickly oversubscribed through an outpouring of small contributions from people of modest means—workers, shopkeepers, teachers, and white-collar professionals. He also took over and reorganized the FAZ itself, bringing it out of the Lower East Side—literally, by relocating the office from Grand Street to Fifth Avenue—and symbolically, by inserting the Zionist story into a larger American narrative (claiming the chalutzim were akin to Pilgrims and pioneers). He painted Palestine as a progressive-paradise-in-the-making, where farmers and workers would be freed from the curse of bigness and the public utilities would be commonly owned.

Brandeis worked closely with Stephen Wise, who had returned to New York in 1906 but been preoccupied with creating the Free Synagogue. After his own Zionism had been reinvigorated by a 1913 trip to the Holy Land, Wise helped Brandeis rebirth the FAZ as a disciplined membership organization, based on individuals not groups, which in 1918 was formally renamed the Zionist Organization of America (ZOA). By then the ZOA, nearly

150,000 strong, had become the undisputed spokesgroup for US Zionism. With the PEC it had also raised millions for relief, and in the process, New York replaced Europe as the indispensable source and funnel of financial support to the Yishuv.

The war also transformed the situation in Palestine itself. Imperial Britain had been eyeing it as a strategic Middle Eastern plum that might be plucked from the weakened fingers of the Ottoman Empire. Its acquisition might also offer—or so suggested Chaim Weizmann, Britain's leading Zionist—a way to help draw a reluctant US into the war. Weizmann told Arthur James Balfour, Britain's secretary of state for foreign affairs, that if England supplanted the Turks and promised Palestine to the Zionists, it might incentivize American Jews (like the powerful Brandeis, whom Wilson in 1916 had elevated to the Supreme Court) to push for American entry. Accordingly, the Balfour Declaration was issued on November 2, 1917, stating that "His Majesty's government view with favour the establishment in Palestine of a national home for the Jewish people, and will use their best endeavors to facilitate the achievement of this object." (Balfour added that "nothing shall be done which may prejudice the civil and religious rights of existing non-Jewish communities in Palestine"—a glancing reference to the Palestinian Arabs, who constituted nearly 90 percent of the population but apparently had no *political* rights that England felt bound to respect.) When this pronouncement was soon followed by Britain's capture of Jerusalem, and its postwar receipt of a League of Nations Mandate to administer Palestine with assistance from the now London-based World Zionist Organization (of which Weizmann became president in 1920), it seemed to Palestinian Jews they were on the verge of entering the promised land.

Paradoxically this potential victory undermined their supporters in New York. With the war emergency over, and a "homeland" on the way, membership in the ZOA plummeted by 1921 to 25,000 and donations dropped off too. The city's wider Jewish community did, however, give generously when Weizmann came to town with specific requests, and it was also drawn to a couple of "practical" projects spearheaded by two New Yorkers.

In 1918 Henrietta Szold established a Hadassah Medical Unit of twenty doctors, twenty nurses, and enough equipment to outfit a fifty-bed hospital intended to serve both Jew and Arab; in 1920, she herself moved to Jerusalem to manage its development. At the same time, Judah Magnes pushed for creation of a Hebrew University of Jerusalem, similarly conceived as a bicultural institution. Construction began in 1918, thanks to significant funding from non-Zionist Felix Warburg, and in 1922 Magnes also emigrated to Palestine, where in 1925 he became the university's first chancellor.

Few New Yorkers followed in their footsteps, despite the rise in anti-Semitism, reflected in quotas, and immigration restriction laws that were aimed in no small part at halting the influx of Jews. The children of Gotham's turn-of-the-century immigrants, believing they could flourish in the city, preferred to do their pioneering in Brooklyn and the Bronx.

The new laws, ironically, worked to Zionism's advantage, as would-be émigrés from Eastern Europe, finding the Golden Door slammed shut, switched their destination to Palestine, where Great Britain was providing protection and promising a future homeland. The Yishuv's population, which by war's end had dropped to 50,000, sprang to 160,000 in 1928, when it constituted 20 percent of the Palestinian total, with Muslims now down to 70 percent and the remaining 10 percent being Christians.

Weizmann and the WZO were pleased. Their strategy was to encourage the slow but steady growth of Jewish settlements, creating little by little a new set of demographic facts on the ground, without triggering an Arab backlash.

A general goods store on the Lower East Side serving primarily Jewish residents, ca. 1940s. (Photo by Charles Phelps Cushing. ClassicStock / Alamy Stock Photo)

This was also the approach of the rising new generation of Palestinian Jews led by David Ben-Gurion. The Polish-born Ben-Gurion, an early convert to socialism and Zionism, left for Palestine in 1906, where he worked as a farmhand and became active in Poale Zion. Expelled from the country in 1915, he relocated to New York, where he lived for three years, working with the local Poale Zion to build up the American branch. He also haunted the New York Public Library, poring over histories of US political parties, guides to shaping public opinion, and manuals on management techniques. And he read everything available, in multiple languages, on the history and potential of Palestine, work summarized in a book he coauthored in 1918, *Eretz Israel in the Past and in the Present*; published in Yiddish by Poale Zion, it sold a remarkable 25,000 copies.

In 1918 Ben-Gurion returned to Palestine to join the Jewish Legion—a set of five volunteer battalions under British army command (one composed largely of Jews from the

US)—and helped take Palestine from the Turks. Rising quickly in the ranks of labor and politics, in 1921 he became general secretary of the Histadrut, the General Federation of Jewish Workers in the Land of Israel, which was the dominant force in the Yishuvian economy; and he worked to forge a merger of Poale Zion and other labor groups, succeeding in 1930 with the formation of Mapai (the Labor Party), which became the dominant player in Yishuvian politics. At first Ben-Gurion followed Weizmann's little-by-little approach and hewed to the official Labor line—that there was no insuperable conflict between Jews and Arabs. Even in 1920 and '21, when Palestinian Arabs attacked Jewish settlements, Ben-Gurion set it down to the Arab masses being stirred up by British authorities or Islamic fanatics.

A very different response came from Odessa-born Vladimir (Ze'ev) Jabotinsky, a nationalist in the mold of his heroes Mazzini and Garibaldi, who had been the driving force behind creation of the Jewish Legion. In 1923 Jabotinsky published an article, "The Iron Wall," that confronted the Arab-Jewish question head on. "We are white settlers colonizing the land of the native people," he declared, "and there is no chance whatsoever that the natives will resign themselves to this voluntarily." Little-by-little Laborites seemed to think "the Arabs are either fools, whom we can deceive by masking our real aims, or that they are corrupt and can be bribed to abandon their claim to priority in Palestine." The Arabs were perfectly aware that continuing immigration was "the way by which the Jews would gradually become the majority, and then a Jewish Government would follow automatically, and the future of the Arab minority would depend on the goodwill of the Jews; and a minority status is not a good thing, as the Jews themselves are never tired of pointing out." If Zionist colonization was to proceed, it could do so "only under the protection of a power that is independent of the native population—behind an iron wall, which the native population cannot breach." Laborites were in effect relying on the British; Jabotinsky urged Zionists to rely on themselves.

Jabotinsky urged WZO president Weizmann to promote not trickle-in immigration but an immediate and massive flood from Europe and to fight as well for a Jewish army. Laborites nonetheless refused to acknowledge the necessity of wielding military force if Zionism was to achieve its objectives, though they did establish the Haganah, a labor Zionist self-defense militia. Jabotinsky pressed ahead on his own, establishing (in 1923) a militant and brown-shirted youth movement—Betar—whose members engaged in weapons training and steeped themselves in the history and poetry of blood sacrifice. In 1925 he founded a faction inside the WZO to push for a revision of policy—the Union of Revisionist Zionists—and in 1926 he went to New York to sow Revisionist seeds (and to raise Revisionist funds) by going on a national speaking tour arranged by impresario Sol Hurok. After more than five months he'd won a beachhead, with the help of Elias Ginsburg, an old comrade in arms, now a banker in Brooklyn, and had established an American Revisionist headquarters in the office of the Palestine Import Company on Union Square (a Betar branch arrived in 1930, a summer camp in 1932). When 133 Jews died in 1929 in another Arab uprising, Ginsburg and other veterans in Jabotinsky's organization mobilized a protest demonstration of 35,000 people at the British Consulate in Manhattan.

Jewish militarism was not the only conceivable response to Arab protest. Judah Magnes declared in a 1929 speech at Hebrew University that a Jewish national home "built up on bayonets and oppression" was "not worth having, even though it succeed," and called for negotiations leading to a binational rather than a Jewish state; power sharing in a joint parliament. Equal rights and cultural autonomy for each side were parts of the mix. While Magnes won some supporters—Henrietta Szold of Hadassah was one, the left-wing socialists of

Hashomer Hatzair were another—opposition in Palestine (from Arabs and Jews) and New York was overwhelming.

The 1929 Crash delivered a massive jolt to the Zionist movement, followed by a sequence of other shocks—the Depression, the ascension of Hitler, the Arab Revolt of 1936–39, Britain's backpedaling from Balfour, and the outbreak of war—all of which, taken together, bound New York's and Palestine's Zionists ever more tightly together.

The Crash and Depression pummeled Gotham's Zionist organizations. Many in the ZOA, Hadassah, Poale Zion, and Mizrachi, strapped for cash, couldn't pay their dues. By 1932, the ZOA had $8 in its treasury. Membership rolls shrank dramatically. By 1932, the ZOA was down to 8,800, Hadassah to 20,000. The result, Rabbi Wise observed, was a "complete lull in things Zionistic in America."

This free fall was checked, then dizzyingly reversed, by Hitler's arrival to power. By 1939 the ZOA had climbed to 43,000 (on its way to 200,000 six years later), and Hadassah hit 66,000. Fascism also engendered rethinking among non-Zionists. The Central Conference of American Rabbis (Reform Judaism's central body), while holding fast against a Jewish state, acknowledged that Palestine could be a port in the storm. In 1937, modifying its 1885 position, it urged Jews to aid in building a "homeland" there. The non-Zionist Joint Distribution Committee (JDC) raised large sums to help tens of thousands flee Germany between 1933 and 1939, many of whom made their way to Palestine. And in January 1939, the JDC (at 270 Madison and 40th Street) joined forces with the Zionists' United Palestine Appeal (two blocks away at 41 East 42nd Street) in a fundraising umbrella group, the United Jewish Appeal (UJA). Stormy disputes would rage inside the UJA over allocation of the income pie, but the pie itself grew dramatically.

Similarly, while New York garment workers and their Jewish Labor Committee continued to reject the goal of a Jewish state, they supported the Zionists' demand for opening Palestine's immigration floodgates. Some of their publications began urging political support, too, especially now that the congenial Ben-Gurion and his Labor Party had assumed effective control of the Yishuv quasi-state in 1935. Palestine's liberal climate also appealed to Gotham's New Deal Democrats, who encompassed most of the city's Jewish population. For his part, Ben-Gurion assiduously cultivated the New York–Jerusalem connection, visiting Gotham every other year between 1933 and 1939.

Jabotinsky, conversely, had trouble gaining traction in New York. Not only had he split from the World Zionist Organization in 1935 and set up a rival New Zionist Organization (NZO), he had vociferously criticized Palestine's powerful Jewish trade union, Histadrut. Given the dangerous global situation, Jabotinsky argued, organized labor should put national goals above class interest and abandon the right to strike. The Histadrut—backed by Gotham's Jewish unionists, reform rabbis, and New Deal labor activists—rejected this as smacking of Mussolini-style corporatism. Nor did they like the Revisionist focus on armed preparedness, its veneration of biblical warriors, or the way its Betar youths in Palestine served as strike breakers and in New York paraded about in brown shirts (changing to blue shirts after the Nazis adopted the style). Jabotinsky was patently anti-Nazi; he was among the first to warn a tidal wave was about to break over European Jewry. But there were sufficient similarities in verbal and visual style to provoke Stephen Wise into declaring that "revisionism is a species of fascism, uttering its commands in the Hebrew language," and the labor-left *Jewish Frontier* to denounce the "fuehrer Jabotinsky." When he visited again in 1935, most New York liberals kept their distance or denounced him outright. He did, however, have strong support in "national" Orthodox circles, like the Young Israel movement, chiefly located in outer-borough working-class neighborhoods where Zionist lectures were a staple of daily life (Manhattan's Wise spoke derisively—in private—of the "pesterers and preachers" of "a thousand Brooklyn street corners").

Nineteen thirty-six brought more Arab upheavals in Palestine. Throughout the early 1930s, European refugees had been pouring in. Annual arrivals had leapt from fewer than 5,000 in 1931 to over 60,000 in 1935, and by 1936, the Yishuv was 400,000 strong. The local Arabs, infuriated by the inundation, launched a countrywide general strike that evolved into an all-out rebellion against the British authorities and the Zionist settlements, which continued until 1939.

In Gotham, many on Zionism's liberal left argued the uprising had been incited by Arab "effendis" (Turkish for "noblemen"). These rich feudal landowners were seeking to drive a wedge between Jewish and Arab workers and peasants who were, insisted Greenberg of the *Jewish Frontier*, natural class allies. Zionism, it was argued, was good for the Arabs. It had made the desert bloom and brought modern health care, education, and prosperity. Such assessments skipped lightly over the fact that Zionists had been buying land from these same effendis and driving out tenants who had been cultivating it for generations; or the fact that many newly created jobs were reserved for "Hebrew labor only."

Facts like these—which underlay Arab fears of becoming second-class citizens in a Jewish land—were more apparent in Palestine itself. During the revolt, Ben-Gurion publicly came round to Jabotinsky's way of thinking (without ever acknowledging the borrowing). Both Jews and Arabs, he admitted, wanted undivided control of Palestine, and given the Arabs' overwhelming numerical superiority, only force could accomplish the Zionist project. Ben-Gurion and his colleagues expanded the Haganah, acquiring foreign arms and transforming the militia into a nascent army. He rejected, however, retaliation against Arabs for attacks on Jewish civilians, so as not to alienate Britain, still the Yishuv's ultimate protector. Some Haganah fighters, chafing under this restraint, hived off and joined what would become known as the Irgun Tsva'i-Leumi (National Military Organization), which launched scores of "eye-for-an-eye" attacks, including the bombing of Arab civilian targets. Betar recruits loomed steadily larger in the Irgun ranks until by 1937 it had become in effect the military arm of the NZO, and Jabotinsky its effective commander.

By 1939, the British had crushed the rebellion. However, doing so had tied down roughly 40 percent of the total British field force in Palestine, a diversion of troops that Whitehall, facing the possibility of war with Germany, Italy, and Japan, felt it could ill afford. To ease Arab concerns, the Mandatory power began throttling back on Jewish immigration, and in May 1939 a British White Paper slashed the quota to a total of 75,000 over the next five years and halted Jewish land purchases almost completely. Jabotinsky, convinced catastrophe in Europe was imminent, defied these restrictions, and the Irgun began running in refugees in leaky old boats. Some got through, but the Royal Navy was ruthlessly effective, and it now seemed—given the virtual closure of US doors—that any Jews who managed to escape Hitler's Europe would find there was no place where, in Robert Frost's definition of home, "if you had to go there, they had to take you in."

Jews in Palestine and Gotham saw this placatory policy as appeasement, on a par with Chamberlain's concessions to the Nazis at Munich months before. The Irgun retaliated by bombing British targets in Jerusalem and Haifa in May and June 1939, until they were put down by the British Army. In New York, Zionist organizations and their allies denounced the British retreat and pressed for reopening immigration to Palestine (though they were unwilling to similarly pressure the US).

Then war came, in September 1939, putting Zionists in a tough spot. Not supporting England against Hitler was unthinkable. Yet England—even after Churchill assumed power in 1940—continued to bar refugees from Palestine. Leading Zionists, accordingly, sought another savior. They believed the US would enter the war, replace Britain at the helm of global affairs, and, if properly cultivated, might defend Jewish claim. Which is why Zionists of all stripes began descending on New York.

On March 13, 1940, having tried and failed to win British backing for a Second World War version of his First World War Jewish Legion, Ze'ev Jabotinsky arrived in Gotham on a Cunard liner (the *Samaria*, no less). He was soon joined by New Zionist Organization aides, notably Benzion Netanyahu, founder and former editor of the Revisionists' daily paper in Jerusalem. Also to town came a handful of Irgun officers, nominally under Jabotinsky's control, who had been directing *aliyah bet* (illegal immigration) operations in Europe but had been ordered to New York to raise money.

Jabotinsky's goal was to win political and financial backing for a fully independent Jewish army, one that would fight in Europe as well as Palestine and not disarm after the war but become the military of a Jewish state-to-be. On March 19, 1940, 5,000 packed the Manhattan Center (at 34th and 8th) to hear him call for a massive evacuation of European Jewry (at the rate of 300,000 a year), establishment of a Jewish army, and creation of a provisional Jewish government in exile. Later NZO literature would call for establishing "suicide squads" to undertake commando raids in the heart of Germany, and for training Jewish pilots to make bombing raids on German cities.

Jabotinsky's proposals got a widespread and sympathetic hearing in the US press but cut no ice with mainstream Zionist forces. In addition to their long-standing antipathy to Revisionists, they feared being labeled as warmongers and provoking the wrath of the goyim. "I have never seen American Jewry so scared of local antisemitism," wrote Jabotinsky in 1940, an assessment echoed that year by Columbia University professor Salo Baron—the nation's premier historian of Jewish history—who agreed that the "Jews in this country have worked themselves into a state of panic verging on catastrophic despair."

Jabotinsky did, however, retain his corps of supporters in New York, the legacy of his former organizational efforts. Rallies in late March and April drew Jewish war veterans, Betar youths, and, despite Jabotinsky's being nonobservant, religious Zionists from Young Israelites to orthodox rabbis. One of the latter, Rabbi Charles Kahane, often hosted Jabotinsky in his Bensonhurst home (on West Second Street between Quentin Road and Kings Highway), where Kahane's eight-year-old son Meir hero-worshipped the Revisionist chieftain and in a few years would join the Betar youth group. And it was while visiting a Betar summer camp in the Catskills, in Hunter, New York, that in August 1940 Jabotinsky died of a heart attack. Thousands followed his hearse as it traced its way through the streets of the Lower East Side, before heading out to New Montefiore Cemetery in Farmingdale, leaving the American branch of the NZO—and the little band of New York Irgunists—for the moment in disarray.

Four months later, in December 1940, Ben-Gurion again arrived in town. Since the Arab Revolt and British White Paper, the Yishuv leader had moved farther away from Weizmann's gradualism and reliance on England. Convinced that the US, not London, would soon control the destiny of Palestine, he wanted to unite the entire Zionist camp, and then the entire US Jewish community, behind a campaign to win American support for a Jewish army and a Jewish state, thus enabling postwar Palestine to receive the 4–5 million surviving European Jews (a number at that point plausible) who would doubtless be homeless at war's end.

Ben-Gurion, too, got nowhere at first. Like Jabotinsky, he remarked on the widespread fear of speaking out among US Jews. Wise argued that fear was not the issue; it was instead the disinclination of Jews—like the Roosevelt Administration—to lean on the British, the only anti-Nazi force in the field in 1940, when its back was to the wall. Wise agreed with Ben-Gurion's goals, though found his rhetoric over-militant.

So things remained until Pearl Harbor, when a new voice blared out from Gotham's crowded Zionist field. At the end of 1941, the five young Irgun officers who had come to harvest money in New York—now cut off from Palestine by German subs and the British Navy—decided to collaborate with Benzion Netanyahu, Jabotinsky's former aide, in launching a new entity, the Committee for a Jewish Army (CJA). Its leader was the twenty-six-year-old Hillel Kook, nephew of the chief rabbi of Palestine, who now assumed the alias of Peter Bergson. The Lithuanian-born Bergson had grown up in Palestine, become active in the Irgun, and been organizing *aliyah bet* in Poland when tapped for the mission to New York. His CJA (headquartered at 285 Madison) would collaborate with the nearby NZO (55 West 42nd), of which Netanyahu became executive director, in putting the Jewish Army scheme on the US radar screen.

They did so by winning high-profile coverage in the keep-a-low-profile *New York Times*, through the simple yet novel expedient of buying their way in. *Times* publisher Sulzberger filtered his news and editorial columns for excessively Jewish content, but his ad pages were open to all paying customers, including anti-Semites publicizing "restricted" resorts, and now Zionists promoting a Jewish Army. On January 5, 1942, a full-page ad appeared in the *Times*, blazoned across the top with the bold-faced slogan: "Jews Fight for the Right to Fight." Coined by Netanyahu, it echoed, wittingly or no, A. Philip Randolph's March on Washington call of almost precisely a year earlier ("We loyal Negro Americans demand the right to work and fight for our country"). The ad's text proposed recruiting a 200,000-man army, consisting of Palestinian Jews and stateless Jewish refugees scattered throughout the world who would fight alongside the Allies. The ad said nothing about the future status of Palestine; made no complaints about the British; issued no calls of doubtful legality urging US citizens to sign up. All it proposed was that foreign Jews be allowed to fight in a war that four weeks before had become America's own.

To the call was appended a lengthy list of signers. It included the few actual CJA organizers (including Jabotinsky's son, Eri), several well-known Zionist activists, and even non-Zionist Jews who could comfortably back an ad stripped of Zionist pitches. More startling, the list was festooned with non-Jewish names, and very distinguished ones at that: lawyers, actors, journalists, scientists, retired admirals, college professors, university presidents, Protestant bishops, ministers and theologians (including Reinhold Niebuhr and Paul Tillich), civic leaders (like William Jay Schieffelin), plus three senators, fourteen congressmen, and one secretary of war—Henry Stimson himself—whose telegram to the CJA (quoted in the ad) declared unambiguously: "Free men everywhere are arming for the defense of democracy. I send my best wishes for the success of your movement."

This was just the first in a barrage of increasingly hard-hitting ads (reminiscent of those turned out by the Office of War Information), written primarily by Ben Hecht, the celebrated journalist turned playwright and screenwriter (*The Front Page*, *Scarface*, *Gone with the Wind*). Bergson, who had a good eye for local talent, had spotted a *PM* article in which Hecht had blistered Jews who failed to speak out loudly and immediately recruited him to turn up the volume. Successive ads featured ever longer and weightier lists of endorsers, including several dozen senators, over 100 congressmen, and assorted governors, mayors, and labor leaders.

Bergson was not creating a mass membership organization—these luminaries were asked for little more than their signatures; he was constructing a media-driven PR machine. The young Irgunists, having grasped New York advertising techniques, broke boldly with conventional Zionist tactics—or lack of tactics, as the Zionist Organization of America had no propaganda department, no PR staff, no lobbyists in Washington, and didn't want any. The Bergson Boys had dragged Zionism out of the back pages of the Yiddish press and into the national arena.

Far from being pleased, the leading organizations were furious. Wise and others not only rejected Bergson's proposal to collaborate in the CJA campaign, they actively tried to sabotage it, writing backers like Mayor La Guardia and urging them to disaffiliate. Partly they feared Bergson's flamboyant and provocative style would alarm the goyim (though Christians were signing up in droves); partly they were convinced the Irgunists were closet fascists, using the CJA as a front group to dupe ignorant liberals; partly they were incensed the CJA was deliberately finessing the issue of a Jewish state; and partly they saw Bergson and his comrades as upstarts, answerable to nobody, refusing to accept the "discipline" of the established organizations and instead competing with them—all too successfully. Still, it was hard to badmouth the CJA's proposed Jewish Army, which was very similar to what Ben-Gurion was proposing. And many in their own ranks saw the feisty Bergson Boys as providing a welcome whiff of resistance. Hadassah leaders privately praised the initiative; the Kings County Council of Jewish War Veterans unanimously endorsed the Bergson plan.

Fear of losing followers to the CJA, along with pressure from Ben-Gurion, a threatened invasion of Palestine itself by Rommel's Afrika Korps, and, crucially, US entry into the war which precluded their being attacked as warmongers—all helped spur the Zionists to action. In May 1942, they summoned nearly 600 delegates to New York's Hotel Biltmore for what amounted to the first World Zionist Conference on the American strand. With eminences like Weizmann and Ben-Gurion in attendance, Gotham, at least for the moment, had become the center of the global movement. Spurred on by the Yishuv leader, delegates adopted a platform embodying his "combative Zionism." It called for unrestricted immigration to Palestine, a Jewish military force under its own flag, and the establishment of a Jewish Commonwealth in Palestine, not as a distant aspiration but an immediate postwar demand. Biltmore was the watershed point at which US Zionism moved beyond philanthropy to politics.

Then came the Holocaust. While the immediate threat to Palestine as checked at the first Battle of El Alamein in July 1942, and mated after the second one in November, that same month brought official confirmation of the death camps. The horror, rather than solidifying Zionist forces, drove them in different directions. The mainstream organizations redoubled their efforts to win a state as the long-term solution to anti-Semitism, while the Bergson Boys launched an all-out effort for short-term rescue.

The Bergson group set up a new single-issue pressure group, the Emergency Committee to Save the Jewish People of Europe. Its first project was inspired not by Madison Avenue but by Broadway. On March 9, 1943, "We Will Never Die"—a pageant aimed at (literally) dramatizing the German war of extermination—played two performances in Madison Square Garden. Against a backdrop of two 42-foot-high Ten Commandments tablets, actors including Paul Muni, Edward G. Robinson, Sylvia Sidney, and Stella Adler reprised major events of Jewish history, recalled Jewish contributions to civilization, and recounted the Nazi massacres, before closing with a choir singing Kaddish, the prayer for the dead. The pageant— scripted by Ben Hecht, scored by Kurt Weill, produced by Billy Rose, and directed by Moss

Hart—received extensive press and newsreel coverage, then went off on national tour, much to the dismay of organized Zionism. Bergson had invited thirty-three Jewish groups to participate, but though some had applauded the message, none would work with the messenger. Wise himself tried and failed to get Hecht to cancel the project, then sought to undercut its supporters. When Governor Dewey declared March 9 a Day of Mourning for European Jewry, Wise led a delegation to Albany and threatened him with a loss of the Jewish vote if he didn't break with "dangerous and irresponsible racketeers." Dewey pressed ahead.

Advertisement for a memorial for European Jews at Madison Square Garden, 1943. Artwork by Arthur Szyk. (Posen Library of Jewish Culture & Civilization)

So did Bergson. In July 1943 he pulled 1,500 people to an Emergency Conference at the Hotel Commodore. The potpourri of speakers and sponsors included Mayor La Guardia, Dorothy Parker, Max Lerner, Herbert Hoover, Harold Ickes, William Randolph Hearst, and Langston Hughes. Panels of experts discussed detailed plans for rescue and the development of havens in neutral countries, Palestine, Africa, and the Americas; La Guardia even argued the US must open its doors. The Conference concluded by calling on the Roosevelt Administration to set up a government agency charged with facilitating rescue. This effort, too, received major media attention.

Three months farther on, Bergson organized a March on Washington. Appeals to Zionist and Jewish organizations to participate were rejected by all except the Orthodox, whose Vaad Hatzalah had expanded its rescue efforts from yeshivas to all Europe's Jewry. On October 6, 1943, over 400 bearded, black-garbed, and black-hatted rabbis—most from the New York area—trained down to Washington's Union Station, from where they marched solemnly to the White House bearing a petition asking the president "to form a special agency to rescue the remainder of the Jewish nation in Europe." Wise, however, had gotten there first, and it was on his advice, and that of FDR speech writer and adviser Samuel Rosenman (a prominent member of the American Jewish Committee), that Roosevelt—who considered liberals or moderates the true spokesmen of American Jewry—absented himself that day, leaving Vice President Henry Wallace to greet the aggrieved Orthodox leaders. It would be the only public protest on behalf of European Jewry by Jewish leaders in the US capital during the Holocaust.

Wise and his colleagues, meanwhile, had launched their own response to the Holocaust, focused less on rescue efforts—which many had painfully concluded were unlikely to be significantly effective given Hitler's grip on Europe—than on winning a Jewish state in Palestine, to bring to a close, forever, the centuries, millennia, of persecution of which Nazism was only the most recent and horrific instance. One month after Bergson's Hotel Commodore Emergency Conference, the mainstream Zionist forces sponsored an American Jewish Conference (August 29–September 2, 1943) at the Waldorf Astoria, aimed at effectuating the call for a Commonwealth adopted at the Biltmore in 1942. This precipitated a struggle within the wider Jewish community along lines of class, politics, and urban geography, in which Gotham figured as a casus belli.

The Waldorf conference organizers, seeking to gain a mandate from the wider Jewish world, arranged for polling the memberships of sixty-four national organizations and 375 regional conferences. The balloting produced 501 delegates to a conference that now represented not just the four core Zionist groups (with together under 200,000 members) but a national constituency of over two million Jews (roughly half the US total).

For all this focus on democratic outreach, organizers remained convinced that inclusion of the AJC was vital, though it numbered only a few hundred; the power and affluence of its German Jewish membership made it unavoidable. So Wise of the AJCongress negotiated with Proskauer of the AJC, able to circumvent their organizations' long-standing rivalry in part because the two had known one another in Gotham's political circles since the 1920s, when both had been advisers to Al Smith. Proskauer agreed to AJC participation in the Conference, though only if any discussion of a Jewish state was taken off the table and the focus kept on demanding unrestricted immigration to Palestine.

All went according to plan, with each presenter carefully skirting the elephant in the hall, until Rabbi Abba Hillel Silver, who'd been kept off the list of speakers, seized the podium. The Lithuanian-born activist, leader of a major Reform congregation in Cleveland

and head of the United Palestine Appeal, proceeded to give a scorching speech that blew away the Wise-Proskauer arrangement. Recounting the long train of anti-Semitic abuses over the centuries, down to the current Nazi butchery, Silver thundered that only a Jewish state could put "a final end to all of this, a sure and certain end." Delegates chafing under the ban exploded in an emotional ovation, sang the Zionist anthem "Hatikvah" repeatedly, and with near unanimity ratified the Biltmore program unconditionally.

The American Jewish Committee resigned from the Conference. Many bid them good riddance; Silver denounced them as "vestigial oligarchs." Proskauer's intransigence in the face of onrolling calamity now precipitated a storm of negative publicity. Ten percent of the AJC's own members quit in protest. When the dust settled, the group's virtual veto over communal policy had been broken. Money would continue to talk but would increasingly do so in the language of Zionism; soon even Proskauer would be supporting a Jewish state.

This class revolt had had a geographic dimension, with Cleveland's Silver prepared to torpedo the Wise/Proskauer deal because he stood outside the New York nexus. A similar spatial correlative marked the confrontation between Silver and Wise over the latter's fierce loyalty to Franklin Roosevelt, despite the president's unwillingness to challenge either Britain, the US Congress, or the State Department on their respective immigration-restriction policies. To some extent his devotion to Roosevelt simply mirrored that of American Jewry. It was rooted, too, in a Gotham-based personal and political association begun back when FDR was governor and Wise a battler against municipal corruption.

This place-based relationship had deepened over the years and extended to encompass the next generation as Wise's daughter, Justine Wise Polier, grew steadily closer to Eleanor Roosevelt. They first met in the 1920s around Women's Trade Union League issues, then worked together in 1938–39 trying to win admittance for refugee children. They joined forces again in 1941 when Polier became ER's right-hand woman in the Office of Civilian Defense, and she became, like her father, a repeat visitor to Hyde Park. For all the Rabbi's fulminations against the AJC's reliance on *Shtadlanut* (quiet backstage diplomacy), and for all his willingness to mount rallies and marches, Wise cherished his personal presidential connection and was convinced of its efficacy—even though it entailed a reluctance to criticize Roosevelt, lest the link to power be snapped.

From Silver's perspective this was altogether too cozy. "It is too late for Court Jews," he said of Wise—and he had a "Put-not-your-trust-in-princes" attitude toward Roosevelt himself. Backstage diplomacy hadn't delivered much for Zionism, he believed; worse, it had underdeveloped, even atrophied, the movement's political muscles, engendering a political passivity that stood in marked contrast to the energetic Bergson Boys for whom Silver had developed an admiration. Unconstrained by the New York ties that bound Wise to Roosevelt, the Midwesterner could and did call for "loud diplomacy"—a mammoth lobbying initiative to make the Biltmore goals a reality.

In August 1943 the Zionist leadership forced Wise to accept Silver as cochair of what became known as the American Zionist Emergency Council (AZEC). It promptly set about constructing a grass-rooted national organization that used professional mobilization techniques to harness the energy of hundreds of thousands of American Jews.

The AZEC mechanism had two poles, an extremely efficient headquarters in New York (at 342 Madison, near Grand Central), and a countrywide network of local Emergency Councils (by January 1944 there were over 200 of them, a year later, 380). New York dispatched to the councils memoranda on the situation in Europe and ready-to-print editorials; addresses by Wise or Silver and speeches by supportive congressmen; position papers, petition drive forms, and manuals on how to organize and lobby. Once up and running, a phone call from Gotham could set them in motion: flooding Congress with petitions, letters, and telegrams; mobilizing clubs, synagogues, and associations to do likewise; hounding local editors to run favorable pieces or deluging them with letters if they ran unfavorable ones; arranging forums in churches, schools, and civic groups; turning out for talks by anti-Zionists who they would question or critique from the floor; and holding rallies and conferences, though New York handled the really big events, like Madison Square Garden conclaves. Headquarters would also arrange for advertising in the press and access to radio. In 1944, AZEC bought time on 182 stations across the country for a thirty-nine-week series of fifteen-minute programs called "Palestine Speaks," featuring stars of stage and screen. New York also reached out to more than 3,000 non-Jewish but supportive institutions: unions, churches, civic groups, fraternal and business societies, ministers' associations, and agrarian granges.

Against the backdrop of unremitting horror in Europe, this disciplined campaign had a terrific impact. By 1944 local Emergency Councils had secured pro-Zionist resolutions from thirty-nine state legislatures, hundreds of municipalities, and 411 out of 535 members of Congress. Eighty-six percent of the Senate and 75 percent of the House resolved that Jews should have the right to settle in Palestine unhampered by the restrictions in Britain's White Paper. By 1945, three-quarters of the US Congress was recorded as supporting a Jewish commonwealth in Palestine.

Silver also helped work a transformation in Zionism's approach to party politics. Arguing that slavish adherence to FDR and the Democratic Party had deprived Jews of leverage, he argued that both parties should be made to vie for Jewish support. This was an insight more readily attainable in Cleveland than in New York, as, like much of the Midwest, the former was dominated by the Republican Party while the latter was a Democratic stronghold. Silver had voted twice for FDR, but he endorsed Willkie in 1940; and while not officially a Republican himself, he had opened lines to Ohio's powerful Senator Robert Taft and to New York's Governor Dewey, the other two leading candidates for the 1944 Republican nomination. That summer, Silver was able to get a pro-Zionist plank into the platform of the Republican Party, much to Wise's chagrin, as it denounced FDR for not challenging England's pro-Arab tilt in Palestine.

The prize all eyed was not just the Zionist vote, not even the generic Jewish vote, but the 47 electoral votes to be cast by New York State, far and away the country's biggest bloc of those peculiar ballots. Since 1876, no candidate (with one exception) had been elected president without carrying New York, one reason it was a rare contest in which one of the nominees for the top two offices did not hail from the Empire State. (In 1944, the Democratic, Republican, and Socialist candidates for president would all be New Yorkers.) And while Jews constituted only 3 percent of the national population, they accounted for 14 percent of New York State and 25 percent of New York City. Thanks to AZEC, moreover, they were mobilized as never before.

With Republicans bidding ardently for these voters, some Zionist analysts of the "Jewish Street" thought a massive electoral shift was possible. Eri Jabotinsky reported in December 1943 that "it is felt in Democratic as well as in Republican circles" that the Administration might lose "a good million of Jewish votes, especially in New York City." While this assessment was wildly overstated—New York Jews were not about to jump FDR's ship en masse—there was enough unhappiness and fluidity in the community to give knowledgeable politicians pause, including in the end FDR himself. The president would decide to make an overture to the Jews—not on statehood, about which he talked out of both sides of his mouth, but on rescue.

In November 1943, Bergson arranged for a resolution to be introduced into the House and Senate that called on FDR to create an agency of diplomatic, economic, and military experts charged with rescue. Then he launched an advertising blitz to promote its passage. Bergson's gambit got FDR's attention. What pushed the president to finally act, however, was an intervention by Secretary of the Treasury Henry Morgenthau Jr., a longtime FDR intimate and a member of his New York inner circle.

Morgenthau, the only Jew in the Cabinet, had mostly kept hands off Jewish-related issues, deemed the purview of the State Department. At the end of 1943 it came to his attention that Breckenridge Long, whom he'd long since pegged as an anti-Semite, had blocked a Treasury-facilitated plan to help rescue 70,000 Romanian Jews and had also ordered consular officials in Switzerland to cease transmitting reports of new atrocities. His staff now drew up a fully documented study—*Report to the Secretary on the Acquiescence of This Government in the Murder of the Jews*—which Morgenthau handed to the president on January 15, 1944. Even more compelling was Morgenthau's oral briefing in which, at the suggestion of FDR adviser Ben Cohen, he underscored the politics of the issue.

As Roosevelt well knew, Willkie and Dewey, his likeliest Republican opponents, were avidly pursuing Jewish votes. The former had endorsed statehood, the latter backed unlimited immigration to Palestine. Sam Rosenman, no alarmist, was predicting a possibly serious falloff in the New York Jewish Democratic vote. And Winston Churchill had recently responded to FDR's concern about not alienating the Arabs by noting that "there were more Jews than Arab votes in the Anglo-Saxon countries and we could not afford to ignore such practical considerations." In this context, when Morgenthau suggested the president could either risk a nasty pre-election confrontation with the American Jewish community (and with Congress, where Bergson's resolution was making headway), or establish the requested rescue agency, the correct decision seemed luminously clear.

On January 22, 1944, by Executive Order, Roosevelt established the War Refugee Board (WRB). Its mission would be to develop plans and programs for rescuing victims of enemy oppression in imminent danger of death. Like the Fair Employment Practices Commission—another agency wrung from Roosevelt by public pressure—it lacked cabinet-level status or powers, had a small staff, and virtually no budget. In this instance (as with the State Department's earlier turn to Gotham's Council on Foreign Relations for staffing and financing of its planning division), the work of the Washington-based WRB would be underwritten by New Yorkers; private Jewish organizations would fund 91 percent of the agency's lifesaving work.

Securing this grudging concession on the rescue issue—one that was clearly too little and too late—was not matched by an equivalent advance on the question of a Jewish state. But an extraordinary transformation had nevertheless been wrought. Long resistant to or agnostic about the Zionist project, in the space of a few years, driven by the unspeakable news arriving from Europe, the New York Jewish community had swung dramatically and near unanimously behind the Zionist position. It had, moreover, mobilized the political muscle and wider national support that would, in a few years more, be fundamental to creation of the State of Israel.

In addition, the genocide had worked a psychic transformation in New York Jewry, which abandoned head-down timidity for unapologetic assertiveness in the public sphere. Having found its voice in the process of aiding Jews in trouble abroad, the community began to raise it on its own behalf in Gotham.

124

Trouble at Home

Anti-Semitism in New York and the US during the war years was mostly a matter of talk—ignorant, malicious, and slanderous, and without lethal consequence. One bit of talk that made the rounds was the accusation that not only had Jews gotten the US into the war—Coughlin began banging this drum soon after Pearl Harbor—but shirked their duty to fight in it. This was the burden of a ditty set to the Marines' Hymn ("From the Halls of Montezuma..."), some stanzas of which ran:

> From the shores of Coney Island/Looking eastward to the sea/Stands a kosher air-raid warden/Wearing a V for victory.
> And the gentle breezes fill the air/With the hot dogs from Cohen's stand/Only Christian boys are drafted/From Coney Island's sands.
> Oh, we Jews are not afraid to say/We'll stay home and give first aid/Let the Christian saps go fight the Japs/In the uniforms we made.
> So it's onward into battle/Let us send the Christian slobs/When the war is done and victory won/All us Jews will have their jobs.

This despite the fact that at war's end there were 550,000 Jews in the military, with Jewish men constituting 8 percent of those in uniform—about twice their percentage of the population as a whole—and 340,000 Jewish women were volunteering in one capacity or another.

It was also galling that in 1944, when a National Opinion Research Center poll asked respondents which group they believed constituted the greatest "threat" to America, 6 percent said the Germans, 9 percent the Japanese, 11 percent cited Negroes, and 24 percent fingered the Jews. Or that a 1945 survey found 58 percent of the public believed Jews had "too much power in the United States," *up* from the 41 percent who'd thought so in 1938. Or that in December 1944, a poll showed that a majority of Americans, while accepting that Hitler had killed some Jews, refused to believe the Nazis had methodically murdered millions—and this two years after official US acknowledgment of the genocide and two months after the Hungarian deportations to Auschwitz.

Anti-Semitic graffiti in the Bronx in support of Thomas E. Dewey's presidential campaign. (Photo by FPG/Archive Photos/Getty Images)

Still, what US Jews faced was grumbling, not pogrom-ing; opinions not actions. A Gallup poll taken back in 1939 had found that 12 percent would have supported "a widespread campaign against the Jews in this country," and another 20–25 percent would have "sympathized" with such an initiative. Nothing of the sort happened. What did take place, chiefly in New York (and Boston), was verbal menacing and low-level violent assaults on property and people, perpetrated chiefly by Irish adolescents—the remnants of the Christian Front and members of wartime gangs like the Shamrocks and Amsterdams. By 1944 almost every synagogue in northern Manhattan had been desecrated, windows smashed, buildings and tombstones defaced with swastikas, and services interrupted by groups of boys yelling "Kill the Jews!" Irish youths physically attacked Jewish youngsters in Washington Heights and Inwood. When police refused to afford protection—Irish officers tended to belittle the attacks—Jewish War Veterans began escorting the children to school. Protests got the city's commissioner of investigation William B. Herlands to start a formal inquiry in fall 1942. Released in January 1944, his *Investigative Report on Anti-Semitism in New York City* criticized police laxity and inaction; only then did Commissioner Valentine take steps to combat vandalism and abuse.

What also rankled—especially given the crack about Jews taking Christian jobs—was the rampant discrimination in employment. The Fair Employment Practices Committee hearing in Gotham in February 1942 produced compelling evidence of bias against Jews by banks and law firms; medical schools had quotas in place, and the American Dental Association called on Columbia Dental School to follow suit, lest New York be swamped by Jewish dentists. Access to defense work was impeded as well, notably in aviation plants where German and Scandinavian foremen believed Jews incapable of mastering mechanical problems. About 30 percent of the want ads in the *New York Times* and *Herald Tribune* baldly expressed their preference for Protestants or Catholics. *PM* commenced a crusade against such advertising, pairing a photo of a *Juden Verboten* sign in Vienna with an ad from the *Times*, and bills were introduced in the state legislature to outlaw the practice.

Near war's end, however, it was decided by leaders in the Jewish community to go much farther and fight for legislation that would ban workplace discrimination altogether. This would be an immense and hotly contested undertaking, whose success clearly demanded allies. When the leadership cast their eyes about for potential partners, the likeliest candidate, despite a friction-filled history, was Gotham's African American community.

JEWS AND BLACKS

A pamphlet for a 1938 exhibition by the Nazi party on "degenerate music," organized by Nazi official Dr. Hans Ziegler. (Album / Alamy Stock Photo)

125

Jews and Blacks Allied

"If Mussolini's fascism and Hitler's Nazism can join forces," asked the Gotham-based weekly *American Hebrew* in 1936, "why shouldn't their joint victims, Negroes and Jews, ally to fight them?"

To some of the city's Jews, the need and basis for such an alliance seemed self-evident. Rabbi Stephen Wise had already suggested this in a 1934 address to the NAACP entitled "The Parallel Between Hitlerism and the Persecution of Negroes in America." In 1938 the Central Conference of American Rabbis invoked "the proverbial friendship of our two peoples." And in 1939 the lawyer for the Scottsboro boys, Samuel Leibowitz, told Harlem's Negro Elks: "Both of us are in the same boat together."

To which some of the city's African Americans in effect replied, "What you mean 'we,' kemo sabe?"

Adam Clayton Powell Jr., for one, *did* believe Jews and Blacks should unite to fight fascism. However, the activist minister rejected the notion they were boatmates in other respects. In July 1938, in the midst of his renewed struggle to wrest jobs for Blacks from recalcitrant Harlem businesses, many of them Jewish-owned, Powell told the *Amsterdam News*: "Everybody knows that the Jew on the way up, when he has to scuffle or scramble for pennies among his Negro neighbors, can say he is a friend to the Negro. However, once he is free of the shackles of poverty, the Jew turns white."

Where Jews saw themselves as vulnerable outsiders, Blacks encountered them as powerful insiders in virtually all the binary relationships of daily life: Jewish employers, Black employees; Jewish housewives, Black maids; Jewish principals and teachers, Black pupils; Jewish union leaders, Black dressmakers; Jewish social workers, Black clients; Jewish shopkeepers, Black customers; Jewish lenders, Black borrowers; and, perhaps the most contentious of these unequal and often antagonistic dyads, Black tenants and Jewish landlords—or, more precisely, Jewish *agents* of landlords (given that most of Harlem was owned by white, Christian-run institutions such as banks, insurance companies, estates, and churches), to whom fell such friction-filled tasks as collecting rents, refusing repairs, and arranging evictions.

Still, many Gotham Jews had long defined themselves as racial liberals. Rabbi Wise and other Jews had helped found the NAACP in 1909, had spoken out against lynching and discrimination, and had argued, with the *Jewish Frontier*, that "both self-interest and our holiest traditions demand our making common cause with the Negro in his fight for equality." While some Jews distanced themselves from white racism, others proved susceptible to its shibboleths, as evidenced by the repeated urgings of Jewish leaders that their coreligionists shed derogatory attitudes toward "the schwartzes." Lawrence D. Reddick, curator of Harlem's Schomburg Collection of Negro Literature, speculated in an essay that many Jews felt it was only "by assuming the characteristics of the members of the dominant majority that they would achieve complete absorption into American life"—would become, in a word, truly *white*.

The Depression exacerbated tensions all along the city's Black/Jewish frontiers—stresses made starkly manifest during the Harlem riot of 1935—and, at first, the triumph of fascism in Germany only aggravated them. Like whites in general, Blacks—suffering from massive unemployment—were seldom responsive to the plight of Jewish refugees. Once "off the boat," worried Powell in 1938, "most of them would settle in the Bronx Alps," then look for work with relatives, and some would wind up on 125th Street, holding jobs denied to Negroes. The country was too poor and too crowded to grant them asylum, said the *Amsterdam News* that same year; and in 1939, when WPA rolls were cut back, tossing still more Harlemites out of work, the paper declared that all aliens should have been dismissed before one Black American was laid off.

Afro-Gothamites also saw the surge of sympathy for Jewish suffering as diverting attention from Black oppression; they resented that Jews had, as it were, jumped the victims'

The NAACP pickets a conference on crime in Washington, DC, December 11, 1934. (Photo by International News Photos/Library of Congress/Corbis/VCG via Getty Images)

queue. A 1938 NAACP *Crisis* editorial seconded US government protests of Nazi barbarism but wished the authorities "could be equally indignant at the lynching, burning alive and torture with blowtorches of Negroes by American mobs on American soil which have shamed America before the world for a much longer time than persecution under Hitler." Adam Clayton Powell Jr. challenged local Jews to "stop crying over German Jews and get an anti-lynch law passed."

Many Black activists deployed anti-Nazi rhetoric, though largely to spotlight racial practices in the US South. *Crisis* editorials tagged Mississippi's white supremacist senators Theodore Bilbo and James Eastland as "America's Hitler and Goebbels," and cartoons depicted Hitler as a Klansman, and Klansmen as storm troopers. Such analogizing, intended to tar American racism with the brush of Nazi anti-Semitism, did collaterally underscore what Blacks had in common with Jews. But analogizing could be deployed to opposite effect as well. The African American *New York Age*, referring to a 125th Street department store, argued that "if the Jewish merchants in Germany treated German workers as Blumsteins treat the people of Harlem, then Hitler is right." A Black employee of a Jewish-owned sweatshop groused that "Jews in Germany don't get kicked around like Negroes in Harlem." And Chandler Owen overheard African Americans saying, "Well, Hitler did one good thing: he put these Jews in their place." Popular anti-Semitism—a facet of local Black thinking at least since Garvey's day—was on the upswing in Black New York on the eve of war, hindering formation of a Black–Jewish coalition.

The beginnings of a turnaround came with the events of 1938 and 1939: Kristallnacht's disturbing preview of Nazi intentions; promulgation by Mussolini's regime of a *Manifesto of the Racist Scientists*, branding Semites and Africans as inherently inferior and denouncing Italian interbreeding with either; US polls listing Blacks (first) and Jews (second) as the "most disliked" groups in America; and the outbreak of war in Europe. Over the next two years, in this context of heightened and interlinked danger, leaders of the nation's major Black and Jewish organizations began to reach out to one another—an effort facilitated by sheer proximity, as virtually all of them lived and worked on Manhattan Island.

Leading Jewish papers—the *Forward*, the *Day*, the *Jewish Morning Journal*—appealed for an alliance, and Black spokespersons responded positively. After Kristallnacht, Walter White told the *Amsterdam News* that "we must join with all those condemning Nazi terror because what happens to one minority can happen to others—a lesson which Jews, Negroes, and all other minorities must learn."

Joint conversations took place—like a conference at Columbia University, cosponsored by Randolph's Brotherhood of Sleeping Car Porters and the Jewish Labor Committee, to discuss mitigating racial tensions.

Coalition groups were established, like the City-Wide Citizens Committee on Harlem, to dismantle Jim Crow in the Black quarter and throughout the metropolis. City-Wide attracted New York's preeminent African Americans: Adam Clayton Powell Sr. and his son (and city councilman) Adam Clayton Powell Jr.; Walter White and Roy Wilkins of the NAACP; A. Philip Randolph of the March on Washington Movement; Lester Granger of the Urban League; Frank Crosswaith (ILGWU official and head of the Negro Labor Committee); and Hulan Jack (St. Lucian–born Tammany man and, since 1940, Harlem's representative in the New York State Assembly). Prominent members of the city's Jewish community also came on board: Dr. David de Sola Pool (since 1907 minister of Congregation Shearith Israel); Robert K. Straus (Macy's heir, New Dealer, and city councilman); housing activist Charles Abrams; and liberal Republican councilman Stanley Isaacs (active in the American Jewish Committee and United Jewish Appeal).

Pearl Harbor accelerated expressions of mutual solidarity. In February 1942, the *Amsterdam News* asserted: "The Black man must realize that his natural ally is the Jewish race.... Every instinct of self-preservation demands that both groups in America get together into an offensive and defensive alliance for the common good." The NAACP Board of Directors pledged "unqualified and unlimited effort on behalf of the persecuted Jews of the world, which includes anti-Semitism in the United States as well as slaughter in Poland." A. Philip Randolph told a Madison Square Garden assemblage in June 1942 that "no Negro is secure from intolerance and race prejudice so long as one Jew is a victim of anti-Semitism." And that summer the first issue of a new Harlem journal, the *Negro Quarterly* (of which Ralph Ellison was managing editor, and to which Langston Hughes and Richard Wright contributed), ran two articles, one exploring Negro anti-Semitism, the other Jewish anti-Negroism; both pieces concluded their respective problems were surmountable.

For their part, Jewish leaders urged their community to back Blacks in their battle against discrimination; stressed the commonality of needs and goals (a *Jewish Survey* cartoon depicted a sign reading "Help Wanted—No Negroes, No Jews"); and called for the elimination of anti-Negro feelings and practices in their own ranks. American Jewish Congress youth groups sponsored interracial forums and circulated petitions protesting racial discrimination, while the Bronx Rabbinic Council joined with the National Council of Jewish Women to campaign for fair treatment of Black domestics.

Then came US acknowledgment that genocide was under way, relayed to the public by Rabbi Wise at his November 1942 press conference. This galvanized a new round of support from Black leaders, with the NAACP announcing it was "appalled at the cold-blooded campaign of extermination of the Jews," and the Urban League donating money for the relief of overseas Jewry as "another means of building goodwill between American Negroes and their fellow-citizens of Jewish faith." Several prominent African Americans—including Powell Jr., Randolph, W.E.B. Du Bois, Langston Hughes, and Canada Lee—backed rescue, Jewish army, or Zionist initiatives, particularly those of the militant Bergsonite variety.

The riot that erupted in Harlem in August 1943 interrupted this growing comity—it was notable, however, that the irate crowds clamored against "the white man," not "the Jews"—though not for long. Indeed the outburst ignited still another round of organizing, beginning with the Citizens Emergency Conference for Interracial Unity in September, at which Walter White argued that "here in New York City a deliberate campaign is being conducted, not only against the Negroes, but against another minority group—the Jews." (This referred to the smears about a supposed Jewish unwillingness to fight—belied, said White, by the "all too prominent" number of "Bernsteins and Cohens and Greenbaums" on the casualty lists).

Halfway through the war, then, a climate of cooperation had largely displaced Depression-era distrust. Still, what, exactly, apart from jawboning their own community to respect the other, were these new allies to do?

126

Fighting Prejudice

One thing they decided to do was get a better handle on exactly what they were up against. At one level the answer seemed obvious—it ran a gamut from fascist exterminism to Mississippi-style segregation to the discriminations against Blacks and Jews still commonplace in New York. What drew their interest was the possibility that these disparate practices had a common origin.

This emerging hypothesis took shape in Gotham's social science community, as evidenced by the phenomenal popularity of work by such Boas protégées as Ashley Montagu, whose *Man's Most Dangerous Myth: The Fallacy of Race* was a bestseller in 1942, or Ruth Benedict and Regina Weltfish, whose popularizing pamphlet *Races of Mankind* of 1943 was widely circulated as well. By war's end, racism had been stripped of intellectual respectability, and the remaining true believers, their convictions now bereft of basis in reason or reality, were adjudged to be governed by "prejudice."

But exactly what was "prejudice"? How was it created, sustained? Could it be eliminated, like typhus, with proper treatment or prophylaxis? Could wartime unity be attained without suppressing diversity? The need for serious study of these issues seemed clear, not least to FDR, who believed that "if civilization is to survive, we must cultivate the science of human relationships—the ability of all peoples, of all kinds, to live together and work together in the same world, at peace."

Members of the Columbia Psychology Department grouped in the Society for the Psychological Study of Social Issues (SPSSI), as well as academic psychologists at City College and Teachers College, and a variety of distinguished émigré intellectuals. The ensuing work by these psycho-social scholars would be underwritten by the city's leading Jewish organizations, by major Gotham foundations (notably the Carnegie Corporation), and by the Office of War Information and other federal agencies interested in overcoming intergroup conflicts (like the 1943 riot) that they deemed divisive and dangerous in wartime.

One of the first groups to take up the challenge was the American Jewish Committee—not surprisingly, given how successful had been its underwriting of Boasian anthropology. In 1944 the Committee invited a "who's who" of the country's top psychologists, psychoanalysts, and sociologists to a conference in New York to probe "the factors that contribute to prejudice against religions, racial and ethnic groups." This led to the establishment of a Department of Scientific Research, charged with producing what would become a series of volumes collectively entitled *Studies in Prejudice*. The project represented an odd coupling of the conservative American Jewish Committee with the radical Institute for Social Research, whose Frankfurt School Marxists had been exiling in Manhattan. During the war their leader, Max Horkheimer, relocated (for health reasons) to Southern California, followed by his colleague Theodor Adorno; there, with others, the Frankfurters subcontracted to work on the Committee's mammoth enterprise. Preliminary results suggested that prejudice was an aspect of something larger, an authoritarian personality type, one predisposed to ethnocentrism, indeed fascism; they believed, too, that latent tendencies toward such authoritarianism might perhaps be revealed by psychological tests they were inventing and thus be made susceptible to therapeutic intervention.

In the meantime, given the war-spawned need for immediate results, the Committee acted on the more optimistic presumption that prejudice—at least prejudice-lite—was rooted in mere misinformation, hence capable of being more swiftly addressed by education. Specifically, the Committee (with the Anti-Defamation League) assumed financial responsibility for Rachel DuBois's Service Bureau for Intercultural Education (BIE)—though they deleted DuBois herself from the project she'd founded. The BIE promoted the teaching of tolerance, and the cultivation of harmonious intergroup relations, in public schools throughout the country.

The intercultural education movement also supported inspirational talks, pamphlets, posters, and mass-media interventions. And here, once again, the conservative Committee's approach dovetailed with that of the left, which had a similar penchant for using propaganda to overcome prejudice. Perhaps the most famous instance was a ten-minute 1945 film, *The House I Live In*, a Popular Front–style collaboration between a trio of New York communist artists and a clutch of liberal Hollywood filmmakers. In the movie, Frank Sinatra rescues a small boy from a youthful gang intent on pummeling him because "we don't like his [unspecified] religion." Sinatra tells the urchins their intolerant behavior is "fascist" in nature and explains that the country's essence lies in its pluralism. He then sings the title song, which includes the line: "All races and religions, that's America to me," and the lads, their mental fog dispelled, depart with their former intended victim, now newfound friend.

A lot of heavy hitters were involved in producing this lightweight piece of agitprop. The title song's lyrics were by Lewis Allan (pseudonym of Abel Meeropol, who had composed "Strange Fruit"); the music was composed by Earl Robinson (of "Ballad for Americans" and "Joe Hill" fame); and the screenplay was by Brooklyn-born, Columbia-educated dramatist Albert Maltz, who had written for the Theater Union and Group Theater in the 1930s, before moving to Hollywood in 1941 to work on films like *Casablanca*. The short was released by RKO for screening in children's matinees and then distributed in 16mm by Young America Films to schools in every state of the union.

In the meantime, the Committee's old rival, the American Jewish Congress, had entered the antiprejudice lists. Its leader, Rabbi Wise, had decided to focus more attention on domestic matters, in part because his efforts on the international front had been so sadly unavailing. As usual, Wise and the Congress opted for a more activist strategy than did the Committee, adopting an approach suggested by Kurt Lewin, one of the most influential social psychologists of the day. The German-born exile argued that relying on education and exhortation to fight prejudice was futile, so long as official discrimination policies remained in place. State-backed segregation statutes, or institutionally imposed quotas, defined a racial or religious group as a *sanctioned* target. These formal caste barriers legitimated and fostered informal prejudice. Only when the former were dismantled would education have some hope of success of eradicating the latter. Attacking prejudice, therefore, was *not* the key to attacking discrimination, as the Committee thought; rather, attacking discrimination was the key to attacking prejudice.

Lewin's two-part tactical proposal to Wise (in July 1944) flowed from this strategic analysis. He suggested the Congress establish a research division that would consist of community sociologists, cultural anthropologists, opinion analysts, group and individual psychologists, and statisticians. This body would investigate the cause, nature, and cure of both anti-Semitic and racial prejudice and undertake "action research" initiatives by going out into communities and studying intergroup relations in the field.

Alongside this analytical team Lewin argued for setting up an "operational division"—a secular arm, composed of attorneys, that would undertake to bring down discriminatory structures through litigation and lobbying.

Enthused by this vision of activist lawyers and social scientists mounting a double-barreled assault on the barricades of bias, Wise announced in February 1945 that the American Jewish Congress would fund, for the next five years, a Commission on Community Interrelations (CCI) to operate as Lewin had proposed.

To work on the complementary outlawing-of-discrimination piece, the Congress formed the Commission on Law and Social Action (CLSA), headed by two distinguished attorneys, Will Maslow and Alexander Pekelis.

Maslow had studied law at Columbia and then, finding the doors of Wall Street firms firmly closed to Jews, went to work for the New Deal—first as a trial attorney for the National Labor Relations Board, and then as director of field operations for the Fair Employment Practices Commission.

Pekelis, born in Russia, spent most of his adult life in Italy and France as a professor of jurisprudence before fleeing to New York in 1941, where he accepted a professorship at the New School. Pekelis argued that because in the US anti-Semitism was subtler than ham-fisted racial segregation, lawyers intent on challenging it needed the sorts of data that only social science could provide: "Law without a knowledge of society is blind," he aphorized, and "sociology without a knowledge of law, powerless."

The CLSA hired seven civil rights lawyers and set up shop as a private-sector attorney general's office—at a time when the US Justice Department had no civil rights division at all—ready to do battle on behalf not just of Jews but of all minorities. As the Congress promised African Americans in 1945: "In all the causes for which they struggle they can count upon finding the Jews and the American Jewish Congress on the side of justice."

AFRICAN AMERICANS WERE, IN FACT, way ahead of them. The NAACP had set up a civil rights litigation operation in the early 1930s, one whose roots ran back to the late 1920s when the left-wing Garland Fund—at the urging of James Weldon Johnson, a Garland trustee who was also executive secretary of the NAACP—had given the organization a substantial grant to undertake a "large-scale, widespread, dramatic campaign to give the Southern Negro his constitutional rights." Specifically, the NAACP envisioned a frontal challenge to the separate-but-equal doctrine of *Plessey v. Ferguson* on the grounds that segregated facilities were inherently unequal.

To run this campaign the NAACP decided to start with a series of suits against professional schools that refused to accept Blacks, beginning with a challenge to the University of

Maryland Law School, which in January 1935 had rejected an African American applicant on avowedly racial grounds. The case was turned over to Thurgood Marshall, a Black Maryland attorney, who had relocated to Gotham in October 1936, where he moved into a two-room apartment at 149th and Bradhurst Avenue, just north of City College, shifting later to Sugar Hill's 409 Edgecombe, where Walter White, Roy Wilkins, and W.E.B. Du Bois—the NAACP high command—resided at various times. Over the next two years Marshall proceeded effectively to create the job of civil rights lawyer, combining courtroom activity with managerial, fundraising, and public-relations duties. "Lean, hard, and Hollywood-handsome"—some called him "the black Ronald Colman"—Marshall was a charismatic speaker, much in demand, and he spent a great deal of time on the road.

Under Marshall's direction the NAACP won its first major victory in 1938 when the Supreme Court decided that the state of Missouri had a constitutional obligation to provide a legal education to Lloyd Gaines, an African American. In March 1939 Marshall—given charge of all the association's legal activities—began hiring young assistants, mostly Black New Yorkers with local law degrees like Franklin Williams (Fordham) and Constance Baker Motley (Columbia). In 1940 he was also made chief counsel for the newly created NAACP Legal Defense and Educational Fund, an advocacy body that was admitted to practice before the Supreme Court.

Marshall and NAACP chief Walter White understood that litigation was a slow and limited vehicle and that the push for desegregation required developing public pressure as well. During the war years, accordingly, the organization ramped up its organizing activities. Much of this work was spearheaded by Ella Baker, who during the 1930s had been a journalist (coauthoring the 1935 exposé of the Bronx "slave markets"), an organizer of Black consumer cooperatives, a teacher in the WPA's Worker's Education Project, and founder of the Harlem YWCA's Negro History Club. In 1941 she joined the NAACP staff as a field secretary, traveling through the South for roughly six months of every year, recruiting new members and supporting local antidiscrimination campaigns, at times putting her life in danger. In March 1941 Baker launched a membership drive in Birmingham, Alabama, the domain of racist police chief Bull Connor, and in 1942–'43 she partnered with left-wing CIO unions in areas where organizers had been found beaten half to death after they'd linked economic and racial issues. In 1943 she was appointed national director of branches, supervising the New York National Office's dealings with local groups and field secretaries.

Though Baker worked closely with her friend Thurgood Marshall, she thought the NAACP's emphasis on legal initiatives had made the organization too bureaucratic, too hierarchical, too Gotham-centric, and too oriented to middle-class concerns. In 1944, she began to bring local southern organizers up to New York for leadership conferences. These offered training in how to mount propaganda and education campaigns, bring political pressure to bear on local officials, institute legal action, and organize mass protests. Then she held similar workshops in the South itself, to further decentralize the organizing process. At one in Atlanta, in March 1945, attendees included two activists from Montgomery, Alabama—E. D. Nixon, an organizer for Randolph's Brotherhood of Sleeping Car Porters, and Rosa Parks, the local chapter secretary (the Atlanta event was Parks's first venture outside the Montgomery area). Between 1940 and 1945, in no small part thanks to Baker's efforts, the NAACP's membership expanded from 50,000 to roughly 450,000.

IN 1945, THEREFORE, WHEN THE American Jewish Congress's new Commission on Law and Social Action (CLSA) was launched, it was in effect playing catch-up with the NAACP, which had long since geared up its campaign to combat discrimination in the courts. In deciding to closely involve social scientists, however, the Congress's Commission on Community Interrelations (CCI) was running slightly ahead of the curve. While African American social psychologists—chiefly Kenneth Clark and his wife, Mamie Phipps Clark—had begun investigating the impact of segregation on African American psyches, their work had yet to be integrated into NAACP legal initiatives.

In 1939–'40, the Clarks had followed up on studies by Eugene and Ruth Horowitz, another psychologist couple who'd trained at Columbia. In the mid-1930s the Horowitzes had studied the genesis of racial prejudice in white children and demonstrated (in Boasian fashion) that it was a learned, not an inborn behavior. They also discovered that New York City schoolchildren absorbed dominant racist attitudes no matter whether their institutions were all-white or mixed-race; only the pupils in a Gotham communist commune appeared to have been inoculated against those biases, seemingly by their institution's or their parents' antiracist ideology.

Following the Horowitz-blazed trail, the Clarks in 1938 and 1939 looked at when and how *Black* children became aware of their racial identity and in 1940 began research on what those children *thought* about that identity. They did so by presenting three-to-seven-year-old subjects with dolls—identical in all but skin color—which the children were asked to characterize. When they described the Black dolls negatively and the white dolls positively, the Clarks hypothesized that Black children absorbed the same prejudices white children did, which in their case fostered a negative self-image. By 1944, their preliminary findings suggested that the American racial order inflicted psychological damage on African American personality structures. In his work that year as part of the CCI's Coney Island task force, Kenneth Clark noted that 30 percent of Blacks interviewed had unfavorable attitudes toward their own group, compared to 21 percent of Italians and 14 percent of Jews—seemingly additional confirmation that significant numbers of Blacks were accepting the negative evaluations imposed by dominant whites.

Clark came to a similar conclusion in his 1945 analysis of the 1943 Harlem riot. Racial prejudice and segregation and their attendant feelings of isolation had, he believed, produced a warped personality type, one lacking in empathy for other individuals or in respect for private property. Racist dehumanization was coming home to roost and hatching societal disturbances. Still, if Clark's diagnoses were psychological, his prescriptions were structural. In his 1942 government-sponsored survey of Black morale ("The Negro Looks at the War"), he insisted the country had to demolish its barriers of discrimination if they wanted Blacks wholeheartedly on board with the war effort.

Some of the Clarks' work-in-progress made its way into *An American Dilemma*, a two-volume tome by Gunnar Myrdal that summed up the war era's most massive investigation of prejudice. Brought out by Harper & Brothers in 1944, it had its roots in the aftermath of the Harlem Riot of 1935, when Newton Baker, a Carnegie Corporation trustee, first proposed a major study of US race relations that would pay particular attention to the condition of Blacks in northern cities. In 1938 the New York Foundation, seeking to provide some fresh and outside thinking, had brought in Myrdal, a Swedish social scientist and social democrat, and started him off with a quarter-million-dollar grant. Myrdal had spent most of the next four years in and out of Gotham (the project office was on the 46th floor of the Chrysler Building) overseeing the work of seventy-five researchers, some of them renowned social scientists (like Columbia's Otto Klineberg, Kenneth Clark's mentor), others younger investigators, many of them African American (including Clark himself).

Myrdal tended to psychologize racism, rooting it less in political, economic, or social structures than in the white American mind, which Myrdal saw as torn between democratic principles and discriminatory practices—which Myrdal documented abundantly—rooted in prejudices lodged deeply in the "heart of every American." This conflict between equality and racism created the American dilemma—a mental discomfort, a guilty conscience—and part of Myrdal's goal was to heighten this tension by appealing to the better angels of the country's nature. That there were grounds for optimism about such an approach seemed evident to him: "The gradual destruction of the popular theory behind race prejudice," Myrdal argued, "is the most important of all social trends in the field of interracial relations." And now, with war, hopefully the tension between fighting racism abroad while practicing it at home would precipitate a favorable resolution of the contradiction.

Myrdal was considerably more pessimistic about the *Black* American mind, and African American culture in general. Following (and over-extrapolating from) Clark and others he grew convinced that Black culture had been irretrievably damaged by white racism. Boas had been right to consider race a social construction not a biological one, Myrdal thought, but wrong to uncritically celebrate the variety of cultures his new landscape revealed, because some cultures were not independent, not genuine. Not only did African American children get infected in the cradle with white prejudice, but Black culture as a whole was determined—sickened—by the dominant white culture. This seemed evident to Myrdal from what he considered to be the instability of Black families, the emotionalism of the Negro church, the unwholesomeness of Black recreational activity, and the community's high crime rate. Ignoring positive assessments by Du Bois and others of the strengths of African American culture, Myrdal pronounced it "pathological," containing virtually nothing worth saving. The only way forward was through total assimilation: Blacks needed to "acquire the traits held in esteem by the dominant white Americans."

Whites, for their part, needed to live up to their creed and grant Blacks full civil rights and equality of economic opportunity. To achieve this, Myrdal (and his sponsor, the Carnegie Corporation) stressed the importance of education in correcting white prejudices: "Subjecting them to rigorous examination in the light of the factual evidence" would, in time, lead to a readjustment of white "value hierarchies," and hence, still farther down the road, a change in white behavior. Yet Myrdal also sprinkled his text with references to the many *material* benefits whites received from the system of racial supremacy, including superior access to jobs, housing, education, health care, and political power. And though these references were subordinate to the main line of his analysis, their presence made clear that he did not believe that education or propaganda about the "brotherhood of man" would be sufficient to convince whites to do what they should do (and what they claimed to believe was right). His own evidence suggested, rather, that many whites were perfectly prepared to live in a state of permanent dilemmahood.

Accordingly, as a believer in "social engineering," Myrdal also promoted steelier brands of intervention. Rejecting William Graham Sumner's argument that "folkways" couldn't be altered by "stateways," Myrdal called for outlawing segregation and discrimination and praised the NAACP's strategy for accomplishing it. More remarkably, he noted—and applauded—the way Black leaders, Randolph and White especially, had used the antifascist war to "demand full civic, political and economic equality more strongly than ever." He specifically endorsed Randolph's ringing assertion that "freedom is never granted, it is won. Justice is never given, it is exacted"; and he applauded Randolph's March on Washington Movement's mix of mass meetings and orderly trade unionism tactics. Indeed, he hoped a wide spectrum of Black organizations would take the field and employ a variety of means, from conservative legalism to militant radicalism, "to advance the cause of social and religious freedom."

Myrdal's one caveat was that while rallying the Black masses would no doubt require some degree of appeal to "racial chauvinism," US power realities made it essential to "engage as many white groups as possible as allies in the struggle against caste." It was imperative, therefore, that Blacks join with whites—especially in the labor movement and the political party system—to jointly pursue "specific and limited practical aims."

By the time Myrdal's *American Dilemma* rolled from the presses, initiatives similar to those he proposed were being vigorously advanced in New York. To the north (Harlem) and the south (Union Square) of his midtown Manhattan eyrie, overlapping constituencies (political, labor, racial, religious) were constructing coalitions intent on accumulating sufficient power to win passage of "practical" legislation. But the Negro leader who had emerged as a prime mover, and some of the "white groups" with which he allied, were not ones the Swede would have chosen if he'd had his druthers.

127

Politics

Adam Clayton Powell Jr. was a hard man to pigeonhole. Some saw him as a principled battler against injustice, others as an arrogant opportunist and irresponsible demagogue. Black journalist and author Roi Ottley, who had worked with Powell and was a shrewd commentator on the political scene, suggested he was all the above, and more. In his 1943 book, *"New World A-Coming": Inside Black America*, Ottley suggested that Powell was "an incredible combination of showman, black parson, and Tammany Hall...at once a salvationist and a politician, an economic messiah and a super-opportunist, an important mass leader and a light-hearted playboy." This was true enough, though it missed Powell's larger political significance. His very flexibility enabled him to forge links between a constantly shifting assortment of players and thus help sustain an alliance that, while unquestionably benefiting Adam Powell, benefited its varied constituencies too. And it was the needs and predilections of those constituencies—ultimately, the city's Black and Jewish working classes—that kept the coalition sailing, despite the occasional tack and turn, in a left-by-liberal direction.

Powell stood at the center of a series of concentric social circles. His core base was situated quite precisely at 138th Street between Lenox and Seventh, in the 8,000-strong congregation of the Abyssinian Baptist Church. No sooner had Powell ascended to its prestigious pulpit in 1937 than he set about fashioning an alliance with other power players in his second circle of concern, the Harlem community itself. In 1938 he had established the Greater New York Coordinating Committee for Employment (GNYCC), an umbrella group embracing activist organizations of varied politics and demographics—including other church leaders, Garveyites, Communists, southern Blacks, and West Indians—who were prepared to work together toward more or less mutual local goals, crucially, winning jobs for African Americans.

Powell was perfectly aware, however, long before Myrdal suggested it, that to make progress in the third circle, encompassing the entire city—much less the fourth and widest circle, embracing the entire country (particularly southern Blacks)—he would have to make common cause with white allies, yet not lose touch with his base. So Powell championed Blackness but opposed Black separatism, calling it "ridiculous," on the ground that no minority could afford to isolate itself. He even challenged Randolph's all-Black March on Washington Movement on this score, though Randolph, a longtime Garvey opponent, was patently no nationalist.

Powell also reached out to whites, quite successfully, his initiatives facilitated, perhaps, by his own appearance. Scion of a genetically complex family, he had virtually white skin, blue eyes, an aquiline nose, and straight almost-blond hair. None of which bothered his parishioners, who laughingly called him their "Great White Hope"; it certainly didn't bother the ladies who tended to swoon in his tall, light, and handsome presence. Powell, however, didn't link up with any and all whites—only those of a congruent political persuasion, one based (though not rigidly) in common class interests.

Powell's conceptual basis for such a linkage was not theoretically rigorous, but compelling enough for his purposes. When he founded his newspaper *The People's Voice* in February 1942, he called it a "working class paper," which was particularly suited to African American readers because, he explained, "we are a working class race." Given that Black Gothamites were overwhelmingly employed as maids and porters and factory workers—higher status/income opportunities being blocked by racist glass ceilings—the appellation was apposite. At the same time, "working class" served as a rough guide for picking allies, pointing toward organizations of left-leaning whites interested in economic and racial justice.

For Powell this included the Communist Party, then enjoying something of a resurgence in post–German-Soviet-pact wartime Gotham in general and Harlem in particular. Powell was certainly not a member. He professed no fascination with (much less allegiance to) Moscow-style models. And though latitudinarian on matters theological, the Baptist preacher had his differences with secular Marxists. Yet Powell was quick to point out that "there is no group in America including the Christian church that practices racial brotherhood one tenth as much as the Communist Party." Whatever its motivation, the CPUSA was the only major party that formally opposed racial segregation, encouraged minority leadership in its own ranks, and devoted considerable resources to the antidiscrimination struggle. No surprise, then, that the pragmatic Powell declared himself "nationally a Democrat, locally a Republican, theoretically a Socialist, but practically a Communist," or that he worked closely with the left wing of the American Labor Party (led in Manhattan by Vito Marcantonio) and with left-wing CIO unions.

There was another bloc of white New Yorkers whose overall interests he believed overlapped those of his Black base: Gotham's Jews, especially since the ascendancy of fascism and the outbreak of war. Powell had been caustic about Jews during the Depression, but his ire had been class-specific, directed against discriminatory merchants and employers. He knew perfectly well that most New York Jews were of working-class background and that both the American Labor Party (the ALP, founded by Jewish garment workers) and the Communist Party drew significantly from their ranks.

From 1938 on, Powell was unwavering in his efforts to forge a Black–Jewish alliance to "smash Hitlerism, both domestic and foreign." Partly this was because in that year his jobs campaign had come to a successful conclusion. In a deal struck with Harlem retail establishments, it was agreed that no white clerical or sales workers would be fired, but as they left, their places would go to Blacks until African Americans held one-third of such positions; in return, Black militants pledged not to picket, boycott, or demonstrate against a store unless charges of discrimination were sustained by arbitration. This settlement diminished anti-Semitic sentiment, so much so that when Bundesführer Fritz Kuhn came to 135th Street with a proposal that Nazis and Blacks band together against the Jews he was shouted down by hecklers.

Over the next few years Powell lashed out repeatedly at anti-Semitism, which he called a "deadly virus," and in one Madison Square Garden rally brought a Jewish crowd to its feet by declaring the US could not fight Nazism abroad while permitting anti-Semites "to spew their hate on the streets of New York." He joined the National Committee to Boycott German Products, urged parishioners to donate money to help Jewish refugees, and backed Zionist calls (especially by the Bergsonites) for a Jewish army and for "the immediate opening of Palestine." In a Madison Square Garden fundraiser, Powell hopped from his seat, pulled a C-note from his pocket, and bellowed, "If a black man will give a hundred dollars for freedom, what will you Jews do?" spurring an immediate surge in contributions. In 1943 he received an award from the American Committee of Jewish Writers, Artists, and Scientists—whose honorary chair was Albert Einstein—for his efforts toward bettering relations between Blacks and Jews.

Drawing on these circles of support, Powell entered the political arena. In 1941 he won his City Council seat by pairing the People's Committee's mostly Black network of more than 200 member organizations with the organizational capabilities of left-wing unions and the ALP, their alliance facilitated by the city's proportional representation system.

Almost immediately after taking office in January 1942, Powell decided to shoot for higher office. The State Legislature was then under tremendous pressure to reapportion US congressional districts. The 1940 census had revealed glaring inequities in the apportionment formulas, dating to 1911, which gave Upstate rural districts of 20,000 the same status as Gotham districts of 350,000. Upstate Republican legislators, understandably, had dragged their heels on rearranging the electoral map, but finally, with Governor Lehman and Congress itself threatening action, they got to work. And in Manhattan, they carved out a district almost coterminous with Harlem, making it all but certain a Black candidate would carry it in the upcoming 1944 election. Lehman signed the reapportionment bill in May 1942. In June, Powell made known his intention of running for Congress.

In 1943 Powell announced he would not seek reelection to the City Council and urged the torch be passed to a Black Communist leader, Benjamin J. Davis Jr. The Georgia-born-and-bred Davis had gone north to school (Amherst College, Harvard Law), then returned south in 1930 to practice in Atlanta. In 1932 he'd been brought in by the Gotham-based International Labor Defense (ILD), legal arm of the Communist Party, to represent Angelo Herndon, a nineteen-year-old Black communist. Herndon, having organized a demonstration by unemployed Black and white workers that succeeded in wresting relief benefits from local authorities, was convicted in 1933 of attempting to incite an insurrection, under a statute descended from antebellum Georgia's efforts at discouraging slave rebellions. Herndon's conviction was overturned in 1937 after a struggle in the courts during which Davis boldly challenged white-only juries, and an ILD campaign in the court of public opinion that made Herndon as much a household name as the Scottsboro boys. Davis, radicalized by the experience, joined the Communist Party himself and, now a marked man for his challenge to the racial and economic order, moved to Harlem. There he worked as a journalist, rising to become editor of the *Daily Worker*. Herndon also relocated to New York, where he would later join Ralph Ellison in editing the *Negro Quarterly*.

Davis's 1943 campaign for the City Council provided an impressive display of the electoral firepower the CPUSA and its ALP and CIO affiliates could muster among both Black and white Manhattanites—the latter's support being crucial as under proportional representation

Billie Holiday with Ben Webster and other musicians in Harlem, 1935. (Granger Historical Picture Archive)

voting was borough-wide. A Negro Freedom Rally in June filled and overflowed Madison Square Garden, at which Powell, Marcantonio, and the Black National Maritime Union official Ferdinand Smith spoke, Paul Robeson sang, and Canada Lee performed a monologue. Uptown venues like the Golden Gate and the Renaissance were similarly crammed during the fall, a testimony to Davis's popularity and to the support he mustered from Black celebrities like writer Richard Wright, boxer Joe Louis, and an armada of jazz musicians, including Count Basie, Cab Calloway, Duke Ellington, Ella Fitzgerald, Lionel Hampton, Coleman Hawkins, Billie Holiday, Lena Horne, Art Tatum, Josh White, and Teddy Wilson—and Hazel Scott, a West Indian–born and New York–raised Café Society singer with whom Powell began an affair and whom he would soon marry. The CP and its affiliates also provided electoral shock troops (with Black women playing a prominent part), including close to a thousand canvassers, and whole brigades of poll watchers (including 100 sailors sent over by the NMU) to ward off vote theft on election day. Davis's victory total of 44,000 votes included 23,000 from white (primarily Jewish working-class) districts, demonstrating whites would vote for Blacks even if red.

Powell's congressional campaign the following year proved something of a Davis rerun, with one major exception. As before, the left turned out its battalions. The ALP gave Powell its nomination; the Greater New York CIO (500,000 strong) endorsed him; and the NMU's Smith convened a meeting of Black trade union leaders to mobilize canvassers and organize events (including another Negro Freedom rally in Madison Square Garden). Powell didn't put all his electoral eggs in one basket, however. He also arranged to get the Democratic Party nomination from Tammany Hall (which, in 1943, had done its anticommunist best to steal the election from Davis).

The Democratic Party had undergone something of a revolution in its internal racial arrangements. The old United Colored Democracy—whose Black leaders, handpicked by white bosses, had had no local territory, no autonomous base—had ruled (profitably) over

Gotham's Black politics until La Guardia arrived in 1933. He starved it of patronage, and it soon went out of business. Harlem Democrats then began taking over the local apparatus, with West Indian businessman Herbert Bruce becoming the first elected Black district leader in 1935. Yet Bruce was no radical, and in 1943 he made it clear that the first-ever Black representative from New York State should not be a "Communist-controlled rabble-rouser" whose policies "may lead to bloodshed between Negroes and whites in this country."

Powell, however, had an up-and-coming Tammany man on *his* side—a Bruce rival named J. Raymond Jones. The St. Thomas–born Jones, who had mastered the machine arts of grass-roots organizing and constituency care, appreciated Powell's proven ability to mobilize the Black masses, even if on an extra-party basis. Hoping to draw the minister's troops into the Democratic camp, he struck up an alliance of convenience. At Powell's suggestion, Jones tried to knock Bruce out of Powell's way by dethroning him as leader. The effort failed, Bruce being still too powerful. But the new Uptown players had impressed the Downtown Tammany bosses, and Jones was able to convince the high command to award Powell the nomination.

Bruce resisted the official designation and decided to contest it in the upcoming (August 1944) Democratic primary. He desperately tried to get A. Philip Randolph to run against Powell, appealing to the former's anticommunist convictions, but Randolph declined, and in the end Bruce was forced to go with Sara Speaks, an unknown Black social worker. (Speaks ran against Powell in the Republican primary as well—the Abyssinian's minister having decided to cover all major party bases.) Her strategy was chiefly to denounce Powell's "inflammatory approach" to politics. In fact, a fiery (even flamboyant) exponent was exactly what Harlemites craved. They didn't want a backstage bargainer in Congress, they wanted someone who could—as Powell promised he would—go toe to toe with Senator Bilbo. Powell won both primaries in August, adding the Democratic and Republican candidacies to his ALP nomination, and loped home unopposed in November. In January 1945 he joined Marcantonio, who had won his own multiparty re-election, determined to help bring civil rights issues to the floor of the US Congress. Indeed, in February 1945, scant weeks after taking office, Powell introduced an Anti–Jim Crow bill that would make it a federal crime for any railroad, bus, or airline to segregate Negro passengers.

For all the real and symbolic significance of Powell's rise to power, more important still was his masterly feat of coalition-building. The network Powell had helped create and energize was itself a subset of a wider matrix of left and liberal New York activists—a reconstructed, post-Pact Popular Front *après la lettre*—most of whom were well known to one another from years of path-crossing in the metropolis. In the last years of the war, a series of ad hoc coalitions would be drawn from this pool of lawyers and politicians, social scientists and consumer advocates, journalists and unionists, communists and Democrats, ALP-ers and liberal Republicans, actors and artists, Black groups and Jewish organizations. The composition of each would vary with the issue tackled and the methods employed, but each would mount a "practical" campaign to topple a particular discriminatory barrier, with the greatest firepower directed against those impeding equal access to housing and jobs in New York.

128

Housing

One flashpoint that attracted a swarm of activists was the April 1943 announcement by Mayor La Guardia and Fred Ecker, head of Metropolitan Life, that Stuyvesant Town would be for whites only—generating a countervailing wave of dismay. And the fact that Commissioner Robert Moses (who had midwifed the deal) and Mayor La Guardia (who had signed off on it) had not only acquiesced in a segregated project but agreed to underwrite it with taxpayer dollars provoked first fury, then action.

The case for demanding revision of the contract Moses had worked out with Ecker was laid out by City Councilman Stanley Isaacs at a May 1943 City Planning Commission (CPC) hearing. Isaacs labeled the proposed complex "a medieval walled city, privately owned, in the heart of New York." Its 13-story ramparts, he argued, were intended to keep at bay not only Blacks but all Lower East Side neighbors, including many who would be evicted from the site to make way for privileged newcomers. Indeed, Ecker's refusal to include a public school, a nursery, a library, a public park, or any other facility to which the surrounding community had right of access, bespoke his intention to preclude transgression by outsiders.

In a first bid at redrafting, Councilman Isaacs teamed up with Councilman Adam Clayton Powell Jr. to introduce a resolution demanding the Met contract be redrawn to include a provision guaranteeing Stuyvesant Town would not discriminate in renting, on either racial or religious grounds. Moses counterattacked by arguing that any such requirement would torpedo the deal. Indeed, Moses warned, given the unwillingness of other insurance companies to get involved at all, even on these terms, it would ring the death knell for private investment in badly needed city housing. Moses won. The City Planning Commission, on May 20, approved the existing arrangement 5–1. Stuyvesant Town had cleared its first hurdle.

The second was a Board of Estimate hearing in June, in anticipation of which a host of critics now entered the fray. The Greater New York Industrial Union Council of the CIO urged the Board to reject a contract that supported what it called, picking up on Isaacs's critique, "a walled city for the privileged." The Citizens Housing Council argued that "if the city countenances a precedent under which discrimination is to be subsidized . . . it will open the door to further incursions on civil rights." Former solicitor general Henry Epstein echoed the point, saying: "Today's Stuyvesant bars Negroes. Tomorrow's will bar Jews. The next day it will bar Catholics." The New York Civil Liberties Union joined the fight against a "race-biased project." *PM* declared its opposition. So, too, did the American Labor Party, which called it a "hasty and ill-considered project." Scores more spoke out against it at a Board of Estimate hearing, including City Council President Newbold Morris, who countered Ecker's argument that nonwhite tenants would drag down property values. "Being 'desirable' doesn't hinge on racial origins."

Moses battled back with an ad hominem blow, asserting that critics seeking to bar discrimination were "obviously looking for a political issue and not for results in the form of actual slum clearance." The Board backed Moses, 11–5.

Now Mayor La Guardia was the last resort. He was bombarded with appeals to veto the deal from the NAACP, the CIO, the ALP, the NMU, the State County and Municipal Workers, various Jewish organizations, and the Communist Party, whose Benjamin Davis presented a petition of protest.

La Guardia was convinced that segregation was the price he had to pay to entice private capital into slum redevelopment. So he compromised his ideals. And he adopted Moses's strategy of sneering off his critics by impugning their motives: "Those who try to use this issue to manufacture a problem," the mayor said, are only trying "to give themselves a cause, an interest and perhaps even a livelihood." Walter White, who had considered La Guardia a friend as well as an ally, felt personally wounded by La Guardia's greenlighting a racially restricted project. Powell, who had never been part of the mayor's inner circle, was simply enraged, and he called for La Guardia's impeachment.

Nor did the coalition give up. In the summer of 1943, the Citizens Housing Council issued a thoroughgoing report on Stuyvesant Town, adding a variety of other critiques—including unacceptable and probably illegal congestion—to the basic charge that the project inscribed divisions and inequalities in the landscape. A coalition of organizations began planning lawsuits.

Moses did not give up either. On August 1, 1943, he published a lengthy counterblast in the *New York Times Sunday Magazine*. The "brickbats, mud, and epithets flung at the Metropolitan by long-haired critics, fanatics and demagogues," Moses fulminated, ignored the realities the corporation faced. Recent history demonstrated clearly that "the infiltration of colored people into many areas previously white, especially in Brooklyn and the Bronx, has caused a drop in values, deterioration of buildings, retirement of responsible owners and mortgage holders, [and] substitution of undesirable landlords without a corresponding decrease in rents." It was unfortunate that "sensible projects must run the gamut of hysterical attacks and insane criticism from perfectionists, day dreamers and fanatics of a dozen breeds." Even worse than the "crackpots" and "irresponsible enthusiasts" who infested the housing and city planning fields were the African American "demagogues," who prefer "to shout for immediate social equality than to work for attainable objectives."

On a tear, Moses widened his attack to include activist Jews. He admitted that, like Blacks, his coreligionists faced discrimination. "Jews are still frozen out of certain business concerns as well as clubs, and there are quarters in which Italians and even Irish are not entirely welcome." Such discrimination, however, was only intensified by "professional agitators who propose to fix everything by passing a law." Moses recalled proudly that at the last State Constitutional Convention, when some who were "intent on attracting religious and racial blocs" put forward an antidiscrimination clause, he, Moses, had staunchly opposed it, saying: "You cannot legislate tolerance," and if you try, you will only "fan the very flames you seek to quench."

That very evening in August, as it turned out, Harlem was engulfed in flames. And while the riot did not lead Moses to reconsider his position—if anything, it affirmed it—La Guardia was not as obdurate. Within days of the outbreak, he sent a stiff (if belated) letter to Metropolitan officials warning he would oppose discrimination in Stuyvesant Town, and he promised as well to fight residential segregation in future such projects. Encouraged by the new climate, Stanley Isaacs asked attorney and housing reformer Charles Abrams (high on Moses's list of "crackpots") to help write an antidiscrimination ordinance. As established law held that the rental of property was a private affair—a market transaction between landlord and tenant in which the state could not intrude—Abrams's draft was directed only against landlords (redevelopment corporations) who received tax exemptions; these were prohibited from denying accommodations on grounds of race, color, creed, or religion. It also required that should such discrimination be discovered after the housing had been built, the tax exemptions were to be terminated forthwith. In February 1944 Stanley Isaacs and Ben Davis (Powell's successor) put Abrams's proposed law into the City Council's hopper.

Moses responded by arguing that the era of public housing was likely coming to an end; that private capital was essential to meet the city's housing needs; and that the Davis–Isaacs bill would scare such capital away. This time, however, the Council dissented and passed the bill (after amending it to apply only to future projects); La Guardia signed it into law in July.

This settled the principle but left Stuyvesant Town free to discriminate, since its contract had been already approved. Abrams decided to fight on by launching a legal challenge to Moses and the Met. Thus began a long slog through the courts that would draw to Abrams's side: Will Maslow of the American Jewish Congress Commission on Law and Social Action; Thurgood Marshall of the NAACP's Legal Defense and Educational Fund; and a cast of supporting characters that included the New York ACLU, the Citizens Housing Council, the City-Wide Committee on Harlem, and the Greater New York Industrial Council of the CIO.

The key point of legal attack—quite apart from the assault on gated communities as bad social policy—was Moses's claim that Stuyvesant Town was a private project. Only "fanatics and demagogues," Moses railed, "refuse to recognize the difference between public and private enterprise." For Abrams, giving the Metropolitan the right to use eminent domain in evicting 10,000 residents, and granting it a partial tax exemption for twenty-five years that added up to $53 million in foregone revenue, clearly made the public a partner in creating Jim Crow housing. And this violated the equal protection clause of the Fourteenth Amendment. If this practice was not struck down, it would open the door to city and state governments ousting minorities and the poor from their homes willy-nilly, to make way for housing the wealthier and whiter in "restricted" private developments.

The courts proved resistant to such arguments, in part because a formidable coalition was vehemently opposed to them—not just the Met and Moses, but Gotham's entire real estate industry (developers, builders, construction unions, brokers) and its financial enablers (bankers, mortgage associations, and the federal government). All believed firmly that racially homogeneous housing was the surest guarantee of profitability, and all worked in perfectly legal ways to achieve it. Bankers routinely denied mortgages on racial or religious grounds. Indeed, the Mortgage Conference of Greater New York, which included most of the city's leading bank and trust companies, created, and kept current, maps of Gotham showing the blocks on which Blacks resided; member banks then refrained from making mortgage loans on properties in such "red-lined" areas, or made them only to Blacks. White would-be home-buyers, moreover, would only be granted mortgages for houses whose property deed included a "restrictive covenant" which obligated the new owners not to sell or rent to African Americans. This had the collateral benefit of helping confine Blacks to overcrowded ghettoes, where their hyper-demand for housing drove up rents far higher than those for comparable properties elsewhere in the city.

As the National Urban League noted in a 1945 analysis, this policy had the full support of the Federal Housing Administration. The FHA Underwriters Manual—which served as a guide for bankers and appraisers throughout the nation—declared that "if a neighborhood is to retain stability, it is necessary that properties shall continue to be occupied by the same social and racial class." High valuations, accordingly, should be given only where zoning or "effective restrictive covenants" exist, as these were the "surest protection against undesirable encroachment."

Aware of what they were up against, the coalition fighting for "open housing" launched a corollary campaign to overturn covenants. In January 1945 Harlem's state assemblyman Hulan Jack introduced a bill to ban racial or religious covenants (which was beaten back), and Charles Abrams and Thurgood Marshall initiated lawsuits (commencing a lengthy series of defeats and appeals).

Arguably the biggest victory chalked up by the liberal/left coalition on the housing front during the war was its winning of rent control in the immediate aftermath of the 1943 riot. Earlier, it had been pushed on a reluctant Office of Price Administration (OPA) by City Councilman Powell, whose People's Committee had collected 100,000 signatures on a petition to have Harlem declared a "war emergency area," hence subject to immediate controls. Lawyers for the Harlem-based Consolidated Tenants League had presented evidence that Harlem landlords were consistently violating the OPA's call for voluntary restraints. Communist Party clubs, left-wing unions, and the American Labor Party had joined the call for rent control by collecting petitions among their followers, establishing "tenant clinics," organizing rent strikes in individual buildings, and pushing it in the electoral arena (ALP candidates Mike Quill, Benjamin Davis, and Peter Cacchione made it an issue in their campaigns).

The riot on August 1 had many roots, but fury at the artificially created housing crunch was one of the deepest. Powell traced the explosion to the "unusual high rents and cost of living forced upon Negroes in Harlem." Almost immediately after the fires died down, the OPA opened a branch office on 135th Street and began monitoring Harlem rents. The Consolidated Tenants League and People's Committee flooded the new office with documented hikes. And La Guardia, sensitive to the combined clout of the ALP, the Harlem community, the CIO unions, and female consumer activists, escalated his pressure on the OPA during September, calling for city-wide controls. The Real Estate Board of New York (REBNY) fought back with equal vigor, claiming rising rents were largely a consequence of high taxes—themselves a function of the mayor's "outrageous" budget—and claimed La Guardia was seeking rent control only to divert attention from his own extravagances. Nonetheless, on September 29, 1943, the OPA announced it was instituting rent control in all five boroughs.

# 129

Jobs

On the job front, the initial goal was to preserve, and if possible extend, the powers of the Fair Employment Practice Committee (FEPC), which A. Philip Randolph had extracted from Roosevelt back in 1941. Under assault by opponents from the moment of its birth, the FEPC was on the verge of being smothered in its cradle when Randolph organized a counterassault. Assembling an interracial and interreligious coalition, whose catchment was much wider than his all-Black March on Washington Movement, he mounted "Save FEPC" rallies around the country. One flyer for a "Monster Mass Meeting" in New York—aimed at "Catholics! Negroes! Jews!"—was emblazoned with the call: "Those Asked to Die for America, Ask to Live in America!"

FDR got the message. In spring 1943 he rescued FEPC from its enemies, gave it more money, and allowed it to build up a professional staff, though their enforcement capabilities remained if not toothless then more on the order of baby teeth. Still, together with the burgeoning demand for labor in the booming war plants, FEPC interventions helped win a steady African American advance, climbing from 3 percent of the labor force in war industries in 1942, toward 7.5 percent in 1944, approaching the Black wedge of the population pie. And as Black workers came to feel the benefits of federal involvement, so did Jews, especially in Gotham, where 43 percent of the complaints filed with the New York FEPC came from Jewish workers.

Having been resuscitated, the FEPC faced a deeper problem: it was slated to expire at war's end. Randolph tackled this issue, too, setting up (in September 1943) a National Council for a Permanent Fair Employment Practices Commission. Not a mass organization, the Council was a more traditional lobbying operation, one that drew on representatives from white as well as Black constituencies. Its roster of civil rights activists, religious leaders, and (non-communist) labor leaders included cadre from the ILGWU, the American Jewish Congress, the American Jewish Committee, the NAACP, and the ACLU, among a growing list of others.

The social composition of this movement for a permanent FEPC did not escape the attention of US Senator Bilbo of Mississippi—bigot incarnate and proud of it—who told his colleagues in that august body in 1945 that "the niggers and the Jews of New York are working hand in hand on this damnable, Communist, poisonous piece of legislation." (A similar assessment of the Roosevelts' political base was embodied in a popular bit of doggerel, supposedly a missive from Franklin to Eleanor, which ran: "You kiss the Niggers / I'll kiss the Jews / And we'll stay in the White House / As long as we choose.") In the end, however, it was the combination of southern racists and northern businessmen that won this round: the FEPC lost half its funding in 1945 and would be dismantled the following year.

The liberal/left coalition, accordingly, shifted its attention to the state level. New York had constructed its own fair-employment apparatus back in 1941, when Governor Lehman had appointed a Committee on Discrimination in Employment, the first in the US. Yet its powers were even weaker than those of its federal counterpart, being limited to persuasion, and its writ ran only till war's end. Hence a constellation of forces coalesced behind a campaign to win formation of a permanent and robust federal FEPC-style agency. The potpourri of players was even broader in that it included communist-affiliated organizations, admixing entities who disagreed on many issues but could come together on this one—among them the City-Wide Committee on Harlem, Negro Labor Victory Committee, Marshall's NAACP-LDEF, the American Labor Party and the new breakaway Liberal Party, the YWCA and a brace of faith-based organizations, and unions of both CIO and AFL persuasions.

The movement even won some Republican support. The great bulk of Upstate legislators (and some Downstate ones sensitive to business interests) were opposed. But liberals in the party entertained hopes of winning back the Black voters who had decamped to the Democrats in 1936, and they, along with politicos who had statewide or national ambitions and had to appeal to minorities, leaned in the opposite direction. The Republicans' national platform contained a civil rights plank stronger than that of the Democrats, and Governor Dewey, his eye on the 1944 presidential nomination, was mindful of this. On the other hand, he was also angling for southern votes. So he temporized by setting up a committee (in June 1944) to study the issue.

The ungainly named New York State Temporary Commission Against Discrimination (TCAD), chaired by Assembly minority leader Irving Ives (Republican of Norwich, in Upstate Chenango County), included legislators and representatives of business, labor, civil rights, and religious organizations. It signaled its inclinations early on by circulating copies of Gunnar Myrdal's *An American Dilemma*, published earlier in the year. And indeed, its report, issued in January 1945 (the election safely over) proposed creation of a five-member State Commission against Discrimination (SCAD), to be appointed by the governor. It would have a strong "educational" (jawboning) component, but also the power to investigate complaints of unlawful discrimination in hiring and promotion, on racial or religious grounds, by any employer, union, or job agency. It could also issue legally enforceable cease-and-desist orders and require the hiring, reinstating, or upgrading of a worker—or some other "affirmative action." Discrimination was made a misdemeanor subject to a $500 fine or up to a year in jail.

Ives now joined with Democratic State Senator Elmer F. Quinn to introduce the TCAD proposal as a bill. Dewey backed it strongly, saying he wanted to put the state "in the forefront of the nation in the handling of this vital issue." Shocked, a range of employer groups—chambers of commerce, boards of trade, manufacturers and merchants and realtors associations—as well as some trade-union brotherhoods mobilized to halt the bill's momentum. Led by Senator Frederic Coudert Jr., the Manhattan Republican who had run the anti-communist investigation of Gotham's public colleges, they persuaded conservative and

Upstate Republicans to demand a showdown hearing in Albany, at which they were determined to roll back the proposed legislation.

On February 20, 1945, hundreds packed the New York State Assembly Chamber in Albany, and opponents delivered a devastating indictment. The proposed law was unnecessary. The scope and severity of discrimination was being overblown. Existing laws were sufficient to deal with whatever existed. It was, in any event, "as impossible to destroy prejudice and discrimination by law," argued lawyer Charles C. Burlingham, as it had been "to control opinion or morals" during Prohibition. The bill, declared the New York State Bar Association, was unconstitutional and would conflict with the "traditional right of the employer to use his own judgment in selection of his employees." It would, said the New York State Chamber of Commerce, give "disgruntled" employees the leverage to "blackmail" employers. It could lead to the "enforced employment of undesirable persons." It could lead to a mass exodus of employers, crippling the state's economy. It could force Jews to hire Nazi butlers. It could provoke race riots and pogroms.

The most inflammatory charge of the day was lobbed by Robert Moses. The New York City Planning Commissioner insisted that the legislation would lead a nervous employer to forestall legal challenges to his hiring practices by choosing his employees in proportion to the division of races and religion in his district. He would be forced, that is, "to establish quotas of his own based upon the anticipated point of view, the practices and the decisions of the new commission." This in turn would mean the "death knell of selection and advancement on the basis of talent."

In invoking the specter of "quotas," Moses was tapping into long-standing Jewish concerns about attempts to limit their admission to colleges and universities. Moses might have been sincerely concerned about unintended consequences of the bill on his coreligionists—though he himself had never been particularly active in Jewish communal life—but he might also have been engaged in fearmongering, or even assaying a canny effort at driving a wedge between Blacks and Jews. Lest anyone miss what he was driving at, Moses got in touch with columnist Westbrook Pegler, who whipped off a nationally syndicated piece claiming that the proposed law would "result in the Hitlerian rule of quotas by which Jews in schools and the professions were restricted in proportion to their number in the entire population."

This collective indictment, for all its ferocity, failed to carry the day, because the bill's proponents had organized a massive and unprecedented show of support. Representatives of more than two hundred groups had braved the winter weather to come forward and testify, and a parade of backers—outnumbering opponents 8 to1—defended Ives–Quinn in the most aggressive terms. La Guardia led off with a sent-in refutation of the arguments of his old sparring partner Moses. The mayor pointed out the obvious fact that the bill not only "does not compel an employer to employ quotas or to employ a less efficient person because of race, creed, color, or religion, but it specifically prohibits discrimination solely on these grounds." Now came a procession of heavyweights—Thurgood Marshall of the NAACP, Stephen S. Wise of the American Jewish Congress, Joseph Proskauer of the American Jewish Committee, Algernon Black of the CWCCH, Stanley Isaacs of the United Neighborhood Houses, Reinhold Niebuhr of the Union for Democratic Action, Charles Evans Hughes Jr. of the Mayor's Unity Committee, Communist Councilman Benjamin Davis, and representatives from the New York State CIO, the State Federation of Labor, Congressman Adam Powell's Peoples Committee, Randolph's Brotherhood of Sleeping Car Porters, the Transport Workers Union, the ILGWU, the National Urban League, the New York State Catholic Welfare Committee, the Methodist Federation for Social Service, and on and on. Algernon

Black's pithy formulation came close to capturing the nub of the collective argument: "A man's right to a job should not have to wait until his neighbors get educated enough to be fair to him." Moreover, now was just the right time, as the nation drove toward conclusion of its mighty war on fascism, to overcome a legacy of discrimination that, in the words of the bill's preamble, "menaces the institutions and foundations of a free democratic state."

Here was a concentration of firepower that legislators could only ignore at their peril. The army of proponents represented an agglomeration of political force that could ruin careers. And when the smoke of battle cleared, and tallies were taken, the grandly titled "Law Against Discrimination" cleared the Assembly by 109–32 and the Senate by 49–6. All the negative votes came from Republicans, but the majority of the party decided it was unwise to vote against the principle of fair employment. Signed by Dewey in March 1945, the Ives–Quinn Law became the first in the nation to explicitly prohibit racial and religious discrimination in private establishments.

Soon the Commission was striking discriminatory language from union rules to job application forms to want-ads—though Sulzberger's *New York Times* took a while before complying with warnings that running ads for house sales or rentals in neighborhoods described as "restricted" was no longer kosher—and rivulets of new faces began appearing in accustomed work sites. Within two years, for example, the percentage of Black women employed in clerical and sales quadrupled—and in places like Alexander's, Macy's, Bloomingdale's, and B. Altman. Within a year of Ives–Quinn's signing, New York Telephone had hired 200 Black switchboard operators (out of only 230 in the entire country). These ordinary working people were the big winners, and though individual triumphs were at times singled out for recognition, perhaps with a story in the Black press, theirs was a collective advance, generally appreciated on a statistical basis. Nonetheless, the ripples spreading out from the law's passage occasionally fostered the arrival of a new face, to a new work site, of such high visibility that the event was plastered all over the front pages.

130

Game Changer

On April 6, 1945, sports reporters Joe Bostic and Nat Low took two Negro league baseball players (one from the Newark Eagles, the other from the New York Cubans) up to the Brooklyn Dodgers' spring training camp at Bear Mountain, New York, about forty miles up the Hudson River just below West Point (preseason train trips to Florida having been precluded for the duration). Arriving unannounced—they had given no prior warning—the party asked to see Dodger president and general manager Branch Rickey. When Rickey arrived, Low explained why they'd come. As Mr. Rickey surely knew, the Ives–Quinn law had been passed only a few weeks before, and though technically it wouldn't take effect until July 1, they wanted to test the law there and then. They were, accordingly, asking that Rickey give the players a tryout.

The mousetrapped manager was furious. Rickey angrily berated the journalists (who had a photographer in tow) for their confrontational approach. Still, he understood that things had changed, that refusing to consider hiring a player on racial grounds—as had long been customary—had suddenly become fraught with serious consequences. Rejected job applicants could submit a formal complaint to the State Committee against Discrimination. Penalties could ensue. The law, Rickey acknowledged, "has teeth in it." So he gave the two players their shot; then passed them up on grounds of talent and age, not color, and dismissed the affair as a mere publicity stunt. It was in fact a momentous development in a decades-long struggle to desegregate the work sites—aka baseball diamonds—of America's national pastime.

The sport had long since settled into a segregated status quo, with Black players relegated to the Negro leagues, despite their often brilliant qualifications for the majors. Major league team owners (in New York, the Dodgers, Giants, and Yankees), and organized baseball's officialdom (since 1920 personified by Commissioner Kenesaw Mountain Landis), blamed white audiences and white players—claiming the former would not come, and the latter would refuse to play, if Blacks were added to the mix. Nor did owners see any apparent economic benefits to integration, especially as they were able to harvest Black patronage by renting their stadiums to homeless Negro League teams (the New York Cubans, the New York Black Yankees), and to African American outfits that barnstormed around the country: African Americans would head for the Polo Grounds in droves if they heard Satchel Paige was pitching.

Pressures to change had emerged in the early 1930s when attacks on baseball's racial arrangements were launched from two quarters. First, the Afro-American press, notably Black sportswriters like the *Pittsburgh Courier*'s Wendell Smith, the *Chicago Defender*'s (and later *Baltimore Afro-American*'s) Sam Lacy, and, from 1942, Joe Bostic of Adam Clayton Powell's *People's Voice*. Second, the communist press, especially the *Daily Worker*'s sports editor Lester Rodney, a Jewish American from Brooklyn (Jews would be particularly prominent in the CPUSA's desegregation drive); when Rodney was in the army, *Worker* writers Bill Mardo and Nat Low took up the torch. These journalists were backed up by the Party's formidable ability to mobilize popular support.

From 1936 on, when the *Daily Worker* initiated a regular sports page, Rodney kept up a steady drumbeat of protest. He and readers wrote letters to owners and officials urging the majors to hire Negro League stars like Paige and Josh Gibson. He dispatched delegations to major league teams demanding tryouts for Black players (Bostic's '45 foray was far from the first). He undermined the owners' denigration of Black players, as when in 1937 he interviewed

A march in support of integrating Major League Baseball. (Science History Images / Alamy Stock Photo and Tamiment Library & Wagner Labor Archives, New York University)

Joe DiMaggio, who told Rodney: "Satchel Paige is the greatest pitcher I ever batted against." Nowhere was the Party's campaign higher powered than in Gotham, partly because of the supportive socio-political climate, partly because the target teams loomed so large in the baseball universe: from 1933 to 1943 a New York nine occupied ten of the available twenty-two World Series slots, and three of those duels (1936, 1937, 1941) were "subway series," entirely intramural affairs. Particularly from 1939 on, campaigners began showing up at New York parks, handing out antidiscrimination pamphlets at games. They also circulated petitions calling for an end to the ban on Blacks, which they sent periodically to Commissioner Landis, who stood staunchly in the stadium door, guarding the color line.

In January 1942, soon after Pearl Harbor, FDR ended fears he might suspend the national pastime, saying it was best for the country to keep the game going. In some ways the war proved a boon to baseball, as rising incomes and diminished spending options, coupled with curtailments on car travel and the accessibility of stadiums to mass transit, led to increased attendance. On the other hand, the selective service ravaged the ranks of players, leaving behind teams stuffed with retirement-age vets, pre–draft age adolescents, athletes of minor-league abilities, or men with 4-F impairments. Yet despite the desperate need for players, organized baseball continued to spurn Negro League athletes. As the war against fascist racism underscored the hypocrisy of all this, pressures accelerated again. Why keep Black stars at bay, Rodney demanded of Landis in 1942, "when we are at war and Negroes and whites are fighting and dying together to end Hitlerism?" In the same year, the Greater New York CIO unions—citing the president on the "importance of ending discrimination to ensure victory"—called on Landis to "end Jim-Crow in the big league baseball now." By mid-July 1942 over a million signatures had landed on the commissioner's desk.

In 1943, the Harlem riot notched up the pressure. Rodney himself was off at war, but his associates Low and Mardo continued the campaign, besieging Branch Rickey, who had arrived in 1942 to pilot the Dodgers, with telephone calls, telegrams, and letters of petition on behalf of Black ball players. Bostic of the *People's Voice* paid special attention to the Bronx Bombers, as in his Christmas 1943 column "No Room at the Yankee Inn."

The Yankees became even more a target a year later when Larry MacPhail, who had been helming the Dodgers before going off to war, returned in January 1945 and bought the Yankees (along with Del Webb and Dan Topping), becoming president as well as co-owner. MacPhail was notoriously opposed to integration, and he condemned "political and social-minded drum beaters" for stirring up the issue. Instead, he proposed strengthening the Negro leagues—which might collapse if Black players were allowed to jump to the white majors, costing the Yankees substantial rental revenues—and perhaps someday, when a few Blacks established their "ability and character," they might be allowed to advance to the big leagues.

Rickey, however, despite his tantrum at Bear Mountain, had already decided that a wave of change was coming and the smart thing to do was ride it. More than most wartime teams, the Dodgers were having trouble fielding talented players and indeed had sunk to seventh place in the 1944 National League season, drawing down on Rickey an avalanche of criticism. However, where MacPhail and others refused to open the door to Black players, Rickey saw them as a source of possible salvation.

Back in the 1920s, when Rickey had been managing the St. Louis Cardinals, he had purchased several minor league outfits and converted them into "farm teams," dedicated to raising crops of talented players that could in due time be harvested by the home team, a strategy that proved brilliantly successful. Eyeing the Negro leagues through this lens, Rickey envisioned them as pools of talented players, who could be gotten cheap and could rebuild the Dodgers, even give them an edge for years to come. Already in 1943, he had consulted the president of the Brooklyn Trust Company, which governed the team through its possession of Ebbets family stock, and gotten approval for a rebuilding plan that might possibly include hiring African American players. The passage of Ives–Quinn, from this perspective, was a plus, as it put the law behind integrationist strategy, which is why on the day Dewey signed the legislation Rickey exulted to his wife, "They can't stop me now!" Still, given the rigid opposition of baseball's ruling regime, he decided to keep his strategy a secret.

In the meantime, pressure from the New York integrationists continued to build. In April 1945, in addition to the Bear Mountain visitation, Congressman Marcantonio introduced a resolution in the House of Representatives that would direct the Secretary of Commerce to investigate the employment policies of professional baseball. Councilman Benjamin Davis with other activists organized a Citizens' Committee to End Jim Crow in Baseball, which set about picketing the city's three baseball stadiums, distributing a flyer with images of two Black men, one a dead soldier, the other a ball player, above the caption: "Good enough to die for his country, but not good enough for organized baseball." On May 1 Davis introduced and the City Council passed a resolution condemning the clubs' racial practices and demanding a formal investigation. He also promised to make the sport's integration a major issue in the coming fall elections.

One week later, on May 7, 1945, Rickey called a press conference and made a surprise announcement. Seemingly aligning himself with MacPhail and others, he denounced the recent agitation for integration as communist-inspired (which was true enough) and not only urged improving the Negro leagues instead but declared the Dodgers were going to sponsor an all-Black team of their own. The Brooklyn "Brown Dodgers," moreover, would be part of a new six-team, all-Black United States League, to be launched in June. Some saw this as a subterfuge to evade Ives–Quinn, others saw it as a chance to create a lucrative tenant (the Brown Dodgers would play in Ebbets Field when the white Dodgers were on the road). In truth it also served a clandestine third function in that it allowed his expanded team of scouts to search out top Black players without creating suspicion that it was on behalf of the Dodgers themselves.

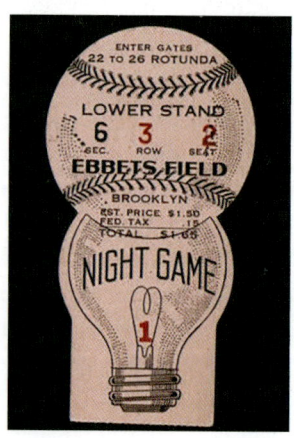

Ticket for a Dodgers night game on June 15, 1938. This was the first-ever night game in Major League Baseball. (Milo Stewart Jr./National Baseball Hall of Fame)

By early summer, most of Rickey's key scouts were sending back enthusiastic reports about Jackie Robinson, who was playing shortstop for the Kansas City Monarchs. Robinson, who had been an outstanding four-sport athlete at UCLA, not only displayed exceptional talent but exceptional character. The previous year, on July 6, 1944, Robinson, then serving as a second lieutenant in the Army in Fort Hood, Texas, had refused to obey an order from a civilian driver of a military bus to "get to the back of the bus where the colored people belong," which led to his being court-martialed for insubordination. But the Army had recently banned segregation on its bases and buses—a fact of which Robinson was aware at the time—and Army judges, ruling he was in his rights, acquitted him. To Rickey, this was proof of spirit—Robinson was "a battler"—which would be as necessary as his baseball skills if the Dodger manager's plan was to succeed.

Then, on August 11, La Guardia announced the creation of a Mayor's Committee on Baseball. It was a subcommittee of the Committee on Unity that he had set up to investigate discrimination after the 1943 riot in Harlem, whose executive director was Dr. Dan Dodson, an NYU sociologist. La Guardia tapped both MacPhail and Rickey for the committee, which was to study the problem, and in the meantime urged all three city teams to comply with the Ives–Quinn Act and start signing Black players. Benjamin Davis's Committee to End Jim Crow in Baseball, underwhelmed by the idea of yet more study and exhortation, announced it would begin mass demonstrations at local stadiums on August 18, though La Guardia, pressed by Rickey and Dodson, prevailed on them to hold off for a spell.

On August 13, Rickey, with two associates, purchased the 50 percent of Dodger stock owned by the Ebbets estate. One partner (and the chief "angel") was John L. Smith, president of the Brooklyn penicillin manufacturer Charles Pfizer & Company; the other was a lawyer for Brooklyn Trust, Walter F. O'Malley.

On August 28, Rickey had Robinson brought to Brooklyn, the latter assuming he was being considered for the Brown Dodgers team. At the meeting in his 215 Montague Street office, Rickey told Robinson he wanted him to play for the Montreal Royals, the Dodgers AAA farm team in the International League, and if all went well, to come the following year to Brooklyn. Rickey conveyed to Robinson the tremendous and likely vicious animosity this would likely engender among fans and other players and said he was counting on Robinson to have guts enough to turn the other cheek (he gave him a copy of a life of Christ and asked him to read the sections on nonresistance). When Robinson agreed, the deal was done, though kept under wraps. Rickey wanted to wait and spring the news the following January, giving him time to sign up more Negro League stars—he was thinking of catcher Roy Campanella and pitcher Don Newcombe—and then announce them as a package.

If Rickey wanted to present his decision as being uncoerced by either communists, Black groups, or government officials, time was rapidly running out. In October, a state delegation investigating violations of Ives–Quinn called on the city's three major club owners and demanded they sign a pledge not to discriminate in future hiring. They all refused—Rickey along with MacPhail and the Giants' Horace Stoneham—with the latter denouncing the officials for trying to force the issue at election time.

Which was exactly what La Guardia was planning to do. His Committee on Baseball was prepared to issue a statement that "there was never a more propitious moment" to integrate Negroes "on the basis of their abilities" than the present, "when we are just concluding a terrible World War to suppress the theory of racial supremacy." Indeed, La Guardia was preparing to make this the theme of his regular Sunday afternoon radio address on October 18. Rickey, hinting at a forthcoming breakthrough, got La Guardia to hold off a week. Then he called Robinson, told him to report to Montreal for a press conference, and on October 23, 1945, the epochal news that a Black man had cracked the color line in professional baseball was flashed to the world.

ON THE TOWN

New Years Eve, 1936, in the Bowery. The original caption reads: "Salami sandwiches and beer were as appreciated here as the caviar and champagne uptown, and if the paper hats were only a dime a hundred they served their purpose." (Bettmann / Contributor / Getty Images)

131

Sex and the City

New York's arts sector had a spectacular war. Local musicians, painters, playwrights, and dancers—spurred by creative encounters with an émigré population that included many of the greatest artists in the world—produced work marked by tremendous vitality and revolutionary innovations. The closely associated entertainment industry had an equally brilliant run from 1940 to 1945. The city's nightclubs, museums, galleries, and theaters were besieged—and galvanized—by a newly flush wartime citizenry and a tidal flux of literally millions of American and Allied soldiers, fliers, sailors, and marines who passed through town, some for a last fling before heading off to combat, others back on R&R leave from the front.

There was a plethora of places such guys might go, from up in the Bronx to down at the Battery, but almost certainly their first choice would have been Times Square.

The crossroads of the world at war were choked with record-breaking crowds. In 1943 it was estimated that the nickel-a-ride subway and bus systems delivered a daily average of nearly a million people to its precincts. And no wonder.

By day it was an endless spectacle. The ambling throngs could take in the giant reproduction of the Statue of Liberty (one-third the height of the original); the 40-foot-tall cash register on the 43rd Street traffic island, which rang up the day's war bond sales; the Camel cigarettes sign belching smoke rings; the glow (until lights-out) from 65 miles of neon; the free noontime stage shows; the jitterbuggers in the streets; the colossal stores (like Bond's, the biggest men's wear emporium on earth); the cheap entertainments (peep shows, shooting galleries, flea circuses, grinders, cheap eateries) and carnivalesque atmosphere (complete with hucksters and hustlers) bequeathed by the Depression decade: all in all a cornucopia of sensations, which could be savored, then reported instantaneously to distant friends and relations via the area's thick concentration of public phones (the 370,000 calls made each day from Times Square made it the busiest communication center in the city).

Nighttime was party time—even in its new dimmed-down incarnation (signmeister Douglas Leigh estimated the Army's edict had subtracted 8,582,200 watts per hour from

Times Square illumination). Uncountable thousands shuffled up and down the "Great Dim Way" and eddied into shadowy side streets, groping their way forward from one under-the-marquee pool of light to the next, some wielding Safe-T-Canes that spread an approved amount of soft red glow in the pedestrian's path. Once inside any of the area's 53 nightclubs and cabarets, 39 legitimate theaters, 44 movie houses (many now air-conditioned), or its vast array of restaurants and bars, they found smoky, friendly, jam-packed joints jumping with people determined to have a good time tonight, for who knew what tomorrow would bring?

One of the major motivating factors that attracted vast numbers of men in uniform to Times Square on almost a 24/7 basis was a pent-up desire to get laid. Which was mighty easy to do in a hot town at a hot time. As playwright Arthur Laurents recalled, "New York in wartime was the sexiest city in the world." Prostitutes worked the square, and its nearby brothels and hotels, and of course the many other parts of town where crowds of soldiers or male war workers clustered, like the strip along Brooklyn's Sands Street, just outside the Navy Yard's main gate.

Not that there weren't impediments to making commercial carnal connections. Remembering the First World War's epidemic of venereal disease (VD), social purity organizations (ardently) and the Armed Services (more ambivalently) had pressured Congress into passing the May Act in July 1941, which forbade sale of sex—or liquor: Prohibition redivivus—within "moral" zones drawn around troop concentrations. Federal officials, shocked and panicked by early reports that prostitution had nevertheless jumped 64 percent between 1941 and 1942, launched a "Blitz on the Brothels," festooning the country with posters warning of syphilis and gonorrhea, and labeling prostitutes de facto enemy agents. In Times Square, hawk-eyed Army MPs (Military Police) and Navy SPs (Shore Patrols) cruised curbsides, scanning for sexual traffickers, though Washington relied mainly on local governments to enforce the May Act edicts. Commissioner Valentine's NYPD made occasional raids on some high-profile bordellos (Polly Adler's place was hit repeatedly); hauled in street-walkers (most of them African Americans, relegated by racism to the pavement trade); and shadowed hotel lobbies day and night to forestall dangerous liaisons. Though selling sex was only a misdemeanor, women suspected of doing so were often committed to reformatories for six-to-eighteen-month stretches.

Antiprostitution warriors also deployed epidemiological weapons. In addition to using the wonder drug penicillin (turned out in huge quantities after 1943 by Pfizer's Marcy Avenue plant in Brooklyn) to treat infected GIs, Health Department officers were authorized to take their recent sexual histories and seize and detain any woman a soldier named as the possible source of his contagion. These "contact tracing" analyses led to a startling finding. Early in the war, public health officials had estimated 80 percent of infections were contracted via commercial intercourse. It turned out that precisely that percentage was in fact due to dallying with "promiscuous teen-age girls." As Gotham's health commissioner, Dr. Ernest Stebbins, put it in a 1943 speech to the Women's City Club, the increase in venereal disease in New York came not from "organized houses of prostitution" but from "unorganized individual vice."

In fact, prostitutes were having a difficult war, for they faced a formidable body of competitors. One soldier, remarking on New Yorkers' generosity to visiting warriors, noted appreciatively that "even if you got money, they don't let you spend it"; something of the sort applied to sex as well. Young women, often in their teens, flocked to Times Square, to bus and train stations, to parks and amusement centers, to any place they could hook up with military personnel. So while police or MPs camped out in hotel lobbies to forestall commercial encounters, the lawns of Central Park were strewn with girls in summer dresses making out with sailors and soldiers, while couples copulated behind its tennis courts. Dimouts after dark made parks especially amorous settings.

The phenomenon generated widespread speculation about its causes. It was generally agreed that these women—known variously as "Khaki-Wackies," "Cuddle Bunnies," "Victory Girls" (as noted earlier), or "Pickups"—were seeking not cash but companionship. Some argued they were motivated by patriotic enthusiasm ("patriotutes" was another descriptor); other analysts insisted they were simply pursuing short-term pleasure. Others still pointed to the wartime shortage of men—"They're Either Too Young or Too Old," as one popular song had it—and suggested desperation was the root of the matter, with the girls aggressively seeking soldiers for a whirlwind romance, hopefully to be capped by marriage.

There was much puzzlement over the fact that girls of "good" (i.e., middle-class) families engaged in the practice, though there shouldn't have been. Since the 1910s, when American courtship venues had begun shifting from parentally supervised church socials and front parlors to harder-to-monitor commercial sites like dance halls and movie theaters, young women—first working-class girls, then their middle-class sisters—had increasingly been having premarital sex, usually, though by no means always, on the assumption that a wedding would soon follow. By the early 1940s, nearly 50 percent of all US women had had premarital intercourse, and prostitution had been substantially marginalized. The wartime spike in noncommercial sex was thus an exaggeration of a long-in-development trend, facilitated by disordered wartime conditions.

Nevertheless the rising levels of "sexual delinquency"—a category applied only to women—seemed shocking, both on moral grounds (preachment not having kept pace with practice), and practical ones: the growing number of sexual encounters was accompanied by a leap in the rates of illegitimate births, of divorce (many hothouse marriages came swiftly unglued), and of venereal disease (in part because these ardent amateurs, unlike the professionals, had not wised up to the value of prophylaxis).

Differences in diagnoses were matched by differences in prescription. Social purity types simply expanded the category of "bad women" beyond play-for-pay prostitutes to include "loose women" who offered themselves free of charge and broadened their suppression efforts accordingly. Posters now appeared depicting a delighted Hitler and Hirohito saying "Ja! We should giff medals to der pickups. They put soldiers out of action better than ve could yet"; or warning that "Over 40% of the Pickups are Diseased." Victory Girls (though not their partners) were frequently arrested, inspected, and convicted of morals violations (rates doubled between 1940 and 1944). The War Department, however, broke ranks with purity crusaders, and abandoned First World War–style efforts at enjoining men as well as women to chastity. Instead, it revived the double standard, assumed male promiscuity to be inevitable, and sought to make sex safer by handing out millions of condoms, ignoring outraged protests from purity activists who wanted another abstinence-only campaign. Despite indignant congressional and clerical demands to know why "our boys" were not "safe" in Times Square, New York remained a paradise of possibility for horny heterosexuals.

Even more alarming to such complainants was the fact that Times Square was also a great place for boys to meet boys. There was a wide range of places where assignations could

Cartoon of a Navy seaman approaching a sex-worker, depicted as "Venereal Carrier." Artwork by C. D. Batchelor for the American Social Hygiene Association. (University of Minnesota Libraries, Social Welfare History Archives)

have been arranged with male prostitutes or, far more likely, with local lads out for a good time. These ranged from Bryant Park (favored by highly flamboyant working-class queens) to the balconies of 42nd Street movie theaters, to the various Horn & Hardart automated restaurants, to the standing room section at the Metropolitan Opera House (where even outlandish attire was acceptable, given the august establishment's invulnerability to raids). There were also gay beaches (Fire Island's Ocean Beach/Cherry Grove featured Duffy's, a pioneering gay hostelry); gay bathhouses (the Mount Morris Baths up in Harlem catered to a gay and interracial crowd); gay galas (Harlem's Fun Makers Social Club still hosted its annual drag ball); and gay bars (like the Dizzy Club—the "low dive" where Auden penned his poem *September 1, 1939*); some of these were run by the mob.

Gays who were gals—on leave, perhaps, from duties in the Women's Army Corps—might also have repaired to Duffy's or headed to more strictly lesbian hangouts in Greenwich Village, such as the Howdy Club (47 West 3rd Street), Club 181 (at 181 Second Avenue), or the Moroccan Village on 8th Street.

Transient GIs might also meet congenial companions at servicemen's hotels, dormitories, and residence clubs, especially the YMCA's immense (1,400-room) Sloane House (at 34th Street and Ninth Avenue), founded in 1930 for members of the armed forces; making new friends there was facilitated by the Sloane's wartime policy—given the tremendous demand for housing—of having enlisted men double up in the same room, even the same bed.

Officers preferred more discreet precincts, those frequented by jacket-and-tie civilians, like the Plaza Hotel's Oak Room, opened in 1907 as a male-only oasis, or the Oval Bar at Times Square's Astor Hotel (Seventh Avenue and 45th Street), known nationally since the 1910s as a gay rendezvous. The Astor was at its zenith during the Second World War. Its management welcomed the hundreds of men who packed in six deep on the Oval's gay side, so long as their self-presentation was sufficiently understated—red tie and matching handkerchief would do the trick—that the straights on the bar's *other* side would remain unaware of their presence. The cigarette girls knew the score, however, and liked to circulate through the gay side, crying "Cigars, cigarettes, hairpins...." Officers were welcome, too, at gay-friendly high-society venues like Tony's Trouville on 52nd Street, where the elite of New York's homosocial world assembled to hear lesbian songstress Madame Spivy perform; and at Spivy's Roof as well, her penthouse nightclub at 139 East 57th, which drew headliners like seasoned café singer Mabel Mercer and fledgling performer Walter Liberace.

Finally, there were the streets themselves. Tennessee Williams loved to cruise Times Square with Donald Windham, making "very abrupt and candid overtures, phrased so bluntly that it's a wonder they didn't slaughter me on the spot." Usually, he reported, the soldiers burst into laughter, then as often as not accepted. Similar encounters transpired along Riverside Drive, in Pershing Square, or on Third Avenue under the El. As Gore Vidal recalled, "Everybody was released by the war; people were doing things they hadn't dreamed of in the villages from whence they came."

Perhaps "everybody" is excessive, with queer bashers and thieves preying on both military and civilian gays. James Baldwin, a teenaged Harlemite Pentecostal preacher, decided in 1941 (at seventeen) to become a writer and moved down to Greenwich Village, where he was regularly beaten up for being a "faggot" (being Black didn't help). And Mayor La Guardia launched another crackdown on homosexuality in public, slapping a 10:00 p.m. curfew on Bryant Park to rid it of "undesirables," though he succeeded only in boosting attendance at grinders along the Deuce, two blocks farther west on 42nd Street.

La Guardia did better at suppressing sexualized entertainment, as when, in 1942, he drove the last nails into burlesque's coffin. Since his closure of Minsky's and most of its counterparts at the behest of clerical critics during his 1937 re-election campaign, the mayor had suffered a few survivors to remain, settling for regulation rather than abolition. In February 1942, Archbishop Spellman and Bishop Manning, the duo that had driven Bertrand Russell out of town, took to the warpath again, though this time attacking on completely opposite grounds. Where in 1937 they had argued burlesque would turn male patrons into violent sex fiends, they now suggested it would turn them into wimps (presumably through overdoses of masturbation), and, by imperiling the virility of servicemen, undermine the war effort. In a March '42 radio address, Spellman likened Broadway producers who promoted the "venal, venomous, diabolical debauching of our boys" to Fifth Columnist saboteurs in factories, and a Catholic Theater Movement, aided by Irish Catholic policemen, harassed playhouses featuring fare they deemed immoral. La Guardia went along with this prudery-is-patriotic line—denouncing the "endless debauches in undressing" as "indecent and obscene"—and Commissioner Moss duly refused to renew expiring licenses of the Gaiety, Eltinge, and Republic theaters.

Burlesque fans could at first take comfort from the fact that hard upon these closures producer Mike Todd opened *Star and Garter*, an elegant burlesque review at the Music Box

Theater (controlled by potentates Lee Shubert and Irving Berlin). The show featured the erudite and witty megastar stripper Gypsy Rose Lee—now also a published author (*The G-String Murders*)—but with tickets at $4.40 (compared to its 35¢ predecessors), her charms were on display only to the affluent. This perhaps explains the failure of Catholic activists to shut it down; indeed, *Star and Garter* completed a run of 605 performances. *Wine, Women, and Song*, a more daring striptease revival at the Shubert Ambassador, came a-cropper later in 1942. Scandalized by "Garbo of the Lowbrows" Margie Hart's willing response to pleas from a "soldier," "sailor," and "marine" planted in the audience that she take off various items whose constituent materials were needed by the War Production Board, Spellman led a denunciatory charge, the show shut down, and its producer was jailed on Rikers Island. Encouraged on the stage front, the Legion of Decency tenaciously went after the film version of Lee's mystery novel—*Lady of Burlesque*, starring Barbara Stanwyck, which opened at the Capitol in 1943. In this case their efforts proved unavailing, but nevertheless they won the larger war: burlesque for the masses, with its combination of sexual display and sexual humor, had been effectively banished from the Gotham nightscape.

The old saw "be careful what you wish for" again proved its perspicacity when, almost immediately, the repressed began to return: hard-core strip shows popped up, like weeds in a new-mown lawn, around the fringes of Times Square (one Zorita, an "exotic snake dancer," was nabbed by police), and a nascent pornography industry stepped up production. Wartime entrants into the new "girlie" magazine sweepstakes, with titles like *Laff* (1939), *See* (1941), *Eyeful* (1943), *Titter* (1943), *Sir* (1944), and *Hit* (1945), were readily available under the counter at Times Square newsstands, bookstores, even penny arcades, despite the best efforts of the Catholic-led National Organization for Decent Literature.

132

Nightclubs

Those seeking to satisfy less carnal urges could have had dinner, taken in a floor show, and gone dancing at any of the hundreds of Gotham's nightclubs, packed with GIs on a farewell spree, suddenly prosperous war workers, and big-spender defense contractors. People went out at night far more than they ever had in the fabled 1920s, seeking respite from worry when war news was bad, or a place to celebrate when tidings turned glad. The *New York Times* in 1945 estimated the combined annual patronage of Gotham's 1,100 nightclubs (presumably defining the term broadly) to have risen to 2,500,000 that year, up from a mere half million in 1939. As this constituted more than a tenth of the US total, New York clearly deserved its reputation as the nation's premier party town; given conditions in competing European capitals, it could claim the world title too.

Novice pleasure-seekers probably headed straight to a Times Square night spot, especially one of the high volume peoples' palaces that had sprung up along Broadway after Repeal. And why not? They offered decent liquor, reasonably priced dinners, plush decor, big bands, top comics, the fanciest floor shows since Ziegfeld, and were distinctly soldier/sailor-friendly (*Time* magazine estimated that patrons in uniform constituted up to 50 percent of the total at the area's establishments). One likely first stop might have been Billy Rose's Diamond Horseshoe at 235 West 46th, just west of Broadway. The nostalgic Gay Nineties–themed venue was famed for its high-kicking chorus lines and barely draped girls, but though the level of public nudity approached that of now banned burlesque, Valentine's cops never raided the Horseshoe: drawing 7,500 customers and clearing $40,000 each week, the club was clearly big business, hence exempt from moralistic pettifoggery. It was even celebrated enough to spawn its own movie: *Billy Rose's Diamond Horseshoe*, starring Betty Grable, which opened at the Roxy in 1945.

More venturesome souls might have opted to stroll two blocks farther north to the Latin Quarter, on the south side of 48th Street between Broadway and 7th Avenue. Modeled on Paris's Moulin Rouge, and run by former vaudeville booker Lou Walters and a staff of 250, the LQ offered chorus girls, two dance orchestras, five to a dozen acts, and grossed over $3 million a year. Pushing on a block farther north would have brought them to the Hurricane

Club, in the Brill Building (the music world's mecca) at 1619 Broadway (between 49th and 50th), where operator David Wolper laid on dancers, singers, magicians, and comedians and featured bands like Duke Ellington's.

Also on offer were stage shows that featured top comics and big bands (though foregoing dinner or dancing) sandwiched between movie screenings at the nearby Roxy, Paramount, Capitol, and Strand Theaters. A ferocious competition for headliners would have almost guaranteed that someone on the order of Jack Benny, Bob Hope, Milton Berle, Danny Kaye, Sophie Tucker, Jimmy Durante, The Andrews Sisters, The Ink Spots, Benny Goodman, or Tommy Dorsey would have been performing.

For all that, some GIs' first choice might well have been the Stage Door Canteen, a night spot dedicated to them and their military colleagues. The American Theatre Wing (ATW)—an organization run by New York's thespian industry—did relief work, sold war bonds, and created touring shows for troops overseas and factory workers at home (like *Lunchtime Follies*, produced by Kurt Weill). The ATW also ran canteens for servicemen in eight cities, with Gotham's located at Times Square in a subterranean space, donated by the Shubert Brothers, that ran below the 44th Street Theater and Sardi's Restaurant. The Canteen, open seven nights a week, was operated by over 1,700 Broadwayite volunteers—actors, designers, directors, staffers—who catered to as many as 4,000 uniformed men per evening, 500 at any given time. Stars and starlets waited on tables, danced with troops, and dispensed coffee at the food counter—served, perhaps, by Katharine Cornell—while Alfred Lunt scraped plates in the kitchen. It, too, had the megawattage to warrant a movie version—1943's *Stage Door Canteen*, replete with scores of cameo appearances.

Had visitors headed east across the Fifth Avenue frontier, their options would have gotten pricier and tonier. East Side clubs offered a svelter kind of entertainment, too: no chorus lines, perhaps a vocalist and a combo; patrons here came primarily to see and be seen by one another. Gowns and black tie still prevailed at East 50's boîtes like El Morocco, aka "Elmo" (154 East 54th), with its zebra-striped banquettes and red stars a-twinkle in an electric blue sky; or Le Coq Rouge (65 East 56th); or Le Ruban Bleu (Blue Ribbon) at 4 East 56th, which Frenchman Herbert Jacoby created to bring a bit of Parisian elegance to New York. In 1943 Jacoby left to open the even more elegant Blue Angel (152 East 55th), featuring walls upholstered in black patent leather, and crème-de-la-crème acts like cabaret singer Bobby Short. Such settings drew debutantes and their pre–draft-age socialite brothers, newly rich defense tycoons, and titled émigrés (assorted duchesses and barons). Officers (and enlisted men) were present too—*Time* estimated that a quarter of East Side habitués were men in uniform—but our mariners would probably have felt more comfortable at the most famous spot of all.

The Stork Club (3 East 53rd) was having a fabulous war. Sherman Billingsley (too old for military service) and his 200 employees presided over consistently packed houses, averaging two thousand guests per weeknight, three thousand on the weekends; in 1943 the Stork grossed $1.25 million. Customers supped, sipped, and danced; there was no floor show beyond that provided by the guests themselves. As one contemporary noted, the "common people" people came to the Stork to look at celebrities, and celebrities came to look in a mirror (of which there were plenty). Why settle for gossip columns when one could scope out the gossippees in the flesh? And the gossipers too: Winchell was still the presiding deity of the Cub Room, and he kept Billingsley's establishment in the headlines. Roaming photogs wielding Speed Graphics provided newspapers and magazines with publicity shots of celebrity attendees—among them Alex Korda and his wife, Merle Oberon, George Burns and Gracie Allen, Bob Hope and Bing Crosby, J. Edgar Hoover and Clyde Tolson, Claudette Colbert,

Leo Durocher, Jim Farley, Robert Benchley, Billy Rose, Monty Woolley, George Balanchine, Ernest Hemingway, Herbert Bayard Swope, William Randolph Hearst Jr., Moss Hart, Fred Astaire, Alfred Hitchcock, Adolphe Menjou, Jimmy Durante, Georgie Jessel, Milton Berle, Sam Goldwyn, Al Smith, Ray Bolger, Gary Cooper, Orson Welles, Edward G. Robinson, Averell Harriman, and the Duke and Duchess of Windsor—whom Winchell snubbed for their Nazi sympathies. Hollywood did its promotional share with *The Stork Club* (1945), featuring Betty Hutton as a hat-check girl belting out "Doctor, Lawyer, Indian Chief."

Officers were prominent—especially those with celebrity credentials like Lieutenant Commander Jack Dempsey, Lieutenant Franklin Roosevelt Jr., Lieutenant Alfred Gwynne Vanderbilt, and Lieutenant John F. Kennedy, who recuperated at the Stork after his *PT-109* got sunk at sea in '43. (Top brass also headed for the equally posh precincts of the 21 Club—located anomalously on *West* 52nd [right latitude, wrong longitude]—as humorist Robert Benchley discovered one rainy night when a uniformed man at 21's door, whom he'd asked to call a cab, drew himself up and said: "Sir, I am an admiral in the United States Navy." "Good," Benchley replied, "call me a boat.")

For all the Stork's glamor, rank-and-file lads would also have been welcome to join the party. Indeed, Billingsley featured their presence and publicized the club's accessibility. A month after Pearl Harbor, Rita Hayworth posed there with boys from the Army, Navy, Coast Guard, and Marines, a photo front-paged by the *Daily Mirror*. On almost any night thereafter, the likes of Joan Blondell, Lana Turner, Peter Lorre, or Greer Garson could be

A Naval officer and his date dance together at the Stage Door Canteen, October 25, 1942. (Bettmann / Contributor / Getty Images)

found buying drinks for servicemen at the bar; at times the club seemed a glitzier version of the Stage Door Canteen across town. Billingsley freely dispensed his own autograph, talked on the phone to soldiers' folks back home, and put out a publication (*Stork Club Talk*) that was air-lifted to the front—initiatives that reaped dividends, ranging from bombers christened *Stork Club* to the little Stork Clubs that sprang up wherever GIs planted the flag. There were limits to his hospitality, however: Sherm made no secret of the fact that Blacks were unwelcome; on one occasion he even refused entry to the Maharaja of Jaipur, remarking: "I don't want none of those colored men in here."

Any who objected to such discrimination could have subwayed down to Barney Josephson's Café Society in Greenwich Village. The *anti*-Stork on Sheridan Square was still catering to mixed-race patrons—Caucasian customers who complained about Paul Robeson's dancing with a white woman were politely shown the door—and it continued to feature stellar Black performers (many pipelined in by John Hammond). Josephson, an admirer of sophisticated European cabaret, might start off an evening with a comic like the politically

The 2nd Avenue Theatre, part of the Yiddish Theater District, or the "Rialto." (Photo by Archive Photos/Stringer/Getty Images)

edgy Zero Mostel or sharp-pointed satirist Imogene Coca; move to a vocalist like Billie Holiday or Lena Horne or Hazel Scott; switch to the syncopated barrelhouse piano pounding of boogie-woogie greats (and Café Society regulars) Meade "Lux" Lewis, Albert Ammons, and old master James P. Johnson; then bring on a jazz combo for dancing, led perhaps by Teddy Wilson or Art Tatum.

Four blocks up Seventh Avenue South one could find the equally sophisticated environs of Max Gordon's Village Vanguard, just below 11th Street. Fifteen steps down from street level awaited a pastiche of performances, and several of the same performers. An evening at the Vanguard offered a mix of social satire, comedy sketches, poetry readings (notably by Yiddish lefties), some jazz, and dinner. The *Revuers* were regulars here, a quintet that included Betty Comden, Adolph Green, and Judith Tuvim (later Judy Holliday, "tuvim" meaning "holiday" in Hebrew); they served up sharp and hilarious skits about Gotham show biz and city life in general.

Gordon also gave a significant boost to the folk-music movement that Alan Lomax and the Almanac Singers, among others, had been fostering for several years now. The Almanacs, tacking closely with the Communist Party, had dropped their "Yanks Are Not Coming" musicology after Hitler invaded Russia—"Well I guess we're not going to be singing any more of them peace songs," Woody Guthrie wrote Pete Seeger—and were having a short burst of popularity. However, while their voices could now be heard on NBC and CBS, the radical balladeers were still living cheaply and communally at the Almanac House's latest

Woody Guthrie playing at McSorley's Old Ale House, 1943. (Woody Guthrie Center)

incarnation on West 10th Street near Sixth Avenue. Gordon, looking around for a new act, consulted Nicholas Ray, a Vanguard regular then bunking at the Almanac. Ray noted that Huddie ("Leadbelly") Ledbetter, a country-blues singer who had been recording songs for the Library of Congress, had just arrived in town. Ray suggested pairing him with Josh White, the Black South Carolinian who had come to Gotham in 1931 and helped introduce city folk to rural folk, blues, and gospel music. By 1941, White had become a recording and radio star, had worked with Ray, Lomax, and Guthrie on the folk music radio series *Back Where I Come From*, and had costarred with Paul Robeson in the short-lived *John Henry* on Broadway. Now Ray produced the duo's engagement at the Village Vanguard. Their opening night, Gordon remembered, had teemed with guitarists like Guthrie, Seeger, Burl Ives, Richard Dyer-Bennett, and Millard Lampel, and it proved as epochal a moment as Seeger's 1940 debut at the first "hootenanny": the two men garnered rave reviews, recording and film dates, and a six-month run of sold-out shows at the Vanguard.

Both proprietors—Josephson and Gordon—proved to be subversive influences on the New York musical scene, infiltrating their Downtown talent Uptown, and ensconcing them in night spots they themselves established. Josephson twinned his club by opening the Café Society Uptown (128 East 58th Street, near Park Avenue) and Gordon opened his second front by partnering with Jacoby in the Blue Angel venture on 55th Street. But if folk and radical cabaret songs got added to the mid-Manhattan mix, they remained marginal, having little impact on the reigning music of the day. It was Big Band swing that provided the soundtrack for the Second World War, and when sailors and soldiers went jiving it would have been to the brassy sounds of Tommy Dorsey, Harry James, or Glenn Miller. Still, at the tail end of 1942, a different kind of musical challenge blew in from Jersey, and this one proved more disruptive to the status quo.

133

The Voice

It's not likely the military had been in attendance at the Paramount on December 31 as virtually every seat in the Times Square theater was filled with teenaged girls. Benny Goodman's band was the featured stage attraction, his six sets a day alternating with screenings of *Star-Spangled Rhythm*, featuring crooner Bing Crosby. The list of accompanying acts included, as an "extra added attraction," a skinny twenty-seven-year-old from Hoboken, who Harry James had discovered in 1939 singing in a roadhouse in Alpine, New Jersey, and who Tommy Dorsey had wooed away from James in 1940; he had gone on to draw considerable attention, being named top male band vocalist by *Billboard* in May 1941. In September 1942 he'd gone out on his own but reaped only modest success. After a foray to Hollywood netted him only a bit part, he'd returned to Jersey and been doing local gigs. He finally landed a date in a major theater, the Newark Mosque, where Paramount's manager, coaxed out by his agent, caught his act and was impressed enough to inquire about his New Year's Eve availability. Replying that he hadn't been able to get a booking anywhere, the singer leapt at the offer of an appearance on Broadway, even bottom billing. And he was as startled as anyone when after the King of Swing's laconic introduction—"And now, Frank Sinatra"—the stage was hit by a deafening tsunami of sound from the huge audience of screaming teens. "What the fuck was that?" exclaimed Benny Goodman, baton frozen in air. *That*, it would soon be apparent, was a major nail in the Big Band coffin.

Sinatra stayed on for eight more weeks at the Paramount, playing to ever larger and more hysterical crowds of moaning, shrieking "bobbysoxers." His career, meanwhile, underwent a meteoric ascent. He was signed by George Washington Hill, American Tobacco Company president, to the coast-to-coast radio show his Lucky Strike brand sponsored—*Your Hit Parade*—the biggest plum in broadcasting for a vocalist. By the time of his first broadcast on February 6, 1943, Sinatra had an RKO movie contract in his pocket as well; in April he was a smash at the Riobamba Room, a sophisticated East Side club; and in June he signed a record deal with Columbia. Over the next year his star climbed ever higher and grew ever brighter, with his ascension capped, in October 1944, when he both wowed the Park

Young Frank Sinatra fans at his performance at the Paramount Theater, October 12, 1944. (Bettmann/Getty Images)

Avenue set in the Waldorf's Wedgwood Room and drew 30,000 mostly twelve-to-sixteen-year-old girls to his return engagement at the Paramount, requiring a massive police presence to cope with the crush of frantic teens, desperate to get inside, the most astonishing demonstration of fandom since Valentino's funeral.

"Sinatramania" it was called, and journalists, sociologists, and psychologists vied in speculating about its causes. The girls (said the socially oriented) were mostly children of the poor, and likely identifying with a kid from Hoboken who'd gotten the breaks. They were also largely children of immigrants, and worshiping Frankie was a way of asserting their Americanism. Sinatramania could also be seen as a generational demarcator, rather like bobby socks. Psychologically inclined analysts suggested the girls were displaying mothering urges triggered by his boyish frame, gaunt face, and a voice "like the plaintive cry of a hungry child." Or perhaps the singer was a stand-in for absent sweethearts; Sinatra himself signed on to this one: "I was the boy on every corner, the boy who'd gone off to war."

Others thought his blue-eyed, curly-locked appeal considerably more sexual in nature, noting the swooning, the moaning in sheer rapture, the waving of doffed panties, and the massive wetting of panties that stayed in place—there was more pee on the seats and carpets, ushers reported, than in the toilets. ("When I hear Frankie sing, I have to let go," said one pubescent.) In this reading the girls were, at least metaphorically, the younger sisters of the Victory Girls who were throwing themselves, not just their underwear, at potential partners.

The exterior of the Paramount Theater for Sinatra's performance, October 12, 1944. (Bettmann/Getty Images)

Sinatra mobbed by adoring fans, ca. early 1940s. (Copyright © Peter Martin)

It was the music, others insisted. As Bing Crosby famously put it: "A talent like Sinatra's comes along once in a lifetime," adding, not entirely in jest: "Why did it have to be my lifetime?" In truth Frank had crafted a style quite different from Bing's, one rooted in his appreciation of the Italian bel canto operatic tradition, and his mastery of such difficult vocal techniques as *appoggiatura* and *portamento*. He also produced a beauty of tone comparable to that of Billie Holiday who, Sinatra said, "I first heard in 52nd Street clubs in the early thirties, [and] who was and still remains the greatest single musical influence on me."

What he was singing was as much an element in Sinatramania as how he sang it. War songs—as would-be Cohan clones and the Office of War Information had discovered—were not on people's wish list. Sentimental, mellow, nostalgic songs were. People wanted "sweet" music, the vocal equivalent of stringed instruments, not the blaring brass of swing—and none more so than teenage girls. They wanted romantic love songs, and Sinatra gave them what they wanted. But this was a two-way transaction. While many saw the girls as bewitched victims—Sinatra as Pied Piper was a popular explanatory trope—they were in fact displaying a very considerable degree of power. It was *they*, after all, who put *him* on the map with their screams. And with their money: they were the ones who bought his records, and jammed his concerts, and fed the jukeboxes, and in doing so they collectively constituted themselves as a formidable new presence in the musical marketplace.

Their purchasing power was itself an artifact of war. As older teenaged girls flocked into defense jobs in factories and shipyards, their younger sisters moved into the retail and wholesale positions they had vacated. By the war's end, four times the number of fourteen-to-fifteen-year-old girls were gainfully employed as had been at its start, reversing a long decline in child labor. And while this was grounds for alarm in some quarters—between 1940 and 1943 citations for violation of the child labor laws jumped 400 percent in New York—for others the girls' spending priorities became matters of urgent attention and immediate action. *Billboard* began polling the musical preferences of high-school students in June 1944, and in September of that year *Seventeen* magazine was launched to cater to the fantasies of, and sell commodities to, young girls; the first issue sold 400,000 copies in six days.

No one was more attentive to this new market than the record industry, and it would be developments in the music biz that gave Sinatra's career a critical boost. On August 1, 1942, James Petrillo's American Federation of Musicians went on strike to address the threat to live music from jukeboxes—rapidly replacing musicians in small restaurants and taverns—and radio, where "disc jockey" shows like Martin Block's *Make Believe Ballroom* on WNEW spun records provided free by the recording industry. Unable to boycott the broadcasters, who could riposte by shifting completely to records, Petrillo targeted the record companies, demanding they pay higher fees into a fund to hire unemployed musicians to put on free public concerts. When they refused, he ordered his 130,000 union members out of the studios (except for sessions to produce V-Discs for the Armed Forces). The companies held firm at first, but their stockpiles dwindled, and by mid-1943 (when Columbia signed Sinatra) they were circumventing the ban by recording crooners and using choral rather than instrumental accompanists. While the big bands were sidelined, Sinatra was in the studio; seven of the nine songs he recorded between June and November 1943 made the hit list, helping pave the way for an era of balladeering that would eclipse the era of Swing.

134

Bop

A second challenge to Swing's preeminence could be found a few blocks north of Times Square, on 52nd Street, between Sixth and Fifth Avenues, where the string of basement jazz clubs (née speakeasies) was still going strong. On many evenings thousands of servicemen and civilians could be found meandering from the Three Deuces to the Onyx to the Downbeat Club, drinks in hand, serially taking in the music.

Some things were changing, though, notably the racial composition of the performers. When Billie Holiday first sang at the Famous Door in 1935 she had not been permitted to mingle with the clientele (among whom on occasion was the young and unknown Sinatra); instead she'd had to sit, between sets, next to the toilets upstairs. As the Depression decade wore on, Black artists like Coleman Hawkins, Mabel Mercer, and Count Basie had begun showing up in greater numbers, and during the war years they became a major presence; Holiday herself returned triumphant from her Downtown sojourn at Café Society and became a roaring Midtown success, resplendent in white gown and gardenia. But when a set of serious young Black men—among them Dizzy Gillespie, Thelonious Monk, and Charlie Parker—began arriving on The Street toward the end of the war, playing an astonishing new music, it seemed they had exploded out of nowhere.

In fact, they'd been up in Harlem, jamming in clubs like Minton's Playhouse at 218 West 118th (between Seventh and St. Nicholas Avenues) and Clark Monroe's Uptown House (198 West 134th Street), places to which Black sidemen repaired after working all evening in all-white venues, seeking an antidote to the boring riffs required of all but featured soloists in the big Swing bands. Stultified by the orchestral rigidity—it was, they said, like working on an assembly line or being in the Army—they headed back up to Harlem (home to most), where they could shed their iridescent green monogrammed uniforms and play till the wee hours, honing their skills all the while.

Increasingly, innovators who'd been working out novel techniques began showing up. Word-of-mouth about exciting developments spread, attracting still other musicians, eager to hear their peers' ideas and perhaps participate in the making of a new music. They came from around town, and around the country, drawn to "the Apple" (their name for Harlem), or the "Big Apple" (their nickname for Gotham, which they'd appropriated from horse-racing aficionados)—as the ultimate proving ground for their profession.

One such newcomer was South Carolinian Dizzy Gillespie. Born in 1917, young Gillespie began teaching himself the trumpet and trombone at thirteen, after hearing a broadcast from Harlem's Savoy Ballroom that featured Roy Eldridge playing trumpet in Teddy Hill's Orchestra. Later he won a music scholarship to a Black industrial school in North Carolina—its band had needed a trumpeter—and learned some musical theory. After graduating he moved in 1935 with his family to Philadelphia, where he committed all of Eldridge's solos to memory and began playing in local bands. In 1937 he moved to New York and haunted the Savoy, trumpet in hand, until Hill chose him to replace the departing Eldridge and took him along on the *Ile de France* with the Hill Orchestra, and the Cotton Club's chorus line, for a two-month tour in England and France.

On returning, while waiting for a union card, Gillespie played gigs here and there, including Communist Party dances in Brooklyn and the Bronx, then rejoined Hill's group, where he soon riled colleagues by breaking away from basic swing rhythm and introducing difficult phrasings. In 1939 he moved to Cab Calloway's orchestra, one of the highest-paying Black bands in the country, where he began composing his own pieces, radically different in beat from the metronomic tempo the band demanded. After an onstage fracas with Calloway in September 1941, involving a small knife, he was summarily fired and back on the street. But word of his talent had gotten around, and Gillespie was snapped up by some of the biggest name bands in the city, those of Hawkins and Ellington, Ella Fitzgerald and Benny Carter.

His real work began when such shows ended at 11:00 p.m.; round about midnight he was on the bandstand up at Minton's, where he jammed until dawn. The house band was

Duke Ellington plays guitar while Cab Calloway plays piano at a private party hosted by Hearst political cartoonist Burris Jenkins, 1939. (Photo by Charles Peterson/Hulton Archive/Getty Images)

organized by drummer Kenny Clarke, who had rebelled against having to thump out four beats per bar and been fired for doing so. Clarke in turn brought in another dissident soul, Thelonious Monk. Born the same year as Dizzy in adjacent North Carolina, Monk had been brought to Gotham in 1922 and raised on West 63rd Street in the Phipps Houses, built early in the century for African American tenants in the then-Black neighborhood of San Juan Hill. Manhattanite Monk, inspired by such masters of New York stride piano as Willie "The Lion" Smith, had gone on to develop an aggressively dissonant keyboard style. A shy and enigmatic man with a linebacker's physique, he nevertheless got on famously with the ebullient Dizzy.

Author Ralph Ellison recalled that he and fellow patrons "thought of Minton's as a sanctuary" where in "music-and-drink lulled suspension of time they could retreat from the wartime tensions of the town." For Gillespie, Clarke, Monk, and others, it was a working laboratory, and often they'd keep at it until after sun-up, and then adjourn for more to Gillespie's apartment four blocks away at 2040 7th Avenue. Scrapping the linear melodies and mechanical rhythms of the commercial music scene, these young musicians resurrected the small ensembles of the 1920s, trading extended improvisational solos in conversational interaction, drawing on African American musical idioms like call and response. They were swapping a steady (and danceable) beat for difficult and purposely complex music; characterized by frenetic intensity, irregular beats, jarring dissonance, and a blistering tempo, it was accessible only to a coterie of extremely virtuosic musicians. Indeed, the inner circle conspired to

From left to right, Thelonious Monk, Howard McGhee, Roy Eldridge, and Teddy Hill outside Minton's Playhouse. (Library of Congress, Prints and Photographs Division. Photograph by William P. Gottlieb)

screen out those Gillespie called "no-talent guys" by playing impossibly difficult riffs, flatted fifths flying, whenever one approached the bandstand. Monk, more baldly, said he wanted to create music that conventional musicians "can't steal because they can't play it." As Gillespie noted, the creativity level reached a "fantastic" pitch, and "guys from all parts of the country and all parts of the world used to converge on New York" to play at Minton's and Monroe's.

One who blew in from Kansas City in 1942 was Charlie Parker. Three years younger than Gillespie, Parker was born in 1920 in Kansas City, Kansas, to working-class parents. He left school at fourteen and picked up the alto sax, inspired by Lester Young. But in the summer of 1936, when Young invited him to sit in with the band, Parker failed to keep pace and was humiliatingly hooted off stage. As a result he hunkered down to a period of "woodshedding" up in the Ozarks, studying and mastering Young's style (as Gillespie had that of Eldridge), then serving a rigorous apprenticeship in the dance halls, bars, grills, and chili houses of Kansas City, a Depression-era jazz mecca; he picked up a heroin habit at the same time. After a crackdown closed local nightclubs, drying up jobs, Parker made his first foray to New York in early 1939, on the heels of Buster Smith, a Kansas City saxophonist mentor. While crashing at Smith's apartment he worked as a dishwasher in Jimmy's Chicken Shack, a Harlem nightclub, where he listened to house pianist Art Tatum playing in the front room. He also worked his first Gotham music gig at a taxi-dancer hall, and studied and jammed with guitarist Biddy Fleet at Monroe's and at Dan Wall's Chili House at Seventh Avenue and 139th/140th Street. Trying to transcend the stereotypical chord voicings then in use—"I kept thinking there's bound to be something else," Parker recalled—he discovered it one night in December 1939 while improvising on the tune "Cherokee."

Parker returned to Kansas City in 1940, his father having died, and began working in the Jay McShann Orchestra, playing "Cherokee" as a solo feature and coming up with arrangements and compositions, some of them recorded by Decca records, that had a powerful impact on musicians around the country. He toured extensively with the group over the next two years, in the process acquiring the nickname "Bird," short for "Yardbird" (southern for chicken). According to McShann, on route to a concert one of the band's cars ran over a chicken and Parker leapt out, took the roadkill to their destination, and had it cooked for dinner. Gillespie was touring then, too, with Cab Calloway, and in 1940, in Kansas City, had a fateful first meeting with Parker at which musical sparks flew. When Parker and the McShann band traveled to New York and debuted at Harlem's Savoy Ballroom, on February 13, 1942, Gillespie was invited to sit in.

Parker began attending the sessions at Monroe's and Minton's with Dizzy and soon decided that only in Gotham could he consummate his musical revolution. As he later noted, "When I came to New York and went to Monroe's, I began to listen to that real advanced New York style." He heard trumpet men "outblowing each other all night long," doing "things I'd never heard," and it was this experience "that caused me to quit McShann and stay in New York."

Gotham also put him in proximity to avant-garde modernists like Béla Bartók and Igor Stravinsky. Bartók had arrived in 1940, fleeing Hungarian fascism, and would produce a final set of masterpieces in New York; he was living on 57th Street, a block from Carnegie Hall, when he died of leukemia in 1945. Parker never met Bartók, though they overlapped in wartime Gotham, but he listened carefully to the music, as he similarly absorbed the work of Stravinsky, who had settled on the West Coast but was in and out of town during the Second World War, guest-conducting programs of his modernist oeuvre.

Still, the biggest influence on Dizzy was Bird, and vice versa; appropriately enough the phrase "he was the other half of my heartbeat" has been variously attributed to one or the other of the duo. It was in 1943, when both joined the Earl Hines orchestra and toured Army bases across the country, and in 1944 when both worked in Billy Eckstine's band, that they really began to swap and develop ideas. And they in turn were part of a larger group of mavericks that was rapidly coalescing into an artistic community with a distinct identity.

The jazzmen adopted a new style of personal presentation as well. Serious professionals, they slipped into tailored suits, sported shades and berets, adopted a cool insider bearing and an arcane jive vocabulary. With this hipster identity they drew a line between themselves and the world of squares—just as their music drew a line between Swing and what they called "modern jazz"—and in this they paralleled the assertive anti-assimilationism of African American youths on the streets around them, also expressed in language and dress. Ironically, hip Harlem talk—helpfully translated by Cab Calloway in his *Hepster's Dictionary* (several editions of which appeared during the war)—was quickly copied by young with-it whites and would become the style of New York's avant-garde.

Drugs were part of this new cultural style, too. Not heroin so much, despite Parker's case, though it was beginning to overtake opium in popularity because the Japanese invasion of China had cut off supplies; thus Billie Holiday, an opium user, switched to heroin. But reefer remained the drug of choice. Jazz musicians glamorized its usage in songs like "Sweet Marijuana Brown," "Reefer Song," and "That Funny Reefer Man," and weed was smoked so freely on 52nd Street that one laid-back cop asked a club owner to keep the marijuana smokers indoors because his horses were getting stoned.

The new cohort and their music remained virtually unknown to the wider public during the incubation period Uptown, their invisibility and inaudibility enhanced by Petrillo's 1942–44 job action, which kept them off records and radio. When they finally took the D (and F) train to 52nd Street, they arrived fully formed, stunning civilians and servicemen auditors alike. One of their first downtown forays came in November 1943, when a small combo led by Gillespie and bassist Oscar Pettiford played the Onyx Club. In the spring Dizzy and drummer Max Roach moved across the Street to the Yacht Club, formerly the Famous Door, and then on to the Downbeat. Though responses were decidedly mixed, the new guys were the talk of the block, and their sessions drew listeners. Club owners decided the unique sound—now termed "be-bop" (after the nonsense syllables found in scat lyrics)—was a marketable commodity, especially as small combos were cheaper than big bands. In March 1945 Parker joined Gillespie and three others in an engagement at the Three Deuces, and on June 22, 1945, the quintet performed in Town Hall, a concert emceed by radio host Symphony Sid Torin.

The Town Hall program—which included "Bebop," "Salt Peanuts," "Groovin' High," "52nd Street Theme," and "A Night in Tunisia" (a reference to the Allied invasion of North Africa)—was recorded by parties unknown on acetate disks that only surfaced sixty years later. Other records had also appeared at the time, thanks in part to the strike that had left them under a cone of silence. In September 1943 Decca records broke ranks with the other majors and settled with Petrillo's union; Columbia and RCA Victor hung tough for another fourteen months, until November 1944. During this period, a host of small independent companies, recently or just now formed, made their own deals with the American Federation of Musicians, then raced to horn in on the holdouts' markets, staking out niche sectors, of which Bebop was an appealing example. The labels included Milt Gabler's Commodore (founded in 1938, and being of a Popular Front inclination, it had recorded Billie Holiday's "Strange Fruit"); Blue Note (set up in 1939 by Alfred Lion, a refugee from Nazi Germany);

OUT OF THE WORLD (ADJ)—perfect rendition. Ex.—"That sax chorus was out of the world".
OW—an exclamation with varied meaning. When a beautiful chick passes by, it's "Ow!"; and when someone pulls an awful pun, it also is "Ow!"

P

PAD (N)—bed.
PECKING (N)—a dance introduced at the Cotton Club in 1937.
PEOLA (N)—light person, almost white.
PIGEON (N)—a young girl.
POPS (N)—salutation for all males (see gate and Jack).
POUNDERS (N)—policemen.

Q

QUEEN (N)—a beautiful girl.

R

RANK (V)—to lower.
READY (ADJ)—100 per cent in every way. Ex.—"That fried chicken was ready".
RIDE (V)—to swing, to keep perfect tempo in playing or singing.
RIFF (N)—hot lick, musical phrase.
RIGHTEOUS (ADJ)—splendid, okay. Ex.—"That was a righteous queen I dug you with last black".
ROCK ME (V)—send me, kill me, move me with rhythm.
RUFF (N)—quarter, twenty five cents.
RUG CUTTER (N)—a very good dancer, an active jitterbug.

S

SAD (ADJ)—very bad. Ex.—"That was the saddest meal I ever collared".
SADDER THAN A MAP (ADJ)—terrible. Ex.—"that man is sadder than a map."
SALTY (ADJ)—angry, ill-tempered.
SAM GOT YOU (ADJ)—drafted into the army.
SEND (V)—to arouse the emotions (joyful). Ex.—"That sends me!"
SET OF SEVEN BRIGHTS (N)—one week.
SHARP (ADJ)—neat, smart, tricky. Ex.—"That hat is sharp as a tack".
SIGNIFYING (V)—to declare yourself, to brag, to boast.
SKIN (N)—drums.
SKIN-BEATER (N)—drummer (see hide-beater).
SKY PIECE (N)—hat.
SLAVE (V)—to work, whether arduous labor or not.
SLIDE YOUR JIB (V)—to talk freely.
SNATCHER (N)—detective.
SO HELP ME—it's the truth, that's fact.
SOLID (ADJ)—great, swell, okay.
SOUNDED OFF (V)—began program or conversation.
SPOUTIN' (V)—talking too much.
SQUARE (N)—an un-hep person (see icky and jeff).
STACHE (V)—to file, to hide away, to secrete.
STAND ONE UP (V)—play one cheap, to assume one is a cut-rate.

Three covers and an interior of Cab Calloway's *"Hepster's Dictionary."* (Seller images; Indiana State Library)

Savoy Records (which entered the lists in 1942, in Newark); and Apollo Records. Apollo, operating out of the Rainbow Music Shop in Harlem, near the Apollo Theater, was launched in February 1944 by a pair of New Jersey jukebox operators named Bess and Ike Berman, whose uncle owned a record-pressing plant, a handy connection given that as we've seen recording shellac was rationed during the war. And it was Apollo that on February 16, 1944, recorded what was arguably the first Bebop record, with Gillespie and a crew from Coleman Hawkins Orchestra doing "Bu-Dee-Daht" and Dizzy's "Woody'n You."

Center label for a 78 of Billie Holiday's "Strange Fruit," published by Commodore Records. (PD-US-no notice)

The sudden visibility of Black beboppers on 52nd Street raised hackles on some white necks. The newcomers were not there as subordinate adjuncts to white bands, they were running their own groups, indeed had white apprentices. Black businessmen arrived, too, notably Clark Monroe, who came down from Harlem to open the Spotlight at #56 in December 1944, and advertised in the city's African American press, attracting still more Blacks to the audiences, including bold young hipsters. Most rattling of all was the growing amount of socializing in the clubs between Black men and white women. Southern white military men in the audience set out to forcibly reimpose white supremacist etiquette, touching off a number of violent altercations. On one occasion Gillespie and Pettiford were standing at Sixth Avenue near the 50th Street subway entrance talking to Madame Bricktop, a red-haired, light-skinned, African American singer, when "three cracker sailors" (Gillespie recalled) came up and demanded to know: "What you niggers doin' talkin' to this white woman!" A fight broke out. Other sailors jumped in and joined the pounding. Dizzy ran down into the subway with ten seamen in hot pursuit, then edged out onto the catwalk that allowed entry to only one at a time and held them off with his horn until the SPs came and carted them away.

Many listeners were distressed by the new music itself. The popular press attacked it as "low," "dirty," and "degenerate." And the academic establishment—even those who defended modernist music of a classical stripe—accused Bebop of inaccessibility and avant-garde posturing. Support came only from a tiny handful of critic-advocates, most notably Leonard Feather, an Anglo-Jewish composer and music producer, coaxed across the Atlantic in 1935 by John Hammond, the tribune of Swing. However, Hammond balked at Bebop, and it was left to Feather to hail it in the pages of *Esquire* and *Metronome*, arguing in one 1945 article that "there is a revolution taking place in jazz circles."

This was even truer than Feather realized. In the next year or so, the world of Swing would abruptly collapse. Weakened by the strike, the rise of vocalists, and the shift in taste to sweet tunes or hard bop that made the big bands seem suddenly old-fashioned, one after another bit the dust, including those of Tommy Dorsey, Harry James, Woody Herman, Les Brown, and Jack Teagarden; Black bands like those of Duke Ellington, Lionel Hampton, and Count Basie proved more durable.

Fifty-second Street did not long outlast Swing as a musical mecca. For all its prominence as a crucible of jazz, The Street had always purveyed other forms of entertainment, notably liquor and sex, and when the musical component sagged toward the very end of the war, the others expanded to replace it. In particular, the block witnessed a springtime for strippers, those whom reformers had believed they'd banished forever. Already in February 1943 police had raided the Famous Door and arrested Zorita, the exotic snake dancer, as part of a crackdown against female "performers" mingling with servicemen. But the publicity simply lured more of those GIs who preferred action to music, and profit-maximizing club owners adjusted their offerings accordingly. By 1945 some were calling the block "Stripty-Second Street," and prostitution and heroin peddling were growing apace as well.

Before The Street succumbed to sleaze, however, Bop musicians had taken wing and come to earth again, less than two blocks farther west, at the point where 52nd Street ambled into Times Square country. Here they came to roost in a new establishment, at 1678 Broadway, named, appropriately enough, Birdland, and it would be in this new home that Bop would bloom into a national and international phenomenon.

Remarkably—even in a city famed for striking juxtapositions—Birdland would sit just one block away from another musical temple, the Palladium, into which would flow yet another set of world-class innovators, those who had been busy during the war years inventing Latin Jazz. Like the boppers, this group of artists contained immigrants—not from the South and Midwest but from the Caribbean and South America (chiefly Cuba and Puerto Rico, Argentina and Brazil). It also included people already on the scene in Harlem—albeit East (Spanish) Harlem rather than West (Black) Harlem—and a budding offshoot in the Bronx. These Latino newcomers and old-timers—in creative interaction with one another—collectively fashioned a third musicological movement that, along with crooners and boppers, evolved out of Swing and hastened its departure.

135

Rumbamania

During the Depression decade, Puerto Ricans escaping hardship and upheaval continued to leave their island for New York, though not in torrential numbers, Gotham having its own problems; their demographic presence swelled gently from 44,908 in 1930 to 61,462 by 1940. As in the 1920s, settlement centered predominantly in East Harlem, just south of Italian territory, fanning out from the northeast corner of Central Park. By 1935 they so noticeably outnumbered remaining Jewish residents that the neighborhood was becoming known as Spanish Harlem (and was so designated in 1939's *WPA Guide to New York City*).

The Puerto Rican community's cultural footprint grew as well. In particular, a musical infrastructure flowered out of Almacenes Hernández, the first Puerto Rican–owned record store. Victoria Hernández had planted it back in 1927 at 1735 Madison, where her brother Rafael Hernández had composed *Lamento Borincano*. Among the newer venues was the Park Plaza, a catering hall for wealthy Jewish professionals on 110th Street at Fifth Avenue, whose proprietress, Anna Hersh, began renting it out to the newcomers for Saturday night dances, along with a downstairs hall known as the Park Palace. In 1934 Marcial Flores, a wealthy *boletero* (numbers runner), opened El Club Cubanacán on 114th and Lenox (WMCA broadcast the music live from its premises). A few months later Flores rented the Mount Morris Theater, at 116th and Fifth, and renamed it El Campoamor (later El Teatro Hispano). In the meantime, the Photoplay Theater at 110th and Fifth had morphed in 1931 into El Teatro San José, which intermixed Spanish-language movies with live stage shows. Some of these survived into the war years, and Hispanics enamored of Latin dancing might well have made the Park Plaza their port of call.

Also in the early 1940s, Latin Manhattan began expanding into the East Bronx along the IRT lines that branched north and east from Spanish Harlem. Victoria Hernández was once again a pioneer—opening a new record shop, Casa Hernández, at 786 Prospect Avenue, one block east of Westchester Avenue. By 1945 the overflow community had become dense enough to support new halls like the Tropicana Ballroom on Westchester Avenue and the Hunts Point Palace on Southern Boulevard and 163rd Street, both of which opened that year.

Dances and performances at such venues—along with a need for entertainers at rent parties—created employment for part-time musicians, most of whom continued to rely mainly on day jobs as factory hands, house painters, porters, and dishwashers. Community demand also underwrote modest record sales for neighborhood trios and quartets, who could stop by Tatay's Spanish Music Center, just around the corner from the Park Plaza, and have its owner, Gabriel Oller, a Puerto Rican sound engineer, make them audition records to take to a major label.

A good percentage of these musicians were Cubans. Even though Gotham's Puerto Ricans now far outnumbered its Cubans, *Borinqueños* were drawn even more to Cuban *sones* and *danzónes* than to their native *plenas* and *bombas*. Not atypically, when Marcial Flores wanted a house band for his Cubanacán he hired a group led by the elegant Afro-Cuban flautist Alberto Socarrás.

Cuban music made Depression-era inroads Downtown as well, beginning with the spectacular opening of Don Azpiazú and his Havana Casino Orchestra at the RKO Palace (at Broadway and 47th) on April 26, 1930. Azpiazú's performance of "*El Manisero* (The Peanut Vendor)"—billed as a "rumba" though in fact a type of Afro-Cuban *son* called a *pregón*, a Havana street vendor song—was presented with vaudevillian flair, with the singer throwing bags of peanuts to the audience and a team of dancers demonstrating the steps. Rooted in Afro-Cuban culture, the music featured an array of authentic island instruments—maracas, claves, guiros, bongos, and timbales—and though RCA Victor recorded a 78-rpm rendition on May 13, they sat on it for seven months, thinking it too weird for American ears. When released, however, it became an instant sensation, its sheet music topping the national charts. "The Peanut Vendor"'s use as background music in the 1931 Warner Brothers film *Cuban Love Song* led to a coast-to-coast tour for Azpiazú's group. In 1932 George Gershwin, antennae a-quiver, wrote an orchestral piece called *Rumba* (later retitled *Cuban Overture*) in which he deployed the novel percussion instruments. Tin Pan Alleyites began churning out knockoffs. Music publisher Edward Marks, who had bought the rights to "El Manisero," soon had hundreds of Latin songs in his catalog. The developing craze was boosted along by the 1935 movie *Rumba*, staring George Raft and Carole Lombard.

As rumba's star rose, tango's declined, though its downward trajectory was halted momentarily by the arrival in New York in 1933 of the French-born Argentinian Carlos Gardel. Already a major cultural figure in the Spanish-speaking world, Gardel was in town to fulfill a broadcasting contract with NBC when Paramount offered to set him up with his own production company, then distribute his films. In 1934 he shot his first two, at the Astoria studios, including *El tango en Broadway*, whose set piece—"*Rubias de New York*"—had Gardel, surrounded by four of the titular blondes, singing at a window overlooking the Flatiron Building. He made two more movies in early 1935, one of which included the magnificent tango "*Volver* (Return)." When these films were acclaimed ecstatically in Latino New York (people lined up at El Campoamor to see them) and throughout Latin America, Paramount decided to make him a crossover star. Gardel proved unable to master English, returned to Argentina, and died shortly afterward in a plane crash, mourned by millions; and US tangomania went back to subsiding.

The man who best bridged the tango and rumba manias was the Catalonian Xavier Cugat. Born in Spain in 1900, his family brought him to Cuba when he was five. A child prodigy, he trained and performed as a classical violinist, and to earn money he accompanied silent films. According to Cugat, he was discovered by Enrico Caruso, at whose urging he moved from Havana to New York in 1921. Caruso died shortly thereafter, Cugat's Carnegie

Hall debut did not go well, and he eventually abandoned his plans for a concert career, switching to popular music. Shifting to Los Angeles, he met Rudolph Valentino, who encouraged him to form a tango orchestra. With the craze still at flood tide in the mid-1920s, Xavier Cugat and His Gigolos did well in clubs, then moved adroitly into talkies at decade's end and segued into feature films. Invited to play at the Waldorf Astoria's Starlight Roof in 1933, he moved back to Gotham and soon settled in as leader of the hotel's house band.

Like the Castles before him, Cugat served as a cultural transformer, stepping down the voltage of imported music for his domestic audience. Convinced that his society listeners couldn't handle Cuba's "intricate and intoxicating rhythms," he played them "at a much slower tempo until they could be comprehended and appreciated" and only "gradually insinuated" the more exotic instruments. "I gave the Americans a Latin music that had nothing authentic about it," he wrote, and later "began to change the music and play more legitimately." He also knew that Americans "were crazy for a personality" and so became one, crafting a vivid stage presence while fronting his band with attractive women, beginning with Margarita Carmen Cansino, the Brooklyn-born daughter of a Spanish flamenco dancer and an English-Irish-American Ziegfeld girl, soon to be better known, after a painful de-Latinization process dictated by Columbia Pictures, as Rita Hayworth.

Another part of Cugat's palatability was that he came across as "white," and so did his band. While he did draw upon New York's community of Hispanic musicians, employing many of the same people who played the Uptown clubs, he at first—again catering to Midtown racial sensibilities—hired only light-skinned artists, not Afro-Cubans like Socarrás, no matter how talented.

Demand for the real McCoy built steadily through the 1930s, primarily because of an immense increase in south-of-the-border tourism. In the Prohibition-era 1920s, pleasure cruises to wide-open Havana and its new American-oriented resorts had drawn flocks of Café Society celebrities and Wall Street tycoons. During the Depression, they were joined by a substantial stratum of the middle class which, priced out of European grand tours, opted for less expensive excursions to Havana, Mexico City, Rio de Janeiro, and Buenos Aires. The number of cruise passengers climbed from 2,567 in 1929, to 10,217 in 1931, to 30,222 in 1933, to 64,103 in 1937. Many came back with their musical tastes sharpened and were delighted when new clubs popped up in Gotham that catered to their more sophisticated desires. In 1938, the La Conga Club opened its doors at 209 West 51st, and the Havana-Madrid debuted at 1650 Broadway, right around the corner; both brought up musicians from Cuba and points south, regardless of color.

The outbreak of war in 1939 effectively shut down remaining European tourism; at the same moment air travel brought more of Latin America into practicable reach from New York. In 1940 Pan Am announced its flying boats could now make Rio and Buenos Aires in three days. Air visits to Havana expanded dramatically, finessing U-boat-infested waters. And by 1941, an average of 3,000 vacation-bound passengers were winging their way south each week.

Shifting tastes summoned forth another clutch of lavish Latin nightclubs—inspired, perhaps, by the spectacular Tropicana Club that opened in Havana in December 1939. The Brazilian-themed Copacabana (10 East 60th Street), launched in October 1940, featured gorgeous Samba Sirens ("the best girl show in town," said Winchell) and white ceramic palm trees with velveteen leaves, which became a favored backdrop for fashion shoots promoting the new Latin sartorial vogue. ("The gaucho shirt," the *Times* opined, "is now considered eligible for parties.") In 1941 the Club Cuba set up shop at 125 East 54th. And in December

1942 Ecuador took the spotlight with the Riobamba Room, named after a small town in that Andean nation; as war shortages required using fabrics for decor, the Riobamba's palm trees were less substantial than the Copa's, being made of white satin and lace.

War was also accompanied by Roosevelt administration efforts, as part of its Good Neighbor policy, to foster a deeper appreciation of Latin American culture—initiatives carried out most assiduously by Coordinator of Inter-American Affairs Nelson Rockefeller. These included events like Inter-American Music Day in May 1941 and a Latin American Fair in January 1942. Hosted by Macy's, the fair offered its over 50,000 visitors "authentic" South American musics, which in turn were broadcast to the hemisphere by CBS's new Network of the Americas. Gimbels, as was its wont, followed suit with an "Ancient Arts and Crafts of South America" exhibition, featuring "native Cuzco Indian" music and dancing.

All in all, the *Times* reported, New Yorkers "have completely gone daffy about Latin-American music, dances and entertainment." There were now "more and better rumba clubs in Manhattan than there are in Havana," along with the "finest Brazilian samba singers, the most celebrated Mexican and Argentinian love crooners, [and] the nimblest Cuban rumbaists." Even clubs and hotel ballrooms that lacked a Latin focus began hiring Cuban-style relief bands to alternate with their swing orchestras.

Swept in on this tide were musics and performers who would further erode the color line. The work of Miguelito Valdés—vocalist, composer, instrumentalist, and bandleader—had a particularly large impact on the Gotham music scene, albeit at first from a distance. By 1937, when he established the Orquesta Casino de la Playa, Valdés, a Cuban *mestizo* (Spanish father, Mayan mother) had absorbed a wide range of African traditions from the Black santeros in his Cuyo Hueso district in Havana, and from the blind Afro-Cuban composer and tres player Arsenio Rodríguez. Nineteen thirty-seven was also the year that *congas*—groups that danced (often drunkenly) in the streets on Carnival days—were legalized again in Cuba, having been forbidden by the Gerardo Machado dictatorship, as was public usage of the Afro-Cuban conga drum (both dance and drum originally imported in slave ships from the Congo). From 1937 to 1939, Valdés and the Orquesta waxed about ninety 78 RPM records for RCA Victor, one of which—"*Babalú*"—was recorded in 1939 and promptly took Gotham by storm.

The person who initially capitalized on the new Afro-Cuban rhythm, however, was not Miguelito Valdés in Cuba, but Desi Arnaz in New York. Born in 1917, Desiderio Alberto Arnaz y de Acha III was the scion of a white and wealthy Cuban family; his father was mayor of Santiago de Cuba under Machado (in which capacity he oversaw suppression of conga dancing). When Fulgencio Batista overthrew Machado in 1933, he jailed the elder Arnaz and confiscated the family's money and property, forcing his wife and sixteen-year-old son to flee to Miami. Desi, who barely spoke English, struggled through high school and did odd jobs to help pay the rent. In 1937 he got a job singing at a Miami Beach hotel, where Cugat spotted him and brought him to the Waldorf as a vocalist. By 1939 Arnaz had formed his own group and was headlining at La Conga, performing "*Babalú*" incessantly, and demonstrating the Conga Line—drawing on the street dances his father had banned—which soon had droves of New Yorkers lining up behind a drummer and snaking around the floor with a one-two-three-kick rhythm, bellowing "Hi yi, Hi yi!"

Unlike Cugat, Arnaz knew little about the music he was popularizing, but he was young, charming, handsome—he looked great in a ruffled rumba shirt—and white. He was soon noticed by Broadway producer George Abbot, who gave him a lead role in the 1939 Rodgers and Hart revue *Too Many Girls*, as a conga-playing South American exchange student at a

US college. The show wrote Arnaz's conga dance into the first act (along with lyrics like "Ev'ry Latin has a temper / Latins have no brain"). It—and Arnaz—were both hits. RKO bought the film rights and invited him to do the movie version, pairing him with RKO contract actress Lucille Ball; in November 1940, when they again crossed paths while performing in New York, they tied the connubial knot.

By this time, Valdés, tired of working for peanuts while Arnaz was on a roll, had taken Cugat up on his offer of a job in New York and arrived in May 1940. By now Gotham was ready for the real thing, and Miguelito promptly rocketed to stardom. With Cugat's orchestra, he rerecorded many of the hits he had sung in Havana (including *Babalú*); performed at the Paramount and the Waldorf's Starlight Roof and on the Camel-sponsored radio show *Rumba Revue*; snared the cover of *Billboard*; joined Fred Astaire and Rita Hayworth in the 1942 movie *You Were Never Lovelier*; and left Cugat to become the top act at nightspots like La Conga and Havana-Madrid.

Another newcomer, the exuberant samba singer and dancer Carmen Miranda, had already achieved fame as a film, radio, and recording star in Brazil before arriving in New York in 1939 to appear in the Abbott and Costello revue *On the Streets of Paris*. Her showstopping song and dance number, "South American Way," performed in a fruited headdress, made her an instant star in Gotham. Saks Fifth Avenue came out with line of Miranda-inspired turbans and jewelry; comic Imogene Coca did a takeoff called "Soused American Way"; and Miranda hit the nightclub circuit, starting at the Waldorf's Sert Room. Hollywood lofted her yet higher—she was one of the highest-paid women in the US in 1945—with a series of wartime movies that included *Down Argentine Way*, *That Night in Rio*, *Weekend in Havana*, and, later, *Copacabana*.

For all the deepening appreciation of Latin-American music wrought by arriving artists, the war years' truly revolutionary transformation (musically speaking) was engendered by two Afro-Cubans—vocalist Frank "Machito" Grillo and trumpeter-arranger Mario Bauzá—who linked up in Gotham with Afro-American counterparts—most critically, Dizzy Gillespie—to create a fusion of two dynamic musics.

Frank Grillo, son of a cigar manufacturer, became a professional musician in his teens before emigrating to New York in 1937 to live with his sister Estrella and her husband, Mario Bauzá. Cugat, once again playing the role of facilitator (and employer) of newly arrived talents, hired Machito as a singer and made some recordings with him as well. Grillo also did vocals in 1938 for Noro Morales, the Puerto Rican pianist, singer and portly (275-pound) bandleader, who had arrived in Spanish Harlem from San Juan in 1935. Finally, Grillo went out on his own, forming the band Machito and His Afro-Cubans, which debuted uptown at the Park Plaza/Palace in December 1940.

The following month he was joined by his brother-in-law. Bauzá, another child prodigy, had played clarinet with the Havana Philharmonic at the age of nine. Later he picked up the trumpet, too, and when he arrived in New York in 1930, aged nineteen, he began playing his horn in dance bands. By 1933 he had landed the position of first trumpet in Chick Webb's pace-setting orchestra and was playing gigs at the Savoy; when Gillespie first arrived in New York in 1937 Webb occasionally let him sit in, and he would play alongside Bauzá. In 1939 Mario moved to Cab Calloway's orchestra, where Dizzy was his bandmate in the trumpet section (and roommate on road tours).

Bauzá tutored Gillespie in Cuban polyrhythms, deepening the introduction to Latin music Dizzy had gotten in 1938 from Albert Socarrás, when they were working the same band, including the principle of the "clave" (a propulsive five-beat pattern at the heart of

Cuban music), and the way to play the maracas; "I became enthralled with [Latin music], when I met Bauza," Dizzy recalled.

When Machito started up the Afro-Cubans, Bauzá left Calloway and signed on as the band's musical director and began intermixing Afro-Cuban and Afro-American phrasing; incorporating trumpets and saxophones with bongós, congas, timbales, and maracas; and recruiting Black jazz musicians along with Cubans and Puerto Ricans. After playing mostly venues in Spanish Harlem, the group finally came downtown to the La Conga nightclub at 51st Street—a move that paralleled that of Gillespie and Parker from Harlem to 52nd Street.

Noro Morales similarly shuttled around Manhattan's musicscape. Starting with uptown Latin locations like El Campoamor and the Park Plaza, he worked in Black jazz spots like the Savoy and Cotton Club and eventually came Downtown, in his case to the Stork Club: Winchell touted Morales in his column, Morales returned the favor by writing the "Walter Winchell Rumba." Though Morales's was known as a Puerto Rican band, and Machito's as a Cuban one, the congenial contenders for the title of most popular Latin band were in fact both mixed ensembles.

In 1941 Bauzá and Machito, who himself married the Puerto Rican Hilda Torres, brought on board a sixteen-year-old timbales player named Ernest Anthony "Tito" Puente, a second-generation Puerto Rican, whose father was a foreman at the Gem Razor Blade Company in Brooklyn. Born in Harlem Hospital in 1923, Puente spent most of his boyhood at 53 East 110th Street, between Madison and Park. His mother encouraged him to develop his talents, enrolling him in the New York School of Music branch at 125th Street, providing him drum lessons, arranging piano lessons with Victoria Hernández, and showcasing his talents in "Stars of the Future," a group she helped start at La Milagrosa Catholic Church (Lenox and 115th). Tito began playing timbales, studying Cuban rhythms, playing at neighborhood dances and church socials, and hanging around the Park Plaza. In 1939 he dropped out of high school to pursue music professionally, his first paying gig being a one-night stand with Morales's band at the Stork Club, and in 1940 he joined Morales full time, appearing in several of his soundies—including the Gay Ranchero, *Mexican Jumping Bean*, and *Cuban Pete*. In 1941 he shifted to Machito and Bauzá, who brought Puente and his timbales stage front, featuring him as a soloist and launching his Downtown career in earnest.

The Afro-Cubans were so well received at La Conga that they stayed on for three years, during which time they recorded (for Decca) the 1943 Bauzá composition *Tanga*, the first Latin jazz tune ever written. Dizzy Gillespie had been at the Park Palace when *Tanga* was first played, and he and Bauzá would continue the cross-pollination they'd begun up in Spanish and Black Harlem when, a few years later, each had settled into his respective temple in mid-Manhattan.

Gillespie (along with boppers Parker, Monk, Clarke, Roach, and countless other giants of modern jazz) would hang his hat in Birdland, on the east side of Broadway between 52nd and 53rd; Bauzá (along with Machito, Puente, Valdés, Rodríguez, Morales, and countless other giants of Latin jazz) would cluster in the former taxi-dance hall reformatted as the Palladium Ballroom, on the east side of Broadway between 53rd and 54th; and high-voltage musical electricity would crackle across 53rd Street.

136

Art of This Century

In May 1943, a few blocks north of 53rd Street, another cultural revolution was under way as Peggy Guggenheim was hosting a "Spring Salon for Young Artists" at the Art of This Century Gallery (30 West 57th Street).

Guggenheim, who had inherited a modest portion of the family's mining fortune, had opened an art gallery in London in 1938. With the aid of advisers like Marcel Duchamp, it had been a succès d'estime, and she decided to establish a museum of contemporary art. In August 1939 Guggenheim set out for Paris to arrange loans for an opening exhibit. With the outbreak of war in September she abandoned the project and shifted into full-scale collecting mode, buying up paintings and sculptures, at a great clip, from the likes of Picasso, Max Ernst, Magritte, Brancusi, Giacometti, Dalí, Kandinsky, Mondrian, Tanguy, and Chagall (some of whom sold at fire-sale prices to raise cash to flee the country). When the Nazis approached Paris in 1940, she herself fled south with her collection and spent the next year in Vichy France. In Marseille she struck up an affair with Ernst. She also aided Varian Fry's smuggling of artists and intellectuals out of France and herself underwrote the flight of a small group, including Ernst, that departed Lisbon by flying boat, arriving at La Guardia's Marine Air Terminal on July 14, 1941. Ernst, a German national, was detained on Ellis Island but was liberated through her efforts and those of Alfred Barr, director of the Museum of Modern Art (MOMA).

Guggenheim moved into a huge townhouse at 440 East 51st Street, just off Beekman Place overlooking the East River (the neighborhood reminded her of Paris), and installed Ernst therein. She offered him board (and bed), provided him a studio, and chauffeured him around town, but he refused to wed. Until Pearl Harbor made him an enemy alien—a status, Guggenheim pointed out, that included the possibility of being sent to an internment camp. Three weeks later he deigned to submit to marriage.

It wouldn't last long. Still, in the meantime, the couple's elegant establishment became the center of a swirl of some of the greatest artists of Europe, dozens of whom had made their way to Gotham. (As Yehudi Menuhin noted: "One of the great war aims is to get to New York.") André Breton, surrealist chieftain, was in her inner circle; indeed, she had paid for his escape from France and guaranteed him a $200 a month stipend for his first year, in exchange for which he helped catalog her massive art collection, which she'd had shipped across the Atlantic, labeled as "household goods." Breton reconstituted his court around Guggenheim's townhouse, and the surrealists were liberally represented at the lavish parties she threw. More generally, the presence of Chagall, Mondrian, Tanguy, Ernst, Léger, Lipchitz, Breton, and Duchamp, among many others, made it possible for New York to claim that it had—at least temporarily—supplanted Paris as capital of the art world.

The émigrés—fourteen of whom Pierre Matisse (Henri's son) collectively fêted in a glittering "Artists in Exile" show at his 57th Street gallery in March 1942—for the most part did well in New York. They had important spokespersons here, access to the press, connections to private collectors, and relations (in some cases of long standing) with art dealers who exhibited and sold their work. Thus Ernst's representative, surrealist champion Julien Levy, kept him in the public eye, and Pierre Matisse, who looked after Chagall, gave him a monthly allowance of $350, rising to $700, and arranged for major showings (despite Chagall's having raised J. Edgar Hoover's hackles by his cozy relations with the Yiddish Communists around *Morgyn Frayhayt*).

Perhaps no one was as creatively energized by the wartime city as Piet Mondrian. The Dutch artist, who arrived in September 1940 at the age of sixty-eight, fell immediately in love with New York's architecture and flashing neon, its jazz clubs and dance halls. He was particularly fond of barrelhouse pianists Meade Lux Lewis and Albert Ammons, whose propulsive music he heard Downtown at Café Society. They inspired (as did galvanic Gotham itself) dynamic new works like *Broadway Boogie-Woogie* (1942–43), whose buoyant network of interwoven strips pulsing with primary colors suggested an aerial view of Manhattan's rush hour traffic a-honk with yellow taxis. An ardent abstractionist who sought (as did Lévi-Strauss) to discern universal structures beneath the buzzing confusion of surface appearances,

Piet Mondrian, *Broadway Boogie-Woogie*, 1942. (PD-US-expired; PD-US-no notice)

Mondrian was enthralled by New York's grid, that underlying matrix which channeled random urban phenomena into orderly circulatory patterns.

Mondrian and Breton represented opposite ends of the modern art spectrum—the abstract and the surreal—but in New York these European differences seemed less compelling. Guggenheim actively worked to reconcile prior aesthetic conflicts, wearing one earring by Tanguy and one by Calder, "in order," she said, "to show my impartiality between surrealist and abstract art." More importantly, her new Art of This Century Gallery (ATC) adopted a similarly catholic approach. For her initial exhibition she culled from her massive collection 171 works by artists of every major twentieth-century tendency. She was aided in this by experts like Duchamp, Barr, James Johnson Sweeney (director of MOMA's Department of Painting and Sculpture), and Howard Putzel (the critic, collector, and gallery owner who since 1938 had been one of her closest advisers). The result was a spectacular show that celebrated the rescue of Europe's avant-garde culture and proposed, implicitly, the suitability of New York as its possible new home. The ATC's launch was made even more spectacular by Guggenheim's having hired Frederick Kiesler, an innovative Viennese architect, to transform her seventh-floor loft into an exhibit space that upended traditional ways of presenting and appreciating art. Works were shown unframed; or supported by suspension columns; or mounted on sawn-off baseball bats protruding from curved gum wood walls; or (like seven paintings by Paul Klee) placed on a wheel that revolved when a visitor tripped a light beam. Gotham had never seen anything like it.

Interior of Peggy Guggenheim's gallery, Art of This Century. Photo by Berenice Abbott, 1942. (Syracuse University Art Museum / Bridgeman Images)

More daring still, in the spring of 1943 Guggenheim expanded her embrace to include local New York artists who been largely dismissed as uninteresting provincials by the snooty Surrealists. In part this was because she had recently quarreled with Breton and been ditched by Ernst for a young painter. She was also urged in this direction by her New York advisers Putzel and Sweeney, and by the now-resident Chilean painter Roberto Matta Echaurren, universally known as Matta, who though part of the Surrealist set spoke excellent English and was friendly with young American painters. In April 1943, accordingly, she announced that the ATC would hold a competitive salon in May for American artists under thirty-five. Crowds of them showed up at 57th Street carrying canvases they hoped would be considered by a jury that consisted of Guggenheim's New York experts and two Europeans, Duchamp and Mondrian.

On judgment day, Mondrian was the first to arrive, and the elegantly attired Dutchman began perambulating the paintings. At one point he stopped walking and began staring at a particular work. Guggenheim wandered over. "Pretty awful, isn't it?" she asked. "That's not painting, is it?" Mondrian did not respond. She walked away. Twenty minutes later she returned to find him still rooted before the same painting, his right hand thoughtfully stroking his chin. Guggenheim again distanced herself from the work and the artist. "There is absolutely no discipline at all," she complained. "This young man has serious problems... and painting is one of them. I don't think he's going to be included... and that is embarrassing because Putzel and Matta think very highly of him." Finally, the mesmerized Mondrian responded: "Peggy," he said, "I have a feeling that this may be the most exciting painting that I have seen in a long, long time, here or in Europe." Guggenheim, astounded but nimble, turned on the proverbial dime. She raced off and began dragging other jurors over to the painting, saying: "I want you to see something very exciting. It's by someone called Pollock."

Jackson Pollock, a farm boy from rural Wyoming, had been living in New York since 1930 when he had come, aged eighteen, to study at the Art Students League with Thomas Hart Benton. He'd also (not having much money) been attracted to the free art courses offered by the Greenwich and Henry Street settlement houses. As the Depression deepened, Pollock, unable to make ends meet, was rescued, like many other floundering artists, by a governmental lifeline. In early 1935 he was hired by the Parks Department to restore civic monuments (he scoured, among others, the Firemen's Memorial at Riverside Drive and 100th Street and the equestrian Washington in Union Square). Later that year he was taken on board by the Works Progress Administration's Federal Art Project (FAP) as a mural assistant, a regularly salaried position that, with occasional interregnums, would provide him with economic security for most of the next seven years.

During this period Pollock soaked up the host of artistic influences then to be found in the cornucopic metropolis.

He was captivated by the Mexican muralists. In 1930 Pollock had met José Clemente Orozco while he was working on murals for the New School cafeteria at 66 West 12th Street (and in 1936 he would travel up to Dartmouth College to see the Orozcos there). In 1933 he watched Diego Rivera paint his doomed mural at Rockefeller Center. In 1936 he joined the Experimental Workshop—billed as "A Laboratory of Modern Techniques in Art"—that David Alfaro Siqueiros set up in his huge loft at 5 West 14th Street; members worked with new industrial materials like Duco (a synthetic resin paint developed for automobiles), pouring it onto panels laid out on the floor, or using sticks to splatter and drip it on the surface below.

He visited all the great MOMA exhibitions—"Cubism and Abstract Art," "Fantastic Art, Dada, Surrealism," and the Picasso retrospective (as well as *Guernica* at the Dudensing Gallery, returning to see it repeatedly). He was fascinated, too, by MOMA's colossal "Twenty Centuries of Mexican Art" exhibition of 1940, arranged with help from Nelson Rockefeller. It featured pre-Columbian artifacts but also brought Orozco back to New York, just after the Nazis blitzkrieged France, to paint in public a portable mural called *Dive Bomber and Tank*, with Pollock among the onlookers. The Westerner attended, as well, the next year's mammoth "Indian Art of the United States" exhibition, watching as Navajo artists executed sand paintings, allowing sand of various colors to trickle through their hands to the galley floor. Deeply taken with Indian art, he immersed himself, too, in Boas's Northwest Coastal collection at the Museum of Natural History and the Heye Collection's trove of artifacts, from whose Bronx storehouse Ernst, Lévi-Strauss, and Breton were making withdrawals. And he prowled the Midtown galleries, too, attending the Expressionist shows of Klee, Wassily Kandinsky, and Max Beckmann at Paul Rosenberg's; the exhibitions of Joan Miró at the Valentine and the Matisse; and the displays of Surrealists Ernst and Tanguy at Julien Levy's.

If his intake was rich and varied, his output, though occasionally remarkable, remained inchoate and intermittent. He engaged in self-destructive drunken binges, bar brawls, and violent outbursts during which he might carve up his own canvasses; alternating these with extensive periods of depression, alcoholic stupor, and nights spent sleeping in the gutter. In 1937 he began four years of Jungian psychotherapy. In 1938, at his brother's urging, he quasi-voluntarily institutionalized himself as a charity patient at New York Hospital's asylum in White Plains, where affluent Gotham families sent their black sheep to dry out; he resumed drinking as soon as he left. In '41, after his latest therapist wrote his draft board suggesting Pollock be referred for a medical examination, he was found psychiatrically unfit to serve and declared 4F.

Nineteen forty-one, however, was the year his life began to turn around, thanks to making some crucial metropolitan connections. The previous year he had encountered John Graham, a painter, critic, collector, and dealer of some notoriety in New York. Descended from minor Polish nobility, Graham (né Dombrowski) had adopted Russia as his homeland, served the Czar as a cavalry officer, then fled to Gotham after the Revolution. In the 1920s he took up painting, first studying under John Sloan at the Art Students League, then traveling frequently to Paris, where he became a devotee of Cubism and (so he claimed) an intimate of Picasso. His embellished autobiography, eccentric opinions, and dandyish self-presentation gave him cosmopolitan cachet among status-anxious local artists, among whom he promoted Surrealist techniques like "automatic writing." However, what really secured Graham's reputation was his ability to spot many of the city's most promising young painters before others did and then promote them. He was not only the first to acclaim Pollock a genius in the rough, he acted on that assertion by including the artist in an exhibition pairing French and American painters, held at the McMillen Gallery (148 East 55th) in January 1942, hanging his work alongside that of Picasso and Matisse.

That same McMillen exhibition included another emerging New York artist, Lee Krasner, who introduced herself to Pollock, promptly fell in love with him, and proceeded to take him in hand (at considerable cost to her own career). Born Lena Krassner in 1908 to an immigrant Russian-Jewish couple in East New York, Krasner had studied art at Washington Irving High School, the Women's Art School at Cooper Union, the Art Students League, and the National Academy of Design. In 1926 she departed Brooklyn to begin life as an artist in Manhattan, only to be confronted, in 1929, with collapsing stock and art markets. After supporting herself for a time as a model and waitress, she was hired in 1934 by the Public Works of Art Project, then taken on by the Federal Art Project as a mural assistant. Shortly after she met Pollock, the FAP was reorganized as the Graphics Section of the War Services Division, and in the summer of 1942 Krasner was set to designing window displays promoting courses at city colleges; she picked Pollock as her assistant. In October she was redeployed to creating Navy recruiting posters; she hired Pollock for the team.

Krasner, far better wired into the New York art world than Pollock, also began introducing him to influential figures, starting with her teacher Hans Hofmann. A celebrated German émigré painter, who really *had* been a friend of Picasso and Matisse, Hofmann had moved to Gotham in 1932 and in 1933 opened a school/atelier at 52 West Eighth Street at which he began transmitting to New York artists the modernist principles of Munich and Paris. Krasner then arranged visits to other members of Hofmann's circle, which led, in spring 1942, to a visit to Pollock's studio from MOMA's James Johnson Sweeney, followed by another that summer by Howard Putzel, and subsequently to Peggy Guggenheim's invitation to her 1943 Spring Salon.

That invitation came just in time, as in October 1942 (when Guggenheim was opening her gallery) the WPA was being terminated, and in January 1943 both Krasner and Pollock were pitched into unemployment. In extremis, Pollock turned to the Baroness Hilla Rebay, a German artist who while painting a portrait of Solomon R. Guggenheim, Peggy's uncle, had convinced him to establish a Museum of Non-Objective Art that would feature artists like Kandinsky, Klee, and Mondrian—and to appoint her its director. Opened in 1939 in a former automobile showroom at 24 East 54th Street, it was to be a temple of high art, with piped-in Bach, the utter opposite of Guggenheim's flashy gallery; the Baronness loathed Peggy, believing she'd sullied the family name by propagating "mediocrity, if not trash." To help run a museum that would in time, she hoped, unblot the Guggenheim escutcheon, Rebay hired young artists. Pollock—after penning, with Krasner's help, a suitably ingratiating letter—was taken on to make frames and run the freight elevator. He started work May 8, 1943.

Days later, lightning struck when—now koshered by Mondrian—Guggenheim adopted him as a protégé, and he began a spectacular ascent to stardom. First she signed a contract guaranteeing him a year's-worth of $150-a-month cash payments against future sales, which allowed him to quit the Baroness before she could fire him for going over to the enemy. She also commissioned Pollock to paint a nineteen-foot-long mural for the entrance hall of her new 61st Street duplex apartment. And she gave him his first solo show (the first for any American artist at the ATC), which opened November 8, 1943. His exhibit garnered favorable reviews—Robert Coates called him "an authentic discovery" in the *New Yorker*—as did the mural, which he painted with volcanic speed in a fifteen-hour all-nighter early in January 1944. In April 1944, Sweeney penned a laudatory article for *Harper's Bazaar* called "Five American Painters," putting Pollock in his featured quintet and providing a full-color reproduction of *The She-Wolf*, one of his solo exhibition's offerings. In May that same painting was purchased by the Museum of Modern Art (thanks more to Sweeney than to Barr, whose troth remained plighted to Europe).

Pollock now acquired a personal champion. Clement Greenberg, formerly a literary critic at *Partisan Review*, had switched in 1942 to doing art criticism for *The Nation*. To prepare for his new calling he took a summer crash course at the Art Students League, attended lectures by Hans Hofmann at his Eighth Street atelier, and was taken around Gotham's galleries by Hofmann's pupil Lee Krasner, who, of course, introduced him to Pollock. Greenberg

Jackson Pollock, *The She-Wolf*, 1943. (© 2019 Pollock-Krasner Foundation / Artists Rights Society (ARS), New York)

became a fierce partisan, especially after seeing his mural for Guggenheim and his second ATC show, held in April 1945, after which he pronounced Pollock "the strongest painter of his generation." In no small part this was because he saw Pollock as an agent of his own ferocious ambition for American art—to counter the humiliating authority of European art by eclipsing it. "I wanted," Greenberg recalled, "to see somebody come along who could match the French so we could stop being minor painters over here." This nationalist ambition, while not shared by Pollock himself, resonated strongly among other critics in the jingoistic war years. Pollock's "abstractions are free of Paris," *ArtNews* declared, "and contain a disciplined American fury." Greenberg was not alone is seeing the glowering Westerner as a good candidate for the role of Great American Painter.

POLLOCK WOULD NOT HAVE TO bear such burdensome expectations alone, because he was no more an *isolated* genius than Charlie Parker was. He was, rather, part of a generation of young Downtown painters—similar to the set of young Uptown musicians of which Parker was but one. It was the cohorts, not the individuals, that would transform their respective terrains. (Parker's bop revolution, Pollock told Krasner, "was the only other really creative thing happening in this country.")

Each member of what critic Coates would at war's end call the Abstract Expressionists, soon aka the New York School, had come to Gotham for different but often overlapping reasons. And once here, their mutual encounters spawned a network of friendships and associations that would gel into something more than the sum of its parts.

Some started out in New York, like Lee Krasner, though for her, as for the literary critic Alfred Kazin, the journey across the East River from Brooklyn was itself as momentous a migration as any that passed through Ellis Island. Barnett Newman and Adolph Gottlieb were second-generation Manhattanites, the former born on Cherry Street in 1905 to Russian Jewish immigrants, the latter born in 1903 on East 10th Street, across from Tompkins Square, to immigrant Jewish Czechs. Most, however, started elsewhere. Willem de Kooning, born in Rotterdam in 1904, arrived in Newport News, Virginia, in 1926, as a stowaway on an English ship, and made his way north to Hoboken's Dutch community, where he worked for five months as a house painter before moving to Manhattan in 1927. Vosdanik Manoog Adoian, born around 1904, fled with his family from their home village in Turkish Armenia to escape the genocide; he arrived in the US in 1920 and in Greenwich Village in 1924, having adopted the name Arshile (after Achilles) Gorky (after the writer). William Baziotes, born in 1912 to Greek parents in Pittsburgh, was working in a glass factory in Reading, Pennsylvania, when he visited New York in 1931, saw a comprehensive Matisse exhibition at MOMA, then packed up in 1933 and moved to Gotham to study painting. Marcus Rothkowitz, born in 1903 in Dvinsk, Russia, escaped his Cossack-ridden country to the US in 1913, when his father emigrated to avoid the draft; he arrived in New York in 1923 to work in the garment industry and in 1940 changed his name to Mark Rothko, fearing the surging anti-Semitism of his adopted country. Robert Motherwell hailed from Aberdeen, Washington, where he was born in 1915; his father, director of the Wells Fargo Bank, could afford to send him to study philosophy at Stanford and then Harvard, but in 1940 he shifted his focus to art history and moved to New York to study at Columbia with Meyer Schapiro, who encouraged him to become a painter himself.

Like Pollock, many of these would-be artists were drawn to Gotham to study art, and many attended the city's formal institutions like the Art Students League, National Academy of Design, New School of Design, Parsons School of Design, Cooper Union, Grand Central School of Art, Educational Alliance Art School, and the New School for Social Research's print workshop, Atelier 17—places where they could work with New York artists of the preceding generation like Robert Henri, John Sloan, and Max Weber.

They also established links to unaffiliated artists like John Graham, who in addition to mentoring Pollock was an important influence on de Kooning, Gorky, Gottlieb, Krasner, Newman, and Rothko. Hans Hofmann was held in similarly high regard. So was Milton Avery (Gottlieb, Newman, and Rothko were among those who regularly gathered at Avery's home to study his work and participate in sketching sessions). And so was Matta, who introduced Baziotes to Motherwell, both of whom, together with Pollock and Krasner, met at his studio to collaborate on collective "automatic" drawings, Pollock less enthusiastically than the others.

New York's museums and galleries were another great draw. They provided crucial portals to European modernist masters (de Kooning said seeing *Guernica* was crucial to his development) and to alternative cultural traditions (most flocked to the MOMA's Mexican and Indian Art exhibitions).

More practically they were attracted by Gotham's cheap housing. They settled, overwhelmingly, into downtown Manhattan, where they rented (at times shared) rooms in the cold-water flats and walk-up apartments of Chelsea, Union Square, and Greenwich Village—the bohemian haunt of artists and writers since the 1890s. Here they could drop in on one another's studios and chat about work in progress (few had phones), then continue their conversation at nearby cheap eateries, some of hoary vintage, like the Pepper Pot, MacDougal Tavern, Jumble Shop, and Romany Marie's, as well as various Village coffee shops, local Syrian, Greek, and Italian restaurants, and cafeterias like the Waldorf (on Eighth Street and Sixth Avenue) or Stewarts (at 23rd and Seventh). More serendipitously, given the density of artists per square mile, they might run into one another ambling around Washington Square, which was where de Kooning first encountered Rothko, when the two sat down coincidentally on the same park bench.

The city also provided fledgling artists with jobs—as cutters or bookkeepers in the garment biz, as art teachers at professional or public schools, or as commercial artists, itself a vast and varied field in Gotham. Thus de Kooning held down jobs at Eastman Brothers, an all-purpose design factory that crafted and constructed anything from stage sets for nearby Broadway theaters to Art Deco stained glass windows; at A. S. Beck, a chain of shoe stores for which he whipped up window displays; at assorted outfits that needed stenciling or sign painting; and he produced occasional ads, like a fashion display of cameo busts with different hairstyles for *Harper's Bazaar*, and a come-on for Model Pipe Tobacco in *Life Magazine*.

During the Depression, when jobs for artists turned scarce, New York and the feds provided governmental aid. The Treasury Relief Art Project (TRAP), which commissioned quality works to decorate federal buildings, selected (among others) Rothko, Avery, de Kooning, Pollock, and Gorky along with Ad Reinhardt, David Smith, and Louise Nevelson. The WPA's Federal Art Project employed (besides Krasner and Pollock) Gorky (who painted murals for Newark Airport), Baziotes (who taught children art at the Queens Museum), and de Kooning (who worked on murals in Williamsburg), among many others. The WPA did more than keep food on the table. It allowed many artists, for the first time in their lives, to practice their craft full time. And by bringing them together in such numbers, it midwifed an artistic community where before there had been only isolated circles and provided its members with a degree of confidence and empowerment they had never experienced, thus facilitating their great leap forward during the war years.

All was not sweetness and light in this FAP community, however. It was wracked by many of the same divisions that cleft the Popular Front. The Moscow Trials and Nazi-Soviet Pact and invasion of Finland schismed the art world, with Philip Evergood, Max Weber, Raphael Soyer, Hugo Gellert, and Stuart Davis generally on one side, while Rothko, Gottlieb, Newman, and Avery were among those who followed Meyer Schapiro out of the CP-dominated American Artists' Congress and into a rival Federation of Modern Painters and Sculptors. While turned off partly by personal discomfort at dogmatic rhetoric and cultural diktats, the fissuring ran along aesthetic fault lines as well, with one side combining modern expressionist techniques with a social justice narrative, the other finding that linkage an artistic dead end. When Matta asked, "Are there any guys on the WPA who are interested in modern art and not in all that social realist crap?" it was members of the nascent New York School who responded affirmatively. In a 1943 manifesto Rothko and Gottlieb placed "social pictures" in the same cornball category as "pictures for the home," pictures "for over the mantle," and "pictures of the American scene." When the socially conscious artists denounced the abstractionists as ivory tower esthetes in retreat from political engagement, the latter responded by calling them "social realists"—linking them nominologically to Soviet-style "socialist realism" with which they had little in common—and branding their art as mere pictorial propaganda, ineffective even on its own terms. As had Trotsky, in his 1938 *Partisan Review* essay "Art and Politics," they argued that only an unfettered independent art could subvert customary ways of seeing and thus be truly revolutionary. Hitler could live with representational art, they noted; it was the avant-garde he hated and feared.

During the war years, this combination of physical proximity, aesthetic propinquity, shared workplace and WPA experiences, and similar political sensibilities helped the Downtown artists coalesce into a community. Its members encouraged one another's innovations and mutually validated artistic practices that broke in significant ways from Depression-era

Poster for the New York at War parade. (Collection of the Boston Athenæum)

realism and European-style modernism. Finding their own voice just as the Europeans arrived allowed them (like their generational peers in the field of physics) to be invigorated and validated rather than undercut and overwhelmed by the eminent émigrés.

The war was also the moment when artists lost government sponsorship and were forced to rely on the private art market. The transition, though long foreseen, was still disruptive, and made more jarring by the way WPA artworks were jettisoned as unceremoniously as were WPA artists. In December 1943 the government removed thousands of FAP oil paintings from their stretchers and auctioned them off, by the pound, at a Flushing warehouse. A plumber bought the entire lot to use for insulating pipes, only to discover that when pipes got hot the paint began to stink. He sold the canvases to a junk dealer, who then sold them to the Roberts Book Company on Canal Street, where they were heaped on long tables in the back room, from which canvases by socially conscious artists like Alice Neel, and those of

Pollock, Avery, and Rothko, could be picked up by buyers—in some cases the artists themselves—for $3 a pop.

As government patronage ended, the private art market took off, powered by wartime prosperity. With shopping expeditions to Europe foreclosed, wealthy art collectors were obliged to buy locally. So were investors seeking shelter from rising inflation, and ordinary consumers with money to spend but with ever fewer commodities (given wartime rationing) on which to spend it. Their collective purchases triggered an "art boom" in New York, the first one not tied in some way to Paris. Parke-Bernet's public sales shot from $2.5 million in 1939 to $4 million in 1942, to $6.5 million in 1945. Private gallery sales jumped 37 percent between 1944 and 1945.

The Downtown artists did reasonably well in this climate, thanks in large part to Peggy Guggenheim, who had the money and prestige to force the market to pay attention to them. She continued to promote Pollock among her circle of wealthy collectors and patrons, though she did find her protégé "rather difficult." He "drank too much," she recalled, "and became so unpleasant, one might say devilish," that he seemed "like a trapped animal who should never have left the prairies of Wyoming." Somewhat to his dismay, Guggenheim started touting other "discoveries," giving solo debut shows in 1944–45 to Baziotes, Motherwell, Rothko, and others, while Julien Levy launched Gorky, and Howard Putzel promoted Gottlieb at his new Gallery 67.

Several tastemakers and market leaders, noting the Downtowners filtering into Midtown, called attention to the phenomenon itself. Greenberg argued that a revolution was in progress in the art world and claimed that the future of American painting rested in the hands of artists like Pollock, Baziotes, and Motherwell.

Samuel Kootz agreed. Formerly an advertising and public relations executive, then a silk converter (in which role he'd commissioned Stuart Davis to do designs for scarves), and then a patron and dealer with Baziotes and Motherwell his first protégés, Kootz in 1943 declared, in his book *New Frontiers in American Painting*, that American art was in the thick of a "revolution." Similarly, Sidney Janis, a former shirt manufacturer turned art collector (he owned works by Picasso, Matisse, and Mondrian), had begun by visiting the individual studios of de Kooning, Gorky, and Pollock, when they were still largely unknown, and in 1944, he wrote about their movement as a whole. In his book *Abstract and Surrealist Art in America*, Janis unapologetically discussed works by Baziotes, de Kooning, Gottlieb, Hofmann, Motherwell, Pollock, and Rothko alongside those of Braque, Chagall, Kandinsky, Mondrian, and Picasso.

By 1945, encouraged by such critical certification, wealthy collectors—many of them (as Meyer Schapiro noted) "young people with inherited incomes"—were purchasing Abstract Expressionists. Both Janis and Kootz would soon open galleries that catered to this demographic.

Museums were slower to climb on the AbEx bandwagon. MOMA people did like to define their institution as young, liberal, and dynamic—especially in contrast to the fusty Metropolitan, which they referred to as the "mausoleum uptown." (There was little love lost from north to south either: Metropolitan chief Francis Henry Taylor referred to MOMA as "that warehouse on 53rd Street.") But the Modern remained Eurocentric, to the dismay of avant-garde radicals in the Federation of Modern Painters and Sculptors, which picketed MOMA in 1942, 1943, and 1944, denouncing it as insufficiently inclusive of American modernists. Still, the mandate of heaven was shifting somewhat, as evidenced by MOMA-mounted exhibitions, like one on Alexander Calder, about which the artist would say that "whatever my success has been, [it was] greatly as a result of the show I had at MOMA in 1943."

The new artists did less well in the emerging middle-class art market, which, having been summoned into being by the many WPA shows aimed at popular audiences, was now spurred onward by war-related activities.

In January 1942, twenty-one of the city's leading arts institutions, following the lead of their English counterparts, came together to form Artists for Victory, Inc., whose goal was to "render effective the talents and abilities of artists" in prosecuting the war. Headquartered at 101 Park Avenue and headed by Hobart Nichols (president of the National Academy of Design), the group, which represented over 10,000 painters, sculptors, designers, and printmakers nationwide, proceeded to canvass, recruit, and classify its members, then connect them with military, business, and governmental agencies in need of war-related art work.

Artists for Victory also sponsored competitive exhibitions aimed at keeping the arts alive and boosting national morale. The initial one, opened on the first anniversary of Pearl Harbor, was held at the Metropolitan, which set up a $52,000 fund to purchase forty-two works for its collection from among the winners. An immense undertaking—1,418 works, in all media, flooded in from across the country—it filled twenty-eight of the museum's galleries, which had been largely emptied out when its own works had been bundled off to Whitemarsh Hall, an estate in Pennsylvania, for safekeeping; they would not return until 1944.

Another Artists for Victory competition, for printmakers only, focused on "America in the War," with artists invited to contribute works in any of five categories: "Heroes of the Fighting Front, Action on the Fighting Front, Heroes of the Home Front, The Enemy, and The Victory and Peace to Follow." When it opened on October 4, 1943, at the Kennedy Galleries, many of the contributions came from first-time exhibitors, almost a third of them women.

MOMA did much the same. It launched an Armed Services Program that—often under contract to the Office of War Information or Rockefeller's OIAA—mounted exhibits like "Wartime Housing," "Anti-hoarding Pictures by New York School Children," and, in June 1942, "Road to Victory," which featured photographic images assembled by Lieutenant Commander Edward Steichen (on loan from the Navy), accompanied by poems from Steichen's brother-in-law Carl Sandburg. It drew 100,000 visitors (men in uniform were admitted free) and received exultant reviews from critics ranging from the *New York Times* to *PM* and the *Daily Worker*.

Some art dealers, eyeing these audiences, set out to develop sales methods that could reach such markets. Realizing that unsophisticated buyers were reluctant to go to galleries, where they might be outsmarted and fleeced, they sought ways of desanctifying art objects and turning them into ordinary consumer goods: advertisements, sales through artists cooperatives, buying by mail, working with popular magazines like *Life*, or allying with department stores. Sam Kootz collaborated with Macy's on a 1942 exhibition and sale of "Contemporary American Paintings," which had clerks selling to customers, rather than gallery experts selling to clients. The ads promised there would be "MANY WELL-KNOWN ARTISTS!" and also "SOME BRILLIANT DISCOVERIES," among the 179 canvases by seventy-two artists, including "expressionists, surrealists, abstractionists" and members of "many other schools." And while the paintings were on sale at rock-bottom prices, ranging from $24.97 to $249 (the two Rothkos were priced at under $200 apiece), buyers could nevertheless "be assured that any one you choose will possess real merit." Gimbels riposted with a sale of William Randolph Hearst's art collection (that fetched over

$4 million); Macy's volleyed back with a show of Old Masters (one third down, take months to pay); and Gimbels responded by opening a permanent art department that featured a Rembrandt for only $9,999.

It would remain to be seen if Greenberg and others were correct in believing that New York might replace Paris as the capital of modern art, or if Guggenheim's coterie of artists would supplant their socially conscious rivals. However, what did seem clear was that Gotham might well emerge as the supreme *marketplace* for contemporary artists and that the war-engendered expansion of the fine-art business might allow it to take its place as the seventh component—alongside radio, recording, press, publishing, music, and drama—of the city's burgeoning culture industry.

137

Book Boom

As the city's banking, advertising, and music industries recovered strongly from the Depression, so did its book trade, whose spine was Publishers Row—the stretch of Fourth Avenue (not yet renamed Park Avenue South) between 34th Street and Union Square—along or nearby which clustered many of New York's leading houses, like the venerable Harper & Brothers at 49 East 33rd. Book Row, home of secondhand stores, continued along Fourth Avenue below Union Square, on down to Astor Place, where the Bible House—original fount of New York's book business, and still host to several used book shops—served as southern anchor.

The roots of publishing's turnaround in the 1940s could be traced to innovations launched in the 1930s. As hard times put downward pressure on prices—threatening to force abandonment of the customary $2.50 charged for new novels—the industry had responded by expanding the number of reprints. One of the first modern firms to specialize in reissuing other companies' products in cheaper format was Grosset & Dunlap, which got its start by doing in the twentieth century what the Harpers had done in the nineteenth: reprinting books without providing so much as a by-your-leave to the original house, much less author's royalties or publisher's fees. This piratical approach evolved over the decades into Messrs. G. & D. buying the rights to sell inexpensive knockoffs of a publisher's first-edition title whenever sales income slackened; this was done by obtaining overprint sheets and binding them or buying the original plates and running off a new edition.

By the 1920s, some publishers had created their own reprint operations. Doubleday, Page established the Garden City Publishing Company, directed from 1925 by Robert Fair de Graff, an innovative salesman who was also the cousin of publisher Nelson Doubleday. De Graff originated Garden City's popular line of inexpensive Star Dollar reprints. Then, in 1930, not long after the Crash, a consortium of four publishers—Harper & Brothers; Dodd, Mead; Harcourt Brace; and Little, Brown—set up Blue Ribbon Books (in 386 Fourth Avenue, at 27th Street) and gave it the right to sell reprints of their nonfiction titles. Which it did, quite successfully, for a quarter of the original cover price, sometimes less. In 1933, de

Graff jumped from Garden City to Blue Ribbon, buying the company and becoming its president.

Industry leaders grew alarmed at the rapid spread of reprints. Grosset & Dunlap and Garden City each produced about 3,000,000 per annum, flooding bookstore "remainder" tables and exacerbating the more general Depression-era problems of overproduction/underconsumption and consequent price cutting. Indeed, a few publishers dropped their $2.50 novels to $1.00, spurred by the popularity of reprints. In 1932 W. Warder Norton headed up a committee of eight publishers (including Alfred Knopf) that urged cooperative action to restrict output—a tack in tune with the National Recovery Act philosophy to come—and to halt reckless bidding for certain authors, with its correlative "best-sellerism"—concentrating promotional attention on a few books at the expense of the others.

What the industry was *not* prepared to do, even to generate new audiences, was publish paperbacks—widely considered beyond the pale of respectability, given their long and often lurid history in New York. Back in the 1840s, story papers like *Brother Jonathan* had gleefully pirated British and European authors, printing up their latest works as "extras," hawking them in the streets, and selling them through the mails at newspaper rates, until squelched by postal authorities. From the 1860s on through the nineteenth century, Erasmus Beadle and his competitors had churned out dime novels in paperback format, concentrating on Wild West adventures and detective stories, an approach and subject matter extended into the early twentieth century by Street & Smith's pulp novels, pumped out from its literary factory at 79 Seventh Avenue in Manhattan. Even Harper had essayed the form with its Franklin Square Library, making paperback versions of popular works available for a pricier but still alluring 25 to 35 cents. By the First World War, however, increased costs, exhausted formulas, moral castigation of paperback-associated vulgarity by clerics and educators, and rivalry from magazines (which Americans bought in the millions) and lending libraries (which rented out novels for pennies)—all had led to a slow fadeout of the cheap paper format.

Paperbacks did resurge in the twenties, though that was due almost entirely to the efforts of one man—the socialist, feminist, and atheist publisher E. Haldeman-Julius—and the astounding popularity of his Little Blue Books. The Philadelphia-born Emanuel Julius had moved to Gotham in 1909, at the age of twenty, becoming a reporter for the socialist *New York Call* and rising to an editorial position. In 1915 he relocated to Girard, Kansas, to edit the waning but still important socialist paper, the *Appeal to Reason*. There he married Marcet Haldeman, a banker's daughter and feminist (they adopted each other's name) and segued into producing paperback books for the masses. He intended to reprint classics of literature, history, science, and philosophy, along with original tracts on socialism, free thought, sexuality, and birth control (beginning with one by Margaret Sanger)—that together would constitute a "University in Print"; to this list he would add popular romances, adventures, mysteries, and self-improvement books. Using the *Appeal to Reason*'s presses and subscription base, he did just that. He ran off "pocket sized" booklets, ranging from 32 to 128 pages, in a 3½-by-5-inch format, with pale blue paper covers, then priced them at a nickel and sold them through the mail (minimum order: twenty titles). By 1928, Haldeman-Julius had sold over one hundred million copies of over one thousand titles; by 1932, his list included 1,725 of these booklets, along with larger-format Big Blue Books.

This phenomenon did not go unnoticed by the publishing industry. Already in 1923 *Publishers Weekly* had declared that for sheer quantity Haldeman-Julius (aka the "Henry Ford of Literature") had created "the greatest publishing business ever in existence." But few in the book biz were inclined to follow suit. His catalog, after all, had racy and radical overtones (attracting the attention of J. Edgar Hoover); his product was marketed by mail rather than bookstores; his Blues seemed more booklet than book. A few venturesome New York firms were inspired in some way by Haldeman-Julius. Dick Simon and Max Schuster sought his advice when he visited Gotham in 1925, and they accepted his suggestion of hardbacking the work of Little Blue Book author Will Durant; the publication next year of *The Story of Philosophy* was the foundation of their (hardcover) empire. Charles Boni, another entrepreneurial New York publisher, started up a handsome line of paperbound books, available by subscription (twelve books a year for $5); but by 1931 his project had fallen victim to the Depression. Thus even into the 1930s, as book-world denizens searched for life rafts to keep them afloat in hard times, they spurned a turn to paperbacks: librarians and book lovers disliked paper bindings, cultural arbiters thought paperbacks smacked of Beadleism, bookstores wouldn't carry them, respectable houses wouldn't print them.

The impetus to rethink paper came from abroad. In Germany, the Leipzig publisher Tauchnitz had—since 1841—been producing inexpensive English-language reprints of American and British authors, uniformly bound in white paper. Tauchnitz had done so, moreover, on the up and up, paying those authors royalties (including Dickens, who'd been feted in New York but found his antipiracy pleas ignored), with the proviso that works by American writers (editions of Irving, Poe, and Melville came out early on) could not be sold inside the US. By 1860, there were 500 Tauchnitz reprints in circulation; by the mid-1930s, more than 5,000, and these paperbacks were beloved by Anglo-Americans who traveled on the Continent.

This pioneering produced few disciples until 1931, when Albatross Modern Continental Library stepped into the reprint lists to challenge Tauchnitz and displayed a competitive ingenuity that quickly commanded attention. Albatross—cofounded by Kurt Enoch, scion of a German publishing family, along with British and German partners—brought out British and German fiction and nonfiction in a fresh and modern format. The crisp paper covers were color coded to identify the contents: blue for romance, red for crime, gray for plays and poetry, purple for biographies and histories. The Albatross logo, a silhouette of the long narrow bird, was soon spotted in most major European cities. By 1934 the youthful and energetic Albatross firm had in effect merged with and taken editorial control of Tauchnitz; Enoch himself focused on expanding the distribution of the conjoint companies.

In England, the success of Enoch and his colleagues caught the eye of Allen Lane, head of The Bodley Head publishing house, which in its heyday had brought out Oscar Wilde and Anatole France and was now in serious decline. Plunging into paperbacks, Lane imitated the Albatross cover design and color-coding scheme and picked a penguin for his logo. Lane's special breakthrough came in distribution. Seeking alternatives to bookstores, he made a presentation to the giant chain discounter, F. W. Woolworth, which to Lane's surprise and delight placed an order for 63,000 books, enough to get his project off the ground. Established in 1935, by March 1936 Penguin Books had printed one million books. By 1939 the papermeisters Penguin and Tauchnitz-Albatross were between them selling 25,000,000 a year.

New York publishers, eyeing these European developments, had begun jumping into the lucrative waters. In 1937, Richard Storrs Childs launched Modern Age Books. In an introductory advertisement he noted that paper reprints had been successful abroad for a century, and he would make them profitable here, too, by deploying mass-production and mass-distribution techniques. His strategy was to hitch a ride on the magazine highway by winning the right to set up countertop steel display cabinets in nearly 500 magazine outlets in greater New York, and then heavily advertising his line—which was weighty with mysteries and contemporary politics—and trumpeting its moderate price, between 35 and 50 cents. Childs failed, partly because he got caught in a Depression downdraft, partly because he wasted money trying to disguise his books as hardcovers (complete with dust jacket). Large losses forced him to raise prices to nearer the $1 level—hardcover reprint country—and the company finally dissolved during the war. Also in 1937 *American Mercury* magazine created American Mercury Books, in this case packaging books to look like magazines and leaving titles on periodical stands for a month max; this, too, proved a losing strategy.

The winning one was devised by Mr. Reprint himself, Robert Fair de Graff, who in 1938 resigned from Blue Ribbon to see if he could come up with an appealing 25-cent paperback and a way to mass market it. De Graff undertook an exhaustive investigation of what readers wanted, assessed various approaches to design and distribution, studied the failures of Modern Age and the successes of Penguin and Albatross, then went to work. He paid an artist $50 to design a logo: breaking with birds, he opted for a bespectacled kangaroo holding a book in one hand and bearing another in its pouch. He came up with a paper cover that featured a shiny, eye-catching, and waterproof "Dura-Gloss" finish, durable and handsome enough to warrant adding a book so nicely covered to one's library, the aura of respectability bolstered by spiffy red end sheets. To end-run paperbacks' sleazy associations, de Graff hired the author and historian Philip Van Doren Stern to advise on selecting titles. To cut costs, he decided that where Modern Age had paid a 10 percent royalty, he would look for publishers and authors willing to settle for 4 percent, and a $500 advance to be divided equally; and where Modern Age offered dealers the standard 40 to 50 percent discount, he would offer 30 percent, tops. He would cut printing costs by opting for press runs ten times those of Modern Age, by gluing the pages instead of stitching them, and by trimming the size to $4\frac{1}{4} \times 6\frac{1}{2}$ inches—a genuinely "pocket-sized book" (hence the company name: Pocket Books)—yet with type big enough to be genuinely readable. For financial backing, he turned to the still-adventurous Simon & Schuster, longtime admirers of Haldeman-Julius and now close followers of Lane's successes in England. De Graff put up $16,000 (and kept 51 percent of the shares). Dick Simon, Max Schuster, and S&S treasurer Leon Shimkin pooled another $14,000 (and 49 percent ownership). With this fund de Graff set up a two-room office at 386 Fourth Avenue, where both Simon & Schuster and Blue Ribbon had long rented space. And in late 1938, he undertook to test drive the new format, using Pearl Buck's *The Good Earth*, a bestseller whose reprint rights he obtained from Blue Ribbon. When sales and responses to a market survey questionnaire proved promising, he undertook a bigger tryout, confined to Gotham and vicinity.

On June 19, 1939, the *New York Times* ran a $2,000 full-page ad, emblazoned: "OUT TODAY—THE NEW POCKET BOOKS THAT MAY REVOLUTIONIZE NEW YORK'S READING HABITS." (De Graff had wanted "WILL" not "MAY," but his partners advised caution.) On offer were ten thoughtfully diversified titles of proven hardback popularity. Five were novels: James Hilton's *Lost Horizon*, Emily Brontë's *Wuthering Heights*, Thornton Wilder's *The Bridge of San Luis Rey*, Thorne Smith's *Topper*, Samuel Butler's *The Way of All Flesh*. There was also one each of drama and poetry: Shakespeare's *Five Great Tragedies* and Dorothy Parker's *Enough Rope*. A mystery: Agatha Christie's *The Murder of Roger Ackroyd*. A self-helper: Dorothea Brande's *Wake Up and Live*. And a children's book: Felix Salter's *Bambi*. De Graff ran off 10,000 copies of each. Predictably, bookstores were not keen to handle them; Brentano's, Putnam's, and Scribner's each took a mere one hundred, on a returnable basis. But de Graff, like Lane, was mainly after unorthodox outlets, and here he scored big. The Liggett Drug Store chain, hoping to duplicate Woolworth's success with

Penguin, jumped in with both feet, its Grand Central store alone taking 5,000. Union News, a major distributor, agreed to put Pocket Books on newsstands all around the city. Cigar store chains bought in too. And de Graff, to his surprise and delight, managed to bag the elephant—Macy's, then the city's biggest outlet for hardcover books in the city—which took 10,000 and scattered them about its premises.

Sales were phenomenal. The Liggetts were besieged. So were the newsstands (at Grand Central, even the "train butchers"—boys who usually hawked papers to passengers—did great business with books). Macy's moved thousands (moving Gimbels to put copies in their window). Perhaps most telling, the small cigar stand near de Graff's office sold 110 copies; and the bookstores reordered, noting that new customers had been lured. The 100,000 sold out in three weeks.

In July the high command launched a nationwide test, with 25,000 of each title, having lined up 10,000 outlets, compared to the max 1,200 traditional sites available to the average publisher. By the end of the 1939 calendar year, Pocket Books had sold over 1.5 million copies; by the end of their first full year, 6 million. In 1940, they relocated to Rockefeller Center. In 1941 de Graff signed up 600 independent wholesalers who integrated Pocket Books into their magazine distribution networks, providing it with 52,000 outlets, which took 70 percent of its offerings, the other 30 percent going to drug or cigar chains and department stores. In 1941, sales jumped to 9 million. In 1942, they reached 20 million. By war's end the company had moved more than 100 million copies since the *Times* ad had hesitantly promised a revolution. In 1944, Pocket Books, initially capitalized at $30,000, was purchased for $3,000,000 by Marshall Field III, who acquired Simon & Schuster at the same time.

Before the launch, traditional book publishers had been skeptical. One had said: "We are cooperating because of all the agitation for cheap books and the success of cheap books in Europe. We feel we ought to give it a chance—to show that it won't work here." Now they were frightened that paperbounds would fatally undercut hardcovers. To soothe these concerns, de Graff did another test, this time in Texas, where Pocket released a 25-cent paper reprint of Dale Carnegie's *How to Win Friends and Influence People* (1940) while the hardback original (at $1.95) was still on the bestseller list. Within two years the quarter edition had sold 900,000 copies. However, hardcover profits had soared as well, demonstrating to general satisfaction that the new books were tapping into a vast new clientele, creating a rising tide that was lifting even pricier boats.

Now competitors emerged from everywhere, particularly from companies that had experience in or access to the magazine trade. Avon Books was founded in 1941 by the American News Corporation, itself a distributor. George T. Delacorte Jr.'s Dell—since the 1920s one of the largest magazine publishers—started up Dell Paperbacks in 1943.

Some came all the way from Europe. Allen Lane sought to access the American market as early as 1939, when he set up American Penguin Books, putting in charge one Ian Ballantine, a twenty-two-year-old New Yorker who had done his senior thesis at Columbia College on the possibilities of paperback printing, then gone to the London School of Economics, where a professor had introduced him to Lane. Lane just wanted Ballantine to distribute British Penguin product, and when Ian and his wife, Betty, arrived back in town on the *Nieuw Amsterdam*, they promptly rented a loft in an office building at East 17th, just off Fifth, to store the first shipment of 50,000 books (109 titles). Penguins, like Pockets, were priced at 25 cents—or "two bits," from the Colonial Era–practice of cutting up dollar coins into eight pie-shaped slices to make change; two of these made a quarter; hence Pockets and Penguins became known as "two-bit books."

There could not, however, have been a worse moment to launch a venture totally dependent on transatlantic shipments. U-boats scuttled some parcels, and those that arrived were of rapidly deteriorating quality, given the paper shortage in England. So in 1941, when Lane paid a visit to New York, he decided to accept a proposal to have American Penguin start producing books locally, a proposal Lane took seriously, as it came from one of the era's master paperbackers, Kurt Enoch of Albatross-Tauchnitz. Enoch, Jewish, had read the writing on the wall early on and relocated to France in 1936, from where he began distributing French books to England, and during which time he first met Allen Lane. When the Nazis took Paris in 1940—the same moment they ordered Tauchnitz to stop printing books in English—Enoch fled south to Marseille, then escaped, via Portugal, to New York. With help from local publisher connections (like Ben Huebsch, Charles Scribner, and Bennett Cerf), he started up his own company in Gotham, then decided that working with Lane and Ballantine to salvage the faltering Penguin enterprise would be a better bet. He put up some capital toward production costs (borrowed from fellow refugee Kurt Wolff) in return for being made vice president of American Penguin and getting a 5 percent equity share. Enoch and Ballantine together brought out Penguin's first American product—*What's That Plane?* (an aircraft recognition primer)—which became its first big seller, too.

Kurt Wolff, meanwhile, had opened up a very different kind of publishing venture—producing hardcover titles aimed largely at the refugee community in New York. Wolff had entered publishing as an editor for the Leipzig house of Rowohlt, where he published the then-unknown Franz Kafka. After buying out and renaming the company Kurt Wolff Verlag in 1912, he went on to promote the work of many German Expressionist writers, and the house flourished until shuttered by the Depression. In 1933 the Jewish Wolff and his wife, Helen Mosel, went into exile in France and finally fled to New York, in March 1941, with the help of Varian Fry. In 1942 the Wolffs incorporated Pantheon Books, housed it in their apartment at 41 Washington Square South, and began issuing small-run, fine editions of German authors.

They quickly added French texts, having formed a partnership with another refugee publisher, the Russian-born Jacques Schiffrin, who had founded Edicions de la Pléiade in France in 1922. In 1936 Schiffrin's now-renowned series of literary classics merged with Edicions Gallimard, the most prestigious firm in Paris. In 1940, to placate German occupiers, Gallimard fired the high-profile Jewish editor, who fled with his wife and young son to Marseille. From there, with Fry's help, they made their way to Gotham, arriving five months after the Wolffs. In 1942, he, too, established a tiny publishing house, Jacques Schiffrin & Cie., which published an underground account of the French resistance, some war poems by Louis Aragon, André Gide's account of the occupation of Tunis, and writings by his old friend the aviator Antoine de Saint-Exupéry (who lived in New York until he returned to fight for the Free French). Eagerly read by fellow exiles, such titles had tiny sales outside New York, so Schiffrin joined forces with Wolff, taking charge of the list's French offerings. During the war years, Pantheon published in French, German, and English the works of André Gide, Stefan George, Albert Camus, Herman Broch, and Robert Musil. For bread-and-butter sales they turned to as-yet untranslated European authors, whom they found in the New York Public Library; their publication of the complete edition of Jacob and Wilhelm Grimm's *Fairy Tales* received enthusiastic endorsements from W. H. Auden in the *New York Times Book Review* and Edmund Wilson in the *New Yorker*. Pantheon's sales figures were never startling, but the house, by opening another pipeline to Europe, had burnished Gotham's credentials as point of entry for cutting-edge literature of the highest quality.

Still, the sensational story about the city's book trade in the war years was the spectacular explosion in mass-market sales. Only a few years before, no one would have dreamed—not even de Graff—that a paperbound book, *any* book, would ever sell a million copies in a single month, as did the Pocket Book edition of 1942's *See Here, Private Hargrove*. More than two-thirds of the increased volume was thought attributable to the tremendous increase in affordability and availability of two-bit books. Much of the rest was thought due to the growing unavailability of competing leisure-time pursuits: thus, gasoline rationing had put the kibosh on Sunday driving, time now filled by reading, or by the singalongs around the piano that were simultaneously boosting sheet music sales. The war itself provided subject matter that drew new readers, with *Hargrove*—a good-natured account about (and for many a primer on) basic training—being a good example. War cartography provided another case in point. On Friday, February 20, 1942, FDR suggested Americans have a map of the world in front of them when he gave his first post–Pearl Harbor fireside chat on Monday evening. This triggered a stampede to the stores. The sales manager of C. S. Hammond & Company, on 43rd Street, went to the downtown warehouse in the morning and brought back 2,000 copies of a new atlas, to augment stock; by closing time, all were gone. And when FDR spoke, over 61 million adults were at their radios, many with maps spread before them.

Ironically, just as New York's book biz saw its wildest dreams coming true, the industry—so Random House President Bennett Cerf noted—found itself unable to keep up with the torrential demand. Countless men in printing plants, binderies, and the publishing houses themselves had been drafted. The government was requisitioning printing plates and melting them down for war. Most critically, paper was getting steadily scarcer. The shortage started in the forests where woodcutters abandoned their saws and headed for the defense plants, where they could earn far more; it was worsened by the diversion of large quantities to military use (every 75-mm shell, for example, had to be packed in its own paper carton). In the fall of 1942, accordingly, the War Production Board began allocating each publishing firm a percentage of what it had used in 1941. At first 90 percent, the quota dropped to 80 percent in 1943, and 65 percent in 1944, even as the demand expanded exponentially. Equally distressing, the product itself, given the shortage of chlorine, mutated steadily from white to gray or yellow.

To deal with this conundrum of famine amid feast, and to make the book trade essential to the war effort, representatives of publishers, booksellers, educators, librarians, and authors groups convened on April 15, 1942, and organized the Council on Books in Wartime (CBW). A board of luminaries, chaired by W. Warder Norton, selected a Council motto ("Books Are Weapons in the War of Ideas"). It also decided to promote the idea that the free selection and reading of books—and the publishing industry so essential a part of that process—were vital to American liberty and the antithesis of German fascism, which by then had banned eighteen categories of books, totaling 4,175 titles, as well as the complete works of 565 authors. The CBW launched this public initiative the following month, when, to commemorate the shameful Nazi book burnings of May 10, 1933, the Council supported a dramatic radio reading of Stephen Vincent Benét's poem "They Burned the Books." In 1943, on the episode's tenth anniversary, the Council, now solidly established, orchestrated a nationwide day of remembrance at bookstores, schools, and libraries; in New York, Ralph Bellamy read passages of Benét before a crowd gathered in front of the New York Public Library, its flag at half-mast.

The Council also promoted war-related books. In 1943 it presented "Words at War," a series of dramatized adaptations on NBC, produced by Erik Barnouw working with

> **Books cannot be killed by fire.**
>
> People die, but books never die. No man and no force can put thought in a concentration camp forever. No man and no force can take from the world the books that embody man's eternal fight against tyranny. In this war, we know, books are weapons. —Franklin D. Roosevelt
>
> **BOOKS ARE WEAPONS IN THE WAR OF IDEAS**

Poster attributed to S. Broder depicting Nazis burning books. (Library of Congress, Prints and Photographs Division)

individual directors like Joseph Losey, and on WQXR it presented "Books Are Bullets," a program of interviews with authors. The Council also backed key titles—labeled "Imperative"—all seven of which were runaway national bestsellers; one of them—Wendell Willkie's travel memoir, *One World* (1943)—sold over two million copies in less than two years. Still, boosting sales didn't address (even worsened) the key problem of wartime demand pressing hard on shrinking supply.

The solution, like the problem, was generated by the war itself, when the military assembled one of the biggest mass markets imaginable—the multimillion members of the US Armed Forces—and the publishing industry, with government backing, decided to follow the troops. Polls showed early on that many soldiers and sailors, faced with the extensive periods of inactivity characteristic of war, were distressed at the paucity of available books. The American Library Association had spearheaded a massive book drive in 1942, and civilians had donated ten million hardback and paperback volumes, but the vast jumble of randomly sized rectangles was awkward to ship and distribute to a planet's worth of battlefields.

The Council on Books in Wartime came up with an alternative. If the government provided all the bookmaking matériel free of charge—including such scarce commodities as paper and printing plates—and paid a modest one-cent royalty fee to the publishing firms and their authors, the book business would print up an immense number of uniformly-sized, easy-to-ship paperbacks on rotary presses, typically used for magazines rather than books, using thin paper and substituting stapled for glued spines. These Armed Services Editions (ASEs) would include first-run bestsellers and highbrow classics, along with lowbrow humor and mysteries and Westerns, at a cost of less than six cents per copy, to be distributed free to servicemen.

In truth, when the idea was first broached, there'd been grumbling in the publishing ranks, from businessmen fearful these overseas freebees might work their way back into the continental book stream and undercut their own commercial offerings, if not immediately, then after the war. W. W. Norton directly addressed these concerns in 1943, noting that the same lightweight throwaway construction that made the ASEs so convenient for troops also made them convenient for the industry, in that such books were all but guaranteed to self-destruct after multiple uses. Not only had the Council worked out a plan for "keeping them wholly out of the civilian economy," but booksellers "who have examined this plan," Norton insisted, "are of the conviction that civilian sales will, if anything, be increased," because the troops' massive exposure to books whose copyright they controlled constituted, in effect, a form of free advertising. In the long run, Norton added, "the very fact that millions of men will have an opportunity to learn what a book is and what it can mean is likely now and in postwar years to exert a tremendous influence."

And millions did: in the end, what the *Saturday Evening Post* described in 1945 as "the greatest book-publishing project in history" produced over 123 million copies of some 1,322 titles, avidly read under astonishingly diverse and difficult conditions. A. J. Liebling, who covered D-Day for the *New Yorker*, found soldiers engrossed in ASE volumes from the American marshaling areas along the southern coast of England to the shores of Normandy. These men (and women) would indeed carry the habit of reading back into civilian life and provide legions of buyers for offerings from Publishers Row. But long before V-J Day, Gotham's book trade, turbocharged by war, had already entered the domain of big business.

138

Broadway

After a terrible first war year (six hits, fifty-four flops), Broadway was booming again. Theaters were packed with newly flush war workers and armies of soldiers, the latter having been handed free tickets by the United Service Organizations (USO), allowing many to attend their first play.

Once settled in their seats there was a fair chance they'd see themselves up on stage, as in *Winged Victory* (1943), Moss Hart's rousing tribute to US Army Air Force, which starred real servicemen—utter novices apart from a sprinkling of promising professionals like Private Edmond O'Brien, Private Lee J. Cobb, Corporal Gary Merrill, and Private Karl Malden. Irving Berlin offered *This Is the Army* (1942), a drumbeating update of his *Yip Yip Yaphank* with an all-soldier cast. An instant hit, critics raved at its gender-bending bevy of husky men in dresses, and especially the stellar impersonation of Gypsy Rose Lee by one Private Oshins. "It has everything except girls," said the *Herald Tribune*, "and the terrible truth is that you don't miss them."

After its Broadway run, Berlin's show toured military encampments around the country, then headed out to play the front lines in Europe, North Africa, and the Pacific. In taking to a "road" gone global, these soldier-actors were following a trail blazed by professional entertainers. In 1941, the USO (chaired by Lord & Taylor's Walter Hoving and headquartered in the Empire State Building) had set up a subsidiary—Camp Shows, Inc. Operating out of a half-dozen floors in 8 West 40th Street, it began dispatching Broadway shows and big bands, comics and pop singers, opera stars and classical musicians to perform for the millions of servicemen parked in embarkation camps around the United States. From 1943 onward they trooped out to theaters of operation in Italy, North Africa, and New Guinea, along with the military entertainers sent out by Armed Forces agencies, which also set up shop in Gotham. The city thus emerged as the center of a planetary "circuit," headquarters of the most gigantic entertainment enterprise in world history, one in which some soon-to-be-famous New York actors and producers discovered their callings.

Actors like Burton Lancaster. Born in 1913 to Irish Protestants, Lancaster had grown up in an East Harlem sea of Italian Catholics, endlessly battling. He was saved from gangsterdom by the Union Settlement House on East 104th, where he starred in its children's choir, Christmas pageants, and amateur but innovative theatricals (a learning trajectory similar to that of another East Side city boy, Jimmy Cagney, over at the Lenox Hill Settlement). Lancaster was also taught gymnastics at Union, a skill he put to use in the Depression, when he joined a truck-and-wagon circus touring the country. On returning to Gotham, he worked as an acrobat with the WPA Circus (part of the Federal Theater Project), touring the five boroughs and delighting audiences of children (sometimes numbering in the thousands) assembled from settlements, orphanages, and detention houses. After New Deal opponents killed the Theatre Project in 1939, Lancaster went back to commercial gymnastics but sank slowly down through small-time vaudeville and burlesque circuits to odd jobs and unemployment, until he was drafted, in 1942, and made an "entertainment specialist." Deployed in a mobile unit of performers (complete with a Steinway Victory piano) he was sent off to Casablanca, then across North Africa, then up Italy to liberated Rome, following and entertaining the troops. It was in the skits and in-drag chorus lines of these soldier shows that Lancaster got his first on-stage speaking roles, accumulating the acting experience that made possible his transition from circus to screen—accomplished with legendary speed when, on returning to New York, he was "discovered" by Broadway, then snatched away by Hollywood.

Another beneficiary of on-the-war-job training was Joseph Papirofsky, born in Williamsburg in 1921 to a very poor orthodox Jewish family. When they later relocated to Brownsville, Papirofsky attended Eastern District High School, where he sang in the glee club, garnered the male lead in many a school play, became president of the Dramatic Society, was taken to see Shakespeare on Broadway, and was voted "most talented" by his 370 classmates. Those talents were at first channeled mainly into politics, performing as a Young Communist League street orator during the Spanish Civil War. But in November 1942, after enlisting in the Navy, Papirofsky got involved in organizing skits in boot camp barracks. As a result, when he was posted to duty on an aircraft carrier, he was asked to organize shipboard entertainment. He wrote and emceed vaudeville-style routines in which he had sailors do imitations of Cagney, Edward G. Robinson, and Jimmy Stewart; and lip synch to Andrews Sisters' records while wearing mops on their heads. By 1945 he had been put in charge of organizing a mobile unit of musicians, singers, and dancers, which flew from island to island in the Pacific, boosting morale. On demobilization, he enlisted immediately in the world of theater (where he would become better known as Joe Papp).

Soldier-performers were also deployed in New York itself, to bring the war back home by staging dramatic reenactments that supplemented reports from radio and press correspondents. In June 1944, as part of a war-bond drive, the Army Quartermaster Corps presented daily re-creations in Central Park, every hour on the half hour, of a battle between American and German forces. In June 1945, 30,000 civilians crammed Ebbets Field to watch "Here Is Your Infantry," in which soldiers equipped with machine guns, mortars, automatic rifles, bazookas, and smoke grenades reprised an attack on a Japanese pill box on Bougainville, fighting their way through the ten truckloads of brush and sand that had been brought in for the stage setting. The audience, the *Times* reported, sat mesmerized, "as though at the front lines."

On March 31, 1943, visiting soldiers who wanted a break from war-related themes could have witnessed the dawning of the golden age of musicals at the St. James Theater's thunderously triumphant opening of *Oklahoma!* The ecstatic response amazed many industry-watchers who had been skeptical of its chances, given that almost everyone connected with the new play was untested or unsuccessful. The Theatre Guild (its producer) had fallen on hard times, and the desperate gamble to recoup its fortunes by reviving a play about the turn-of-the-century Oklahoma Territory, which had failed the first time the Guild had offered it back in 1931, seemed seriously wrongheaded to Broadway mavens. The chosen librettist, Oscar Hammerstein II, was famous as the creator (with Jerome Kern) of *Show Boat*. Still, this had been back in 1927, and Hammerstein hadn't had a hit for about ten years. Richard Rodgers—tunesmith to Hammerstein's wordsmith—had been doing great in his partnership with Lorenz Hart, concocter of martini-dry lyrics. That pairing, however, was foundering on the rocks of Hart's psychic and alcoholic decline; when Hart refused to participate in *Oklahoma!* there were those who wondered if Rodgers could really work in harness with Hammerstein, whose style—he leaned toward sentimental operettas—was so drastically different. And while choreographer Agnes de Mille—the Harlem-born granddaughter of Henry George and niece of film mogul Cecil B. DeMille—had just won kudos for creating and dancing in *Rodeo* (1942), a cowboy ballet with music by Aaron Copland, de Mille had never done a theater piece. Ticket brokers who went up to the tryout in New Haven came back predicting bad reviews because the collaborators had not provided what was expected from Broadway musicals. As producer Mike Todd had purportedly put it, when walking out after the first act: "No legs, no jokes, no chance."

Oklahoma! was, in fact, boldly unconventional. It was not the usual clothesline with "showstopping" songs pegged on; it had a no-name cast; it didn't lead with a razzmatazzy production number featuring high-stepping chorines but instead opened on a Beautiful Morning with Aunt Eller churning butter while, offstage, cowboy Curly waxed rhapsodic about elephant-eye-high cornfields. Messrs. R & H didn't *want* to use songs and dances to stop the show, they wanted them to arise out of the dramatic action and to carry it further along. They intended to—and did—pick up the project of seamlessly integrating book and music on which Hammerstein and Kern had embarked with *Show Boat*. They even went a step further by integrating ballet into the narrative; where dance had previously played a peripheral role, de Mille planted it front and center. Together these departures added up to a new template for musicals, a transformation as revolutionary in its field as the innovations of Parker and Machito and Pollock were in theirs.

Given its glorious music and amazing choreography, *Oklahoma!*'s record-smashing success—it ran for five years on Broadway (four times longer than any musical predecessor) and ten on tour—was no surprise. But the play's spectacular popularity—Decca sold over a million copies of the original cast recording, the first-ever album of an entire musical—rested on yet another foundation, the intellectual and emotional messages it provided wartime audiences about America's past, present, and future.

Both Rodgers and Hammerstein were Fighting Liberals. Hammerstein in particular had been active since the mid-1930s in the antifascist movement, and in 1942 had joined Rex Stout on the War Writers Board, where he took his morale-building duties very seriously. Both believed they could contribute to the war effort by offering theatergoers a healthy dollop of exuberant optimism. They did so by bathing the Oklahoma Territory's problematic history in a bright golden haze—no hint here of the 1907 extinguishment of the once-coterminous Indian Territory—and painting it as a bucolic Arcadian landscape. This feel-good past made inexplicable Oklahoma's all-too-recent troubles—the Dust Bowl devastation, rooted in abusive farming practices as well as drought, which had sent "Okies" (a derogatory term) fleeing toward their miserable rendezvous with California, the story famously recounted in Steinbeck's Joads-on-the-road novel, *The Grapes of Wrath*.

A parade of circus elephants. (Photo by George Marks/Retrofile/Getty Images)

Oklahoma! excised all such unpleasantries, offering a prelapsarian vision of a time when social tensions had (supposedly) been subsumed in the name of patriotic comity: the farmer and the cowman (and even the merchant) would be friends in the new state of Oklahoma. Analogically, in 1943, Depression-era class conflicts and pre–Pearl Harbor battles over intervention could and should be set aside for the patriotic higher good. Even the growing wartime anti-Semitism that so troubled the two Jewish artists from New York was transcended in the magical space of the St. James Theater: Ali Hakim, the alien peddler character who was billed as Persian but played as Jewish (by veteran Yiddish theater actor Joseph Buloff), got assimilated into the folk community, demonstrating to audiences the virtues of toleration.

At the same time, Rodgers and Hammerstein made clear there were unabsorbable evils in the world of *Oklahoma!*—and by extension the wartime world—that could not be accommodated, only crushed. Jud Fry, the degenerate hired hand, whose wickedness is made patent by the quasi-pornographic *Police Gazettes* he hangs on his walls, is a snake in Eden, a man who defies (as did contemporary fascists) accepted rules of civilized behavior. In the end he's destroyed, allowing the community to enter its radiant future ("You're doin' fine Oklahoma: Oklahoma, OK!"), and allowing the audience to exit feeling that theirs was a country worth fighting for.

Toward war's end soldiers and civilians might have caught Tennessee Williams's Broadway debut with his *Glass Menagerie* at the Playhouse Theatre, another instance of fruitful wartime interaction between local talent and exile émigrés—though this one proved a good deal bumpier than those between Mondrian and Pollock, or Lévi-Strauss and Boas, or Fermi and Rabi. The overseas arrival in this case was the renowned German producer-director Erwin Piscator, who back in Weimar days had helped launch Berlin's proletarian theater movement, ofttimes in collaboration with Bertolt Brecht. Noted for his political commitment (he was a member of the German Communist Party) and experimental stagecraft (he used film projections, constructivist sets, and documentary formats), Piscator's techniques had inspired New York's Group Theatre and the city's "living newspaper" movement. In 1933 he fled Hitler to Moscow; in 1936 he fled Stalin to Paris; in 1939, he moved with his Jewish wife, Maria Ley, to Gotham (arriving in January on the same boat that carried Fermi and his Jewish wife).

In May of that year, at the age of forty-six, Piscator—armed with letters of introduction from the likes of Albert Einstein and Sinclair Lewis—approached the New School's Alvin Johnson with a proposal to, in effect, transplant his avant-garde, politically engaged theater to New York. Johnson was eager to work with such a distinguished and experienced figure, but he insisted Piscator tone down his talk about "revolutionary" theater and modulate his criticisms of "bourgeois society," terms to which the émigré agreed. Piscator proceeded to establish the Dramatic Workshop. It would prepare students for careers in all aspects of theatrical production, through courses and workshops, and by having them participate in the work of the Studio Theatre, which Piscator also created. A fully professional operation, the Studio Theatre employed top-notch actors and aimed to produce cutting-edge plays not likely to find a home on Broadway.

By spring 1940, when Dramatic Workshop classes began, Piscator had assembled a stellar (and trans-Atlantic) teaching staff. Some were old Weimar associates (Hanns Eisler, Erich Leinsdorf); others were drawn from the Group Theater (Harold Clurman, Stella Adler); and his invited guest lecturers included Charlie Chaplin, Robeson, and Bertolt Brecht. Adler taught the acting class (though as a staunch Stanislavskian her motto was: "Don't act. Behave"). John Gassner—the eminent theater historian, teacher, critic, and chief play reader for the Theatre Guild—handled playwriting. Eisler did composition. Brooks Atkinson, drama critic for the *New York Times*, taught criticism. Piscator himself looked after directing. By fall 1940, the Studio Theatre was also up and running; housed somewhat uncomfortably in the New School's 12th Street building, it would move in 1945 to its own quarters in the small President Theatre on 48th Street.

Remarkable students arrived.

In 1943 Marlon Brando gusted into town, a Nebraska stud sporting a red fedora and hyper-tight blue jeans, whose self-professed goal was "to knock New York on its ass!" Adler not only instructed Brando, she introduced him to some of Gotham's most important actors, writers, and composers. Piscator (whom Brando mocked behind his back for his Teutonic mannerisms and heavy accent) cast him in several Studio Theatre productions, beginning with Shaw's *St. Joan*, which afforded him (on October 29, 1943) his first appearance on a New York stage. But Piscator was too autocratic, and Brando too rebellious, for the teacher/pupil relationship to last, though in the end it was Brando's sexual rambunctiousness and omnivorousness that led Piscator to expel him, when, in 1944, Brando's serial deflowering of virgins in the summer-stock troupe Piscator ran out in Sayville, Long Island, helped stoke the level of unbridled fornication to disruptive heights. No sooner was Brando cut loose than he was reeled in by a talent scout who'd spotted him in Sayville. This led to his Broadway debut on October 19, 1944—in *I Remember Mama*—which ignited his meteoric takeoff to stardom. Still, there were plenty of other up-and-coming actors already (or soon to clamber) on board the Dramatic Workshop, including Elaine Stritch, Harry Belafonte, Walter Matthau, Rod Steiger, Shelley Winters, Tony Curtis, Ben Gazzara, and Judith Malina.

John Gassner's playwriting class, meanwhile, had attracted an up-and-coming playwright from out of town. What originally drew Thomas Lanier Williams III to New York was an announcement by the Group Theatre in 1938 of its contest for playwrights under twenty-five. Williams, having been born in 1911 (in Mississippi) simply lied about his age. He misstated his name and address too. Williams's deeply troubled family had moved to St. Louis in 1918, and after Tom graduated from the University of Iowa in 1938, having written a considerable number of plays, he returned to Missouri, though he was living in New Orleans when he sent off his application to New York in December 1938. For his return address, however, he gave his grandparents' house in Memphis, and he called himself "Tennessee" to project a persona he thought would be more appealing in New York. On March 20, 1939, six days before his twenty-eighth birthday, a wire arrived from Harold Clurman, Irwin Shaw, and Molly Day Thacher, awarding him not the $500 prize—that went to someone else—but a special prize of $100 in recognition, Thacher explained, of his unique talents.

Of far greater consequence for Williams's career, Thacher recommended him to a prominent New York literary agent, Audrey Wood, who agreed to take him on. When he checked in to Gotham's 63rd Street "Y" to meet her in September of 1939, she began plugging him into the theatrical profession. Over the next months, she (and Thacher) arranged to have him sit in on Group Theatre rehearsals of Clifford Odets's new play, *Night Music*, directed by Clurman and featuring actor Elia Kazan (Thacher's husband). Wood also shepherded him to a host of Broadway performances, taking in Tallulah Bankhead in Lillian Hellman's *Little Foxes* and Paul Robeson in *John Henry*. "I'm afraid this city would not do for me to write in," he epistled his mother, "there are too many diverting things going on." (He did not mention that these diversions included a wholesale plunge into the world of gay New York.) In December 1939 Williams won a $1,000 Rockefeller Fellowship, granted through the Dramatists' Guild of the Authors League of America, for which he had applied at Wood's suggestion.

The indefatigable Wood also helped him get a scholarship to the Dramatic Workshop, where she was on Piscator's faculty, and in January 1940 Williams enrolled in Gassner's semester-long Playwrights' Seminar. Quite apart from what he might get from the classes, Wood knew that Gassner, who vetted plays for the Theatre Guild, might help get Williams's latest play produced. In fact he did, and *Battle of Angels* went into production, only to have his takeoff sputter out when the play bombed in Boston in January 1941. Over the next year Williams worked on revisions, hoping the Guild would give him another chance; when they did not, Wood got Piscator to consider mounting a run at the Studio Theatre. Playwright and producer began negotiations over revisions in January 1942; these proved disappointing. As Williams wrote his mother in February, the "terribly dictatorial German" was "trying to force me to turn the play into a dry, didactic sermon on social injustice, representing the South as a fascist state." Worse, he reported to Wood in July, Piscator had accused *him* of having "written a Fascist play," charging that "all of your characters are selfishly pursuing their little personal ends and aims in life with a ruthless disregard for the wrongs and sufferings to the world about them."

Battle of Angels went unstaged, though Williams continued to work with Piscator. He assisted him in a production of *War and Peace* (during January to April 1942). He watched the director stage (in May 1942) Williams's one-act play, *This Property Is Condemned*. And he pushed to get a job reading plays for the Studio Theatre. In August 1942 Piscator wrote that "it is far more important for you to be perfectly free to write your own plays." Thus ended their encounter, with the young American having learned much about stagecraft from the older European but, perhaps equally important, having developed the confidence to stand his literary ground.

Over the next difficult year—his career seemingly washed up—Williams resisted even stronger pressures than Piscator's, notably exhortations to write plays that would contribute to the war effort. (Williams himself remained a civilian; having undergone repeated cataract operations, he had been classified 4F.) The New York stage was inundated with dramas treating military themes and the problems of home-front society; Williams argued that to deem only war-related dramas acceptable meant "that for the duration, you have committed your theatre to the creation of only sham and claptrap." Instead, he concentrated on finishing *The Glass Menagerie*, a play that had almost nothing to do with war. Nor could its content and focus have been less responsive to Piscator's prescriptions (though Williams did call for Piscator-like touches, such as projecting slides that commented on the action, instructions ignored by the producer-director). Rather, it was a heavily autobiographical memory drama, the story—recounted by a narrator—almost Noh-like in being constructed out of fragments of remembered experience. The play broke with the rituals of "realistic" dramaturgy—the "genuine Frigidaire and authentic ice-cubes" approach, as Williams put it—calling instead for a "new, plastic theater" that rejected "photographic likeness" for "poetic imagination" and thus revitalized "the exhausted theatre of realistic conventions" (an assessment and agenda that bore resemblance to exactly contemporary calls, elsewhere in the city, for superseding "realism" in the world of art and music).

Wood took it to the independent producer-director and former song-and-dance man Eddie Dowling—attracted by his reputation for backing highly praised but commercially risky ventures. After checking with his friend the critic George Jean Nathan, Dowling agreed to mount it, gambling also on Nathan's suggestion of a once-great but now often-inebriated actress, Laurette Taylor, for the starring role. For whatever reason—Williams's poetic prose, a magnificent performance by Taylor, superb scenery by Jo Mielziner, music by Paul Bowles—the final curtain on opening night, March 31, 1945, was greeted with clapping, shouting, whistling, and shrieking approval from an audience that demanded twenty-four curtain calls. When soon thereafter the New York Drama Critics Circle voted *Glass Menagerie* the season's Best Play, Williams's career, fueled by popular and critical acclaim, achieved war time lift-off.

139

Toward a Fashion-Industrial Complex

The Nazi occupation of Paris on June 14, 1940, was treated in New York as the calamity it was, but in certain quarters it was also seen as a breathtaking opportunity. Within a matter of days, the idea was being bruited about that—as there would be no manikins sashaying down Parisian runways that fall or in the foreseeable future—Gotham should seize the moment to replace the city-by-the-Seine as the capital of couture. "No doubt about it," one style observer told the *New York Times* on August 9, "this is the 1776 of the fashion world, and revolution is afoot."

The rebel high command—virtually all women—embarked on a frenzy of consultations that summer. The locus of strategic planning was The Fashion Group, Inc., an organization of female professionals that had been formed back in 1930 by industry titanesses. Among the seventy-five founding members had been editors and critics Edna Woolman Chase (*Vogue*), Carmel Snow (*Harper's Bazaar*), Virginia Pope (*New York Times*), and Julia Coburn (*Ladies' Home Journal*); cosmetics moguls Elizabeth Arden and Helena Rubinstein; designers Claire McCardell, Clare Potter, and Lilly Daché; publicist Eleanor Lambert and department store executive Dorothy Shaver; and Eleanor Roosevelt, wife of the then-governor. By the end of 1931, the Fashion Group had attracted 375 members, representing all facets of the industry—designers, retailers, critics, editors, manufacturers, educators, and buyers—and had become a female networking vehicle, especially at mammoth Hotel Biltmore luncheons. In 1940, a decade older and stronger than ever, the Fashion Group would become GHQ of a campaign to wrest the crown from Paris.

The major male ally of this female phalanx was himself anything but a fashion plate, but Fiorello La Guardia knew a once-in-a-lifetime opening for a crucial metropolitan industry when he saw one. Even before Paris fell, he had told a Fashion Group meeting, "I don't see why we have to take our fashion from any other country," adding that as "New York City is the center of fashion of the entire world"—wish fathering thought—he hoped "to see the time come when people will be copying New York models." Now, in the critical summer of

1940, the mayor was raring to make this a reality, and he summoned a dozen fashion honchas to his City Hall office to plot strategy. Among them was the woman who would emerge as commander-in-chief of Gotham's forces, Virginia Pope, fashion editor of the *New York Times*, whose advertising income was intimately linked to the prosperity of the garment industry in general, and the great department stores in particular.

A key problem, quickly identified, was that New York didn't lavish attention on its designers as the French did on theirs. On July 11—scant days after France surrendered—one expert underscored the implications for hundreds of Fashion Groupers at a Biltmore conclave. When we think of Paris couture, she said, what comes to mind is not the city but "individuals—vivid personalities, who helped make their designs fascinating to us," but "when we talk about Seventh Avenue, it is with complete anonymity." This, in turn, was rooted in a long-standing division of labor between New York and Paris—the former focused on production, the latter on design—which dated back at least to the 1858 opening of the House of Worth at No. 7 Rue de la Paix.

Parisian couturiers liked to say they were artists, not tradespeople—and they were indeed masters of the dressmaking art—but their endeavor was also rooted in the structure of their industry. Originally, because their patrons were wealthy members of the nobility, haute bourgeoisie, or demi-mondaine, they could take their time, experiment with creative designs, use the most luxurious fabrics, seek to please the most sophisticated tastes. A century later they were still pampered—by rich patrons, a benevolent state, and French textile mills—and still possessed of the time and resources to produce fabulous original designs for an elite market.

Twice a year, however, buyers, designers, merchants, manufacturers, publicists, and journalists from New York flocked to the Parisian salons, where they were welcomed warmly, being a major source of revenue for the couture industry. There they would buy dresses to bring back, copy, manufacture, and sell in gross lots. For their part, Seventh Avenue designers labored in obscurity, interpreting French designs to maximize their appeal to American consumers, generally following whatever trends the French were promoting—lowering the waistline with Coco Chanel, raising it again with Elsa Schiaparelli, obscuring the body, or revealing its curves through the magic of Madeleine Vionnet's bias cut.

New York did have a dozen creators of the first rank, people whom industry insiders believed stood shoulder pad to shoulder pad with Schiaparelli and Chanel—Elizabeth Hawes, Claire McCardell, Valentina, Nettie Rosenstein, Clare Potter, and Hattie Carnegie, along with milliners like Lilly Daché and Sally Victor. They produced original designs for mass production—being particularly innovative at crafting easy-to-wear, easy-to-manufacture, and affordable sportswear—but some also created more luxurious lines for the custom trade, items sold in high-end shops and department stores.

Some of these auteurs of apparel did gain public visibility, though often for collateral accomplishments. Hawes, before leaving the business in 1940 for *PM* and consumer activism, had been a polemical and popular writer, as well as a top-notch designer; her *Fashion Is Spinach* (1938) was a sharp attack on an industry based on planned obsolescence. Valentina confected glamorous and expensive evening wear for wealthy women but became renowned for her stage costumes—she designs clothes "that act before a line is spoken," enthused drama critic Brooks Atkinson—notably the ensemble she created for Katharine Hepburn in the 1939 play *The Philadelphia Story*. Sophie Gimbel of Saks, head custom designer of the store's Salon Moderne, got her name on the brand in part because she was married to Adam Gimbel, the store's owner. In general, however, New York designers were kept discreetly in the background, their collections released to the public (or the trade) unsigned and uncelebrated by the openings that were de rigueur in Paris. Stores branded themselves, not their employees; besides, enforcing anonymity made it less likely their designers would be wooed by competitors and thus gain an edge in salary negotiations. Even if Seventh Avenue *had* lavished credit where due, New York's fashionista institutions—magazines, schools, retailers—might not have paid attention, being overwhelmingly focused on Paris.

Condé Nast's *Vogue*, still piloted by Edna Chase, was slowly updating its look—with help from photographer Edward Steichen and art directors Mehemed Fehmy Agha and his assistant (soon successor), the émigré Alex Liberman. Chase hewed to *Vogue*'s traditional Francophilia; despite an occasional cover story on American fashion and the American garment industry, the magazine seldom mentioned local designers. Hearst's *Harper's Bazaar*, under the formidable quartet of Carmel Snow, Diana Vreeland, Alexey Brodovitch, and action-photographer Martin Munkacsi, had leapfrogged past Chase's *Vogue* in the brilliance of its layout, photography, and commissioned art and fiction; but Snow's heart, too, belonged to Paris. Both editors promoted Parisian designers, vied to get ads from Parisian houses, personally attended Parisian openings. Snow adored the Paris scene and loved trumpeting its qualities. In 1937, introduced by Edward R. Murrow, she made the first fashion broadcast direct from Paris. Snow traveled to Paris in early 1940, not easy to do at that point, to see the February collections and express solidarity with the couturiers.

Schools were similarly Paris-oriented. The New York School of Fine and Applied Art had a branch in Paris, and faculty and students shuttled back and forth between the two schools. So tight was the connection that longtime president Frank Alvah Parsons was made a *Chevalier* of the Legion of Honor for improving Franco-American relations. The establishment was renamed the Parsons School of Design in 1941.

Equally besotted with Paris were the exclusive specialty shops on and off Fifth Avenue in the 50s and 60s, notably along the perpendicular axis of 57th Street, which was not known as "New York's Rue de la Paix" for nothing. The stretch between Fifth and Sixth Avenues alone housed Sally Milgrim at Number 6, Henri Bendel at Number 10, and Jay Thorpe at Number 24–26. Nearby was hat confectioner Lilly Daché, who had opened her own seven-story building at 18 East 56th, with separate fitting rooms for brunettes and blonds, and Hattie Carnegie's establishment at 42–44 East 49th—the size of a small department store, it employed a thousand people. Out-of-town buyers came to these shops to check out not just the goods, but the promotional methods used to sell them—window displays, floor layouts, merchandising operations—and they would hardly have missed that these temples were devoted to the worship of French design.

When the Parisian head was abruptly severed from its New York body in 1940, some on Seventh Avenue thought they could make up the sudden design deficit by relying on émigré talent. Perhaps there would be a flood of couturiers arriving from France, shipmates of the disembarking French artists and anthropologists. Exhibit A for this strategy was the designer known as Mainbocher, who landed in September 1939, trailing clouds of Parisian glamor; by November 1940 he had reopened for business at 4–6 East 57th Street, adjoining Tiffany's. His shop reproduced the ambience of his former atelier—the vendeuse who narrated runway showings spoke in French-tinged English—to the degree that one old acquaintance at the opening exclaimed: "It's just like a Paris showing!" The House of Mainbocher immediately became New York's finest and most exclusive cathedral of couture.

But Mainbocher was a special case. For one thing, he was an American, né Main Bocher (pronounced like "rocker"), who had come to New York from his native Chicago to study at the Art Student's League. After serving in France during the Great War, Bocher stayed on in Paris, working as a fashion illustrator for *Harper's Bazaar* and later as fashion editor for French *Vogue* (he'd been hired by Carmel Snow, then still at Condé Nast). In 1930, the now elided Mainbocher established his own fashion house, designing expensive, elegant gowns (an admirer of Vionnet, he borrowed her bias-cut technique). His first customers were American émigrés, like socialite Wallis Simpson, with whom he hit the jackpot in 1937: when the Duke of Windsor married the woman he loved, she was wearing a Mainbocher gown.

After arriving in Gotham, Mainbocher cannily seconded Manhattan buzz—Paris was finished and New York was slated to be the world's fashion capital—while also declaring himself "very proud of his American citizenship." In 1940, this combination of impeccable Parisian credentials with irreproachable American pedigree acted like cultural catnip to the city's social and entertainment world elite, and Mainbocher's star ascended accordingly. His situation was all but unique. Less than a handful of European designers arrived. The leading Parisians either stayed home and spent the war dealing with the Nazis in various ways, or went elsewhere in Europe, or shut down altogether (Mme. Vionnet closed her doors in 1939).

One superstar did arrive: Elsa Schiaparelli flew in on the Yankee Clipper in July 1940 and would spend most of the war in New York. She came not to design but to give lectures, and what she had to say was not encouraging. In her first speech, to a crowd of 2,000 assembled in Lord & Taylor's, she poured cold water on local aspirations. Paris, for all its troubles, was still the center of fashion, and Gotham would not—*could* not—ever replace it because "the demands of mass production put artists and designers under great handicaps." Seventh Avenue creativity was hobbled by the imperatives of profit and the untutored taste of American women, who "fail to appreciate fine workmanship and high quality materials." Schiaparelli did acknowledge the US did well at sportswear, and she had a kind word for fur. Still, New York shouldn't get its hopes up. Paris—her listeners should "be assured"—would retain "its place as the center of artistic creation in fashion," because only there was commerce kept in check, and designers given free rein.

"Poppycock," said Virginia Pope (metaphorically); she and her legions weren't buying any of this. Consider, she argued in the *Times*, what New York could offer Couture. Fashion must start at the top of the social heap—"Society" sets the style for society—and America's Society lived in Manhattan. Fashion was also the mistress of luxury, said Pope; she went where her whims could be paid for. Well, luxury had decamped from Paris and was alive and well and living in New York, and the international smartset refugees (who could be found nightly at Le Ruban Bleu) would provide local designers all the sophisticated patronage they needed. New York also had drop-dead backdrops, a crucial asset, as "styles are as much dependent on where and how women wear clothes as what clothes they wear." Gotham was a city of renowned hotels, famed restaurants, and lavish nightclubs where "society and fashion crowd the foyers, eager to see or be seen." New York was an entertainment and media capital, too—"a city of first nights, where gowns make news for the entire country."

Sources of design inspiration? It was true that Parisian couturiers had been able to draw on the work of contemporary artists, and, through access to the Louvre, a treasury of past masterpieces. However, in a happy conjunction of events, Pope observed, "the artistic axis of the world has now shifted to New York," and the rich collections of Gotham's libraries and museums would afford the requisite historical models. Indeed, just recently, in 1937, theater-oriented civic leaders led by philanthropist Irene Lewisohn had inaugurated a Museum of Costume Art, a trove of spectacular garments including material from the last three hundred years. The Museum, ensconced in new Rockefeller Center quarters, held exhibitions like the

"Sources of Fashion Inspiration" show, dedicated precisely to "further strengthening New York's distinction as the fashion center of the world."

Still, if such abundant resources were a necessary precondition of capital-ship, they weren't a sufficient one, Pope agreed, so she and her colleagues got to work turning on spotlights and ramping up runways. That fall of '40, between September 3 and 7, leading stores staged an unprecedented show blitz, a coordinated and sequential series of openings whose glamor quotient matched the "luxurious atmosphere of the Paris previews." Bergdorf-Goodman, Saks Fifth Avenue, Jay Thorpe, Milgrim, Hattie Carnegie, and Bonwit Teller collectively unveiled 800 original American designs. Macy's hailed the event with a full-page ad—blazoned "The Importance of New York!"—which read "Macy's bows low to New York... undisputed fashion capital of the world." Pope seconded that emotion: "For the first time," she applauded, "New York stepped out of the position of understudy and took over the stellar role."

That winter, in January 1941, the Fashion Group followed up the fall foray with a glittering "Fashion Futures" extravaganza, a showing-cum-champagne-supper for 1,500 industry professionals, held in the Grand Ballroom of the Hotel Astor. The committee running the event consisted of Edna Chase of *Vogue*, Carmel Snow of *Harper's Bazaar*, Tobé Coller Davis (publisher since 1927 of the *Tobé Report*, a weekly fashion update for retailers), and Dorothy Shaver (first vice president of Lord & Taylor), who announced their goal was "to develop taste." Honorary Chair La Guardia told those present that "New York from tonight on is and will continue to be the fashion center of the world."

And indeed, from then on, the city fairly bristled with fashion shows from September to May, some for professionals only, some open to the public, most increasingly large and lavish. Looking back on the first year's effort, Pope was pleased at how the pageant of exhibits had filled in "the void left by the conquest of Paris." Formerly, she said, "we in America took our cue from the Rue de la Paix, but "today it is the voice of New York that is heard."

And that voice, it was finally acknowledged, was composed of the many voices of previously unsung American designers. To end the anonymity, Lord & Taylor announced a Designers' Shop, with labels bearing the couturiers' names. Bergdorf-Goodman followed suit with its first "All-American collection" and Arnold Constable with its "American Creators" line. Townley Frocks began selling "Claire McCardell Clothes by Townley," and when Diana Vreeland credited McCardell in *Harper's Bazaar* as the originator of an "American Look," she became one of the city's first fashion stars. *Vogue* announced that "for the first time in fashion history," American designers had demonstrated their ability to turn out goods "without the direct inspiration of Paris," and in February 1941 it showcased them in its first all-American issue, "U.S.A. Fashion on Its Own." Not to be outdone, the *New York Times*, despite wartime paper shortages, launched a "Fashion Forecasts" section that featured interviews with (and photographs of) local couturiers who, "freed from any foreign influence," are "creating authentic all-American styles."

Other Gotham institutions jumped in to the capital-building project. In January 1942 the fragrance firm Coty, Inc., then chaired by Grover A. Whalen, created a Coty American Fashion Critics Award. At the suggestion of a Fashion Group stalwart, publicist Eleanor Lambert, it would go annually to a designer who set a trend which the industry then followed. The first award—presented by Mayor La Guardia in 1941—went to Norman Norell, a Parsons- and Pratt-trained designer who had worked for Paramount (costuming Gloria Swanson), nightclubs (dressing Ziegfeld Follies and Cotton Club stars), and Hattie Carnegie (anonymously), before venturing out on his own in the new designer-friendly era; the Coty

Award put him on the map. Citations were also handed out to McCardell, Mainbocher, and Valentina, among others, in the fashion trade's version of the Academy Awards.

The educational base expanded, too. The Tobé-Coburn School, established in 1937 to train women for executive positions in fashion retailing, advertising, and merchandising, came into its own during the war. The school was a collaboration between Tobé Coller Davis, publisher of the *Tobé Report*, and Julia Coburn, who resigned as fashion editor of *Ladies' Home Journal* to become the school's executive director (in 1940 she was elected president of The Fashion Group). The faculty of well-known academics and business executives produced graduates who were snapped up by department stores and fashion organizations.

Perhaps inspired by the Tobé-Coburn's success, a group of apparel manufacturers and labor leaders formed a foundation to create "an MIT for the fashion industries." In September 1944, in cooperation with the Board of Education, it opened the Fashion Institute of Design and Technology. Housed in the top two floors of the Central High School of Needle Trades, 225 West 24th Street, the two-year technical institute quickly became a major supplier of designers, patternmakers, and merchandisers to the New York rag trade.

Manufacturers and unions had good reason to collaborate on promoting Gotham as a fashion center. Clothing was still New York's biggest manufacturing sector. The city's thousands of dress, suit, coat, accessory, lingerie, and fur houses employed roughly 400,000 people and generated $1.3 billion of annual output—just under half the national industry's total of $3 billion in 1940 (an output comparable to that of steel, autos, oil, meat packing, and electrical machinery). In some areas, New York's proportion was higher still: 70 percent of all dresses American women wore came from Gotham, and about the same percentage of suits and coats. Fifty-five percent of the nation's hats were produced here, as was 27 percent of its perfume and jewelry. And with the wartime shutdown of the Moscow and London auctions, New York emerged as the world's largest market for furs.

Yet New York's share (by value) of manufactured apparel products had been declining steadily, as manufacturing decamped to (or confronted new rivals in) Chicago, Kansas City, and now the South, where the armed forces were building modern mechanized plants. It was clear that Gotham's retention rate was highest for firms tightly tied to fashion. Plain vanilla garments could be made en masse anywhere. But tastes in women's clothing varied so greatly, and styles changed so quickly, that producers would pay a premium (in rent, labor, and taxes) to stay inside the matrix of New York's design and production process. When a new style emerged, buyers ordered, jobbers responded, and small factories mushroomed; came the next season, the fashion changed, the factories disappeared, and the cycle began anew. It was thus transparently clear to manufacturers and unions alike that making New York the fashion capital would be good for jobs and business.

In July 1941 the International Ladies Garment Workers Union (ILGWU) and a congeries of clothing firms jointly established the New York Dress Institute to promote the city as design center. One project was to sew labels into each dress reading "New York Creation" and "Made under standards of I.L.G.W.U." The Institute also sponsored a National Press Week which, starting in 1943, brought fashion editors to town from across the country twice a year, to see the latest fashions.

With all this apparatus set in place to boost New York designers, what did they actually come up with? Did Seventh Avenue create an "American" or a "New York" look? Yes and no. Some of what they did, as so often the case with wartime fashions, was to deploy military, masculine, and patriotic motifs. Coats acquired a military cut. Shoulder pads were everywhere. Colors ran to navy blue, highlighted by red and white. The sailor hat made a comeback. More novel was Seventh Avenue's fashionizing of the military, or at least its new female divisions. Mainbocher designed smart ensemble uniforms for the Waves and the Women's Marine Corps; available at women's clothing stores, they could be individually fitted. Civilian battalions were similarly well clad: Elizabeth Hawes created the uniform for Red Cross aides and Claire McCardell designed the Civilian Defense Volunteer Organization outfit. The industry took a hand in smartening up war workers as well: in 1942, Vera Maxwell, a leading designer of women's sportswear, came up with a one-piece coverall for Sperry Gyroscope women, using thirty-one specifications contributed by the women themselves, and Lilly Daché turned out a companion headdress—a turban with tiny pillbox crown made out of blue plastic straw, edged with white braid.

More daring was the exploration of Latin America as a source of inspiration. The "swing of the rhumba and the tango," Virginia Pope reported, had already "made New Yorkers look to the South." Now interest escalated in what was being worn by the women of Cuba and Mexico; artists were dispatched to record the costumes of Peru, Bolivia, and Argentina; and "the flash of Indian colors and the charm of Spanish cavalier designs" began making an appearance on the runways. This "frank genuflection to South America," moreover, aided in increasing exports: Latin America, Pope argued, "now looks to New York, as it formerly did to Paris, for its fashions."

The biggest fashion change—a dramatic move toward simplicity—came in response to a government edict. The War Production Board (WPB) was as concerned about supplies of wool and cotton as it was stocks of rubber and aluminum. To ensure the availability of the millions of pounds needed for millions of uniforms, the WPB—on March 8, 1942—issued Limiting Order L-85, imposing an array of restrictions on how clothes could be made. The goal was to discourage women from buying new outfits—which would increase civilian demand and curtail military supply—by assuring them that "their present wardrobes will not be made obsolete by radical fashion changes." To accomplish this, the WPB's Textile Division chief, Dallas retailer H. Stanley Marcus (of the Neiman-Marcus company), issued precise instructions.

If made of wool or any other fiber necessary for the war effort, the descent of women's skirts was halted (on average) 17 inches off the ground and limited circumferentially to 72 inches. Jackets were to be no longer than 25 inches. Blouses could not have turned-back cuffs, double yokes, sashes, scarves, or hoods. Balloon or leg-of-mutton sleeves were deleted from the repertoire, belts were made thinner, billowing bathing skirts were banished and a two-piece format encouraged. Men's clothing was restricted to single-breasted, two-piece suits (no vests), slightly shorter jackets, narrower lapels, and no patch pockets. Pants were to be cuffless and pleatless, and only one pair was to be sold with suits instead of the customary two. These restrictions applied to everything but wedding gowns, maternity apparel, infants and children's clothing up to four years, religious vestments, and burial shrouds.

Seventh Avenue responded to L-85 rather as architects had to the Zoning Law of 1916: by figuring out how to work within the assigned framework in a creative and imaginative way. Building on their strength in sportswear and casual-but-elegant styles, designers evolved a new pegtop silhouette, sleek, slim, and functional, that emphasized suits with collarless jackets, long tight sleeves, and mannish topcoats. In August 1942 Marcus argued that American design had been "stimulated by the restrictions." While to some degree this was putting the best face on things—L-85 didn't lead to epochal breakthroughs on the order of the setback skyscrapers—the fashions were competent enough to render plausible the claim that New York had reconstituted itself from manufacturing hub to fashion center. Certainly, the garment industry prospered. Women's wear sales in department stores rose 85 percent between 1939 and 1943. The total dollar volume of manufactured apparel grew from the $1.3 billion of 1940 to $2 billion by 1943. The exodus of shops was arrested. And the size of the sector's payroll jumped from $279.4 million to $425.5 million.

The surge certainly galvanized La Guardia, who in August 1943 set up a mayoral committee to explore ways to lock in these gains and position the city for further expansion. On June 27, 1944, he laid out the group's proposal before a Waldorf Astoria gathering of the fashion and allied industries, sponsored by the New York Board of Trade. Just as Gotham had taken the global lead in music, art, and medicine, so it had a chance to cement its position as capital of couture. The way to do so was to build, after victory, a colossal World Fashion Center (WFC) that would combine all the showrooms of the apparel trades, and a good deal more. The WFC would occupy a set of six to ten structures, estimated to cost roughly $45 million, on land worth $18 million, situated in two parcels bordering the Garment District: a westerly one between Broadway and Sixth Avenue (bounded by 24th and 30th Streets), and an easterly portion between Broadway and Fifth Avenue (from 25th and 27th Streets). The city and state would help out with land costs and necessary street widenings, while a public corporation would be established to issue bonds and oversee development. The WFC would create a well-knit and highly organized industry, capable of meeting competition from other US cities, and from any revanchist effort from Paris to regain its global preeminence. The chair of the Mayor's Committee for a World Fashion Center—the seemingly ubiquitous Grover A. Whalen—was slightly more circumspect, telling the assembled businesspeople only that given the tremendous purchasing power of the United States market, "New York might properly cultivate the ambition to become the fashion authority of the world."

Such caution proved warranted when two months later Paris was liberated and began preparing to resume showings. Many in Gotham's fashion industry—for all their recent New York boosterism—couldn't restrain their enthusiasm at the impending return of couture. Fifth Avenue was festooned with French tricolors from the minute the news arrived, and Carmel Snow wangled permission from Harry Hopkins to make a flying visit to Paris even while the Battle of the Bulge was under way in December 1944.

The French quickly staged a brilliant reassertion of their cultural authority. The Chambre Syndicale de la Couture Parisienne brought together 150 super-talents to collectively create a Théâtre de la Mode. This was an assemblage of two hundred wire-frame dolls, each two feet tall, each dressed to perfection by one or another Parisian giant (Schiaparelli, Worth, Lucien Lelong), down to the tiniest detail—hats, shoes, matching accessories, jewels (a fortune's worth, by Cartier, Van Cleef and Arpels, et al.)—then arranged (by famed Ballets Russes choreographer Boris Kochno) on fifteen 9-by-4-foot mini-theaters (designed by artists like Cocteau), such as the Paris Opera, the Place Vendôme, a Parisian street fair, a bridge on the Seine, a Parisian bistro.

The Théâtre opened March 27, 1945, in Paris, then went on the road in Europe. It would arrive in New York the following spring and draw vast throngs from the retail and fashion worlds and the general public to the Whitelaw Reid House at 451 Madison. It engendered wild enthusiasm in the fashion press—there was particular enthusiasm for some startling New-Look dolls by one Christian Dior (Snow had already spotted him as a comer). "We have come merely to get you back to France," said Jacques Worth, with disarming candor. Henri Bonnet, the French ambassador, more diplomatically, suggested rather that the rivalry between the Parisian and New York fashion establishments was a "reciprocal enrichment" by which both could "profit mutually."

At war's end, this assessment seemed closest to the mark. Snow's enthusiasm for the return of Paris was widely shared. The dress editor of the *Tobé Report*, while decrying the "premature and unfortunate publicity" that Paris styles had received since the Liberation, admitted that "Paris is still a magic word." Nonetheless, Virginia Pope kept up her Fashion of the Times show, department stores continued to feature American designers, designers like Mainbocher and McCardell said that while they would certainly drink at the well of Parisian fashion, they would continue to work in New York. Seventh Avenue, accordingly, rallied around the more defensible proposition, advanced at a Fashion Group gathering in October 1944, that the center of couture would henceforth be bi-polar: "Paris plus New York."

140

On the Town

Clearly, uniformed visitors had a variety of epochal theatrical evenings from which to choose. In the end, however, they would probably have been most pleased by *On the Town*, a play at least as authentically American as *Oklahoma!*, albeit set in an urban not rural terrain, and in its own way as innovative as Tennessee Williams's work, representing as it did an astonishing mixture of individuals and influences.

Its progenitor—the ballet *Fancy Free*—had been choreographed and danced by Jerome Robbins, himself a product of the city's eclectic cultural scene. He had been born Jerome Wilson Rabinowitz in 1918 at the Jewish Maternity Hospital (270 East Broadway) in the heart of immigrant Lower East Side. His father, Harry, had arrived in the US in 1904, aged fifteen, from a shtetl near Pinsk; his mother, Lena, had arrived in 1893, aged four, from the city of Minsk. Harry and his brothers opened a kosher deli uptown, on East 97th Street, in still largely Jewish East Harlem. It did well; they sold it; Harry moved his family to Weehawken, New Jersey; and he opened a modest manufactory—the Comfort Corset Company (for "stylish stouts")—in nearby Union City.

The Rabinowitz children were recognized as prodigies, his sister Sonia in dance, Jerry in music—at 3½ he was composing pieces for piano and had his first recital, in Manhattan's Aeolian Hall—but during his high school years he grew more intrigued by his sister's blooming dance career. In 1936, reverses in Harry's corset business forced Jerry to leave NYU after one semester. Faced with factory work on foundation garments, he opted for dance instead.

Rabinowitz auditioned that year for the Dance Center group, where his sister had taken classes. It was run by Senia Gluck Sandor and his wife, Felicia Sorel, in a small studio theater atop a garage in the West 50s. The Harlem-born Sandor had studied with Mikhail Fokine and danced at the Metropolitan Opera but also performed in Vaudeville and Broadway during the 1920s. In 1932 Sandor used his profits to open the Dance Center, which he hoped would do for dance what the Theatre Guild had for drama: provide progressive art to adventurous audiences. Sandor also served as choreographer and dance adviser to the Group Theatre, so when he accepted Rabinowitz, he was able to arrange a job for him with the Group.

Sandor also advised adopting a non-Jewish stage name, so it was as Jerome Robbins that he began his multifaceted education. Apart from his Dance Center work, Robbins took classes in Spanish and Asian dance; studied modern dance at the New Dance Group, a left-wing collective; and looked into ballet at the WPA, though reluctantly, and only at Sandor's insistence, as Robbins shared the antipathy toward ballet of Martha Graham and her modern dance disciples, who considered it an artificial, hierarchical, patriarchal, formulaic, and individualistic form. One evening at the Met watching Alexandra Danilova, the *prima ballerina assoluta* who had trained at the Russian Imperial Ballet School, brought him around sharply, and he set out to find the best available teacher. He tried to enter the School of American Ballet that Kirstein and Balanchine had opened at 59th and Madison in 1934—Balanchine and Danilova having defected together to the West in 1924 to join Diaghilev's Ballets Russes—but Balanchine's school did not offer scholarships. So Robbins began studies with a highly regarded teacher, Ella Daganova, who taught him classical Russian techniques in exchange for his doing her windows and floors.

Robbins's first sustained contact with professional theater people, and first paid work as a dancer, came the following year when he was hired for a ten-week stint at Camp Tamiment. Situated on a lake in a 2,200-wooded-acre tract in the Pocono Mountains, Tamiment had opened in 1921 as a summer retreat for faculty and students at the Rand School of Social Science, the workers school founded by the Socialist Party in 1906. By 1938 it had taken on many of the trappings of a Borscht Belt resort—social directors, dances, and entertainments. It offered its audience of vacationing Jewish white-collar workers a full-fledged Broadway-caliber revue every Saturday night, and informal cabaret shows throughout the week, with actors, dancers, and comedians like Danny Kaye and Imogene Coca, the saucer-eyed Carol Channing and the sad-eyed Jules Munshin, and Jerome Robbins, who over four summers at Tamiment worked his way up from ensemble parts, to solo turns, to creating and choreographing dances, often on radical themes, such as *Death of a Loyalist* (about the Spanish Civil War), and a pas de deux set to Billie Holiday's "Strange Fruit," both done in 1939.

Tamiment also provided Robbins a ticket to Broadway that year, when Lee and J. J. Shubert mounted a fall musical, entitled *Straw Hat Revue*, based on that summer's sketches. *Straw Hat* made Kaye a star, boosted Coca's career (she rolled out her Carmen Miranda knockoff, *The Soused American Way*), and led Robbins to other dance turns in Broadway vehicles like *Stars in Your Eyes* (with Jimmy Durante and Ethel Merman) and *Keep off the Grass*, choreographed by Balanchine, then moonlighting on musicals (he even choreographed elephants for a Ringling Brothers and Barnum & Bailey war benefit).

In 1940, Robbins became a member of the Ballet Theatre. A quasi-national repertory company, it had a roster of principals and corps members that mingled natives with refugees arriving from war-torn Europe; a schedule that alternated a New York season with a national road show; and a diverse basket of offerings, including works by Russian, English, and American choreographers. The American wing notably included Agnes de Mille, who had one foot in modern dance, the other in ballet. The Russian wing was dominated by Michel Fokine himself, still vigorous and creative in his sixties. Their grandly scaled approach caught Gotham's fancy: its first performance, on January 11, 1940, sold out all 3,500 seats of Rockefeller Center's Center Theatre.

Robbins pressed hard to join this distinguished troupe and in June 1940 was accepted for the corps de ballet. By 1941, after having been directed by Fokine (in his *Carnaval*) and de Mille (in her *Three Virgins and a Devil*), he was promoted to soloist and proceeded to burnish his growing reputation with roles in *Helen of Troy*, *Petrouchka*, and *Romeo and Juliet*.

The war created a problem for the Ballet Theatre. The European-based Ballet Russe de Monte Carlo had been doing tours in the United States since 1933, under the aegis of impresario Sol Hurok. With war in 1939, the company relocated to New York and became a very formidable competitor. The Ballet Theater responded by having Hurok take them under his wing as well. In addition to handling bookings and publicity, the Russophiliac Hurok used his position to boost the company's Russian wing and undercut the American camp.

Robbins, furious at the Russomaniacal focus ("for a whole year I did not get out of boots, Russian bloomers, and a peasant wig"), began writing stories and scenarios for short ballets on American themes, as had de Mille with her Western-based *Rodeo* (whose massive success at the rival Ballet Russe, which mounted it over Hurok's objections, was widely seen as proof positive that a ballet did not have to be Russian to sell well). Robbins's scenarios were more local still—set in New York itself—and they reflected "the way we dance today and how we are." He envisioned a "blackout ballet" featuring an air raid warden; a comic-book ballet starring Superman and Little Orphan Annie; a ballet set in Times Square with a score featuring traffic sounds and police whistles; a pageant-ballet that recounted New York's history; and a ballet about East Side kids that echoed the Group Theater's *Dead End* of 1935.

Then fellow actor Mary Hunter recommended Robbins look at Paul Cadmus's raunchy 1934 painting, *The Fleet's In*, which had created a firestorm over its sensual depiction of sailors on leave lustily cruising girls (and being cruised, it seemed, by a wavy-haired Adonis whose red tie implied same-sex proclivities). Though the Cadmus canvas gave Robbins the idea of doing a ballet on the theme, he insisted that he had "inwardly rejected" the painting and would sternly distance himself from any unseemly sexuality. His ballet would "show that the boys in the service are healthy, vital boys: there is nothing sordid or morbid about them." This public posturing likely reflected private turmoil over his sexual identity, for though he had taken full advantage of the theatrical world's tolerance for unconventional sexual orientations, his own remained a source of confusion and guilt: "Please save me from being gay," he scrawled in his journal.

Nevertheless, after seeing *The Fleet's In*, and perhaps also Cadmus's 1938 *Sailors and Floosies*, Robbins now "watched sailors, and girls, too, all over town." He observed, among

Paul Cadmus, *The Fleet's In!*, 1934. (PD-US-no notice. Public Works of Art Project)

A man does the Lindy Hop at the Savoy Ballroom in Harlem, 1941. (Photo by Charles Peterson/Hulton Archive/Getty Images)

other things, how often the men went around in threes, "strutting down the avenue," their "eyes and mouths open to all the sights." He observed how they went "dancing in bars." He studied the dances themselves, like the Lindy Hop and the Shorty George, which were being done all around Times Square, right next door to the Metropolitan Opera House where the Ballet Theatre performed. He asked Madeleine Lee, a young actress, communist organizer, and great dancer, to teach him the street steps he needed; she did, and also helped initiate him into the CP, which he would formally join at the end of 1943. And then in the spring of 1943 he wrote a scenario for a ballet—*Fancy Free*—that described, he said, "World War II as it appeared in the streets of New York," and it promptly won Ballet Theatre approval.

Now he needed the music. Robbins had clear ideas about what he wanted, a jazzy score that would incorporate the boogie-woogie and rumba rhythms to which his peers were dancing. For a composer he thought first of Marc Blitzstein, who'd scored *The Cradle Will Rock*, but Blitzstein was in London. Pianist and composer Morton Gould, who had worked in radio, vaudeville, and movie theaters as well as concert halls, was another candidate, but also unavailable. Gould suggested a student of Serge Koussevitzky, recently hired as an assistant conductor by the New York Philharmonic, who could probably use the money, but no one seemed to know where this Leonard Bernstein lived. Finally, Oliver Smith, the Ballet Theatre's scenic designer, provided the lead. Smith's cousin was Paul Bowles—a Jamaica, Queens–born composer of incidental music for theater (he would shortly be commissioned to work on Tennessee Williams's *Glass Menagerie*) and a music critic (he worked for Virgil Thomson at the *Herald Tribune*). Bowles knew Aaron Copland; Copland knew Leonard Bernstein; and indeed Copland was in large measure responsible for Bernstein's being in New York.

Bernstein was born in Lawrence, Massachusetts, in 1918 to a family at the bottom of the immigrant Jewish ladder. His father, Sam, worked his way up from cleaning fish to running the Samuel Bernstein Hair Company which, unlike corsets, did OK in the Depression, so Sam, though he took a dim view of professional musicians, could pay for Leonard's piano lessons at the New England Conservatory of Music, as well as Boston Latin School and Harvard, which he entered in 1935. In 1937, the nineteen-year-old Bernstein had his professional debut in Cambridge playing Ravel's Piano Concerto and made a foray down to New York to attend the November 14 debut, at the Guild Theater, of Anna Sokolow—a member of Martha Graham's company, now branching out on her own—on whom Bernstein had developed a crush. By happenstance, he found himself seated next to Aaron Copland, whose music he adored but whom he'd never met and didn't recognize until they were introduced by the poet Muriel Rukeyser. It was Copland's birthday, and the composer invited Bernstein to an after-recital party at his loft above a candy factory on West 63rd Street, where Lincoln Center State Theater now stands; it was Copland's work space, he lived just down the block at the Empire Hotel. When Bernstein told Copland he knew his Piano Variations, the composer dared him to play it. He did, and spectacularly, leaving drop-jawed the glittering assemblage of poets, photographers, filmmakers, writers, and composers (including Virgil Thomson and Paul Bowles).

Bernstein was equally agog, not just because he was a lad from the provinces mingling with a salonful of New York's artistic elite, but also because it became clear that many in the room, starting with Copland, were emancipated homosexuals, living a guilt-free and uncloseted life. Bernstein himself was muddled about his own sexual orientation and worried about his family's likely response to any sign he had strayed from the straight and narrow. Copland himself provided an alternative model, managing with discretion his serial relationships with younger men. No one knows if Bernstein was among them, but they quickly proved to be kindred spirits, and it would be Copland who became Bernstein's closest composition adviser and musical inspiration. When he wrote his senior thesis the following year, his topic was "The Absorption of Race Elements into American Music," in which he argued that US composers, preeminently New Yorkers Gershwin and Copland, had created a new national musical style by responding to jazz and Latin-American influences.

In July 1939, sidestepping his father's request that he join the family firm, Bernstein accepted an invitation from Adolph Green to share an East Village sublet on East 9th Street (complete with Steinway grand). The Bronx-born Green was the graduate of De Witt Clinton High and New York University who had put together the *Revuers* with Betty Comden (whom he'd met at NYU, where both majored in drama). He had been working in 1937 at a summer camp outside Pittsfield where Bernstein was hired as music counselor, and they hit it off. Bernstein now alternated between palling around with Green's group (often accompanying their Village Vanguard skits on piano) and hanging out with Copland's highbrow crowd on the Upper West Side. He tried for a Juilliard conducting fellowship but missed the deadline, so enrolled instead at the Curtis Institute in Philadelphia. In the summer of 1940, he studied composing with Copland, and conducting with Serge Koussevitzky, at the newly established Berkshire Music Center at Tanglewood, the country estate (near Lenox, Massachusetts) of the Tappan family, descendants of New York's merchant-abolitionist Lewis Tappan. In September 1940 Bernstein returned to Philly but traveled almost weekly to Gotham, visiting his Uptown and Downtown friends, until in September 1942 he moved up permanently, writing a former teacher: "I have come to the Big City, finally, to seek my fortune."

Fortune proved elusive at first. Copland advised nightclub work, and Bernstein played occasionally for the *Revuers* at the Vanguard and Café Society Uptown. He shared an apartment on West 52nd Street (the same block that housed the *Leon and Eddies*, *Onyx*, *Three Deuces*, and *Famous Door*), where he coached singers, rehearsed dancers, gave piano lessons, and composed his first symphony. He got a job with music publisher Harms-Witmark transcribing jazz improvisations recorded by noted musicians such as Coleman Hawkins—providing him a thorough grounding in the workings of Tin Pan Alley. He was squeaking by on $25 a week when, in August 1943, aged twenty-five, he was hired by Artur Rodzinki, the Philharmonic's conductor, as his assistant—other US candidates having been drafted and Bernstein having been deferred as asthmatic. He was now making $125 a week and was offered a one-room efficiency (#503) in the warren of studios above Carnegie Hall, where he was living when Jerome Robbins came knocking in the fall.

When Robbins asked what kind of music he wrote, Bernstein played some of his still unperformed First Symphony, and its jazzy syncopated dissonance proved to be precisely what the choreographer was looking for. And when he explained he wanted music that would capture the spirit and dances of wartime New York, Bernstein trotted out a tune he'd jotted down on a napkin at the Russian Tea Room, just that afternoon, and Robbins closed the deal on the spot. The two young men (both the same age) clicked on many levels, sharing a Russian-Polish-Jewish heritage, disapproving fathers, conflicted sexuality, and a love for admixing cultures high and low.

The collaboration, if exhilarating, was difficult, as Robbins had to tour with the Ballet Theatre, while Bernstein was tied down in New York by his assistant conductorship which, on November 14, 1943, thrust him into the national spotlight. Bruno Walter had been subbing for the vacationing Rodzinski when Walter had taken ill, and with Rodzinski out of town, the twenty-five-year-old Bernstein, with short notice, had taken the floor at Carnegie Hall. The nationally broadcast concert was an enormous triumph, partly because he gave a magnificent performance (even the orchestra cheered him), partly because the boy-conductor-makes-good story was terrific wartime copy. Journalists—tipped off in advance by the Philharmonic's PR person—played up the angle that an all-American (albeit Jewish) Harvard grad, who did sambas and congas, loved baseball, and read Dick Tracy, had scored big in a field (classical music) hitherto dominated by foreigners. (His ascension came at just the moment Jackson Pollock was being elevated as a culture hero, and for overlapping reasons.) The born-in-the-USA Bernstein, hailed as a potential rival to Toscanini and Stokowski, was interviewed by all the leading magazines, invited to appear (as had Willkie) on *Information Please*, and had a party thrown for him by *Post* columnist Leonard Lyons, at which he met, among many others, Ethel Barrymore, Bernard Baruch, Joe DiMaggio, Moss Hart, and John Steinbeck.

Despite such heady distractions, Bernstein kept at his scoring, mailing off installments to Robbins on the road. Once they were agreed, Bernstein recorded piano renditions (backed by Copland on a second instrument) and sent them off to his distant collaborator so he could rehearse the Ballet Theatre dancers in nightclubs and deserted ballrooms across the country.

In the meantime, Hurok had hired the Met for the Ballet Theatre's spring season. And there, on April 18, 1944, three happy-go-lucky sailors on shore leave (one of them Robbins himself) cartwheeled onto the stage set designed by Oliver Smith, its stylized twinkling skyscrapers backdropping a city street, a lamppost, and a Hopper-like *Nighthawk*-type bar. The boisterous, exuberant trio swagger about on the hot summer night, looking for a good time. A Blonde and a Redhead arrive—Victory girls, fast but respectable. The guys perform dazzling dances to gain their attention (Robbins's sailor moves in a Latin mode). The competition turns into a brawl. The girls split, the guys make up and have a beer, then swagger off in pursuit of a Blonde. It was all done at a sizzling pace—"the kids who dance in it dance like mad," wrote the *Times*'s John Martin in his rave review (he found *Fancy Free* to be "ten degrees north of terrific"). Audience and critics alike were thrilled to see this highbrow form incorporating such vernacular and familiar images: the ballet, said the *World Telegram*, was "right up-to-date" and "strictly New York from the sidewalk up." Robbins himself stressed in "Ballet Puts on Dungarees," a *Times* piece he published, that a dance form which had been the "orchidaceous pet of the Czars, has come out of the hothouse and become a people's entertainment in our energetic land." Hurok extended the season to accommodate the crush, but the crowds broke Met records anyway, with all 3,300 seats consistently filled and standees packed three deep. Quickly added to the Ballet Theatre's national tour, *Fancy Free* was performed 162 times in the following year and became the company's signature piece.

Oliver Smith now urged Bernstein and Robbins to turn the ballet into a Broadway musical and offered to be its producer. The three collaborators agreed to integrate the story, music, dance, sets, and lyrics, as had *Oklahoma!* Bernstein's friends Comden and Green were brought on board to write the book (and play parts as well), after the composer took Robbins and Smith to catch their act at the Blue Angel. The two writers set out to create characters (they recalled) who possessed "the qualities and attitudes of the servicemen we had seen coming into the city for the first time and at least touch on the frantic search for gaiety and love, and the terrific pressure of time that war brings." Money proved hard to come by until veteran Broadway director George Abbott signed on to captain the crew of twenty-somethings, and his awesome reputation for bringing in hit shows unlocked a floodgate of funding. Comden and Green wrote it up between June and December of 1944, their spirits perhaps buoyed by the Normandy invasion and the liberation of Rome and Paris.

When *On the Town* opened on December 28 at the Adelphi Theatre on 54th Street, it was clearly a very different product than *Fancy Free*, in many more ways than the obvious changes in form and length. Not a note of the original score remained; instead there was Bernstein's racy and sophisticated melange of Stravinsky and Copland with the driving boogie-woogie that had so attracted Mondrian, music that evoked Gotham's edgy excitement from the very first four skyward-leaping notes of "New York, New York." Smith's settings were different too, now grounded in real New York sites rather than the abstract street scene he had concocted for *Fancy Free*: his backdrops conjured up Times Square, the Brooklyn Navy Yard, Central Park, Carnegie Hall, a subway car, Coney Island—a dozen in all—constituting a cityscape through which the principals undertake their picaresque journey.

The narrative, too, was different. There were still three guys, and "just one day," but now three gals too, and the guys (partly because they all paired off) don't compete, they cooperate. The three sailors—romantic Gabey, serious-minded Chip, and happy-go-lucky Ozzie (played by Adolph Green)—set out from the Brooklyn Navy Yard on their twenty-four-hour adventure. They arrive by subway at Times Square just as a bill-sticker is pasting up a poster announcing the attractive Ivy Smith has been chosen this month's "Miss Turnstiles"—a nod to the real "Miss Subways," elected by New York passengers, whose face was displayed in each car. Gabey, instantly smitten, vows to find and woo her; the others agree to help; and they each set off to follow the clues provided in the poster: Ivy studies at Carnegie Hall, paints at the Museum of Modern Art, and frequents the club scene. They will rendezvous back in Times Square at 11:00 p.m.

Ozzie gets sidetracked when he goes to the Museum of Natural History (which he confuses with MOMA) and is diverted by the amorous anthropologist Claire DeLoone (played by Comden); after the two accidentally demolish a dinosaur skeleton they flee to Claire's for serious convivializing. Chip never gets beyond the Checkered cab of Brunhilde (Hildy) Esterhazy, the feisty and brazen driver who determinedly carries him off to her place. Gabey actually finds Ivy in a Carnegie Hall studio, taking singing lessons with Madam Dilly, and she agrees to meet him in Times Square. Ivy pays for her high-culture studies by working as a lowdown cootch dancer at Coney Island, and her instructresses informs Ivy she'd better not dally this evening or there'll be no Dilly in the morning; besides, she says, one can't have love and perfect one's art, too, so Ivy reluctantly agrees to stand up Gabey and bump and grind instead.

So, when Gabey arrives in Times Square, his buddies and their girls are there, but no Ivy. To cheer up their disconsolate comrade they take him on a tour of New York's nightclubs—stopping at watering holes like *Diamond Eddie's*, the *Congacabana*, and the *Slam-Bang*—at which they do all kinds of popular dances. Finally, they subway down to Coney, where Gabey discovers Ivy in deshabille, but true love conquers respectability, and dawn finds all six back at the Yard. The male trio clambers up the gangplank—it's poignantly unclear if they'll ever see the ladies again—just as another threesome dashes down to commence their own twenty-four-hour encounter with New York, New York, clearly one helluva town.

141

The Theater at the Center of the World

One person not enthralled by Bernstein's sailor-centric composing was Serge Koussevitzky, who saw it as diverting Bernstein from his true calling: conducting. After *Fancy Free* was launched, the maestro had called Mayor La Guardia and asked to have Bernstein conduct some of the city's summer concerts at Lewisohn Stadium, which is why July 14, 1944, had found Bernstein, baton in hand, leading the Philharmonic before a crowd of 10,000 in his debut at the City College venue. Yet almost immediately afterward, to Koussevitzky's dismay, Bernstein had again hared off toward Broadway. Now, in 1945, with *On the Town* up and running, Koussevitzky again contacted La Guardia with a proposal to have Bernstein appointed as conductor of Gotham's recently established New York City Symphony, itself only part of the mayor's far grander project of launching a municipal culture complex.

La Guardia had proposed establishing something of the sort once before, in 1935, and indeed had collected fourteen million dollars in pledges from private donors toward creating a Civic Art Center, just north of Rockefeller Center, that would, he hoped, bring together the Metropolitan Opera, the Philharmonic, and the Museum of Modern Art. MOMA had opted out, preferring to build its own edifice, and the enterprise never happened. The mayor did, however, manage to establish that year two cognate projects—the High School of Music & Art on 135th Street and Convent Avenue, and (with WPA assistance) the country's first municipal art gallery, in an old brownstone at 62 West 53rd Street. For the remainder of the Depression decade, the mayor relied on federal spending—particularly the art, theater, and music projects of the WPA—to advance his goal of making cultural offerings accessible to popular audiences. The huge consequent turnout for free or low-priced performances amply demonstrated widespread middle- and working-class interest.

With the wind-down of WPA funding in the early war years, La Guardia's thoughts again turned toward the city's assuming some responsibility for cultural development, in modest emulation of European cities' centuries-old tradition of public support for the arts. What made it seem conceivable again was Gotham's acquisition in 1942 (for nonpayment of taxes) of the Mecca Temple at 135 West 55th Street, which had housed the Ancient Arabic Order of the Nobles of the Mystic Shrine (aka the Masonic Shriners). City Council President Newbold Morris, with La Guardia's support, developed a plan to convert the neo-Moorish structure into an art center that would offer high culture at low prices.

In July 1943 La Guardia announced the city would lease the building to a nonprofit organization—the City Center of Music and Drama, Inc.—charging it only the equivalent of property taxes and providing $65,000 to transform the auditorium into a theater and the various lodge rooms into rehearsal halls and studios. While "New York has become, by force of circumstances, the world center of creative and interpretive art," the mayor explained, at least a million citizens could not share in this bounty because high-culture temples like the Metropolitan Opera or Carnegie Hall were way beyond their means. The new City Center, he said, would provide concerts, plays, ballets, and more at popular prices—and at hours when working people could attend—and it would do so without municipal subsidy. The American Federation of Musicians and the Dramatists Guild (among others) would adjust wage and royalty scales downward. And any operating deficits would be covered by the incorporators, who included prominent citizens in business and the professions (like Morton Baum, Howard S. Cullman, John D. Rockefeller Jr., and Marshall Field), and the arts (such as John Hammond, Paul Robeson, Elmer Rice, and Lillian Gish). The new organization also included institutions (notably labor unions) whose members would be major arts consumers (like the Amalgamated, the ILGWU, the Greater New York City Council of Industrial Unions, and the Workmen's Circle). And the city's major arts institutions—the Met, the Philharmonic, the ballet companies, and Broadway producers—accepted the argument that the new City Center would not be a rival, but, rather, a feeder organization that would develop new audiences and new talents (as had the WPA).

On December 11, 1943, La Guardia (on his sixty-first birthday) presided over the structure's opening performance, featuring the Philharmonic, with Rodzinski conducting Tchaikovsky, Gershwin, and "Happy Birthday." All 2,800 seats were filled, prices ranging from 55 cents to $1.10, with David Dubinsky's garment workers and Joe Curran's seamen much in evidence, and traditional opening night fancy dress attire barely to be seen at all. The mayor praised the new venture as a marvelous beginning but stubbornly declared he still hoped to return to his mid-'30s vision—which some had wrongly dismissed as "grandiose"—of a "great Art Center" that would bring together many cultural institutions on a permanent basis. After all, he again underscored, "New York City is the center of music and the theatre and the arts, not only of our country but, it may be said, of the entire world."

That same year La Guardia and an assortment of civic leaders began to move toward fulfilling that vision, when the New York City Opera was founded—with conductor László Halász as general director—to make high-quality opera widely available to City Center audiences (tickets were priced between 75 cents and $2.20). The company launched its first season in February 1944 (with a performance of *Tosca*) and quickly won a reputation as a platform for young singers (particularly Americans)—Halász supported the notion of mounting operas in English translation—and for a repertory that included new works as well as old classics.

Mayor La Guardia conducts the New York Philharmonic, ca. 1940. (Photo by Irving Haberman/IH Images/Getty Images)

The year 1944 also brought formation of the New York City Symphony when Leopold Stokowski, his contract with the NBC Symphony Orchestra having been cancelled (largely at Toscanini's urging), acceded to La Guardia's request that he create an orchestra for the new arts center. Stokowski agreed to serve as conductor-director without pay, indeed put $20,000 of his own money into improving the acoustics. Then he set about rounding up young musicians (the older ones were in the Army), fully one-third of whom were women, an utterly unique statistic in the history of symphonic music. Tickets maxed out at $1.80, and despite serious budgetary constraints, the 1944–45 season was a success with audience and critics alike.

The City Center became the place where ballet companies (notably the Ballet Russe de Monte Carlo), Broadway shows, operettas, jazz bands, modern dance companies, choirs, and lecturers (notably Orson Welles) came to present their wares at reduced prices to sell out audiences, who rapidly included out of towners as well as New Yorkers. In the first two years roughly a million paying customers turned out.

Still, given the absence of municipal subsidy—of the sort extended to several museums and libraries—it was always a scramble to make ends meet. And when budget cuts were announced in the summer of 1945, Stokowski decided to move on, and the position of music director of the New York City Symphony Orchestra at City Center was offered to Leonard Bernstein. He agreed to do so, also without pay, for several reasons: the egalitarian nature of the venture, an opportunity to shape an orchestra, the chance to mount new or seldom heard works—all of which would keep him in the public eye and increase his long-term chances of winning command of one of the nation's great orchestras. Plus, there was the sense—one increasingly common in the wartime city—that a momentous transformation was under way, that the global spotlight was swinging across the Atlantic from Europe to Gotham. "America is now definitely the cultural center of the world," Bernstein argued, echoing La Guardia, "and New York is the cultural center of America, hence of the world." Given that "there should be a fountain-head in the city for music and art," and given that "the City Center fills that need," it seemed to Bernstein that there could be no more spotlit a podium than the one he was about to occupy.

PLANNING THE POSTWAR CITY

Robert Moses with a model of lower Manhattan and his proposed Brooklyn-Battery Bridge. (Bettmann / Contributor / Getty Images)

142

Presenting the Future: A Public Plan

On May 1, 1944, Fiorello La Guardia inaugurated an exhibition called *NYC Postwar Program.* The show displayed projects the city intended to build, once the global conflict came to its inevitably victorious conclusion. On entering 500 Park Avenue, visitors moved through a space—designed by the up-and-coming architectural firm of Skidmore, Owings & Merrill—that was reminiscent of General Motors' Futurama exhibit at the 1939–1940 New York World's Fair. Traversing a semicircular ramp, exhibit-goers could gaze down at a 50-by-20-foot floor-map-and-model of New York City, studded with three-dimensional icons marking the sites of proposed public works. Red crosses indicated new hospitals, writing slates suggested schools, blue-coated mini-cops stood for police stations, bright green swatches forecast parks and playgrounds. Other totems promised the arrival or rehabilitation of markets and museums, zoos and libraries, bridges and beaches, tunnels and prisons, fire houses and courthouses, health centers and housing projects, sewage treatment plants, parkways, expressways, and more.

This was no dreamy wish list. Three-quarters of the projects were in various stages of planning and development. Twenty-one percent were ready to build. Visitors could view a profusion of blueprints, renderings, maps, and models in successive gallery spaces. Some undertakings—Idlewild Airport, the Delaware Aqueduct, the Brooklyn Queens Expressway—were colossal multimillion-dollar affairs. Others were minute and particular: a soap-making machine for Rikers Island Penitentiary; a new roof for the Botanical Garden's manure shed. An accompanying booklet, with an introduction by the mayor, meticulously set down and toted up the price tags. The tab came to roughly $1.25 billion. As one reviewer noted, this was "the most gigantic postwar program as yet undertaken by any city." In fact, it was unmatched at either the state or federal level.

Yet for all its immensity, and the impressiveness of its component parts, the charts, models, graphs, and columns of figures did not set the blood to racing, partly because they were not conjoined to any larger economic or social strategy, not components of an overarching metropolitan plan embedded in a soaring vision of the city's future.

Its justifications were strictly narrow gauge.

First and foremost, it was portrayed as an emergency plan to deal with the downturn expected when troops and war workers returned to the civilian job market. If unemployment surged, Gotham could quickly set to work over 200,000 men (it was very male-oriented), nearly as many as the 240,000 hired by the WPA. A photo-mural depicted New York soldiers and workers, the future beneficiaries of their municipality's foresight.

Second, the program was presented as an exercise in municipal housekeeping, a simple replacing or refurbishing of items fallen into disrepair or obsolescence over the long years of depression and war.

If the *Postwar Program* had all the moral grandeur of a line-item budget, that was exactly the way Robert Moses wanted it, and it was Robert Moses whom Mayor La Guardia had put in charge of designing New York's future.

Moses was now casting himself as a sober, safe, and practical alternative to Rexford Tugwell, the former chairman of the City Planning Commission (CPC), whom Moses had more or less run out of town in 1941 by smearing him, seriatim, as a long-haired wimp, an ivory-tower dreamer, a stalking horse for Lewis Mumford's dream of disaggregating the city, a power-mad would-be dictator, and a "planning Red" whose aim was "to reconstruct the entire city and with it our economic and political systems."

Having toppled Tugwell, Moses had taken his place. Back in 1937 he'd made the mistake of declining the chairmanship of the CPC, a body mandated by the revised City Charter of 1936 to fashion a Master Plan for Gotham. Convinced the new office would prove powerless, Moses had let it pass to Tugwell, who turned out to be a dangerous rival, daring even to intrude on his park-and-parkway turf. Now, with its potential enhanced by the 1938 housing provisions of the New York State Constitution, Moses realized that by controlling the CPC he could expand his domain to include public housing, a territory he'd previously tried and failed to annex.

Accordingly, on November 27, 1941, Moses accepted La Guardia's offer to join the CPC (while keeping his job as parks commissioner). Though not its chair, Moses quickly dominated the agency through his commanding personality, political connections, and ideological rigor.

One of the first things he did was deep-six Tugwell's Master Plan. The commission declared itself "opposed to the adoption of general plans of land use which suggested to some persons [principally Moses himself] drastic and revolutionary changes in ownership, use and taxation of private property."

Then, immediately after Pearl Harbor, when Regional Plan Association board chairman George McAneny urged the mayor to undertake postwar planning, Moses moved fast. Taking a leaf from the New Deal's National Resources Planning Board, he proposed creating "a reservoir of public works." La Guardia endorsed the idea and in effect anointed him coordinator of all postwar planning ("I have leaned heavily on Commissioner Bob Moses," the mayor would acknowledge in the 1944 exhibition booklet). RM's great enemy FDR may have sidelined him from the nation's antifascist effort, but in New York, World War II would be the making of Robert Moses.

True to his disdain for Master Plans, Moses set about compiling a Master List instead. He called on all city departments, borough presidents, and other public agencies to assess postwar needs in their domain and propose ways to meet them. (Bureaucrats lacking technical resources were supplied with engineers and other experts from Moses's Parks Department and Triborough Bridge Authority.) Suggestions for schools, precinct houses, roadways, and sewer lines were added to the list. Rezonings or changes in land-use regulations were off the table. Moses rested the program's legitimacy not on its furtherance of some larger urban vision but on its prophylactic power to ward off unemployment. "Failure to prepare for peace," he declared, "is quite as serious as failure to prepare for war."

Neither Moses nor La Guardia believed their billion-plus program could be paid for wholly or even mainly out of municipal coffers. They were counting on support from the state and federal governments.

In Albany, Governor Dewey had been accumulating surplus revenue in a Postwar Reconstruction Fund and had shelled out over half a million dollars to aid Gotham's planning process. When he lost New York to FDR in the 1944 presidential sweepstakes, Dewey decided he hadn't been liberal enough and proceeded to set aside still more money for postwar housing, highway, and health-care needs.

But the bottom line ran through Washington, DC. The success of the city's public works initiative, La Guardia said forthrightly, was "entirely dependent upon what the Federal Government does." What it *should* do, he told Congress in 1944, was pay 50 percent of the cost of postwar construction (nationally, not just in New York), and cover 75 percent of the bill for the planning process, monies he wanted delivered directly to municipalities.

La Guardia was counting on the Second Coming of the New Deal. The *NYC Postwar Program* booklet gave pride of place to a signed letter from Franklin Roosevelt in which the president heartily endorsed Gotham's "pioneering" work on postwar planning, urged other cities and states to "follow New York's example," and called on Congress to foot part of the bill. The 1944 election campaign—in full swing during the exhibit's run—gave the mayor grounds for hope that a postwar liberal resurgence was in the works, as evidenced by the CIO Political Action Committee's agenda, by FDR's Economic Bill of Rights, and by Roosevelt's liberal heir apparent, Henry Wallace, having taken up the president's call for sixty million postwar jobs. More generally, the successful marshalling of public resources behind prosecution of the war had bolstered faith in the possibilities of government-directed planning.

The same events that revitalized La Guardia's determination to promote the social democratic project, however, also enhanced the determination of local business elites to assert private control of the public agenda.

143

"Two Million Plans!"

On May 2, 1944, one day after La Guardia and Moses launched their exhibition on postwar public works, Al Smith held a press conference. The aged warrior announced that the Committee for Economic Development (CED), whose Gotham chapter Smith now chaired, would *also* tackle the postwar re-employment problem, emphasizing the private sector's role.

Five months later, on October 10, 1944, over 1,000 representatives of New York's economic high command—potentates from industry, commerce, and finance—assembled in the Waldorf Astoria to hear what the CED proposed. This time, Al Smith was not presiding. The former governor had died a week earlier—the gathering stood for a minute of silent homage—and the chairmanship had passed to the omnipresent Grover Whalen.

The new CED leader, aided by several economic experts, laid out the challenge facing the assembled businessmen. If Gotham's returning veterans and displaced war workers were to find jobs awaiting them, the local economy would have to generate 550,000 more positions than had been available back in 1940, when 2,840,000 had been gainfully employed. This boost of roughly 20 percent in job openings would in turn require (the number-crunchers calculated) an increase of 35 percent in annual production and sales over prewar levels. Given pent-up consumer purchasing power, they thought this an eminently attainable target. Indeed, the economists were sanguine that the metropolitan private sector might well pull off an "economic triumph," not only providing jobs for all but raising the standard of living by a third.

The gathering ratified the CED's proposed sectoral targets (New York should shoot for 885,000 manufacturing jobs, 736,000 service slots, etc.) and adopted the rousing slogan: "35% More." The meeting adjourned without presenting a plan for *how* such targets were to be hit. Quite the opposite: Paul Hoffman, the CED's national chairman, specifically ruled out any centralized planning beyond suggesting job quotas and exhorting businesses to meet them. The CED, he explained, rejected the notion "that one big over-all plan to integrate all business activities was the way to provide" the requisite new jobs, not least because it would require an unacceptably "high degree of regimentation." Instead, the CED called for "not one plan but 2,000,000 plans!"—roughly the number of businesses in the country—"a bold, smart plan for every enterprise, large or small." In the real world, however, there were decisive limits on the ability of any one company, no matter how big, to shape its own destiny, apart from making tactical adjustments to the conditions in which it found itself. The CED's approach in effect left economic actors to their own devices.

Mayor La Guardia, an invited guest, warned that the road ahead might be rockier than assumed, and that preplanned public works were essential. Hoffman agreed that public works had their place but believed that "mass Government employment" was as dangerous as "mass unemployment." The only "sound method" of providing jobs was "through an expansion of business and its output of goods and services." Beardsley Ruml (of the CED, Macy's, and the New York Fed) allowed that some postwar public works might be a necessary short-term expedient, at least for the construction trades, but certainly weren't "a general cure-all for the business cycle." Ruml's preferred cure-all was to cut taxes; this would serve as "a giant arm to lift us to high peacetime production."

Business fundamentalists, unlike the CED elite, thought the La Guardia/Moses program constituted government competition with "free enterprise" and was hence unwarranted, illegitimate, and dangerous. What particularly irked them was the *cost* of the program, especially as part would be paid from their pockets. The Citizens Budget Commission (CBC)—still captained (as since its formation in 1932) by Columbia University president Nicholas Murray Butler—was, despite its grass-roots name, the creation of banking and real-estate interests whose unremitting goal was to hack away at the municipal budget. Not surprisingly it branded the postwar program "a grandiose scheme which will run the city into a financial blind alley." The CBC also complained bitterly (and not incorrectly) that it would entail higher real estate taxes, a concern vigorously echoed by REBNY (the Real Estate Board of New York) and the CIA (Commerce and Industry Association).

Property taxes became the bête noire of a new businessmen's group—the Committee of Fifteen, organized in 1940 by Paul Windels. Formerly La Guardia's corporation counsel, Windels had grown increasingly apprehensive in the late 1930s about the growth of municipal government and the correlative influence of communists. (As chief counsel of the Rapp Coudert investigation he'd helped win dismissal of nearly fifty teachers and clerks for "subversive activities.") The city's $1.25 billion program seemed to Windels a giant leap in the wrong direction and one that, given the tax structure, would unjustly burden real estate owners. The city was not allowed to levy taxes on anything but real property, and its debt ceiling was fixed at 10 percent of that property's assessed value. Windels charged that Gotham officials, to cover normal expenses (much less the proposed new exactions), had lofted assessed values to "high and fictitious levels," a move amounting to "illegal extortion." If assessments were calculated honestly, he claimed, "we wouldn't have a single dollar of borrowing capacity left under the constitutional formula."

Moses had tried to find a middle ground in this debate over the propriety of state intervention. In a sense he succeeded, as the exhibition embodying his plan was criticized both for doing too little and doing too much.

Among those who deplored its lack of vision and depth was Columbia University architectural historian Talbot Hamlin, who chastised Moses's City Planning Commission for answering the question of "what the new city is to be" only with promises of "more of the same—a billion dollars more." Hamlin decried the almost "complete failure of human imagination" evidenced in the program; it was a plan without a plan. Another critic complained that "the city's post-war program does not reach to those fundamental factors of land use, land values, tax assessments, rents and building costs which really determine the growth of a city. The program is a handsome poultice, standing ready to be slapped on the face of old New York."

Moses wasted little time on reasoned defense, though he did note en passant that the massive surgical intervention such critics presumably favored would entail a bureaucratic government "reaching into our very vitals, and that the city might not recover from the shock of the operation." (This from a "bureaucratic government" man who knew whereof he spoke, having just finished, in 1941, ramming 4 miles of the Gowanus Expressway through Sunset Park, ripping down every building on one side of Third Avenue between 39th and 63rd Streets, evicting 1,300 families and demolishing 100 plus stores in the process. In 1945, in a more candid mood, Moses said that "it had been my lot to use the axe where other methods failed.")

Instead, he launched another smear offensive against "long-haired planners," expanding his targets beyond long-time nemesis Lewis Mumford and long-gone rival Rex Tugwell to assault "foreign revolutionaries" who were foisting alien notions of planning and land use on naive locals. ("They make the TNT for those who throw the bombs.") In sharp xenophobic contrast to the welcoming reception afforded arriving European counterparts by most American physicists, playwrights, producers, and professors, Moses lit into Walter Gropius, Eliel Saarinen, and Eric Mendelsohn—architects and planners he deemed badly lacking in gratitude to the country which had given them shelter, as evidenced by their (Moses-fantasized) efforts to subvert private property and impose communal land ownership.

Moses was more placatory to those on his right. In January 1942, with the war scarcely begun, he had expressed sympathy with the business-class concern that, at the conflict's conclusion, "a government grown great on the red meat of war" might be "reluctant to return to a bland diet of limited authority." On the other hand, he couldn't agree with the "sunny optimists" who urged that the future be left entirely in the market's invisible hands. "There is a tendency on the part of big business," he told the American Institute of Steel Construction, to assume that "private initiative and capital can take care of the entire post-war employment problem. The sooner your industry and others get away from this hokum, the better off you will be." Serious unemployment was coming and was "not to be laughed off by fine phrases." Veterans of *this* war, he warned, would not "be trifled with," they would not settle for selling apples on street corners.

Moses was particularly caustic about penny-pinching critics "who shudder at a 2-mill rise in the tax rate, who denounce post-war public works, [and] who threaten the town with bankruptcy and ruin if municipal services are not drastically cut." He was particularly exasperated with their short-sightedness and undertook to tutor them on their own self-interest. Early in 1945, he had an epistolary exchange with Alfred P. Sloan Jr., chairman of the board of General Motors. Sloan, a business fundamentalist, wrote Moses, insisting that driving up the debt to pay for public works done "on an enormous scale for the sake of producing jobs for somebody" would endanger the dollar. Moreover, the "free enterprise system"—unaided—could and would provide full employment after the war. Moses replied he did not believe "that business can do the entire job"; that public works programs to ward off unemployment were "a legitimate and necessary field of government expenditure"; and that it was "preposterous" to suggest that relatively modest public programs would result in inflation. Furthermore, couldn't Sloan see that public expenditures underwrote private profitability? "I still do not understand how your cars and trucks and buses can be of any real use to the people to whom you sell them," he lectured the auto chief, "unless there are first-rate roads for them to run on, and I don't by the same token see why an expenditure for automobile manufacture is constructive and wise and one for new and improved roads is wasteful and ill-timed." Moses urged Sloan and his fellow fundamentalists to uncloud their minds. "I advocate a sensible attitude on the part of business toward necessary government expenditure and enterprises and deprecate what I honestly believe to be the reactionary, ultraconservative, and Bourbon attitude of some of our big bankers and industrialists. It is the Bourbons of business and banking that make the Henry Wallaces."

In a lecture the following year, Moses transmuted his colloquy with Sloan into a general proposition, one long understood by most New York businessmen, and still acceptable to contemporary corporate liberals, but forgotten by fundamentalists in their frenzied opposition to the New Deal: "Without public enterprise and public works, as well as public law and regulation, all private enterprise would be as healthy and about as attractive as the dead Lazarus in the Bible," Moses said. "Government not only keeps order. It paves the way for private risk and profit." Without streets, parks, and utilities—no speculative buildings. Without publicly dredged channels and public docks—no shipping industry. Without massive government subsidies for airports—no aviation business. "Those who make a sharp distinction between public works, which they label as waste, and private enterprise, which alone in their philosophy is constructive, are just about as silly as the radicals who denounce free enterprise as fascism and monopoly and demand that the government plan and run everything."

These three perspectives—New Dealer, corporate liberal, business fundamentalist—threaded their way through the many strategic-level conversations under way in New York about the future of certain sectors of the city's economy. In the real world, the lines of division between them were not so clear cut. Public and private approaches got intertwined in complicated and unexpected ways, nowhere more so than in debates over postwar housing.

144

Housing: The Specter of Suburbanization, the Battle against Blight

In October 1944 the *Saturday Evening Post* ran an article entitled "They'll Build Neighborhoods, Not Houses." It drew heavily on an interview with Abraham Levitt who, with his sons Alfred and William, had flourished during the Depression, constructing upscale suburban developments out in Nassau County. In 1941 Levitt & Sons had won a government contract to build 1,600 homes for defense workers in Norfolk. The job proved unprofitable but instructive. Union workers, they decided, asked too much and did too little, and the construction industry itself was mired in antiquated methods. For a second round of 750 units, the Levitts broke the house-building process down into twenty-seven different steps, which were assigned to twenty-seven different teams, diminishing the need for skilled (and unionized) carpenters. They also standardized and preassembled as many components as possible. It was, Abraham explained, the equivalent of shifting from custom tailoring to mass production of ready-to-wear (it bore comparison as well to the war-spurred transformation of shipbuilding then under way).

As soon as his son Bill (the firm's president and sparkplug) returned from the Pacific, where since 1943 he'd been building airfields for the Navy as a Seabee Lieutenant (JG), Levitt & Sons—Abraham told the *SEP*—was going to apply its assembly-line techniques to mass producing low-cost housing for veterans. (*Some* veterans: these would be "stabilized" communities, Levitt explained, thanks to "effective restrictions which can be fixed in deeds with a view to establishing for the associated property owners something like a perpetual guardianship over their neighborhoods against the kind of decay which has attacked much city real estate.")

The family firm had already taken out an option on a thousand acres of Long Island potato farmland (agriculturally decommissioned due to golden nematode infestation) and were busy buying more tracts near Hempstead. This suburban commercial hub lay 29 miles east of Manhattan and was within five miles in any direction of Grumman, Republic, Sperry, or Liberty Aircraft; convenient, therefore, both to the Emerald City and to Long Island's incipient military industrial complex. There they were planning to modernize, standardize, and vertically integrate the house production process—supplying their own concrete, cutting their own lumber, making their own nails. And thanks to the just-passed GI Bill they would be able to count on the availability of government-guaranteed mortgages. "We had known all along we could mass-produce houses if there was a market for them and credit for builders," Bill recalled thinking as he headed home in 1945. "Now the market was there and the Government was ready with the backing. How could we lose?"

A worrisome question indeed for those who had sunk vast sums in Manhattan real estate and were concerned that a postwar exodus would further diminish land values. As in cities across the country, Downtown property owners and developers, banks and insurance firms, realtors and retailers, and a municipal government dependent on property taxes—all were distressed by "the Specter of decentralization."

In April 1940, the Urban Land Institute (ULI), a real estate industry think tank, had published "Decentralization: What Is It Doing to Our Cities?" The collective answer gleaned from 500 brokers and appraisers was: Nothing Good. Their premium clients were heading for the urban exits, while the impecunious lower classes were staying behind, lodged in steadily deteriorating neighborhoods, many of which were adjacent to Central Business Districts (CBDs). This proximity put enormous investments at risk, threatened municipal solvency, and endangered "much of what we now prize as civilization." We cannot afford, the ULI report concluded forcefully, "to let our cities destroy themselves through uncontrolled decentralization."

New York was better buffered against decentralization than many cities, but here, too, the process was under way. One of the first to notice had been Nelson Rockefeller, sensitized by Rockefeller Center's disturbingly low occupancy rates. "Property owners in Manhattan," he'd told a radio audience back in 1936, "lulled into a false sense of security by rising land values, have awakened to find those values declining while adjacent suburban residential communities have experienced an increased demand." Rockefeller warned that "a decentralization movement has set in, which unless it is checked will involve the very future of this great island."

Soon more "scientific" assessments appeared, notably those commissioned from Homer Hoyt, one of the country's leading real estate economists. In 1941 Hoyt produced, with Robert H. Armstrong, a scholarly monograph for the Urban Land Institute, *Decentralization in New York City*. In it they suggested that FHA-underwritten building of groups of houses in Nassau County "has been a powerful factor in draining families out of the central city," and called for "curbing the excessive trend towards residential decentralization." In a 1943 follow-up article, "Rebuilding American Cities after the War," Hoyt warned that something worse was in the offing: "a chaotic, hit-or-miss building boom after the war which will suck most of the remaining values from the property within the corporate limits of our present cities." Given its size, New York was better positioned to withstand this outflow, as space was available for suburban development *inside* the city limits, notably in Queens (though that would require costly infrastructure). Analysts at the City Planning Commission took little comfort from this. "To put it bluntly," then-chairman Rexford Tugwell had announced in 1940, New York like other cities had "almost stopped growing," and in the future "either we are going to have to bring the population back from the suburbs or we are going to have to allow the city itself to be ruined."

These chilling assessments sent shivers through Gotham's biggest stakeholders. In January 1942, after extensive consultation with local real estate and financial interests, the Citizens Budget Commission—declaring "the fundamental purpose of a city is centralization"—insisted that Gotham's center could and must be held. "After the war," they believed, "New York will assume world leadership in many spheres and expand or rehabilitate its facilities." The privately propertied should do the same and opt not for "flight from devalued areas but rather restoration of values by modernizing the neighborhood."

Even the Regional Plan Association (RPA) was having second thoughts. In the 1920s and 1930s its planners had argued for an orderly relocation of industrial factories (and their workers) to the outer boroughs or New Jersey, and of Central Business District managers and professionals to leafy, auto-accessible enclaves on Long Island or in Westchester. This would relieve congestion in the center, affording room for office and retail expansion. Now, with dispersal increasingly deemed counterproductive, the RPA was torn. Paul Windels, who in 1943 became the organization's president (George McAneny retained the chairmanship), still found the idea of a multicentered metropolitan region appealing. But he also worried and wondered, "How can we stop the drift away from the city and maintain valuations in older areas?"

How indeed? While little could be done about the growing attraction of suburban competitors, maybe making Manhattan comelier could enhance *its* gravitational pull. This would require tackling what Levitt called the "decay which has attacked much city real estate," and what New York's propertied elite called "blight." A "blighted neighborhood" was one that, like Levitt's potato field, had succumbed to some baleful influence that sickened it, arrested its growth, withered its hopes and prospects. "Blight" was a vague and fuzzy term, however. A blighted section might look seriously decrepit, or merely down at the heels, or even perfectly healthy. The most important metrics were not physical and social—like those (abandonment, mortality, and crime) applied in defining "slums"—but economic and financial indices, like declining (or simply static) rent rolls, land values, and tax receipts.

The blighted areas that principally concerned the real estate industry were those nearest a CBD. Brownsville and Harlem were not on their mind. Downtown Brooklyn and the Lower East Side were. Four-fifths of the building stock abutting Brooklyn's CBD predated 1900, and much of it was in disrepair; the district was dotted with boarded-up brownstones. The Lower East Side had lost half its population in the good times of the 1920s, when tenants fled squalid old-law tenements to better accommodations in Brooklyn and the Bronx. In the 1930s, those remaining had been pummeled by hard times, as had their landlords when rent rolls plummeted and vacancy rates soared still higher. With war, the hemorrhaging of rentier profits had been momentarily stanched by the demand for housing, but realtors were sure the bleeding would resume with the expected postwar hejira to the suburbs.

The ideal thing would be to fix up these blighted districts and put them back in the black by bringing in a better class of tenant. Few landlords dared to advocate this strategy as forthrightly as did Carol Aronovici, a planner at Columbia who suggested "we should quit trying to rehabilitate lower Manhattan for the poor and give it back to the well-to-do by building expensive, luxurious and well planned apartment houses in which they could live close to the financial district."

Easier said than done. Assembling large tracts of land in Manhattan or Brooklyn CBDs was murderously difficult. Ownership of a single block might well be splintered among dozens of lot holders. And slum landlords were notorious for demanding outrageous prices, even when the properties on them were seriously dilapidated. Some had jammed in so many tenants that profits were high; others, whose assets were nonperforming (i.e., worthless dumps) nevertheless dreamed that one day they'd bring in big bucks for their location, location, location. Banks helped sustain these high values, unwilling to write down mortgages, lest that lower the book value of their assets. And the city government was reluctant to lower assessed values, lest that reduce their revenues. Even if a would-be assembler could get the government to condemn takeover targets using eminent domain, their owners still had to be paid the "fair market price," usually obscenely more than the land was worth if measured by the income it actually generated.

Nor was it easy to get the city to raze "blighted" property, especially if it meant evicting the poor to house the well-off. Where was the requisite "public purpose" in that? One answer lay in the 1944 argument of Homer Hoyt, now director of economic studies for the Regional Plan Association, that blight was contagious ("Like a cancer, blight spread[s] through all the tissues of the urban body"). Infected districts, Hoyt asserted, were occupied by low-income groups whose crime, disease, and mobility rates were high. Such neighborhoods emitted a steady "filtration of families, contaminated by the vicious environment," into adjacent areas and thus "threatened the stability of residential investments in the rest of the city." The degenerative forces destroying the inner core would no doubt gain momentum after the war, Hoyt believed, and surround the CBDs with "jungles of crime," accelerating out-migration. "Cities with spreading blighted areas at their cores," Hoyt concluded, "are facing a flight to the suburbs," and drastic measures were warranted to stop this, as the "urban organism," once blighted, was "unable to cure itself except by a major surgical operation."

Unfortunately, the two instances where major operations were undertaken—Manhattan's Stuyvesant Town and Brooklyn's Civic Center—highlighted the obstacles awaiting would-be surgeons.

In her 1943 novel, *The Fountainhead*, Ayn Rand included a slum-clearance fairy tale in which she solved the property-assembly problem by conjuring up a munificent millionaire. Her Hearstian stand-in, Gail Wynand, tells Rand's Promethean architect-hero, Howard Roark, that over the years he had bought up ten square blocks of slum in the middle of Hell's Kitchen. This "grimy desolation of tenements," this "malignant growth of decomposition," was now going "to be torn down, Howard. All of it. Razed off." Then, once cleared, he would engage Roark to erect thereon a tower in a park.

Also in 1943, Robert Moses and Fiorello La Guardia found themselves a millionaire, Fred Ecker, predident of Metropolitan Life, who offered to "raze off" eighteen blocks of slum in the middle of the Gas House District and erect thereon many towers in a park. Their millionaire was not as munificent as Rand's: Ecker demanded the authorities provide him with substantial subsidies, the use of eminent domain, and support for his "whites only" policy before he would proceed. Ecker was not easily replicable. Not only did he have the deepest pockets around—Metropolitan Life was then the largest private corporation in the United States, with assets approaching $6 billion—but his headquarters tower lay a scant five blocks west of the proposed project; for Ecker, building Stuyvesant Town would do double duty, generating profits *and* protecting his industry's CBD from encroaching blight. Other insurance giants or banks, lacking such resources or special needs, declined to follow Ecker's lead, fearing that tenants would be siphoned off by suburbs.

In downtown Brooklyn a constellation of local businessmen and politicians took a different tack. Yearning to demolish blighted lofts and tenements near Borough Hall, the group— which included Borough President John Cashmore, the Brooklyn Real Estate Board, the Brooklyn Heights Association, and a group of local savings banks—called for a massive clearance program to remake the area as a Civic Center, replete with dignified public buildings, parks, monuments, plazas, and (included in the mix) a private upscale housing component. The City Planning Commission, spurred on by Cleveland Rodgers—*Brooklyn Eagle* editor and himself a CPC member—developed a "completely integrated plan" for over forty-five acres. Comparable in scale to the City Beautiful proposals advanced before the First World War, it would be the largest civic center to come out of the Second World War.

The initiative received powerful backing from Joseph D. McGoldrick, the city comptroller (and a resident of Sunset Park), who wanted to use downtown Brooklyn as a "test case" for Hoyt's theory. "If blighted areas are to be restored to health," McGoldrick agreed, "we must cut out the whole cancer and not leave any diseased tissue." This meant tearing out the grid itself—a constraining remnant from horse-and-buggy days—and substituting modern super-blocks. "If we are to translate the super-block into reality," said McGoldrick, we must "achieve a consolidation of land ownership, including the city streets."

This was accomplished in 1945 when twenty-three blocks (bounded by Sands, Jay, Fulton, and Washington Streets) were condemned in one of the largest uses of eminent domain in the history of the city. Included in the package was a 7.4-acre parcel (Sands, Jay, Tillary, and Adams) set aside for Concord Village, a private middle-income project. The Concord piece alone was assessed at roughly a million dollars, which the city paid to the original owners. It got the money back, however, in a prearranged deal, when they resold the land to a consortium of Brooklyn savings banks, who kicked in another 5 percent, confident

T. A. Morgan, president of the Sperry Corporation, speaks with turret lathe operator Sayde R. Carter at the plant in Lake Success, Long Island, April 3, 1943. (Hagley Museum)

the housing they would build could attract well-heeled tenants, given the de-blighted downtown location. This operation, too, was not readily replicable. One couldn't build a civic center every time one needed to establish a public purpose or wanted to guarantee investors a secure environment. Indeed, if this model prevailed, and potential buyers/builders were required to pony up whatever slumlords could win in court, *plus* 5 percent, the financial bar to clearance would have been set even higher.

WHILE PRIVATE CAPITAL (ARMED WITH eminent domain) battled blight, a second phalanx, rooted in the civic and public sectors, also sought to reshape the cityscape. A loose alliance of tenant groups, social workers, city planners, settlement workers, housing reformers, liberal Democratic and American Labor Party activists, civic, religious and philanthropic organizations, federal officials, architects, and liberal realtors similarly urged a massive clearance campaign, also using eminent domain. But this one would replace razed tenements with public housing for working-class tenants, including displaced residents of the about-to-be-demolished structures. The emphasis was less on restoring property values and profits downtown than on providing decent accommodations for the city's ill-housed, wherever they might live.

This coalition had deep roots in Gotham. It was grounded in the turn-of-the-century reform movements for tenement regulation and model housing, which in the 1930s had shifted to urging government construction of low-income housing, a campaign that triumphed with passage of the Housing Act of 1937. Under federal aegis and with federal financing, the New York City Housing Authority (NYCHA) had generated the first wave of clearance and construction. Working at first principally in the outer boroughs, where it was cheaper to assemble and clear land, it had shifted its focus to more densely peopled locales, building taller to offset higher land costs. This transformation had culminated in the 1941 East River Houses in East Harlem, whose 10- and 11-story towers-in-a-park provided a blueprint for Gotham's future, one inspired by modernist European working-class housing, and 1920s-era New York apartment complexes like Tudor City and London Terrace.

No sooner did war suspend this slum-clearance-cum-public-housing program than the coalition began to campaign for its postwar revival. No one was a more ardent advocate than Mayor La Guardia, who in 1944 chanted: "Tear down the old. Build up the new. Down with rotten, antiquated rat holes. Down with hovels. Down with disease. Down with crime. Down with firecraft. Let in the sun. Let in the sky. A new day is dawning. A new life. A new America!"

Proponents insisted such rebuilding needed to be done on a larger scale than ever before. Maxwell Stewart, a *Nation* editor, argued this case in *Building for Peace at Home and Abroad* (1943). In a chapter entitled "Rebuilding Our Cities," Stewart called for remaking entire neighborhoods at a blow—perhaps even a square mile at a time—taking slum land through eminent domain, closing streets, and putting up modern tower housing on cleared superblocks large enough to not be overwhelmed by the old tenement district.

The drumbeat climaxed during May 1944 with "Housing Week," organized by the Citizens Housing Council and 150 other organizations, with La Guardia and Wagner as honorary chairs. This concatenation of events, in scores of venues across the five boroughs, included radio programs, conferences, tours, department store displays, film screenings at Loew's theaters, exhibitions, tours of public housing projects, and "Farewell to the Slums" block parties.

The movement's sails were further billowed by the city's terrific housing crunch. In 1945, of an estimated 2,255,850 dwellings in Gotham, there were only 2,000 vacancies to be found. Restrictions were clamped on Manhattan hotels: transients could occupy a room for no more than five days. This touched off a citywide game of musical beds. Losers could join the growing ranks of the homeless hunkering down in Bryant Park and Union Square. Moves were afoot to legalize long-outlawed practices, like renting out basements. Others urged appropriating barracks for civilian use or ordering up Quonset huts. In this context, the rapid mass production of government housing seemed a no-brainer. Its prestige had never been higher and its spaces never more in demand; in Brooklyn alone 20,000 applicants awaited an opening.

BETWEEN THESE TWO FORCES—THE REALTY-CONSTRUCTION complex and the public housers—Moses again self-presented as the man in the middle. His primary goals and political temperament were more akin to those of the businessmen. The construction commando in him longed to tear down slums, but more to restore property values than to improve housing for residents. And he forthrightly opposed the "radical housing boys, who don't want private capital horning into their field," finding them "obsessed with the idea that only public housing is the answer to slum clearance."

Yet Moses had done his best to cajole private capital into building affordable housing, and, in the main, had failed. Also, it was obvious to him that the housing crunch would worsen when the troops returned. Veterans would not go back to overcrowded slum tenements. And with the GI Bill they wouldn't have to; they could head for the Levitts' ex-potato fields instead. Government-backed public housing seemed the only option on the table that could compete with government-backed suburbs. It also seemed there'd be money to pay for public housing, and Moses always followed the funding stream. Accordingly, while keeping a channel open to the private builders (especially rhetorically), he threw in his lot with the public housers.

In 1944, La Guardia and Moses announced plans to *double* the public-housing sector within three years, for an estimated cost of $260,000,000. NYCHA had designed sixteen new projects, drawing on some of the city's top architects, and visitors to the *NYC Postwar Program* exhibition were given a preview.

The densest concentration of new public housing would be planted along the East River, running north from the Brooklyn Bridge, intermingling there with earlier public and private projects to create something of a red brick waterfront rampart. Twelve 16-story towers of the future Governor Alfred E. Smith Houses (sited atop Smith's South Street birthplace) would stretch up to Catherine Street, from where Fred French's 1934 Knickerbocker Village carried on to the Manhattan Bridge. On the other side, between Gouverneur to Grand, lay the 15-acre, twenty-building, prewar Vladeck Houses (slated for a postwar extension). At Grand Street would arise the Hillman Houses, three 12-story co-op buildings to be sponsored by the Amalgamated Clothing Workers, co-operator guru Abraham Kazan having won Moses's approval. Rounding Corlears Hook and passing under the Williamsburg Bridge a shore walker would come to the 17-acre superblock site running from Houston to Sixth Street on which would go the Lillian D. Wald Houses, sixteen five-winged buildings, 10-to-13 stories tall. Sixth Street would in turn mark the lower border of the Jacob Riis Houses, whose nineteen buildings, 6-to-14 stories in height, would span two superblocks and end at 13th Street. At 14th Street the vast red brick forest would roll north again with mammoth Stuyvesant Town running up to 20th Street, from where its sister development, Peter Cooper Village, would carry on to 23rd Street, the two together encompassing 80 acres and fifty-six buildings. All this would indeed be a mighty city in the city.

A sketch proposing the Elliot Houses.   (PD-US-no notice. New York City Housing Authority Collection, LaGuardia and Wagner Archives)

Elsewhere in Manhattan coverage was to be spottier: Chelsea would get the John Lovejoy Elliott Houses (named for the founder of the Hudson Guild settlement), four 11-to-12-story buildings between 25th and 27th; higher up the West Side an expansion of the Amsterdam Houses (between 61st and 64th) was planned; and Harlem would get the James Weldon Johnson project (112th/115th), and the Abraham Lincoln Houses (132nd/135th), each with fourteen buildings sited on 12 acres.

IN THE BRONX, SAINT MARY'S Park Houses would have six 21-story buildings on thirteen acres and the more modest Morrisania Houses two towers of 16 floors each. Brooklyn encampments would include the twenty-seven buildings of Brownsville Houses, the twenty-seven of Marcy Houses, the fourteen of Gowanus Houses, and a 25-story extension to Kingsborough. In Queens, the Astoria Houses would splay out on 32.3 acres at Hallet's Cove, while South Jamaica was slated to receive sixteen additional structures.

By late 1945, evictions and demolitions at several of these sites were already well under way, to general—though not unanimous—applause. Some found the designs dreary, stark, and monotonous; the density levels too high; the facilities mean-spirited (no closets, skip-stop elevators, and a newly decreed ban on shops, so as not to compete with private enterprise). Others were disturbed that while the public housing was not officially white-only (like Stuyvesant Town), the projects (despite some token integration) in effect accepted and strengthened existing racial boundaries.

Some critics feared slum clearance would simply mean slum displacement, given that, as a June 1945 Community Service Society study found, no more than 3 percent of the existing Gas House District residents could afford Stuy-town rents. (This, of course, was not news to the evictees: "Stuyvesant Town is not for working people like us," said one; it was all about "putting the poor people out," said another.) More troublesome, only 22 percent were eligible for public housing, which meant the uprooted families would have to seek shelter in one or another of New York's slums, aggravating overcrowding elsewhere. Nevertheless, so powerful was the conviction that Gotham was in desperate need of a drastic makeover that almost all the housing reformers, from the Citizens Housing Council to the largely left-wing Tenant Leagues, put up only token resistance as vast amounts of affordable (if often wretched) housing vanished under the wrecker's ball.

What did worry the public housers was whether funding would be available to complete this enormous and enormously expensive program. The Gordian financial knot remained intact: to make way for superblock tracts, slumlords would have to be bought off. True, the program could certainly be started up with city and state money. Capital spending having been halted for the duration, La Guardia had used the money to retire much old debt, so the municipality's legal borrowing capacity had expanded again, allowing it to issue new housing construction bonds. And in Albany, Dewey pumped money into Gotham's public housing program, allowing several postwar projects to get off the ground. But La Guardia and Moses had been counting on federal money to cover roughly half the costs, and it was not immediately in the offing.

The indefatigable Senator Wagner, father of the 1937 Housing Act, went back to the federal well in 1943, proposing that the national government underwrite slum clearance programs if linked to public housing. This touched off a firestorm of opposition from home builders and their allies on the grounds that public housing constituted unfair competition and imperiled their industry. In truth, public housing operated in a low-income market that private builders had never pretended to serve as it didn't pay, a fact La Guardia underlined. All the proposed projects, said the mayor, were "in undesirable areas where there is not the slightest possibility of rehabilitation through private enterprise."

Builders feared that if public housing caught on for low-income tenants, it might spread (like blight) up the class ladder. And indeed, during the war NYCHA—under pressure from the Citizens Housing Council, labor unions, tenant associations, and local politicians—had raised the maximum income residents were allowed to make before being asked to vacate their premises and granted similar exemptions to veterans. It quickly became evident that middle-class families were perfectly delighted to live in such affordable housing, and builders and bankers were quick to suss out the threat to profitability.

Real estate interests also presented the fight as an ideological showdown between "free enterprise" and "socialism" (or "communism," for the more perfervid). More concretely, they saw it as a face-off between the private, individualist, single-family, home-and-mortgage system, and the New Deal–nurtured vision of modern mass public housing being promoted by the Wagnerians. (This was the industry whose official spokesgroup, the National Association of Real Estate Boards, had successfully insisted that Lanham Act government-built housing for war workers should be sold off, cheap, to the private sector after victory. Or, better yet, torn down—*pace* the tremendous demand for shelter—so that private industry could build it again for a profit.)

Builders and realtors were backed by nearly the entire business community. The Commerce and Industry Association of New York and the National Association of Manufacturers (NAM) denounced the whole idea of federal aid for city rebuilding: that should remain a local responsibility. Raiding the national treasury to assist the cities would lead to further centralization of power in Washington, more extravagance and waste, and, worst of all, higher taxes. Business lobbyists easily gained the ear of congressional conservatives, appalled at the notion of channeling money to big cities for "socialistic experiments."

Wagner's proposal was swiftly imprisoned in congressional committees and might have died there, except for a startling volte face by the free enterprisers.

THE REAL ESTATE INDUSTRY HAD been chewing on the problem of the astronomical land costs demanded by slumlords. This seemed an insuperable obstacle to rescuing their downtown investments. And then a solution emerged, more or less simultaneously, in several venues, but most critically (if counterintuitively) from NAREB's Committee on Housing and Blighted Areas. In this redoubt of opposition to federal involvement, big-city realtors came up with an unprecedented proposal, brilliant in its simplicity if startling in its hypocrisy, a plan so radical that had it been advanced by long-haired Europeans it would have been condemned out of hand as a communist contrivance. In a nutshell, it called on Congress to authorize local redevelopment agencies to condemn and buy blighted properties at whatever exorbitant "fair market" price slumlords could get the courts to approve. The agency would then turn around and sell the land to private developers, but *not* (as in Brooklyn) at a price high enough to cover the condemnation award. Instead, it would "write down" the value of the blighted property, puncturing its inflated "fair market" price, and bringing it down to a level based on actual or realistically prospective earning power, *with the federal government covering most of the cost of bridging the gap*. Then, with the Gordian knot neatly sliced, and the cost of buying out slumlords laid off on the taxpayer, a new set of builders and bankers and realtors could profitably begin construction on government-cleared land. This tactic also severed slum clearance from public housing. Developers would be allowed to build private housing for an affluent clientele. Urban renewal could now mean subsidizing the transmutation of lower-class residencies into shelter for the city's middle and upper classes.

Now it was the public housers turn to protest. Senator Wagner denounced the hypocrisy of "those who are perfectly willing to advocate and favor governmental assistance in the accomplishment of their own objective, but who look with disfavor upon governmental assistance to ill-housed families of very low income, including veterans." Housing reformer Catherine Bauer would frame a more complete critique: "It is proposed to bail out with Federal subsidy the owners of slum and blighted property—not in order to rehouse their present tenants properly, but to stimulate another wave of speculative overbuilding for [the] well-to-do and thus, it is naively hoped, to turn the tide of decentralization and preserve downtown property values based on high densities and even higher hopes."

The result was a standoff between New Dealers, still in command of the national executive, and business fundamentalists, predominant in the national legislature. But both sides agreed on one thing—they wanted access to federal money, one group to pay for public housing, the other to pave the way for private investment. So, in 1945, three senators, representing the three congressional power blocs, decided to form an odd-trio alliance and pursue a political compromise. Wagner (the ur-urban liberal), Allen Ellender (a white supremacist from Louisiana), and Robert Taft (the Ohioan arch opponent of the welfare state) jointly introduced the Wagner-Ellender-Taft bill (WET). One of its titles (sections) provided continued and expanded financing for public housing. Another authorized federal aid for "land assembly for participation by private enterprise in development or redevelopment programs." WET did not bring an instant resolution. Many in the camps so uncomfortably yoked together refused to go along. Too much federal control, conservatives worried; not enough federal control, fretted the public housers. The measure passed the Senate but was blocked in the House.

The ultimate contours of New York's postwar housing program would depend on if and how that impasse got resolved.

145

Rubber and Rails

When Robert Moses told General Motors chieftain Alfred P. Sloan that his cars and trucks and buses weren't likely to get sold "unless there are first-rate roads for them to run on," he was at that moment preparing to put the public's money where his mouth was. This was immediately apparent to visitors at the *Postwar Program* exhibit, festooned as it was with maps devoted to plans for expanding New York's arterial tapestry. The maps used thick black lines to indicate the city's existing highway network; planned additions were delineated in bright red. Moses was determined to convert red to black at top speed, with particular emphasis on the three concentric loops he'd already largely completed with New Deal money.

The innermost route encircled Manhattan. When the new stretches were in place, traffic coming off the George Washington Bridge could cruise east underneath Washington Heights through the prewar 178th Street Tunnel (a 179th Street twin was planned) and then turn south, onto the proposed Harlem River Drive, to the Triborough Bridge, continuing on down to lower Manhattan via the existing East River Drive. There autos could swoop around the island's bottom over a new South Street Viaduct and under a new Battery Park Tunnel, before flowing up onto the old Miller Elevated (West Side) Highway, on which motorists could travel north, segueing to the extant Henry Hudson Parkway, and arrive back at the George Washington Bridge.

The Belt Parkway, cinched around the city's middle, had, with one major exception, been completed before the wartime construction cutoff. In 1945, a circumferentially inclined driver coming off the Triborough from Manhattan could roll onto a limited access parkway composed of contiguous segments, each with its own name, starting with the Grand Central Parkway. Heading east on the GCP past La Guardia Field our motorist could proceed via Whitestone Parkway to the Cross Island Parkway. Here the Belt hung a right and headed south, hugging the Nassau County line, until reaching the Laurelton, Southern State, and Shore Parkways, where it swung west, affording spectacular views across the Narrows. From there our driver could torque north up to Owl's Head Park in Bay Ridge. At this point the

Belt glided up onto the recently opened ('41) elevated Gowanus Parkway, which darkened the sky over Third Avenue on its way north to Hamilton Avenue, the future point of entry to the still uncompleted Brooklyn-Battery Tunnel.

Ahead lay a great traffic-choked chunk of territory that would be crossed by the Brooklyn-Queens Connecting Highway. This stretch of road, like the Gowanus which fed into it, was to be a six-lane expressway, much of it elevated, that would dispense with the grace notes of Moses's prewar ribbon parkways. The new road, and indeed virtually all proposed postwar highways, would trade in landscaped borders and medians for wider lanes, longer sightlines, and broader shoulders. Unlike the parkways, which had banned commercial traffic, the new expressways would be truck user–friendly.

The B-Q highway had been slated to run along Hicks Street, bisecting South Brooklyn and Brooklyn Heights. The latter community had enough muscle to force Moses into detouring the route around the Heights's East River–facing periphery, which he did brilliantly by double-decking the road and roofing it with a glorious public esplanade, creating a world-class view of Manhattan. Once out of genteel territory, Moses sent the expressway shooting east along Park Avenue below the Navy Yard, then angled it northeast, slicing willy-nilly through industrial and residential Brooklyn neighborhoods, crossing into Queens over the Kosciuszko Bridge; then he rammed it north, heedless of protests, until it reached the Triborough, its point of departure.

Moses would work, too, on an outer loop, that would include the northern and southernmost boroughs. Starting out from the George Washington Bridge drivers would be able to follow a projected Cross Bronx Expressway that plowed its way due east, traversing the borough's ridges and valleys, until reaching the recently completed Bronx-Whitestone Bridge, and from there gain access to Long Island's Belt Parkway. Following the Belt down and around to the Narrows, it reached the point where eventually either a tunnel or bridge (not part of the postwar plan) would provide them access to Staten Island. Once across, future motorists could proceed due west on a proposed Clove Lakes Expressway to Goethals Bridge, or head south via a projected Richmond Parkway to Outerbridge Crossing. Both bridges linked Staten Island to New Jersey, where, via various roads, travelers could wend their way back north to the George Washington Bridge.

From each of these urban ringways, red spokes radiated outward, heading away from the center city. To the north, many of the established highways threading through Westchester County were slated for expansion and were soon to be joined by major new arteries, the New York State and New England Thruways. To the east, the exhibit plan depicted a Queens Midtown Expressway linking the Queens–Midtown Tunnel with Horace Harding Boulevard (itself being considered for an upgrade to expressway), which speared on into Long Island's Nassau County, straight into the jaws of suburbia.

Which raises a question: did Moses not see a contradiction between providing so many exit routes to outlying areas, and protecting the city itself from dispersal? The Commissioner did, after all, agree with Central Business District grandees on the need to resist centrifugal pressures: "Nothing," he said, "is more destructive than decentralization." Indeed, he urged municipal efforts against "letting trade and population drift away and continuing a trend toward suburban dormitory living and commuting." Did it never occur to him he might be complicit in that process? Some contemporaries thought it obvious that his roads and bridges were facilitating flight by auto-equipped middle-class Gothamites. By "shortening driving time from rim to hub," argued an official of the National Association of Real Estate Boards, highways "entice people to live further and further out."

Moses doesn't seem to have reflected on the matter, and a variety of things inclined him toward pouring a fresh torrent of concrete. Huge amounts of money had already been invested in forging these roadway chains; it would have been unimaginable not to provide the last missing links. True, the Regional Plan Association, which back in the 1920s had mapped out nearly every roadway that Moses was now preparing to build, had gotten cold feet and was in mid-paradigm shift, but their faithful executor remained doggedly determined to stick to the original model. For all his animus toward plans and planners, Moses was fast in the grip of both.

The roads, moreover, would do more than facilitate commuting; they would address commercial complaints that clogged arteries were blocking the flow of freight, making imports and exports more expensive.

Moses worshiped flow and detested bottlenecks. Whenever he diagnosed auto-constipation he immediately prescribed another dose of laxative engineering. He was obsessed, too, with connecting things. It was as if he could *feel* the George Washington Bridge yearning to make contact with the Bronx Whitestone, Brooklyn pining to embrace Staten Island. This was more than a personal quirk, but rather a New York state of mind, part of the city's cultural inheritance. Since at least since the opening of the Erie Canal, Gothamites had turned out in great numbers for Festivals of Connection (the arrival of the *Great Western*, the inauguration of the Atlantic Cable, Lindbergh's flight), hailing the city's latest suturing to the wider world, in the well-founded belief that municipal prosperity was contingent on enhanced accessibility.

There would also be *money* available for urban roadways. New government funding streams were being allocated to linking city and country—on military grounds. In 1941, Roosevelt had appointed a National Interregional Highway Committee, which proposed a 40,000-mile National System of Interstate Highways, "so located, as to connect by routes, direct as practical, the principal metropolitan areas, cities, and industrial centers, to serve the National Defense." (Moses had advanced the same rationale at the municipal level, insisting that new highways were essential to evacuating the city or moving munitions through it.) The trucking industry had added its two cents, arguing that Washington's long-standing focus on building country highways needed rethinking: the key obstacles to rubber-wheeled commerce were no longer muddy rural roads but rather snarled city streets. Urban renewal forces had also climbed on the bandwagon, even claiming that highways could facilitate re-centralization. If routed strategically—right through "cramped, crowded and depreciated" sections, thus taking out "long-standing eyesore[s] and blight"—they could, FDR told Congress, provide a "key to the functional rebuilding of our cities." Congress concurred, and its $1.5 billion Federal-Aid Highway Act of 1944 made "urban extensions" of intercity highways eligible for federal aid. Given the likelihood that more roads were imminent, La Guardia worried less about the people they might possibly usher out than those the vehicles would surely usher in. In January 1944 the mayor declared publicly his fear that after the war, when Detroit resumed mass production of ever-cheaper cars, their growing numbers—together with a burgeoning influx of interstate trucks and buses—would soon paralyze the city center, already alarmingly congested. In a 1942 survey, the Regional Plan Association had found that in 1940, of the 3.3 million people who on an average day entered Manhattan south of 61st Street, nearly a quarter (roughly 750,000) had come by car. The resulting traffic jams and dearth of parking spaces had been decried by retailers, shoppers, manufacturers, workers, tourists, and residents alike. Wartime restrictions on driving relieved the pressure somewhat. Informed opinion agreed with La Guardia: an auto-inundation was coming, and it might prove cataclysmic.

Looking for preemptive solutions, La Guardia turned, as so often, to Robert Moses, appointing him head of a committee to study the problem. Moses's response, delivered in July 1944, was to suggest that more traffic could best be handled by...building more roads. In this case, he urged creating crosstown arteries to "loosen up congestion." His favorite candidate was a lower Manhattan expressway (another Regional Plan Association idea from the 1920s) that would connect the Holland Tunnel with the Williamsburg and Manhattan bridges, diverting through traffic from Downtown streets. Others urged a counterpart crossing through midtown Manhattan that would link the Lincoln Tunnel with the Queens Midtown Tunnel. Given that both would require hacking through a forest of skyscrapers and other obstacles, neither was in the immediate offing.

Into this idea vacuum rushed New Yorkers bearing parking plans, most of which were quickly deemed problematic by other New Yorkers. Many urged constructing commercial garages and lots, though this ran up against the land assembly problem. Some counseled creation of a Parking Authority with power to condemn land and build car-care facilities. Private interests beat this back, decrying unfair competition. Legalization of parking meters, it was argued, would increase turnover of curb parking. This in turn was criticized by retailers. Providing cab stands and prohibiting cruising didn't sit well with the taxi industry. Requiring new apartment houses and public structures to include parking facilities had merit but was only a long-term solution. In the short run, the best La Guardia could come up with (in October 1945) was a basket of stopgap administrative measures: designating some crosstown streets as express lanes, requiring that car owners answer traffic summonses in person, imposing tougher fines, towing illegally parked cars to new auto pounds, and permitting trucks to load only when their cargos were ready.

It was left to the Port Authority of New York to promote more ambitious quasi-public interventions, aimed at rationalizing interstate bus and truck transportation.

Since that agency's Lincoln Tunnel had opened in 1937, the earlier stream of long-distance buses had steadily swelled. By 1944 an average of 3,000 cross-Hudson trips were being made each day. In 1945, the tunnel would open a second tube. Another increase in traffic was expected. This bode ill. Most buses, on emerging at 39th and Tenth Avenue, fanned out across Midtown, heading to one or another of the eight terminals scattered between Fifth/Eighth Avenues and 34th/51st Streets, stopping to disgorge passengers, royally tying up traffic. In 1944, Austin Tobin, since 1942 the Port Authority's executive director, announced plans to build the world's largest union bus terminal, a counterpart Grand Central. Under its immense roof would be gathered all existing terminals (hence "union"). To be sited at Eighth/Ninth Avenues and 40th/41st Streets, it would be ramped directly into the Lincoln Tunnel. Accommodating 2,500 buses a day, it would dramatically curtail bus street presence.

This idea, too, ran into opposition. The Greyhound Corporation, biggest bus operator in the city, had long occupied a prime location on 34th Street between Seventh and Eighth Avenues, right next to Macy's and Penn Station. It was planning on expanding its own facilities and had no interest in joining the hoi polloi in a way west venue. The Port Authority responded that its project was contingent on universal participation, and La Guardia proposed supporting the PA by outlawing bus terminals east of Eighth Avenue. Greyhound fought back. Remarkably, Moses backed Greyhound, perhaps because the union terminal had been proposed by his great rival. With these behemoths at loggerheads, the outcome remained murky.

The Port Authority made more headway on the truck front. These vehicles had made considerable wartime inroads on the city's lighter-and-car float system. When the rail lines failed to muster enough water-based equipment to handle the immense wartime flow, truckers had charged into the breach. By 1945 their conveyances were carrying about two-thirds of the merchandise freight entering and departing New York. The Port Authority welcomed the change, in part because each load crossing the harbor by road meant a toll in PA pockets, whereas water-borne commerce earned them nothing.

To help alleviate the resulting crush, the Port Authority announced it would build a Downtown union truck terminal, on the scale of its proposed venue for buses. In 1944 La Guardia approved construction of a thousand-foot structure between Washington and Greenwich, Spring and Houston—right next to the Holland Tunnel, the Hudson ship piers, and the St. John's Park freight terminal of the New York Central (at West, Washington, Clarkson, Spring). Here, long-haul vehicles could pull into one of 136 street bays, and by means of cranes and an overhead circular chain-conveyor, exchange goods with local delivery trucks, and vice versa.

Even if all these lubricating measures were put in place, some argued they would be insufficient to deal with the impending crisis. The only way the city could avoid drowning in rubber-wheeled vehicles, according to this school of thought, was to revivify steel-wheeled transit. This set the stage for another battle in the now decades-long war between road and rail.

World War II raised railroad companies' hopes of making a comeback. Gains in rail-based efficiency, and restrictions on gas-vehicle competitors, helped them recapture much of the freight traffic lost to trucks. It also allowed their passenger services to run in the black for the first time in many years. Convinced this winning streak would outlast the war, in 1945 New York Central executives, with incautious zeal, ordered 420 new air-conditioned streamliner cars, the biggest purchase in the history of American railroading. Also in 1945, spiffing themselves up for an expected passenger crush, the company restored Grand Central Terminal's zodiacal ceiling to its original starry brilliance.

The smart money thought train people were deluding themselves. Once Detroit began cranking out cars again—GM et al. had already announced a production target of 2.1 million autos for the first peacetime year—commuters would desert trains in droves. Long-distance freight handling was a stronger suit, less so in Gotham, where the lines confronted a geographical obstacle (the Hudson River) and political resistance to surmounting it. Since Mayor Hylan's day there'd been talk of building a cross-harbor tunnel between Staten Island and Brooklyn (it had been in the Port Authority's original charge), but Moses was dead set against it, determined to reserve the Narrows for an auto-only bridge. Antirail animus was prevalent inside metropolitan borders as well. La Guardia continued his war to the death against the trolley. In Manhattan, only the Third Avenue Railway's cars had survived the mass conversion to buses in 1936. The mayor had hounded the line mercilessly until in 1939 it agreed to trade in its perpetual trolley franchise for a fifty-year bus franchise. Then the war granted a temporary reprieve. In 1942 the Office of Defense Transportation halted conversion, because electric rail vehicles conserved essential gas and rubber. But in 1945 La Guardia returned to the attack. The Third Avenue line was forced to order 200 buses from General Motors. Its old cars were reluctantly sold off to Bombay, Vienna, Lima, and São Paulo. And within two years trolley service in Manhattan was history, leaving Brooklyn as its last redoubt.

A 1943 poster for the New York Central System. (Artwork by Leslie Ragan)

In 1936, just as Manhattan succumbed to buses, the Brooklyn and Queens Transit Corporation (BQT), a subsidiary of the still independent Brooklyn-Manhattan Transit Corporation (BMT), had defiantly placed the first order for Presidents' Conference Committee (PCC) trolleys. Belying its awkward name, the PCC was a modernized, streamlined, vastly improved version, cheaper to run than buses and longer lasting, too. Then the 1940 consolidation brought the BQT under La Guardia's sway. Eschewing expert opinion, he announced: "I do not approve of trolleys and would recommend the substitution of buses."

By 1942, with new purchases blocked, and one rail route after another eliminated, it was clear that a trolley-based solution to the looming traffic crisis was definitively off the table.

La Guardia had decreed the death of elevateds, too, considering them old, obsolete, and obstructive of auto traffic. And in truth their departure was far less lamented than that of the trolleys, as neighboring residents found them forbidding and noisy, and property owners saw them as drags on development. Down they came, one by one. Service on the Sixth Avenue El ended in December 1938, and it was demolished by April 1939. The Ninth Avenue and the Second Avenue (though only the piece from 60th Street up to the Harlem River) were shut down in June 1940, at the time of consolidation. This was in accord with one of the merger's goals, eliminating redundancies by shifting elevated riders to parallel subway lines, and in due course Ninth and Sixth Avenue El riders moved over to the Eighth and Sixth Avenue subways.

Second Avenue was a different—and larger—story. The Downtown portion from 59th Street to Chatham Square was spared the axe in 1940 thanks to vociferous protests from well-organized riders in Queens. Subway lines from Astoria and Flushing ran through Queensboro Plaza and over the Queensboro Bridge, then continued down the Second Avenue El track, giving them a one-seat ride to downtown Manhattan they were loath to lose. La Guardia agreed the El could stay until replaced by a projected Second Avenue Subway. However, the influential First Avenue Association—consisting of realtors, bankers, and property owners along the more fashionable thoroughfare—didn't want to wait. They were out to diminish auto traffic by diverting it to their Second Avenue neighbor, which in turn required losing the

E. M. Bofinger, *Broadway from 52nd Street, Elevated Train*, April 25, 1938. (WPA FWP Photo, New York City Municipal Archives)

El. The outbreak of war gave them the upper hand over Queens diehards. The Firsters pointed out that the structure and rails of the Second Avenue El could be transmuted into three 35,000-ton battleships; the War Production Board agreed; and by October 1942 the El was scrap metal. One realtor, Harry B. Helmsley, proposed to celebrate the arrival of light and air with a tree-planting campaign that would, not incidentally, bring "higher grade tenants" to the avenue. Queens riders were placated with free transfers to the Third Avenue El, which received a stay of execution until the promised Second Avenue subway arrived to replace it.

But the Second Avenue subway, which in 1942 had topped the Board of Transportation's wish list of proposed system extensions, had by 1945 been put on indefinite hold, on the grounds that the city could not afford it. How had this come to pass?

La Guardia had promoted consolidation because he thought it would produce significant operating economies, allowing the system to become self-supporting without raising the nickel fare. In one respect it worked. During the war, the New York subway system—the biggest in the world—was also the most heavily used. It carried six million passengers a day, more than most railroads did in a year. With that volume of business, the subway generated an operating surplus each wartime year. People did complain it was horribly crowded—rush hour was known as the "daily riot"—but La Guardia rejoiced at the packed trains. "Any time we don't have crowding during the rush hour," he said in 1943, "there'll be a receiver sitting in the mayor's chair and New York will be a ghost town. Why, they talk about the rush hour and the crush and noise. Why, listen, don't you see that's the proof of our life and vitality? Why, why, that is New York City!"

True, though misleading. Expenses were down in part because, given the wartime lack of material and personnel, it was impossible to invest in improvements. That meant that cars, tracks, and stations, all of which had deteriorated through the 1930s, kept getting worse. Meanwhile other costs were escalating—notably wages, which went up 27 percent during the war—cutting into operating surpluses, which shrank each year. And if ridership were to decline after the war, when auto competition returned, those operating surpluses would swiftly turn to deficits.

In truth the subway system as a whole was *already* in deficit, because municipalization, in bailing out stockholders of bankrupt companies, had saddled the city with $326 million in new debt. By 1944, the annual debt service on this was $37 million, which negated the operating surplus and put the subways in the red.

There were two basic but antagonistic solutions to the transit fiscal crisis. The first of these was to raise the fare. In 1944 Paul Windels formed the Citizens' Transit Committee—another demotic-sounding entity dominated by the real estate complex—to lobby for hiking the nickel fare to ten cents. That, he calculated, would cover debt service, allow the purchase of new aluminum or stainless-steel cars (with air conditioning), brighten up dreary stations, provide ten million annually to the municipal treasury, and, not least, enable a lower tax rate.

This represented a sharp change of position by the development community. Earlier in the century it had championed mass transit as a way to stimulate residential construction in outlying areas. Now real estate men were either worried about decentralization, hence not keen on enhancing access to the periphery; or themselves engaged in suburban development, in which case they favored roadways over subways because autos opened up more territory. Either way they had lost interest in public transit. Worse, they saw it as an unaffordable extravagance that inflated their tax bills. The subways were a business, said Windels, and should be run in a businesslike way. Costs should be covered by customer-riders. And a

Transit Authority should be established, with the power to raise fares—unhampered by popular opposition—whenever necessary to provide good service.

Liberals, labor, socialists, and communists opposed this. Councilman Stanley M. Isaacs became the nickel fare's ablest defender, in part because as a real estate tax lawyer he knew whereof he criticized. Isaacs rejected the notion that the subway was a business that should be self-supporting. It was, rather, a vital municipal service, akin to schools, sanitation pickups, fire protection, and street repairs, for which the city did not and should not charge user fees. Moreover, it was important to remember "that those who want [the fare] changed are the very real estate men who profited most by unloading their property because, as they advertised, it was within reach of the very heart of Manhattan for five cents." Channeling Henry George, Isaacs asserted that "the capital charges of those subways which had built up real estate values should be carried by real estate."

Isaacs accused proponents of a higher fare of wanting to rob Peter to pay Paul. Boosting fares and eliminating the subway deficit would also free up city credit, enabling the municipality to borrow money to finance postwar highway construction. This was doubly unfair to poor and working-class New Yorkers, most of whom didn't own a car and couldn't use the new highways. Why, asked Isaacs, should subway riders be forced to "indirectly subsidize the motorist"?

La Guardia, for all his autophilia, agreed. "Rapid transit is as necessary to New York City and its people as water and air," he declared in 1945. "Rapid transit has made the City." Windels's attack forced him to do what he had never done before: explicitly define the subways as a public service that should be subsidized by tax revenues. In 1944 he called on the state to legislate a broad-based "transportation tax"—a levy on rents, mortgage interest, and commuters—to spread the subway's costs to all who enjoyed its benefits. And in 1945 he asked for an additional three-year 1 percent sales tax, to fund a $100 million crash rehabilitation program of surface and subway lines. An official of REBNY (the Real Estate Board of New York), joining the issue squarely, declared that, to the contrary, "the people who should pay the subway costs are the people who use the subways."

The two sides fought the issue to a draw. In the end, the Legislature refused either to create an Authority to raise the fare, or to authorize a transportation or commuter tax. This left the city in 1945 looking at a following-year subway deficit of $46 million. It was in this context that the proposal to spend $250 million on a new Second Avenue Subway never got off (or under) the ground. The line was important, La Guardia admitted; building it would allow demolition of the Third Avenue El; but "we must be realistic." Indeed, all proposed subway expansions were now put on ice, the mayor saying, "It is necessary that we pause for a while and improve, rehabilitate and reconstruct the vast area of our city now developed and settled," before opening up more territory: "This is not time for new frontiers within the city limits."

In 1945, City Hall Station, from which Mayor McClellan and a train full of dignitaries had set out on the IRT's opening day back in 1904, was shut down, having been deemed uneconomic. Four decades of subway expansion had come to an end, at least for the moment. It was not clear when, if ever, Gotham's underground would begin to grow again.

146

Sea

The port of New York had been having a great war. In 1944 it handled the largest volume of export traffic in its history, or, for that matter, the history of any port on earth. Yet what of the future? On this score there were optimistic and pessimistic predictions.

The optimists realized that wartime levels of traffic—which included vast quantities of military hardware—were not sustainable. They believed that when the transition to peace was finally effected, New York's trade with Europe, Africa, and South America would still be 20–25 percent higher than it had been in 1940. One reason for this positive assessment was that war had wrought major improvements in the port's operation. Under command of the War Shipping Administration, railroads and shippers had transcended ruinous competition between (and among) themselves and through pooling and coordination had achieved dramatic increases in efficiency. The head of the Maritime Association of the Port of New York believed the lessons learned "can be carried over to peacetime." The president of the Foreign Commerce Club agreed. "The port's position in international commerce is stronger today than ever before," he said in 1944, "and benefits from this strengthening will be reaped for years to come."

The other major ground for optimism was the likelihood of a great postwar revival of international commerce, with the United States as sparkplug. Already in 1943, the *Herald Tribune* had announced that the US—"the one great source of supply for the world"—will be the center of "a global trade, to dwarf anything of the kind in the country's history." As a corollary, the paper said, New York "seems certain to become by all odds the world's greatest seaport and busier than it ever dreamed of being."

Governor Thomas Dewey agreed that the port's magnificent war record "holds huge promise for postwar trade" and decided to assist in its realization. Galvanized perhaps by San Francisco's 1945 plan to erect a huge World Trade Center on twelve city blocks near the Embarcadero, Dewey approved a bill the following year to establish a World Trade Center Corporation in New York and appointed Winthrop Aldrich, chairman of Chase National Bank, to head it. The legislature advanced $100,000 to examine the feasibility of creating a version of Germany's 700-year-old Leipzig Trade Fair, one that would make Gotham the "central market place for the world." Plans were sketched for an enormous twenty-one-building complex, spread over ten square blocks, that would bring together shippers and bankers and manufacturers and farmers, from every country, to display and exchange and promote and finance the sale of every imaginable kind of good.

More pessimistic voices noted that the war had also strengthened port competitors. "All good things have imitators and provoke jealousies," said the president of the New York Dock Company in December 1944, in warning that Gotham's postwar maritime supremacy was by no means guaranteed. To the south, when the coastwise route had been disrupted by U-boat attacks early in the conflict, New Orleans and other Gulf of Mexico ports had leapt to modernize their shipping services and siphoned off some of New York's trade with the Caribbean and Central and South America. To the west, Los Angeles, Seattle, and San Francisco would be the beneficiaries should postwar China's economy take off. (San Francisco, aiming to become the "New York of the Pacific," planned to devote four buildings in its World Trade Center to four trading targets—the Pacific, the "Orient," Latin America, and even Europe.) Perhaps the scariest scenario envisioned land-locked Chicago emerging as a potent rival, if visions for a St. Lawrence Seaway were ever realized. The Seaway, promoted by midwestern and Canadian interests since 1919, had been opposed by New Yorkers for an equal length of time, and efforts to block US government participation were still going strong in 1940s Gotham. The West Side Association of Commerce, in particular, trumpeted the danger that the Seaway might divert hundreds of millions of dollars of export and import business in grain and autos, while also threatening New York's manufacturing base and the billions in real estate values dependent on commercial and industrial primacy.

As for the port's improvements in efficiency, some worried they might falter without the guiding hand of government, or that the major improvements needed to match modernizing rivals might not be forthcoming. Howard Cullman, chairman of the Port Authority, was in the optimists' camp in terms of possibilities—he told the Foreign Commerce Club that the city might even triple its prewar business—but that winning this trade would require that Gotham dramatically enhance its marine facilities and end midtown traffic congestion, and it wasn't at all clear that either would happen.

The Dock Department had plans afoot to build six new piers on the North River (Hudson), reconstruct others, and perhaps raise a new shipping terminal at the foot of Atlantic Avenue in Brooklyn. But there were few signs that New York would or could come up with the requisite funds to undertake more substantial renewal, given its other needs and debts. The Port Authority also worried that Gotham might engage in ruinous interstate competition with its New Jersey harbor-mates, rather than cooperating to develop their mutual assets. And should the postwar port lapse back into archaic prewar competition, driving up the costs of doing business, the consequent loss of foreign trade to competing cities, the Authority feared, might well precipitate a collapse in Gotham "akin to that of Nantucket after the whaling trade dried up." In 1943, scouting for alternatives, the Port Authority prepared a postwar planning paper—kept secret lest the PA be accused of seeking "supergovernment" status—that mulled the possibility of the agency's taking control of rundown Port Newark, and of all Gotham's piers, and developing them conjointly as a New York–New Jersey megaport.

There was, however, another set of transport watchers who believed the port's most dangerous future competition would not come from other seaports but from out of the blue. Grover Loening, a leading aeronautical engineer with Grumman Aircraft, presented this perspective to the Foreign Commerce Club in a May 1942 talk at the Hotel Astor. Immediately after the war, Loening declared, airplanes would replace oceangoing vessels, both for passenger service and heavy freight. Cargo ships lumbering along at 10 miles per hour would be swiftly outmatched by cargo planes zooming along at 250. This inevitable development "will strip New York harbor of its commanding trade position," he prophesied. "There is no shoreline in the air," hence no reason why Detroit "cannot be a European port also." Ditto for South America: Why should rubber be lugged from Brazil to New York, then railed to Akron, when it could be landed at an Akron runway adjacent to a tire factory consignee? The Panama Canal was about to lose its raison d'être; perhaps Gotham would too.

If true, it was fortunate indeed that nowhere were New York's postwar energies more powerfully engaged than in extending its transport preeminence into the coming Air Age.

147

Sky

Amid the many commodities Madison Avenue dangled before wartime's balked consumers, few had quite the pizzazz of the personal airplane. At MOMA's immensely popular 1943 exhibition "Airways to Peace," a promo film produced by the Sikorsky Helicopter Company depicted a man taking off in his private chopper from the roof of a New York apartment building, heading for his office, only to return, moments later, to hover motionless a few feet in the air, while his wife handed through the cockpit window the lunch he'd forgotten to take. Polls suggested a crowded peacetime sky. One in September 1945 showed that 32 percent of the adult US population wanted their own plane, and 7 percent definitely planned to buy one. New Yorkers who wanted to browse the possibilities could have headed to Macy's where, in 1945, elevator operators arriving at the fifth floor chimed out: "Ladies' girdles, gentlemen's socks, airplanes, and household appliances." Here shoppers could check out the $2,994 all-metal, two-seater Ercoupe.

Whether or not this fad would fly, it would soon be possible to head for the nearest airport and clamber aboard a commercial airliner headed to distant climes—a more collective but still exciting prospect. Where that airport would *be* was still somewhat up in the air. In 1944 six East Coast cities vied at a Civil Aeronautics Board hearing for designation as a terminus for trans-Atlantic air routes. New York reps pressed the case that geography was still destiny. Gotham was closest to key European cities, allowing for the quickest flights (fourteen hours to London, seventeen to Berlin, eighteen to Rome). Commercially too, New York made most sense. Expert testimony suggested that established travel patterns—before the war 70 percent of overseas departures left from Gotham—indicated that a route would attain "maximum development" if the New York district was made its "principal United States terminal," a rationale that applied to international air freight as well.

A similar case was made for southbound traffic. Prewar travelers heading to the Caribbean and beyond had voyaged to Miami and transferred there to a flying boat for the over-water part of their trip. However, according to an azimuthal map showing great circle ("as the crow flies") distances—which the Port Authority published in 1944—a direct flight from New York to almost anywhere in the West Indies and South America was several hundred miles

A Macy's advertisement for an Ercoupe private plane, 1945. (David Winters)

shorter than one that deviated from the great circle path by stopping off at a southern port. And given the war-proven ability of the new four-engine planes (like the Douglas C-54) to make it safely all the way, there was no longer a need to change at Miami.

For all its theoretical advantages, Gotham's postwar air supremacy was far from being assured. La Guardia Field, virtually from its inception the busiest airport in the United States, was patently incapable of handling the expected postwar travel boom. Some estimates suggested the number of regularly scheduled flights to foreign countries might expand by a factor of fifty. Already in 1945 domestic and international airlines were clamoring for terminal facilities. But La Guardia, hemmed in between Grand Central Parkway and Flushing Bay, had no room for expansion. In addition to being maxed out volume-wise, it had a weight problem to contend with. La Guardia's runways, built on sand, had been sinking slowly into the bay when they had only had 35-ton planes to contend with; 70-ton air ships (surplus C-54s) were on the way, and 200-tonners were on the planning boards. Last, certainly not least, was the safety issue. With too few runways and too much traffic, the often-fogbound skies above La Guardia could seem as congested as midtown Manhattan. It was a testimony to the skill of the field's air-traffic controllers that there had been virtually no crashes, much less collisions, in the field's history to that point.

All these limitations were about to be spectacularly transcended, as the world's largest airport was then rising from the marshlands of Jamaica Bay and the sandy links of Idlewild Golf Course. Ever since the Navy had commandeered Floyd Bennett Field in 1941, La Guardia had been condemning and purchasing swampy acres. By 1945 he'd accumulated 4,527 of them, roughly the size of Manhattan from Battery Park to Times Square, and nearly ten times the size of his eponymous field. Since 1942, engineers had been preparing a colossal foundation, under the direction of the Department of Docks and Aviation (the new name for the old Department of Docks, mirroring the city's shift in attention). In the greatest land-reclamation project in American history, floating dredges were set to scooping up sand from the floor of the bay and spreading it atop the marshy areas, compressing and squeezing out the water. This technology could move more fill in an hour than an army of men with wheelbarrows and mule-drawn dumpcarts had moved in a day, twenty years earlier. By 1945, workers had poured forty-one million cubic yards of sand over seven square miles, and before they were finished they had moved enough to cover every street in Manhattan to a depth of eight feet. Behind them came those who laid sewers, power and communication lines, 70 miles of

A ticket reservation board for United Airlines, ca. 1945. (SFO Museum Collection, Gift of United Airlines)

storm drains to control tidal flow, and vast spillways—pipes as big as the Holland Tunnel—to deal with rain on runways. Once topped with Long Island beach grass, the site was ready for runways, aprons, loading docks, buildings, parking lots—the surface stuff of airports.

But the stuff was expensive. Foundation preparation for Idlewild Airport (as it would be called) had cost $71 million; finishing it might could cost $100 million more, some said twice that. La Guardia insisted that in the long run it would pay for itself. In the short run, given the limits on city taxing authority, from where was the money to come?

Moses proposed establishing a New York City Airport Authority (CAA) which, like his Triborough Bridge Authority, would be empowered to issue bonds and finish the airport. To back the bonds, he would tear up the leases La Guardia had signed with the airline companies, arguing correctly the mayor had charged too little for renting hangar and terminal space. As elsewhere in the nation, aviation firms played off rival cities one against the other—here New York and Newark—and La Guardia had won by lowballing his bid. Moses declared he would jack up these fees 600 percent, which put him on a collision course with the airlines; Eddie Rickenbacker of Eastern stormed out of a meeting with Moses, saying, "I'm going to Newark."

Moses faced a wilier opponent in Austin Tobin, who proposed that his Port Authority of New York take over Idlewild (and La Guardia), too, and run them in cooperative tandem with Newark. This proposal infuriated city officials, loath to give the governor of New Jersey any say in running their airports, and Moses, who saw it as a power grab. Tobin rowed to his objective with muffled oars, pointing out to investment bankers and airline executives that *his* Authority was a far better credit risk, as it was rolling in toll money. Car and truck traffic would keep surging across his bridges and tunnels, while New York's CAA would have no equivalent income stream, unless it hiked its rental fees, which Tobin promised not to do. Moses had met his match. The banks and airlines leaned on municipal officials, the deal was done, and Idlewild could proceed to completion.

148

Infrastructure

While attending to Gotham's transportation synapses—seeking to lubricate the flow of people and commodities into and out of the city—postwar planners also concentrated on refurbishing New York's life-support systems, which channeled water, food, power, and sewage into and out of the city. Upgrading or transforming networks that sustained multiple millions were *long durée* projects, and most were in medias res during the war years.

The decision to increase Gotham's water supply by tapping the headwaters of the Delaware River had been approved in 1928. Work on the Delaware Aqueduct and its supporting dams and reservoirs commenced in 1937. By 1943, the 18-foot-diameter Aqueduct was nearing completion. Intended to channel 540 million gallons per day (mgd) from Rondout Reservoir, to Hill View Reservoir, to the metropolis via City Tunnel No. 2, the 85-mile-long Aqueduct, bored through rock lying 300–1000 feet below the surface, would be by far the longest continuous deep rock tunnel on earth. The war interrupted the larger water supply project, but the Aqueduct was pushed forward, partly as an emergency measure, to supplement the bomb-or-sabotage-vulnerable Croton and Catskill systems, and partly because the city had been experiencing periodic water shortages since 1941. The spigot was opened in April 1944, and an interim supply of 100 mgd of Delaware water soon filled the city's reservoirs to the brim. With the postwar plan budgeting $75,000,000 to complete phase 2, aqueous abundance seemed assured.

Food, if anything, was overabundant; or, more precisely, the system for receiving the daily deluge of meat, milk, poultry, fruits, and vegetables was overloaded, particularly in the case of perishable produce.

Few New York supply nodes had changed as little, in either place or modus operandi, as the Washington Market, which dealt in fruits and vegetables. The same patch of ground, bounded by Fulton, Washington, Vesey, and West Streets (in the northwest corner of the World Trade Center site where building #6 once stood), had been the locus of retail produce marketing since the late eighteenth century. At first an open-air affair, it was later housed in a structure that was built in 1813, replaced in 1884, modernized inside in 1915, and given an exterior facelift in 1940–41.

Wholesale trading in the same goods—among them grapes, apples, plums, pears, lettuce, peppers, radishes, and string beans—was also situated where it had been for well over a century, in the choked and narrow streets just above the retail market, stretching north along West, Washington, and Hudson, up to Laight (just below Canal, where the Holland Tunnel entered Manhattan). This 58-acre territory, also called the Washington Market, was what most people understood by the term. Here wholesale jobbers and commission men did business out of old Federal and Greek Revival brownstones, with wooden shed roofs that jutted from the second floor forming the sidewalk stalls wherein they worked.

Congestion had been a fact of market life since at least the 1850s, though shifts in the way that goods arrived had newly clogged its arteries. As late as the 1920s, the overwhelming bulk of produce had arrived by boat or train. Car floats operated by the Erie Lackawanna, New York Central, and Pennsylvania railroads (among others), together with steamships that sailed up the East Coast, or down the Hudson, had deposited foodstuffs at the great covered piers adjacent to the market. There, together with additional loads brought in via the New York Central's West Side freight line, the goods were unloaded and laid out each night, ready for wholesalers to buy. Smaller quantities were carried from the pier by hand cart or horse truck to the jobbers' stalls that lined streets to the east, and there piled high along the sidewalks. Buyers—jobbers from New Jersey, Connecticut, and New York's secondary

The Wallabout Market in Brooklyn, September 1940. World Telegram & Sun photo by Al Aumuller. (Library of Congress, Prints and Photographs Division)

markets—arrived in motor trucks, made their transactions from 1:00 a.m. to 5:00 a.m., and by early morning sidewalk stocks were depleted.

By the 1940s, this pattern had altered. Trains and boats still predominated, but motorized transport now accounted for 40 percent of deliveries, and much wholesaling had shifted from piers to street stalls. Late each night, hundreds of farm trucks poured into the market blocks from as far north as Maine and as far south as Florida, most arriving via the nearby Holland Tunnel. After 2:00 a.m. a second wave was allowed into the district—hundreds of buyers' trucks from an equally far-flung hinterland, many of which jumped the gun, trapping first-wave trucks attempting to exit. The result—a "pushing, swearing, tooting bedlam"—was glorious to behold but costly to sustain. Inefficiencies and delays led to higher prices, which ricocheted across the country, as in 1945 the Washington Market supplied food to thirteen million people, nearly one-tenth the US population, and prices set in lower Manhattan determined values elsewhere.

Market men and city officials had been dreaming of unsnarling Washington Market since at least the 1850s, but one plan after another had fallen through. La Guardia, alluding to this dismal record, declared: "We are not going to fool around this time. We are going to get action." In 1943 he announced preliminary plans for "the largest, most modern primary terminal market in the entire country." By 1945 the specifications were in place. For forty-two million dollars—most of it for land acquisition so the private market could be taken public—a brand-new market, covering sixty acres (from Murray to Vestry, Greenwich to the Hudson River), would feature eight long and spacious market buildings, separated by streets one hundred feet wide, and laid out east to west, down to the river, where new bulkheads would unload forty car floats at a time. As with many of his more ambitious postwar plans, the mayor was counting on federal support. Promisingly, Congress, concerned about bottlenecks at the nation's largest produce exchange, had coughed up $750,000 for the plan to eliminate them.

Big plans were afoot as well for completing an in-progress citywide attack on harbor pollution. Talked about since the 1903 report of the New York Bay Pollution Commission, it had commenced in earnest with the 1935 opening of the first modern sewage treatment plant, at Coney Island. By 1945, as sanitary engineer Richard H. Gould—the city's point man on sewage disposal—told the Public Health Association of New York City, there were thirteen plants in operation (seven recent, six vintage), which together constituted about 30 percent of what the city's master sanitation plan called for. These had made major progress in cleaning up the Harlem and East Rivers, but raw sewage still floated up on many city beaches. To finish the cleanup, the postwar program proposed five new plants, plus nine extensions and additions, which together would bring fulfillment up to 94 percent and solve the problem of Gotham's harbor pollution. If all went well, some believed, people would again be boating, swimming, and fishing in the city's rivers and bays. "All going well" included obtaining federal financing. While the city had paid for some of its plants, it had also been mightily helped by New Deal funding. As with other projects, La Guardia was counting on Washington making sewage-disposal systems a national responsibility, as he told a Planning Conference on Sanitation for the Post-War Period, at the Engineers Club in 1943.

THE FUTURE OF THE CITY'S power supply was less mapped out than other life-support systems. Coal remained king during the war years and was even boosted by military developments. Consolidated Edison and its subsidiary New York Steam Corporation imported roughly seven million tons of coal each year, with a million being used to manufacture gas, somewhat less to make steam, and the rest to generate electricity. Brooklyn Union Gas imported another million. Most was anthracite brought in by rail from Pennsylvania mines to Bayonne, then shipped across the bay to company docks. There was also bituminous coal, up from the so-called Pocahontas fields of Virginia and West Virginia, that came via Hampton Roads on self-propelled colliers or tug-drawn barges. U-boats bit into the latter traffic early in the war, but supplies were swiftly shifted to rail and carried up to the Greenville Yards in Jersey City for transfer to harbor barges. Occasional miner strikes had a disruptive impact, but the power companies and Coal Merchants Association (at 90 West Street) seldom reported a less than sixty-day supply on hand in the city. Nor was electricity ever cut off, despite the increased diversion of coal to war production (notably to power-hungry aluminum plants, which alone devoured two million additional tons).

Submarine warfare battered oil deliveries as well. When diminished supplies led to rationing, large-scale consumers of fuel oil—urged on by federal war agencies—responded by switching to coal-generated steam. Hundreds of big buildings shut down their oil burners and signed up with the New York Steam Corporation, which by 1943 was piping "street steam" through underground mains to roughly 2,500 structures between 92nd Street and the Battery, including hotels, apartment houses, restaurants, hospitals, theaters, factories, small businesses, and office skyscrapers (among them Rockefeller Center and the Empire State). Its six plants along the East River, flagshipped by the Kips Bay Station at East 35th Street, the largest central station steam plant in the world, were fed by nearly a million tons of barged coal and could draw when necessary on the Waterside and 14th Street stations of its Consolidated Edison parent to keep its customers toasty.

There was, however, an increase in the amount of bituminous being burned, especially in war plants in New Jersey, from which emanated toxic clouds that floated across the Arthur Kill to lay waste to Staten Island strawberry fields. More generally, increased coal usage in dwellings and plants, locomotives and ships, subway and Con Ed power stations, all contributed their share of sooty air to growing air pollution. When City Councilman Joseph T. Sharkey, an early champion of anti-smoke-and-soot legislation, introduced a bill curtailing atmospheric emissions in 1942, it was rejected as an obstacle to war production.

Perhaps the major wartime impact on the mix of power streams feeding New York City was on the manufactured-gas industry, which dated back to the 1820s and on which the city was unusually reliant. Gothamites consumed approximately 40 percent of all such gas manufactured in the US. But as many gas makers used oil as well as coal in their manufacturing process, cutbacks in fuel oil supplies forced a reduction in output. The arrival of the Big Inch pipeline restored the flow of oil, and by early 1944, 300,000 barrels a day were surging into the New York area, ending constraints on gas production. Ironically, the pipelines proved the local industry's undoing, as they opened the door to postwar delivery of natural gas direct from Texas to Gotham.

Another potential rival to coal, hydroelectric power, was stymied by virtue of its association with the St. Lawrence Seaway project. In 1931, then Governor Roosevelt had helped create a state Power Authority to develop the generating capabilities of the St. Lawrence River. However, because the hydroelectric generators had to be integrated with the larger Seaway system of canals, dams, and locks, the commercial interests that blocked the waterway project in effect blocked the power project as well. La Guardia favored the

Seaway, despite its likely negative impact on city shipping interests, because he wanted to lower electric rates in the city, and he was convinced that the real opposition to the Seaway came from private power interests who dreaded the coming of TVA-style public power at lower rates.

These public/private conundrums marked debates about other aspects of the metropolitan future—concerning issues more intangible than houses, trolleys, autos, airplanes, and coal barges—none more ethereal than money.

149

Washington or Wall Street?

On July 22, 1944, the would-be architects of a new world financial order rested, after three weeks of labor in the Mt. Washington Hotel, nestled below New Hampshire's White Mountains (postal address: Bretton Woods). Although representatives were present from all forty-four Allied nations, the key clashes were those between Harry Dexter White, the US Treasury's man, and John Maynard Keynes, leader of the British delegation. The principal outcome of their negotiations were linked proposals to establish an International Bank for Reconstruction and Development (IBRD) and an International Monetary Fund (IMF). The IRBD (or World Bank as it was popularly known) would make long-term loans to war-shattered Europe and to developing and decolonizing countries. The IMF would make short-term loans intended to shore up weakened currencies and avoid the competitive devaluations that had fueled economic warfare in the 1930s.

President Roosevelt and Secretary of the Treasury Morgenthau (White's boss) were pleased with the results of the Bretton Woods conclave—results which, given the respective strengths of the contending parties, largely embodied the US government's position.

Similarly pleased were powerful New York institutions like the Council on Foreign Relations which, as early as February 1942, had urged creating just such institutions to serve as pillars of a revamped international order. The Committee for Economic Development also approved the Bretton Woods schema, and, like the CFR, would push Congress to approve US participation.

Gotham's banking community, however, was distinctly unhappy, and it set out to revise the terms of American participation or scuttle it altogether. The campaign was led by Winthrop Aldrich, chair of Chase National Bank, president of the prestigious Economic Club of New York, and a good bet to become secretary of the treasury in any Tom Dewey administration.

Aldrich and the Wall Street fraternity, in seeing the proposed World Bank as an assault on their prerogatives, could point to Secretary Morgenthau's closing address to the Bretton Woods conference, in which he declared that the IBRD would "limit the control which certain private bankers have in the past exercised over international finance." Even more disturbing was the New Dealer's assertion that the Bank would "provide capital for those who need it at lower interest rates than in the past" and thus drive "usurious money lenders from the temple of international finance." In the end, however, the Wall Streeters acquiesced in the IBRD, as Morgenthau also offered assurances that its ultimate purpose would be "to guarantee private loans made through the usual investment channels," and that it would expand their own lending opportunities while minimizing their credit risks. Besides, as the great bulk of the IBRD's capital would have to be raised on New York's financial markets, Wall Street would have considerable sway over its lending policies and priorities.

The IMF seemed considerably more objectionable. Under its provisions, member countries would be entitled to automatic borrowing privileges. This, the bankers believed, would lead to loans being made without regard to creditworthiness or ability to repay. As the US would provide the bulk of the funds, the IMF might well become a sluiceway for channeling dollars to wily and profligate Europeans.

Henry Hazlitt, an economic fundamentalist, backed Aldrich on this. In his *New York Times* column, Hazlitt argued that IMF managers should have complete authority to withhold credit from any country that indulged in undue deficit financing, currency expansion, or trade discrimination. This would give the IMF power to force borrowers into adopting policies the bankers deemed "reasonable," like balanced budgets.

Hazlitt and the New York bankers were also upset by an IMF provision that "members may exercise such controls as are necessary to regulate international capital movements." This clause was intended to curb the flow of speculative "hot money"—funds that whipped in and out of countries in response to interest-rate differentials—which had proved so destabilizing in the interwar era. Both Keynes and the New Dealers were equally determined to allow interventionist welfare states the leeway to take whatever domestic measures they deemed necessary to succor their unemployed or provide them with jobs, without having their hands tied by assaults on their currencies. Wall Street bankers objected to such constraints on capital flows, partly because they had made a lot of money in the 1930s when Eurocapital fled to Manhattan, and partly because they thought speculative attacks on weakened currencies a good way to force a reversal of the "unsound" policies that had weakened them in the first place.

Rather than creating an IMF—in their view a typically New Dealish impediment to the rational and efficient working of the marketplace over which they presided—Aldrich and his allies (including the American Bankers Association, the *Wall Street Journal*, and the US Chamber of Commerce) proposed an alternative. The US should resume gold payments, pegging the dollar to gold; and then stabilize the pound–dollar rate by granting Great Britain an enormous loan with which to shore up its economy. The end result would be that the dollar "would constitute a sure anchorage for the currencies of other nations and would become a generally acceptable international medium of exchange." Short-term currency adjustments could be handled as needed not by an international agency but by central bankers united behind New York's leadership. Informal control of international monetary and financial policy would, in this scenario, be returned to lower Manhattan.

Morgenthau, furious, embarked on a drive (piloted by Senator Wagner) to win congressional acceptance of the Bretton Woods agreements. Backed by the Independent Bankers Association (representing "country bankers") and industrial exporters (notably auto makers), and by the CFR, CED, and CIO, the Treasury successfully repelled efforts by New York bankers, deemed to be "pursuing selfish ends," to control postwar finance.

As one senator put it, Aldrich wanted the US to "abandon Government regulation of our money system and return it to the hands of the private bankers who led us into the orgy of speculation in the twenties." In the end, with memories of the Crash still vivid, it proved impossible for Wall Street to convince Congress of the superior efficacy of private over public regulation. US participation in the Fund and Bank was signed into law in August 1945.

One last issue remained—the location of these new institutions. The British hoped it might be London, or some European capital. They were bluntly informed by Harry White that with the US anteing up two or three times more money than the others, "it is preposterous that the head office should be any place else." The alternatives—a Committee on Site reported early the following year—boiled down to New York or Washington.

The Brits wanted Gotham. In an odd inverse echo of the eighteenth-century debate between Hamilton and Jefferson over where to put the US capital, in which Jefferson had worked to remove it from the corrupting influence of New York money men, Keynes wanted the Fund and Bank kept clear of "the politics of Congress and the nationalistic whispering gallery of the Embassies and Legations." New York being the preeminent economic city— Harry White agreed that "New York has become the financial center of the world"—it would provide a more businesslike atmosphere, one free from overweening dominance by the American government.

The US position was precisely the opposite. The Fund and Bank would not be private businesses, but government enterprises; not profit-making institutions (for which Gotham was the appropriate venue) but policy-making institutions (which should be kept in Washington to minimize improper influence from private interests). The Committee on Site reported that "in recent years there has been a shift from New York to Washington of international financial policy making." The US delegation, seeing the Gotham gambit as an attempt to reverse this trend, promptly squelched it. Henry Morgenthau was thrilled by what he considered the successful culmination of what he called his and FDR's twelve-year struggle "to move the financial center of the world from London and Wall Street to the United States Treasury."

It remained to be seen whether Morgenthau's triumph would be as long-lived as he assumed, the borders between NY and DC having already proved more permeable than prior planners had imagined. Wall Street, after all, had handily survived the establishment of the Washington-based Federal Reserve Board. But for the moment Gotham's financial wings seemed trimmed, if not clipped.

The New York banking community—both its commercial and investment branches— had been circumscribed in other, more immediate ways, by wartime developments. International finance was practically dormant. Before the conflict, National City Bank had had one hundred offices around the world. By 1942, most NCB offices in Asia (and all in China) had been shuttered; all its European branches were closed (except for one in London); and with over three-fourths of all loans to Latin America in default, there was no interest in lending to most of the Western Hemisphere either.

Nor was much domestic lending happening—though not for lack of money to lend. Given the surge in wartime savings, the great commercial banks were rolling in assets. National City and Chase, the two "Rockefeller banks," headed the list of those flush with cash. Chase, long connected to the John D. Senior side of the family (Aldrich himself was Rockefeller Jr.'s brother-in-law), was in first place, with $6.1 billion in 1945. National City, the preferred venue for Senior's brother William's descendants, was the close runner-up, at

$5.6 billion. The Morgans, who had fared least well in the New Deal reform era, had restructured and beefed up their position.

Capital wasn't in short supply; borrowers were. Loan demand plummeted because corporations could borrow from the government or self-finance out of profits. So, instead, banks loaned to the government, buying bonds to help finance the war. Of NCB's $5.6 billion in assets, $2.9 billion were in US government obligations. Chase, too, took on a lot of federal debt, and J. P. Morgan, after it went public, also became a major participant. Profits were small but virtually guaranteed.

In this context there was little need and less inclination to engage in risk-taking. Such private sector loans as the banks did extend were closely scrutinized, and most were short term and self-liquidating, used to finance trade. The combination of low but stable interest rates, heavy government regulation, and lingering memories of the traumatic Thirties, led commercial bankers to retreat into a cautious, conservative mode, with a conservative culture to match. Offices were somber, wood-paneled and walnut-desked. Senior bankers (most still Anglo-Saxon Protestants) wore stiff detachable collars, had their shoes shined by the bootblacks in front of Trinity—unless it was summer, when white shoes were de rigueur (and soon an adjective)—and lunched at the Downtown Association (60 Pine). Firms recruited Harvard, Yale, Williams men. Commercial banking was settling into a "3-6-3" culture: borrow at 3 percent, lend at 6 percent, get to the golf course by 3:00 p.m.

The investment banking side of the industry was similarly running in low gear. The Treasury Department asked underwriters to desist from new bond issues, so as not to compete with war bond drives, but there were precious few requests for their services in the first place. Giant US corporations expanded profits dramatically while holding dividend payouts steady, partly at government command, partly to accumulate earnings for a postwar surge. Rather than taking on new debts, many companies paid off old ones and bought back their own common stock. By 1944 they were extremely solvent. Instead of selling securities or investing on their own account, leading investment houses like Morgan Stanley (the other half of the old House of Morgan) and Dillon, Read concentrated on providing financial advice to a small circle of blue chip clients. Like their commercial cousins, investment bankers, too, adopted a conservative genteel style, though their ranks were ethnically more varied and included members like "Bobbie" Lehman of Lehman Brothers, Sidney Weinberg of Goldman Sachs, and refugee André Meyer, who assumed control at Lazard Frères.

The New York Stock Exchange itself remained similarly somnolent, as Crash-scarred investors kept their distance, though the improving military situation did trigger some fitful rallies in 1943 and 1944 and a steeper rise in prices and volume during 1945 (when the price of a seat on the Exchange exceeded 1942 levels). There wasn't a lot of steam behind the surges, however. Caution remained the watchword, and NYSE quotes continued to lag behind soaring profits in the corporate world. The mood was bullish, though the bull seemed disinclined to snort.

Finance would certainly be an important profit center for the city's postwar economy. Exactly how vigorous a driver it would be remained unclear.

150

Manufacturing: Tide Going Out or Tide Coming In?

Wartime Gotham remained by far the largest manufacturing center in the nation, unsurpassed in diversity of industries, number of factories, and aggregate volume. Would it stay that way? Some argued industrial New York had peaked, others that the best was yet to come.

One of the gloomier prognoses—that of the Hanes Committee commissioned by Governor Dewey in November 1942—was written during a low point in the city's fortunes, when unemployment was still high, Gotham wasn't getting its fair share of war contracts, workers were leaving town, and small enterprises were going under. This distressing present looked worse in the light of the recent depressed past. Between 1929 and 1939 the city's percentage of total US manufacturing had dropped, the number of factories and wage earners had declined, wages and value added by manufacturing had slid. Some industries had experienced only a relational slippage—they'd been overtaken by more rapidly growing areas—but others (printing, men's outerwear) had experienced an absolute loss. To the worried Hanes analysts, it seemed such trends were continuing and that unless strong measures were taken, "New York City may expect to continue to lose ground relative to the rest of the nation in the future as it has in the past."

In scouting the reasons for this deterioration, the Hanes Committee fastened first on taxes, particularly those on real estate and corporations, which (it believed) militated against expansion of existing industries and discouraged the emergence of new ones. This assessment was seconded by the Commerce and Industry Association of New York and the Real Estate Board of New York. The Regional Plan Association, in its *Economic Status of the New York Metropolitan Region in 1944*, similarly called on the federal government to provide "a favorable climate for free enterprise by repealing the excess profits tax and by reducing the high wartime surtax rates on personal incomes in the higher brackets," as these were siphoning off the capital needed to expand business.

Other explanations in the Hanes report for manufacturing's decline included high labor costs, antiquated factories, obsolete machinery, insufficient parking, and congested transport (or its converse: printing had left town when trains and trucks made it possible to take advantage of lower costs elsewhere while keeping in touch with clients in the city). High rents barely made the list. All these impediments, it was held, placed New York plants at a competitive disadvantage with those in the war boomtowns of the Midwest and South. The New York Board of Trade warned the mayor that "one industry after another" was leaving the city. It was imperative, the Hanes report concluded, "to remove the handicaps which now stifle business."

The La Guardia administration bristled at these assessments, criticizing the Hanes analysis as superficial, called its "alarming generalizations" based on out-of-date data and hearsay evidence, saw its "unduly dark" conclusions as a function of their having viewed the situation through distorted interpretive lenses. As for reports of manufacturers rushing for the exits, the mayor branded these as "cheap propaganda" and "a malicious, deliberate lie."

To back up these criticisms, La Guardia asked his Business Advisory Committee (in November 1943) to set up a Postwar Industrial Committee to study the manufacturing situation in detail. It included representatives from the New York Central and Pennsylvania railroads, Con Ed, New York Telephone, Brooklyn Union Gas, and Gulf Oil, among others; and these firms loaned engineers and executives to the survey team. By February 1944, the committee had interviewed managers at 1,335 concerns, of which only fourteen planned to leave the city or go out of business when the war ended. Eight hundred seventy-eight had laid plans for postwar expansion. Twenty-eight million dollars-worth of orders had been placed for as-soon-as-available delivery, orders that constituted only part of the $1.5 billion in reported anticipated outlays.

As to the putative throttling of enterprise, a "surprisingly small" number complained of taxes, labor legislation, or government interference. Taxes, in particular, were not considered onerous enough to warrant leaving otherwise desirable locations. As to the cost of labor, Commissioner of Investigations Herlands observed that one of New York's "greatest assets is its reservoir of skilled labor which is naturally entitled to higher wages." Perhaps most telling was Con Ed's contribution, a report on the number of factories that had disconnected or added electric service. Between January and June of 1944, it turned out, 203 new manufacturing concerns had been established in New York, while only 21 had thrown in the towel, making a net gain of 182 industrial plants. Finally, the Regional Plan Association's own data—which analyzed the 22-county New York Metropolitan Area rather than only the five boroughs—suggested a more heartening reading. In 1944, the region produced 50 percent more manufactured goods than did Chicago; twice the output of Detroit; and four times that of Pittsburgh. Moreover, since war orders had gotten under way, industrial production had grown more rapidly in the New York region than it had in Chicago, Detroit, or Philadelphia.

Still, the critical question was what would happen once those war contracts stopped coming. It was generally agreed that ship and airplane production might well plummet by 90 percent; Seattle, Portland, San Francisco, and San Diego, which had mushroomed as industrial centers during the war, were where the future of those industries likely lay. Yet there were substantial grounds for thinking that Gotham might well remain the supreme manufacturing center, partly by fulfilling ongoing military demand, and partly by providing commodities (traditional and novel) to civilian markets.

The military, especially the Navy, had established a close relationship with a network of industrial suppliers, a connection that many in the high command, notably Secretary

Forrestal, wanted to sustain. New York's small and highly specialized plants excelled in making precision instruments, electronic components, and a great variety of high-tech hardware. Given that military technology had been developing at a breathtaking pace during the conflict, and would likely continue to mutate in unpredictable ways, the arms business bore more than passing resemblance to the quicksilver, fashion-driven ladies' garment trade—for which Gotham's industrial ecosystem, capable of rapid response to changing styles and designs, had proven singularly well adapted. New York's military contractors could offer the newly completed Pentagon a supple and flexible mix of firms—a matrix of contractors and subcontractors jumbled together in convenient proximity—linked to pools of engineering and academic expertise, outside services like testing labs and machine shops, and a profusion of workers skilled in a great variety of trades.

Gotham was especially dense with engineering talent. Not only did local schools produce prodigious numbers of (especially electrical) engineers—NYU, Brooklyn Polytechnic, Cooper Union, Columbia, City College, Pratt Institute, Manhattan College, Long Island University, and Stevens Institute—but graduates were inclined to stay in the city (and those from other states to locate here) because of the ready availability of jobs, the opportunities for continuing education, and the manifold sources of intellectual and cultural stimulation.

Scientists, both theoretical and applied, were also thick on the ground. Some of the major corporate research and development giants, strapped for expansion space, had moved out of the center city during the war but hadn't gone far. In 1941 a large component of Bell Labs relocated from West Street to Murray Hill, New Jersey, thirty miles west of Manhattan, and by 1945 its staff had nearly doubled, to 8,000 people. Most were focused on radar research. By 1944, however, Mervin J. Kelly, the new executive vice president, was turning attention elsewhere. Convinced that electron tubes had reached the limit of their capacities, Kelly wanted electrons sent flowing through crystalline semiconductors rather than problematic vacuum tubes. In July 1945 he began setting up a task force, with the aid of physicist William Shockley, that would undertake the fundamental research in solid state physics necessary for further progress.

New York was also well positioned on the front line of advancing computer technology, as Columbia University, in collaboration with IBM, had opened the Thomas J. Watson Scientific Computing Laboratory on West 116th Street in 1945. Columbia took strides as well in nuclear physics research, though not in Morningside Heights, where there was neither space nor community tolerance for facilities that might spew radioactive material. Isidor Rabi spearheaded the campaign by a consortium of universities that won federal financing for establishing the Brookhaven Research Laboratory, fifty miles east of Manhattan, on the site of the US Army's Camp Upton (where Irving Berlin had hated to get up in the morning).

Despite all these desirable qualities and qualifications, Gotham could not *count* on remaining a major center of military manufacturing. Such decisions would ultimately be made in Washington and be subject (via Congress) to political pressure from contending cities. But civilian production was another story. Here New York had something going for it that no other place could match. It was—in the words of a 1945 Regional Plan Association report on the *Resources and Purchasing Power of the New York Region*—"the center of the greatest concentration of buying power the world has ever known." These massed purchasers, said the RPA, constituted an "enormous deferred demand for hundreds of lines of consumer goods which form such an important part of New York's industrial output." And while the city's longstanding specialization in such goods had slowed conversion to production of military hardware, it would—conversely—facilitate postwar reconversion, as rejiggered factories could simply revert to traditional pursuits. Thus, the General Bronze Corporation of Long Island City, which had been making machine gun cradle assemblies, was gearing up to mass-produce aluminum window frames for an expected postwar housing boom.

The most exciting, promising, and near-term developments, however, were likely to come in consumer electronics. Metropolitan area corporate laboratories—such as Bell Labs, RCA Labs (in Princeton since 1942), CBS Labs (still at Madison Avenue), and the Sylvania Electric Products research center (which the company had been given the go-ahead to construct in Bayside, Queens)—were poised to extend the city's longstanding front-runner status in entertainment and communication commodities.

Topping the list was television, hailed in 1943 by *Fortune* magazine as "one of the brightest stars in the heaven of the postwar planners...the hope and beacon of a great new industry."

After its 1939 public debut at the World's Fair, TV's promoters had pressed ahead with trial-run programming—like the telecast over NBC's experimental station W2XBS of the Republican convention in June 1940—while waiting for the government to establish industry-wide technical standards. Finally, in March 1941, the Federal Communications Commission approved a 525-lines-per-screen, thirty-frames-per-second, and FM-audio package. On July 1, 1941, the first three stations to be granted commercial licenses began transmitting from rival towers: W2XBS (now WNBT) was atop the Empire State Building; CBS's W2XAB (reminted as WCBW) surmounted the Chrysler Building; and upstart Allen B. DuMont's station (W2XWV now WABD) bestrode 515 Madison (a 42-story structure at 53rd Street).

On its first day on the air, WNBT broadcast the world's first television commercial, just before a Dodgers–Phillies game. The ten-second spot for Bulova watches, for which the company paid $4 (plus $5 for "facilities and handling"), displayed the picture of a Bulova clock face, superimposed on a map of the United States, which ticked off the seconds as a voice-over intoned: "America runs on Bulova time." According to a National Association of

RCA executives watch a prototype of the television, 1939. (Carl Mydans The LIFE Picture Collection/Shutterstock)

Broadcasters estimate, roughly 7,000 television sets were in operation at the time, 5,000 of them in the New York metropolitan area.

This proved a false dawn. By fall 1941, with manpower and materials draining away into defense work, production of TV sets had begun dropping and in April 1942 was banned altogether. Commercial broadcasts were canceled, cameras reassigned to training air-raid wardens. RCA researchers, placed at the Navy's disposal, worked on developing a TV-guided missile. This led to invention of the image orthicon, a highly light-sensitive camera tube which, though of doubtful wartime value (it's not clear any TV-missile ever hit its target), would prove of immense peacetime utility.

During 1943–44, with commercial operations in suspension, CBS pushed hard to reopen the technical standards decision. In particular, Bill Paley's people wanted to shift television broadcasting from the VHF (very high frequency) range of the wavelength spectrum to the UHF (ultrahigh frequency) portion. The UHF location would allow for more stations (40 rather than 13) and higher-definition pictures (1,000 not 515 lines). It would also better facilitate broadcasting in color, which CBS engineer (and 1933 transplant to Gotham) Peter Goldmark had recently developed and had demonstrated by transmitting color images from the Chrysler spire to CBS headquarters at 485 Madison. RCA's David Sarnoff deprecated Goldmark's technology as merely mechanical, and given that the electronic version might take another five years to develop, he argued that it would be a disservice to the public to wait so long, when black and white was ready to roll. In addition, shifting to UHF would render obsolete the existing VHF equipment in which consumers had invested.

Less emphasized by Sarnoff was the fact that RCA had a lot of money riding on the decision. As things stood, his company received 3/5ths of one percent of the wholesale price of every TV set sold by his competitors, because RCA controlled the major patents on VHF technology. It had not, however, sewn up the UHF frequencies. Insisting that the FCC should stick with what many believed an inferior standard for the sake of RCA's bottom line was not a promising strategy.

Sarnoff argued instead that immediate release of VHF machines would be good for the postwar economy. The conflict had galvanized war-related radio production; by 1945, according to one RCA executive, over 300,000 people were so employed. But the peacetime radio industry could not absorb all these war workers. The new TV industry, however, might well be able to hire large numbers of veterans and thus provide a cushion against unemployment and depression.

This more public-spirited approach was echoed in new New York media about mass media, like *Television* magazine, which premiered in spring 1944. An outrigger argument was advanced by *Sponsor* magazine

A boy watches a television in the window of an appliance store, 1948. (Ralph Morse The LIFE Picture Collection/Shutterstock)

(a journal for broadcast advertisers). It suggested that television was more than a consumer product *for* the home, it was an advertising showroom *in* the home, capable of promoting many other consumer products. Given that warding off a postwar depression would require a surge of consumer spending (said an RCA executive in 1944), how fortunate it was that "television has the power to create consumer demand and buying of goods and services beyond anything we have heretofore known." Another company man underscored the implication for postwar spending: "Television has the power to create in the minds of the people a greater desire for merchandise than they have for their hoarded cash."

In May 1945, the FCC reaffirmed the VHF decision. New York was now poised to become Television City.

Still, in 1945, the future of manufacturing in Gotham remained unclear. Both pessimists and optimists had reasonable ground on which to stand. There was a third attitude abroad in the city, which proposed that neither outcome—neither failure nor success—would be crucial to New York's well-being, as it would have been decades earlier. The city's central economic sinews, in this reading, were based on white-collar smarts not blue-collar brawn. From this vantage point, it was certainly fine to keep a place at the table for industrial plants—preferably on the periphery, as the RPA had proposed back in the 1920s—but the real business of New York City was business.

151

Headquarters

In May 1943, William Edward Robinson, advertising director of the *New York Herald Tribune*, wrote a series of editorials for the paper attacking critics who claimed the metropolis "is at last slipping"—critics like the Hanes Committee, whose report had just come out in April. Whatever losses New York may or may not have suffered in manufacturing, Robinson insisted, had been more than recouped by gains in "business management"— which he called "the city's hidden industry," its workshops not in lofts and factories but in Gotham's great towers.

Robinson traced this sector's emergence to the mergers of the 1890s and consolidations of the 1920s. Before these seismic transformations in American capitalism, most US manufacturing had been directed from within the works themselves; blue and white collars commingled. After the emergence of giant nationwide corporations, however, many under banker overlordship, centralized managements grew up to coordinate far-flung manufacturing components and to interface with financial overseers. More and more companies opted to keep plants near raw materials or markets but to move management to New York. Even after banker control weakened, Gotham was still where the money was. It was also (Robinson noted) "the pivotal point of global economic influence" (especially important for export-oriented firms). And it was where other corporations had already gone, firms from across the country having gravitated, in immigrant-style serial migration, to office buildings in Gotham's Downtown and Midtown business districts.

Corporate managers found it convenient to cluster together, as did diamond merchants or vegetable wholesalers. Proximity afforded easy access to other companies and to clients. Here, too, were essential adjuncts: lawyers versed in the statutes and decisions governing large corporations; accountants who kept records and prepared taxes; advertisers and wholesalers and retailers who hawked and stored and moved their wares; and a plethora of skilled professionals and office workers—draftsmen, engineers, market researchers, chemists, statisticians, stenographers, secretaries, clerks.

By the mid-1940s, Robinson pointed out, New York was the nation's preeminent headquarters city. Of the one hundred largest American corporations, forty-one had their national offices in Gotham, with another fifty-three maintaining local branches. Here, too, were chambers of commerce, business associations, think tanks, promotional and informational bureaus, and headquarters of industrial organizations and trade groups. New York was also the predominant wholesale market of the United States for a spectacular array of commodities—women's and children's clothing, notions, millinery, watches, diamonds, oils and greases, home furnishings, toys, china, glassware, crockery, toilet articles, cameras, and on and on. In 1945 there were 24,000 wholesale establishments in the metropolitan area, along with 115,000 retail outlets; together they accounted for one quarter of all employment.

In short, Robinson concluded, New York was the world's greatest center of organization, operation, and distribution. And whatever might be happening to manufacturing, the business of business management was undeniably growing.

La Guardia was so pleased with this take on tomorrow that he ordered 50,000 reprints. Robinson's assessment was also music to real estate industry ears. If business management was going to expand, it would need more office towers; and if the ranks of better-paid managers and professionals grew, so would demand for luxury apartment houses. It had been a long dry spell for developers (and the construction trades). Few skyscrapers or apartment towers had gone up since the early 1930s. The bust, coming on the heels of the twenties' overbuilding, had bequeathed high vacancy rates and low rents, even at signature structures like Rockefeller Center. Add in residential and commercial rent control, banker reluctance to lend, and the wartime construction freeze, and the result was a New York real estate scene that was weary, stale, flat, and unprofitable. Major players contented themselves with buying, selling, or managing existing properties, basically biding their time.

Gotham's real estate complex was still largely a network of families, dominated either by descendants of nineteenth-century land barons or those who had entered the field during the 1920s boom.

Of the old primarily Protestant landed-money crowd—those who had prospered for a century by buying Uptown lots in advance of northward migration and exacting tribute from new arrivals—only the Astors and Goelets remained seriously active. Vincent Astor—great-great-grandson of John Jacob Astor—flew the flag for the former family, while the latter (after the passing of the fabulously wealthy Robert Walton Goelet in 1941) relied on more institutionalized incarnations, like the Goelet Realty Company and the Goelet Estate.

Many of the speculative builders who had dominated development in the 1920s—the Lefcourts, Frenches, Chanins—had died or withdrawn from the scene during the Depression, but others were still active or were passing their torches to the next generation. Julius Tishman & Sons had survived the death of Julius in 1935 in part because the family had established a corporate persona, going public in 1928. In the 1940s, the Tishman Realty and Construction Company was run by three of the sons, David, Paul, and Norman. Also active were the Rudins—Sam and his sons Lew and Jack (both in the military)—who ran the Rudin Management Company (1925); the Urises, with Harris's sons Percy and Harold having assumed the reins (the former looking after financial affairs, the latter attending to construction); and the Dursts, with Joseph passing the business on to his sons Seymour, Royal, and David. Joe Durst, routinely referred to as "operator and realty dealer," did extensive buying and selling, sometimes in conjunction with Charles F. Noyes, the city's premier real estate broker, who (with his daughter) was also one of the largest individual investors in Manhattan.

This generally Jewish real-estate complex also embraced key architectural firms, to whom many of the builder families had long turned. At Emery Roth & Sons, the elder Roth was still at work, though the sons, Richard and Julian, were now senior partners. In 1940, Ely Jacques Kahn (in whose office Ayn Rand boned up on the profession), had joined with a new young partner, Robert Allan Jacobs, and the Kahn & Jacobs firm was active in wartime housing and planning, designing among other things the parabolic exterior of the East River Drive's Municipal Asphalt Plant.

This network of clients, developers, builders, brokers, and architects all kept in touch, awaiting postwar developments with hope but for the nonce proceeding cautiously (like the bankers), remembering the recent disastrous past. It was left to one of the newest developers, in tandem with one of the oldest, to focus more forcefully on the future.

William Zeckendorf, born in Illinois, was brought to New York in 1908 at the age of three. He attended public elementary schools, then De Witt Clinton High School, then NYU for three years before dropping out to work—first managing an office building for an uncle, then drudging in a real-estate agency for a decade. In 1938 he became a partner in Webb & Knapp, a run-of-the-mill brokerage founded in 1922, which now began a rapid expansion, and Zeckendorf a rapid rise.

In 1942, the year he became executive vice president, Webb & Knapp was contacted by attorneys for Vincent Astor, now a commander in the Naval Reserve. Astor was about to enter active duty on the staff of the Eastern Sea Frontier and wanted someone to look after his real estate investments for the duration. An interview was arranged in Astor's penthouse at 120 East End Avenue. Zeckendorf critically reviewed Astor's $50 million debt-free real estate portfolio. Though it was enormous—ranging from blue-chip properties like the St. Regis Hotel, through Midtown apartments and brownstones, Downtown lofts and office buildings, to Bowery tenements and rundown West Side housing—he noted that these vast holdings were bringing in only a paltry 1 percent annual return. Zeckendorf proposed a vigorous campaign to shed unprofitable holdings and acquire new improved ones, not necessarily in New York, given its doldrums. Astor gave Webb & Knapp a free hand.

Overnight, Zeckendorf—hitherto a bit player—became the hottest dealmaker in town. Holding a fifty-million-dollar empire in his hands, he proceeded to play his cards brilliantly. (One example: he sold off less-desirable properties in a way that hiked the value of others by setting a high purchase price but asking only a little cash down, and then taking back a large second mortgage; in the press, however, which Zeckendorf assiduously courted, it was the high selling price that got the headlines and created a profitable buzz.) Profits were immediately rolled over into dozens of Byzantine deals and intricate swaps. In his first year he increased the value of Astor's holdings by several million, earning an initial fee (of $350,000) from a grateful commander. By the time he turned the properties back to Astor in 1945, Zeckendorf had completed 152 transactions, increased the estate's value by ten million, turned Webb & Knapp into a capital-rich operator, and done some strategic buying on his own account.

Zeckendorf disparaged the wartime Manhattan market but was convinced it would take off again after the war. The trick was to figure out where, and then get there first. His candidate for the next hot office spot was Park Avenue above 42nd Street, still the main line venue for top-of-the-line apartment houses. There were several reasons for this assessment. First and foremost—and here he agreed with his patron Commander Astor—the days of luxury living on Park Avenue seemed numbered. For Astor the problem was that depression and the financial reforms on Wall Street wrought by his close friend Franklin Roosevelt had diminished the number of finance industry titans who could afford $2,000-a-month rentals. For Zeckendorf rent control was the key factor: not only had a lot of those high-priced flats dropped considerably during hard times (down 25 percent, said realtor Douglas L. Elliman), but rent control, passed in 1943, was threatening to make those reductions permanent. Park Avenue apartment buildings increasingly looked like white elephants.

Zeckendorf's solution was to tear them down and replace them with office buildings, which would be in demand should the postwar economy take off. This was, to a degree, simply extrapolating from a long-in-process transformation. Offices and lofts had arrived in the 1890s on Fourth Avenue between 17th and 32nd Streets (the strip that would later be called "Park Avenue South") and crept north from there on Park proper during the 1910s and '20s. North of the New York Central Building, however, from 47th up, Park had remained purely residential. Then, in 1929, at the tail end of the Twenties boom, the city rezoned Park between 50th and 57th. Immediately a developer announced plans for a 50-story tower to rise at 53rd. The Depression drove a stake through that, and all subsequent such notions, and indeed many expected that any postwar office boom might well happen in the suburbs. But to Zeckendorf, the fortuitous combination of rent control and commercial zoning made this stretch of Park Avenue an irresistible alternative.

Using Astor money, he did some buying and leasing from Grand Central to 59th Street. Then, in July 1945, Webb & Knapp announced it had taken a lease (from the New York Central Corporation) on the luxurious Marguery Hotel at 270 Park, erected in 1918 by Charles Paterno. Zeckendorf declared his intention to raze it, together with the other 12-story buildings in the residential complex that filled the Park/Madison/47th/48th block, and thereupon put up a skyscraper. The *Times* was not alone in believing that this redevelopment project "may mark the start of transition" of the "choice residential section along Park Avenue north of Grand Central Terminal" to "business use."

Dave Tishman was thinking the same way. He, too, spotted the potential of the Park Avenue strip. Getting in touch with Kahn and Jacobs, they worked out a plan for a 22-story building that would replace several apartment buildings on the east side of Park between 56th and 57th. Late in 1945 Tishman announced plans for 445 Park, which he hoped would be the city's first postwar commercial tower. It was to have the first fully automatic elevators and would be the first fully air-conditioned building; this would allow the use of 80 percent of the floor space, rather than the usual 65 percent, and Tishman hired Richard Roth, Emery's son, to design adjustable interior offices. In short order Percy and Harold Uris would buy property at Park and 59th, commissioning Roth to design a 21-story structure at #505. The avenue was off and running.

Sixth Avenue, a would-be running mate, hoped to extend its commercial stretch southward—from Rockefeller Center's lower frontier at 47th down to 34th street—having been freed (in 1939) of its elevated incubus. To hasten redevelopment, the Sixth Avenue Association (SAA) set out (in 1941) to rebrand down-at-the-heels Sixth as a tonier "Avenue of the Americas." Despite some opposition—it was an awful mouthful, critics said—the City Council and Mayor La Guardia approved the change in September 1945. More than just a name-lift, the SAA saw the new moniker as the linguistic foundation for a Latin-themed allée, one that could tap into the popularity of President Roosevelt's Good Neighbor policy and exploit the connections being newly forged with Latin America by Coordinator of Inter American Affairs (and former Rockefeller Center rental agent) Nelson Rockefeller.

Sixth Avenue Association organizer and early name-change advocate V. Clement Jenkins envisioned making the thoroughfare into a "central marketplace for the Americas," even the "commercial capital of the Western Hemisphere." The notion was to have all twenty-one Latin American republics move their consulates from the Whitehall Building at Manhattan's lower tip, where most had long hung their hats, to the congenially renamed Avenue of the Americas. In one variant of this vision, each would have their own (distinctively themed) structure, containing not only diplomatic bureaus but exhibition halls in which to display their national wares, and office space for nationals engaged in international trade. Hotels would no doubt spring up to accommodate visitors from south of the border, and themed restaurants and other entertainment venues would be encouraged. Major architects tried their hand at master plans—Edward Durell Stone came up with one, Ely Jacques Kahn another, Harvey Wiley Corbett designed a Hemisphere Trade Center—and in 1945 plans were announced for a Good Neighbor Building, a 57-story skyscraper, at 52nd Street. Whether or not any of this would come to pass remained to be seen, but for the moment the fizz and ferment lent credibility to Robinson's vision of the city's future as the great directing center of global webs of commerce and industry.

PLANNING THE POSTWAR NATION

Times Square celebrations on V-J Day. (Photo by Hulton Archive/Getty Images)

152

Dueling Planners

In 1943, at a press conference held three days after Christmas, President Roosevelt was asked about rumors he'd decided the term "New Deal" no longer accurately described his administration's policies. Did this mean that if FDR decided to run again in 1944—the real question on reporters' minds—he'd back away from his own record? Nothing of the sort, Roosevelt replied in effect, and proceeded to explain what he'd meant.

Back in 1932, there had been "an awfully sick patient called the United States," who "was suffering from a grave internal disorder—he was awfully sick—he had all kinds of internal troubles." So they sent for Dr. New Deal. It took a few years, but the good doctor's remedies—and here the president rattled off about thirty federal programs—had gotten the patient back on his feet; he was now "all right internally." Then, two years ago, "on the seventh of December, he got into a pretty bad smashup—broke his hip, broke his leg in two or three places, broke a wrist and an arm"—so Dr. New Deal, a specialist in internal medicine, turned the patient over to his partner, the orthopedic surgeon Dr. Win-the-War. Happily, the new physician's methods seemed to be doing the trick, though the patient was still not out of danger.

Did this mean Dr. New Deal had been cashiered, removed from the roster of physicians on call? Of course not. There was the future to think about. What if the Depression was only in remission? What if, when the troops came home and war production ceased, unemployment and homelessness again stalked the land? Then one would need the internist's skills. Indeed, Roosevelt argued, it would be wise and prudent to *plan* for such an eventuality and attempt to forestall it. "We must plan for, and help to bring about, an expanded economy," he told the assembled press, one that "will result in more security, in more employment, in more recreation, in more education, in more health, in better housing for all of our citizens, so that the conditions of 1932 and the beginning of 1933 won't come back again."

Roosevelt had not abandoned the New Deal's goals. Social Security, deposit insurance, public works projects—these were not just prescriptions for illness, they were intrinsic social goods. FDR was a supremely canny politician. He was all too aware his programs had been stymied since 1938 by Congressional opponents. But his commitment to a social-justice agenda remained intact. Indeed, he had escalated his ambitions by embedding the Four Freedoms' social entitlements at the core of the nation's war aims. He'd proposed a New Deal for the World.

The war had also enhanced the liberals' confidence in the possibilities of planning. The national economy—in large measure planned, financed, regulated, and directed by government—had not only clambered out of crisis but was producing at levels spectacularly higher than any ever achieved by the private sector, when left to its own devices. The Keynesian pumping of billions of dollars into government-overseen programs—far vaster than any the New Deal had undertaken—had wiped out unemployment, sent the gross national product soaring, developed a new industrial base, and was winning a world-wide war. Why not use the kind of state-guided stimulus that had equipped and fielded mighty armies to underwrite economic growth in peacetime, thereby securing full employment and enhancing social welfare?

THE WAR HAD ALSO RE-NERVED the New Deal's opponents, particularly the dollar-a-year corporate leaders and lawyers who had been instrumental in running the government-led war effort. This capitalist elite, whose self-confidence and social authority had been badly undermined by the Depression, had been refreshed in spirit by a spectacular flow of dollars into corporate coffers: even after subtracting stiff wartime taxes, the profits of prime contractors had doubled since the war began. Yet the business class was divided into two camps over how to explain these wartime successes and what they implied for postwar policy.

One group stressed that government, if in trustworthy hands (their own), could be good for business. Its members—some of whom had come to terms with the New Deal back in the thirties—were now seriously worried about postwar collapse; it was not at all clear that capitalism could survive another massive breakdown. Some sort of planning on a national scale seemed imperative to ward one off, especially given the war-wrought leap in the economy's scale and complexity. These corporate pragmatists, accordingly, were open to making the national state, if tucked securely under their wing, into a useful adjunct. Its authority and credit could be deployed to shore up consumer demand, diminish entrepreneurial risk, build infrastructure that would underwrite private accumulation, and stabilize the system in times of crisis.

A second section of the corporate community—top heavy with those who had detested the New Deal from its inception—argued that the triumphs of wartime production had been accomplished by the private sector; that the war had facilitated a dangerous accretion of power in federal hands, particularly those of the president; that statism was irredeemably evil, a threat to liberty (and their own freedom of operation); that most of the New Deal and its wartime elaborations should be dismantled; that direction of the national economy should be handed back to the revivified corporate (and small-business) domain; that businessmen could be trusted to ensure the Depression would not return; that planning was not only unnecessary but would lead inevitably to dictatorship or totalitarianism.

The boundaries between these three camps were not rigid; there was personal and intellectual traffic across the frontiers. However, in general: Rooseveltian liberals planned to rely heavily on Dr. New Deal after the war; corporate pragmatists were prepared to resort to him from time to time, especially in extremis; and business fundamentalists wanted to drive a stake through his heart.

New Yorkers—those at home and those on loan to Washington—were in the forefront of all three camps, participating as vigorously in debates over domestic postwar planning as in those about the planet's future. Gotham was home to the liberals, leftists, and labor unions that championed expanding the New Deal. It headquartered the corporations, foundations, think tanks, and media that supported business-directed planning. And it was a major redoubt of anti–New Deal trade associations, banks, and pro-capitalist economists—the latter's hitherto minuscule ranks now enhanced by incoming émigrés.

These three-way debates, moreover, were anything but academic exercises. The question of how to shape the postwar domestic order—given urgency by the imminence of peace and possibility of postwar crisis—was now thrown into the cockpit of national politics, where it would dominate the 1944 elections. Here, too, New York would be at the vortex of things. Once again, it would provide the campaign its leading contenders: the presidential race would be yet another Subway Series. And it was a race in whose outcome the city was vitally interested, because it would provide the political context within which Gotham was to plan its own future.

153

Paging Dr. New Deal

On March 10, 1943, FDR sent a fat package of documents down Pennsylvania Avenue to the Capitol for congressional consideration. It included a 640-page tome entitled *Security, Work and Relief Policies*, and a slimmer almost pamphlet-size text called *Post-War Plan and Program*. Both were products of the National Resources Planning Board (NRPB)—itself a descendent of the National Planning Board (NPB), the New Deal's institutionalized brain trust, which Roosevelt had established in 1933. Back then, the NPB had been headed by Frederic A. Delano, a pioneering planner who had worked with Daniel Burnham on the Chicago City Plan in the 1900s and overseen the New York Regional Plan during the 1920s. Appointed by his nephew—Franklin Delano Roosevelt—"Uncle Fred" had stayed at the helm of the president's planning agency through its various incarnations and was still in charge in 1941 when FDR added postwar planning to Delano's portfolio.

The NRPB planning manifestos drew on many minds—*Post-War Plan and Program* relied heavily on Alvin Hansen of Harvard, and the principal author of *Security, Work and Relief Policies* was Columbia University economist Eveline M. Burns—and reflected the NRPB's twin priorities of underwriting economic development and enhancing social welfare. The former proposed the federal government "guarantee a job for every man released from the armed forces and the war industries at the close of the war, with fair pay and working conditions," and back up this commitment by developing a shelf-load of ready-to-build public works projects. Should the economic weather turn stormy, they could be taken down and used by a federal work agency to hire those whom the private sector could not or would not employ. The latter called for greatly expanding existing New Deal programs and creating new ones—notably in the spheres of health, housing, and education. It made the Keynesian case that welfare initiatives like Social Security, public assistance, and unemployment insurance, valuable in themselves, also helped counter capitalism's tendency toward underconsumption by bolstering the purchasing power of low-income Americans.

In his cover note transmitting the NRPB documents to Congress, FDR declared that "we can all agree" about the proposition "that work, fair pay, and social security after the war is won must be firmly established for the people of the United States." This, as Roosevelt well knew, was an utterly unwarranted profession of confidence.

Liberals, to be sure, loved the NRPB report. Labor unions, farm organizations, church and civil rights groups, the liberal media—all hailed its call for a "high-income, full-employment economy." The *New Republic* applauded it as "an American Beveridge Plan," referring to the proposal recently put forward (in December 1942) by a British commission, headed by Sir William Beveridge of the London School of Economics, which, if adopted, would provide the scaffolding for a postwar welfare state. There were indeed similarities between the two blueprints (though significant divergences as well), and mutual admiration flowed between the US and British planners. But the reception accorded the plans by their respective countries was quite different. Beveridge's proposals, though primarily taken up by the Labour Party, were accepted by many employers and Conservatives (even Churchill, albeit grudgingly) as the basis for a postwar consensus. Nothing resembling such agreement existed in the US.

Without question, the vast majority of the population favored NRPB-style liberal programs. A *Fortune* magazine poll in July 1942 found that 57 percent backed government regulation of banks, 58 percent wanted unemployment compensation, 68 percent sought public sector jobs for everyone who couldn't find private sector employment, 74 percent supported old age pensions for every citizen over sixty-five, and 74 percent urged medical care be made available to all who needed it. And while 40 percent of a national sample were opposed to "socialism" in the US, 25 percent *favored* it, and 34 percent retained "an open mind." Such sentiments grew stronger during the war years.

Ranged against the NRPB proposals were powerful economic elites: corporate pragmatists, who could live with pieces of the package but not the whole of it, and business fundamentalists, who were dead set against any and all of it. In the political arena, their clout could overbear mere numbers.

154

Dr. New Deal: Call Only When Needed

In September 1942, when a score of corporate leaders had established the Committee for Economic Development (CED), most of them were what William Benton, former New York advertising executive and one of the CED's chief progenitors, called "liberal, progressive businessmen." Many were heads of large corporations. A majority were members of the Business Advisory Council (BAC), set up during the Depression inside the Commerce Department to garner the views of businessmen who, if critical of this or that New Deal policy, nevertheless believed some government intervention an urgent necessity.

For help in getting started they turned to Secretary of Commerce Jesse Jones. As head of the Reconstruction Finance Corporation and its many wartime subsidiaries, Jones had presided over a stupendous amount of government intervention, pumping $10 billion into New Deal projects. He would channel another $40 billion into the war effort, constructing an armada of war plants that could conceivably serve as the chrysalis of a socialist or state capitalist order. Yet Jones, a conservative Texas banker, was committed to the restoration of private capitalism. However, he insisted that US businessmen had better start taking a long-term perspective on their economic order. "Private initiative must be ready to occupy its rightful place when the war is over," he told the fledgling CED operation. But "if it is to do this, it must have plans." Business must work "to avoid another post-war depression" by promoting a vigorous economic expansion. "The attainment and maintenance of high employment after the war," CED founders agreed, "dare not be left to chance."

Jones helped the fledgling CED, providing funding and free office space in the Commerce Department's DC building. Yet if the CED was to be a credible counterweight to state planners, it had to be privately financed and visibly independent. So, the following year it left the government nest and moved to New York, the nation's business capital. Two hundred eighty-five Madison Avenue now became the headquarters of a consortium of businessmen organized not around specific trade interests but around the proposition that—as Columbia economist John Clark put it in a CED monograph—a businessman was "not effectively safeguarding his individual business unless he is also working effectively to keep the system of which it is part in good working order."

Swiftly the CED set up committees of businessmen at community, county, state, district, and regional levels. By February 1944 there were 1,354 such committees (1,230 at the local level, and 124 at one or another of the higher orders). These committees embraced 24,500 businessmen who collectively represented three-quarters of the industrial capacity of the United States. Before the year was out membership had jumped to 65,000 businessmen, who confabulated in more than 2,900 venues.

Often under discussion were the latest proposals issued by the CED's Research and Policy committee—a corporate sector brain trust whose most fecund idea man was the protean Beardsley Ruml. Trained as a psychologist, Ruml had switched to philanthropic management in 1922, when he was appointed to head the Laura Spelman Rockefeller Memorial Fund of New York. There he funded programs that used social science to address social problems; most notably he helped get the Manhattan-based Social Science Research Council up and running by 1924. In 1931 he became dean of the Division of Social Sciences at the University of Chicago. In 1934 he segued from the academy to the business world (and back to Gotham), becoming treasurer of R. H. Macy & Company, where, not surprisingly, he developed a keen interest in how to maintain consumer purchasing power in the Depression. In 1935 Ruml joined Delano's board, straddling the public-private planning divide. And in 1937 he became a director of the Federal Reserve Bank of New York, then served as its chair from 1941 through war's end.

Ruml was a sophisticated conservative who appreciated the role of government. In 1937, when the economy dropped back into deep depression after Roosevelt prematurely chopped spending (at budget-balancers' behest), Ruml helped Harry Hopkins convince the president to reverse himself. Ruml told the historically minded FDR that for all the business-class blather about American "free enterprise," the country's "competitive capitalist system has been sustained from the beginning by federal intervention to create purchasing power." In 1938, citing Ruml's argument, FDR went back to deficit spending.

During the war, Ruml and CED leaders continued to contest free marketeers. Paul Hoffman, president of the Studebaker Corporation and the CED's chairman, said a modern industrial economy couldn't be left to laissez faire–istas. Business groups who thought "all that is necessary is to 'unshackle free enterprise' " were guilty of "loose, irresponsible talk"; and those who thought government had no role to play in managing the economy "have their heads in the sand." Business cycles were not the product of ineluctable and incontestable forces, they were man-made and could be modified or mitigated by government action. On the other hand, CED officials denied they were a "long-haired, starry-eyed" group aiming to regiment the economy; they promised their organization "in no sense will attempt over-all national planning." Rather, it would suggest ways business and government might respond to postwar needs and opportunities.

CED planners calculated that if discharged soldiers and laid-off war workers were to be reabsorbed into the civilian economy—thus avoiding a postwar crisis that could trigger collectivist responses—US business would have to provide fifty-five million peacetime jobs, nine million more than had been employed in 1940. This would require enlarging production and sales by 30–45 percent over 1940 levels. And doing that would require roughly $10 billion in new investments.

The CED was relatively optimistic about the private sector's ability to meet such targets because wartime conditions had fostered a voracious consumer demand. Since 1939, per capita income had risen more than 40 percent but there hadn't been much to spend it on. Many commodities (autos, houses, appliances) were not produced at all; many of those available (meat, sugar, gas) were strictly rationed. Therefore, people saved more, roughly a quarter of their income. By the end of 1944, such savings had collectively swollen to more than $100 billion. There the money sat, burning holes in bank accounts, while advertisers dangled before one and all visions of commodities to come ("After Total War Can Come Total Living," promised the Revere Copper Company). Consumers, it was presumed, would break from the gate and race to the stores the minute the guns went silent. And in the unlikely event their desire flagged, New York's ad industry was standing by, ready to wave them on. Admen in the American Association of Advertising Agencies (headquartered in the Graybar Building)—having successfully justified their industry's existence by selling the war—now promised to "insure a level of consumption equal to the level of production."

Yet despite these glorious prospects, the CED worried about its members' entrepreneurial spirits, which seemed subdued. Indeed, the CED had been struggling, said its field director, "to rekindle in the hearts of American businessmen a flame of adventure." But why wasn't the lure of postwar profits sufficient motivation? It appeared to be a matter of "climate." Entrepreneurs would do the job, said Chairman Hoffman, but only if "the business climate in the post-war world is favorable to expansion of enterprise." The weather report could be changed for the better if government would stop competing with private business, and, somewhat contradictorily, start creating "incentives to restore the desire for risk-taking in the business community."

One such incentive envisioned the state selling off to entrepreneurs, at bargain-basement prices, the war plants Jesse Jones had built at taxpayer expense. The "basic objective," said John F. Fennelly (the CED's executive director) in September 1944, "must be to get these plants into operation under private management"—especially given the "danger" that if hard times returned the government might staff their factories with the unemployed. (Fennelly did acknowledge a possible speed bump on the road to privatization: "If [the plants] are sold at prices low enough to justify their purchase on a business basis, the political outcry is certain to be terrific and in the long run may be very harmful to business.")

In the end the best way to achieve the "restoration of rewards for risk-taking" was to cut taxes. In September 1944 Beardsley Ruml called for slashing rates on corporate profits and dividends. While some saw the CED tax plan as selfishly aimed at the "relief of business," it was really, Ruml argued, a way of "getting more money to the people." Corporations, after all, shifted their tax burden to consumers (via higher prices) and workers (through lower wages). This shrank aggregate demand, led to unemployment, and required costly government intervention. "Why not leave at home, for the individual to spend, the income that otherwise might have to be pumped out again in order to maintain high employment?" Cutting taxes on business would also make more money available to corporations to devote to industrial reconversion and expansion and thus generate more jobs. This seemed a win-win solution to Ruml, though he did allow that "corporations might withhold earnings, which if done would be self defeating," and he asked for ideas on how one could prevent corporations from hogging the tax breaks for themselves.

Ruml's proposed reductions were not, however, aimed at starving the federal government beast, thus forcing it to cut social programs. He had, after all, invented the withholding tax in order to guarantee government revenues. Ruml and the CED allowed that government should be adequately financed so it could meet its legitimate responsibilities. In 1944, the CED estimated (and supported) postwar federal spending at a level of $18 billion a year, whereas the largest annual federal expenditure in New Deal days had been $8.5 billion in 1939.

The CED also accepted—as Jones had argued during their first public conference, held at the Waldorf Astoria in April 1943—that government "must complement and supplement the activities of private business in the maintenance of high production and high employment." It should do so, Jones said, "through an explicit fiscal and monetary policy," stepping in whenever "business, as business, cannot act to sustain employment and effective demand." The great goal, said John Fennelly, was "ironing out the peaks and valleys of the business cycle." To this end Ruml proposed that government budgets be balanced not on a short-term, fiscal-year basis, but on a long-term, business-cycle basis. Taxation levels, money supply, and government spending on public works should be constantly adjusted so that deficits during hard times were offset by surpluses accrued during periods of prosperity.

The bottom-line strategic consideration from the CED's perspective was that the US could not afford more wild economic fluctuations. Accordingly, said Chairman Hoffman, though business concerns should not be unduly hampered in their freedom of action, corporate leaders should "look one important fact squarely in the face—that the Federal Government has a vital role to play in our capitalistic system."

155

Dr. New Deal: Wanted, Dead or Alive, Preferably Dead

The reply lobbed from National Association of Manufacturers (NAM) headquarters (at 14 West 49th just off Fifth) the nine blocks down to CED central (at Madison between 40th and 41st) was, in effect, "Nonsense!" Publisher Walter D. Fuller, the chairman of NAM's board, insisted that "private enterprise can provide all the jobs the post-war period will demand," and there was absolutely no need for "government spending on fantastic scales." Fuller's downtown colleagues concurred. Both the *Wall Street Journal* and the president of the New York Stock Exchange declared that private industry could and should be trusted to handle the nation's economic affairs.

More than unnecessary, government planning was an abomination. The NRPB's proposals, said the *Journal*, constituted a "totalitarian plan" for building a "halfway house to socialism." NAM agreed: federal planning and spending would pave the way to tyranny and bankruptcy. In the view of these business-class fundamentalists, the country faced a stark choice between whether (as Fuller put it) "we go ahead as free enterprisers or under a State-controlled economy." Their clear preference was to cut back or dismantle as much of the New Deal state as possible.

No group laid out a road map for reaction more straightforwardly than did the Commerce and Industry Association of New York (CIA). Headquartered in the Woolworth Building across from City Hall Park, the CIA was composed of top executives from Gotham's finance, real estate, utilities, transportation, manufacturing, advertising, and corporate law sectors. The CIA's Post-war Planning Committee, chaired by Bankers Trust director Fred I. Kent, included leaders from the Real Estate Board of New York, Con Ed, the Pennsylvania Railroad, the Dodge Corporation, J. Walter Thompson, and Winthrop, Stimson, Putnam and Roberts. Their report—*Winning the War and the Peace: A Program of Legislative Action* (1944)—called for halting the expansion of government into the sphere of private enterprise; eliminating agencies, bureaus, departments, and commissions that competed with private enterprise; and shutting down all federal departments, agencies, and activities not essential to the war effort or the nation's future economic welfare. They wanted to change the labor laws, revise Social Security, and block schemes to "socialize" medicine. They also sought to restore the gold standard, balance the postwar budget, and cut taxes. On the last point they agreed with the CED's Ruml but also believed he hadn't gone far enough. In addition to chopping taxes on corporate income, the country should end the capital gains tax and slash inheritance and gift taxes. If Washington needed more money, it could inaugurate a general sales tax (a regressive imposition that would fall on the bulk of population). Nor did the CIA go along with the CED's fear, laid out by its executive director John Fennelly, that because a postwar Oklahoma Land Rush–style shopping spree might lead to inflation, "thoughtful students" recognized the "necessity of maintaining many of our present wartime controls on prices, wages, rents, etc., for some time after the close of hostilities." On the contrary, said the CIA: sweep the controls away and the nation will "grow spiritually and will prosper economically."

Such revanchism proved a hard sell. The social authority of the business class had been shattered by the 1929 collapse of a prosperity for which they had taken full credit and further pulverized by the ensuing decade of depression. It was all fine and well for NAM's Fuller to claim that "the mistakes which irked the public were not the fault of the system but were departures from the ideals of that system," but this was not a case that made itself. Worse, it seemed that government-directed wartime prosperity had misled (or corrupted) the citizenry into thinking that Rooseveltian planning might be a better bet for their future than handing the country back to those who'd laid it low. Even Fuller admitted on occasion that business couldn't simply urge a return to "the good old days" because those days "just weren't good enough." NAM conducted a vigorous campaign—a carryover from Depression-era initiatives—touting the virtues of "free enterprise" and the grave dangers of creeping "socialism," bombarding Americans with press releases, radio programs, and advertisements. According to a study commissioned by General Electric and circulated to other large corporations, it seemed to "leave the people cold."

Part of the problem was that the classical economic liberalism they were hawking had been in retreat since the surge of progressivism and social gospelism earlier in the century. Ideological forebears like Herbert Spencer, William Graham Sumner, and E. L. Godkin, if remembered at all, were recalled as fusty figures from a fast-receding past. The naked class self-interest on display in the CIA program needed to be dressed up in more appealing raiment. But business fundamentalists lacked the intellectual firepower to contest the Keynesianism that was sweeping all before it. They needed a pitch more compelling than sloganeering about "free enterprise."

Providentially, at just this moment, some theoretically sophisticated and staunchly antisocialist economists arrived in town, part of the great wartime migration of European intellectuals and artists. Like their refugee counterparts in physics, anthropology, drama, painting, music, publishing, and architecture, these economists would soon link up with like-minded colleagues in Gotham, with the city again serving as a combustion chamber in which the confluence of Europeans and Americans would have propulsive consequences.

In this instance the incoming economists made contact not with counterpart academics—New York universities were practically bereft of their right-wing ilk—but with a smattering of Gotham-based economic journalists, some of whom occupied influential niches. Perhaps the best-placed was Henry Hazlitt, since 1934 financial editor, book reviewer, and editorialist for the *New York Times*. From this pulpit Hazlitt regularly held forth on the virtues of free market capitalism, the fallacies of Keynesian economics, the stupidity of socialism, and the ill effects of wartime price controls and unionization. Isabel Paterson, similarly, was a popular book reviewer working for Irita Van Doren at the *Herald Tribune*; a self-professed Spencerian, Paterson held that the Depression had been caused by government, that stricken economies were best left to recover on their own, and that planning produced omnipotent states which undermined individual liberty—themes presented at book length in her *The God of the Machine* brought out by G. P. Putnam's Sons in 1943.

Many in this anti–New Deal camp had trekked across the political spectrum only recently, during the mid-Thirties and early Forties. John Chamberlain had been a self-described "New York literary liberal" before he shifted rightward while working for Luce's *Fortune* (1936–1941), and *Life* magazine (during the war). Whittaker Chambers, former Communist spy, had come in from the cold to a warm reception at *Time*, whose rightward-sidling publisher made him a senior editor in 1943 and gave him oversight of the foreign news desk in 1944. By 1941, Max Eastman had completed the long journey away from *The Masses* to his new home at the *Reader's Digest*. John T. Flynn had been a financial editor of the *New York Globe* and a prominent economic columnist ("Other People's Money") for the *New Republic*, before his role in America First led to a parting of the ways; and in 1944 Flynn published *As We Go Marching*, his critique of a perceived US drift toward statism. Eugene Lyons, a one-time employee of TASS (the Soviet news agency), assumed editorship of the Mencken-founded *American Mercury* in 1939 and in 1941 issued *The Red Decade*, an exposé of "Stalinist penetration" of American life. Westbrook Pegler, who early on had supported FDR, switched to penning dipped-in-vitriol columns for the *New York World-Telegram* and the Scripps-Howard chain, until he moved to the Hearst syndicate in 1944 and grew even more acidic. Finally, George Sokolsky, a enthusiast of Alexander Kerensky and his provisional government, who had gone to Petrograd in 1917 to edit an English-language paper, spent much of 1935–40 attacking the New Deal (particularly Social Security) in the pages of the *New York Herald Tribune*, before moving to the *New York Sun* in 1940. He also became a well-paid "industrial consultant"—giving speeches and doing a radio show for the National Association of Manufacturers. NAM was about to retain a thinker far more high-powered than George Sokolsky, or indeed any of these Gotham-based scribes.

On August 3, 1940, Ludwig von Mises and his wife, Margit, disembarked in New York City. An internationally known theoretician of the Austrian school of economics—Marxism's most penetrating academic antagonists—Mises, of Jewish descent, had left Vienna for Geneva in 1934, convinced (correctly) that Austria was ripe for Nazi takeover. He taught in Switzerland until 1940, then moved on to Manhattan, where many of his relatives, friends, colleagues, students, and even his family doctor had taken shelter. Mises found himself unable to secure an academic appointment, however, even at the New School for Social Research, which had absorbed so many social scientists from Central Europe. This was partly because, at fifty-eight, he was getting on in years, and partly because his views on the beneficence of the free market were even more out of intellectual fashion in Gotham's universities than they had been back in Austria's.

The University of Vienna, Mises's alma mater, had never granted him a full-time salaried post. He had been, rather, a *privatdozent*, paid from student fees—a not-unusual position in the Austrian academy for those deemed overly innovative (Freud among them)—and he ran a private seminar, unconnected to the university, that met in Vienna's restaurants and cafés. His major post, from 1909 until he left Austria, was as an economist with the city's Chamber of Commerce—not an organization of private business interests but a quasi-official body that advised the government. Here he promoted his gospel of government noninterference in the economy. More: in works like *Socialism* (1922), Mises argued that socialistic alternatives to capitalism were unattainable because, lacking the kind of pricing mechanism provided by the market, they could not efficiently allocate resources. Even after the arrival of the Depression, he opposed government meddling, urging the economy be left to eliminate distortions he believed had been imposed by government in the first place. With views such as these, Mises was unlikely to seek a post in New Deal agencies like the National Resources Planning Board, or in a wartime entity like the Office of Price Administration (where he would have worked under the young John Kenneth Galbraith).

In the short term, Mises was rescued by the Rockefeller Foundation, which gave the New York–based National Bureau of Economic Research (NBER) a grant of $2,500 to put Mises on its payroll for a year, allowing him and his wife to move into a three-bedroom (rent-controlled) apartment at 777 West End Avenue. Starting at the end of 1940, he gave a seminar at the NBER's "Hillside" estate, overlooking the Hudson at Riverdale. The grant, extended for a year, was not further renewed, but by then Mises had hooked up with ideological allies in the journalistic community.

His first call for help had gone to Henry Hazlitt, who in 1938, reviewing the English edition of *Socialism* for the *New York Times*, had called it an "economic classic in our time." Through Hazlitt's good offices, Mises was taken on to write occasional articles for the paper on world economic problems. These helped bring him to the attention (in January 1943) of the National Association of Manufacturers, which hired Mises as a consultant (at $3,000 a year). He became a member of NAM's Economic Policy Advisory Group, and its Economic Principles Commission, and began lecturing about free enterprise to groups of leading industrialists.

Hazlitt also helped him edge into academia. In 1944 he got Yale University Press to publish two translated Mises works, *Bureaucracy* and *Omnipotent Government*. In the same year other admirers, notably Lawrence Fertig, an NYU trustee who owned an advertising firm and was himself an economic columnist, tackled NYU on his behalf. Fertig arranged for the Graduate School of Business Administration to make Mises a visiting professor, his salary to be paid from private funds. Participants in Mises's NYU economic seminar would, in the Viennese manner, follow their classroom session by joining the professor in Child's Restaurant and then moving on to the Café Lafayette.

As Mises's star began to rise, he was outshone in the intellectual firmament by one of his former students. Friedrich Hayek had entered the University of Vienna in 1918, becoming a protégé of Mises's and an analyst of the business cycle. In 1923–24 he had worked in New York as a research assistant for an NYU professor and sat in on lectures at Columbia by Wesley Mitchell (head of the NBER) on the history of economics. He became fluent in English, which soon came in handy. In the early 1930s Hayek's challenge to underconsumptionist explanations of capitalist crises caught the attention of anti-Keynesians at the London School of Economics. They brought him to England in 1931 as a potential champion. Hayek argued, with Adam Smith, that an unfettered economy tended toward stability. Keynes thought a free market prone to crises that required remedial government action, particularly by stimulating aggregate demand. Hayek riposted that such interventions merely created artificial and short-lived booms and that government should leave well enough alone. As the Depression deepened, Keynes waxed, Hayek waned, and the latter withdrew (for the moment) from the theoretical field. Instead, he launched a counterattack in the public rather than the professional arena, with the publication in Britain in March 1944 of *The Road to Serfdom*.

In September 1944, shortly before the US presidential election, an American edition meteored across the Atlantic and was met—to Mises's delight, as well as Hayek's—with a huge, immediate, and quite unexpected success. To some degree this was thanks to *Road*'s promotion by the city's coterie of anti–New Deal journalists and industrialists. It was forewarded by John Chamberlain; reviewed glowingly by Hazlitt in the *Times Book Review*; republished by Max Eastman in a *Reader's Digest* condensed version; and business groups, thrilled at the appearance of a "scientific" yet accessible explication of their doctrine, bought and distributed it in bulk. *Road*'s success was also a testimonial to the undogmatic way in which Hayek preached and extended the Misean gospel.

Being "soft on government" did, however, open Hayek to ferocious attack from an unexpected quarter. *The Road to Serfdom* was denounced as "pure poison" and its author branded a "pernicious enemy" and "an ass, with no conception of a free society at all"—by someone who had staked out a position much farther along the rightwing road than even Hayek was willing to travel—a point that arguably marked that road's ideological terminus. This someone was not a trained economist, nor even an economic journalist, but rather a novelist, Ayn Rand, whose 1943 book *The Fountainhead*—written and set in New York—shot past *Road to Serfdom* on the bestseller lists of 1944 and 1945.

In a December 1943 interview Rand recalled sailing into Gotham's harbor seventeen years earlier, agog at her first sight of Manhattan. "There was one skyscraper," she said—probably referring to the Woolworth Building, in 1926 still the world's tallest—"that stood out ablaze like the finger of God, and it seemed to me the greatest symbol of free man." Then and there, she claimed, "I made a mental note that someday I would write a novel with the skyscraper as a theme." *The Fountainhead* was, among many other things, a valentine to the New York skyline, praised both for its inherent beauty and as a metaphor for the glories of capitalism and "individualism."

Back in 1926 Rand—née Alisa Rosenbaum—had been boating away from Bolshevism, with which she'd had rocky encounters. She had been born in 1905 in St. Petersburg to a moderately prosperous Jewish family—her father owned a pharmacy—but their fortunes plummeted in 1918 when the St. Petersburg (now "Petrograd") Red Guards nationalized their shop, pitching them into privation. The expropriation had been made in the name of building a better society, but the high-mindedness seemed to the Rosenbaums a rhetorical cover for banditry. The Bolsheviks did, however, liberalize admission policy to the University, and their opening of access to women and Jews, together with provision of free tuition, allowed Alisa to join the flood of new students. She got a BA, then studied film at the State Institute for Cinematography, screening hundreds of American movies, sitting through multiple showings of any that contained images of the Gotham skyline. When an opportunity to emigrate to the US emerged, Rosenbaum grabbed it, departing Petrograd (now "Leningrad") bound for Hollywood, by way of New York and Chicago, having changed her own name (now "Rand") in transit.

Rand got a job reviewing literary properties for Cecil B. DeMille, then worked in the wardrobe department at RKO, got married, and tried her hand at writing stories, plays, and film scripts. In 1933 she completed a play that was picked up by a Broadway producer, and in November 1934 she and her husband relocated to New York to assist in its 1935 staging.

By then she had also completed a novel, *We the Living*, a heavily autobiographical and rabidly anticommunist story set in Petrograd, which her agent had difficulty in selling. When finally Macmillan brought it out in 1936, it was trashed by reviewers, as much for its politics as its prose. Rand blamed her reception on the hostility of the communists who were prevalent in the city's literary culture: "You have no idea," she wrote a friend, "how radical and pro-Soviet New York is."

Increasingly she was drawn into anti–New Deal politics. Though she'd voted for FDR in 1932, by 1936 she saw his rapid expansion of the federal government as tantamount to an armed communist revolution. In 1940, smitten with the Republican candidate, she volunteered full time for the New York Willkie Club, which brimmed with writers, editors, and the literati of Irita Van Doren's circle, as well as distinguished members of Gotham's business elite—all committed to a defense of free enterprise.

After Willkie's defeat, seeking to keep a more stoutly pro-capitalist version of the Willkie Club going, Rand began reaching out to the circle of New York intellectuals and businessmen committed to free markets. To attract their attention, she wrote a broadside in early 1941 (provocatively entitled "To All Fifth Columnists") arguing that the US, under Roosevelt, was skiing down a slippery slope at the bottom of which lay "Totalitarian America, a world of slavery, of starvation, of concentration camps and firing squads." She followed this clang of the alarm bell with a "Manifesto of Individualism," which rejected the (supposedly now dominant) idea that the State was superior to the individual and instead celebrated capitalism as "the noblest, cleanest and most idealistic system of all." This attracted some right-leaning journalists, but not the right-leaning businessmen she was after. Many of these thought that NAM was a sufficiently stalwart defender of their interests. Not true, Rand insisted. People needed to be taught not just what free enterprise was but "why we should believe in it and fight for it." Someone had to provide "a spiritual, ethical, philosophical groundwork for the belief in the system of private enterprise," and she appointed herself to the task.

Her chosen vehicle was a novel. She would circulate her credo, she wrote a friend, "as the Reds do...in the form of fiction...because it arouses the public." The plot revolved around a Gotham architect, Howard Roark (as in York). In preparation she read up on architectural history, guided by an annotated bibliography prepared for her by the New York Public Library in 1936. In 1937 she worked as a volunteer in the office of Ely Jacques Kahn for six months, learning the business from the drafting room up. Roark, an inner-directed individualist and modernist (very loosely modeled on Frank Lloyd Wright), is surrounded by "second-hander" mediocrities still recycling old-fashioned historicism.

Roark agrees to design Cortlandt Homes, a government housing project slated for Astoria, Queens, fronting on the East River. Though he despises public housing, or public anything, he has some innovative notions on how to build attractive and inexpensive low-rent housing and undertakes the commission solely to satisfy himself. Predictably, "second handers" and do-gooders muck up his sleek and efficient design—starting with an opportunistic social worker who declares the absence of a gymnasium an affront to children of the poor. A gym is accordingly added, and she acquires a permanent job as director of social recreation. Hack architects and bureaucrats pile on more changes. Roark's gorge rises higher and higher. Until one night, he dynamites the as-yet unoccupied buildings.

At his ensuing trial he directs his own defense, arguing he was justified in demolishing the structures because his rights as their creator had been violated. (The architect giveth, the architect can taketh away.) But Roark/Rand spins a larger argument. The second handers thought they were entitled to "improve" his plans because "the altruistic purpose of the building" superseded his rights. Now the real target swims into view: altruism itself, the perverse notion that virtue consists in selflessness, in living for others. But altruism is in truth "a weapon of exploitation," its practitioners "parasites" who feed off the needs of others, and indeed need those others to remain dependent on their "benefactors." The really virtuous man is independent of others. "True creators" (like himself) are "self-sufficient, self-motivated, self-generated" able to be "a first cause, a fount of energy, a life force, a Prime Mover" and thus able to "achieve the things which are the glory of mankind." It is selfishness, not selflessness, that is productive of the highest social good.

Arrayed against the creative individual are the massed second handers, the "collectives" who profess to act altruistically, in the name of the "common good." In reality, "every major horror of history was committed in the name of an altruistic motive." "Leaders of collectivist movements," Roark declaims, start with declarations of love for mankind and end up producing "a sea of blood." Now collectivism "has broken loose and is running amuck.... It has reached a scale of horror without precedent.... It has swallowed most of Europe. It is engulfing our country."

Having successfully equated blowing up a housing project with resistance to Nazism, Roark is acquitted and promptly receives a hero's reward. A millionaire private developer buys the ruins of Cortlandt Homes from the government, tears down what's left, and hires Roark to rebuild it properly; he does so with such admirably strict economy that the developer is able to rent the apartments inexpensively yet provide himself "a comfortable margin of profit." Soon another millionaire—a Hearst-like publisher—commissions him to build nothing less than the tallest building on earth. The magnate, born and raised in Hell's Kitchen, has bought up piecemeal a great rectangle two blocks wide and five blocks long, between Ninth and Eleventh Avenues, fill with grimy and desolate tenements in a "malignant growth of decomposition." He plans to evict the denizens and have Roark build a staggering skyscraper in a park, a Promethean eruption from Manhattan's schist, set off in splendid isolation, "ablaze like the finger of God."

Rand's tribute to creativity, capitalism, and the New York skyline was published in May 1943. *The Fountainhead* got strongly positive reviews in the *Times* and the *Herald Tribune*. By year's end the nearly 700-page book had sold almost 50,000 copies. Warner Brothers bought the rights and hired her to come to Hollywood and script it, which she did, braving what she called "the disgusting California sunshine." She reached out again to NAM executives, arguing that it would be in their interest for her to become the right-wing equivalent of John Steinbeck. "Let our side now build me into a 'name'—then let me address meetings, head drives, and endorse committees," she said. That way she could help break the "Pink-New-Deal-Collectivist blockade" that prevented their views from being heard.

Something of the sort was in the works in '43, but not on an individual basis. Rather it was an interplay between American entrepreneurs and émigré intellectuals that generated the first substantial institution, a pro-capitalist think tank.

In 1943, Ludwig von Mises was invited by Leonard Read—NAM having put them in touch—to lecture in California on free-market economics. Read, a self-made businessman, a champion of laissez-faire, and manager of the Los Angeles Chamber of Commerce, was mightily impressed by Mises. Persuaded by the Austrian's argument that America's future would be determined by "the outcome of the intellectual combat between the supporters of socialism and those of capitalism," Read set out to organize his side's warriors. In April 1945 he moved east, and with backing from New York businessmen like David Goodrich, president of B. F. Goodrich Company, he set up the Foundation for Economic Education (FEE). Substantial funds flowed in from major corporations—Chrysler, Monsanto, US Steel, General Motors, Halliburton—for an institution to promote free enterprise through research, lectures, and publications. It would be, said Read, "an intellectual lighthouse that persons may be attracted from the sea of socialistic error," with Mises (and Hazlitt) hired on to provide the high-wattage illumination.

Ayn Rand was an ardent FEE supporter, in part because she, too, admired Mises (as he appreciated her contributions to the cause). But her support did not survive publication of the FEE's inaugural pamphlet, an attack on New York's rent-control law, coauthored by economist Milton Friedman. Rand's problem was not with the exemplary choice of target but with the bowmanship employed in hitting it. Friedman, a Brooklyn-born and Rahway-raised economist who had worked during the war in Columbia University's Statistical Research Group, had suggested dispassionately that rent control was inefficient. By interfering with the free market (he and his coauthor argued), the law removed incentives to build more housing, thus worsening rather than alleviating the shortage. It simply failed to accomplish its stated goal. What aroused Rand's ire was the duo's refusal to challenge the goal itself. Worse, they had even spoken favorably of the rent controllers' motivations. This didn't bother the anti–rent control National Association of Real Estate Boards, which delightedly distributed half a million copies of the tract. Rand was infuriated by their failure to ground their case in moral principle and by the dry academic tone in which they made it. They *should* have said, loudly, that rent control, like all government infringements of individual rights, was not just inefficient but tyrannical. The FEE pamphlet, she fumed in a letter to a friend, contained "not one word about the inalienable right of landlords and property owners," just "humanitarian...concern for those who can find no houses." Blazing mad, she told Read that the publication in effect "advocates the nationalization of private homes"; that it was "the most pernicious thing ever issued by an avowedly conservative organization"; and that she would have nothing further to do with him or his operation.

Still, if the fledgling right was not without its internecine struggles (as was the left), it had established itself as an intellectual and political presence on the New York scene, just in time to add its voice to the debate on the New Deal which lay at the heart of the 1944 campaign.

156

Rightist Thrust...

The 1942 congressional elections had handed New Deal opponents a major victory, with Republicans gaining forty-seven seats in the House and nine in the Senate. This was primarily due to diminished Democratic presence on the eligible voter rolls. US troops were now scattered all over the world, and many industrial workers had moved to where the war plants were. Election procedures, controlled by the states, required soldiers to register in person or get an absentee ballot; both were virtually impossible to accomplish under wartime conditions. The states also required relocated war workers to establish residency in their new communities; this was often a lengthy process. As those on the battlefields and assembly lines—workers, ethnics, the young, and the poor—were more likely to vote Democratic than Republican, the Roosevelt Administration was facing de facto disfranchisement of much of its base. A federal Soldier Voting Act was proposed to ease these obstacles to eligibility. Congressional opponents delayed passage in the name of "states' rights" until September 1942—too late to affect the November election. As a result, only 28,051 soldier ballots were cast, roughly one-half of one percent of the five million active-duty service personnel. This, coupled with restraints on war workers, helped drive turnout down from the 67 percent of the adult population (excluding southern Blacks) who had voted in 1940, to 40 percent in 1942.

The resulting influx of conservative Republicans galvanized congressional efforts to move beyond blocking new liberal laws to rolling back old ones. Still, Republicans were a minority in both houses. They would need the votes of their sometime allies, the Southern Democrats. Southern elites, however, did not share the Midwesterners' ideological opposition to an assertive national state. They had been partners in the New Deal coalition and had profited handsomely from many of its programs.

Southern senators and representatives were, however, increasingly disaffected from the Roosevelt regime because they believed its support for their race-based civilization was slackening. Throughout the '30s, FDR had tailored his programs to suit their specifications, denying African Americans benefits that might have strengthened their hand vis-à-vis Southern whites and overriding protests from the party's northern liberal wing in order to keep the South solidly in the Democratic column.

The war altered this dynamic. Southern oligarchs faced new threats to their grip on political power. They had long used Jim Crow devices like the poll tax and white primary to bar Blacks from voting and to filter out enough poor whites to make the electorate manageable. Efforts by northern Black and white liberals to outlaw the poll tax had been beaten back using the filibuster. But in 1942 opponents had gotten a provision into the Soldier Voting Act, exempting military personnel from the pay-to-vote requirement—a worrisome shot across segregation's bow. Then in April 1944 the Supreme Court accepted Thurgood Marshall's argument that banning Blacks from the Texas Democratic Party primary was unconstitutional, and the S.S. *Segregation* began taking on water.

Equally alarming were assaults on the South's labor regime. One of the regional economy's only advantages was its low-wage labor force, an asset sustained by encouraging racial divisions and beating off unions. Now, often with federal help, textile, mine, tobacco, and fur and leather organizers were again gaining footholds. And employers of farm labor (according to one government report) were complaining that they had to "pay a higher price than they planned to pay" because "the Negroes are becoming too independent."

Many oligarchs blamed the Roosevelt administration for their woes. The federal War Labor Board protected organizers, the federal Fair Employment Practices Commission defended Blacks, federal bureaucrats were seeking to extend Social Security coverage to (mostly Black) domestic and agricultural laborers, and Mrs. Roosevelt was fraternizing altogether too much with Negroes. Birmingham, Alabama's, commissioner of public safety—Eugene "Bull" Connor as his stationery styled him—fired off a letter to the president in 1942 declaring that outside agitation was making Blacks "impudent, unruly, arrogant, law breaking, violent and insolent." Further federal pressure on the segregationist regime, he warned, would lead to "the Annihilation of the Democratic Party in this section of the Nation."

Southern elites were also convinced that the source of their troubles lay as much in New York as in Washington. Gotham was headquarters to the NAACP, the International Ladies Garment Workers Union, and the Communist Party–affiliated International Fur and Leather Workers Union that had been organizing Southern tanneries. It was home to Vito Marcantonio, the most vigorous supporter of the FEPC in the House and leader of efforts to abolish the poll tax. Arch segregationist Congressman John Rankin of Mississippi blamed a cabal of New York Jewish communists and labor organizers for the Soldiers Vote Act and other assaults on the racial oligarchy. And Governor Eugene Talmadge campaigned in 1944 against "Moscow-Harlem zoot suiters trying to take over Georgia."

These assertions, if overheated, were in fact on target. New York, which all in all had been the South's most trustworthy Northern ally for most of the preceding century, was now home to forces that considered the South an international embarrassment and a drag on national progress and were determined to use federal power to remake the region's racial regime.

Facing challenges that they believed the Democratic administration had permitted or fostered, the Southern elite joined Midwestern Republicans in a full-throated counteroffensive. Though wary of tackling agencies in charge of popular or useful New Deal programs—Social Security, farm price supports, infrastructure development—the 78th Congress found plenty of more vulnerable entities to cut from the herd and bring down. Some were terminated altogether: the Civilian Conservation Corps, the Works Progress Administration, and the National Youth Agency (which was recruiting and training Black workers for war industries). Others were partially defunded, like the Rural Electrification Administration and the Farm Security Administration (which was protecting agricultural laborers from their employers). The coalition also went after liberal war agencies. It slashed the budget of the domestic arm of the Office of War Information for having over-lauded Roosevelt and having published Chandler Owen's *Negroes and the War*. And it hamstrung the Office of Price Administration by driving its leaders Leon Henderson and John Kenneth Galbraith (both labeled "communistic") out of office.

The allies lit into labor as well. Howard Smith, the Virginia congressman who had authored the Smith Act and led the fight against the National Labor Relations Board, teamed up with Tom Connally, the Texas senator who had led the war against repeal of the poll tax, to win passage on June 25, 1943, over a presidential veto, of the Smith Connally Act. The law—in part a response to a wave of wildcat strikes—allowed the federal government to seize and operate industries threatened by actions that would interfere with war production, and it prohibited unions from contributing to candidates for federal office.

Finally, the coalition decapitated what it considered the hydra's chief head—the National Resources Planning Board (NRPB). When FDR sent over the NRPB's postwar plans in March 1943, Ohio Republican Frederick C. Smith attacked them as a "communistic program" aimed at "the complete destruction of all free enterprise." More temperately, the NRPB was denounced for seeking to usurp legislative authority by expanding executive prerogatives—a defensible charge, as the NRPB did indeed propose vesting considerable new powers in the White House. Declaring it wanted no part of an American Beveridge Plan, the Congress cut off the agency's funding altogether. By the end of 1943 the NRPB had ceased to exist.

Next on the target list was President Roosevelt himself.

157

...Liberal Riposte

The liberal riposte to the right-wing thrust began in New York, at 15 Union Square West, headquarters of the Amalgamated Clothing Workers of America (ACWA). Sidney Hillman had returned to his post as union president in the summer of 1942, after two difficult years in Washington as labor's chief representative. Back in the political fray as well, Hillman witnessed close up the electoral debacle of 1942 and its consequences. His assessment—"the forces of reaction were organized for political action; the progressives were not organized"—suggested his response: progressives had better *get* organized. Hillman proposed that the CIO construct a political machine powerful enough to take on Republicans, Dixiecrats, machine bosses, and corporate lobbyists, powerful enough to re-elect Roosevelt and win Congress back to a liberal-labor agenda.

In July 1943 Hillman reported to FDR that the CIO was creating a Political Action Committee—the country's primal PAC—with headquarters at 205 East 42nd Street and branch offices across the United States. Assembling a formidable staff of professionals and volunteers, the CIO-PAC began building an immense mobilization operation. A funding base was established too: end-running the Smith Connally Act's prohibition on union contributions to federal candidates, the PAC sought and got voluntary donations directly from union members, rather than union treasuries. Opponents howled, but the gambit passed legal muster.

In the meantime, their presumed candidate raised his own battle standard. On January 11, 1944, Roosevelt proposed in his State of the Union address the adoption of an "Economic Bill of Rights." The idea had been suggested back in August 1939 by his planning chief Frederic Delano, who had urged FDR to expand the definition of rights from the political to the economic arena. The president had given Uncle Fred the go-ahead to draft such a call; it had gone through several iterations; and now it was taken public.

"This Republic had its beginning, and grew to its present strength, under the protection of certain inalienable political rights," Roosevelt told his radio listeners, "among them the right of free speech, free press, free worship, trial by jury, freedom from unreasonable searches and seizures." Yet over time, he continued, it had become clear "that true individual freedom cannot exist without economic security and independence," and that "people who are hungry and out of a job are the stuff of which dictatorships are made."

Accordingly, the president proposed assertion of an additional set of rights "under which a new basis of security and prosperity can be established for all—regardless of station, or race or creed." These included the right to a "useful and remunerative job"; the right "to earn enough to provide adequate food and clothing and recreation"; the right of businessmen to be free "from unfair competition and domination by monopolies at home or abroad"; the right "of every family to a decent home," to "adequate medical care," to "a good education," and to "protection from the economic fears of old age, and sickness, and accident and unemployment."

Unlike political rights—things states should not be allowed to do—economic rights required positive government action. "After this war is won," he suggested, "we must be prepared to move forward, in the implementation of these rights," which meant planning should begin immediately. This task, said the president, was the responsibility of Congress. Would that body have the political will to secure these rights? Roosevelt noted "the grave dangers of 'rightist reaction' in this Nation," which he characterized as an effort "to return to the so-called 'normalcy' of the 1920's." He urged that the country "not repeat the excesses of the wild twenties when this Nation went for a joy ride on a roller coaster which ended in a tragic crash." Giving in to the right would constitute more than an economic error, he warned bluntly (if hyperbolically), it would mean that "even though we shall have conquered our enemies on the battlefields abroad, we shall have yielded to the spirit of Fascism here at home."

Fortunately, he added, well-thought-out suggestions about how to move forward "are already before committees of the Congress in the form of proposed legislation." And in fact, New York's indefatigable Senator Wagner had joined with colleagues the previous June to put the Wagner-Murray-Dingell (WMD) bill into the legislative hopper. An omnibus 200-page document, WMD drew heavily upon the National Resources Planning Board's March 1943 proposals in laying out key components of a postwar American welfare state: expanded old age and unemployment insurance, national health insurance, etc. Wagner et al.'s proposal had gone nowhere in a Congress preoccupied with dismantling New Deal programs and signing the NRPB's death warrant.

FDR, perfectly aware of the situation, had not expended much political capital on Wagner's initiative. Instead, he cannily trumpeted yet another NRPB initiative, in the works since 1942, that would have the federal government take responsibility for reintegrating veterans into the postwar economy and society. In July 1943, Roosevelt had gone public with this notion in a fireside chat (rather than taking it straight to Congress), insisting that America's men and women in uniform must not be mustered out "to a place on the breadline or on a corner selling apples. We must, this time, have plans ready—instead of waiting to do a hasty, inefficient and ill-considered job at the last moment." FDR of course had just such a plan ready, a package of social and educational benefits for veterans largely decanted from Wagner's bill and proposals of the recently executed NRPB.

Rightists fumed—Taft called it a transparent bid for the 1944 soldiers' vote—but opposition was suicidal, especially after the American Legion jumped into the fray. Concurrently with Roosevelt's Economic Bill of Rights speech, the three-million-strong veterans' organization proposed "a bill of rights for G.I. Joe and G.I. Jane," soon shortened to "GI Bill of Rights." Though the Legion was in general anti–New Deal, its bill's provisions built on those

Roosevelt had advanced and were even *more* generous—offering veterans up to four years of government-paid education instead of the Administration's one.

The right wing in Congress was convinced (correctly) that liberals saw the GI Bill as a way for the New Deal to make a comeback, to put its foot in the legislative door, and it did its utmost to delimit the program. Eschewing the Legion's "bill of rights" language as a rhetorical Trojan horse, they dubbed the legislation the Servicemen's Readjustment Act and worked to define its benefits, duration, and eligibility requirements as stringently as possible (even civilian war workers and the merchant marine were excluded, though the mortality rates of both were higher than those of the military).

Still, the bill Roosevelt signed in June 1944, amid the Normandy invasion, constituted a model demonstration project for an American welfare state. It provided health-care benefits, government-sponsored education, low-cost loans for buying a home, unemployment insurance, and more, to sixteen million veterans, Blacks as well as whites, women as well as men, a cohort that would soon, together with their families, amount to nearly one-third the population.

The CIO-Political Action Committee now set out to make such a package of rights and benefits available to *all* Americans, and their call for construction of a US social democratic state became the centerpiece of their 1944 campaign.

On June 17, 1944, almost coincident with passage of the GI Bill, the first national conference of CIO-PAC approved a 4,000 word "People's Program of 1944." It borrowed much from various NRPB plans, from FDR's economic bill of rights, and from the GI Bill, but added still other proposals, many long advanced by various reforms groups in Gotham, to come up with a charter of American liberalism. Items on its lengthy list included construction of 1.5 million public housing units a year for ten years, the extension and expansion of Social Security coverage to include medical insurance, federal aid to education, infrastructure initiatives, urban redevelopment, permanent status for the Fair Employment Practices Commission, equal pay for equal work, federally subsidized child care, abolition of the poll tax, an antilynching law, the retention of rent and price controls, an increase in the minimum wage, and a call for guaranteeing a full employment economy after the war.

This last—part and parcel of the larger issue of how to reconvert from a wartime to a peacetime economy—had been a particularly hot-button item since May 1944. The US Navy had cancelled production, on three days' notice, of the Corsair fighter planes being produced at the Long Island City plant of the Brewster Aeronautical Corporation, throwing roughly 13,000 people out of work. They did not go quietly. Local 365 of the United Auto Workers staged a "stay-in." Eight thousand workers, at least a quarter of them women, occupied the former Ford Building on the south side of Northern Boulevard and unfurled banners from windows, one of which read: "We've Got the Tools. We've Got the Ability. We've Got the Experience. We've Got the Will. But We Ain't Got the Work." The protest, which lasted little more than a day, made headlines across the country, it being patently obvious that massive overnight firings would certainly happen elsewhere if plans were not set in place to minimize reconversion disruptions.

More fundamentally, as the CIO-PAC argued in *Jobs for All after the War*, the wartime "miracle of production" had made clear that unemployment itself was unnecessary. "Full employment at fair wages" could be assured by establishing a joint government-business planning board with power to initiate compensatory public works spending in the event of a slump. Some also suggested that government-owned plants should not be auctioned off on the cheap and instead retained for public use.

To rally support for the People's Program, the CIO-PAC made common cause with other liberal organizations in New York, one of which it created itself. During the summer of 1944, Sidney Hillman organized the National Citizens PAC, also housed in 205 East 42nd. Reaching beyond the organized working class, it tapped into Gotham's opinion-making circles, drawing in literati, publicists, professionals, academics, businessmen, theologians, journalists, and representatives of fraternal and ethnic groups. The 142-member board included Reinhold Niebuhr, Max Lerner, Arthur Schlesinger Jr., Orson Welles, Dorothy Parker, and Freda Kirchwey. Twenty-two on its roster were African Americans, including A. Philip Randolph and Paul Robeson.

The National Citizens PAC, in turn, overlapped with the Union for Democratic Action (UDA), another city-based liberal organization (situated across town at 202 West 40th). Led by James Loeb, who had cofounded it (with Niebuhr) in 1941, it included many former members of the Socialist Party who had broken with SP leader Norman Thomas on foreign policy issues. The UDA, like Hillman's PACs, wanted to preserve and extend threatened New Deal programs. In a joint supplement issued with the *New Republic*—*A Congress to Win the War and the Peace*—the UDA vitriolically attacked right-wing Democrats and Republicans, almost accusing them of treason for attempting to "sabotage" administration policies during wartime.

This constellation of New York liberals—institutions marshaled, platform planks in place—now marched into the national political arena.

158

The Last Subway Series

At the Democratic National Convention, held July 19–21 in Chicago, the right couldn't, wouldn't, block Roosevelt's being nominated for a fourth term; he was patently the party's strongest possible candidate. Instead, they poured their ire and energy into warding off renomination of Henry Wallace as vice president, a crucial position given FDR's obviously deteriorating health. The CIO and its PAC, the Union for Democratic Action (UDA), and 65 percent of the Democratic Party's rank and file in a Gallup Poll, strongly backed Wallace, the liberals' tribune. He was serenaded when he arrived by UDA members to the tune of "Joshua Fit the Battle of Jericho" ("Wallace Fought the Battle for the Common Man, Common Man, Common Man…"), and he received an ovation from liberal delegates when he addressed the convention (no olive brancher he, his speech called for abolishing the poll tax).

Southerners countered with James Byrnes of South Carolina, a strong New Dealer who had been entrusted by FDR with major mobilization tasks, winning him the appellation "Assistant President." In South Carolinian terms Byrnes was a racial moderate; in his various campaigns for congressman and then senator he had stressed his economic contributions to the state, avoiding white supremacist demagoguery. However, the Southerners in his corner—particularly segregationist factions in Texas, Virginia, Mississippi, Louisiana, Oklahoma—were threatening to secede from the party, taking their votes and money with them, unless the Democrats came out against things like a permanent FEPC (which New York's Wagner was pushing in the Senate). The wilder-eyed among them were demanding a convention commitment to segregation itself.

The critical figures in preventing this donnybrook from tearing the party apart were Democratic National Committee chieftains and Northeastern urban bosses, most notably Ed Flynn of the Bronx. The politicos thought Wallace too radical and believed he would drag down the ticket, but they also understood that labor and African Americans found Byrnes utterly unacceptable. Black organizations had recently taken out an ad in the *New York Times*—signed by Walter White, Thurgood Marshall, and A. Philip Randolph, among others—stating that no candidate, of either party, would get the Black vote if it did not support a permanent FEPC. This was a position Byrnes would not survive endorsing. Flynn accordingly told Roosevelt that running with Byrnes would lose him 200,000 Black votes in New York alone, costing him the state and the general election.

The compromise candidate put forward was Harry Truman—border state senator, protégé of the Kansas City Pendergast machine, and a politician more or less acceptable to Southern bourbons and northern liberals. At a private meeting with party leaders considering alternatives to Wallace, FDR was rumored to have told the Democratic Party National Chairman to "clear it with Sidney." This was widely taken as a sign of Hillman's (and liberalism's) clout. Yet while it did demonstrate that the liberal faction had won veto power over the vice presidential pick, the fact remained the left hadn't been strong enough to block the right from forcing Wallace's removal.

Still, Franklin Roosevelt was Admiral of the Democratic Fleet and his flagship still sailed under liberal colors.

The Republican convention, held three weeks earlier on June 26–28, also in Chicago, had been a relatively tranquil affair, because the analogous showdown—oddly, for such a heartland-centered party, a duel between two New Yorkers—had been fought beforehand.

The initial front runner had been Wendell Willkie, the 1940 standard bearer. But Willkie, who had alienated party professionals in his last outing, had since moved to the left, alienating much of the rank and file. For many Republicans, the line between Willkie and Roosevelt was ever harder to discern. While Willkie had returned to the practice of corporate law in Gotham, joining a sixty-year-old Broad Street firm in 1940, and while he did continue to attack big government from that Wall Street perch, he spent at least as much time challenging Republican pieties. He became an all-out internationalist and proposed a form of global government in his *One World* (1943). He called for full employment and welfare policies in language uncomfortably similar to FDR's. He derided much of the talk about "free enterprise" as "just propaganda on the part of powerful groups who have not practiced real enterprise in a generation." And he developed a close working relationship with the NAACP, urging civil rights initiatives that congressional Republicans opposed almost as vigorously as did Southern Democrats. As Willkie's party-popularity tobogganed downward, particularly in the Midwest, he decided to enter the Wisconsin primary in April, promising to drop out if he didn't make a strong showing. When he failed to win a single delegate, he removed his hat from the ring.

Conservative Republicans who found Willkie to be as liberal as Roosevelt would have felt amply confirmed in their judgment had they known about a secret meeting between the failed candidate and FDR aide Samuel Rosenman. Roosevelt, having learned that Willkie was interested in a realignment of the parties, dispatched Rosenman to convey his complete agreement that "the time has come for the Democratic Party to get rid of its reactionary elements in the South and to attract to it the liberals of the Republican Party." "We ought," he added, "to have two real parties—one liberal and the other conservative." The two-hour talk took place on July 5, at the St. Regis Hotel on 55th and Fifth, just down the avenue from Willkie's apartment across from the Met. It went well, and the parties agreed to continue the conversation after the election, looking toward possibly effecting a major change by 1948. The moment never came. On October 8 the fifty-two-year-old Willkie died of a heart attack in Lenox Hill Hospital, and the next day 60,000 filed through the Fifth Avenue Presbyterian Church (kitty corner from the St. Regis) to pay their respects.

The beneficiary of Willkie's flameout was not a Midwestern conservative. Taft had announced he was not a candidate and backed instead Governor John Bricker of Ohio, a sentimental favorite of Republican delegates but clearly no match for FDR. Instead, the party went with Tom Dewey, another New Yorker. The Midwesterners acquiesced because they believed the Republicans couldn't defeat Roosevelt unless they carried New York, and Dewey, who had won election as governor in 1942, had a better chance of doing so than anyone else. Also, Gotham was where the money was; or, as the furious *Chicago Tribune* put it, Dewey's nomination had been "bought by the prospect of millions for his campaign fund from New York bankers."

And Dewey was not Willkie. He had positioned himself to the right of the New Dealers and to the left of the business-class fundamentalists, more or less in the spot occupied by the corporate liberals running the Committee for Economic Development. Dewey was a private enterprise man. Government would never be able to adequately provide Americans with security from economic hazards, he said; only a "vigorous and productive economic system" could do that. He underscored that "long-haired braintrusters" hadn't been able to end the Depression. And he insisted they shouldn't be allowed (and couldn't be trusted) to oversee the postwar conversion from a state-directed to a private economy, one that he, too, was confident would be satisfactorily powered by pent up consumer demand.

On the other hand, there was no going back to the 1920s. Dewey, like the Committee for Economic Development, accepted the basic New Deal transformation. He held no brief for those who would simply dismantle its programs. What he called "modern republicanism" (and what others called "liberal Republicanism") would, rather, manage those programs more efficiently, less expensively, with fewer regulations, and lower taxes. As governor of New York, he had overhauled the Workmen's Compensation system and reorganized the Social Welfare and the Health Departments—modernizing hospitals that were unsafe for human habitation and which had been "left to me by those who claimed to be liberals." Nor had he shied away from providing subsidies to low-income housing or hesitated to reform private power companies.

Like the CED, Dewey believed in planning. Early on he had reviewed the economy of New York with an eye toward ensuring its postwar economy would be strong enough to absorb 1.5 million veterans. He had set up a Postwar Planning Committee to commission designs for new housing projects, additions to crowded hospitals, and a vast network of highways. He established a Postwar Reconstruction Fund and channeled millions into it and had the Department of Commerce devise a system of unemployment insurance for returning vets.

With Dewey as the Republican candidate, the race that now got under way in earnest was shaping up as a contest between New Deal and corporate liberal approaches, with business fundamentalists having no entrant in the presidential race apart from Bricker, whom the convention had tapped to be Dewey's running mate.

Fittingly, for one thought to be the most progressive Republican candidate since Theodore Roosevelt, Dewey moved the party's national headquarters from Chicago to New York's Roosevelt Hotel—named for Teddy not Franklin—leaving only a regional office behind to placate Midwesterners suspicious of the Eastern establishment. The sop didn't help much. Taft groused throughout the campaign that Dewey suffered from "too much of the New York viewpoint.... He sees the group opinions there as a lot more important than they are." One Dewey supporter worried similarly about political myopia, seeing the candidate as being surrounded by "a small group of very intelligent New York men, ill equipped to understand Americans beyond the eastern seaboard."

Yet Dewey was quite professional, as was his campaign manager, Herbert Brownell Jr., the Lord Day & Lord attorney who had run his gubernatorial race. They relied on polling organizations to provide opinion sampling, which they used to make mid-course adjustments in tactics. And they paid attention to specific constituencies—farmers, labor, young Republicans, Jews (Dewey courted the Zionist vote), and Blacks (he proposed the first state FEPC in the nation, though stalled its passage until after the election so as not to rile Southern Republicans).

These efficient Republicans were, however, up against a formidable new force, much of the Democratic ground game having been turned over to Hillman's CIO-PAC. PAC professionals in Gotham wrote weekly bulletins for distribution to 1,500 labor papers and 255 Black ones; produced radio programs; printed color posters (like Ben Shahn's stirring series); and ran off millions of slickly produced pamphlets ("Back to the Breadlines with Dewey"), which were shipped out at the rate of nearly ten million a week from New York headquarters to fourteen CIO-PAC distribution centers throughout the US. From there campaign material flowed on to 14,000 union locals, the base camps for registration and education initiatives that were organized down to precinct and block levels and which reached into living rooms of union families and the war plants and shipyards where they worked. In preparation for election day, get-out-the-vote blitzes were readied, with union volunteers (20,000 in New York alone) ready to staff phone banks and carpools. It had been a while since wheezy Democratic machines had been capable of such an effort.

And in FDR they had a brilliant public performer. For all his war distractions and health problems, the candidate ably promoted the People's Program, as much as that of the Democratic Party, even upping the ante at times. In an October speech in Chicago, Roosevelt promised to fashion a postwar economy capable of providing sixty million jobs (five million more than the CED was promising private industry could come up with); those who scoffed at such a "fantastic" number were reminded they'd said the same about his 1940 vow to build 50,000 war planes, a promise on which he'd more than delivered. Barnstorming the country, FDR painted a beguiling picture of the future—based not on the availability of shiny new commodities but on the guarantee of new economic rights.

The contrast between the avuncular president and the prickly governor was telling, too. Dewey's personal liabilities were the converse of his abilities: Mr. Efficiency Man came across as arrogant and bossy, his carefully planned presentations as dull and robotic. He attracted quips like flies—he was a man "who could strut sitting down"; "You can't really dislike Tom Dewey until you get to know him."

When all was said and done, the biggest obstacle to a Dewey presidency was not being out-organized, or out-charmed, but rather, as it were, out-generaled. As the campaign rolled on, American forces kept racking up smashing successes in Europe and the Pacific, from the liberation of Paris in August to the Battle of Leyte Gulf in October, making a political triumph for the victorious commander-in-chief all but inevitable. Unless Roosevelt's opponents could come up with a truly formidable game-changing strategy they would all too soon be toast.

It was at this point that the right reached for the club of anticommunism.

159

Enter: "Red Menace"

Dewey was not antilabor. He rejected the use of "gunfire and gas bombs" to settle organizing disputes and endorsed the principles of the Wagner Act. But the entry of organized labor into organized politics was something else again. Dewey and the Republicans and Southern Democrats were dismayed by the emergence and seeming effectiveness of the CIO's Political Action Committee. They went after it with everything they had.

At first, they focused on its chief, Sidney Hillman, a man who in his being and bearing ruffled the prejudices of many middle Americans. Hillman's opponents, boosted by media emperors like Hearst and Luce, did their best to deepen heartland anxieties, pounding away at the PAC-man's foreign birth and foreign accent, his Jewish faith and racial egalitarianism, his radical associations and supposed criminal ones. Not since Al Smith's demonization back in the twenties had a New York liberal been singled out for such national opprobrium, with the important difference that Tom Dewey was in no position to run against his own city.

What gave such nativist and anti-Semitic sentiments traction was that Hillman, through his CIO-PAC, had become something of a power. Had not Roosevelt said: "Clear it with Sidney"? (Perhaps he hadn't, but the phrase was a godsend to the right, and they made extravagant use of it.) Herbert Brownell promoted the idea that the CIO had a stranglehold on the Democratic Party, allowing Hillman to hold the White House hostage. Republican billboards blazoned forth a new slogan: "It's Your Country—Why Let Sidney Hillman Run It."

Peeking out from behind the menace of organized labor, in this scenario, was a far more potent antagonist, the Communist Party. The argument was straightforwardly syllogistic. The CIO-PAC was a Communist operation; the PAC now dictated Democratic Party policy; therefore the Communists were running the Democratic Party. The key premise was the initial one, and the strongest case for it had come not from Republican or Dixiecratic ranks but from the Jewish left-wing labor movement in New York itself.

Back in January 1944, when Hillman was mapping out an electoral strategy, he concluded that winning New York was vital to winning the White House. This raised a worrisome problem. The American Labor Party (ALP), which he counted on to anchor CIO-PAC's Gotham operation, had (he believed) hogtied itself by marginalizing the biggest and most powerful unions in the city—the CIO-affiliated organizations, linked to the Communist Party, of the maritime, transport, office, professional, electrical, and fur workers.

Back in 1939, during the Nazi-Soviet pact period, Hillman himself had been a co-architect of this arms-length policy, together with David Dubinsky, his collaborator in founding the ALP. When the Communists, then in their Yanks-are-not-coming phase, tried to deny Labor Party backing to the "warmongering" Roosevelt, the two union chiefs had teamed up to freeze left-wing unions out of leadership positions, though welcoming their members in the rank and file. Since then, the ban had remained in place, leaving Dubinsky (in Hillman's absence) in effective control of the Party's state machinery, though the self-styled "left wing" and "right wing" continued to battle for control of county ALP organizations.

From Hillman's 1944 perspective, the situation had changed, and the policy warranted rethinking. When the Nazis invaded the Soviet Union in 1941, US Communists and their affiliated unions had become superpatriotic advocates of all-out war production, fierce supporters of the no-strike pledge, and ardent backers of a fourth term for Franklin Roosevelt. By early 1944 Earl Browder was even preparing to dissolve the Communist Party and replace it with a Communist Political Association (a mission accomplished by May).

Hillman—no naif—didn't trust the Communists but thought he could use them, marshaling their superb organizing capabilities against the current common foe. Accordingly, he proposed allowing the left-wing CIO unions representation on the State Executive Committee, with voting strength proportional to the size of their membership. To ease right-wing anxieties (and FDR's concern) about potential Communist control, he suggested banning CPUSA members from positions of authority.

Dubinsky, who had also been around the block a few times, flatly rejected the plan, which would end his iron grip on the ALP apparatus, and the issue was in effect put to trial-by-electoral-combat. Because the antagonism between the two generals rested on more than mere principle, the run-up to the March 1944 primary quickly turned vicious.

The central point of contention was certainly the Communist issue. Dubinsky and his associates hated the CP, considered it a totally untrustworthy creature of the Kremlin, and would under no circumstances work with it. Hillman thought the critical enemies lay to the right and he would therefore accept Communists as tactical allies; the Dubinskyites, he believed, had become sectarians, trapped in outdated positions.

The two also divided on electoral strategy. Dubinsky objected to Hillman's making FDR's re-election the be-all-and-end-all, in effect tying labor to the Democratic Party; he wanted to build, state by state, a truly independent labor party that would be free to challenge the Democrats when necessary. Hillman thought promoting a third party, especially during wartime, was delusionary, utopian, and would only blunt labor's political power.

These high-minded stands were exacerbated by personal, organizational, and intra-ethnic rivalries of long standing. The two men had different personal styles (Hillman favored diplomacy, Dubinsky direct action). They moved in different circles (Hillman had become a national figure, Dubinsky remained a local one). Their unions (ACWA and ILGWU) and labor federations (CIO and AFL) were perpetually at loggerheads over jurisdictional disputes. Though both Jewish, they related differently to Jewish issues—Hillman subordinating them to his labor agenda, Dubinsky pouring energy and resources into Jewish Labor Committee rescue initiatives—and they appealed to slightly different strata and neighborhoods in Jewish New York. There were generational differences, as well: Dubinsky's "Old

Guard" were heavily rooted in the early-twentieth-century Social Democratic movement and its institutions (*Daily Forward*, *New Leader*, *Workmen's Circle*); the formative experiences of Hillman's supporters tended to have come in the CIO and New Deal era. Finally, Dubinsky resented Hillman's muscling in on what had become his territory, while Hillman resented Dubinsky's fighting to maintain a dictatorial grip on the ALP. With all these overlapping animosities and non-negotiable issues, the primary turned acrid and rancorous, becoming a zero-sum struggle for control of the party.

For all Dubinsky's claims that the Amalgamated's boss was a "front man for the Communists" who were out to take over the ALP, the Old Guard failed to pin the Red badge on Hillman. On March 28 the left swept all five boroughs and captured most of Upstate as well. Dubinsky and his colleagues, asserting that "Mr. Earl Browder has captured the American Labor Party," seceded and created the Liberal Party, whose platform was all but identical to the one it left behind, on every issue except working with Communists. In the American Labor Party, the Communists did expand their influence, but, *pace* Dubinsky's claims, never controlled it. They remained shut out of the ALP leadership and never challenged Hillman's authority. They did, however, put their members to work in the CIO-PAC and played a critical role in making it efficient and effective. This was the fire behind the smoke that now billowed into the national arena, as the Red Scare fanned by the Old Guard jumped from the world of Gotham's Jewish socialists to the tinderbox of presidential politics. Dubinsky may have lost the argument in New York, but his charges would resonate longest and loudest on the national stage.

The right wing's conflation of unionism, New Dealism, and communism became central to its campaign, its charges growing more inflammatory as election day approached. The *New York Daily Mirror* began writing about "the New Deal-Communist-Left Wing axis." The *New York Daily News* warned a PAC victory would be the "greatest single political triumph ever achieved by the Communists." Clare Boothe Luce said Hillman had admitted "Communist Trojan horses" into American politics; that "Moscow stooges" now controlled the New York CIO and ALP; and that Hillman and the Communists were plotting to "take over the Democratic party" after the election. Senator Taft agreed FDR's re-election would put the country in the hands of the Communists, and the *Chicago Tribune* warned that New Dealers were helping those who "plan to bring Red Terror sweeping down upon America."

Dewey himself had been hesitant to get on board the anticommunist express but, increasingly desperate as his campaign limped into the homestretch, he began linking Browder and Roosevelt. Soon he was arguing that Communists had infiltrated the federal government and that Roosevelt's reelection was "essential to the aims of the Communists." On November 1, days before the election, he went for broke, giving a speech in Boston that was accurately summed up next day by *New York Times* headlines proclaiming: "Dewey Predicts 'Red Menace' Rise if Roosevelt Wins," and "Asserts Communists with Aid of Hillman Seek to Seize Government." As evidence (and cover) for such claims, Dewey declared, "In the words of David Dubinsky, Sidney Hillman is a front for the Communists."

None of this was sufficiently persuasive, however. Too much smoke, not enough fire. Nor were the syllogistic links sufficiently self-evident. As the Jesuit magazine *America* calmly pointed out: yes, no doubt there was a communist presence in the CIO's PAC. Yet most of the People's Program they were promoting "might have been based on Quadragesimo Anno" and other papal teachings. The fact that communists supported a given issue did not ipso facto taint it, nor did their backing it imply that anyone else who did so was under communist compulsion. Those "opposed to Communism," it counseled, "should not play into the Party's hands by firing blindly every time someone yells that he sees a red flag."

Though what if the focus was shifted from the communists in Union Square to their presumed masters in Moscow, from domestic matters to foreign affairs? There, recent developments, notably troubling moves by Stalin in Eastern Europe, did indeed raise issues of considerable moment. Perhaps highlighting these could redirect attention from present military successes to possible future diplomatic failures and help trigger an electoral shift just big enough to ward off impending defeat.

160

Cue: Cold War

Attacking the Russian Red Menace was awkward; it was also, after all, our Heroic Soviet Ally. In February 1943 the six-month nightmare of the Battle of Stalingrad had ended in a crucial Russian triumph over the Nazis, and admiration and gratitude for the Soviets' great victory were still the order of the day. Nowhere more so than in New York, headquarters (at Madison and 37th) of the popular-frontish National Council of American-Soviet Friendship, devoted to building US-SU amity during and after the war. Steered by Corliss Lamont, it assembled giant broad-based rallies in support of the Russian war effort, like the one that had filled Madison Square Garden on November 8, 1942, in mid-Stalingrad, with a spectrum of speakers that included Vice President Wallace, Governor Lehman, Mayor La Guardia, GE chairman Owen Young, AFL head William Green, and Morgan banker (also Corliss's father) Thomas Lamont; additional messages hailing the Red Army's heroism were read out to the wildly cheering crowd from Lieutenant General Dwight Eisenhower and FDR. This tremendous reservoir of goodwill, and the ongoing military partnership, set limits on those who would kindle anti-Soviet fervor.

Also, when those thinking geostrategically about the postwar world order pondered potential obstacles to an American-directed free trade future, the Soviet Union did not rank as high as imperial Britain. Russia seemed less a potential rival than a source of critical raw materials and a likely market for industrial goods. Even among staunch anticommunists, the prevailing sentiment was dislike rather than fear; few worried that Stalin would attempt to impose his system on the west.

Concerns began to arise after the summer of 1943 when, at the Battle of Kursk, the Soviets repelled the Wehrmacht's last Eastern Front offensive and then began driving the Nazis out of occupied Russia, grinding their way west toward Eastern Europe and Germany itself. In June 1944, in tandem with Operation Overlord (the invasion of Normandy), the Soviets launched a colossal offensive along a 300-mile-wide front. Within weeks, the biggest military force on earth, dwarfing those of the Normandy landings, had utterly demolished three entire German armies, cleared fascist forces from Belorussia, and advanced into Poland. With the Red Army thus poised to liberate/occupy the rest of Poland (and likely Romania, Czechoslovakia, Hungary, and Bulgaria) as it marched toward Berlin, formerly abstract geopolitical questions were placed forcefully on the table. If Stalin used his overwhelming military power to set up puppet regimes, what should be the US response? Broadly, there were two realpolitikish approaches. Some argued that Great Powers (even repulsive dictatorships) were entitled to spheres of influence and protective cordons; by these lights, the Russians, especially after repeated invasions from the West, were entitled to as free a hand in Eastern Europe as the US claimed in Latin America (namely various US-backed Caribbean dictatorships, "*our* sons of bitches," as FDR had supposedly characterized them). Others—notably Council on Foreign Relations planners—had been arguing that the US couldn't "afford to see one hundred million Europeans added to the Soviet power."

Roosevelt was largely in the first camp. His principal goal was to maintain harmonious relations with the Russians—both to ensure victory against Germany and Japan today and to achieve postwar stability tomorrow through joint participation in a new international organization. To achieve this, he was prepared to cut Stalin some slack vis-à-vis the countries on Russia's western border, especially as Roosevelt was also an advocate of the non-realpolitik principle—self-determination of peoples—that he'd promulgated in the Atlantic Charter. And with the 1944 election looming, there were domestic politics to consider.

For Polish Americans, the issues at hand were anything but abstract. Their country had been carved up by Nazis and Communists in 1939, and they—like the official Polish Government-in-Exile camped in London—wanted it resurrected and its old boundaries restored. As the Wehrmacht retreated and the Eastern Front lurched west, America's Poles hoped US power would be deployed to protect their homeland.

Roosevelt, caught between his desire to accommodate the Soviets and placate the Poles, tried to do both. At the Churchill-Roosevelt-Stalin conclave in Teheran during November 1943, Churchill and Stalin were agreed that the Soviets should basically be allowed to keep the parts of Eastern Poland they had annexed in 1939, fixing the Russo-Polish border roughly along the old Curzon Line, which had been adopted at Britain's suggestion after World War I. In compensation, Poland should be awarded an equivalent amount of territory on her western frontier, said land to be seized from a defeated Germany. Roosevelt was prepared to live with something like this but not prepared to announce his acquiescence publicly before the next election. As he explained to Stalin in a very-off-the-record meeting, "there were in the United States from six to seven million Americans of Polish extraction, and as a practical man, he did not wish to lose their vote."

Roosevelt overstated the numbers somewhat—in the 1940 census there were about three million Polish Americans who were foreign born, or native born of foreign or mixed parentage—but the higher figure was commonly employed. And the demographic reality was impressive enough: Poles were the third-largest component of the total foreign white stock in the population, exceeded only by the 5.2 million Germans and 4.6 million Italians. Politically, as FDR well knew, they were even more formidable because they were heavily concentrated in six electoral-vote-rich northern states. Poles were particularly numerous in Ohio and Illinois (centered around Chicago), and in Pennsylvania and New York, where a hefty 412,543 (194,163 being foreign born) lived in Gotham alone. They tended, moreover, to bloc vote—as Democrats—but if they ever decided to march en masse to the beat of a Republican drummer, they could do serious damage. Worse, as one Democratic adviser fretted in February 1944: "The Polish Americans may be able to start enough of a rumpus to swing over other groups before November"—namely Irish and Italian fellow Catholics. It was not lost on Roosevelt that Archbishop Spellman was a supporter of the London Poles and an opponent of atheistic Russia.

Yet US Poles had been relatively inert, politically. Their largest organization, the Polish National Alliance, was primarily an association of fraternal and benefit groups; it did not attempt to influence national politics or foreign policy. There was also the Polish American Council, dedicated to coordinating war relief efforts. It had been under its aegis that over two thousand delegates, representing 350,000 members of Polish organizations in the New York metropolitan area, had rallied on September 1, 1939, at the Polish National Home (19–25 St. Mark's Place) to organize the sending of aid—but not to mobilize electorally.

This began to change with the arrival in New York, in September 1941, of Colonel Ignacy Matuszewski, who had been a colonel in the Polish army, a diplomat, a well-known journalist, and a leading member of the hyper-nationalist political faction associated with the legacy of Józef Pilsudski. In 1919–21, Pilsudski, as Poland's chief of state, had warred against the Soviet Union and fought the Bolsheviks to a draw, becoming a national hero. In 1923 he retired from politics, then returned to power in a 1926 coup d'état, and ruled Poland as de facto dictator until his death in 1935. Matuszewski, similarly nationalistic and Russophobic, was shocked to discover Polish American passivity, and he set out to hammer American Polonia into an instrument that could reshape US foreign policy.

Matuszewski—as was the case with wartime émigrés in many other fields—teamed up with like-minded Gothamites, in this instance notably Maksymilian Wegrzynek. Born in Poland in 1892, Wegrzynek had emigrated to New York in 1914, just before the outbreak of war. He studied at Columbia University and in 1922 became the publisher of *Nowy Swiat* (*New World*), the Polish-language magazine, whose offices were at 374 Second Avenue (between 21st and 22nd). Wegrzynek was very active in New York Polish American affairs. He served as vice president of the Kosciuszko Foundation (149 East 67th Street), dedicated to providing exchange scholarships and promoting cultural events; its annual fundraising Polka Ball was where debutantes were presented to Polish American Society. He and Matuszewski were also cofounders of New York's Pilsudski Institute of America.

In June 1942, the two men helped organize the National Committee of Americans of Polish Descent, known by its Polish initials as KNAPP, and housed it in the United Charities Building at 105 East 22nd Street. The KNAPP launched a campaign blasting the fraternals for timidity; criticizing the London government-in-exile for even considering negotiating with the Soviets; berated FDR for failing to take a strong stand; appealed to Congress to support a no-compromise policy on the prewar Russo-Polish frontier; and excoriated not only the Soviet government but the Russian people, whom they considered anti-Christian, little better than the Mongol hordes.

Through 1943, KNAPP gained little favor with either American Poles or the Catholic Church; most of Polonia backed the moderate exile government of Premier Stanislaw Mikolajczyk. But after the Red Army pushed the Germans back across the prewar Russo-Polish border in early January 1944 and formally proposed the Curzon Line boundary to the London government, the major organizations assembled in May to create the Polish American Congress, an umbrella organization intended to be overtly political, and which included KNAPPers in positions of authority. This grabbed the Administration's attention. Assistant Secretary of State Breckinridge Long, responsible for relations with domestic groups interested in foreign policy, wrote that the "Polish question is a great problem for us here," as the Polish vote could hold the balance of power in New York and other key states.

In June, FDR agreed to a White House meeting with Premier Mikolajczyk, though on condition that he make no public speeches and "establish no contacts with Polish Americans." Roosevelt gave assurances of sympathy but no promises of intervention. He made clear that the notion Poles could force the Russians to settle on their terms seemed fanciful to him and counseled more flexibility on the boundary question. Despite this closed-door candor, Mikolajczyk told the press he believed Poland could in the end count on Roosevelt, and the president breathed easier.

Then in late July the Russians advanced deeper into Eastern Poland, liberating Lublin (and the nearby Nazi death camp of Majdanek—the first such to be freed). On August 1 they established in Lublin the headquarters of a newly constituted provisional government, to rival the one in London. On the same day, the Polish Home Army, the London government's military arm, launched an uprising in Warsaw to liberate the city and enhance the likelihood of winning an independent Poland. The Red Army, which had arrived at the eastern suburbs of Warsaw, refused to aid the insurrection, or to cooperate with US and English efforts to do so, partly because they had their hands full with German resistance on nearby fronts, and partly because defeat of the Polish military would weaken the London Poles. As a result, during over two months of savage fighting, 200,000 Poles died, the great majority Warsaw citizens.

It was in this context that Republicans entered the fray, beginning with a series of targeted appeals to Polish Americans and culminating with a surprise appearance by governor and presidential candidate Dewey at New York City's Pulaski Day parade. On October 8, 1944, as an estimated quarter million looked on, 45,000 Polish Americans marched up Fifth Avenue, many in national costumes, many carrying Polish flags with mourning strips affixed to protest the recent slaughter in Warsaw. Dewey spent three hours on the reviewing stand with the Polish ambassador, and he told the Polish American Congress chief that if elected he would firmly oppose Soviet appetites in Eastern Europe, unlike Roosevelt, whose passivity, he said, revolted him. Wegrzynek, a Republican, backed Dewey in his *Nowy Swiat*.

Herald Tribune columnist Walter Lippmann probably voiced what FDR was thinking when he came out against Dewey, in part because of the Republican's effort to capitalize on the Polish issue (a move Lippmann figured was instigated by Dewey's secretary of state-in-waiting, John Foster Dulles). Encouraging the hard-line anti-Soviet faction just at the moment when delicate negotiations were under way between the Russians and Mikolajczyk, was not, Lippmann believed, in Poland's best interest, much less that of the United States.

This was not Roosevelt's public response. Rather, Senator Wagner (also running for re-election) was immediately authorized to tell the Pulaski Day dinner at the Waldorf Astoria that FDR intended to protect the independence and boundaries of Poland. Three days later the president invited a delegation of Polish activists to the White House. Posing with them for photographers in front of a giant map of Poland, its prewar boundaries blatantly intact, FDR again assured them of his adherence to the Atlantic Charter and promised they would be "treated justly at the peace conference." When pushed for specifics he replied evasively only that he wanted Poland reconstituted as "a great nation." But this was enough to win him the endorsement of the Polish American Congress chief (though not the militants) just days before the election. Roosevelt had defused the potential political crisis. He had also created a potentially bigger one. If, after the election, he acknowledged in public the deals to which he had privately agreed at Teheran, he would be vulnerable to being charged with betraying the Poles, which might have incalculable ramifications.

161

Dr. New Deal: Back in the Saddle?

With the collapse of the Polish gambit, the last card Dewey could play was the president's health. "Let's not be squeamish," said the Deweyite *New York Sun*, "six presidents have died in office." It was a valid concern—more than Dewey knew—though the whispering campaigns that had the president dying of cancer or syphilis were off the mark. FDR responded by taking to the hustings in a series of campaign swings dedicated to proving he retained the vigor and vitality the job required. These culminated with a grueling fifty-one-mile motorcade through all five boroughs of New York.

The weather was rotten that Saturday, October 21—a cold wind-lashed rain, the tail end of a northeast storm—but Roosevelt insisted on opening the canvas top of his green Packard so he could wave to the enormous crowds. Toasty at first under a fur robe and heavy Navy cape and a special heater at his legs, he was nevertheless soon drenched, the rain pouring down his cheeks, but he continued to radiate heartiness throughout the five-hour ordeal. Starting from the Brooklyn Army Base the procession drove to the Navy Yard, and then to Ebbets Field, where he hobbled through the rain to a lectern behind second base and urged Senator Wagner's re-election, to a thunderous ovation. After a stop at the Coast Guard's motor pool, where he was lifted from the car, given a brandy, a rubdown, and a dry suit, it was on to Brownsville, then up the Interborough to Queens, over the Triborough to the Bronx (swapping borough presidents at each frontier), where after a pause at the Kingsbridge Armory to review the Waves it was over the Macombs Dam Bridge to Harlem and down Broadway to and through the tumultuous garment workers' district with its huge, sodden, but exuberant crowds (3,500 per block; the police estimated an overall turnout of three million). The party arrived mid-afternoon at Eleanor's apartment at 29 Washington Square West. Though she had leased it two years earlier, for the couple to use as their base in the city after Franklin left the White House, it was the first time he'd seen it. In the Library overlooking the Square, he knocked back three bourbons, had a hot bath and nap, then it was on to the

Waldorf and an evening speech before 2,000 members of the Foreign Policy Association, after which an elevator to the basement lowered him to the waiting presidential train, which chugged up the New York Central tracks to Hyde Park. By the next day, several of the Secret Service had come down with colds, but FDR felt fine. He had, so it seemed, put to bed claims he lacked the stamina for another four years.

Roosevelt won by 25.6 million votes to Dewey's 22.0 million (53.4 percent to 45.9 percent), the closest margin in a presidential race since Wilson beat Hughes in 1916. In the Electoral College, however, the margin was an ample 432–99, with FDR carrying thirty-six of the forty-eight states, including all those in the South, despite a huge drop-off in his popular vote below the Mason-Dixon line, which accounted for much of the decline in his total margin of victory. At the same time, the congressional slide was reversed, with the Democratic Party gaining a total of twenty seats from Republican and other parties (courtesy in part of a newly facilitated soldiers' vote).

Most people, starting with FDR, gave substantial credit to Hillman and his PAC, which had registered millions of voters and gotten them to the polls on time. And while organized labor had not been able to dethrone the reigning coalition of Republicans and Southern Democrats who continued to rule Congress, it had given a significant boost to the liberal wing of the Democratic Party, though by doing so it all but foreclosed the possibility of establishing a national independent labor party in the United States.

Nowhere had the PAC's contribution to victory been more apparent than in New York, where independent parties remained a factor. Despite the Republican Party's hopes (and their reason for giving him the nomination), Dewey lost his home state by 316,000 votes (Willkie had done better four years earlier). He did win Upstate and in key suburban counties, but his plurality was erased by Roosevelt's thumping win in New York City, which gave him a plurality of 718,459.

The two liberal labor parties, spurred on by the CIO-PAC, were essential components of Roosevelt's victory. Statewide, the Republicans' 47.5 percent showing had overmatched the Democrats' 39.4 percent; only when the American Labor Party's 7.9 percent and the Liberal Party's 5.2 percent were added in did the coalition come up with the winning 52.5 percent for Roosevelt. Despite the intramural warfare between the two liberal parties, or perhaps because of it, their combined vote total was higher than ever, and New York was the only state in which FDR's margin of success increased in 1944.

Ethnically, Jews were indispensable to this reinvigorated liberalism. FDR got 87 percent of the vote in heavily Jewish districts (Borough Park handed him 96 percent), delivering 55 percent of it on the Democratic Party line, and 45 percent on either the ALP or LP lines. (The LP did better slightly better in middle- and upper-middle-class Jewish neighborhoods, like the Upper West Side and Washington Heights, the Grand Concourse and West Bronx, East Flatbush, Bensonhurst, and Borough Park. The ALP did somewhat better in lower- and lower-middle-class neighborhoods such as Brownsville, Coney Island, Morrisania, Hunt's Point, and Crotona Park.) The ALP also did well in African American areas—and helped Adam Clayton Powell Jr. win his seat in the House—and in El Barrio, where Marcantonio had galvanized Puerto Ricans.

The election revealed that Gotham's white Catholics were continuing to drift away from New Deal-ish positions. The Irish had given FDR 56 percent of their votes in 1940 but slumped to 49.5 percent in 1944. And Italians gave only 41 percent to the president (despite Generoso Pope's best efforts), and 80 percent of those were delivered on the Democratic line rather than one of the explicitly liberal parties. Dewey also did portentously well in comfortable suburban or quasi-suburban areas, carrying Queens, Staten Island, Nassau, Suffolk, and Westchester, where "Modern Republicanism's" nicely calibrated detente with the New Deal appealed to voters happy to keep benefits they'd gained but unwilling to extend them to those less fortunate.

Yet all in all, Roosevelt's re-election seemed a momentous victory for New Deal liberals—Hillman called it "our Battle of Britain, our Stalingrad"—and they moved quickly to lock in their gains legislatively. In January 1945, liberal Democrats, led by the re-elected Senator Wagner, introduced a Full Employment bill, modeled on proposals of the now-entombed National Resources Planning Board. The bill (echoing FDR's Economic Bill of Rights) proclaimed the *right* to useful, regular, and full-time employment of all Americans who were "able to work and seeking work" and affirmed it was the responsibility of government to guarantee that right. It proposed creation of a permanent planning mechanism that would create an annual "National Production and Employment Budget." The budget would estimate the amount of private and public investment needed to provide full employment, and while encouraging the former would, if necessary, underwrite the latter, countering economic downturns through governmental spending initiatives. If passed as written, the law would in effect institutionalize the wartime-state management of the economy, making Keynesian social planning public policy. The bill—backed as it was by the AFL, CIO, NAACP, the UDA, religious groups, and even Southern politicos (though only if shorn of its "fair employment" provisions)—seemed, in early 1945, destined to become law. Things looked brighter too for the long-stalled Wagner-Murray-Dingell bill, reintroduced in 1945, which would expand existing Social Security programs for those unable to work.

It was true that the right-wing, free enterprise crowd said, "no way." The National Association of Manufacturers and the US Chamber of Commerce and various banking circles were appalled. Warning that the bill portended a socialist future and insisting that the private sector could unaided keep the economy purring, it revved up for an intensive contra lobbying effort.

The corporate liberals in the Committee for Economic Development tried to seize the middle ground. Their leading theoretician, Beardsley Ruml, supported the bill, agreeing that government should affirm its interest in maintaining maximum employment, should set up research machinery to monitor the state of the economy, and should prepare federal public works programs to help stabilize the economy. Opposition to the Full Employment bill "seems to be based entirely on fears and straw men," said Ruml. "Nothing could be more misleading" than charges that the bill was "an attempt to introduce into the American scene the ideas of Sir William Beveridge, or was a plot to fasten a European State socialism on an unsuspecting America."

But—and it was a big "but"—he was not happy with the notion of establishing a *right* to full employment. He thought it a "singularly inept and unnecessary provocative formulation." He preferred a simple assertion that "involuntary unemployment" was a matter of national concern in that it menaced the foundations of a free democratic state. There were other "buts": Ruml worried that the bill tried to do too much, that it might lead to "vast improvised expenditures, unwholesome centralization of power, and ultimately the dependence of a substantial segment...on Federal largess for its employment." And while public works might in a pinch prove necessary, really, the best way to stimulate full employment was by cutting taxes. So the corporate liberal sector favored passage, though only of a much watered down commitment.

As the war entered its last lap, it was not clear which vision of the country's future would prevail. Those planning the future of New York itself could be forgiven for assuming that it was now better-than-even money that some version of New Deal liberalism would retain command of the ship of state and continue to provide the resources upon which Gotham had constructed—and could now expand—the rudiments of a social democratic city.

PLANNING THE POSTWAR WORLD

Facing north over the construction site for the United Nations permanent headquarters. (United Nations Photo)

162

New World A-Comin'

Long before the war was over—in some cases before it even started—a diverse array of New Yorkers were thinking hard about the postwar world. It seemed obvious to many that the future would be profoundly different from the past. The global cataclysm had cracked open customary social, political, economic, and cultural arrangements, fracturing the status quo. At the same time, the successful prosecution of the conflict itself—by 1943 victory seemed a foregone conclusion—heightened people's belief in their ability to alter the course of history. Out of the horrors of combat a tremendous optimism bloomed. In this plastic moment, with the future seemingly up for grabs, everyone rushed to lay down their markers on how tomorrow should look.

This eagerness manifested itself in an explosion of planning. From 1939 on, proposals, projects, and programs tumbled out of research institutes, think tanks, business associations, government agencies, union conventions, religious conferences, racial assemblies, and neighborhood organizations. So many players stuck their oar in the future that scorecards were needed to tell them apart. The Twentieth Century Fund's *Postwar Planning in the United States* for 1942 listed 105 public and private agencies pondering postwar reconstruction; the 1943 edition cited 137; by 1944 there were nearly 200. An even more comprehensive directory issued by the Council on Foreign Relations in 1942 found that 300 organizations were busy sorting out the postwar world.

Plans were promulgated in pamphlets, newspaper stories, magazine articles, town hall symposia, radio forums, conference manifestos, academic studies, government reports, and a torrent of books aimed at a popular audience. Exactly how hot the future was became dazzlingly clear to New York publishers when Simon and Schuster brought out Wendell Willkie's *One World* in 1943. Priced at a dollar, the initial 40,000 print run of the former presidential candidate's visionary musings sold out in two days flat; 200,000 flew out of bookstores in the first week; and two printing presses ran round the clock keeping up with a demand that would gobble up 2,000,000 hardbacks by the end of the book's first year. And while such a volume and velocity of sales was unprecedented, and would remain unmatched during the war, the industry, seeking lightning's second strike, spewed out titles from experts and novices, the famous and the obscure alike. Knopf offered Carl Becker's *How New Will the Better World Be? A Discussion of Post-war Reconstruction*; Macmillan entered the lists with Stuart Chevalier's *War's End and After: An Informal Discussion of the Problems of a Post-war World*; and Harper & Brothers essayed Cleveland Rodgers's *New York Plans for the Future* and Maxwell Stewart's *Building for Peace at Home and Abroad*.

Not every future-oriented volume dwelt on a lofty plane. There were also how-to books like Richard Hart's *Marching Home; Complete War and Post-war Handbook for Service Men and Families*; volumes that drooled over consumption to come, like Norman Carlisle and Frank Latham's *Miracles Ahead! Better Living in the Postwar World*; and responses to the planning craze itself, ranging from Otto Ehrlich's *Planning Jobs and Jobs in Planning* to a spoof by cartoonist Rube Goldberg—the imagineer of contraptions that performed simple tasks in convoluted ways—the cover of whose *Plan for the Post-War World* (1944) was bannered: "Look at the practically perfect shape of things to come!"

Readers overwhelmed by this inundation of texts could turn to aids that helped them navigate: abstracts, digests, bibliographies, surveys, manuals, reading lists, discussion guides, and yet more books, like *Church Literature of Post-War Planning*, assembled by the Inter-Council Committee on Postwar Planning, or *Plans for a Post-war World*, put together by compiler extraordinaire Julia Johnsen for the H. W. Wilson Company's Reference Shelf series.

The great bulk of these plans were fashioned in New York. Not that Gotham was alone in its frenzied preoccupation with the future. Washington was a major player, home to the White House, Congress, and specialized entities like the National Resources Planning Board and the Committee for Economic Development—though the former was stocked with men who had cut their planning teeth in Gotham, and the latter, not long after its DC founding, relocated to New York because (said its leader) "we can accomplish much more in this city." Economists from Harvard, political scientists from Chicago, lawyers and officials in Washington, politicians from the South, and industrialists from the Midwest were among the many who would make important contributions to the conversation. The fountainhead was Gotham.

As so often, and in so many areas, New York pioneered in the present because it had in the past. The city—partial to purposiveness since the grid and the Erie Canal—had inherited a culture and infrastructure of planning. As a result, the social and foreign-policy complexes that had hammered out the New Deal and fashioned the nation's war aims now segued comfortably into designing the postwar era. Gotham's penchant for planning was rooted in something more substantial than a handed-down sensibility. It was sustained by the interests and inclinations of the tremendous number of commercial, civic, and political organizations that made their home in the city of headquarters.

At the apex of the metropolitan and national economies, the city's great corporations, banks, and law firms—capable of concerted as well as competitive behavior—underwrote the great macro-policy think tanks. These included the flourishing and long-established Council on Foreign Relations (CFR, at 45 East 65th Street), whose purview was planetary; and burgeoning newcomers like the transplanted Committee for Economic Development (CED, at 285 Madison, near Grand Central), which enlisted virtually the entire corporate and financial elite in an effort to recapture the national planning initiative from New Dealers.

Gotham was also home to a multitude of less grand-scale planners—more tacticians than strategists—such as the host of trade associations that undertook wartime studies of their sector, then recommended postwar courses of action to their constituent companies.

Thus the National Foreign Trade Council (26 Beaver Street) collaborated with the American Maritime Council (nearby at 11 Broadway) in surveying the war's impact on shipping and shipbuilding and suggesting appropriate next steps. The National Association of Manufacturers (14 West 49th) set up a Post-War Problems Committee that brought out both cheery tracts like *Today Production for Victory, Tomorrow Opportunity, Jobs, Freedom* and more pragmatic pamphlets like *Guide to Postwar Product Development* and *Guide to Postwar Sales Planning*. The Commerce and Industry Association of New York (headquartered in the Woolworth Building across from City Hall Park) had a Post-war Planning Committee that issued the cautiously titled *Program to Aid the War Effort That Should Make for Post-war Employment*. And the country's grocers, grouped in the National Retail Dry Goods Association (101 West 31st), formed a Retailers' Committee for Post-War Economy that issued compendia of suggestions like *Planning the Store of Tomorrow*.

Farther down the business chain came ever more narrowly focused organizations, like the National Electrical Manufacturers Association (155 East 44th Street), whose Postwar Planning Committee promoted an expanding power grid; and the fashion industry, which, still plotting to replace Paris, collaborated on a 1944 mayoral report: *The World Fashion Center, New York City's Post War Business Project No. 1*. There was also the Association of Cotton Textile Merchants of New York (40 Worth Street), which asked *Shall Post-war Markets for Cotton Textiles Expand or Contract?*; the Institute of Carpet Manufacturers of America (soon to relocate to the Empire State Building), which issued a *Post War Plan of an Industry Important to Your Store*; and the Association of American Soap and Glycerine Products (381 Fourth Avenue)—whose ranks included Colgate-Palmolive-Peet, Lever Brothers, and Procter & Gamble—which proposed a postwar push for cleanliness.

The nation's professionals, headquartered in New York, were equally future-facing. The American Institute of Accountants (in their own building at 13 East 41st) brought out *Accounting Problems in War Contract Termination, Taxes, and Postwar Planning*. The American Society of Mechanical Engineers and the American Society of Civil Engineers (both housed in the dedicated Engineering Societies Building at 29 West 39th) set their Postwar Planning Committees to proposing projects. Educators moved the fastest: the Progressive Education Association (221 West 57th) set up its postwar committee a month before Pearl Harbor; the Association of American Colleges (19 West 44th) established a Commission on Colleges and Post-War Problems, also in 1941; and Columbia Teachers College's Commission on Postwar Training and Adjustment issued a report on *The Educational Problems of Returning Soldiers, Sailors, and Displaced War Industry Workers* in 1942, when the objects of their concern had only just been drafted or hired.

New York was also home to a plethora of not-for-profit institutions that focused on tomorrow, starting with the state and city governments. In 1942, Albany's Temporary State Commission for Post-war Public Works Planning issued, not surprisingly, *Postwar Public Works Planning in New York State*, and in the same year Gotham's City Planning Commission promulgated its *Proposed Post-war Works Program*. Veteran professional planning groups like the Regional Plan Association weighed in with studies like the *Economic Status of the New York Metropolitan Region in 1944*, which sought to discern present trends to project.

Local leftists and liberals—inveterate planners—were avid contributors to the conversation. The city's socialists were swiftest off the mark. The day after Pearl Harbor, Norman Thomas dissolved his Keep America Out of War Congress, then phoenixed from its ashes the Post War World Council (operating from the same stand at 112 East 19th Street, near Union Square); its vigorous publications program was soon issuing works like Thomas's *What is Our*

Destiny? Communist chief Earl Browder offered his thoughts on the future in *The Road Ahead to Victory and Lasting Peace.* The liberal Twentieth Century Fund (330 West 42nd) issued a series of popular books by Stuart Chase under the rubric *When the War Ends*, and Freda Kirchwey, *Nation* editor (and wife of the Fund's director, Evans Clark), featured planning pieces in the magazine, her own 1944 *Program of Action* being a notable one.

The country's major religious denominations chimed in from their New York headquarters. The Federal Council of Churches (297 Fourth Avenue) established a Commission to Study the Bases of a Just and Durable Peace. The American Jewish Committee (386 Fourth Avenue) set up a Research Institute on Peace and Post-war Problems (which issued a pamphlet series on *Jews and the Post-war World*). The American Jewish Congress and World Jewish Congress set up a parallel Institute of Jewish Affairs (330 West 42nd), chaired by Horace Kallen, which among other things studied the postwar rehabilitation and resettlement of refugees. The National Conference of Christians and Jews (300 Fourth Avenue) sponsored conferences like Religion and the Post-War World. And Archbishop and Military Vicar Francis Spellman wrote on the spiritual prerequisites for lasting peace in *The Road to Victory*.

In addition, the many metropolitan advocacy organizations that focused on issues of gender, race, or class made significant interventions. Among these were the Committee on the Participation of Women in Post War Planning (itself an umbrella outfit covering a dozen national women's groups); the Planned Parenthood Federation of America (501 Madison), which in 1945 issued *Planning to Have a Baby?*; the National Urban League, which brought out studies like *Racial Aspects of Reconversion*; and union confederations like the Congress of Industrial Organizations, which produced *Jobs for All after the War*, and the American Federation of Labor, whose Post-War Planning Committee issued a *Post-war Program* in December 1942.

Finally, ready with the resources to sustain such initiatives, were the city's great foundations, notably such treasuries of accumulated capital as the Rockefeller Foundation and the Carnegie Corporation of New York, the Carnegie Endowment for International Peace, and others in the Carnegie family of funding agencies.

For all this welter of plans and programs, put forward with sunny optimism by businessmen and Four Freedoms proponents alike, a dark plume of pessimism, even panic, underlay much of the frantic attention paid to tomorrow. There were, after all, two great question marks hovering over the pending postwar order, queries so conducive to pessimistic answers that they might well have been called the Two Fears. Everyone knew that only war had ended the Depression: mightn't peace usher in a return of hard times? And everyone recalled how swiftly postwar dreams of a peaceful world had given way to renascent nationalism and another conflagration: mightn't World War III be lurking just around the corner? These were not matters that could safely be left to tomorrow to address. Looming on the horizon were some certain sure events. War orders would end, troops would march home, and these in turn would lay on the table two inescapable and interlinked issues: how to reorganize the economy and how to ward off another cataclysm. It was all but universally agreed that such momentous matters could not be safely left to the "free market"—businessmen were amongst the busiest of planners—or to those who would muddle through with politics-as-usual. The stakes were too high. Hence the rush to draw up road maps. Yet the road ahead was full of forks, and there were serious differences of opinion between (and within) the business and the New Dealer camps about which path to take.

New Yorkers were centrally involved in the debates on reshaping the national and metropolitan orders and constructing a new world order. When businessmen and New Dealers saw eye to eye on a project, plans morphed into reality with relative ease and speed. When they adopted different stances—as in contouring a new global economy—the road got bumpy. And when it came to settling the fate of empires and colonies, a tumultuous debate erupted, one that flowed far beyond the elite planners conclaved in their business boardrooms and liberal think tanks. Indeed, it might spill out of Lower and Midtown Manhattan into far-flung Gotham neighborhoods where residents were personally interested in the outcome. By war's end, the postwar global planning process would have drawn in a potpourri of New Yorkers who were no longer drawn exclusively from prewar ranks (Irish, Italians, Germans, Jews) but now included those of Indian, Chinese, or Puerto Rican descent. The initial encounter, however, would be a veritable slugfest between the two principal Anglo-economies, that of Oil and Aviation.

163

An Empire of Free Trade

In the Council on Foreign Relations (CFR) reading of recent history, while the Depression had been a disaster, the *responses* to it had been demonstrably worse. Countries had opted for autarchic defense tactics (hunkering down behind tariff battlements) and bugger-thy-competitor policies (like repeated currency devaluations). Skirmishes had escalated into all-out economic warfare that presaged, and galvanized, its military equivalent.

The key to forestalling depressions and their disastrous remedies—in the opinion of the CFR—was free trade. The planners were emphatically clear that the "economy of the United States is geared to the export of certain manufactured and agricultural products, and the import of numerous raw materials and foodstuffs." Despite the enormous size of the country's internal market, autarchy was not an option, even with access to the markets and resources of the Western Hemisphere. That was why the CFR had counseled going to war—to forcibly turn back Germany and Japan's efforts at locking up Europe and Asia. And that is why they argued it would be equally essential, after victory, to throw doors open all over the world, eliminating any barriers blocking access to markets and raw materials and lifting any constraints on the free flow of investment capital.

When Gotham's corporate planners surveyed possible postwar obstacles to this vision of flux and flow, most seemed superable.

Tariffs had been a major problem in the thirties, primarily those passed by the US itself (at the insistence of manufacturers). Such import taxes had triggered tit-for-tat retaliation abroad, which hindered exports. The Depression had worked a sea change among corporate managers in the formerly protectionist heartland. They now recognized that access to foreign markets was essential if they themselves were to avoid another catastrophe. Some holdouts remained. The American Tariff League (19 West 44th Street), which had been promoting protective barriers since the 1880s, branded "free trade" a peril, and warned (in 1943) of a postwar flood of imports that would undermine "our wage and living standards." Gotham's dominant business interests were, however, adamantly opposed to trade restrictions—a New York state of mind since the seventeenth century—and most of the country was now prepared to follow their lead.

International monetary instability was another potential problem. A return to competitive currency devaluations and mutually exclusive currency blocs would be disastrous. The CFR seemed confident that a new financial architecture could be designed and built, one that would provide predictability through fixed exchange rates and free convertibility of currencies. Perhaps an international monetary fund could be set up to provide loans to countries with temporary balance-of-payments problems; then they would not have to resort to currency depreciation or tariff barriers. More orthodox New York banking circles (led by Chase Bank's Winthrop Aldrich) preferred a return to the gold standard, but this was an intramural dispute that could be sorted out.

There was, however, one obstacle looming on the postwar horizon that was not so easily dislodged or finessed—the empires of Europe, into whose vast territories US access was delimited or denied. While French, Dutch, Portuguese, and Belgian possessions were matters of some concern, and while there was still a war to be won before Germany's (and Japan's) dominions were reopened to all comers, the preeminent roadblock on the path to a new world order—the door that remained most obstinately closed—was the empire of Great Britain, our major wartime ally.

New York commerce and capital had long been bumping heads with British rivals—and losing as often as winning, given England's overweening military and financial power. The war, however, strengthened the US economy tremendously, while badly undercutting that of besieged Britain. As a result, the determination of Gotham's merchants, manufacturers, and bankers to restructure global economic relationships was heightened by fears of another depression, and by new possibilities opened up by the war itself.

The aviation industry was a case in point. In 1938, Great Britain had conducted half of all international aviation traffic, the US only one-ninth. England's premier carrier, Imperial Airways, which linked the British Empire to the mother country, outpaced New York's Pan American Airways, which dominated the Western hemisphere and spanned both Atlantic and Pacific. The war, however, severed Imperial's routes to the Mediterranean and Far East, and the company's resources, diverted to the anti-Nazi effort, were badly overstretched. In 1941, when the British desperately needed an air-transport service to supply troops in the Middle East, the British Overseas Airways Corporation (BOAC)—into which Imperial was folded after 1939—tried and failed to establish one across British West Africa. At which point Juan Trippe proposed to Churchill that Pan Am be hired to do the job of constructing airfields and running the resulting network. Despite deep reluctance in his cabinet at allowing the US a toehold in their empire, Churchill, back to the wall, agreed.

When the US entered the war, it agreed to furnish Britain with transport aircraft, allowing it to focus on developing war planes. A sensible wartime division of labor, this also allowed American industry to leap ahead in the development, production, and operation of airliners that could become the backbone of a postwar commercial fleet. Fueled by government funding that underwrote construction of 17,000 aircraft, and marshaled by the Air Transport Command, US carriers, Pan Am foremost, all but eclipsed their competitors. By 1943, Britain was down to 12 percent of all international traffic, while the US was flying high with 72 percent.

The British had an ace up their sleeves: the enormous land mass of the British Empire. The Americans, to solidify their routes to Asia and Africa, needed to obtain landing and flyover rights from the British. Using their imperial holdings as leverage, the British proposed formation of a postwar international authority that would regulate rates and scheduling. Such a body, by imposing on Pan Am pricing comparable to BOAC's, would neutralize the

US company's technological and financial superiority and give English aviation a chance to catch up. Assistant Secretary of State Berle countered with an "open skies" proposal that would allow any airline to fly (and land) anywhere on Earth—secure in the knowledge that in the resulting free-for-all, US planes and money would dominate the world's air routes. The ensuing dogfight drew in Roosevelt and Churchill, with the former hinting to the latter that England's Lend Lease financing might be jeopardized if he wasn't more amenable, but the British bulldog held out, and stalemate ensued.

Still, US companies had begun dreaming of a limitless postwar future; American Airlines (which had transferred its national headquarters from Chicago to New York's La Guardia airport in 1939) began running ads featuring air maps of a world without borders.

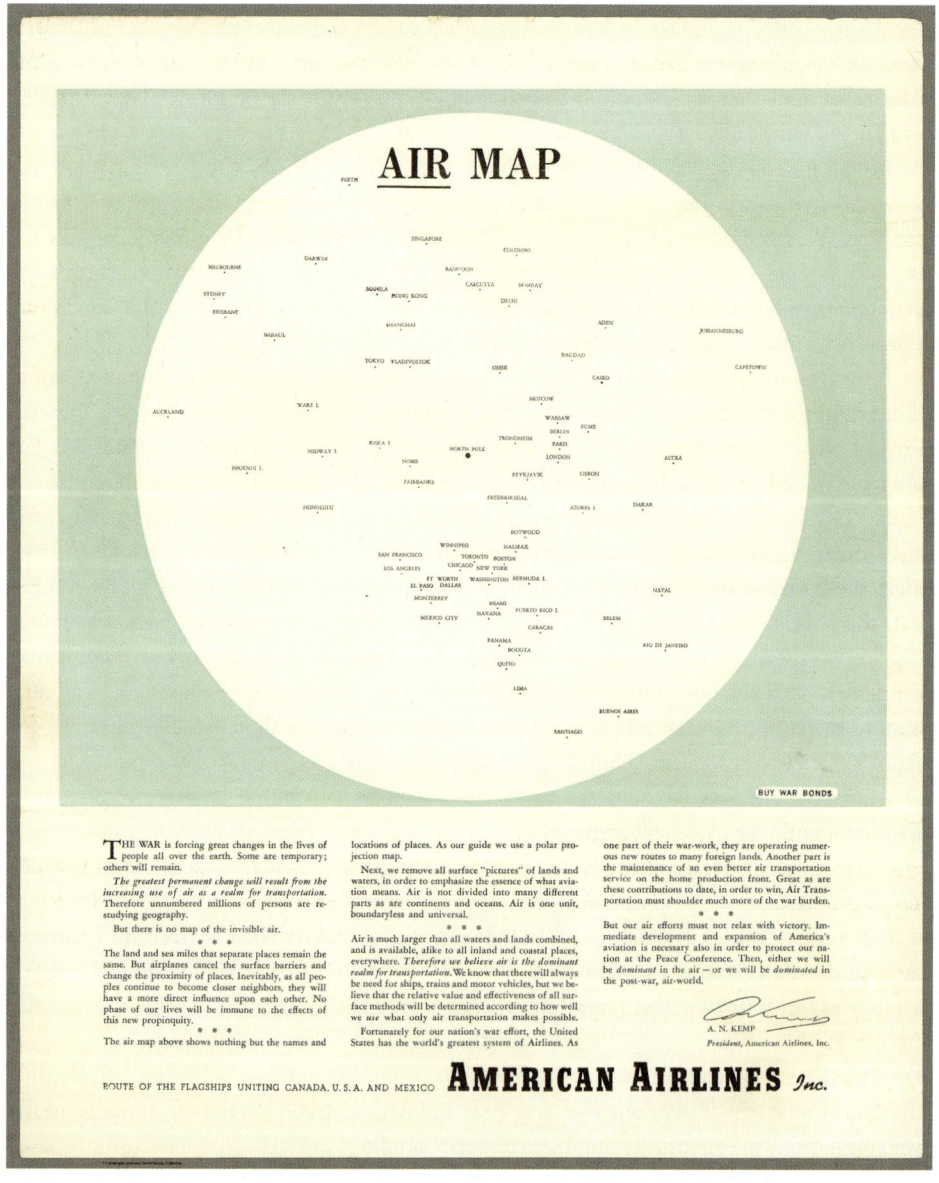

American Airlines war bonds advertisement, 1943, depicting only major cities, with no land nor water. (PD-US-not renewed)

The British Empire was equally obstructionist, from the New York point of view, in an even more vital and potentially super-profitable industry—the oil business.

The war forced a new appreciation of oil's importance as a critical strategic commodity. For New Yorkers, the degree to which a mechanized military had become completely dependent on oil products had been brought home, all too literally, by the 1941–42 U-boat attacks on oil tankers at their harbor's mouth, a campaign that nearly knocked Britain out of the war. Similarly, in 1944, Allied bombers pinpointing Nazi-controlled refineries were able to paralyze German panzers and ground the Luftwaffe; and when Patton's Third Army dashed across Europe that fall, outracing supply lines, it literally ran out of gas.

So also, some feared, had the US oil industry. Mobilized and coordinated by the government, it had produced almost 90 percent of the oil used by the Allies, though in the process domestic reserves had been badly depleted. At the same time, auxiliary hemispheric sources of supply had become more expensive, after Mexico's expropriation of US oil holdings in 1938 and Venezuela's successful exaction of a fifty-fifty profit split in 1943. That was why the oil industry, led by Gotham behemoths Standard Oil of New Jersey (ensconced in Rockefeller Center) and Standard Oil of New York (still downtown at 26 Broadway), had been focusing intently on the Middle East—hitherto a chiefly British preserve.

England's Anglo-Persian Oil Company had monopolized Iranian supplies ever since the first big strike in 1908. And before the First World War, the British and other Europeans had moved quickly to lock up rights to neighboring Mesopotamia, via the jointly owned Turkish Petroleum Company (after 1929, the Iraq Petroleum Company). Vigorous US demands that the Iraqi door be pried open for American capital did win a 23.75 percent share for a syndicate of US firms, primarily Jersey Standard and SOCONY. Once in, however, the two giants locked the door behind them and joined the Europeans in an exclusive cartel. To ward off overproduction, members pledged (in the 1928 Red Line Agreement) not to independently seek new oil sources in a vast area that included most of the Arabian Peninsula (excluding Kuwait, a British protectorate).

This left smaller American companies, like Standard Oil of California (SOCAL), free to cut independent deals. In 1933 SOCAL won a concession from Saudi Arabia's Ibn Saud to develop his kingdom's oil resources. In 1936, the California company partnered with another non–New York independent, the Texas Oil Company (Texaco), in a joint venture of exploration. In 1938 they discovered an ocean of oil beneath the desert outside Dhahran, Saudi Arabia, on the Persian Gulf. By 1940, the SOCAL/Texaco subsidiary (soon to be called the Arabian-American Oil Company, or Aramco) was pumping five million barrels a year. By 1945, Saudi output was approaching that of Iraq, and Britain's hitherto overwhelming dominance was under serious challenge.

So, too, was the status of the New York "majors," Jersey Standard and SOCONY, which were prohibited by the Red Line Agreement from entering Saudi Arabia. In May 1945, the oil-rich Aramco independents—needing $200 million to build a Trans-Arabian Pipeline to carry Saudi crude from the Persian Gulf to the Mediterranean coast—offered the capital-rich Gotham giants a piece of Aramco in exchange for financing. The two firms now began a full-court press to extricate themselves from the ties that bound them, in the process rediscovering a principled commitment to open doors.

The British considered such free-market rhetoric to be verbal sheep's clothing disguising wolfish intentions. Already in 1944 Churchill had written Roosevelt: "There is apprehension in some quarters here that the United States has a desire to deprive us of our oil assets in the Middle East," adding, bluntly, that some feel "we are being hustled." Roosevelt denied the

US was "making sheep's eyes at your oil fields in Iraq or Iran" but said he himself was "disturbed about the rumor that the British wish to horn in on Saudi Arabian oil reserves." Churchill shot back that "we have no thought of trying to horn in upon your interests or property in Saudi Arabia" but warned that Britain "will not be deprived of anything that belongs to her . . . so long as your humble servant is entrusted with the conduct of her affairs." For the moment, another stalemate.

Clearly, Franklin Roosevelt was not opposed to expanding the reach of US corporations in the postwar world, from the skies above to the oil below. He, too, favored dismantling European empires because they hampered American profits and sinned against free trade, the world's best hope for peace and prosperity. FDR also opposed traditional colonialism on grounds not dreamt of in the business-class philosophy, grounds rooted in political principles rather than commercial ethics.

In drafting the 1941 Atlantic Charter, FDR insisted on its endorsing "the right of all peoples to choose the form of government under which they will live." The document underscored the Allies' "wish to see sovereign rights and self-government restored to those who have been forcibly deprived of them." Churchill had tried hard to strike out or water down sentences that so frontally challenged Britain's imperial prerogatives. Having failed to do so, he simply ignored them, claiming they applied only to victims of German or Japanese expansion. Roosevelt insisted he had called for decolonization throughout the world, and the now-official war aim resonated far and wide.

The liberal community, heavily concentrated in New York, helped spread the anticolonial gospel. On May 8, 1942, Vice President Henry Wallace was invited to address a meeting at the Commodore Hotel of the Free World Association (another liberal internationalist group directed by Clark Eichelberger and run out of 8 West 40th). Wallace argued that, *pace* Henry Luce, the war would not, and should not, usher in an "American Century" but rather a "century of the common man," in which there "must be neither military nor economic imperialism," and "no nation will have the God-given right to exploit other nations." Wendell Willkie followed suit in arguing that "a true world outlook is incompatible with a foreign imperialism, no matter how high-minded the governing country." Mayor La Guardia seconded the president's insistence that the Atlantic Charter, *pace* Churchill, "guaranteed the right of self-determination" to colonies which "have had little or no say in their own destiny, in their own government."

If this version of decolonization unsettled the business community, conceived as it was from the vantage point of the colonized, Roosevelt's collateral notion of how to develop lands liberated from European overlords—by applying New Deal principles and programs on a global scale—struck them as truly appalling. FDR had included in the Atlantic Charter a call for a postwar order "which will afford assurance that all the men in all the lands may live out their lives in freedom from fear and want." Worse, the document got down to specifics, proposing "the fullest collaboration between all nations in the economic field with the object of securing, for all, improved labor standards, economic advancement and social security."

Here, too, FDR's vision was fleshed out by other liberals. Wallace's "century of the common man" would feature full employment, internationally agreed-upon workplace conditions, and a decent standard of living for all (with every child on earth guaranteed at least a pint of milk a day). To achieve this happy state of affairs, Wallace proposed a global investment fund to develop infrastructure in the postcolonial world and rebuild war-torn Europe, drawing inspiration from such initiatives as the Tennessee Valley Authority, the Rural Electrification Administration, and the Reconstruction Finance Corporation. One critic got it exactly right when he complained that Wallace wanted "to extend the New Deal throughout the earth"—and many New York liberals, like *Nation* editor Freda Kirchwey, began to call forthrightly for "a New Deal for the World."

Resistance to all this would be fierce and come from many directions, not just 10 Downing Street. Much of the criticism was predictable—a matter of imperial interests defending profits they'd been extracting for decades if not centuries—and this kind of attack New Dealers were well equipped to contest from years of battling Wall Street bankers. Yet the assault on colonialism challenged interests that were not simply economic. Colonizers were nearly always white, the colonized nearly always people of color; and the sides were divided on lines of race as well as class. This made decolonization a heavier lift for liberals. Upsetting the global racial status quo meant doing so inside the United States as well and thus alienating domestic powers—like southern senators and cotton exporters—who hadn't minded critiquing foreign empires on free trade grounds.

Some white liberals—those who had long battled domestic racism—simply plowed ahead, adopting the attack on overseas colonialism as a cognate struggle. Wendell Willkie declared in *One World* that Americans "have practiced within our own boundaries something that amounts to race imperialism." "The attitude of the white citizens of this country toward the Negroes," he explained, "has undeniably had some of the unlovely characteristics of an alien imperialism—a smug racial superiority, a willingness to exploit an unprotected people." Eleanor Roosevelt stressed the connection between colonialism and racism—and the need to overturn both—with clarity and ferocity. Few of her peers, and certainly not her husband, were prepared to tell a southern racist (as she did in 1942) that white Americans had better face up to the fact that "unrest among the colored people is part of the world revolution of all colored peoples against the domination of white people." Much less to proclaim boldly, as she had in a September 1941 speech, that "a wind is rising throughout the world of free men everywhere, and they will not be kept in bondage."

ER was as exceptional in this regard as in so many others. It was rare to find liberals as prepared as she to unblinkingly confront the commonalities between domestic racism and foreign colonialism. In part this was because New Dealers, like corporate managers, were overwhelmingly white. No matter how empathetic, they were championing other people's battles, not their own. Yet New York was chock-full of people of color who had a visceral interest in these issues, given their historical and contemporary links to the colonized. It would be in their precincts that planning and promotion of a decolonized postwar world would be most vigorous.

164

Racism and Imperialism

On May 25, 1944, 600 guests joined Eleanor Roosevelt and Wendell Willkie at the Roosevelt Hotel to celebrate Walter White's 25th anniversary with the National Association for the Advancement of Colored People. White had recently returned from a three-month tour of the European and North African theaters of war, as an accredited war correspondent of the *New York Post* and *Life* magazine. He would soon publish an account of his travels in a little book called *A Rising Wind*, its title a hat tip to the First Lady. In it he hailed the heroism of Negro troops while also condemning the abuse they suffered from the many white GIs who carried American racism in their duffle bags, as if determined to transplant it to foreign soils.

White also pointed to a more portentous phenomenon: "World War II," he argued, "has given to the Negro a sense of kinship with other colored—and also oppressed—peoples of the world." More and more African Americans believed that "the struggle of the Negro in the United States is part and parcel of the struggle against imperialism and exploitation in India, China, Burma, Africa, the Philippines, Malaya, the West Indies, and South America."

This awareness of racism and imperialism, and the need to contest both simultaneously, had been an evolutionary development for White himself, and for most members of the National Association for the Advancement of Colored People. Despite its name, before the Second World War, few in the organization's high command had focused on the relationship of African Americans to people of color around the world. By 1942, however, White believed that US Blacks were confronting an international problem—a malignant symbiosis of global capitalism and white supremacy. That required linking the African American fight for civil rights with the Asian and African struggles against colonialism.

In May of 1942, encouraged by Roosevelt's anti-imperial pronouncements, White went so far as to urge the president to consider declaring that "the era of white domination of colored peoples is ended." Over the next two years he had steadily preached the new gospel—telling the NAACP's 1943 annual meeting in New York that racism had become a global rather than a national or sectional phenomenon. In 1944 a State Department report noted that leading Negro journals like *The Crisis*, official organ of the NAACP, as well the relatively conservative *New York Amsterdam News* and the militant left-wing organ the *Peoples Voice*, had conducted a perpetual and bitter campaign against "white imperialism."

During the same years, White, like many Blacks, was heartened by the emergence of a "human rights" movement and a concomitant drive to create an international organization that could guarantee such rights. If such possibilities were to be realized, however, the NAACP would have to jump into the fray. "On every hand there are discussions and plans by groups in and out of the gov[ernmen]t," one correspondent wrote White in 1943, "but none seem to include us." The executive secretary now agreed that African Americans and "other colored peoples throughout the world" had to participate in planning the postwar world, lest the future be built on "white rule and white exploitation" and seeds be sown for a third world war.

But who would represent the NAACP at the table? White needed an expert in international and colonial affairs, someone with theoretical acumen, practical experience, activist credentials, and the gravitas to be a player at the global level. Fortunately, the right person surfaced at just the right moment. Unfortunately, it was White's worst enemy.

Since 1934, when W.E.B. Du Bois had resigned from the organization he'd cofounded, following bitter policy and personal disputes with Walter White, he'd been at Atlanta University. In November 1943 that institution told the seventy-five-year-old legend they intended to retire him, willy-nilly, when his contract expired the following June. White, all too aware that Du Bois was perfect for the job at hand, swallowed hard and hired him back. In September 1944, Du Bois returned to New York and the NAACP, moving into 409 Edgecombe Avenue, where White lived as well, though proximity would not long prevent a resumption of their ideological and personal conflicts.

Du Bois's portfolio included representing the organization at the forthcoming meeting involving the United Nations in San Francisco, where, beginning in April 1945, fifty nations would consider ratification. It was a task for which he prepared by analyzing the charter proposals issued at Dumbarton Oaks (a colonial revival residence in the Georgetown neighborhood of Washington, DC, whose draft charter became the basis for the grand conclave at San Francisco). He quickly discovered, as did many others, that Roosevelt's "human rights" and "self-determination" had both gone missing. Du Bois informed State Department officials that he found the document "intolerable, dangerous" and irreconcilable with democracy, given that the 750 million people of color in the colonial world—a third of humanity—would have no rights or representation in the proposed world body.

Behind the scenes, FDR had tried to make good on his commitments. At his urging the State Department had crafted provisions that would have replaced the League of Nations mandate system with a United Nations trusteeship system that would provide stronger international oversight of colonies and foster a transition to independence. The British, not surprisingly, had objected vehemently. Letting the UN inspect their colonies without their consent, or allowing it to accept petitions of complaint directly from the colonized, was completely unacceptable. Unexpected opposition had also cropped up from the US military. The armed forces had wrested strategic Pacific islands from the Japanese, which they intended to keep and use as postwar military bases. They would not brook UN inspectors stopping by to ensure the inhabitants were being fairly treated, much less moving briskly toward independence. Rather than lock horns with the British *and* the American military, the State Department simply withdrew the proposal. The Dumbarton Oaks conferees followed suit, taking no stand on colonies, and the hot potato passed to San Francisco.

In preparation for that event—to which White and Du Bois (thanks to the intervention of Eleanor Roosevelt) were appointed "consultant" and "associate," respectively—Du Bois set out to line up support for a decolonization push in California.

He had the NAACP pass resolutions demanding that imperial countries provide their subjects with "a voice in their own government" and declare their willingness to eventually either liberate them or integrate them into the "mother country with full rights of citizenship."

He surveyed 151 African American organizations, soliciting their opinions on items to address at San Francisco; overwhelmingly they urged an end to racial discrimination at home and the abolition of colonialism abroad.

He consulted with the New York's premier African specialists, the influential Council on African Affairs (CAA), headquartered at 23 West 26th Street. Cofounded in 1937 by Paul Robeson and Max Yergan, the CAA disseminated information on Africa to liberals and leftists in the US and Europe, notably through its monthly bulletin, *New Africa*. Robeson and Yergan, like White and Du Bois, worried that after the war Europeans would fight to retain their colonies in order to rebuild their own shattered economies. The CAA leaders, both close to the Communist Party, suggested that the Soviets, who had been talking a good anticolonial game, might be key allies in resisting these imperial ambitions (a prospect about which Du Bois was dubious).

He also arranged a Harlem Colonial Conference, on April 6, 1945, at the 135th Street branch of the New York Public Library, which brought together forty-nine representatives from the colonial world and Black America. Present were liberation leaders from Latin America, Asia, and Africa—including the thirty-five-year-old Kwame Nkrumah from the British colony of Gold Coast. Nkrumah had been in New York working with the CAA, attending meetings of Harlem's Blyden Society for the Study of African History, and planning, with Du Bois, for a Fifth Pan-African Congress in Manchester, England, upcoming in October. The conferees recommended that Du Bois urge creation of a UN International Colonial Commission (with colonized peoples included) to facilitate a general move toward independence. And they offered specific strategies for decolonizing specific territories, including Ethiopia, Manchukuo, Formosa, Korea, Nigeria, Rhodesia, and Kenya. Finally, they proposed that in any UN trusteeship program, nations practicing discrimination at home be barred from supervising colonial areas.

In April 1945, Du Bois and White set aside their antagonisms and entrained for California, where the two would be forceful presences. On May 2 they (with Mary McLeod Bethune) presented the NAACP resolutions to the US delegation, asking that the UN Charter support independence for all colonized peoples, on the grounds that the colonial system was undemocratic and that inter-imperial rivalries were a major cause of war. During the consultants' showdown with Edward R. Stettinius over a human rights commission, White spoke up for "the importance of including colonies and other dependent peoples within the concept of human rights."

In the end, their efforts brought very modest results. A few soothing phrases were inserted in the Charter. The Preamble included among the UN's goals the development of "friendly relations among nations based on respect for the principle of equal rights and self-determination of peoples." And the section on "non-self-governing territories"—the euphemism of choice for colonies—declared that the "responsible" countries "accept as a sacred trust the obligation...to develop self-government, to take due account of the political aspirations of the peoples, and to assist them in the progressive development of their free political institutions, according to the particular circumstances of each territory and its peoples and their varying stages of advancement." (Privately, Stettinius averred that independence was appropriate only for people capable of exercising it and that most colonials were simply unable to handle the "strenuous conditions of the modern world.")

All this rhetoric bound the imperial powers to absolutely nothing. Moreover, the trusteeship system set up to oversee the colonizers set no limits on the length of their occupation (some had been in place for five hundred years) and said nothing about working toward (much less requiring) eventual independence—arguably a step backward from the League of Nations' mandate system. It recognized neither the equality of races nor the human rights of the colonized. It failed to include colonials in trusteeship administration. It allowed no independent UN oversight, though the international body could require reports from the colonial power about social and educational conditions in its non-self-governing territory. And apart from countries that had been League mandates or Axis possessions, the only way a colony could be put into trusteeship was if the colonial power did so voluntarily. The odds of this happening could be gauged from Churchill's response on first hearing of the plan, that "not one scrap of British territory" would be included if he could help it. In the end only 3 percent of the colonial world was covered by even these anemic provisions.

Du Bois was incensed. Not only was the plight of colonial peoples not being recognized as the result of "oppression and exploitation" by white capitalists pursuing cheap colored labor, it was blamed on their own inherent inferiority. In truth, Du Bois—no naif—was not stunned that the US "would not take a stand for race equality"; the NAACP and their African American associates had, after all, been trying to create an outside body that could intervene in US domestic affairs to right racial wrongs. Such a strategy would hardly have escaped the attention of the sharp-eyed Texan Tom Connally, who had repeatedly sidetracked antilynching legislation, or John Foster Dulles, who feared an unconstrained UN would launch an investigation of "the Negro question in this country." Du Bois and White and the NGOs and "smaller nations" simply hadn't the juice to overcome such potentates.

There would be other fronts in this decolonization struggle—a war that, like politics, would make strange bedfellows.

165

India

South Asians in America were, like the Chinese, against the law. More precisely, they were in America despite the law's best efforts.

In 1917, Congress, inspired by the success of the Chinese Exclusion Act, had gone whole hog and passed an Immigration Act that created an unambiguously titled "Asiatic Barred Zone." This was an enormous territory, of which all of India was merely a part, whose citizens were to be barred from entering the United States—though a small loophole was left through which merchants, teachers, and students might slip.

In the early 1920s, a larger rent appeared in the exclusionary fabric, one that threatened to unravel the whole cloth. In 1922, when naturalized citizenship was still reserved for "whites" or people of "African" descent, a Japanese man brought suit, not to challenge the racial restrictions, but to argue that Japanese should be classified as "white." That was clearly a nonstarter, ruled the US Supreme Court. Only "Caucasians" were white; Japanese were not Caucasian; ergo Japanese were not "white," hence not eligible for naturalization. Indeed, Justice George Sutherland added for good measure, they were members of an "unassimilable race." Seeing an opening here, one Bhagat Singh Thind, a Punjabi Sikh living in Oregon, claimed that because Indians *were* Caucasians (as was widely acknowledged)—Singh himself was an Aryan, no less, situated at the summit of the world's racial hierarchy, even by emerging Nazi standards—Indians were therefore white, and eligible to become US citizens. Justice Sutherland quickly slapped him down, ruling in a 1923 decision that being Caucasian didn't cut it. In the "understanding of the common man," he opined, "white" clearly denoted a white person of *European* origin. End of story. Or not quite: for their temerity, some forty-five Indians who had managed to win naturalization were stripped of their American citizenship.

Alarmed at this near-catastrophe, immigration restrictionists decided to nail the door shut altogether. In 1924, their banner year, they not only won passage of the national origins quota system (for Europeans) but also secured permanent exclusion of any "alien ineligible for citizenship," which encompassed Indians, having been declared neither "white" nor "black"; and this time the exclusion included the previously acceptable merchants, teachers, and students.

As a result, by the early 1940s, there were at most a few hundred Asian Indians in New York, mostly professionals and businessmen. As a political force, they were nonexistent. Yet as a lobbying force—on behalf of Indian nationalists and the Indian American community—they were not without influence, because they struck up an alliance with the flourishing network of white liberal and Black activist decolonizationists.

Such alliances were a long-established practice for Indian nationalists. Between 1914 and 1919, when Lala Lajpat Rai had run the India Home Rule League out of 1400 Broadway, he had linked up with metropolitan liberals like Norman Thomas, Roger Baldwin, and John Haynes Holmes, and with Black activists like W.E.B. Du Bois. When the exiled revolutionary Tarak Nath Das began a struggle against the 1917 immigration act, he joined with Agnes Smedley, Roger Baldwin, Franz Boas, Du Bois, and others in forming the Friends for Freedom of India (1919), modeled on and tied to the Friends of Irish Freedom (Indian activists even marched in the St. Patrick's Day parade).

The latter-day version of those New York–based Indian militants was Sirdar Jagjit ("J.J.") Singh. A Rawalpindi-born Sikh businessman, Singh migrated to Gotham in 1926, where, unlike most Sikhs, he went native. Discarding his turban, beard, and long hair, over the next decade the handsome six-footer cut a swath through New York's commercial and social worlds—by day selling expensive silks and saris to society ladies at his India Arts and Crafts shop (115 East 57th), by night squiring debutantes to Broadway shows and fancy parties as a personable bachelor and exotic extra man.

In the mid-1930s, Singh underwent a nationalist conversion, inspired by the emergence of Gandhi and Nehru's Indian National Congress as a political force, and by the publication of Nehru's autobiography. Singh returned to India to confer with Nehru and other Congress leaders and, at their urging, founded in New York an Indian Chamber of Commerce to promote bilateral trade. He also set about stirring up support for Indian independence. Singh took over the India League of America, founded in 1938 by intellectuals who had largely confined their activities to dinner discussions at the Ceylon-India Inn (148 West 49th), probably the oldest of the handful of Indian restaurants in Gotham. In 1939, Singh reorganized the organization, pumped money into it, and turned it into a formidable lobbying machine. With terrific energy he went after policy makers and congresspeople and the "blah-blah people who make public opinion"—press columnists, radio commentators, and media moguls like Hearst and Henry Luce (a trip to India that Singh arranged for Clare Boothe Luce led to a *Time* cover story on Nehru). He also started up his own media division in 1940, taking on Dr. Anup Singh to edit a monthly, *India Today*.

All this left Singh well prepared to galvanize a substantial US solidarity campaign when Indian nationalists made a concerted bid for independence. In February 1942, the Japanese captured Singapore, Britain's supposed "Gibraltar of the East." By May they had conquered British Burma and advanced to the Indian frontier. Gandhi announced that Indians would join fully in a British counteroffensive, and the quid pro quo was immediate self-government and eventual independence. In March 1942, the British Parliament had sent Sir Stafford Cripps to negotiate, though Cripps offered only full dominion status at war's end, which the leaders of the Congress and the Muslim league flatly rejected. In April, FDR, trying to make good on his Atlantic Charter call for "self-determination," pushed Churchill hard to make a deal, but the prime minister, infuriated, told him to back off.

(Churchill was convinced, not without reason, that the US was angling to end British imperial preferences, so that American business could barge through the newly opened door.) Rebuffed, Roosevelt reluctantly accepted that India would, for the time being, remain within the British sphere of influence.

On July 1, 1942, a disappointed Gandhi wrote FDR cuttingly that for all the Allies' insistence that they were "fighting to make the world safe for freedom of the individual and for democracy," their assertion "sounds hollow, so long as India, and for that matter, Africa are exploited by Great Britain, and America has the Negro problem in her own home." With US intervention precluded, the nationalists opted for hardball. On August 8, the Congress Party passed a Quit India Resolution, declaring that if the British did not leave, a nonviolent civil disobedience campaign would be launched to make them do so. At dawn on August 9 British forces arrested Gandhi and within twenty-four hours had jailed almost all his fellow leaders. The arrests sparked large-scale protests and demonstrations, peaceful strikes and violent riots. The Raj, as the British colonial system was called, riposted by outlawing the Congress party; and over the next several months its police and army shot hundreds, arrested tens of thousands.

All this provoked an uproar of protest in New York. The India League was very much in the middle of it, though the campaign drew its strength from the liberal and African American communities. No group was stauncher in support for Gandhi and his incarcerated colleagues than the city's Black leadership, whose links with the Mahatma stretched back decades. The day after Gandhi's arrest, White wrote FDR that "one billion brown and yellow peoples in the Pacific will without question consider ruthless treatment of Indian leaders and people typical of what white peoples will do to colored peoples" if they win. On September 2, 1942, over 4,000 attended a Council on African Affairs "Rally for the Cause of Free India" at the Manhattan Center, where Adam Clayton Powell Jr., Channing Tobias of the YMCA, and CAA chief Paul Robeson demanded Nehru's release from prison (Robeson had been a supporter of Nehru since they had met in London in the 1930s).

Black leaders repeatedly drew parallels between the situation of African Americans and Asian Indians. Walter White wrote Anup Singh that "our people understand, perhaps more clearly than any other American group, the conditions forced upon India. They resemble in many respects the proscription suffered by colored Americans." Du Bois tried on the colonial metaphor for size, telling his readers to "remember that we American Negroes are the bound colony of the United States just as India is of England."

India should continue to contend for her rights. And Langston Hughes celebrated their mutual determination in "Jim Crow's Last Stand" (1943):

> Pearl Harbor put Jim Crow on the run.
> That Crow can't fight for Democracy
> And be the same old crow he used to be—
> Although right now, even yet today,
> He tries to act in the same old way.
> But India and China and Harlem, too.
> Have made up their minds Jim Crow is through.

African Americans were well informed about the events in India—the Black press provided saturation coverage—and when a national sample of 10,000 African Americans was asked in October 1942, in the midst of Raj reprisals, "Do you believe in her liberty now?", 87.8 percent answered yes.

There was also widespread agreement that Indians in the United States should do the same. When J. J. Singh—after the Chinese Exclusion Act was abrogated in December 1943—renewed efforts to reverse the ban on citizenship for Indians, liberal and Black support rolled in. It seemed self-evidently true that, as one Asian Indian put it, "America cannot afford to say that she wants the people of India to fight on her side, and at the same time maintain that she will not have them among her immigrant groups."

In April 1944 Singh broached the issue at a Town Hall meeting, asking for the removal of the "stigma of inferiority," as had been recently done for the Chinese.

166

China

During the August 1943 Harlem riot, as a brick-and-bottle-wielding crowd boiled up Eighth Avenue, the owner of Chin Toy's Hand Laundry put a sign in his plate-glass window reading: "ME COLORED TOO." When the rioters came upon the shop and read the sign—as Malcolm Little would later remember—they thought it hilarious and fell about laughing. They also passed it by.

Chin Toy's claim of kinship, after all, had a certain plausibility. Both Chinese American and African American New Yorkers were subject to race-based discrimination, though it took different forms. The local Chinese, even if born here, still lived in the shadow of the Chinese Exclusion Act of 1882 that had all but banned immigration (due to "undesirable qualities"). Three score years later, immigration authorities—whom local Chinese had begun to call "the Gestapo"—were still patrolling New York's borders, often putting Chinese residents, even highly respectable ones, in detention and interrogating them for weeks, and arresting Chinese sailors who tried to take shore leave with their fellows—no *On the Town* for them. More to the point, the exclusion regime shaped the contours of daily life in Chinese American Gotham.

With the arrival of war, this unmarried and childless population became subject (if inadvertently) to a different kind of discrimination. Given that few Chinese had dependents, which would have exempted them from the draft, they were inducted into the military at a far higher rate than any other national group: approximately 40 percent of Gotham's Chinese population was called up.

The community attacked the exclusion laws at the heart of their many problems, denouncing them as racist and undemocratic, yet were powerless to change them. Not only were their numbers tiny—leaving them without political muscle and internally divided. On one side were the workers and small businessmen around the Chinese Hand Laundry Alliance; on the other were the traditional mercantile elites, who dominated the Chinese Consolidated Benevolent Association, the family and regional associations, and the tongs, and who had linked themselves with the Kuomintang—the Nationalists—China's ruling political party.

This New York status quo was about to be challenged by the geo-politics of global war.

Two days after Pearl Harbor and one day after the US declared war on Japan, China followed suit (though of course it had been fighting an undeclared war against Japanese invaders for ten years). With the two countries now formal allies, the US began funneling major financial and military resources to Chiang Kai-shek's Kuomintang regime. Many in the Roosevelt administration were aware its ranks were riddled with corruption. FDR was counting on the Nationalists to keep millions of Japanese troops tied down until the ultimate Allied victory in Europe, after which the US would strike at Japan from bases in China. The United States also wanted to secure an economic inside track in postwar Asia and was eager to guarantee China's support in various intra-Allied wartime conflicts. Roosevelt was so eager that he insisted China be treated as a Great Power, despite being virtually prostrate and dependent on US aid. Indeed, he accorded China the same status as Great Britain and the Soviet Union, to the intense annoyance of both. "That China is one of the world's four great powers, is an absolute farce," snarled Churchill, who well understood that Roosevelt was just seeking "a faggot vote for the United States" (an archaic Anglicism that meant, in essence, a bought-and-paid-for ballot).

No sooner was this US–China alliance struck than Japan set out to wedge it apart, by littering China with leaflets proclaiming: "Americans say they love and admire the Chinese. But can you go to America, can you become citizens? No. Americans do not want you. They just want you to do their fighting. Their Exclusion Act names you and says you are unfit for American citizenship." Whereas the Japanese goal, they proclaimed foxily, was to "liberate East Asia from Anglo-Saxon imperialists" and establish instead a "Greater East Asia Co-Prosperity Sphere," wherein "racial equality and harmony" would reign.

The possibility that America's new reliance on China might afford serious leverage to those opposing US race-based immigration restrictions was duly noted in New York's Chinatown, yet residents were too weak to pursue the opportunity. Others in Gotham—white liberals, white business leaders, and African American activists—would forge an alliance powerful enough to challenge a long entrenched but now embarrassing policy.

At the center of this alliance was a woman on the cusp of two cultures who became the champion of a third. By the time Pearl Buck returned to the United States in 1934, she had spent half her life in China, as the child of Presbyterian missionaries and as a missionary herself. She arrived therefore as an insider-outsider, capable of viewing her native culture with an unusually critical eye. She was also a literary celebrity—author of the Pulitzer Prize–winning *The Good Earth* (1931), a novel that had almost singlehandedly re-engineered American attitudes toward China. Long considered the hive, the point of departure from which swarms of demonic Orientals set out to bedevil the West, China in Buck's pages became a land of wonderfully attractive, earthy, and noble peasants—albeit in need of Christian salvation and Western progress. Not for nothing was Buck known as the most influential Westerner to write about China since Marco Polo.

Back in the US, Buck threw herself into working for a similar transformation of attitudes toward African Americans, becoming a regular contributor to New York journals like the NAACP's *Crisis* and the Urban League's *Opportunity*. Partly she was motivated by a sensitivity to prejudice—developed when she'd been on the receiving end of it in China—which she was dismayed to find so virulent in the US. Partly this was because she had become a Boasian convert, a big fan of Ruth Benedict's work on race. And partly she was hyperaware of how American racism was playing in Asia.

All her sensibilities and convictions came together in a powerful and lengthy letter she published in the *New York Times* on November 15, 1941, in response to the hysteria over the presumed "crime wave" in Harlem. Like other liberal commentators, Buck argued that violent crime was mainly an angry response to being trapped by racial prejudice in a ghetto that left them vulnerable to exploitation in housing and jobs, an anger newly stoked by being excluded from war plants and segregated in the army. Whites saw this seething fury but refused to acknowledge its source—that "our prejudice denies him democracy"—because "we wish to keep him the servant of the white man." If the country intended to maintain this distinction between a "white ruler race and a subject colored race," said Buck, the honest thing would be to "change the Constitution and make it plain that Negroes cannot share the privileges of the white people." Yes, that would mean acknowledging the US was "totalitarian rather than democratic," but at least white Americans would "be relieved of the necessity of hypocrisy and the colored people will know where they are."

This was pretty sharp, but only a way station on her way up to the international level. As Buck saw it, the spreading Black anger, fed by a growing sense they would never win justice or security in their own country, was undermining their patriotism. Some Black leaders, she noted, "prefer Hitler to British imperialism, feeling that if English rule over colored races can be destroyed," Hitler could be dealt with later. "Everywhere in the world," Buck argued, "the colored peoples are asking each other if they must forever endure the arrogant ruling white race," and "we are foolish if we do not realize it."

This text created a sensation—Walter White congratulated her on a "magnificent letter" and had it reprinted and circulated in large quantities—and she pushed the argument still farther after Pearl Harbor brought the US into the war. On February 10, 1942, the 1,700 auditors who had come to the Astor Hotel expecting a conventional literary lunch received a Buck lecture on international racial politics. The Japanese, she reported, were telling the colored races they had "no hope of justice and equality from white peoples because of their unalterable racial prejudice," and there was disturbing evidence that this "weapon of racial propaganda" was "beginning to show signs of effectiveness." As "we cannot win this war, without convincing our colored allies—who are most of our allies—that we are not fighting for ourselves as continuing superior over colored peoples," she continued, "it was essential that Americans abandon 'white supremacy.'" Besides, "if we plan to persist" in discriminating against Blacks, "then we are fighting on the wrong side on this war. We belong with Hitler."

Acting on her own advice, Buck threw herself even more vigorously into the city's antiracist movement. In early 1942 she convinced Roger Baldwin to set up an ACLU Committee Against Racial Discrimination, with herself as chair. She also served on the board of *Common Ground* with Louis Adamic and Langston Hughes, who hailed her as "the current Harriet Beecher Stowe to the Race!" White, too, sang her praises, declaring at a 1942 Madison Square Garden rally that only two white Americans understood the reality of Black life, and both were women: Eleanor Roosevelt and Pearl Buck. (J. Edgar Hoover adding his seal of disapproval, stepping up surveillance of Buck, who he came to hate nearly as much as he loathed ER.)

Buck also worked on transforming the war into an antiracist and anti-imperialist struggle. On April 8, 1942, she joined Paul Robeson at a 4,000-strong interracial rally at Manhattan Center, sponsored by his Council on African Affairs; *Opportunity*'s account was headlined: "Pearl Buck Urges Mobilization of Negro and Colonial Peoples," arguing that the Allies "had no intention of changing the existing organization of empire." The international body they suggested as a response to global political inequality and economic imbalance was but "a poultice put on a cancer."

For all this attention to African American and global-colonial issues, Buck did not ignore either China or the Chinese in the city and country. In November 1940 she and her husband, publisher Richard Walsh, started the China Emergency Relief Committee to raise money for hospitals, medical supplies, food, clothing, and the care of orphans. In the spring of 1941, they joined with several other such groups in a New York–headquartered umbrella organization, United China Relief (UCR). Its leadership—a mixed group of New Dealers and Wall Streeters—included Buck, Eleanor Roosevelt, John D. Rockefeller III, Thomas Lamont (of J. P. Morgan), Wendell Willkie, and another child of Presbyterian missionaries—Henry Luce.

Luce had been born in 1898 (six years after Buck) in Tengchow, a coastal town in Shantung province, and had grown up in China, living mainly in missionary compounds. In 1913, at age fifteen, he was enrolled in Hotchkiss, a Connecticut prep school, where—promptly nicknamed "chink" by his classmates—his inherited revulsion against racial bigotry deepened. From there it was on to Yale (class of '20) and construction of the *Time* empire. Though Luce briefly visited China in 1932, he paid no special attention to his birth-country through the thirties, nor did his magazines cover Japan's invasion any more assiduously than did the US press in general. Indeed until 1941, his overseas attention remained fixed on Europe.

In 1941 Luce got involved with Chinese philanthropy, first aiding Buck's initial effort, then joining her and other luminaries in United China Relief. He soon announced he would spearhead a campaign to raise an unheard-of $5 million and go to China to enlist Madame Chiang Kai-shek's support. He and his wife, Clare Boothe Luce, took a Pan Am clipper to Hong Kong and then traveled on to Chungking and into the middle of the ten-year-old war. Swept away by Chiang—a Methodist convert—Luce called him "the greatest ruler Asia has seen since Emperor Kian Hsi 200 years ago," and "America's best friend" to boot. He was equally blown away by Chiang's wife and became the couple's most tenacious supporter and propagandist, averting his eyes as much as possible from the doings of their kleptocratic family and corrupt government. When Madame Chiang visited the United States in 1942–43, using New York as her base, he splashed her on the covers of his magazines.

Buck, meanwhile, was becoming an increasingly severe critic. She warned of the Nationalists' corruption, inefficiency, repressiveness, and remoteness. She wrote ER that after the war the Chinese people would revolt against their government, though she remained an ardent anticommunist and opponent of Chiang's enemy Mao Tse-tung. Buck and Luce got on effectively in United China Relief, which raised immense sums—$47 million during its first five years—in no small part because many affluent people wanted to be on the sunny side of the publisher of *Time*, *Life*, and *Fortune*.

The duo collaborated as well on another project that bore directly on Chinese Americans, including those in New York.

On November 10, 1942, Buck's husband, Richard Walsh, made a speech at the Town Hall Round Table, urging that the United States repeal the Chinese Exclusion Acts, place Chinese immigration on a quota basis, and make them eligible for American citizenship. The following May, he, Buck, and Henry Luce founded the Citizens Committee to Repeal the Chinese Exclusion. Based in New York, it soon attracted over 250 people to its ranks. None of them, ironically, were Chinese, membership having been limited "to American citizens not of Asiatic origin," so the group wouldn't seem self-interested. Madame Chiang kept mum, too, though her presence during their campaign generated significant support: on the same day she visited Capitol Hill, Manhattan Democrat Martin Kennedy introduced the first repeal bill in Congress.

In May–June of 1943, the House Committee on Immigration and Naturalization held hearings, to which they summoned fifty-one witnesses. American nativists took a vigorous stand against lowering the barrier against Chinese immigration. John Trevor, the New York attorney who had masterminded the 1924 National Origins Act, was now sixty-five but still on the case. His American Coalition of Patriotic Societies, representing approximately one hundred such groups, joined with representatives of the American Federation of Labor and the Veterans of Foreign Wars to strongly oppose repeal—partly on its own supposed demerits, but also because, as Trevor observed, the campaign was "obviously a prelude to undoing the work of twenty years of immigration restrictions" and therefore a "grave peril." Many southern lawmakers saw repeal as a threat to the American racial order, in that it "may encourage the Southern black people to demand equality too."

The bigger battalions, however, were on the other side. In addition to the arguments of Buck and her liberal colleagues, and President Roosevelt's personal appeal that Congress "take the offensive in this propaganda war and repeal the laws that insult our only ally on the mainland of Asia," two powerful forces spoke out for change. A series of military men told the hearings that the Exclusion Act legislation was worth "twenty divisions" to the Japanese army, and its repeal would help the United States win the war quicker. And businessmen came forward to note that if Exclusion was maintained, it might hamper postwar development of the long-dreamed-of China market, whose 400 million potential consumers could help mightily in warding off a postwar depression.

In December 1943, therefore, fifteen explicitly anti-Chinese laws were abrogated, and repeal permitted Chinese resident aliens to become naturalized citizens. On the other hand, Trevor's 1924 immigration quota system remained unaltered, and under its provisions China was allotted a grand total of 105 entrants per year (other Asians remained banned, including America's own colony of the Philippines and England's colony of India). It remained to be seen if repeal would be a trivial adjustment, extorted under duress by wartime exigencies, or, as its opponents feared, a fateful crack in one of the pillars upholding a larger racial edifice.

167

Puerto Rico

Ever since Francisco de Miranda's 1806 expedition sailed from the East River in its doomed attempt to liberate South America from Spanish rule, New York had been the premier base of operations for rebel Latin Americans. Once the Wars of Independence triumphed in the 1820s, leaving Cuba and Puerto Rico as Spain's only hemispheric possessions, an array of exiles, from Félix Varela to José Martí, concentrated on extracting those two remaining colonies from Iberian clutches.

In 1898, the Spanish-Cuban-American War, in large measure launched from New York, had succeeded in wresting Cuba from Spain. Almost immediately, however, the US had donned the Spanish mantle and imposed a protectorate/extractorate, backed by the Marines. Wall Street corporations flocked to Cuba, completing the transfer of economic overlordship from Spain to the US. Americans could still claim, however, that they were not *imperialists*, at least in the old-fashioned European sense, because the US had not taken formal possession of the island.

Such a claim was impossible to sustain in the case of Cuba's neighbor. Puerto Rico remained unambiguously a colony—though squeamish North Americans preferred circumlocutions like "island possession" or "unincorporated territory." To be sure, the 1917 Jones Act had granted Puerto Ricans US citizenship, but it had withheld statehood or real self-governance, much less independence. Soon the island's crucial sugar economy was dominated by just four New York corporations—South Porto Rico Sugar Company, Central Aguirre Associates, Fajardo Sugar Company, and Eastern Sugar Association—themselves controlled by a combination of Wall Street banks (especially National City and the House of Morgan) and sugar-refining interests (notably the Havemeyers). And though the island's Organic Acts of 1900 limited to 500 acres the amount of land any corporation could own for agricultural purposes, Eastern Sugar alone held over 100,000.

In the 1930s, during Puerto Rico's terrible Depression years, when per-capita income fell by a third and the unemployment rate hit 65 percent, the island was roiled by strikes, demonstrations, and boycotts. At the same moment, a militant independence movement emerged to challenge the legal and moral basis of US colonial rule. The hitherto marginal Partido Nacionalista de Puerto Rico (Nationalist Party)—invigorated after 1930 by its new and super-militant leader Pedro Albizu Campos—had burst onto the political scene and reshaped it.

Albizu Campos blamed the economic crisis on the US-installed regime. It had, he argued, fostered a corporate monoculture that displaced small farmers and impoverished the rural working class. Only independence promised a way out of this colonial trap. A free Puerto Rico could curb the sugarocracy, curtail the size of land holdings, and impose tariffs to foster industries oriented to local markets. No socialist, Albizu Campos's goal was an independent capitalist development that would protect a Puerto Rican bourgeoisie and elevate workers into small landholders. As the US would never willingly grant the island liberty, Puerto Ricans would have to win it themselves, and not through the colonial electoral process, which he denounced as a farce. The ruling regime was illegitimate. It had been imposed by force. It must be resisted by force.

Some saw more than a whiff of fascism in Albizu Campos's predilection for violence, hyper-nationalist rhetoric, and creation of a corps of black-shirted paramilitary cadets. He was not easily pigeonholed. If fascism was anything it was antilabor, anticlerical, pro-imperialist, and pro-racist. Albizu Campos supported labor struggles (in fact he led the 1934 general strike by sugarcane workers at their request). He was devoutly Catholic. He denounced not only US imperialism but British rule over India, French atrocities in Algeria, Japan's invasion of China, Italy's occupation of Ethiopia, Germany's treatment of Jews; and, for good measure, he branded the Soviet regime a new form of despotism, one reason, no doubt, Albizu Campos was praised by Trotsky from his Mexican exile. And he was deeply antiracist, not surprisingly, being himself a mulatto who had had bitter encounters with US (and island) discrimination, despite his having earned a BA and law degree from Harvard.

The combination of economic upheaval and nationalist mobilization deeply alarmed local elites and distant corporations. In 1934, the War Department, which still controlled Insular Affairs, appointed as governor (still an unelected position) of Puerto Rico a recently retired general, Blanton Winship, who was expected to rule with a firm hand. Winship appointed as police commissioner another former military officer, Colonel Francis E. Riggs. Preparing for battle, Winship and Riggs increased the number and armament of the insular police force and called in the FBI to investigate the Nationalists. In this inflammatory atmosphere, a series of violent encounters escalated into a major crisis. In October 1935 four nationalist youths were killed by Riggs's police. Albizu Campos swore revenge at their gravesite. In February 1936 two nationalists shot and killed Commissioner Riggs. Captured immediately, they were taken to a San Juan jail and summarily executed. In March Albizu Campos and the top Nationalist leadership were arrested for sedition and "conspiracy to overthrow the government of the United States." In August 1936, they were found guilty (after a hung jury of locals was replaced by a panel of continentals and two Insular subordinates). Albizu Campos was sentenced to ten years, with the possibility of probation after six.

At this point help arrived from New York in the person of Vito Marcantonio, the East Harlem Congressman who responded to his substantial and growing Puerto Rican constituency by becoming the island's de facto representative. Marcantonio flew to San Juan, met with Albizu Campos, offered to assist in legal appeals, and brought in Roger Baldwin and the American Civil Liberties Union (ACLU), which denounced the proceedings as a political trial, not a criminal prosecution. On August 29, 1936, on returning to New York, Marcantonio participated in a huge demonstration, the largest El Barrio had ever seen. Ten thousand

Puerto Ricans—a hefty portion of their citywide population, then approaching sixty thousand—paraded through lower Harlem, arrayed in their varied political and social clubs, chanting "Free Puerto Rico!" and "Down with Yankee Imperialism!" as Blacks and other Hispanics cheered from windows and rooftops.

The marchers spanned a narrow political gamut that ran from *La Junta Nacionalista de Nueva York*—the official New York branch of the Nationalist Party of Puerto Rico—to an assortment of leftwing groups, including El Centro Obrero Español, the Tobacco Workers Union, the Spanish-speaking lodges of the International Workers Order (confederated in the Sociedad Fraternal Cervantes, led by Jesús Colón), and the Harlem sections of the Communist Party (with which Marcantonio was closely connected though not a member). Gotham's nationalists and communists had not always seen eye to eye, as the latter favored concentrating on local not island affairs. Yet now they drew together under the twin banners of anti-imperialism and antifascism. The Spanish Civil War had just gotten under way, and *independentistas* and anti-*Francoistas* commingled in mammoth demonstrations, like the 1937 May Day celebration devoted to supporting the Spanish Republic, which drew 70,000 people, the majority of them Hispanic.

On March 21, 1937, the Palm Sunday marchers had been mown down by Governor Winship's Insular Police, using pistols, rifles, and Thompson submachine guns, with nineteen killed and perhaps 200 wounded. New York Hispanics protested the shootings in April when 3,000 jammed El Barrio's Park Palace Ballroom (110th and Fifth). There they listened to denunciations from Marcantonio and Albizu Campos's other attorney, the twenty-six-year-old Gilberto Concepción de Gracia, who had closed his office in San Juan and moved to New York to press the Nationalists' appeal case. And two weeks after the May Day 1937 march, thousands of Puerto Rican and other Spanish Americans again tramped through lower Harlem, where they heard Marcantonio claim the island was under "the worst form of military terrorism."

Marcantonio's endorsement was explicit. In May 1936 he came out officially for Puerto Rican independence in response to a congressional initiative by Maryland Senator Millard E. Tydings. A close friend of the assassinated Colonel Riggs, Tydings introduced a punitive bill authorizing Puerto Rican independence, if accepted by an island referendum, but imposing ruinous conditions that would subject the liberated colony's sugar exports to full US tariffs and cut off the free flow of immigration (which, Tydings argued privately, was "essential to stop the influx [of Puerto Ricans] into New York"). Marcantonio riposted with his own bill that, if passed, would grant independence but bar tariffs and allow unrestricted immigration. He argued that this would constitute a morally legitimate indemnification for decades of US colonialism, which had produced "the disastrous state of the economy of Puerto Rico and the abysmal poverty of its people." US business, Marcantonio noted, had gobbled up the island—"four large American sugar corporations own over half the good sugar land"—and milked it for hundreds of millions in profits. Neither his nor Tydings's bill passed, but the contending positions had been made clear.

Marcantonio continued to back the prisoners during their long incarceration. He visited them in Atlanta, pushed the Justice Department to provide medical care, and organized an appeal to FDR for clemency (signed by Ernest Hemingway, Ruth Benedict, Sherwood Anderson, Theodore Dreiser, and Pearl Buck). And Albizu Campos was released in June 1943 on four-year probation, during which he could not return to Puerto Rico.

During much of that month FDR, accompanied by his chief of naval operations, Admiral William Leahy, participated in *Fleet Problem XX*—the first US Navy war games ever held in the Caribbean. At Roosevelt's express order, they hypothesized a German naval attack on Puerto Rico. The maneuvers lay bare the island's glaring vulnerabilities, and by extension those of the Panama Canal and Venezuelan oil refineries whose approach ways it guarded. After the exercises, the commander-in-chief caucused on the island of Culebra with all the participating admirals, and it was decided to sharply upgrade the strategic status of Puerto Rico and shore up its military defenses. Clearly, from this moment on, independence was off the table as far as FDR was concerned. Equally clearly, it was imperative to bring stability to the turbulent island if it was to serve as a secure stronghold for the USA's Caribbean defenses. How to achieve this desired tranquility? Roosevelt was nothing if not pragmatic when pursuing order. In the Dominican Republic and Nicaragua, the quest led to deals with dictators—Trujillo and Somoza. In Mexico, it meant overriding US oilmen's pleas that he reverse President Cardenas's nationalization of their companies. In Puerto Rico—Governor Winship's rightist authoritarianism having failed to produce stability, much less loyalty—FDR opted for tacking left.

To win Puerto Rican hearts and minds the president would resuscitate liberal reform initiatives launched in the early 1930s but aborted during the mid-1930s crackdown on nationalists. As a result, at just the moment when FDR's domestic program on the mainland had been checked (if not mated) by conservative and corporate opponents, and just as he was being forced to come to terms with the business community to win its participation in the war effort, Roosevelt moved in precisely the opposite direction in Puerto Rico. There, more than anywhere else in the country, Dr. Win-the-War summoned to his side the supposedly superannuated Dr. New Deal.

Roosevelt acted on his plan with ruthless immediacy. On March 1, 1939, while still returning from the fleet exercises—indeed just as the USS *Houston* was cruising past San Juan—he turned to Leahy and announced that the admiral was to be the next governor of Puerto Rico. By September, Winship was out and Leahy was in. The new governor's most visible task was to oversee a rapid buildup of military fortifications. By year's end, Borinquen Field, built on 3,796 acres of confiscated sugarcane fields, was up and runwaying, home to an Army Air Forces bomber squadron of B-18s. Leahy also commenced construction of Roosevelt Roads—at Ceiba, a site FDR had spotted back when he was assistant secretary of the navy. A Pearl Harbor–sized deepwater base, "Rosey Roads" would be big enough to house the entire British Fleet, should the Nazis conquer England. Together with Culebra and Vieques, it constituted a vast military complex on the island's eastern coast and led to Puerto Rico's becoming known as the "Gibraltar of the Caribbean."

Meanwhile, in the back corridors of power, Leahy was executing a different set of presidential orders—to facilitate a transfer of power from the conservative business interests on whose behalf Winship had been acting to a liberal set of actors who could jolt back to life the now moribund New Deal program that had been launched back in 1934. The most important of these liberal New Dealers were a pair of Gothamites—Luis Muñoz Marín (a leading island politician) and Rexford Guy Tugwell (the Ur-Brain Truster of Roosevelt's First Hundred Days)—who constituted a counterpoint to the *independendista* duo of Albizu Campos and Vito Marcantonio.

Luis Muñoz Marín, born in 1898 in Old San Juan, spent crucial chunks of his first thirty-three years in New York. In 1901 his father, Luis Muñoz Rivera, Puerto Rico's most influential political leader, having been threatened with violence, had established a base for his family in Gotham (at 156 Fifth Avenue). His son always considered the move to the metropolis decisive for his personal development and political career. "I lived two childhoods,"

Muñoz Marín would say, "the one in New York and the one in Puerto Rico." He was totally bilingual—though when back on the island for a time at the age of seven, his schoolmates laughed at his Spanish, tinged as it was with a New York (some said Brooklyn) accent. From 1911 to 1916 his father was resident commissioner in Washington, though even then his wife and son lived mostly in New York. After his father died in 1916, Muñoz Marín darted down to Puerto Rico on occasion but basically hung his hat in Manhattan, or Staten Island, or West Englewood, New Jersey, just across the Hudson, while trying his hand at various jobs and careers, most successfully in journalism. In the 1920s he wrote for *The Nation* and for Mencken's *American Mercury* and became a fixture in New York reform circles, known for anti-imperialist pieces like "Puerto Rico: The American Colony," which argued that independence and land reform were the keys to solving Puerto Rico's problems.

When Muñoz Marín resettled permanently on the island in 1931, he was drawn to Albizu Campos's arguments but put off by Nationalist Party tactics. He opted instead for joining the Liberal Party and assuming editorship of its organ *La Democracia*, a paper his father had founded. In 1933, newly elected to the Puerto Rican Senate, he became an admirer of FDR's New Deal. If extended to the island, he thought, it might not only help deal with the Depression but also restructure the insular economy in a way that might make a future independence viable. He and his colleagues developed a plan that would diminish dependency on sugar by breaking the stranglehold of absentee New York companies and diversifying the island's agriculture and industry. Having been introduced to Eleanor Roosevelt, he urged the First Lady to examine Puerto Rico's problems firsthand. In March 1934 she did so, visiting San Juan's vast and dismal slum, El Fanguito (The Mudhole); confronting rural poverty; and listening to pleas from Muñoz Marín and others to bring the New Deal to the Caribbean.

Equally attentive was Rexford Guy Tugwell, then assistant secretary of agriculture (the department headed at the time by Henry Wallace). Tugwell, who had flown in on the same plane as ER, was exploring ways to curtail sugar production (and so raise prices and farm income). He was taken with a Muñoz Marín plan to buy up bankrupt sugar companies and redistribute the land to *jíbaros* (peasants), who would then produce other kinds of crops. Tugwell recommended that FDR bring a small group of Puerto Rican officials to Washington to design a comprehensive policy for remaking the island. FDR accordingly set up a Puerto Rico Policy Commission, with Tugwell in charge and Muñoz Marín sitting in, which in June 1934 came up with a plan, one that FDR approved, an endorsement he repeated on a July trip to Puerto Rico itself.

Roosevelt now transferred administration of the island from the War Department's Bureau of Insular Affairs—the entity that had dispatched Winship—to a new Division of Territories and Island Possessions, housed at the Interior Department under the watchful eye of New Deal stalwart Harold Ickes. To run it, FDR and Ickes turned to another card-carrying member of the New York liberal community, Ernest Gruening.

Born in 1887 and raised in Gotham, Gruening's parents were wealthy (and nonpracticing) German Jews—they pronounced their name Green-ing—who sent him to Sachs, Hotchkiss, Harvard, and Harvard Med. He opted instead for journalism and worked on various papers, including the New York *Tribune*. In 1919, after wartime service, Gruening edited New York's Spanish-language daily *La Prensa*, which brought him into contact with exiles from the Caribbean, and he became a critic of US military interventionism there. Soon Oswald Garrison Villard hired him away to become managing editor of *The Nation*, in which capacity he spearheaded a campaign to terminate the US occupation of Haiti. Gruening also edited a two-volume symposium, *These United States* (1923–1925), which included a chapter on US colonialism in Puerto Rico written by Muñoz Marín, whom he'd met and befriended in New York. Gruening spent the next five years researching and writing a well-regarded book on the Mexican Revolution, and another five years in reform journalism, before returning to *The Nation* in 1933, where, after penning editorials urging FDR to extend the New Deal to the Caribbean, he was handed the job of doing so.

In Puerto Rico, Gruening swiftly allied with Muñoz Marín, with whom he saw eye to eye on most issues, except independence. Muñoz Marín still favored it, while Gruening, like most New Dealers, believed the island's best bet—especially at a time when many Caribbean countries were groaning under right wing dictatorships—was to remain "under the protection and with the great benefits of American citizenship." The duo worked together promoting land reform and economic diversification. When the conservative parties maneuvered to kill their program, Gruening got FDR to issue an Executive Order, in May 1935, setting up a Puerto Rico Reconstruction Administration, with himself as head, that rapidly expanded to include 53,000 people. There were some substantial achievements—notably rural electrification and health and housing initiatives—but limited financial resources, ongoing opposition, and the crackdown on the Nationalists (which Gruening supported) derailed the liberal enterprise. By 1938, further New Deal initiatives were as blocked on the island as they were on the mainland, with Governor Winship, the local right, and Wall Street sugar interests in command of the field.

Muñoz Marín pressed ahead on his own. Launching a new Popular Democratic Party (Partido Popular Democratico, PPD), he spent 1939 and 1940 barnstorming the island, talking to farmers and workers, promising to set aside the independence issue and focus on alleviating their immediate hardships. He also renewed the drive against Big Sugar, an effort made newly plausible by a March 1940 Supreme Court ruling that authorized the Insular government to enforce the 500-acre limitation. The new party was favored as well by FDR's break with Winship and installation of Admiral Leahy, who frustrated conservative initiatives and oversaw clean elections in November 1940. These the PPD narrowly won, with 40 percent of the votes, enabling it and its allies to control the Senate and elect Muñoz Marín its president.

His mission accomplished, Leahy was recalled by FDR for a diplomatic mission in Europe, followed by service as his top military adviser. Leahy was replaced as governor, after a brief interregnum, by Muñoz Marín's old partner Rexford Tugwell. "Red Rex" had been forced to resign from the administration back in 1936 by ferocious attacks from the right wing—though he wasn't even a socialist, much less a communist. In 1938 Tugwell had been tapped by Mayor La Guardia to head the New York City Planning Commission. Having fared poorly in battles with Robert Moses, he responded with alacrity to Roosevelt's offer of the governorship of Puerto Rico. He assumed the office in September 1941, fully aware that his wartime assignment would be to win "the tranquility, even the loyalty of its people," and to align his government with the PPD in re-launching New Deal style reforms.

After Pearl Harbor, as Roosevelt had feared, the Caribbean was quickly infested with Nazi submarines, which succeeded in all but severing the maritime link between Puerto Rico and the US. Shut off from the major source of its imports and the leading buyer of its exports, its food and oil stockpiles shrank to dangerously low levels while its unemployment rate shot up from 99,100 (in July 1941) to 237,000 (in September 1942). Nevertheless, it was in the midst of this crisis, over the course of roughly a hundred days from February to May 1942, that Muñoz Marín and Governor Tugwell (the latter reliving his role in the original Hundred

Days of 1933) managed to legislate and set in place the infrastructure for a government-led revolution.

Within two years, having started from scratch, they established a Planning Board to design development projects; a Puerto Rico Development Company to build state-run industrial enterprises (organized and headed by Teodoro Moscoso, a young Gotham-educated Tugwell assistant); and a Development Bank to finance such projects, in which local and foreign capital refused to invest. They also launched an array of New Deal–style (and New York–invented) authorities to take charge of key economic sectors: a Power Authority, Communications Authority, Water and Sewage Authority, and Transportation Authority. They built public housing projects, created free public clinics, enacted social and labor laws (while Tugwell halted government repression of strikers), and instituted land reforms that reduced the influence of absentee capital. The money to pay for all this came in large measure from selling rum to the States, where distilleries were pressed into war production and European imports were blocked. The island, moreover, was entitled to keep 70 percent of the taxes levied on such sales, with the result that revenues leapt from $1.7 million in 1941 to $65.8 million in 1944.

In effect, the Muñoz Marín–Tugwell team had set in place a demonstration project, a concrete example of what administration officials had been promulgating as an American war aim—the fashioning of a New Deal for the world.

Not surprisingly it generated hysterical levels of opposition. There were screams of fear and fury from sugar corporations, from local importers opposed to the island increasing its own food production, from private industries incensed at public-sector competition, and from the "better element" panicked at their loss of political dominance. On the mainland, the same forces that had stymied the New Deal in 1938 moved to stamp out its Caribbean resurrection in 1943. Congressmen generated bills to annul the laws authorizing authorities, to take away rum-tax revenues, to evict "Red Rex" from office. Roosevelt, who had given ground elsewhere, here hung tough. The assaults were turned back. And in the 1944 elections, Muñoz Marín's brand of revitalized liberalism won a smashing electoral victory, with the PPD pulling 65 percent of the votes.

The status issue, however, refused to go away. El Congreso Pro-Independencia de Puerto Rico—set up in 1943 to offer an alternative to the use of violence associated with the Nationalist Party—had held a full-scale convention in San Juan that year, in which 1,800 elected delegates, cheered on by an audience of 10,000, sent a demand to FDR "that Puerto Rico become a free and sovereign nation with the cooperation of the friendly people of the United States." Gotham-based *Independentistas*—from Concepción de Gracia's Asociación Pro Independencia de Puerto Rico en Nueva York, to Albizu Campos's Partido Nacionalista, to Congressman Marcantonio's American Labor Party—sent their approval.

In 1944, after the PPDs election triumph, another Pro-Independence Congress was held—this time under the presidency of Concepción de Gracia, who returned from New York to lead this challenge to Muñoz Marín, calling on him to live up to longstanding professions. Even a majority of his PPD members made plain their growing impatience.

The New York Nationalists—whose leadership was barred from returning to the island until 1947—pressed their claims in other venues. Julio Pinto Gandia, who in 1937 had become acting president of the Nationalist Party after Albizu Campos was jailed, only to be himself jailed soon thereafter, joined his comrades in New York after being freed in 1943 and was soon selected as general secretary of the party. Particularly interested in having Puerto Rico included in the conversations around creation of a United Nations, Pinto Gandia approached Du Bois in April 1945 and went on to San Francisco, where he lobbied for including the case of Puerto Rico in the decolonization discussion. The Pro-Independence Congress did likewise, and dispatched Rafael Soltero Peralta to California to argue that "our contribution of blood and sacrifice in defeating the totalitarian powers has made Puerto Rico one of the United Nations whose right in this conference cannot be challenged."

Muñoz Marín again declined to participate in reigniting the anti-imperial argument, holding to the position that for the moment immediate economic issues had to take priority over long term political ones. Privately he was giving serious consideration to a major change in position. For all his political life, Muñoz Marín had argued that Puerto Rico's colonial condition had been disastrous in its humiliating political subordination, and its deleterious economic consequences: overspecialization, mass unemployment, low wages, absentee control, and a systematic outflow of profits. He had also long been sensitive to the dark side of the free trade doctrine so exuberantly exported by Open Door advocates. The notion that the free flow of goods and capital would over time tend to diminish economic disparities between more advanced and less developed trading partners was belied by the US–Puerto Rican experience. Trade had been totally free since 1901, capital (and labor) had come and gone as it pleased, the island had even operated with the US dollar and a Fed-regulated banking system. Free trade had deepened the divide, not bridged it.

And yet, precisely because colonialism had *not* created the economic basis for independence and instead addicted the island to its privileged access to a protected US market, slamming the open door shut would likely be catastrophic (as indirectly evidenced by the U-boat-engendered free fall of 1942–43). Muñoz Marín was also paying more attention to those, chiefly in the business community, who were arguing that the island's difficulties were due not to imperial exploitation but to "overpopulation," and that halting the free flow of Puerto Ricans to New York would deliver yet another body blow to the local economy. It was all fine and well for Marcantonio to draft legislation—as he did again in May 1945—that would hurdle this dilemma by proposing the US free the island *and* continue unrestricted immigration and untaxed imports. It was patently apparent that the US Congress was never going to go along with this, not least because granting Puerto Rico immigration exemptions would challenge the entire restrictionist quota system—compare the experience of Jews, Chinese, and Indians on this score—and because "most favored nation" treaties would force the US to grant its cosignatories whatever it granted Puerto Rico, and that was never going to happen.

If independence would be spiritually, culturally, and politically satisfying, but economically disastrous—as Muñoz Marín was increasingly convinced—there was one conceivably viable alternative (apart from statehood, which had its own set of drawbacks), and it was the one New Dealers had been gently advocating all along. Rexford Tugwell was unusual in his call-a-spade-a-spade willingness to admit that Puerto Rico was a colony and to proclaim independence a desirable goal. Though because, at least for the moment, that goal could not be realized without ruinous consequences, he (like Gruening) argued that a "commonwealth, Dominion—call it anything indicating a half-way relationship" might best reconcile the need for self-rule with maintaining the US connection essential to the island's progress. As a move in that direction, Tugwell promoted the idea of allowing Puerto Ricans to elect their own governor, an idea FDR supported. Up till 1945, Muñoz Marín had concurred completely with Marcantonio's dismissive response to this gesture. When a bill to that effect was introduced in Congress, Marcantonio argued that while admittedly an improvement, the gubernatorial suffrage would be a mere "decoration on the facade of the building of colonialism, whose beams are rotten and whose foundations are crumbling."

Now Muñoz Marín was reconsidering, and not only because he would be a likely candidate for such an elective position. What had changed was the latter-day arrival of the New Deal in Puerto Rico. The blizzard of reform laws looking toward a significant reconstruction of the island's economy, and the provision of real resources by an administration that was also willing to take on and overcome opponents of reform—all this cast traditional categorizations in a different light. It was hard to depict Franklin Roosevelt and Rex Tugwell as imperialist exploiters. So as long as the New Deal was on the scene, and willing to back the kind of social democratic initiatives that might one day put Puerto Rico in a position to survive independence, an autonomist position seemed an almost thinkable thought.

168

Uniting the Nations

In 1934, US internationalists established a command post in an office building at 8 West 40th Street, overlooking the New York Public Library and Bryant Park. Here, on three increasingly crowded floors, resided a steadily multiplying network of interlocking groups seeking US participation in a global organization dedicated to maintaining world peace.

Primacy of place went to the League of Nations Association (LNA), founded in 1923 amid the wreckage of Woodrow Wilson's campaign to have the US join the League. Ever since, the LNA had been fighting to keep Wilson's flickering dream aflame, with little success in a country more suspicious than ever of foreign entanglements. Since 1933 the LNA had been captained by peace activist Clark Mell Eichelberger, who, in pursuit of allies, had steered his vessel into the growing antiwar fleet of militant church groups. After 1939, however, Eichelberger changed course. Convinced that US participation in an antifascist front was imperative, he set up and ran—out of 8 West 40th—the internationalist-minded Committee to Defend America by Aiding the Allies, which in 1940–41 out-argued America First in the court of public opinion. Eichelberger did not abandon his focus on an international organization during this campaign. Rather, in conjunction with an LNA colleague, Columbia history professor James T. Shotwell, he spun off a new entity to deal with it. Shotwell, born of Quaker ancestry in 1874—twenty-two years before Eichelberger—was a seasoned internationalist and scholarly organizer. He had been a core member of the Inquiry, the group that advised the American delegation at the 1919 Paris Peace Conference. And he had edited a mammoth (150-volume) series on the impact of the First World War for the Carnegie Endowment for International Peace. On Sunday, November 4, 1939, resurrecting the Inquiry model, Shotwell invited fifty experts on international relations to the Murray Hill Hotel to think about the aftermath of the war just barely begun. Quickly formalized as the Commission to Study the Organization of Peace (CSOP)—and also housed in 8 West 40th—the group began running even bigger scholarly conclaves on a monthly basis. It also launched a public education campaign promoting a "world organization for peace."

The CSOP was joined in this campaign by another denizen of 8 West 40th, the Foreign Policy Association (FPA). Like the LNA, it had emerged out of the First World War, but with a more liberal tinge. Founded in 1918 as the League of Free Nations Association by Paul Kellogg, editor of *The Survey*, it soon included writers and editors from *The New Republic*, *The Nation*, and *The Independent*, and a brace of activists from Charles Beard to Eleanor Roosevelt. Kellogg's group favored forming an international body open only to governments organized on liberal and democratic principles. Throughout the 1920s and 1930s the FPA ran discussion sessions in New York, and after 1938 added a weekly radio program on international affairs.

Funding for all these initiatives came in part crowded into the 40th Street beehive, the Woodrow Wilson Foundation (WWF). Created in 1921 for the "perpetuation of Wilson's ideals," the foundation aimed to give grants and awards to groups or individuals who performed "meritorious service to democracy, public welfare, liberal thought or peace through justice." Its board included numerous League of Nations proponents, not least among them the WWF's original chairman, Franklin Roosevelt, who as James Cox's vice-presidential candidate in 1920 had given more than 800 speeches promoting US membership.

One recipient of a Wilson Foundation grant was the Council on Foreign Relations, housed a score and more blocks uptown at 45 East 65th Street. In 1939 this high-powered organization, rooted not in the city's liberal intelligentsia but in the highest reaches of its corporate and financial elite, had embarked on the massive *War and Peace Studies* planning project. The Council's checklist of postwar desirables included a League-like international body, one that would bolster an orderly system of state relations—deemed essential to doing international business—by fostering peaceful settlement of disputes between governments.

The Council was convinced that Wilson's generation had won the war but bungled the peace, and its members were determined not to make the same mistake.

This conviction was held most strongly by the elite New Yorkers who had been junior officers in the First World War and were now running the Second. Secretary of War Henry Stimson (much the oldest among them) believed strongly that America's refusal to join the League had been instrumental in bringing on World War II. This opinion was all but universally shared by his younger colleagues at the apex of the wartime state. This cohort of New Yorkers, all born in the 1890s, included Patterson, Forrestal, Edward R. Stettinius, Robert A. Lovett, John Jay McCloy, Averell Harriman, Draper, Eberstadt, A. A. Berle—and Sumner Welles, one of those most responsible for moving an international organization from concept to reality.

Welles was born in 1892 to a wealthy and socially prominent Gotham family—related to Schermerhorns, Astors, and the Oyster Bay Roosevelts, including Eleanor, who chose young Sumner as a page to carry her bridal train when she married Franklin in 1905. Welles attended Groton, where he roomed with Eleanor's brother, and after graduating from Harvard in 1914 joined the foreign service—with a leg-up from FDR, then assistant secretary of the navy, who penned a personal recommendation to Secretary of State William Jennings Bryan. During the war, when he was posted to Tokyo and Buenos Aires, Welles got captivated by "the vision that Woodrow Wilson had held out to us of a world order founded on justice and on democracy." In 1921, he was made head of the State Department's Latin American Affairs Division, though he resigned in 1925 after further advancement was blocked by President Coolidge. He considered joining a Wall Street investment bank and returning to New York, though instead he married a wealthy Washington heiress and settled in DC.

Welles maintained his links to Gotham, however, especially those to Franklin Roosevelt. In the late 1920s, he began drafting foreign affairs position papers for the rising Democratic star, and he entered the city's unofficial foreign policy establishment by joining the CFR and the Woodrow Wilson Foundation. After Roosevelt became governor in 1928, Welles served in his informal cabinet. In 1932 he provided expertise (and a generous financial contribution) to Roosevelt's successful presidential campaign, and FDR appointed him assistant secretary of state for Latin America. In 1936, Roosevelt elevated Welles to the post of undersecretary, over the strenuous objections of Secretary of State Cordell Hull, who was less than pleased to have a number two so well connected to the president. Worse, Hull was a secret sufferer from tuberculosis and diabetes and frequently had to turn the department over to Welles for lengthy periods, during which Roosevelt became ever more reliant on his advice. (Welles was able to help Eleanor, too, notably in aiding Varian Fry's rescue mission.) With the arrival of war in 1939, Undersecretary Welles, like his peers in Gotham's foreign policy complex, was eager to begin planning the postwar order, and particularly keen to start fashioning a new international organization.

So, too, was the economist Leo Pasvolsky, a longtime and loyal Hull adviser whom the secretary appointed to direct departmental planning, in part as a counterweight to Welles. Pasvolsky was another transplanted New Yorker, though from a very different part of town. Born in Russia in 1893, Pasvolsky had been brought to the US in 1905 by his anti-Czarist parents. He attended night school at City College, graduating in 1916, then did graduate work at Columbia. When the Russian Revolution broke out, Pasvolsky lined up with Kerensky and against the Bolsheviks in Gotham's émigré battles (he claimed to have debated Trotsky during the latter's visit to New York). He also did some journalism—serving as editor of the monthly *Russian Review* and the daily *Amerikansky Viestnik*—and in 1919 covered the Paris peace conference for the New York *Tribune* and *Brooklyn Eagle*. In 1922 he joined the economic research staff of the Washington-based Brookings Institution, and in 1936 entered the State Department at Hull's behest. Like Welles, Pasvolsky kept up connections to New York. In 1938 he joined the CFR, and in 1939 began making regular trips up to Gotham for meetings of the *War and Peace Studies*' Economic and Financial Group. And, like Welles, Pasvolsky wanted to get started on planning.

At the end of 1939 Hull established an in-house postwar planning committee, which Welles chaired, but its early efforts at formulating postwar goals were hampered by limited resources and the press of contemporary events. For the time being, planning was in effect outsourced to New York, from where CFR brain trusters shipped memos south.

In August 1941 FDR took Welles (not Hull) to a secret meeting with Churchill, held aboard warships off the coast of Newfoundland, where they worked on an outline of war aims. Churchill suggested (with Welles's enthusiastic support) including a call for an "effective international organization." FDR said no. The old Wilsonian still favored such a body—though his real preference was to have the US, Britain, Russia, and China collectively police the planet—but believed a premature public appeal would arouse "suspicions and opposition." So the document that emerged—which a British journalist dubbed the "Atlantic Charter"—included only a vague reference to a future "permanent system of general security."

Welles and Pasvolsky continued to push for beefing up the State Department's anemic planning capabilities, and after Pearl Harbor, Roosevelt agreed to shift from importing the work of outside experts to importing the experts themselves. Welles now began recruiting New Yorkers to a blandly named Advisory Committee on Post-war Foreign Policy, whose work was to be kept secret.

His first choice, Norman Davis, was a founder and (since 1936) president of the CFR. Another CFR recruit was Hamilton Fish Armstrong, editor of *Foreign Affairs* and vice president of the *War and Peace Studies* project.

In February 1942, the Advisory Committee began sorting out the future of the world. The real work was parceled out to subcommittees, each headed by a trusted Welles ally. Norman Davis led the Subcommittee on Security Problems, Assistant Secretary of State Adolf Berle ran the Subcommittee on Economic Reconstruction, and Welles himself helmed a Subcommittee on Political Problems. The CFR supplied each subcommittee with a research secretary; as each of these simultaneously served a corresponding *War and Peace Studies* group, meetings were scheduled so the secretaries could be in New York the first half of each week, and the second half in Washington.

In June 1942, Welles created one last entity, a subset of his subcommittee. To this elite task force, which included himself and Pasvolsky, he added James T. Shotwell as a member and Clark Eichelberger as a consultant, establishing a link to 40th Street as well as 65th. The State Department was now nearly as hardwired to mid-Manhattan as the War Department was to Wall Street.

One reason Eichelberger was brought on board was that Welles was determined to build advance political support for the a-borning world organization, and given Eichelberger's genius for mass mobilization it seemed smart to give him a hand in creating the product he would soon be asked to sell. In February 1942, Eichelberger had launched a one-thousand-strong Commission to Study the Organization of Peace (CSOP). With funds from the Carnegie Endowment for International Peace, it set up thirteen "International Centres" around the country—distribution points from which a torrent of material sent out from New York was funneled to 900 study groups and the local chapters of sixty national organizations. Among the two million pieces of CSOP literature pumped out by October 1942 were pamphlets Manhattan writers believed well-tailored for specific markets, like one that folksily explained, to presumably isolationist Midwestern farmers, that "Just as pigs need to huddle together on a cold night, the world's many nations need to stick together."

As he moved forward, Eichelberger kept in regular contact with Roosevelt, getting a sense of his thinking, then floating as trial balloons proposals that FDR was not yet prepared to fly in public. The president and his public relations maven discussed tactics as well as strategy, even items like the best organizational name to use. When Eichelberger wondered if his "League of Nations Association" didn't yoke him to a largely discredited organization, FDR agreed it might be better to go with the fresher-sounding "United Nations," the term he had applied to the Allies. Loath to give up on the LNA altogether, Eichelberger in July 1943 nonetheless launched a *new* entity—the United Nations Association (UNA)—to be run by himself and Shotwell and shoehorned into 8 West 40th. The UNA now joined in producing radio shows, arranging thousands of meetings, and distributing millions more pamphlets. In the meantime, the Federal Council of Churches (297 Fourth Avenue) had taken up promoting yet another international body that approached the issue from a theological perspective. In February 1941, John Foster Dulles had accepted the chairmanship of a 100-member Gotham-based Commission to Study the Bases of a Just and Durable Peace (CJDP). Over the next two years the Commission hammered out a set of proposals for a new world order, issued in March 1943 as *The Six Pillars of Peace*. Though primarily Dulles's work, the document drew on realist Protestant theologians (notably CJDP member Reinhold Niebuhr), who argued that sinful aggression must be thwarted by collective international action and that international political affairs should be organized in conformity with moral law.

Six Pillars became the consensus doctrine of mainline Protestant denominations—Methodists, Presbyterians, Episcopalians, Congregationalists, and northern Baptists—who now threw their considerable resources into mobilizing for a world organization, their fervor stoked by the opportunity thus afforded of renewing Protestantism's ability to define America's mission. The FCC kicked off the campaign on October 28, 1943, at the Cathedral of St. John the Divine in Morningside Heights, where Dulles addressed a throng of 5,000. Then it was on, revival style, to over a hundred cities, with programs, preachings, and publications left behind for discussion by local congregants. And it worked: Congress was soon swamped by a flood of mail insisting that backing international cooperation was the Christian thing to do.

Women took the field as well. They had of course been major players in the prewar peace movement, but few of those organizations had survived Pearl Harbor and those that had were seriously shrunken. Membership in the US section of the Women's International League for Peace and Freedom dropped from a prewar high of 14,000 to under 4,000 at war's end. But many other groups stepped up to advance the cause of world peace—and, collaterally, the agenda-setting power of women. Three weeks before the US entered the war, the New York State Federation of Women's Clubs called for involving women in making the peace. In October 1942, representatives of twenty-one national women's organizations met in the headquarters of the YWCA (600 Lexington) to discuss their role in forging tomorrow's world. This led to formation of the Committee on the Participation of Women in Post War Planning, an umbrella group, headquartered in Gotham, that embraced a wide array of affiliates. (These ranged from the American Legion Auxiliary to the National Council of Negro Women and included the National Federation of Business and Professional Women's Clubs, American Association of University Women, the National Council of Jewish Women, the YWCA, and the League of Women Voters.)

The great bulk of this vast and variegated pro-UN armada linked attainment of an international body to the advancement of "human rights." The notion that all individuals had certain inalienable rights—not controvertible by the nation in which they lived—had ancient roots. Though it had never had the winds of a mass movement in its sails until Franklin Roosevelt declared in 1941 that his Four Freedoms—freedom of speech and worship, freedom from want and fear—should be secured not just at home but "everywhere in the world." By insisting that people everywhere were entitled to civil and religious liberty, to prosperity and security—by proposing that, as he perorated, "Freedom means the supremacy of human rights everywhere"—FDR staked out a set of *avant la guerre* war aims that had enormous appeal.

The president's declaring human rights to be a central US aspiration galvanized discussions in peace and social justice circles—nowhere denser than in New York—which had been wrestling with analogous issues on a local level. With amazing speed, a widespread consensus emerged among them that human rights should form the moral and legal foundation of the new postwar order and that it should be guaranteed by a supranational body.

On December 13, 1941, a week after Pearl Harbor and two days before the 150th anniversary of the US Bill of Rights, James Shotwell argued in a radio address that "an International Bill of Rights safeguarding not only personal liberty but freedom of thought, of religion, and of expression" should be made one of the nation's chief war aims. In 1943, Shotwell's CSOP released a report on "Human Rights and the World Order," which argued that securing human rights on a worldwide basis required setting limits on state sovereignty. In 1944, the CSOP urged that, if established, the proposed United Nations should create a permanent international commission, dedicated to protecting "the basic rights of the individual," by applying sanctions when warranted.

Faith-based internationalists adopted a similar stance.

Jews, especially after official confirmation of German genocide, were particularly active. In January 1943, the American Jewish Committee expressed hope "that a world order based on the Four Freedoms and the Atlantic Charter will also find its expression in an International Bill of Rights." As it had in New York, the Committee eschewed arguing narrowly on behalf of beleaguered Jewry, in favor of universalizing its demands, proposing that no religious, racial, or ethnic minority could be secure until all were. As AJC president Joseph Proskauer would put it: "the ultimate safety of the Jewish populations of Europe will rest upon an international enforcement of justice, and equality of treatment to all men of every race and creed."

Also in 1943, thirty-eight Protestant leaders—including such leading city lights as Reinhold Niebuhr, Henry P. Van Dusen, Henry Sloane Coffin, Guy Emery Shipler, and Methodist Bishop Francis J. McConnell (chair)—formed a Christian Conference on War and Peace. Together with the American Council of the World Alliance for International Friendship Through the Churches (70 Fifth Avenue), they pored over statements previously issued by the three major faiths, seeking common elements—a usual ecumenical procedure in New York. Then they put together an interfaith declaration (the "Pattern for Peace") which argued that moral law must govern world order; that nations were subject to the sovereignty of God; that the God-given rights of individuals must be assured; that an "international declaration of rights" and a body of international law (backed by "adequate sanctions") should be developed by an international organization; that racial and religious discrimination should be outlawed; and that the "rights of ethnic, religious and cultural minorities" to economic livelihood, equal opportunity for educational and cultural development, and political equality, should be guaranteed. Finally, they secured the signatures of 144 religious leaders, acting as individuals not official spokesmen, including some of Gotham's preeminent personages.

In the meantime, behind *very* closed doors, Welles's Special Subcommittee—at his urging and that of Shotwell in his capacity as member—was writing a constitution for the proposed world body. Their draft, like many of those circulating out-of-doors, proposed guaranteeing very specific civil and social rights and banning discrimination on grounds of race, nationality, language, political opinion, or religious belief (though not yet gender). The committee, being a governmental body, had to confront the question of precisely how such provisions were to be enforced—given the potential challenges to national sovereignty, starting with America's own. Welles favored some mild form of outside intervention, but as one discussant noted, it was politically unthinkable that an international bar against racial discrimination would be permitted to overrule "the laws of some of our states for the segregation of the races."

No one resisted the human rights clamor more than Cordell Hull (at least when out of the public eye). In the spring of 1943, having grown increasingly bitter at his inability to control postwar planning, the secretary of state assumed full-time chairmanship of the Special Subcommittee, after its forty-seventh meeting. Hull considered himself a "realist" and thought Welles prone to "idealism" and "crusading liberalism." The secretary specifically attacked the international bill of rights notion. No self-respecting nation—he told the others, notably Welles—would allow an international body to determine its relations with its own people. Certainly, the US would oppose any sacrifice of its national sovereignty on the altar of human rights.

The long-smoldering Hull, moreover, was seeking more than a policy override; he wanted Welles's scalp, and he had the knife with which to take it. In September 1940, an intoxicated Welles had allegedly propositioned several Black male porters on a train returning from Alabama—one filed a formal complaint—and again on a train bound for Cleveland. Though the newspapers published not a word, word got around anyway, spread most venomously by William Bullitt, a former ambassador and a resentful rival for the president's favor. It was generally assumed that Welles would be axed, given that homosexual behavior constituted grounds for criminal prosecution, and Welles, a high government official, had thus left himself open to blackmail. Roosevelt, however, considered Welles a friend and an indispensable adviser, so he sat on the story for the next three years, with the aid of J. Edgar Hoover (though the president did agree to have Welles escorted on train trips). Hull had gotten wind of this and, together with Bullitt, struggled to get the press to pay attention. Finally, in 1943, they succeeded in doing so, and in putting Republican congressmen on the scent. Even then it was not until August, when Hull, during a critical moment in international diplomacy, told FDR he would resign if Welles didn't, that Roosevelt, who thought Hull an "old fool" and found Bullitt despicable, acquiesced in Welles's departure.

FDR replaced Welles with Edward R. Stettinius Jr., another member of the New York corporate and social elite. The new undersecretary had been born in Chicago but grew up in a thirteen-room mansion on Staten Island after his father moved the family east to become a Morgan partner. Stettinius would rise to become chairman of the board of United States Steel but had also been a Wall Streeter for Roosevelt, and the president had given him several important wartime positions.

It was Leo Pasvolsky to whom Hull now turned over the responsibility of finishing the largely completed draft charter and amending or deleting those sections of Welles's version Hull found objectionable. Pasvolsky, who also had found it hard to reconcile international rights with national jurisdiction, just left them out altogether. His revised version served as the framework for negotiations between the Big Four (the US, Soviet Union, Britain, and China) at Dumbarton Oaks. This draft charter—which also ignored the issue, apart from a vague pledge to "promote respect for human rights and fundamental freedoms"—became the basis for a grand conclave at San Francisco where, beginning in April 1945, representatives of fifty nations would consider ratification.

Like Du Bois, many of the New Yorkers who had been agitating for human rights viewed the Dumbarton Oaks draft as a betrayal and called vocally for its emendation. John Foster Dulles of the FCC's Commission on a Just and Durable Peace thought the proposed structure smacked of being a "military alliance of a few great powers" out to divide world into "regional spheres of influence," and his CJDP called for including a Commission on Human Rights and Fundamental Freedoms. Proskauer's American Jewish Committee got 1,326 distinguished citizens of all faiths to sign a Declaration of Human Rights. Published on December 14, 1944, it argued that as Hitler's barbarism had shown what could happen when citizens were left to the mercy of their states, "No plea of sovereignty shall ever again be allowed to permit any nation to deprive those within its borders of these fundamental rights on the claim that these are matters of internal concern"—a position to which FDR publicly affirmed adherence. Eichelberger added the CSOP to the list of protesters by getting 150 American *prominenti* to endorse a two-page statement, read aloud over CBS radio on February 5, 1945, which also urged creation of a "Commission on Human Rights and Fundamental Freedoms."

Yet for all the criticisms by Dulles, Proskauer, Eichelberger, and others, the last thing they wanted was to replay 1920 by sinking US participation. So they adopted a two-prong strategy—pushing for revisions but also joining hand-in-hand with the Department of State in a mammoth pro-UN campaign.

It began when Clark Eichelberger brought representatives of forty mass organizations to an October 6, 1944, sit-down in New York—held, inevitably, at 8 West 40th Street—at which time they agreed to act in concert to promote the emerging world organization.

Also in October, the State Department decided to reach out to business, labor, peace, professional, civic, religious, and ethnic advocacy groups, who collectively represented tens of millions of Americans. This new policy would be overseen by Stettinius, whom FDR elevated to secretary of state after ill-health forced Hull to retire at the end of November. (New Yorkers now occupied the top spot at the Departments of State, War, Navy, and Treasury.) In December, Roosevelt persuaded Archibald MacLeish to leave the Library of Congress, to become (the first) assistant secretary of state for public and cultural affairs to direct the UN initiative.

Stettinius and MacLeish turned to the CSOP for help in accessing the world of nongovernmental organizations with which Eichelberger and Shotwell had been working for years. With their assistance, the State Department's new Division of Public Liaison gave over 500 briefings to these groups during the run-up to San Francisco and distributed another million pieces of literature. At the same time the 40th Street–directed network of two score associated groups generated its own blizzard of radio specials, opinion pieces, public lectures, Sunday sermons, school programs, and even comic books (in conjunction with *True Comics Magazine*).

So massive was the demand for 40th Street's resources that Eichelberger added yet another entity to the already bursting complex. In February 1945 the all-but-moribund League of Nations Association was finally renamed, and reconstructed as an essentially new powerhouse, the American Association for the United Nations (AAUN), with Sumner Welles as honorary president. In no time at all the AAUN emerged as the central coordinating body of the drive toward ratification. Its efforts culminated, on the eve of San Francisco, in the ungainly named "Dumbarton Oaks Week" campaign (April 16–22, 1945), marked in Gotham by a joint effort with the New York League of Women Voters to take the struggle to the streets. Corner rallies were held in Chelsea and Greenwich Village, in Wall Street and Union Square, while sound trucks were sent rolling through neighborhoods around town, drumming up support.

The emergence and explosive growth of the AAUN proved to be the last gasp for the impossibly overcrowded 8 West 40th Street complex, and the AAUN, the CSOP, the Woodrow Wilson Foundation, the whole kit and kaboodle, packed up and moved out. On April 17, 1945, amid the frenzy of the drive's final week, the Eichelberger–Shotwell operation formally inaugurated its roomy new quarters at 45 East 65th Street, with President Wilson's widow as guest of honor. The townhouse—henceforth known as Woodrow Wilson House—had been recently vacated by the Council on Foreign Relations, whose even vaster operations had outgrown the space. The CFR had moved a scant three blocks north, to a five-story mansion at 58 East 68th Street, on the corner of Park Avenue. Donated by the widow of Standard Oil of New Jersey partner Harold Irving Pratt, and refurbished with help from John D. Rockefeller Jr., it would be known as the Harold Pratt House. The nation's foreign-policy complex was now consolidated within the ambit of the Upper East Side, wherein dwelt a considerable portion of its membership.

The president of the Wilson Foundation found it fitting that its new center was being dedicated at the very moment when "Wilson's great objective of an international organization is, we hope, about to be fulfilled at the San Francisco Conference." And the signs were indeed propitious. Thanks in part to the all-out campaign, a recent poll found that when asked "Do you think the United States should join a world organization with police power to maintain world peace?" an astounding 81 percent answered "yes."

It also seemed the administration was disposed to move the human rights agenda. American Jewish Committee leaders Proskauer and Jacob Blaustein had met with President Roosevelt on March 20, 1945. They had talked of the death camps in Europe and conveyed their intention to ask the conference to include a commission that would draft an International Bill of Human Rights, a prospect in which (he authorized them to say) he "expressed sympathy and interest." His parting words to them (as Blaustein recalled) were: "Go to San Francisco. Work to get those human rights provisions into the Charter so that unspeakable crimes like those by the Nazis will never again be countenanced by world society."

When the conference began its nine weeks of work on April 25, there were over 5,000 people in attendance, including 850 delegates, 2,600 media, and the 102 advisers to the US delegation. The latter agreed to meet regularly as a group, of which a few New Yorkers became leaders. Shotwell was selected as chair—a natural choice given his seniority and experience and the fact that many of the consultants were long-standing members of his CSOP. Eichelberger assumed the role of unofficial whip, coordinating the activities of the various NGOs, and Proskauer and Frederick Nolde (of the Federal Council of Churches) emerged as the group's most forceful and eloquent spokesmen.

The consultants first met with the US delegation on May 1, 1945, in the Fairmont Hotel. To their dismay, the former were given to understand that the latter had little interest in pressing for inclusion of any human rights machinery in the charter text; they preferred rather to remain at the level of broad principles and frameworks. Eichelberger, Nolde, Shotwell, and Proskauer caucused, decided to protest, drafted a statement on human rights, corralled other advisers to sign it, and got an appointment with Secretary Stettinius for the following day, May 2, at 5:00 p.m., a half hour before the delegation itself would meet to take its final decisions as to what amendments to put forward.

At the ensuing sit-down, Stettinius stressed that efforts to win human rights at Dumbarton Oaks had failed and were unlikely to be any more successful at San Francisco. Nolde replied that their proposals were supported by millions of church members; Proskauer (in an eloquent presentation) argued they reflected the desires of the vast majority of the American people; and others supported the notion that if human rights were not part of the final mix there would be a tremendous backlash against American participation from their massive memberships.

At meeting's end, in Shotwell's recollection: "Secretary Stettinius instantly promised that he would do all he could to have the human rights clauses inserted in the Charter," and, at 5:25 p.m., he hove off to the delegates' meeting, which indeed agreed to sponsor and fight for the consultants' package. Stettinius and the delegates were swayed less by the oratory, which they had heard before, than by a conundrum of their own making. They had counted on the NGO advisers acting as powerful cheerleaders for official policy, but clearly the headstrong New Yorkers would turn into powerful opponents if given nothing whatever. On the other hand, the ultimate goal remained winning Senate confirmation of US participation. That body was ruled by Southern Democrats who would never brook a world organization empowered to break Jim Crow. And a representative of racism was very much on hand, in the person of Texas Senator Tom Connally, an ardent white supremacist and skilled defender of segregation. Connally, who was chair of the Senate Foreign Relations Committee and thus in a key position to decide the UN's fate, was also (not coincidentally) vice chairman of the US delegation at San Francisco, the second most powerful player after Stettinius.

In the end it was John Foster Dulles—also worried that an unconstrained UN would launch a messy and embarrassing investigation of "the Negro question in this country"—who crafted the solution. The drafters would accept provisions calling for human rights—but withhold the power to enforce them.

So it was that the final text began with a Preamble in which signatories declared their "faith in fundamental human rights, in the dignity and worth of the human person, in the equal rights of men and women, and of nations large and small." The Charter's first Article—listing the UN's purposes—included "promoting and encouraging respect for human rights and for fundamental freedoms for all without distinction as to race, sex, language or religion." And Article 68 set up an Economic and Social Council that was in turn mandated to create a commission "for the promotion of human rights."

However, the document also included the countervailing Dulles-drafted Article 2(7), which asserted that "Nothing in the present Charter shall authorize the United Nations to intervene in matters which are essentially within the domestic jurisdiction of any state," a phrase that neatly precluded any outside interference on behalf of threatened citizens (for example, Jews or Blacks).

The human rights references were a remarkable accomplishment for their advocates, but with no International Bill of Rights to specify which rights were included, nor any mandatory mechanisms to enforce them, the victory, for the moment, remained largely rhetorical and hortatory. Secretary Stettinius held a press conference in which he suggested how the "domestic jurisdiction" clause might be overcome in the future. He called on the Charter-mandated Commission on Human Rights to promptly prepare a bill of specific rights, which could then "be accepted by all member nations as an integral part of their own systems of law," rather than being left to a supranational body to enforce.

If action on human rights had been shoved off to the future, liberal Gotham-based proponents could take some comfort in knowing that one of their own would be heavily involved in working on them. A year after San Francisco, when a nine-member committee convened at Hunter College to begin deliberating on the structure and functions of a Commission on Human Rights, its first act was to elect Eleanor Roosevelt as its chairperson.

On July 28, 1945, in a testament to the sustained efforts at building support for the United Nations—the critical thrust having come from New York—the Charter adopted at San Francisco was approved in the Senate by a vote of 89 to 2, with 5 abstentions. The conference then adjourned, though without settling another issue, one in which Gothamites were vitally interested: the question of exactly *where* the United Nations would set up shop. That battle, left for another day, would prove to be as contentious as the founding itself.

EPILOGS

Epilogs

On Thursday, April 12, 1945, Franklin Roosevelt was in good spirits. He had arrived at Warm Springs, Georgia, two weeks earlier, totally exhausted, seeking rejuvenation in its therapeutic waters, as he had so often in the past. It had been a grueling winter—marked notably by a week-long meeting in February with Stalin and Churchill, on the return from which his haggard appearance had been widely noted.

A few leisurely weeks seemed to have perked him up. On that Thursday afternoon he was planning to dictate to his personal secretary, Grace Tully, the first draft of the opening address he would give to the roughly 6,000 delegates, staff, and press—from fifty nations—who on April 25 would gather in San Francisco to establish the United Nations. He settled in, read and signed some pressing documents, and welcomed the artist who had come to sketch his portrait while he worked.

At 1:15 p.m., he complained of a terrific pain at the back of his head and immediately collapsed into unconsciousness. His attending physicians gave him several injections, to no avail. At 3:35 p.m., they declared him dead, victim of a massive cerebral hemorrhage.

At 5:47 p.m., after Eleanor Roosevelt had set off from Washington to retrieve her husband's body, and Vice President Harry Truman had been sworn in, the White House press office sent out an official bulletin that President Franklin Delano Roosevelt had died suddenly two hours before.

In New York, a city whose history was intimately intertwined with his, reactions were stunned, disbelieving. The *Times* reported: "In home communities—Brooklyn, the Bronx, Harlem, Queens—women left their dinners on the stoves to stand in their neighborhoods, passing the word, discussing it with bated breath." Groups of New Yorkers, small at first but ever-growing, gathered in silence wherever a shopkeeper had turned his radio speaker toward the street, the four major stations having cancelled regular programming for full-time coverage. The news flowed through the streets, into office building lobbies and restaurants, and rush-hour subways, where youths ran from car to car, carrying the word. Have you heard? Ten thousand Catholic War Veterans held a memorial service in Duffy Square at 46th and Broadway. Twenty thousand garment workers and employers gathered on Seventh Avenue, between 28th and 29th, the usually cacophonous street hushed to hear cantor M. S. Yardelni intone "El Malei Rachamim," the ancient Hebrew prayer for the dead. Solemn crowds gathered in Times Square, the shock of the news revealed in their faces.

In City Hall a distraught Mayor La Guardia flicked on his WNYC microphone and, pounding his desk, declared that though "our leader had died, he lives on." "His inspiration is with us." "His leadership is with us. We cannot escape it. We must not escape it. An additional duty and responsibility has now been thrust upon us, a duty to carry on." "Centuries and centuries from now. As long as history is recorded, people will know Franklin Delano Roosevelt loved humanity. I call upon all New Yorkers to carry on!"

It turned out there was an immediate way for the city to honor FDR, and La Guardia set about helping organize it. Back in Washington, Eleanor and Truman had arranged for a funeral service to be held in the White House East Wing, the next day, Friday the 13th, at precisely 4:00 p.m. In New York, La Guardia—together with metropolitan leaders of civic, social, economic, cultural, and commercial institutions—set about organizing a temporary cessation of business as usual, to commence precisely at 4:00 p.m. Sector by sector, the gigantic city set about shutting itself down, some for minutes, some for hours, some for a day or a night.

At 4:00 p.m., radios went silent. At 4:00 p.m., the New York Telephone Company momentarily halted service—"Hello, hello, are you there?"—and on resumption, racked up a record 10,002,498 calls for the day. Western Union ceased sending domestic and foreign messages for a brief spell. In newspaper offices teletype machines stopped their clattering, then slowly tapped out seven letters: "S I L E N C E."

At 4:00 p.m., the motormen of the city's 505 subway and elevated trains halted their 3,500 cars in place—in or between stations—and paused there; many passengers folded their newspapers, stood up, and bowed their heads. At La Guardia Airport, planes backed up on the runways, their clearance for take-offs having been temporarily withheld, while arriving planes circled in the air, their pilots instructed to delay landing except in case of emergency.

Most mercantile offices closed for the afternoon or the day. Most war plants suspended production, but only briefly.

Fifth Avenue's department stores shrouded their famed window displays with long black drapes. Thousands of retail cigar stores, shoe shops, and the like stayed closed all day. Groceries and food stores closed between 2 and 5 p.m. Theaters on Broadway cancelled matinees, as did the Ringling Brothers Barnum and Bailey Circus at Madison Square Garden. The city's seven hundred movie theaters closed till six. The 224 members of the Hotel Association of New York City discontinued music, dancing, and entertainment in their establishments, day and night. The Philharmonic cancelled a scheduled performance in Carnegie Hall for the first time since April 22, 1865, the date of Lincoln's assassination.

After the silences, multiple verbal encomiums marked FDR's passing.

La Guardia and Columbia President Nicolas Murray Butler addressed the 50,000 crammed into City Hall Plaza. Archbishop Spellman held forth in St. Patrick's. Episcopal Bishop William T. Manning held a special mass at St. John the Divine. Rabbis offered eulogies at synagogues and rabbinical colleges. Public and parochial schools offered memorial services, as did colleges including City, Brooklyn, Queens, Hunter, NYU, and Columbia elegies. Three thousand students at the Central Commercial High School collected 1,200 plants for the wounded at nearby Army and Navy hospitals. The Second Service Command, headquartered on Governor's Island, held memorial services at all its camps and stations. And the alarm center of the New York Fire Department instructed all firehouses to toll "four fives"—the dreaded signal that a fireman had died in the line of duty.

Newspaper stand the day after Roosevelt's death, April 13, 1945. This was the first photo published by Stanley Kubrick, then sixteen years old. (Stanley Kubrick, photographer, LOOK Magazine Photograph Collection, Library of Congress, Prints & Photographs Division)

THE *NEW YORK TIMES* HEADLINE of May 8, 1945, gave equal attention to these seismic events:

PRESIDENT ROOSEVELT IS DEAD;
TRUMAN TO CONTINUE POLICIES;
9TH CROSSES ELBE, NEARS BERLIN

The Ninth U.S. Army was indeed some fifty miles from Berlin, and it was being urged by Britain's Field Marshal Montgomery to race east and capture the city before the Russians did. But Marshal Zhukov's million-man Red Army was closer still. When Supreme Commander General Dwight Eisenhower asked General Omar Bradley for his opinion, Bradley estimated that a breakthrough might cost upward of 100,000 American lives—"a pretty stiff price to pay for a prestige objective." It was a price Eisenhower wasn't willing to pay, especially as any territory gained would have to be turned over to the Soviets at war's end, as required by the terms of postwar occupation drawn up by the Big Three at Yalta months earlier.

On April 11, 1945, Red Army tanks smashed through Berlin's outer defenses and began battling their way toward the heart of the city—the Reich Chancellery, beneath which lay the Führerbunker, where, on April 30, Adolf Hitler gave Eva Braun, his one-day wife, a capsule of prussic acid, and then blew his brains out with his Walther PPK. Mindful of Mussolini's heel-hanging two days earlier, the Führer had arranged to have their corpses burned to ash and bone, and this was done.

In the early morning hours of Monday, May 7, 1945, the unconditional surrender of the German Third Reich was signed by General Alfred Jodl, Chief of Staff of the German Army, at Eisenhower's headquarters in Reims.

THE NEXT DAY, MAY 8, 1945, the war's end in Europe touched off a frenzied celebration in Gotham. In Times Square 500,000 people poured out of Midtown buildings and generated a vast tsunami of sound. They whooped, whistled, cheered, shouted. They danced in conga lines, stood on their heads, sang, drank, and hugged and kissed strangers, as confetti rained down upon them. There were similar scenes on Wall Street, in the Garment District, and in Rockefeller Center. NBC television covered the victory party from atop the Astor Hotel marquee.

A MONTH LATER, VICTORIOUS VETERANS began arriving from Europe to receive the city's tribute. On June 19, 1945, an astounding four million New Yorkers turned out to hail Supreme Commander Eisenhower. A motorized cavalcade, with La Guardia at his side, bore him through 37 miles of city streets, their sidewalks lined with gigantic crowds, and every window, fire escape, balcony, and rooftop occupied with cheering onlookers. In towering skyscraper districts the procession was pelted with paper snowstorms. The throngs were thickest in the Garment District and Black Harlem and were composed predominantly of women and children, as hundreds of thousands of male New Yorkers were still at the fighting fronts. There were, however, plenty of uniformed men in the crowds, with battle stars on their tunics, some on crutches, others with empty sleeves, all eager to pay tribute to the man who had led them to victory. As Police Commissioner Valentine summed up, it was "unquestionably the largest and most enthusiastic crowd in the history of the city." Also the loudest: a General Electric noise meter assessed the maximum applause as "equivalent to 3,000 loud peals of thunder at the same time."

ON THE FOLLOWING MORNING, JUNE 20, 1945, Britain's 81,235-ton liner, the *Queen Mary*, came steaming up the bay, her foghorn bellowing, bearing 14,526 American servicemen and women, the first big contingent to return from the European Theater of war. Flotillas of lesser vessels sailed out to greet her—tugs, freighters, ferryboats, barges, train flat cars, launchers, lighters, and the 16-knot *Fire Fighter*—the most powerful in the world—spouting plumes of water. Hundreds of ship sirens bellowed as the vessel made its way up the Hudson River to West 50th Street, where it warped into the slip on the north side of Pier 90. From its towering decks and portholes soldiers and sailors waved to the cheering crowds below. But for many of the sailors and soldiers, cries of "Welcome home!" were premature, as most of them were about to be redeployed from the Atlantic to the Pacific front. As La Guardia cautioned the celebrants, "while the evil forces of Nazism and Fascism are destroyed . . . there is still a great deal of fighting and dying yet ahead."

TWO DAYS AFTER HE SPOKE in June, the Navy and Marine Corps finally won a horrific eighty-two-day struggle to control Okinawa, intended to be the base for an amphibious invasion of Japan's Home Islands. It had cost more than ten thousand American lives.

Earlier, in March 1945, the US had begun firebombing Japanese cities. This strategy had been widely adopted in Europe after combatants abandoned the policy of restricting attacks on an enemy's military targets—factories, railroads, ports—that had been adopted after the uproar over the bombing of helpless Guernica.

In the Pacific Theater, the US Army Air Corps' chief of staff, General Harley "Hap" Arnold, followed suit, arguing that "this is a brutal war and...the way to stop the killing of civilians is to cause so much damage and destruction and death that the civilians will demand their government cease fighting." Arnold turned this task over to the head of the XXI Bomber Command, General Curtis LeMay, who had worked closely with Britain's RAF in European aerial campaigns.

ON THE NIGHT OF MARCH 9, 1945, an armada of 334 Boeing B-29 Superfortresses flew 1,500 miles to Tokyo, on which they dropped 1,665 tons of incendiary bomblets, each containing half a million cylinders of napalm and white phosphorus, which ignited when they hit the ground, spewing flames in all directions, creating a firestorm of superheated air and cyclonic winds which roared far beyond the target area with devastating results. Citizens ran through the streets in panic, desperate to escape the searing heat, which reached an unimaginable temperature of 1,800 degrees, sucking the oxygen out of the air, asphyxiating those it did not simply roast to death.

Approximately 100,000 died in a six-hour span, a carnage unlike anything the world had ever seen. It did not, however, produce the desired surrender. So, over the following spring and summer, LeMay's B-29s firebombed one Japanese city after another, until sixty-six had been destroyed and 330,000 residents killed. In addition, LeMay oversaw a campaign—the forthrightly named Operation Starvation—to bomb ports and waterways, further reducing Japan's ability to move its troops or feed its people. The diehard military dictators, and Emperor Hirohito, rejected the American demand for unconditional surrender.

ON AUGUST 6, A SINGLE B-29, the Enola Gay, dropped an atomic bomb on Hiroshima, killing roughly 100,000 people.

ON AUGUST 8, AS AGREED at Yalta, the Soviet Union declared war on Japan and invaded its puppet state of Manchukuo.

ON AUGUST 9, A SECOND atomic bomb was dropped, on Nagasaki, killing roughly 100,000 people.

IN NEW YORK, HOPES OF an impending breakthrough attracted crowds to Times Square. Days passed; the crowds swelled. Then, in the early evening of August 14, fresh rumors suggesting Japan had accepted the Allies' terms drew 750,000 to Broadway between 40th and 48th Streets, their attention riveted on the illuminated Motogram rippling around the New York Times tower. Which at 7:03 p.m. confirmed that it was "OFFICIAL—TRUMAN ANNOUNCES JAPANESE SURRENDER."

At which a huge uproar issued forth, from Herald Square to Columbus Circle. People poured out of theaters, raced in by subway, and by 10:00 p.m. there were two million people in Times Square, whistling, shouting, screaming, dancing, kissing, embracing, snake dancing, playing leapfrog, forming la conga chains, standing on their heads. Fire engines clanged, police sirens wailed, taxi horns blasted. "The victory roar beat upon the eardrums until it numbed the senses," said the *Times*. So boisterous were the crowds—nearly a thousand people were treated for injuries incurred in the celebration—that fourteen thousand police, more than a thousand Navy Shore Patrolmen, and four companies of MPs were called in to suppress "over-exuberance."

THE DAY AFTER V-J DAY, a national Gallup poll revealed that 85 percent of those surveyed approved of the nuclear attacks on Japan. Later that August a Roper survey found that 23 percent regretted that more atomic bombs had not been used before the surrender. But in subsequent weeks and months, as reports from the ruined cities depicting the incredible degree of damage began to circulate, more and more people began to wonder if what had happened to Tokyo and Hiroshima might not happen elsewhere, perhaps, even most likely, in New York.

Hitler, after all, had actually attempted to incinerate Gotham. According to Albert Speer, Hitler's favorite architect, the Führer took great pleasure in watching films in the Reich Chancellery of London burning, and he was intoxicated by the idea of achieving "the downfall of New York" by firebombing the city, turning its skyscrapers "into gigantic burning torches, collapsing onto one another, the glow of the exploding city illuminating the dark sky." Hermann Goering, the Luftwaffe's commander-in-chief, complained bitterly that we "completely lack the bombers capable of round-trip flights to New York with a 4.5-tonne bomb load. I would be extremely happy to possess such a bomber, which would at last stuff the mouth of arrogance across the sea," and he set about obtaining one. Plans for a four-engine, long-range "Amerikabomber" (the Messerschmitt Me 264) began to appear in the spring of 1942, and three prototypes were actually produced. The project was abandoned when priority went to producing fighters with which to fend off Allied bombers.

There had been, too, a long-standing literary predilection for imagining the Destruction of Gotham (the title of an 1886 novel). As of 1945, New York had been repeatedly demolished by earthquakes, by collision with comets, by plagues, or floods of biblical proportion; by class wars and ethnic wars; by being bombed by zeppelins; by collapsing under the weight of its skyscrapers; and by invasion from monsters or Martians. These were obvious fictions.

A real-life connection between Gotham and atomic Armageddon emerged during the 1939 debate among Columbia University physicists about the possibilities and perils of nuclear fission. One set of scholars believed that bombarding uranium atoms with neutrons would release enormous but controllable and even useful energy. The other worried that unleashing a "chain reaction" would have a sensationally explosive effect. This not-yet-secret controversy was widely covered in the press. *New York Times* science writer William L. Laurence reported concerns that cracking a tiny amount of uranium-235 "would blow a hole in the earth 100 miles in diameter," obliterating Gotham completely. "Every building in New York City and every ship at its docks—not to mention its people—would have vanished without a trace."

Six years later, on January 25, 1945, with the nearly completed development of an atomic weapon shrouded in silence, President Roosevelt summoned Edward Stettinius, his recently appointed secretary of state, up to his White House study and told him, "in the utmost secrecy," of "a far-reaching experiment that might revolutionize the world." He was "not sure how long it would take to perfect a new bomb—the atomic bomb—but before too long it might be possible to drop this bomb in New York City at 42nd Street and Broadway. The resulting explosion," the president said, "would lay New York low."

Postwar fantasies of New York's looming destruction focused not on the manner in which atomic bombs were produced but on the ease with which they could be delivered. Curtis LeMay insisted that "we scorched and boiled and baked to death more people in Tokyo on that night of March 9–10 than went up in vapor at Hiroshima and Nagasaki." It's true that both approaches had yielded the same result—each had killed 100,000 Japanese—the striking difference was that LeMay's strategy had required an armada of hundreds of B-29s, while the other needed but a single plane. The bomb had been liberated from its makers, so to speak. And given its portability—the Enola Gay's appropriately named Little Boy was a mere 120 inches in length and 28 inches in diameter (though admittedly it weighed an unwieldly 9,700 pounds)—it could be transported to its target by a ship or train or truck or plane.

Increasingly, that likely target was Gotham. As a piece in the December 1945 issue of the *Reader's Digest* observed, "It is now in the power of the atom-smashers to blot out New York with a single bomb.... Such a bomb can burn up in an instant every creature, can fuse the steel buildings and smash the concrete into flying shrapnel."

In February 1946, Brigadier General Thomas F. Farrell, commander of the first US Army investigating team to enter Hiroshima, testified that in a nuclear attack New York's skyscrapers "would fly apart as though they themselves were bombs and someone had lighted their fuse."

In March 1946 the Federation of American Scientists published *One World or None*, an immediate bestseller. In one chapter of the book, Philip Morrison, an atomic physicist who had also inspected Hiroshima, described a hypothetical bomb attack on New York in moment-by-moment detail. Dropped at 12:07 p.m., it was detonated at 2,600 feet "just above the corner of Third Avenue and East 20th Street, near Gramercy Park." The dead and dying filled streets from Coney Island to Van Cortlandt Park, and many survivors of the blast were later killed by "unstoppable internal hemorrhages" from radiation disease; total deaths he estimated at 300,000.

A 1947 *Reader's Digest* article—"Mist of Death Over New York"—described an explosion in the harbor which sent a deadly radioactive cloud across the city. Those not killed immediately died in great numbers as they attempted to escape their doomed island. In "the worst panic known in all human history," they were crushed to death in subway stations, bridges, and tunnels, or were drowned in the surrounding rivers. Within six weeks, 389,101 New Yorkers were dead or missing.

These speculations about future horrors were matched by detailed accounts of the damage wreaked upon individual Hiroshima citizens, a depiction more gripping than simply counting corpses. The most compelling of these was a special issue of the *New Yorker* magazine devoted entirely to a 30,000-word account by John Hersey, a Pulitzer Prize–winning war reporter, of his visit to Hiroshima in May 1946, where he interviewed six survivors, who recounted—in calm and restrained prose—how each had experienced the day of the bombing. They were a diverse group: two clerics (a German Jesuit missionary and a Japanese Methodist priest); two Japanese women (a widowed seamstress with three young children, and a clerk in the personnel department of the East Asia Tin Works); and two doctors (one a staff surgeon at the modern Red Cross Hospital, the other a physician in a private hospital). They represented a wider social spectrum than the stereotypes usually suggested, and Hersey's prose, free of moralizing, humanized his interviewees.

The result was a spectacular success. The day before its publication the *New Yorker* sent press releases announcing the report to nine major New York newspapers and three international wire services, whetting public interest. Within one hour, 300,000 copies disappeared from newsstands. Papers around the country clamored for reprint rights. Alfred Knopf brought out a first printing of 300,000. The Book-of-the-Month Club told its million members that *Hiroshima* was "destined to be the most widely read book of our generation." In England, Penguin Press published 250,000 copies that sold out within weeks. A dozen translations were hastened to print. Global sales were spectacular. The American Broadcasting Company Radio Network aired a reading of the entire work in four parts on successive evenings, reaching tens of millions more.

Many radio commentators called *Hiroshima* a cautionary tale and warned that soon no one would be exempt from the threat of nuclear war. Bill Leonard, a political analyst for ABC, found the book disturbing. "As I read Mr. Hersey's account it was all too easy...to change the Japanese names to American names, to change the flimsy buildings of Hiroshima to the sturdy buildings of New York." "Read it," he advised his audience, "and then read it again, because this is New York's story." *PM* editor and WOR commentator Max Lerner concurred, telling his listeners, "Don't say it can't happen here. It can."

THE WIDESPREAD CONVICTION THAT A nuclear world war would put an end to civilization led to heightened support for the United Nations, whose charter had been signed in San Francisco on June 26, ratified by the US Senate on July 28, and come into effect on October 24, 1945.

Three days later, on Navy Day (a national holiday since 1922), President Truman came to New York to make what the White House billed as the first major presentation of his approach to foreign policy since he came into office.

On arriving at Penn Station, a motorcade conveyed him to the Brooklyn Navy Yard, where he commissioned a new super-carrier, the *Franklin D. Roosevelt*.

Then it was on to City Hall, where Mayor La Guardia received what was said to be the first visit by a sitting president, and Truman reviewed 2,000 soldiers from the vantage point of the central window facing the plaza—the spot where on July 9, 1776, the Declaration of Independence was read to Continental Army troops, in the presence of General George Washington.

Next he was taken to Central Park's Sheep Meadow, where before a million-strong crowd he laid out his vision of the United Nations' remit, and America's central role in its operation.

"The atomic bombs which fell on Hiroshima and Nagasaki must be made a signal not for the old but for a new era—an era of ever-closer unity and ever-closer friendship among peaceful nations." "We are convinced," he said, "that the preservation of peace between nations requires a United Nations organization composed of all the peace-loving nations of the world who are willing jointly to use force to insure peace."

The United States's sole possession of the atom bomb, Truman declared, was not a threat to any nation. "The world, which has seen the United States in two great recent wars, knows that full well. The possession in our hands of this new power of destruction we regard as a sacred trust. Because of our love of peace, the thoughtful people of the world know that that trust will not be violated, that it will be faithfully executed."

Finally, after lunch aboard the battleship *Missouri*, upon which MacArthur had accepted Japan's surrender, there came a spectacular celebration of the Navy's wartime role and peacetime prowess. Six million people lined the banks of the Hudson along a seven-mile stretch, from 60th Street north to Spuyten Duyvil, where forty-seven warships—aircraft carriers, cruisers, destroyers, submarines—rode at anchor. The president then boarded the destroyer

Renshaw which cruised along the river, receiving a 21-gun salute from each vessel as it passed, two hours of rolling thunder that were matched by a continuous roar from the 1,200 airplanes—fighters and bombers—that soared overhead.

DURING THE FALL OF 1945, the United Nations Preparatory Commission (UNPC), consisting of one delegate from each government that had signed the UN Charter, gathered in London to launch the multinational organization. The first and most contentious issue was where to place its headquarters—Europe or the United States.

The Europeanists, led by England, favored Geneva, home of the League of Nations. Those who favored the USA argued that the League's failure to ward off World War II had stemmed in no small part from America's refusal to join it. Giving the headquarters to the Americans would ensure their participation. As Andrei Gromyko, Russia's ambassador to the US, summarized their position: "The United States is located conveniently between Asia and Europe. The Old World has had it once, and it is time for the New World to have it."

On December 15, 1945, the UNPC announced its decision: "The permanent headquarters of the United Nations should be located in the United States of America."

Next question: where in the USA? Even before this decision was handed down, cities and towns across the country had been dispatching civic boosters to London—without being invited to do so—who offered to host the UN. San Francisco, Chicago, Denver, St. Louis, Atlanta, Philadelphia, Boston, and other major metropolises jostled for attention, joined by a host of equally unbidden lobbyists from the Black Hills of South Dakota, the estate of Abraham Lincoln, Tuskahoma, Oklahoma, and an island at Niagara Falls. Substantial invitations had flowed in from more than forty US locations. Now, with the designation made official, a slew of new offers arrived.

Dismayed by the possibility that the headquarters might be placed too far away from Europe, the British delegates managed to revise the criteria to read: "The site of the permanent headquarters should be in the East [emphasis added] of the United States of America." With one stroke, all western and midwestern venues were rejected. Another bold slash disqualified all states below the Mason-Dixon line on the grounds that racially segregated southern cities might subject delegates from Liberia or India or Ethiopia or China to humiliating treatment. Washington was passed over to avoid political entanglements in the nation's capital. Thus, the strongest remaining candidates for the United Nations' home base were located in Massachusetts (notably Boston), Connecticut (Greenwich, Stamford), Pennsylvania (Philadelphia), and New York State (but not New York City).

Gotham was a no-go territory. The UNPC had decreed that the site "should not be located within or too near a large metropolitan district." The UN desired a vast multi-acre site, at least forty square miles wide, in a rural or suburban setting, within which it could build an international city. Proposed sites were specifically forbidden to come closer than 25 miles from New York City.

To inspect the locations that had been proposed, and investigate promising new candidates, the UNPC created an Interim Headquarters Committee. It included all the Security Council heavyweights—China, France, Great Britain, and the Soviet Union—with the United States opting for neutrality. It was chaired by Stoyan Gavrilovic of Yugoslavia, who described the Committee's mission as finding a place "which will be reserved entirely for the United Nations, a place which will become the Capital of the World."

After a crash course in the delineated regions' topographical, social, and cultural attributes—gleaned by poring through the American Automobile Association's road maps and various WPA Guides—they selected several likely locations to examine and set off on their journey, flying from London to New York, the base of operations from which they would make on-site assessments of the "East's" top candidates. Gotham, pursuant to the 25-mile no-go diktat, was not on their list, but they scheduled a visit on January 8 with Mayor William O'Dwyer in City Hall (Fiorello La Guardia's final term having ended on December 31). Like his predecessor, O'Dwyer dearly wanted the United Nations to settle in the city. It was, he said, "the one great thing that would make New York the center of the world."

O'Dwyer, like La Guardia, was overly sanguine about the city's chances. Fiorello had refused to send emissaries to London to make a case for Gotham. "I am not going to put my city in a position of bidding for it the same as a small-sized city would bid for a national political convention or for the Elks convention or something like that," he had told a CBS radio audience. "I think it is unbecoming." "I advise strongly that we wait and let all the other cities peddle themselves," and "I am sure that when everything is considered—the facilities and communications, and everything that is needed—the United Nations Organization will come to New York City."

This did not mean he had been complacent. La Guardia had worked closely with Robert Moses to prepare a prospectus for the UN's new home in New York. It would be located in Flushing Meadows, Queens, where the 1939 World's Fair had been held. Its still-standing New York City Building—now a roller- and ice-skating rink—would become the domain of the UN's General Assembly. To craft this complex, Moses had enlisted top architects, including Aymar Embury II, who had designed the original structure, and Wallace (Wally) Harrison, whose work included the Fair's dramatic Trylon and Perisphere. The finished proposal—a brochure of architectural drawings and relevant facts and figures—was bound in blue leather and paired with a 10-by-5-foot map.

For his part, O'Dwyer invited to the January 8 meeting several members of the city's business and cultural elite—Grover Whalen, Bernard Baruch, Thomas Watson, Frederick Ecker, Herbert Bayard Swope, and, notably, Nelson Rockefeller, who knew many of the UN delegates from his days attending the San Francisco founding conference. A Roosevelt appointee as assistant secretary of state, he had recently been nudged out of office by the Truman administration. Since then, the thirty-seven-year-old Rockefeller had become increasingly active in city affairs, having been named chairman of the board of the Rockefeller Center complex and would soon be returning to his former position as head of the Museum of Modern Art.

The January 8 meeting lasted only half an hour, long enough for Gavrilovic to make painfully clear that the city would not be considered for the permanent site. But then, unexpectedly, he asked if New York might be willing to serve as a temporary location—housing the UN for three to five years while the permanent headquarters were being constructed elsewhere. O'Dwyer, startled, said he'd have to think about it, and the delegates departed, declining to take the blue book with them.

AFTER SEVERAL WEEKS OF DISCUSSION and consultation, O'Dwyer and Moses decided that serving as interim headquarters might improve Gotham's chances of winning its bid for permanence—by giving the UN members a chance to experience living in the city. The team came up with a formal appraisal of possibilities, and in early February the General Assembly voted New York to be the interim home of the United Nations. It also directed the newly appointed Secretary General Trygve Lie of Norway to oversee its progress. This was a fortunate choice for Gotham, as Lie, though he didn't say so publicly, believed the permanent home should be in New York City. And he thought that once temporary headquarters were established, "human inertia—and the high cost of moving"—would make that outcome more likely.

Lie arrived on March 21 and worked with Moses on acquiring and renovating three temporary locations.

First needed was a home for the Security Council, which would be arriving in March for its inaugural session. Moses suggested the Bronx campus of Hunter College. The two-year women's college had been taken over by the Navy during the war and used as a training camp for WAVES. Now the college was scheduled to reopen, but Moses diverted its four ivy-covered buildings to UN use—overcoming the students' vigorous protests—and deployed 2,000 workmen, who completed a makeover two days before the delegates arrived.

For the General Assembly's meeting place, Moses, not surprisingly, suggested the New York City Building in Flushing Meadows that he'd been promoting for permanence. In the second week of April the city agreed to bear the cost of renovation—2.2 million dollars—and the makeover was completed in a record-breaking two months before the fall arrival of 5,000 delegates and staff.

Third, Moses came up with the now vacant Sperry Gyroscope factory, whose three enormous and modern buildings had, during the war, employed 22,000 workers. It was located in Lake Success, a village in Nassau County, seventeen miles from mid-Manhattan. And it was available to rent.

Meanwhile, on the permanence front, Gavrilovic and his committee had canvassed candidates for non-Gotham dwellings; had been most enthused by several villages along the Connecticut coast, particularly Greenwich; and had staked out a large swath of suburban land above it in Fairfield County (which could be increased from 40 to 172 square miles). In February, the General Assembly established another committee to study the area and report back by the fall.

Things soon began to go south, in both the permanent and temporary initiatives.

The Greenwich countryside of Fairfield County that the inspectors had picked out was dotted with historic villages and large estates that were owned by many of New York's corporate magnates, bankers, lawyers, and publishers—among the most wealthy and powerful families in the country. Many were supporters of the United Nations. However, when told that a thousand of their homes would be confiscated (ten thousand if the expanded version was imposed) and their land would be turned into an enclave that would no longer be United States territory, they hit the roof. Unlike the hundreds of towns and cities who desperately desired to have the UN nearby, denizens of the "Gold Coast" were fiercely determined to fend it off. Protests began early and spread swiftly. On February 5, 1946, the Greenwich Town Meeting, which normally drew a hundred plus residents, now attracted two thousand enraged protesters, and its lawyer members threatened an all-out legal war. When attention shifted to neighboring towns in Westchester County in subsequent months, it was met with even louder howls of resistance.

Faced with terrible press coverage, calls grew for federal intervention. A coalition of eleven national organizations, led by the American Association for the United Nations (headed by Clark Eichelberger), declared the brouhaha a "national disgrace" and called on President Truman to appoint a "high commissioner" to deal with the problem.

In the temporary sector, the several thousand delegates and staff workers complained of a shortage of available housing, cramped office quarters, poor hotel accommodations, and the time wasted in shuttling between its three component parts and Manhattan. Many complaints were issued, and some suggested moving to another city.

To deal with the public relations debacle, O'Dwyer, in late March, sent a telegram to hundreds of New York's most prominent businessmen, philanthropists, and leaders in the entertainment industry, saying that "it gives me great pleasure to appoint you a member of the 'United Nations Committee of the City of New York.'"

His targets included John D. Rockefeller Jr., *New York Times* publisher Arthur Hays Sulzberger, retail giant Bernard Gimbel, banker Winthrop Aldrich, RCA's David Sarnoff, and Broadway producer Billy Rose. Harriet Aldrich, wife of Winthrop Aldrich (and Nelson Rockefeller's aunt), was named to head a women's group, of which Eleanor Roosevelt was honorary chair.

The charm offensive was vigorous. The committee members entertained UN staffers and their families at teas, luncheons, cocktail parties, dinners, and weekend stays at their country homes. They invited them to Broadway shows, the opera and concerts, and arranged to have the city's best galleries open their doors for private showings. They hosted parties at the American Museum of Natural History's Hayden Planetarium, the Metropolitan Museum of Art's Cloisters, the Museum of Modern Art, and hosted a formal supper dance for the UN guests held at the Waldorf Astoria Hotel.

Nevertheless, by late spring of 1946, cities that had been passed over began sending officials to New York, where they buttonholed delegates and implored them to reconsider their selection. When the mayor of San Francisco and the governor of California arrived to do so, the dam broke and the torrent of offers began again.

To assess this new state of affairs, the General Assembly in London created yet another entity, the Permanent Headquarters Committee, chaired by Dr. Zuleta Angel of Colombia.

On October 18, five days before the transplanting General Assembly arrived, the city completed the Flushing Meadows temporary arrangement. At the same time they released the city's (largely Moses's) formal offer of a permanent center, in Flushing Meadows, which would begin by razing the building they had just reconstructed and would cost an estimated 65 million dollars, to be paid for by the United Nations.

Grumblings followed.

Now the US government reversed its neutral stance and agreed to take on a bigger role in helping the UN find a permanent home. On November 1, Warren Austin, head of the United States delegation and a US senator, proposed that serious consideration be given to Westchester's White Plains sites and San Francisco's Crystal Spring area. The Ukrainians then moved to include locations in Europe as well. Four days later, the British urged opening up even more US cities.

So, on November 18, 1946, a newly organized subcommittee of eighteen men boarded a train bound for Philadelphia to begin the search for a permanent United Nations home all over again. By the time they completed their inspections two weeks later, they had toured Philadelphia's Belmont-Roxborough area; San Francisco's Presidio and Crystal Springs; the Blue Hills and Framingham near Boston; and in the New York area, White Plains, Harrison in Westchester, and Flushing Meadows (on which they turned thumbs down after an engineering investigation reported the site might sink into the former garbage dump on which it rested).

On Monday, December 2, the United States announced that President Truman would ask Congress to offer the Army's Presidio to the United Nations free of charge. The other delegations assumed that the US government supported San Francisco. On Thursday, December 5, at a meeting of the Headquarters Committee, Georgi Saksin, the Soviets' representative, charged the United States with "maneuvering" and interfering "inexcusably" with the site debate. In an angry tirade Saksin fumed that "the U.S.S.R. delegation will not, under any circumstances, countenance the selection of the San Francisco site, and will not go there." If the United Nations were to move to California, he said, it would become a second-rate organization with only second-rate delegates whose efforts "cannot lead to anything."

At this point Senator Austin raised the possibility of postponing the search to the next year's General Assembly session, but the by-now thoroughly fed-up committee announced that if it had not come to an agreement by a week hence—on Wednesday, December 11—the United Nations would move to Philadelphia.

Then, on the very next day, Friday, December 6, at mid-morning, Mayor O'Dwyer received a phone call from real estate mogul William Zeckendorf, who had a startling proposal to make.

Back in July 1945, after three years of boosting the value of Commodore Vincent Astor's vast properties, Zeckendorf had gone out on his own, big time. Leasing the luxurious Marguery Hotel, at 270 Park Avenue (between 47th and 48th) from the New York Central Corporation, he had announced his intention to raze it and erect a skyscraper office building in its stead. The hotel's wealthy and powerful tenants had blocked eviction in the courts, but Zeckendorf persevered and in June 1947 would succeed.

In the meantime, he had sniffed another likely target for tearing down and building up. He could hardly have missed it, as the property in question was a scant four blocks east of Park. It ran from 42nd to 48th Streets, between First Avenue and the East River. In the early 1800s, a series of wharves and warehouses had been built along the river's edge, at a cove named Turtle Bay. After the Civil War, the buildings were turned into a string of slaughterhouses, the final destination of cows railed in from the Midwest and flat-barged to their doom. Some were mooed across 46th Street from the West Side docks, in open-air trucks, from which a cow occasionally leapt to freedom and lumbered its way along an avenue until lassoed and corralled by cowboys in the employ of their owners. Turtle Bay became notorious for the noxious effluvia from its stockyards, slaughterhouses, bone-boiling establishments, tanneries, and tallow factories that infused the air with the reek of blood and animal waste which, when the wind was westerly, could reach as far as Third Avenue. The stench drove land values down: surrounding properties fetched $2 to $5 per square foot, compared with $100 to $150 per square foot in other Midtown locations.

The three core companies were owned by the Swift and Wilson meatpacking firms of Chicago. They had long held an irrevocable franchise to operate in Manhattan, but late in 1945 they decided to retire and hired John Dunbar, a real estate broker with Cushman & Wakefield, Inc., to negotiate a sale. Dunbar offered the property at $17 per square foot, which came to $6.5 million. Zeckendorf figured that with the slaughterhouses gone, the property's value might jump to $50, perhaps $100, making a gross profit of $32 million. There were also the value-depressed properties around the slaughterhouses, which would rise in value from their $2 or $5 base.

Zeckendorf agreed to the deal. His real estate company, Webb & Knapp, would put up one million dollars for a one-year option against the total $6.5 million price. At the end of the year—December 11, 1946—he would pay the remaining $5.5 million. If he failed to do so he'd be out a million bucks.

He now began buying as much of the $2- and $5-per-square-foot surrounding property as he could get his hands on—surreptitiously, through third parties, lest would-be sellers charge a higher price. He ultimately acquired most of the land north of the slaughterhouses to 49th Street, and many lots to the west, between First and Second Avenues—in all about seventy-five properties, totaling 17 acres, at an average price of $9 per square foot.

These were the foothills. What to do with the property once the slaughterhouse mountain was leveled? He wanted something soaring, not just a skyscraper or two, but a whole bevy of commercial and residential and cultural structures. To provide a base for such buildings he proposed to erect a seven-block-long, two-block-wide, raised platform of concrete and steel. Stretching from Tudor City to Beekman Place, it overrode the grid of streets and avenues below, allowing city traffic to flow as it did before.

Zeckendorf acknowledged the pioneering work done by previous New York developers. "The prototype of such a platform," he observed, "had been constructed in 1913 when the city forced the New York Central Railroad to cover the ugly network of open railroad tracks lying to the south and north of Grand Central Station. This roofing created Park Avenue, and a fortune in real-estate values, but what I was proposing was a greater and more unified development."

He also cited as a forebear John D. Rockefeller Jr., who leased from Columbia University its extensive midtown properties and developed them into Rockefeller Center, a coherent, multi-acreage, multi-towered complex, a city within the city. Zeckendorf intended to rival it with his "X City"—the working name for his mega-development. It would comprise four 40-story office towers at the south end; three 30-story apartment houses with living facilities for seventy-five hundred families built at the north end; and in between, two 57-story towers, one with offices, and the other a hotel with more than four thousand rooms. In addition to all these tall towers, Zeckendorf proposed a concert hall and home for the Metropolitan Opera, which at that time was planning to leave its West 38th Street address. He would also establish a Television City, with which to rival Rockefeller Center's Radio City—and an airline terminal, a heliport, a marina, and a floating nightclub.

To design this into a credible package he hired Wally Harrison, whose work on Rockefeller Center had brought him a deserved and estimable reputation. Harrison was held in high regard by Robert Moses and other civic leaders, and Zeckendorf considered him a friend, providing him with an apartment in his (still-standing) Marguery Hotel.

Harrison drew a map of his suggested design—a glass-curtained wall-slab tower in a park—which was published in *Life* magazine. Much attention was paid. Yet despite some nibbles from giant banks and corporations—the Aluminum Company of America's chairman offered some support if Zeckendorf would name the entire package Aluminum City (he demurred)—there was no way X-City was going to happen.

His option would expire at midnight, December 11.

The clock was tick-tocking away.

MEANWHILE, THE SQUABBLING OUT IN Flushing Meadows—what with the Russians savaging the Californians—continued. The Headquarters Committee was approaching its deadline—midnight of December 11—after which Philadelphia, not New York, would house the United Nations.

Then, at breakfast on Friday, December 6, Zeckendorf read the report of the debates on the UN site in the *New York Times*. At that moment it occurred to him (as he would later relate) "that we at Webb & Knapp had an ideal site for the UN right here in Manhattan! Turning to Marion, I said, 'I'm going to put those bastards on the platform!' 'Which bastards on what platform?' 'The UN—I'm going to put them on the platform over the slaughterhouses.'"

After consulting with his partners, he called Mayor O'Dwyer and asked if he would like to keep the United Nations in New York. The mayor fervently said that he'd give an arm, a leg, and various other parts of his body for the chance, but that none of them was particularly salable. He then asked O'Dwyer to put Miss Holly, his secretary, on the extension phone as he was going to dictate a statement he could take to the United Nations: "We hereby offer to the United Nations approximately seventeen acres on the East River from Forty-second Street and First Avenue north to Forty-ninth Street for any price they wish to pay." O'Dwyer, taken aback, interrupted to ask how he could possibly say that. "I told him that the matter of the UN site was now so close to the deadline there was no time for trading. Unless I said price was no object, they would think this was a trick by a real-estate operator to stop their Philadelphia negotiations, and then hold them up for millions. It had to be a carte blanche. We would either capture their imagination and start them rethinking, or we would not."

That evening Secretary-General Lie phoned O'Dwyer and Moses to say that unless a better proposition was received quickly it would be all over for New York. Get in touch with Nelson Rockefeller immediately, he advised.

O'Dwyer called Harrison who found Rockefeller (whom he knew well from his work on Rockefeller Center) who was in Mexico City, attending the inauguration of Miguel Aleman. They agreed that Harrison would study the feasibility of transforming X-CITY into UNHQ, and they would bring Senator Austin and Dr. Zuleta Angel into the picture.

News that there was a possibility of New York's finding a solution in its own back yard spread with lightning speed. On Saturday morning, twenty-four hours after Zeckendorf's call to O'Dwyer, a United Press reporter phoned to ask if it was true that he'd offered seventeen acres of Manhattan property to the UN? Zeckendorf said yes and asked if there was any interest. "Interest! There's a revolution! They're going wild down there in the Assembly. Philadelphia is dead. In my opinion they're going to accept!"

Harrison now needed something he could show the Assembly, the Headquarters Committee, and the Rockefellers. There was no time to prepare an elaborate presentation. But the architect realized that his office walls were surrounded by impressive renderings of the site. All he needed to do was demonstrate how the elements of the wall papers could fit into the X-City's spaces. He then erased "Metropolitan Opera" and lettered in "General Assembly"; erased "Philharmonic" and lettered in "Security Council"; the tall Office Building became "Secretariat"; and so forth.

By Tuesday, December 10, Nelson had returned and at 6:30 a.m. had caucused with his father and brothers about the X-City cooptation. He was doubtful that the city could afford what most assumed would be a $25 million cost to buy the property. He suggested instead that the Rockefeller family donate their collective Pocono homesteads. Junior reluctantly agreed but suggested one last consultation with the UN people, who reported that by now they had lost interest in the multi-acre option and much preferred the mini-acre site in mid-Manhattan. What would it cost? Junior then asked. He consulted Harrison who, knowing Zeckendorf's perilous financial situation, surmised that $8.5 million might do the trick. Junior then agreed to offer to buy the property and donate it to the United Nations. Harrison was deputed to track Zeckendorf down; found him in his Monte Carlo nightclub; and asked if he'd give him an option for the UN. He would indeed; asked how much they wanted; agreed to the figure quoted; and scrawled on a document: "$8,500,000 to U.N. December 10 for 30 days 11:11 [p.m.]." Harrison raced back to Junior's office, where they worked on specifics and terms until one o'clock, then reassembled at 7:30 a.m. next morning at Junior's office, where he signed the relevant documents.

At 8 a.m. the delegate members of the UN Permanent Headquarters Committee assembled for what they assumed would be their ratification of Philadelphia. Instead they were addressed by chairman Zuleta Angel, who had just been briefed by Rockefeller and Harrison, who turned the podium over to Senator Austin, who in turn read out loud a letter addressed to them by John D. Rockefeller Jr. in which he said: "It is my belief that this city affords an environment uniquely fitted to the task of the United Nations and that the people of New York would like to have the United Nations here permanently. For these reasons I have ventured to obtain a firm offer covering property located on the East River in the midtown area, which, should it serve your purpose, I would be glad to give to the United Nations." The committee—entranced by the idea of UN skyscraper—set their deadline (and Philadelphia) aside.

Over the next forty-eight hours, a UN group of delegates visited the site, accompanied by Moses and other city officials; the Headquarters Committee approved a resolution accepting the gift; and on December 14, 1946—just eight days after Zeckendorf first called O'Dwyer about a possible land deal—the UN General Assembly voted to make New York City its permanent home.

AT 10:30 A.M. ON DECEMBER 11, about the time Austin was reading the momentous letter, Zeckendorf had gotten a call from Rockefeller. As he later recalled, "Rockefeller's brisk voice crackled, 'Is this Bill Zeckendorf?' 'Yes.' 'We've been up all night patching up the details, but it's going to work. The old man is going to give that 8.5 million dollars to the UN, and they're going to take your property. See you soon.... Good-bye.'"

"I couldn't believe it," Zeckendorf later recalled. "The property was being purchased! I couldn't believe it. I signaled our switchboard operator and told her to find out who it was that had called. She buzzed back to say it had indeed been Rockefeller. I gingerly put on my hat and carried my hangover home. As I came into the apartment, I told Marion, 'We have just moved the capital of the world.'"

Acknowledgments

As decades go by, debts pile up.

My first thanks go to those who plowed through the whole manuscript, commenting on its conceptual underpinnings and pointing out infelicities (and felicities) of presentation: Elizabeth Blackmar, Victoria de Grazia, Joshua Freeman, and Peter-Christian Aigner.

Plaudits, next, to the crack team at Oxford University Press that brought *Gotham at War* from hard drive to hard copy. My exceptional chief editor was Tim Bent, whose talent and dedication can never be praised enough. Others on the production squad included: production editor Amy Whitmer, the sharp-eyed copy editor Joellyn Ausanka, Theodore Reiner, who handled the graphics department, and research assistant Rachel Pitkin. My agent Sam Stoloff handled financial relations with OUP.

Longtime *Gotham* researcher and historian Joel Feingold pored over the manuscript for many years. I asked Feingold to join the project in the fall of 2011—nearly fifteen years ago—when he was my student in a City University of New York graduate seminar, and he has served as researcher and invaluable assistant since: through *Greater Gotham* to the publication of *Gotham at War* in the fall of 2025.

Thanks are due as well to Louise Mirrer, Marci Reaven, Sam Roberts, Phillip Lopate, Richard Kahan, Jeff Madrick, Peter Kwong and Dusanka Miscevic, for reading and critiquing hundreds of these pages.

My gratitude goes out to those who lent me their ears—putting up with me telling stories and trying out formulations, often around a dinner table, feeding all of us with their expertise. I think of them as my verbal commentators, and they include Andrew Fierberg, Anthony and Margo Viscusi, Vicky de Grazia, Phil Lopate, Leina Schiffrin, Salman Rushdie, Michael Sorkin, Naief Yehya, Ted Widmer, James Periconi, James McCourt, Vincent Virga, Pablo Boullosa, and Robert Padgug.

Thanks, too, to friends and family who accompanied me through these years, including Carlos Pereda, Magali Lara, Ana Luisa Liguori, Alberto Quintero, Abraham Neme, Lupina

Becerra, Giuliana Bruno, Julia Preston, Lucia Melgar, Judith Sackoff, Ted Joyce, Dohra Ahmad, Orin Herskowitz, Maria Aura, Juan Aura, Alonso Barrera, Aura Erendira Martinez Oriol, Leon and Leonora Barrera Aura, and Bill Lingle, Penny Wallace, Elaine and Julie Birnbaum, Bob and Claudie Isaacs, Eric, David, Terry, Henry and Hedy.

Last, but definitely not least, my wife, Carmen Boullosa, who, apart from teaching at Macaulay Honors College, CUNY, has also been engaged in a decade-long project, writing (and illustrating) a story that spans some three hundred years, involving priests, merchants, and slaves, and runs from the Philippines and the South Seas, from Mexico to the Iberian Peninsula. Yet she has always been my support helping me through all sorts of unexpected problems, with love and devotion.

Finally, an endnote: I was born in 1942, and my family was involved in the war. Uncle Leon was in the Marianas, on Guam, building air strips; Aunt Betty was making WAC uniforms at the Aywon Dress Company. Uncle Sol, a presser in the garment industry in NYC, was an air raid warden in Brooklyn. And Uncle Joe was in the Army, stationed in England, making Eisenhower jackets. This book tries to do justice to that wartime generation.

References

INTRODUCTION TO SOURCES AND SUGGESTIONS FOR FURTHER READING

This book draws upon thousands of studies made by myriad specialists who in the last two generations have rewritten the city's history. It is they who produced the strands of scholarship that I have woven into a narrative.

In the resource notes that follow, I have space to offer only the most truncated acknowledgment of the immense debt I owe those upon whose research and insights I have relied. The alphabetized author and date listings are intended only to suggest those works I found most valuable in sorting my way through the subject of each particular section. This approach does not allow me to differentiate between those interpretations I support and follow and those with which I disagree but nevertheless consider provocative or informative. Under these circumstances, it is more important than usual to insist that those I cite are to be held blameless for my infelicities of analysis and errors of fact.

NAZIS AND NEW YORK

1. BOYCOTT

Adams, 1986; Bayor, 1978; Black, 1999; Black, 2001; Brenner, 1983; Brody, 1956; Chatfield, 1973; Cohen, 2002a; Curti, 1936; Dawidowicz, 1986; DeBenedetti, 1986; Duke, 2003; Goodman, 1968; Gottlieb, 1982; Gray et al., 1990; Herzstein, 1989; Medoff, 1987; Nolzen, 2003; Noraian, 2001; Urofsky, 1982; Voss, 1968; Wallace, 2003; Wise, 1949

2. BRAIN DRAIN

Baynes, 1981; Black, 1999; Brody, 1956; Chester, 1995; Fleming et al., 1969; Heilbut, 1983; Herzstein, 1989; Jackman et al., 1983; Jay, 1996; Kennedy, 1999; Leff, 2000; Levenstein, 1983; Lowenstein, 1989; Medoff, 1987; Morse, 1968; Persico, 1988; Scott et al., 1999; Strauss, 1971; Strauss, 1981; Sulzberger et al., 1987; Wyman, 1968

3. NAZIS IN NEW YORK

Agusta et al., 1976; Bayor, 1978; Behren, 1998; Canedy, 1990; Carlson, 1943; Diamond, 1974; Esposito et al., 1988; Glazer, 1993; Goodman, 1968; Gottlieb, 1982; Groth, 1983; Herzstein, 1989; Keller, 1971; Kessner, 1989; MacDonnell, 1995; O'Haire, 1977; O'Reilly, 1983; Remak, 1957

4. A FIFTH COLUMN?

Bayor, 1978; Berenbaum, 1993; Breuer, 1989; Cull, 1995; Diamond, 1974; Dinnerstein, 1994;

Farago, 1972; Finan, 2002; Goodman, 1968; Groth, 1983; Haynes et al., 1999; Heilbut, 1983; Hertzberg, 1997; Herzstein, 1989; Kennedy, 1999; MacDonnell, 1995; Medoff, 1987; Urofsky, 1982; Wyman, 1984

5. KRISTALLNACHT

Alpern, 1987; Bayor, 1978; Berenbaum, 1993; Esposito et al., 1988; Groth, 1983; Herzstein, 1989; Jackman et al., 1983; Kazanjian et al., 1993; Kranzler, 1961; Lowenstein, 1989; Medoff, 2004; Urofsky, 1982; Wyman, 1984

6./7. ÉMIGRÉS ARRIVE (MANHATTAN, WILLIAMSBURG)

Davie et al., 1974; Fuchs, 1934; Groth, 1983; Heilbut, 1983; Helmreich, 2000; Hertzberg, 1997; Herzstein, 1989; Horowitz et al., 1959; Israelowitz, 2000; Joselit, 1990; Kennedy, 1999; Kranzler, 1961; Kranzler, 1988; Lingeman, 1970; Lowenstein, 1989; Pfanner, 1984; Porter, 1942; Reiss et al., 2000; Rosenblum et al., 1995; Rosenblum et al., 2001; United States Holocaust Memorial Museum, 2018b

8. ALIENS AND ENEMIES

Bayor, 1978; Breuer, 1989; Britt, 1940; Canedy, 1990; Carlson, 1943; Davenport-Hines, 1995; Diamond, 1974; Fox, 1990b; Fried, 1997; Goodman, 1968; Goodwin, 1994; Gottlieb, 1982; Groth, 1983; Herzstein, 1989; Horten, 2002; Keller, 1971; MacDonnell, 1995; Perrett, 1985; Pfanner, 1984; Sandeen, 1979; Steele, 1984; Steele, 1991; Troy, 1996

ITALIANS

9. DUCE! DUCE!

Bayor, 1978; Britt, 1940; Cannistraro, 1985a; Cannistraro, 1985b; Cannistraro et al., 2003; Catino, 2003; Collomp, 2005; Diggins, 1972; Douglas, 1987; Fraser, 1991; Gallagher, 1988; Godfried, 2001; Jaker et al., 1998; Lombardi, 1980; Luconi, 2001a; Luconi, 2004; Martin, 2005; Miller, 1978; Miller, 2005; Nasaw, 2000; Olmsted, 2002; Pozzetta, 1995; Salvemini et al., 1940; Schnapper, 1938; Smith, 1987; Tyler, 1995; Ventresco, 1980; Walker, 1990

10. ITALIAN ANTI-FASCISTS

Bayor, 1978; Borstelmann, 2001; Cannistraro, 1985a; Catino, 2003; Conyer et al., 2004; Diggins, 1972; Esposito et al., 1988; Gallagher, 1988; Greenberg, 1991; Hamilton, 1991; Kanawada, 1982; Kennedy, 1999; Kessner, 1989; Luconi, 2001a; Meyer, 1989; Miller, 1978; Nugent, 1971; Perrett, 1985

11. HANDS OFF ETHIOPIA!

Martin, 1986; Plummer, 1996; Powell, 1971a; Ross, 1972; Scott, 1992; Ventresco, 1980

12. AMBLING ALP V. BROWN BOMBER

Bak, 1998; Breslin, 1991; Daniel, 1950; Durso, 1979; Edmonds, 1973; Gallico, 1938; Hamilton, 1991; Hietala, 2002; Kearns et al., 1966; Kelley, 1994; Louis et al., 1947; Mullally, 2000; Naison, 1984; Nasaw, 2000; Nown, 1987; Riess, 1988; Riess, 1989; Ritter, 1998; Sammons, 1988; Taylor, 1991

13. "THE EAGLES OF ROME HAVE DEVOURED THE LION OF JUDAH"

Naison, 1984; Plummer, 1996

14. ITALIANS AND JEWS: 1938–1941

Baughman, 1987; Bayor, 1978; Britt, 1940; Cannistraro, 1985a; Cannistraro, 1985b; Carnevale, 2003; Catino, 2003; Diggins, 1972; Esposito et al., 1988; Gallagher, 1988; Luconi, 2001a; Luconi, 2001b; Luconi, 2004; Meyer, 1989; Pozzetta, 1995; Vecoli, 1978a

15. LOUIS V. SCHMELING

Bak, 1998; Berg, 2004; Blum, 1976; Capeci, 1977b; Carlson, 1943; Daniel, 1950; Diggins, 1972; Duberman, 1988; Edmonds, 1973; Finkle, 1975; Gallicchio, 2000; Garfinkel, 1959; Greenberg, 1991; Kapur, 1992; Kelley, 1994; Marquis, 1986; Naison, 1984; Plummer, 1996; Polenberg, 1972; Riess, 1988; Sammons, 1988; Schuyler, 1966; Scott, 1992; Spivey, 1985

THE IRISH

16. THE WANING OF THE GREEN

Almeida, 2001; Bayor, 1978; Blanshard, 1951; Bradshaw, 2004; Cadegan, 2001; Casey, 1996; Casey, 1998; Cheney, 2013a; Cheney, 2013b; Council for Scholarly Evaluation of Gaelic Gotham, 1997; Erie, 1988; Foley, 1968; Freeman, 1989; Friedman, 1996; Garrett, 1961; Gerson, 1990; Glazer et al., 1963; Gleason, 2000; Greeley, 1981; Hoopes, 1985; Kessner, 1989; Koppes et al., 1990; Kroessler, 1991; Lardner et al., 2000; Martin, 2005; McNickle, 1996; Miller, 1996; Moore, 1994; Morris, 1997; New York City WPA Writers' Project, 1941; O'Brien, 1968; O'Dwyer et al., 1987; Reeves, 2001; Schroth, 2002; Sharp, 1954; Skinner, 1993; Tully, 2004; Ultan et al., 1985; Walkowitz, 1999; Walsh, 1996; Zeitz, 2007

17. CATHOLIC NEW YORK

Bayor, 1978; Blanshard, 1951; Blantz et al., 1993; Brown, 1983; Brown et al., 1997; Cadegan, 2001; Coles, 1987; Cooney, 1984; Corrin, 2002; Critchlow et al., 1998; Desmond, 2008; Finan, 2002; Fraser, 1991; Freeman, 1989; Gannon, 1962; Glaze et al., 1963; Gleason, 1995b; Greeley, 1995; Marcus, 1973; McGreevy, 1996; McGreevy, 2003; McNickle, 1996; McVetty, 1995; Morris, 1997; Moscow, 1948; O'Brien, 1968; O'Grady, 1930; *Official Catholic Directory*, 1939; Reeves, 2001; Sharp, 1954; Shea, 1966; Shelley, 1999; Van Allen, 1974; "Vatican over Hollywood," 1936; Wainwright, 1986; Walsh, 1960; Wentz, 1962; Zeitz, 200

18. A CHURCH BESIEGED

Callahan, 2004; Carroll, 1996; Corrin, 2002; Crosby, 1971; Foley, 1968; Lash, 1971; Mabry, 1978; Meyer, 1976; Pérez de Urbel, 1993; Seldes, 1994; Thomas, 1961; Traina, 1968; Van Allen, 1974

19./20. WAR IN SPAIN/¡VIVA LA QUINCE BRIGADA!

Blanco, 2003; Carroll, 1994; Crosby, 1971; Fernandez, 2005; Howson, 1999; MacDonald, 1987; Navarro, 2006; New York Public Library Manuscripts and Archives Division, 2015; North American Committee to Aid Spanish Democracy, 1937; Packer, 2005; Payne, 2004; Pérez de Urbel, 1993; Taylor, 1971; Thomas, 1961; Tierney, 2004; Traina, 1968; Weintraub, 1968

21. GREENS AND REDS: THE TRANSPORT WORKERS UNION

Cohen, 1991; Cuff, 1989; Doig, 1966; Fotsch, 2007; Freeman, 1983; Freeman, 1989; Schrag, 2000

22. CATHOLICS v. "COMMUNISTS"

Freeman, 1983; Massa, 1999; Rosswurm, 2001; Pope Pius XI, 1937

23. THE CHRISTIAN FRONT

Bayor, 1978; Brinkley, 1982; Carlson, 1943; Dawley, 1991; Diamond, 1974; Dinnerstein, 1994; Fogarty, 2003; Garraty, 1986; Herzstein, 1989; Kessner, 1989; Kurth, 1990; Lavine, 1940; Luconi, 2004; Marcus, 1973; McGreevy, 1996; McNickle, 1996; Miller, 1973; Morris, 1997; O'Brien, 1968; O'Dwyer et al., 1987; "Spellman Warned on Christian Front," 1939; Van Allen, 1974; Wechsler, 1939; Wentz, 1962; Zitron, 1969

24. ENTER SPELLMAN

Birmingham, 1973; Brown, 1983; Chernow, 1990; Cohalan, 1983; Cooney, 1984; Cornwell, 1999; Douglass, 1954; Ellis, 1983;

Fogarty, 1982; Fogarty, 2003; Gannon, 1962; Glazer et al., 1963; Marcus, 1973; Morris, 1997; Morris, 1987; Reeves, 2001; Tittmann, 2004; Van Allen, 1974; Wills, 1984

25. SPELLMAN TAKES COMMAND

Cooney, 1984; Fogarty, 1982; Ford, 1969; McGreevy, 2003; Morris, 1997; Wills, 1984

26. THE CROSS AND THE FLAG

Bayor, 1978; Blanshard, 1951; Braudy, 2003; Brown, 1983; Buhle, 1990; Casey, 1998; Clines, 1998; Cohalan, 1983; Cooney, 1984; Douglass, 1954; Duggan, 1985; Durkan, 1998; Dwyer, 1973; Dwyer, 1977; Dwyer, 1988; Fels, 2001; Fogarty, 1982; Fogarty, 2003; Gannon, 1962; Gerstle, 2001; Greeley, 1981; Herzstein, 1989; Kessner, 1989; Lukas, 1978; Marcus, 1973; McKean, 2004; Milkman, 1997; Morris, 1997; Muller, 1998; O'Brien, 1968; O'Dwyer, 1979; Pula, 1995; Raymond, 1980; Raymond, 1983; Raymond, 1985; Reeves, 2001; Tully, 2004; Van Allen, 1974; Wicker, 1995; Wills, 1984

27. POLONIA

Bukowczyk, 1987; Pienkos, 1991; Wytrwal, 1977

ASIAN NEW YORK

28. JAPANESE NEW YORK

Anderson, 1997; Bonner, 1997; Borstelmann, 2001; Conn, 1996; Dower, 1986; Finkle, 1975; Friedman, 1968; Friedman, 1995b; Gallicchio, 2000; Glickman, 2005; Horne, 2004; Isaacs, 1980; Kearney, 1998; Kennedy, 1999; Kwong, 1979; LaFeber, 1997; Lewis, 2000; Ottley, 1968; Plummer, 1996; Rampersad, 1986; Sawada, 1996; Stephan, 1984; Yu, 1992

29. CHINESE GOTHAM

Bonner, 1997; Chen, 1941; Chen, 2003; Conn, 1996; Department of State, 1943; Dower, 1986; Friedman, 1968; Gallicchio, 2000; Glickman, 2005; Horne, 2004; Isaacs, 1980; Jespersen, 1996; Kearney, 1998; Kennedy, 1999; Kwong, 1979; LaFeber, 1997; Lai, 1991; Lee, 2002; Lewis, 2000; Light, 1974; Plummer, 1996; Yu, 1992

IN UNO PLURES

30. PLURALISTS

Adamic, 1936; Akam, 2002; Bendersky, 2000; Blake, 1990; Facing History and Ourselves, 2002; Federal Writers' Project, 1938; Gleason, 1992; Higham, 1984a; Hutchison, 2003; Kallen et al., 1956; Kallen et al., 1987; Konvitz, 1994; Kronish, 1987; Lichtenstein, 1988; Michaels, 1995; Mirel, 2002; Ribuffo, 2004; Rosenwaike, 1972; Sayers et al., 1942; Schlesinger, 2000; Shpak-Lisak, 1989; Sollors, 1986b; Steele, 1989; Strauss, 1996; Toll, 1997; Tucker, 2002; Walzer, 1992; Wissot, 1975; Zucker, 2001

31. CULTURE WARRIOR

Adamic, 1936; Allen, 1986; Baker, 2004; Banner, 2003; Barkan, 1992; Barkan, 1988; Benedict et al., 1977; Black, 2003; Boas, 1934; Caffrey, 1989; Cohen, 1972; Dikötter, 1998; Facing History and Ourselves, 2002; Fee, 1973; Fee, 1979; Frank, 1997; Friedman, 1995b; Gleason, 1992; Goldschmidt, 1959; Goldstein et al., 1995; Handler, 1990; Hart, 2000; Hegerman, 1998; Hutchison, 2003; Hyatt, 1990; Jackson, 2001; Janiewski et al., 2004; Kenny, 2002; Kirshenblatt-Gimblett, 1995; Kirshenblatt-Gimblett, 2001; Kirshenblatt-Gimblett, 2005; Krook, 1993; Kühl, 1994; Landman, 1934; Lapsley, 1999; Lesser, 2004; Lewis, 2000; MacDonald, 1998; McCaughey, 2003; McDaniel, 1997; Mead, 1979; Modell, 1983; Montalto, 1982; Pathé, 1989; Pierpont, 2004; Roediger, 2005; Samelson, 1978; Selig, 2001; Southern, 1998; Spiro, 2000; Steele, 1989; Stocking, 1982; Stoddard, 1940; Svonkin, 1997; Tompkins, 2006; Tucker, 2002; Weiss, 1979; Williams, 1996; Yans-McLaughlin, 1986; Yans, 2004; Young, 2005b

32. BUILDING BROTHERHOOD

Cohen, 1972; Cohen, 2002a; Hutchison, 2003; Kraut, 1988; Kraut, 1989; Montalto, 1982; Pitt, 1955; Selig, 2001; Svonkin, 1997

33. FÊTEING THE FOLKS

Abramovitch, 1996; Baron et al., 1992; Cantwell, 1992; Glassberg, 1990; Montalto, 1982; Selig, 2001; Shpak-Lisak, 1989

34. TEACHING TOLERANCE

Abramovitch, 1996; Adamic, 1934; Carbone, 1977; Cinotto, 2004; Cook, 1999; Covello, 1936; Covello, 1958; Cremin, 1961; Davis, 1999; Diner, 1995; DuBois, 1984; FitzGerald, 1979; García et al., 2002; Gelfand, 1976; Gerstle, 1996; Gerstle, 1997; Gleason, 1992; Goodenow et al., 1977; Gutek, 1984; Higham, 1955; Johnson, 2002; Kallen, 1924; Kazal, 1995; Lasker, et al., 1957; Lewis, 2000; Montalto, 1982; Nash et al., 1997; Peebles, 1978; Perrone et al., 1998; Pitt, 1955; Powell, 1971b; Ravitch, 2000; Roche, 1963; Rugg et al., 1922; Samelson, 1978; Selig, 2001; Shaffer, 1996; Shpak-Lisak, 1989; Sorin, 2002; Svonkin, 1997; Tucker, 2002; Ueda, 1996; Vickery et al., 1943; Weiss, 1979; Westbrook, 1991; Whitfield, 1998a; Wissot, 1975; Zimmerman, 2002

35. AMERICANS ALL

Barnouw, 1966; Blue, 2002; DuBois, 1984; Gleason, 1981; Gleason, 1992; Johnson, 2002; Kammen, 1996; Leach, 1983; McChesney, 1993; Mirel, 2002; Montalto, 1982; Savage, 1999; Shaffer, 1996; Svonkin, 1997; Weiss, 1979

36. IMMIGRANTS ALL

Adamic, 1936; Benet, 1936; Blumberg et al., 1985; Higham, 1984b; Higham, 1988; Koed, 1992; McNickle, 1993; Montalto, 1982; "Roosevelt's Address at the Statue of Liberty," 1936; "Roosevelt Urges Guarding of Peace: Speaking at Statue of Liberty, He Rededicates Nation to Ideal It Represents," 1936; Weiss, 1979

37. BALLADEERS FOR BROTHERHOOD

Blue, 2002; Buhle et al., 1990; Buhle, 1987; Cantwell, 1996; Cosgrove, 1981; Cosgrove, 1985; Denning, 1996; Duberman, 1988; Gleason, 1992; Gobel, 1988; Kazan, 1997; Kennedy, 1999; Mirel, 2002; Orenstein, 2001; Ottanelli, 1991; Robeson, 1958; Robeson, 1965; Savage, 1999; Schickel, 2005; Shteir, 1997; Walker, 1991; Warren, 1999

38. COMMON GROUND

Adamic, 1934; Adamic, 1936; Adamic, 1940; Adamic, 1976; Allen, 1986; Bendersky, 2000; Beyer, 1995; Bullert, 2002; Carlson, 1943; Chafee, 1969; Christian, 1968; Denning, 1996; Duberman, 1988; DuBois, 1984; Ehrt et al., 1933; Facing History and Ourselves, 2002; Gerstle, 1989; Gerstle, 2001; Gleason, 1992; Harney, 1986; Hollinger, 1995; Johnson, 2002; Kennedy, 1999; Kuznick, 1987; Lee, 2000; "Louis Adamic: His Life, Work, Legacy," 1982; Montalto, 1982; Patterson, 1977; Perrett, 1985; Peterson, 2003; Pierpont, 2004; Roediger, 2005; Sayers et al., 1946; Schlesinger, 2000; Selig, 2001; Shiffman, 2003; Slotkin, 2005; Sollors, 1986a; Sollors, 1986b; Steele, 1989; Svonkin, 1997; Toll, 1997; Tompkins, 2006; Tucker, 2002; Vecoli, 1978b; Walzer, 1992; Warren, 1999; Weiss, 1979; Wyman, 1968

STUDY WAR NO MORE

39. THE RENUNCIATOR

Abbott, 1994; Fosdick, 1934; Fosdick, 1956; Handy, 1987; Miller, 1985

40. ANTIWARRIORS

Abbott, 1994; Addison, 2004; "Anti-War Pledge

Given by Fosdick," 1934; Arnold, 1969; Balanoff, 1985; Bennett, 2003; Buhle, 1999; Bullert, 2002; Chatfield, 1973; Cohen, 1993; Coles, 1987; Coulter, 1997; D'Emilio, 2003; Danielson, 2003; Deats, 2001; Dekar, 2005a; Engelbrecht et al., 1934; Ferrell, 1968; Fox, 1997; Fox, 1985; Gregg, 1934; Harrington, 2007; Holmes, 1933; Holmes, 1959; Johnpoll, 1970; Kapur, 1992; Kosek, 2005; Lippy, 2000; McConnell, 1952; McNeal, 1992; Miller, 1958; Miller, 1985; Miller, 1982; Morison, 1947; New York City Chapter of the American Guild of Organists, 2006; Pijl, 1984; Roberts, 1984b; Schmidt, 1978; Seldes, 1934; Sifton, 2003; Singer, 1975; Sprecher, 2002; Swanberg, 1976; Swarthmore College Peace Collection, 2006; Van Kirk, 1934; Voss, 1964; "War Is Renounced by 240 Clergymen: Jews and Christians Accept 'Covenant of Peace' as 800 in Church Rise in Approval," 1935; Wilz, 1963; Wittner, 1969

41. AGAINST WAR AND FASCISM

Addison, 2004; Blue, 2002; Buhle, 1999; Carroll, 1994; Chatfield, 1973; Cohen, 1993; Dekar, 2005a; Draper, 1967a; Duke, 2003; Fox, 1985; Handy, 1987; Howe et al., 1957; Jaffe, 1975; Johnpoll, 1970; Klehr et al., 1992; Kutulas, 1995; Miller, 1985; Naison, 1993; Ottanelli, 1991; Rossinow, 2004; Rossinow, 2005; Rudy, 1949; Sifton, 2003; Smith et al., 2005; Wald, 1987; Wittner, 1969

42. PEACE CRUSADE

Bélanger, 2004; Bennett, 2003; Chatfield, 1973; Cohen, 1993; Dekar, 2005a; Divine, 1967; Eichelberger, 1977; Johnstone, 2006; McCaughey, 2004; Miller, 1985; Rosenthal, 2006; Schaffer, 1966; Shotwell, 1961; Swarthmore College Peace Collection, 2016a; Swarthmore College Peace Collection, 2016b; Wittner, 1969

43. UNPOPULAR FRONTS
44. SPANISH NEW YORKERS

Aaron, 1961; Addison, 2004; Banner, 2003; Bennett, 2003; Blanco, 2003; Brookeman, 1984; Carroll, 1994; Centro de Estudios Puertorriqueños, 2005d; Chase, 1943; Chatfield, 1973; Cohen, 1993; Colon, 1982; Colón López, 2002; Cook, 1999; Davis, 1993; Denning, 1996; Federal Writers' Project, 1939; Fernandez, 2005; Fox, 1990a; Freeman, 1983; Howson, 1999; Johnpoll, 1970; Kelley, 1994; Koch, 2005; Kovel, 1997; Kutulas, 1995; Kuznick, 1987; Lifka, 1988; Marquis, 1989; McGreevy, 2003; Miller, 1985; Navarro, 2006; Neather, 1995; New York Public Library Manuscripts and Archives Division, 2015; North American Committee to Aid Spanish Democracy, 1937; Ottanelli, 1991; Packer, 2005; Payne, 2004; Perrett, 1985; Rossinow, 2004; Ryan, 1997; Schaffer, 1966; Sifton, 2003; Spanish Benevolent Society Inc., 2001; Stowe, 1994; Taylor, 1971; Tommasini, 1997; Van Hensbergen, 2004; Weintraub, 1968; Wood, 1992; Zitron, 1969

45. PARTISAN VIEWS

Alpers, 2003; Barrett, 1982; Bender, 1987; Bennett, 2003; Bloom, 1986; Brightman, 1992; Bush, 2003; Carroll, 1994; Cohen, 1993; Conquest, 1968; Cooney, 1986; Costello, 1985; Costello et al., 1993; Cotter, 2004; Deacon, 2004; Denning, 1996; Diggins, 1994; Dorman, 2000; Dubinsky et al., 1977; Dvosin, 1977; Greenberg, 1939; Guilbaut, 1984; Guilbaut, 1990; Hook, 1987; Howe et al., 1957; Isserman, 1993; Isserman, 2000; Johnpoll, 1970; Kallen, 1934; Kiernan, 2000; King, 1987; Klehr, 1984; Koch, 2005; Kutulas, 1995; Laskin, 2000; Macdonald et al., 2001; MacDonald, 1987; Maddux, 1977; Maksimov, 1940; Marquis, 1986; McCarthy, 1963; McCarthy, 1992; Neather, 1995; Novack, 1968; Ottanelli, 1991; Pells, 1973; Phelps, 1997; Phillips, 1976; Phillips, 2004b; Ryan, 1997; Schrecker, 1986; Scott et al., 1999; Shaplen et al., 1934; Strouse, 1992; Tanenhaus, 1997; Taylor, 1990; Van Paassen et al., 1934; Wald, 1978; Wald, 1987; Wald, 2002; Warren, 1993; Weintraub, 1968; Westbrook, 1991; Whitfield, 1998b; Wreszin, 1994

46. ANTI-TOTALITARIANISM

Adler et al., 1970; Alpern, 1987; Alpers, 2003; Bennett, 1969; Bloom, 1986; Carroll, 1994; Cook, 1999; Cotter, 2004; Cottrell, 1992; Davis, 1993; Denning, 1996; Fox, 1985; Gleason, 1995a; Goodwin, 1994; Haynes, 2005; Hook, 1939b; Hook, 1987; Howe et al., 1957; Jacoby, 1987; Jaffe, 1975; Kennedy, 1999; Kirchwey, 1939; Klehr et al., 1992; Kutulas, 1995; Kuznick, 1987; League for Cultural Freedom and Socialism, 1939; Levenstein, 1981; Lifka, 1988; Lyons, 1937; Maddux, 1977; McCollam, 2003; Miller, 1985; Morris, 1997; Naison, 1984; Naison, 1993; Nelson, 1988; Ottanelli, 1991; Pells, 1973; Reeves, 2001; Rossinow, 2004; Ryan, 1995; Ryan, 1997; Schaffer, 1966; Schrecker, 1986; Scott-Smith, 2002; Spiro, 1968; Steel, 1980; Taylor, 1990; Van Paassen et al., 1934; Wald, 1987; Warren, 1993; Weidlich, 2000; Westbrook, 1991; Wittner, 1969

47. UNPOPULAR FRONT

American Philosophical Society, 1983; Auerbach, 1976; Bailey, 1982; Baxandall, 1988; "Blanshard Scores Labor Left Wing: Calls Upon Party Membership to Support Right Wingers in Fight on Reds," 1940; Bullert, 2004; Camp, 1995; Chafee, 1969; Cottrell, 1992; Cottrell, 2000; Davis, 1993; Dodd, 1954; Draper, 1967b; Ernst, 1945; Feffer, 2005; Folsom, 1991; Fosdick, 1956; Fraser, 1991; Geisel Library et al., 1998; Gerstle, 2001; Gleason, 1995a; Gleason, 1992; Goodman, 1968; Guilbaut, 1984; Hills et al., 1983; Hook, 1987; Howe et al., 1957; Jacoby, 1987; Johnpoll, 1970; Kessner, 1989; Klehr, 1984; Klehr et al., Kutulas, 1995; Kuznick, 1987; Lamson, 1976; Lerner, 1998; Levenstein, 1981; Miller, 1985; Milner, 1954; Murphy, 1992; Ottanelli, 1991; Parmet, 2005; Pells, 1973; Rossinow, 2004; Rossinow, 2005; Schaffer, 1966; Schrecker, 1986; Schwarz, 1987; Scott et al., 1999; Tompkins, 2006; Wald, 1987; Walker, 1990; Waltzer, 1977; Waltzer, 1980; Waltzer, 1982; Warren, 1993; Wechsler, 1971; Weidlich, 2000; Zitron, 1969

48. RED SCARE LITE

Adamic, 1976; Alpers, 2003; Bailey, 1982; Bayor, 1978; Bouza, 1976; Bullert, 2004; Carbone, 1977; Chamberlain, 1951; Cook, 1999; Davis, 1993; Denning, 1996; Dodd, 1954; Donner, 1981; Donner, 1990; FitzGerald, 1979; Fleming, 2001; Foley, 1968; Gettleman, 1977; Gettleman, 1982; Goodman, 1968; Hook, 1939a; Hook, 1987; Hopkins, 1972; Judis, 1988; Kutulas, 1995; Limpus, 1939; MacDonnell, 1995; Miller, 1985; Murphy, 1992; Naison, 1984; Nash et al., 1997; Ottanelli, 1991; Perrett, 1985; Ravitch, 2000; Rossinow, 2004; Ryan, 1995; Schlesinger, 2000; Schrecker, 1986; Seldes, 1948; Sirgiovanni, 1990; Smith et al., 2005; Theoharis, 1978; Theoharis, 2002; Tompkins, 2006; Veenswijk, 1994; Wald, 1987; Waltzer, 1982; Walzer, 1992; Weidlich, 2000; Zitron, 1969

49. SPIES

Bailey, 1982; Bedacht, 2001; Bentley et al., 1988; Bouza, 1976; Brown et al., 1981; Carroll, 1994; Conquest, 1968; Costello et al., 1993; Dorwart, 1981; Epstein, 1996; Fleming, 2001; Gallagher, 1988; Gallagher, 2006; Gitlow, 1971; Haynes et al., 1999; Haynes et al., 2003; Haynes et al., 2006b;

Hook, 1987; Isserman, 2000; Kessler, 2003; Klehr, 1984; Klehr et al., 1992; Klehr et al., 1998; Klehr et al., 1995; MacDonnell, 1995; Melton et al., 2020; Office of the House Historian et al., 2021; Olmsted, 2002; Ottanelli, 1991; Pernicone, 2005; Peter, 1983; Roberts, 2001b; Ryan, 1997; Ryan, 2002; Schecter et al., 2002; Schrecker, 1999; Schwarz, 1987; Scully, 2003; Sibley, 1999; Sibley, 2004; Tanenhaus, 1997; Waltzer, 1982; Weinstein, 1997; Weinstein et al., 1999

50. THE YANKS ARE NOT COMING?

Addison, 2004; Anderson, 1997; Bennett, 2003; Bloom, 1986; Bloom, 1998; Buhle, 1999; Bullert, 2002; Bullert, 2004; Chafee, 1969; Chatfield, 1973; Cohen, 1993; Coulter, 1997; D'Emilio, 2003; Danielson, 2003; Dekar, 2005a; Dekar, 2005b; Doenecke, 1977; Duberman, 1988; Duke, 2003; Fox, 1997; Freeman, 1989; Goodwin, 1968; Goodwin, 1994; Guthrie et al., 1996; Handy, 1987; Herzstein, 1989; Hook, 1987; Howe et al., 1957; Hyatt, 1990; Jaffe, 1975; Johnpoll, 1970; Kapur, 1992; Kosek, 2005; Kutulas, 1995; Levenstein, 1981; Meyer, 1989; Miller, 1985; Muste, 1967; Muste et al., 1967; Nelson, 1988; Ottanelli, 1991; Pells, 1973; Perrett, 1985; Plummer, 1996; Ravitch, 2000; Robinson, 1981; Rossinow, 2004; Ryan, 1995; Ryan, 2002; Schaffer, 1966; Schlesinger, 2000; Schrecker, 1986; Sifton, 2003; Singer, 1975; Sirgiovanni, 1990; Swanberg, 1976; Thomas et al., 1939; United States Senate, 1976; Wald, 1987; Waltzer, 1982; Warren, 1993; Warren, 1999; Westbrook, 1991; Wittner, 1969; Wreszin, 1994

FIGHTING LIBERALS

51. FDR: COMMON DEFENSE AND GENERAL WELFARE

Blum, 1970; Cook, 1999; Davis, 1993; Feagin et al., 1990; Fleming, 2001; Fraser, 1991; Gleason, 1992; Goodwin, 1994; Heinrichs, 1988; Herzstein, 1989; Huthmacher, 1968; Kennedy, 1999; Kessner, 1989; Klausen, 2002; Klehr, 1984; Koistinen, 1980; LaFeber, 1997; Lakoff, 1998; Levenstein, 1981; Lichtenstein, 1982; Markusen, 1991; Miller, 1978; Mintz, 1985; Moscow, 1968; Ottanelli, 1991; Polenberg, 1972; Roosevelt, 1940a; Rubinstein et al., 2002; Schaffer, 1966; Schwarz, 1981; Schwarz, 1987; Tierney, 2004; Tuttle, 1980; Waddell, 2001; Waltzer, 1977; Waltzer, 1982; Warren, 1999; White, 1980; Winfield, 1994; Zitron, 1969

52. MORAL REARMAMENT

Bennett, 2003; Bullert, 2002; Chatfield, 1973; Chester, 1995; Coulter, 1997; Doenecke, 1995; Duke, 2003; Fowler, 1981; Fox, 1976; Fox, 1985; Handy, 1987; Hook, 1987; Hulsether, 1999; Kutulas, 1995; Martin, 2005; McGreevy, 2003; Miller, 1985; Perrett, 1985; Roberts, 1984b; Robinson, 1981; Schlesinger, 2000; Sifton, 2003; Singer, 1975; Thomas et al., 1939; Warren, 1997; Wittner, 1969; World Council of Churches, 2000

53. MUSCULAR DEMOCRACY

Alpern, 1987; Alpers, 2003; Bennett, 2003; Bullert, 2002; Bunk, 1984; Chester, 1995; Cohalan, 1983; Dewey et al., 1941; Fox, 1976; Gleason, 1992; Kutulas, 1995; Lakoff, 1998; Massa, 2003; McGreevy, 1997; McGreevy, 2003; Milkman, 1997; Miller, 1985; Mirel, 2002; Paton-Walsh, 2002; Pells, 1973; Perrett, 1985; Ribuffo, 1983; Schlesinger, 2000; Schwarz, 1987; Seldes, 1939; Teres, 1996; Wald, 1987; Warren, 1997; Weidlich, 2000; Westbrook, 1990b; Westbrook, 1991; Wittner, 1969; Wreszin, 1994

54. PLAYWRIGHTS AND POETS

Adler et al., 1970; Alpers, 2003; Barber, 1999; Barnouw, 1945; Bernstein et al., 2003; Brown, 1979; Brown et al., 1970; Cull, 1995; Davis, 1993; Donaldson et al., 1992; Fleming, 2001; Herzstein, 1989; Horten, 2002; Kammen, 1996; Kutulas, 1995; Lavine et al., 1972; Lewis, 1978; Lewis, 1991; Perrett, 1985; Steel, 1980; Wertheim, 2004

55. REALITY RADIO

Barnouw, 1978; Blue, 2002; Cloud et al., 1996; Denning, 1996; Douglas, 1999; Fang, 1977; Horten, 2002; Lemann, 2006; Marquis, 1986; Persico, 1988; Steele, 1984

56. MARS INVADES NEW YORK

Blue, 2002; Callow, 1996; Cantril et al., 1940; Douglas, 1999; Fleming et al., 1969; Garfinkel, 1987; Herzstein, 1989; Horten, 2002; "Radio Listeners in Panic, Taking War Drama as Fact," 1938; Robinson, 2006; Wells, 1898

57. WINCHELL CALLING TO ALL SHIPS AT SEA

Alpern, 1987; Alpers, 2003; Aylesworth et al., 1987; Baughman, 1987; Blumenthal, 2000; Chapman, 1961; Cohen, 1972; Cohen, 1993; Cook, 1999; Covert et al., 1984; Cuneo, 1955; Davis, 1993; Donaldson et al., 1992; Douglas, 1999; Gabler, 1994; Gentry, 1991a; Gerber, 1976; Goodwin, 1994; Gordon, 1994; Herr, 1990; Herzstein, 1989; Kutulas, 1995; Lakoff, 1998; Nasaw, 2000; Remnick, 2000; Roosevelt, 1942; Sante et al., 2006; Steele, 1984; Taylor, 1971; Tebbel, 1968; Wald, 1987; Ware, 1982; White, 1979; Winfield, 1994; Wreszin, 1994

58. STERN'S POST, DOLLY'S DAILY

Cohen, 1972; Cuozzo, 1996; MacPherson, 2006; Milkman, 1997; "The New York 'Post' Changes Hands," 1939; Nissenson, 2007; Patner, 1988; Potter, 1976; Rothbard, 1984; Stern, 1962; Waltzer, 1977; White, 1979; Winfield, 1994; Wreszin, 1965

59. PM

Baughman, 1987; Beyer, 1995; Chapman, 1961; Cottrell, 1992; Denning, 1996; Gabler, 1994; Goldberg, 1986; Hess, 1997; Hoopes, 1985; Kozloff et al., 2002; MacPherson, 2006; Milkman, 1997; Minear et al., 1999; Phillips, 2003; Sante et al., 2006; Starr, 1993; Winfield, 1994

60. BRANDS FROM THE BURNING

Berman, 1997; Chester, 1995; Collomp, 2005; Cook, 1999; Davie et al., 1974; Dubinsky et al., 1977; "Emergency Rescue Committee," 2002; Ernst, 1984; Gold, 1980; Goodwin, 1994; Heilbut, 1983; Isenberg, 2001; Jackman et al., 1983; Jacobs, 1996; Kross, 2008; Levenstein, 1983; Lynes, 1973; Malmgreen, 1991; Malmgreen, 1997; Martin, 1976; Noël, 1985; Parmet, 2005; Pfanner, 1984; Renaud, 2005; Rosenblum et al., 1995; Sauvage, 2001; Stevenson, 1976; "Varian Fry, the Saviour of So Many Avant-Garde Artists During the War," 1999; Wyman, 1968

WALL STREET WARRIORS

61. LET'S MAKE A DEAL

Aris et al., 2004; Billstein, 2000; Black, 1999; Black, 2001; Blum, 1976; Britt, 1940; Burk, 1991; Chernow, 1990; Goda, 2004; Grose, 1996b; Herzstein, 1989; Higham, 1983; Hoopes, 1973; Immerman, 1999; Kolko, 1962; Kovel, 1997; Kwong, 1979; Lamont, 1994; Lee, 1980; Lisagor et al., 1988; Loftus et al., 1994; Mosley, 1978; Noraian, 2001; Pauwels, 2003; Phillips, 2004a; Pijl, 1984; Polenberg, 1972; Pruessen, 1982; Rogers, 2002; Rosenberg, 1982; Sampson, 1973; Schulzinger, 1984; Simpson, 1995; Sobel, 1982; Sobel, 1991; Stevenson, 1976; Sutton, 1976; Troy, 1996; Turner, 2005; Wallace, 2003; Warren, 1997; Weitz, 1997; Yergin, 1991

62. CHANGE AGENT

Erdmann, 2005

63. THE VERIEST ROMAN

Becker et al., 2003; Bernstein et al., 1975; Bird,

1992; Bird, 1998; Britt, 1940; Browder et al., 1986; Bundy, 1994; Burch, 1980; Chase, 1943; Chernow, 1990; Chernow, 1998; Clement, 2004; Cull, 1995; Davis, 1993; Divine, 1967; Gottlieb, 1982; Grose, 1996a; Herzstein, 1989; Hodgson, 1990; Horn, 2000; Horowitz, 1969; Isaacson et al., 1986; Johnson, 1968; Kahler, 1993; Kurth, 1993; Leffler, 1992; Lisagor et al., 1988; Martin, 2005; Morison, 1960; Parmar, 1995; Parmar, 1999b; Parmar, 2001; Parmar, 2002a; Parmar, 2002b; Perrett, 1985; Pijl, 1984; Pruessen, 1982; Riebling, 1994; Roberts, 2001a; Rosenberg, 1982; Rothbard, 1984; Schmitz, 2001; Schulzinger, 1984; Schwarz, 1981; Shefter, 1993b; Shoup, 1977; Simpson, 1995; Wala, 1994

64. BANKERS BALKED

65. COUNCIL COUNSEL

66. ANGLOPHILIACS

67. INTREPID

Bryce, 1984; Chester, 1995; Churchill et al., 1975; Cull, 1995; Dorwart, 1981; Dunlop, 1982; Gabler, 1994; Gentry, 1991a; Gilbert, 2005; Harrington, 1999; Herzstein, 1989; Hyde, 1989; Leslie, 1964; Loftus et al., 1994; MacDonnell, 1995; Mahl, 1998; Martin, 1969; Mosley, 1978; Riebling, 1994; Schwarz, 1987; Smith, 1983; Steele, 1984; Stevenson, 1976; Troy, 1996

68. AID THE ALLIES!

Barnouw, 1978; Baughman, 1987; Bilby, 1986; Bird, 1992; Blue, 2002; Brewer, 1997; Browder et al., 1986; Brown, 1979; Brown et al., 1970; Bullert, 2002; Bunk, 1984; Burch, 1980; Chadwin, 1968; Chase, 1943; Chatfield, 1973; Chernow, 1990; Cloud et al., 1996; Conant, 2002; Culbert, 1976; Cull, 1995; Denning, 1996; Doenecke, 1995; Doenecke, 2005; Donaldson et al., 1992; Dubinsky et al., 1977; Eichelberger, 1977; Fielding, 1978; Fleming et al., 1969; Goodwin, 1994; Gordon, 1994; Herzstein, 1989; Herzstein, 1994; Horten, 2002; Isaacson et al., 1986; Johnson, 1944; Kennedy, 1999; Kluger, 1986; Kurth, 1990; Lamont, 1994; Marquis, 1986; Martin, 2005; Masland, 1940; Milkman, 1997; Namikas, 1999; Parmar, 1999b; Parmar, 2004; Paton-Walsh, 2002; Perrett, 1985; Persico, 1988; Peters, 2005; Pijl, 1984; Ribuffo, 1983; Roberts, 2001a; Sanders, 1973; Schlesinger, 2000; Schmidt, 1987; Schulzinger, 1984; Shefter, 1993b; Shotwell, 1961; Shoup, 1977; Sills, 1987; Simpson, 1941; Smith, 1990a; Sperber, 1986; Steel, 1980; Steele, 1984; Stevenson, 1976; Swanberg, 1972; Troy, 1996; Wala, 1994; Waltzer, 1977; Wittner, 1969

69. FIFTH COLUMNIST

Kluger, 1986

70. FIGHTING LIBERALS V. WALL STREET WARRIORS

Chernow, 1990; Cook, 1999; Davis, 1993; Dorwart, 1991; Feagin et al., 1990; Hawley, 1966; Higgs, 1993; Kennedy, 1999; Koistinen, 1980; Lamont, 1994; Lichtenstein, 1982; Pijl, 1984; Polenberg, 1972; Ribuffo, 1983; Schwarz, 1981; Schwarz, 1987; "U.S. Steel Votes Common Dividend: Names New Heads," 1937; Waddell, 2001; Walker, 1963; White, 1980; Winkler, 2000

71. WE WANT WILLKIE!

Alpers, 2003; Bayor, 1978; Bird, 1992; Blum, 1976; Browder et al., 1986; Chadwin, 1968; Chernow, 1990; Cloud et al., 1996; Cull, 1995; D'Emilio, 2003; Davis, 1993; Donaldson et al., 1992; Dorwart, 1991; Duberman, 1988; Eiler, 1997; Finan, 2002; Flynn, 1947; Fraser, 1991; Gabler, 1994; Gallagher, 1988; Gleason, 1995a; Gordon, 1994; Handy, 1987; Herzstein, 1989; Herzstein, 1994; Hodgson, 1990; Hoopes, 1973; Kennedy, 1999; Kluger, 1986; Kurth, 1990; Lamont, 1994; Lichtenstein, 1982; Luconi, 2001a; Madison, 1992; Moscow, 1968; Mosley, 1978; Namikas, 1999; Neal, 1984; Parmar, 1999b; Perrett, 1985; Persico, 1988; Peters, 2005; Pijl, 1984; Pula, 1995; Ribuffo, 1983; Robinson, 1981; Rogin et al., 2003; Smith, 1982; Smith, 1990a; Steel, 1980; Tracy, 1996; Winfield, 1994

72. WAR HAWKS AT WORK

Anderson, 1997; Bennett, 2003; Bird, 1992; Browder et al., 1986; Chadwin, 1968; Chambers, 1987; Clifford et al., 1986; Clifford, 1973; D'Emilio, 2003; Davis, 1993; Dellinger, 1993; Eiler, 1997; Goodwin, 1994; Handy, 1987; Herzstein, 1994; Hodgson, 1990; Hunt, 2006; Kennedy, 1999; Kershaw, 2007; Lichtenstein, 1982; Madison, 1992; Morison, 1960; Moscow, 1968; Mosley, 1978; Mudd Manuscript Library, 2006; Namikas, 1999; Parmar, 1999b; Peters, 2005; Robinson, 1981; Steel, 1980; Wala, 1994

73. MARTIN, BARTON, AND FISH

Alpers, 2003; Baughman, 1987; Browder et al., 1986; Chadwin, 1968; Chernow, 1990; Donaldson et al., 1992; Douglas, 1999; Flynn, 1947; Gabler, 1994; Goodwin, 1994; Gordon, 1994; Herzstein, 1989; Herzstein, 1994; Johnpoll, 1970; Johnson, 1968; Kennedy, 1999; Kershaw, 2007; Kluger, 1986; Kurth, 1990; Lemann, 2006; Luconi, 2001a; Madison, 1992; Moscow, 1968; Paper, 1987; Peters, 2005; Pula, 1995; Smith, 1982; Smith, 1990a; Steel, 1980; Swanberg, 1972; Wall, 2000; Waltzer, 1977

74. ARSENAL OF DEMOCRACY

Baughman, 1987; Browder et al., 1986; Chadwin, 1968; Chernow, 1990; Davis, 1993; Foner, 1998; Gilbert, 2005; Goodwin, 1994; Hogan, 1999; Johnson, 1968; Kennedy, 1999; Kershaw, 2007; Kessner, 1989; Lamont, 1994; MacDonald, 1942; Miller, 1978; Perrett, 1985; Peters, 2005; Polenberg, 1972; Swanberg, 1972; Warren, 1999

75. AMERICA FIRST

Baughman, 1987; Bayor, 1978; Chapman, 1961; Chernow, 1990; Cole, 1953; Davis, 1993; Diggins, 1972; Doenecke, 1977; Doenecke, 1987; Doenecke, 1990; Doenecke, 2000; Gallicchio, 2000; Gerber, 1976; Herzstein, 1989; Johnpoll, 1970; Kennedy, 1999; Kershaw, 2007; Kimball, 1969; Levenstein, 1981; Lisagor et al., 1988; MacPherson, 2006; Miller, 1985; Moser, 2005; Mosley, 1978; Parmar, 1999b; Roberts, 1984b; Skidelsky, 1986; Tebbel, 1968; Wala, 1994

76. SECOND PLATOON

Abramson, 1992; Bird, 1992; Blum, 1976; Burch, 1980; Callahan, 1990; Chadwin, 1968; Chernow, 1990; Colby et al., 1995; Cull, 1995; Dorwart, 1991; Eiler, 1997; Fox, 1990b; Groth, 1983; Herzstein, 1989; Hodgson, 1990; Hooks, 1991; Hopkins, 1997; Isaacson et al., 1986; Kershaw, 2007; Lynes, 1973; Malloy, 2002; Millman, 2006; Morison, 1960; Mosley, 1978; Mudd Manuscript Library, 2006; Nelson, 1946; Perrett, 1985; Persico, 1982; Pijl, 1984; Polenberg, 1972; Reich, 1996; Roberts, 2001a; Rosenberg, 1982; Schwarz, 1994; Shefter, 1993b; Sherwood, 1950; Shoup, 1977; Smith, 1983; Sparrow, 1996; Stevenson, 1976; Swaine, 1946; Troy, 1996; Waddell, 2001; Walker, 1963; Winkler, 2000; Witcover, 1989; Yergin, 1991

77. 007 AND THE STORK CLUB DETECTIVE

Bailey, 1982; Blum, 1976; Bryce, 1984; Chester, 1995; Clarke, 1999; Cull, 1995; Donaldson et al., 1992; Donner, 1990; Dorwart, 1981; Douglas, 1999; Dunlop, 1982; Finnegan et al., 1989; Fleming, 2001; Fox, 1990b; Gabler, 1994; Gary, 1999; Gentry, 1991a; Groth, 1983; Harrington, 1999; Haynes, 2005; Herzstein, 1989; Hyde, 1989; MacDonnell, 1995; Mahl, 1998; Mauch, 2003; Miller,

1978; Mosley, 1978; Ortiz Garza, 2001; Peters, 2005; Reich, 1996; Ribuffo, 1983; Riebling, 1994; Schwarz, 1987; Shulman, 1990; Smith, 1983; Smith, 1972; Steele, 1984; Stevenson, 1976; Tomkins, 1994; Troy, 1996; Waltzer, 1982; Webb, 2005

78. DOWN SOUTH AMERICA WAY

Colby et al., 1995; Cramer et al., 2006; Decherney, 2005; Duberman, 2007; Guilbaut, 1984; Herzstein, 1994; Hiebert, 1966; Kramer, 1981; Lynes, 1973; MacDonnell, 1995; Museum of Modern Art, 1992; Ortiz Garza, 2001; Perrett, 1985; Persico, 1982; Pijl, 1984; Reich, 1996; Rivas, 2002; Rosenberg, 1982; Stevenson, 1976; Weaver et al., 1994; Yergin, 1991

79. YOU GO TO WAR WITH THE CAPITALISTS YOU'VE GOT

Baughman, 1987; Blum, 1976; Chernow, 1990; Collins, 2000; Cook, 1999; Davis, 1993; Dorwart, 1991; Eiler, 1997; Feagin et al., 1990; Fleming, 2001; Foner, 1998; Fraser, 1991; Furer, 1959; Goodwin, 1994; Hawley, 1966; Herzstein, 1989; Higgs, 1993; Hooks, 1991; Hopkins, 1941; Kazin, 1996; Kennedy, 1999; Kershaw, 2007; Koistinen, 1980; Koistinen, 2004; Kramer, 1981; Lamont, 1994; Lichtenstein, 1982; Lingeman, 1970; Mahl, 1998; McJimsey, 1987; Milkman, 1997; Perrett, 1985; Pijl, 1984; Polenberg, 1972; Ribuffo, 1983; Roosevelt, 1940b; Rosenberg, 1982; Schmitz, 2001; Schwarz, 1981; Schwarz, 1987; Schwarz, 1994; Swaine, 1946; "U.S. Steel Votes Common Dividend: Names New Heads," 1937; Waddell, 2001; Walker, 1963; White, 1980; White et al., 1995; Winkler, 2000; Wreszin, 1994

GOTHAM GIRDS FOR WAR

80. CASH AND CARRY

Bayor, 1978; Blumberg, 1979; Colton, 2007; Conn et al., 1960; Furer, 1959; Garraty, 1986; Gerber, 1976; Goodwin, 1994; Greenberg, 1991; Hanes et al., 1944; Hartzell et al., 1949; Ingalls, 1975; Johnson, 1968; Kershaw, 2007; Lane et al., 1951; Mahl, 1998; Martin, 2005; Mitchell et al., 1981; New York City WPA Writers' Project, 1941; Patterson, 1940; Perrett, 1985; Plunz, 1990; Schwarz, 1994; Sobel, 1975; Wilder, 2000; Williams et al., 2001b; Zolotow, 1941

81. BLACK POWER

Anderson, 1997; Biondi, 1997; Black, 1996; Blum, 1976; Blumberg, 1979; Bracey et al., 1991; Capeci, 1977b; City Wide Citizens' Committee on Harlem, 1942; D'Emilio, 2003; Danielson, 2003; Dekar, 2005a; Dekar, 2005b; Edmonds, 1973; Eiler, 1997; Fletcher, 1989; Foner, 1974; Fraser, 1991; Garfinkel, 1959; Goodwin, 1994; Greenberg, 1991; Huthmacher, 1968; Ingalls, 1975; Janken, 2003; Kennedy, 1999; Kessner, 1989; Layton, 2000; Lewis, 2000; McGuire, 1983; Patterson, 1940; Perrett, 1985; Polenberg, 1972; Reed, 1991; Schmitz, 2001; Sklaroff, 2002; Steele, 1991; Tyler, 1999; Wilder, 2000; Williams et al., 2001b; Winkler, 2000

82. ILLIBERAL LIBERALS

Baughman, 1987; Bayor, 1978; Berg, 1998; Bird, 1992; Blue, 2002; Breuer, 1989; Brown et al., 1970; Bullert, 2002; Callow, 1996; Carlson, 1943; Casey et al., 2001; Chadwin, 1968; Chernow, 1990; Chester, 1995; Cole, 1974; Cook, 1984; Davis, 1993; Diggins, 1972; Dinnerstein, 1994; Doenecke, 2000; Doenecke, 2005; Finan, 2002; Finkle, 1975; Fleming, 2001; Foner, 1998; Fox, 1985; Fox, 1990b; Gallagher, 1988; Gallicchio, 2000; Gerber, 1976; Gleason, 1992; Gordon, 2003; Heilbut, 1983; Herzstein, 1989; Herzstein, 1994; Hogan, 1999; Hoopes, 1985; Hopkins, 1941; Hulsether, 1999; Johnpoll, 1970; Keller, 1971; Kurth, 1990; Kutulas, 1995; Levenstein, 1981; Lichtenstein, 1982; Luconi, 2001a; MacDonnell, 1995; MacPherson, 2006; Milkman, 1997; Miller, 1978; Minear et al., 1999; Mirel, 2002; Parmar, 2004; Perrett, 1985; Ribuffo, 1983; Riebling, 1994; Rothbard, 2007; Sanders, 1973; Schlesinger, 2000; Schulzinger, 1984; Sirgiovanni, 1990; Steele, 1984; Wala, 1994; Zunz, 1998

83. BATTLE OF THE ATLANTIC

Air Force Historical Research Agency, 2007; Andrews, 1941; Aylesworth et al., 1987; Blumberg, 1979; Brooklyn Eagle, 1945; Brown, 1999; Buckley, 1999; Carse, 1965; Conn et al., 1964; Conn et al., 1960; Department of the Navy, 2003; Duffy, 1974; Fort Tilden History, 2000; Funigiello, 1978; Gannon, 1990; Gerber, 1976; Gilmore, 1983; Hartzell et al., 1949; Headquarters of the Eastern Sea Frontier, 1942a; Headquarters of the Eastern Sea Frontier, 1942b; Heinrichs, 1988; Herzstein, 1989; Hickam, 1989; Imperial War Museum, 2004; Kennedy, 1999; Kershaw, 2007; Kessner, 1989; Lingeman, 1970; Martin, 2005; Morison, 1947; National Park Service, 1983; Page, 2008; Perrett, 1985; Polaski et al., 2003; Ray et al., 1980; Rowland, 1947; Schelm, 2003; Schwarz, 1994; Smith, 2011; Steele, 1984; UBoatAces, 2006; United States Army, 1944; United States Bureau of Yards and Docks, 1947; Van der Vat, 1988; Walding, 2001; Walding, 2013; Yarnall, 2003; Yergin, 1991

84. CIVILIAN DEFENDER

Bayor, 1978; Bilby, 1986; Brodsky, 2003; Duffy, 1974; Eleanor Roosevelt Papers, 2003; Fort Tilden History, 1999; Fox, 1990b; Funigiello, 1978; Hartzell et al., 1949; Heckscher et al., 1978; Heilbut, 1983; Herzstein, 1989; Kessner, 1989; Lingeman, 1970; Nevins, 1963; Perrett, 1985; Steele, 1984; Thies, 2001; Yellin, 2004

85. LA GUARDIA THIRD TERM?

Anthony, 2006; Bayor, 1978; Bayor, 2018; Biondi, 1997; Block, 1983; Blue, 2002; Brodsky, 2003; Cantwell, 1996; Capeci, 1977a; Capeci, 1977b; Caro, 1974; Cuneo, 1955; Davis, 1993; Farley, 1948; Foner, 1950; Fraser, 1991; Garrett, 1961; Gerber, 1976; Gerson, 1976; Goodman, 1968; Gunther, 1985; Hamburger, 2000; Hamilton, 1991; Haygood, 1993; Heckscher et al., 1978; Hook, 1987; Howe et al., 1957; Huberman, 1941; Kennedy, 1999; Kessner, 1989; Levenstein, 1981; Lichtenstein, 1982; Martin, 2005; Meyer, 1989; Milkman, 1997; O'Dwyer, 1979; O'Dwyer et al., 1987; Powell, 1971a; Pritchett, 1997; Rabinowitz, 1996; "Reles Loan Racket Is Exposed by Amen," 1941; Rockefeller, 2002; Rodgers, 1943; Schulzinger, 1984; Smith, 1982; Special Committee to Investigate Organized Crime in Interstate Commerce, 1951; Turkus, 1951; Valentine, 1947; Wallace, 2018; Walter et al., 1989; Waltzer, 1977; Wittner, 1969; Witwer, 2005

86. PEARL HARBOR

Anderson, 1981; Brodsky, 2003; Brown, 1999; Carse, 1965; Conn et al., 1964; Department of the Navy, 1946b; Douglas, 1999; Fleming, 2001; Fort Tilden History, 1999; Frey et al., 1946; Funigiello, 1978; Gannon, 1990; Goodwin, 1994; Gray, 2001; Hartzell et al., 1949; Headquarters of the Eastern Sea Frontier, 1942a; Heckscher et al., 1978; Hickam, 1989; Kazin, 1996; Kennedy, 1999; Kessner, 1989; Kisseloff, 1995; Lingeman, 1970; Morison, 1947; Museum of the City of New York et al., 2000; Nash, 1968; Rosenberg, 1995; Smith,

2011; Sparr, 2000; Tomkins, 1970; Van der Vat, 1988; Weaver et al., 1994; Winkler, 2000; Yergin, 1991

UNDER THE GUN

87. TURKEY SHOOT

Brown, 1999; Department of the Navy, 1946b

88. SABOTAGE?

Ardman, 1985; Breuer, 1989; Duffy, 1986; Federal Writers' Project, 1938; Foucart et al., 1985; Gallagher, 1988; Gosch et al., 1975; Maxtone-Graham, 2007; Meany, 1994; Mehlman, 2000; Milkman, 1997; Perrett, 1985; Spoto, 1999

89. THE MOB AND THE MILITARY

Ardman, 1985; Block, 1986; Campbell, 1977; Costello, 1985; Costello et al., 1993; Gallagher, 1988; Gosch et al., 1975; Hughes et al., 1977; Joesten, 1955; Lacey, 1991; Meany, 1994; Meyer et al., 1998; Rosenberg, 1995; Stolberg, 1995; Van der Vat, 1988

90. SABOTAGE!

Biddle, 1962; Bird, 1992; Breuer, 1989; Campbell, 1977; Fisher, 2003; Gentry, 1991a; Kennedy, 1999; MacDonnell, 1995; Perrett, 1985; Polenberg, 1972; Rachlis, 1961; Swanberg, 1970; Van der Vat, 1988

91. ALIENS

Alpern, 1987; Bayor, 1978; Block, 1994; Blum, 1976; Bullert, 2002; Campbell, 1977; Carnevale, 2003; Chernow, 1990; Cottrell, 1992; Cramer, 2000; Daniels, 1971; Daniels, 1993; Diggins, 1972; DiStasi, 1997; DiStasi, 2001; Douglas, 1999; Dower, 1986; Fleming, 2001; Foner, 1998; Fox, 1985; Fox, 1990b; Gallagher, 1988; Greenberg, 1995b; Groth, 1983; Harris, 1998; Horten, 2002; Kessner, 1989; Lacey, 1991; Lee, 2007; Lewis, 2000; Luconi, 2001a; May, 1987; Meyer, 1989; Milkman, 1997; Miller, 1978; Minear et al., 1999; "Mission to N.Y. Japs," 1943; Modell, 1995; Pernicone, 2005; Perrett, 1985; Polenberg, 1972; Polenberg, 1995; Pozzetta, 1995; Schmitz, 2001; Seidel, 1988; Steel, 1980; Steele, 1991; Swanberg, 1976; Talese, 1992; Wall, 2000; Winkler, 2000

92. DISSENTERS

Anderson, 1997; Bayor, 1978; Bennett, 1969; Bergman, 1984; Bloom, 1986; Brown, 1983; Carlson, 1943; Cooney, 1984; D'Emilio, 2003; Dower, 1986; Finan, 2002; Finkle, 1975; Fisher, 1989; Gerber, 1976; Johnpoll, 1970; Klejment et al., 1996; McNeal, 1992; Miller, 1982; Mize, 2001; Perrett, 1985; Polenberg, 1972; Polenberg, 1995; Roberts, 1984b; Sibley et al., 1952; Sumner, 1996; Swanberg, 1976; Tracy, 1996; Wald, 1987; Washburn, 1986; Wogaman et al., 1996; Wreszin, 1994; Zeitzer et al., 1986

93. "AS DARK AS HITLER'S HEART"

Brooklyn Eagle, 1945; Campbell, 1977; Castles, 1946; Department of the Navy, 1946b; Duffy, 1974; Fort Tilden History, 2000; Fort Tilden History, 2001a; Fort Tilden History, 2001b; Gerstle, 1989; Goodwin, 1994; Hartzell et al., 1949; Johnson, 1968; Kennedy, 1999; Kessner, 1989; Kisseloff, 1995; Lingeman, 1970; Meany, 1994; Museum of the City of New York et al., 2000; Preston, 1986; Rachlis et al., 1963; Rosenberg, 1995; Stern et al., 1987; Tell, 2007; Tomkins, 1970; United States Bureau of Yards and Docks, 1947; Yergin, 1991

94. CONVOYS

Barlow, 1994; Brooklyn Eagle, 1945; Brown, 1994; Department of the Navy, 1946b; Gannon, 1990; International Registry of Sunken Ships, 2006; Kennedy, 1999; Kershaw, 2007; Kindell, 2012; Love, 1994; Meany, 1994; Morison, 1947; Smith, 2011; Valle, 1994; Van der Vat, 1988; Vego, 1999; Venzi, 2009

95. "NEW YORK AT WAR"

Aylesworth et al., 1987; Brooklyn Eagle, 1945; Department of the Navy, 1946b; Heckscher et al., 1978; Imperial War Museum, 2004; Jaffe, 2012; Kennedy, 1999; Perrett, 1985; Polenberg, 1972; Rigden, 2000; Yergin, 1991

WAR PORT

96. ANCHORS AWEIGH

Arend, 1979; Ballon et al., 2002; Beebe, 2000; Bell, 1961; Biondi, 2003; Bird, 1949; Block, 1986; Boyer, 1947; Brooklyn Eagle, 1945; Brouwer, 1989; Brouwer, 1990; Bukatman, 2007; Byles, 2005; Campbell, 1977; Cape Liberty Cruise Port, 2006; Caro, 1974; Carse, 1965; Castaneda, 1993; Chase, 1943; City of Bayonne, 2005; Condit, 1980; Cuff, 1989; Department of the Navy, 1946b; Diehl, 1985; Dorwart, 1991; Duffy, 1986; Federal Writers' Project, 1938; Fitch, 1977; Fox, 1993; Frees, 1970; Frey et al., 1946; Gabler, 1994; Goddard, 1996; Griffin, 1959; Hartzell et al., 1949; Heckscher et al., 1978; Herbert, 2004; Horne, 2005; "Industrial Development on Long Island," 1967; International Registry of Sunken Ships, 2006; Isaacson et al., 1986; Itzkoff, 1985; Jackson, 1984; Johnson, 1967; Juno Beach Centre, 2022; Kempton, 1955; Kimeldorf, 1988; Koistinen, 1980; Koppes et al., 1990; Kramer, 1943; Lacey, 1991; Lane et al., 1951; Larrowe, 1972; Levenstein, 1981; Martin, 2005; McGowan, 1998; Meany, 1994; Mitchell, 1992; Moran et al., 1956; Morris, 1987; Naison, 1993; Nash, 1968; Nelson, 1988; New York City WPA Writers' Project, 1941; Palmer et al., 2001; Perrett, 1985; Polenberg, 1972; Pomerance, 2007; Popple, 1952; Port of New York Authority, 1941; Roberts, 2013; Rosenberg, 1982; Schlichting, 2001; Schulzinger, 1984; Scullin, 1968; Singer, 1951; Singer, 1952; Sparks, 1930; Tobier, 1988; Toynbee, 1970; "Two Pipelines for Sale?," 1945; United States Bureau of Yards and Docks, 1947; Van der Vat, 1988; Venzi, 2009; White, 1980; Willett, 1985; Yergin, 1991

97. SMALLER WAR PLANTS

Adams, 1994; Adams et al., 1999; Blum, 1976; Blumberg, 1979; "Brewster XF2A-1," 1999; Brinkley, 1989; Brooklyn Eagle, 1945; Capeci, 1977b; Casper et al., 2001; Chandler et al., 2005; Christman, 1971; Citizens Housing and Planning Council et al., 1942; City Planning Commission, 1940; City Planning Commission, 1951; Cohen et al., 1956; Collins, 2000; Davis, 1967; Dorwart, 1991; Duffy, 1986; Fagen et al., 1975; Feagin et al., 1990; Fraser, 1991; Fryer, 2002; Funigiello, 1978; Goodwin, 1994; Greenberg, 1991; Hall et al., 1988; Hanes et al., 1944; Hartmann, 1982; Hartzell et al., 1949; Heckscher et al., 1978; Higgs, 1992; Higgs, 1993; Higgs, 2004; Howard, 2007; Iardella, 1964; "Industrial Development on Long Island," 1967; Jackson, 1984; Jordan, 2000; Jordan, 2005; Kennedy, 1999; Kessner, 1989; Lane et al., 1951; Lichtenstein, 1982; Lieberman, 1995; Lingeman, 1970; Lipsitz, 1994; Lurkis, 1982; Maas, 1985; MacPherson, 2006; Markusen, 1991; Meany, 1994; Mollenkopf, 1983; Moscow, 1968; "Nabisco Foods Group," 1993; National Park Service, 2008; National Urban League, 1945; New York Naval Shipyard, 1951; New York State Department of Commerce, 1957; New York State Department of Commerce et al., 1943; Polenberg, 1972; Quivik, 2004; Regional Plan Association, 1967; Roberts et al., 1993; Rosenberg, 1982; Rossano, 1984; Sachs et al., 1988; Schwartz, 1993; Seyfried, 1982; Shortridge,

References 873

2005; Stoff, 1989; Tillman, 1998; Tobier, 1988; United States Bureau of Yards and Docks, 1947; Waddell, 2001; White, 1980; Wilder, 2000; Willett, 1985; Winkler, 2000

SCIENCE IN THE CITY

98. R&D: RADAR

Adams et al., 1999; Alvarez, 1980; "AT&T Bell Laboratories, Inc. History," 1996; "Bell Labs' First 50 Years: Prelude to Tomorrow," 1975; Bernstein, 1984; Bird et al., 2005; Brittain, 1998; Brooklyn Eagle, 1945; Brown, 1999; Buderi, 1998; Chandler et al., 2000; Chandler et al., 2005; Conant, 2002; Dow, 1954; Genuth, 1988; Goebel, 2020; Hall, 1959; Heppenheimer, 1996; IEEE Virtual Museum, 2004; Lipsitz, 1994; McCaughey, 2003

99. MANHATTAN PROJECT

Badash et al., 1986; Bernstein, 1984; Bilby, 1986; Brennan, 1971; Broad, 2007; Buderi, 1998; Chandler et al., 2000; da Cruz, 2022; Davis, 1967; Ellis, 1966; Frusciano et al., 1997; Grosch, 1991; Hall, 1959; Haynes et al., 2006a; Heppenheimer, 1996; Hewlett et al., 1962; Jackman et al., 1983; Jones, 1985; Kelly, 2007; Kennedy, 1999; Kevles, 1978; Lichello, 1971; Mabon, 1975; McCaughey, 2003; Norris, 2007; Radosh et al., 1997; Reid, 1976; Rezelman et al., 2003; Rhodes, 1986; Rigden, 2000; Roberts, 2001b; Rodgers, 1969; Sarnoff Corporation, 2004; Schwarz, 1994; Seidel, 1992; Stroke, 1995; Szilard, 1969; Thorpe, 2006; Usdin, 2005a; Usdin, 2005b; Weiner, 1969; Weinstein et al., 1999; Wheeler et al., 1998

100. THE ANTHROPOLOGY OF NEW YORK CITY

Bucher et al., 1985; Clifford, 1999; Cohen-Solal, 2000; Fermi, 1968; Fleming et al., 1969; Freed et al., 1983; Heilbut, 1983; Jennings, 2002; Johnson, 2003a; Lévi-Strauss, 1985; Lévi-Strauss, 1992; Lévi-Strauss et al., 1991; MacDonald, 1998; Mehlman, 2000; Pace, 1983; Pierpont, 2004; Scott et al., 1999; Thompson, 2004; Zolberg et al., 1998

SELLING THE WAR

101. "ANY BONDS TODAY?"

Adams, 1994; Blum, 1976; Brooklyn Eagle, 1945; Chernow, 1990; Feagin et al., 1990; Geisst, 2004; Goodwin, 1994; Greider, 1989; Griffith, 1983; Higgs, 2004; Honey, 1984; Hooks, 1991; Horowitz, 1988; Horten, 2002; John W. Hartman Center for Sales, 1999; Keller, 1963; Kennedy, 1999; Kimble, 2006; Lamont, 1994; Leff, 1991; Lichtenstein, 1982; Olson, 1988; Perrett, 1985; Pijl, 1984; Polenberg, 1972; Ritter et al., 1988; Samuel, 1997; Schwarz, 1981; Schwarz, 1994; Seligman, 2003; Sobel, 1975; Sobel, 1980; Stole, 2001; Sweeting, 1994; Tax Policy Center, 2016; Thomas, 1951; Thorndike, 2001; Twight, 1995; Ventry et al., 1997; White, 1980; Winkler, 2000

102. "WHAT THIS WAR IS ALL ABOUT"
103. CLASHING VISIONS OF VICTORY

Adams, 1994; Alonso, 2007; Barnes, 1943; Barnes, 2007; Barnouw, 1968; Batterberry et al., 1999; Baughman, 1987; Belgrad, 1998; Bird, 1998; Blue, 2002; Blum, 1976; Brown et al., 1970; Cohen, 2003a; Cramer et al., 2006; Culver et al., 2000; Donaldson et al., 1992; Fish et al., 2004; Fleming, 2001; Foner, 1998; Fox, 1975; Fox, 1985; Fraser, 1991; Griffith, 1983; Grose, 1996b; Groth, 1983; Hawkins et al., 1943; Heil, 2003; Honey, 1984; Honey, 1995; Horten, 2002; Howell, 1971; Kessner, 1989; Kimble, 2001; Kurth, 1990; Lears, 1994; Lingeman, 1970; MacDonald, 1942; Mauch, 2003; Miller, 1978; Moliski et al., 2007; Morse, 1972; Pfanner, 1984; Pierce, 1979; Pohl, 1989; Polenberg, 1972; Rosenberg, 1982; Rubenstein Library, 2022; Schiffrin, 2007; Schlesinger, 2000; Shulman, 1990; Smith, 1990a; Spiller, 2004; Steele, 1984; Voice of America, 2007; Weaver et al., 1994; Weinberg, 1968; Westbrook, 1990a; White et al., 1995; Wreszin, 1994; Young, 2005a

104. WRITERS ON DEMAND

Aloglazernso, 2007; Ballantine et al., 1989; Batterberry et al., 1999; Blue, 2002; Blum, 1976; Brooklyn Eagle, 1945; "Cheap Books," 1939; DeGruson, 2002; Denning, 1996; Edelman, 2006; Fermi, 1968; Frederick, 1948; French, 1964; Glazer, 1993; Goodwin, 1994; Graham, 2006; Heilbut, 1983; Herder, 1971; Howell, 1971; Hyde Park Books, 2003; Kent et al., 1968; Lee, 2017; Lingeman, 1970; Loss, 2003; MacDonnell, 1995; Mondlin et al., 2004; Morris, 1987; Neavill, 2007; Perrett, 1985; Pfanner, 1984; Radway, 1991; Ribuffo, 1983; Schick, 1958; Schiffrin, 2001; Schiffrin, 2007; Tebbel, 1978; Tebbel, 1981; Tippins, 2005; Volz, 1992; Winkler, 2000

105. WAR SONGS

Costello, 1985; Desmond, 1943; Hajduk, 2003; Jones, 1994; Jones, 2006; Perrett, 1985; Smith, 1996; Smith, 2003; Smith, 1946; Young et al., 2005

106. "SMASHING THRU, CAPTAIN AMERICA CAME FACE TO FACE WITH HITLER"

Andelman, 2015; Andrae, 1987; Andrae, 2007; Benton, 1992; Brooklyn Eagle, 1945; Cull, 1995; DeBona, 1997; Dooley et al., 1987; Eco, 1979; Feiffer, 1965; Fingeroth, 2007; Goulart, 1986; Hartmann, 1982; Jones, 2004; Kane et al., 1989; Lee, 1974; Lingeman, 1970; MacDonnell, 1995; Minganti, 1990; Pearson et al., 1991; Perrett, 1985; Savage, 1990; Simon et al., 2003; "Superman's Dilemma," 1942; Weinstein, 2006; Winkler, 2000; Wright, 2001

HOME FRONT

107. WOMEN AT WORK

Adams, 1994; Anderson, 1981; Bellafaire, 1993; Bentley, 1998; Blantz et al., 1993; Boucher, 2003; Bowers et al., 1986; Brooklyn Eagle, 1945; "Catholics v. WAACs," 1942; Chafe et al., 1991; Costello, 1985; Dratch, 1974; Duffy, 1974; Epstein, 1993; Foner, 1950; Freeman, 1989; Frusciano et al., 1997; Gardner, 1982; Gregory, 1974; Halper, 2001; Hartmann, 1982; Hartzell et al., 1949; Hirsh, 1954; Hodges, 2007; Hodgson, 2000; Honey, 1984; Honey, 1995; Hoogenboom, 1987; Horowitz, 1998; Howard, 1984; Howell, 1971; Kennedy, 1999; Litoff et al., 1996; Martin, 2005; Meany, 1994; Meyer, 1996; Milkman, 1987; National Cemetery Administration, 2022a; National Cemetery Administration, 2022b; New York City Civilian Defense Volunteer Office, 1943; New York City Civilian Defense Volunteer Office, 1946; Office of Civilian Mobilization et al., 1943; Perrett, 1985; Pritchett, 2002; Rodgers, 1969; Rosenberg, 1995; Ross, 1943; Schatz, 1983; Shultz et al., 1959; Smith, 2003; Smith, 1990b; Sparr, 2000; Tilley, 2008; United States Bureau of Yards and Docks, 1947; United States Office of Civilian Defense, 1941; Weatherford, 1990; Winchell, 2004; Winkler, 2012; Wylie, 1942

108. ROSIE AND CHARLIE

Adams, 1994; Anderson, 1981; Arnesen, 2006; Bentley, 1998; Biondi, 1997; Blum, 1976; Blumberg, 1979; Brooklyn Eagle, 1945; Cobble, 2004; Coble, 2006; Cohen, 1996; Columbia Law Review Association, 1946; Costello, 1985; Dabakis, 1993; Daniels et al., 2004; Denning, 1996; Department of the Navy, 1946a; Evans et al., 1942; Foner, 1950; Goodwin, 1994; Gregory, 1998; Harrison, 1988; Hartmann, 1982; Honey, 1984; Hoogenboom, 1987;

Horowitz, 1998; Horten, 2002; Jones, 2004; Kennedy, 1999; Kimble et al., 2006; Lepore, 2014; Lingeman, 1970; Lipsitz, 1994; Meany, 1994; Milkman, 1997; Milkman, 1987; Mollenkopf, 1983; Palmer, 1989; Perrett, 1985; Rupp, 1979; Schatz, 1983; Straub, 1973; War Department, 1946; Ware, 1981; Weatherford, 1990; Weisbord et al., 1970; Wright, 2001

109. "WENCHES WITH WRENCHES"

Adams, 1994; Anderson, 1981; Baxandall, 1988; Bentley, 1998; Bond, 1945; "Catholics v. WAACs," 1942; Cobble, 2004; Coble, 2006; Cohen, 1996; Columbia Law Review Association, 1946; Denning, 1996; Dratch, 1974; Duffy, 1974; Flynn, 1942; Foner, 1950; Funigiello, 1978; Goodwin, 1994; Gregory, 1974; Hartmann, 1982; Hawes, 1943; Honey, 1984; Horowitz, 1998; Kennedy, 1999; Kessler-Harris, 1988; Litoff et al., 1996; Matles et al., 1975; National Library of Medicine, 2018; Polenberg, 1972; Sinai et al., 1948; Sparr, 2000; Tuttle, 1993

110. BAD MOMS

Adams, 1994; Anderson, 1982; Anderson, 1981; Anthony, 1943; Bayor, 1978; Bell, 1961; Blum, 1976; "Catholics v. WAACs," 1942; Chambers, 1944; Cobble, 2004; Costello, 1985; Dratch, 1974; Goodwin, 1994; Gregory, 1974; Gregory, 1998; Harrison, 1988; Hartmann, 1982; Hodgson, 2000; Honey, 1984; Honey, 1995; Kelley, 1992; Kennedy, 1999; Kersten, 2006; Kessler-Harris, 1988; Lichtenstein, 2000; Lingeman, 1970; Lipsitz, 1994; Meyer, 1996; Milkman, 1987; Monkkonen, 2001; Norwood, 2003; Perrett, 1985; Polenberg, 1972; Pozzetta, 1995; Rosenzweig et al., 1994; Schneider, 1999; Sparr, 2000; Tuttle, 1993; Weatherford, 1990; Winkler, 2000

111. CONTROLLING CONSUMPTION

Abadinsky, 1981; Adams, 1994; Ames Historical Society, 2008; Anderson, 1981; Aylesworth et al., 1987; Batterberry et al., 1999; Bayor, 2018; Bentley, 1998; Blue, 2002; Blum, 1976; Blum, 1983; Brecher, 2008; Brooklyn Eagle, 1945; Caro, 1974; Cohen, 2003a; Duffy, 1974; Ernst et al., 2002; Foner, 1950; Gage, 1972; Glickman, 2005; Goodwin, 1994; Greider, 1989; Hartzell et al., 1949; Heckscher et al., 1978; Higgs, 2004; Hodges, 2007; Horowitz, 2004; Howell, 1971; Jacobs, 1997; Jacobs, 2004; Kennedy, 1999; Kessner, 1989; Leff, 1991; Lichtenstein, 2000; Lingeman, 1970; Maas, 1968; Martin, 1953; Meskil, 1973; Miller, 2000; Morris, 1987; Perrett, 1985; Polenberg, 1972; Pritchett, 2002; Raab, 2005; Samuel, 1997; Strasser, 1999; Torro, 2002; Waddell, 2001; Winkler, 2000; Yergin, 1991

112. CONTROLLING RENTS

Chisholm, 1970; Cohen, 2003a; Cooney, 1984; Day, 1999; Friedman et al., 1946; Hartzell et al., 1949; Horne, 2005; Lawson et al., 1986; Roberts, 1984a; Schaffer, 1966; Schwartz, 1986; Shachtman, 1991; Shultz et al., 1959; Smith, 1982; Waltzer, 1977

BLACKS

113. A WHITE FOLKS' WAR?

Anderson, 1982; Blue, 2002; Borstelmann, 2001; Brandt, 1996; Dower, 1986; Finkle, 1975; Garfinkel, 1959; Greenberg, 1991; Gunther, 1985; Jackson, 2001; Kessner, 1989; Markowitz et al., 1996; Ottley, 1942; Polenberg, 1972; Rampersad, 1988; Sklaroff, 2002; United States Office of Facts and Figures et al., 1942

114. "CHECKERBOARDING" WORKSITES

Biondi, 1997; Blumberg, 1979; Boyer, 1947; Brandt, 1996; Capeci, 1977b; Chisholm, 1970; City-wide Citizens' Committee on Harlem, 1942a; Foner, 1974; Freeman, 1978; Garfinkel, 1959; Greenberg, 1991; Gregory, 1998; Hamilton, 1991; Hartmann, 1982; Heilbut, 1983; Horne, 2005; Isserman, 1993; Johnson, 2003b; Kennedy, 1999; Kessner, 1989; Lichtenstein, 2000; Markowitz et al., 1996; Milkman, 1997; Price, 1973; Rampersad, 1988; Reed, 1991; Schneider, 1999; Walkowitz, 1999; Wilder, 2000; Willett, 1985

115. PENNED IN AND PISSED OFF

Biondi, 1997; Brandt, 1996; Capeci, 1977b; City-wide Citizens' Committee on Harlem, 1942b; Friedman, 1995b; Funigiello, 1978; Garfinkel, 1959; Gelfand, 1975; Goldstein, 2006; Greenberg, 1991; Hamilton, 1991; James, 1947; Johanek et al., 2007; Johnson, 2003b; Markowitz et al., 1996; Meyer, 2000; National Urban League, 1945; Perrett, 1985; Petry, 1946; Plunz, 1990; Price, 1973; Rosenzweig et al., 1994; Schneider, 1999; Schwartz, 1993; Smith, 2001; Ultan et al., 1992; Zipp, 2010

116. GI JIM CROW

Bailey et al., 1992; Bentley, 1998; Biondi, 1997; Blum, 1976; Borstelmann, 2001; Brandt, 1996; Capeci, 1977b; Dower, 1986; Finkle, 1975; Johnson, 2003b; Katznelson, 2005; Kennedy, 1999; MacPherson, 2006; Motley, 1987; Perrett, 1985; Rampersad, 1988; Roeder, 1993; Sklaroff, 2002; Washburn, 1986

117. SATYAGRAHA IN MADISON SQUARE GARDEN

Blum, 1976; Callow, 1996; Chatfield, 1973; D'Emilio, 2003; Dekar, 2005a; Foner, 1974; Garfinkel, 1959; Hill, 1995; Hobson, 2005; Isserman, 1993; Kapur, 1992; Kersten, 2007; Kosek, 2005; Naison, 1984; Perrett, 1985; Plummer, 1996; Rampersad, 1988; Rosenberg, 2006; Sitkoff, 1997; Smith, 2004

118. ZOOTS

Anderson, 1982; Blum, 1976; Brandt, 1996; Capeci, 1977b; Cosgrove, 1984; DeCaro, 1996; Dyson, 1995; Gillespie, 1979; Gormley, 2008; Gregory, 1998; Kelley, 1992; Lardner et al., 2000; Leeming, 1994; Lott, 1988; Maggin, 2005; Malcolm X et al., 1992; McGuire, 1983; Perrett, 1985; Rampersad, 1988; Rosenberg, 2006; Shaw, 1977; Shipton, 1999; Sitkoff, 1997; Smith, 1990a; Taylor, 2002; Wilder, 2000

119. CLAMPDOWN

Benjamin, 1974; Bentley, 1998; Biondi, 1997; Blue, 2002; Blum, 1976; Brandt, 1996; Capeci, 1977b; Clark et al., 1945; Cosgrove, 1984; Johnson, 2003b; Katznelson, 2005; Kessner, 1989; Lardner et al., 2000; Leeming, 1994; Malcolm X et al., 1992; Marshall et al., 2003; Rockefeller, 2002; Rucker et al., 2007; Schneider, 1999; Shaw, 1977; Smith, 1990a; Taylor, 2002; Wilder, 2000

120. "GET THE WHITE MAN! GET THE WHITE MAN!"

Anderson, 1982; Baker, 2006a; Benjamin, 1974; Brandt, 1996; Clark et al., 1945; Cohen, 2003a; Greenberg, 1991; Horne, 2005; Jackson, 2001; Janken, 2003; Johnson, 2003b; Kelley, 1992; Lardner et al., 2000; Lott, 1988; Petry, 1946; Polenberg, 1972; Price, 1973; Schneider, 1999; Smith, 2001

121. PASSING THE TORCH

Anderson, 1997; Benjamin, 1974; Biondi, 1997; Capeci, 1977b; D'Emilio, 2003; Farmer, 1985; Finkle, 1975; Flynn, 1984; Gannon, 1962; Garfinkel, 1959; Greenberg, 1995a; Horne, 2008; Janken, 2003; Kosek, 2005; Levine, 2000; Litoff et al., 2000; Metres, 2000; Mjagkij, 2001; Polenberg, 1972; Rosenberg, 2006; Sitkoff, 1997; Southern, 1996

References 875

HOLOCAUST

122. SOUNDS OF DISTANT SLAUGHTER

Bauer, 1981; Berman, 1990; Bird, 1992; Blatman, 2010; Blum, 1976; Borstelmann, 2001; Brecher, 1990; Breitman, 2004; Collomp, 2005; Conroy, 2006; Dawidowicz, 1982; Desbois, 2008; Edelman, 1946; Engel, 1983; Engel, 1990; Fox, 1985; Friedenson et al., 1984; Fry, 1942; Goldstein, 2006; Goodwin, 1994; Grobman, 1998; Grobman, 2004; Gurock, 1998; Herzstein, 1989; Idelson, 2007; Isenberg, 2001; Joint Emergency Committee for European Jewish Affairs et al., 1943; JTA, 2008; Karski, 1944; Kaufman, 1991; Kessin Berman, 1997; Kranzler, 1987; Kranzler, 2002; Leff, 2000; Leff, 2005; Levy, 2002; Malmgreen, 1991; Malmgreen et al., 1997; Medoff, 1987; Medoff, et al., 2004; Penkower, 1983; Penkower, 1994; Penkower, 2002; Radosh et al., 2009; Raider, 1998; Ravel et al., 1980; Remus, 2002; Sauvage, 2001; Schoenbaum, 1993; Shapiro, 2004; Shapiro, 1994; Sitkoff, 2003; Snyder, 2009; United States Holocaust Memorial Museum, 2018a; United States Holocaust Memorial Museum, 2018c; Urofsky, 1982; Wood et al., 1994; Wyman, 1984; Wyman et al., 2002; Zuroff, 2000; Zuroff et al., 2003; Zygielbaum, 2009

123. HOMELAND?

Arens, 2008; Bauer, 1981; Baumel-Schwartz, 2005; Bell, 1996; Berman, 1990; Bierbrier, 1998; Bird, 1992; Blum, 1976; Brecher, 1990; Brenner, 1983; Cohen, 2003b; Cohen, 2000; Dawidowicz, 1982; Dinnerstein, 1994; Feingold, 1992; Fleming, 2001; Friedman, 1990; Gal, 1991; Gelb, 2003; Goldstein, 2006; Goodwin, 1994; Heilbut, 1983; Hertzberg, 1997; Hirschmann, 1962; Idelson, 2007; Jacobs, 2022; Jewish Women's Archive, 2003; Kahane, 2008; Katz, 1996; Kaufman, 1991; Kazin, 1996; Kellogg, 1979; Kennedy, 1999; Kessner, 1989; Kessner, 1994; Kessner, 1989; Khalidi, 2009; Klinger, 2007; Kolsky, 1990; Laqueur, 1972; Leff, 2000; Levy, 2002; Malmgreen, 1991; Malmgreen et al., 1997; Medoff, 1987; Medoff, 1998; Medoff, 2002; Medoff, 2003; Moore, 1987; Morris, 2001; Morris, 2004; Novick, 1999; O'Dwyer et al., 1987; Penkower, 1994; Radosh et al., 2009; Raider, 1989; Raider, 2008; Raider, 2009; Raider et al., 1997; Reinharz, et al., 2005; Rubinstein, 2001; Sanua, 2007; Schechtman, 1986; Schoenbaum, 1993; Shlaim, 2000; Shpiro, 1994; Troen, 2003; United States Holocaust Memorial Museum, 2018a; United States Holocaust Memorial Museum, 2018c; Urofsky, 1987; Urofsky, 2009; Wasserstein, 1987; Wyman, 1984; Wyman et al., 2002; Zuroff et al., 2003

124. TROUBLE AT HOME

Adams, 1994; Bayor, 1978; Blum, 1976; Brecher, 1990; Dawidowicz, 1982; Diner, 2004; Dinnerstein, 1994; Epstein, 1994; Erskine, 1973; Friedman, 1995b; Goldstein, 2006; Horowitz et al., 1959; Kessner, 1989; Lederhendler, 2001; Medoff, 2002; Milkman, 1997; Moore, 2004; Norwood, 2003; Quinley et al., 1979; Shpiro, 1994; Stember et al., 1966; Wyman, 1984; Wyman et al., 2002

JEWS AND BLACKS

125. JEWS AND BLACKS ALLIED

Benjamin, 1974; Biondi, 1997; Blue, 2002; Borstelmann, 2001; Brandt, 1996; Buhle et al., 1997; Capeci, 1977b; Carlson, 1943; City-wide Citizens' Committee on Harlem, 1942a; Dijkstra, 2003; Finan, 2002; Friedman, 1995b; Greenberg, 1995a; Greenberg, 1997; Greenberg, 1998; Greenberg, 2006; Hamilton, 1991; Henderson, 2000; Isaacs, 1967; Jackson, 2001; Jackson, 2002; Kessner, 1989; Laurentz, 1980; Medoff, 1987; Minear et al., 1999; Price, 1973; Rampersad, 1988; Rosenberg, 2006; Ruderman, 1977; Schwartz, 1993; Sitkoff, 2003; Wedlock, 1942; Weisbord et al., 1970; Wyman et al., 2002

126. FIGHTING PREJUDICE

Aptheker, 1946; Borstelmann, 2001; Brandt, 1996; Cherry et al., 2002; Dinnerstein, 1994; Dudziak, 2000; Finison, 1983; Foner, 1998; Friedman, 1995b; Gleason, 1981; Goldstein, 2006; Greenberg, 1995a; Greenberg, 1998; Greenberg, 1994; Idelson, 2007; Jackson, 2000; Jackson, 2001; Jackson et al., 2004; Jackson, 1990; Janken, 2003; King, 2004; Lewis, 2000; Markowitz et al., 1996; McNally, 2008; McNeil, 1983; Meyer, 2002; Meyer, 2003; Myrdal, 1944; Nicholson, 1998; Payne, 1995; Petkov et al., 1995; Polenberg, 1972; Ransby, 2003; Saint-Arnaud et al., 2009; Samson, 1996; Scott, 2004; Short, 1983; Sitkoff, 2003; Svonkin, 1997; Tushnet, 1994; Wiener, 1991

127. POLITICS

Anderson, 1982; Baker, 2002; Biondi, 1997; Brandt, 1996; Buhle et al., 1997; Capeci, 1977a; Capeci, 1977b; City-wide Citizens' Committee on Harlem, 1942a; Clark, 1965; Davis, 1969; Dinnerstein, 1994; Dudziak, 2000; Finkle, 1975; Foner, 1998; Friedman, 1995b; Goldstein, 2006; Greenberg, 1991; Greenberg, 1995a; Griffiths, 2001; Gunther, 1985; Hamilton, 1991; Haygood, 1993; Horne, 1993; Horne, 1994; Idelson, 2007; Jackson, 2001; Kellogg, 1979; Kessner, 1989; Margolick, 2000; Markowitz et al., 1996; Medoff, 2008; Meyer, 1989; Meyer, 2002; Meyer, 2003; Mjagkij, 2001; Naison, 1984; Perrett, 1985; Petkov et al., 1995; Polenberg, 1972; Price, 1973; Rampersad, 1988; Scates, 2006; Schaffer, 1966; Sitkoff, 2003; Smith, 2004; Walter et al., 1989; Waltzer, 1977; Weisbord et al., 1970; Wintz et al., 2004

128. HOUSING

Adams, 1994; Biondi, 2003; Blum, 1976; Boyer, 1983; Brandt, 1996; Capeci, 1977b; Cohalan, 1983; Cohen, 2003a; Friedman, 1995b; Gelfand, 1975; Greenberg, 1991; Greenberg, 1994; Hamilton, 1991; Henderson, 2000; Isaacs, 1967; James, 1947; Kessner, 1989; Lawson et al., 1986; National Urban League, 1945; Plunz, 1990; Pritchett, 2002; Schwartz, 1993; Simon, 1970; Stern et al., 1987; Winkleman, 1986; Zipp, 2010

129. JOBS

Bayor, 2018; Bentley, 1998; Berman, 1990; Biondi, 1997; Brandt, 1996; Chen, 2006; Chen, 2009; Foner, 1974; Friedman, 1995b; Garfinkel, 1959; Gelb, 2003; Goldstein, 2006; Greenberg, 1991; Greenberg, 1995a; Hartzell et al., 1949; Henderson, 2000; Kellogg, 1979; Kennedy, 1999; Kersten, 2007; Lynn, 1992; Milkman, 1997; Moscow, 1948; Murray, 1945; Schultz, 2008; Sitkoff, 2003; Smith, 1982; Waltzer, 1977; Yale Law Journal, 1947

130. GAME CHANGER

Bérubé, 1990; Biondi, 1997; Bird, 1992; Blum, 1976; Brandt, 1996; Burk, 2001; Dodson, 1954; Dorinson et al., 1998; Edmonds, 1973; Fetter, 2001; Fetter, 2007; Goodwin, 1994; Hiss, 2006; Horne, 1993; Lamb, 2004; Lanctot, 2004; Lester, 2001; Lowenfish, 2009; Mardo, 1998; Mead, 1985; Naison, 1985; Norwood et al., 1995; Peterson, 1992; Polner, 2007; Rodney, 1998; Rusinack, 1998; Schaffer, 1966; Silber et al., 2003; Sitkoff, 2003; Sullivan, 2002; Tygiel, 1984; Tygiel, 2003; Tygiel, 2008

ON THE TOWN

131. SEX AND THE CITY

Bérubé, 1990; Bianco, 2004; Bitter Queen, 2007;

Blum, 1976; Caldwell, 2005; Clement, 2006; Costello, 1985; D'Emilio, 1983; Friedman, 1996; Funigiello, 1978; Gavin, 2006; Gustav-Wrathall, 1998; Hegarty, 1998a; Hegarty, 1998b; Hegarty, 2008; Hurewitz, 1997; Jackson, 1984; Kaiser, 1997; Kornblum, 1978; Lingeman, 1970; Meany, 1994; Morris, 1987; Peretti, 2007; Polenberg, 1972; Robinson, 1943; Sherman, 1995; Shteir, 2004; Starr et al., 1998; Stone, 1982; Traub, 2004

132. NIGHTCLUBS

Aylesworth et al., 1987; Batterberry et al., 1999; Bell, 1961; "Better Late Than Never," 1943; Blumenthal, 2000; Caldwell, 2005; Charters et al., 1962; Cohen, 2002b; Duberman, 1988; Durante et al., 1931; Feinberg, 1945; Gabler, 1994; Gavin, 2006; Gordon, 1980; Kaytor, 1975; Kessner, 1989; Lingeman, 1970; Margolick, 2000; Morris, 1987; Peretti, 2007; Scott et al., 1999; Shaw, 1977; Shteir, 2004; Stone, 1982; Stowe, 1998

133. THE VOICE

Bergreen, 1997; Chevigny, 1991; Collier, 1989; Collis, 2001; Ehrenreich, 2007; Ehrenreich et al., 1992; Firestone, 1993; Friedwald, 1995; Hamill, 1998; Jones, 2006; Massoni, 2006; Petkov et al., 1995; Schrum, 1998; Smith, 2003; Traub, 2004; Turner, 2004

134. BOP

Belgrad, 1998; Burke, 2008; Charters et al., 1962; Chevigny, 1991; Collier, 1989; DeVeaux, 1988; Erenberg, 1998; Gentry, 1991b; Giddins, 1994; Giddins, 1998; Gillespie, 1979; Gitler, 1985; Gregory, 1998; Kelley, 1992; Kenney, 1999; Kisliuk, 2002; Lott, 1988; Lynes, 1973; MacAdams, 2001; Margolick, 2000; McWilliams, 1990; Peretti, 2007; Schneider, 2004; Schuller, 1989; Scott et al., 1999; Shapiro et al., 1955; Shaw, 1977; Shipton, 1999; Shteir, 2004; Stern et al., 1987; Stowe, 1994; Stump, 1998; Sylvester, 1956; Woideck, 1996

135. RUMBAMANIA

Baggelaar, 2006; Belgrad, 1998; Collier, 1986; Federal Writers' Project, 1938; Figueroa, 2007a; Figueroa, 2007b; Figueroa, 2010; Fletcher, 2009; Gitler, 1985; Glasser, 1990; Glasser, 1995; Gonzalez, 2004; Groppa, 2004; Loza, 1999; On2 Productions, 1999; Pérez, 1999; Perrett, 1985; Powell, 2007; Puente et al., 2000; Roberts, 1999; Salazar, 1998; Salazar, 2002; Schuller, 1989; Shipton, 1999; Sublette, 2004; Zolotow, 1940

136. ART OF THIS CENTURY

Alloway et al., 1981; Ashton, 1992; Belgrad, 1998; Comenas, 2008; Conrad, 1984; Crane, 1987; Dearborn, 2004; Ernst, 1984; Federal Writers' Project, 1938; Fermi, 1968; Friedman, 1995a; Gill, 2003; Glazer, 1993; Goodrich, 1983; Guggenheim, 1946; Guggenheim, 1960; Guilbaut, 1984; Harshav, 2004; Heilbut, 1983; Herrera, 2003; Hills et al., 1983; Hobbs, 1985; Horowitz, 1988; Jackman et al., 1983; Kazanjian et al., 1993; Kleeblatt et al., 2008; Landau et al., 1983; Lawton, 1998; Levin, 1996; Lorance, 2002; Lynes, 1973; Mark Borghi Fine Art Inc., 2007; Mayor, 1942; Morris, 1987; Naifeh et al., 1989; Noël, 1985; O'Connor, 1984; Perrett, 1985; Polcari, 1992; Rosenberg, 1959; Russell, 2002; Sandler, 1970; Sawin, 1995; Schjeldahl, 2006; Scott et al., 1999; Shefter, 1993a; Solomon, 2003; Solomon, 1987; Stern et al., 1987; Stevens et al., 2004; Tomkins, 1970; Varnedoe et al., 1998; Wald, 1987; Wallock et al., 1988; Zolberg, 1993

137. BOOK BOOM

"Cheap Books," 1939; DeGruson, 2002; Edelman, 2006; Frederick, 1948; French, 1964; Graham, 2006; Herder, 1971; Howell, 1971; Hyde Park Books, 2003; Kent et al., 1968; Lee, 2017; Loss, 2003; Mondlin et al., 2004; Neavill, 2007; Radway, 1991; Schick, 1958; Schiffrin, 2001; Schiffrin, 2007; Volz, 1992

138. BROADWAY

Buford, 2000; Devlin et al., 2000; Duberman, 2007; Easton, 1996; Filmer et al., 1999; Fordin, 1977; Gassner, 1948; Gill, 1990; Kirle, 2003; Kramer, 2002; Lawrence, 2001; Leiter, 1993; Lingeman, 1970; Mordden, 1992; Mordden, 1999; Peyser, 1998; Pollack, 1999; Porter, 2006; Probst, 1991; Secrest, 1994; Sheed, 2007; Stone, 1982; Vaill, 2006; Wertheim, 2004; Willett, 1978; Wright, 2003

139. TOWARD A FASHION-INDUSTRIAL COMPLEX

Baker, 2006b; Blum, 1976; Brooklyn Eagle, 1945; Brown, 1942; Buckland, 1996; Buckland, 2005; Chase et al., 1954; Conover, 1978; Dwight, 2002; Emery, 1998; Faderman, 1991; Fashion Group International, 2007; Fashion Institute of Technology, 2003; Goodwin, 1994; Gross, 1995; Hall, 1959; Hartmann, 1982; John Robert Powers Agency, 2008; Kazanjian et al., 1993; Kennedy, 1999; Kozloff et al., 2002; Laurentz, 1980; Lingeman, 1970; Mayor's Committee for World Fashion Center, 1944; Meyer, 1996; Milbank, 1985; Milbank, 1989; Morris, 1987; Perrett, 1985; Pochna, 1996; Rantisi, 2004; Rowlands, 2006; Salvador Dalí Museum, 2005; Schweitzer, 2008; Seidman, 1942; Semple, 1994; Snow et al., 1962; Strasser, 1999; Tomkins, 1994; Vintage Fashion Guild, 2010; Wingfield et al., 1997; Winkler, 2000

140. ON THE TOWN

Amberg, 1949; Aylesworth et al., 1987; Berman, 2006; Bérubé, 1990; Bianco, 2004; Blue, 2002; Brooklyn Eagle, 1945; Buckle et al., 1988; Buford, 2000; Bukatman, 2007; Burton, 1994; Cooney, 1984; Devlin et al., 2000; Duberman, 1988; Duberman, 2007; Easton, 1996; Epstein, 1994; Filmer et al., 1999; Fordin, 1977; Garafola, 1988; Garrett, 1961; Gassner, 1948; Gill, 1990; Graff, 1997; Heckscher et al., 1978; Heilbut, 1983; Horowitz, 1988; Howell, 1971; Jackman et al., 1983; Kazin, 1996; Kirle, 2003; Kramer, 2002; Lawrence, 2001; Leeming, 1994; Leiter, 1993; Leverich, 1995; Lingeman, 1970; Litoff et al., 1996; Long, 2001; Lynes, 1973; Manso, 1994; Mordden, 1992; Mordden, 1999; Morris, 1987; Perrett, 1985; Peyser, 1998; Pollack, 1999; Porter, 2006; Probst, 1991; Scott et al., 1999; Secrest, 1994; Sheed, 2007; Sherry, 2007; Smith, 2003; Smith, 1990b; Stone, 1982; Susman, 1984; Vaill, 2006; Wertheim, 2004; Willett, 1978; Wright, 2003

141. THE THEATER AT THE CENTER OF THE WORLD

PLANNING THE POSTWAR CITY

142. PRESENTING THE FUTURE: A PUBLIC PLAN

Ballon, 2007; Bayor, 2018; Bloom, 2008; Brinkley, 1996; Chase et al., 1942; Fishman, 2007; Fitch, 1993; Foner, 1998; Funigiello, 1978; Galloway et al., 1942; Gandy, 2002; Gelfand, 1985; Goodman et al., 1944; Gutfreund, 2007; Hanes et al., 1944; Hartzell et al., 1949; Heckscher et al., 1978; Hood, 2004; Jackson, 2007; Kessner, 1989; La Guardia, 1944; McGoldrick, 1944; McGowan, 1944; Morris, 1987; Moses, 1942; Moses, 1944; Moses, 1970; Namorato, 1988; "New York Opens Its Post-War Exhibit," 1944; New York State Department of Commerce et al., 1943; New York State Postwar Public Works Planning Commission, 1944; Perrett, 1985; Rankin,

1939; Rodgers, 1943; Schwartz, 1993; Schwartz, 2007; Smith, 2006; Smith, 1982; Stein, 1943; Stern et al., 1995; Stewart, 1942; Stewart, 1943a; Stewart, 1943b; Tugwell, 1940

143. "TWO MILLION PLANS!"

144. HOUSING: THE SPECTER OF SUBURBANIZATION, THE BATTLE AGAINST BLIGHT

Abu-Lughod, 1994; Ballon, 2007; Batterberry et al., 1999; Baxandall et al., 2000; Bloom, 2008; Boyer, 1983; Capeci, 1977b; Chase et al., 1942; City Wide Citizens' Committee on Harlem, 1942; Cooperative Village, 2015; Eisenstadt, 2010; Finan, 2002; Fishman, 2007; Fitch, 1993; Fogelson, 2001; Funigiello, 1978; Gandy, 2002; Gelfand, 1975; Gelfand, 1985; Halberstam, 1993; Hanes et al., 1944; Hartzell et al., 1949; "Housing: Up from the Potato Fields," 1950; Hoyt, 1943; Jackson, 1985; Kazin, 1996; Kelly, 1993; Lasner, 2007; Levittown Historical Society, 2001; Losey et al., 2010; McGoldrick, 1944; McGoldrick, 1945; Mock et al., 1945; Morris, 1987; Perrett, 1985; Plunz, 1990; Polenberg, 1972; Pritchett, 2002; Rankin, 1939; Rodgers, 1943; Schwartz, 1993; Schwartz, 2007; Scott, 1969; Smith, 2006; Sparkes, 1944; Stern et al., 1987; Stern et al., 1995; Stewart, 1943a; Tugwell, 1940; United States Department of Agriculture, 2008; Wilder, 2000; Winkler, 2000; Wolfe, 1981; Zipp, 2010

145. RUBBER AND RAILS

Ballon et al., 2007; Belle et al., 2000; Bloom, 2008; Buttenwieser, 1987; Cohen, 2001; Cohen, 1988; Cohen, 1991; Doig, 1966; Doig, 2001; Fishman, 2007; Fitch, 1993; Fogelson, 2001; Fotsch, 2007; Gandy, 2002; Goddard, 1996; Goodman et al., 1944; Gurin, 1977a; Gurin, 1977b; Gutfreund, 2004; Gutfreund, 2007; Hodges, 2007; Hood, 2004; Hudson Waterfront Museum et al., 1992; Itzkoff, 1985; Kessner, 1989; Kramer, 2001; Miller, 2000; Rankin, 1939; Rodgers, 1943; Rose, 1979; Schlichting, 2001; Schrag, 2000; Schwartz, 1993; Stelter et al., 1995; Stern et al., 1995; U.S. Department of Transportation et al., 2009; Weiner, 2008; Yago, 1984; Zipp, 2010

146. SEA

Bone et al., 1997; California State Reconstruction and Reemployment Commission, 1945; Davis, 2003; Doig, 2001; Fitch, 1993; Hartzell et al., 1949; Horne, 2005; Kessner, 1989; Kimeldorf, 1988; Levinson, 2006; Miller, 2000; Miller, 2003; New York City WPA Writers' Project, 1941; Port of New York Authority, 1958; Rankin, 1939; Regional Plan Association, 1944; Scullin, 1968; Stern et al., 1995; Todd Shipyards Corporation, 1942; Willoughby, 1961

147. SKY

Aylesworth et al., 1987; Bender et al., 1982; Benson, 2001; Bone et al., 1997; Corn, 2002; Doig, 2001; Douglas, 1996; Fox, 2006; Gelb, 2003; Kaplan, 1994; Kessner, 1989; Kluger, 1986; Miller, 2000; Morris, 1987; Rankin, 1939; Regional Plan Association, 1944; Rosenberg, 1982; Scullin, 1968; Stern et al., 1995; Stoff, 1989

148. INFRASTRUCTURE

Bard, 1939; Bloom, 2008; Blum, 1976; Bone, 2006; Bulletin of the American Warehousemen's Association, 1916; Castaneda, 1993; Corey, 1994; Dewey, 1995; Dewey, 2000; Dolkart et al., 2009; Galloway et al., 1942; Gandy, 2002; Gould, 1946; Granick, 1991; Greenwich Village Society for Historic Preservation, 2002; Kurlansky, 2006; Landmarks Preservation Commission, 2003; Lieber, 1968; Lurkis, 1982; Miller, 2000; Miller, 2003; New York City Department of Parks & Recreation, 2014; Rankin, 1939; Regional Plan Association, 1944; Rodgers, 1943; Smith, 1982; Stern et al., 1995; Tangires, 2008; "Two Pipelines for Sale?," 1945; Waldman, 1999; Willcox et al., 1920

149. WASHINGTON OR WALL STREET?

Andrews, 2003; Bendix, 1945; Casey, 2001; Chernow, 1990; "Closing Address by Secretary of the Treasury Henry Morgenthau, July 22, 1944," 1946; de Vries et al., 1969; Dormael, 1978; Eakins, 1969; Frieden, 1987; Geisst, 2001; Helleiner, 1994; Higgs, 1992; Higgs, 2004; Horsefield, 1969; Hudson, 2003; Ikenberry, 1993; Johnson, 1968; Mason et al., 1973; Morris, 1987; Perrett, 1985; Regional Plan Association, 1944; Reich et al., 1983; Shoup, 1977; Skidelsky, 1986; Sobel, 1965; Sobel, 1975; Zweig, 1995

150. MANUFACTURING: TIDE GOING OUT OR TIDE COMING IN?

Alonso, 2007; Aylesworth et al., 1987; Ballon, 2007; Bannister, 2001; Bernstein, 1984; Bilby, 1986; Black, 2001; Bloom, 2008; Blue, 2002; Blum, 1976; Boddy, 1990; Chandler et al., 2000; Garrett, 1961; Hall, 1959; Hanes et al., 1944; Heppenheimer, 1996; Hooks, 1991; Jackson, 2007; Kessner, 1989; Kisseloff, 1995; McCaughey, 2003; Morris, 1987; Perrett, 1985; Rankin, 1939; Regional Plan Association, 1944; Rigden, 2000; Samuel, 2001; Schwartz, 1993; Scott et al., 1999; Shurkin, 2006; Stein, 1943; Sterling et al., 2002; Stern et al., 1995; Stewart, 1943a; Udelson, 1982; Von Schilling, 2003

151. HEADQUARTERS

Avery Architectural & Fine Arts Library et al., 2009; Blum, 1976; Chase et al., 1942; Fogelson, 2001; Hanes et al., 1944; Hellman, 1976; Ingham, 1983; Jessie Smith Noyes Foundation, 2010; Kahn, 1951; Kluger, 1986; Landmarks Preservation Commission, 2010; Nash et al., 2010; New York Herald Tribune, 1943; Rankin, 1939; Regional Plan Association, 1944; Rose-Redwood, 2008; Ruttenbaum, 1986; Schwartz, 1993; Shachtman, 1991; Stein, 1943; Stern et al., 2006; Stern, et al., 1995; Trager, 1990; Wallace, 2010; Zeckendorf et al., 1987

PLANNING THE POSTWAR NATION

152. DUELING PLANNERS

Brinkley, 1996; Greider, 1989; Jeffries, 1990; Klausen, 2002; Roosevelt, 1944

153. PAGING DR. NEW DEAL

Amenta et al., 1988; Blum, 1976; Borstelmann, 2001; Bowles, 1946; Boyer, 1983; Brinkley, 1989; Brinkley, 2000; Chase et al., 1942; Foner, 1998; Fraser, 1991; Gelfand, 1975; Geyer, 2002; Horowitz, 1969; Janken, 2003; Jeffries, 1990; Katznelson et al., 1991; Kennedy, 1999; Kersten, 2006; Klausen, 2002; Milkman, 1997; National Resources Planning Board et al., 1942; Perrett, 1985; Pijl, 1984; Polenberg, 1972; Reagan, 1999; Skidelsky, 1986; Williams, 1996

154. DR. NEW DEAL: CALL ONLY WHEN NEEDED

Baughman, 1987; Bernstein, 1987; Blum, 1976; Boyer, 1983; Brick, 1986; Burch, 1980; Clark, 1944; Cohen, 2003a; Collins, 1978; Collins, 1981; Committee for Economic Development et al., 1946; Eakins, 1969; Foner, 1998; Fones-Wolf, 1994; Foster et al., 1989; Fraser, 1991; Greider, 1989; Griffith, 1983; Hendrickson et al., 2004; Higgs, 2009; Horten, 2002; Kennedy, 1999; Klausen, 2002; Leff, 1991; Lichtenstein, 1982; Oakes, 1944; Perrett, 1985; Pijl, 1984; Raucher, 1985; Reagan, 1999; Stein, 1969; Stole, 2001; Waddell, 2001; Young, 2005a

155. DR. NEW DEAL: WANTED, DEAD OR ALIVE, PREFERABLY DEAD

Anderson, 2001; Baughman, 1987; Bjerre-Poulsen, 2002; Blum, 1976; Burns, 2009; Chase et al., 1942; Commerce and Industry Association of New York, 1944; Doherty, 2007; Drury, 1997; Ebenstein, 2001; Ebenstein, 2007; Eow, 2007; Fermi, 1968; Fleming, 2001; Foner, 1998; Fones-Wolf, 1994; Fraser, 1991; Freeman, 1978; Friedman et al., 1946; Gerber, 1976; Gill, 1990; Gleason, 1995a; Hayek, 1944; Hülsmann, 2007; Kennedy, 1999; Klausen, 2002; Lichtenstein, 1982; Marchand, 1998; Mayhew, 2007; Moser, 2005; Nash, 2006; Perrett, 1985; Phillips-Fein, 2009; Rockwell, 2007; Rothbard, 1988; Schleier, 2002; Schleier, 2009; Scott, et al., 1999; Sheppard, 2006; Stole, 2001; Tuck, 1995; Zuckert et al., 2006

156./157. RIGHTIST THRUST...LIBERAL RIPOSTE

Abt et al., 1993; Adams, 1994; Altschuler et al., 2009; Anderson, 2001; Black, 1996; Blum, 1976; Borstelmann, 2001; Brinkley, 2000; Buhite et al., 1992; Cantril et al., 1943; Chase et al., 1942; Congress of Industrial Organizations Political Action Committee (CIO-PAC), 1944; Donaldson, 1999; Fleming, 2001; Foner, 1998; Foner, 1950; Fox, 1985; Fox, 1993; Fraser, 1991; Freeman, 1978; Geyer, 2002; Goodwin, 1994; Hine, 1977; Huthmacher, 1968; Isserman, 1993; Janken, 2003; Jeffries, 1990; Katznelson et al., 1991; Kennedy, 1999; Klausen, 2002; Kleinman, 2000; Laurentz, 1980; Levenstein, 1981; Lichtenstein, 1982; Madison, 1992; Mettler, 2005; Meyer, 1989; Milkman, 1997; Moscow, 1948; O'Donnell, 2002; Perrett, 1985; Polenberg, 1972; Reagan, 1999; Severo et al., 1989; Shefter, 1993b; Sirgiovanni, 1990; Smith, 1982; State of New Jersey Commission on Post-War Economic Welfare, 1944; Sunstein, 2004; Waddell, 2001; Waltzer, 1977; Willett, 1985; Winkler, 2000; Wolf et al., 2001

158. THE LAST SUBWAY SERIES

Black, 1996; Blum, 1976; Davis, 1967; Duberman, 1988; Fleming, 2001; Flynn, 1947; Foner, 1998; Fraser, 1991; Galloway et al., 1942; Garrett, 1961; Goodwin, 1994; Hertzberg, 1997; Hutchinson, 1970; Huthmacher, 1968; Levenstein, 1981; Lichtenstein, 1982; Madison, 1992; Milkman, 1997; Pohl, 1989; Robertson, 1994; Rosswurm, 2001; Sirgiovanni, 1990; Smith, 1982; Tuck, 1995; Waltzer, 1977; Washburn, 1986; White et al., 1995; Winkler, 2000

159. ENTER: "RED MENACE"

Block, 1983; Blum, 1976; Duberman, 1988; Fraser, 1991; Fried, 1980; Kavieff, 2005; Levenstein, 1981; Lichtenstein, 1982; Link, 2006; Moscow, 1948; Parmet, 2005; Rosswurm, 2001; Sirgiovanni, 1990; "That Lepke," 1944; Tuck, 1995; Waltzer, 1977; Winkler, 2000

160. CUE: COLD WAR

Baughman, 1987; Blejwas, 1998; Bukowczyk, 1996; Bukowczyk, 2008; Drąg-Korga, 2007; Glendon, 2001; Hammersmith, 1977; Hoopes, 1973; Immerman, 1999; Irons, 1973; Isaacson et al., 1986; Kennedy, 1999; Kovel, 1997; Lamont, 1994; Lukas, 1978; Lukas, 1982; Medoff, 1987; Misse, 1980; Pijl, 1984; Pula, 1995; Rosenwaike, 1972; Shoup, 1977; Steel, 1980; Szymczak, 1984; Tuck, 1995; Wytrwal, 1977

161. DR. NEW DEAL: BACK IN THE SADDLE?

Anderson, 2001; Asbell, 1961; Collins, 1981; Ferrell, 1998; Fleming, 2001; Fones-Wolf, 1994; Fraser, 1991; Goodwin, 1994; Huthmacher, 1968; Janken, 2003; Katznelson et al., 1991; Kleinman, 2000; Lichtenstein, 1982; Link, 2006; Luconi, 2001a; Moody, 1988; Moscow, 1948; Perrett, 1985; Pierson, 1946; Polenberg, 1972; Smith, 1982; Waddell, 2001; Wallace, 1945; Waltzer, 1977; Williams et al., 2001a; Williams, 1996; Zeitz, 2007

PLANNING THE POSTWAR WORLD

162. NEW WORLD A-COMIN'

American Sociological Association, 1943; Book Publishers Bureau, 1944; Bowles, 1946; Chase et al., 1942; Chester, 1995; Clark et al., 1943; Fraser, 1991; Galloway et al., 1942; Howell, 1971; Inter-Council Committee on Post-War Planning, 1944; Johnsen, 1942; Kersten, 2006; Klausen, 2002; Litoff et al., 2000; Schulzinger, 1984; Shapiro, 1994; Spitz et al., 2006; Sturmthal, 1943; University of Southampton Libraries, 2010

163. AN EMPIRE OF FREE TRADE

Barnet et al., 1974; Baughman, 1987; Benson, 2000; Block, 1977; Blum, 1976; Borgwardt, 2005; Boyne, 2002; Colby et al., 1995; Collomp, 2005; Demirmen, 2003a; Demirmen, 2003b; Dormael, 1978; Herzstein, 1994; Horowitz, 1969; Ikenberry, 1993; Immerman, 1999; Isaacson et al., 1986; Khalidi, 2009; Kolko et al., 1972; Kovel, 1997; Lairson, 1998; Lamont, 1994; Leffler, 1992; Little, 1990; Little, 2002; Palan, 1998; Paul, 2002; Perrett, 1985; Pijl, 1984; Randall, 2005; Rickard, 1999; Rosenberg, 1982; Roxborough, 1998; Shoup, 1977; Simpson, 1995; Skidelsky, 1986; Standard Oil Company, 1944; Swanberg, 1972; Tuck, 1995; Venn, 2000; Waddell, 2001; Yergin, 1991

164. RACISM AND IMPERIALISM

Anderson, 2003; Black, 1996; Blum, 1976; Borgwardt, 2005; Borstelmann, 2001; Dower, 1986; Duberman, 1988; Dudziak, 2000; Fleming, 2001; Foner, 1998; Glendon, 2001; Greenberg, 1994; Horne, 1986; Janken, 2003; Kennedy, 1999; Lee et al., 2002; Lewis, 2000; Normand et al., 2008; Plummer, 1996; Rampersad, 1988; Rosenberg, 2006; Von Eschen, 1997; Von Eschen, 2000

165. INDIA

Anderson, 2003; Blum, 1976; Brandt, 1996; Brinkley, 2010; Chen, 2003; Conn, 1996; Daniels, 1971; Daniels, 1988; Dower, 1986; Dudziak, 2000; Gallicchio, 2000; Herzstein, 1994; Hing, 1993; Isaacs, 1980; Jacobson, 1998; Kwong, 1979; Lai, 1991; Leong, 2005; Li, 2006; Ma, 1998; Ma, 2000; Pakula, 2009; Perrett, 1985; Price, 1973; Rampersad, 1988; Reimers, 1998; Robeson et al., 1978; Swanberg, 1972; Ueda, 1996; Wright, 2001; Yu, 1990; Zhao, 2002

166. CHINA

Anderson, 1997; Borgwardt, 2005; Chary, 1995; Duberman, 1988; Fenton, 1988; Gould, 2006; Hess, 1969; Hess, 1971; Hing, 1993; Horne, 2008; Janken, 1998; Janken, 2003; Kapur, 1992; Khagram, 2001; Kim, 1999; Kux, 1992; Ng, 1998; Pelinka et al., 2003; Perrett, 1985; Plummer, 1996; Prashad, 2000; Rampersad, 1988; Rosenberg, 2006; Sathasivam, 2005; Shaplen, 1951; Singh, 2009; Sinha, 2006; Slate, 2012; Von Eschen, 1997; Weigold, 2008

167. PUERTO RICO

Ayala, 1999; Ayala et al., 2007; Burgos et al., 1997; Cancel Miranda, 1998; Centro de Estudios Puertorriqueños, 2003; Centro de Estudios Puertorriqueños, 2005a; Centro de Estudios Puertorriqueños, 2005b; Centro de Estudios Puertorriqueños, 2005c; Centro de Estudios Puertorriqueños, 2021; Centro de Estudios Puertorriqueños et al., 2007; Colby et al., 1995; Delgado,

2005; Dietz, 1986; Gatell, 1958; Horne, 1986; Johnson, 1997; Johnson, 1998; Kanellos, 1990; Kanellos et al., 2002; Kessner, 1989; Kovel, 1997; Lefebvre, 2007; Maldonado, 2006; Marcantonio, 2002; Matos-Rodriguez et al., 2001; Meyer, 1984; Meyer, 1989; Namorato, 1988; Negrón-Muntaner et al., 1997; Rivas, 2002; Robeson et al., 1978; Rodriguez-Fraticelli, 1992; Rodriguez-Morazzani, 1995; Rodríguez Beruff, 2009; Ruiz et al., 2006; Thomas, 2002; Thomas, 2010; Villaronga, 2004; Zwickel, 1998

168. UNITING THE NATIONS

Anderson, 2003; Anderson, 2005; Blum, 1976; Borgwardt, 2005; D'Itri, 1999; Dennis, 2002; Dennis, 2005; Eisenberg, 1996; Galloway et al., 1942; Glendon, 2001; Goodwin, 1994; Gowan, 2003; Grose, 1996a; Guilbaut, 1984; Hilderbrand, 1990; Hoopes, 1973; Howell, 1971; Ignatieff et al., 2003; Immerman, 1999; Johnstone, 2006; Johnstone, 2009; Johnstone, 2010; Josephson, 1974; Killough, 1991; Kolko et al., 1972; Korey, 2001; Kovel, 1997; Kuehl et al., 1997; Lauren, 2003; League of Free Nations Association, 1918; League to Enforce Peace, 1918; Litoff et al., 2000; Lynn, 1992; Mitoma, 2008; Morsink, 1999; Mosley, 1978; Normand et al., 2008; Nurser, 2003; O'Sullivan, 2008; Parmar, 1999a; Parmar, 2001; Perrett, 1985; Pijl, 1984; Ryan, 2002; Schlesinger, 2003; Schulzinger, 1984; Shotwell, 1961; Shoup, 1977; Singer, 1975; Skard, 2008; Traer, 1991; United Nations Association of the United States of America, 2009; Wala, 1994; Warren, 1997; Welles, 1997; White et al., 1995; Woodrow Wilson Foundation, 1922

EPILOGS

Asbell, 1961; Berman, 2006; Bird, 1992; Boyer, 1985; Caro, 1974; Davis, 2000; Dower, 1999; Kessner, 1989; Klara, 2010; Koegel, 1971; Le Corbusier, 1947; Leffler, 1992; Luard, 1982; Milhaud, 1946; Mires, 2013; Morris, 1960; Newhouse, 1989; Rockefeller, 2002; Sert, 1947; Stern et al., 1987; Stern et al., 1995; Wertheim, 2020; Zeckendorf et al., 1987; Zipp, 2010

Bibliography

Aaron, Daniel. (1961) *Writers on the Left: Episodes in American Literary Communism.* New York.

Abadinsky, Howard. (1981) *Organized Crime.* Boston, MA.

Abbott, Zane Allen. (1994) "Radio Preaching in the World War Two Era: The Cases of Harry Emerson Fosdick and Charles Coughlin on War and Peace." PhD diss., Southern Baptist Theological Seminary.

Abramovitch, Ilana. (1996) "America's Making Exposition and Festival (New York, 1921): Immigrant Gifts on the Altar of America." PhD diss., New York University.

Abramson, Rudy. (1992) *Spanning the Century: The Life of W. Averell Harriman, 1891–1986.* New York.

Abt, John J., and Michael Myerson. (1993) *Advocate and Activist: Memoirs of an American Communist Lawyer.* Urbana, IL.

Abu-Lughod, Janet L. (1994) *From Urban Village to East Village: The Battle for New York's Lower East Side.* Cambridge, MA.

Adamic, Louis. (1934) "Thirty Million New Americans." *Harper's Magazine,* November.

———. (1936) "Aliens and Alien-Baiters." *Harper's Magazine,* November.

———. (1976) *My America, 1928–1938.* New York.

Adams, David. (1986) *The American Peace Movements: History, Root Causes, and Future.* New Haven, CT.

Adams, Michael C. C. (1994) *The Best War Ever: America and World War II.* Baltimore, MD.

Adams, Stephen B., and Orville R. Butler. (1999) *Manufacturing the Future: A History of Western Electric.* New York.

Addison, Barbara E. (2004) "Pragmatic Pacifist: Devere Allen and the Interwar Peace Movement, 1918–1940." *Peace & Change* 29: 81–105.

Adler, Les K., and Thomas G. Paterson. (1970) "Red Fascism: The Merger of Nazi Germany and Soviet Russia in the American Image of Totalitarianism, 1930's–1950's." *American Historical Review* 75: 1046–1064.

Agusta, Phillip P., Walter J. Hutter, et al. (1976) *Our Community, It's [sic] History and People: Ridgewood, Glendale, Maspeth, Middle Village, Liberty Park.* Queens, NY.

Air Force Historical Research Agency. (2007) "Numbered Air Forces." *Research Division: Organizational History Branch,* November 21.

Akam, Everett Helmut. (2002) *Transnational America: Cultural Pluralist Thought in the Twentieth Century.* Lanham, MD.

Allen, Garland E. (1986) "The Eugenics Record Office at Cold Spring Harbor, 1910–1940: An Essay in Institutional History." *Osiris* 2: 225–264.

Alloway, Lawrence, Adolph Gottlieb, et al. (1981) *Adolph Gottlieb: A Retrospective.* New York.

Almeida, Linda Dowling. (2001) *Irish Immigrants in New York City, 1945–1995.* Bloomington, IN.

Alonso, Harriet Hyman. (2007) *Robert E. Sherwood: The Playwright in Peace and War.* Amherst, MA.

Alpern, Sara. (1987) *Freda Kirchwey: A Woman of the Nation.* Cambridge, MA.

Alpers, Benjamin Leontief. (2003) *Dictators, Democracy, and American Public Culture: Envisioning the Totalitarian Enemy, 1920s–1950s.* Chapel Hill, NC.

Altschuler, Glenn C., and Stuart M. Blumin. (2009) *The G.I. Bill: A New Deal for Veterans.* New York.

Alvarez, Luis W. (1980) *Alfred Lee Loomis, 1887–1975: A Biographical Memoir.* Washington, DC.

Amberg, George. (1949) *Ballet in America: The Emergence of an American Art.* New York.

Amenta, Edwin, and Theda Skocpol. (1988) "Redefining the New Deal: World War II and the Development of Social

Provision in the U.S." In *The Politics of Social Policy in the United States*, edited by Margaret Weir and Ann Shola Orloff. Princeton, NJ.

American Philosophical Society. (1983) "Photocopies of F.B.I. Files on Boas, 1939–1950." In *Boas Family Papers: MSS.B.B6If*, edited by Stephen Catlett. Philadelphia, PA.

American Sociological Association. (1943) "A Selected Bibliography on Postwar Goals and Reconstruction." *Journal of Educational Sociology* 17: 183–192.

Ames Historical Society. (2008) *Rationing on the US Homefront*. Ames, IA.

Andelman, Bob. (2015) *Will Eisner: A Spirited Life*. Raleigh, NC.

Anderson, Carol. (2003) *Eyes Off the Prize: The United Nations and the African American Struggle for Human Rights, 1944–1955*. New York.

Anderson, Jervis. (1982) *Harlem: The Great Black Way, 1900–1950*. New York.

———. (1997) *Bayard Rustin: Troubles I've Seen: A Biography*. New York.

Anderson, Karen. (1981) *Wartime Women: Sex Roles, Family Relations, and the Status of Women During World War II*. Westport, CT.

Anderson, Lisa. (2005) "James T. Shotwell: A Life Devoted to Organizing Peace." In *Living Legacies at Columbia*, edited by William Theodore de Bary, Jerry Kisslinger, and Tom Mathewson. New York.

Anderson, Michael. (2001) "Politics, Patriotism, and the State: The Fight over the Soldier Vote, 1942–1944." In *Politics and Progress: American Society and the State since 1865*, edited by Andrew Edmund Kersten and Kriste Lindenmeyer. Westport, CT.

Andrae, Thomas. (1987) "From Menace to Messiah: The History and Historicity of Superman." In *American Media and Mass Culture: Left Perspectives*, edited by Donald Lazere. Berkeley, CA.

———. (2007) *Masters of Comic Art*. New Castle, PA.

Andrews, Adolphus. (1941) "Status of Naval Defense of the North Atlantic Naval Coastal Frontier." In *War Diary: North Atlantic Naval Coastal Frontier, December 1941*, edited by Headquarters of the Eastern Sea Frontier. New York.

Andrews, David M. (2003) "The Myth of Bretton Woods." Paper presented at 8th EUSA Biennial International Conference. Nashville, TN.

Anthony, David Henry. (2006) *Max Yergan: Race Man, Internationalist, Cold Warrior*. New York.

Anthony, Susan Brownell. (1943) *Out of the Kitchen, into the War: Woman's Winning Role in the Nation's Drama*. New York.

"Anti-War Pledge Given by Fosdick." (1934) *New York Times*, May 8.

Aptheker, Herbert. (1946) *The Negro People in America*. New York.

Ardman, Harvey. (1985) *Normandie: Her Life and Times*. New York.

Arend, Geoffrey. (1979) *Air World's Great Airports: La Guardia, 1939–1979*. New York.

Arens, Moshe. (2008) "The Development of the Narrative of the Warsaw Ghetto Uprising." *Israel Affairs* 14: 6–28.

Aris, Ben, and Duncan Campbell. (2004) "How Bush's Grandfather Helped Hitler's Rise to Power." *The Guardian*, September 25.

Arnesen, Eric. (2006) *Encyclopedia of U.S. Labor and Working-Class History*. New York.

Arnold, Wade. (1969) *A Brief Narrative History of the Broadway United Church of Christ*. New York.

Asbell, Bernard. (1961) *When F.D.R. Died*. New York.

Ashton, Dore. (1992) *The New York School: A Cultural Reckoning*. Berkeley, CA.

"AT&T Bell Laboratories, Inc. History." (1996) In *International Directory of Company Histories: Vol. 13*, edited by Tina Grant. Detroit, MI.

Auerbach, Jerold S. (1976) *Unequal Justice: Lawyers and Social Change in Modern America*. New York.

Avery Architectural & Fine Arts Library and Department of Drawings & Archives. (2009) "Finding Aid." In *Percy and Harold D. Uris Papers, 1901–2003*, edited by Columbia University. New York.

Ayala, César J. (1999) *American Sugar Kingdom: The Plantation Economy of the Spanish Caribbean, 1898–1934*. Chapel Hill, NC.

Ayala, César J., and Rafael Bernabe. (2007) *Puerto Rico in the American Century: A History since 1898*. Chapel Hill, NC.

Aylesworth, Thomas, and Virginia Aylesworth. (1987) *New York: The Glamour Years (1919–1945)*. New York.

Badash, Lawrence, Elizabeth Hodes, et al. (1986) "Nuclear Fission: Reaction to the Discovery in 1939." *Proceedings of the American Philosophical Society* 130: 196–231.

Baggelaar, Kristin. (2006) *The Copacabana*. Charleston, SC.

Bailey, Beth, and David Farber. (1992) *The First Strange Place: The Alchemy of Race and Sex in World War II Hawaii*. New York.

Bailey, Percival. (1982) *The Case of the National Lawyers Guild, 1939–1958*. Philadelphia, PA.

Bak, Richard. (1998) *Joe Louis: The Great Black Hope*. Dallas, TX.

Baker, Kevin. (2006a) "Jitterbug Days." *New York Times*, January 22.

Baker, Lee D. (2004) "Franz Boas out of the Ivory Tower." *Anthropological Theory* 4: 29–51.

Baker, Nancy Kovaleff. (2002) "Abel Meeropol (A.K.A. Lewis Allan): Political Commentator and Social Conscience." *American Music* 20: 25–79.

Baker, Therese Duzinkiewicz. (2006b) "Valentina." In *Encyclopedia of Fashion*, edited by Thomson Gale. Stamford, CT.

Balanoff, Elizabeth. (1985) "Norman Thomas: Socialism and the Social Gospel." *The Christian Century*, January 30.

Ballantine, Ian, and Betty Ballantine. (1989) "From the Two-Bit Beginning." *New York Times*, April 30.

Ballon, Hilary. (2007) "Robert Moses and Urban Renewal: The Title I Program." In *Robert Moses and the Modern City: The Transformation of New York*, edited by Hilary Ballon and Kenneth T. Jackson. New York.

Ballon, Hilary, and Kenneth T. Jackson. (2007) *Robert Moses and the Modern City: The Transformation of New York*. New York.

Ballon, Hilary, and Norman McGrath. (2002) *New York's Pennsylvania Stations*. New York.

Banner, Lois W. (2003) *Intertwined Lives: Margaret Mead, Ruth Benedict, and Their Circle*. New York.

Bannister, Jennifer Burton. (2001) "From Laboratory to Living Room: The Development of Television in the United States, 1920–1960." PhD diss., Carnegie Mellon University.

Barber, David. (1999) "Archibald Macleish's Life and Career." In *American National Biography*, edited by John Arthur Garraty and Mark C. Carnes. New York.

Bard, Erwin Wilkie. (1939) *The Port of New York Authority*. New York.

Barkan, Elazar. (1988) "Mobilizing Scientists against Nazi Racism." In *Bones, Bodies, Behavior: Essays on Biological Anthropology*, edited by George W. Stocking Jr. Madison, WI.

Barkan, Elazar. (1992) *The Retreat of Scientific Racism: Changing Concepts of Race in Britain and the United States between the World Wars*. Cambridge, UK.

Barlow, Jeffrey G. (1994) *The Views of Stimson and Knox on Atlantic Strategy and Planning*. Boulder, CO.

Barnes, Joseph. (1943) "Fighting with Information: OWI Overseas." *The Public Opinion Quarterly* 7: 34–45.

Barnes, Michael. (2007) "American Attitudes toward the Japanese, Part 2: Pearl Harbor in Music." *The Authentic History Center: Primary Sources from American Popular Culture*, February 2.

Barnet, Richard J., and Ronald E. Müller. (1974) *Global Reach: The Power of the Multinational Corporations*. New York.

Barnouw, Erik. (1945) *Radio Drama in Action: Twenty-Five Plays of a Changing World*. New York.

———. (1966) *A Tower in Babel: A History of Broadcasting in the United States, to 1933*. Vol. 1. New York.

———. (1968) *The Golden Web: A History of Broadcasting in the United States, 1933 to 1953*. Vol. 2. New York.

———. (1978) *The Sponsor: Notes on a Modern Potentate*. New York.

Baron, Robert, Nicholas R. Spitzer, et al. (1992) *Public Folklore*. Washington, DC.

Barrett, William. (1982) *The Truants: Adventures among the Intellectuals*. Garden City, NY.

Batterberry, Michael, and Ariane Ruskin Batterberry. (1999) *On the Town in New York: The Landmark History of Eating, Drinking, and Entertainments from the American Revolution to the Food Revolution*. New York.

Bauer, Yehuda. (1981) *American Jewry and the Holocaust: The American Jewish Joint Distribution Committee, 1939–1945*. Detroit, MI.

Baughman, James L. (1987) *Henry R. Luce and the Rise of the American News Media*. Boston, MA.

Baumel-Schwartz, Judith Tydor. (2005) *The "Bergson Boys" and the Origins of Contemporary Zionist Militancy*. Syracuse, NY.

Baxandall, Rosalyn F. (1988) *Words on Fire: The Life and Writing of Elizabeth Gurley Flynn*. Piscataway, NJ.

Baxandall, Rosalyn Fraad, and Elizabeth Ewen. (2000) *Picture Windows: How the Suburbs Happened*. New York.

Baynes, Norman Hepburn. (1981) *The Speeches of Adolf Hitler, April 1922–August 1939: An English Translation of Representative Passages*. New York.

Bayor, Ronald H. (1978) *Neighbors in Conflict: The Irish, Germans, Jews, and Italians of New York City, 1929–1941*. Baltimore, MD.

———. (2018) *Fiorello La Guardia: Ethnicity, Reform, and Urban Development*. Hoboken, NJ.

Becker, William H., and William M. McClenahan. (2003) *The Market, the State, and the Export-Import Bank of the United States, 1934–2000*. New York.

Bedacht, Max. (2001) "Max Bedacht on Whittaker Chambers." In *The Alger Hiss Story*, edited by Jeff Kisseloff. New York.

Beebe, John L. (2000) "'This Is Sheepshead Bay.'" In *American Merchant Marine at War*, edited by T. Horodysky. Eugene, OR.

Behren, David. (1998) "Hitler's LI Legion." *Newsday*, May 3.

Bélanger, Damien-Claude. (2004) "James Thomson Shotwell (1874–1965)." In *Biographies of Prominent Quebec and Canadian Historical Figures*, edited by Damien-Claude Bélanger. Westmount, Quebec.

Belgrad, Daniel. (1998) *The Culture of Spontaneity: Improvisation and the Arts in Postwar America*. Chicago, IL.

Bell, Daniel. (1961) *The End of Ideology*. New York.

Bell, J. Bowyer. (1996) *Terror out of Zion: The Fight for Israeli Independence*. New Brunswick, NJ.

"Bell Labs' First 50 Years: Prelude to Tomorrow." (1975) In *Bell Laboratories Record, Vol. 53, January 1975*, edited by Bell Laboratories. Murray Hill, NJ.

Bellafaire, Judith. (1993) *The Army Nurse Corps: A Commemoration of World War II Service*. Washington, DC.

Belle, John, and Maxinne Rhea Leighton. (2000) *Grand Central: Gateway to a Million Lives*. New York.

Bender, Marylin, and Selig Altschul. (1982) *The Chosen Instrument: Pan Am, Juan Trippe, the Rise and Fall of an American Entrepreneur*. New York.

Bender, Thomas. (1987) *New York Intellect: A History of Intellectual Life in New York City, from 1750 to the Beginnings of Our Own Time*. New York.

Bendersky, Joseph W. (2000) *The 'Jewish Threat': Anti-Semitic Politics of the U.S. Army*. New York.

Bendix, Ludwig. (1945) *Planning for the Future: Current Economic Problems, Finance and the Stock Exchange*. New York.

Benedict, Ruth. (1943) "Recognition of Cultural Diversities in the Postwar World." *Annals of the American Academy of Politican and Social Science* 227: 101–107.

Benedict, Ruth, and Margaret Mead. (1977) *An Anthropologist at Work: Writings of Ruth Benedict*. Westport, CT.

Benet, James. (1936) "Mother of Exiles." *New Republic*, November 25.

Benjamin, Gerald. (1974) *Race Relations and the New York City Commission on Human Rights*. Ithaca, NY.

Bennett, David Harry. (1969) *Demagogues in the Depression: American Radicals and the Union Party, 1932–1936*. New Brunswick, NJ.

Bennett, Scott H. (2003) *Radical Pacifism: The War Resisters League and Gandhian Nonviolence in America, 1915–1963*. Syracuse, NY.

Benson, Erik. (2000) "Suspicious Allies: Wartime Aviation Developments and the Anglo-American International Airline Rivalry, 1939–45." *History and Technology* 17: 21–42.

———. (2001) "Flying Down to Rio: American Commercial Aviation, the Good Neighbor Policy and World War Two, 1939–45." *Essays in Economic and Business History* 19: 61–73.

Bentley, Amy. (1998) *Eating for Victory: Food Rationing and the Politics of Domesticity*. Urbana, IL.

Bentley, Elizabeth, and Hayden B. Peake. (1988) *Out of Bondage: The Story of Elizabeth Bentley*. New York.

Benton, Mike. (1992) *Superhero Comics of the Golden Age: The Illustrated History*. Dallas, TX.

Berenbaum, Michael. (1993) *The World Must Know: The History of the Holocaust as Told in the United States Holocaust Memorial Museum*. Boston, MA.

Berg, A. Scott. (1998) *Lindbergh*. New York.

Berg, Emmett. (2004) "Fight of the Century." *Humanities* 25: 1–4.

Bergman, Jerry. (1984) *Jehovah's Witnesses and Kindred Groups: A Historical Compendium*

and *Bibliography*. New York.
Bergreen, Laurence. (1997) *Louis Armstrong: An Extravagant Life*. New York.
Berman, Aaron. (1990) *Nazism, the Jews, and American Zionism, 1933–1948*. Detroit, MI.
Berman, Elisabeth Kessin. (1997) "Moral Triage or Cultural Salvage?: The Agendas of Varian Fry and the Emergency Rescue Committee." In *Exiles + Emigrés: The Flight of European Artists from Hitler*, edited by Stephanie Barron et al. Los Angeles, CA.
Berman, Marshall. (2006) *On the Town: One Hundred Years of Spectacle in Times Square*. New York.
Bernstein, Bernard, and Richard D. McKinzie. (1975) "Oral History Interview with Bernard Bernstein." Harry S. Truman Presidential Library and Museum, July 23.
Bernstein, Jeremy. (1984) *Three Degrees above Zero: Bell Labs in the Information Age*. New York.
Bernstein, Mark, and Alex Lubertozzi. (2003) *World War II on the Air: Edward R. Murrow and the Broadcasts That Riveted a Nation*. Naperville, IL.
Bernstein, Michael A. (1987) *The Great Depression: Delayed Recovery and Economic Change in America, 1929–1939*. New York.
Bérubé, Allan. (1990) *Coming out under Fire: The History of Gay Men and Women in World War Two*. New York.
"Better Late Than Never." (1943) *Time*, March 22.
Beyer, William C. (1995) "Creating 'Common Ground' on the Home Front: Race, Class, and Ethnicity in a 1940s Quarterly Magazine." In *The Home-Front War: World War II and American Society*, edited by Kenneth Paul O'Brien

and Lynn H. Parsons. Westport, CT.
Bianco, Anthony. (2004) *Ghosts of 42nd Street: A History of America's Most Infamous Block*. New York.
Biddle, Francis. (1962) *In Brief Authority*. Garden City, NY.
Bierbrier, Doreen. (1998) "The American Zionist Emergency Council: An Analysis of a Pressure Group." In *American Zionism: Mission and Politics*, edited by Jeffrey S. Gurock. New York.
Bilby, Kenneth W. (1986) *The General: David Sarnoff and the Rise of the Communications Industry*. New York.
Billstein, Reinhold. (2000) *Working for the Enemy: Ford, General Motors, and Forced Labor in Germany During the Second World War*. New York.
Biondi, Martha. (1997) "The Struggle for Black Equality in New York City." PhD diss., Columbia University.
———. (2003) *To Stand and Fight: The Struggle for Civil Rights in Postwar New York City*. Cambridge, MA.
Bird, Frederick L. (1949) *A Study of the Port of New York Authority*. New York.
Bird, Kai. (1992) *The Chairman: John J. McCloy and the Making of the American Establishment*. New York.
———. (1998) *The Color of Truth: McGeorge Bundy and William Bundy, Brothers in Arms: A Biography*. New York.
Bird, Kai, and Martin J. Sherwin. (2005) *American Prometheus: The Triumph and Tragedy of J. Robert Oppenheimer*. New York.
Birmingham, Stephen. (1973) *Real Lace: America's Irish Rich*. New York.
Bitter Queen. (2007) "History of Gay Bars in New York City." BitterQueen.Typepad.com, December 26.

Bjerre-Poulsen, Niels. (2002) *Right Face: Organizing the American Conservative Movement 1945–65*. Copenhagen, Denmark.
Black, Allida M. (1996) *Casting Her Own Shadow: Eleanor Roosevelt and the Shaping of Postwar Liberalism*. New York.
Black, Edwin. (1999) *The Transfer Agreement: The Dramatic Story of the Pact between the Third Reich and Jewish Palestine*. Cambridge, MA.
———. (2001) *IBM and the Holocaust: The Strategic Alliance between Nazi Germany and America's Most Powerful Corporation*. New York.
———. (2003) *War against the Weak: Eugenics and America's Campaign to Create a Master Race*. New York.
Blake, Casey Nelson. (1990) *Beloved Community: The Cultural Criticism of Randolph Bourne, Van Wyck Brooks, Waldo Frank & Lewis Mumford*. Chapel Hill, NC.
Blanco, Francisco A. (2003) "Proyección de la Falange en los Estados Unidos (1936–39)." In *Rastro de la Historia*, edited by Asociación Cultural Rastro de la Historia. Madrid, Spain.
Blanshard, Paul. (1951) *American Freedom and Catholic Power*. Boston, MA.
"Blanshard Scores Labor Left Wing: Calls Upon Party Membership to Support Right Wingers in Fight on Reds." (1940) *New York Times*, March 3.
Blantz, Thomas E., and George Naumann Shuster. (1993) *George N. Shuster: On the Side of Truth*. Notre Dame, IN.
Blatman, Daniel. (2010) "Bund." In *YIVO Encyclopedia of Jews in Eastern Europe*, edited by YIVO. New York.
Blejwas, Stanislaus A. (1998) "The Republic of Poland and the Origins of Polish American Congress." *Polish American Studies* 55: 23–33.

Block, Alan A. (1983) *East Side, West Side: Organizing Crime in New York, 1930–1950*. New Brunswick, NJ.
———. (1986) "A Modern Marriage of Convenience: A Collaboration between Organized Crime and US Intelligence." In *Organized Crime: A Global Perspective*, edited by Robert J. Kelly. Totowa, NJ.
———. (1994) "Fascism and Organized Crime: The Assassination of Carlo Tresca." In *Space, Time & Organized Crime*, edited by Alan A. Block. New Brunswick, NJ.
Block, Fred L. (1977) *The Origins of International Economic Disorder: A Study of United States International Monetary Policy from World War II to the Present*. Berkeley, CA.
Bloom, Alexander. (1986) *Prodigal Sons: The New York Intellectuals and Their World*. New York.
Bloom, Jon. (1998) "Muste, A. J." In *Encyclopedia of the American Left*, edited by Mari Jo Buhle, Paul Buhle, and Dan Georgakas. New York.
Bloom, Nicholas Dagen. (2008) *Public Housing That Worked: New York in the Twentieth Century*. Philadelphia, PA.
Blue, Howard. (2002) *Words at War: World War II Era Radio Drama and the Postwar Broadcasting Industry Blacklist*. Lanham, MD.
Blum, John Morton. (1970) *Roosevelt and Morgenthau*. Boston, MA.
———. (1976) *V Was for Victory: Politics and American Culture During World War II*. New York.
———. (1983) "United Against: American Culture and Society During World War II." Paper presented at the Harmon Memorial Lectures in Military History. United States Air Force Academy, CO.
Blumberg, Barbara. (1979) *The New Deal and the Unemployed: The View*

from New York City. Lewisburg, PA.

Blumberg, Barbara, and United States National Park Service. (1985) *Celebrating the Immigrant: An Administrative History of the Statue of Liberty National Monument, 1952–1982.* Boston, MA.

Blumenthal, Ralph. (2000) *The Stork Club: America's Most Famous Nightspot and the Lost World of Cafe Society.* Boston, MA.

Boas, Franz. (1934) "Nordic Propaganda." *New Republic,* March 7.

Boddy, William. (1990) *Fifties Television: The Industry and Its Critics.* Urbana, IL.

Bond, Elsie. (1945) "Day Care of Children of Working Mothers in New York State During the War Emergency." *New York History* 26: 51–57.

Bone, Kevin. (2006) "The Delaware System." In *Water-Works: The Architecture and Engineering of the New York City Water Supply*, edited by Kevin Bone, Gina Pollara, and Albert F. Appleton. New York.

Bone, Kevin, Mary Beth Betts, et al. (1997) *The New York Waterfront: Evolution and Building Culture of the Port and Harbor.* New York.

Bonner, Arthur. (1997) *Alas! What Brought Thee Hither? The Chinese in New York, 1800–1950.* Madison, NJ.

Book Publishers Bureau, War Committee. (1944) *The Essentiality of Books in Wartime and in the Post-War World.* New York.

Borgwardt, Elizabeth. (2005) *A New Deal for the World: America's Vision for Human Rights.* Cambridge, MA.

Borstelmann, Thomas. (2001) *The Cold War and the Color Line: American Race Relations in the Global Arena.* Cambridge, MA.

Boucher, Joanne. (2003) "Betty Friedan and the Radical Past of Liberal Feminism." *New Politics* 9: 23–32.

Bouza, Anthony V. (1976) *Police Intelligence: The Operations of an Investigative Unit.* New York.

Bowers, Jane M., and Judith Tick. (1986) *Women Making Music: The Western Art Tradition, 1150–1950.* Urbana, IL.

Bowles, Chester. (1946) *Tomorrow without Fear.* New York.

Bowman-Kruhm, Mary. (2003) *Margaret Mead: A Biography.* Westport, CT.

Boyer, M. Christine. (1983) *Dreaming the Rational City: The Myth of American City Planning.* Cambridge, MA.

Boyer, Paul S. (1985) *By the Bomb's Early Light: American Thought and Culture at the Dawn of the Atomic Age.* New York.

Boyer, Richard Owen. (1947) *The Dark Ship.* Boston, MA.

Boyne, Walter J. (2002) *Air Warfare: An International Encyclopedia.* 2 vols. Santa Barbara, CA.

Bracey, John H., Jr., and August Meier. (1991) "Allies or Adversaries?: The NAACP, A. Philip Randolph and the 1941 March on Washington." *Georgia Historical Quarterly* 75: 1–17.

Bradshaw, Harry. (2004) "The James Morrison Story." Morrison.ie, August 3.

Brandt, Nat. (1996) *Harlem at War: The Black Experience in WWII.* Syracuse, NY.

Braudy, Susan. (2003) *Family Circle: The Boudins and the Aristocracy of the Left.* New York.

Brecher, Frank W. (1990) "David Wyman and the Historiography of America's Response to the Holocaust: Counter-Considerations." *Holocaust and Genocide Studies* 5: 423–446.

Brecher, Jeremy. (2008) "Doctor Wall Street: How the US Health-Care System Got So Sick." *Z Magazine,* June.

Breitman, Richard. (2004) *U.S. Intelligence and the Nazis.* Washington, DC.

Brennan, Jean Ford. (1971) *The IBM Watson Laboratory at Columbia University: A History.* New York.

Brenner, Lenni. (1983) *Zionism in the Age of the Dictators.* Westport, CT.

Breslin, Jimmy. (1991) *Damon Runyon.* New York.

Breuer, William B. (1989) *Hitler's Undercover War: The Nazi Espionage Invasion of the U.S.A.* New York.

Brewer, Susan A. (1997) *To Win the Peace: British Propaganda in the United States During World War II.* Ithaca, NY.

"Brewster XF2A-1." (1999) *Air to Air Combat,* December 25.

Brick, Howard. (1986) *Daniel Bell and the Decline of Intellectual Radicalism: Social Theory and Political Reconciliation in the 1940s.* Madison, WI.

Brightman, Carol. (1992) *Writing Dangerously: Mary McCarthy and Her World.* New York.

Brinkley, Alan. (1982) *Voices of Protest: Huey Long, Father Coughlin, and the Great Depression.* New York.

———. (1989) "The New Deal and the Idea of the State." In *The Rise and Fall of the New Deal Order, 1930–1980*, edited by Gary Gerstle and Steve Fraser. Princeton, NJ.

———. (1996) "World War II and American Liberalism." In *The War in American Culture: Society and Consciousness During World War II*, edited by Lewis A. Erenberg and Susan E. Hirsch. Chicago, IL.

———. (2000) "The National Resources Planning Board and the Reconstruction of Planning." In *The American Planning Tradition: Culture and Policy*, edited by Robert Fishman. Washington, DC.

———. (2010) *The Publisher: Henry Luce and His American Century.* New York.

Britt, George. (1940) *The Fifth Column Is Here.* New York.

Brittain, James. (1998) "Scanning the Past: Frank B. Jewett and the Bell Telephone Laboratories." *Proceedings of the IEEE* 86: 463–465.

Broad, William J. (2007) "Why They Called It the Manhattan Project." *New York Times,* October 30.

Brodsky, Alyn. (2003) *The Great Mayor: Fiorello La Guardia and the Making of the City of New York.* New York.

Brody, David. (1956) "American Jewry, the Refugees and Immigration Restriction, 1932–1942." *Publications of the American Jewish Historical Society* 45: 219–247.

Brookeman, Christopher. (1984) *American Culture and Society since the 1930s.* New York.

Brooklyn Eagle. (1945) *Staging Area—Brooklyn: A Section of the Brooklyn Eagle, Sunday, December 9, 1945.* Brooklyn, NY.

Brouwer, Norman. (1989) "Improving Conditions for Seamen Ashore and Afloat." *Seaport,* Fall.

———. (1990) "Fortress New York." *Seaport,* Summer.

Browder, Robert Paul, and Thomas G. Smith. (1986) *Independent: A Biography of Lewis W. Douglas.* New York.

Brown, Alden V. (1983) *The Tablet: The First Seventy-Five Years.* New York.

Brown, Anthony Cave, and Charles Brown MacDonald. (1981) *On a Field of Red: The Communist International and the Coming of World War II.* New York.

Brown, Dorothy M., and Elizabeth McKeown. (1997) *The Poor Belong to Us: Catholic Charities and American Welfare.* Cambridge, MA.

Brown, J. David. (1994) "The Battle of the Atlantic, 1941–1943: Peaks and Troughs." In *To Die Gallantly: The Battle of*

the Atlantic, edited by Timothy J. Runyan, and Jan M. Copes. Boulder, CO.
Brown, John Mason. (1979) The Worlds of Robert E. Sherwood: Mirror to His Times, 1896–1939. Westport, CT.
Brown, John Mason, and Robert E. Sherwood. (1970) The Ordeal of a Playwright: Robert E. Sherwood and the Challenge of War. New York.
Brown, Louis. (1999) A Radar History of World War II: Technical and Military Imperatives. Philadelphia, PA.
Brown, Vivian. (1942) "How to Lead a Model Life." Washington Post, November 12.
Bryce, Ivar. (1984) You Only Live Once: Memories of Ian Fleming. Frederick, MD.
Bucher, Bernadette, and Claude Lévi-Strauss. (1985) "An Interview with Claude Lévi-Strauss, 30 June 1982." American Ethnologist 12: 360–368.
Buckland, Sandra Stansbery. (1996) "Promoting American Fashion 1940 through 1945: From Understudy to Star." PhD diss., Ohio State University.
———. (2005) "Promoting American Designers, 1940–1944: Building Our Own House." In Twentieth-Century American Fashion, edited by Linda Welters and Patricia A. Cunningham. New York.
Buckle, Richard, and John Taras. (1988) George Balanchine, Ballet Master: A Biography. New York.
Buckley, John. (1999) Air Power in the Age of Total War. Bloomington, IN.
Buderi, Robert. (1998) The Invention That Changed the World: The Story of Radar from War to Peace. London.
Buford, Kate. (2000) Burt Lancaster: An American Life. New York.
Buhite, Russell D., and David W. Levy. (1992) FDR's Fireside Chats. Norman, OK.
Buhle, Mari Jo, Paul Buhle, et al. (1990) Encyclopedia of the American Left. New York.
Buhle, Paul. (1987) Marxism in the U.S.A.: From 1870 to the Present Day. New York.
———. (1990) "Louis B. Boudin." In Encyclopedia of the American Left, edited by Mari Jo Buhle, Paul Buhle, and Dan Georgakas. New York.
———. (1999) "David McReynolds: Socialist Peacemaker." Nonviolent Activist: The Magazine of the War Resisters League, March–April.
Buhle, Paul, and Robin D. G. Kelley. (1997) "Allies of a Different Sort: Jews and Blacks in the Amertican Left." In Struggles in the Promised Land: Toward a History of Black-Jewish Relations in the United States, edited by Jack Salzman and Cornel West. New York.
Bukatman, Scott. (2007) "A Day in New York: On the Town and The Clock." In City That Never Sleeps: New York and the Filmic Imagination, edited by Murray Pomerance. New Brunswick, NJ.
Bukowczyk, John J. (1987) And My Children Did Not Know Me: A History of the Polish-Americans. Bloomington, IN.
———. (1996) Polish Americans and Their History: Community, Culture, and Politics. Pittsburgh, PA.
———. (2008) A History of the Polish Americans. New Brunswick, NJ.
Bullert, Gary B. (2002) "Reinhold Niebuhr and the Christian Century: World War II and the Eclipse of the Social Gospel." Journal of Church & State 44: 271–290.
———. (2004) "From Dewey to Hook: World War II and the Crisis of Democracy." In Sidney Hook Reconsidered, edited by Matthew J. Cotter. Amherst, NY.
Bulletin of the American Warehousemen's Association. (1916) "About the Washington Market, New York." Bulletin of the American Warehousemen's Association 17: 25–28.
Bundy, William P. (1994) "Notes on the History of Foreign Affairs." CFR.org, July 18, 2006: 1–10.
Bunk, William Killeen. (1984) "Lewis Mumford and the World Wars." PhD diss., State University of New York at Albany.
Burch, Philip H. (1980) Elites in American History: The New Deal to the Carter Administration. Vol. 3. New York.
Burgos, Julia de, and Jack Agüeros. (1997) Song of the Simple Truth: Obra Completa Poética: The Complete Poems. Willimantic, CT.
Burk, Kathleen. (1991) "The House of Morgan in Financial Diplomacy, 1920–1930." In Anglo-American Relations in the 1920's: The Struggle for Supremacy, edited by B. J. C. McKercher. London.
Burk, Robert Fredrick. (2001) Much More Than a Game: Players, Owners, & American Baseball since 1921. Chapel Hill, NC.
Burke, Patrick Lawrence. (2008) Come in and Hear the Truth: Jazz and Race on 52nd Street. Chicago, IL.
Burns, Jennifer. (2009) Goddess of the Market: Ayn Rand and the American Right. New York.
Burton, Humphrey. (1994) Leonard Bernstein. New York.
Bush, Clive. (2003) "Left-Wing Isolationalism, Literature and Ideology in America During the Run-up to World War II." Comparative American Studies 1: 131–152.
Buttenwieser, Ann L. (1987) Manhattan, Water-Bound: Planning and Developing Manhattan's Waterfront from the Seventeenth Century to the Present. New York.
Byles, Jeff. (2005) Rubble: Unearthing the History of Demolition. New York.
Cadegan, Una M. (2001) "Guardians of Democracy or Cultural Storm Troopers? American Catholics and the Control of Popular Media, 1934–1966." Catholic Historical Review 87: 252–282.
Caffrey, Margaret M. (1989) Ruth Benedict: Stranger in This Land. Austin, TX.
Caldwell, Mark. (2005) New York Night: The Mystique and Its History. New York.
California State Reconstruction and Reemployment Commission. (1945) Apparel Manufacturing in California. Sacramento, CA.
Callahan, David. (1990) Dangerous Capabilities: Paul Nitze and the Cold War. New York.
Callahan, William James. (2004) "Archivo Gomá: Documentos de la Guerra Civil by José Andrés-Gallego and Antón M. Pazos." Catholic Historical Review 90: 341–344.
Callow, Simon. (1996) Orson Welles: The Road to Xanadu. Vol. 1. New York.
Camp, Helen C. (1995) Iron in Her Soul: Elizabeth Gurley Flynn and the American Left. Pullman, WA.
Campbell, Rodney. (1977) The Luciano Project: The Secret Wartime Collaboration of the Mafia and the U.S. Navy. New York.
Cancel Miranda, Rafael. (1998) Puerto Rico: Independence Is a Necessity: On the Fight against U.S. Colonial Rule. New York.
Canedy, Susan. (1990) America's Nazis: A Democratic Dilemma: A History of the German American Bund. Menlo Park, CA.
Cannistraro, Philip V. (1985a) "Generoso

Pope and the Rise of Italian American Politics, 1925–1936." In *Italian Americans: New Perspectives in Italian Immigration and Ethnicity*, edited by Lydio F. Tomasi. Staten Island, NY.

———. (1985b) "Luigi Antonini and the Italian Anti-Fascist Movement in the United States, 1940–1943." *Journal of American Ethnic History* 5: 21–40.

Cannistraro, Philip V., and Gerald Meyer. (2003) *The Lost World of Italian American Radicalism: Politics, Labor, and Culture*. Westport, CT.

Cantril, Hadley, and John Harding. (1943) "The 1942 Elections: A Case Study in Political Psychology." *Public Opinion Quarterly* 7: 222–241.

Cantril, Hadley, Howard Koch, et al. (1940) *The Invasion from Mars: A Study in the Psychology of Panic*. Princeton, NJ.

Cantwell, Robert. (1992) "Feasts of Unnaming: Folk Festivals and the Representation of Folklife." In *Public Folklore*, edited by Robert Baron, Nicholas R. Spitzer and American Folklore Society. Washington, DC.

———. (1996) *When We Were Good: The Folk Revival*. Cambridge, MA.

Cape Liberty Cruise Port. (2006) "History." *CruiseLiberty.org*, September 1.

Capeci, Dominic J. (1977a) "From Different Liberal Perspectives: Fiorello H. La Guardia, Adam Clayton Powell, Jr., and Civil Rights in New York City, 1941–1943." *Journal of Negro History* 62: 160–173.

———. (1977b) *The Harlem Riot of 1943*. Philadelphia, PA.

Carbone, Peter F. (1977) *The Social and Educational Thought of Harold Rugg*. Durham, NC.

Carlson, John Roy. (1943) *Under Cover: My Four Years in the Nazi Underworld of America: The Amazing Revelation of How Axis Agents and Our Enemies within Are Now Plotting to Destroy the United States*. New York.

Carnevale, Nancy C. (2003) "'No Italian Spoken for the Duration of the War': Language, Italian American Identity, and Cultural Pluralism in the World War II Years." *Journal of American Ethnic History* 22: 3–33.

Caro, Robert. (1974) *The Power Broker: Robert Moses and the Fall of New York*. New York.

Carroll, Peter N. (1994) *The Odyssey of the Abraham Lincoln Brigade: Americans in the Spanish Civil War*. Stanford, CA.

Carroll, Warren Hasty. (1996) *The Last Crusade*. Front Royal, VA.

Carse, Robert. (1965) *The Long Haul: The United States Merchant Service in World War II*. New York.

Casey, Dennis, and Air Intelligence Agency at Lackland Air Force Base, Texas. (2001) "Tables Turn on Hitler's Spy Plan: Blackmailed Spies Are First to Become Disloyal." *Spokesman Online*, October.

Casey, Kevin M. (2001) *Saving International Capitalism During the Early Truman Presidency: The National Advisory Council on International Monetary and Financial Problems, 1945–1948*. New York.

Casey, Marion R. (1996) "From the East Side to the Seaside: Irish Americans on the Move in New York City." In *The New York Irish*, edited by Ronald H. Bayor and Timothy J. Meagher. Baltimore, MD.

———. (1998) "Ireland, New York, and the Irish Image in American Popular Culture, 1890–1960." PhD diss., New York University.

Casper, Scott E., and Lucinda M. Long. (2001) *Moving Stories: Migration and the American West, 1850–2000*. Reno, NV.

Castaneda, Christopher James. (1993) *Regulated Enterprise: Natural Gas Pipelines and Northeastern Markets, 1938–1954*. Columbus, OH.

Castles, Mrs. John V. (1946) *History of the Civilian Defense Volunteer Office in the City of New York, 1941–1945*. New York.

"Catholics v. WAACs." (1942) *Time*, June 15.

Catino, Martin Scott. (2003) "Mussolini's March on America: Italian Americans and the Fascist Experience, 1922–1941." PhD diss., University of Southern Mississippi.

Centro de Estudios Puertorriqueños. (2003) *Guide to the Emelí Vélez De Vando Papers*. New York.

———. (2005a) "Biographical Note." In *Guide to the Erasmo Vando Papers*, edited by Pedro Juan Hernández and Nélida Pérez. New York.

———. (2005b) *Guide to the Clemente Soto Vélez and Amanda Vélez Papers*. New York.

———. (2005c) *Guide to the Juanita Arocho Papers*. New York.

———. (2005d) "Historical/Biographical Note." In *Guide to the Jesús Colón Papers, 1901–1974 (Bulk 1920–1970)*, edited by Archives of the Puerto Rican Diaspora at Hunter College. New York.

———. (2021) "Biographical / Historical." In *Ruth M. Reynolds Papers*, edited by Pedro Juan Hernández and Nélida Pérez. New York.

Centro de Estudios Puertorriqueños and Ramón Bosque-Pérez. (2007) *FBI Files on Puerto Ricans: The Serrano Initiative*. New York.

Chadwin, Mark Lincoln. (1968) *The Hawks of World War II*. Chapel Hill, NC.

Chafe, William H. (1991) *The Paradox of Change: American Women in the 20th Century*. New York.

Chafee, Zechariah. (1969) *Free Speech in the United States*. New York.

Chamberlain, Lawrence H. (1951) *Loyalty and Legislative Action*. Ithaca, NY.

Chambers, Bradford. (1944) "Boy Gangs of New York: 500 Fighting Units." *New York Times Magazine*, December 10.

Chambers, John Whiteclay II. (1987) *To Raise an Army: The Draft Comes to Modern America*. New York.

Chandler, Alfred D., and James W. Cortada. (2000) *A Nation Transformed by Information: How Information Has Shaped the United States from Colonial Times to the Present*. New York.

Chandler, Alfred D., Takashi Hikino, et al. (2005) *Inventing the Electronic Century: The Epic Story of the Consumer Electronics and Computer Industries*. Cambridge, MA.

Chapman, John. (1961) *Tell It to Sweeney: The Informal History of the New York Daily News*. New York.

Charters, Samuel, and Leonard Kunstadt. (1962) *Jazz: A History of the New York Scene*. Garden City, NY.

Chary, M. Srinivas. (1995) *The Eagle and the Peacock: U.S. Foreign Policy toward India since Independence*. Westport, CT.

Chase, Allan. (1943) *Falange: The Axis Secret Army in the Americas*. New York.

Chase, Edna Woolman, and Ilka Chase. (1954) *Always in Vogue*. Garden City, NY.

Chase, Stuart, and Twentieth Century Fund. (1942) *Goals for America: A Budget of Our Needs and Resources; Guide Lines to America's Future as Reported to the Twentieth Century Fund*. New York.

Chatfield, Charles. (1973) *For Peace and Justice: Pacifism in America, 1914–1941*. Boston, MA.

"Cheap Books." (1939) *Time*, July 10.

Chen, Anthony S. (2006) "'The Hitlerian Rule of Quotas': Racial Conservatism and the Politics of Fair Employment Legislation in New York State, 1941–1945." *Journal of American History* 92: 1238–1264.

———. (2009) *The Fifth Freedom: Jobs, Politics, and Civil Rights in the United States, 1941–1972.* Princeton, NJ.

Chen, Julia I. Hsuan. (1941) "The Chinese Community in New York: A Study in Their Cultural Adjustment, 1920–1940." PhD diss., American University.

Chen, Pei-Yao. (2003) "The 'Isolation' of New York City Chinatown: A Geo-Historical Approach to a Chinese Community in the United States." PhD diss., City University of New York.

Cheney, David M. (2013a) "Archdiocese of New York." *Catholic-hierarchy.org,* March 16.

———. (2013b) "Diocese of Brooklyn." *Catholic-hierarchy.org,* March 16.

Chernow, Ron. (1990) *The House of Morgan: An American Banking Dynasty and the Rise of Modern Finance.* New York.

———. (1998) *Titan: The Life of John D. Rockefeller, Sr.* New York.

Cherry, Frances, and Catherine Borshuk. (2002) "Social Action Research and the Commission on Community Interrelations." *Journal of Social Issues* 54: 119–142.

Chester, Eric Thomas. (1995) *Covert Network: Progressives, the International Rescue Committee, and the CIA.* Armonk, NY.

Chevigny, Paul. (1991) *Gigs: Jazz and the Cabaret Laws in New York City.* New York.

Chisholm, Shirley. (1970) *Unbought and Unbossed.* Boston, MA.

Christian, Henry Arthur. (1968) "Louis Adamic: Immigrant and American Liberal." PhD diss., Brown University.

Christman, Calvin Lee. (1971) "Ferdinand Eberstadt and Economic Mobilization for War, 1941–1943." PhD diss., Ohio State University.

Churchill, Peregrine, Julian Mitchell, et al. (1975) *Jennie, Lady Randolph Churchill: A Portrait with Letters.* New York.

Cinotto, Simone. (2004) "Leonard Covello, the Covello Papers, and the History of Eating Habits among Italian Imigrants in New York." *Journal of American History* 91: 497–521.

Citizens Housing and Planning Council and Division of Defense Housing Coordination. (1942) *Wartime Housing in the New York Metropolitan Area: What the Federal and State Agencies Are Doing, and, What They Ask Local Public Bodies and Civic Organizations to Do.* New York.

City-wide Citizens' Committee on Harlem. (1942a) *Preliminary Report of the Sub-Committee on Employment of the City-Wide Citizens' Committee on Harlem.* New York.

———. (1942b) *Report of the Sub-Committee on Housing of the City-Wide Citizens' Committee on Harlem.* New York.

City of Bayonne. (2005) "History of Bayonne." *BayonneNJ.com,* November 8.

City Planning Commission. (1940) "Reports: Master Plan." *Minutes of Meeting of the City Planning Commission,* May 29, 1940: 317–394.

———. (1951) *Planning Progress in New York City, 1940–1950.* New York.

Clark, Evans, and Twentieth Century Fund. (1943) *Wartime Facts and Postwar Problems: A Study and Discussion Manual.* New York.

Clark, John Maurice. (1944) *Demobilization of Wartime Economic Controls.* New York.

Clark, Kenneth B., and James Barker. (1945) "The Zoot Effect in Personality: A Race Riot Participant." *Journal of Abnormal and Social Psychology* 40: 143–148.

Clark, Kenneth Bancroft. (1965) *Dark Ghetto: Dilemmas of Social Power.* New York.

Clarke, Nick. (1999) *Alistair Cooke: A Biography.* New York.

Clement, Elizabeth Alice. (2006) *Love for Sale: Courting, Treating, and Prostitution in New York City, 1900–1945.* Chapel Hill, NC.

Clement, Piet. (2004) "'The Touchstone of German Credit': Nazi Germany and the Service of the Dawes and Young Loans." *Financial History Review* 11: 33–50.

Clifford, J. Garry, and Samuel R. Spencer. (1986) *The First Peacetime Draft.* Lawrence, KS.

Clifford, James. (1999) "On Collecting Art and Culture." In *The Cultural Studies Reader,* edited by Simon During. New York.

Clifford, John G. (1973) "Grenville Clark and the Origins of Selective Service." *Review of Politics* 35: 17–40.

Clines, Francis X. (1998) "Paul O'Dwyer, New York's Liberal Battler for Underdogs and Outsiders, Dies at 90." *New York Times,* June 25.

"Closing Address by Secretary of the Treasury Henry Morgenthau, July 22, 1944." (1946) In *Pillars of Peace: Documents Pertaining to American Interest in Establishing a Lasting World Peace, January 1941–February 1946,* edited by Book Department of the Army Information School. Carlisle Barracks, PA.

Cloud, Stanley, and Lynne Olson. (1996) *The Murrow Boys: Pioneers on the Front Lines of Broadcasting Journalism.* Boston, MA.

Cobble, Dorothy Sue. (2004) *The Other Women's Movement: Workplace Justice and Social Rights in Modern America.* Princeton, NJ.

Coble, Alana Erickson. (2006) *Cleaning Up: The Transformation of Domestic Service in Twentieth Century New York City.* New York.

Cohalan, Rev. Msgr. Florence D. (1983) *A Popular History of the Archdiocese of New York.* Yonkers, NY.

Cohen, Abby J. (1996) "A Brief History of Federal Financing for Child Care in the United States." *The Future of Children* 6: 26–40.

Cohen, Alexander Nobler. (2001) "Fallen Transit: The Loss of Rapid Transit on New York's Second Avenue." *The Third Rail,* July 2.

Cohen, James K. (1988) "Capital Investment and the Decline of Mass Transit in New York City, 1945–1981." *Urban Affairs Quarterly* 23: 369–388.

———. (1991) "Structural Versus Functional Determinants of New York's Fiscal Policies Towards Metropolitan Transportation, 1904–1990." *Social Science History* 15: 177–198.

Cohen, Lizabeth. (2003a) *A Consumers' Republic: The Politics of Mass Consumption in Postwar America.* New York.

Cohen, Naomi W. (1972) *Not Free to Desist: The American Jewish Committee, 1906–1966.* Philadelphia, PA.

———. (2002a) "The Transatlantic Connection: The American Jewish Committee and the Joint Foreign Committee in Defense of German Jews, 1933–1937." *American Jewish History* 90: 353–384.

———. (2003b) *The Americanization of Zionism, 1897–1948.* Hanover, MA.

Cohen, Raya. (2000) "Against the Current: Hashomer Hatzair in the Warsaw Ghetto." *Jewish Social Studies* 7: 63–80.

Cohen, Robert. (1993) *When the Old Left Was Young: Student Radicals and America's First Mass Student Movement*. New York.

Cohen, Ronald D. (2002b) *Rainbow Quest: The Folk Music Revival and American Society, 1940–1970*. Amherst, MA.

Cohen, Stuart, Stanley Kogan, et al. (1956) "Brooklyn Industrial Development." *Progressive Architecture*, December.

Cohen-Solal, Annie. (2000) "'Claude L. Strauss' in the United States." *Partisan Review* 47: 252–260.

Colby, Gerard, and Charlotte Dennett. (1995) *Thy Will Be Done: The Conquest of the Amazon: Nelson Rockefeller and Evangelism in the Age of Oil*. New York.

Cold Spring Harbor Laboratory, New York Public Library, et al. (2003) *Seeking the Secret of Life: The DNA Story in New York*. New York.

Cole, Wayne S. (1953) *America First: The Battle against Intervention, 1940–1941*. New York.

———. (1974) *Charles A. Lindbergh and the Battle against American Intervention in World War II*. New York.

Coles, Robert. (1987) *Dorothy Day: A Radical Devotion*. Reading, MA.

Collier, James Lincoln. (1989) *Benny Goodman and the Swing Era*. New York.

Collier, Simon. (1986) *The Life, Music & Times of Carlos Gardel*. Pittsburgh, PA.

Collins, Robert M. (1978) "Positive Business Responses to the New Deal: The Roots of the Committee for Economic Development, 1933–1942." *Business History Review* 52: 369–391.

———. (1981) *The Business Response to Keynes, 1929–1964*. New York.

———. (2000) *More: The Politics of Economic Growth in Postwar America*. New York.

Collis, John. (2001) *The Musicians' Bible 2002: The Complete Guide to the Music Business*. London.

Collomp, Catherine. (2005) "The Jewish Labor Committee, American Labor, and the Rescue of European Socialists, 1934–1941." *International Labor and Working-Class History* 68: 112–133.

Colon, Jesus. (1982) *A Puerto Rican in New York and Other Sketches*. New York.

Colón López, Joaquín. (2002) *Pioneros Puertorriqueños en Nueva York: 1917–1947*. Houston, TX.

Colton, Tim. (2007) "Bethlehem Steel Corporation, Staten Island NY: WWII Construction Record." In *ColtonCompany.com/ShipbuildingHistory.com*, edited by Tim Colton. Delray Beach, FL.

Columbia Law Review Association, Inc. (1946) "N.Y. Labor Law, Section 199-A: 'Equal Pay for Equal Work'." *Columbia Law Review* 46: 442–452.

Comenas, G. (2008) "1943: Search for a Symbol." *The Abstract Expressionism Chronology*, July 25.

Commerce and Industry Association of New York. (1944) *Winning the War and the Peace: A Program of Legislative Action Proposed by Post-War Planning Committee*. New York.

Committee for Economic Development and Melvin G. De Chazeau. (1946) *Jobs and Markets: How to Prevent Inflation and Depression in the Transition*. New York.

Conant, Jennet. (2002) *Tuxedo Park: A Wall Street Tycoon and the Secret Palace of Science That Changed the Course of World War II*. New York.

Condit, Carl W. (1980) *The Port of New York: The History of the Rail & Terminal System from the Beginnings to Pennsylvania Station*. Vol. 2. Chicago, IL.

Congress of Industrial Organizations Political Action Committee (CIO-PAC). (1944) *Jobs for All after the War*. New York.

Conn, Peter J. (1996) *Pearl S. Buck: A Cultural Biography*. New York.

Conn, Stetson, Rose C. Engelman, et al. (1964) *Guarding the United States and Its Outposts*. Washington, DC.

Conn, Stetson, and Byron Fairchild. (1960) *The Framework of Hemisphere Defense*. Washington, DC.

Conover, Carole. (1978) *Cover Girls: The Story of Harry Conover*. Englewood Cliffs, NJ.

Conquest, Robert. (1968) *The Great Terror: Stalin's Purge of the Thirties*. London.

Conrad, Peter. (1984) *The Art of the City: Views and Versions of New York*. New York.

Conroy, Melvyn. (2006) *The Terrible Choice: Some Contemporary Jewish Responses to the Holocaust*. New York.

Conyer, James L., and Julius Eric Thompson. (2004) *Pan African Nationalism in the Americas: The Life and Times of John Henrik Clarke*. Trenton, NJ.

Cook, Blanche Wiesen. (1984) "First Comes the Lie: C. D. Jackson and Political Warfare." *Radical History Review* 31: 42–71.

———. (1999) *Eleanor Roosevelt: Volume Two, the Defining Years, 1933–1938*. New York.

Cooney, John. (1984) *The American Pope: The Life and Times of Francis Cardinal Spellman*. New York.

Cooney, Terry A. (1986) *The Rise of the New York Intellectuals: Partisan Review and Its Circle, 1934–1945*. Madison, WI.

Cooperative Village. (2015) "A Brief History of Cooperative Housing on the Lower East Side." *coopvillage.coop*, March 27.

Corey, Steven Hunt. (1994) "King Garbage: A History of Solid Waste Management in New York City, 1881–1970." PhD diss., New York University.

Corn, Joseph J. (2002) *The Winged Gospel: America's Romance with Aviation*. Baltimore, MD.

Corner, George Washington. (1964) *A History of the Rockefeller Institute, 1901–1953: Origins and Growth*. New York.

Cornwell, John. (1999) *Hitler's Pope: The Secret History of Pius XII*. New York.

Corrin, Jay P. (2002) *Catholic Intellectuals and the Challenge of Democracy*. Notre Dame, IN.

Cosgrove, Stuart. (1981) "Cabaret and Counter-Culture: The Anti-Fascist Theatre in New York." *Theatre Quarterly* 10: 49–60.

———. (1984) "The Zoot-Suit and Style Warfare." *History Workshop Journal* 18: 77–91.

———. (1985) "From Shock Troupe to Group Theatre." In *Theatres of the Left, 1880–1935: Workers' Theatre Movements in Britain and America*, edited by Raphael Samuel, Ewan MacColl, and Stuart Cosgrove. London.

Costello, John. (1985) *Virtue under Fire: How World War II Changed Our Social and Sexual Attitudes*. Boston, MA.

Costello, John, and Oleg Tsarev. (1993) *Deadly Illusions: The KGB Orlov Dossier Reveals Stalin's Master Spy*. New York.

Cotter, Matthew J. (2004) *Sidney Hook Reconsidered*. Amherst, NY.

Cottrell, Robert C. (1992) *Izzy: A Biography of I. F. Stone*. New Brunswick, NJ.

———. (2000) *Roger Nash Baldwin and the American*

Civil Liberties Union. New York.

Coulter, Matthew Ware. (1997) *The Senate Munitions Inquiry of the 1930s: Beyond the Merchants of Death.* Westport, CT.

Council for Scholarly Evaluation of Gaelic Gotham. (1997) *The Gaelic Gotham Report.* New York.

Covello, Leonard. (1936) "A High School and Its Immigrant Community—a Challenge and an Opportunity." *Journal of Educational Sociology* 9, no. 6: 331–346.

———. (1958) *The Heart Is the Teacher.* New York.

Covert, Catherine L., and John D. Stevens. (1984) *Mass Media between the Wars: Perceptions of Cultural Tension, 1918–1941.* Syracuse, NY.

Cramer, Gisela, and Ursula Prutsch. (2006) "Nelson A. Rockefeller's Office of Inter-American Affairs (1940–1946) and Record Group 229." *Hispanic American Historical Review* 86: 785–806.

Cramer, Richard Ben. (2000) *Joe DiMaggio: The Hero's Life.* New York.

Crane, Diana. (1987) *The Transformation of the Avant-Garde: The New York Art World, 1940–1985.* Chicago, IL.

Cremin, Lawrence A. (1961) *The Transformation of the School: Progressivism in American Education, 1876–1957.* New York.

Critchlow, Donald T., and Charles H. Parker. (1998) *With Us Always: A History of Private Charity and Public Welfare.* Lanham, MD.

Crosby, Donald F. (1971) "Boston Catholics and the Spanish Civil War." *New England Quarterly* 44: 82–100.

Cuff, Robert D. (1989) "United States Mobilization and Railroad Transportation: Lessons in Coordination and Control, 1917–1945." *Journal of Military History* 53: 33–50.

Culbert, David Holbrook. (1976) *News for Everyman: Radio and Foreign Affairs in Thirties America.* Westport, CT.

Cull, Nicholas John. (1995) *Selling War: The British Propaganda against American "Neutrality" in World War II.* New York.

Culver, John C., and John Hyde. (2000) *American Dreamer: The Life and Times of Henry A. Wallace.* New York.

Cuneo, Ernest L. (1955) *Life with Fiorello: A Memoir.* New York.

Cuozzo, Steven. (1996) *It's Alive! How America's Oldest Newspaper Cheated Death and Why It Matters.* New York.

Curti, Merle. (1936) *Peace or War: The American Struggle, 1636–1936.* New York.

D'Emilio, John. (1983) *Sexual Politics, Sexual Communities: The Making of a Homosexual Minority in the United States, 1940–1970.* Chicago, IL.

———. (2003) *Lost Prophet: The Life and Times of Bayard Rustin.* New York.

D'Itri, Patricia Ward. (1999) *Cross Currents in the International Women's Movement, 1848–1948.* Bowling Green, OH.

da Cruz, Frank. (2022) *Columbia University Computing History: A Chronology of Computing at Columbia University.* New York.

Dabakis, Melissa. (1993) "Gendered Labor: Norman Rockwell's Rosie the Riveter and the Discourses of Wartime Womanhood." In *Gender and American History since 1890*, edited by Barbara Melosh. London.

Daniel, Daniel M. (1950) *The Mike Jacobs Story.* New York.

Daniels, Les, and Chip Kidd. (2004) *Wonder Woman: The Complete History.* San Francisco, CA.

Daniels, Roger. (1971) *Concentration Camps USA: Japanese Americans and World War II.* Hinsdale, IL.

———. (1988) *Asian America: Chinese and Japanese in the United States since 1850.* Seattle, WA.

———. (1993) *Prisoners without Trial: Japanese Americans in World War II.* New York.

Danielson, Leilah C. (2003) "'In My Extremity I Turned to Gandhi': American Pacifists, Christianity, and Gandhian Nonviolence, 1915–1941." *Church History* 72: 361–388.

Davenport-Hines, R. P. T. (1995) *Auden.* New York.

Davie, Maurice R., and Committee for the Study of Recent Immigration from Europe. (1974) *Refugees in America: Report of the Committee for the Study of Recent Immigration from Europe.* Westport, CT.

Davis, Benjamin J. (1969) *Communist Councilman from Harlem: Autobiographical Notes Written in a Federal Penitentiary.* New York.

Davis, Colin J. (2003) *Waterfront Revolts: New York and London Dockworkers, 1946–61.* Urbana, IL.

Davis, Kenneth S. (1993) *FDR: Into the Storm, 1937–1940: A History.* New York.

———. (2000) *FDR, the War President, 1940–1943: A History.* New York.

Davis, Kenneth Sydney. (1967) *The American Experience of War, 1939–1945.* London.

Davis, O. L. (1999) "Rachel Davis DuBois: Intercultural Education Pioneer." In *'Bending the Future to Their Will': Civic Women, Social Education, and Democracy*, edited by Margaret Crocco and O. L. Davis. Lanham, MD.

Dawidowicz, Lucy S. (1982) "American Jews and the Holocaust." *New York Times Magazine*, April 18.

———. (1986) *The War against the Jews, 1933–1945.* New York.

Dawley, Alan. (1991) *Struggles for Justice: Social Responsibility and the Liberal State.* Cambridge, MA.

Day, Jared N. (1999) *Urban Castles: Tenement Housing and Urban Landlord Activism in New York City, 1890–1943.* New York.

de Vries, Margaret G., and J. Keith Horsefield. (1969) *The International Monetary Fund, 1945–1965: Twenty Years of International Monetary Cooperation. Volume II: Analysis.* Washington, DC.

Deacon, Desley. (2004) "Cruel and Barbarous Teatment: The Marriage of Mary McCarthy and Edmund Wilson." *Australian Feminist Studies* 19: 103–115.

Dearborn, Mary V. (2004) *Mistress of Modernism: The Life of Peggy Guggenheim.* Boston, MA.

Deats, Richard. (2001) "The Rebel Passion: Eighty-Five Years of the Fellowship of Reconciliation." *FOR's Blog*, March 29.

DeBenedetti, Charles. (1986) *Peace Heroes in Twentieth-Century America.* Bloomington, IN.

DeBona, Guerric. (1997) "The Canon and Cultural Studies: Culture and Anarchy in Gotham City." *Journal of Film and Video* 49: 52–65.

DeCaro, Louis A. (1996) *On the Side of My People: A Religious Life of Malcolm X.* New York.

Decherney, Peter. (2005) "The Museum of Modern Art and the Roots of the Cultural Cold War." In *Hollywood and the Culture Elite: How the Movies Became American*, edited by Peter Decherney. New York.

DeGruson, Gene. (2002) "Transcript: Little Blue Books." In *KTWU. Washburn.edu*, edited by Jim Kelly. Topeka, KS.

Dekar, Paul R. (2005a) *Creating the Beloved Community: A Journey with the Fellowship of Reconciliation.* Telford, PA.

———. (2005b) "The Harlem Ashram 1940–1947: Gandhian *Satyagraha* in the United States." In *Gandhiinstitute.org*, edited by M. K. Gandhi Institute for Nonviolence.

Delgado, Linda C. (2005) "Jesus Colon and the Making of the New York City Community, 1917 to 1974." In *The Puerto Rican Diaspora: Historical Perspectives*, edited by Carmen Teresa Whalen and Víctor Vázquez-Hernández. Philadelphia, PA.

Dellinger, David T. (1993) *From Yale to Jail: The Life Story of a Moral Dissenter*. New York.

Demirmen, Ferruh. (2003a) "Oil in Iraq: The Byzantine Beginnings, Part I: The Quest for Oil." *Global Policy Forum*, April 25.

———. (2003b) "Oil in Iraq: The Byzantine Beginnings, Part II: The Reign of a Monopoly." *Global Policy Forum*, April 26.

Denning, Michael. (1996) *The Cultural Front: The Laboring of American Culture in the Twentieth Century*. New York.

Dennis, Donald P. (2002) *Foreign Policy in Democracy: The Role of the Foreign Policy Association*. New York.

———. (2005) "The League of Free Nations Association, the First Organized Attempt to Move Policy toward a Union of Democracies." In *Annual Meeting, Society of Historians of American Foreign Relations: Atlanticism in 20th Century US Foreign Policy*, edited by Streit Council for a Union of Democracies, Tiziana Stella, and the Office of the Historian of the Foreign Service Institute (United States Department of State). Washington, DC.

Department of State. (1943) *Peace and War: United States Foreign Policy, 1931–1941*. Washington, DC.

Department of the Navy. (1946a) *State Summary of War Casualties from World War II for Navy, Marine Corps, and Coast Guard Personnel from New York*. Washington, DC.

———. (1946b) *United States Naval Administration in World War II: Commandant, Third Naval District*. Vols. 1 & 2. Washington, DC.

———. (2003) "Historical Narrative of Port Director: New York Third Naval District, 15 October 1939 to 14 August 1945." In *United States Naval Administration in World War II: Commandant, Third Naval District, Vol. 2*, edited by Naval Historical Center.

Desbois, Patrick. (2008) *The Holocaust by Bullets: A Priest's Journey to Uncover the Truth Behind the Murder of 1.5 Million Jews*. New York.

Desmond, John. (1943) "Tin Pan Alley Seeks the Song." *New York Times*, June 6.

Desmond, Tim. (2008) "Roman Catholic Churches of Brooklyn, N.Y." *Desmondcorp.com*, February 22.

DeVeaux, Scott. (1988) "Bebop and the Recording Industry: The 1942 AFM Recording Ban Reconsidered." *Journal of the American Musicological Society* 41: 126–165.

Devlin, Albert J., and Nancy Marie Patterson Tischler. (2000) *The Selected Letters of Tennessee Williams*. New York.

Dewey, John, and Horace Meyer Kallen. (1941) *The Bertrand Russell Case*. New York.

Dewey, Scott Hamilton. (1995) "Discovering Smog: The New York City Press and the Battle for Air Pollution Control, 1945–1965." Paper presented at Annual Meeting of the National Council on Public History. Washington, DC.

———. (2000) *Don't Breathe the Air: Air Pollution and U.S. Environmental Politics, 1945–1970*. College Station, TX.

Diamond, Sander A. (1974) *The Nazi Movement in the United States, 1924–1941*. Ithaca, NY.

Diehl, Lorraine B. (1985) *The Late, Great Pennsylvania Station*. New York.

Dietz, James L. (1986) *Economic History of Puerto Rico: Institutional Change and Capitalist Development*. Princeton, NJ.

Diggins, John P. (1972) *Mussolini and Fascism: The View from America*. Princeton, NJ.

———. (1994) *The Promise of Pragmatism: Modernism and the Crisis of Knowledge and Authority*. Chicago, IL.

Dijkstra, Bram. (2003) *American Expressionism: Art and Social Change, 1920–1950*. New York.

Dikötter, Frank. (1998) "Race Culture: Recent Perspectives on the History of Eugenics." *American Historical Review* 103: 467–478.

Diner, Hasia R. (1995) *In the Almost Promised Land: American Jews and Blacks, 1915–1935*. Baltimore, MD.

———. (2004) *The Jews of the United States, 1654 to 2000*. Berkeley, CA.

Dinnerstein, Leonard. (1994) *Antisemitism in America*. New York.

DiStasi, Lawrence. (1997) "How World War II Iced Italian American Culture." In *MultiAmerica: Essays on Cultural Wars and Cultural Peace*, edited by Ishmael Reed. New York.

———. (2001) *Una Storia Segreta: The Secret History of Italian American Evacuation and Internment During World War II*. Berkeley, CA.

Divine, Robert A. (1967) *Second Chance: The Triumph of Internationalism in America During World War II*. New York.

Dodd, Bella V. (1954) *School of Darkness*. New York.

Dodson, Dan. (1954) "The Integration of Negroes in Baseball." *Journal of Educational Sociology* 28: 73–82.

Doenecke, Justus D. (1977) "Non-Interventionism of the Left: The Keep America out of the War Congress, 1938–1941." *Journal of Contemporary History* 12: 221–236.

———. (1987) "The Anti-Interventionism of Herbert Hoover." *Journal of Libertarian Studies* 8: 311–340.

———. (1990) *In Danger Undaunted: The Anti-Interventionist Movement of 1940–1941 as Revealed in the Papers of the America First Committee*. Stanford, CA.

———. (1995) "Reinhold Niebuhr and His Critics: The Interventionist Controversy in World War II." *Anglican and Episcopal History* 64: 459–481.

———. (2000) *Storm on the Horizon: The Challenge to American Intervention, 1939–1941*. Lanham, MD.

———. (2005) "Committee to Defend America by Aiding the Allies, 1940–1942: Primary Source Microfilm." In *War, Peace, and Democracy in America: Series 1*, edited by Seeley G. Mudd Manuscript Library. Princeton, NJ.

Doherty, Brian. (2007) *Radicals for Capitalism: A Freewheeling History of the Modern American Libertarian Movement*. New York.

Doig, Jameson W. (1966) *Metropolitan Transportation Politics and the New York Region*. New York.

———. (2001) *Empire on the Hudson: Entrepreneurial Vision and Political Power at the Port of New York Authority*. New York.

Dolan, Jay P. (2002) *In Search of an American Catholicism: A History of Religion and Culture in Tension*. New York.

Dolkart, Andrew, Matthew A. Postal, et al. (2009) *Guide to New York City Landmarks*. Hoboken, NJ.

Donaldson, Gary. (1999) *Truman Defeats Dewey*. Lexington, KY.

Donaldson, Scott, and R. H. Winnick. (1992) *Archibald MacLeish: An American Life*. Boston, MA.

Donner, Frank J. (1981) *The Age of Surveillance: The Aims and Methods of America's Political Intelligence System*. New York.

———. (1990) *Protectors of Privilege: Red Squads and Police Repression in Urban America*. Berkeley, CA.

Dooley, Dennis, and Gary D. Engle. (1987) *Superman at Fifty! The Persistence of a Legend*. Cleveland, OH.

Dorinson, Joseph, and Joram Warmund. (1998) *Jackie Robinson: Race, Sports, and the American Dream*. Armonk, NY.

Dormael, Armand van. (1978) *Bretton Woods: Birth of a Monetary System*. London.

Dorman, Joseph. (2000) *Arguing the World: The New York Intellectuals in Their Own Words*. New York.

Dorwart, Jeffery M. (1981) "The Roosevelt-Astor Espionage Ring." *New York History* 62: 307–322.

———. (1991) *Eberstadt and Forrestal: A National Security Partnership, 1909–1949*. College Station, TX.

Douglas, Deborah Gwen. (1996) "The Invention of Airports: A Political, Economic, and Technological History of Airports in the United States, 1919–1939." PhD diss., University of Pennsylvania.

Douglas, Susan J. (1987) *Inventing American Broadcasting, 1899–1922*. Baltimore, MD.

———. (1999) *Listening In: Radio and the American Imagination*. New York.

Douglass, Paul. (1954) *Six Upon the World: Toward an American Culture for an Industrial Age*. Boston, MA.

Dow, W. G. (1954) *Report on Visits to European Electron Tube Laboratories, 1953*. Ann Arbor, MI.

Dower, John W. (1986) *War without Mercy: Race and Power in the Pacific War*. New York.

———. (1999) *Embracing Defeat: Japan in the Wake of World War II*. New York.

Drąg-Korga, Iwona. (2007) "The Information Policy of the Polish Government-in-Exile toward the American Public During World War II." *Polish American Studies* 64: 27–45.

Draper, Hal. (1967a) "The Student Movement of the Thirties: A Political History." In *As We Saw the Thirties: Essays on Social and Political Movements of a Decade*, edited by Rita James Simon. Urbana, IL.

Dratch, Howard. (1974) "The Politics of Child Care in the 1940s." *Science & Society* 38: 167–204.

Drury, Shadia B. (1997) *Leo Strauss and the American Right*. New York.

Duberman, Martin B. (1988) *Paul Robeson*. New York.

———. (2007) *The Worlds of Lincoln Kirstein*. New York.

Dubinsky, David, and A. H. Raskin. (1977) *David Dubinsky: A Life with Labor*. New York.

DuBois, Rachel Davis. (1984) *All This and Something More: Pioneering in Intercultural Education, an Autobiography*. Bryn Mawr, PA.

Dudziak, Mary L. (2000) *Cold War Civil Rights: Race and the Image of American Democracy*. Princeton, NJ.

Duffy, Francis J. (1986) *The New York Harbor Book*. Falmouth, ME.

Duffy, John. (1974) *A History of Public Health in New York City, 1866–1966*. Vol. 2. New York.

Duggan, John P. (1985) *Neutral Ireland and the Third Reich*. Totowa, NJ.

Duke, David Nelson. (2003) *In the Trenches with Jesus and Marx: Harry F. Ward and the Struggle for Social Justice*. Tuscaloosa, AL.

Dunlop, Richard. (1982) *Donovan, America's Master Spy*. Chicago, IL.

Durante, Jimmy, and Jack Kofoed. (1931) *Night Clubs*. New York.

Durkan, Frank. (1998) "Eulogy for Paul O'Dwyer." *New York Irish History* 12: 7–9.

Durso, Joseph. (1979) *Madison Square Garden: 100 Years of History*. New York.

Dvosin, Andrew James. (1977) "Literature in a Political World: The Career and Writings of Philip Rahv." PhD diss., New York University.

Dwight, Eleanor. (2002) *Diana Vreeland*. New York.

Dwyer, T. Ryle. (1973) "The United States and Irish Neutrality, 1939–1945." PhD diss., North Texas State University.

———. (1977) *Irish Neutrality and the USA, 1939–47*. Totowa, NJ.

———. (1988) *Strained Relations: Ireland at Peace and the USA at War, 1941–45*. Totowa, NJ.

Dyson, Michael Eric. (1995) *Making Malcolm: The Myth and Meaning of Malcolm X*. New York.

Eakins, David W. (1969) "Business Planners and America's Postwar Expansion." In *Corporations and the Cold War*, edited by David Horowitz. New York.

Easton, Carol. (1996) *No Intermissions: The Life of Agnes de Mille*. Boston, MA.

Ebenstein, Alan O. (2001) *Friedrich Hayek: A Biography*. New York.

———. (2007) *Milton Friedman: A Biography*. New York.

Eco, Umberto. (1979) "The Myth of Superman." In *The Role of the Reader: Explorations in the Semiotics of Texts*, edited by Umberto Eco. Bloomington, IN.

Edelman, Hendrik. (2006) "Kurt Wolff and Jacques Schiffrin: Two Publishing Giants Start over in America." *Logos* 17: 76–82.

Edelman, Marek. (1946) *The Ghetto Fights*. New York.

Edmonds, Anthony O. (1973) *Joe Louis*. Grand Rapids, MI.

Ehrenreich, Barbara. (2007) *Dancing in the Streets: A History of Collective Joy*. New York.

Ehrenreich, Barbara, Elizabeth Hess, et al. (1992) *Beatlemania: Girls Just Want to Have Fun*. New York.

Ehrt, Adolf, and Gesamtverband deutscher antikommunistischer Vereinigungen. (1933) *Communism in Germany: The Truth About the Communist Conspiracy on the Eve of the National Revolution*. Berlin.

Eichelberger, Clark M. (1977) *Organizing for Peace: A Personal History of the Founding of the United Nations*. New York.

Eiler, Keith E. (1997) *Mobilizing America: Robert P. Patterson and the War Effort, 1940–1945*. Ithaca, NY.

Eisenberg, Carolyn. (1996) *Drawing the Line: The American Decision to Divide Germany, 1944–1949*. New York.

Eisenstadt, Peter R. (2010) *Rochdale Village: Robert Moses, 6,000 Families, and New York City's Great Experiment in Integrated Housing*. Ithaca, NY.

Eleanor Roosevelt Papers. (2003) "Office of Civilian Defense." In *Teaching Eleanor Roosevelt*, edited by Allida Black and June Hopkins. Hyde Park, NY.

Ellis, Edward R. (1966) *The Epic of New York City*. New York.

Ellis, John Tracy. (1983) *Catholic Bishops: A Memoir*. Wilmington, DE.

"Emergency Rescue Committee." (2002) In *The Eleanor Roosevelt Papers: The Eleanor Roosevelt and Human*

Rights Project, edited by George Washington University. Washington, DC.

Emery, Carla. (1998) "Case History: Candy Jones." In *Secret, Don't Tell: The Encyclopedia of Hypnotism*, edited by Carla Emery. Clare, MI.

Engel, David. (1983) "An Early Account of Polish Jewry under Nazi and Soviet Occupation Presented to the Polish Government-in-Exile, February 1940." *Jewish Social Studies* 45: 1–16.

——. (1990) "Jan Karski's Mission to the West, 1942–1944." *Holocaust and Genocide Studies* 5: 363–380.

Engelbrecht, H. C., and Frank Cleary Hanighen. (1934) *Merchants of Death: A Study of the International Armament Industry*. New York.

Eow, Gregory Teddy. (2007) "Fighting a New Deal: Intellectual Origins of the Reagan Revolution, 1932–1952." PhD diss., Rice University.

Epstein, Cynthia Fuchs. (1993) *Women in Law*. Urbana, IL.

Epstein, Edward Jay. (1996) *Dossier: The Secret History of Armand Hammer*. New York.

Epstein, Helen. (1994) *Joe Papp: An American Life*. Boston, MA.

Erdmann, Martin. (2005) *Building the Kingdom of God on Earth: The Churches' Contribution to Marshal Public Support for World Order and Peace, 1919–1945*. Eugene, OR.

Erenberg, Lewis A. (1998) *Swingin' the Dream: Big Band Jazz and the Rebirth of American Culture*. Chicago, IL.

Erie, Steven P. (1988) *Rainbow's End: Irish-Americans and the Dilemmas of Urban Machine Politics, 1840–1985*. Berkeley, CA.

Ernst, Daniel R., and Victor Jew. (2002) *Total War and the Law: The American Home Front in World War II*. Westport, CT.

Ernst, Jimmy. (1984) *A Not-So-Still Life: A Memoir*. New York.

Ernst, Morris Leopold. (1945) *The Best Is Yet*. New York.

Erskine, Hazel. (1973) "The Polls: Corruption in Government." *Public Opinion Quarterly* 37: 628–644.

Esposito, David M., and Jackie R. Esposito. (1988) "LaGuardia and the Nazis, 1933–1938." *American Jewish History* 78: 38–53.

Evans, Redd, and John Jacob Loeb. (1942) *Rosie the Riveter: Words and Music*. New York.

Facing History and Ourselves. (2002) "The Nazi Connection." In *Race and Membership in American History: The Eugenics Movement*, edited by Joseph Blumenthal et al. New York.

Faderman, Lillian. (1991) *Odd Girls and Twilight Lovers: A History of Lesbian Life in Twentieth Century America*. New York.

Fagen, M. D., Amos E. Joel, et al. (1975) *A History of Engineering and Science in the Bell System*. Vols. 2–7. New York.

Fang, Irving E. (1977) *Those Radio Commentators!* Ames, IA.

Farago, Ladislas. (1972) *The Game of the Foxes: The Untold Story of German Espionage in the United States and Great Britain During World War II*. New York.

Farley, James A. (1948) *Jim Farley's Story: The Roosevelt Years*. New York.

Farmer, James. (1985) *Lay Bare the Heart: An Autobiography of the Civil Rights Movement*. New York.

Fashion Group International. (2007) "Fashion Group History." *FGI Archives: Archive Room*, December 4.

Fashion Institute of Technology. (2003) "History / Mission." *About FIT*, December 28.

Feagin, Joe R., and Kelly Riddell. (1990) "The State, Capitalism, and World War II: The U.S. Case." *Armed Forces and Society* 17: 53–79.

Federal Writers' Project. (1938) *New York Panorama: A Comprehensive View of the Metropolis*. New York.

——. (1939) *New York City Guide: A Comprehensive Guide to the Five Boroughs of the Metropolis: Manhattan, Brooklyn, the Bronx, Queens, and Richmond*. New York.

Fee, Elizabeth. (1973) "The Sexual Politics of Victorian Social Anthropology." *Feminist Studies* 1: 23–29.

——. (1979) "Nineteenth Century Craniology: The Study of the Female Skull." *Bulletin of the History of Medicine* 53: 415–433.

Feffer, Andrew. (2005) "The Presence of Democracy: Deweyan Exceptionalism and Communist Teachers in the 1930s." *Journal of the History of Ideas* 66: 79–97.

Feiffer, Jules. (1965) *The Great Comic Book Heroes*. New York.

Feinberg, Alexander. (1945) "The Why of Night Clubs." *New York Times Magazine*, May 20.

Feingold, Henry L. (1992) *A Time for Searching: Entering the Mainstream, 1920–1945*. Baltimore, MD.

Fels, Bradley E. (2001) "That Poland Might Be Free: Polish-American and Polish Efforts to Gain American Support for Poland During the Second World War." PhD diss., University of Kansas.

Fenton, John Y. (1988) *Transplanting Religious Traditions: Asian Indians in America*. New York.

Fermi, Laura. (1968) *Illustrious Immigrants: The Intellectual Migration from Europe, 1930–41*. Chicago, IL.

Fernandez, James D. (2005) "Nueva York." In *Facing Fascism: New Yorkers Remember the Spanish Civil War*, edited by Museum of the City of New York. New York.

Ferrell, Robert H. (1968) *Peace in Their Time: The Origins of the Kellogg-Briand Pact*. Hamden, CT.

——. (1998) *The Dying President: Franklin D. Roosevelt, 1944–1945*. Columbia, MO.

Fetter, Henry D. (2001) "The Party Line and the Color Line: The American Communist Party, the *Daily Worker*, and Jackie Robinson." *Journal of Sport History* 28: 375–402.

——. (2007) "From 'Stooge' to 'Czar': Judge Landis, the Daily Worker and the Integration of Baseball." *American Communist History* 6: 29–63.

Fielding, Raymond. (1978) *The March of Time, 1935–1951*. New York.

Figueroa, Frank M. (2007a) "Miguelito Valdés: 'Mr. Babalú': Act I, Cuban Roots." *Latin Beat Magazine*, October.

——. (2007b) "Miguelito Valdés: 'Mr. Babalú': Act II, New York Transplant." *Latin Beat Magazine*, November.

——. (2010) "New York's Latin Music Landmarks." In *Hispanic New York: A Sourcebook*, edited by Claudio Iván Remeseira. New York.

Filmer, Paul, Val Rimmer, et al. (1999) "Oklahoma! Ideology and Politics in the Vernacular Tradition of the American Musical." *Popular Music* 18: 381–395.

Finan, Christopher M. (2002) *Alfred E. Smith, the Happy Warrior*. New York.

Fingeroth, Danny. (2007) *Disguised as Clark Kent: Jews, Comics, and the Creation of the Superhero*. New York.

Finison, Lorenz J. (1983) "The Society for the Psychological Study of Social Issues, Peace Action, and Theories of

Conflict: 1936–1950." *American Psychologist* 38: 1250–1252.

Finkle, Lee. (1975) *Forum for Protest: The Black Press During World War II*. Rutherford, NJ.

Finnegan, John Patrick, and Romana Danysh. (1998) *Military Intelligence*. Washington, DC.

Firestone, Ross. (1993) *Swing, Swing, Swing: The Life & Times of Benny Goodman*. New York.

Fish, Richard, John Weber, et al. (2004) "Program Details: We Hold These Truths." *NormanCorwin.com*, November 18.

Fisher, James Terence. (1989) *The Catholic Counterculture in America, 1933–1962*. Chapel Hill, NC.

Fisher, Louis. (2003) *Nazi Saboteurs on Trial: A Military Tribunal and American Law*. Lawrence, KS.

Fishman, Robert. (2007) "Revolt of the Urbs: Robert Moses and His Critics." In *Robert Moses and the Modern City: The Transformation of New York*, edited by Hilary Ballon and Kenneth T. Jackson. New York.

Fitch, Robert. (1977) "Planning New York." In *The Fiscal Crisis of American Cities: Essays on the Political Economy of Urban America with Special Reference to New York*, edited by Roger E. Alcaly and David Mermelstein. New York.

———. (1993) *The Assassination of New York*. New York.

FitzGerald, Frances. (1979) *America Revised: History Schoolbooks in the Twentieth Century*. Boston, MA.

Fleming, Donald, and Bernard Bailyn. (1969) *The Intellectual Migration: Europe and America, 1930–1960*. Cambridge, MA.

Fleming, Thomas J. (2001) *The New Dealers' War: Franklin D. Roosevelt and the War within World War II*. New York.

Fletcher, Marvin. (1989) *America's First Black General: Benjamin O. Davis, Sr., 1880–1970*. Lawrence, KS.

Fletcher, Tony. (2009) *All Hopped up and Ready to Go: Music from the Streets of New York, 1927–77*. New York.

Flynn, Edward J. (1947) *You're the Boss*. New York.

Flynn, Elizabeth Gurley. (1942) *Women in the War*. New York.

Flynn, George Q. (1984) "Selective Service and American Blacks During World War II." *Journal of Negro History* 69: 14–25.

Fogarty, Gerald P. (1982) *The Vatican and the American Hierarchy from 1870 to 1965*. Stuttgart, Germany.

———. (2003) "Roosevelt and the American Catholic Hierarchy." In *FDR, the Vatican, and the Roman Catholic Church in America, 1933–1945*, edited by David B. Woolner and Richard G. Kurial. New York.

Fogelson, Robert M. (2001) *Downtown: Its Rise and Fall, 1880–1950*. New Haven, CT.

Foley, James E. (1968) *The Knights of Columbus in the State of New York, 1891–1968*. New York.

Folsom, Franklin. (1991) *Impatient Armies of the Poor: The Story of Collective Action of the Unemployed, 1808–1942*. Niwot, CO.

Foner, Eric. (1998) *The Story of American Freedom*. New York.

Foner, Philip S. (1950) *The Fur and Leather Workers Union: A Story of Dramatic Struggles and Achievements*. Newark, NJ.

———. (1974) *Organized Labor and the Black Worker, 1619–1973*. New York,.

Fones-Wolf, Elizabeth A. (1994) *Selling Free Enterprise: The Business Assault on Labor and Liberalism, 1945–60*. Urbana, IL.

Ford, George Barry. (1969) *A Degree of Difference*. New York.

Fordin, Hugh. (1977) *Getting to Know Him: A Biography of Oscar Hammerstein II*. New York.

Fort Tilden History. (1999) "Nazi U-Boats Attack New York Shipping!" *The History of Fort Tilden NY—1917 to 1974*, November 14.

———. (2000) "Selected Excerpts Pertaining to the Defenses of the Southern New York Harbor." *War Diary of the Eastern Sea Frontier: December 1941–September 1943*, October 23.

———. (2001a) "Fort Tilden's Harbor Entrance Control Post (Advance HECP #2)." *The History of Fort Tilden NY—1917 to 1974*, January 24.

———. (2001b) "Fort Tilden's Mine Casemate." *The History of Fort Tilden NY—1917 to 1974*, September 6.

Fosdick, Harry Emerson. (1934) *The Secret of Victorious Living: Sermons on Christianity Today*. New York.

———. (1956) *The Living of These Days, an Autobiography*. New York.

Foster, John Bellamy, Hannah Holleman, et al. (2008) "The U.S. Imperial Triangle and Military Spending." *Monthly Review*, October 1.

Fotsch, Paul Mason. (2007) *Watching the Traffic Go By: Transportation and Isolation in Urban America*. Austin, TX.

Foucart, Bruno, and François Robichon. (1985) *Normandie: Queen of the Seas*. New York.

Fowler, Dorothy Ganfield. (1981) *A City Church: The First Presbyterian Church in the City of New York, 1716–1976*. New York.

Fox, Daniel M. (2006) "The Significance of the Milbank Memorial Fund for Policy: An Assessment at Its Centennial." *Milbank Quarterly* 84: 5–36.

Fox, Frank W. (1975) *Madison Avenue Goes to War: The Strange Military Career of American Advertising, 1941–45*. Provo, UT.

Fox, Richard G. (1997) "Passage from India." In *Between Resistance and Revolution: Cultural Politics and Social Protest*, edited by Richard Gabriel Fox and Orin Starn. New Brunswick, NJ.

Fox, Richard Wightman. (1976) "Reinhold Niebuhr and the Emergence of the Liberal Realist Faith, 1930–1945." *Review of Politics* 38: 244–265.

———. (1985) *Reinhold Niebuhr: A Biography*. New York.

———. (1990a) "Tragedy, Responsibility, and the American Intellectual, 1925–1950." In *Lewis Mumford: Public Intellectual*, edited by Thomas P. Hughes and Agatha Hughes. New York.

Fox, Stephen. (1990b) *The Unknown Internment: An Oral History of the Relocation of Italian Americans During World War II*. Boston, MA.

———. (1993) *Blood and Power: Organized Crime in Twentieth-Century America*. New York.

Frank, Gelya. (1997) "Jews, Multiculturalism, and Boasian Anthropology." *American Anthropologist* 99: 731–745.

Fraser, Steve. (1991) *Labor Will Rule: Sidney Hillman and the Rise of American Labor*. New York.

Frederick, John T. (1948) "The Quarter Books." *College English* 9: 407–413.

Freed, Stanley A., and Ruth S. Freed. (1983) "Clark Wissler and the Development of Anthropology in the United States." *American Anthropologist, New Series* 85: 800–825.

Freeman, Joshua. (1978) "Delivering the Goods: Industrial Unionism

During World War II." *Labor History* 19: 570–593.

Freeman, Joshua B. (1983) "Catholics, Communists, and Republicans: Irish Workers and the Organization of the Transport Workers Union." In *Working-Class America: Essays on Labor, Community, and American Society*, edited by Daniel J. Walkowitz and Michael H. Frisch. Urbana, IL.

———. (1989) *In Transit: The Transport Workers Union in New York City, 1933–1966*. New York.

Frees, William A. (1970) "Labor Racketeering in the International Longshoremen's Association and Its Impact on the Port of New York." PhD diss., John Jay College of Criminal Justice, City University of New York.

French, Warren. (1964) "The First Year of the Paperback Revolution." *College English* 25: 255–260.

Frey, John Weaver, and H. Chandler Ide. (1946) *A History of the Petroleum Administration for War, 1941–1945*. Washington, DC.

Fried, Albert. (1980) *The Rise and Fall of the Jewish Gangster in America*. New York.

———. (1997) *McCarthyism: The Great American Red Scare*. New York.

Frieden, Jeffrey A. (1987) *Banking on the World: The Politics of American International Finance*. New York.

Friedenson, Joseph, and David Kranzler. (1984) *Heroine of Rescue: The Incredible Story of Recha Sternbuch Who Saved Thousands from the Holocaust*. Brooklyn, NY.

Friedman, Andrea. (1996) "The Habitats of Sex Crazed Perverts: Campaigns against Burlesque in Depression Era New York City." *Journal of the History of Sexuality* 7: 203–238.

Friedman, B. H. (1995a) *Jackson Pollock: Energy Made Visible*. New York.

Friedman, Donald J. (1968) *The Road from Isolation: The Campaign of the American Committee for Non-Participation in Japanese Aggression, 1938–1941*. Cambridge, MA.

Friedman, Milton, and George Joseph Stigler. (1946) *Roofs or Ceilings? The Current Housing Problem*. Irvington-on-Hudson, NY.

Friedman, Murray. (1995b) *What Went Wrong? The Creation and Collapse of the Black-Jewish Alliance*. New York.

Friedman, Robert I. (1990) *The False Prophet: Rabbi Meir Kahane: From FBI Informant to Knesset Member*. Brooklyn, NY.

Friedwald, Will. (1995) *Sinatra! The Song Is You: A Singer's Art*. New York.

Frusciano, Thomas J., and Marilyn H. Pettit. (1997) *New York University and the City: An Illustrated History*. New Brunswick, NJ.

Fry, Varian. (1942) "The Massacre of the Jews." *New Republic*, December 21.

Fryer, Heather. (2002) "Enclosed Worlds in Open Space: Federal Communities and Social Experience in the American West." PhD diss., Boston College.

Fuchs, Daniel. (1934) *Summer in Williamsburg*. New York.

Funigiello, Philip J. (1978) *The Challenge to Urban Liberalism: Federal-City Relations During World War II*. Knoxville, TN.

Furer, Julius Augustus. (1959) *Administration of the Navy Department in World War II*. Washington, DC.

Gabler, Neal. (1994) *Winchell: Gossip, Power, and the Culture of Celebrity*. New York.

Gage, Nicholas. (1972) *Mafia, U.S.A.* Chicago, IL.

Gal, Allon. (1991) *David Ben-Gurion and the American Alignment for a Jewish State*. Bloomington, IN.

Gallagher, Dorothy. (1988) *All the Right Enemies: The Life and Murder of Carlo Tresca*. New Brunswick, NJ.

———. (2006) *Strangers in the House: Life Stories*. New York.

Gallicchio, Marc S. (2000) *The African American Encounter with Japan and China: Black Internationalism in Asia, 1895–1945*. Chapel Hill, NC.

Gallico, Paul. (1938) *Farewell to Sport*. New York.

Galloway, George B., and Twentieth Century Fund. (1942) *Postwar Planning in the United States: An Organizational Directory*. Vols. 1–3. New York.

Gandy, Matthew. (2002) *Concrete and Clay: Reworking Nature in New York City*. Cambridge, MA.

Gannon, Michael. (1990) *Operation Drumbeat: The Dramatic True Story of Germany's First U-Boat Attacks Along the American Coast in World War II*. New York.

Gannon, Robert I. (1962) *The Cardinal Spellman Story*. Garden City, NY.

Garafola, Lynn. (1988) "Toward an American Dance: Dance in the City." In *New York: Culture Capital of the World 1940–1965*, edited by Leonard Wallock. New York.

Garcia, Ofelia, and Joshua A. Fishman. (2002) *The Multilingual Apple: Languages in New York City*. New York.

Gardner, Deborah S. (1982) *Marketplace: A Brief History of the New York Stock Exchange*. New York.

Garfinkel, Herbert. (1959) *When Negroes March: The March on Washington Movement in the Organizational Politics for FEPC*. Glencoe, IL.

Garfinkel, Simson L. (1987) "Radio Research, McCarthyism, and Paul F. Lazarsfeld." PhD diss., Massachusetts Institute of Technology.

Garraty, John A. (1986) *The Great Depression: An Inquiry into the Causes, Course, and Consequences of the Worldwide Depression of the Nineteen-Thirties, as Seen by Contemporaries and in the Light of History*. San Diego, CA.

Garrett, Charles. (1961) *The La Guardia Years: Machine and Reform Politics in New York City*. New Brunswick, NJ.

Gary, Brett. (1999) *The Nervous Liberals: Propaganda Anxieties from World War I to the Cold War*. New York.

Gassner, John. (1948) "Tennessee Williams: Dramatist of Frustration." *College English* 10: 1–7.

Gatell, Frank Otto. (1958) "Independence Rejected: Puerto Rico and the Tydings Bill of 1936." *Hispanic American Historical Review* 38: 25–44.

Gavin, James. (2006) *Intimate Nights: The Golden Age of New York Cabaret*. New York.

Geisel Library and University of California San Diego. (1998) "David Lasser Papers: Background." In *David Lasser Papers, 1931–1994: MSS 0322*, edited by Mandeville Special Collections Library. San Diego, CA.

Geisst, Charles R. (2001) *The Last Partnerships: Inside the Great Wall Street Money Dynasties*. New York.

———. (2004) *Wall Street: A History: From Its Beginnings to the Fall of Enron*. New York.

Gelb, Arthur. (2003) *City Room*. New York.

Gelfand, Lawrence E. (1976) *The Inquiry: American Preparations for Peace, 1917–1919*. Westport, CT.

Gelfand, Mark I. (1975) *A Nation of Cities: The Federal Government* and Urban America, 1933–1965. New York.

———. (1985) "Rexford G. Tugwell and the Frustration of Planning in New York City." *Journal of the American Planning Association* 51: 151–160.

Gentry, Curt. (1991a) *J. Edgar Hoover: The Man and the Secrets.* New York.

Gentry, Tony. (1991b) *Dizzy Gillespie.* New York.

Genuth, Joel. (1988) "Microwave Radar, the Atomic Bomb, and the Background to U. S. Research Priorities in World War II." *Science, Technology, & Human Values* 13: 276–289.

Gerber, Michele Stenehjem. (1976) *An American First: John T. Flynn and the America First Committee.* New Rochelle, NY.

Gerson, Jeffrey Nathan. (1990) "Building the Brooklyn Machine: Irish, Jewish and Black Political Succession in Central Brooklyn, 1919–1964." PhD diss., City University of New York.

Gerson, Simon W. (1976) *Pete: The Story of Peter V. Cacchione, New York's First Communist Councilman.* New York.

Gerstle, Gary. (1989) *Working-Class Americanism: The Politics of Labor in a Textile City, 1914–1960.* New York.

———. (1996) "Interpreting the 'American Way.'" In *The War in American Culture: Society and Consciousness During World War II*, edited by Lewis A. Erenberg and Susan E. Hirsch. Chicago, IL.

———. (1997) "Liberty, Coercion and the Making of Americans." *Journal of American History* 84: 524–558.

———. (2001) *American Crucible: Race and Nation in the Twentieth Century.* Princeton, NJ.

Gettleman, Marvin E. (1977) *Communists in Higher Education: CCNY and Brooklyn College on the Eve of the Rapp-Coudert Investigation, 1935–1939.* New York. Unpublished manuscript, cited with permission.

———. (1982) "Rehearsal for McCarthyism: The New York State Rapp-Coudert Committee and Academic Freedom, 1940–1941." Paper presented at Annual Meeting of the American Historical Association. Washington, DC.

Geyer, Martin H. (2002) "Social Rights and Citizenship During World War II." In *Two Cultures of Rights: The Quest for Inclusion and Participation in Modern America and Germany*, edited by Manfred Berg and Martin H. Geyer. Washington, DC.

Giddins, Gary. (1994) "Leonard Feather: 1914–1994." *Village Voice*, October 11.

———. (1998) *Visions of Jazz: The First Century.* New York.

Gilbert, Martin. (2005) *Churchill and America.* New York.

Gill, Anton. (2003) *Art Lover: A Biography of Peggy Guggenheim.* New York.

Gill, Brendan. (1990) *A New York Life: Of Friends and Others.* New York.

Gillespie, Dizzy. (1979) *To Be, or Not . . . To BOP: Memoirs.* Garden City, NY.

Gilmore, Russell Stanley. (1983) *Guarding America's Front Door: Harbor Forts in the Defense of New York City, with a Guide to the Surviving Structures.* Brooklyn, NY.

Gitler, Ira. (1985) *Swing to Bop: An Oral History of the Transition in Jazz in the 1940s.* New York.

Gitlow, Benjamin. (1971) *The Whole of Their Lives: Communism in America: A Personal History and Intimate Portrayal of Its Leaders.* Freeport, NY.

Glassberg, David. (1990) *American Historical Pageantry: The Uses of Tradition in the Early Twentieth Century.* Chapel Hill, NC.

Glasser, Ruth. (1990) "Paradoxical Ethnicity: Puerto Rican Musicians in Post World War I New York City." *Latin American Music Review/Revista de Música Latinoamericana* 11: 63–72.

———. (1995) *My Music Is My Flag: Puerto Rican Musicians and Their New York Communities, 1917–1940.* Berkeley, CA.

Glazer, Nathan. (1993) "The National Influence of Jewish New York." In *Capital of the American Century: National and International Influence of New York City*, edited by Martin Shefter. New York.

Glazer, Nathan, and Daniel P. Moynihan. (1963) *Beyond the Melting Pot: The Negroes, Puerto Ricans, Jews, Italians, and Irish of New York City.* Cambridge, MA.

Gleason, Abbott. (1995a) *Totalitarianism: The Inner History of the Cold War.* New York.

Gleason, Philip. (1981) "Americans All: World War II and the Shaping of American Identity." *Review of Politics* 43: 511–515.

———. (1992) *Speaking of Diversity: Language and Ethnicity in Twentieth-Century America.* Baltimore, MD.

———. (1995b) *Contending with Modernity: Catholic Higher Education in the Twentieth Century.* New York.

———. (2000) "The Catholic Church in American Public Life in the Twentieth Century." *Logos: A Journal of Catholic Thought and Culture* 3: 85–99.

Glendon, Mary Ann. (2001) *A World Made New: Eleanor Roosevelt and the Universal Declaration of Human Rights.* New York.

Glickman, Lawrence B. (2005) "'Make Lisle the Style': The Politics of Fashion in the Japanese Silk Boycott, 1937–1940." *Journal of Social History* 38: 573–608.

Gobel, Thomas. (1988) "Becoming American: Ethnic Workers and the Rise of the CIO." *Labor History* 29: 173–198.

Goda, Norman. (2004) "Banking on Hitler: Chase National Bank and the *Ruckwanderer* Mark Scheme, 1936–1941." In *U.S. Intelligence and the Nazis*, edited by Richard Breitman. Washington, DC.

Goddard, Stephen B. (1996) *Getting There: The Epic Struggle between Road and Rail in the American Century.* Chicago, IL.

Godfried, Nathan. (2001) "Struggling over Politics and Culture: Organized Labor and Radio Station WEVD During the 1930s." *Labor History* 42: 347–369.

Goebel, Greg. (2020) *The Wizard War: WW2 & the Origins of Radar.* Loveland, CO.

Gold, Mary Jayne. (1980) *Crossroads Marseilles, 1940.* Garden City, NY.

Goldberg, Vicki. (1986) *Margaret Bourke-White: A Biography.* New York.

Goldschmidt, Walter Rochs. (1959) *The Anthropology of Franz Boas: Essays on the Centennial of His Birth.* Menasha, WI.

Goldstein, Eric L. (2006) *The Price of Whiteness: Jews, Race, and American Identity.* Princeton, NJ.

Goldstein, Sidney, and Alice Goldstein. (1995) *Jews on the Move: Implications for Jewish Identity.* Albany, NY.

Gonzalez, Evelyn Diaz. (2004) *The Bronx.* New York.

Goodenow, Ronald K., and Wayne J. Urban. (1977) "George S. Counts: A Critical Appreciation." *The Educational Forum* 41: 167–174.

Goodman, Percival, and Paul Goodman. (1944) "A Master Plan for New York." *New Republic*, November 20.

Goodman, Walter. (1968) *The Committee: The Extraordinary Career of the House Committee on Un-American Activities.* New York.

Goodrich, Lloyd. (1983) *Edward Hopper.* New York.

Goodwin, Doris Kearns. (1994) *No Ordinary Time: Franklin and Eleanor Roosevelt: The Home Front in World War II*. New York.

Gordon, David. (2003) "America First: The Anti-War Movement, Charles Lindbergh and the Second World War, 1940–1941." Paper presented at Joint Meeting of the Historical Society and the New York Military Affairs Symposium. New York.

Gordon, Lynn. (1994) "Why Dorothy Thompson Lost Her Job: Political Columnist and the Press Wars of the 1930s and 1940s." *History of Education Quarterly* 34: 281–304.

Gordon, Max. (1980) *Live at the Village Vanguard*. New York.

Gorham, L. Whittington. (1952) "The Tenth Anniversary of the Public Health Research Institute of the City of New York, Inc." *Bulletin of the New York Academy of Medicine* 28: 827–832.

Gormley, Beatrice. (2008) *Malcolm X: A Revolutionary Voice*. New York.

Gosch, Martin A., and Richard Hammer. (1975) *The Last Testament of Lucky Luciano*. Boston, MA.

Gottlieb, Moshe R. (1982) *American Anti-Nazi Resistance, 1933–1941: An Historical Analysis*. New York.

Goulart, Ron. (1986) *Ron Goulart's Great History of Comic Books*. Chicago, IL.

Gould, Harold A. (2006) *Sikhs, Swamis, Students, and Spies: The India Lobby in the United States, 1900–1946*. New Delhi.

Gould, Richard H. (1946) "Post-War Program for Abatement of Pollution in New York Harbor." *American Journal of Public Health* 36: 1293–1298.

Gowan, Peter. (2003) "US: UN." *New Left Review* 24: 5–28.

Graff, Ellen. (1997) *Stepping Left: Dance and Politics in New York City, 1928–1942*. Durham, NC.

Graham, Gordon. (2006) "Kurt Enoch: Paperback Pioneer." *Logos* 17: 28–34.

Granick, Harry. (1991) *Underneath New York*. New York.

Gray, Christopher. (2001) "New York City: December 7, 1941." *City Review*, November 3.

Gray, Wendy, and Robert Knight Barney. (1990) "Devotion to Whom? German-American Loyalty on the Issue of Participation in the 1936 Olympic Games." *Journal of Sport History* 17: 214–231.

Greeley, Andrew M. (1981) *The Irish Americans: The Rise to Money and Power*. New York.

Greeley, Dawn. (1995) "Beyond Benevolence: Gender, Class and the Development of Scientific Charity in New York, 1882–1935." PhD diss., State University of New York at Stony Brook.

Greenberg, Cheryl Lynn. (1991) *'Or Does It Explode?': Black Harlem in the Great Depression*. New York.

———. (1995a) "Ambivalent Allies: African Americans and American Jews after World War II." In *Black Resistance Movements in the United States and Africa, 1800–1993: Oppression and Retaliation*, edited by Felton O. Best. Lampeter, Wales.

———. (1995b) "Black and Jewish Responses to Japanese Internment." *Journal of American Ethnic History* 14: 3–37.

———. (1997) "Negotiating Coalition: Black and Jewish Civil Rights Agencies in the Twentieth Century." In *Struggles in the Promised Land: Toward a History of Black-Jewish Relations in the United States*, edited by Jack Salzman and Cornel West. New York.

———. (1998) "Pluralism and Its Discontents: The Case of Blacks and Jews." In *Insider/Outsider: American Jews and Multiculturalism*, edited by David Biale, Michael Galchinsky, and Susannah Heschel. Berkeley, CA.

———. (2006) *Troubling the Waters: Black-Jewish Relations in the American Century*. Princeton, NJ.

Greenberg, Clement. (1939) "Avant-Garde and Kitsch." *Partisan Review* 6: 34–49.

Greenberg, Jack. (1994) *Crusaders in the Courts: How a Dedicated Band of Lawyers Fought for the Civil Rights Revolution*. New York.

Greenwich Village Society for Historic Preservation. (2002) "Gansevoort Market: A New York City Walking Tour." In *Save Gansevoort Market*, edited by Greenwich Village Society for Historic Preservation. New York.

Gregg, Richard Bartlett. (1934) *The Power of Non-Violence*. Philadelphia, PA.

Gregory, Chester W. (1974) *Women in Defense Work During World War II: An Analysis of the Labor Problem and Women's Rights*. New York.

Gregory, Steven. (1998) *Black Corona: Race and the Politics of Place in an Urban Community*. Princeton, NJ.

Greider, William. (1989) *Secrets of the Temple: How the Federal Reserve Runs the Country*. New York.

Griffin, John Ignatius. (1959) *The Port of New York*. New York.

Griffith, Robert. (1983) "The Selling of America: The Advertising Council and American Politics, 1942–1960." *Business History Review* 57: 388–412.

Griffiths, Frederick T. (2001) "Ralph Ellison, Richard Wright, and the Case of Angelo Herndon." *African American Review* 35: 615–636.

Grobman, Alex. (1998) "What Did They Know? The American Jewish Press and the Holocaust, 1 September 1939–17 December 1942." In *America, American Jews, and the Holocaust*, edited by Jeffrey S. Gurock. New York.

———. (2004) *Battling for Souls: The Vaad Hatzala Rescue Committee in Post-Holocaust Europe*. Jersey City, NJ.

Groppa, Carlos G. (2004) *The Tango in the United States: A History*. Jefferson, NC.

Grosch, Herbert R. J. (1991) *Computer: Bit Slices from a Life*. Novato, CA.

Grose, Peter. (1996a) *Continuing the Inquiry: The Council on Foreign Relations from 1921 to 1996*. New York.

———. (1996b) *Gentleman Spy: The Life of Allen Dulles*. Amherst, MA.

Gross, Michael. (1995) *Model: The Ugly Business of Beautiful Women*. New York.

Groth, Michael. (1983) "The Road to New York: The Emigration of Berlin Journalists, 1933–1945." PhD diss., University of Iowa.

Guggenheim, Peggy. (1946) *Out of This Century: The Informal Memoirs of Peggy Guggenheim*. New York.

———. (1960) *Confessions of an Art Addict*. New York.

Guilbaut, Serge. (1984) *How New York Stole the Idea of Modern Art: Abstract Expressionism, Freedom, and the Cold War*. Chicago, IL.

———. (1990) *Reconstructing Modernism: Art in New York, Paris, and Montreal, 1945–1964*. Cambridge, MA.

Gunther, Lenworth A. (1985) "Flamin' Tongue: The Rise of Adam Clayton Powell, Jr., 1908–1941." PhD diss., Columbia University.

Gurin, David. (1977a) "Trolley Transit in New York: Part I." *National Railway Bulletin* 42, no. 1: 4–14.

———. (1977b) "Trolley Transit in New York: Part II." *National Railway Bulletin* 42, no. 2: 12–42.

Gurock, Jeffrey S. (1998) *America, American*

Jews, and the Holocaust. New York.

Gustav-Wrathall, John Donald. (1998) *Take the Young Stranger by the Hand: Same-Sex Relations and the YMCA.* Chicago, IL.

Gutek, Gerald Lee. (1984) *George S. Counts and American Civilization: The Educator as Social Theorist.* Macon, GA.

Gutfreund, Owen D. (2004) *Twentieth Century Sprawl: Highways and the Reshaping of the American Landscape.* New York.

———. (2007) "Rebuilding New York in the Auto Age: Robert Moses and His Highways." In *Robert Moses and the Modern City: The Transformation of New York*, edited by Hilary Ballon and Kenneth T. Jackson. New York.

Guthrie, Woody, Leadbelly, et al. (1996) *Almanac Singers: That's Why We're Marching.* Washington, DC.

Hajduk, John C. (2003) "Tin Pan Alley on the March: Popular Music, World War II, and the Quest for a Great War Song." *Popular Music and Society* 26: 497–512.

Halberstam, David. (1993) *The Fifties.* New York.

Hall, Max. (1959) *Made in New York: Case Studies in Metropolitan Manufacturing.* Cambridge, MA.

Hall, Peter Geoffrey, and Paschal Preston. (1988) *The Carrier Wave: New Information Technology and the Geography of Innovation, 1846–2003.* London.

Halper, Donna L. (2001) *Invisible Stars: A Social History of Women in American Broadcasting.* Armonk, NY.

Hamburger, Philip. (2000) *Matters of State: A Political Excursion.* Washington, DC.

Hamill, Pete. (1998) *Why Sinatra Matters.* Boston, MA.

Hamilton, Charles V. (1991) *Adam Clayton Powell, Jr.: The Political Biography of an American Dilemma.* New York.

Hammersmith, Jack L. (1977) "Franklin Roosevelt, the Polish Question, and the Election of 1944." *Mid-America* 59: 5–17.

Handler, Richard. (1990) "Boasian Anthropology and the Critique of American Culture." *American Quarterly* 42: 252–273.

Handy, Robert T. (1987) *A History of Union Theological Seminary in New York.* New York.

Hanes, John W., David Dubinsky, et al. (1944) "Report of Dewey Committee on Employment." In *Public Papers of Thomas E. Dewey: Fifty-First Governor of the State of New York, 1943*, edited by State of New York. Albany, NY.

Hanson, Elizabeth. (2000) *The Rockefeller University: Achievements: A Century of Science for the Benefit of Humankind 1901–2001.* New York.

Harney, Robert F. (1986) "E Pluribus Unum: Louis Adamic and the Meaning of Ethnic History." *Journal of Ethnic Studies* 14: 29–46.

Harrington, Dale. (1999) *Mystery Man: William Rhodes Davis, Nazi Agent of Influence.* Washington, DC.

Harrington, Donald Szantho. (2007) "John Haynes Holmes: The Community Church of New York (1879–1964)." In *Notable American Unitarians, 1936–1961*, edited by Herbert Vetter. Cambridge, MA.

Harris, Benjamin. (1998) "The Perils of a Public Intellectual." *Journal of Social Issues* 54: 79–118.

Harrison, Cynthia Ellen. (1988) *On Account of Sex: The Politics of Women's Issues, 1945–1968.* Berkeley, CA.

Harshav, Benjamin. (2004) *Marc Chagall and His Times: A Documentary Narrative.* Stanford, CA.

Hart, Mitchell Bryan. (2000) *Social Science and the Politics of Modern Jewish Identity.* Stanford, CA.

Hartmann, Susan M. (1982) *The Home Front and Beyond: American Women in the 1940s.* Boston, MA.

Hartzell, Karl Drew, and New York State War Council. (1949) *The Empire State at War: World War II.* Albany, NY.

Hawes, Elizabeth. (1943) *Why Women Cry; or, Wenches with Wrenches.* New York.

Hawkins, Lester G., Jr., and George S. Pettee. (1943) "OWI-Organization and Problems." *Public Opinion Quarterly* 7: 15–33.

Hawley, Ellis Wayne. (1966) *The New Deal and the Problem of Monopoly: A Study in Economic Ambivalence.* Princeton, NJ.

Hayek, Friedrich A. von. (1944) *The Road to Serfdom.* Chicago, IL.

Haygood, Wil. (1993) *King of the Cats: The Life and Times of Adam Clayton Powell, Jr.* Boston, MA.

Haynes, John Earl. (2005) "The American Communist Party as an Auxiliary to Espionage: From Asset to Liability." Paper presented at Raleigh International Spy Conference. Raleigh, NC.

Haynes, John Earl, and Harvey Klehr. (1999) *Venona: Decoding Soviet Espionage in America.* New Haven, CT.

———. (2003) *In Denial: Historians, Communism & Espionage.* San Francisco, CA.

———. (2006a) *Early Cold War Spies: The Espionage Trials That Shaped American Politics.* New York.

———. (2006b) "The Historiography of Soviet Espionage and American Communism: From Separate to Converging Paths." Paper presented at European Social Science History Conference. Amsterdam.

Headquarters of the Eastern Sea Frontier. (1942a) *War Diary: North Atlantic Naval Coastal Frontier, February 1942.* New York.

———. (1942b) *War Diary: North Atlantic Naval Coastal Frontier, January 1942.* New York.

Heckscher, August, and Phyllis C. Robinson. (1978) *When La Guardia Was Mayor: New York's Legendary Years.* New York.

Hegarty, Marilyn E. (1998a) "Patriot or Prostitute? Sexual Discourses, Print Media, and American Women During World War II." *Journal of Women's History* 10: 112–136.

———. (1998b) "Patriots, Prostitutes, Patriotutes: The Mobilization and Control of Female Sexuality in the United States During World War II." PhD diss., Ohio State University.

———. (2008) *Victory Girls, Khaki-Wackies, and Patriotutes: The Regulation of Female Sexuality During World War II.* New York.

Hegerman, Susan. (1998) "Franz Boas and Professional Anthropology: On Mapping the Borders of the Modern." *Victorian Studies* 41: 455–484.

Heidelberger, Michael. (1952) "Introductory Remarks: The Public Health Research Institute of the City of New York, Inc." Paper presented at Celebration of Tenth Anniversary of Founding of the Institute. New York.

Heil, Alan L. (2003) *Voice of America: A History.* New York.

Heilbut, Anthony. (1983) *Exiled in Paradise: German Refugee Artists and Intellectuals in America, from the 1930s to the Present.* New York.

Heinrichs, Waldo H. (1988) *Threshold of War: Franklin D. Roosevelt and American Entry into World War II.* New York.

Helleiner, Eric. (1994) *States and the Reemergence of Global Finance: From Bretton Woods to the 1990s.* Ithaca, NY.

Hellman, Geoffrey T. (1976) "You've Simply Got to

Go out and Raise the Scratch." *New Yorker*, October 18.
Helmreich, William B. (2000) *The World of the Yeshiva: An Intimate Portrait of Orthodox Jewry*. Hoboken, NJ.
Henderson, A. Scott. (2000) *Housing & the Democratic Ideal: The Life and Thought of Charles Abrams*. New York.
Hendrickson, Kenneth E., Jr., Michael L. Collins, et al. (2004) *Profiles in Power: Twentieth-Century Texans in Washington*. Austin, TX.
Heppenheimer, T. A. (1996) "What Made Bell Labs Great." *American Heritage's Invention and Technology* 12: 46–56.
Herbert, Brian. (2004) *The Forgotten Heroes: The Heroic Story of the United States Merchant Marine*. New York.
Herder, Dale M. (1971) "Haldeman-Julius, the Little Blue Books, and the Theory of Popular Culture." *Journal of Popular Culture* 4: 881–892.
Herr, Michael. (1990) *Walter Winchell: A Novel*. New York.
Herrera, Hayden. (2003) *Arshile Gorky: His Life and Work*. New York.
Hertzberg, Arthur. (1997) *The Jews in America: Four Centuries of an Uneasy Encounter: A History*. New York.
Herzstein, Robert Edwin. (1989) *Roosevelt & Hitler: Prelude to War*. New York.
———. (1994) *Henry R. Luce: A Political Portrait of the Man Who Created the American Century*. New York.
Hess, Gary R. (1969) "The 'Hindu' in America: Immigration and Naturalization Policies and India, 1917–1946." *Pacific Historical Review* 38: 59–79.
———. (1971) *America Encounters India, 1941–1947*. Baltimore, MD.
Hess, John L. (1997) "Pro-Union, Anti-Fascist, No Ads." *Nation*, July 14.
Hewlett, Richard G., and Oscar E. Anderson. (1962) *The New World, 1939/1946, Volume I: A History of the United States Atomic Energy Commission*. University Park, PA.
Hickam, Homer H. (1989) *Torpedo Junction: U-Boat War Off America's East Coast, 1942*. Annapolis, MD.
Hiebert, Ray Eldon. (1966) *Courtier to the Crowd: The Story of Ivy Lee and the Development of Public Relations*. Ames, IA.
Hietala, Thomas R. (2002) *The Fight of the Century: Jack Johnson, Joe Louis, and the Struggle for Racial Equality*. Armonk, NY.
Higgs, Robert. (1992) "Wartime Prosperity? A Reassessment of the U.S. Economy in the 1940s." *Journal of Economic History* 52: 41–60.
———. (1993) "Private Profit, Public Risk." In *The Sinews of War: Essays on the Economic History of World War II*, edited by Geofrey T. Mills and Hugh Rockoff. Ames, IA.
———. (2004) "Wartime Socialization of Investment: A Reassessment of U.S. Capital Formation in the 1940s." *Journal of Economic History* 64: 500–520.
———. (2009) "Military Keynesianism to the Rescue?" *The Independent Institute*, January 2.
Higham, Charles. (1983) *Trading with the Enemy: An Exposé of the Nazi-American Money Plot, 1933–1949*. New York.
Higham, John. (1955) *Strangers in the Land: Patterns of American Nativism, 1860–1925*. New Brunswick, NJ.
———. (1984a) "Ethnic Pluralism in Modern American Thought." In *Send These to Me: Immigrants in Urban America*, edited by John Higham. Baltimore, MD.
———. (1984b) *Send These to Me: Immigrants in Urban America (Revised Edition)*. Baltimore, MD.
———. (1988) *Strangers in the Land: Patterns of American Nativism, 1860–1925 (Second Edition)*. New Brunswick, NJ.
Hilderbrand, Robert C. (1990) *Dumbarton Oaks: The Origins of the United Nations and the Search for Postwar Security*. Chapel Hill, NC.
Hill, Robert A. (1995) *The FBI's RACON: Racial Conditions in the United States During World War II*. Boston, MA.
Hills, Patricia, and Raphael Soyer. (1983) *Social Concern and Urban Realism: American Painting of the 1930s*. Boston, MA.
Hine, Darlene Clark. (1977) "Blacks and the Destruction of the Democratic White Primary 1935–1944." *Journal of Negro History* 62: 43–59.
Hing, Bill Ong. (1993) *Making and Remaking Asian America through Immigration Policy, 1850–1990*. Stanford, CA.
Hirschmann, Ira Arthur. (1962) *Caution to the Winds*. New York.
Hirsh, Joseph. (1954) *Saturday, Sunday, and Everyday: The History of the United Hospital Fund of New York*. New York.
Hiss, George L. (2006) *The Joe Bostic Story: First Black American Radio Announcer*. Bloomington, IN.
Hobbs, Robert C. (1985) "Early Abstract Expressionism and Surrealism." *Art Journal* 45: 299–302.
Hobson, Christopher Z. (2005) "*Invisible Man* and African American Radicalism in World War II." *African American Review* 39: 355–376.
Hodges, Graham Russell. (2007) *Taxi! A Social History of the New York City Cabdriver*. Baltimore, MD.
Hodgson, Godfrey. (1990) *The Colonel: The Life and Wars of Henry Stimson, 1867–1950*. New York.
———. (2000) *The Gentleman from New York: Daniel Patrick Moynihan: A Biography*. Boston, MA.
Hogan, M. J. (1999) "The American Century: A Roundtable, Part I: Editor's Introduction." *Diplomatic History* 23: 157.
Hollinger, David A. (1995) *Postethnic America: Beyond Multiculturalism*. New York.
Holmes, John Haynes. (1933) "For India's Freedom." *Nation*, February 8.
———. (1959) *I Speak for Myself: The Autobiography of John Haynes Holmes*. New York.
Honey, Maureen. (1984) *Creating Rosie the Riveter: Class, Gender, and Propaganda During World War II*. Amherst, MA.
———. (1995) "Remembering Rosie: Advertising Images of Women in World War II." In *The Home-Front War: World War II and American Society*, edited by Kenneth Paul O'Brien and Lynn H. Parsons. Westport, CT.
Hood, Clifton. (2004) *722 Miles: The Building of the Subways and How They Transformed New York*. Baltimore, MD.
Hoogenboom, Olive. (1987) *The First Unitarian Church of Brooklyn, One Hundred Fifty Years: A History*. Brooklyn, NY.
Hook, Sidney. (1939a) "Academic Freedom and 'the Trojan Horse' in American Education." *Bulletin of the American Association of University Professors* 25: 550–555.
———. (1939b) "Manifesto." *Nation*, May 27.
———. (1987) *Out of Step: An Unquiet Life in the 20th Century*. New York.
Hooks, Gregory Michael. (1991) *Forging the Military-Industrial Complex: World War II's Battle of the Potomac*. Urbana, IL.
Hoopes, Roy. (1985) *Ralph Ingersoll: A Biography*. New York.
Hoopes, Townsend. (1973) *The Devil and John Foster Dulles*. Boston, MA.
Hopkins, Ernest Jerome. (1972) *Our Lawless Police: A Study of the Unlawful

Enforcement of the Law. New York.
Hopkins, Harry. (1941) *The New Deal of Mr. Roosevelt Is the Designate and Invincible Adversary of the New Order of Hitler.* Washington, DC.
Hopkins, June. (1997) "The First and Final Task: Harry Hopkins and the Development of the American Welfare System." PhD diss., Georgetown University.
Horn, Martin. (2000) "A Private Bank at War: J. P. Morgan & Co. And France, 1914–1918." *Business History Review* 74: 85–112.
Horne, Gerald. (1986) *Black and Red: W.E.B. Du Bois and the Afro-American Response to the Cold War, 1944–1963.* Albany, NY.
———. (1993) "The Red and the Black: The Communist Party and African-Americans in Historical Perspective." In *New Studies in the Politics and Culture of US Communism*, edited by Michael E. Brown. New York.
———. (1994) *Black Liberation/Red Scare: Ben Davis and the Communist Party.* Newark, DE.
———. (2004) *Race War: White Supremacy and the Japanese Attack on the British Empire.* New York.
———. (2005) *Red Seas: Ferdinand Smith and Radical Black Sailors in the United States and Jamaica.* New York.
———. (2008) *The End of Empires: African Americans and India.* Philadelphia, PA.
Horowitz, Chaim Morris, and Lawrence J. Kaplan. (1959) *The Jewish Population of the New York Area, 1900–1975.* New York.
Horowitz, Daniel. (1998) *Betty Friedan and the Making of the Feminine Mystique: The American Left, the Cold War, and Modern Feminism.* Amherst, MA.
———. (2004) *The Anxieties of Affluence: Critiques of American Consumer Culture, 1939–1979.* Amherst, MA.
Horowitz, David. (1969) *Corporations and the Cold War.* New York.
Horowitz, Joseph. (1988) *Understanding Toscanini: How He Became an American Culture-God and Helped Create a New Audience for Old Music.* Minneapolis, MN.
Horsefield, J. Keith. (1969) *The International Monetary Fund, 1945–1965: Twenty Years of International Monetary Cooperation. Volume I: Chronicle.* Washington, DC.
Horten, Gerd. (2002) *Radio Goes to War: The Cultural Politics of Propaganda During World War II.* Berkeley, CA.
"Housing: Up from the Potato Fields." (1950) *Time*, July 3.
Howard, Ella. (2007) "Skid Row: Homelessness on the Bowery in the Twentieth Century." PhD diss., Boston University.
Howard, Jane. (1984) *Margaret Mead, a Life.* New York.
Howe, Irving, and Lewis A. Coser. (1957) *The American Communist Party: A Critical History, 1919–1957.* Boston, MA.
Howell, Robert Thomas. (1971) "The Writers' War Board: Writers and World War II." PhD diss., Louisiana State University and Agriculture and Mechanical College.
Howson, Gerald. (1999) *Arms for Spain: The Untold Story of the Spanish Civil War.* New York.
Hoyt, Homer. (1943) "Rebuilding American Cities after the War." *Journal of Land & Public Utility Economics* 19: 364–368.
Huberman, Leo. (1941) *The Great Bus Strike.* New York.
Hudson, Michael. (2003) *Super Imperialism: The Origin and Fundamentals of U.S. World Dominance.* Sterling, VA.
Hudson Waterfront Museum, Robert Foster, et al. (1992) *The Lighterage System in the New York/New Jersey Harbor.* Jersey City, NJ.
Hughes, Terry, and John Costello. (1977) *The Battle of the Atlantic.* New York.
Hulsether, Mark. (1999) *Building a Protestant Left: Christianity and Crisis Magazine, 1941–1993.* Knoxville, TN.
Hülsmann, Jörg Guido. (2007) *Mises: The Last Knight of Liberalism.* Auburn, AL.
Hunt, Andrew E. (2006) *David Dellinger: The Life and Times of a Nonviolent Revolutionary.* New York.
Hurewitz, Daniel. (1997) *Stepping Out: Nine Tours through New York City's Gay and Lesbian Past.* New York.
Hutchinson, John. (1970) *The Imperfect Union: A History of Corruption in American Trade Unions.* New York.
Hutchison, William R. (2003) *Religious Pluralism in America: The Contentious History of a Founding Ideal.* New Haven, CT.
Huthmacher, J. Joseph. (1968) *Senator Robert F. Wagner and the Rise of Urban Liberalism.* New York.
Hyatt, Marshall. (1990) *Franz Boas, Social Activist: The Dynamics of Ethnicity.* New York.
Hyde, H. Montgomery. (1989) *The Quiet Canadian: The Secret Service Story of Sir William Stephenson (Intrepid).* London.
Hyde Park Books. (2003) "Index of Modern Paperback Publishing Houses." *Paperback Books*, May 13.
Iardella, Albert B. (1964) *Western Electric and the Bell System: A Survey of Service.* New York.
Idelson, Shirley. (2007) "Justine Wise Polier and the American Jewish Congress." Paper presented at Seminar in American History, Graduate Center, City University of New York. New York.
IEEE Virtual Museum. (2004) "Bell Labs." *IEEE Virtual Museum*, September 1.
Ignatieff, Michael, and Lukas Haynes. (2003) "Mobilizing Public Support for the United Nations." *Center for Public Leadership Working Paper Series* 03–02: 53–83.
Ikenberry, G. John. (1993) "Creating Yesterday's New World Order: Keynesian 'New Thinking' and the Anglo-American Postwar Settlement." In *Ideas and Foreign Policy: Beliefs, Institutions, and Political Change*, edited by Judith Goldstein and Robert O. Keohane. Ithaca, NY.
Immerman, Richard H. (1999) *John Foster Dulles: Piety, Pragmatism, and Power in U.S. Foreign Policy.* Wilmington, DE.
Imperial War Museum. (2004) *The Battle of the Atlantic: Online Exhibitions.* London.
"Industrial Development on Long Island." (1967) In *A History of Long Island Maps*, edited by Preston R. Bassett, Myron H. Luke, and Harriet Stryker-Rodda. Brooklyn, NY.
Ingalls, Robert P. (1975) *Herbert H. Lehman and New York's Little New Deal.* New York.
Ingham, John N. (1983) *Biographical Dictionary of American Business Leaders.* Westport, CT.
Inter-Council Committee on Post-War Planning. (1944) *Post-War Plans of National Interdenominational Agencies.* New York.
International Registry of Sunken Ships. (2006) "Convoy Routes: WW1 & WW2." *A Guide to Sunk, Missing and Wrecked Ships*, February 2.
Irons, Peter H. (1973) "'The Test Is Poland': Polish Americans and the Origins of the Cold War."

Polish American Studies 30: 5–63.

Isaacs, Edith S. (1967) *Love Affair with a City: The Story of Stanley M. Isaacs.* New York.

Isaacs, Harold Robert. (1980) *Scratches on Our Minds: American Views of China and India.* White Plains, NY.

Isaacson, Walter, and Evan Thomas. (1986) *The Wise Men: Six Friends and the World They Made.* London.

Isenberg, Sheila. (2001) *A Hero of Our Own: The Story of Varian Fry.* New York.

Israelowitz, Oscar. (2000) *Synagogues of New York City: History of a Jewish Community.* Brooklyn, NY.

Isserman, Maurice. (1993) *Which Side Were You On?: The American Communist Party During the Second World War.* Urbana, IL.

———. (2000) "Disloyalty as a Principle: Why Communists Spied." *Foreign Service Journal* 77: 29–38.

Itzkoff, Donald M. (1985) *Off the Track: The Decline of the Intercity Passenger Train in the United States.* Westport, CT.

Jackman, Jarrell C., and Carla M. Borden. (1983) *The Muses Flee Hitler: Cultural Transfer and Adaptation, 1930–1945.* Washington, DC.

Jackson, John P., Jr. (2000) "Blind Law and Powerless Science: The American Jewish Congress, the NAACP, and the Scientific Case against Discrimination, 1945–1950." *Isis* 91: 89–116.

———. (2001) *Social Scientists for Social Justice: Making the Case against Segregation.* New York.

Jackson, John P., Jr., and Nadine M. Weidman. (2004) *Race, Racism, and Science: Social Impact and Interaction.* Santa Barbara, CA.

Jackson, Kenneth T. (1984) "The City Loses the Sword: The Decline of Major Military Activity in the New York Metropolitan Region." In *The Martial Metropolis: U.S. Cities in War and Peace,* edited by Roger W. Lotchin. New York.

———. (1985) *Crabgrass Frontier: The Suburbanization of the United States.* New York.

———. (2007) "Robert Moses and the Rise of New York: The Power Broker in Perspective." In *Robert Moses and the Modern City: The Transformation of New York,* edited by Hilary Ballon and Kenneth T. Jackson. New York.

Jackson, Lawrence Patrick. (2002) *Ralph Ellison: Emergence of Genius.* New York.

Jackson, Walter A. (1990) *Gunnar Myrdal and America's Conscience: Social Engineering and Racial Liberalism, 1938–1987.* Chapel Hill, NC.

Jacobs, Emma. (2022) "Garden Cafeteria (Former, Now Wing Shoon Restaurant)." *Place Matters,* September 24.

Jacobs, Jack. (1996) "A Friend in Need: The Jewish Labor Committee and Refugees from the German Speaking Lands, 1933–1945." *Yivo Annual* 23: 391–417.

Jacobs, Meg. (1997) "'How About Some Meat?': The Office of Price Administration, Consumption Politics, and State Building from the Bottom Up, 1941–1946." *Journal of American History* 84: 910–941.

———. (2004) *Pocketbook Politics: Economic Citizenship in Twentieth-Century America.* Princeton, NJ.

Jacobson, Matthew Frye. (1998) *Whiteness of a Different Color: European Immigrants and the Alchemy of Race.* Cambridge, MA.

Jacoby, Russell. (1987) *The Last Intellectuals: American Culture in the Age of Academe.* New York.

Jaffe, Philip J. (1975) *The Rise and Fall of American Communism.* New York.

Jaffe, Steven H. (2012) *New York at War: Four Centuries of Combat, Fear, and Intrigue in Gotham.* New York.

Jaker, Bill, Frank Sulek, et al. (1998) *The Airwaves of New York: Illustrated Histories of 156 AM Stations in the Metropolitan Area, 1921–1996.* Jefferson, NC.

James, Marquis. (1947) *The Metropolitan Life: A Study in Business Growth.* New York.

Janiewski, Dolores E., and Lois W. Banner. (2004) *Reading Benedict/Reading Mead: Feminism, Race, and Imperial Visions.* Baltimore, MD.

Janken, Kenneth Robert. (1998) "From Colonial Liberation to Cold War Liberalism: Walter White, the NAACP, and Foreign Affairs, 1941–1955." *Ethnic and Racial Studies* 21: 1074–1095.

———. (2003) *White: The Biography of Walter White, Mr. NAACP.* New York.

Jay, Martin. (1996) *The Dialectical Imagination: A History of the Frankfurt School and the Institute of Social Research, 1923–1950.* Berkeley, CA.

Jeffries, John W. (1990) "The 'New' New Deal: FDR and American Liberalism, 1937–1945." *Political Science Quarterly* 105: 397–418.

Jennings, Eric. (2002) "Last Exit from Vichy France: The Martinique Escape Route and the Ambiguities of Emigration." *Journal of Modern History* 74: 289–324.

Jespersen, T. Christopher. (1996) *American Images of China, 1931–1949.* Stanford, CA.

Jessie Smith Noyes Foundation. (2010) "Charles Floyd Noyes: Dean of Real Estate." *Noyes.org,* June 20.

Jewish Women's Archive. (2003) "Henrietta Szold." *Exhibit: Women of Valor,* September 7, 2003.

Joesten, Joachim. (1955) *Dewey, Luciano, and I.* Great Barrington, MA.

Johanek, Michael C., and John L. Puckett. (2007) *Leonard Covello and the Making of Benjamin Franklin High School: Education as If Citizenship Mattered.* Philadelphia, PA.

John Robert Powers Agency. (2008) "Success Stories." *John Robert Powers School System,* August 20.

John W. Hartman Center for Sales, Advertising & Marketing History. (1999) "Brief History of World War Two Advertising Campaigns: War Loans and Bonds." In *Rare Book, Manuscript & Special Collections Library: Ad*Access,* edited by Duke University. Durham, NC.

Johnpoll, Bernard K. (1970) *Pacifist's Progress: Norman Thomas and the Decline of American Socialism.* Chicago, IL.

Johnsen, Julia E. (1942) *Plans for a Post-War World.* New York.

Johnson, Arthur Menzies. (1967) *Petroleum Pipelines and Public Policy, 1906–1959.* Cambridge, MA.

———. (1968) *Winthrop W. Aldrich: Lawyer, Banker, Diplomat.* Boston, MA.

Johnson, Christopher. (2003a) *Claude Lévi-Strauss: The Formative Years.* New York.

Johnson, Lauri. (2002) "'Making Democracy Real': Teacher Union and Community Activism to Promote Diversity in the New York City Public Schools, 1935–1950." *Urban Education* 37: 566–587.

Johnson, Marilynn S. (2003b) *Street Justice: A History of Police Violence in New York City.* Boston, MA.

Johnson, Robert David. (1997) "Anti-Imperialism and the Good Neighbor Policy: Ernest Gruening and Puerto Rican Affairs, 1934–1939." *Journal of Latin American Studies* 29: 89–110.

———. (1998) *Ernest Gruening and the American Dissenting Tradition*. Cambridge, MA.

Johnson, Walter. (1944) *The Battle against Isolation*. Chicago, IL.

Johnstone, Andrew. (2006) "Clark Eichelberger and the Negotiation of Internationalism During World War II." In *The US Government, Citizen Groups and the Cold War*, edited by Helen Laville and Hugh Wilford. Abingdon-on-Thames, UK.

———. (2009) *Dilemmas of Internationalism: The American Association for the United Nations and US Foreign Policy, 1941–1948*. Burlington, VT.

———. (2010) "Americans Disunited: Americans United for World Organization and the Triumph of Internationalism." *Journal of American Studies* 44: 1–18.

Joint Emergency Committee for European Jewish Affairs, Stephen S. Wise, et al. (1943) "Letter to Under Secretary of State Sumner Welles, April 14, 1943." In *Excerpt from a Plan for Rescue of Refugees That Was Submitted to the Bermuda Conference by Jewish Leaders*, edited by PBS.org.

Jones, Delilah. (1994) *Sentimental Journey: Songs of the World War II Era*. New York.

Jones, Gerard. (2004) *Men of Tomorrow: Geeks, Gangsters, and the Birth of the Comic Book*. New York.

Jones, John Bush. (2006) *The Songs That Fought the War: Popular Music and the Home Front, 1939–1945*. Waltham, MA.

Jones, Vincent C. (1985) *Manhattan, the Army and the Atomic Bomb*. Washington, DC.

Jordan, Corey C. (2000) "P-47 Thunderbolt: Aviation Darwinism." *The Cradle of Aviation Series: Seversky Aircraft & Republic Aviation*, February 9.

———. (2005) "Grumman's Ascendency." *The Cradle of Aviation Series: The Grumman Story, 1930–1945*, December 25.

Joselit, Jenna. (1990) *New York's Jewish Jews: The Orthodox Community in the Interwar Years*. Bloomington, IN.

Josephson, Harold. (1974) *James T. Shotwell and the Rise of Internationalism in America*. Rutherford, NJ.

JTA. (2008) "About: History." *JTA.org*, December 17.

Judis, John B. (1988) *William F. Buckley, Jr., Patron Saint of the Conservatives*. New York.

Juno Beach Centre. (2022) *Canada in the Second World War*. Courseulles-sur-Mer, France.

Kahane, Libby. (2008) *Rabbi Meir Kahane: His Life and Thought*. Jerusalem.

Kahler, Miles. (1993) "New York City and the International System: International Strategy and Urban Fortunes." In *Capital of the American Century: The National and International Influence of New York City*, edited by Martin Shefter. New York.

Kahn, E. J. (1951) "Big Operator: Part II." *New Yorker*, December 15.

Kaiser, Charles. (1997) *The Gay Metropolis: 1940–1996*. Boston, MA.

Kallen, Horace M. (1924) *Culture and Democracy in the United States*. New York.

Kallen, Horace M., and Stanley H. Chapman. (1956) *Cultural Pluralism and the American Idea; an Essay in Social Philosophy*. Philadelphia, PA.

Kallen, Horace M., and Milton Ridvas Konvitz. (1987) *The Legacy of Horace M. Kallen*. Rutherford, NJ.

Kallen, Horace Meyer. (1934) *A Free Society*. New York.

Kammen, Michael G. (1996) *The Lively Arts: Gilbert Seldes and the Transformation of Cultural Criticism in the United States*. New York.

Kanawada, Leo V. (1982) *Franklin D. Roosevelt's Diplomacy and American Catholics, Italians, and Jews*. Ann Arbor, MI.

Kane, Bob, and Tom Andrae. (1989) *Batman & Me: An Autobiography*. Forestville, CA.

Kanellos, Nicolás. (1990) *A History of Hispanic Theatre in the United States: Origins to 1940*. Austin, TX.

Kanellos, Nicolás, Kenya Dworkin y Méndez, et al. (2002) *Herencia: The Anthology of Hispanic Literature of the United States*. New York.

Kaplan, James. (1994) *The Airport: Terminal Nights and Runway Days at John F. Kennedy International*. New York.

Kapur, Sudarshan. (1992) *Raising up a Prophet: The African-American Encounter with Gandhi*. Boston, MA.

Karski, Jan. (1944) *Story of a Secret State*. Boston, MA.

Katz, Shmuel. (1996) *Lone Wolf: A Biography of Vladimir (Ze'ev) Jabotinsky*. Vols. 1 & 2. New York.

Katznelson, Ira. (2005) *When Affirmative Action Was White: An Untold History of Racial Inequality in Twentieth-Century America*. New York.

Katznelson, Ira, and Bruce Pietrykowski. (1991) "Rebuilding the American State: Evidence from the 1940s." *Studies in American Political Development* 5: 301–339.

Kaufman, Menahem. (1991) *An Ambiguous Partnership: Non-Zionists and Zionists in America, 1939–1948*. Detroit, MI.

Kavieff, Paul R. (2005) *The Life and Times of Lepke Buchalter: America's Most Ruthless Labor Racketeer*. Fort Lee, NJ.

Kaytor, Marilyn. (1975) *"21": The Life and Times of New York's Favorite Club*. New York.

Kazal, Russell A. (1995) "Revisiting Assimilation: The Rise, Fall, and Reappraisal of a Concept in American Ethnic History." *American Historical Review* 100: 437–471.

Kazan, Elia. (1997) *Elia Kazan: A Life*. New York.

Kazanjian, Dodie, and Calvin Tomkins. (1993) *Alex: The Life of Alexander Liberman*. New York.

Kazin, Alfred. (1996) *New York Jew*. Syracuse, NY.

Kearney, Reginald. (1998) *African American Views of the Japanese: Solidarity or Sedition?* Albany, NY.

Kearns, Jack, and Oscar Fraley. (1966) *The Million Dollar Gate*. New York.

Keller, Morton. (1963) *The Life Insurance Enterprise, 1865–1910: A Study in the Limits of Corporate Power*. Cambridge, MA.

Keller, Phyllis. (1971) "George Sylvester Viereck: The Psychology of a German-American Militant." *Journal of Interdisciplinary History* 2: 59–108.

Kelley, Robin D. G. (1992) "The Riddle of the Zoot: Malcolm Little and Black Cultural Politics During World War II." In *Malcolm X: In Our Own Image*, edited by Joe Wood. New York.

———. (1994) *Race Rebels: Culture, Politics, and the Black Working Class*. New York.

Kellogg, Peter J. (1979) "Civil Rights Consciousness in the 1940s." *Historian* 42: 18–41.

Kelly, Barbara M. (1993) *Expanding the American Dream: Building and Rebuilding Levittown*. Albany, NY.

Kelly, Cynthia C. (2007) *The Manhattan Project: The Birth of the Atomic Bomb by Its Creators, Eyewitnesses, and Historians*. New York.

Kempton, Murray. (1955) *Part of Our Time: Some Ruins and Monuments of the Thirties*. New York.

Kennedy, David M. (1999) *Freedom from Fear: The American People* in Depression and War, 1929–1945. New York.

Kenney, William Howland. (1999) *Recorded Music in American Life: The Phonograph and Popular Memory, 1890–1945.* New York.

Kenny, Michael G. (2002) "Toward a Racial Abyss: Eugenics, Wickliffe Draper, and the Origins of the Pioneer Fund." *Journal of History of the Behavioral Sciences* 38: 259–283.

Kent, Allen, Harold Lancour, et al. (1968) *Encyclopedia of Library and Information Science.* New York.

Kershaw, Ian. (2007) *Fateful Choices: Ten Decisions That Changed the World, 1940–1941.* New York.

Kersten, Andrew Edmund. (2006) *Labor's Home Front: The American Federation of Labor During World War II.* New York.

———. (2007) *A. Philip Randolph: A Life in the Vanguard.* Lanham, MD.

Kessin Berman, Elizabeth. (1997) "Moral Triage or Cultural Salvage? The Agendas of Varian Fry and the Emergency Rescue Committee." In *Exiles + Émigrés: The Flight of European Artists from Hitler*, edited by Stephanie Barron et al. Los Angeles, CA.

Kessler, Lauren. (2003) *Clever Girl: Elizabeth Bentley, the Spy Who Ushered in the McCarthy Era.* New York.

Kessler-Harris, Alice. (1988) *A Woman's Wage: Historical Meaning and Social Consequences.* Lexington, KY.

Kessner, Carole S. (1994) *The "Other" New York Jewish Intellectuals.* New York.

Kessner, Thomas. (1989) *Fiorello H. La Guardia and the Making of Modern New York.* New York.

Kevles, Daniel J. (1978) *The Physicists: The History of a Scientific Community in Modern America.* New York.

Khagram, Sanjeev. (2001) "Seen, Rich, but Unheard: The Politics of Asian Indians in the United States." In *Asian Americans and Politics: Perspectives, Experiences, Prospects*, edited by Gordon H. Chang. Stanford, CA.

Khalidi, Rashid. (2009) *Sowing Crisis: The Cold War and American Dominance in the Middle East.* Boston, MA.

Kiernan, Frances. (2000) *Seeing Mary Plain: A Life of Mary McCarthy.* New York.

Killough, Patrick. (1991) "Clark Mell Eichelberger: Mobilizer Extraordinaire of American Public Opinion." wiki/User:John_Z/drafts/Clark_M._Eichelberger, July 26.

Kim, Hyung-chan. (1999) *Distinguished Asian Americans: A Biographical Dictionary.* Westport, CT.

Kimball, Warren F. (1969) *The Most Unsordid Act: Lend-Lease, 1939–1941.* Baltimore, MD.

Kimble, James J. (2001) "Mobilizing the Home Front: War Bonds, Morale, and the U.S. Treasury's Domestic Propaganda Campaign, 1942–1945." PhD diss., University of Maryland.

———. (2006) *Mobilizing the Home Front: War Bonds and Domestic Propaganda.* College Station, TX.

Kimble, James J., and Lester C. Olson. (2006) "Visual Rhetoric Representing Rosie the Riveter: Myth and Misconception in J. Howard Miller's 'We Can Do It!' Poster." *Rhetoric & Public Affairs* 9: 533–569.

Kimeldorf, Howard. (1988) *Reds or Rackets? The Making of Radical and Conservative Unions on the Waterfront.* Berkeley, CA.

Kindell, Don. (2012) "British and Other Navies in World War 2 Day-by-Day: Naval Events, January 1942 (Part 2 of 2)." *Naval History Homepage*, August 4.

King, Richard H. (1987) "Modernism and Mass Culture: The Origins of the Debate." *European Contributions to American Studies* 12: 120–142.

———. (2004) *Race, Culture, and the Intellectuals: 1940–1970.* Washington, DC.

Kirchwey, Freda. (1939) "'Red Totalitarianism.'" *Nation*, May 27.

———. (1944) "Program of Action." *Nation*, March 11.

Kirle, Bruce. (2003) "Reconciliation, Resolution, and the Political Role of *Oklahoma!* In American Consciousness." *Theatre Journal* 55: 251–274.

Kirshenblatt-Gimblett, Barbara. (1995) "Introduction." In *Life Is with People: The Culture of the Shtetl*, edited by Mark Zborowski and Elizabeth Herzog. New York.

———. (2001) "Imagining Europe: The Popular Arts of American Jewish Ethnography." In *Divergent Jewish Cultures: Israel and America*, edited by Deborah Dash Moore and S. Ilan Troen. New Haven, CT.

———. (2005) "The Corporeal Turn." *Jewish Quarterly Review* 95: 447–461.

Kisliuk, Bill. (2002) "Apollo Landings: Delmark Unveils a Treasure Trove." *Boston Phoenix*, May 30.

Kisseloff, Jeff. (1995) *The Box: An Oral History of Television, 1920–1961.* New York.

Klara, Robert. (2010) *FDR's Funeral Train: A Betrayed Widow, a Soviet Spy, and a Presidency in the Balance.* New York.

Klausen, Jytte. (2002) "Did World War II End the New Deal? A Comparative Perspective on Postwar Planning Initiatives." In *The New Deal and the Triumph of Liberalism*, edited by Sidney M. Milkis and Jerome M. Mileur. Amherst, MA.

Kleeblatt, Norman L., Maurice Berger, et al. (2008) *Action/Abstraction: Pollock, de Kooning, and American Art, 1940–1976.* New Haven, CT.

Klehr, Harvey. (1984) *The Heyday of American Communism: The Depression Decade.* New York.

Klehr, Harvey, and John Earl Haynes. (1992) *The American Communist Movement: Storming Heaven Itself.* New York.

Klehr, Harvey, John Earl Haynes, et al. (1995) *The Secret World of American Communism.* New Haven, CT.

Kleinman, Mark L. (2000) *A World of Hope, a World of Fear: Henry A. Wallace, Reinhold Niebuhr, and American Liberalism.* Columbus, OH.

Klejment, Anne, and Nancy L. Roberts. (1996) *American Catholic Pacifism: The Influence of Dorothy Day and the Catholic Worker Movement.* Westport, CT.

Klinger, Jerry. (2007) "Richard Gottheil: The Reluctant Father of American Zionism." *Jewish Magazine*, November.

Kluger, Richard. (1986) *The Paper: The Life and Death of the New York Herald Tribune.* New York.

Koch, Stephen. (2005) *The Breaking Point: Hemingway, Dos Passos, and the Murder of José Robles.* New York.

Koed, Elizabeth. (1992) "A Symbol Transformed: How 'Liberty Enlightening the World' Became 'the Mother of Exiles,'" *The Social Contract*, Spring 1992: 134–142.

Koegel, Otto E. (1971) "The Selection of the Headquarters Site of United Nations in New York in 1946, the Participation Therein by a Westchester County Special Committee and the Conclusion of the Matter by the Late John D. Rockefeller, Jr., in Purchasing a Site on the East River and Presenting It to the United Nations."

New York Public Library Call No. JLF 75–655, 1–237.

Kohler, Robert E. (1976) "The Management of Science: The Experience of Warren Weaver and the Rockefeller Foundation Programme in Molecular Biology." *Minerva* 14: 279–306.

Koistinen, Paul A. C. (1980) *The Military-Industrial Complex: A Historical Perspective*. New York.

———. (2004) *Arsenal of World War II: The Political Economy of American Warfare, 1940–1945*. Lawrence, KS.

Kolko, Gabriel. (1962) "American Business and Germany, 1930–1940." *Western Political Quarterly* 15: 713–728.

Kolko, Joyce, and Gabriel Kolko. (1972) *The Limits of Power: The World and United States Foreign Policy, 1945–1954*. New York.

Kolsky, Thomas A. (1990) *Jews against Zionism: The American Council for Judaism, 1942–1948*. Philadelphia, PA.

Konvitz, Milton Ridvas. (1994) "Horace M. Kallen." In *The "Other" New York Jewish Intellectuals*, edited by Carole S. Kessner. New York.

Koppes, Clayton R., and Gregory D. Black. (1990) *Hollywood Goes to War: How Politics, Profits, and Propaganda Shaped World War II Movies*. Berkeley, CA.

Korey, William. (2001) *NGOs and the Universal Declaration of Human Rights: A Curious Grapevine*. New York.

Kornblum, William. (1978) *West 42nd Street Study: "The Bright Light Zone."* New York.

Kosek, Joseph Kip. (2005) "Richard Gregg, Mohandas Gandhi, and the Strategy of Nonviolence." *Journal of American History* 91: 1318–1348.

Kovel, Joel. (1997) *Red Hunting in the Promised Land: Anticommunism and the Making of America*. Washington, DC.

Kozloff, Max, Karen Levitov, et al. (2002) *New York: Capital of Photography*. New Haven, CT.

Kramer, Frederick A. (2001) *Unifying the Subways: New York City's Rapid Transit System from Unification to the Transit Authority*. New York.

Kramer, Paul. (1981) "Nelson Rockefeller and British Security Coordination." *Journal of Contemporary History* 16: 73–88.

Kramer, Richard. (2002) "'The Sculptural Drama': Tennessee Williams's Plastic Theater." *Tennessee Williams Annual Review* 5: 1–14.

Kramer, Roland L. (1943) "War and Our Merchant Marine." *Annals of the American Academy of Political and Social Science* 230: 48–53.

Kranzler, David. (1987) *Thy Brother's Blood: The Orthodox Jewish Response During the Holocaust*. New York.

———. (2002) "Orthodoxy's Finest Hour: Rescue Efforts During the Holocaust." *Jewish Action* 63: 1–10.

Kranzler, George. (1961) *Williamsburg: A Jewish Community in Transition*. New York.

Kranzler, Gershon. (1988) *Williamsburg Memories*. Lakewood, NJ.

Kraut, Benny. (1988) "Towards the Establishment of the National Conference of Christians and Jews: The Tenuous Road to Religious Goodwill in the 1920s." *American Jewish History* 77: 388–412.

———. (1989) "A Wary Collaboration: Jews, Catholics, and the Protestant Goodwill Movement." In *Between the Times: The Travail of the Protestant Establishment in America, 1900–1960*, edited by William R. Hutchison. New York.

Kroessler, Jeffrey A. (1991) "Building Queens: The Urbanization of New York's Largest Borough." PhD diss., City University of New York.

Kronish, Ronald. (1987) "Horace M. Kallen and John Dewey on Cultural Pluralism and Jewish Education." In *The Legacy of Horace M. Kallen*, edited by Milton Ridvas Konvitz. Rutherford, NJ.

Krook, Susan Pennington. (1993) "An Analysis of Franz Boas' Achievements and Work Emphasis During the Last Five Years of His Life." PhD diss., University of Colorado at Boulder.

Kross, Peter. (2008) "Varian Fry: The American Schindler." *HistoryNet*, February 13, 2008. 1–4.

Kuehl, Warren F., and Lynne Dunn. (1997) *Keeping the Covenant: American Internationalists and the League of Nations, 1920–1939*. Kent, OH.

Kühl, Stefan. (1994) *The Nazi Connection: Eugenics, American Racism, and German National Socialism*. New York.

Kurlansky, Mark. (2006) *The Big Oyster: New York on the Half Shell*. New York.

Kurth, James R. (1993) *Between Europe and America: The New York Foreign Policy Elite*. New York.

Kurth, Peter. (1990) *American Cassandra: The Life of Dorothy Thompson*. Boston, MA.

Kutulas, Judy. (1995) *The Long War: The Intellectual People's Front and Anti-Stalinism, 1930–1940*. Durham, NC.

Kux, Dennis. (1992) *India and the United States: Estranged Democracies, 1941–1991*. Washington, DC

Kuznick, Peter J. (1987) *Beyond the Laboratory: Scientists as Political Activists in 1930s America*. Chicago, IL.

Kwong, Peter. (1979) *Chinatown, New York: Labor and Politics, 1930–1950*. New York.

La Guardia, Fiorello H. (1944) "New York City's Postwar Program." In *NYC Postwar Program: Exhibit of New York City's Post War Program, 500 Park Avenue*, edited by New York City Board of Estimate, New York City Council and New York City Planning Commission. New York.

Lacey, Robert. (1991) *Little Man: Meyer Lansky and the Gangster Life*. Boston, MA.

LaFeber, Walter. (1997) *The Clash: A History of U.S.–Japan Relations*. New York.

Lai, Him Mark. (1991) "The *Kuomintang* in Chinese American Communities before World War II." In *Entry Denied: Exclusion and the Chinese Community in America, 1882–1943*, edited by Sucheng Chan. Philadelphia, PA.

Lairson, Thomas D. (1998) "Revising Postrevisionism: Credibility and Hegemony in the Early Cold War." In *Rethinking the Cold War*, edited by Allen Hunter. Philadelphia, PA.

Lakoff, Sanford A. (1998) *Max Lerner: Pilgrim in the Promised Land*. Chicago, IL.

Lamb, Chris. (2004) *Blackout: The Untold Story of Jackie Robinson's First Spring Training*. Lincoln, NE.

Lamont, Edward M. (1994) *The Ambassador from Wall Street: The Story of Thomas W. Lamont, J. P. Morgan's Chief Executive*. New York.

Lamson, Peggy. (1976) *Roger Baldwin, Founder of the American Civil Liberties Union: A Portrait*. Boston, MA.

Lanctot, Neil. (2004) *Negro League Baseball: The Rise and Ruin of a Black Institution*. Philadelphia, PA.

Landau, Ellen G., and Library of Congress. (1983) *Artists for Victory: An Exhibition Catalog*. Washington, DC.

Landman, J. H. (1934) "Eugenic, Cacogenic and Socially Inadequate

Tendencies in Our Population." In *International Eugenics Congress: A Decade of Progress in Eugenics*, edited by Henry Farnham Perkins and Harry Hamilton Laughlin. Baltimore, MD.

Landmarks Preservation Commission. (2003) *Gansevoort Market Historic District Designation Report*. New York.

———. (2010) *Look Building Designation Report*. New York.

Lane, Frederic Chapin, and United States Maritime Commission. (1951) *Ships for Victory: A History of Shipbuilding under the U.S. Maritime Commission in World War II*. Baltimore, MD.

Lapsley, Hilary. (1999) *Margaret Mead and Ruth Benedict: The Kinship of Women*. Amherst, MA.

Laqueur, Walter. (1972) *A History of Zionism*. London.

Lardner, James, and Thomas A. Reppetto. (2000) *NYPD: A City and Its Police*. New York.

Larrowe, Charles P. (1972) *Harry Bridges: The Rise and Fall of Radical Labor in the United States*. New York.

Lash, Joseph P. (1971) *Eleanor and Franklin: The Story of Their Relationship, Based on Eleanor Roosevelt's Private Papers*. New York.

Lasker, Bruno, and Louis M. Starr. (1957) *The Reminiscences of Bruno Lasker*. Columbia University Oral History Research Office. New York.

Laskin, David. (2000) *Partisans: Marriage, Politics, and Betrayal among the New York Intellectuals*. New York.

Lasner, Matthew Gordon. (2007) "No Lawn to Mow: Co-Ops, Condominiums, and the Revolution in Collective Homeownership in Metropolitan America, 1881–1973." PhD diss., Harvard University.

Lauren, Paul Gordon. (2003) *The Evolution of International Human Rights: Visions Seen*. Philadelphia, PA.

Laurentz, Robert. (1980) "Racial/Ethnic Conflict in the New York City Garment Industry, 1933–1980." PhD diss., State University of New York at Binghamton.

Lavine, Harold. (1940) *Fifth Column in America*. New York.

Lavine, Harold, and James Arthur Wechsler. (1972) *War Propaganda and the United States*. New York.

Lawrence, Greg. (2001) *Dance with Demons: The Life of Jerome Robbins*. New York.

Lawson, Ronald, and Mark D. Naison. (1986) *The Tenant Movement in New York City, 1904–1984*. New Brunswick, NJ.

Lawton, Rebecca E. (1998) *Heroic America: James Daugherty's Mural Drawings from the 1930's*. Poughkeepsie, NY.

Layton, Azza Salama. (2000) *International Politics and Civil Rights Policies in the United States, 1941–1960*. New York.

Le Corbusier. (1947) *UN Headquarters*. New York.

Leach, Eugene E. (1983) "Tuning out Education: The Cooperation Doctrine in Radio, 1922–38." *Current*, August 1983: 1–20.

League for Cultural Freedom and Socialism. (1939) "Manifesto and Appeal." *Nation*, July 15.

League of Free Nations Association. (1918) "Statement of Principles." *The Dial*, November 30.

League to Enforce Peace. (1918) "New Platform of the League to Enforce Peace." *The World Court* 4: 725–726.

Lears, T. J. Jackson. (1994) *Fables of Abundance: A Cultural History of Advertising in America*. New York.

Lederhendler, Eli. (2001) *New York Jews and the Decline of Urban Ethnicity, 1950–1970*. Syracuse, NY.

Lee, Albert. (1980) *Henry Ford and the Jews*. New York.

Lee, Erika. (2002) "The Chinese Exclusion Example: Race, Immigration, and American Gatekeeping, 1882–1924." *Journal of American Ethnic History* 21: 36–62.

Lee, Fred I. (2007) "The Japanese Interment and the Racial State of Exception." *Theory & Event* 10: 1–22.

Lee, Martin A. (2000) *The Beast Reawakens*. New York.

Lee, Paul, and Runoko Rashidi. (2002) "The Making of a Pan-African: Kwame Nkrumah in America." *The Global African Community: History Notes*, April 25, 2002: 1–5.

Lee, R. Alton. (2017) *Publisher for the Masses, Emanuel Haldeman-Julius*. Lincoln, NE.

Lee, Stan. (1974) *Origins of Marvel Comics*. New York.

Leeming, David Adams. (1994) *James Baldwin: A Biography*. New York.

Lefebvre, Andrew. (2007) "Puerto Rico: Quiet Participant." In *Latin America During World War II*, edited by Thomas M. Leonard and John F. Bratzel. Lanham, MD.

Leff, Laurel. (2000) "A Tragic 'Fight in the Family': *The New York Times*, Reform Judaism and the Holocaust." *American Jewish History* 88: 3–51.

———. (2005) *Buried by the Times: The Holocaust and America's Most Important Newspaper*. New York.

Leff, Mark H. (1991) "The Politics of Sacrifice on the American Home Front in World War II." *Journal of American History* 77: 1296–1318.

Leffler, Melvyn P. (1992) *A Preponderance of Power: National Security, the Truman Administration, and the Cold War*. Stanford, CA.

Leiter, Samuel L. (1993) "Theatre on the Home Front: World War II on New York's Stages, 1941–1945." *Journal of American Drama and Theatre* 5: 47–70.

Lemann, Nicholas. (2006) "The Murrow Doctrine." *New Yorker*, January 23, 2006, 38–43.

Leong, Karen J. (2005) *The China Mystique: Pearl S. Buck, Anna May Wong, Mayling Soong, and the Transformation of American Orientalism*. Berkeley, CA.

Lepore, Jill. (2014) *The Secret History of Wonder Woman*. New York.

Lerner, James. (1998) "American League against War and Fascism." In *Encyclopedia of the American Left*, edited by Mari Jo Buhle, Paul Buhle, and Dan Georgakas. New York.

Leslie, Anita. (1964) *The Remarkable Mr. Jerome*. New York.

Lesser, Alexander. (2004) "Franz Boas." In *Totems and Teachers: Key Figures in the History of Anthropology*, edited by Sydel Silverman. Walnut Creek, CA.

Lester, Larry. (2001) *Black Baseball's National Showcase: The East-West All-Star Game, 1933–1953*. Lincoln, NE.

Levenstein, Aaron. (1983) *Escape to Freedom: The Story of the International Rescue Committee*. Westport, CT.

Levenstein, Harvey A. (1981) *Communism, Anti-Communism, and the CIO*. Westport, CT.

Leverich, Lyle. (1995) *Tom: The Unknown Tennessee Williams*. New York.

Lévi-Strauss, Claude. (1985) *The View from Afar*. New York.

———. (1992) *Tristes Tropiques*. New York.

Lévi-Strauss, Claude, and Didier Eribon. (1991) *Conversations with Claude Lévi-Strauss*. Chicago, IL.

Levin, Gail. (1996) "Edward Hopper's 'Nighthawks', Surrealism, and the War." *Art Institute of Chicago Museum Studies* 22: 180–195.

Levine, Daniel. (2000) *Bayard Rustin and the Civil Rights Movement.* New Brunswick, NJ.

Levinson, Marc. (2006) *The Box: How the Shipping Container Made the World Smaller and the World Economy Bigger.* Princeton, NJ.

Levittown Historical Society. (2001) "A Brief History of Levittown, New York." LevittownHistoricalSociety.org, February 13.

Levy, David B. (2002) "Levy on Zuroff, 'The Response of Orthodox Jewry in the United States to the Holocaust: The Activities of the Vaad Ha-Hatzala Rescue Committee, 1939-1945.'" *H-Judaic*, February 2002: 1–21.

Lewis, Alfred Allan. (1978) *Man of the World: Herbert Bayard Swope: A Charmed Life of Pulitzer Prizes, Poker and Politics.* New York.

Lewis, David Levering. (2000) *W. E. B. Du Bois, 1919–1963: The Fight for Equality and the American Century.* New York.

Lewis, Tom. (1991) *Empire of the Air: The Men Who Made Radio.* New York.

Li, Laura Tyson. (2006) *Madame Chiang Kai-Shek: China's Eternal First Lady.* New York.

Lichello, Robert. (1971) *Enrico Fermi, Father of the Atomic Bomb.* Charlotteville, NY.

Lichtenstein, Nelson. (1982) *Labor's War at Home: The CIO in World War II.* New York.

———. (1988) "The Making of the Postwar Working Class: Cultural Pluralism and Social Structure in World War II." *The Historian* 51: 42–63.

———. (2000) "Class Politics and the State During World War Two." *International Labor and Working-Class History* 58: 261–274.

Lieber, Harvey. (1968) "The Politics of Air and Water Pollution Control in the New York Metropolitan Area." PhD diss., Columbia University.

Lieberman, Richard K. (1995) *Steinway & Sons.* New Haven, CT.

Lifka, Thomas E. (1988) *The Concept 'Totalitarianism' and American Foreign Policy, 1933–1949.* 2 vols. New York.

Light, Ivan. (1974) "From Vice District to Tourist Attraction: The Moral Career of American Chinatowns, 1880–1940." *Pacific Historical Review* 43: 367–394.

Limpus, Lowell M. (1939) *Honest Cop, Lewis J. Valentine: Being a Chronicle of the Commissioner's Thirty-Six Years in the New York Police Department.* New York.

Lingeman, Richard R. (1970) *Don't You Know There's a War On? The American Home Front, 1941–1945.* New York.

Link, Daniel J. (2006) "'Every Day Was a Battle': Liberal Anticommunism in Cold War New York, 1944–1956." PhD diss., New York University.

Lippy, Charles H. (2000) *Pluralism Comes of Age: American Religious Culture in the Twentieth Century.* Armonk, NY.

Lipsitz, George. (1994) *Rainbow at Midnight: Labor and Culture in the 1940s.* Urbana, IL.

Lisagor, Nancy, and Frank Lipsius. (1988) *A Law Unto Itself: The Untold Story of the Law Firm of Sullivan & Cromwell.* New York.

Litoff, Judy Barrett, and David C. Smith. (1996) *American Women in a World at War: Contemporary Accounts from World War II.* Wilmington, DE.

———. (2000) *What Kind of World Do We Want? American Women Plan for Peace.* Wilmington, DE.

Little, Douglas. (1990) "Pipeline Politics: America, TAPLINE, and the Arabs." *Business History Review* 64: 255–285.

———. (2002) *American Orientalism: The United States and the Middle East since 1945.* Chapel Hill, NC.

Loftus, John. and Mark Aarons. (1994) *Secret War against the Jews: How Western Espionage Betrayed the Jewish People.* New York.

Lombardi, Vincent. (1980) "Italian American Workers and the Response to Fascism." In *Pane E Lavoro, the Italian American Working Class: Proceedings of the Eleventh Annual Conference of the American Italian Historical Association Held in Cleveland, Ohio, October 27 and 28, 1978 at John Carroll University*, edited by George E. Pozzetta. Toronto, Canada.

Long, Robert Emmet. (2001) *Broadway, the Golden Years: Jerome Robbins and the Great Choreographer-Directors: 1940 to the Present.* New York.

Lorance, Nancy. (2002) "History and the New Deal Art Projects." *W.P.A.—New Deal Art During the Great Depression*, May 24, 2002: 1–3.

Losey, John E., Antonio DiTommaso, et al. (2010) "Regulatory Control: Golden Nematode." *Integrated Pest Management: Cornell University IPM 444*, Fall 2010: 1–2.

Loss, Christopher P. (2003) "Reading between Enemy Lines: Armed Services Editions and World War II." *Journal of Military History* 67: 811–834.

Lott, Eric. (1988) "Double V, Double-Time: Bebops Politics of Style." *Callaloo* 11: 597–605.

"Louis Adamic: His Life, Work, Legacy." (1982) *Spectrum* 4: 1–16.

Louis, Joe, Chester L. Washington, et al. (1947) *My Life Story.* London.

Love, Robert W., Jr. (1994) "The U.S. Navy and Operation Roll of Drums, 1942." In *To Die Gallantly: The Battle of the Atlantic*, edited by Timothy J. Runyan and Jan M. Copes. Boulder, CO.

Lowenfish, Lee. (2009) *Branch Rickey: Baseball's Ferocious Gentleman.* Lincoln, NE.

Lowenstein, Steven M. (1989) *Frankfurt on the Hudson: The German-Jewish Community of Washington Heights, 1933–1983, Its Structure and Culture.* Detroit, MI.

Loza, Steven Joseph. (1999) *Tito Puente and the Making of Latin Music.* Urbana, IL.

Luard, Evan. (1982) *A History of the United Nations.* New York.

Luconi, Stefano. (2001a) "Generoso Pope and Italian-American Voters in New York City." *Studi Emigrazione* 38: 399–422.

———. (2001b) "The Response of Italian Americans to Fascist Antisemitism." *Patterns of Prejudice* 35: 3–23.

———. (2004) "*Il Grido Della Stirpe* and Mussolini's 1938 Racial Legislation." *Shofar: An Interdisciplinary Journal of Jewish Studies* 22: 67–79.

Lukas, Richard C. (1978) *The Strange Allies, the United States and Poland, 1941–1945.* Knoxville, TN.

———. (1982) *Bitter Legacy: Polish-American Relations in the Wake of World War II.* Lexington, KY.

Lurkis, Alexander. (1982) *The Power Brink: Con Edison, a Centennial of Electricity.* New York.

Lynes, Russell. (1973) *Good Old Modern: An Intimate Portrait of the Museum of Modern Art.* New York.

Lynn, Susan. (1992) *Progressive Women in Conservative Times: Racial Justice, Peace, and Feminism, 1945 to the 1960s.* New Brunswick, NJ.

Lyons, Eugene. (1937) *Assignment in Utopia.* New York.

Ma, Xiaohua. (1998) "A Democracy at War: The American Campaign to Repeal Chinese Exclusion in 1943." *Japanese Journal* of American Studies 9: 121–142.

———. (2000) "The Sino-American Alliance During World War II and the Lifting of the Chinese Exclusion Acts." *American Studies International* 38: 39–61.

Maas, Jim. (1985) "Fall from Grace: The Brewster Aeronautical Corporation, 1932–1942." *American Aviation Historical Society Journal* 30: 118–135.

Maas, Peter. (1968) *The Valachi Papers*. New York.

Mabon, Prescott C. (1975) *Mission Communication: The Story of Bell Laboratories*. Murray Hill, NJ.

Mabry, Donald J. (1978) "Mexican Anticlerics, Bishops, Cristeros, and the Devout During the 1920s: A Scholarly Debate." *Journal of Church and State* 20: 81–92.

MacAdams, Lewis. (2001) *Birth of the Cool: Beat, Bebop, and the American Avant-Garde*. New York.

Macdonald, Dwight. (1942) "The (American) People's Century." *Partisan Review* 9: 294–310.

Macdonald, Dwight, and Michael Wreszin. (2001) *A Moral Temper: The Letters of Dwight Macdonald*. Chicago, IL.

MacDonald, Kevin B. (1998) *The Culture of Critique: An Evolutionary Analysis of Jewish Involvement in Twentieth-Century Intellectual and Political Movements*. Westport, CT.

MacDonald, Nancy. (1987) *Homage to the Spanish Exiles: Voices from the Spanish Civil War*. New York.

MacDonnell, Francis. (1995) *Insidious Foes: The Axis Fifth Column and the American Home Front*. New York.

MacPherson, Myra. (2006) *All Governments Lie: The Life and Times of Rebel Journalist I. F. Stone*. New York.

Maddux, Thomas R. (1977) "Red Fascism, Brown Bolshevism: The American Image of Totalitarianism in the 1930s." *The Historian* 40: 85–103.

Madison, James H. (1992) *Wendell Willkie: Hoosier Internationalist*. Bloomington, IN.

Maggin, Donald L. (2005) *Dizzy: The Life and Times of John Birks Gillespie*. New York.

Mahl, Thomas E. (1998) *Desperate Deception: British Covert Operations in the United States, 1939–44*. Washington, DC.

Maksimov, Grigorii Petrovich. (1940) *The Guillotine at Work: Twenty Years of Terror in Russia*. Chicago, IL.

Malcolm X and Alex Haley. (1992) *The Autobiography of Malcolm X*. New York.

Maldonado, A. W. (2006) *Luis Muñoz Marín: Puerto Rico's Democratic Revolution*. San Juan, PR.

Malloy, Sean Langdon. (2002) "The Reluctant Warrior: Henry L. Stimson and the Crisis of 'Industrial Civilization." PhD diss., Stanford University.

Malmgreen, Gail. (1991) "Labor and the Holocaust: The Jewish Labor Committee and the Anti-Nazi Struggle." *Labor's Heritage: Quarterly of the George Meany Memorial Archives* 3: 20–35.

———. (1997) "Jewish Labor and the Holocaust." In *NYU.edu/Library*, edited by Robert F. Wagner Labor Archives and Jewish Labor Committee. New York.

Malmgreen, Gail, and Tamiment Library & Robert F. Wagner Labor Archive. (1997) "Introduction." In *Jewish Labor Committee Collection*, edited by New York University Library. New York.

Manso, Peter. (1994) *Brando: The Biography*. New York.

Marcantonio, Vito. (2002) "Puerto Rico and the Puerto Rican People 1935–1950." In *I Vote My Conscience: Debates, Speeches and Writings of Vito Marcantonio, 1935–1950*, edited by Annette T. Rubinstein. Queens, NY.

Marchand, Roland. (1998) *Creating the Corporate Soul: The Rise of Public Relations and Corporate Imagery in American Big Business*. Berkeley, CA.

Marcus, Sheldon. (1973) *Father Coughlin: The Tumultuous Life of the Priest of the Little Flower*. Boston, MA.

Mardo, Bill. (1998) "Robinson-Robeson." In *Jackie Robinson: Race, Sports and the American Dream*, edited by Joseph Dorinson and Joram Warmund. Armonk, NY.

Margolick, David. (2000) *Strange Fruit: Billie Holiday, Café Society, and an Early Cry for Civil Rights*. Philadelphia, PA.

Mark Borghi Fine Art Inc. (2007) "Hilla Rebay, 1890–1967." *Inventory*, January 11, 2008: 1–2.

Markowitz, Gerald E., and David Rosner. (1996) *Children, Race, and Power: Kenneth and Mamie Clark's Northside Center*. Charlottesville, VA.

Markusen, Ann R. (1991) *The Rise of the Gunbelt: The Military Remapping of Industrial America*. New York.

Marquis, Alice Goldfarb. (1986) *Hopes and Ashes: The Birth of Modern Times, 1929–1939*. New York.

———. (1989) *Alfred H. Barr, Jr.: Missionary for the Modern*. Chicago, IL.

Marshall, Thurgood, and J. Clay Smith. (2003) *Supreme Justice: Speeches and Writings: Thurgood Marshall*. Philadelphia, PA.

Martin, George Whitney. (1976) *Madam Secretary, Frances Perkins*. Boston, MA.

———. (2005) *CCB: The Life and Century of Charles C. Burlingham, New York's First Citizen, 1858–1959*. New York.

Martin, Ralph G. (1969) *Jennie: The Life of Lady Randolph Churchill*. Englewood Cliffs, NJ.

Martin, T. R. (1953) "Inflation: The Second World War." *Current History* 24: 295–301.

Martin, Tony. (1986) *Race First: The Ideological and Organizational Struggles of Marcus Garvey and the Universal Negro Improvement Association*. Dover, MA.

Masland, John W. (1940) "The 'Peace' Groups Join Battle." *Public Opinion Quarterly* 4: 664–673.

Mason, Edward S., and Robert E. Asher. (1973) *The World Bank since Bretton Woods: The Origins, Policies, Operations, and Impact of the International Bank for Reconstruction and Development and the Other Members of the World Bank Group: The International Finance Corporation, the International Development Association, [and] the International Centre for Settlement of Investment Disputes*. Washington, DC.

Massa, Mark Stephen. (1999) *Catholics and American Culture: Fulton Sheen, Dorothy Day, and the Notre Dame Football Team*. New York.

———. (2003) *Anti-Catholicism in America: The Last Acceptable Prejudice*. New York.

Massoni, Kelley. (2006) "'Teena Goes to Market': Seventeen Magazine and the Early Construction of the Teen Girl (as) Consumer." *Journal of American Culture* 29: 31–42.

Matles, James J., and James Higgins. (1975) *Them and Us: Struggles of a Rank-and-File Union*. Boston, MA.

Matos-Rodriguez, Felix V., and Pedro Juan Hernandez. (2001) *Pioneros: Puerto Ricans in New York City, 1892–1948*. Charleston, SC.

Mauch, Christof. (2003) *The Shadow War against Hitler: The Covert Operations of America's Wartime Secret Intelligence Service*. New York.

Maxtone-Graham, John. (2007) *Normandie: France's Legendary Art Deco Ocean Liner*. New York.

May, Lary. (1987) "Making the American Way: Moderne Theatres, Audiences, and the Film Industry, 1929–1945." *Prospects* 12: 107–111.

Mayhew, Robert. (2007) *Essays on Ayn Rand's 'The Fountainhead'*. Lanham, MD.

Mayor, A. Hyatt. (1942) "The Artists for Victory Exhibition." *The Metropolitan Museum of Art Bulletin*, New Series, Vol. 1: 141–143.

Mayor's Committee for World Fashion Center. (1944) *The World Fashion Center: New York City's Post War Business Project No. 1*. New York.

McCarthy, Mary. (1963) *Theatre Chronicles, 1937–1962*. New York.

——. (1992) *Intellectual Memoirs: New York, 1936–1938*. New York.

McCaughey, Robert A. (2003) *Stand, Columbia: A History of Columbia University in the City of New York, 1754–2004*. New York.

——. (2004) "Columbia College Student Life: The Curriculum and the Extra-Curriculum, 1754–2004." In *C250: Columbia's 250th Anniversary*, edited by Roger Lehecka and Kathy Anderson. New York.

McChesney, Robert Waterman. (1993) *Telecommunications, Mass Media, and Democracy: The Battle for the Control of U.S. Broadcasting, 1928–1935*. New York.

McCollam, Douglas. (2003) "Should This Pulitzer Be Pulled?" *Columbia Journalism Review* 42: 43–48.

McConnell, Francis John. (1952) *By the Way: An Autobiography*. New York.

McDaniel, George. (1997) "Madison Grant and the Racialist Movement: The Distinguished Origins of Racial Activism." *American Renaissance* 8: 1–13.

McGoldrick, Joseph D. (1944) "The Super-Block Instead of the Slums." *New York Times Magazine*, November 19.

——. (1945) "City Building and Renewal." *Annals of the American Academy of Political and Social Science* 242: 96–100.

McGowan, Kathleen. (1999) "The Waterfront." *City Limits*, January 1.

McGowan, Sam. (1998) "ATC: Air Transport Command." In *Airlift USA*, edited by Sam McGowan. Houston, TX.

McGreevy, John T. (1996) *Parish Boundaries: The Catholic Encounter with Race in the Twentieth-Century Urban North*. Chicago, IL.

——. (1997) "Thinking on One's Own: Caholicism in the American Intellectual Imagination, 1928–1960." *Journal of American History* 84: 97–131.

——. (2003) *Catholicism and American Freedom: A History*. New York.

McGuire, Phillip. (1983) "Desegregation of the Armed Forces: Black Leadership, Protest and World War II." *Journal of Negro History* 68: 147–158.

McJimsey, George. (1987) *Harry Hopkins: Ally of the Poor and Defender of Democracy*. Cambridge, MA.

McKean, David. (2004) *Tommy the Cork: Washington's Ultimate Insider from Roosevelt to Reagan*. South Royalton, VT.

McNally, Karen. (2008) *When Frankie Went to Hollywood: Frank Sinatra and American Male Identity*. Urbana, IL.

McNeal, Patricia. (1992) "Dorothy Day: Origins of Catholic Pacifism." *Mid-America* 74: 149–170.

McNeil, Genna Rae. (1983) *Groundwork: Charles Hamilton Houston and the Struggle for Civil Rights*. Philadelphia, PA.

McNickle, Chris. (1993) *To Be Mayor of New York: Ethnic Politics in the City*. New York.

——. (1996) "When New York Was Irish, and After." In *The New York Irish*, edited by Ronald H. Bayor and Timothy J. Meagher. Baltimore, MD.

McVetty, Suzanne. (1995) "Catholic Cemeteries in New York City." *The Irish at Home and Abroad* 3: 38–41.

McWilliams, John C. (1990) *The Protectors: Harry J. Anslinger and the Federal Bureau of Narcotics, 1930–1962*. Newark, DE.

Mead, Margaret. (1979) "Anthropological Contributions to National Policies During and Immediately after World War II." In *The Uses of Anthropology*, edited by Walter Rochs Goldschmidt. Washington, DC.

Mead, William B. (1985) *Baseball Goes to War*. Washington, DC.

Meany, Joseph F., Jr. (1994) "Port in a Storm: The Port of New York in World War II." In *To Die Gallantly: The Battle of the Atlantic*, edited by Timothy J. Runyan and Jan M. Copes. Boulder, CO.

Medoff, Rafael. (1987) *The Deafening Silence: American Jewish Leaders and the Holocaust*. New York.

——. (1998) "The Emergence of American Zionism, by Mark A. Raider." *American Jewish History* 86: 367–376.

——. (2002) *Militant Zionism in America: The Rise and Impact of the Jabotinsky Movement in the United States, 1926–1948*. Tuscaloosa, AL.

——. (2003) "The Day the Rabbis Marched on Washington." David S. Wyman Institute for Holocaust Studies, October.

——. (2004) "America's Response to Kristallnacht." David S. Wyman Institute for Holocaust Studies, November.

——. (2008) "The Forgotten Whistle-Blower Who Saved Jews from Hitler." *The Jewish Press*, August 20.

Medoff, Rafael, and William J. vanden Heuvel. (2004) "Should the Allies Have Bombed Auschwitz? William J. Vanden Heuvel vs. Rafael Medoff." *History News Network*, March 29.

Mehlman, Jeffrey. (2000) *Emigré New York: French Intellectuals in Wartime Manhattan, 1940–1944*. Baltimore, MD.

Melton, H. Keith, Robert Wallace, et al. (2020) *Spy Sites of New York City: A Guide to the Region's Secret History*. Washington, DC.

Meskil, Paul. (1973) *Don Carlo, Boss of Bosses*. New York.

Metres, Philip. (2000) "Confusing a Naive Robert Lowell and Lowell Naeve: 'Lost Connections' in 1940s War Resistance at West Street Jail and Danbury Prison." *Contemporary Literature* 41: 661–692.

Mettler, Suzanne. (2005) *Soldiers to Citizens: The G.I. Bill and the Making of the Greatest Generation*. New York.

Meyer, Gerald. (1984) "The FBI's Surveillance of Congressman Vito Marcantonio." *Our Right to Know*, Fall/Winter.

——. (1989) *Vito Marcantonio: Radical Politician, 1902–1954*. Albany, NY.

——. (2002) "Frank Sinatra: The Popular Front and an American Icon." *Science & Society* 66: 311–335.

——. (2003) "When Sinatra Came to Italian Harlem: The 1945 'Race Riot' at Benjamin Franklin High School." In *Are Italians White? How Race Is Made in America*, edited by Jennifer Guglielmo and Salvatore Salerno. New York.

Meyer, Jean A. (1976) *The Cristero Rebellion: The Mexican People between Church and State, 1926–1929*. New York.

Meyer, Kathryn, and Terry M. Parssinen. (1998) *Webs of Smoke: Smugglers, Warlords, Spies, and the History of the International Drug Trade*. Lanham, MD.

Meyer, Leisa D. (1996) *Creating GI Jane: Sexuality and Power in the Women's Army Corps During World War II*. New York.

Meyer, Stephen Grant. (2000) *As Long as They Don't Move Next Door: Segregation and Racial Conflict in American Neighborhoods*. Lanham, MD.

Michaels, Walter Benn. (1995) *Our America: Nativism, Modernism, and Pluralism*. Durham, NC.

Milbank, Caroline Rennolds. (1985) *Couture: The Great Designers*. New York.

——. (1989) *New York Fashion: The Evolution of American Style*. New York.

Milhaud, Edgard. (1946) *Plural Headquarters of U. N. O.? Washington-London-Moscow-Paris-Nanking-Geneva*. Geneva, Switzerland.

Milkman, Paul. (1997) *PM: A New Deal in Journalism, 1940–1948*. New Brunswick, NJ.

Milkman, Ruth. (1987) *Gender at Work: The Dynamics of Job Segregation by Sex During World War II*. Urbana, IL.

Miller, Benjamin. (2000) *Fat of the Land: Garbage of New York—The Last Two Hundred Years*. New York.

——. (2003) "Missing the Train: Gotham's Three-Century Quest for a Continental Connection." Paper presented at the Seminar on Post-WWII New York City. Gotham Center at the Graduate Center of the City University of New York.

Miller, James. (1978) "A Question of Loyalty: American Liberals, Propaganda, and the Italian-American Community, 1939–1943." *Maryland Historian* 9: 49–71.

Miller, Jeff. (2005) *History of American Broadcasting*. Pasco County, FL.

Miller, Rebecca. (1996) "Irish Traditional and Popular Music in New York City: Identity and Social Change, 1930–1975." In *The New York Irish*, edited by Ronald H. Bayor and Timothy J. Meagher. Baltimore, MD.

Miller, Robert Moats. (1958) *American Protestantism and Social Issues, 1919–1939*. Chapel Hill, NC.

——. (1985) *Harry Emerson Fosdick: Preacher, Pastor, Prophet*. New York.

Miller, William D. (1973) *A Harsh and Dreadful Love: Dorothy Day and the Catholic Worker Movement*. New York.

——. (1982) *Dorothy Day: A Biography*. New York.

Millman, Chad. (2006) *The Detonators: The Secret Plot to Destroy America and an Epic Hunt for Justice*. New York.

Milner, Lucille Bernheimer. (1954) *Education of an American Liberal: An Autobiography*. New York.

Mindich, Leonard. (2010) "A Subjective History of the Public Health Research Institute." *Public Health Research Institute Center*, September 7, 2010: 1–3.

Minear, Richard H., and Art Spiegelman. (1999) *Dr. Seuss Goes to War: The World War II Editorial Cartoons of Theodor Seuss Geisel*. New York.

Minganti, Franco. (1990) "'1939: Flying Eyes—Flight, Metropolis, and Icons of Popular Imagination." *Storia Nordamericana* 7: 93–103.

Mintz, Frank P. (1985) *Revisionism and the Origins of Pearl Harbor*. Lanham, MD.

Mirel, Jeffrey. (2002) "Civic Education and Changing Definitions of American Identity, 1900–1950." *Educational Review* 54: 143–152.

Mires, Charlene. (2013) *Capital of the World: The Race to Host the United Nations*. New York.

Misse, Fred B. (1980) "Franklin Roosevelt and the Polish Vote in 1944." *Midwest Quarterly* 21: 317–332.

"Mission to N.Y. Japs." (1943) *Newsweek*, March 8.

Mitchell, C. Bradford, and Edwin K. Linen. (1981) *Every Kind of Shipwork: A History of Todd Shipyards Corporation, 1916–1981*. New York.

Mitchell, Joseph. (1992) *Up in the Old Hotel and Other Stories*. New York.

Mitoma, Glenn Tatsuya. (2008) "Civil Society and International Human Rights: The Commission to Study the Organization of Peace and the Origins of the UN Human Rights Regime." *Human Rights Quarterly* 30: 607–630.

Mize, Sandra Yocum. (2001) "We Are Still Pacifists: Dorothy Day's Pacifism During World War II." In *Dorothy Day and the Catholic Worker Movement: Centenary Essays*, edited by William J. Thorn, Phillip M. Runkel, and Susan Mountin. Milwaukee, WI.

Mjagkij, Nina. (2001) *Organizing Black America: An Encyclopedia of African American Associations*. New York.

Mock, Elizabeth B., and Susanne Wasson-Tucker. (1945) "Tomorrow's Small House: Models and Plans." *Bulletin of the Museum of Modern Art* 12: 3–19.

Modell, John. (1995) "Did the 'Good War' Make Good Workers?" In *The Home-Front War: World War II and American Society*, edited by Kenneth Paul O'Brien and Lynn H. Parsons. Westport, CT.

Modell, Judith Schachter. (1983) *Ruth Benedict, Patterns of a Life*. Philadelphia, PA.

Moliski, Mary, and Ray Boomhower. (2007) "About Elmer Davis." *Coutant.org*, October 16.

Mollenkopf, John H. (1983) *The Contested City*. Princeton, NJ.

Mondlin, Marvin, Roy Meador, et al. (2004) *Book Row: An Anecdotal and Pictorial History of the Antiquarian Book Trade*. New York.

Monkkonen, Eric H. (2001) *Murder in New York City*. Berkeley, CA.

Montalto, Nicholas V. (1982) *A History of the Intercultural Education Movement, 1924–1941*. New York.

Moody, Kim. (1988) *An Injury to All: The Decline of American Unionism*. New York.

Moore, Deborah Dash. (1987) "A New American Judaism." In *Like All the Nations? The Life and Legacy of Judah L. Magnes*, edited by William M. Brinner and Moses Rischin. Albany, NY.

——. (2004) *GI Jews: How World War II Changed a Generation*. Cambridge, MA.

Moore, R. Laurence. (1994) *Selling God: American Religion in the Marketplace of Culture*. New York.

Moran, Eugene F., and Louis Reid. (1956) *Tugboat: The Moran Story*. New York.

Mordden, Ethan. (1992) *Rodgers & Hammerstein*. New York.

——. (1999) *Beautiful Mornin': The Broadway Musical in the 1940s*. New York.

Morison, Elting Elmore. (1960) *Turmoil and Tradition: A Study of the Life and Times of Henry L. Stimson*. New York.

Morison, Samuel Eliot. (1947) *History of United States Naval Operations in World War II*. Boston, MA.

Morris, Benny. (2001) *Righteous Victims: A History of the Zionist-Arab Conflict, 1881–2001*. New York.

——. (2004) *The Birth of the Palestinian Refugee Problem Revisited*. New York.

Morris, Charles R. (1997) *American Catholic: The*

Morris, Jan. (1987) *Manhattan '45*. New York.

Morris, Joe Alex. (1960) *Nelson Rockefeller: A Biography*. New York.

Morse, Arthur D. (1968) *While Six Million Died: A Chronicle of American Apathy*. Woodstock, NY.

Morse, John D. (1972) *Ben Shahn*. New York.

Morsink, Johannes. (1999) *The Universal Declaration of Human Rights: Origins, Drafting, and Intent*. Philadelphia, PA.

Moscow, Warren. (1948) *Politics in the Empire State*. New York.

——. (1968) *Roosevelt and Willkie*. Englewood Cliffs, NJ.

Moser, John E. (2005) *Right Turn: John T. Flynn and the Transformation of American Liberalism*. New York.

Moses, Robert. (1942) "Remarks of Robert Moses on a Public Works Reservoir." In *State Committee on Post War Employment: January 8, 1942*, edited by New York State Post War Employment Committee. New York.

——. (1944) "Mr. Moses Dissects the 'Long Haired Planners': The Park Commissioner Prefers Common Sense to Their Revolutionary Theories." *New York Times Magazine*, June 25.

——. (1970) *Public Works: A Dangerous Trade*. New York.

Mosley, Leonard. (1978) *Dulles: A Biography of Eleanor, Allen and John Foster Dulles and Their Family Network*. New York.

Motley, Mary Penick. (1987) *The Invisible Soldier: The Experience of the Black Soldier, World War II*. Detroit, MI.

Mudd Manuscript Library. (2006) "Biography of Howard C. Petersen." In *Howard C. Petersen Papers, 1915–1995 (Bulk 1935–1970): Finding Aid*, edited by Princeton University Library. Princeton, NJ.

Mullally, Frederic. (2000) *Primo: The Story of 'Man Mountain' Carnera*. Parkwest, NY.

Muller, Jane. (1998) "Paul O'Dwyer, in His Own Words." *New York Irish History* 12: 12–15.

Murphy, Marjorie. (1992) *Blackboard Unions: The AFT and the NEA, 1900–1980*. Ithaca, NY.

Murray, Pauli. (1945) "The Right to Equal Opportunity in Employment." *California Law Review* 33: 388–433.

Museum of Modern Art. (1992) "Historical Note." In *Department of Circulating Exhibitions Records in the Museum of Modern Art Archives: 1931–1990*, edited by Rona Roob and Rachel Wild. New York.

Museum of the City of New York, Jan Seidler Ramirez, et al. (2000) *Painting the Town: Cityscapes of New York: Paintings from the Museum of the City of New York*. New Haven, CT.

Muste, A. J. (1967) "My Experience in the Labor and Radical Struggles of the Thirties." In *As We Saw the Thirties: Essays on Social and Political Movements of a Decade*, edited by Rita James Simon. Urbana, IL.

Muste, A. J., and Nat Hentoff. (1967) *The Essays of A. J. Muste*. Indianapolis, IN.

Myrdal, Gunnar. (1944) *An American Dilemma: The Negro Problem and Modern Democracy*. New York.

"Nabisco Foods Group." (1993) In *International Directory of Company Histories: Vol. 7*, edited by Paula Kepos. Detroit, MI.

Naifeh, Steven, and Gregory White Smith. (1989) *Jackson Pollock: An American Saga*. New York.

Naison, Mark D. (1984) *Communists in Harlem During the Depression*. New York.

——. (1985) "Lefties and Righties: The Communist Party and Sports During the Great Depression." In *Sport in America: New Historical Perspectives*, edited by Donald Spivey. Westport, CT.

——. (1993) "Remaking America: Communists and Liberals in the Popular Front." In *New Studies in the Politics and Culture of US Communism*, edited by Michael E. Brown. New York.

Namikas, Lise. (1999) "The Committee to Defend America and the Debate between Internationalists and Interventionalists, 1939–1941." *The Historian* 61: 843–863.

Namorato, Michael V. (1988) *Rexford G. Tugwell: A Biography*. New York.

Nasaw, David. (2000) *The Chief: The Life of William Randolph Hearst*. Boston, MA.

Nash, Eric Peter, and Norman McGrath. (2010) *Manhattan Skyscrapers*. New York.

Nash, Gary B., Charlotte A. Crabtree, et al. (1997) *History on Trial: Culture Wars and the Teaching of the Past*. New York.

Nash, George H. (2006) *The Conservative Intellectual Movement in America since 1945*. Wilmington, DE.

Nash, Gerald D. (1968) *United States Oil Policy, 1890–1964: Business and Government in Twentieth Century America*. Pittsburgh, PA.

National Cemetery Administration. (2022a) "Cypress Hills National Cemetery." *National Cemetery Administration*, September 12, 2022: 1–6.

——. (2022b) "Long Island National Cemetery." *National Cemetery Administration*, September 12, 2022: 1–8.

National Institutes of Health. (2004a) "Fluorescence to the Rescue (1941–1945)." In *The AMINCO-Bowman SPF*, edited by National Institutes of Health. Bethesda, MD.

——. (2004b) "Goldwater." In *The AMINCO-Bowman SPF*, edited by National Institutes of Health. Bethesda, MD.

National Library of Medicine. (2018) "Index of Physicians." In *Changing the Face of Medicine: Celebrating America's Women Physicians*, edited by Elizabeth Fee, Patricia Tuohy, and Ellen S. More. Bethesda, MD.

National Park Service. (1983) *National Register of Historic Places: Governors Island Nomination Form*. Washington, DC.

——. (2008) "Liberty Ships." *Determining the Facts*, April 13, 2008: 1–3.

National Resources Planning Board and Committee on Long-range Work and Relief Policies. (1942) *Security, Work, and Relief Policies*. Washington, DC.

National Urban League. (1945) *Racial Aspects of Reconversion: A Memorandum Prepared for the President of the United States by the National Urban League*. New York.

Navarro, Vicente. (2006) "How Spain's Church Still Pushes Fascist Agenda." *Counterpunch*, July 19, 2006: 1–7.

Neal, Steve. (1984) *Dark Horse: A Biography of Wendell Willkie*. Garden City, NY.

Neather, Andrew E. (1995) "Twentieth-Century Communism and Anticommunism: The View after the Cold War." *Reviews in American History* 23: 336–341.

Neavill, Gordon B. (2007) "Publishing in Wartime: The Modern Library Series During the Second World War." *Library Trends* 55: 583–596.

Negrón-Muntaner, Frances, and Ramón Grosfoguel. (1997) *Puerto Rican Jam: Rethinking Colonialism and Nationalism*. Minneapolis, MN.

Nelson, Bruce. (1988) *Workers on the Waterfront:*

Seamen, Longshoremen, and Unionism in the 1930s. Urbana, IL.

Nelson, Donald Marr. (1946) *Arsenal of Democracy: The Story of American War Production.* New York.

Nevins, Allan. (1963) *Herbert H. Lehman and His Era.* New York.

"The New York 'Post' Changes Hands." (1939) *Nation,* July 1.

New York City Chapter of the American Guild of Organists. (2006) "The Community Church of New York (Unitarian Universalist Association)." *NYCAGO. org,* February 21.

New York City Civilian Defense Volunteer Office. (1943) *Block Service Leader's Kit, New York City.* New York.

———. (1946) *History of the Civilian Defense Volunteer Office of the City of New York, 1941–1945.* New York.

New York City Department of Parks & Recreation. (2014) "Soundview Park." *NYC Parks: Official Website of the New York City Department of Parks & Recreation,* December 5.

New York City WPA Writers' Project. (1941) *A Maritime History of New York.* New York.

New York Herald Tribune. (1943) "New York Marches On: I. The City's Greatest Industry; II. Why Management Comes Here; III. Its Leadership in Design; IV. The Bright Prospect Ahead." *New York Herald Tribune,* May 5–8.

New York Naval Shipyard. (1951) *A Journal of Progress through a Century and a Half of Service to the Fleet.* Brooklyn, NY.

"New York Opens Its Post-War Exhibit." (1944) *The American City,* May.

New York Public Library Manuscripts and Archives Division. (2015) "Biographical/Historical Information." In *American Friends of Spanish Democracy Records,* *1935–1939,* edited by New York Public Library Manuscripts and Archives Division. New York.

New York State Department of Commerce. (1957) "Brooklyn as an Industrial Center." *New York State Commerce Review* 11: 1–8.

New York State Department of Commerce and M. P. Catherwood. (1943) *New York at Work for Victory and the Future.* New York.

New York State Postwar Public Works Planning Commission. (1944) *Approved State and Municipal Projects.* Albany, NY.

Newhouse, Victoria. (1989) *Wallace K. Harrison, Architect.* New York.

Ng, Franklin. (1998) *The History and Immigration of Asian Americans.* New York.

Nicholson, Ian A. M. (1998) "'The Approved Bureaucratic Torpor': Goodwin Watson, Critical Psychology, and the Dilemmas of Expertise, 1930–1945." *Journal of Social Issues* 54: 29–52.

Nissenson, Marilyn. (2007) *The Lady Upstairs: Dorothy Schiff and the New York Post.* New York.

Noël, Bernard. (1985) *Marseille, New York: Une Liaison Surréaliste.* Marseille.

Nolzen, Armin. (2003) "The Nazi Party and Its Violence against the Jews, 1933–1939: Violence as a Historiographical Concept." *Yad Vashem Studies* 31: 245–285.

Noraian, Monica Cousins. (2001) "The American Business Press and Business Community's Reaction to German Aggression, 1932–1940." *Essays in Economic and Business History* 19: 163–177.

Normand, Roger, and Sarah Zaidi. (2008) *Human Rights at the UN: The Political History of Universal Justice.* Bloomington, IN.

Norris, Robert S. (2007) "Manhattan Project Sites in Manhattan." In *The Manhattan Project: The Birth of the Atomic Bomb by Its Creators, Eyewitnesses, and Historians,* edited by Cynthia C. Kelly. New York.

North American Committee to Aid Spanish Democracy. (1937) *American Democracy vs. The Spanish Hierarchy.* New York.

Norwood, Stephen H. (2003) "Marauding Youth and the Christian Front: Antisemitic Violence in Boston and New York During World War II." *American Jewish History* 91: 233–267.

Norwood, Stephen H., and Harold Brackman. (1995) *Going to Bat for Jackie Robinson: The Jewish Role in Breaking Baseball's Color Line.* Champaign, IL.

Novack, George. (1968) "Radical Intellectuals in the 1930s." *International Socialist Review* 29: 21–34.

Novick, Peter. (1999) *The Holocaust in American Life.* Boston, MA.

Nown, Graham. (1987) *The English Godfather.* London.

Nugent, John Peer. (1971) *The Black Eagle.* New York.

Nurser, John. (2003) "The 'Ecumenical Movement' Churches, 'Global Order,' and Human Rights: 1938–1948." *Human Rights Quarterly* 25: 841–881.

O'Brien, David J. (1968) *American Catholics and Social Reform: The New Deal Years.* New York.

O'Connor, Francis V. (1984) "Review: Fifty Years of Government Versus Art." *Art Journal* 44: 393–400.

O'Donnell, Mary Ann. (2002) "The G.I. Bill of Rights of 1944 and the Creation of America's Modern Middle Class Society." PhD diss., St. John's University.

O'Dwyer, Paul. (1979) *Counsel for the Defense: The Autobiography of Paul O'Dwyer.* New York.

O'Dwyer, William, and Paul O'Dwyer. (1987) *Beyond the Golden Door.* Jamaica, NY.

O'Grady, John. (1930) *Catholic Charities in the United States: History and Problems.* Washington, DC.

O'Haire, Hugh. (1977) "When the Bund Strutted in Yaphank." *New York Times,* May 8, 1977.

O'Reilly, Kenneth. (1983) *Hoover and the Un-Americans: The FBI, HUAC, and the Red Menace.* Philadelphia, PA.

O'Sullivan, Christopher D. (2008) *Sumner Welles, Postwar Planning, and the Quest for a New World Order, 1937–1943.* New York.

Oakes, Walter J. (1944) "Toward a Permanent War Economy?" *Politics,* February 1944: 11–17.

Office of Civilian Mobilization and New York State War Council. (1943) *Fighting the War at Home.* New York.

Office of the House Historian and Office of the Senate Historian. (2021) "Dickstein, Samuel." *Biographical Directory of the United States Congress,* November 22, 2021: 1.

Official Catholic Directory. (1939) New Providence, NJ.

Olmsted, Kathryn S. (2002) *Red Spy Queen: A Biography of Elizabeth Bentley.* Chapel Hill, NC.

Olson, James Stuart. (1988) *Saving Capitalism: The Reconstruction Finance Corporation and the New Deal, 1933–1940.* Princeton, NJ.

On2 Productions. (1999) "The History of Mambo/Salsa." *On2Productions. com,* June 26, 1999, 1–2.

Orenstein, Claudia. (2001) "Agitational Performance, Now and Then." *Theater* 31: 139–151.

Ortiz Garza, José Luis. (2001) "Propaganda Warfare in Mexican Radio During Second World War." *OldRadio.com,* October 22.

Ottanelli, Fraser M. (1991) *The Communist Party of*

the United States from the Depression to World War II. New Brunswick, NJ.

Ottley, Roi. (1942) "A White Folks' War?" *Common Ground* 2: 28–31.

———. (1968) *New World a-Coming*. New York.

Pace, David. (1983) *Claude Lévi-Strauss, the Bearer of Ashes*. Boston, MA.

Packer, George. (2005) "The Spanish Prisoner." *New Yorker*, October 23.

Page, Max. (2008) *The City's End: Two Centuries of Fantasies, Fears, and Premonitions of New York's Destruction*. New Haven, CT.

Pakula, Hannah. (2009) *The Last Empress: Madame Chiang Kai-Shek and the Birth of Modern China*. New York.

Palan, Ronen. (1998) *After the Cold War: International Relations in the Period of the Latest 'New World Order.'* Philadelphia, PA.

Palmer, Jerrell Dean, and John G. Johnson. (2001) "Big Inch and Little Big Inch." In *The Handbook of Texas Online*, edited by Texas State Historical Association. Austin, TX.

Palmer, Phyllis M. (1989) *Domesticity and Dirt: Housewives and Domestic Servants in the United States, 1920–1945*. Philadelphia, PA.

Paper, Lewis J. (1987) *Empire: William S. Paley and the Making of CBS*. New York.

Parascandola, John. (2001) "John Mahoney and the Introduction of Penicillin to Treat Syphilis." *Pharmacy in History* 43: 3–13.

Parmar, Inderjeet. (1995) "The Issue of State Power: A Case Study of the Council on Foreign Relations." *Journal of American Studies* 29: 73–95.

———. (1999a) "The Carnegie Corporation and the Mobilization of Opinion in the United States' Rise to Globalism, 1939–45." *Minerva* 37: 355–378.

———. (1999b) "Mobilizing America for an Internationalist Foreign Policy: The Role of the Council on Foreign Relations." *Studies in American Political Development* 13: 337–373.

———. (2001) "Resurgent Academic Interest in the Council on Foreign Relations." *Politics* 21: 31–39.

———. (2002a) "Anglo-American Elites in the Interwar Years: Idalism and Power in the Intellectual Roots of Chatham House and the Council of Foreign Relations." *International Relations* 16: 53–75.

———. (2002b) "To Relate Knowledge and Action: The Impact of the Rockefeller Foundation on Foreign Policy Thinking During America's Rise to Globalism, 1939–1945." *Minerva* 40: 235–263.

———. (2004) "'...Another Important Group That Needs More Cultivation': The Council on Foreign Relations and the Mobilization of Black Americans for Interventionism, 1939–1941." *Ethnic and Racial Studies* 27: 710–731.

Parmet, Robert D. (2005) *The Master of Seventh Avenue: David Dubinsky and the American Labor Movement*. New York.

Pathé, Ruth E. (1989) "Gene Weltfish (1902–1980)." In *Women Anthropologists: Selected Biographies*, edited by Ute Gacs. Urbana, IL.

Patner, Andrew. (1988) *I. F. Stone: A Portrait*. New York.

Paton-Walsh, Margaret. (2002) *Our War Too: American Women against the Axis*. Lawrence, KS.

Patterson, Orlando. (1977) *Ethnic Chauvinism: The Reactionary Impulse*. New York.

Patterson, Robert P. (1940) "Statement of Policy Submitted by Robert P. Patterson, Assistant Secretary of War and Approved by President Roosevelt: October 9, 1940." *AFRO-Americ@*, October 16, 2002: 1–2.

Paul, James A. (2002) "Great Power Conflict over Iraqi Oil: The World War I Era." *Global Policy Forum*, October.

Pauwels, Jacques R. (2003) "Profits *über Alles*! American Corporations and Hitler." *Labour/Le Travail* 51: 223–249.

Payne, Charles M. (1995) *I've Got the Light of Freedom: The Organizing Tradition and the Mississippi Freedom Struggle*. Berkeley, CA.

Payne, Stanley G. (2004) *The Spanish Civil War, the Soviet Union, and Communism*. New Haven, CT.

Pearson, Roberta E., and William Uricchio. (1991) *The Many Lives of the Batman: Critical Approaches to a Superhero and His Media*. New York.

Peebles, Robert. (1978) "Leonard Covello: A Study of an Immigrant's Contribution to New York City. New York.

Pelinka, Anton, and Renée Schell. (2003) *Democracy Indian Style: Subhas Chandra Bose and the Creation of India's Political Culture*. New Brunswick, NJ.

Pells, Richard H. (1973) *Radical Visions and American Dreams: Culture and Social Thought in the Depression Years*. New York.

Penkower, Monty Noam. (1983) *The Jews Were Expendable: Free World Diplomacy and the Holocaust*. Urbana, IL.

———. (1994) *The Holocaust and Israel Reborn: From Catastrophe to Sovereignty*. Urbana, IL.

———. (2002) *Decision on Palestine Deferred: America, Britain and Wartime Diplomacy, 1939–1945*. London.

Peretti, Burton W. (2007) *Nightclub City: Politics and Amusement in Manhattan*. Philadelphia, PA.

Pérez de Urbel, Justo. (1993) *Catholic Martyrs of the Spanish Civil War, 1936–1939*. Kansas City, MO.

Pérez, Louis A. (1999) *On Becoming Cuban: Identity, Nationality, and Culture*. Chapel Hill, NC.

Pernicone, Nunzio. (2005) *Carlo Tresca: Portrait of a Rebel*. New York.

Perrett, Geoffrey. (1985) *Days of Sadness, Years of Triumph: The American People, 1939–1945*. Madison, WI.

Perrone, Vito, and Leonard Covello. (1998) *Teacher with a Heart: Reflections on Leonard Covello and Community*. New York.

Persico, Joseph E. (1982) *The Imperial Rockefeller: A Biography of Nelson A. Rockefeller*. New York.

———. (1988) *Edward R. Murrow: An American Original*. New York.

Peter, Jozsef. (1983) "The Witnesses." In *The Alger Hiss Story*, edited by Jeff Kisseloff. New York.

Peters, Charles. (2005) *Five Days in Philadelphia: Wendell Willkie, Franklin Roosevelt, and the 1940 Convention That Saved the Western World*. New York.

Peterson, Dale E. (2003) "The American Adamic: Immigrant Bard of Diversity." *Massachusetts Review* 44: 233–250.

Peterson, Robert. (1992) *Only the Ball Was White: A History of Legendary Black Players and All-Black Professional Teams*. New York.

Petkov, Steven, and Leonard Mustazza. (1995) *The Frank Sinatra Reader*. New York.

Petry, Ann. (1946) *The Street*. Boston, MA.

Peyser, Joan. (1998) *Bernstein: A Biography: Revised & Updated*. New York.

Pfanner, Helmut F. (1984) *Exile in New York: German and Austrian Writers after 1933*. Detroit, MI.

Pfizer Inc. (2004) "Timeline: 1900–1950." *Exploring*

Our History, October 2, 2007: 1–3.
Phelps, Christopher. (1997) *Young Sidney Hook: Marxist and Pragmatist*. Ithaca, NY.
Phillips, Kevin. (2004a) *American Dynasty: Aristocracy, Fortune, and the Politics of Deceit in the House of Bush*. New York.
Phillips, Stephen Bennett. (2003) *Margaret Bourke-White: The Photography of Design, 1927–1936*. New York.
Phillips, William. (1976) "How 'Partisan Review' Began." *Commentary* 62: 42–46.
———. (2004b) *A Partisan View: Five Decades of the Politics of Literature*. New Brunswick, NJ.
Phillips-Fein, Kimberly. (2009) *Invisible Hands: The Making of the Conservative Movement from the New Deal to Reagan*. New York.
Pienkos, Donald E. (1991) *For Your Freedom through Ours: Polish-American Efforts on Poland's Behalf, 1863–1991*. New York.
Pierce, Robert Clayton. (1979) "Liberals and the Cold War: Union for Democratic Action and Americans for Democratic Action, 1940–1949." PhD diss., University of Wisconsin–Madison.
Pierpont, Claudia Roth. (2004) "The Measure of America: How a Rebel Anthropologist Waged War on Racism." *New Yorker*, March 8.
Pierson, John Herman Groesbeck. (1946) *Full Employment in Practice*. New York.
Pijl, Kees van der. (1984) *The Making of an Atlantic Ruling Class*. London.
Pitt, James E. (1955) *Adventures in Brotherhood*. New York.
Plummer, Brenda Gayle. (1996) *Rising Wind: Black Americans and U.S. Foreign Affairs, 1935–1960*. Chapel Hill, NC.
Plunz, Richard. (1990) *A History of Housing in New York City: Dwelling Type and Social Change in the American Metropolis*. New York.
Pochna, Marie-France. (1996) *Christian Dior: The Man Who Made the World Look New*. New York.
Pohl, Frances K. (1989) *Ben Shahn: New Deal Artist in a Cold War Climate, 1947–1954*. Austin, TX.
Polaski, Leo, and Glen Williford. (2003) *New York City's Harbor Defenses*. Charleston, SC.
Polcari, Stephen. (1992) "Orozco and Pollock: Epic Transfigurations." *American Art* 6: 36–57.
Polenberg, Richard. (1972) *War and Society: The United States, 1941–1945*. New York.
———. (1995) "World War II and the Bill of Rights." In *The Home-Front War: World War II and American Society*, edited by Kenneth Paul O'Brien and Lynn H. Parsons. Westport, CT.
Pollack, Howard. (1999) *Aaron Copland: The Life and Work of an Uncommon Man*. New York.
Polner, Murray. (2007) *Branch Rickey: A Biography*. Jefferson, NC.
Pomerance, Murray. (2007) *City That Never Sleeps: New York and the Filmic Imagination*. New Brunswick, NJ.
Pope Pius XI. (1937) *Divini Redemptoris: On Atheistic Communism*. The Vatican.
Popple, Charles Sterling. (1952) *Standard Oil Company (New Jersey) in World War II*. New York.
Port of New York Authority. (1941) *The Port of New York*. New York.
———. (1958) *The Port of New York: Port of Progress*. New York.
Porter, Darwin. (2006) *Brando Unzipped: Bad Boy, Megastar, Sexual Outlaw*. New York.
Porter, S. F. (1942) "Refugee Gold Rush." *American Magazine* 134: 46–47, 88–89.
Potter, Jeffrey. (1976) *Men, Money & Magic: The Story of Dorothy Schiff*. New York.
Powell, Adam Clayton. (1971a) *Adam by Adam: The Autobiography of Adam Clayton Powell, Jr.* New York.
Powell, James H. (1971b) "The Concept of Cultural Pluralism in American Social Thought, 1915–1965." PhD diss., University of Notre Dame.
Powell, Josephine. (2007) *Tito Puente: When the Drums Are Dreaming*. Bloomington, IN.
Pozzetta, George E. (1995) "'My Children Are My Jewels': Italian-American Generations During World War II." In *The Home-Front War: World War II and American Society*, edited by Kenneth Paul O'Brien and Lynn H. Parsons. Westport, CT.
Prashad, Vijay. (2000) *The Karma of Brown Folk*. Minneapolis, MN.
Preston, Douglas J. (1986) *Dinosaurs in the Attic: An Excursion into the American Museum of Natural History*. New York.
Price, David H. (2008) *Anthropological Intelligence: The Deployment and Neglect of American Anthropology in the Second World War*. Durham, NC.
Price, Isabel Boiko. (1973) "Black Responses to Anti-Semitism: Negroes and Jews in New York, 1880 to World War II." PhD diss., University of New Mexico.
Pritchett, Wendell Eric. (1997) "From One Ghetto to Another: Blacks, Jews and Public Housing in Brownsville, Brooklyn, 1945–1970." PhD diss., University of Pennsylvania.
———. (2002) *Brownsville, Brooklyn: Blacks, Jews, and the Changing Face of the Ghetto*. Chicago, IL.
Probst, Gerhard F. (1991) *Erwin Piscator and the American Theatre*. New York.
Pruessen, Ronald W. (1982) *John Foster Dulles: The Road to Power*. New York.
Public Health Research Institute. (1942) *Annual Report of the Public Health Research Institute of the City of New York, Inc.* New York.
Puente, Tito, and Jim Payne. (2000) *Tito Puente's Drumming with the Mambo King*. Milwaukee, WI.
Pula, James S. (1995) *Polish Americans: An Ethnic Community*. New York.
Quinley, Harold E., and Charles Y. Glock. (1979) *Anti-Semitism in America*. New York.
Quivik, Fredric L. (2004) *Kaiser's Richmond Shipyards with Special Emphasis on Richmond Shipyard No. 3*. Richmond, CA.
Raab, Selwyn. (2005) *Five Families: The Rise, Decline, and Resurgence of America's Most Powerful Mafia Empires*. New York.
Rabinowitz, Victor. (1996) *Unrepentant Leftist: A Lawyer's Memoir*. Urbana, IL.
Rachlis, Eugene. (1961) *They Came to Kill: The Story of Eight Nazi Saboteurs in America*. New York.
Rachlis, Eugene, and John E. Marqusee. (1963) *The Landlords*. New York.
"Radio Listeners in Panic, Taking War Drama as Fact." (1938) *New York Times*, October 31.
Radosh, Allis, and Ronald Radosh. (2009) *A Safe Haven: Harry S. Truman and the Founding of Israel*. New York.
Radosh, Ronald, and Joyce Milton. (1997) *The Rosenberg File*. New Haven, CT.
Radway, Janice A. (1991) *Reading the Romance: Women, Patriarchy, and Popular Literature*. Chapel Hill, NC.
Raider, Mark A. (1998) *The Emergence of American Zionism*. New York.
———. (2008) "The Aristocrat and the Democrat: Louis Marshall, Stephen Wise and the Challenge of American Jewish Leadership." *American Jewish Journal* 94: 91–113.

———. (2009) "Idealism, Vision, and Pragmatism: Stephen S. Wise, Nahum Goldmann, and Abba Hillel Silver in the United States." In *Nahum Goldmann: Statesman without a State*, edited by Mark A. Raider. Albany, NY.

Raider, Mark A., Jonathan D. Sarna, et al. (1997) *Abba Hillel Silver and American Zionism*. London.

Rampersad, Arnold. (1986) *The Life of Langston Hughes. Volume I: 1902–1941. I, Too, Sing America*. New York.

———. (1988) *The Life of Langston Hughes. Volume II: 1941–1967. I Dream a World*. New York.

Randall, Stephen J. (2005) *United States Foreign Oil Policy since World War I: For Profit and Security*. Montréal, Canada.

Rankin, Rebecca B. (1939) *New York Advancing: World's Fair Edition: The Result of Five Years of Progressive Administration in the City of New York, F. H. La Guardia, Mayor*. New York.

Ransby, Barbara. (2003) *Ella Baker & the Black Freedom Movement: A Radical Democratic Vision*. Chapel Hill, NC.

Rantisi, Norma M. (2004) "The Ascendance of New York Fashion." *International Journal of Urban and Regional Research* 28: 86–106.

Rasmussen, Nicolas. (2002) "Of 'Small Men,' Big Science, and Bigger Business: The Second World War and Biomedical Research in the United States." *Minerva: A Review of Science, Learning and Policy* 40: 115–146.

Raucher, Alan R. (1985) *Paul G. Hoffman: Architect of Foreign Aid*. Lexington, KY.

Ravel, Aviva, and Szmul Zygielbojm. (1980) *Faithful Unto Death: The Story of Arthur Zygielbaum*. Montreal, Quebec.

Ravitch, Diane. (1976) *The Great School Wars: New York City, 1805–1973*. New York.

———. (2000) *Left Back: A Century of Failed School Reforms*. New York.

Ray, Max A., and First United States Army. (1980) *The History of the First United States Army from 1918 to 1980*. Fort Meade, MD.

Raymond, R. J. (1980) "The Economics of Neutrality: The United States, Great Britain, and Ireland's War Economy, 1937–1945." PhD diss., University of Kansas.

———. (1983) "American Public Opinion and Irish Neutrality, 1939–1945." *Eire/Ireland* 18: 20–45.

———. (1985) "David Gray, the Aiken Mission, and Irish Neutrality, 1940–41." *Diplomatic History* 9: 55–71.

Reagan, Patrick D. (1999) *Designing a New America: The Origins of New Deal Planning, 1890–1943*. Amherst, MA.

Reed, Merl Elwyn. (1991) *Seedtime for the Modern Civil Rights Movement: The President's Committee on Fair Employment Practice, 1941–1946*. Baton Rouge, LA.

Reeves, Thomas C. (2001) *America's Bishop: The Life and Times of Fulton J. Sheen*. San Francisco, CA.

Regional Plan Association. (1944) *The Economic Status of the New York Metropolitan Region in 1944*. New York.

———. (1967) *The Region's Growth: A Report of the Second Regional Plan*. New York.

Reich, Cary. (1996) *The Life of Nelson A. Rockefeller: Worlds to Conquer, 1908–1958*. New York.

Reich, Cary, and André Meyer. (1983) *Financier, the Biography of André Meyer: A Story of Money, Power, and the Reshaping of American Business*. New York.

Reid, Constance. (1976) *Courant in Göttingen and New York: The Story of an Improbable Mathematician*. New York.

Reimers, David M. (1998) *Unwelcome Strangers: American Identity and the Turn against Immigration*. New York.

Reinharz, Shulamit, and Mark A. Raider. (2005) *American Jewish Women and the Zionist Enterprise*. Waltham, MA.

Reiss, Marcia, and Brooklyn Historical Society. (2000) *Williamsburg Neighborhood History Guide*. Brooklyn, NY.

"Reles Loan Racket Is Exposed by Amen." (1941) *New York Times*, January 25.

Remak, Joachim. (1957) "'Friends of the New Germany': The Bund and German-American Relations." *Journal of Modern History* 29: 38–41.

Remnick, David. (2000) *Life Stories: Profiles from the New Yorker*. New York.

Remus, Ina. (2002) "Agency History." In *An Inventory to the Records of the World Jewish Congress: 1918–1982*, edited by American Jewish Archives et al. Cincinnati, OH.

Renaud, Terence. (2005) *The Genesis of the Emergency Rescue Committee, 1933–1942*. Boston, MA.

Rezelman, David, F. G. Gosling, et al. (2003) "The Manhattan Project: An Interactive History." In *Office of History & Heritage Resources*, edited by United States Department of Energy.

Rhodes, Richard. (1986) *The Making of the Atomic Bomb*. New York.

Ribuffo, Leo P. (1983) *The Old Christian Right: The Protestant Far Right from the Great Depression to the Cold War*. Philadelphia, PA.

———. (2004) "If We Are All Multiculralists Now, Then What?" *Reviews in American History* 32: 463–470.

Rickard, John Nelson. (1999) *Patton at Bay: The Lorraine Campaign, September to December, 1944*. Westport, CT.

Riebling, Mark. (1994) *Wedge: The Secret War between the FBI and CIA*. New York.

Riess, Steven A. (1988) "Only the Ring Was Square: Frankie Carbo and the Underworld Control of American Boxing." *International Journal of the History of Sport* 5: 29–52.

———. (1989) *City Games: The Evolution of American Urban Society and the Rise of Sports*. Urbana, IL.

Rigden, John S. (2000) *Rabi, Scientist and Citizen*. Cambridge, MA.

Ritter, Lawrence S. (1998) *East Side, West Side: Tales of New York Sporting Life, 1910–1960*. New York.

Ritter, Lawrence S., and Mark Rucker. (1988) *The Babe: A Life in Pictures*. New York.

Rivas, Darlene. (2002) *Missionary Capitalist: Nelson Rockefeller in Venezuela*. Chapel Hill, NC.

Roberts, Allen. (1984a) *Robert Francis Kennedy: Biography of a Compulsive Politician*. Brookline Village, MA.

Roberts, Jerry, and Larry Sowinski. (1993) "The Battle of the Atlantic." *Sea History: Journal of the National Maritime Historical Society* 66: 8–15.

Roberts, John Storm. (1999) *The Latin Tinge: The Impact of Latin American Music on the United States*. New York.

Roberts, Nancy L. (1984b) *Dorothy Day and the Catholic Worker*. Albany, NY.

Roberts, Priscilla. (2001a) "'The Council Has Been Your Creation': Hamilton Fish Armstrong, Paradigm of the American Foreign Policy Establishment?" *Journal of American Studies* 35: 65–94.

Roberts, Sam. (2001b) *The Brother: The Untold Story of Atomic Spy David Greenglass and How He

Sent His Sister, Ethel Rosenberg, to the Electric Chair. New York.
———. (2013) *Grand Central: How a Train Station Transformed America.* New York.
Robertson, David. (1994) *Sly and Able: A Political Biography of James F. Byrnes.* New York.
Robeson, Paul. (1958) *Ballad for Americans (and Great Songs of Faith, Love and Patriotism).* New York.
———. (1965) *Paul Robeson Sings Ballad for Americans, and Carnegie Hall Concert.* Vol. 2. New York.
Robeson, Paul, and Philip S. Foner. (1978) *Paul Robeson Speaks: Writings, Speeches, Interviews, 1918–1974.* New York.
Robinson, Gertrude J. (2006) "The Katz/Lowenthal Encounter: An Episode in the Creation of *Personal Influence.*" *Annals of the American Academy of Political and Social Science* 608: 76–96.
Robinson, Jo Ann. (1981) *Abraham Went Out: A Biography of A. J. Muste.* Philadelphia, PA.
Robinson, Victor. (1943) *Morals in Wartime.* New York.
Rocchio, David M. (2005) "Thunderstorms and Landscapes." *Judevine Mountain Emailite,* October 10.
Roche, John Pearson. (1963) *The Quest for the Dream: The Development of Civil Rights and Human Relations in Modern America.* New York.
Rockefeller, David. (2002) *Memoirs.* New York.
Rockwell, Llewellyn H., Jr. (2007) "A Biography of Henry Hazlitt." *Mises.org,* August.
Rodengen, Jeffrey L. (1999) *The Legend of Pfizer.* Fort Lauderdale, FL.
Rodgers, Cleveland. (1943) *New York Plans for the Future.* New York.
Rodgers, William. (1969) *Think: A Biography of the Watsons and IBM.* New York.

Rodney, Lester. (1998) "White Dodgers, Black Dodgers." In *Jackie Robinson: Race, Sports and the American Dream,* edited by Joseph Dorinson and Joram Warmund. Armonk, NY.
Rodríguez Beruff, Jorge. (2009) "From Winship to Leahy: Crisis, War, and Transition in Puerto Rico." In *The Colonial Crucible: Empire in the Making of the Modern American State,* edited by Alfred W. McCoy and Francisco A. Scarano. Madison, WI.
Rodriguez-Fraticelli, Carlos. (1992) "Pedro Albizu Campos: Strategies of Struggle and Strategic Struggles." *En Centro Bulletin* 4: 25–33.
Rodriguez-Morazzani, Roberto P. (1995) "Linking a Fractured Past: The World of the Old Puerto Rican Left." *Centro: Journal of the Center of Puerto Rican Studies* 7: 20–30.
Roeder, George H. (1993) *The Censored War: American Visual Experience During World War Two.* New Haven, CT.
Roediger, David R. (2005) *Working toward Whiteness: How America's Immigrants Became White: The Strange Journey from Ellis Island to the Suburbs.* New York.
Rogers, Toby. (2002) "Heir to the Holocaust: Prescott Bush, $1.5 Million, and Auschwitz: How the Bush Family Wealth Is Linked to the Holocaust." *Clamor* 14: 1–9.
Rogin, Michael P., and Kathleen Moran. (2003) "Mr. Capra Goes to Washington." *Representations* 84: 213–248.
"Roosevelt's Address at the Statue of Liberty." (1936) *New York Times,* October 29.
Roosevelt, Eleanor. (1942) "My Day." *St. Petersburg Times,* December 12.
Roosevelt, Franklin Delano. (1940a) "Fireside Chat:

May 26, 1940." In *Franklin D. Roosevelt, 32nd President of the United States: 1933–1945,* edited by American Presidency Project. Santa Barbara, CA.
———. (1940b) *The Great Arsenal of Democracy: Radio Address.* December 29, 1940. Washington, DC.
———. (1944) "Platform for 1944." *Time,* January 10.
"Roosevelt Urges Guarding of Peace: Speaking at Statue of Liberty, He Rededicates Nation to Ideal It Represents." (1936) *New York Times,* October 29.
Rose, Mark H. (1979) *Interstate: Express Highway Politics, 1941–1956.* Lawrence, KS.
Rose-Redwood, Reuben S. (2008) "'Sixth Avenue Is Now a Memory': Regimes of Spatial Inscription and the Performative Limits of the Official City-Text." *Political Geography* 27: 875–894.
Rosenberg, Elliot. (1995) "Fiorello's Army." *Seaport Magazine,* Summer.
Rosenberg, Emily. (1982) *Spreading the American Dream: American Economic and Cultural Expansion, 1890–1945.* New York.
Rosenberg, Harold. (1959) *The Tradition of the New.* New York.
Rosenberg, Jonathan. (2006) *How Far the Promised Land? World Affairs and the American Civil Rights Movement from the First World War to Vietnam.* Princeton, NJ.
Rosenblum, Yonason, and David Kranzler. (1995) *They Called Him Mike: Reb Elemelech Tress, His Era, Hatzalah, and the Building of an American Orthodoxy.* Brooklyn, NY.
Rosenblum, Yonason, and Aharon Sorski. (2001) *Reb Shraga Feivel: The Life and Times of Rabbi Shraga Feivel Mendlowitz, the Architect of Torah in America.* Brooklyn, NY.
Rosenthal, Michael. (2006) *Nicholas Miraculous: The

Amazing Career of the Redoubtable Dr. Nicholas Murray Butler.* New York.
Rosenwaike, Ira. (1972) *The Population History of New York City.* Syracuse, NY.
Rosenzweig, Roy. and Elizabeth Blackmar. (1994) *The Park and the People: A History of Central Park.* New York.
Ross, Nancy Wilson. (1943) *The WAVES: The Story of the Girls in Blue.* New York.
Ross, Rodney A. (1972) "Black Americans and Italo-Ethiopian Relief, 1935–1936." *Ethiopia Observer* 15: 122–131.
Rossano, Geoffrey. (1984) "Suburbia Armed: Nassau County Development and Rise of the Aerospace Industry, 1909–1960." In *The Martial Metropolis: U.S. Cities in War and Peace,* edited by Roger W. Lotchin. New York.
Rossinow, Doug. (2004) "The Model of a Model Fellow Traveler: Harry F. Ward, the American League for Peace and Democracy, and the 'Russian Question' in American Politics." *Peace & Change* 29: 177–220.
———. (2005) "The Radicalization of the Social Gospel: Harry F. Ward and the Search for a New Social Order, 1898–1936." *Religion and American Culture* 15: 63–106.
Rosswurm, Steve. (2001) "Communism and the CIO: Catholics and the 1944 Presidential Campaign." *U.S. Catholic Historian* 19: 73–86.
Rothbard, Murray N. (1984) "Wall Street, Banks, and American Foreign Policy." *World Market Perspective,* August.
———. (1988) *Ludwig von Mises: Scholar, Creator, Hero.* Auburn, AL.
———. (2007) *The Betrayal of the American Right.* Auburn, AL.
Rowland, Buford. (1947) "Revolution in Nets: An Unglamorous but Essential Phase of Naval

Warfare." *Military Affairs* 11: 149–158.

Rowlands, Penelope. (2006) *A Dash of Daring: Carmel Snow and Her Life in Fashion, Art, and Letters.* New York.

Roxborough, Ian. (1998) "Cold War, Capital Accumulation, and Labor Control in Latin America: The Closing of a Cycle, 1945–1990." In *Rethinking the Cold War*, edited by Allen Hunter. Philadelphia, PA.

Rubenstein Library. (2022) "Collection Guide." In *Walter Weir Papers, 1909–1996 and Undated, Bulk 1950–1990*, edited by Duke University Libraries. Durham, NC.

Rubinstein, Annette T., and Gerald Meyer. (2002) *I Vote My Conscience: Debates, Speeches and Writings of Vito Marcantonio, 1935–1950.* New York.

Rubinstein, William D. (2001) "Saving Remnant: The Response of Orthodox Jewry in the United States to the Holocaust: The Activities of the Vaad-Ha-Hatzalah Rescue Committee, 1939–1945, by Ephraim Zuroff." *First Things*, May.

Rucker, Walter C., and James N. Upton. (2007) *Encyclopedia of American Race Riots.* Westport, CT.

Ruderman, Terry Schwartz. (1977) "Stanley M. Isaacs: The Conscience of New York." PhD diss., City University of New York.

Rudy, S. Willis. (1949) *The College of the City of New York: A History, 1847–1947.* New York.

Rugg, Harold, Emma Schweppe, et al. (1922) *America and Her Immigrants.* New York.

Ruíz, Vicki, and Virginia Sánchez Korrol. (2006) *Latinas in the United States: A Historical Encyclopedia.* Bloomington, IN.

Rupp, Leila J. (1979) "Woman's Place Is in the War: Propaganda and Public Opinion in the United States and Germany, 1939–1945." In *Women of America: A History*, edited by Carol Berkin and Mary Beth Norton. Boston, MA.

Rusinack, Kelly E. (1998) "Baseball on the Radical Agenda: The *Daily Worker* and *Sunday Worker* Journalistic Campaign to Desegregate Major League Baseball, 1933–1947." In *Jackie Robinson: Race, Sports and the American Dream*, edited by Joseph Dorinson and Joram Warmund. Armonk, NY.

Russell, John. (2002) "Modern Art Groupie: *Art Lover: A Biography of Peggy Guggenheim*, by Anton Gill." *New York Review of Books*, June 27, 2002, 23.

Ruttenbaum, Steven. (1986) *Mansions in the Clouds: The Skyscraper Palazzi of Emery Roth.* New York.

Ryan, Alan. (1995) *John Dewey and the High Tide of American Liberalism.* New York.

Ryan, James Gilbert. (1997) *Earl Browder: The Failure of American Communism.* Tuscaloosa, AL.

———. (2002) "Socialist Triumph as a Family Value: Earl Browder and Soviet Espionage." *American Communist History* 1: 125–142.

Sachs, Charles L., and Nancy H. Waters. (1988) *Made on Staten Island: Agriculture, Industry, and Suburban Living in the City.* Staten Island, NY.

Saint-Arnaud, Pierre, and Peter Feldstein. (2009) *African American Pioneers of Sociology: A Critical History.* Toronto, Canada.

Salazar, Max. (1998) "50th Anniversary of Cubop." *Latin Beat Magazine*, November.

———. (2002) *Mambo Kingdom: Latin Music in New York.* New York.

Salvador Dalí Museum. (2005) "Pollock to Pop: America's Brush with Dalí." *Dexigner*, December 10.

Salvemini, Gaetano, William Yandell Elliott, et al. (1940) *Italian Fascist Activities in the U.S.* Washington, DC.

Samelson, Franz. (1978) "From 'Race Psychology' to 'Studies in Prejudice': Some Observations on the Thematic Reversal in Social Psychology." *Journal of the History of the Behavioural Sciences* 14: 265–278.

Sammons, Jeffrey T. (1988) *Beyond the Ring: The Role of Boxing in American Society.* Urbana, IL.

Sampson, Anthony. (1973) *The Sovereign State of ITT.* New York.

Samson, Gloria Garrett. (1996) *The American Fund for Public Service: Charles Garland and Radical Philanthropy, 1922–1941.* Westport, CT.

Samuel, Lawrence R. (1997) *Pledging Allegiance: American Identity and the Bond Drive of World War II.* Washington, DC.

———. (2001) *Brought to You By: Postwar Television Advertising and the American Dream.* Austin, TX.

Sandeen, Eric J. (1979) "Confessions of a Nazi Spy and the German American Bund." *American Studies* 20: 69–81.

Sanders, Marion K. (1973) *Dorothy Thompson: A Legend in Her Time.* Boston, MA.

Sandler, Irving. (1970) *The Triumph of American Painting: A History of Abstract Expressionism.* New York.

Sante, Luc, Cynthia Young, et al. (2006) *Unknown Weegee.* Göttingen, Germany.

Sanua, Marianne Rachel. (2007) *Let Us Prove Strong: The American Jewish Committee, 1945–2006.* Waltham, MA.

Sarnoff Corporation. (2004) "Background of Facility." *Sarnoff Corporation: About: History*, August 23.

Sathasivam, Kanishkan. (2005) *Uneasy Neighbors: India, Pakistan, and US Foreign Policy.* Aldershot, UK.

Sauvage, Pierre. (2001) "Varian Fry in Marseille." In *Remembering for the Future: The Holocaust in an Age of Genocide*, edited by John K. Roth and Elisabeth Maxwell. New York.

Savage, Barbara Dianne. (1999) *Broadcasting Freedom: Radio, War, and the Politics of Race, 1938–1948.* Chapel Hill, NC.

Savage, William W. (1990) *Comic Books and America, 1945–1954.* Norman, OK.

Sawada, Mitziko. (1996) *Tokyo Life, New York Dreams: Urban Japanese Visions of America, 1890–1924.* Berkeley, CA.

Sawin, Martica. (1995) *Surrealism in Exile and the Beginning of the New York School.* Cambridge, MA.

Sayers, Michael, and Albert Eugene Kahn. (1942) *Sabotage! The Secret War against America.* New York.

———. (1946) *The Great Conspiracy: The Secret War against Soviet Russia.* Boston, MA.

Scates, Shelby. (2006) *Maurice Rosenblatt and the Fall of Joseph McCarthy.* Seattle, WA.

Schaffer, Alan. (1966) *Vito Marcantonio: Radical in Congress.* Syracuse, NY.

Schatz, Ronald W. (1983) *The Electrical Workers: A History of Labor at General Electric and Westinghouse, 1923–1960.* Urbana, IL.

Schechtman, Joseph B. (1986) *The Life and Times of Vladimir Jabotinsky.* Vols. 1 & 2. Silver Spring, MD.

Schecter, Jerrold L., and Leona Schecter. (2002) *Sacred Secrets: How Soviet Intelligence Operations Changed American History.* Washington, DC.

Schelm, Gerold M. (2003) "Coastal Radars." *The Golf Sierra PX/Montauk Link Archive Project*, February 19.

Schick, Frank Leopold. (1958) *The Paperbound Book in America: The*

History of Paperbacks and Their European Background. New York.

Schickel, Richard. (2005) Elia Kazan: A Biography. New York.

Schiffrin, André. (2001) The Business of Books: How International Conglomerates Took over Publishing and Changed the Way We Read. New York.

———. (2007) A Political Education: Coming of Age in Paris and New York. Hoboken, NJ.

Schjeldahl, Peter. (2006) "American Abstract." New Yorker, July 31.

Schleier, Merrill. (2002) "Ayn Rand and King Vidor's Film 'The Fountainhead': Architectural Modernism, the Gendered Body, and Political Ideology." Journal of the Society of Architectural Historians 61: 310–331.

———. (2009) Skyscraper Cinema: Architecture and Gender in American Film. Minneapolis, MN.

Schlesinger, Arthur M. (2000) A Life in the Twentieth Century. Boston, MA.

Schlesinger, Stephen C. (2003) Act of Creation: The Founding of the United Nations: A Story of Superpowers, Secret Agents, Wartime Allies and Enemies, and Their Quest for a Peaceful World. Boulder, CO.

Schlichting, Kurt C. (2001) Grand Central Terminal: Railroads, Engineering, and Architecture in New York City. Baltimore, MD.

Schmidt, Hans. (1987) Maverick Marine: General Smedley D. Butler and the Contradictions of American Military History. Lexington, KY.

Schmidt, William J. (1978) Architect of Unity: A Biography of Samuel McCrea Cavert. New York.

Schmitz, David F. (2001) Henry L. Stimson: The First Wise Man. Wilmington, DE.

Schnapper, M. B. (1938) "Mussolini's American Agents." Nation, October 15.

Schneider, Eric. (2004) "'You Had to Get High to Play': Jazz and the Rise of New York's Postwar Heroin Epidemic." Paper presented at City Seminar, Columbia University. New York.

Schneider, Eric C. (1999) Vampires, Dragons, and Egyptian Kings: Youth Gangs in Postwar New York. Princeton, NJ.

Schoenbaum, David. (1993) The United States and the State of Israel. New York.

Schrag, Zachary M. (2000) "'The Bus Is Young and Honest': Transportation Politics, Technical Choice, and the Motorization of Manhattan Surface Transit, 1919–1936." Technology and Culture 41: 51–79.

Schrecker, Ellen. (1986) No Ivory Tower: McCarthyism and the Universities. New York.

———. (1999) "The Spies Who Loved Us?" Nation, May 6.

Schroth, Raymond A. (2002) Fordham: A History and Memoir. Chicago, IL.

Schrum, Kelly. (1998) "'Teena Means Business': Teenage Girls' Culture and 'Seventeen' Magazine, 1944–1950." In Delinquents and Debutantes: Twentieth-Century American Girls' Cultures, edited by Sherrie A. Inness. New York.

Schuller, Gunther. (1989) The Swing Era: The Development of Jazz, 1930–1945. Vol. 2. New York.

Schultz, Kevin M. (2008) "The FEPC and the Legacy of the Labor-Based Civil Rights Movement of the 1940s." Labor History 49: 71–92.

Schulzinger, Robert D. (1984) The Wise Men of Foreign Affairs: The History of the Council on Foreign Relations. New York.

Schuyler, George Samuel. (1966) Black and Conservative: The Autobiography of George S. Schuyler. New Rochelle, NY.

Schwartz, Joel. (1986) "Tenant Unions in New York City Low-Rent Housing, 1934–1949." Journal of Urban History 12: 414–443.

———. (1993) The New York Approach: Robert Moses, Urban Liberals, and Redevelopment of the Inner City. Columbus, OH.

———. (2007) "Robert Moses and City Planning." In Robert Moses and the Modern City: The Transformation of New York, edited by Hilary Ballon and Kenneth T. Jackson. New York.

Schwarz, Jordan A. (1981) The Speculator: Bernard M. Baruch in Washington, 1917–1965. Chapel Hill, NC.

———. (1987) Liberal: Adolf A. Berle and the Vision of an American Era. New York.

———. (1994) The New Dealers: Power Politics in the Age of Roosevelt. New York.

Schweitzer, Marlis. (2008) "American Fashions for American Women: The Rise and Fall of Fashion Nationalism." In Producing Fashion: Commerce, Culture, and Consumers, edited by Regina Lee Blaszczyk. Philadelphia, PA.

Scott, Daryl Michael. (2004) "Postwar Pluralism, Brown v. Board of Education, and the Origins of Multicultural Education." Journal of American History 91: 69–82.

Scott, Mel. (1969) American City Planning since 1890. Berkeley, CA.

Scott, William R. (1992) The Sons of Sheba's Race: African-Americans and the Italo-Ethiopian War, 1935–1941. Bloomington, IN.

Scott, William, and Peter Rutkoff. (1999) New York Modern: The Arts and the City. Baltimore, MD.

Scott-Smith, Giles. (2002) The Politics of Apolitical Culture: The Congress for Cultural Freedom, the CIA and Post-War American Hegemony. London.

Scullin, George. (1968) International Airport: The Story of Kennedy Airport and U.S. Commercial Aviation. Boston, MA.

Scully, Eileen. (2003) "Scully on Olmsted, 'Red Spy Queen: A Biography of Elizabeth Bentley.'" H-Women, April.

Secrest, Meryle. (1994) Leonard Bernstein: A Life. New York.

Seidel, Michael. (1988) Streak: Joe DiMaggio and the Summer of '41. New York.

Seidel, Robert. (1992) "The Origins of the Lawrence Berkeley Laboratory." In Big Science: The Growth of Large-Scale Research, edited by Peter Galison and Bruce William Hevly. Stanford, CA.

Seidman, Joel Isaac. (1942) The Needle Trades. New York.

Seldes, George. (1934) Iron, Blood and Profits: An Exposure of the World-Wide Munitions Racket. New York.

———. (1939) The Catholic Crisis. New York.

———. (1948) One Thousand Americans. New York.

———. (1994) "The Roman Church and Franco." The Human Quest, March–April.

Selig, Diana Marcia. (2001) "Cultural Gifts: American Liberals, Childhood, and the Origins of Multiculturalism, 1924–1939." PhD diss., University of California, Berkeley.

Seligman, Joel. (2003) The Transformation of Wall Street: A History of the Securities and Exchange Commission and Modern Corporate Finance. New York.

Semple, Mildred. (1994) "New York Fashion: The Tobé-Coburn School, 1937–1967." PhD diss., State University of New York at Binghamton.

Sert, Jose Luis. (1947) "U.N. Headquarters: Le Corbusier. Reinhold Publishing Corp., 330 W. 42nd St., New York 18, NY, 1947. 80 pp., illus. by the author. $3.50." *Progressive Architecture,* October.

Severo, Richard, and Lewis Milford. (1989) *The Wages of War: When America's Soldiers Came Home—from Valley Forge to Vietnam.* New York.

Seyfried, Vincent F. (1982) *Queens, a Pictorial History.* Norfolk, VA.

Shachtman, Tom. (1991) *Skyscraper Dreams: The Great Real Estate Dynasties of New York.* Boston, MA.

Shaffer, Robert. (1996) "Multicultural Education in New York City During World War II." *New York History* 77: 301–332.

Shapiro, Chaim. (2004) "Rabbi Avraham Kalmanowitz: The Last of His Kind." *Tzemach Dovid,* June 22.

Shapiro, David H. (1994) *From Philanthropy to Activism: The Political Transformation of American Zionism in the Holocaust Years, 1933–1945.* New York.

Shapiro, Nat, and Nat Hentoff. (1955) *Hear Me Talkin' to Ya: The Story of Jazz by the Men Who Made It.* New York.

Shaplen, Joseph, and David Shub. (1934) *Socialism, Fascism, Communism.* New York.

Shaplen, Robert. (1951) "One Man Lobby." *New Yorker,* March 24.

Sharp, John Kean. (1954) *History of the Diocese of Brooklyn, 1853–1953: The Catholic Church on Long Island, Vol. 2.* New York.

Shaw, Arnold. (1977) *52nd Street, the Street of Jazz.* New York.

Shea, Sister Mary Margretta. (1966) "Patrick Cardinal Hayes and the Catholic Charities in New York City." PhD diss., New York University.

Sheed, Wilfrid. (2007) *The House That George Built: With a Little Help from Irving, Cole, and a Crew of About Fifty.* New York.

Shefter, Martin. (1993a) *Capital of the American Century: The National and International Influence of New York City.* New York.

——. (1993b) "New York City and American National Politics." In *Capital of the American Century: National and International Influence of New York City,* edited by Martin Shefter. New York.

Shelley, Msgr. Thomas J. (1999) "Proud Legacy." *Catholic New York,* December 23.

Sheppard, Eugene R. (2006) *Leo Strauss and the Politics of Exile: The Making of a Political Philosopher.* Waltham, MA.

Sherman, Janann. (1995) "'The Vice Admiral': Margaret Chase Smith and the Investigation of Congested Areas in Wartime." In *The Home-Front War: World War II and American Society,* edited by Kenneth Paul O'Brien and Lynn H. Parsons. Westport, CT.

Sherry, Michael S. (2007) *Gay Artists in Modern American Culture: An Imagined Conspiracy.* Chapel Hill, NC.

Sherwood, Robert Emmet. (1950) *Roosevelt and Hopkins, an Intimate History.* New York.

Shiffman, Dan. (2003) *Rooting Multiculturalism: The Work of Louis Adamic.* Madison, NJ.

Shipton, Alyn. (1999) *Groovin' High: The Life of Dizzy Gillespie.* New York.

Shlaim, Avi. (2000) *The Iron Wall: Israel and the Arab World.* New York.

Short, K. R. M. (1983) *Film & Radio Propaganda in World War II.* Knoxville, TN.

Shortridge, Bud. (2005) "Development of the Liberty & Victory Ships." *The U.S. Maritime Commission in WW II,* March 29.

Shotwell, James T. (1961) *Autobiography.* Indianapolis, IN.

Shoup, Laurence H. (1977) *Imperial Brain Trust: The Council on Foreign Relations & US Foreign Policy.* Lincoln, NE.

Shpak Lisak, Rivka. (1989) *Pluralism & Progressives: Hull House and the New Immigrants, 1890–1919.* Chicago, IL.

Shteir, Rachel. (1997) "Workers Laboratory Theatre." *Nation,* July 14.

——. (2004) *Striptease: The Untold History of the Girlie Show.* New York.

Shulman, Holly Cowan. (1990) *The Voice of America: Propaganda and Democracy, 1941–1945.* Madison, WI.

Shultz, Earle, and Walter Simmons. (1959) *Offices in the Sky.* Indianapolis, IN.

Shurkin, Joel N. (2006) *Broken Genius: The Rise and Fall of William Shockley, Creator of the Electronic Age.* New York.

Sibley, Katherine A. S. (1999) "Soviet Industrial Espionage against American Military Technology and the US Response, 1930–1945." *Intelligence and National Security* 14: 94–123.

——. (2004) *Red Spies in America: Stolen Secrets and the Dawn of the Cold War.* Lawrence, KS.

Sibley, Mulford Quickert, and Philip E. Jacob. (1952) *Conscription of Conscience: The American State and the Conscientious Objector, 1940–1947.* Ithaca, NY.

Sifton, Elisabeth. (2003) *The Serenity Prayer: Faith and Politics in Times of Peace and War.* New York.

Silber, Irwin, and Lester Rodney. (2003) *Press Box Red: The Story of Lester Rodney, the Communist Who Helped Break the Color Line in American Sports.* Philadelphia, PA.

Sills, David L. (1987) *Paul F. Lazarsfeld, 1901–1976: A Biographical Memoir.* Washington, DC.

Simon, Arthur R. (1970) *Stuyvesant Town, U.S.A.: Pattern for Two Americas.* New York.

Simon, Joe, and Jim Simon. (2003) *The Comic Book Makers.* New York.

Simpson, Christopher. (1995) *The Splendid Blond Beast: Money, Law, and Genocide in the Twentieth Century.* Monroe, ME.

Simpson, Smith. (1941) "The Commission to Study the Organization of Peace." *American Political Science Review* 35: 317–324.

Sinai, Nathan, and Odin W. Anderson. (1948) *EMIC (Emergency Maternity and Infant Care): A Study of Administrative Experience.* New York.

Singer, C. Gregg. (1975) *The Unholy Alliance.* New Rochelle, NY.

Singer, Michael. (1951) "Who Killed Pete Panto?" *Daily Worker,* April 11.

——. (1952) "Panto's Killer Walks out Free after Probe." *Daily Worker,* December 22.

Singh, Inder. (2009) "Indians in America: Settling in the States." *India Empire* 1: 1–4.

Sinha, Mrinalini. (2006) *Specters of Mother India: The Global Restructuring of an Empire.* Durham, NC.

Sirgiovanni, George. (1990) *An Undercurrent of Suspicion: Anti-Communism in America During World War II.* New Brunswick, NJ.

Sitkoff, Harvard. (1997) "African American Militancy in the World War II South." In *Remaking Dixie: The Impact of World War II on the American South,* edited by Neil R. McMillen. Jackson, MS.

——. (2003) "African Americans, American Jews, and the Holocaust." In *The Achievement of American Liberalism: The New Deal and Its Legacies,* edited by William Henry Chafe. New York.

Skard, Torild. (2008) "Getting Our History

Right: How Were the Equal Rights of Women and Men Included in the Charter of the United Nations?" *Forum for Development Studies* 1: 37–60.

Skidelsky, Robert. (1986) *John Maynard Keynes, Vol. 3: Fighting for Freedom, 1937–1946.* New York.

Skinner, James M. (1993) *The Cross and the Cinema: The Legion of Decency and the National Catholic Office for Motion Pictures, 1933–1970.* Westport, CT.

Sklaroff, Lauren Rebecca. (2002) "Constructing G.I. Joe Louis: Cultural Solutions to the 'Negro Problem' During World War II." *Journal of American History* 89: 958–983.

Slate, Nico. (2012) "Nonviolence and the Nation." In *Colored Cosmopolitanism: The Shared Struggle for Freedom in the United States and India*, edited by Nico Slate. Cambridge, MA.

Slotkin, Richard. (2005) *Lost Battalions: The Great War and the Crisis of American Nationality.* New York.

Smith, Beverly A. (2001) "Ann Petry's *In Darkness and Confusion* and the Harlem Riot of 1943: Fictional Insights into the Causes and Nature of Collective Violence." *Women & Criminal Justice* 12: 1–20.

Smith, Bradley F. (1983) *The Shadow Warriors: O.S.S. & the Origins of the C.I.A.* New York.

Smith, Carol, Stephen Brier, et al. (2005) *The Struggle for Free Speech at CCNY, 1931–1942.* New York.

Smith, Gordon. (2011) "Battle of the Atlantic— Its Development: Part of 1 of 2, 1939–1942." *Naval History Homepage*, August 7.

Smith, Jason Scott. (2006) *Building New Deal Liberalism: The Political Economy of Public Works, 1933–1956.* New York.

Smith, Kathleen E. R. (1996) "'Goodbye Mama, I'm Off to Yokohama': The Office of War Information and Tin Pan Alley in World War II." PhD diss., Louisiana State University and Agricultural and Mechanical College.

———. (2003) *God Bless America: Tin Pan Alley Goes to War.* Lexington, KY.

Smith, Mapheus. (1946) "The Differential Impact of Selective Service Inductions on Occupations in the United States." *American Sociological Review* 11: 567–572.

Smith, Mona Z. (2004) *Becoming Something: The Story of Canada Lee.* New York.

Smith, Page. (1987) *Redeeming the Time: A People's History of the 1920's and the New Deal.* New York.

Smith, R. Harris. (1972) *OSS: The Secret History of America's First Central Intelligence Agency.* Berkeley, CA.

Smith, Richard N. (1982) *Thomas E. Dewey and His Times.* New York.

Smith, Sally Bedell. (1990a) *In All His Glory: The Life of William S. Paley, the Legendary Tycoon and His Brilliant Circle.* New York.

Smith, William Ander. (1990b) *The Mystery of Leopold Stokowski.* Rutherford, NJ.

Snow, Carmel, and Mary Louise White Aswell. (1962) *The World of Carmel Snow.* New York.

Snyder, Timothy. (2009) "Holocaust: The Ignored Reality." *New York Review of Books*, July 16.

Sobel, Robert. (1965) *The Big Board: A History of the New York Stock Market.* New York.

———. (1975) *N.Y.S.E.: A History of the New York Stock Exchange, 1935–1975.* New York.

———. (1980) *The Last Bull Market: Wall Street in the 1960's.* New York.

———. (1982) *I.T.T.: The Management of Opportunity.* New York.

———. (1991) *The Life and Times of Dillon Read.* New York.

Sollors, Werner. (1986a) *Beyond Ethnicity: Consent and Descent in American Culture.* New York.

———. (1986b) "A Critique of Pure Pluralism." In *Reconstructing American Literary History*, edited by Sacvan Bercovitch. Cambridge, MA.

Solomon, Andrew. (2003) "The Picasso of Washington Square: Arshile Gorky: His Life and Work, by Hayden Herrera." *New York Times*, September 28.

Solomon, Deborah. (1987) *Jackson Pollock: A Biography.* New York.

Sorin, Gerald. (2002) *Irving Howe: A Life of Passionate Dissent.* New York.

Southern, David W. (1996) *John LaFarge and the Limits of Catholic Interracialism, 1911–1963.* Baton Rouge, LA.

———. (1998) "Rethinking Race: Franz Boas and His Contemporaries by Vernon J. Williams." *American Historical Review* 103: 984–985.

Spanish Benevolent Society Inc. (2001) "'La Nacional': Fundada en 1868." LaNacional.org, June 5.

Sparkes, Boyden. (1944) "They'll Build Neighborhoods, Not Houses." *Saturday Evening Post*, October 28.

Sparks, N. (1930) *The Struggle of the Marine Workers.* New York.

Sparr, Arnold. (2000) "Looking for Rosie: Women Defense Workers in the Brooklyn Navy Yard, 1942–1946." *New York History* 81: 313–340.

Sparrow, Bartholomew H. (1996) *From the Outside In: World War II and the American State.* Princeton, NJ.

Special Committee to Investigate Organized Crime in Interstate Commerce. (1951) *Third Interim Report Pursuant to S. Res. 202, 81st Congress, a Resolution to Investigate Gambling and Racketeering Activities.* Washington, DC.

"Spellman Warned on Christian Front." (1939) *New York Times*, September 26.

Sperber, A. M. (1986) *Murrow, His Life and Times.* New York.

Spiller, James. (2004) "This Is War! Network Radio and World War II Propaganda in America." *Journal of Radio Studies* 11: 55–72.

Spiro, Herbert J. (1968) "Totalitarianism." In *International Encyclopedia of the Social Sciences*, edited by David L. Sills. New York.

Spiro, Jonathan Peter. (2000) "Patrician Racist: The Evolution of Madison Grant." PhD diss., University of California, Berkeley.

Spitz, Fortuna, Luis Spitz, et al. (2006) *The Evolution of Clean: A Visual Journey through the History of Soaps and Detergents.* Washington, DC.

Spivey, Donald. (1985) *Sport in America: New Historical Perspectives.* Westport, CT.

Spoto, Donald. (1999) *The Dark Side of Genius: The Life of Alfred Hitchcock.* New York.

Sprecher, Paul. (2002) "John Haynes Holmes." In *The Dictionary of Unitarian and Universalist Biography*, edited by Unitarian Universalist Historical Society. Dedham, MA.

Standard Oil Company. (1944) *Oil for the World.* New York.

Stapleton, Darwin H. (2004) *Creating a Tradition of Biomedical Research: Contributions to the History of the Rockefeller University.* New York.

Starr, Roger. (1993) "PM: New York's Highbrow Tabloid." *City Journal*, Summer.

Starr, Tama, and Ed Hayman. (1998) *Signs and Wonders: The Spectacular Marketing of America.* New York.

State of New Jersey Commission on Post-War Economic Welfare. (1944) *A New Jersey Program for the Post-War Period.* Trenton, NJ.

Steel, Ronald. (1980) *Walter Lippmann and the American Century.* Boston, MA.

Steele, Richard W. (1984) "The Great Debate: Roosevelt, the Media, and the Coming of the War, 1940–1941." *Journal of American History* 71: 69–92.

———. (1989) "The War on Intolerance: The Reformulation of American Nationalism, 1939–1941." *Journal of American Ethnic History* 9: 11–33.

———. (1991) " 'No Racials': Discrimination against Ethnics in American Defense Industry, 1940–1942." *Labor History* 32: 66–90.

Stein, Clarence S. (1943) "The Future of New York." *Post War Planning News Digest,* July 19.

Stein, Herbert. (1969) *The Fiscal Revolution in America.* Chicago, IL.

Stelter, Lawrence, Lothar Stelter, et al. (1995) *By the El: Third Avenue and Its El at Mid-Century.* New York.

Stember, Charles Herbert, Marshall Sklare, et al. (1966) *Jews in the Mind of America.* New York.

Stephan, John J. (1984) *Hawaii under the Rising Sun: Japan's Plans for Conquest after Pearl Harbor.* Honolulu, HI.

Sterling, Christopher H., and John M. Kittross. (2002) *Stay Tuned: A History of American Broadcasting.* Mahwah, NJ.

Stern, Jewel, and John A. Stuart. (2006) *Ely Jacques Kahn, Architect: Beaux-Arts to Modernism in New York.* New York.

Stern, Julius David. (1962) *Memoirs of a Maverick Publisher.* New York.

Stern, Robert A. M., Gregory Gilmartin, et al. (1987) *New York 1930:* *Architecture and Urbanism between the Two World Wars.* New York.

Stern, Robert A. M., Thomas Mellins, et al. (1995) *New York 1960: Architecture and Urbanism between the Second World War and the Bicentennial.* New York, NY.

Stevens, Mark, and Annalyn Swan. (2004) *de Kooning: An American Master.* New York.

Stevenson, William. (1976) *A Man Called Intrepid: The Secret War.* New York.

Stewart, Maxwell Slutz. (1942) *After the War?* New York.

———. (1943a) *Building for Peace at Home and Abroad.* New York.

———. (1943b) *When I Get Out? Will I Find a Job?* New York.

Stocking, George W., Jr. (1982) "Franz Boas and the Culture Concept in Historical Perspective." In *Race, Culture, and Evolution: Essays in the History of Anthropology,* edited by George W. Stocking Jr. Chicago, IL.

Stoddard, Lothrop. (1940) *Into the Darkness: Nazi Germany Today.* New York.

Stoff, Joshua. (1989) *The Aerospace Heritage of Long Island.* Interlaken, NY.

Stolberg, Mary M. (1995) *Fighting Organized Crime: Politics, Justice, and the Legacy of Thomas E. Dewey.* Boston, MA.

Stole, Inger L. (2001) "The 'Salesmanship of Sacrifice': The Advertising Industry's Use of Public Relations During the Second World War." *Advertising & Society Review* 2: 1–17.

Stone, Jill. (1982) *Times Square: A Pictorial History.* New York.

Stowe, D. W. (1998) "The Politics of Cafe Society." *Journal of American History* 84: 1384–1406.

Stowe, David W. (1994) *Swing Changes: Big-Band Jazz in New Deal America.* Cambridge, MA.

Strasser, Susan. (1999) *Waste and Want: A Social History of Trash.* New York.

Straub, Eleanor Ferguson. (1973) "Government Policy toward Civilian Women During World War II." PhD diss., Emory University.

Strauss, Herbert A. (1971) "The Immigration and Acculturation of the German Jew in the United States of America." *Leo Baeck Institute Yearbook* 16: 63–94.

———. (1981) "Jewish Immigration from Germany: Nazi Policies and Jewish Responses, Part 2." *Leo Baeck Institute Yearbook* 26: 343–409.

Strauss, Lauren. (1996) "Staying Afloat in the Melting Pot: Constructing an American Jewish Identity in the 'Menorah Journal' of the 1920s." *American Jewish History* 84: 315–331.

Stroke, H. Henry. (1995) *The Physical Review, the First Hundred Years: A Selection of Seminal Papers and Commentaries.* New York.

Strouse, Jean. (1992) "Making the Facts Obey." *New York Times Book Review,* May 24.

Stump, Roger W. (1998) "Place and Innovation in Popular Music: The Bebop Revolution in Jazz." *Journal of Cultural Geography* 18: 11–34.

Sturmthal, Adolf Fox. (1943) *A Survey of Literature on Postwar Reconstruction.* New York.

Sublette, Ned. (2004) *Cuba and Its Music: From the First Drums to the Mambo.* Chicago, IL.

Sullivan, Dean A. (2002) *Late Innings: A Documentary History of Baseball, 1945–1972.* Lincoln, NE.

Sulzberger, Iphigene Ochs, and Susan W. Dryfoos. (1987) *Iphigene: My Life and the New York Times: The Memoirs of Iphigene Ochs Sulzberger as Written by Susan W. Dryfoos.* New York.

Sumner, Gregory D. (1996) *Dwight Macdonald and the Politics Circle: The Challenge of Cosmopolitan Democracy.* Ithaca, NY.

Sunstein, Cass R. (2004) *The Second Bill of Rights: FDR's Unfinished Revolution and Why We Need It More Than Ever.* New York.

"Superman's Dilemma." (1942) *Time,* April 13.

Susman, Warren. (1984) *Culture as History: The Transformation of American Society in the Twentieth Century.* New York.

Sutton, Antony C. (1976) *Wall Street and the Rise of Hitler.* Seal Beach, CA.

Svonkin, Stuart. (1997) *Jews against Prejudice: American Jews and the Fight for Civil Liberties.* New York.

Swaine, Robert Taylor. (1946) *The Cravath Firm and Its Predecessors: The Cravath Firm since 1906.* Vol. 2. New York.

Swanberg, W.A. (1970) "The Spies Who Came in from the Sea." *American Heritage* 21: 66.

———. (1972) *Luce and His Empire.* New York.

———. (1976) *Norman Thomas, the Last Idealist.* New York.

Swarthmore College Peace Collection. (2006) "Historical Background." In *John Nevin Sayre Papers, 1885–1982 (Bulk 1922–1967), Collection: DG 117,* edited by Swarthmore College Peace Collection. Swarthmore, PA.

———. (2016a) "Historical Background." In *Emergency Peace Campaign Records, 1936–1937, Collection: DG 012,* edited by Swarthmore College Peace Collection. Swarthmore, PA.

———. (2016b) "Historical Background." In *New York Peace Society Records, 1818–1940, Collection: DG 026,* edited by Swarthmore College Peace Collection. Swarthmore, PA.

Sweeting, George Vincent. (1994) "Building the

Arsenal of Democracy: The Government's Role in Expansion of Industrial Capacity, 1940 to 1945." PhD diss., Columbia University.

Sylvester, Robert. (1956) *No Cover Charge: A Backward Look at the Night Clubs.* New York.

Szilard, Leo. (1969) "Reminiscences." In *The Intellectual Migration: Europe and America, 1930–1960,* edited by Donald Fleming and Bernard Bailyn. Cambridge, MA.

Szymczak, Robert. (1984) "A Matter of Honor: Polonia and the Congressional Investigation of the Katyn Forest Massacre." *Polish American Studies* 41: 25–65.

Talese, Gay. (1992) *Unto the Sons.* New York.

Tanenhaus, Sam. (1997) *Whittaker Chambers: A Biography.* New York.

Tangires, Helen. (2008) *Public Markets.* New York.

Tax Policy Center. (2016) "Major Enacted Tax Legislation, 1940–1949." *Laws & Proposals,* April 10.

Taylor, Clarence. (2002) *Black Religious Intellectuals: The Fight for Equality from Jim Crow to the Twenty-First Century.* New York.

Taylor, F. Jay. (1971) *The United States and the Spanish Civil War.* New York.

Taylor, S. J. (1990) *Stalin's Apologist: Walter Duranty, the New York Times's Man in Moscow.* New York.

Taylor, William R. (1991) "Broadway: The Place That Words Built." In *Inventing Times Square: Commerce and Culture at the Crossroads of the World,* edited by William R. Taylor. New York.

Tebbel, John William. (1968) *An American Dynasty: The Story of the McCormicks, Medills, and Pattersons.* New York.

———. (1978) *A History of Book Publishing in the United States, Volume III: The Golden Age between Two Wars, 1920–1940.* New York.

———. (1981) *A History of Book Publishing in the United States, Volume IV: The Great Change, 1940–1980.* New York.

Tell, Darcy. (2007) *Times Square Spectacular: Lighting up Broadway.* New York.

Teres, Harvey M. (1996) *Renewing the Left: Politics, Imagination, and the New York Intellectuals.* New York.

"That Lepke." (1944) *Time,* January 10.

Theoharis, Athan G. (1978) *Spying on Americans: Political Surveillance from Hoover to the Huston Plan.* Philadelphia, PA.

———. (2002) *Chasing Spies: How the FBI Failed in Counterintelligence but Promoted the Politics of McCarthyism in the Cold War Years.* Chicago, IL.

Thies, Jochen. (2001) "Bomben Auf Manhattan: Wie Hitler Und Seine Militärs New York in Schutt Und Asche Legen Wollten." *Die Zeit,* September 17.

Thomas, Hugh. (1961) *The Spanish Civil War.* London.

Thomas, Lorrin Reed. (2002) "Citizens on the Margins: Puerto Rican Migrants in New York City, 1917–1960." PhD diss., University of Pennsylvania.

———. (2010) *Puerto Rican Citizen: History and Political Identity in Twentieth-Century New York City.* Chicago, IL.

Thomas, Norman Mattoon, and Bertram David Wolfe. (1939) *Keep America out of War.* New York.

Thomas, Woodlief. (1951) "Lessons of War Finance." *American Economic Review* 41: 618–631.

Thompson, Bob. (2004) "Return of the Native: In a Collection from a 'Dying Culture,' Rick West Finds a Life's Work." *Washington Post,* March 18.

Thorndike, Joseph J. (2001) "Wartime Tax Legislation and the Politics of Policymaking." *Tax History Project,* October 25.

Thorpe, Charles. (2006) *Oppenheimer: The Tragic Intellect.* Chicago, IL.

Tierney, Dominic. (2004) "Franklin D. Roosevelt and Covert Aid to the Loyalists in the Spanish Civil War, 1936–1939." *Journal of Contemporary History* 39: 299–313.

Tilley, John A. (2008) "A History of Women in the Coast Guard." *Coast Guard History: Historian's Office,* July 21.

Tillman, Barrett. (1998) "Before There Were Cats." *Flight Journal* 3: 72–78.

Tippins, Sherill. (2005) *February House.* Boston, MA.

Tittmann, Harold H. (2004) *Inside the Vatican of Pius XII: The Memoir of an American Diplomat During World War II.* New York.

Tobier, Emanuel. (1988) "Manhattan's Business District in the Industrial Age." In *Power, Culture, and Place: Essays on New York City,* edited by John H. Mollenkopf. New York.

Todd Shipyards Corporation. (1942) "Battle-Front... U.S.A. Todd Shipyards Corporation, N.Y." *National Geographic,* June.

Toll, William. (1997) "Horace M. Kallen: Pluralism and American Jewish Identity." *American Jewish History* 85: 57–74.

Tomkins, Calvin. (1970) *Merchants and Masterpieces: The Story of the Metropolitan Museum of Art.* New York.

———. (1994) "The World of Carmel Snow." *New Yorker,* November 7.

Tommasini, Anthony. (1997) *Virgil Thomson: Composer on the Aisle.* New York.

Tompkins, Daniel P. (2006) "The World of Moses Finkelstein: The Year 1939 in M. I. Finley's Development as a Historian." In *Classical Antiquity and the Politics of America,* edited by Michael Meckler. Waco, TX.

Torro, Kenny. (2002) "Carlo Gambino." *Mafia International,* August 18, 2002: 1–2.

Toynbee, Arnold. (1970) *Cities on the Move.* London.

Tracy, James. (1996) *Direct Action: Radical Pacifism from the Union Eight to the Chicago Seven.* Chicago, IL.

Traer, Robert. (1991) *Faith in Human Rights: Support in Religious Traditions for a Global Struggle.* Washington, DC.

Trager, James. (1990) *Park Avenue: Street of Dreams.* New York.

Traina, Richard P. (1968) *American Diplomacy and the Spanish Civil War.* Bloomington, IN.

Traub, James. (2004) *The Devil's Playground: A Century of Pleasure and Profit in Times Square.* New York.

Troen, S. Ilan. (2003) *Imagining Zion: Dreams, Designs, and Realities in a Century of Jewish Settlement.* New Haven, CT.

Troy, Thomas F. (1996) *Wild Bill and Intrepid: Donovan, Stephenson, and the Origin of CIA.* New Haven, CT.

Tuck, Jim. (1995) *McCarthyism and New York's Hearst Press: A Study of Roles in the Witch Hunt.* Lanham, MD.

Tucker, William H. (2002) *The Funding of Scientific Racism: Wickliffe Draper and the Pioneer Fund.* Urbana, IL.

Tugwell, Rexford G. (1940) "Planning in New York City." *Journal of the American Institute of Planners* 6: 33–34.

Tully, John Day. (2004) "Identities and Distortions: Irish-Americans, Ireland, and the United States, 1932–1945." PhD diss., Ohio State University.

Turkus, Burton B. (1951) *Murder, Inc.: The Story of "the Syndicate."* New York.

Turner, Henry Ashby. (2005) *General Motors and the Nazis: The Struggle for Control of Opel, Europe's Biggest Carmaker.* New Haven, CT.

Turner, John Frayn. (2004) *Frank Sinatra.* Dallas, TX.

Tushnet, Mark V. (1994) *Making Civil Rights Law: Thurgood Marshall and the Supreme Court, 1936–1961.* New York.

Tuttle, Dwight William. (1980) "Harry L. Hopkins and Anglo-Soviet Relations, 1941–1945." PhD diss., Washington State University.

Tuttle, William M. (1993) *"Daddy's Gone to War": The Second World War in the Lives of America's Children.* New York.

Twight, Charlotte. (1995) "Evolution of Federal Income Tax Withholding: The Machinery of Institutional Change." *Cato Journal* 14: 359–395.

"Two Pipelines for Sale?" (1945) *Fortune* 31: 125–129, 242, 245–246.

Tygiel, Jules. (1984) "The Court-Martial of Jackie Robinson." *American Heritage* 35: 34.

———. (2003) "Press Box Red by Lester Rodney and Irwin Sibler: An Introduction and a Chapter." *American Communist History* 2: 95–113.

———. (2008) *Baseball's Great Experiment: Jackie Robinson and His Legacy.* New York.

Tyler, Bruce M. (1999) "The Black Double V Campaign for Racial Democracy During World War II." *Journal of Kentucky Studies* 8: 79–108.

Tyler, Gus. (1995) *Look for the Union Label: A History of the International Ladies' Garment Workers' Union.* Armonk, NY.

UBoatAces. (2006) "America Joins the War." *German U-Boats and Battle of the Atlantic,* December 31, 2006: 1–3.

Udelson, Joseph H. (1982) *The Great Television Race: A History of the American Television Industry, 1925–1941.* University, AL.

Ueda, Reed. (1996) "The Changing Path to Citizenship: Ethnicity and Naturalization During World War II." In *The War in American Culture: Society and Consciousness During World War II,* edited by Lewis A. Erenberg and Susan E. Hirsch. Chicago, IL.

Ultan, Lloyd, and Gary Hermalyn. (1985) *The Bronx in the Innocent Years, 1890–1925.* The Bronx, NY.

———. (1992) *The Bronx: It Was Only Yesterday, 1935–1965.* Bronx, NY.

United Nations Association of the United States of America. (2009) "About UNA-USA." unausa.org, February 26.

United States Army. (1944) *History of the New York and Philadelphia Coastal Defenses.* Washington, DC.

United States Bureau of Yards and Docks. (1947) *Building the Navy's Bases in World War II: History of the Bureau of Yards and Docks and the Civil Engineer Corps, 1940–1946.* Vols. 1 & 2. Washington, DC.

United States Department of Agriculture. (2008) "Golden Nematode." *APHIS Factsheet: Plant Protection and Quarantine,* April.

United States Holocaust Memorial Museum. (2018a) "American Jewish Joint Distribution Committee and Refugee Aid." In *Holocaust Encyclopedia,* edited by United States Holocaust Memorial Museum. Washington, DC.

———. (2018b) "German Jewish Refugees, 1933–1939." In *Holocaust Encyclopedia,* edited by United States Holocaust Memorial Museum.

———. (2018c) "Stephen W. Wise." In *Holocaust Encyclopedia,* edited by United States Holocaust Memorial Museum. Washington, DC.

United States Office of Civilian Defense. (1941) *A Civil Defense Volunteer Office, an Official Arm of the Local Defense Council: What It Is, How to Organize It, What It Does.* Washington, DC.

United States Office of Facts and Figures and National Opinion Research Center. (1942) *The Negro Looks at the War: Attitudes of New York Negroes toward Discrimination against Negroes and a Comparison of Negro and Poor White Attitudes toward War-Related Issues; Based on a Series of Questions Asked of 1008 Negroes and 501 Whites in New York City.* Denver, CO.

United States Senate. (1976) *Final Report of the Select Committee to Study Governmental Operations with Respect to Intelligence Activities: The Church Committee Report.* Vol. 3. Washington, DC.

U.S. Department of Transportation and Federal Highway Administration. (2009) "Dwight D. Eisenhower National System of Interstate and Defense Highways." fhwa.dot.gov, January 7.

"U.S. Steel Votes Common Dividend: Names New Heads." (1937) *New York Times,* October 27.

University of Southampton Libraries. (2010) "Administrative/Biographical History." In *Papers of the Institute of Jewish Affairs,* edited by Special Collections. Southampton, UK.

Urofsky, Melvin I. (1982) *A Voice That Spoke for Justice: The Life and Times of Stephen S. Wise.* Albany, NY.

———. (1987) "Two Paths to Zion: Magnes and Stephen S. Wise." In *Like All the Nations? The Life and Legacy of Judah L. Magnes,* edited by William M. Brinner and Moses Rischin. Albany, NY.

———. (2009) *Louis D. Brandeis: A Life.* New York.

Usdin, Steven T. (2005a) *Engineering Communism: How Two Americans Spied for Stalin and Founded the Soviet Silicon Valley.* New Haven, CT.

———. (2005b) "Tracking Julius Rosenberg's Lesser Known Associates." *Studies in Intelligence* 49: 1–20.

Vaill, Amanda. (2006) *Somewhere: A Life of Jerome Robbins.* New York.

Valentine, Lewis Joseph. (1947) *Night Stick: The Autobiography of Lewis J. Valentine.* New York.

Valle, James E. (1994) "United States Merchant Marine Casualties." In *To Die Gallantly: The Battle of the Atlantic,* edited by Timothy J. Runyan and Jan M. Copes. Boulder, CO.

Van Allen, Rodger. (1974) *The Commonweal and American Catholicism: The Magazine, the Movement, the Meaning.* Philadelphia, PA.

Van der Vat, Dan. (1988) *The Atlantic Campaign: World War II's Great Struggle at Sea.* New York.

Van Hensbergen, Gijs. (2004) *Guernica: The Biography of a Twentieth-Century Icon.* New York.

Van Kirk, Walter W. (1934) *Religion Renounces War.* New York.

Van Paassen, Pierre, and James Waterman Wise. (1934) *Nazism: An Assault on Civilization.* New York.

"Varian Fry, the Saviour of So Many Avant-Garde Artists During the War." (1999) *artcult,* January.

Varnedoe, Kirk, and Pepe Karmel. (1998) *Jackson Pollock.* New York.

"Vatican over Hollywood." (1936) *Nation,* July 11.

Vecoli, Rudolph J. (1978a) "Girolamo Valenti." In

Il Movimento Operaio Italiano: Dizionario Biografico, 1853–1943, Volume 5, edited by Franco Andreucci and Tommaso Detti. Rome.

———. (1978b) "Louis Adamic and the Contemporary Search for Roots." *Ethnic Studies* 2: 29–35.

Veenswijk, Virginia Kays. (1994) *Coudert Brothers: A Legacy in Law: The History of America's First International Law Firm, 1853–1993*. New York.

Vego, Milan N. (1999) *Naval Strategy and Operations in Narrow Seas*. Portland, OR.

Venn, Fiona. (2000) "A Struggle for Supremacy? Great Britain, the United States and Kuwaiti Oil in the 1930s." In *Working Paper Series: Working Paper II*, edited by University of Essex Department of History. Colchester, UK.

Ventresco, Fiorello B. (1980) "Italian-Americans and the Ethiopian Crisis." *Italian Americana* 6: 4–27.

Ventry, Dennis, Jr., and Joseph J. Thorndike. (1997) "The Plan That Slogans Built: The Revenue Act of 1943." *Tax History Project*, September 1.

Venzi, Maureen. (2009) "A Tribute to the Merchant Seamen of World War Two: Parts One & Two." *Allied Merchant Navy of WWII*, September 10 and September 15.

Vickery, William E., and Stewart Grant Cole. (1943) *Intercultural Education in American Schools: Proposed Objectives and Methods*. New York.

Villaronga, Gabriel. (2004) *Toward a Discourse of Consent: Mass Mobilization and Colonial Politics in Puerto Rico, 1932–1948*. Westport, CT.

Vintage Fashion Guild. (2010) "New York Creation." *Label Resource*, July 16.

Voice of America. (2007) "The Beginning: An American Voice Greets the World." *VOA History*, March 14.

Volz, Barbara. (1992) "History of the Council on Books in Wartime." In *Council on Books in Wartime Records, 1942–1947: Finding Aid*, edited by Seeley G. Mudd Manuscript Library. Princeton, NJ.

Von Eschen, Penny M. (1997) *Race against Empire: Black Americans and Anticolonialism, 1937–1957*. Ithaca, NY.

———. (2000) "Who's the Real Ambassador? Exploding Cold War Racial Ideology." In *Cold War Constructions: The Political Culture of United States Imperialism, 1945–1966*, edited by Christian G. Appy. Amherst, MA.

Von Schilling, James A. (2003) *The Magic Window: American Television, 1939–1953*. New York.

Voss, Carl Hermann. (1964) *Rabbi and Minister: The Friendship of Stephen S. Wise and John Haynes Holmes*. Cleveland, OH.

———. (1968) "Let Stephen Wise Speak for Himself." *Dimensions in American Judaism* 3: 35–39.

Waddell, Brian. (2001) *The War against the New Deal: World War II and American Democracy*. DeKalb, IL.

Wainwright, Loudon. (1986) *The Great American Magazine: An Insider History of Life*. New York.

Wala, Michael. (1994) *The Council on Foreign Relations and American Foreign Policy in the Early Cold War*. Providence, RI.

Wald, Alan M. (1978) *James T. Farrell: The Revolutionary Socialist Years*. New York.

———. (1987) *The New York Intellectuals: The Rise and Decline of the Anti-Stalinist Left from the 1930s to the 1980s*. Chapel Hill, NC.

———. (2002) *Exiles from a Future Time: The Forging of the Mid-Twentieth-Century Literary Left*. Chapel Hill, NC.

Walding, Roger. (2001) *Anti-Submarine Indicator Loop Stations in the United States*. Wynnum, Australia.

———. (2013) "Anti-Submarine Indicator Loop Stations in the United States: Fort Tilden, New York." *Indicator Loops: Around the World*, October 23.

Waldman, John R. (1999) *Heartbeats in the Muck: The History, Sea Life, and Environment of New York Harbor*. New York.

Walker, Richard L. (1963) "E. R. Stettinius, Jr." In *The American Secretaries of State and Their Diplomacy: Vol. 14*, edited by Robert H. Ferrell and Samuel Flagg Bemis. New York.

Walker, Samuel. (1990) *In Defense of American Liberties: A History of the ACLU*. New York.

Walker, Thomas Joseph Edward. (1991) *Pluralistic Fraternity: The History of the International Worker's Order*. New York.

Walkowitz, Daniel J. (1999) *Working with Class: Social Workers and the Politics of Middle-Class Identity*. Chapel Hill, NC.

Wall, Wendy L. (2000) "America's 'Best Propagandists': Italian Americans and the 1948 'Letters to Italy' Campaign." In *Cold War Constructions: The Political Culture of United States Imperialism, 1945–1966*, edited by Christian G. Appy. Amherst, MA.

Wallace, Henry A. (1945) "Transform Liberal Words into Concrete Action: We Must Prove Idealism More Practical Than Common Sense." In *Testimonial Dinner under the Auspices of the Union for Democratic Action and the 'New Republic,' January 29, 1945*, edited by Vital Speeches of the Day. New York.

Wallace, Max. (2003) *The American Axis: Henry Ford, Charles Lindbergh, and the Rise of the Third Reich*. New York.

Wallace, Mike. (2010) "Nueva York, the Back Story: New York City and the Spanish-Speaking World from Dutch Days to the Second World War." In *Nueva York, 1613–1945*, edited by Edward J. Sullivan. New York.

———. (2018) "Gangbusters: La Guardia, Dewey, O'Dwyer." Paper presented at John Jay College, October 25, 2018. New York.

Wallock, Leonard, Dore Ashton, et al. (1988) *New York, Culture Capital of the World, 1940–1965*. New York.

Walsh, Frank. (1996) *Sin and Censorship: The Catholic Church and the Motion Picture Industry*. New Haven, CT.

Walsh, Marie de Lourdes. (1960) *The Sisters of Charity of New York, 1809–1959*. New York.

Walter, John C., and J. Raymond Jones. (1989) *The Harlem Fox: J. Raymond Jones and Tammany, 1920–1970*. Albany, NY.

Waltzer, Kenneth. (1977) "The American Labor Party: Third Party Politics in New Deal-Cold War New York, 1936–1954." PhD diss., Harvard University.

———. (1980) "The Party and the Polling Place: American Communism and an American Labor Party in the 1930s." *Radical History Review* 23: 104–129.

———. (1982) "The FBI, Congressman Vito Marcantonio, and the American Labor Party." In *Beyond the Hiss Case: The FBI, Congress, and the Cold War*, edited by Athan G. Theoharis. Philadelphia, PA.

Walzer, Michael. (1992) *What It Means to Be an American*. New York.

War Department. (1946) *World War II Honor List of Dead and Missing Army* and Army Air Forces Personnel from New York. Washington, DC.

"War Is Renounced by 240 Clergymen: Jews and Christians Accept 'Covenant of Peace' as 800 in Church Rise in Approval." (1935) *New York Times*, May 3.

Ware, Susan. (1981) *Beyond Suffrage: Women in the New Deal*. Cambridge, MA.

———. (1982) *Holding Their Own: American Women in the 1930s*. Boston, MA.

Warren, Frank A. (1993) *Liberals and Communism: The 'Red Decade' Revisited*. New York.

———. (1999) *Noble Abstractions: American Liberal Intellectuals and World War II*. Columbus, OH.

Warren, Heather A. (1997) *Theologians of a New World Order: Reinhold Niebuhr and the Christian Realists, 1920–1948*. New York.

Washburn, Patrick Scott. (1986) *A Question of Sedition: The Federal Government's Investigation of the Black Press During World War II*. New York.

Wasserstein, Bernard. (1987) "The Arab-Jewish Dilemma." In *Like All the Nations? The Life and Legacy of Judah L. Magnes*, edited by William M. Brinner and Moses Rischin. Albany, NY.

Weatherford, Doris. (1990) *American Women and World War II*. New York.

Weaver, Pat, and Thomas M. Coffey. (1994) *The Best Seat in the House: The Golden Years of Radio and Television*. New York.

Webb, G. Gregg. (2005) "Intelligence Liaison between the FBI and State, 1940–44: Effective Interagency Collaboration." *Studies in Intelligence* 49: 1–14.

Wechsler, James A. (1939) "The Coughlin Terror." *Nation*, July 22.

———. (1971) *Reflections of an Angry Middle-Aged Editor*. Freeport, NY.

Wedlock, Lunabelle. (1942) *The Reaction of Negro Publications and Organizations to German Anti-Semitism*. Washington, DC.

Weidlich, Thom. (2000) *Appointment Denied: The Inquisition of Bertrand Russell*. Amherst, NY.

Weigold, Auriol. (2008) *Churchill, Roosevelt, and India: Propaganda During World War II*. New York.

Weinberg, Sydney. (1968) "What to Tell America: The Writers' Quarrel in the Office of War Information." *Journal of American History* 55: 73–89.

Weiner, Charles. (1969) "Refugees and American Physics." In *The Intellectual Migration: Europe and America, 1930–1960*, edited by Donald Fleming and Bernard Bailyn. Cambridge, MA.

Weiner, Edward. (2008) *Urban Transportation Planning in the United States: History, Policy, and Practice*. New York.

Weinstein, Allen. (1997) *Perjury: The Hiss-Chambers Case*. New York.

Weinstein, Allen, and Alexander Vassiliev. (1999) *The Haunted Wood: Soviet Espionage in America: The Stalin Era*. New York.

Weinstein, Simcha. (2006) *Up, up, and Oy Vey! How Jewish History, Culture, and Values Shaped the Comic Book Superhero*. Baltimore, MD.

Weintraub, Stanley. (1968) *The Last Great Cause: The Intellectuals and the Spanish Civil War*. London.

Weisbord, Robert G., and Arthur Stein. (1970) *Bittersweet Encounter: The Afro-American and the American Jew*. Westport, CT.

Weiss, Richard. (1979) "Ethnicity and Reform: Minorities and the Ambience of the Depression Years."

Journal of American History 66: 566–585.

Weitz, John. (1997) *Hitler's Banker: Hjalmar Horace Greeley Schacht*. Boston, MA.

Welles, Benjamin. (1997) *Sumner Welles: FDR's Global Strategist: A Biography*. New York.

Wells, H. G. (1898) *The War of the Worlds*. New York.

Wentz, F. K. (1962) "American Catholic Periodicals React to Nazism." *Church History* 31: 400–420.

Wertheim, Albert. (2004) *Staging the War: American Drama and World War II*. Bloomington, IN.

Wertheim, Stephen. (2020) *Tomorrow, the World: The Birth of U.S. Global Supremacy*. Cambridge, MA.

Westbrook, Robert B. (1990a) "'I Want a Girl, Just Like the Girl That Married Harry James': American Women and the Problem of Political Obligation in World War II." *American Quarterly* 42: 587–614.

———. (1990b) "Lewis Mumford, John Dewey, and the 'Pragmatic Acquiescence.'" In *Lewis Mumford: Public Intellectual*, edited by Thomas P. Hughes and Agatha Hughes.

———. (1991) *John Dewey and American Democracy*. Ithaca, NY.

Wheeler, John Archibald and Kenneth William Ford. (1998) *Geons, Black Holes, and Quantum Foam: A Life in Physics*. New York.

White, E. B. (1946) *The Wild Flag: Editorials from the New Yorker on Federal World Government and Other Matters*. Boston, MA.

White, Gerald Taylor. (1980) *Billions for Defense: Government Financing by the Defense Plant Corporation During World War II*. Tuscaloosa, AL.

White, Graham J. (1979) *FDR and the Press*. Chicago, IL.

White, Graham J., and J. R. Maze. (1995)

Henry A. Wallace: His Search for a New World Order. Chapel Hill, NC.

Whitfield, Stephen J. (1998a) "Introduction to the Transaction Edition." In *Culture and Democracy in the United States*, edited by Horace Meyer Kallen and Stephen J. Whitfield. New Brunswick, NJ.

———. (1998b) "A Tale of Two Critics." *American Jewish History* 86: 1–25.

Wicker, Tom. (1995) "World War I: Five Films." In *Past Imperfect: History According to the Movies*, edited by Mark C. Carnes. New York.

Wiener, Jon. (1991) "When Old Blue Eyes Was Red." In *Professors, Politics, and Pop*, edited by Jon Wiener. New York.

Wilder, Craig Steven. (2000) *A Covenant with Color: Race and Social Power in Brooklyn*. New York.

Willcox, William Russell, and New York & New Jersey Port and Harbor Development Commission. (1920) *Joint Report with Comprehensive Plan and Recommendations*. Albany, NY.

Willett, Donald Edward. (1985) "Joe Curran and the National Maritime Union, 1936–1945." PhD diss., Texas A&M University.

Willett, John. (1978) "Erwin Piscator: New York and the Dramatic Workshop, 1939–1951." *Performing Arts Journal* 2: 3–16.

Williams, Arthur R., Michael P. Barrett, et al. (2001a) "Cutting the Deck: New Deal, Fair Deal, and the Employment Act of 1946: Problems of Study and Interpretation." In *Franklin D. Roosevelt and Congress: The New Deal and Its Aftermath, Vol. 2*, edited by Thomas P. Wolf, William D. Pederson, and Byron W. Daynes. Armonk, NY.

Williams, Jeannette, and Yolande Dickerson. (2001b) *The Invisible Cryptologists: African Americans, WWII to 1956*. Center for Cryptologic

History at the National Security Agency. Fort Meade, MD.

Williams, Vernon J. (1996) *Rethinking Race: Franz Boas and His Contemporaries.* Lexington, KY.

Willoughby, William R. (1961) *The St. Lawrence Waterway: A Study in Politics and Diplomacy.* Madison, WI.

Wills, Garry. (1984) "Cardinal Sins." *New Republic,* December 10.

Wilz, John Edward. (1963) *In Search of Peace: The Senate Munitions Inquiry, 1934–36.* Baton Rouge, LA.

Winchell, Meghan K. (2004) "'To Make the Boys Feel at Home': USO Senior Hostesses and Gendered Citizenship." *Frontiers: A Journal of Women Studies* 25: 190–211.

Winfield, Betty Houchin. (1994) *FDR and the News Media.* New York.

Wingfield, Valerie, and New York Public Library. (1997) *The Fashion Group International Records c. 1930–1997: Finding Aid.* New York.

Winkleman, Michael. (1986) *The Fragility of Turf: The Neighborhoods of New York City.* Albany, NY.

Winkler, Allan M. (2000) *Home Front U.S.A.: America During World War II.* Wheeling, IL.
———. (2012) *Home Front U.S.A.: America During World War II.* Wheeling, IL.

Wintz, Cary D., and Paul Finkelman. (2004) *Encyclopedia of the Harlem Renaissance.* New York.

Wise, Stephen Samuel. (1949) *Challenging Years: The Autobiography of Stephen Wise.* New York.

Wissot, Jay. (1975) "John Dewey, Horace Meyer Kallen and Cultural Pluralism." *Educational Theory* 25: 186–196.

Witcover, Jules. (1989) *Sabotage at Black Tom: Imperial Germany's Secret War in America, 1914–1917.* Chapel Hill, NC.

Wittner, Lawrence S. (1969) *Rebels against War: The American Peace Movement, 1941–1960.* New York.

Witwer, David. (2005) "Westbrook Pegler and the Anti-Union Movement." *Journal of American History* 92: 527–552.

Wogaman, J. Philip, and Douglas M. Strong. (1996) *Readings in Christian Ethics: A Historical Sourcebook.* Louisville, KY.

Woideck, Carl. (1996) *Charlie Parker: His Music and Life.* Ann Arbor, MI.

Wolf, Thomas P., William D. Pederson, et al. (2001) *Franklin D. Roosevelt and Congress: The New Deal and Its Aftermath.* Vol. 2. Armonk, NY.

Wolfe, Alan. (1981) *America's Impasse: The Rise and Fall of the Politics of Growth.* New York.

Wood, E. Thomas, and Stanislaw M Jankowski. (1994) *Karski: How One Man Tried to Stop the Holocaust.* New York.

Wood, Julie K. (1992) "Identities in Conflict: New York Irish Catholics' Response to the Spanish Civil War, 1936–1939." *New York Irish History* 7: 5–10, 36–47.

Woodrow Wilson Foundation. (1922) *The Woodrow Wilson Foundation: A Tribute to a Great American.* New York.

World Council of Churches. (2000) *A Half-Century of Service.* Geneva, Switzerland.

Wreszin, Michael. (1965) *Oswald Garrison Villard, Pacifist at War.* Bloomington, IN.
———. (1994) *A Rebel in Defense of Tradition: The Life and Politics of Dwight Macdonald.* New York.

Wright, Bradford W. (2001) *Comic Book Nation: The Transformation of Youth Culture in America.* Baltimore, MD.

Wright, Jill Yvonne Gold. (2003) "Creating America on Stage: How Jewish Composers and Lyricists Pioneered American Musical Theater." PhD diss., Claremont Graduate University.

Wylie, Philip. (1942) *Generation of Vipers.* New York.

Wyman, David S. (1968) *Paper Walls: America and the Refugee Crisis, 1938–1941.* Amherst, MA.
———. (1984) *The Abandonment of the Jews: America and the Holocaust, 1941–1945.* New York.

Wyman, David S., and Rafael Medoff. (2002) *A Race against Death: Peter Bergson, America, and the Holocaust.* New York.

Wytrwal, Joseph Anthony. (1977) *Behold! The Polish-Americans.* Detroit, MI.

Yago, Glenn. (1984) *The Decline of Transit: Urban Transportation in German and U.S. Cities, 1900–1970.* New York.

Yale Law Journal. (1947) "The New York State Commission against Discrimination: A New Technique for an Old Problem." *Yale Law Journal* 56: 837–863.

Yans, Virginia. (2004) "On the Political Anatomy of Mead-Bashing, or Re-Thinking Margaret Mead." In *Reading Benedict/Reading Mead: Feminism, Race, and Imperial Visions,* edited by Dolores E. Janiewski and Lois W. Banner. Baltimore, MD.

Yans-McLaughlin, Virginia. (1986) "Science, Democracy, and Ethics: Mobilizing Culture and Personality for World War II." In *Malinowski, Rivers, Benedict, and Others: Essays on Culture and Personality,* edited by George W. Stocking Jr. Madison, WI.

Yarnall, Paul R. (2003) "Locations of the United States Army Air Force: December 7, 1941." *NavSource Naval History,* November.

Yellin, Emily. (2004) *Our Mothers' War: American Women at Home and at the Front During World War II.* New York.

Yergin, Daniel. (1991) *The Prize: The Epic Quest for Oil, Money, and Power.* New York.

Young, Dannagal Goldthwaite. (2005a) "Sacrifice, Consumption, and the American Way of Life: Advertising and Domestic Propaganda During World War II." *Communication Review* 8: 27–52.

Young, Virginia Heyer. (2005b) *Ruth Benedict: Beyond Relativity, Beyond Pattern.* Lincoln, NE.

Young, William H., and Nancy K. Young. (2005) *Music of the Great Depression.* Westport, CT.

Yu, Renqiu. (1990) "Little Heard Voices: The Chinese Hand Laundry Alliance and the *China Daily News'* Appeal for Repeal of the Chinese Exclusion Act in 1943." *Chinese America: History and Perspectives* 4: 21–35.
———. (1992) *To Save China, to Save Ourselves: The Chinese Hand Laundry Alliance of New York.* Philadelphia, PA.

Zeckendorf, William, and Edward A. McCreary. (1987) *Zeckendorf: The Autobiography of William Zeckendorf.* Chicago, IL.

Zeitz, Joshua. (2007) *White Ethnic New York: Jews, Catholics, and the Shaping of Postwar Politics.* Chapel Hill, NC.

Zeitzer, Glen, and Charles F. Howlett. (1986) "Political Versus Religious Pacifism: The Peace Movement of 1943." *The Historian* 48: 375–393.

Zhao, Xiaojian. (2002) *Remaking Chinese America: Immigration, Family, and Community, 1940–1965.* New Brunswick, NJ.

Zimmerman, Jonathan. (2002) "Ethnics against Ethnicity: European Immigrants and Foreign-Language Instruction, 1890–1940." *Journal of American History* 88: 1383–1404.

Zipp, Samuel. (2010) *Manhattan Projects: The*

Rise and Fall of Urban Renewal in Cold War New York. New York.

Zitron, Celia Lewis. (1969) The New York City Teachers Union, 1916–1964: A Story of Educational and Social Commitment. New York.

Zolberg, Aristide R., and Agnès Callamard. (1998) "The École Libre at the New School, 1941–1946." Social Research 65: 921–951.

Zolberg, Vera L. (1993) "New York Culture: Ascendant or Subsident?" In Capital of the American Century: National and International Influence of New York City, edited by Martin Shefter. New York.

Zolotow, Maurice. (1940) "South of the Border–on Broadway: A Latin-American Craze Sweeps All before It in Theatres and Night Clubs." New York Times Magazine, February 18.

———. (1941) "Broadway Rose." Saturday Evening Post, September 20.

Zucker, Bat-Ami. (2001) "Frances Perkins and the German-Jewish Refugees, 1933–1940." American Jewish History 89: 35–59.

Zuckert, Catherine H., and Michael P. Zuckert. (2006) The Truth About Leo Strauss: Political Philosophy and American Democracy. Chicago, IL.

Zunz, Olivier. (1998) Why the American Century? Chicago, IL.

Zuroff, Efraim. (2000) The Response of Orthodox Jewry in the United States to the Holocaust: The Activities of the Vaad Ha-Hatzala Rescue Committee, 1939–1945. New York.

Zuroff, Efraim, and David Kranzler. (2003) "Orthodox Rescue Revisited." Jewish Action 63: 1–8.

Zweig, Phillip L. (1995) Wriston: Walter Wriston, Citibank, and the Rise and Full of American Financial Supremacy. New York.

Zwickel, Jean Wiley. (1998) Voices for Independence: In the Spirit of Valor and Sacrifice: Portraits of Notable Individuals in the Struggle for Puerto Rican Independence. Pittsburg, CA.

Zygielbaum, Joseph L. (2009) The Odyssey of a Partisan. Scotts Valley, CA.

Index of Names

Figures are indicated by "f" following page numbers. A separate Index of Subjects follows this Index of Names.

Abbot, George, 648, 695
Abbott, Berenice, 653f
Abel, Lionel, 173
Abrams, Charles, 591, 607, 608
Abzug, Bella, 484
Acheson, Dean, 266, 279
Adamic, Louis, 142–43, 822
Adler, Cyrus, 10, 121, 122
Adler, Polly, 622
Adler, Stella, 578, 677
Adoian, Vosdanik Manoog, 658
Adonis, Joe, 364, 376
Adorno, Theodor, 11–12, 594
Agee, James, 173
Agha, Mehemed Fehmy, 682
Aiken, Frank, 97
Akhmerov, Itzhak, 192, 193, 195
Albert, Heinrich, 243–45, 247
Albizu Campos, Pedro, 826–29, 831
Aldrich, Harriet, 490, 858
Aldrich, Winthrop, 259, 265, 286, 302, 342, 345, 729, 741–43, 807, 858
Aleman, Miguel, 861
Alexander II (czar of Russia), 568

Allan, Lewis (pen name of Abel Meeropol), 594
Allen, Clemon, 529
Allen, Devere, 150–51, 158, 198
Allen, Gracie, 628
Alsop, Joseph, 266
Altschul, Frank, 254, 269, 274, 276
Ameche, Don, 218–19
Ammons, Albert, 630, 652
Anastasia, Albert, 345, 346, 351, 363
Anastasio, Tough Tony, 363
Anderson, Marian, 322, 323f, 329
Anderson, Maxwell, 173, 454
Anderson, Sherwood, 332, 827
Andrews, Adolphus "Dolly," 335–36, 338, 353, 359, 362, 386–87, 391, 404
Angel, Zuleta, 858, 861
Annenberg, Ivan, 231
Antonini, Luigi, 41–42, 54, 56, 375
Aragon, Louis, 669
Arden, Elizabeth, 680
Arendt, Hannah, 236
Armstrong, Hamilton "Ham" Fish, 255, 256, 263, 264, 266, 269, 327, 328, 837
Armstrong, Robert H., 711
Arnaz, Desi, 648–49
Arnold, Benedict, 166
Arnold, Harley "Hap," 851
Arnold, Matthew, 117, 275
Aronovici, Carol, 712
Ascoli, Max, 56, 228, 236, 375
Astaire, Fred, 629, 649
Astor, John Jacob, 445, 752
Astor, Nancy (Lady Astor), 257
Astor, Vincent, 297, 302, 752–54, 859
Atkinson, Brooks, 151, 218, 538, 677, 681
Attucks, Crispus, 130
Auden, W. H., 35, 624, 669
Aumuller, Al, 737f
Austin, Warren, 858, 861–62
Autry, Gene, 469
Avery, Milton, 658, 659, 661
Ayer, William Ward, 491
Azpiazú, Don, 646

Backer, George, Jr., 227, 228
Baer, Max, 47, 66
Bailey, Bill, 74
Baker, Ella, 514, 596
Baker, Newton, 122, 597

Balanchine, George, 307, 629, 690
Baldwin, James, 551, 625
Baldwin, Roger, 12, 149, 152–53, 161, 168, 180, 198, 237, 369, 817, 822, 826
Balfour, Arthur James, 571, 574
Ball, Lucille, 649
Ballantine, Betty, 668
Ballantine, Ian, 668, 669
Bandy, Robert, 546, 548
Bankhead, Tallulah, 183, 327, 678
Barnes, Joseph F., 303, 460, 461
Barnett, Claude, 549
Barnouw, Erik, 465, 670–71
Baron, Salo, 576
Barr, Alfred, 165, 236, 651, 653, 656
Barringer, Emily Dunning, 484
Barrymore, Ethel, 694
Barrymore, Lionel, 453
Bartholdi, Frédéric Auguste, 136
Bartók, Béla, 640
Barton, Bruce, 275, 284
Baruch, Bernard, 270–71, 294, 409, 511, 694, 856

Index of Names

Basie, Count, 160, 603, 637, 644
Batchelor, C. D., 624f
Batista, Fulgencio, 648
Bauer, Catherine, 719
Baum, Morton, 698
Baumgartner, Leona, 501, 502
Bauzá, Estrella, 649
Bauzá, Mario, 649–50
Bazarov, Boris, 192
Baziotes, William, 658, 659, 661
Beadle, Erasmus, 665
Beard, Charles, 10, 12, 835
Beard, Mary, 515
Beaverbrook, Lord, 228
Bechtel, Steven, 316
Beck, A. S., 659
Becker, Carl, 802
Beckmann, Max, 655
Bedacht, Max, 193
Behn, Sosthenes, 243, 245, 246
Belafonte, Harry, 677
Bel Geddes, Norman, 228
Bell, Alexander Graham, 426
Bellamy, Ralph, 670
Benchley, Robert, 212, 295, 629
Bendel, Henri, 682
Bendix, William, 410
Benedict, Ruth, 119, 127, 141, 163, 185, 439, 593, 821, 827
Benét, Stephen Vincent, 218, 332, 454, 670
Ben-Gurion, David, 572–78
Benjamin, Walter, 238
Benny, Jack, 327, 628
Bentley, Elizabeth Terrill, 195
Benton, Thomas Hart, 654
Benton, William, 231, 764
Bergen, Edgar, 219
Bergson, Henri, 248
Bergson, Peter, 577–80, 583
Beria, Lavrenty, 195
Berle, Adolf, 184, 204–5, 210, 224, 300, 302, 307, 343, 808, 835, 837
Berle, Milton, 628, 629
Berlin, Irving, 276, 327, 329, 447, 467–69, 626, 673, 747
Berlin, Isaiah, 262
Berman, Bess, 642
Berman, Ike, 642
Bernays, Edward L., 209
Bernstein, Leonard, 692–95, 697, 699–700
Bernstein, Sam, 693
Berry, Abner, 45
Bethe, Hans, 423
Bethune, Mary McLeod, 538, 814
Beveridge, William, 763, 797
Biddle, Francis, 141, 370, 373, 375, 536
Bilbo, Theodore, 591, 604, 609–10

Billings, John Shaw, 229
Billingsley, Sherman, 224, 225, 628–30
Bishop, William Gerald, 96
Black, Algernon, 198, 543, 611–12
Black, Julian, 48
Blackburn, Jack "Chappie," 48
Blake, Eubie, 161
Blaustein, Jacob, 842
Blitzstein, Marc, 159, 160, 218, 692
Block, Martin, 636
Blondell, Joan, 629–30
Boas, Franz, 11, 95, 117–22, 127, 134, 141, 161, 163, 184–85, 187–88, 197, 438–40, 527, 560, 593, 598, 655, 676, 817
Boas, Marie, 117
Bocher, Main.
  See Mainbocher
Bofinger, E. M., 712f
Bogart, Humphrey, 272
Bohn, Frank, 237, 238
Bohr, Niels, 422, 425, 429
Bolger, Ray, 629
Boni, Charles, 666
Bonnet, Henri, 687
Borgongini Duca, Francesco, 89
Bostic, Joe, 613–15
Boudin, Louis, 96–97
Bourke-White, Margaret, 231, 515
Bourne, Randolph, 113–14, 116, 118, 127, 143, 196, 197, 209, 379
Bowles, Chester, 231, 292, 511–12, 514, 518
Bowles, Paul, 679, 692, 693
Braddock, James, 57, 58
Bradley, Omar, 849–50
Brady, Anthony N., 89
Brady, Genevieve Garvan, 89–91
Brady, John F., 84
Brady, Nicholas F., 89, 93
Brancusi, Constantin, 651
Brande, Dorothea, 667
Brandeis, Louis Dembitz, 570, 571
Brando, Marlon, 677
Braque, Georges, 661
Braun, Eva, 850
Brecht, Bertolt, 677
Brennan, Walter, 453
Brent, George, 99
Breton, André, 174, 236, 238–39, 439, 441, 456–57, 651–55
Breuer, Joseph, 27
Brewster, Kingman, Jr., 290, 291
Bricker, John, 784–85
Bricktop, Madame, 643
Bridges, Harry, 406–7

Britt, George, 35
Broch, Herman, 669
Broder, S., 671f
Brodovitch, Alexey, 682
Brontë, Emily, 667
Broun, Heywood (father), 177
Broun, Heywood Hale (son), 232
Browder, Earl, 152–53, 157, 166, 168, 176, 181–83, 187, 192, 193, 195, 406, 788, 789, 804
Brown, Adele, 295
Brown, Claude, 547
Brown, Les, 644
Brownell, Herbert, Jr., 785–87
Bruce, Herbert, 604
Brundage, Avery, 8
Bryan, William Jennings, 835
Brynner, Yul, 456
Buber, Martin, 11
Buchalter, Lepke, 345–47, 378
Buck, Pearl, 667, 821–24, 827
Budenz, Louis, 182
Bullitt, William, 840
Buloff, Joseph, 676
Buñuel, Luis, 306
Burke, John S., 93
Burlingham, Charles Culp, 208, 279, 344, 345, 399, 611
Burnham, Daniel, 762
Burnham, Philip, 87
Burns, Eveline M., 762
Burns, George, 628
Burr, Aaron, 166
Bush, Prescott, 244, 253
Bush, Vannevar, 426–27, 432
Butler, Nicholas Murray, 11, 119, 156, 157, 345, 707, 848
Butler, Samuel, 667
Buttinger, Joseph, 236
Bykov, Boris, 192–95
Byrnes, James, 783–84

Cacchione, Peter, 351, 518, 608
Cadman, S. Parkes, 123
Cadmus, Paul, 691, 691f
Cagney, Jimmy, 99–100, 475, 674
Calder, Alexander, 653, 661
Caldwell, Erskine, 230
Calles, Plutarco Elías, 69, 70
Calloway, Cab, 160, 603, 638, 638f, 640–41, 642f, 649–50
Calverton, V. F., 170, 227, 282
Camp, Florence, 34
Campanella, Roy, 617
Campbell, Harold, 141
Camus, Albert, 669
Caniff, Milton, 474
Canning, William Martin, 189

Cansino, Margarita Carmen.
  See Hayworth, Rita
Cantor, Eddie, 327, 329, 345
Cantril, Hadley, 221
Capra, Frank, 275
Cárdenas, Juan F., 163
Cárdenas, Lázaro, 177, 304, 828
Carlebach, Julius, 441
Carlisle, Norman, 802
Carman, Harry J., 154
Carnegie, Dale, 668
Carnegie, Hattie, 681, 682, 684
Carnera, Primo, 47–50
Carpentier, Georges, 47
Carter, Benny, 638
Carter, Boake, 216
Carter, Sayde R., 714f
Caruso, Enrico, 646–47
Carver, George Washington, 126
Casals, Pablo, 160, 238
Cashmore, John, 713
Cassidy, John F., 86, 87, 96
Castroviejo, Ramon, 163
Cavert, Samuel McCrea, 207
Celler, Emanuel, 9, 24, 303, 410, 564
Cerf, Bennett, 95, 669, 670
Chadwick, James, 428
Chagall, Marc, 236, 239, 651, 652, 661
Chalmers, Allan Knight, 148, 198
Chamberlain, John, 770, 772
Chamberlain, Neville, 212, 217, 575
Chambers, Whittaker, 193–94, 770
Chanel, Coco, 681
Channing, Carol, 690
Chaplin, Charlie, 677
Chase, Edna Woolman, 680, 682, 684
Chase, Stuart, 804
Chevalier, Stuart, 802
Chiang Kai-shek, 106–7, 821, 823
Childs, Richard Storrs, 666–67
Christie, Agatha, 667
Chrysler, Walter, 407
Churchill, Randolph, 260
Churchill, Winston, 96, 232, 234, 260, 261, 278, 286, 293, 297, 299, 303, 386, 392, 400, 566, 576, 583, 763, 792, 807–10, 815, 817–18, 821, 836, 847
Clark, Evans, 804
Clark, Grenville, 276, 279, 294, 295
Clark, John, 765
Clark, Kenneth Bancroft, 524, 527, 551, 597, 598
Clark, Mamie Phipps, 597
Clarke, John Henrik, 44

Index of Names

Clarke, Kenny, 639, 650
Clinchy, Everett, 122, 128, 130
Clurman, Harold, 677, 678
Coates, Robert, 656, 657
Cobb, Lee J., 673
Coburn, Julia, 680, 685
Coca, Imogene, 630, 649, 690
Cocteau, Jean, 687
Coffin, Henry Sloane, 122, 207, 208, 266, 280, 292, 839
Cohan, George M., 196, 329, 332, 467
Cohen, Ben, 583
Cohen, Elliot, 169
Cohen, Irene, 17
Cohen, Morris Raphael, 12, 176, 187
Colbert, Claudette, 628
Coleman, John, 93
Collado, Benito, 163
Collado, Tomas, 163
Collingswood, Charles, 222
Collins, Ella, 540, 541
Collins, James, 546
Colon, Jesus, 162
Colón, Jesús, 827
Comden, Betty, 631, 693, 695, 696
Compton, Arthur H., 432
Compton, Karl, 425, 427, 432
Concepción de Gracia, Gilberto, 827, 831
Connally, Tom, 778, 815, 843
Connolly, James, 77
Connolly, Maurice, 65
Connor, Eugene "Bull," 596, 777
Conroy, Jack, 169
Coolidge, Calvin, 250, 835
Cooper, Gary, 629
Copernicus, Nicolaus, 421
Copland, Aaron, 139, 160, 307, 675, 692–95
Coralnik, Abe, 5
Corbett, Harvey Wiley, 755
Cornell, Katharine, 628
Corwin, Norman, 139, 453, 454
Costello, Frank, 363, 364
Costigan, William J., 84
Coudert, Fred (father), 188
Coudert, Frederic R. "Fritz," Jr. (son), 188, 189, 610–11
Coudert, Frederic René (grandfather), 188
Coughlin, Charles E., 85, 87, 90, 94–96, 98, 132, 156, 164, 210, 232, 330, 373, 550, 584
Counts, George, 127, 130, 163, 168, 185, 209
Courant, Richard, 435
Covello, Leonard, 128–31, 142, 530
Cowles, Gardner "Mike," Jr., 454–55, 457, 460

Cowley, Malcolm, 177, 180, 210
Cox, James R., 87, 835
Cravath, Paul, 254
Creel, George, 303
Cripps, Stafford, 817
Criscuolo, Luigi, 40
Croker, Richard, 65
Crosby, Bing, 469, 628, 633, 636
Crosswaith, Frank, 322, 591
Cugat, Xavier, 646–49
Cullen, John, 366
Cullman, Howard S., 698, 730
Cuneo, Ernest, 223–25, 261–62
Curran, Edward Lodge, 75, 78–79, 82–84, 94, 98–99, 232, 374
Curran, Joe, 109, 407, 408, 526, 698
Curry, John, 65
Curtis, Cyrus H. K., 226
Curtis, Tony, 677
Cuse, Robert, 164

Daché, Lilly, 680–82, 686
Daganova, Ella, 690
Daladier, Édouard, 217
Dalí, Salvador, 651
Daly, John, 352
Danaher, Daniel, 65
Danilova, Alexandra, 690
D' Annunzio, Gabriele, 40
D' Annunzio, Ugo Veniero, 40
Darlan, François, 360
Darlan, Jean, 460
Das, Tarak Nath, 817
Dasch, George John, 366–67
Davenport, Charles, 118
Davenport, Russell, 274–75
Davies, John R., 344–45
Davis, Benjamin J., Jr., 518, 602–3, 606–8, 611, 616, 617
Davis, Benjamin O., Sr., 321, 535–36
Davis, Elmer, 222, 266, 454, 457, 459–61
Davis, Jefferson, 166
Davis, John W., 254, 258, 259, 328
Davis, Norman, 529, 837
Davis, Stuart, 659, 661
Davis, Tobé Coller, 684, 685
Davisson, Clinton, 426
Day, Dorothy, 75, 81, 87, 92, 99, 377
Deatherage, George E., 87
Debs, Eugene Victor, 5
De Forest, Lee, 416, 422, 426
De Gaulle, Charles, 436, 440, 460
De Graff, Robert Fair, 664–65, 667–68, 670
De Haas, Jacob, 569, 570

De Kooning, Willem, 657–59, 661
Delacorte, George T., Jr., 668
Delano, Frederic A., 762, 765, 779
Dellinger, David, 280
DeMange, Big Frenchy, 47
DeMille, Agnes, 675, 690, 691
DeMille, Cecil B., 675, 772
Dempsey, Jack, 47, 48, 57, 66, 629
De Valera, Éamon, 63, 96, 97
Devany, John A., Jr., 83
Dewey, John, 10–12, 81, 122, 127, 161, 163, 168, 176–80, 185–89, 194, 197, 198, 209, 210, 282
Dewey, Thomas, 34, 54, 150, 189, 272–74, 276, 343, 345, 346, 363, 364, 365, 375, 411, 414, 501, 519–20, 548, 579, 582, 583, 585f, 610, 612, 616, 705, 718, 729, 741, 745, 785–87, 789, 794–97
DeWitt, John L., 369, 372
Diaghilev, Sergei, 690
Diaz, Manuel, 163, 164
Dickens, Charles, 251, 666
Dickstein, Samuel, 9–10, 16, 20–21, 24, 194, 564
Dieckhoff, Hans Heinrich, 19
Dies, Martin, 20–21, 187, 188, 191
Dietrich, Marlene, 360
Dillon, Clarence, 296
DiMaggio, Joe, 66, 374–75, 454, 615, 694
Dimitrov, Georgi, 181
Dior, Christian, 687
Divine, Father, 50
Dodd, Bella, 189
Dodson, Dan, 617
Donenfeld, Harry, 474, 476
Dönitz, Karl, 334, 335, 338, 357, 359, 364, 386, 387, 392–93, 427
Donovan, William "Wild Bill," 35, 93, 99, 100, 279, 299, 302–3, 307, 352, 456, 458
Dooling, Peter J., 65
Dore, Jerome, 529
Dorsey, Tommy, 628, 632, 633, 640
Dos Passos, John, 12, 159, 176, 178, 236
Dostoevsky, Fyodor, 169
Douglas, Aaron, 128
Douglas, Alta, 128
Douglas, Lewis, 265, 266, 274, 279, 282
Douglass, Frederick, 537, 552
Dowling, Eddie, 679
Downey, Wallace, 415

Draper, Wickliffe Preston, 119, 835
Dreiser, Theodore, 142, 152, 176, 177, 180, 827
Drum, Hugh A., 336, 340, 353, 372, 383, 391
Dubinsky, David, 12, 41, 152, 161, 168, 184, 204, 234, 237, 264, 265, 283, 328, 345, 392, 411, 557–58, 698, 788–89
DuBois, Rachel Davis, 126–34, 142, 143, 185, 530, 594
Du Bois, W. E. B., 44, 45, 51, 126, 128, 133, 325, 369, 523, 524, 549, 592, 596, 598, 813–15, 817, 818, 832, 840
Duchamp, Marcel, 236, 239, 651–54
Duchin, Eddy, 327
Dudensing, Valentine, 165
Duffy, Big Bill, 47
Duffy, Francis Patrick, 99–100
Duggan, Stephen, 11, 163
Dulles, Allen, 247–48, 254–56, 266, 279, 303, 456
Dulles, John Foster, 246–51, 254, 273, 279, 290–91, 331, 794, 815, 837–38, 840–41, 843
DuMont, Allen B., 748
Dunbar, John, 859
Dunn, John J., 5
Dunn, Johnny "Cockeye," 364, 365, 406
Dunn, Leslie, 11, 120
Dunnigan, John J., 188
Dunning, John R., 423, 429–30, 430f, 432, 438
Dupee, Fred, 169, 171–73, 180
Durant, Will, 666
Durante, Jimmy, 628, 629, 690
Duranty, Walter, 168, 179
Durocher, Leo, 327, 629
Durst, David, 752
Durst, Joseph, 752
Durst, Royal, 752
Durst, Seymour, 752
Dyer-Bennett, Richard, 632

Early, Steve, 320, 321, 324
Eastland, James, 591
Eastman, Max, 770, 772
Eaton, Fred, 310
Eberstadt, Ferdinand, 244, 296–98, 308, 409–11, 835
Eccles, Marriner, 451
Echaurren, Roberto Matta, 654, 658, 659
Ecker, Frederick H., 532, 605, 713, 856
Eckert, Wallace J., 436
Eckstine, Billy, 641

Eddy, Sherwood, 208
Edel, Leon, 230
Edelman, Marek, 562
Edison, Thomas, 416, 422, 430
Edward VIII (king of England), 258
Efron, David, 122
Ehrlich, Otto, 802
Eichelberger, Clark Mell, 156, 157, 264, 266, 279, 810, 834, 837, 840–42, 857
Einstein, Albert, 12, 23, 238, 422, 423, 425, 429–31, 440, 602, 677
Eisenhower, Dwight, 359, 436, 460, 533, 791, 849–50
Eisler, Hanns, 677
Eisner, Will, 475, 477
Elchanan, Isaac, 30
Eldridge, Roy, 638–40, 639*f*
Elena (queen of Italy), 51
Eliot, T. S., 169, 170, 213
Elizabeth (wife of George VI), 257, 258
Ellender, Allen, 719
Elliman, Douglas L., 754
Ellington, Duke, 59, 160, 469, 603, 628, 638, 638*f*, 644
Elliott, John Lovejoy, 717
Ellison, Ralph, 547, 592, 602, 639
Embury, Aymar, II, 856
Emmet, Thomas Addis, 212
Emy, Sabro, 370
Englebrecht, H. C., 150
Enoch, Kurt, 666, 669
Epstein, Henry, 606
Ernst, Max, 236, 238–39, 441, 651, 652, 654, 655
Ernst, Morris, 300
Evans, Redd, 493
Evergood, Philip, 659

Fadiman, Clifton, 275, 465
Falconer, Bruce M., 422
Farley, James Aloysius, 65, 204, 205, 347, 629
Farmer, Frances, 109
Farmer, James, 325
Farrell, James T., 172–74, 180
Farrell, John, 93
Farrell, Thomas F., 853
Fastenberg, Arnold, 224–25
Feather, Leonard, 643
Feeney, Harry, 345
Feiner, Leon, 562, 564–65
Feininger, Andreas, 382*f*
Feinstein, Isidor. *See* Stone, I. F.
Feklisov, Aleksandr, 434, 435
Fellig, Usher (Weegee), 231
Fennelly, John F., 766, 767, 769
Fermi, Enrico, 423, 428–32, 430*f*, 435, 438, 676, 677

Fermi, Laura, 428–29
Fertig, Lawrence, 771
Feuchtwanger, Lion, 236, 238
Field, Marshall, III, 230, 234, 668, 698
Fields, Gracie, 334
Finkelstein, Max, 22
Finkelstein (later Finley), Moses I., 120, 184, 185, 189
Fish, Hamilton, Jr., 284, 330, 373, 534–35
Fitzgerald, Ella, 603, 638
Fitzgerald, F. Scott, 169
Flaubert, Gustave, 173
Fleet, Biddy, 640
Fleischer, Max, 475
Fleming, Ian, 302–3
Flores, Marcial, 645, 646
Flynn, Edward J., 65, 205, 283, 783–84
Flynn, Elizabeth Gurley, 78, 502, 503
Flynn, John Thomas, 291–93, 330, 333, 770
Fokine, Mikhail, 689, 690
Foner, Jack, 189
Foner, Philip, 189
Fontanne, Lynn, 212, 327
Ford, Edsel, 243
Ford, George Barry, 92
Ford, Henry, 5, 16, 85, 245
Ford, James, 45
Forrestal, James Vincent, 228, 244, 295–98, 305, 308, 324, 409, 411, 747, 835
Forster, Arnold, 224–25
Fosdick, Harry Emerson, 122, 123, 147–49, 157, 163, 188, 197, 292
Foster, William Z., 78, 187
Fox, Victor, 474
France, Anatole, 666
Francisco, Don, 457
Franco, Francisco, 20, 72–76, 86, 158, 163–66, 178, 183, 213, 229, 232, 238, 245, 251, 266, 407
Frank, Karl, 207, 235–38
Frank, Waldo, 168, 176, 209
Frankfurter, Felix, 276
Freeman, Joseph, 167, 169, 170
French, Fred, 716
Friedan, Betty Goldstein, 502–3
Friedan, Carl, 503
Friedman, Milton, 775
Frisch, Otto Robert, 429
Fromm, Erich, 11–12
Frost, Robert, 575
Fry, Varian, 237–39, 269, 439, 557, 565, 651, 669, 836
Fuchs, Daniel, 28
Fuchs, Klaus, 434, 435

Fuller, Walter D., 464, 768, 769
Fulton, Robert, 431

Gabler, Milt, 641
Gaines, Lloyd, 596
Gaines, Maxwell Charles, 495
Galante, Carmine, 375
Galbraith, John Kenneth, 771, 778
Gambino, Carlo, 512
Gandhi, Mohandas K., 5, 59, 149–51, 326, 379, 538, 817, 818
Gannon, Robert I., 81, 283, 374
Garbo, Greta, 94
Garcia, Marcelino, 163, 164
Gardel, Carlos, 646
Gardiner, Muriel, 236
Garibaldi, Giuseppe, 573
Garland, Judy, 398, 506
Garofalo, Frank, 375
Garson, Greer, 629–30
Garvey, Marcus, 44, 526, 537, 538, 591, 601
Gasparri, Pietro, 89
Gassner, John, 677, 678
Gates, Artemus, 298
Gavrilovic, Stoyan, 855–57
Gay, Edwin F., 226
Gazzara, Ben, 677
Geisel, Theodor Seuss (Dr. Seuss), 231, 369, 370*f*
Gellert, Hugo, 659
Gellhorn, Martha, 164–65
Geoghan, William F. X., 81
George VI (king of England), 257, 258, 299
George, Henry, 675, 728
George, Stefan, 669
Gernsback, Hugo, 421
Gershwin, George, 646, 693, 698
Gershwin, Ira, 467
Gerson, Simon W., 82, 83
Giacometti, Alberto, 651
Gibson, Josh, 614
Gide, André, 238, 669
Gilbert, Cass, 401
Gildersleeve, Dean Virginia, 342
Gillespie, Dizzy, 541, 542, 637–43, 649–50
Gimbel, Adam, 681
Gimbel, Bernard, 858
Gimbel, Elinor S., 230, 500–503
Gimbel, Sophie, 681
Ginsburg, Elias, 573
Gish, Lillian, 698
Gleason, Lev, 477
Godfrey, John H., 302–3
Godkin, E. L., 769
Goebbels, Joseph, 6, 7, 14, 16, 57, 58, 113, 229
Goelet, Robert Walton, 752

Goerdeler, Karl, 19
Goering, Hermann, 4, 16, 332, 852
Goetz, Karl, 18
Gold, Harry, 434, 435
Gold, Mike, 167, 174
Gold, Zev Wolf, 569
Goldberg, Rube, 802
Goldmann, Nahum, 558, 567
Goldmark, Peter, 749
Goldsborough, Laird "Goldie," 213, 229, 266
Goldstein, Abe "Hymie," 541
Goldstein, Betty, 502–3
Goldstein, Herbert S., 206
Goldstein, Israel, 565–67
Goldstein, Sidney, 198
Goldwyn, Sam, 629
Golos, Jacob, 193, 195, 435
Gomá, Isidro, 74
Gonzalez Malo, Jesus, 165
Goodman, Benny, 160, 628, 633
Goodman, Martin, 474–77
Goodman, Paul, 379
Goodrich, David, 774
Gordon, Max, 631–32
Gorky, Arshile, 165, 658, 659, 661
Gorky, Maxim, 169
Gottheil, Richard, 569
Gottlieb, Adolph, 657–59, 661
Gould, Morton, 160, 692
Gould, Richard H., 738
Grable, Betty, 627
Grace, J. Peter, 93
Grace, William Russell, 65
Graham, John, 655, 658
Graham, Martha, 161, 690, 693
Granger, Lester B., 322, 552, 591
Grant, Madison, 114, 118–19
Grant, Ulysses S., 336
Gray, David, 96
Grebanier, Bernard, 189
Green, Adolph, 631, 693, 695
Green, William, 5, 237, 563, 791
Greenberg, Clement, 174, 175, 656–57, 661, 663
Greenberg, Hayim, 559, 562, 575
Greenberg, Ivan. *See* Rahv, Philip
Greenglass, David, 434, 435
Gregg, Richard, 149
Griebl, Ignatz Theodor, 14, 21
Griffin, William, 373
Grillo, Frank "Machito," 649–50, 675
Grimm, Jacob, 669
Grimm, Wilhelm, 669
Gromyko, Andrei, 855
Gropius, Walter, 708

Groves, Leslie R., 433
Gruening, Ernest, 829–30, 832
Guggenheim, Harry F., 505
Guggenheim, Peggy, 238, 484, 651–54, 653*f*, 656–57, 661, 663
Guggenheim, Simon, 422
Guggenheim, Solomon R., 656
Guildersleeve, Virginia C., 484
Guinzburg, Harold, 266
Gurfein, Murray, 364, 365
Guthrie, Woody, 335, 454, 631–32, 631*f*
Gutzeit, Peter, 194

Haffenden, Charles, 364, 365, 376, 406
Hagen, Uta, 533
Hahn, Otto, 429
Halász, László, 698
Haldeman-Julius, Emanuel, 665–67
Haldeman-Julius, Marcet, 665
Hall, Helen, 514
Hall, Richard B. W., 228
Halle, Hiram, 11
Hamilton, Alexander, 226, 743
Hamlin, Talbot, 707
Hammerstein, Oscar, II, 465, 467, 468, 675, 676
Hammett, Dashiell, 95, 180, 229, 230
Hammond, John, 160, 630, 643, 698
Hampton, Lionel, 603, 644
Hand, Augustus, 294
Hand, Learned, 250, 294
Handy, W. C., 160
Hanes, John W., 411
Hansen, Alvin, 762
Hanzelin, Helen, 483
Hardegen, Reinhard, 354, 357–58
Harkness, Edward Stephen, 257–58
Harriman, Averell, 228, 244, 271, 294, 295, 297, 415, 629, 835
Harriman, E. H., 294
Harriman, Marie, 295
Harrison, Hubert Henry, 44
Harrison, Wallace, 856, 860–61
Hart, Lorenz, 675
Hart, Margie, 626
Hart, Moss, 95, 578–79, 629, 673, 694
Hart, Richard, 802
Hartmann, George Wilfried, 379
Harvey, George U., 65, 84
Hatzair, Hashomer, 574

Hawes, Elizabeth, 109, 232, 501, 503, 681, 686
Hawkins, Coleman, 603, 637, 638, 642, 694
Hayek, Friedrich, 771, 772
Hayes, Carlton J. H., 123
Hayes, Helen, 327
Hayes, Patrick Joseph, 67, 68, 70, 75, 84, 91, 92
Hayworth, Rita, 629, 647, 649
Hazlitt, Henry, 742, 769–72, 775
Hearst, William Randolph, 156, 177, 186, 223, 225, 229, 230, 282, 332, 347, 454, 529, 580, 662, 682, 770, 787, 817
Hearst, William Randolph, Jr., 629
Hecht, Ben, 173, 230, 327, 577–79
Height, Dorothy, 497
Heisenberg, Werner, 120, 422, 423, 425
Held, Adolph, 565–66
Heller, Joseph, 227
Hellman, Lillian, 159, 177, 178, 183, 229, 230, 232, 295, 332, 515, 678
Helmsley, Harry B., 727
Hemingway, Ernest, 159, 165, 178, 180, 230, 360, 629, 827
Henderson, Leon, 511–12, 778
Henri, Robert, 658
Hepburn, Katharine, 131, 681
Herlands, William B., 33–34, 586, 746
Herman, Woody, 469, 644
Hernández, Almacenes, 645
Hernández, Rafael, 645
Hernández, Victoria, 645, 650
Herndon, Angelo, 602
Hersey, John, 853–54
Hersh, Anna, 645
Herzl, Theodor, 568–70
Hess, Rudolf, 13
Heydrich, Reinhard, 391
Heye, George, 441
Hicks, Granville, 166, 170, 180, 182
Hill, George Washington, 633
Hill, T. Arnold, 320
Hill, Teddy, 638, 639*f*
Hillman, Sidney, 184, 204, 283, 297, 309–10, 323, 344, 345, 392, 411, 779, 782, 784, 786–89, 796, 797
Hillquit, Morris, 176
Hilton, James, 667
Himmler, Heinrich, 562
Hindenburg, Paul von, 3
Hines, Earl, 641

Hirohito (emperor of Japan), 623, 851
Hitchcock, Alfred, 362, 629
Hitler, Adolf, 3–4, 6, 7, 12–14, 16–20, 25, 33–35, 39, 40, 42*f*, 43, 55, 57–60, 70, 72–75, 81, 85, 86, 118, 121–23, 130, 152–54, 164, 168, 179, 181, 185, 198, 202, 204, 209, 210, 212, 216–17, 224, 229–30, 232, 236, 237, 243–45, 248–50, 252–53, 255, 256, 260, 264–69, 273, 276, 278, 281, 282, 295, 297, 299, 303, 310, 332, 334–35, 357, 359, 360, 364, 379, 390, 390*f*, 392, 423, 428, 429, 434, 475–77, 513, 538, 544, 560, 566, 574–76, 580, 584, 589, 591, 623, 631, 659, 677, 822, 840, 850, 852
Hochman, Julius, 519
Hoffman, Paul, 706–7, 765–67
Hoffman, Theodore H., 35
Hofmann, Hans, 656, 658, 661
Hogan, Frank, 362, 364
Holiday, Billie, 541, 603, 603*f*, 630, 636–37, 641, 643*f*, 690
Holmes, John Haynes, 17, 149, 151, 157, 158, 163, 168, 179, 188, 197, 198, 282, 291, 345, 378, 817
Hook, Sidney, 176–78, 180, 184–89, 191, 194, 196–97, 379
Hoover, Herbert, 9, 85, 135, 250–51, 290, 294, 580
Hoover, J. Edgar, 21, 35, 95–96, 181, 185, 197, 224, 249, 261, 300–303, 301*f*, 329, 330, 367, 370, 536, 539, 549, 628, 652, 666, 822, 840
Hope, Bob, 223, 628
Hopkins, Harry, 204, 212–14, 287, 296, 297, 305, 307, 310, 328, 341, 343, 453, 687, 765
Horkheimer, Max, 11–12, 594
Horne, Lena, 603, 630
Horowitz, Eugene, 597
Horowitz, Ruth, 597
Hoskins, N. K., 437
Houghteling, Laura Delano, 24
Houseman, John, 218, 219, 456, 460, 461, 538
Houser, George, 280, 325
Hoving, Walter, 673
Howard, Leslie, 237
Howard, Roy, 223, 225, 230
Howe, Irving, 379
Hoyt, Homer, 711, 713, 714
Huberman, Leo, 232

Huebsch, Ben, 669
Huggins, Willis Nathaniel, 44, 50, 51
Hughan, Jessie, 158, 197, 377
Hughes, Charles Evans, Jr., 123, 611, 796
Hughes, John, 69
Hughes, Langston, 51, 524, 536, 545, 580, 592, 818, 822
Hugo, Victor, 218
Hull, Cordell, 17–18, 237, 249, 836, 839–40
Hunter, Mary, 691
Hurok, Sol, 160, 329, 573, 691, 694–95
Huston, Walter, 453
Hutton, Betty, 629
Hylan, John Francis, 422, 724

Ibn Saud (king of Saudi Arabia), 809
Ickes, Harold, 76, 225, 271, 272, 275, 344, 580, 829
Iger, Jerry, 475
Ingersoll, Ralph McAllister "Mac," 229–32, 234, 360–61, 369
Ingersoll, Robert, 229
Irving, Washington, 666
Isaacs, Stanley M., 82–83, 109, 591, 605, 607, 611, 728
Iselin, Louise, 342
Ivens, Joris, 159, 165
Ives, Burl, 632
Ives, Irving, 610–13, 616, 617

Jabotinsky, Eri, 577, 582
Jabotinsky, Vladimir "Ze'ev," 573–77
Jack, Hulan, 591, 608
Jackson, C. D., 328
Jackson, John Glover, 44
Jacobi, Mary Putnam, 484
Jacobs, Joe, 57
Jacobs, Mike, 48, 58
Jacobs, Robert Allan, 753
Jacoby, Herbert, 628, 632
Jacquet, Lloyd, 474
Jakobson, Roman, 440, 441
James, Harry, 632, 633, 644
James, Henry, 169
Janis, Sidney, 165, 661
Jefferson, Thomas, 743
Jenkins, Burris, 638*f*
Jenkins, V. Clement, 754–55
Jerome, Jennie, 260
Jerome, Leonard, 260
Jessel, Georgie, 629
Jewett, Frank B., 426, 427
Jodl, Alfred, 850
Johnsen, Julia, 802
Johnson, Alvin, 10–11, 236, 440, 677
Johnson, Hugh, 271
Johnson, Jack, 48

Index of Names

Johnson, James P., 630
Johnson, James Weldon, 128, 130, 325, 595
Johnsrud, Harold, 172
Jones, Dora, 497
Jones, J. Raymond, 604
Jones, Jesse, 764, 766, 767
Jones, Spike, 468–69
Jordan, Max, 216
Jordan, Robert, 86
Josephson, Barney, 630, 632
Josephson, Matthew, 180
Joyce, James, 173

Kafka, Franz, 669
Kahane, Charles, 576
Kahane, Meir, 576
Kahlo, Frida, 177, 484
Kahn, Ely Jacques, 753, 755, 773
Kahn, Otto H., 93, 254
Kaiser, Henry J., 316, 415–16
Kallen, Horace, 113–14, 116, 118, 122, 127, 142, 168, 187, 804
Kalmanowitz, Avraham, 559, 564
Kaltenborn, H. V., 216, 217, 222, 454
Kandinsky, Wassily, 236, 238, 651, 655, 656, 661
Kaplan, Mordecai, 122, 128
Karski, Jan, 564–65
Kaye, Danny, 628, 690
Kazan, Abraham, 716
Kazan, Elia, 139, 678
Kazin, Alfred, 657
Keelan, Joseph, 529
Kelley, Frank, 65, 345
Kelley, Mervin J., 747
Kellogg, Paul, 835
Kelly, John, 65
Kemp, Ira, 45, 50, 51
Kennedy, John F., 629
Kennedy, Joseph P., 90, 93, 299, 518–20
Kennedy, Martin, 824
Kent, Fred I., 768
Kent, Rockwell, 138
Kenyon, Teddy, 500
Kerensky, Alexander, 770, 836
Kern, Jerome, 465, 467, 675
Kern, Paul J., 80, 82
Kerr, Florence, 341
Keynes, John Maynard, 741–43, 771
Kheel, Theodore W., 511
Kieran, John, 48–49
Kiesler, Frederick, 653
Kilgallen, Dorothy, 231
King, Ernest J., 338, 386–87
Kingdon, Frank, 235, 330
Kirby, Jack (pen name of Jacob Kurtzberg), 474–77
Kirchwey, Freda, 12, 180, 183, 227, 234, 328, 373, 459, 515, 782, 804, 811
Kirov, Sergei, 166, 179

Kirstein, Lincoln, 237, 307, 690
Klauber, Edward, 216, 461
Klee, Paul, 653, 655, 656
Klineberg, Otto, 597
Knopf, Alfred, 665, 802, 854
Knox, Frank, 295, 299, 310, 320, 321, 344, 362, 387–88
Knudsen, William, 297, 308, 310, 323, 344
Koch, Howard, 219
Kochno, Boris, 687
Kook, Hillel, 577
Kootz, Samuel, 661, 662
Korda, Alex, 628
Kotler, Aharon, 559
Koussevitzky, Serge, 692, 693, 697
Kracauer, Siegfried, 236
Kranzler, Gershon, 31
Krasner, Lee, 655–59
Krock, Arthur, 274
Kronenberger, Louis, 232
Kuhn, Fritz, 16–21, 33, 34, 40, 86, 130–31, 269, 601–2
Kurtzberg, Jacob (pen name Jack Kirby), 474–77
Kvasnikov, Leonid, 433–35
Kyser, Kay, 493

Lacy, Sam, 614
Lafayette, Marquis de, 130
La Guardia, Fiorello, 17–18, 22, 33–34, 42, 47, 54, 65, 80, 88, 116, 130, 131, 144, 150, 165, 205, 208, 224, 226, 228, 231, 232, 250, 258, 264, 265, 283, 292–93, 314, 317, 324, 328–29, 334, 338–45, 347, 349–54, 361, 369, 371–72, 374, 381, 383, 384, 392, 399, 400, 411–12, 449, 453, 457, 477, 482, 483, 485, 497, 501–2, 507, 513, 514, 518, 519, 525, 531–32, 543, 545, 547–49, 563, 580, 604–8, 611, 617, 625, 666–67, 684, 687, 697–700, 699f, 703–7, 713, 715, 716, 718, 722–28, 734–35, 738–40, 746, 752, 754, 791, 810, 830, 848, 850, 854, 856
Lambert, Eleanor, 680, 684
Lamont, Corliss, 167, 168, 177, 180, 183, 791
Lamont, Thomas W., 156, 167, 226, 252–54, 258, 264, 265, 272, 274–77, 791, 823
Lamour, Dorothy, 219
Lampel, Millard, 632
Lancaster, Burton, 673–74
Land, Emory Scott, 402–3, 406, 407, 415
Landau, Jacob, 559, 560
Landis, James M., 354, 393
Landis, Kenesaw Mountain, 613, 615

Lane, Allen, 666–69
Lane, Layle, 322
Lang, Hermann, 330
Lansky, Meyer, 363, 365, 406
Lanza, Joseph "Socks," 364, 365
Larkin, Joseph J., 93
LaRoche, Chester "Chet," 448
Larsen, Roy Edward, 266
Lascher, James, 183
Lash, Joseph, 153, 155, 158, 183, 236
Lasker, Bruno, 127–28, 142
Latham, Frank, 802
Latham, Natalie Wales, 259
LaTouche, John, 139, 276
Laughlin, Harry, 118, 119, 141
Laurence, William L., 852
Laurents, Arthur, 622
Laval, Pierre, 460
Lawrence, Ernest, 423
Lazareff, Pierre, 456–57
Lazarsfeld, Paul, 221
Lazarus, Emma, 136
Ledbetter, Huddie "Leadbelly," 631
Lee, Canada, 538, 539, 542, 592, 603
Lee, Gypsy Rose, 626, 673
Lee, Madeleine, 692
Lee, Stan (pen name of Stanley Martin Lieber), 477
Leffingwell, Russell, 254, 286
Léger, Fernand, 652
Lehman, Bobbie, 744
Lehman, Herbert, 8, 32, 34, 40–42, 54, 65, 82, 83, 88, 100, 186, 205, 258, 264, 265, 272, 274, 299, 322, 343, 344, 374, 375, 411, 563, 602, 610, 791
Lehman, Irving, 4, 121
Leibowitz, Samuel, 589
Leigh, Douglas, 384, 621–22
Leinsdorf, Erich, 677
Lelong, Lucien, 687
LeMay, Curtis, 851, 853
Lemkin, Rafael, 561
Lenin, Vladimir, 167, 168, 172
Leonard, Bill, 854
Lerner, Max, 177, 180, 230, 580, 782, 854
Levin, Chaim Avraham Dov, 31
Lévi-Strauss, Claude, 438–41, 457, 652, 655, 676
Levitt, Abraham, 710
Levitt, Alfred, 710
Levitt, Helen, 231
Levitt, William, 710–12
Levy, Julien, 652, 655, 661
Lewin, Kurt, 11, 594–95
Lewis, John L., 137, 204

Lewis, Meade "Lux," 630, 652
Lewis, Sinclair, 142, 268, 269, 677
Lewis, William B., 453, 467
Lewisohn, Irene, 683
Ley, Maria, 677
Libby, Fred, 198
Liberace, Walter, 625
Liberman, Alex, 682
Libsohn, Sol, 365f
Lie, Trygve, 856–57, 861
Lieber, Stanley Martin (pen name Stan Lee), 477
Liebling, A. J., 231, 672
Liebowitz, Jack, 476
Lincoln, Abraham, 273, 287, 454, 855
Lindbergh, Anne Morrow, 331
Lindbergh, Charles, 292f, 330–33, 349, 369, 465, 722
Lindsay, Howard, 465
Linton, Ralph, 439
Lion, Alfred, 641
Lipchitz, Jacques, 236, 239, 652
Lippmann, Helen, 490
Lippmann, Walter, 256, 266–67, 269, 275, 279, 282, 289, 369, 794
Little, Malcolm, 540–42, 545, 551, 820
Lloyd, Norman, 362
Locke, Alain, 133
Loeb, James, 782
Loeb, John Jacob, 493
Loening, Grover, 730–31
Loesser, Frank, 468
Lomax, Alan, 631–32
Lombard, Carole, 646
Long, Breckinridge, 236–38, 583, 793
Longworth, Alice Roosevelt, 276
Lonkowski, Wilhelm, 21
Loomis, Alfred Lee, 424–25, 427
Lorre, Peter, 629–30
Losey, Joseph, 671
Lothian, Lord, 260, 286
Lotti, E. A., 437
Louis, Joe, 48–50, 57–59, 59f, 66, 603
Lovestone, Jay, 198, 265
Lovett, Robert A., 294–95, 297, 409, 835
Lovett, Robert S., 294
Low, Nat, 613–15
Lowell, Robert, 378
Lowenthal, Leo, 11–12
Lowie, Robert, 438, 439, 441
Lucchese, Thomas, 47
Luce, Clare Boothe, 109, 789, 817, 823
Luce, Henry, 18, 172, 174, 194, 213, 223, 229–30, 258, 266–67, 272, 274, 275,

Index of Names

278–79, 282, 288–89, 306, 328, 332, 458, 459, 770, 787, 810, 817, 823
Luciano, Lucky, 47, 273, 363–65, 375, 376
Lunt, Alfred, 212, 628
Lusk, Clayton, 83, 188
Lynd, Helen, 515
Lyons, Eugene, 179, 770
Lyons, Leonard, 225, 694

MacArthur, Charles, 327
MacArthur, Douglas, 100, 408, 854
MacCormack, Daniel W., 135
Macdonald, Dwight, 169, 171–75, 180, 229, 379, 459
Machado, Gerardo, 648
Mackay, Clarence, 93
Maclean, Donald, 434
MacLeish, Archibald, 159, 213–14, 217–19, 229, 234, 282, 295, 324, 332, 453, 454, 841
MacPhail, Larry, 615–17
Madden, Owney, 47
Madigan, Michael J., 298
Magnes, Judah, 569–71, 573
Magoon, Blue Jaw, 345
Magritte, René, 651
Mahoney, Jeremiah T., 8, 18
Mainbocher, 682–83, 685, 686, 688
Malden, Karl, 673
Malina, Judith, 677
Malraux, André, 238
Maltz, Albert, 594
Mangano, Vince, 512
Mann, Erika, 235
Mann, Heinrich, 238
Mann, Thomas, 235, 236
Manning, William T., 5, 163, 329, 625, 848
Mao Tse-tung, 823
Marcantonio, Vito, 54, 56, 82, 130, 196, 197, 204, 300–301, 329, 343, 374, 375, 501, 518, 601, 603, 604, 616, 777, 796, 826–28, 831–33
Marconi, Guglielmo, 425
Marcus, H. Stanley, 686
Marcuse, Herbert, 11–12
Mardo, Bill, 614, 615
Maritain, Jacques, 11, 75, 236, 456
Markin, Valentin, 192, 193
Marks, Edward, 646
Marshall, George, 336, 359, 387, 483
Marshall, James C., 432
Marshall, Louis, 121
Marshall, Thurgood, 544, 596, 607, 608, 610, 611, 777, 783
Marston, William Moulton, 495

Martí, José, 825
Martin, Joe, 284
Martin, John, 125, 695
Martin, William McChesney, Jr., 316, 317
Marx, Karl, 169
Maslow, Will, 595, 607
Matisse, Henri, 236, 238, 652, 655, 656, 658, 661
Matisse, Pierre, 652
Matthau, Walter, 677
Matuszewski, Ignacy, 793
Maurin, Peter, 377
Maxwell, Vera, 686
Mazzei, Filippo, 130
Mazzini, Giuseppe, 573
McAneny, George, 399, 704, 712
McCardell, Claire, 680, 681, 684–86, 688
McCarthy, Mary, 169, 172–73, 177, 178, 216
McClellan, George, 728
McCloy, John J., 254, 265, 295–97, 330, 369, 409, 535, 835
McConnell, Francis J., 160, 839
McCooey, John H., 65
McCormick, Anne O' Hare, 12, 269
McCormick, Robert, 223, 290
McDermott, Michael, 192
McDonnell, T. Murray, 92
McGhee, Howard, 639f
McGoldrick, Joseph D., 714
McIntyre, James Francis A., 87, 92
McKelway, St. Clair, 225
McNaboe, John J., 83
McNeil, Harry, 87
McNicholas, John T., 91
McNutt, Paul, 493
McShann, Jay, 640
McWilliams, Joseph Ellsworth, 86, 87
Mead, Margaret, 118, 119, 127, 439
Meany, Tom, 232
Meeropol, Abel (pen name Lewis Allan), 594
Meitner, Lise, 429
Melville, Herman, 174, 666
Mencken, H. L., 770, 829
Mendelsohn, Eric, 708
Mendlowitz, Shraga Feivel, 30, 31
Menjou, Adolphe, 629
Menuhin, Yehudi, 651
Mercer, Johnny, 467
Mercer, Mabel, 625, 637
Meredith, Burgess, 327
Merman, Ethel, 327, 690
Merrill, Gary, 673
Merrill, William P., 148
Merton, Robert K., 450
Meyer, André, 744

Michaux, Lewis H., 550
Michelson, Albert A., 426
Mielziner, Jo, 679
Mikolajczyk, Stanislaw, 793–94
Milgrim, Sally, 682, 684
Millay, Edna St. Vincent, 218, 466
Miller, Arthur, 218
Miller, Francis P., 264, 266
Miller, Glenn, 469, 632
Minnelli, Vincente, 398
Miranda, Carmen, 327, 649, 690
Miranda, Francisco de, 825
Miró, Joan, 655
Mises, Ludwig von, 770–72, 774–75
Mises, Margit von, 770
Mitchell, Dana P., 430f
Mitchell, Wesley, 11, 771
Molloy, Thomas Edmund, 67, 75, 84, 87, 94
Mondrian, Piet, 651–54, 652f, 656, 661, 676
Monk, Thelonious, 637, 639–40, 639f, 650
Monroe, Clark, 643
Monroe, Lucy, 392
Monsky, Henry, 565–66
Montagu, Ashley, 593
Montgomery, Bernard, 849
Mooney, James D., 243, 245
Moore, Fred, 533
Morales, Noro, 649, 650
Moran, Edmond J., 405–6
Morgan, J. P., 277, 293
Morgan, Jack, 252–53, 257–59
Morgan, Pierpont, 252
Morgan, T. A., 714f
Morgenthau, Hans J., 11
Morgenthau, Henry, Sr., 570
Morgenthau, Henry, Jr., 122, 205, 305, 446–52, 560, 583, 741–43
Morris, George Lovett Kingsland, 172, 173
Morris, Lewis, 172
Morris, Newbold, 331, 353, 606, 698
Morrison, Philip, 853
Morrow, Dwight, 69, 331
Morse, Samuel F. B., 359, 422
Moscoso, Teodoro, 831
Moses, Anne, 488f
Moses, Robert, 80, 283, 370–71, 399–400, 507–8, 531–32, 605–7, 611, 704–9, 713, 716, 718, 720–24, 735, 830, 856–58, 860–62
Moss, Paul, 625
Motherwell, Robert, 658, 661
Motley, Constance Baker, 596
Mowrer, Edgar Ansel, 35, 262, 299
Mulzac, Hugh, 526, 527

Mumford, Lewis, 176, 209–11, 214, 234, 264, 265, 704, 708
Mundelein, George, 91
Muni, Paul, 578
Munkacsi, Martin, 682
Muñoz Marín, Luis, 828–33
Muñoz Rivera, Luis, 828
Munshin, Jules, 690
Murphy, Gardner, 527
Murray, Thomas E., 93
Murrow, Edward R., 11, 215–17, 222, 281–82, 565, 682
Musil, Robert, 669
Mussolini, Benito, 39–45, 42f, 48–56, 53f, 70, 72, 74, 75, 85, 90, 130–31, 150, 164, 179, 215, 232, 248, 252, 256, 267, 269, 333, 364, 369, 374–75, 429, 454, 512, 538, 589, 591, 850
Mussolini, Vittorio, 51
Muste, A. J., 177, 197, 198, 282, 325, 377–78
Myers, Pauline, 538
Myrdal, Gunnar, 597–600, 610

Napoleon Bonaparte, 431
Nathan, George Jean, 679
Neel, Alice, 660
Nehru, Jawaharlal, 817, 818
Nelson, Donald, 409, 411, 448
Netanyahu, Benzion, 576, 577
Neumann, John von, 436
Nevelson, Louise, 484, 659
Nevins, Allan, 121
Newcombe, Don, 617
Newell, William H., 315
Newman, Barnett, 657–59
Nichols, Hobart, 662
Niebuhr, Reinhold, 12, 122, 206–9, 211, 234, 235, 248, 264, 265, 280, 282, 292, 328, 341, 373, 459, 577, 611, 782, 837, 839
Nin, Andres, 178
Ninfo, Ralph, 55
Nitze, Paul, 296–97
Nixon, E. D., 596
Nkrumah, Kwame, 44, 814
Nolde, Frederick, 842
Norell, Norman, 684
Norton, W. Warder, 665, 670, 672
Noyes, Charles F., 752
Nye, Gerald, 150, 155, 164

Oberon, Merle, 628
Obolensky, Serge, 228
O' Brien, Edmond, 673
O' Brien, John L., 65
O' Brien, John Patrick, 4, 14
O' Brien, Pat, 99–100
Ochs, Adolph, 559
O' Connell, James, 529
O' Connell, William, 89, 90

O' Day, Caroline, 163
Odegard, Peter, 452
Odets, Clifford, 109, 139, 180, 232, 678
O' Donnell, John, 373
O' Dwyer, Paul, 96–97, 347
O' Dwyer, William, 87, 96, 345–49, 346*f*, 351, 856, 858–62
Ogden, Josephine, 296
O' Keeffe, Georgia, 165
Oller, Gabriel, 646
O' Malley, Walter F., 617
O' Neill, Eugene, 232, 538
Oppenheimer, J. Robert, 423, 433
Oram, Harold, 235, 238
O' Reilly, Gerald, 161
O' Reilly, Tom, 232
Orozco, José Clemente, 654, 655
Osborn, Henry Fairfield, 118
Ottley, Roi, 348, 523, 600
Ovakimian, Gaik Badalovich, 192, 194, 195, 434
Owen, Chandler, 460, 591, 778

Pacelli, Eugenio Maria Giuseppe Giovanni. *See* Pius XII
Paige, Satchel, 614, 615
Paley, Dorothy, 216
Paley, William, 165, 215–17, 222, 281–82, 307, 332, 749
Panto, Peter, 345–46, 406
Papirofsky, Joseph, 674
Papp, Joe, 674
Parker, Charlie, 541, 637, 640–41, 650, 657, 675
Parker, Dorothy, 95, 177, 212, 230, 295, 515, 580, 667, 782
Parks, Rosa, 596
Parsons, Frank Alvah, 682
Parsons, Wilfred, 122
Pasvolsky, Leo, 836, 837, 840
Paterno, Charles, 27, 754
Paterson, Isabel, 770
Patterson, Joseph, 223, 231, 290
Patterson, Robert, 294, 296–98, 308–10, 320, 321, 324, 409, 835
Patton, George, 809
Peale, Norman Vincent, 147–48
Pecora, Ferdinand, 40
Pegler, Westbrook, 225, 408, 549, 611, 770
Pegram, George B., 422, 423, 429, 430, 432
Pekelis, Alexander, 595
Perkins, Frances, 135, 236, 271
Pershing, John J. "Black Jack," 279, 299
Pétain, Phillipe, 460
Peters, Josef, 192, 193

Petersen, Howard C., 279
Petrillo, James, 636, 641
Petry, Ann, 528–29
Pettiford, Oscar, 641, 643
Phillips, William, 169–70, 172, 173, 176, 180, 379
Picasso, Pablo, 165, 236, 238, 651, 655, 656, 661
Pilsudski, Józef, 793
Pinto Gandia, Julio, 831–32
Pinza, Ezio, 51, 374
Piscator, Erwin, 676–79
Pius XI (pope), 70, 75, 80, 89–91
Pius XII (pope), 74, 90–91, 93
Planck, Max, 120
Poe, Edgar Allan, 666
Polakoff, Moses, 365
Polier, Justine Wise, 581
Polite, Marjorie, 546
Polk, Frank, 254, 345
Pollock, Jackson, 654–59, 657*f*, 661, 675, 676, 694
Ponselle, Rosa, 51
Pool, David de Sola, 591
Pope, Generoso, 40–43, 47, 51–56, 91, 130, 135, 284, 333, 375, 376, 451, 796
Pope, Virginia, 680, 681, 683–84, 686, 687
Porter, Cole, 108, 360, 469
Posner, Louis, 130
Potter, Clare, 680, 681
Pound, Dudley, 387
Pound, Ezra, 213
Powell, Adam Clayton, Sr., 44, 550–51, 591
Powell, Adam Clayton, Jr., 50, 116, 152, 322, 348–51, 518, 524, 527, 528, 532, 536, 538, 543, 544, 549, 550, 589–92, 600–608, 611, 614, 796, 818
Powell, Dawn, 159
Poyntz, Juliet Stuart, 194, 195
Pratt, Harold Irving, 841
Pratt, Phyllis, 296
Proskauer, Joseph M., 4, 121, 566, 580–81, 611, 839–42
Proust, Marcel, 173
Puente, Ernest Anthony "Tito," 650
Pulaski, Casimir, 130
Pupin, M. I., 422, 429, 430*f*, 432
Putzel, Howard, 653–54, 656, 661

Quezon, Manuel L., 391
Quill, Mike, 77–78, 78–79*f*, 184, 347, 348, 518, 608
Quinn, Elmer F., 610–13, 616, 617
Quiñonez, Carmen, 485

Rabi, Isidor Isaac, 421–24, 427–30, 433, 435, 438, 676, 747

Rabinowitz, Harry, 689
Rabinowitz, Jerome Wilson. *See* Robbins, Jerome
Rabinowitz, Lena, 689
Rabinowitz, Sonia, 689
Raeder, Erich, 334, 335, 357
Raft, George, 646
Ragan, Leslie, 725*f*
Rahv, Philip, 169–70, 172, 173, 180, 196, 379
Rai, Lala Lajpat, 817
Rains, Claude, 327
Rand, Ayn, 713, 753, 772–75
Randolph, A. Philip, 60, 128, 264, 265, 320–25, 328, 347, 411, 459, 525, 537–39, 549, 552, 577, 591, 592, 596, 598, 601, 604, 609, 611, 782, 783
Rankin, John E., 224, 533, 777
Rapp, Herbert, 188, 189
Rasin, Jacob. *See* Golos, Jacob
Raskob, John J., 90, 93
Ravel, Maurice, 693
Ray, Nicholas, 139, 631–32
Raymond, Alex, 474
Raymond, Natalie, 119
Read, Leonard, 774–75
Reading, Stella, 341
Rebay, Hilla, 656
Reddick, Lawrence D., 590
Reid, Arthur, 45, 50, 51
Reid, Helen Rodgers, 268, 269, 274, 282
Reid, Ogden, 268
Reinhardt, Ad, 659
Reinicke, F. G., 336, 404–5
Reles, Abe "Kid Twist," 345–47, 350*f*, 351, 482
Rembrandt, 663
Revel, Bernard, 30
Reynolds, John J., 92, 519
Ribbentrop, Joachim von, 243
Rice, Elmer, 236, 698
Rickenbacker, Eddie, 735
Rickey, Branch, 613, 615–17
Ridder, Bernard, 13–14, 20
Ridder, Herman, 13
Ridder, Joseph, 13–14, 20
Ridder, Victor, 13–14, 20, 345
Rieber, Torkild, 243, 245
Riegner, Gerhart, 558, 563, 564
Riggs, Francis E., 826, 827
Ritter, Nikolaus, 329–30
Rivera, Diego, 174, 177, 304, 654
Rivet, Paul, 440
Roach, Max, 641, 650
Robbins, Jerome, 689–92, 694–95
Roberts, Florine, 546
Robeson, Paul, 139–40, 144, 325, 453, 524, 533, 603,

630, 632, 677, 678, 698, 782, 814, 818, 822
Robinson, Bill "Bojangles," 327, 329
Robinson, Earl, 139, 140, 276, 594
Robinson, Edward G., 453, 578, 629, 674
Robinson, Frederick, 154–55, 154*f*
Robinson, Jackie, 616, 617
Robinson, James Harvey, 10
Robinson, William Edward, 751–52, 755
Robles, José, 178
Rockefeller, John D., Sr., 743
Rockefeller, John D., Jr., 245, 254, 258, 265, 272, 286, 295, 422, 698, 743, 841, 858, 860–62
Rockefeller, John D., III, 823
Rockefeller, Nelson, 303–7, 454, 457, 648, 655, 662, 711, 754, 856, 858, 861, 862
Rockefeller, William, Jr., 743
Rockwell, Norman, 493
Rodgers, Cleveland, 802
Rodgers, Richard, 465, 467, 675, 676
Rodman, Nancy, 172
Rodman, Selman, 172
Rodney, Lester, 614–15
Rodríguez, Arsenio, 648
Rodzinki, Artur, 694, 698
Rogers, Will, 273
Rommel, Erwin, 392, 578
Roosevelt, Eleanor, 76, 131, 157, 164–65, 204, 223, 236–37, 268, 269, 320, 322–24, 323*f*, 341, 482, 501, 514, 557, 581, 610, 680, 777, 795, 811, 812, 814, 822, 823, 829, 835–36, 843, 847–48, 858
Roosevelt, Franklin D., 5, 18, 22–24, 32, 33, 35, 51–54, 56, 58, 65, 76, 85, 90, 91, 94, 96–99, 109, 120, 121, 123, 135–37, 139, 141, 150, 164–65, 181–82, 184, 191, 198, 201–5, 208, 212–16, 222–28, 230, 231, 234, 236, 249, 251, 253, 255, 256, 258, 261, 264–67, 269–73, 275, 276, 278–79, 282–97, 288*f*, 299–305, 307–8, 314, 316, 320–21, 323–24, 330–35, 340, 341, 343–44, 347, 349, 353, 354, 359, 362, 367–69, 372–75, 378, 386–87, 392, 397, 399–400, 402, 408, 409, 411, 426, 431–32, 446, 447, 449, 453, 454, 456–61, 464, 475, 485, 491, 501, 510–12, 525, 526, 536–37, 543, 560, 563, 566, 580–83, 593, 609, 610, 615,

Index of Names 935

648, 670, 704, 705, 722, 739, 741, 743, 753, 754, 759–63, 765, 773, 776–81, 783–89, 791–97, 808–13, 817–18, 821, 824, 827–33, 835–38, 840–42, 847–49, 849*f*, 852
Roosevelt, Franklin, Jr., 629
Roosevelt, James, 307
Roosevelt, Kermit, 302
Roosevelt, Theodore, 22, 122, 250, 302, 785
Roosevelt, Theodore, Jr., 302
Root, Elihu, 156, 250, 275
Root, Elihu, Jr, 276
Root, Oren, Jr., 275–76
Rose, Alex, 184
Rose, Billy, 327, 329, 467, 578, 627, 629, 858
Rosen, Joseph, 346–47
Rosenbaum, Alisa. *See* Rand, Ayn
Rosenberg, Anna, 305, 307, 323, 344
Rosenberg, Ethel, 160, 434
Rosenberg, Israel, 565–66
Rosenberg, Julius, 160, 434–35, 437
Rosenberg, Paul, 655
Rosenfeld, Leon, 429
Rosenheim, Jacob, 559, 564
Rosenman, Samuel, 24, 121, 212–14, 453, 580, 583, 784
Rosenstein, Nettie, 681
Ross, Colin, 18
Ross, Harold, 225
Roth, Emery, 753, 754
Roth, Henry, 177
Roth, Julian, 753
Roth, Richard, 753, 754
Rothkowitz (later Rothko), Marcus, 658, 659, 661, 662
Rougemont, Denis de, 456
Roxborough, John, 48
Royal, John, 307
Rubinstein, Annette T., 500–501, 503
Rubinstein, Helena, 680
Rublee, George, 279
Rudin, Jack, 752
Rudin, Lew, 752
Rudin, Sam, 752
Rugg, Harold Ordway, 127, 187
Rukeyser, Muriel, 693
Ruml, Beardsley, 305, 707, 765–67, 769, 797
Rumrich, Guenther Gustave, 21
Russell, Bertrand, 186–88, 625
Russell, Bob, 469
Rustin, Bayard, 44, 324–26, 377–78
Rustin, Julia, 325
Ruth, Babe, 450
Rutherford, J. F., 378
Ryan, Joe, 364, 406

Saarinen, Eliel, 708
Sachs, Alexander, 269, 431
Saint-Exupéry, Antoine de, 669
Saksin, Georgi, 858–59
Salomon, Haym, 130
Salter, Felix, 667
Salvemini, Gaetano, 56
Sandburg, Carl, 662
Sandor, Senia Gluck, 689–90
Sanger, Margaret, 80, 665
Sarnoff, David, 215, 307, 329, 332, 380, 416, 436, 749, 858
Saroyan, William, 332
Sayre, John Nevin, 157, 197
Scanlan, Patrick, 75, 76, 80, 81, 87, 91, 94, 98, 292, 490–91
Schacht, Hjalmar Horace Greeley, 247
Schachtman, Max, 177
Schapiro, Meyer, 169, 180, 193, 194, 658, 659, 661
Schappes, Morris, 189
Schiaparelli, Elsa, 681, 683, 687
Schieffelin, William Jay, 23, 354, 577
Schiff, Adele, 227
Schiff, Dorothy "Dolly," 227–28
Schiff, Jacob Henry, 103, 227, 570
Schiff, Mortimer, 227
Schiffrin, Jacques, 236, 669
Schlesinger, Arthur, Jr., 332, 782
Schmeling, Max, 57–59, 59*f*
Schneersohn, Yosef Yitzchak, 31, 32
Schneerson, Chaya Mushka, 32
Schneerson, Menachem Mendel, 32
Schneiderman, Rose, 342, 518
Schomburg, Arthur, 44, 524
Schorr, Gedaliah, 29–31
Schulte, Eduard, 563
Schultz, Dutch, 47
Schuster, Max, 666, 667, 801
Schwartz, Delmore, 173
Schwartz, Hilda G., 484
Schwartzbart, Ignacy, 565
Scopes, John, 187
Scott, Edmund, 361, 362
Scott, Hazel, 603, 630
Scribner, Charles, 669
Seabury, Samuel, 17, 205, 343, 344
Sebold, William, 330
Seeger, Pete, 335, 454, 631–32
Seger, Gerhart Heinrich, 14
Selassie, Haile, 45, 50, 53
Seldes, George, 150, 210
Seldes, Gilbert, 132, 133
Seligman, Eustace, 248

Semenov, Semyon, 434, 435
Serge, Victor, 239
Seuss, Dr. *See* Geisel, Theodor Seuss
Sevareid, Eric, 221–22
Seversky, Alexander de, 414
Sforza, Carlo, 56
Shahn, Ben, 460, 786
Shakespeare, William, 667, 674
Shannon, Claude, 439
Sharkey, Jack, 57
Sharkey, Joseph T., 739
Shaver, Dorothy, 680, 684
Shaw, George Bernard, 677
Shaw, Irwin, 678
Sheen, Fulton, 81, 82, 122–23
Shepardson, Whitney, 264, 265
Sherman, John, 193
Sherwood, Robert Emmet, 212–14, 232, 234, 264–66, 295, 303, 306, 307, 329, 332, 453, 456, 458, 460, 461
Shimkin, Leon, 667
Shipler, Guy Emery, 95, 839
Shirer, William L., 215–17
Shockley, William, 747
Short, Bobby, 628
Shotwell, James T., 156, 157, 834, 837–39, 841, 842
Shridharani, Krishnalal, 326
Shubert, J. J., 690
Shubert, Lee, 626, 690
Shulman, Irving, 505, 540–41
Shuster, George N., 75–76, 236, 333
Shuster, Joe, 471, 477
Sidney, Sylvia, 578
Siegel, Jerry, 471, 477
Silver, Abba Hillel, 580–82
Silverman, Sidney, 563
Simon, Dick, 666, 667, 801
Simon, Joe, 474–77
Simpson, Wallis, 683
Sinatra, Frank, 594, 633–37, 634–35*f*
Sinclair, Upton, 236
Singh, Anup, 818
Singh, Sirdar Jagjit "J.J.," 379, 817, 819
Siqueiros, David Alfaro, 654
Sissle, Noble, 160
Sloan, Alfred P., Jr., 246, 708–9, 720
Sloan, James, 321
Sloan, John, 172, 282, 655, 658
Smedley, Agnes, 817
Smith, Adam, 771
Smith, Alfred E., 4, 5, 17, 65, 84, 87, 93, 122, 123, 226, 274, 328, 333, 580, 629, 706, 716, 787
Smith, Buster, 640

Smith, David, 659
Smith, Ferdinand, 526, 533, 548, 603
Smith, Frederick C., 778
Smith, Howard K., 222
Smith, Howard W., 778
Smith, John L., 617
Smith, John Thomas, 93
Smith, Kate, 276, 329, 450
Smith, Oliver, 692, 694–95
Smith, Thorne, 667
Smith, Wendell, 614
Smith, Willie "The Lion," 639
Snow, Carmel, 680, 682–84, 687–88
Socarrás, Alberto, 646, 647, 649–50
Socrates, 187
Sokolow, Anna, 161, 693
Sokolsky, George, 275, 770
Solomon, Charles, 150
Solow, Herbert, 169
Soltero Peralta, Rafael, 832
Somoza, Anastasio, 828
Sorel, Felicia, 689
Sothern, Ann, 494
Soyer, Raphael, 659
Spanknoebel, Heinz, 13, 14
Speaks, Sara, 604
Speer, Albert, 246, 852
Spellman, Francis Joseph, 88–100, 232–33, 283, 329, 377, 519, 625, 626, 793, 804, 848
Spencer, Herbert, 769
Sperling, Benjamin, 3
Spivy, Madame, 625
Spock, Benjamin, 232
Sprague, J. Russell, 414
Stalin, Joseph, 81, 153, 166, 168, 175, 177–79, 181, 185, 194, 204, 232, 267, 297, 402, 414, 434, 677, 790–92, 847
Stanton, Frank, 221
Stanwyck, Barbara, 626
Stark, Johannes, 120
Stebbins, Ernest, 622
Steichen, Edward, 662, 682
Steiger, Rod, 677
Steinbeck, John, 675, 694, 774
Steingut, Irwin, 65
Stephenson, William, 261–62, 299, 302–3
Stern, David, 226–28
Stern, Philip Van Doren, 667
Sternbuch, Isaac, 559, 564
Sternbuch, Recha, 559, 564
Stettinius, Edward R., Jr., 271, 297, 814–15, 835, 840–43, 852
Steuben, Friedrich Wilhelm von, 130
Stevens, Wallace, 173
Stewart, Jimmy, 275, 453, 674
Stewart, Maxwell, 715, 802

Stewart, William Rhinelander, 302
Stimson, Henry, 163, 250–52, 254, 257, 265, 276, 279, 280, 294–97, 302, 305, 308–10, 320–21, 323, 324, 331, 344, 369, 372, 387, 409, 424, 425, 427, 453, 461, 535–36, 543, 577, 835
Stoddard, Lothrop, 330
Stokowski, Leopold, 454, 484, 694, 699
Stolberg, Benjamin, 185
Stolper, Gustave, 431
Stone, Edward Durell, 755
Stone, I. F., 180, 183, 226–27, 231, 308, 309, 503
Stone, Marc, 503
Stoneham, Horace, 617
Stout, Rex, 327, 331, 465–66, 493–94, 675
Stowe, Harriet Beecher, 822
Strassmann, Fritz, 429
Straus, Nathan, 570
Straus, Oscar S., 122
Straus, Percy S., 6, 227
Straus, Robert K., 591
Straus, Roger W., 121, 122
Strauss, Anna Lord, 342
Strauss, Lewis, 298
Strauss, Phil, 347
Stravinsky, Igor, 640, 695
Streit, Clarence K., 258
Stritch, Elaine, 677
Strölin, Karl, 18
Stuart, Douglas, Jr., 290
Studebaker, John, 132–33
Stuyvesant, Peter, 532
Sullivan, Ed, 57
Sullivan, John, 66
Sullivan, Tim, 65
Sulzberger, Arthur Hays, 10, 559–60, 577, 612, 858
Sulzberger, Iphigene, 10, 132–33
Sumner, William Graham, 598, 769
Sun Yat-sen, 106, 107
Sutherland, George, 816
Swanson, Gloria, 684
Sweeney, James Johnson, 653–54, 656
Sweezy, Paul, 177
Swing, Raymond Gram, 235, 328
Swope, Herbert Bayard, 212, 296, 297, 629, 856
Sylvester, Harry, 87
Syrkin, Marie, 562
Szilárd, Leo, 428–33, 435, 438
Szold, Henrietta, 569–71, 573
Szyk, Arthur, 579f

Taft, Robert, 272, 276, 277, 282, 332–33, 582, 719, 780, 784, 785, 789

Taft, William Howard, 250
Talbot, Francis X., 75, 76
Talmadge, Eugene, 777
Tanguy, Yves, 651–53, 655
Tannenbaum, Tick Tock, 345
Tappan, Lewis, 693
Tatum, Art, 603, 630, 640
Taubman, Howard, 140
Taylor, Francis Henry, 661
Taylor, Laurette, 679
Tchaikovsky, Pyotr Ilyich, 698
Teagarden, Jack, 644
Teller, Edward, 423, 431
Thacher, Molly Day, 678
Thatcher, Thomas, 279
Thind, Bhagat Singh, 816
Thomas, J. Parnell, 187
Thomas, Lowell, 487
Thomas, Norman, 6, 149–52, 155, 157, 158, 164, 168, 178, 188, 198, 208, 236, 237, 282, 291–93, 331–33, 369, 373, 378–79, 782, 803–4, 817
Thompson, Dorothy, 236, 268–69, 275, 282, 292, 328, 330, 331
Thomson, Virgil, 159, 160, 692, 693
Thorkelson, Jacob, 224
Thorne, Landon, 424, 425
Thorpe, Jay, 682, 684
Thurber, James, 230
Tillich, Paul, 11, 179, 577
Tishman, David, 752, 754
Tishman, Julius, 752
Tishman, Norman, 752
Tishman, Paul, 752
Tobias, Channing, 322, 348, 818
Tobin, Austin, 723, 735
Todd, Jane, 499
Todd, Mike, 625–26, 675
Tolson, Clyde, 224, 300–301, 628
Topping, Dan, 615
Torin, Sid, 641
Torres, Hilda, 650
Toscanini, Arturo, 450, 694, 699
Trager, Frank, 185
Tresca, Carlo, 41, 194, 375
Tress, Elimelech Gavriel "Mike", 30, 31
Trevor, John B., 113–15, 118, 119, 135, 141, 143, 197, 824
Trilling, Lionel, 169, 173
Trippe, Juan, 306, 807
Trombetta, Domenico, 39–40, 55, 373
Trotsky, Leon, 166, 168, 173–74, 177, 659, 826, 836
Trout, Bob, 216, 217
Trujillo, Rafael, 828
Truman, Harry S., 309, 784, 847–48, 851, 854–58

Trumbo, Dalton, 230
Tucker, Sophie, 628
Tugwell, Rexford Guy, 204, 343, 704, 708, 711, 828–33
Tully, Grace, 847
Tunney, Gene, 57, 66, 261
Turkus, Burton, 351
Turner, Lana, 629–30
Turrou, Leon, 21, 34
Tuvim, Judith, 631
Tydings, Millard E., 827

Ulanovsky, Aleksandr, 191–92
Ulanovsky, Nadya, 191
Untermyer, Samuel, 5–7, 16, 17, 21, 58, 121
Urban, Joseph, 11
Urey, Harold, 120, 424, 432, 434, 435
Uris, Harold, 752, 754
Uris, Harris, 752
Uris, Percy, 752, 754

Valachi, Joe, 512
Valdés, Miguelito, 648–50
Valenti, Girolamo, 41, 56
Valentina, 681, 685
Valentine, Lewis Joseph, 47, 301–2, 340, 352, 531, 586, 622, 627, 850
Valentino, Rudolph, 634, 647
Vallee, Rudy, 453
Vanderbilt, Alfred Gwynne, 629
Van Doren, Carl, 274
Van Doren, Irita, 274, 770, 773
Van Doren, Mark, 450
Van Dusen, Henry P., 207, 208, 248, 265, 266, 280, 292, 839
Van Kirk, Walter W., 150, 157
Van Kleek, Mary, 177, 180
Varela, Félix, 825
Vargas, Getúlio, 256
Vayo, J. Alvarez del, 236
Veblen, Thorstein, 10
Vecchiotti, Gaetano, 40, 54
Victor, Sally, 681
Vidal, Gore, 625
Viereck, George Sylvester, 330
Villard, Henry, 226
Villard, Oswald Garrison, 12, 168, 197, 226, 291, 292, 333, 829
Vionnet, Madeleine, 681, 683
Vladeck, Baruch Charney, 7, 12
Vreeland, Diana, 682, 684

Wagner, Robert F., 5, 24, 32, 88, 141, 163, 204, 319, 411, 510–11, 519, 715, 718–19, 742, 780, 783, 794, 795, 797

Wagner, Robert F., Jr., 35, 333
Wald, Lillian, 163, 177, 570
Waldman, Morris, 121
Walker, George Herbert, 244
Walker, Jimmy, 42, 65, 343, 449
Walker, Robert, 398, 506
Wall, Dan, 640
Wallace, Dewitt, 306
Wallace, Henry, 204, 458–59, 580, 705, 709, 783, 784, 791, 810–11, 829
Wallace, Lila Acheson, 306
Wallach, Sidney, 121, 123
Waller, Fats, 160
Waller, Willard, 506
Walsh, Edward James, 81
Walsh, Michael F., 81
Walsh, Patrick J., 361–62
Walsh, Richard, 823
Walter, Bruno, 694
Walters, Lou, 627
Warburg, Edward M., 558
Warburg, Felix, 123, 235, 571
Warburg, Ingrid, 235
Warburg, James P., 266, 327, 331, 460, 461
Warburg, Paul, 254
Ward, Harry, 153, 160, 163, 180, 183
Ware, Harold, 193
Warner, Jack, 99
Washington, George, 33, 75, 204, 269, 454, 854
Watson, Edwin "Pa," 431
Watson, Thomas A., 426
Watson, Thomas J., 244–46, 249, 436, 856
Weaver, Sylvester "Pat," 457
Webb, Chick, 649
Webb, Del, 615
Weber, Max, 658, 659
Webster, Ben, 603f
Webster, Edwin Sibley, Jr., 291
Wechsler, James, 153, 155, 183, 230
Weegee (Usher Fellig), 231
Wegrzynek, Maksymilian, 793, 794
Weill, Kurt, 327, 578, 628
Weinberg, Sidney J., 298, 744
Weir, Walter, 448, 462–63
Weiss, Emanuel "Mendy," 346–47
Weitzman, Martin, 403f
Weizmann, Chaim, 571, 573, 576, 578
Welles, Orson, 213–14, 218–21, 280, 332, 341, 453, 456, 538, 629, 699, 782
Welles, Sumner, 236, 563–65, 835–37, 839–41
Wells, H. G., 219, 220, 428
Weltfish, Regina, 593
Werfel, Franz, 238

Wertheim, Maurice, 565–66
West, Rebecca, 274
Westrick, Gerhardt, 243–47, 249, 262
Whalen, Grover A., 389, 684, 687, 706, 856
Wheeler, Burton, 262
White, Harry Dexter, 741, 743
White, Josh, 325, 603, 631–32
White, Walter, 45, 51, 532, 536, 538, 544, 550, 552, 591, 592, 596, 598, 606, 783, 812–15, 818, 822
White, William (NAACP leader), 320, 322–24
White, William Allen (CDAAA chair), 264, 265, 292
Whitman, Walt, 103
Whitney, Jock, 230
Whitney, John Hay, 306
Whittier, John Greenleaf, 481
Wigner, Eugene, 431

Wilde, Oscar, 666
Wilder, Thornton, 667
Wilkins, Roy, 45, 543–44, 591, 596
Williams, Aubrey, 323
Williams, Franklin, 596
Williams, Tennessee, 625, 676, 678–79, 689, 692
Willkie, Edith, 273
Willkie, Wendell, 273–84, 286, 301, 321, 328, 331, 343, 344, 424, 459, 475, 582, 583, 671, 694, 773, 784, 785, 796, 801, 810–12, 823
Wilson, Edmund, 173, 669
Wilson, Teddy, 603, 630
Wilson, Woodrow, 165, 263, 271, 321, 523, 570, 571, 796, 834, 835, 841–42
Winchell, Walter, 86, 223–25, 230, 234, 243, 261, 262, 269, 282, 301, 301*f*, 329, 330, 379, 408, 628, 629, 647, 650

Windels, Paul, 188, 189, 707, 712, 727–28
Windham, Donald, 625
Winship, Blanton, 826–30
Winters, Shelley, 677
Wise, James Waterman, 131
Wise, Stephen S., 4–7, 9, 24, 55, 58, 121, 163, 329, 558, 560, 563–66, 569, 570, 574–75, 577–82, 589–90, 592, 594–95, 611
Wissler, Clark, 438
Wittfogel, Karl, 11–12
Wolff, Helen Mosel, 236, 669
Wolff, Kurt, 236, 669
Wolper, David, 628
Wood, Audrey, 678
Wood, Robert E., 290
Wood, Robert W., 424–25
Woodring, Harry, 276
Woodward, Clark, 314
Woolley, Monty, 629
Worth, Jacques, 687
Wright, Frank Lloyd, 773

Wright, Richard, 538, 592, 603
Wylie, Philip, 494

Yakovlev, Anatoli, 434, 435
Yardelni, M. S., 848
Yeats, William Butler, 173
Yergan, Max, 189–90, 348, 548, 814
Young, James Webb, 305–6, 447–48, 457, 462, 464
Young, John Orr, 275
Young, Lester, 640
Young, Owen, 791
Young, Ruth, 498, 500, 501, 503

Zarubin, Vassily, 434
Zeckendorf, William, 753–54, 859–62
Zhukov, Georgy, 849
Zorita (exotic snake dancer), 626, 644
Zygielbojm, Arthur, 557–58, 562, 564, 565, 567

Index of Subjects

Figures are indicated by "f" following page numbers. A separate Index of Names precedes this index.

Abe Lincoln in Illinois (Sherwood), 212
Abwehr (German Military Intelligence), 21, 192, 329–30, 366
Abyssinia. *See* Ethiopia
Abyssinian Baptist Church, 44, 45, 348
Academic freedom, 17, 153, 177, 186, 189
Adolescents. *See* Children and adolescents
Advisory Committee on Post-war Foreign Policy, 836–37
African Americans: 1940 presidential election and, 284; 1941 mayoral election and, 347–48, 350–51; 1944 presidential election and, 796; all-Black rally (1942), 537–39; alliance with Jews, 553, 589–92; antifascism and, 50, 56, 59; boxing and, 47–49, 57–59; bus boycott by, 348; civil rights movement and, 320–24, 525–26, 537, 538, 552, 610, 612, 616; communism and, 45; education and, 524, 527; FDR's policies and, 776; ghetto subculture, 528–30, 540; Hitler and, 60, 544; on Italian conquest of Ethiopia, 43–45, 50–51, 53; labor unions and, 525–26; migration to NYC, 528; nationalism and, 44, 45, 48, 50; police brutality against, 543, 544; poverty among, 527–29; in San Juan Hill neighborhood, 104, 639; Spanish Civil War and, 74; Tammany Hall and, 348; voting rights for, 777; World War I and, 523; World War II and, 319–20, 523–24, 533–36, 543, 812; Zoot suits and, 540–42. *See also* Jim Crow; National Association for the Advancement of Colored People; Racism; Segregation
African Patriotic League, 44, 45
Agudath Israel (Union of Israel), 29–32, 559, 564
Airplanes and airports, 732–35, 733–34f. *See also* Aviation industry
Air pollution, 739
Air Raid (MacLeish), 218, 219

60, 544; on Italian conquest of Ethiopia, 43–45, 50–51, 53; labor unions and, 525–26; migration to NYC, 528; nationalism and, 44, 45, 48, 50; police brutality against, 543, 544; poverty among, 527–29; in San Juan Hill neighborhood, 104, 639; Spanish Civil War and, 74; Tammany Hall and, 348; voting rights for, 777; World War I and, 523; World War II and, 319–20, 523–24, 533–36, 543, 812; Zoot suits and, 540–42. *See also* Jim Crow; National Association for the Advancement of Colored People; Racism; Segregation
Air Transport Command, 807
Albatross Modern Continental Library, 666, 667
Alien Enemy Act of 1798, 368
Alien Registration Act of 1940 (Smith Act): as domestic totalitarianism, 187; proof of compliance with, 329; requirements of, 35–36, 109, 141, 203, 368
All-Chinatown Anti-Japanese Salvation Association, 107
Allied Relief Fund, 259
Amalgamated Clothing Workers of America (ACWA), 7, 283, 392, 450, 698, 716, 779, 788–89
Amateur Athletic Union (AAU), 8
America (Jesuit magazine), 68, 75, 76, 163, 789
America First Committee (AFC), 290–93, 292f, 301, 330–33, 335, 378
American Aid for Ethiopia, 50
American Airlines, 808, 808f
American Association Against Communism, 78–79

American Association for the Advancement of Science, 117
American Association for the United Nations (AAUN), 841
American Association of Advertising Agencies, 766
American Ballet Caravan, 307
American Civil Liberties Union (ACLU), 12, 141, 152–53, 177, 300, 369, 391, 607, 826; Committee Against Racial Discrimination, 822
American Coalition of Patriotic Societies, 113, 824
American Committee against Communism (ACC), 75, 84
American Committee for Anti-Nazi Literature, 119–20
American Committee for Democracy and Intellectual Freedom (ACDIF), 120, 122, 184–85, 187–88
American Committee for the Defense of Leon Trotsky (ACDLT), 177

American Committee on the Ethiopian Crisis, 50
American Council of the World Alliance for International Friendship Through the Churches, 839
American Cystoscope, 412
"American Declaration of Tolerance and Equality" (CAIA), 131
American Federation of Labor (AFL): anti-Nazi boycott and, 5, 7; on Black access to defense jobs, 526; "The Case of Civilization Against Hitler" mock trial and, 17; immigration policies supported by, 24, 824; "New York at War" parade and, 392; New York State Federation of Labor, 347; on postwar planning, 804; rescue movements and, 12, 237, 238
American Federation of Musicians, 698
American Federation of Teachers (AFT), 185, 322
American Female Guardian Society, 128
American Friends of German Freedom (AFGF), 207, 235–37
American Friends of Irish Neutrality (AFIN), 96–97
American Friends of Spanish Democracy, 161, 164
American Friends of the Chinese People, 108, 109
American Friends Service Committee (AFSC), 157, 198
American Institute of Accountants, 803
Americanization. *See* Assimilationism
American Jewish Committee: ACDIF supported by, 185; "Americans All, Immigrants All" and, 132; on anti-Nazi protests, 4, 5, 7, 24; Boas supported by, 121, 122; on human rights, 839, 840; on internment of Japanese Americans, 369; on Jewish immigration to US, 10; pluralism supported by, 130–31, 143; on postwar planning, 804; Survey Committee, 121
American Jewish Congress (AJC): on anti-Nazi protests, 4–7, 24; boxing match protested by, 58; "The Case of Civilization Against Hitler" mock trial and, 17; Commission on Law and Social Action, 607; interracial forums sponsored by, 592; on postwar planning, 804; Women's Division, 17
American Labor Party (ALP): 1941 mayoral election and, 343–45; 1944 presidential election and, 796; anticommunism of, 184; Browder and, 789; Dubinsky and, 789; FDR and, 204, 283, 285, 350, 788; on housing discrimination, 606; interventionism and, 328; members of, 78, 80, 227; on Powell for City Council, 348, 349; rent control and, 518, 608; on slum clearance, 715; socialism and, 282
American League Against War and Fascism (ALWF), 7, 45*f*, 51, 108, 152–53, 195
American League for India's Freedom, 149
American League for Peace and Democracy (ALPD), 95, 160, 183
American Legion, 83, 126, 141, 187, 189, 392, 564, 780, 838
American Maritime Council, 803
American Medical Bureau, 159–60*f*, 161
American Mercury Books, 667
American Mercury (magazine), 142, 179, 667, 829
American Museum of Natural History, 118, 434, 438, 439
American Peace Mobilization, 196, 197
American Physical Society (APS), 422
"Americans All, Immigrants All" (radio series), 132–34, 133*f*, 138, 143, 144
American Society of Civil Engineers, 803
American Society of Composers, Authors, and Publishers (ASCAP), 467, 469, 470
American Society of Mechanical Engineers, 803
American Student Union (ASU), 74, 155, 157–60, 183, 189–90
American Tariff League, 806
American Women's Association Clubhouse, 194
American Women's Voluntary Services (AWVS), 340, 449
American Workers Party (AWP), 177
Amity and Commerce Treaty (1858), 103
Amsterdam Houses, 717
Amtorg Trading Agency, 191
Ancient Order of Hibernians (AOH), 77, 83, 96
Anglo-Persian Oil Company, 809
Anglophiles, 257–59, 262, 265–66, 273, 291, 292, 331
Anschluss (1938), 20, 23, 120, 210, 216–17, 266
Anthropology, 117–19, 127, 144, 184, 438–41, 593, 769
Anticlericalism, 69, 71, 74, 81, 90, 826
Anticommunism: 1944 presidential election and, 787–90; American Labor Party and, 184; Catholic Church and, 70, 82–85, 99; Christian Front and, 85–87; discrediting of movement, 187; rallies in support of, 84. *See also* Red Scare
Anti-Defamation League (ADL), 224–25
Antifascism: of academic refugees, 10, 25; African Americans and, 50, 56, 59; anti-Nazi boycott and, 6, 8; German consulate bomb threat by, 22; Italian Americans and, 41–43, 50, 51, 54, 56; labor unions and, 41–42; of La Guardia, 17, 42, 347, 457; literature on, 119–21, 213–14; of Murrow, 281–82; newspapers and, 41, 227; NYC as bastion of, 12; rallies in support of, 14; of Stalin, 168
Anti-Fascist Alliance of North America, 41
Anti-imperialism, 44, 378, 553, 822, 827, 829
Anti-Semitism: Boasian campaign against, 118; of Christian Front, 86, 87, 95–96, 120; criminalization of, 180; of John Foster Dulles, 249; in education, 10, 421; in employment, 586; employment discrimination, 586; fascism and, 55; of Henry Ford, 5, 85; of German American Bund, 17; graffiti and, 585*f*; Irish Americans and, 585–86; isolationism and, 24; Italian Americans and, 55, 56; juvenile delinquency and, 505; Kristallnacht and (1938), 22–24, 27, 31, 33, 131, 266, 591; of Lindbergh, 332, 333; in Nazi Germany, 3–8, 10–12, 14, 17, 22–25, 237; *Oklahoma!* demonstrating toleration, 676; pogroms and, 9, 12, 22–23, 169, 266, 568; propaganda in promotion of, 121, 184; in science, 120; street violence and, 232; unemployment and, 23. *See also* Genocide against Jews
Antitrust law, 309
Antiwar movement. *See* Pacifism
Appeal to Reason (socialist paper), 665
Aramco, 809
Arma Corporation, 315, 319
Army. *See* United States Army
Army Navy Munitions Board (ANMB), 296, 409, 410
Artists for Victory, 369, 484
Artists Union, 169*f*
Art Students League, 172, 174
Asian Americans. *See* Chinese Americans; Japanese Americans
Assimilationism: coercive, 114, 143; criticisms of, 113–14; German Americans and, 13, 14, 18, 19, 27; Irish Americans and, 99; Italian Americans and, 128–29; Jews and, 4, 27, 29, 121, 122; refugees and, 11, 27; World War I campaigns for, 203
Association of American Colleges, 803
Association of American Railroads (AAR), 397
Association of American Soap and Glycerine Products, 803
Association of Cotton Textile Merchants of New York, 803
Astor Hotel, 4–5, 17, 35, 68, 80, 364, 684, 731
Astoria: General Aircraft Corporation in, 413; German American Bund in, 16, 20
As We Go Marching (Flynn), 770
Atlantic Charter (1941), 392, 794, 810, 817, 836
Atomic bombs, 417, 428–36, 433*f*, 851–53

Aufbau/Reconstruction (journal), 27
Austria: Anschluss (1938), 20, 23, 120, 210, 216–17, 266; anti-Nazi protests in, 5; fascism in, 152; Jewish immigrants from, 25; pogroms in, 22; US immigration quota for, 23, 25
Autarchy, 291, 806
Authoritarianism, 12, 107, 267, 594, 828. *See also* Totalitarianism
Authors' League, 465, 678
Automobile industry: assembly-line technique in, 295; Model T and, 5; projected sales growth, 308; Stalin's toast to, 402; World War II production stoppages, 398
Avant-garde, 57, 173–75, 640–41, 653, 659, 661, 677
Avenue of the Americas, Sixth Avenue as, 754–55
Aviation industry, 413–15, 807–8. *See also* Airplanes and airports
Avon Books, 668

Ballad for Americans (Robinson & LaTouche), 139–40, 144, 276, 453
Ballet Russe de Monte Carlo, 691, 699
Ballet Theatre, 690–92, 694–95
Bankers Trust, 92, 425, 445, 768
Banking industry: exchange rates, 807; postwar order, 741–44
Barnard College, 157
Baseball, 66, 374–75, 450
Battery Park, 6, 399, 734
Battery Park Tunnel, 720
Battles. *See specific names of battles*
Bayonne Bridge, 283
Belasco Theater, 109
Belgium: anti-Nazi boycott in, 5; Jewish immigrants from, 26, 32; Nazi invasion of (1940), 26, 201, 202; uranium stockpile in Belgian Congo, 431
Bell Labs, 381, 425–27, 435–37, 439, 747–48
Belt Parkway, 720–21
Bendix Aviation Corporation, 414–15
Benjamin Franklin High School, 130, 325, 530
Bergdorf-Goodman, 165, 684
Berkshire Music Center at Tanglewood, 693

Berlin: book burnings in, 6; ICC meeting in (1937), 245; Jewish population in, 25; Olympic Games (1936), 8, 18; Russian troops taking at end of WWII, 849–50
Beth Elohim congregation, 28
Bethlehem Steel, 295, 310, 314, 319, 415
Bias. *See* Discrimination and stereotypes
Bible House, 149, 173, 664
Big Blue Books, 665–66
Big Inch pipeline, 739
Biltmore Hotel, 283
Birth control, 76, 80–81, 210, 665
Black Americans. *See* African Americans
Black Tom munitions depot explosion (1916), 295
Blue Ribbon Books, 664–65, 667
Blyden Society for the Study of African History, 44, 814
B'nai B'rith, 4, 7, 224, 563, 566
Bodley Head publishing house, 666
Bolsheviks: conspiracy theories involving, 33, 74; Stalin's show trials and purge of, 166–68. *See also* Soviet Union
Bonds. *See* War bonds
Bonwit Teller, 165, 684
Boogie-woogie, 630, 652, 692, 695
Book burnings in Nazi Germany, 670, 671*f*
Books. *See* Literature; Publishing industry; *specific titles*
"Books Are Bullets" (radio interviews with book authors), 671
Borough Park, 28, 796
Boroughs. *See specific names of boroughs*
Boxing, 47–49, 57–59, 59*f*, 66, 68
Boycotts: anti-Nazi, 3–8, 6*f*, 13–14, 16–17, 23, 182, 227; of buses by African Americans, 348; of Italian American merchants, 45, 50; of Japanese goods, 108–9, 158, 172; of Model T cars, 5; by Orthodox Jews, 30
Braddock Hotel, 541, 544
Bretton Woods agreements, 741–42
Breuers (K'hal Adath Jeshurun), 27
Brewster Aeronautical Corporation, 413, 781

Britain: aviation industry, 807; Battle of Britain (1940), 208, 281–82, 334; destroyers-for-bases swap with US, 278–79; espionage networks, 260–62, 300, 302; evacuation of children from, 24, 259; Hitler on invasion of, 276, 278, 281, 299; imperialism and, 59–60, 204, 282, 328; Irish independence from, 63; Lend Lease program and, 286–93, 297, 313, 334–35; Munich Agreement (1938), 20, 221; pacifist movements in, 153; at Paris Peace Conference (1919), 248; Spanish Civil War and, 72; US relations with, 257–61. *See also* Anglophiles; Churchill, Winston; London
Britain, Battle of (1940), 208, 281–82, 334
British American Ambulance Corps, 259
British Overseas Airways Corporation (BOAC), 807
British Press Service (BPS), 262
British Secret Intelligence Service (SIS), 260–61
British Security Coordination (BSC), 261–62, 299, 302–3
Broadcast Music, Inc. (BMI), 469
Broadway, 673–79; Army Quartermaster Corps presenting war reenactments in Central Park, 674; biggest entertainment enterprise in world history created in NYC, 673; Camp Shows, Inc., 673; dramas by Tennessee Williams, 676, 678–79; Group Theatre playwriting contest, 678; musicals, 674–76; soldier-performers deployed in NYC, 674; Studio Theatre, 677, 678; tours of shows and entertainment to military bases, 673–74; USO handing out free tickets, 673; war-related themes, 673
Bronx: anti-Semitism in, 585*f*; birth control services in, 80; Catholic Church in, 67, 82, 87, 92–93; Christian Front in, 86; Christian Mobilizers in, 86–87; Democratic Party

in, 205; dim-outs of streetlamps in, 381; Friends of the New Germany in, 13; German American Bund in, 16; housing projects in, 531, 532, 717; Irish Americans in, 64, 65, 531; Jewish population in, 31, 170, 174, 590; Latinos/Latinas in, 162; manufacturing industry in, 412; "slave market" in, 232. *See also specific neighborhoods and locations*
Bronx Rabbinic Council, 592
Brookhaven Research Laboratory, 747
Brooklyn, 115*f*; America First rallies in, 292; blighted downtown and slum clearance in, 712–15; Bush Terminal in, 109; Catholic Church in, 67, 68, 82, 87, 284; Christian Front in, 86, 96; Civic Center development, 713–15; Concord Village development, 714–15; congressmen from, 9; dim-outs of streetlamps in, 381; eminent domain in, 714; German American Bund in, 16, 18, 20; housing market in, 518, 531; Irish Americans in, 64, 65, 284; Jewish population in, 3, 28–32, 284; manufacturing industry in, 412; public housing in, 717; raiding parties in, 372; Wallabout Market in, 28, 314, 737*f*. *See also specific neighborhoods and locations*
Brooklyn and Queens Transit Corporation (BQT), 725
Brooklyn-Battery Tunnel, 283, 399–400, 720
Brooklyn Bridge, 162, 337, 437, 441, 716
Brooklyn College, 155, 157, 189
Brooklyn Eagle (newspaper), 216, 225, 231, 277
Brooklyn Labor Lyceum, 51
Brooklyn-Manhattan Transit Corporation (BMT), 78, 227
Brooklyn Navy Yard: employment, 103, 314; Lend Lease program and, 313; Pearl Harbor attack and, 352; tenement district near, 28; World War II and, 201, 314, 415
Brooklyn Queens Expressway, 703, 721

Index of Subjects   941

Brooklyn Rapid Transit Company, 89
Brooklyn Tablet (newspaper), 68, 75–76, 79, 82, 87, 163, 292, 332, 374
Brotherhood Day and Brotherhood Week, 123
Brotherhood of Sleeping Car Porters (BSCP), 320, 325, 591
Brownsville: criminal arrests in, 345; Jewish population in, 424; protests against Italian conquest of Ethiopia in, 51; Soviet espionage network in, 192
Building for Peace at Home and Abroad (Stewart), 715
Bundles for Britain, 259
Bureaucracy and Omnipotent Government (Mises), 771
Bureau of Fascists Abroad, 39
Bureau of Public Relations (BPR), 533
Bushwick, 18, 176
Business Advisory Council (BAC), 764
Bus transportation and terminal, 723–26

Café Society, 295–96, 325, 603, 630, 632, 637, 647, 652, 694
Cameo Theater, 95
Campaign in Poland (film), 35
Camp Shows, Inc., 673
Camp Tamiment (Poconos), 690
Capitalism: America Firsters on, 290; benignity of, 305; class struggle under, 206; commercialism and, 174; crisis of, 12, 153, 760; free trade and, 246; global, 255, 812; imperialism and, 150; Marxist critiques of, 168; military-industrial complex and, 309
Capuchins, 67, 88
Cardinal Hayes Memorial High School for Boys, 92–93
Carlyle Hotel, 243
Carmelite Church, 97
Carnegie Corporation, 254, 593, 804
Carnegie Endowment for International Peace, 156–57, 804, 834, 837
Carnegie Foundation, 132, 143, 424
Carnegie Hall: anti-Nazi rally, 22; Emergency Peace Campaign meeting, 157; fundraising events, 160–61; "Keep America Out of War" meeting, 150;

League of American Writers conference, 159, 213; "New York's Answer to the Bund" meeting, 33; Peace Now rally, 379
Carnegie Institution, 118, 141
Cars. *See* Automobile industry; Highways and roads
Casa de España, 163, 164
Casa Italiana, 40, 128, 129
Castle Village, 27
Catholic Digest (magazine), 68
Catholics and Catholic Church: 1944 presidential election and, 796–97; anticommunism of, 70, 82–85, 99; on birth control, 80–81, 210; Capuchins, 67, 88; Cristero War and (1926–1929), 69–71; Dominicans, 67, 88; education and, 68, 69, 81–82, 92–93; films proscribed by, 94, 210; Franciscans, 67, 88; German Americans and, 16; in Great Depression, 68; immigration policy and, 24; Irish Americans and, 67–69, 75, 93–100, 284; Jesuits, 67, 71, 75, 88–89, 122, 163, 789, 853; labor unions and, 78–79; Lateran Accord and (1929), 70; on Nazi anti-Semitism, 5; NCCJ and, 122–23; newspapers and magazines of, 68, 75–76, 81, 82, 87, 99, 163; nuns in, 69, 70, 72, 87, 92, 93, 266; *PM* attacks on, 232–33; Polish Americans and, 98; Reich Concordat and (1933), 70, 75; Ridder family connections with, 14; social services provided by, 68, 92; Spanish Civil War and, 71–72, 74–76, 163–65; Spellman as New York Archbishop, 88–100, 232–33, 283, 329, 377, 519, 625–26, 793, 804, 848; totalitarianism and, 187, 210; Vatican, 45, 69–70, 74, 89–91, 93. *See also specific churches*
Catholic War Veterans, 83
Catholic Worker (newspaper), 75, 87, 99, 377
Catholic World (magazine), 68
CBS, 748, 749
Central Conference of American Rabbis, 80, 157, 589
Central Opera House, 51

Central Park: British royals visiting, 258; German population and, 14; "I Am An American Day" rally, 328–29, 344; Jewish population and, 169; Upper West Side and, 26
Central Trades and Labor Council, 347
Century Group, 265–67, 269, 274, 278–79, 290, 299, 303, 327, 453
Cervantes Fraternal Society, 138, 162
Chambre Syndicale de la Couture Parisienne's Théâtre de la Mode, 687
Charles Pfizer & Co., Inc., 412, 413*f*
Chase Bank, 90, 253, 259, 286, 302, 342, 445, 527, 729, 743–44, 807
Chelsea, 64, 360, 501, 658, 717, 841
Chicago: anti-Nazi protests in, 5; city planning for, 762; pacifist movements in, 148, 154; St. Lawrence Seaway and, 730
Chicago Tribune (newspaper), 223, 290
Children and adolescents: air raid drills for, 341; Catholic organizations for, 68; child labor, 228; evacuation from Britain, 24, 259; fascist organizations for, 40; in German American Bund, 16; Hitler Youth, 16, 40, 565; juvenile delinquency, 504–6; latchkey, 504; Orthodox Judaism and, 29; working moms, 504–6. *See also:* Education
China, 820–24; Buck and, 821–23; communism in, 106–7; declaring war on Japan (WWII), 821; Japanese invasion of (1937), 107–9, 108*f*, 202, 207, 250–52; Kuomintang and, 106–7, 820–21; Qing (Manchu) dynasty in, 106
Chinese Americans, 104–9, 114, 370, 820, 823–24
Chinese Consolidated Benevolent Association (CCBA), 105–7, 370, 820
Chinese Exclusion Act of 1882, 105, 816, 820, 824
Chinese Hand Laundry Alliance (CHLA), 106–8, 820
Christian Conference on War and Peace, 839
Christian Front, 85–87, 95–96, 120, 210, 292, 300, 347, 374, 505

Christian Mobilizers, 86–87, 292, 331
Christians and Christianity: anticlericalism and, 69, 71, 74, 81, 90, 826; on anti-Nazi boycott, 23; on anti-Semitism, 5, 6, 22; Ethiopia's adoption of, 44; human rights and, 838–39; realism and, 206–8. *See also:* Federal Council of Churches; *specific denominations*
Churches. *See specific names of churches*
Churchill, Winston: Atlantic Charter (1941), 392; on British Empire and India, 808–10, 815, 817–18, 821; BSC and, 261, 303; on China's status as Great Power, 821; Donovan's meeting with, 299; family background, 260; FDR and, 278, 286, 293, 297, 386, 400, 836; on Irish neutrality during World War II, 96; media coverage of, 232, 234; on postwar planning, 763; propaganda deployed by, 261; at Tehran Summit (1943), 792; at Yalta Conference (1945), 847, 850
Church Literature of Post-War Planning (Inter-Council Committee on Postwar Planning), 802
Citizens Budget Commission (CBC), 707, 712
Citizens Emergency Conference for Interracial Unity, 592
Citizens Housing Council, 605–7, 715, 718
Citizens' Transit Committee, 727
City Center of Music and Drama, Inc., 698–99
City College of New York (CCNY): antifascist protests, 154, 154*f*; antiwar protests, 154–55; graduates of, 9, 170, 176, 379, 438; professors, 11, 189, 190, 422; Young Communist League and, 325, 434
City Defense Council, 339–40, 342
City Hall: anti-Nazi march to, 4; City Defense Council meeting, 339; Einstein's visit to, 422; newspaper reporters at, 82; reviewing stand, 6; Smith Act registration site, 36
City Planning Commission (CPC), 204, 605, 704, 707, 711, 714, 803, 830

City-Wide Citizens Committee on Harlem, 528, 591, 607
City-Wide Tenants Council, 517
Civil Aeronautics Board, 732
Civil disobedience, 5, 151, 377–79, 538, 552, 818
Civilian Conservation Corps, 377, 777
Civilian Defense Volunteer Office (CDVO), 342, 353
Civilian Defense Volunteer Organization, 686
Civilian Public Service (CPS), 377–78
Civil rights movement, 320–24, 525–26, 537, 538, 552, 610, 612, 616
Civil Service Commission., 80, 82, 174
Clan na Gael, 63, 64, 77–78, 161
Claridge Hotel, 384, 384*f*
Coal Merchants Association, 739
Coast Guard. *See* United States Coast Guard
Cold War, 791–94
Colleges. *See* Education; *specific institutions*
College Teachers Union (CTU), 185, 190
Colonialism. *See* Imperialism
Columbia Teachers College's Commission on Postwar Training and Adjustment, 803
Columbia University: anthropology department, 117–19, 127, 438; antiwar protests, 154, 157; chaplains, 92; computer technology, 747; Einstein lectures, 422; English language studies, 192; Faculty Club, 11, 119, 439; German academics, 11–12; graduate studies, 176, 195, 274; Law School, 296; Low Library, 258; physics department, 409, 429; psychology department, 524, 527; Teachers College, 81, 126–27, 130, 185
Columbus Day celebrations, 40, 41, 51, 54, 376
Comintern, 72, 73, 152, 181, 192
Commerce and Industry Association of New York (CIA), 718, 745; Post-war Planning Committee, 768, 803
Commission to Study the Bases of a Just and Durable Peace (CJDP), 804, 837, 840

Commission to Study the Organization of Peace (CSOP), 834–35, 837, 838, 840–41
Committee for Cultural Freedom (CCF), 180, 184, 185
Committee for Economic Development (CED), 706–7, 764–67, 769, 785, 797, 802
Committee for Ethiopia, 50
Committee of Catholics to Fight Anti-Semitism, 87
Committee on Discrimination in Employment, 610
Committee on Militarism in Education, 157
Committee on the Participation of Women in Post War Planning, 804, 838
Committee to Defend America by Aiding the Allies (CDAAA), 264–65, 269, 278–79, 290, 292, 330, 334, 834
Commodore Hotel, 235
Common Council for American Unity (CCAU), 143
Common Ground (magazine), 143, 523, 822
Commonweal (magazine), 68, 75–76, 81, 87, 99
Communication Act of 1934, 132
Communism: African Americans and, 45; in China, 106–7; education threatened by, 186–90; internment of Japanese Americans and, 369; Irish Americans and, 77–78; Italian Americans and, 41; Jews and, 7, 8, 14, 85, 182; labor unions and, 184–85, 189, 788; pacifism and, 148, 152, 158; pluralism and, 138–39; popular culture initiatives, 175; red-baiting, 177, 234, 347; Red Scare and, 83, 185, 187, 300, 787–90; Reichstag fire blamed on, 3; in Soviet Union, 69, 166–68, 180, 183; Spanish Civil War and, 73, 75, 76, 158, 178; State Department on Hitler as bulwark against, 7.
See also: Anticommunism; Red Scare
Communist Political Association, 788
Community Church of New York, 17, 149, 378

Community Service Society, 717
Computer technology, 747
Comstock Laws, 80
Concentration camps, 14, 22, 197, 210, 300, 390–91, 584
Coney Island, 227, 338, 345, 354, 358, 381–82
Confederated Spanish Societies, 162, 165
Confessions of a Nazi Spy (film), 34
Congress of Industrial Organizations (CIO): aid for Spanish Civil War, 161; *Ballad for Americans* as unofficial anthem of, 140; on Black access to defense jobs, 526; calls for investigation of, 21; Democratic Party and, 787; FDR supported by, 204, 216; Greater New York Industrial Union Council, 347; on housing discrimination, 606, 607; "New York at War" parade and, 392; "People's Program of 1944," 781–82, 789; Political Action Committee (CIO-PAC), 705, 779, 781–82, 786, 787, 796; on rent control, 518; on suppression of political opponents, 82; Transit Workers Union and, 78
A Congress to Win the War and the Peace (UDA & *New Republic*), 782
Conscientious objectors (COs), 280, 377–78
Conscription (draft), 269, 279–80, 319–20, 372, 505, 820
Conservative right, 776–78
Consolidated Edison, 739
Consolidated Shipbuilding Corporation, 415
Consolidated Tenants League, 518, 608
Consumer electronics manufacture, 748
Contraception. *See* Birth control
Convent of the Sacred Heart School, 93
Cooper Union, 98, 436
Corporate headquarters, 751–55
Coty, Inc., 684
Coty American Fashion Critics Award, 684–85
Council Against Intolerance in America (CAIA), 33, 131, 330
Council for Democracy, 328
Council of National Defense, 297

Council on African Affairs (CAA), 814, 818, 822
Council on Books in Wartime (CBW), 670–71
Council on Foreign Relations (CFR), 254–58, 263–66, 269, 274, 297, 741, 792, 801, 802, 806, 807, 835–37, 841
Covenant of Peace Group, 148
Crane Shipbuilding, 310, 314
Creole Petroleum, 304–5
Crime waves, 529–31, 530*f*
Crisis (magazine), 45, 53, 528, 544, 591, 812
Cristero War (1926–1929), 69–71
Cross Bronx Expressway, 721
Crown Heights, 28, 32, 65
C. S. Hammond & Company, 670
Cuba, 825
Cultural diversity. *See* Pluralism; Race and ethnicity
Cultural freedom, 179–80, 184
Currency, 742, 807
Czas (newspaper), 98
Czechoslovakia, 5, 20, 21

Daily Worker (newspaper), 82, 95, 169, 539
Dance Center, 689–90
Dante Alighieri Society, 40
Das Schwarze Korps (newspaper), 18
Daughters of the American Revolution (DAR), 137, 141, 187, 322
Dawes Plan, 244, 252
Decentralization in New York City (Hoyt & Armstrong), 711
Decolonization. *See* Imperialism
Defense Plant Corporation (DPC), 309, 316, 402, 436–37, 445
Delaware Aqueduct, 703
Dell Paperbacks, 668
Delmonico Hotel, 47
Democracy: Brotherhood Day and, 123; fascism vs., 210, 251, 287, 303, 326, 454; of nationalities, 114; Nazi crimes against, 17; pacifist movement on, 147, 153; Pan American, 391; publications advocating for, 106; safeguards for, 188, 211; social, 205, 287, 459; threats to, 197, 198; totalitarianism compared to, 179; workers', 177; World War II and, 59, 196, 287, 291, 303

Democratic Party: CIO and, 787; Foreign Language Citizens Committee, 53–54, 135; Irish Americans and, 65, 77, 284; Italian Americans and, 40, 53–55, 375; Jewish community and, 18, 55, 65, 284; National Convention (1944), 783; New Deal wing of, 203–5, 216, 283, 776; Ridder family connections with, 14; Southern, 776–77. *See also* Roosevelt, Franklin
Demonstrations. *See* Protests and demonstrations
Department stores: anti-Nazi boycott and, 6–7; Jewish-owned, 86, 591. *See also specific stores*
Destroyers-for-bases deal, 278–79
Dewey, Thomas: 1940 presidential candidate for nomination, 272–76; 1944 presidential election, 375, 785–87, 789, 795–97; anti-communist stance of, 789; civil rights and anti-discrimination legislation, 610, 612, 616; Hanes Committee and, 745; Harlem riots and, 548; Italian American voters and, 54; Jewish vote and, 579, 582–83, 585*f*; La Guardia endorsed by, 345; as NY District Attorney, 34, 150, 189, 363, 364; as NY Governor, 365, 411, 501; Polish Americans and, 794; Port of New York and, 729; public housing and, 718; rent control and, 519–20; welfare services and, 705
DeWitt Clinton High School, 128–29
Diamond industry, 7, 26, 32, 751–52
Discrimination and stereotypes: countering through education, 126, 128; in education, 527; in housing, 232, 528, 531–32, 605–8; immigrant stereotypes, 56, 133, 142, 284; Latino/Latina stereotypes, 306; as learned behavior, 127–28; propaganda in promotion of, 120; protests against, 319–22; redlining and, 528, 608; religious, 120, 232; sexism, 119, 502–3. *See also* Anti-Semitism; Employment discrimination; Racism

Diversity. *See* Pluralism; Race and ethnicity
Divorce rates, 505, 506
Dominican Republic, 828
Dominicans, 67, 88
Donovan's Hall, 86, 87
Doubleday (publishers), 664
"Double V for Victory" rally,, 534*f*
DOW Chemical, 246
Downey Shipbuilding Corporation, 415
Downtown Music School, 139
Draft. *See* Conscription; Selective Service Act
Dramatic Workshop, 677, 678
Dramatists' Guild, 678, 698
Duce Fascist Alliance of New York, 40
Dumbarton Oaks negotiations and draft, 813, 840

East River Drive, 720
East River public housing, 716
Ebbets Field, 84
Ebling's Casino, 16, 86
Economic Bill of Rights, 705, 779–80
Economic journalism, 769–70
Economic Status of the New York Metropolitan Region in 1944 (RPA), 745, 803
Edicions Gallimard, 669
Edison Electric Institute, 276
Education: academic freedom and, 17, 153, 177, 186; African Americans and, 524, 527; anti-Semitism in, 10, 421; Catholic, 68, 69, 81–82, 92–93; communist threats to, 186–90; discrimination in, 527; in Great Depression, 10; industrial training schools, 319; intercultural, 126–31, 185, 530; parochial schools, 26, 68, 69, 81–82, 86, 93; School Defense Council, 381; social reconstructionist views of, 127; student exchange programs, 11; yeshivas, 27, 29–32, 559, 580. *See also* Public schools; *specific institutions*
El Congreso Pro-Independencia de Puerto Rico, 831
Elections: 1942 congressional, 776; 1944 congressional, 796; Black vote and, 777. *See also* Roosevelt, Franklin D.

Electricity, 739–40, 803
Electronics industry, 416–17, 435–37
Elevateds (trains), 726–27, 726*f*
Elliott Houses (John Lovejoy Elliott Houses), 717, 717*f*
Ellis Island, 136, 142–43, 329, 352, 374, 651, 657
Elysée Hotel, 144
Emergency Committee for War-Torn Yeshivoth. *See* Vaad Hatzalah
Emergency Committee in Aid of Displaced German Scholars, 11
Emergency Peace Campaign (EPC), 157, 325
Emergency Rescue Committee (ERC), 235–39, 269
Emery Roth & Sons, 753
Eminent domain to fight blight, 714, 715
Empire State Building, 284, 340, 384
Employment: child labor, 228; engineering jobs, 747; of immigrants, 63–65, 103–6, 116; postwar, 704–7, 776; racial and ethnic trends in, 116, 319; R&D jobs, 747; of refugees, 26, 27, 31–32, 215; in sweatshops, 421, 591; of women, 26, 63, 65, 504–6; World War II and, 314; in WPA, 317, 320, 325, 527. *See also* Employment discrimination; Labor unions; Unemployment
Employment discrimination: anti-Semitism and, 586; Committee on Discrimination in Employment, 610; in defense industry, 317–19, 374, 525; in Latin America, 305; March on Washington movement and, 322–24; in municipal jobs, 65, 80, 526. *See also* Fair Employment Practice Committee
Engineering talent, 747
England. *See* Britain
English-Speaking Union, 258
Enola Gay, 851, 853
Entertainment industry, 689–96; City Center of Music and Drama, Inc., 698–99; dance, 689–92; music scoring and conducting, 692–94; New York City Opera, 698; New York City Symphony,

699–700. *See also* Broadway
Equality (magazine), 95, 120
España Libre (newspaper), 165
Espionage: British, 260–62, 300, 302; German, 21, 34, 192, 243–44, 262, 295, 300, 329–30; Italian, 192; Japanese, 262; Soviet, 186, 187, 191–95, 262, 300, 434–35
Ethiopia: Christianity adopted in, 44; Italian conquest of, 42–45, 45*f*, 50–53, 52–53*f*, 150, 215, 248, 252
Ethnicity. *See* Race and ethnicity; *specific ethnic group*
Ethnology, 438, 439
Ethyl Gasoline Corporation, 245
Eugenics, 114, 118–19, 141, 197, 332
Export Control Act of 1940, 109
Expressways, construction of, 720–22

Fair Employment Practice Committee (FEPC), 324, 347–48, 525–26, 537, 586, 610, 777, 781, 783–84, 786
The Fall of the City (MacLeish), 213–14, 218
Fancy Free (ballet), 689, 692, 694–95
Farmingdale, 21, 35, 414, 576
Farm Security Administration, 777–78
Fascism: anti-Semitism and, 55; Austrian, 152; boxing and, 48, 57; as enemy of democracy, 210, 251, 287, 303, 326, 454; global threat of, 56; internment of Japanese Americans and, 369; Italian, 11, 39–40, 48, 90, 154, 178, 195; kitsch and, 174–75; master-race, 113, 144; in Nazi Germany, 4, 11, 12, 19, 209–10; pluralism in contrast to, 113, 116, 144, 454, 596; propaganda in support of, 39, 40, 56, 163; protests against, 42*f*, 154, 154*f*, 169*f*; Spanish Civil War and, 20, 71–73, 75, 165, 178; in US, 18–21, 27, 33, 35, 39–40, 56, 113. *See also* Antifascism
Fascist League of North America, 39
The Fashion Group, Inc., 680, 684, 685, 688

Index of Subjects

Fashion industry, 680–88; clothing as biggest manufacturing sector in city, 685, 687; dethroning Paris as capital of couture, 680–81, 803; educational institutions dedicated to, 685; émigré talent and, 682–83; Fifth Avenue specialty shops, 682; furs and, 685; Latin America as source of inspiration for, 686; military look during wartime, 685–86; Museum of Costume Art, 683–84; New York Dress Institute, 685; Parisian couture and, 680–82; Parsons School of Design, 682; return of Parisian domination at war's end, 687–88; supply shortages of wool and cotton, 686; unions and, 685. *See also* Garment District
Fashion Institute of Design and Technology, 685
Fashion Is Spinach (Hawes), 681
Federal-Aid Highway Act of 1944, 722
Federal Arts Project, 170, 365*f*, 403*f*
Federal Bureau of Investigation (FBI): Christian Front and, 95–96; collaboration with British intelligence, 260–61; Custodial Detention List compiled by, 197; espionage networks uncovered by, 21, 195, 329–30; FDR and, 300–302, 373, 536; on Fifth Columnists, 35; General Intelligence Division, 300; German American Bund and, 16, 372; on USS *Lafayette* fire, 362; Manhattan Project and, 433–34; Nazi sabotage plots uncovered by, 367; Pearl Harbor attack and, 352; on Pope's political activities, 56, 333
Federal Communications Commission (FCC), 55, 216, 284, 332, 374
Federal Council of Churches (FCC): on birth control, 80; Commission on International Justice and Good Will, 150; domestic agenda of, 153; ecumenical cooperation and, 207; Goodwill Committee, 122; international initiatives, 248; at National Peace Conference, 157; Nazi subversion investigations supported by, 21; postwar planning and, 804; *Six Pillars of Peace* (John Foster Dulles) and, 837–38; World War II and, 208
Federal Housing Administration (FHA), 528, 608, 711
Federal postwar planning, 759–67; CIA's Post-war Planning Committee reaction to, 768–69; Committee for Economic Development proposals, 764–67; conservative right and, 776–78; GI Bill, 716, 780–81; government and, 759–63; liberalism and, 779–82; NAM reaction to, 768; social and educational benefits for veterans, 780; tax cuts and federal spending, 766–67; war plants, sale to private sector, 766
Federal Radio Project (FRP), 132
Federal Reserve, 85, 93, 95, 251, 446, 743
Federal Shipbuilding and Drydock Corporation, 21, 310, 314, 414
Federal Theater Project (FTP), 139, 276, 455*f*, 538–39, 539*f*, 674
Federal Trade Commission (FTC), 447
Federal Writers Project, 269
Federation of American Scientists, 853
Federation of Irish Societies, 65
Federation of Jewish Women, 80
Fellowship of Reconciliation (FOR), 149–52, 158, 197–98, 325, 377–78
Fenians, 63, 78
Fifth Column: BSC leaks on, 262; defense industry and, 317–18; FDR on, 35, 141, 203, 236, 284, 299; German American Bundists as, 20–21, 34; Italian Americans and, 363; in Latin America, 256; NYPD concerns regarding, 56; surveillance of, 210
Fight for Freedom Committee (FFC), 327–28, 330–31, 453, 465
The Fighting 69th (film), 99–100
Films: antifascist themes in, 121; Catholic Church on, 94, 210; Latino/Latina stereotypes in, 306; portrayals of Hitler in, 34; propaganda, 35. *See also specific films*
Fireside chats, 35, 58, 202–3, 234, 286, 297, 670
First Avenue Association, 726
First National Bank, 92, 425
First World War. *See* World War I
Flatbush, 16, 28, 64, 796
The Fleet's In (Cadmus's painting), 691, 691*f*
Flushing, 65, 501, 660, 726
Folk-arts movement, 124–25
Folk Festival Council (FFC), 124–25, 129
Food supply, 736–38, 737*f*
Football, 352, 450
Fordham neighborhood, 64, 86
Fordham University, 75, 81, 86–87, 89, 91, 96, 283–84, 345
Ford Motor Company, 243–45, 309
Foreign Affairs (magazine), 255, 256, 269
Foreign Agents Registration Act of 1938, 330
Foreign Commerce Club, 729–31
Foreign Information Service (FIS), 303, 456
Foreign Language Citizens Committee, 135
Foreign Language Information Service (FLIS), 124, 143
Foreign Policy Association (FPA), 156, 796, 835
Fort Totten, 21, 337, 353
Fort Tryon Park, 27
Fortune (magazine), 24, 172, 213, 229–30, 273–75, 424, 763
Foundation for Economic Education (FEE), 774–75
The Fountainhead (Rand), 713, 772, 773–74
Four Freedoms speech (1941), 287–89, 378, 379, 838, 839
France: Huguenots expelled from, 11; invasion of (1940), 56, 201, 202, 210, 252, 264; Munich Agreement (1938), 20, 221; at Paris Peace Conference (1919), 248; refugees in, 9, 235–39; Spanish Civil War and, 72, 165; Vichy government in, 235, 238, 360, 439–40, 460, 651
France, Battle of (1940), 264
Franciscans, 67, 88
Francophones, 440, 456
Frankfurt School, 175
Franklin Square Library, 665
Freedom: academic, 17, 153, 177, 186, 189; cultural, 179–80, 184; Four Freedoms speech (1941), 287–89, 378, 379, 838, 839; religious, 70, 123, 208, 287, 599; of speech, 33, 154, 188, 210, 287, 330, 373, 838
Free market system and competition, 765, 770–71, 774–75, 806–11
Free speech. *See* Speech, freedom of
Free trade system, 832
Free World Association, 810
French resistance, 669
Frente Popular (newspaper), 162, 165
Friendly Sons of St. Patrick, 77, 81, 333
Friends for Freedom of India, 817
Friends of Ethiopia, 51
Friends of the New Germany, 13–16, 15*f*, 21
Friends of the Soviet Union, 167
Fulton Fish Market, 136, 364
Fusion Movement, 343–45, 349

F. W. Woolworth, 666

Gaelic American (newspaper), 64, 374
Garden City Publishing Company, 664–65
Garibaldi-American Fraternal Society, 40, 41
Garment District, 23*f*, 26, 283, 315, 687
Gay persons. *See* Homosexuality
Gender: immigration laws and, 105–6; Orthodox Judaism and, 30–31. *See also* Men; Women
General Aircraft Corporation (GAC), 413
General Bronze Corporation, 748
General Electric (GE), 244, 245, 427, 448, 769
General Jewish Council, 24
General Motors: chairmen of, 93, 246; Futurama exhibit at World's Fair, 703; general counsel for, 93; new roads needed to sell cars, 720; overseas operations, 243–46; welfare programs, 271
Genocide against Jews (later called Holocaust), 14, 22,

197, 210, 300, 390–91, 557–67, 583–84, 592, 658, 839
Gentile Manual Training High School, 421
Gentlemen's Agreement (1907–1908), 104
George Washington Bridge, 720–21
George Washington High School, 527
German Air Force. *See* Luftwaffe
German American Bund, 16–21, 27, 33–35, 34*f*, 55, 86, 121, 269, 330–31, 372
German American Congress for Democracy, 35, 237
German Americans: 1940 presidential election and, 284; 1941 mayoral election and, 349; assimilationism and, 13, 14, 18, 19, 27; Catholic Church and, 16; Jewish, 4–5, 9–12, 14; Nazi outreach to, 13–19, 15*f*, 35, 39, 43; repression during World War I, 13; support for Hitler, 14, 16, 19, 33, 297; on US involvement in World War II, 35, 36; World War II raids on, 329, 372–73
German American Vocational League, 372–73
German Day celebrations, 13, 14, 16, 18, 21, 40
German Expressionists, 669
German Foreign Institute (DAI), 18
German Military Intelligence (Abwehr), 21, 192, 329–30, 366
Germany: espionage networks, 21, 34, 192, 243–44, 262, 295, 300, 329–30; Red Cross in, 249; Reichstag, 3, 14, 428, 431; reparations imposed upon, 244, 247, 248; Weimar theater movement, 676–77; World War I and, 5, 16. *See also* Berlin; Nazi Germany
Gestapo, 14, 22, 35, 192, 235, 299, 391, 557
GI Bill, 716, 780–81
Gimbels department store, 7, 140, 513, 648, 662–63, 668
The Glass Menagerie (Williams), 676, 679, 692
Global postwar planning, 801–5; books devoted to, 801–2; leadership of NYC in, 802; leftists and liberals on, 803–4; metropolitan advocacy organizations, 804; professional associations, 803; religious denominations, 804; state agencies, 803; think tanks, 802; trade associations, 802–3
The God of the Machine (Paterson), 770
Goelet Realty Company, 752
Gold standard, 742, 807
Golf, 57, 482, 734, 744
The Good Earth (Buck), 667, 821
Governor Alfred E. Smith Houses, 716
Governors Island, 336, 359, 548
Grand Central Station: Pearl Harbor attack and, 353; restoration of, 724; World War I veteran gathering in, 100
Great Depression: Catholic Church during, 68; education during, 10; immigration during, 10, 39, 64; industry, collapse of, 28, 64; Marxism and, 170; measures to combat, 7, 9, 255; race riots during, 590; racial and ethnic differences in, 18; unemployment, 86, 106, 169, 174, 203; Wall Street and, 64, 291, 296, 299, 317
Great War. *See* World War I
Greenwich Village: espionage in, 191; MacLeish in, 213; nightclubs in, 163; Roosevelt apartment in, 131, 795; syndicalist atmosphere of, 441
Greyhound Corporation, 723–24
Greystone Hotel, 32
Grimm's *Fairy Tales*, 669
Grosset & Dunlap, 664–65
Group Theatre, 678, 689
Grumman Aircraft Engineering Corporation, 413–14
GRU (Soviet Military Intelligence), 192–95, 434
Guernica (Picasso), 165

Half Moon Hotel, 345, 346, 350*f*, 351
Hamburg-American shipping line, 6, 21, 191
Hanes Committee, 745–46, 751
Hapag Lloyd shipping line, 73
Harlem: Black nationalism, 44, 45, 50; Blyden Society, 44, 814; crime wave, 529, 530*f*; Gandhi receiving support from, 59; housing, 128, 517, 518, 531, 715; intercultural education, 130–31; Italian Americans in, 45, 50, 53, 530; juvenile delinquency, 504; Latinos/Latinas in, 162; public housing, 717; race riots, 45, 531, 544–45, 590, 592, 608, 820; Savoy Ballroom, 541, 544, 638, 640, 692*f*; YMCA, 44, 320, 523; Zoot suits, 540–41, 777
Harlem Colonial Conference (1945), 814
Harlem History Club, 44
Harlem Hospital, 14, 650
Harlem Labor Committee, 322
Harlem River Drive, 720
Harold Pratt House, 841
Harper & Brothers, 664–65
Harper's Bazaar magazine, 143, 656, 682, 683, 684
Hasidic Orthodox Judaism, 30–32
Hattie Carnegie, 681, 682, 684
Hearn's Department Store, 6, 487
Hebrew Sheltering and Immigrant Aid Society of America (HIAS), 9, 26
Hell's Kitchen, 57, 64, 713, 774
Henry Street Settlement, 128, 228, 434
"Here Is Your Infantry" performance (Ebbets Field), 674
High School of Music & Art, 697
High schools. *See* Education; *specific institutions*
Highways and roads, construction of, 720–23; National System of Interstate Highways, 722
Hillman Houses, 716
Hindenburg airship, 58, 219, 220*f*
Hippodrome, 54, 84, 161, 177, 198
Hiroshima atomic bombing, 851
Hiroshima (Hersey), 853–54
Hispanics. *See* Latinos; Puerto Rico and Puerto Ricans
Hitler, Adolf: on African Americans, 60, 544; Anschluss and, 20, 216–17; anti-Semitic campaigns, 3, 25, 237; atomic bomb and, 428, 429, 434; Blitzkrieg and, 35, 59, 210, 260; boxing supported by, 57–58; on British invasion, 276, 278, 281, 299; as bulwark against communism, 7; cartoon depictions, 232, 591; "The Case of Civilization Against Hitler" mock trial, 17; Catholic views of, 81; Christian Front and, 86; commercial relations with US companies, 243–46, 249; death of (1945), 850; democratic socialism and, 379; eugenics and, 118, 119; German American support for, 14, 16, 19, 33, 297; Hollywood portrayals of, 34; House of Morgan's relationship with, 252–53; interviews with, 255, 268; La Guardia on, 17–18; Latin America and, 256; in *Life*'s "Speaking of Dictators" photo montage, 267; *Mein Kampf*, 55; movements against, 3, 6, 121, 122, 154, 198, 207, 212, 250, 264–65, 310; Mussolini's relationship with, 55, 364, 589; "New York at War" parade and, 390, 390*f*, 392; nonaggression pact with Stalin, 181, 204; Order of the German Eagle with Star, 332; outreach to German Americans, 18, 39, 43; personal hit list of, 236; physics programs shut down by, 423; political prisoners held by, 42*f*; propaganda campaigns, 303; purge of radical Nazis by, 168; Reich Concordat with Catholic Church, 70, 75; on reparations following World War I, 248; response to Lend Lease, 334; rise to power, 3, 4, 13, 123, 130, 152, 252, 266; *Social Justice* profiles of, 85; Spanish Civil War and, 72–75, 164; submarine warfare and, 334, 335, 357, 359; Sudetenland annexation and, 20; threat posed by, 153, 185, 202, 209, 224, 255–56, 267, 269, 273, 282, 295, 584; as *Time* magazine's Man of the Year, 229–30; totalitarianism of, 179; on US immigration laws, 12; Vichy government and, 360. *See also* Nazi Germany
Hitler Youth, 16, 40, 565
Holland, 5, 7, 201, 203, 249
Hollywood. *See* Films
Holocaust. *See* Genocide against Jews

946   Index of Subjects

Homelessness, 317, 411, 716
Homosexuality, 119, 325, 378, 490, 624–25, 678, 691–93, 840
Horni Manufacturing Company, 412
Horst Wessel Song, 17
Hotels: Fifth Column activity in, 35; for refugees, 26; residential, 26. *See also: specific hotels*
House Committee on Immigration and Naturalization, 9, 824
House of Morgan, 244, 252–53, 257, 270, 275
House Un-American Activities Committee (HUAC), 16, 21, 187, 194
Housing: blighted neighborhoods and slum landlords, 712–14; for defense workers, 414; discrimination in, 232, 528, 531–32, 605–8; government-backed public housing, 716–17; in Great Depression, 64; for immigrants, 26–29, 31, 104, 105, 128; New Deal and, 28–29, 531; postwar planning, 710–19; for refugees, 26–28, 31; rent control, 517–20, 608, 752, 754, 775; restrictive covenants, 608; settlement houses, 115, 124, 128, 228, 434, 654, 674; shortage at end of war, 716; suburban development, 710–11. *See also* Public housing; Tenements
Housing Act of 1937, 715, 718
How New Will the Better World Be? A Discussion of Post-war Reconstruction (Becker), 802
How to Win Friends and In?uence People (Carnegie), 668
Hudson View Gardens, 27
Human rights: FDR on, 838, 842; La Guardia on, 17; Non-Sectarian Anti-Nazi League and, 6, 6f, 7, 21, 58, 121; religious groups advocating for, 837–39; UN Charter's Preamble and, 843
"Human Rights and the World Order" (CSOP report), 838
Hunter College, 76, 236, 283, 307, 333, 483–84, 843, 857
Hydroelectric power, 739–40

"I Am An American Day" rally, 328–29, 344
IBM, 244–46, 249, 392, 436, 747
Idiot's Delight (Sherwood), 212
Idlewild Airport, 703, 734–35
If This Be Treason (Holmes), 151
Il Giornale d'Italia (newspaper), 55
Il Grido della Stirpe (newspaper), 40, 55, 373
Il Martello (newspaper), 41, 178, 375
Il Nuovo Mondo (newspaper), 41
Il Progresso Italo-Americano (newspaper), 40–42, 54–56, 333
Immigrants and immigration: alienation of, 17, 129, 130; anti-Chinese laws abrogated, 824; Asian Indians and, 816–17; Asiatic Barred Zone, 816; employment of, 63–65, 103–6, 116; folk-arts movement and, 124–25; in Great Depression, 10, 39, 64; housing for, 26–29, 31, 104, 105, 128; laws on, 9–10, 23, 39, 104–6, 113; mutual aid societies for, 27, 162; nativist views of, 113–19, 124, 129, 133, 787, 824; New Deal policies and, 135; Puerto Ricans, 827, 832, 835; quota system, 9, 12, 23–26, 300, 816, 824; Statue of Liberty and, 135–37; stereotypes of, 56, 133, 142, 284. *See also* Alien Registration Act of 1940; Assimilationism; Chinese Exclusion Act; Refugees; *specific ethnic groups*
Immigration Act of 1917, 817
Imperial Airways, 807
Imperialism: anti-imperialism, 44, 378, 553, 822, 827, 829; British, 59–60, 204, 282, 328, 807; capitalism and, 150; Japanese, 523–24; postwar world and, 807–11; racism and, 811, 812–15; UN Charter and, 814–15; UN trusteeship system for transition to independence, 813–15; World War II and, 198
India: civil disobedience in, 5, 818; Gandhi's movement for independence, 149, 816–19; World War II and, 817–18
India League of America, 379, 817–18
India Today (magazine), 817
Industrial Union of Marine and Shipbuilding Workers, 310
Influenza epidemic (1918), 114, 172
Infrastructure projects, 736–40
Institute for Social Research, 11, 594
Institute of Carpet Manufacturers of America, 803
Institute of International Education (IIE), 11, 157, 215
Institute of Jewish Affairs, 804
Institute of Scrap Iron and Steel, 109
Intercultural education, 126–31, 185, 530
Interior Department, Division of Territories and Island Possessions, 829
International Bill of Human Rights, 842, 843
International Brigades, 72–74
International Catholic Truth Society (ICTS), 75, 83
International Chamber of Commerce (ICC), 244–45
International finance, 741–42
International Fur and Leather Workers Union, 97, 777
International Ladies' Garment Workers Union (ILGWU), 7, 12, 41–42, 56, 139, 283, 375, 392, 527, 685, 698, 777, 788
International Longshoremen's Association (ILA), 361, 363–64, 406
International Monetary Fund (IMF), 741–42
International Relief Association (IRA), 12
International Telephone and Telegraph (ITT), 243–46
International Workers Order (IWO), 138, 139, 162
Internment camps, 165, 329, 368–69
Investment banking, 743–44
Inwood, 64, 501, 586
Iraq Petroleum Company, 809
Ireland: civil war in (1922–1923), 63; Easter Rising in (1916), 63, 77, 97; immigration to US from, 63, 64; neutrality during World War II, 96–97; War of Independence (1919–1921), 63
I Remember Mama (play), 677
Irish Advocate (newspaper), 64
Irish Americans: 1940 presidential election and, 284; 1941 mayoral election and, 349; 1944 presidential election and, 796; anti-Semitism and, 585–86; assimilationism and, 99; Catholic Church and, 67–69, 75, 93–100, 284; Christian Front and, 85–86; communism and, 77–78; Democratic Party and, 65, 77, 284; employment of, 63–65, 116; Great Depression and, 64; on Irish neutrality during World War II, 96–97; labor unions and, 77–79; Republican Party and, 65, 77; Tammany Hall and, 65–66, 80, 135
Irish Echo (newspaper), 64, 96
Irish Republican Army (IRA), 63, 64, 77, 79, 161
Irish Transport and General Workers Union, 77
Irish World (newspaper), 64, 374
Isolationism: anti-Semitism and, 24; pacifism vs., 148, 156; Stimson's criticisms of, 251; on US neutrality during World War II, 99
Italian Americans: 1940 presidential election and, 284; 1941 mayoral election and, 349; 1944 presidential election and, 796–97; America First Committee and, 292; antifascism and, 41–43, 50, 51, 54, 56; anti-Semitism and, 55, 56; assimilationism and, 128–29; Black boycotts against merchants, 45, 50; boxing and, 47, 48; Columbus Day celebrations, 40, 41, 51, 54, 376; communism and, 41; Democratic Party and, 40, 53–55, 375; employment of, 116; Fifth Column and, 363; Great Depression and, 39; housing for, 128; Mussolini's outreach to, 39–40, 42–43, 53, 56, 375; socialism and, 282;

stereotypes of, 56, 284; on US involvement in World War II, 36; World War I service of, 51; World War II raids on, 329, 372
Italian Library of Information, 39, 40
Italian Socialist Federation, 282
Italy: Catholic Church in, 70, 90; espionage networks, 192; Ethiopia conquest by, 42–45, 45*f*, 50–53, 52–53*f*, 150, 215, 248, 252; fascism in, 11, 39–40, 48, 90, 154, 178, 195; France invasion (1940), 56, 252; House of Morgan's relationship with, 252; Latin America and, 256; military alliance with Japan, 109; Red Cross in, 51; totalitarianism in, 180, 264. *See also* Mussolini, Benito

Jacob Riis Houses, 716
Jacques Schiffrin & Cie. (French publishing house), 669
Jamaica (neighborhood), 16
Japan: Amity and Commerce Treaty (1858), 103; boycott against goods from, 108–9, 158, 172; China invasion (1937), 107–9, 108*f*, 202, 207, 250–52; espionage networks, 262; Gentlemen's Agreement (1907–1908), 104; House of Morgan's relationship with, 252; imperialism and, 523–24; military alliance with Italy and Nazi Germany, 109; Mukden Incident and (1931), 250, 252; *Panay* sinking by (1937), 109; at Paris Peace Conference (1919), 523; Pearl Harbor attack (1941), 352–54, 357, 447–48; Russo-Japanese War (1904–1905), 523; submarine warfare and, 368; totalitarianism in, 180; US export of war materials to, 109, 150. *See also* World War II
Japanese American Committee for Democracy, 372
Japanese Americans: employment of, 103–4; housing for, 104; internment during World War II, 368–69; *Life* magazine on Chinese Americans vs., 370; Pearl Harbor attack and, 352–53; as percentage of population, 114, 371; unemployment during World War II, 372
Japanese Association of New York, 104
Japan Society, 103
Jarama, Battle of (1937), 74
Jehovah's Witnesses, 378
Jesuits, 67, 71, 75, 88–89, 122, 163, 789, 853
Jewish Daily Forward (newspaper), 7, 40, 95, 557
Jewish Frontier (magazine), 559, 562, 574, 575, 590
Jewish Labor Committee (JLC): American Friends of German Freedom and, 207; anti-Nazi boycott and, 7; Black–Jewish conference sponsored by, 591; Counter-Olympics held by (1936), 8; Emergency Rescue Committee and, 236, 788; on Nazi assault on labor rights, 12
Jewish Theological Seminary, 22, 30, 128, 157, 559, 569
Jewish War Veterans (JWV), 3–4, 392, 560, 586
Jewish Welfare Board, 28
Jews: 1940 presidential election and, 284; 1941 mayoral election and, 347, 350; 1944 presidential election and, 579, 582–83, 786, 796; on anti-Nazi boycott, 3–7; assimilationism and, 4, 27, 29, 121, 122; Black alliance with, 553, 589–92; communism and, 7, 8, 14, 85, 182; conspiracy theories involving, 8, 11, 33, 74, 85; Democratic Party and, 18, 55, 65, 284; Eastern European, 4, 30, 570; employment of, 65, 116; genocide and concentration camps (later called Holocaust), 14, 22, 197, 210, 300, 390–91, 557–67, 583–84, 592, 658, 839; German American, 4–5, 9–12, 14; immigration to US, 9–12, 23–32, 236; *kehillas* (caring communities), 27, 569; NCCJ and, 122–23; NYPD's all-Jewish detail, 22; *Oklahoma!* demonstrating toleration, 676; Orthodox, 4, 26–32, 139, 236, 421, 568, 674; pogroms against, 9, 12, 22–23, 169, 266, 568; public school attendance by, 29, 30, 170; real-estate complex, 753; Reconstructionist, 128; Reform, 4, 28, 29, 559, 574; as refugees, 3, 9–11, 23–33, 66, 119, 269, 300, 431, 577, 590, 602; socialism and, 4, 7, 12, 138, 282–83; Spanish Civil War and, 74, 163; Spanish expulsion of, 11; World War I service of, 4; World War II service of, 584; yeshivas and, 27, 29–32, 559, 580; Young Israel movement, 29, 574–76; Zionism, 4–5, 7, 29, 169, 592. *See also* American Jewish Committee; American Jewish Congress; Anti-Semitism; *specific congregations and temples*
Jim Crow, 320, 523–25, 591, 607, 777, 842. *See also* Lynchings; Segregation
"Jim Crow's Last Stand" (Hughes's poem), 818
Jobs. *See* Employment
Jobs for All after the War (CIO-PAC), 781, 804
John Reed Club, 169, 169*f*, 170
Jones Act of 1917, 825
Jukeboxes, 365, 468, 470, 636, 642
Juvenile delinquency, 504–6

Kahn & Jacobs ?rm, 753
Keep America Out of War Congress (KAOWC), 198, 282, 291–93, 378, 803
Kehillas (caring communities), 27, 569
Keynesianism, 741–43, 760, 762, 769, 771, 797
KGB, 178, 192–95, 434–35
K'hal Adath Jeshurun (Breuers), 27
Kingsbridge, 64, 795
King's Crown Hotel, 429
Kitsch, 174–75
Knights of Columbus, 68, 79, 81–83, 188
Knights of Malta, 93, 99
Kristallnacht (1938), 22–24, 27, 31, 33, 131, 266, 591
Ku Klux Klan, 5, 70, 75, 544
Kuomintang (KMT), 106–7, 820–21
Kyffhaeuser Bund, 372

Labor unions: African Americans and, 525–26; antifascism and, 41–42; anti-Nazi boycott and, 5, 7; campaign fundraising and, 779; Catholic Church and, 78–79; Chinese Americans and, 106, 107; communism and, 184–85, 189, 788; Irish Americans and, 77–79; Latinos/Latinas and, 525; New Deal and, 310; "New York at War" parade and, 392; on NRPB report, 763; rescue movements and, 12; South's labor force and, 777; strikes by, 78, 310, 347, 778. *See also specific unions*
USS *Lafayette*, 74, 165, 360–63, 361*f*
La Guardia, Fiorello: 1933 mayoral election, 17, 42, 65, 130; 1937 mayoral election, 18; 1941 mayoral election, 347–51; airport construction and, 734–35; on Anglo-American relations, 258; antifascism of, 17, 42, 347, 457; on anti-Nazi boycott, 17; Atlantic Charter and, 810; Bernstein and, 697; at boxing matches, 47; Brooklyn Navy Yard expansion and, 314; budget cuts by, 399; at CDAAA meetings, 265, 334; civilian defense and, 338–42, 344, 353–54, 381, 383–84, 453; civil rights and, 526; Columbus Day celebrations and, 54; conducting orchestra, 699*f*; on corporate headquarters choosing city location, 752; crime waves and, 531; criticisms of, 17–18, 226, 543; Eisenhower victory parade and, 850; employees of, 208, 224; expressway construction and parking plans and, 723; on Fair Employment Practice Committee, 324, 347–48; fashion industry and, 680–81, 684, 687; FDR and, 18, 205, 343–44, 349, 354, 411; on FDR's death, 847; on freedom of speech, 33; German American Bund investigation by, 33–34; on *Guernica* committee, 165; on homelessness, 317; housing discrimination and, 532, 605–7; on human rights, 17; "I Am An American Day" rally organized by, 328–29, 344; impeachment calls, 532; on Japanese Americans, 369, 371–72; at "Keep America Out of War" meeting, 150; on USS *Lafayette* fire, 361;

La Guardia, Fiorello: (*continued*)
on Lend Lease program, 292–93; mass transit and, 724–26; "New York at War" parade and, 392; nicknames for, 17, 250; on Non-Partisan Committee for Peace, 264; *NYC Postwar Program* exhibition (1944), 703–5; NYPD's all-Jewish detail created by, 22; opening of employment categories by, 116; Pearl Harbor attack and, 352–54; on pluralism, 144; *PM* and, 231, 232; political appointments by, 80, 228; Postwar Industrial Committee and, 746; postwar planning and, 703–5, 707; poverty mitigation measures, 412; propaganda generated by, 457; public housing and, 716, 718; on race riots, 545; radio program of, 374; on rent control, 518, 519, 608; sewage treatment plant and, 738; Sixth Avenue name change and, 754; slum clearance and, 715; at Spellman's investiture as Archbishop, 88; on subway revenue and construction plans, 727–28; Tammany Hall and, 42, 283, 343–45; transit hubs and, 400, 723; truck terminal, construction of, 724; Truman and, 854; United Nations location and, 856; on World's Fair (1939), 17–18, 131
La Guardia Field, 733–34
La Junta Nacionalista de Nueva York, 827
La Stampa Libera (newspaper), 41
Latchkey children, 504
Lateran Accord (1929), 70
Latin America: consulates, 755; fashion influence from, 686; Fifth Columnists in, 256; German influence in, 255–56, 302, 305–6; Italian immigrants in, 256; oil production in, 304, 387; propaganda in, 306–7, 457; rebels in NYC, 825; Spanish Civil War refugees in, 165; US dominance of, 255–56, 305–7. *See also specific countries*
Latinos: labor unions and, 525; on Spanish Civil War, 162–63; stereotypes of, 306; Zoot suits and, 541–42, 544. *See also* Puerto Rico and Puerto Ricans
League Against Totalitarianism, 178–80
League of American Writers (LAW), 159, 163–64, 168, 170, 184, 213
League of Free Nations Association, 835
League of Nations, 45, 50–52, 250–51, 258, 264, 835
League of Nations Association (LNA), 156, 157, 264, 834, 837, 841
Legion of Decency, 94
Lehigh Valley Railroad, 401
Lehman, Herbert: anti-communist legislation and, 83, 186; British king (George VI) visit and, 258; CDAAA and, 265; employment discrimination and, 322, 610; genocide of Jews and, 563; Harlem reapportionment bill and, 602; Irish American voters and, 65, 82; Italian American voters and, 40–42, 54, 375; La Guardia and, 343–44, 349; Non-Partisan Committee for Peace and, 264; as NY Governor, 8, 32; Red Army's heroism celebrated by, 791; at Spellman's investiture as Archbishop, 88; war preparation and, 205
Lend Lease program, 286–93, 297, 313, 334–35, 386, 808
Lesbians. *See* Homosexuality
Levittown housing, 710–11, 716
Liberalism, 779–82, 784; 1944 presidential election and, 797; liberal Republicanism of Dewey, 785; postwar planning and, 803–4
Liberal Party, 789, 796
Lictor Federations, 39–40
Life (magazine): on America Firsters, 330; "The American Century," 288–89; "The American Destiny," 266–67, 289; "The Case against Roosevelt," 283; on Chinese vs. Japanese Americans, 370; "Christmas in Naziland," 266; general manager of, 328; Ingersoll and, 229, 230; interracial photos in, 533; on National War Posters exhibition, 371*f*; on Willkie, 275
Liggett Drug Store chain, 667–68
Lillian D. Wald Houses, 716
Lilly Daché, 680, 681, 682, 686
Lincoln Tunnel, 401, 723
Lindy Hop, 692, 692*f*
Literature: antifascist, 119–21, 213–14; anti-Nazi, 119–20, 227, 236; book burnings, 6, 187; Federal Writers Project, 269; on Fifth Column activity, 35; worker-literature movement, 169–72; Writers' War Board, 465–66. *See also* Publishing industry; *specific works*
Little Blue Books, 665–66
London: air raids in, 281–82, 339; anti-Nazi boycott in, 5; ecumenical Protestantism in, 207; as global financial center, 255
Long Island Railroad, 16, 366, 398, 414
Look (magazine), 56, 455
Lord & Taylor's, 683, 684
Lower East Side: as blighted neighborhood, 712; housing projects, 531–32; industrial clusters, 437; Jewish population, 9, 28, 30; Popular Front and, 139; Roosevelt Park, 136, 283
Lower West Side, 406, 437
Loyal Americans of German Descent, 333
Luftwaffe (German Air Force), 21, 74, 244–45, 281, 295, 339, 380, 414
L'Unita del Popolo (newspaper), 41
L'Unita Operaia (newspaper), 41
Lynchings, 140, 178, 232, 233*f*

Macy's department store: airplanes and, 732, 733*f*; anti-Nazi boycott and, 6, 227; book sales, 668; executive training program, 171–72; fashion and, 684
Madison Avenue Presbyterian Church, 207
Madison Square Garden: ACC rally, 75; all-Black rally, 537–39; American Medical Bureau meeting, 161; anti-Nazi rally, 4, 5; boxing matches, 48, 57–58; "The Case of Civilization Against Hitler" mock trial, 17; CDAAA rally, 334; communist gatherings, 166; FDR campaign speech, 284, 321; FFC "Fun to Be Free" spectacular, 327–28; fundraising events, 162; German American Bund rally, 33, 269; German Day celebrations, 14, 16, 18; "Hands Off Ethiopia" rally, 51; ILGWU anniversary celebration, 42; Italian-American rallies, 51, 53; Japanese silk boycott rally, 108; mock air raid staged, 341; socialist-communist brawl, 152, 176; Willkie campaign speech, 284
Magazines: Catholic, 68, 75–76, 81, 87, 99, 163; ethnic-based, 13; suppression during World War II, 373. *See also specific publications*
Manchu (Qing) dynasty, 106
Manhattan: America First rallies in, 292, 292*f*; birth control services in, 80; Catholic Church in, 67, 82; congressmen from, 9; dim-outs of streetlamps in, 381; Irish Americans in, 64, 65; Japanese Americans in, 104; Jewish population in, 26–27; Latinos/Latinas in, 162; manufacturing industry in, 412. *See also specific neighborhoods and locations*
Manhattan Bridge, 283, 381, 401, 436, 716, 723
Manhattan Hotel, 192
Manhattan Lyceum, 74
Manhattan Project, 431–45, 433*f*
Manufacturing industry, 412–13; corporate management and, 751–52; postwar, 745–50. *See also* Fashion industry; Publishing industry
Marching Home; Complete War and Post-war Handbook for Service Men and Families (Hart), 802
The March of Time film series, 35, 262, 266, 278, 306, 332, 456
March on Washington Movement (MOWM), 322–25, 348, 537–38, 552
Marines. *See* United States Marine Corps
Maritime Association of the Port of New York, 404, 729

Marriage: divorce rates, 505, 506; interracial, 55, 119
Marseilles Hotel, 26, 570
Marxism: on capitalism, 168; economic determinism and, 176; Great Depression and, 170; modernism and, 173; Spanish Civil War and, 74; theoreticians and, 96–97
Mass transit. *See* Bus transportation and terminal; Railroad industry; Subway
Master-race ideology, 113, 114, 116, 144, 469
Mazzini Society, 56, 375
McAlpin Hotel, 21
Mecca Temple, 293, 698
Melting Pot metaphor, 113–14, 129, 136, 143, 534
Men: conscription into military, 269, 279–80, 319–20, 372, 505; patriarchy, 26, 30, 690. *See also* Gender
Mercury Theatre, 218, 538
Methodist Federation for Social Service, 153
Metropolitan Life, 93, 451, 527, 531–32, 605–7, 713
Mexico: Cristero War in (1926–1929), 69–71; FDR seeking stable relations with, 828; oil production in, 256, 304; Spanish Civil War refugees in, 165; Trotsky in, 177
Meyer's Hotel, 364
Midway, Battle of (1942), 387, 388
Milburn Hotel, 26
Military: conscription for, 269, 279–80, 319–20, 372, 505; segregation of, 319–21, 325, 379, 533–35; voting rights for personnel in, 776–77. *See also specific branches of the military*
Military-industrial complex, 296–98, 308–10
Military Intelligence Division (MID), 300–302
Ministers No War Committee, 292
Minkoff Bill of 1938, 517
Miracles Ahead! Better Living in the Postwar World (Carlisle & Latham), 802
Mitchel Airfield, 21
Mob, 363–65, 375–76, 406
Modern Age Books, 666, 667
Modern Monthly (magazine), 170, 227
Morgan Stanley, 744
Morningside Heights, 11–12, 126, 157, 207, 747, 838

Morris High School, 128
Morse Shipbuilding, 310, 314
Moses, Robert: airports, control of, 735; Brooklyn-Battery Tunnel shutdown and, 508; bus transportation and terminal, 723–24; City Planning Commission and, 704; demolition and construction plans thwarted, 399–400; employment discrimination legislation opposed by, 611; expressway construction and, 721–23; FDR and, 283, 399, 400, 704; housing shortage at end of war and, 716; Japanese Pavilion in Flushing Meadow Park demolished, 370; on Kern's possible communist leanings, 80; loss of construction funding and drop in toll revenues, 399; postwar planning and, 400, 704–9; public housing and, 716, 718; railroad access and, 724; raw materials salvaging and, 507–8; Redevelopment Company Law and, 531–32; slum clearance and, 606, 713, 715–19; Stuyvesant Town and, 532, 605–7; UN headquarters location and, 857, 862; xenophobia of, 708
Motherhood and momism, 494, 504–6. *See also* Children and adolescents
Movies. *See* Films
Mt. Neboh Temple sisterhood, 26
Mukden Incident (1931), 250, 252
Multiculturalism. *See* Pluralism; Race and ethnicity
Munich Agreement (1938), 20, 207–8, 221, 224, 249, 428
Murder, Incorporated, 345, 347, 363, 378
Murray Hill Hotel, 274, 276
Museum of Costume Art, 683–84
Museum of Modern Art (MOMA), 165, 231, 235, 304, 306–7, 369–70, 697; "Airways to Peace" exhibition, 732
Music: country music, 469; jukeboxes, 365, 468, 470, 636, 642; race music, 469; scoring and conducting,

692–94; Tin Pan Alley, 174, 467–68, 470, 493, 646, 694; war songs, 467–70. *See also* Broadway
Music Box Theatre, 151
Music Industries War Council, 467
Music War Committee, 467
Mussolini, Benito: African Americans on, 49, 50; anticlerical campaign, 90; antifascist opposition to, 41, 42, 50, 51, 56; on boxing as fascist means of self-expression, 48; cartoon depictions, 232, 369; death of, 850; Ethiopia conquest by, 42–45, 50–53, 53*f*, 150, 215, 248, 252; FDR and, 52, 56, 333, 374; Hitler's relationship with, 55, 364, 589; House of Morgan's relationship with, 252; Italian American support for, 39–40, 42–43, 53, 56, 375; Italian nationalism and, 130; Lateran Accord with Catholic Church, 70; Latin America and, 256; League of Nations condemnation of, 51; in *Life*'s "Speaking of Dictators" photo montage, 267; outreach to Italian Americans, 39–40, 42–43, 53, 56; political prisoners held by, 42*f*; propaganda in support of, 39, 40; on race, 429, 591; rise to power, 269; *Social Justice* profiles of, 85; Spanish Civil War and, 72, 74, 75, 164, 248; totalitarianism of, 179
Mutual aid societies, 27, 162

Nagasaki atomic bombing, 851
The Nation (magazine): BSC propaganda and, 262; contributors to, 12, 168, 169, 183, 227; editorial staff, 274; "An End to Illusions," 208; on fascist publications, 373; Gruening as managing editor, 829; "The Irresponsibles," 214; on League Against Totalitarianism, 179–80; Muñoz Marín writing for, 829; "Our Critics, Right or Wrong" series, 172; on Spanish Civil War, 178; on Stalin's show trials, 168
National Academy of Sciences, 120, 426

National Association for the Advancement of Colored People (NAACP): on all-Black rally, 537; ALWF conference and, 152; Board of Directors, 592; campaigns against racial exclusion, 320, 322; crime conference picket, 590*f*; *Crisis* magazine and, 45, 53, 528, 544, 591, 812, 821; Du Bois and, 813–14; FEPC and, 525, 526; on Harlem crime wave, 529; headquarters of, 777; on housing discrimination, 606; imperialism in conjunction with racism, opposition to, 812; intercultural education and, 130; on internment of Japanese Americans, 369; on Italian conquest of Ethiopia, 45, 51, 53; Jewish contributions to, 589, 590; Legal Defense and Educational Fund, 607; on race mixing in social settings, 544; Willkie and, 784
National Association of Manufacturers (NAM), 187, 718, 768, 770, 771, 774, 797; Post-War Problems Committee, 803
National Association of Real Estate Boards, 718, 719, 721, 775
National Bureau of Economic Research (NBER), 771
National Catholic Youth Organization, 68
National Citizens PAC, 782
National City Bank, 244, 445, 743–44
National Committee of Americans of Polish Descent (KNAPP), 793
National Conference of Christians and Jews (NCCJ), 122–23, 128, 130, 140, 804
National Council of American-Soviet Friendship, 791
National Council of Catholic Men, 68
National Council of Catholic Women, 68, 515
National Council of Jewish Women, 157, 592
National Defense Advisory Commission (NDAC), 297
National Defense Research Committee (NDRC), 426–27, 432, 439

National Electrical Manufacturers Association, 803
National Foreign Trade Council, 803
National Interregional Highway Committee, 722
Nationalism: Black, 44, 45, 48, 50; Caribbean, 59; Chinese, 107; economic, 156; German, 246, 389; Italian, 39, 130; pan-nationalism, 248; Protestant, 207
Nationalist Party of Puerto Rico, 826–27, 829, 831
National Labor Relations Board, 78, 309, 778
National Lawyers Guild (NLG), 97, 300
National Maritime Union (NMU), 109, 392, 407–8, 525–26, 533, 606
National Negro Congress, 518, 525
National Origins Act of 1924, 104, 824
National Peace Conference (NPC), 157
National Planning Board (NPB), 762
National Recovery Act of 1933, 665
National Recovery Administration (NRA), 397, 431
National Resources Planning Board (NRPB), 704, 762–63, 768, 778, 780, 797, 802
National Retail Dry Goods Association, 803
National Rifle Association, 87
National Socialist Transocean Agency, 14
National Student League (NSL), 153–55
National Student Strike Against War, 154
National Union for Social Justice, 330
National United Italian Associations (NUIA), 40
National Urban League, 804
National Wartime Music Committee, 467
National Youth Agency, 777
Native Son (Wright), 538–39
Nativism, 113–19, 124, 129, 133, 787, 824
Nature (journal), 120
Naval Limitation Treaty (1936), 314
Navy. *See* United States Navy
Nazi Germany: Anschluss (1938), 20, 23, 120, 210, 216–17, 266; anti-Semitism in, 3–8, 10–12, 14, 17, 22–25, 237; Blitzkrieg (1940), 35, 59, 201, 204, 206, 210, 234, 236, 249, 260, 271, 273, 426; book burnings in, 670, 671*f*; boycott against, 3–8, 6*f*, 13–14, 16–17, 23, 182, 227; brain drain in, 10–12; commercial relations with US companies, 243–49, 309; espionage networks, 21, 34, 192, 329–30; eugenics practiced in, 118; fascism in, 4, 11, 12, 19, 209–10; genocide against Jews and concentration camps, 14, 22, 197, 210, 300, 390–91, 583–84, 592, 658, 839; Gestapo in, 14, 22, 35, 192, 235, 299, 391, 557; Horst Wessel Song as unofficial anthem of, 17; House of Morgan's relationship with, 252–53; Jewish immigrants from, 9–12, 23–29; Kristallnacht in (1938), 22–24, 27, 31, 33, 131, 266, 591; Latin America and, 255–56, 302, 305–6; military alliance with Japan, 109; Munich Agreement (1938), 20, 207–8, 221, 224, 249, 428; nonaggression pact with Soviet Union, 181–85, 204, 227; Nuremberg Laws (1935), 12; outreach to German Americans, 13–19, 15*f*, 35, 39, 43; pogroms in, 12, 22–23, 266; Poland invasion (1939), 31–32, 56, 59, 98–99, 181, 208; propaganda by, 14, 16, 35, 58, 303; protests against, 3–8, 17, 22–24, 23*f*; sabotage plots, 366–67; Soviet Union invasion (1941), 325, 335, 344, 788; Soviet Union victory over (1943), 791; Spanish Civil War and, 58, 72–74; submarine warfare and, 96, 278, 334–38, 354, 357–59, 363–64, 386–88, 393; Sudetenland annexation (1938), 20, 21; suppression of political opponents in, 82; surrender (May 7, 1945), 850; totalitarianism in, 179, 180, 264, 282; Transfer Agreement with Zionists (1933), 7; underground resistance in, 12; unemployment in, 3, 10; US immigration quota for, 9, 23, 25. *See also* Berlin; Hitler, Adolf
Negroes and the War (Owen), 777
Negro Labor Victory Committee (NLVC), 526
Neutrality Act of 1935, 35, 51, 150–51, 157, 164, 202, 251
Neutrality Act of 1937, 256
Neutrality Act of 1939, 335
"The New Colossus" (Lazarus), 136
New Dance Group, 690
New Deal: criticisms of, 187, 216, 269, 272, 273; Democratic Party and, 203–5, 216, 283, 776; expansion of, 287, 309, 760, 761; Federal Radio Project, 132; housing and, 28–29, 531; immigrant concerns and, 135; labor unions and, 310; postwar planning and, 759–67; social and economic reforms of, 271; Spellman on, 91. *See also* Works Progress Administration; *specific programs and legislation*
New Masses (magazine), 166, 169–73, 193
New Republic (magazine): on America Firsters, 330; antifascism and, 210, 211; BSC propaganda and, 262; "Call to Arms," 210; *A Congress to Win the War and the Peace* (with UDA), 782; on fascist publications, 373; on immigration, 136; MacLeish speeches printed in, 214; on National Resources Planning Board report (1943), 763; on NRPB report, 763; "Other People's Money" column in, 291; on Stalin's show trials, 168; on totalitarianism, 183; on Wall Street, 308
New School for Social Research: Dramatic Workshop, 677, 678; journal of, 179; Lévi-Strauss on faculty, 439–40; Mazzini Society and, 56; Schiff as student, 228; University in Exile, 10–11, 440
Newspaper Guild, 172, 225, 227, 230, 234, 392
Newspapers: antifascist, 41, 227; Catholic, 68, 75, 76, 82, 87, 99, 163; ethnic-based, 13–14, 40, 64, 98, 115; fascist, 40, 55, 373; for Orthodox Jews, 30; suppression during World War II, 373. *See also specific publications*
Newsweek (magazine), 457, 565
New York Age (newspaper), 523, 526, 533, 535, 549, 591
New York American (newspaper), 177, 229
New York Amsterdam News, 348, 524, 532, 536–37, 544, 550, 552, 589–92, 813
"New York at War" parade, 389–92, 390*f*
New York Bar Association, 251, 279, 297
New York Bay Pollution Commission, 738
New York Board of Trade, 687, 746
New York Chinese Anti-Japanese Society, 107
New York City Board of Aldermen, 106, 135, 422
New York City Board of Education, 130, 131
New York City Housing Authority (NYCHA), 715, 716, 718
New York City Opera, 698
New York City Planning Commission. *See* City Planning Commission
New York City Police Department (NYPD): Alien Squad, 21; all-Jewish detail, 22; Black officers, 321; at boxing matches, 47; brutality against Blacks, 543, 544; Bureau of War Operations, 380; on fascist threat in US, 56; Irish Americans and, 80, 87, 116; juvenile delinquency and, 505; O'Dwyer as member of, 345; at protests, 34*f*, 51, 53; race riots and, 544–45; Radical-Alien Squad, 192; Sabotage Squad, 300, 302
New York City Symphony, 699–700
New York Daily Mirror, 48, 223, 225, 230, 282, 347, 349, 789
New York Daily News: on boxing matches, 59; FDR supported by, 223; on Harlem crime wave, 529; on La Guardia's reelection, 345; on Lend Lease program, 290; local news coverage by, 231; on Powell for City Council,

Index of Subjects 951

349; on unionism and communism, 789; Winchell and, 225
New York Department of Docks, 403f, 730, 734
New York Dock Company, 730
New York Dress Institute, 685
New York Edison Company, 89
New York Herald Tribune (newspaper): anti-Semitic want ads in, 586; BSC propaganda and, 262; on corporate headquarters as city's hidden industry, 751–52; on destroyers-for-bases swap, 279; on Dewey's attempt to manipulate Polish American vote, 794; economic journalism of, 770; on La Guardia's reelection, 345; literary section of, 274; *My Day* column in, 131, 223, 268; Paris edition of, 222; on postwar global trade, 729; on Powell for City Council, 349; *On the Record* column in, 269; on totalitarianism, 179; Waldorf-Astoria forum sponsored by, 186; on Westrick's corporate visitors, 243; on Willkie, 275
New York Kehillah, 569
New York Labor Temple, 197
New York Peace Society, 156
New York Port of Embarkation (NYPE), 401–2
New York Post, 21, 225–28, 812
New York Public Library, 156, 169–70, 192, 353, 389, 392, 421, 439–40, 670
New York School of Fine and Applied Art, 682
New York Steam Corporation, 739
New York Stock Exchange (NYSE), 93, 316–17, 354, 445, 744
New York Times: on ACDIF, 184; on all-Black rally, 539; anti-Semitic want ads in, 586; on atomic bomb, 430–31; on *Ballad for Americans*, 140; boxing matches covered by, 48–49; BSC propaganda and, 262; Buck's letter on American racism, 822; on civilian defense, 354; "Defense Contracts in Day," 315; on destroyers-for-bases swap,

279; economic journalism of, 769–70; fashion industry and, 681, 684; on FDR's death, 847, 849; female columnists for, 269; on folk-arts movement, 125; on Harlem crime wave, 529; on Hitler and anti-Semitism, 12, 237; on *If This Be Treason*, 151; on IMF, 742; on La Guardia's reelection, 345; on Lend Lease program, 293; local news coverage by, 231; objectivity of reporting in, 216; on Powell for City Council, 349; on Spellman's preparedness for war, 99; Stimson's opinion pieces on isolationism, 251; Sulzberger family and, 10, 132; on Ukraine famine, 179; on Willkie, 275
New York University (NYU): antiwar protests, 155; intercultural education training courses, 131; KGB agents and, 192; OSRD contracts awarded to, 435; professors, 170, 176, 177, 435; School of Education, 129
New York Volks-Zeitung (newspaper), 14
New York World-Telegram, 35, 223, 227, 296, 345, 349
Nicaragua, 828
Night Music (play), 678
Nippon Club, 103, 352–53
Non-Partisan Committee for Peace, 264
Non-Partisan Labor Defense, 177
Non-Sectarian Anti-Nazi League to Champion Human Rights, 6, 6f, 7, 21, 58, 121
Normandie. See USS *Lafayette*
North American Committee to Aid Spanish Democracy (NAC), 159–60f, 160–65
North German Lloyd shipping line, 21, 22, 191
Nowy Świat (newspaper), 98
Nuns, 69, 70, 72, 87, 92, 93, 266
Nuremberg Laws (1935), 12
NYC Postwar Program exhibition (1944), 703–5, 716
NYPD. *See* New York City Police Department

Office buildings, 752–55
Office of Civilian Defense (OCD), 341, 344, 353, 354, 393, 453

Office of Defense Transportation, 397, 724
Office of Facts and Figures (OFF), 453
Office of Naval Intelligence (ONI), 300, 301, 376
Office of Price Administration (OPA), 517–18, 525, 608, 778
Office of Production Management (OPM), 297, 298, 308, 309
Office of Radio Research (ORR), 221
Office of Scientific Research and Development (OSRD), 432, 435–36
Office of Strategic Services (OSS), 35, 456
Office of the Coordinator of Inter-American Affairs (OCIAA), 305–7, 454, 457
Office of War Information (OWI): budget cuts to, 778; Domestic Branch, 454–56; Overseas Branch, 456; propaganda and, 457; radio surveillance by, 373; war song competition, 467–70; writers available to, 465–66
Oil industry, 809–10
Oklahoma! (musical), 674–76, 689, 695
Olympic Games (Berlin, 1936), 8, 18
One World or None (Federation of American Scientists), 853
One World (Willkie), 671, 784, 801, 811
On the Town (musical), 689, 695
Open skies, 808, 808f
Opera Nazionale Ballila, 40
Orbach's department store, 86
Order Sons of Italy in America, 129
Orthodox Judaism, 4, 26–32, 139, 236, 421, 568, 674
Oxford Pledge, 153–55, 157, 158

Pacifism: communism and, 148, 152, 158; conscientious objectors and, 280, 377–78; Gandhian ashram project and, 325–26; gospel-based, 99, 149, 150, 206–8, 280; isolationism vs., 148, 156; Neutrality Act and, 150, 151; Oxford Pledge and, 153–55, 157, 158; Popular Front and, 152, 213; Protestantism and, 147–50, 157, 164, 165, 206–8; socialism and, 148–50, 152,

158–59, 176, 198; Spanish Civil War and, 157–59; student uprisings in support of, 153–55, 157, 325; theatrical works on, 212; in World War I, 126, 149; in World War II, 197–98, 291, 377–79
Palestine, Jewish population in, 7, 31, 169
Pan-Africanism, 44, 46f, 814
Panama Canal, 405, 527, 731, 828
Pan American Airways, 807
Panay sinking (1937), 109
Pantheon Books, 669
Parisian couture, 680–81
Paris Peace Conference (1919), 248, 523, 834
Park Avenue development, 753–54
Park Avenue Presbyterian Church, 248
Park Central Hotel, 163
Park Slope, 64, 96, 194, 421
Parsons School of Design, 682
Partisan Review (magazine), 170–76, 171f, 180, 196, 379
Patriarchy, 26, 30, 690
Paulist Fathers, 78, 83, 85
Peace movement. *See* Pacifism
Peace Now, 379
Pearl Harbor attack (1941), 352–54, 357, 447–48
Penguin Books, 666, 668
Penn Station, 16, 224, 353, 398, 398f, 723, 854
Pennsylvania Hotel, 109
People's Voice (newspaper), 528, 536, 543, 550, 601, 614, 615, 813
Peter Cooper Village, 716
The Philadelphia Story (play), 681
Physics, 422–29, 440, 485, 660, 747, 769
Pilgrims Society, 257–58, 260
Pioneer Fund, 119
Pipeline construction, 402, 404f
Plan for the Post-War World (Goldberg), 802
Planned Parenthood Federation of America, 804
Planning Jobs and Jobs in Planning (Ehrlich), 802
Plans for a Post-war World (Johnsen), 802
Plaza Hotel, 243, 258, 260, 330, 345
Pluralism: Adamic on, 143; Boasian views of, 118, 119, 127; Catholic Church and, 71; communism and,

Pluralism: (*continued*) 138–39; ethnic neighborhoods and, 115–16; fascism in contrast to, 113, 116, 144, 454, 594; FDR on, 136–37, 139, 203; folk-arts movement and, 124–25; intercultural education and, 126–31, 530; La Guardia on, 144; Melting Pot metaphor vs., 113–14; "New York at War" parade and, 389; Popular Front and, 138–40; in World War II, 142, 389

PM (newspaper): on America Firsters, 330; on anti-Semitic want ads, 586; BSC propaganda and, 262; contributors to, 282; on defense production, 308; history of, 230–34; on housing discrimination, 606; on USS *Lafayette*, 360–62; on La Guardia's reelection, 345; on Powell for City Council, 349

Pocket Books, 667–68

Pogroms, 9, 12, 22–23, 169, 266, 529, 568, 611

Poland: anti-Nazi protests, 5; Jewish ghettoes, 31, 557; Jewish immigrants from, 26, 28, 236; Nazi invasion (1939), 31–32, 56, 59, 98–99, 181, 208; Red Cross, 98; Soviets driving Nazis from, 792. *See also* Warsaw

Police department. *See* New York City Police Department

Polish American Congress, 793, 794

Polish Americans, 98, 284, 792–94

Polish National Alliance, 793

Polish National Council, 98, 565

Polish National Home, 98, 793

Popular Democratic Party (Puerto Rico), 830

Popular Front: *Ballad for Americans* as unofficial anthem of, 140; collapse of, 166, 178, 181, 183, 196; consumer activism and, 232; journalism and, 139, 170, 227, 231; pacifism and, 152, 213; pluralism and, 138–40; Spanish Civil War and, 71, 165, 245

Port Authority of New York, 397, 723–24, 730, 732, 735

Port of New York, 729–31

Post-War Plan and Program (NRPB), 762–63

Postwar planning, 703–5; airplanes and airports, 732–35, 733–34*f*; corporate headquarters, 751–55; employment of returning soldiers, 704–7, 765; housing, 710–19, 717*f*; infrastructure projects, 736–40; manufacturing, 745–50; Port of New York, 729–31; taxation and, 707, 708; transit, 720–26, 726*f*. *See also* Federal postwar planning; Global postwar planning

Postwar Planning in the United States (Twentieth Century Fund), 801

Postwar Reconstruction Fund, 705

Post War World Council, 378, 803

Poverty: of African Americans, 527–29; of Britain, 293; of Jews, 29, 31, 169; mitigation measures, 412

Power supply, 738–40

Prejudice. *See* Discrimination and stereotypes

Presidential elections. *See specific candidates and political parties*

Presidents' Conference Committee (PCC) trolleys, 725

Program to Aid the War Effort That Should Make for Post-war Employment (CIA's Post-war Planning Committee), 803

Progressive Education Association, 127, 131, 803

Prohibition, 299, 512

Propaganda: anti-Hun, 4–5; anti-Semitic, 121, 184; fascist, 39, 40, 56, 163; kitsch and, 175; in Latin America, 306–7, 457; by Nazi Germany, 14, 16, 35, 58, 303; in public schools, 39, 82; racist, 120, 184; in Spanish Civil War, 163–64; for women, 506; in World War I, 4–5, 260; in World War II, 35, 85, 97, 261–62, 265, 300, 303, 327–28, 466

Proposed Post-war Works Program (City Planning Commission), 803

Prospect Hall, 20

Prostitution, 544

Protestantism: ecumenical, 207; human rights and, 838–39; immigration policy and, 24; liberal, 122, 147, 149, 206, 237, 248; NCCJ and, 122–23; pacifism and, 147–50, 157, 164, 165, 206–8; Spanish Civil War and, 76. *See also* Christians and Christianity; Federal Council of Churches; *specific denominations*

Protests and demonstrations: antifascist, 42*f*, 154, 154*f*, 169*f*; anti-Nazi, 3–8, 17, 22–24, 23*f*; antiwar, 154–55, 157; boxing matches and, 58; civil disobedience, 5, 151, 377–79, 538, 552, 818; discrimination and, 319–22; German American Bund rally, 33, 34*f*; immigration laws and, 10; internment of Japanese Americans and, 369; Italian conquest of Ethiopia and, 45*f*, 50–51, 53; mass transit construction/demolition and, 726; Negro Freedom Rally, 603; nonviolent, 149, 197; Spanish Civil War and, 73, 74, 164; of US war material exports to Japan, 109; Zoot suit as form of, 541. *See also* Boycotts

Provisional Committee for the Defense of Ethiopia (PCDE), 45, 50

Public housing: City Planning Commission and, 704; in ethnic neighborhoods, 115, 130; Moses and, 607, 716; New Deal and, 531; postwar, 715–19, 717*f*

Public schools: British, 257; Catholic criticisms of, 81–82; communist threats to, 186, 188; in ethnic neighborhoods, 115; intercultural education in, 128–31, 530; Jewish attendees, 29, 30, 170; propaganda in, 39, 82; secularism of, 29, 69, 71, 81–82

Publishing industry, 664–72; Armed Services Editions of books for soldiers, 671–72; cartography and maps as big sellers during war, 670; dime novels, 665; German and French refugees as publishers, 669; lending libraries and, 665; mass-production and mass-market sales, 666–68, 670; paperbacks, 665–68; paper shortage and, 670; Publishers Row, 664; reprints, 664–65, 666; turnaround in 1940s, 664; war-related topics producing high sales, 670–71

Puerto Rico and Puerto Ricans, 825–33; 1944 presidential election and, 796; Development Bank, 831; El Congreso Pro-Independencia de Puerto Rico, 831; FDR policies, 827–28; free trade system and, 832; land reform and economic diversification, 830; Marcantonio as de facto representative, 826–27; Muñoz Marín's positions on autonomy and economy, 828–31; nationalist mobilization, 825–26; rum sales to US, 831; self-elected governor, 832–33; strategic importance of island in WWII, 827–28; US citizenship, 825; WWII severing maritime link with US, 830

Pujo Committee, 5, 270

Pulaski Day celebrations, 98, 794

Pupin cyclotron, 429, 430*f*

Quakers, 126, 149, 198, 325, 377, 379

Quantum mechanics, 422, 423

Queens: Catholic Church in, 67, 82; Christian Front in, 86; dim-outs of streetlamps, 381; German American Bund in, 18; housing development, 711, 717; Irish Americans in, 65; Latinos/Latinas in, 162; manufacturing industry, 412–13; raiding parties, 372. *See also specific neighborhoods and locations*

Queens Bridge Housing Development, 283

Queens College, 30

Rabbi Isaac Elchanan Theological Seminary (RIETS), 30

Race and ethnicity: Boasian views of, 117–18, 370; employment and, 116, 319; folk-arts movement and, 124–25; Great Depression and, 18; interrracial marriages, 55, 119; music associated with, 469; myth of white invincibility, 523; neighborhoods based on, 115–16, 717; newspapers based on, 13–14, 40, 64, 98, 115. *See also* Immigrants and immigration; Pluralism; Racism; *specific racial and ethnic groups*

Race riots, 45, 531, 544–45, 550, 552, 590, 592, 608, 611, 820

Racism: anti-Asian, 369–72, 820; in education, 527; in employment, 45, 319; eugenics and, 114, 118–19, 141, 197, 332; in immigration laws, 104, 105; imperialism and, 811, 812–15; Ku Klux Klan and, 5, 70, 75, 544; master-race ideology, 113, 114, 116, 144, 469; media coverage of, 232; postwar world and, 811; propaganda in promotion of, 120, 184; scientific, 116, 117, 120, 122, 591; structural forms of, 144; UN Charter and, 815; US soldiers and, 812; xenophobia, 113, 135, 143, 236, 708. *See also* Segregation; White supremacy

Radar, 359, 386, 393, 417, 425–27, 433, 436–37, 747

Radio: "Americans All, Immigrants All" series, 132–34, 133*f*, 138, 143, 144; antifascist series, 120; anti-Nazi rally broadcast, 5; broadcast journalism and, 215–17, 221–22, 269, 281–82; Coughlin broadcasts, 85, 164; drama series, 213–14, 218–22; FDR's fireside chats, 35, 58, 202–3, 234, 286, 297, 670; Federal Radio Project, 132; Nazi programming, 14, 175; Office of Radio Research, 221; "Speaking of Liberty" series, 328; Spellman's investiture as Archbishop, 88; surveillance during World War II, 373–74; *This Is War!* series, 454; Voice of America, 456; War Emergency Radio Service, 385

Radio City Music Hall, 35, 275, 412

Radio Corporation of America (RCA), 216, 245, 392, 405, 427, 436, 748*f*, 749–50

Railroad industry, 16, 366, 397–99, 401, 414, 724, 725*f*

A Raising Wind (White), 812

Randall's Island, 8, 35, 158

Random House, 21, 670

Rand School of Social Science, 690

Real Estate Board of New York (REBNY), 518–20, 608, 707, 728, 745

Real estate development: corporate headquarters, impact of, 752–55. *See also* Housing

Rebel Arts Group, 233*f*

"Rebuilding American Cities after the War" (Hoyt), 711

Reconstruction Finance Corporation (RFC), 309, 316

Reconstructionist Judaism, 128

Recreational camps, 16–17, 20, 280

Red-baiting, 177, 234, 347

Red Cross, 51, 98, 249, 340, 385, 392, 533, 686

Red Hook, 75, 162, 329, 487*f*

Red Line Agreement (1928), 809

Redlining, 528, 608

Red Scare, 83, 185, 187, 300, 787–90

Reform Judaism, 4, 28, 29, 559, 574

Refugees: academic, 10–11, 25, 26; assimilationism and, 11, 27; demographic profile of, 25–27; dispersal throughout Europe, 3, 9; Emergency Rescue Committee for, 235–39, 269; employment of, 26, 27, 31–32, 215; housing for, 26–28, 31; Jewish, 3, 9–11, 23–33, 66, 119, 269, 300, 431, 577, 590, 602; "New York at War" parade and, 390; opposition to, 23, 24, 33, 119; settlement in US, 25–32, 66; from Spanish Civil War, 165; visas for, 236–37, 557, 836

Regional Plan Association (RPA), 712–13, 722, 723, 745–46, 750, 803

Reich Concordat (1933), 70, 75

Religion: discrimination based on, 120, 232; freedom of, 70, 123, 208, 287, 599; inter-religious harmony promotion, 122–23. *See also specific religions and denominations*

Rent control, 517–20, 608, 752, 754, 775

Republican Party: 1940 National Convention, 140, 272, 276–77; 1942 congressional elections, 776; 1944 presidential election, 785–87; fundraisers held by, 162, 274; Irish Americans and, 65, 77; mayoral candidates from, 84; National Finance Committee, 274; New Deal criticized by, 187, 272, 273; progressives within, 150, 275

Republic Aviation, 414, 435

Resources and Purchasing Power of the New York Region (RAP 1945 report), 747

Restrictive covenants, 608

Revenue Act of 1942, 446

Revuers, 693, 694

Ridgewood, 18, 20, 26, 284, 329

Ritz-Carlton Hotel, 163, 164, 329

Riverside Church, 123, 147, 149

The Road Ahead to Victory and Lasting Peace (Browder), 804

The Road to Rome (Sherwood), 212

The Road to Serfdom (Hayek), 771–72

The Road to Victory (Spellman), 804

Rockefeller Center: British Empire Building, 303; BSC headquarters, 261, 302–3; FFC headquarters, 327; International Building, 261; Italian consulate, 56; occupancy rates, 711, 752; OSS headquarters, 456; relocation of businesses to, 245, 266

Rockefeller Foundation: International Division, 305; Lévi-Strauss assisted by, 439; Mises assisted by, 771; Office of Radio Research and, 221; physicists assisted by, 423; on postwar planning, 804; University in Exile and, 11, 440; War and Peace Studies Project funded by, 263

Rodeo (ballet), 675

Roland German-American Democratic Society, 35

Roosevelt, Eleanor: 1940 presidential campaign, 204; Marian Anderson concert and, 322, 323*f*; China Emergency Relief Committee and, 823; civilian defense and, 341, 482; as civil rights advocate, 320, 322–24, 497, 610, 777, 814, 822; as Commission on Human Rights chairperson, 843; emergency visas for European refugees, advocating for, 236–37, 557, 836; FDR's death and, 847–48; Hoover's dislike of, 822; as human rights advocate, 811–12; intercultural education and, 131; Lanham Act and, 501; *My Day* column, 131, 223, 268; Neutrality Act passage and, 157; NYC apartment of, 131, 795; Puerto Rico and, 829; rationing and, 514; Spanish Civil War and, 76, 164–65; UN headquarters location and, 858; Welles and, 835–36

Roosevelt, Franklin D. (FDR): 1932 presidential election, 65, 135, 204, 226, 275, 291, 297, 759; 1936 presidential election, 52–54, 91, 135, 204, 223, 228, 275, 297; 1940 presidential election, 98, 203–4, 223, 272–73, 275, 283–85, 291, 399; 1944 presidential election, 411, 705, 761, 783–86, 795–96; Alien Enemy Act invoked by, 368; on Anglo-American relations, 258, 261; Atlantic Charter (1941), 392; Black engagement with, 320–21, 323–24, 347, 525–26, 536, 537, 543; Boas tribute by, 120; boxing supported by, 58; Bretton Woods institutions and, 741; on Brotherhood Day, 123; CDAAA and, 264–65; China as WWII ally and, 821; Churchill and, 278, 286, 293, 297, 386, 400, 836; communist views of, 181, 182, 184; Bull Connor's letter to, 777; on Coughlin, 85, 90, 96; Council on Foreign Relations and, 255, 256; criticisms of, 330, 331, 372; death and funeral of (1945), 847–48; denunciation of Nazi excesses by, 249; destroyers-for-bases deal with Britain, 278–79; disenfranchisement of

Roosevelt, Franklin D. (FDR): *(continued)* base, 776; Economic Bill of Rights, 705, 779–80; ethnic constituencies for, 135, 375; on European empires' dismantling, 810; Export Control Act and, 109; FBI and, 300–302, 373, 536; on Fifth Columnists, 35, 141, 203, 236, 284, 299; fireside chats, 35, 58, 202–3, 234, 286, 297, 670; *Fleet Problem XX* and, 827–28; Four Freedoms speech (1941), 287–89, 378, 379, 838, 839; German American Bund on, 33; on House of Morgan, 253; on human rights, 838, 842; Hyde Park residence of, 90, 91, 204, 228, 258; immigration policy, 23, 24; on internment of Japanese Americans, 369; on Italian conquest of Ethiopia, 51–52; Jewish community and, 32, 121, 284; on USS *Lafayette* fire, 362; La Guardia and, 18, 205, 343–44, 349, 354, 411; on Latin America, 304, 305, 307; as League of Nations proponent, 835; Lend Lease program, 286–93, 297, 313, 334–35, 386; Manhattan Project and, 431, 432; map of the world sales from fireside chats, 670; media coverage of, 222–27, 230, 231, 267, 332, 454; Robert Moses and, 400, 704; Mussolini and, 52, 56, 333, 374; on Nazi anti-Semitism and genocide, 5, 22, 842; on Nazi sabotage plots, 367; on Nazi–Soviet nonaggression pact, 181; NDRC created by, 426; OCD created by, 341; on overseas intelligence units, 456; Pearl Harbor attack and, 353; on pluralism, 136–37, 139, 203; postwar planning by, 759–63, 778; private sector initiatives, 409; propaganda campaigns, 303; Puerto Rico's status and, 827–28; radio readings of speeches by, 457; on railroad industry, 397; replacing Wallace as VP, 783; seamen honored by, 408; Soviet Union recognized by, 191; Spanish Civil War and, 76, 164, 165, 202, 251; speech writing team for, 212–14; Spellman and, 90, 91, 94, 97, 99; Stalin and, 297, 792; on Stimson as secretary of war, 276, 344; on submarine warfare, 335, 359; at Tehran Summit (1943), 792; Dorothy Thompson and, 269, 282; Unlimited National Emergency proclaimed by, 340; on US export of war materials to Japan, 150; war bonds and, 446, 447, 449; war preparation and rearmament, 198, 201–6, 208, 253, 270–71, 288*f*, 294–98, 308–10, 314–16, 387, 402, 453; at Yalta Conference (1945), 847, 850. *See also* New Deal

Roosevelt Park, 136, 283

Rowohlt (German publisher), 669

Rudin Management Company, 752

Rural Electrification Administration, 777

Russia. *See* Soviet Union

Russian Revolution (1917), 85, 166, 177, 836

Russo-Japanese War (1904–1905), 523

Saks Fifth Avenue, 6, 649, 681, 684

Salvage ethnology, 438

Same-sex relationships. *See* Homosexuality

San Francisco: anti-Nazi protests in, 5; defense spending in, 315; World Trade Center in, 729, 730

San Francisco Conference on the United Nations, 813, 814, 832, 840–43

San Juan Hill, 104, 639

Saturday Evening Post, 672, 710

Satyagraha (nonviolent resistance), 537–39, 552

Savoy Ballroom, 541, 544, 638, 640, 692*f*

School. *See* Education; *specific institutions*

Schwaben Hall, 18, 86

Scientific racism, 116, 117, 120, 122, 591

Scientists' Manifesto (1938), 120

Seafarers International Union (SIU), 392, 407, 408, 525

Second Avenue Subway, 727–28

Second World War. *See* World War II

Securities Exchange Act of 1934, 291

Security, Work and Relief Policies (Burns), 762

See Here, Private Hargrove (Pocket Book edition), 670

Segregation: of blood plasma for transfusions, 533; in boxing, 48; in employment, 320, 527, 777; escalation of, 543–44; in housing, 528, 531–32, 605–8, 717; media coverage of, 232; of military, 319–21, 325, 379, 533–35; redlining and, 528, 608; in restaurants, 144; Stuyvesant Town, 532, 605–7, 713, 716–17. *See also* Jim Crow

Selective Service Act of 1940, 279–80, 319, 372, 377, 505

Seminary of the Immaculate Conception, 67

Service Bureau for Intercultural Education, 130–32, 142

Servicemen's Readjustment Act of 1944. *See* GI Bill

Settlement houses, 115, 124, 128, 228, 434, 654, 674

Seversky Aircraft Corporation, 21, 414

Sewage disposal, 738

Seward Park High School, 30, 434

Sex and sexuality: birth control, 76, 80–81, 210, 665; homosexuality, 119, 325, 378, 490, 624–25, 678, 691–93, 840; prostitution, 544; silk boycott and, 108–9; Victory Girls and, 504

Sexism, 119, 502–3

Sexually transmitted diseases. *See* Venereal disease

Shipbuilding industry, 21, 310, 314–16, 319, 402, 415–16

Shomrin Society, 22

Show Boat (musical), 675

Sikorsky Helicopter Company, 732

Simon and Schuster, 666–68

Sing Sing Prison, 34, 347, 363

The Six Pillars of Peace (John Foster Dulles), 837–38

Sixth Avenue Association, 754

Skidmore, Owings & Merrill, 703

Smaller War Plants Corporation (SWPC), 411

Smith, Alfred E., 716, 787; in 1941 supporting idea of America entering the war, 333; anti-communist stance, 84; as Brotherhood Day sponsor, 123; as Committee for Economic Development local chair, 706; on Committee of Catholics to Fight Anti-Semitism, 87; death of (1944), 706; "Democrats for Willkie" endorsed by, 274; as "I-Am-An-American Day" rally sponsor, 328; on Irish share of political jobs, 65; at Madison Square Garden rally against Hitler, 17; on Nazi persecution of Jews, 5; Protestants in opposition to, 122; Spellman and, 93; at Stork Club, 629

Smith Act. *See* Alien Registration Act of 1940

Smith Connally Act of 1943, 778, 779

Social Creed of the Churches (1908), 153

Social Darwinism, 117–18

Social Democrats, 10, 168, 207, 235, 434, 789

The Social Frontier (journal), 127

Social Gospel movements, 149, 150, 153, 160, 206–8, 210, 280

Socialism: democratic, 379, 459; Italian Americans and, 282; Jews and, 4, 7, 12, 138, 282–83; Kuomintang and, 106; National Socialist Transocean Agency, 14; pacifism and, 148–50, 152, 158–59, 176, 198; Red Scare and, 83; Spanish Civil War and, 158–59; World War II and, 291

Socialism (Mises), 771

Social Justice (magazine), 85, 373

Social Security, 269, 497, 759, 762, 769–70, 777, 781, 797

Society for the Prevention of World War III, 466

Society of Friends. *See* Quakers

Soldier Voting Act of 1942, 776, 777

Sons of Italy, 40

Southern Democrats and lawmakers, 776–77, 824

Soviet Union: Chinese alliance with, 106; communism in, 69, 166–68, 180, 183; espionage networks, 186, 187, 191–95, 262, 300, 434–35; FDR's recognition

of, 191; GRU and, 192–95, 434; Jewish immigrants from, 26, 28, 30, 236; KGB and, 178, 192–95, 434–35; Lend Lease program and, 335, 386; Nazi invasion of (1941), 325, 335, 344, 788; nonaggression pact with Nazi Germany, 181–85, 204, 227; pogroms in, 9, 568; Spanish Civil War and, 72, 178; totalitarianism in, 179, 180, 184. *See also* Bolsheviks; Stalin, Joseph; World War II
Spain: Jews expelled from, 11; Latin American colonies, 825; totalitarianism in, 180; Treaty of Tordesillas (1493), 244
Spanish Civil War (1936–1939): casualties, 74; Catholic Church and, 71–72, 74–76, 163–65; fascism and, 20, 71–73, 75, 165, 178; FDR on, 76, 164, 165, 202, 251; fundraising efforts for, 160–62; Guernica bombing, 58, 74, 75, 163, 164; Hitler and, 72–75, 164; International Brigades and, 72–74; Latinos/Latinas on, 162–63; media coverage of, 213, 216; Mussolini and, 72, 74, 75, 164, 248; pacifist movement and, 157–59; Popular Front and, 71, 165, 245; propaganda, 163–64; protests, 73, 74, 164; refugees from, 165
Spanish-Cuban-American War, 825
The Spanish Earth (film), 159, 165, 178, 213
"Speaking of Liberty" radio series, 328
Speech, freedom of, 33, 154, 188, 210, 287, 330, 373, 838
Sperry Gyroscope, 315, 319, 414, 435–36, 486, 500, 525, 686, 857
Spies. *See* Espionage
Sports: baseball, 66, 374–75, 450; boxing, 47–49, 57–59, 59f, 66, 68; equipment manufacturers, 231; football, 352, 450; golf, 57, 482, 734, 744; Olympic Games (Berlin, 1936), 8, 18; tennis, 89, 295
St. Catherine of Alexandria School, 82

St. George Hotel, 68
St. George's Episcopal Church, 208
St. John's University, 81, 96, 224, 225
St. Joseph's Seminary, 67
St. Lawrence Seaway, 730, 739–40
St. Nicholas Arena, 157
St. Patrick's Cathedral, 88, 97, 98
St. Paul's Church, 85
St. Stephen's Church, 75
St. Vincent's Hospital, 93, 375
Staats-Zeitung (newspaper), 13–14, 20–21, 27, 35, 374
Stage Door Canteen, 469–70, 628, 630
Stalin, Joseph: antifascism of, 168; anti-Stalinists, 169–70, 172, 178, 180, 194, 205; cartoon depictions, 232; Catholic views of, 81; FDR and, 297, 792; kitsch deployed by, 175; in *Life*'s "Speaking of Dictators" photo montage, 267; nonaggression pact with Hitler, 181, 204; show trials and purges by, 166–68, 177, 414, 434; at Tehran Summit (1943), 792; threat posed by, 185, 194; toast to automobile industry, 402; totalitarianism of, 179, 186; Harry Ward on, 153; at Yalta Conference (1945), 847, 850
Standard Aircraft Products, 437
Standard Oil, 244–46, 251, 257, 296, 304, 369, 809
State Department, US: Bureau of Intelligence, 300; diplomatic immunity granted by, 32; Ethiopia supporters' lobbying of, 45; on FBI collaboration with British intelligence, 261; on Hitler as bulwark against communism, 7; on immigration, 10, 23, 236–38; on moral embargo against Japan, 109; on Nazi anti-Semitism, 5; pro-UN campaign of, 841; United Nations charter and, 813; Yeshiva College recognized by, 31
Staten Island: Catholic Church in, 67; dim-outs of streetlamps in, 381; German American Bund in, 16; highways and bridges, 721; manufacturing industry

on, 412; shipbuilding industry in, 314; St. George ferry and, 283. *See also specific neighborhoods and locations*
Statue of Liberty, 135–37, 357, 382
Steinway & Sons, 413
Stereotypes. *See* Discrimination and stereotypes
Steuben Society of America, 13–14, 16, 18, 35–36, 284, 292
Stimson, Henry: background of, 250–51; British-US relations and, 257; CDAAA meetings and, 265; on civil rights and Black troops, 320–21, 323, 324, 535–36, 543; conscription law and, 279; Council on Foreign Relations and, 254; Italian and German aliens in US and, 372; Japanese American internment and, 369; on League of Nation's failure, 835; Loomis and, 424–25; McCloy and, 295; oil tankers sinking and, 387; on public support for US intervention in war, 453; radar and, 427; as secretary of war, 276, 279, 344; Spanish Civil War and, 163; War Department and, 294–97; war production and, 308–10, 409, 461; on Zionists and Jewish Army, 577
Stimson Doctrine (1932), 251
Stork Club, 159, 223–25, 301, 301f, 628–30, 650
Strand Theatre, 34, 100
Straw Hat Revue, 690
Strike for Peace (1935), 154–55
Structural anthropology, 441
Student Congress Against War, 153
Student League for Industrial Democracy (SLID), 153–55
Studio Theatre, 677, 678
Stuyvesant Town, 532, 605–7, 713, 716–17
Submarine warfare, 96, 278, 334–38, 354, 357–59, 363–64, 386–88, 393
Suburban development, 710–11
Subway, 726–28
Sudetenland, Nazi annexation of (1938), 20, 21
Suez Canal, 53
Sugar industry, 825, 830, 831

Sweatshops, 421, 591
Sylvania Electric Products, 748
Syphilis, 435, 504, 622, 795

Taft Hotel, 192
Tammany Hall, 42, 65–66, 80, 135, 274, 283, 343–45, 348
Tariffs, 806
Tauchnitz (German publisher), 666, 669
Taxation, 316, 518, 608, 707, 708, 745, 746; postwar federal tax cuts and federal spending, 766–67; Victory Tax, 446
Teachers Guild, 177, 185
Teachers Union (TU), 177, 185, 189
Tehran Summit (1943), 792
Television, 132, 284, 380, 416–17, 748–50, 748f, 850
Temporary Commission Against Discrimination (TCAD), 610
Temporary Committee on Discrimination in Employment, 322–23
Temporary National Economic Committee (TNEC), 270, 309
Temporary State Commission for Post-war Public Works Planning, 803
Tenant Leagues, 718
Tenements: Chinese Americans in, 105; clearance of blighted areas, 711–19; Italian Americans in, 128; Orthodox Jews in, 28, 29, 31; rent control, 517
Tennessee Valley Authority (TVA), 273
Tennis, 89, 295
Texaco (Texas Company), 243, 245, 809
Theater. *See* Broadway
Theatre Arts Committee, 139
Theatre Guild, 674–75
Theresa Hotel, 322, 537, 543
These United States (Gruening, ed.), 830
"They Burned the Books" (Benét), 670
Think tanks, 802
Third International Congress of Eugenics (1932), 118
Third Reich. *See* Nazi Germany
This Is the Army (Berlin), 673
This Is War! radio series, 454
This Property Is Condemned (Williams), 678

Time (magazine): on destroyers-for-bases swap, 279; Hitler named Man of the Year by, 229–30; on La Guardia, 18; in Latin America, 306; on Muste, 197; on Spanish Civil War, 213, 266; staff writers for, 194; Streit on cover of, 258; on Willkie, 275
Times Square, 382*f;* billboards in, 131; celebrations at end of war in Europe and in Pacific, 850, 851; Christian Front in, 86; Claridge Hotel in, 384, 384*f;* dim-outs and rapid reaction shutdowns in, 381–84, 383*f;* fundraising efforts in, 160; German espionage network in, 330; Smith Act registration site, 36; Stage Door Canteen in, 469–70, 628, 630; Strand Theatre in, 34, 100; Taft Hotel in, 192
Tin Pan Alley (TPA), 174, 467–68, 470, 493, 646, 694
Tishman Realty and Construction Company, 752
Tobé-Coburn School, 685
Todd Shipyards Corporation, 310, 314, 316, 335
Torah Vodaath Yeshiva and Mesivta, 30–32
Tordesillas, Treaty of (1493), 244
Totalitarianism: Alien Registration Act and, 187; Catholic Church and, 187, 210; democracy in contrast to, 179; in Italy, 180, 264; in Japan, 180; League Against Totalitarianism, 178–80; in Nazi Germany, 179, 180, 264, 282; Selective Service Act and, 280; in Soviet Union, 179, 180, 184; in Spain, 180; in United States, 186, 187, 196–97, 272
Townley Frocks, 684
Trade Union Relief for Spain, 161
Trade unions. *See* Labor unions
Trans-Arabian Pipeline, 809
Transfer Agreement (1933), 7
Transit Workers Union (TWU), 78, 78–79*f,* 161, 184, 347–48
Treaties. *See specific names of treaties*
A Tree Grows in Brooklyn (film), 64*f*

Triboro Palace, 86
Triborough Bridge, 258, 399, 705
Truck terminal, construction of, 724
Two-Faced Woman (film), 94

U-boats. *See* Submarine warfare
Ukraine, 169, 179
Unemployment: anti-Semitism and, 23; Great Depression and, 86, 106, 169, 174, 203; Japanese Americans and, 372; in Nazi Germany, 3, 10; as political issue, 411; postwar concerns regarding, 704, 781; rationing and growth in, 410
Union for Democratic Action (UDA), 328, 332, 341, 782, 783
Union News newsstands, 668
Union of Israel (Agudath Israel), 29–32, 559, 564
Union of Orthodox Rabbis, 31
Union Pacific, 294, 295
Union Parts Manufacturing Company, 392
Unions. *See* Labor unions
Union Theological Seminary (UTS), 22, 153, 157, 179, 206–7, 280, 292, 325
United Aid for Ethiopia, 51
United Anti-Fascist Committee, 41, 42*f*
United Auto Workers, 781
United Electrical, Radio, and Machine Workers of America (UE), 392, 525, 526
United German Societies, 13, 14, 18
United Hebrew Trades, 7
United Kingdom. *See* Britain
United Libertarian Organizations, 178
United Nations, 813, 837–43; Charter, 814–15, 843; Commission on Human Rights, 843; early name of United Nations Association (UNA), 837; Economic and Social Council, 843; location of headquarters, 855–62; Preparatory Commission, 855; trusteeship system, 813–15
United Service Organizations (USO), 673
United States Army: African Americans in, 319–20,

533–36; Air Corps, 245, 295, 336–37, 359, 391; Air Transport Command, 400; Armed Services Editions of books for soldiers, 671–72; book drive to provide reading material to soldiers, 671–72; Coast Artillery Corps, 337; Corps of Engineers, 432–33; Military Intelligence Division, 300–302; "New York at War" parade and, 391; Northeast Defense Command, 336; Quartermaster Corps presenting war reenactments in Central Park, 674; Quartermaster's Department, 317; Regular Army, 279
United States Coast Guard: Air Station, 336; USS *Lafayette* and, 360, 361*f;* Pearl Harbor attack and, 353; ships detained by, 164; submarine warfare and, 337, 338; training station for, 407
United States Marine Corps, 166f, 320, 483, 535, 672, 851; Women's Marine Corps, 686
United States Maritime Commission (USMC), 402, 405, 407, 415
United States Maritime Service, 337, 407, 485
United States Naval Clothing Depot, 315
United States Navy: African Americans in, 320; cancellation of Corsair fighter planes order (1944), 781; coastal defense operations, 336; *Fleet Problem XX* (war games), 827–28; industrial suppliers and, 746–47; "New York at War" parade and, 391; Office of Naval Intelligence, 300, 301, 376; submarine warfare and, 321, 337–38, 359, 386–88, 393; Waves uniforms, 686
Universal Negro Improvement Association, 44
Universities. *See* Education; *specific institutions*
University in Exile, 10–11, 440
Upper East Side, 275, 296, 441, 841
Upper West Side, 26, 31, 32, 171, 693, 796
Urban Land Institute (ULI), 711

Urban League, 319–20, 322, 526, 529, 537, 552, 608, 821

Vaad Hatzalah, 31, 558–59, 564, 580
Variety (magazine), 454, 468, 469
Vatican, 45, 69–70, 74, 89–91, 93. *See also* Catholics and Catholic Church
Venereal disease (VD), 341, 504, 544, 622–23
Veterans. *See* Postwar planning
Veterans of Foreign Wars, 392, 824
Victory Girls, 504, 623, 634, 694
Victory Tax, 446
Vladeck Houses, 716
Vogue magazine, 682, 683, 684
Voice of America, 456
Volunteer Christian Committee to Boycott Nazi Germany, 23
Voting rights, 776–77

W. W. Norton (publisher), 672
Wagner, Robert F.: Bretton Woods agreements and, 742; Emergency Price Control Act of 1942 and, 510–11; FDR campaigning for reelection of (1944), 795; FDR's rearmament drive supported by, 204; Full Employment bill introduced by (1945), 797; immigration quota, attempt to raise, 24; Jewish immigrants from Nazi Germany and, 32; Laughlin's ban on nonwhite immigration and, 141; on Nazi persecution of Jews, 5; Polish American vote and, 794; public housing and, 718–19; racial discrimination in military opposed by, 319; rent control and, 519; slum clearance and, 715; Smaller War Plants Corporation proposal by, 411; Spanish Civil War and, 163; at Spellman's arrival in city, 88; Wagner-Murray-Dingell bill on welfare programs, 780, 797
Waldorf-Astoria Hotel, 68, 100, 243, 262, 282, 290, 437, 544

Index of Subjects   957

Wallabout Market, 28, 314, 737f
Wall Street: concentration of power on, 270; Coughlin's attacks against, 85; Great Depression and, 64, 291, 296, 299, 317; interventionism and, 198, 239, 263–67, 282, 286, 290–91; postwar order, 741–44; war preparation and rearmament, 294–98, 308–10, 316
Wall Street Journal, 227, 308–9, 768
War and Peace Studies Project, 263–64, 836, 837
War bonds, 375, 378, 449–51, 459–66, 481, 621, 628, 808f
War contracts, 745, 747
War Department, 270, 294–97, 321, 354, 368, 543, 623; Bureau of Insular Affairs, 826, 829; Bureau of Public Relations, 533
War Emergency Radio Service, 385
War Industries Board (WIB), 270, 294
War Labor Board, 777
Warner Brothers, 34, 90, 99, 646, 774
War Production Board (WPB): Brooklyn-Battery Tunnel and, 399; Controlled Materials Plan, 409–11; El as scrap metal for, 727; fashion industry and, 686; paper shortage and, 670; Pearl Harbor attack and, 448; pipeline construction and, 402; rationing of materials, 398, 413, 541; Textile Division, 686
War Resisters League (WRL), 158, 197, 198, 377
War Resources Board (WRB), 270–71, 297
Warsaw: anti-Nazi boycott, 5; Jewish ghetto, 557; Nazi invasion (1939), 32
War's End and After: An Informal Discussion of the Problems of a Post-war World (Chevalier), 802
War Shipping Administration (WSA), 402–8, 486, 729
War songs, 467–70
Washington, DC: anti-Nazi protests in, 5; population growth in, 298; World Bank and IMF located in, 743
Washington Heights: anti-Semitism in, 586; Christian Front in, 86;

Irish Americans in, 64, 86; Jewish population in, 27, 31, 66, 86; juvenile delinquency in, 504–5; Latinos/Latinas in, 162
Washington Market, 736–38
Water supply, 736
Webb & Knapp, 753–54
Welfare Department, 80, 320, 385, 411
Welfare initiatives, 762–63
Welfare Island penitentiary, 65
West Side Association of Commerce, 730
West Side Highway, 720
What's That Plane? (Penguin's first American book), 669
Wheeler-Lea Act in 1938, 447
When the War Ends series (Chase), 804
White supremacy, 59, 525, 591, 643, 719, 783, 812, 816, 822, 843
Williamsburg: Great Depression and, 28; housing in, 28–29, 31; Jewish population in, 28–32, 176, 236; raiding parties in, 329
Williamsburg Bridge, 28, 716, 723
Willkie, Wendell: 1940 presidential campaign and loss to FDR, 281–84; 1940 presidential nominee of Republican Party, 273–77; 1944 hopeful for presidential nomination, 784–85, 796; China Emergency Relief Committee and, 823; civil rights and, 321; death of (1944), 784; destroyers-for-bases deal and, 278–79, 286; Jewish vote and, 582, 583; La Guardia and, 328, 344; Loomis and, 424; *One World*, 671, 784, 801, 811; on racism and imperialism, 810–12; Rand and, 773; Selective Service Act and, 279–80
Windsor Palace Ballroom, 97
Winged Victory (Hart), 673
Winning the War and the Peace: A Program of Legislative Action (CIA), 768–69
WNBT TV broadcasting, 748
Woman's Christian Temperance Union (WCTU), 157
Women: AJC division for, 17; birth control for, 76,

80–81, 210, 665; in civilian defense, 340–42; Committee on the Participation of Women in Post War Planning, 838; employment of, 26, 63, 65, 504–6; The Fashion Group, Inc. and, 680; in German American Bund, 16; homosexuality among, 119; in Italian conquest of Ethiopia, 51; in journalism, 268–69; motherhood and, 494, 504–6; in New York City Symphony, 699; as nuns, 69, 70, 72, 87, 92, 93, 266; propaganda aimed at, 506; sexism and, 119, 502–3; Victory Girls, 504, 623, 634, 694. *See also* Gender; Sex and sexuality
Women's International League for Peace and Freedom (WILPF), 126, 157, 198, 838
Women's Trade Union League (WTUL), 228, 518
Women's Voluntary Services for Civil Defense (WVS), 340, 341
Woodbury High School, 126
Woodrow Wilson Foundation (WWF), 835, 836
Woodrow Wilson House, 841
Woolworth's department store, 7, 667–68
Worker-literature movement, 169–72
Workers. *See* Employment; Labor unions
Workers Laboratory Theatre, 139
Workmen's Circle, 7, 138, 698
Works Progress Administration (WPA): "Americans All, Immigrants All" and, 132; Circus, 674; Community Service Projects, 341; cultural offerings underwritten by, 697; employment through, 317, 320, 325, 527; Federal Arts Project, 170, 365f, 403f; Federal Theater Project, 139, 276, 455f, 538–39, 539f; Federal Writers Project, 269; harbor fort refurbishment by, 337; intercultural education and, 130; Living Newspaper, 390; municipal art gallery and, 697; termination of, 777
World Bank, 741–42

World Congress Against War, 152
World Council of Churches, 207
The World Fashion Center, New York City's Post War Business Project No. 1, 803
World Jewish Congress, 156
World Peace Foundation, 156
World's Fair (1939), 17–18, 98, 131, 142, 258, 329, 357, 703
World Trade Center Corporation, 729
World War I: African Americans and, 523; anti-Hun hysteria, 4–5, 36; assimilation campaigns, 203; casualties, 189; espionage, 243–44; German American repression, 13; Italian American service, 51; Jewish participation in, 4; munitions production, 150; pacifist movement, 126, 149; Paris Peace Conference (1919), 248, 523; propaganda, 4–5, 260; reparations following, 244, 247, 248; US involvement in, 24, 206, 270; veterans of, 4, 16, 72, 99–100, 142, 147, 192, 209, 250, 261, 294–96
World War II: African Americans and, 319–20, 523–24, 533–36; conscription, 269, 279–80, 319–20, 372, 505; democracy and, 59, 196, 287, 291, 303; employment available, 314; Hiroshima atomic bombing, 851; internment of Japanese Americans, 368–69; Irish neutrality, 96–97; Japanese surrender ending war in Pacific, 851–52; Jewish participation in, 584; Lend Lease program, 286–93, 297, 313, 334–35, 386; Nagasaki atomic bombing, 851; Nazi surrender ending war in Europe, 850; Operation Overlord (Normandy invasion), 791; Operation Starvation (Japan), 851; Pacific Theater (1945), 851; pacifist movement, 197–98, 291, 377–79; Paris occupation, 680; Pearl Harbor attack (1941), 352–54, 357, 447–48; propaganda, 35, 85, 97, 261–62, 265, 300, 303, 327–28, 466; Russian triumph over Nazis, 791;

World War II: (*continued*)
Russian war on Japan, 851; submarine warfare in, 96, 278, 334–38, 354, 357–59, 363–64, 386–88, 393; US-British destroyers-for-bases swap, 278–79; US entrance into, 353; US neutrality, 35, 56, 60, 98–99, 196–98, 202, 278. *See also* Nazi Germany; *specific battles*

Writers' War Board (WWB), 465–66

Xenophobia, 113, 135, 143, 236, 708

Yalta Conference (1945), 847, 850
Yankee Stadium, 25, 47, 48, 58
Yeshiva College, 30, 31
Yeshivas, 27, 29–32, 559, 580
YMCA (Young Men's Christian Association), 44, 68, 157, 320, 523, 531
Yokohama Specie Bank, 103
Yorkville, 13–14, 16–17, 20, 26, 34–35, 284, 329, 372–74
Young Communist League (YCL), 325, 434
Young Israel movement, 29, 574–76
Young Plan, 244, 252

Youth. *See* Children and adolescents
YWCA (Young Women's Christian Association), 68
YWHA (Young Women's Hebrew Association), 26

Zionism, 4–5, 7, 29, 169, 592
Zoot suits, 540–42, 544, 777